# EXPLANATION

I.  Example of entry under artist:
    (1) **BELLOWS**, George Wesley, 1882-1925
    (2)     **Children on the porch** (On the porch)  OCo
    (3)         DN.  Bellows
    (4)         Time.  300 years (col)
    (5)     **On the porch.**  See Children on the porch

### EXPLANATION

(1) Name of painter, surname in capitals
(2) Title used followed (in parentheses) by alternative title and by symbol
    giving location of painting.  Meaning of symbol is given in Key to
    Symbols, pages 21-3.
(3)-(4) Names of books in which reproductions may be found.  Full entry for
    these books is given in List of Works Indexed, pages 9-20.
(5) Reference from alternative title to title used


II.  Example of title entry:
     **Children** on the porch by G. W. Bellows
     **On** the porch by G. W. Bellows

### EXPLANATION

All titles entered in their alphabetical places in index, first word in boldface type


III.  Example of subject entry:
      **Bridges**
          Moses, A. M. R.  Sunday (The covered bridge)
          Whistler, J. A. M.  Old Battersea bridge

### EXPLANATION

To find books in which reproductions occur, consult the main entries under
Moses and under Whistler

# INDEX TO REPRODUCTIONS

## OF

# AMERICAN PAINTINGS

## FIRST SUPPLEMENT

By the Same Authors

INDEX TO REPRODUCTIONS OF EUROPEAN PAINTINGS

# INDEX TO REPRODUCTIONS

## OF

# AMERICAN PAINTINGS

## FIRST SUPPLEMENT

*A guide to pictures occurring in more than four hundred works*

BY

ISABEL STEVENSON MONRO

AND

KATE M. MONRO

THE H. W. WILSON COMPANY

NEW YORK                    1964

# PREFACE

This supplement to INDEX TO REPRODUCTIONS OF AMERICAN PAINT-INGS, published in 1948, continues the earlier index through 1961. It lists the paintings of artists reproduced in more than 400 general books on art, books on individual artists, and catalogs of museums and of special exhibitions.

Material indexed was chosen by the compilers and was selected because it introduced names of new and older artists and of additional reproductions. A few books issued before 1948 have been included as they were published while the original volume was in process of printing or because they were suggested for inclusion. Many small publications, even of pamphlet size, have been indexed, since otherwise the names of some newly-discovered or rather obscure artists might not appear. In fact, this index may be particularly valuable in identifying some of these less-known names.

The word *American* in the title of this index refers to artists of the United States, not only native-born, but also foreign-born who have become naturalized or who have lived and worked in the United States so that their later work is regarded as American. Artists are regarded as American when they are so identified in museum catalogs and exhibitions.

As in the foundation volume, paintings are entered (1) under name of artist, followed by his dates when obtainable, by title of picture, and by an abbreviated entry for the book in which the reproduction may be found; (2) under distinctive titles; and (3) in some cases under subjects. Locations of paintings in permanent collections have been indicated by symbols following the title of the picture whenever such information has been available.

*Symbols.* Symbols follow the form used in the previous index. They are usually formed by taking the first letter from the name of the state, the second from the city or town, and the third from some distinguishing letter for the museum or other institution where the original is located. For example, the letters *NUM* represent *N* for New York, *U* for Utica, *M* for Munson-Williams-Proctor Institute. A few exceptions occur in the use of *MM* for the Metropolitan Museum, New York; of *MMA* for the Museum of Modern Art, New York; and *WMAA* for the Whitney Museum of American Art, New York.

*Subjects.* Subjects, such as Boxers and wrestlers, Children, Circus, and place names, are given for paintings where such groupings might be helpful in identifying the pictures or interesting in themselves. Names of individuals occurring as sitters are always given as subjects. Married women have usually been entered under their married names with references from their maiden names unless such references would follow immediately under the subjects.

*Titles.* Titles are given in their alphabetical order if they seem distinctive enough to be brought out or if such titles might be remembered and so traced to the artist. In the case of two titles found for the same

picture, both are given under the artist with reference from the alternative title unless it follows immediately below.  The alternative title is also listed in its alphabetical order followed by the name of the painter.  For example, under Chase, William Merritt, the title *Turkish page* occurs, followed by the alternative title in parentheses (*Boy feeding a cockatoo*).  The title *Boy feeding a cockatoo* also appears as a title under Chase with the reference See *Turkish page*.  Both titles are also given in their alphabetical place in the index.

*Unidentified artists.*  Under the entry Unidentified artists, reproductions are listed for those that have a subject value, such as names of individuals or places, or for those that have distinctive titles, as *Quilting Party.*

The compilers are very grateful to the many museums and libraries that have lent or given material for indexing.  Although these organizations cannot all be listed, the compilers wish to mention the Library of the University of North Carolina for the many courtesies extended to them.

I. S. M.
K. M. M.

Winter Park, Florida

May 1964

# CONTENTS

# LIST OF WORKS INDEXED

The abbreviated forms in boldface type are those used in the index. Full name of author, or museum, publisher, place, and date follow in roman type.

**Art since 1945**—Art since 1945 by Marcel Brion and others. N.Y. Harry N. Abrams, 1958

**Ashton. Philip Guston**—Ashton, Dore. Philip Guston. N.Y. Grove press, 1960

**ATeS. Collection**—Arizona state college, Tempe. Collection of American art. Tempe, The college, 1954

**ATU. Coll of Amer art.** University of Arizona. Collection of American art. Tucson, The university, 1947

**Barker. Amer ptg**—Barker, Virgil. American painting, history and interpretation. N.Y. The Macmillan co. 1950

**Barker. From realism**—Barker, Virgil. From realism to reality in recent American painting. Lincoln, University of Nebraska press, 1959

**Barr. Masters of modern art.** See MMA. Masters

**Barr. Painting and sculpture.** See MMA. Ptg and sculpture

**Barr. What is mod ptg 1956**—Barr, Alfred Hamilton. What is modern painting. rev (i.e. 6th) ed. N.Y. Museum of modern art, 1956 (Introduction to the modern arts 2)

**Baur. Amer ptg**—Baur, John Ireland Howe. American painting in the nineteenth century: main trends and movements. N.Y. Frederick A. Praeger, 1953

**Baur. Balcomb Greene**—Baur, John Ireland Howe. Balcomb Greene. N.Y. American federation of arts, 1961

**Baur. Bradley Walker Tomlin**—Baur, John Ireland Howe. Bradley Walker Tomlin. N.Y. The Macmillan co. 1957

**Baur. Charles Burchfield**—Baur, John Ireland Howe. Charles Burchfield. N.Y. The Macmillan co. 1956

**Baur. George Grosz**—Baur, John Ireland Howe. George Grosz. N.Y. Whitney museum of American art, 1954

**Baur. MacIver and Pereira**—Baur, John Ireland Howe. Loren MacIver; I. Rice Pereira. N.Y. The Macmillan co. 1953

**Baur. Nature**—Baur, John Ireland Howe. Nature in abstraction, the relation of abstract painting and sculpture to nature in twentieth century American art. N.Y. The Macmillan co. 1958

**Baur. New art**—Baur, John Ireland Howe, ed. New art in America: fifty painters of the twentieth century by J. I. H. Baur, ed., Lloyd Goodrich, D. C. Miller, J. T. Soby, F. S. Wight. N.Y. New York Graphic society, 1957

**Baur. Philip Evergood**—Baur, John Ireland Howe. Philip Evergood. N.Y. Published for the Whitney museum of American art by Frederick A. Praeger, 1960

**Baur. Revolution**—Baur, John Ireland Howe. Revolution and tradition in modern American art. Cambridge, Harvard university press, 1951

**Baur. William Zorach**—Baur, John Ireland Howe. William Zorach. N.Y. Published for the Whitney museum of American art by Frederick A. Praeger, 1959

**Baur. Young America 1957.** See WMAA. Young America 1957

**Bazin**—Bazin, Germain. History of modern painting. N.Y. The Hyperion press, 1951

**Bazin. History of art**—Bazin, Germain. A history of art from prehistoric times to the present. Boston, Houghton Mifflin co. 1959

**Belknap**—Belknap, Waldron Phoenix. American colonial painting: materials for a history. Cambridge, Harvard university press, 1959

**Benton**—Benton, Thomas Hart, An artist in America. New and rev ed. N.Y. University of Kansas City press, 1951

**Biddle. Yes and no**—Biddle, George. The yes and no of contemporary art, an artist's evaluation. Cambridge, Harvard university press, 1957

**Blesh**—Blesh, Rudi. Modern art, U.S.A. men, rebellion, conquest, 1900-1956. N.Y. Alfred A. Knopf, 1956

**Blesh. Stuart Davis**—Blesh, Rudi. Stuart Davis. N.Y. Grove press, 1960

**Bolton. Ezra Ames**—Bolton, Theodore and Cortelyou, Irwin F. Ezra Ames of Albany, portrait painter, craftsman, Royal arch mason, banker. N.Y. New-York Historical society, 1955

**Born**—Born, Wolfgang. American landscape painting, an interpretation. New Haven, Yale university press, 1948

**Breeskin. Milton Avery**—Breeskin, Adelyn. Milton Avery. N.Y. The American federation of arts, 1960

**Brion, Marcel. Art since 1945.** See Art since 1945

**Brooks. John Sloan**—Brooks, Van Wyck. John Sloan, a painter's life. N.Y. E. P. Dutton & co. 1955

**Brown. Amer ptg.**—Brown, Milton Wolf. American painting from the Armory show to the depression. Princeton, Princeton university press, 1955

**Brussels. Exposition**—Brussels. Exposition universelle et internationale, 1958. American art: four exhibitions. 17 April to October 18, 1958. N.Y. American federation of arts, 1958

**Bywaters. Andrew Dasburg**—Bywaters, Jerry. Andrew Dasburg. N.Y. American federation of arts, 1959

**Canaday**—Canaday, John. Mainstreams of modern art. N.Y. Simon and Schuster, 1959

**CanO. Hirshhorn coll**—National gallery of Canada, Ottawa. Some American paintings from the collection of Joseph H. Hirshhorn. 2d ed. Ottawa, The gallery, 1957

**Carlson. Gallery**—Carlson, Raymond, ed. Gallery of western paintings. N.Y. McGraw-Hill Book co. 1951

**Cheney. Expressionism 1948 ed.**—Cheney, Sheldon. Expressionism in art. rev ed. Liveright publishing co. 1948

**Cheney. New world history**—Cheney, Sheldon. A new world history of art. N.Y. The Viking press, 1956

**Cheney. Primer 1958 ed**—Cheney, Sheldon. A primer of modern art. 13th rev ed. N.Y. Liveright publishing corp. 1958

**Cheney. Story 1958 ed**—Cheney, Sheldon. The story of modern art. rev and enl mid-century ed. N.Y. The Viking press, 1958

**Chew. 250 years of art**—Chew, Paul A. comp. and ed. Two hundred and fifty years of art in Pennsylvania. Greensburg, Pa. The Westmoreland county museum of art, 1959

**CLA. 35 ptgs**—Los Angeles county museum. Thirty-five paintings from the collection of the Los Angeles county museum. n.p. 1950 (Picture book no 1)

**Coates. Walter Quirt**—Coates, Robert M. Walter Quirt. N.Y. The American federation of arts, 1960

**Cortelyou. Ezra Ames supp**—Cortelyou, Irvin W. A supplement to the catalogue of pictures by Ezra Ames of Albany. N.Y. New-York historical society, 1957

**CoS. New accessions USA**—Colorado Springs fine arts center. New accessions USA, 1946-1960. Colorado Springs, 1946-1960

**Cowdrey**—Cowdrey, Mary Bartlett. American academy of fine arts and American art-union. Exhibition record 1816-1852. N.Y. New-York historical society, 1953 2v

**Craven. Rainbow book**—Craven, Thomas. The rainbow book of art. Cleveland, The World publishing co. 1956

**Craven. Treasury 1952 ed.**—Craven, Thomas. A treasury of art masterpieces from the renaissance to the present day. rev and enl. N.Y. Simon and Schuster, 1952

**CSB. Illusion**—Santa Barbara museum of art. Illusion and reality in contemporary American art. Santa Barbara, The museum, 1956

**CSB. Impressionism**—Santa Barbara museum of art. Impressionism and its influence in American art . . . n.p. 1954

**CSFP. Annual ex**—California Palace of the Legion of Honor, San Francisco. Annual exhibition, 1946-1952. San Francisco, The palace, 1946-1952

**CSFP. Annual exhibition of contemporary American painting.** See CSFP. Annual ex, 1950/51; Annual ex, 1952

**CSFP. First spring annual ex.** See CSFP. Annual ex, 1946

**CSFP. Handbook**—California Palace of the Legion of Honor, San Francisco. Handbook of the collections. San Francisco, The palace, 1960

**CSFP. Illusionism**—California Palace of the Legion of Honor, San Francisco. Illusionism & trompe l'oeil, an idea illustrated by an exhibition held May 3—June 12, 1949. San Francisco, The palace, 1949

**CtHW. Durrie**—Wadsworth atheneum, Hartford, Conn. George Henry Durrie, Connecticut painter of American life. Special loan exhibition March 12-April 13, 1947. Hartford, The atheneum, 1947

**CtHW. Handbook**—Wadsworth atheneum, Hartford, Conn. Handbook. Hartford, 1958

**CtHW. Thomas Cole**—Wadsworth atheneum, Hartford, Conn. Thomas Cole 1801-1848: one hundred years later. A loan exhibition, Wadsworth atheneum . . . Whitney museum of American art. Hartford, The atheneum, 1949

**CtHW. Trumbull**—Wadsworth atheneum, Hartford, Conn. John Trumbull: painter—patriot, an exhibition organized to honor the bicentennial of the artist's birth. October 10-November 25, 1956. Hartford, The atheneum, 1956

**CtY. Portrait index**—Yale university, New Haven, Conn. Portrait index, 1701-1951. New Haven, Yale university press, 1951

**CtY. Soc Anonyme**—Yale university, New Haven, Conn. Gallery of fine arts. Collection of the Société anonyme. 1920. New Haven, 1950

**CtY. Yale alumni**—Yale university, New Haven, Conn. Pictures collected by Yale alumni. Exhibition May eight to June eighteen, 1956. New Haven, 1956

**Davidson v1, v2.**—Davidson, Marshall B. Life in America. Boston, Houghton Mifflin co. 1951 2v

**DC. Amer ptrs of the South**—The Corcoran gallery of art, Washington, D.C. American painters of the South, April 23-June 5, 1960. Washington, The gallery, 1960

**DC. Biennial ex.**—The Corcoran gallery of art, Washington, D.C. Biennial exhibition of contemporary American painting, 1947-1961. Washington, The gallery, 1947-1961

**DC. De gustibus**—The Corcoran gallery of art, Washington, D.C. De gustibus, an exhibition of American paintings illustrating a century of taste and criticism, January 9 through February 20, 1949. Washington, The gallery, 1949

**DC. Halpert collection**—The Corcoran gallery of art, Washington, D.C. A loan exhibition from the Edith Gregor Halpert collection, January 16-February 26, 1960. Washington, The gallery, 1960

**DC. Masterpieces**—The Corcoran gallery of art, Washington, D.C. Masterpieces of the Corcoran gallery of art. Washington, The gallery, 1959

DC. Privately owned—The Corcoran gallery of art, Washington, D.C. Privately owned, a selection of works of art from collections in the Washington area, February tenth-March thirtieth, 1952. Washington, The gallery, 1952

DC. Ryder—The Corcoran gallery of art, Washington, D.C. Albert Pinkham Ryder, April 8-May 12, 1961. Washington, The gallery, 1961

De Mare. G. P. A. Healy—De Mare, Marie. G. P. A. Healy, American artist: an intimate chronicle of the nineteenth century. N.Y. David McKay co. 1954

Dickson. John Wesley Jarvis—Dickson, Harold E. John Wesley Jarvis, American painter, 1780-1840 with a checklist of his works. N.Y. New-York historical society, 1949

DN. Amer primitive ptgs—U.S. National gallery of art, Washington, D.C. American primitive paintings from the collection of Edgar William and Bernice Chrysler Garbisch. Washington, The gallery, 1954-1957 (2 parts)

DN. Bellows—U.S. National gallery of art, Washington, D.C. George Bellows, a retrospective exhibition, January 19 through February 24, 1957. Washington, The gallery, 1957

DN. Homer—U.S. National gallery of art, Washington, D.C. Winslow Homer, a retrospective exhibition: National gallery of art, Metropolitan museum of art. Washington, The gallery, 1958

DN. Mellon collection—U.S. National gallery of art, Washington, D.C. Paintings and sculpture from the Mellon collection. Washington, The gallery, 1940

DNC. Gellatly coll, 1954—Smithsonian institution. National collection of fine arts, Washington, D.C. Catalog of American and European paintings in the Gellatly collection. 4th ed. Washington, The institution, 1954

Donahue. William Pachner—Donahue, Kenneth. William Pachner. N.Y. The American federation of arts, 1959

DP. Catalogue—The Phillips collection, Washington, D.C. Catalogue, 1952. n.p., n.d.

Ebersole. Fletcher Martin—Ebersole, Barbara. Fletcher Martin. Gainesville, University of Florida press, 1954

Eliot. Art of our time—Eliot, Alexander. Art of our time, 1950-1960: painting, architecture, sculpture. N.Y. Omicron books, 1959

Eliot. Three hundred years of American painting. See Time. 300 years

Evans—Evans, Grose. Benjamin West and the taste of his times. Carbondale, Southern Illinois university press, 1959

Faulkner. Art today, 1956—Faulkner, Ray Nelson. Art today, an introduction to the fine and functional arts. 3d ed. N.Y. Henry Holt & co. 1956

50 years of modern art—50 years of modern art, introduction by Emile Langui. N.Y. Frederick A. Praeger, 1959

Fleischman collection. See WiMiA. Amer ptg, 1760-1960

Flexner. Amer ptg—Flexner, James Thomas. The pocket history of American painting. N.Y. Pocket books, 1957

Flexner. Copley—Flexner, James Thomas. John Singleton Copley. Boston, Houghton Mifflin co. 1948

Flexner. First flowers—Flexner, James Thomas. First flowers of our wilderness. Boston, Houghton Mifflin co. 1947 (American painting v1)

Flexner. Light of distant skies—Flexner, James Thomas. The light of distant skies, 1760-1835. N.Y. Harcourt, Brace and co. 1954 (American painting v2)

Flexner. Short history—Flexner, James Thomas. A short history of American painting. Boston, Houghton Mifflin co. 1950

Foote. John Smibert—Foote, Henry Wilder. John Smibert, painter, with a descriptive catalogue of portraits and notes on the work of Nathaniel Smibert. Cambridge, Harvard university press, 1950

Ford. Edward Hicks—Ford, Alice Elizabeth. Edward Hicks, painter of The peaceable kingdom. Philadelphia, University of Pennsylvania press, 1952

Ford. Pictorial folk art—Ford, Alice Elizabeth. Pictorial folk art, New England to California. N.Y. Studio publications, 1949

Frankenstein. After the hunt—Frankenstein, Alfred. After the hunt: William Harnett and other American still life painters 1870-1900. Berkeley, University of California press, 1953

Frankenstein. Two journeyman ptrs—Frankenstein, Alfred and Healy, Arthur K. D. Two journeyman painters. Middlebury, Vt. Sheldon museum, 1950

Gardner. 1959 ed—Gardner, Helen. Art through the ages. 4th ed rev under the editorship of Sumner McK. Crosby by the Department of the history of art, Yale university. N.Y. Harcourt, Brace and co. 1959

GAtM. Holbrook collection—Georgia museum of art, Athens, Ga. The Eva Underhill Holbrook memorial collection. Athens, University of Georgia, 1953

Genauer—Genauer, Emily. Best of art. N.Y. Doubleday & co. 1948

Getlein. Abraham Rattner. Getlein, Frank. Abraham Rattner. N.Y. The American federation of arts, 1960

Goodrich. Amer art—Goodrich, Lloyd and Baur, John Ireland Howe. American art of our century. N.Y. Published for the Whitney museum of American art by F. A. Praeger, 1961

Goodrich. Edward Hopper—Goodrich, Lloyd. Edward Hopper. Baltimore Penguin books, 1949 (The Penguin modern painters)

Goodrich. John Sloan—Goodrich, Lloyd. John Sloan. N.Y. Published for the Whitney museum of American art by The Macmillan co. 1952

Goodrich. Max Weber—Goodrich, Lloyd. Max Weber. N.Y. Published for the Whitney museum of American art by The Macmillan co. 1949

Goodrich. Pioneers of modern art in America. See WMAA. Pioneers

Goodrich. Reginald Marsh. See WMAA. Marsh

Goodrich. Ryder—Goodrich, Lloyd. Albert P. Ryder. N.Y. George Braziller, 1959 (Great American artists series)

Goodrich. Winslow Homer—Goodrich, Lloyd. Winslow Homer. N.Y. George Braziller, 1959 (Great American artists series)

Goodrich. Yasuo Kuniyoshi—Goodrich, Lloyd. Yasuo Kuniyoshi. N.Y. Published for the Whitney museum of American art by The Macmillan co. 1948

Goossen. Stuart Davis—Goossen, Eugene C. Stuart Davis. N.Y. George Braziller, 1959 (Great American artists series)

Gordon. Karl Schrag—Gordon, John. Karl Schrag. N.Y. The American federation of arts, 1960

Gregory. The world of Whistler—Gregory, Horace. The world of James McNeill Whistler. N.Y. Thomas Nelson & sons, 1959

Gruskin—Gruskin, Alan D. Painting in the U.S.A. N.Y. Doubleday & co. 1946

Habasque—Habasque, Guy. Cubism. Geneva, Skira, 1959 (Taste of our time series)

Helm. John Marin—Helm, MacKinley. John Marin. Boston, Pelligrini & Cudahy in association with the Institute of contemporary art, 1948

Hess. Abstract ptg—Hess, Thomas B. Abstract painting, background and American phase. N.Y. Viking press, 1951

Hess. Willem De Kooning—Hess, Thomas B. Willem de Kooning. N.Y. George Braziller, 1959 (Great American artists series)

Hunter. Jackson Pollock. See MMA. Jackson Pollock

Hunter. Mod Amer ptg—Hunter, Sam. Modern American painting and sculpture. N.Y. Dell publishing co. 1959 (Laurel edition)

IaDa. Silver jubilee—Davenport municipal art gallery, Davenport, Iowa. Silver jubilee exhibition of 100 contemporary painters. Davenport, 1950

IaDa. 30th anniversary—Davenport municipal art gallery, Davenport, Iowa. Thirtieth anniversary exhibition of 100 contemporary American paintings. n.p., 1955

IaDa. Wood—Davenport municipal art gallery, Davenport, Iowa. Grant Wood and the American scene. February 3-24, 1957. n.p., n.d.

ICA. Abstract and surrealist art. See ICA. Annual ex, 1947/48

ICA. Amer artists paint the city—Chicago. Art institute. American artists paint the city. XXVIIIth biennale, Venice, 1956. Chicago, The institute, 1956

ICA. American exhibition: paintings, sculpture. See ICA. Annual ex.

ICA. Annual ex—Chicago, Art institute. American exhibition: paintings, sculpture. v56, 1945/46-v64, 1961 (lacking: v57, 1946/47; v59, 1949/50) Chicago, The institute, 1945-1961. 6 numbers

ICA. From colony to nation—Chicago. Art institute. From colony to nation, an exhibition of American painting, silver and architecture from 1650 to the War of 1812. Chicago, The institute, 1949

InIJ. Chase centennial—John Herron art museum, Indianapolis, Ind. Chase centennial exhibition . . . November 1-December 11, 1949 n.p., n.d.

InIJ. 105 ptgs—John Herron art museum, Indianapolis, Ind. 105 paintings in the John Herron art museum. Indianapolis, Art association of Indianapolis, 1951

InTH. Catalogue—Sheldon Swope art gallery, Terre Haute, Ind. Catalogue 1951 Terre Haute, The gallery, 1951

IU. Contemp Amer ptg—Illinois. University. College of fine and applied arts. Exhibition of contemporary American painting, 1948-1952. Urbana, The university, 1948-1952. 5 numbers

IU. Contemp Amer ptg & sculp—Illinois. University. College of fine and applied arts. Contemporary American painting and sculpture, 1953-1961. Urbana, The university, 1953-1961. 9 numbers

IU. 20th century—Illinois. University. College of fine and applied arts. 20th century works of art from the permanent collection . . . 1957. Urbana, The university, 1957

Janis—De Kooning—Janis, Harriet Grossman and Blesh, Rudi. De Kooning. N.Y. Grove press, 1960

Janson. Key monuments—Janson, Horst Woldemar, ed. Key monuments of the history of art, a visual survey ed by H. W. Janson with Dora Jane Janson. Englewood Cliffs, N.J. Prentice-Hall and Harry N. Abrams, 1959

Janson. Picture history—Janson, Horst Woldemar and Janson, Dora Jane. Picture history of painting from cave painting to modern times. N.Y. Harry N. Abrams, 1957

Jean. Surrealist ptg—Jean, Marcel. The history of surrealist painting, with the collaboration of Arpad Mezei. Tr from the French by S. W. Taylor. N.Y. Grove press, 1959

Jetté. Amer heritage collection—Jetté, Edith Kemper and Jetté, Ellerton Marcel. A group of paintings from the American heritage collection. Waterville, Me. Colby college press, 1956

John Marin—John Marin memorial exhibition with a foreword by Duncan Phillips; appreciation by William Carlos Williams and Dorothy Norman; conclusion to a biography by MacKinley Helm; John Marin—frontiersman by F. S. Wight. Los Angeles, University of California, 1955. (Organized by the Art galleries of the University of California, Los Angeles, Cleveland, Minneapolis, Boston, Phillips, San Francisco)

**Jones. New-found folk art**—Jones, Agnes Halsey and Jones, Louis C. New-found folk art of the young republic. Cooperstown, N.Y. State historical assn. 1960

**Jones. Rediscovered ptrs**—Jones, Agnes Halsey. Rediscovered painters of upstate New York 1700-1875. Utica, Munson-Williams-Proctor institute, 1958. (Exhibition sponsored by N.Y. state historical assn; Albany institute; Munson-Williams-Proctor institute; New-York historical society, 1958-1959)

**Kallir. Amer primitive ptgs**—Kallir, Otto. American primitive paintings. Washington, Smithsonian institution, 1958

**KLU. Benton**—University of Kansas. Museum of art, Lawrence. Thomas Hart Benton; a retrospective exhibition, April 12 to May 18, 1958. Lawrence, The university, 1958

**KLU. Wood**—University of Kansas. Museum of art, Lawrence. Grant Wood, 1891-1942, a retrospective exhibition, April 12 to May 30, 1959. Lawrence, The university, 1959

**KyLS. Kentucky port gall**—The J. B. Speed art museum, Louisville, Ky. A preliminary catalogue of the Kentucky portrait gallery, Louisville, 1949

**Langui, Emile.** See 50 years of modern art

**Larkin**—Larkin, Oliver W. Art and life in America. N.Y. Rinehart & co. 1949

**Larkin rev ed**—Larkin, Oliver W. Art and life in America. rev and enl ed. N.Y. Holt, Rinehart and Winston, 1960

**Lee. Art then and now.**—Lee, Kathryn Dean and Burchwood, Katharine Tyler. Art then and now. N.Y. Appleton-Century Crofts. 1949

**Leepa**—Leepa, Allen. The challenge of modern art. N.Y. Beechhurst press, 1949

**Leeper. Everett Spruce**—Leeper, John Palmer. Everett Spruce. N.Y. The American federation of arts, 1959

**Lewis. Russell Smith**—Lewis, Virginia E. Russell Smith, romantic realist. Pittsburgh, University of Pittsburgh press, 1956

**Lewisohn**—Lewisohn, Sam A. Painters and personality. N.Y. Harper & brothers, 1947

**Lipman. Primitive ptrs**—Lipman, Jean and Winchester, Alice, eds. Primitive painters in America 1750-1950: an anthology. N.Y. Dodd Mead & co. 1950

**MB. Great Americans**—Boston museum of fine arts. Great Americans from the Revolution to the Civil war. Meriden, Meriden gravure co. 1954 (Picture book no 1)

**MB. Karolik coll**—Boston museum of fine arts. M. and M. Karolik collection of American paintings, 1815-1865. Cambridge, Harvard university press, 1949

**MB. Lane**—Boston museum of fine arts. Fitz Hugh Lane. Boston, The museum, 1956 (Picture book no 8)

**MB. New England miniatures**—Boston museum of fine arts. New England miniatures. Boston, The museum. 1957

**MB. Prendergast**—Boston museum of fine arts. Maurice Prendergast by Hedley Howell Rhys. Cambridge, Harvard university press, 1960

**MB. Ptgs in water color**—Boston museum of fine arts. Catalogue of paintings and drawings in water color. Boston, The museum, 1949

**MBIC. Jack Levine**—Boston. Institute of contemporary art. Jack Levine with an essay by F. S. Wight and a foreword by Lloyd Goodrich. N.Y. Whitney museum of American art, 1955

**MBIC. Salemme**—Boston. Institute of contemporary art. Salemme. Boston, 1955?

**MBIC. View 1960**—Boston. Institute of contemporary art. View 1960. Boston, The institute, 1960

**MBIC. Villon and Feininger**—Boston. Institute of contemporary art. Jacques Villon. Lyonel Feininger . . . N.Y. Chanticleer press, 1949?

**McCausland. A. H. Maurer**—McCausland, Elizabeth. A. H. Maurer, 1868-1932. Minneapolis, Walker art center, 1949

**McCausland. Marsden Hartley**—McCausland, Elizabeth. Marsden Hartley. Minneapolis, University of Minnesota press, n.d.

**McClintock**—McClintock, Gilbert S. Valley views of northeastern Pennsylvania. Wilkes-Barre, The Wyoming historical and genealogical society, 1948

**McCracken. Charles M. Russell**—McCracken, Harold. The Charles M. Russell book: the life and work of the cowboy artist. Garden City, Doubleday & co. 1957

**McCracken. George Catlin**—McCracken, Harold. George Catlin and the old frontier. N.Y. The Dial press, 1959

**McCracken. Portrait of the old west**—McCracken, Harold. Portrait of the old west with a biographical check list of western artists. N.Y. McGraw-Hill book co. n.d.

**McCracken. Remington**—McCracken, Harold. A catalogue of the Frederic Remington collection with chronology and notes. N.Y. Knoedler galleries (for the Remington art memorial, Ogdensburg N. Y.) 1954

**McCurdy**—McCurdy, Charles, ed. Modern art, a pictorial anthology. N.Y. The Macmillan co. 1958

**McDermott. G. C. Bingham**—McDermott, John Francis. George Caleb Bingham, river portraitist. Norman, University of Oklahoma press, 1959

**McDermott. Samuel Seymour**—McDermott, John Francis. Samuel Seymour: pioneer artist of the plains and the Rockies. Washington, Government printing office, 1951 (Smithsonian publication 4043)

**McKibben. Sargent's Boston**—McKibben, David. Sargent's Boston with an essay & biographical summary & a complete checklist of Sargent's portraits. Boston, Boston museum of fine arts, 1956

**McKinney**—McKinney, Roland Joseph. Famous American painters. N.Y. Dodd, Mead & co. 1955 (Famous biographies for young people)

**MdBMu. Rendezvous**—Baltimore. Municipal museum. Rendezvous for taste: Peale's Baltimore museum, 1814 to 1830: Exhibition celebrating the 25th anniversary of the Peale museum 1931-1956. Baltimore, n.d.

**MeC. Inaugural ex**—Colby college art collection. Inaugural exhibition including gifts acquired through the Friends of arts at Colby. Waterville, Me. The college, 1959

**Mendelowitz**—Mendelowitz, Daniel Marcus. A history of American art. N.Y. Holt, Rinehart and Winston, 1960

**MiA. Root coll**—University of Michigan, Ann Arbor. Selection from the Edward Root collection, the Munson-Williams-Proctor institute, Utica, N.Y., Circulated by the Smithsonian institution, 1959-60. n.p. n.d.

**MiC. Zoltan Sepeshy**—Cranbrook academy, Bloomfield Hills, Mich. Zoltan Sepeshy, April 28-May 14, 1950. Bloomfield Hills, The academy, 1950

**MiD. Coll in progress**—Detroit institute of arts. Collection in progress: selections from the Lawrence and Barbara Fleischman collection of American art. Detroit, The institute, 1955

**MiD. Ports of the Pitts family**—Detroit institute of arts. Portraits of eight generations of the Pitts family from the seventeenth to the twentieth century. Detroit, The institute, 1959

**MiD. Ptg in America**—Detroit institute of arts. Painting in America, the story of 450 years [exhibition] April 23 through June 9, 1957. Detroit, The institute, 1957

**MiD. Travelers in Arcadia**—Detroit institute of arts. Travelers in Arcadia, American artists in Italy 1830-1875. Detroit, The institute, 1951; Toledo museum of art, 1951 (Text by E. P. Richardson and Otto Wittmann, jr.)

**MiD. Treasures**—Detroit institute of arts. Treasures from the Detroit institute of arts. Detroit, 1960

**Middleton. Jeremiah Theus**—Middleton, Margaret Simons. Jeremiah Theus, colonial artist of Charles Town. Columbia, University of South Carolina press, 1953

**Miller, A. J. The West**—Miller, Alfred Jacob. The West of Alfred Jacob Miller (1837) from the notes and water colors in the Walters art gallery with an account of the artist by Marvin C. Ross. Norman, University of Oklahoma press, 1951

**Miller, D. David G. Blythe**—Miller, Dorothy. Life and work of David G. Blythe. Pittsburgh, University of Pittsburgh press, 1950

**MM. Amer ptg today**—Metropolitan museum of art. N.Y. American painting today, a national competitive exhibition, 1950. N.Y. The museum, 1950

**MM. 100 Amer ptrs**—Metropolitan museum of art. N.Y. 100 American painters of the 20th century, works selected from the collections of the Metropolitan museum of art with an introduction by R. B. Hale. N.Y. The museum, 1950

**MMA. Abstract**—N.Y. Museum of modern art. Abstract painting and sculpture in America by Andrew Carnduff Ritchie. N.Y. The museum, 1951

**MMA. Contemp ptrs**—N.Y. Museum of modern art. Contemporary painters [by] James Thrall Soby. N.Y. The museum, 1948

**MMA. Demuth**—N.Y. Museum of modern art. Charles Demuth by Andrew Carnduff Ritchie. N.Y. The museum, 1950

**MMA. Edward Hopper.** See Goodrich, Lloyd. Edward Hopper

**MMA. Ernst**—N.Y. Museum of modern art. Max Ernst, ed by William S. Lieberman. N.Y. The museum, 1961

**MMA. Fifteen**—N.Y. Museum of modern art. 15 Americans, ed by Dorothy C. Miller. N.Y. The museum, 1952

**MMA. Fourteen**—N.Y. Museum of modern art. 14 Americans, ed by Dorothy C. Miller. N.Y. The museum, 1946

**MMA. Jackson Pollock**—N.Y. Museum of modern art. Jackson Pollock; text by Sam Hunter. N.Y. The museum. Distributed by Simon and Schuster, 1956/7

**MMA. Masters**—N.Y. Museum of modern art. Masters of modern art, ed by Alfred H. Barr, jr. 3d ed rev. N.Y. The museum, 1958

**MMA. New Amer ptg**—N.Y. Museum of modern art. The new American painting as shown in eight European countries 1958-1959. N.Y. The museum, 1959

**MMA Ptg and sculpture**—N.Y. Museum of modern art. Painting and sculpture collection [by Alfred H. Barr, jr.] N.Y. Erich S. Herrmann, 1950

**MMA. Rothko**—N.Y. Museum of modern art. Mark Rothko [by Peter Selz] N.Y. The museum, 1961

**MMA. Shahn**—N.Y. Museum of modern art. Ben Shahn. N.Y. The museum, 1947 (Special bulletin, summer, 1947)

**MMA. Sixteen**—N.Y. Museum of modern art. Sixteen Americans, ed by Dorothy C. Miller with statements by the artist and others. N.Y. The museum, 1959

**MMA. Soby collection**—N.Y. Museum of modern art. The James Thrall Soby collection of works of art pledged or given to the museum. N.Y. The museum, 1961

**MMA. 12 Americans**—N.Y. Museum of modern art. 12 Americans, ed by Dorothy C. Miller with statements by the artists and others. N.Y. The museum, 1956

**MMA. Watkins**—N.Y. Museum of modern art. Franklin C. Watkins by A. C. Ritchie. N.Y. The museum, 1950

**MMA. What is modern painting.** See Barr. What is modern painting

**MMA. Yves Tanguy**—N.Y. Museum of modern art. Yves Tanguy by James Thrall Soby. N.Y. The museum, 1955

**MnMW. Classic tradition**—Walker art center, Minneapolis, Minn. The classic tradition in contemporary art, April 24 through June 28, 1953. Minneapolis, University of Minnesota, 1953

MnMW. Contemporary—Walker art center, Minneapolis, Minn. Contemporary American painting and sculpture collected by Mr. and Mrs. Roy R. Neuberger, May 25th through August 10th, 1952. Minneapolis, The center, 1952

MnMW. Eighty works—Walker art center, Minneapolis, Minn. Eighty works from the Richard Brown Baker collection, March 12-April 16, 1961. n.p. n.d.

MnMW. Expressionism 1900-1955—Walker art center, Minneapolis, Minn. Expressionism 1900-1955: Walker art center; Institute of contemporary art; San Francisco museum of art; Cincinnati art museum and Contemporary art center; Baltimore museum of art; Albright art gallery. n.p. 1956

MnMW. Precisionist view—Walker art center, Minneapolis, Minn. The precisionist view in American art. Minneapolis, The center, 1960 (Exhibition held in cooperation with Whitney, Detroit, Los Angeles, San Francisco museums)

MnMW. Reality and fantasy—Walker art center, Minneapolis, Minn. Reality and fantasy, May 23 through July 2, 1954. Minneapolis, The center, 1954

MnMW. Roszak—Walker art center, Minneapolis, Minn. Theodore Roszak [by H. H. Arnason]. Minneapolis, The center, 1956 (In collaboration with the Whitney museum)

MnMW. 60 Amer ptrs—Walker art center, Minneapolis, Minn. 60 American painters 1960; abstract expressionist painting of the fifties, April 3-May 8, 1960. Minneapolis, The center, 1961

MnMW. Stuart Davis—Walker art center, Minneapolis, Minn. Stuart Davis, an exhibition organized by the Walker art center in collaboration with the Des Moines art center, San Francisco museum of art and the Whitney museum of American art. n.p. [1957]

MNS. Homer—Smith college museum of art, Northampton, Mass. Winslow Homer, illustrator. Catalogue of the exhibition with a checklist of wood engravings and a list of illustrated books by Mary Bartlett Cowdrey. Northampton, The college, 1951

MnU. Arnold Blanch—University of Minnesota. Department of art. Arnold Blanch, the years 1924-1949. Minneapolis, The university, 1949

MnU. 40 Amer ptrs—University of Minnesota. Department of art. 40 American painters, 1940-1950. June 4-August 30, 1951. Minneapolis, the university, 1951

MnU. Philip Guston—University of Minnesota. Department of art. Philip Guston, April 10-May 12, 1950. n.p., n.d.

Mocsanyi. Karl Knaths—Mocsanyi, Paul. Karl Knaths. Washington, The Phillips gallery, 1957

Moderns and their world—The moderns and their world, with an introduction by John Rothenstein. London, Phoenix house, 1957?

MoKN. Handbook—William Rockhill Nelson gallery of art, Kansas City, Mo. Handbook of the collections in the William Rockhill Nelson gallery of art and Mary Atkins museum of fine arts. 4th ed. Kansas City, 1959

Morgan—Morgan, Lewis Henry. The Indian journals, 1859-62. Ann Arbor, University of Michigan press, 1959

Morley. Carl Morris—Morley, Grace L. Carl Morris. N.Y. The American federation of arts, 1960

Moses—Moses, Anna Mary (Robertson) Grandma Moses, American primitive. N.Y. Doubleday & co. 1947

MoSL. Beckman—St. Louis. City art museum. Max Beckman, retrospective exhibition: City art museum of St Louis, Los Angeles county museum, Detroit institute of arts, Baltimore museum of art, Minneapolis institute of arts. n.p., n.d.

MoSL. Contemporary Amer ptg—St Louis. City art museum. Contemporary American painting, November 12 to December 10, 1951. St Louis, The museum, 1951

MoSL. 50 masterworks—St Louis. City art museum. Fifty masterworks from the City art museum of St Louis [at Wildenstein, Nov. 5, 1958] n.p., n.d.

MoSL. 40 masterpieces—St Louis. City art museum. 40 masterpieces, a loan exhibition of paintings from American museums 6 October to 10 November, 1947. Fortieth anniversary exhibiton. n.p., n.d.

MoSL. Handbook 1953—St Louis. City art museum. Handbook of the collections. St Louis, The museum, 1953

Mount. John Singer Sargent—Mount, Charles Merrill. John Singer Sargent, a biography. N.Y. W. W. Norton & co. 1955

MSE. Catalogue of ports, 1950—Essex institute, Salem, Mass. Additions to the catalogue of portraits in the Essex institute received since 1936. Compiled by R. L. Jackson. Salem, The institute, 1950?

MSM. Handbook—Springfield, Mass. Museum of fine arts. Handbook. 2d ed. Springfield, The museum, 1958

MSt. Country art—Little, Nina Fletcher. Country art in New England, 1790-1840. Sturbridge, Mass. 1960 (Old Sturbridge village booklet series)

Munsterberg—Munsterberg, Hugo. Twentieth century painting. N.Y. Philosophical library, 1951

Murphy. John James Audubon—Murphy, Robert Cushman. John James Audubon, an evaluation of the man and his work. N.Y. New-York Historical society, 1956

MWA. Checklist of portraits—Massachusetts antiquarian society, Worcester, Mass. Checklist of the portraits in the library of the American antiquarian society by F. L. Weis. Worcester, The society, 1947

MWiS. Ex 4 and 7—Sterling and Francine Clark art institute, Williamstown, Mass. Exhibit four and exhibit seven. n.p. [1958]

**MWM. Georgia O'Keeffe**—Worcester art museum. An exhibition by Georgia O'Keeffe. October 4 through December 4, 1960 n.p., n.d.

**Myers**—Myers, Bernard Samuel. Modern art in the making. N.Y. McGraw-Hill book co. 1950

**Myers. Art**—Myers, Bernard Samuel. Art and civilization. N.Y. McGraw-Hill book co. 1917

**NAD. Amer tradition.** National academy of design, N.Y. The American tradition, 1800-1900. N.Y. The academy, 1951

**NAD. Annual ex**—National academy of design, N.Y. Annual exhibition, v 120 (2d half) 1946-v 136, 1961. N.Y. The academy, 1946-1961. 19 numbers.

**NAD. Special ex, 1956**—National academy of design, N.Y. Special exhibition: contemporary prints and watercolors, November 15-December 2, 1956. N.Y. The academy, 1956

**NAI. Hudson valley**—Albany institute of history and art, Albany, N.Y. Hudson valley paintings 1700-1750. Albany, The institute, 1959

**NBuA. Acquisitions 1954-57**—Buffalo fine arts academy. Contemporary art acquisitions 1954-1957. Buffalo, The academy, 1957. 4 numbers

**NBuA. Acquisitions 1957-58.** Buffalo fine arts academy. Contemporary art acquisitions 1957-1958. Buffalo, The academy, 1959

**NBuA. Acquisitions 1959-1961**—Buffalo fine arts academy. Contemporary art acquisitions 1959-1961. Buffalo, The academy, 1961

**NBuA. Catalogue of the ptgs**—Buffalo fine arts academy. Catalogue of the paintings and sculpture in the permanent collection, ed by A. C. Ritchie. Buffalo, The academy, 1949

**NBuA. Contemporary ptgs**—Buffalo fine arts academy. Catalogue of contemporary paintings and sculpture, ed by A. C. Ritchie. Buffalo, The academy, 1949

**NBuA. Eugene Speicher**—Buffalo fine arts academy. Eugene Speicher, a retrospective exhibition of oils and drawings . . . 1908-1949. Held September 29-October 26, 1950. Buffalo, The academy, 1950

**NBuA. Expressionism**—Buffalo fine arts academy. Expressionism in American painting, May 10-June 29, 1952, Albright art gallery, Buffalo, N.Y. Buffalo, The academy, 1952

**NBuA. Fifty ptgs**—Buffalo fine arts academy. Fifty paintings, 1905-1913, the fiftieth anniversary exhibition May 14-June 12, 1955. Buffalo, The academy, 1955

**NBuA. Still**—Buffalo fine arts academy. Paintings by Clyfford Still, Nov. 5-Dec. 13, 1959. n.p., n.d.

**Newmeyer**—Newmeyer, Sarah. Enjoying modern art. N.Y. Reinhold publishing corporation, 1955

**NHMC. Alexander James**—Currier gallery of art, Manchester, N.H. Memorial exhibition: Alexander James, 1890-1946. Manchester, The gallery, 1947

**NHMC. Andrew Wyeth**—Currier gallery of art, Manchester, N.H. Paintings and drawings by Andrew Wyeth. Manchester, The gallery, 1951

**NHMC. Paul Sample**—Currier gallery of art, Manchester, N.H. Paul Sample retrospective exhibition July 15 to September 15, 1948. Manchester, The gallery, 1948

**NIC. Arthur G. Dove**—Cornell university, Ithaca, N.Y. Andrew Dickson White museum of art. Arthur G. Dove, 1880-1946: a retrospective exhibition, November 1954. Ithaca, The university, 1954

**NJMo. Forty years**—The Montclair art museum, Montclair, N.J. Forty years of collecting. An exhibition presenting the major American paintings in the permanent collection of The Montclair art museum. Montclair, The museum, 1953

**NJMo. Your Montclair art museum**—The Montclair art museum, Montclair, N.J. Your Montclair art museum, its collections, activities, services. Summit, N.J. John F. McKenna co. 1955

**NJN. Early N.J. artists**—The Newark museum of art, Newark, N.J. Early New Jersey artists, 18th and 19th centuries. March 7-May 10. Newark, The museum, 1957

**NJN. Weber**—The Newark museum, Newark, N.J. Max Weber retrospective exhibition October 1-November 15, 1959. Newark, The museum, 1959

**NJP. Amer folk art**—Princeton University. American folk art, a collection of paintings presented in 1958 by Edward Duff Balken . . . to the art museum of Princeton university. n.p., n.d.

**NNHS. Lockman**—The New-York historical society. De Witt McClellan Lockman memorial exhibition March 14-May 15, 1958. N.Y. The society, 1958

**NNHS. Waldron Phoenix Belknap coll**—The New-York historical society. The Waldron Phoenix Belknap, jr. collection of portraits and silver . . . Cambridge, Harvard university press, 1955

**NNSG. Handbook**—The Solomon R. Guggenheim museum, N.Y. A handbook to the collection. N.Y. The museum, 1959

**NNSG. Younger Amer ptrs**—The Solomon R. Guggenheim museum, N.Y. Younger American painters; a selection, May 12 to July 25, 1954. N.Y. The museum, 1954

**NoCR. Catalogue**—North Carolina museum of art, Raleigh. Catalogue of paintings including three sets of tapestries by W. R. Valentiner. Raleigh, The museum, 1956

**NSP. Sportscapes**—The Parrish art museum, Southampton, N.Y. Sportscapes: hunting—fowling—angling. A loan exhibition. July 25-August 24, 1959. Southampton, The museum, 1959

NSP. **William Merritt Chase**—The Parrish art museum, Southampton, N.Y. William Merritt Chase, 1849-1916: a retrospective exhibition, June 30-July 27, 1957. Southampton, The museum, 1957

NSyE. **The Eight**—Everson museum of art of Syracuse and Onondaga county, N.Y. The Eight. Syracuse, 1958

NUM. **Art across America**—Munson-Williams-Proctor institute, Utica, N.Y. Art across America, a selection of American art from collections open to the public in communities of one hundred thousand or less. Utica, The institute, 1960

NUM. **Root bequest**—Munson-Williams-Proctor institute, Utica, N.Y. Edward Wales Root bequest. Utica, The institute, 1961

NYG. **Fine art**—New York graphic society —Fine art reproductions: old and modern masters. N.Y. The society, 1946 (and supplement, 1948) Consecutively paged with 3 indexes

OCiM. **Guide**—Cincinnati art museum. Guide to the collections, 1950? n.p., n.d.

OCiM. **Ptgs by the Peale family**—Cincinnati art museum. Paintings by the Peale family [exhibited] October 1 to 31, 1954. Cincinnati, The museum, 1954

OCiM. **Rediscoveries**—Cincinnati art museum. Rediscoveries in American painting. Cincinnati, The museum, 1955

OCl. **Feininger**—Cleveland museum of art. The work of Lyonel Feininger, catalogue of an exhibition sponsored by The Print club of Cleveland and The Cleveland museum of art, November 2-December 9, 1951. Cleveland, The museum, 1951

OCl. **Handbook**—Cleveland museum of art. Handbook. Cleveland, The museum, 1958

OCl. **Keller**—Cleveland. Institute of art. The Henry G. Keller memorial exhibition . . . sponsored by The Cleveland institute of art and The Cleveland museum of art. Cleveland, The museum, 1950

OCl. **Portrait miniatures**—Cleveland museum of art. Portrait miniatures: the Edward B. Greene collection. Cleveland, The museum, 1951

OCl. **Some contemporary works**—Cleveland museum of art. Some contemporary works of art. Cleveland, The museum, 1958

OCl. **Sommer**—Cleveland museum of art. The William Sommer memorial exhibition . . . Cleveland, The museum, 1950

OCo. **George Bellows**—Columbus gallery of fine arts. Paintings by George Bellows, March 21 to April 21, 1957. n.p., n.d.

O'Hara. **Jackson Pollock**—O'Hara, Frank. Jackson Pollock. N.Y. George Braziller, 1959 (Great American artists series)

O'Neal—O'Neal, William B. Primitive into painter, life and letters of John Toole. Charlottesville, University of Virginia press, 1960

OrPA. **C. S. Price**—Portland art museum and the Walker art center. C. S. Price, a memorial exhibition . . . Portland, Ore. Portland art association, 1951

OrPA. **Ptgs & sculptures**—Portland art museum, Portland, Ore. Paintings and sculptures of the Pacific northwest: Oregon, Washington, British Columbia, Portland, The museum, 1959

OT. **Contemp Amer ptgs**—Toledo museum of art. Contemporary American paintings: The Mau collection. Toledo, The museum, 1947

OT. **John Sloan**—See Goodrich. John Sloan

OT. **Travelers in Arcadia.** See MiD. Travelers in Arcadia

OYB. **Accessions**—Butler institute of American art, Youngstown, Ohio. Special exhibit of accessions during the past two years. Youngstown, The institute, 1956-1958

OYB. **Annual**—Butler institute of American art, Youngstown, Ohio. Annual midyear show, 1948-1960. Youngstown, The institute, 1948-1960 (1948-1952 has title Annual new year show) 12 numbers

OYB. **Blythe**—Butler institute of American art, Youngstown, Ohio. An exhibition of the work of David G. Blythe. Youngstown, The institute, 1947

OYB. **Catalogue, 1951**—Butler institute of American art, Youngstown, Ohio. Catalogue of the permanent collection of American art. Youngstown, The institute, 1951

OYB. **Supplement**—Butler institute of American art, Youngstown, Ohio. Supplement to the collection of the permanent collection of American art, Youngstown, The institute, 1951

OYB. **Supplement, 1959**—Butler institute of American art. Supplement to the Catalogues of the permanent collection (published October 1951 and October 1954) Youngstown, The institute, 1959

PA. **Annual ex, 1947-1961**—Pennsylvania academy of the fine arts, Philadelphia. Annual exhibition of painting and sculpture, 1947-1961, Philadelphia, The academy, 1947-1961. 13 numbers

PA. **Carles**—Pennsylvania academy of the fine arts and the Philadelphia museum of art. Memorial exhibition, Arthur B. Carles, March 18 through April 12, 1953. n.p., n.d.

Pearson. **Mod renaissance**—Pearson, Ralph M. Modern renaissance in American art presenting the work and philosophy of 54 distinguished artists. N.Y. Harper & brothers, 1954

Pearson, H. **The man Whistler**—Pearson, Hesketh. The man Whistler. N.Y. Harper & brothers, 1952

Pierson—Pierson, William Henry and Davidson, Martha, eds. Arts of the United States, a pictorial survey. N.Y. McGraw-Hill book co. 1960

Ponente. **Mod ptg, 1960**—Ponente, Nello. Modern painting, contemporary trends. N.Y. Skira, 1960

Porter. Thomas Eakins—Porter, Fairfield. Thomas Eakins. N.Y. George Braziller, 1959 (The great American artists series)

Pousette-Dart. Amer ptg—Pousette-Dart, Nathaniel. American painting today. N.Y. Hastings house, 1958

PPC. Amer classics—Carnegie institute, Pittsburgh. American classics of the nineteenth century. Pittsburgh, The institute, 1957

PPC. International ex, 1950-1961/62. Carnegie institute, Pittsburgh. Dept of fine arts. The Pittsburgh international exhibition of paintings. Pittsburgh, The institute, 1950-1961. (1958 entitled: The 1958 Pittsburgh bicentennial international exhibition of contemporary painting and sculpture) 6 numbers

PPC. Ptg in the U.S. 1949—Carnegie institute, Pittsburgh. Painting in the United States, 1949. Pittsburgh, The institute, 1949

PPhM. Arensberg coll—Philadelphia museum of art. The Louise and Walter Arensberg collection: v 1: 20th century section. Philadelphia, The museum, 1954

PPhM. Gallatin coll—Philadelphia museum of art. A. E. Gallatin collection, "Museum of living art." Philadelphia, The museum, 1954

PR. Catalogue—Reading public museum and art gallery, Reading, Pa. Catalogue of paintings. 4th ed. Reading, The museum, 1953

Pulitzer—Pulitzer, Louise and Pulitzer, Joseph. Modern painting, drawing & sculpture collected by Louise and Joseph Pulitzer. Cambridge, Fogg art museum, 1958 2v

Rathbone—Rathbone, Perry Townsend, ed. Westward the way: the character and development of the Louisiana Territory as seen by artists and writers of the nineteenth century. St Louis, City art museum, 1954

Rathbun—Rathbun, Mary Chalmers and Hayes, Bartlett, H. Layman's guide to modern art: paintings for a scientific age. N.Y. Oxford university press, 1949

Raynal. History v3—Raynal, Maurice. History of modern painting, v3: from Picasso to surrealism. Geneva, Skira, 1950

Read. Art now 1948—Read, Herbert. Art now; an introduction to the theory of modern painting and sculpture. new ed. N.Y. Pitman publishing co., 1948

Read. Concise history—Read, Herbert. A concise history of modern painting. N.Y. Frederick A. Praeger, 1959

Rewald. History of impressionism—Rewald, John. The history of impressionism. 2d ed. N.Y. The museum of modern art, 1946

Richardson. Ptg in America—Richardson, Edgar Preston. Painting in America: the story of 450 years. N.Y. Thomas Y. Crowell co. 1956 (Growth of America series)

Richardson. Travelers in Arcadia. See MiD. Travelers in Arcadia

Richardson. Washington Allston—Richardson, Edgar Preston. Washington Allston, a study of the romantic artist in America. Chicago, University of Chicago press, 1948

Riley. Your art heritage—Riley, Olive Lasette. Your art heritage. N.Y. McGraw-Hill book co. 1952

Ritchie, Andrew Carnduff. Abstract ptg and sculpture. See MMA. Abstract

Ritchie, Andrew Carnduff. Demuth. See MMA. Demuth

Ritchie, Andrew Carnduff. Watkins. See MMA. Watkins

Robb. Art 1953 ed—Robb, David Metheny and Garrison, Jesse James. Art in the western world. 3d ed. Harper & brothers, 1953

Robb. Harper history—Robb, David Metheny. The Harper history of painting: the occidental tradition. N.Y. Harper & brothers, 1951

Roberts. Mark Tobey—Roberts, Colette. Mark Tobey. N.Y. Grove press, 1959

Robertson. Jackson Pollock—Robertson, Bryan. Jackson Pollock. N.Y. Harry H. Abrams, 1960

Rodman. Horace Pippin—Rodman, Selden. Horace Pippin, a Negro painter in America. N.Y. Quadrangle press, 1947

Rodman. Portrait of the artist—Rodman, Selden. Portrait of the artist as an American: Ben Shahn; a biography with pictures. N.Y. Harper & brothers, 1951

Roos—Roos, Frank John. An illustrated handbook of art history. rev ed N.Y. The Macmillan co. 1954

Rosenblum—Rosenblum, Robert. Cubism and twentieth-century art. N.Y. Harry N. Abrams, 1961

Schwabacher. Arshile Gorky—Schwabacher, Ethel K. Arshile Gorky. With a preface by Lloyd Goodrich and an introduction by Meyer Schapiro. N.Y. Published for the Whitney museum of American art by The Macmillan co. 1957

Sears. Highlights—Sears, Clara Endicott. Highlights among the Hudson river artists. Boston, Houghton Mifflin co. 1947

Seiberling—Seiberling, Frank. Looking into art. N.Y. Henry Holt and co. 1959

Sellers. C. W. Peale v2—Sellers, Charles Coleman. Charles Willson Peale, v2: later life, 1790-1827. Philadelphia. American philosophical society, 1947

Selz. Mark Rothko. See MMA. Rothko

Selz. New images—Selz, Peter. New images of man with statements by the artists. N.Y. Museum of modern art in collaboration with the Baltimore museum of art, 1959

Sewall. History of western art—Sewall, John Ives. A history of western art. N.Y. Henry Holt and co. 1953

Shahn—Shahn, Ben. Ben Shahn, his graphic art. Text by James Thrall Soby. N.Y. George Braziller, 1957

**Sizer. John Trumbull**—Sizer, Theodore. Works of Colonel John Trumbull, artist of the American revolution. New Haven, Yale university press, 1950

**Soby. Ben Shahn**—Soby, James Thrall. Ben Shahn. N.Y. Museum of modern art, 1947 (Penguin modern painters)

**Sweet**—Sweet, Frederick A. Sargent, Whistler and Mary Cassatt: The Art institute of Chicago. Jan. 14 through Feb. 25, 1954; the Metropolitan museum of art, March 25 through May 23, 1954. Chicago, The institute, 1954

**Taylor. Fifty centuries, 1954 ed.** Taylor, Francis Henry. Fifty centuries of art. N.Y. Harper & brothers, 1954

**Time. 300 years**—Time, the weekly news magazine. Three hundred years of American painting by Alexander Eliot. N.Y. 1957

**Tolman**—Tolman, Ruel Pardee. The life and works of Edward Greene Malbone. N.Y. The New-York historical society, 1958. (New-York historical society: The John Divine Jones Fund series XIII)

**UNESCO. 1860-1949**—United nations educational, scientific and cultural organization. Catalogue of colour reproductions of painting from 1860 to 1949. Paris, UNESCO, 1949

**UNESCO. 1860-1955**—United nations educational, scientific and cultural organization. Catalogue of colour reproductions of paintings—1860 to 1955. 3d ed. Paris, UNESCO, 1955

**UNESCO. 1860-1959**—United nations educational, scientific and cultural organization. Catalogue of colour reproductions of paintings—1860 to 1959. 5th ed. Paris, UNESCO, 1959

**UNESCO. Prior to 1860**—United nations educational, scientific and cultural organization. Catalogue of colour reproductions of paintings prior to 1860. Paris, UNESCO, 1950

**UNESCO. Prior to 1860 3d ed.**—United nations educational, scientific and cultural organization. Catalogue of colour reproductions of paintings prior to 1860, 3d ed. Paris, UNESCO, 1955

**UNESCO. Prior to 1860 5th ed.**—United nations educational, scientific and cultural organization. Catalogue of colour reproductions of paintings prior to 1860. 5th ed. Paris, UNESCO, 1960

**Upjohn**—Upjohn, Edward Miller; Wingert, P. S.; and Mahler, J. G. History of world art. N.Y. Oxford university press, 1949

**U.S. National Capital sesquicentennial com**—U.S. The National Capital sesquicentennial commission. American processional 1492-1900. Washington, Corcoran gallery of art, 1950

**Vail. Stuyvesant ports**—Vail, Robert William Glenroie. The case of the Stuyvesant portraits. N.Y. New-York historical society, 1958

**VR. Amer ptg**—Virginia museum of fine arts, Richmond. American painting. 1954, 1958. Richmond, The museum, 1954, 1958

**VR. Biennial ex**—Virginia museum of fine arts, Richmond. Biennial exhibition of contemporary American paintings, v6, 1948. Richmond, The museum, 1948

**VR. Healy's sitters**—Virginia museum of fine arts, Richmond. A souvenir of the exhibition entitled Healy's sitters . . . between the years 1837 and 1899. Richmond, The museum, 1950

**VRV. William James Hubard**—Valentine museum, Richmond. William James Hubard, 1807-1862, a concurrent survey and exhibition, January, 1948. Richmond, The museum, 1948

**VWR. Amer. folk art**—The Abby Aldrich Rockefeller folk art collection, Williamsburg, Va. American folk art. Williamsburg, Colonial Williamsburg, 1959

**VWR. Folk art**—The Abby Aldrich Rockefeller collection, Williamsburg, Va. Folk art collection, a descriptive catalogue by Nina Fetcher Little. Williamsburg, Colonial Williamsburg, 1957

**Walker. Ptgs from America**—Walker, John. Paintings from America. Baltimore, Penguin books, 1951 (Penguin modern painters)

**Weir. Recollections**—Weir, John Ferguson. Recollections, ed by Theodore Sizer. N.Y. New-York historical society, 1957

**Wight. Arthur G. Dove**—Wight, Frederick Stallknecht. Arthur G. Dove. Berkeley, University of California press, 1958

**Wight. Hans Hofmann**—Wight, Frederick Stallknecht. Hans Hofmann. Berkeley, University of California press, 1957

**Wight. Hyman Bloom**—Wight, Frederick Stallknecht. Hyman Bloom: Albright art gallery, Institute of contemporary art, Lowe gallery, M. H. De Young memorial museum, Whitney museum of American art. Boston, Institute of contemporary art, 1954

**Wight. Milestones**—Wight, Frederick Stallknecht. Milestones of American painting in our century. N.Y. Chanticleer press, 1948

**Wight. Milton Avery**—Wight, Frederick Stallknecht. Milton Avery: The Baltimore museum of art, The Institute of contemporary art, Loew gallery, Phillips gallery, Wadsworth atheneum. Baltimore, Baltimore museum of art, 1952?

**Wight. Morris Graves**—Wight, Frederick Stallknecht; Baur, John I. H.; and Phillips, Duncan. Morris Graves. Berkeley, University of California press, 1956

**WiMiA. Amer ptg 1760-1960**—Milwaukee art center, Milwaukee, Wis. American painting 1760-1960; a selection of 125 paintings from the collection of Mr and Mrs Lawrence A. Fleischman, Detroit. Milwaukee art center, March 3rd through April 3rd, 1960. Milwaukee, The center, 1960

**WiMiA. Crawford**—Milwaukee art center, Milwaukee, Wis. Ralston Crawford, February 6-March 9, 1958. Milwaukee, The center, 1958

**WiMiA. Raphaelle Peale**—Milwaukee art center, Milwaukee, Wis. Raphaelle Peale, exhibition January 15th, through February 15th 1959; M. Knoedler & co., N.Y. March 2nd through March 31st, 1959. n.p., n.d.

**WMAA. Annual ex**—Whitney museum of American art. Annual exhibition: sculpture, paintings, watercolors, drawings, 1948-1959. N.Y. The museum 1948-1959. 11 numbers

**WMAA. Arshile Gorky.** See Schwabacher. Arshile Gorky

**WMAA. Blakelock**—Whitney museum of American art. Ralph Blakelock centenary exhibition in celebration of the centennial of the City college of New York. April 22 to May 22, 1947. N.Y. The museum, 1947

**WMAA. Contemp Amer ptg**—Whitney museum of American art. Annual exhibition of contemporary American painting, 1955/56-1959/60. N.Y. The museum, 1956-1960. 5 numbers

**WMAA. Four Amer expressionists**—Whitney museum of American art. Four American expressionists: Doris Caesar; Chaim Gross; Karl Knaths; Abraham Rattner. N.Y. The museum, 1959

**WMAA. George Grosz.** See Baur. George Grosz

**WMAA. Hyman Bloom.** See Wight. Hyman Bloom

**WMAA. John Sloan.** See Goodrich. John Sloan

**WMAA. Juliana Force**—Whitney museum of American art. Juliana Force and American art, a memorial exhibition Sept. 24-Oct. 30, 1949. N.Y. The museum, 1949

**WMAA. Marsh**—Whitney museum of American art. Reginald Marsh. Exhibition and catalogue: Whitney, Columbus, Detroit, St Louis, Dallas, Los Angeles, Santa Barbara. N.Y. The museum, 1955 (Text by Lloyd Goodrich)

**WMAA. Maurer.** See McCausland. Maurer

**WMAA. Max Weber.** See Goodrich. Max Weber

**WMAA. Museum and its friends, 1958**—Whitney museum of American art. The museum and its friends: twentieth century American art from collections of the friends of the Whitney museum, 1958. N.Y. The museum, 1958

**WMAA. Museum and its friends, 1959**—Whitney museum of American art. The museum and its friends: eighteen living American artists selected by the friends of the Whitney museum. N.Y. The museum, 1959

**WMAA. Neuberger collection**—Whitney museum of American art. Roy and Marie Neuberger collection: modern American painting and sculpture. n.p. 1955?

**WMAA. New decade**—Whitney museum of American art. New decade: 35 American painters and sculptors. N.Y. The museum, 1955

**WMAA. New images of man.** See Selz. New images

**WMAA. Pioneers**—Whitney museum of American art. Pioneers of modern art in America. April 9-May 19, 1946. N.Y. The museum, 1946

**WMAA. Ryder**—Whitney museum of American art. Albert P. Ryder, Centenary exhibition October 18 to November 30, 1947. N.Y. The museum, 1947

**WMAA. Sara Roby**—Whitney museum of American art. The collection of the Sara Roby foundation, April 29-June 14, 1959. N.Y. The museum, 1959

**WMAA. Young America 1957**—Whitney museum of American art. Young American art—Young America 1957; thirty American painters and sculptors under thirty-five. N.Y. The museum, 1957

**WMAA. Young America 1960**—Whitney museum of American art. Young America 1960; thirty American painters under thirty-six. N.Y. The museum, 1960

**WMAA. Zorach**—Whitney museum of American art. William Zorach. N.Y. The museum, 1959

# KEY TO SYMBOLS USED FOR LOCATIONS
## OF PAINTINGS

**AP** Phoenix art museum, Phoenix, Ariz.

**ATeS** Arizona state college, Tempe, Ariz.

**ATU** University of Arizona, Tucson, Ariz.

**CanO** National gallery of Canada, Ottawa

**CLA** Los Angeles county museum of history, science and art, Los Angeles, Calif.

**CLAU** University of California, Los Angeles, Calif.

**CLAUS** University of Southern California, Los Angeles, Calif.

**CoD** Denver art museum, Denver, Colo.

**CoS** Colorado Springs fine arts center, Colorado Springs, Colo.

**CP** Pasadena art institute, Pasadena, Calif.

**CSB** Santa Barbara museum of art, Santa Barbara, Calif.

**CSC** Crocker art gallery, Sacramento, Calif.

**CSD** Fine arts society of San Diego, San Diego, Calif.

**CSFD** M. H. De Young memorial museum, San Francisco, Calif.

**CSFM** San Francisco museum of art, San Francisco, Calif.

**CSFP** California palace of the legion of honor, San Francisco, Calif.

**CtHW** Wadsworth atheneum, Hartford, Conn.

**CtLH** Litchfield historical society, Litchfield, Conn.

**CtNB** New Britain institute, New Britain, Conn.

**CtNH** New Haven colony historical society, New Haven, Conn.

**CtNL** Lyman Allyn museum, New London, Conn.

**CtY** Yale university, New Haven, Conn.

**DC** The Corcoran gallery of art, Washington, D.C.

**DCap** The Capitol, Washington, D.C.

**DeW** Wilmington society of the fine arts, Wilmington, Del.

**DeWin** Henry Francis Du Pont Winterthur museum, Greenville, Del.

**DF** Freer gallery of art, Washington, D.C.

**DN** National gallery of art, Washington, D.C.

**DNC** Smithsonian institution. National collection of fine arts, Washington, D.C.

**DP** Phillips collection, Washington, D.C.

**DW** The White house, Washington, D.C.

**ELK** Kensington palace, London, England

**ELN** National gallery, London, England

**ELNP** National portrait gallery, London, England

**ELT** Tate gallery, London, England

**FaW** Norton gallery and school of art, West Palm Beach, Fla.

**FPL** The Louvre, Paris, France

**FPP** Petit palais, Paris, France

**GAtM** Georgia museum of art, Athens, Ga.

**GST** Telfair academy, Savannah, Ga.

**HaH** Honolulu academy of arts, Honolulu, Hawaii

**IaDa** Davenport municipal art gallery, Davenport, Iowa

**IaDM** Des Moines art center, Des Moines, Iowa

**IaIU** University of Iowa, Iowa City, Iowa

**IBM** International business machines corporation, New York, N.Y.

**ICA** Art institute of Chicago, Chicago, Ill.

**ICH** Chicago historical society, Chicago, Ill.

**ICN** Newberry library, Chicago, Ill.

**InBu** Indiana university, Bloomington, Ind.

**InIJ** John Herron art institute, Indianapolis, Ind.

**InR** Richmond art association, Richmond, Ind.

**InTH** Sheldon Swope art gallery, Terre Haute, Ind.

**IU** Krannert art museum, University of Illinois, Urbana, Ill.

**KLU** Museum of art, University of Kansas, Lawrence, Kans.

**KW** Wichita art museum, Wichita, Kans.

**KyLS** J. B. Speed memorial, Louisville, Ky.

**MAC** Amherst college, Amherst, Mass.

**MAP** Addison gallery of American art, Phillips academy, Andover, Mass.

| | | | |
|---|---|---|---|
| **MB** | Boston museum of fine arts, Boston, Mass. | **MoSLH** | Missouri historical society, St Louis, Mo. |
| **MBA** | Boston athenaeum, Boston, Mass. | **MoSLM** | Mercantile library association of St Louis, Mo. |
| **MBF** | Faneuil hall, Boston, Mass. | **MoSLW** | Washington university, St Louis, Mo. |
| **MBH** | Massachusetts historical society, Boston, Mass. | **MoSp** | Springfield art museum, Springfield, Mo. |
| **MBIC** | Institute of contemporary art, Boston, Mass. | **MPB** | Berkshire athenaeum and museum, Pittsfield, Mass. |
| **MBT** | Trinity church, Boston, Mass. | **MSE** | Essex institute, Salem, Mass. |
| **MCH** | Harvard university, Cambridge, Mass. Same symbol for Fogg art museum. | **MSG** | George Walter Vincent Smith art gallery, Springfield, Mass. |
| **MCoL** | Free public library, Concord, Mass. | **MSM** | Springfield museum of fine arts, Springfield, Mass. |
| **MdAn** | United States naval academy, Annapolis, Md. | **MSP** | Peabody museum, Salem, Mass. |
| **MdBH** | Maryland historical society, Baltimore, Md. | **MSt** | Old Sturbridge Village, Sturbridge, Mass. |
| **MdBM** | Baltimore museum of art, Baltimore, Md. | **MWA** | American antiquarian society, Worcester, Mass. |
| **MdBMu** | Municipal museum (Peale museum), Baltimore, Md. | **MWiC** | Williams college, Williamstown, Mass. |
| **MdBP** | Peabody institute, Baltimore, Md. | **MWiS** | Sterling and Francine Clark institute, Williamstown, Mass. |
| **MdBW** | Walters art gallery, Baltimore, Md. | **MWM** | Worcester art museum, Worcester, Mass. |
| **MdHW** | Washington county museum of fine arts, Hagerstown, Md. | **NAD** | National academy of design, New York, N.Y. |
| **MeB** | Bowdoin college, Brunswick, Me. | **NAI** | Albany institute of history and art, Albany, N.Y. |
| **MeC** | Colby college, Waterville, Me. | **NAS** | New York State capitol, Albany, N.Y. |
| **MeR** | William A. Farnsworth library and art museum, Rockland, Me. | **NBH** | Long Island historical society, Brooklyn, N.Y. |
| **MexS** | Supreme court building, Mexico, D.F. | **NBM** | Brooklyn museum, Brooklyn, N.Y. |
| **MiA** | University of Michigan, Ann Arbor, Mich. | **NBuA** | Albright-Knox art gallery, Buffalo, N.Y. |
| **MiC** | Cranbrook academy, Bloomfield Hills, Mich. | **NCa** | Canajoharie library and art gallery, Canajoharie, N.Y. |
| **MiD** | Detroit institute of fine arts, Detroit, Mich. | **NCB** | National museum of baseball, Cooperstown, N.Y. |
| **MiM** | Hackley art gallery, Muskegon, Mich. | **NCHA** | New York State historical society, Cooperstown, N.Y. |
| **MLL** | William Lane foundations, Leominster, Mass. | **NeL** | University of Nebraska, Lincoln, Nebr. |
| **MM** | Metropolitan museum of art, New York, N.Y. | **NeO** | Joslyn art museum, Omaha, Nebr. |
| **MMA** | Museum of modern art, New York, N.Y. | **NHD** | Dartmouth college, Hanover, N.H. |
| **MnMI** | Minneapolis institute of arts, Minneapolis, Minn. | **NHMC** | Currier gallery of art, Manchester, N.H. |
| **MnMW** | Walker art center, Minneapolis, Minn. | **NHP** | Warner house association, Portsmouth, N.H. |
| **MNS** | Smith college, Northampton, Mass. | **NIC** | Cornell University, Ithaca, N.Y. |
| **MnSH** | Minneapolis historical society, St Paul, Minn. | **NJF** | Monmouth county historical society, Freehold, N.J. |
| **MnSJ** | Jerome Hill reference library, St Paul, Minn. | **NJMo** | Montclair art museum, Montclair, N.J. |
| **MnU** | University of Minnesota, Minneapolis, Minn. | **NJN** | Newark museum association, Newark, N.J. |
| **MoKN** | William Rockhill Nelson gallery of art, Kansas City, Mo. | **NJP** | The Art museum, Princeton university, Princeton, N.J. |
| **MonH** | State capitol, Helena, Mont. | **NKS** | Senate house museum, Kingston, N.Y. |
| **MoSL** | City art museum, St Louis, Mo. | | |
| **MoSLB** | Boatmen's national bank, St Louis, Mo. | **NMS** | New Mexico museum of art, Santa Fe, N.M. |

| | | | |
|---|---|---|---|
| NNAJ | American Jewish historical society, New York, N.Y. | PA | Pennsylvania academy of the fine arts, Philadelphia, Pa. |
| NNAM | American museum of natural history, New York, N.Y. | PH | Historical society of Pennsylvania, Philadelphia, Pa. |
| NNCH | New York. City Hall, New York, N.Y. | PMB | Barnes foundation, Merion, Pa. |
| | | PPC | Carnegie institute, Pittsburgh, Pa. |
| NNCo | Cooper union, New York, N.Y. | PPD | Duquesne club, Pittsburgh, Pa. |
| NNHS | New-York historical society, New York, N.Y. | PPhA | American philosophical society, Philadelphia, Pa. |
| NNMC | Museum of the City of New York, New York, N.Y. | PPhI | Independence hall, Philadelphia, Pa. |
| NNPL | New York public library, New York, N.Y. | PPhJ | Jefferson medical college, Philadelphia, Pa. |
| NNSG | Solomon R. Guggenheim museum, New York, N.Y. | PPhL | Library company of Philadelphia, Philadelphia, Pa. |
| NNSL | St Luke's hospital, New York, N.Y. | PPhM | Philadelphia museum of art, Philadelphia, Pa. |
| NNSR | New school of social research, New York, N.Y. | PPhU | Union league of Philadelphia, Pa. |
| | | PPhUn | University of Pennsylvania, Philadelphia, Pa. |
| NNU | Union league club, New York, N.Y. | PR | Reading museum, Reading, Pa. |
| NoCG | University of North Carolina. Greensboro, N.C. | PW | Westmoreland county museum of art, Greensburg, Pa. |
| NoCR | North Carolina museum of art, Raleigh, N.C. (Formerly North Carolina State art gallery) | RNH | Newport historical society, Newport, R.I. |
| | | RNR | Redwood library and athenaeum, Newport, R.I. |
| NOR | Remington art memorial, Ogdensburg, N.Y. | RPAt | Providence athenaeum, Providence, R.I. |
| NR | Rochester memorial art gallery, Rochester, N.Y. | RPB | Brown university, Providence, R.I. |
| NScU | Union college, Schenectady, N.Y. | RPHS | Rhode Island historical society, Providence, R.I. |
| NSP | Parrish art museum, Southampton, N.Y. | RPS | Rhode Island school of design, Providence, R.I. |
| NStS | Suffolk museum, Stony Brook, N.Y. | SCCG | Gibbes art gallery, Charleston, S.C. |
| NSU | Syracuse university, Syracuse, N.Y. | ScG | Glasgow art gallery and museum, Glasgow, Scotland |
| NSyE | Everson museum of art of Syracuse and Onondaga county, Syracuse, N.Y. | SwB | Kunstmuseum, Basel, Switzerland |
| | | TMB | Brooks memorial art gallery, Memphis, Tenn. |
| NUM | Munson-Williams-Proctor institute, Utica, N.Y. | TNF | Fisk university, Nashville, Tenn. |
| NWP | United States military academy, West Point, N.Y. | TxD | Dallas museum of fine arts, Dallas, Tex. |
| OCiM | Cincinnati art museum, Cincinnati, Ohio | TxF | Fort Worth museum of art, Fort Worth, Tex. |
| OCiT | Taft museum, Cincinnati, Ohio | TxH | Houston museum of fine arts, Houston, Tex. |
| OCl | Cleveland museum of art, Cleveland, Ohio | TxSa | Witte memorial museum, San Antonio, Tex. |
| OCo | Columbus gallery of fine arts, Columbus, Ohio | VCU | University of Virginia, Charlottesville, Va. |
| OCoA | Ohio state archaeological and historical society, Columbus, Ohio | VR | Virginia museum of fine arts, Richmond, Va. |
| | | VRCM | Confederate memorial institute, Richmond, Va. |
| OkNU | University of Oklahoma, Norman, Okla. | VRV | Valentine museum, Richmond, Va. |
| OkT | Philbrook art center, Tulsa, Okla. | VtMS | Sheldon museum, Middlebury, Vt. |
| OkTT | Thomas Gilchrist institute of American history and art, Tulsa, Okla. | VWC | College of William and Mary, Williamsburg, Va. |
| | | VWR | The Abby Aldrich Rockefeller folk art collection, Williamsburg, Va. |
| OOb | Oberlin college, Oberlin, Ohio | | |
| OrPA | Portland art museum, Portland, Ore. | WaS | Seattle art museum, Seattle, Wash. |
| OrPH | Oregon historical society, Portland, Ore. | WaSU | University of Washington, Seattle, Wash. |
| OT | Toledo museum of art, Toledo, Ohio | WiMiA | Milwaukee art center, Milwaukee, Wis. Same symbol for Milwaukee art institute |
| OYB | Butler institute of American art, Youngstown, Ohio | WMAA | Whitney museum of American art, New York, N.Y. |

# LIST OF INSTITUTIONS WITH SYMBOLS
## USED IN THIS BOOK

The Abby Aldrich Rockefeller folk art collection, Williamsburg, Va. VWR

Addison gallery of American art, Phillips academy, Andover, Mass. MAP

Albany institute of history and art, Albany, N.Y. NAI

Albright-Knox art gallery, Buffalo, N.Y. NBuA

American antiquarian society, Worcester, Mass. MWA

American Jewish historical society, New York, N.Y. NNAJ

American museum of natural history, New York, N.Y. NNAM

American philosophical society, Philadelphia, Pa. PPhA

Amherst college, Amherst, Mass. MAC

Arizona state college, Tempe, Ariz. ATeS

Art association of Indianapolis, Ind. InIJ

Art institute of Chicago, Chicago, Ill. ICA

Baltimore, Md. Municipal museum (Peale museum) MdBMu

Baltimore museum of art, Baltimore, Md. MdBM

Barnes foundation, Merion, Pa. PMB

Basel, Switzerland. Kunstmuseum. SwB

Berkshire athenaeum and museum, Pittsfield, Mass. MPB

Boatmen's national bank, St Louis, Mo. MoSLB

Boston athenaeum, Boston, Mass. MBA

Boston museum of fine arts, Boston, Mass. MB

Bowdoin college, Brunswick, Me. MeB

Brooklyn museum, Brooklyn, N.Y. NBM

Brooks memorial art gallery, Memphis, Tenn. TMB

Brown university, Providence, R.I. RPB

Buffalo fine arts academy, Buffalo, N.Y. Albright-Knox art gallery. NBuA

Butler institute of American art, Youngstown, Ohio. OYB

California palace of the legion of honor, San Francisco, Calif. CSFP

Canajoharie library and art gallery, Canajoharie, N.Y. NCa

The Capitol, Washington, D.C. DCap

Carnegie institute, Pittsburgh, Pa. PPC

Carolina art association. Gibbes art gallery, Charleston, S.C. SCCG

Chicago art institute, Chicago, Ill. ICA

Chicago historical society, Chicago, Ill. ICH

Cincinnati art museum, Cincinnati, Ohio OCiM

City art museum, St. Louis, Mo. MoSL

Cleveland museum of art, Cleveland, Ohio. OCl

Colby college, Waterville, Me. MeC

College of William and Mary, Williamsburg, Va. VWC

Colorado Springs fine arts center, Colorado Springs, Colo. CoS

Columbus gallery of fine arts, Columbus, Ohio. OCo

Concord, Mass. Free public library. MCoL

Confederate memorial institute, Richmond, Va. VRCM

Cooper union, New York, N.Y. NNCo

The Corcoran gallery of art, Washington, D.C. DC

Cornell university, Ithaca, N.Y. White art museum. NIC

Cranbrook academy, Bloomfield Hills, Mich. MiC

Crocker art gallery, Sacramento, Calif. CSC

Currier gallery of art, Manchester, N.H. NHMC

Dallas museum of fine arts, Dallas, Tex. TxD

Dartmouth college, Hanover, N.H. NHD

Davenport municipal art gallery, Davenport, Iowa. IaDa

Denver art museum, Denver, Colo. CoD

Des Moines art center, Des Moines, Iowa. IaDM

Detroit institute of arts, Detroit, Mich. MiD

De Young memorial museum, San Francisco, Calif. CSFD

Duquesne club. Pittsburgh, Pa. PPD

Essex institute, Salem, Mass. MSE

Everson museum of art of Syracuse and Onondaga county, Syracuse, N.Y. NSyE

Faneuil hall, Boston, Mass. MBF

Fine arts society of San Diego, San Diego, Calif. CSD

Fisk university, Nashville, Tenn. TNF

Fogg art museum, Harvard university, Cambridge, Mass. MCH

Fort Worth museum of art, Fort Worth, Tex. TxF

Freer gallery of art, Washington, D.C. DF

George Walter Vincent Smith gallery, Springfield, Mass. MSG

Georgia museum of art, Athens, Ga. GAtM

Gibbes art gallery, Charleston, S.C. SCCG

Glasgow art gallery and museum, Glasgow, Scotland. ScG

Guggenheim museum, New York, N.Y. NNSG

Hackley art gallery, Muskegon, Mich. MiM

Harvard university, Cambridge, Mass. MCH

Henry Francis Du Pont Winterthur museum, Greenville, Del. DeWin

Historical society of Pennsylvania, Philadelphia, Pa. PH

Honolulu academy of arts, Honolulu, Hawaii. HaH

Houston museum of fine arts, Houston, Tex. TxH

Independence hall, Philadelphia, Pa. PPhI

Indiana university, Bloomington, Ind. InBU

Institute of contemporary art, Boston, Mass. MBIC

International business machines corporation, New York, N.Y. IBM

J. B. Speed memorial, Louisville, Ky. KyLS

Jefferson medical college, Philadelphia, Pa. PPhJ

Jerome Hill reference library, St Paul, Minn. MnSJ

John Herron art institute, Indianapolis, Ind. InIJ

Joslyn art museum, Omaha, Nebr. NeO

Kensington Palace, London, England. ELK

Krannert art museum, University of Illinois, Urbana, Ill. IU

Kunstmuseum, Basel, Switzerland. SwB

Lane foundation, Leominster, Mass. MLL

Layton art gallery, Milwaukee, Wis. Milwaukee art center. WiMiA

Library company of Philadelphia, Pa. PPhL

Litchfield historical society, Litchfield, Conn. CtLH

Long Island historical society, Brooklyn, N.Y. NBH

Los Angeles county museum of history, science and art, Los Angeles, Calif. CLA

The Louvre, Paris, France. FPL

Lyman Allyn museum, New London, Conn. CtNL

M. H. De Young memorial museum, San Francisco, Calif. CSFD

Maryland historical society, Baltimore, Md. MdBH

Massachusetts antiquarian society, Worcester, Mass. MWA

Massachusetts historical society, Boston, Mass. MBH

Mercantile library association of St Louis, St Louis, Mo. MoSLM

Metropolitan Museum of art, New York, N.Y. MM

Mexico, D.F. Supreme court building. MexS

Milwaukee art center, Milwaukee, Wis. WiMiA

Milwaukee art institute, Milwaukee, Wis. WiMiA

Minneapolis institute of arts, Minneapolis, Minn. MnMi

Minnesota historical society, St Paul, Minn. MnSH

Missouri historical society, St Louis, Mo. MoSLH

Monmouth county historical society, Freehold, N.J. NJF

Montana State capitol, Helena, Mont. MonH

Montclair art museum, Montclair, N.J. NJMo

Municipal museum (Peale museum), Baltimore, Md. MdBMu

Munson-Williams-Proctor institute, Utica, N.Y. NUM

Museum of modern art, New York, N.Y. MMA

Museum of the City of New York, New York, N.Y. NNMC

National academy of design, New York, N.Y. NAD

National gallery, London, England, ELN

National gallery of art, Washington, D.C. DN

National gallery of Canada, Ottawa. CanO

National museum of baseball, Cooperstown, N.Y. NCB

National portrait gallery, London, England. ELNP

New Britain institute, New Britain, Conn. CtNB

New Haven colony historical society, New Haven, Conn. CtNH

New Mexico museum of art, Santa Fe, N.M. NMS

New school of social research, New York, N.Y. NNSR

New York. City Hall, New York, N.Y. NNCH

New York graphic society, New York, N.Y. NYG

New-York historical society, New York, N.Y. NNHS

New York public library, New York, N.Y. NNPL

New York State capitol, Albany, N.Y. NAS

New York State historical society, Cooperstown, N.Y. NCHA

Newark museum association, Newark, N.J. NJN

Newberry library, Chicago, Ill. ICN

Newport historical society, Newport, R.I. RNH

North Carolina museum of art, Raleigh, N.C. NoCR

North Carolina State art gallery. See North Carolina museum of art, Raleigh, N.C.

Norton gallery and school of art, West Palm Beach, Fla. FaW

Oberlin college, Oberlin, Ohio. OOb

Ohio State archaeological and historical society OCoA

Old Sturbridge Village, Sturbridge, Mass. MSt

Oregon historical society, Portland, Ore. OrPH

Parrish art museum, Southampton, N.Y. NSP

Pasadena art institute, Pasadena, Calif. CP

Peabody institute, Baltimore, Md. MdBP

Peabody museum, Salem, Mass. MSP

Peale museum (Municipal museum), Baltimore, Md. MdBMu

Pennsylvania academy of the fine arts, Philadelphia, Pa. PA

Petit palais, Paris, France. FPP

Philadelphia museum of art, Philadelphia, Pa. PPhM

Philbrook art center, Tulsa, Okla. OkT

Phillips academy, Andover, Mass. Addison gallery of American art. MAP

Phillips collection, Washington, D.C. DP

Phoenix art museum, Phoenix, Ariz. AP

Portland art museum, Portland, Ore. OrPA

Princeton university, Princeton, N.J. The Art museum. NJP

Providence athenaeum, Providence, R.I. RPAt

Reading museum, Reading, Pa. PR

Redwood library and athenaeum, Newport, R.I. RNR

Remington art memorial, Ogdensburg, N.Y. NOR

Rhode Island historical society, Providence, R.I. RPHS

Rhode Island school of design, Providence, R.I. RPS

Richmond art association, Richmond, Ind. InR

Rochester memorial art gallery, Rochester, N.Y. NR

St Louis, Mo. City art museum. MoSL

St Luke's hospital, New York, N.Y. NNSL

San Francisco museum of art, San Francisco, Calif. CSFM

Santa Barbara museum of art, Santa Barbara, Calif. CSB

Seattle art museum, Seattle, Wash. WaS

Senate house museum, Kingston, N.Y. NKS

Sheldon museum, Middlebury, Vt. VtMS

Sheldon Swope art gallery, Terre Haute, Ind. InTH

Smith college, Northampton, Mass. MNS

Smithsonian institution, Washington, D.C. National collection of fine arts DNC

Solomon R. Guggenheim museum, New York, N.Y. NNSG

Speed memorial, Louisville, Ky. KyLS

Springfield art museum, Springfield, Mo. MoSp

Springfield museum of fine arts, Springfield, Mass. MSM

Sterling and Francine Clark art institute, Williamstown, Mass. MWiS

Suffolk museum, Stony Brook, N.Y. NStS

Syracuse museum of art, Syracuse, N.Y. See Everson museum of Syracuse and Onondaga county, N.Y.

Syracuse university, Syracuse, N.Y. NSU

Taft museum, Cincinnati, Ohio. OCiT

Tate gallery, London, England. ELT

Telfair academy, Savannah, Ga. GST

Thomas Gilchrist institute of American history and art, Tulsa, Okla. OkTT

Toledo museum of art, Toledo, Ohio. OT

Trinity church, Boston, Mass. MBT

Union college, Schenectady, N.Y. NScU

Union league club, New York, N.Y. NNU

Union league of Philadelphia, Philadelphia, Pa. PPhU

United States military academy, West Point, N.Y. NWP

United States naval academy, Annapolis, Maryland, MdAn

University of Arizona, Tucson, Ariz. ATU

University of California, Los Angeles, Calif. CLAU

University of Illinois, Urbana, Ill. Krannert art museum. IU

University of Iowa, Iowa City, Iowa. IoIU

University of Kansas, Lawrence, Kans. Museum of art. KLU

University of Michigan, Ann Arbor, Mich. MiA

University of Minnesota, Minneapolis, Minn. MnU

University of Nebraska, Lincoln, Nebr. NeL

University of North Carolina, Woman's College, Greensboro, N.C. NoCG

University of Oklahoma, Norman, Okla. OkNU

University of Pennsylvania, Philadelphia, Pa. PPhUn

University of Southern California, Los Angeles, Calif. CLAUS

University of Virginia, Charlottesville, Va. VCU

University of Washington, Seattle, Wash. WaSU

Valentine museum, Richmond, Va. VRV

Virginia museum of fine arts, Richmond, Va. VR

Wadsworth atheneum, Hartford, Conn. CtHW

Walker art center, Minneapolis, Minn. MnMW

Walters art gallery, Baltimore, Md. MdBW

Warner house association, Portsmouth, N.H. NHP

Washington county museum of fine arts, Hagerstown, Md. MdHW

Washington university, St Louis, Mo. MoSLW

Westmoreland county museum of art, Greensburg, Pa. PW

White art museum, Cornell university, Ithaca, N.Y. NIC

The White house, Washington, D.C. DW

Whitney museum of American art, New York, N.Y. WMAA

Wichita art museum, Wichita, Kans. KW

William A. Farnsworth library and art museum, Rockland, Me. MeR

William Lane foundation, Leominster, Mass. MLL

William Rockhill Nelson gallery of art, Kansas City, Mo. MoKN

Williams college, Williamstown, Mass. MWiC

Wilmington society of the fine arts, Wilmington, Del. DeW

Winterthur museum, Greenville, Del. DeWin

Witte memorial museum, San Antonio, Tex. TxSA

Worcester art museum, Worcester, Mass. MWM

Yale university, New Haven, Conn. CtY

# EXPLANATION

I. Example of entry under artist:
    (1) **BELLOWS, George Wesley,** 1882-1925
    (2)     **Children on the porch** (On the porch)   OCo
    (3)     DN. Bellows
    (4)     Time. 300 years (col)
    (5)     **On the porch.** See Children on the porch

### EXPLANATION

(1) Name of painter, surname in capitals
(2) Title used followed (in parentheses) by alternative title and by symbol
    giving location of painting. Meaning of symbol is given in Key to
    Symbols, pages 21-3.
(3)-(4) Names of books in which reproductions may be found. Full entry for
    these books is given in List of Works Indexed, pages 9-20.
(5) Reference from alternative title to title used


II. Example of title entry:
    **Children** on the porch by G. W. Bellows
    **On** the porch by G. W. Bellows

### EXPLANATION

All titles entered in their alphabetical places in index, first word in boldface type


III. Example of subject entry:
    **Bridges**
        Moses, A. M. R. Sunday (The covered bridge)
        Whistler, J. A. M. Old Battersea bridge

### EXPLANATION

To find books in which reproductions occur, consult the main entries under
    Moses and under Whistler

# INDEX TO REPRODUCTIONS OF AMERICAN PAINTINGS

## SUPPLEMENT

**AACH, Herbert,** 1924-
Mesa Grande
  IU. Contemp Amer ptg & sculp, 1961
**Abandoned** by M. Henriksen
**Abandoned** quarry by L. Kroll
**Abandoned** treasures by Y. Kuniyoshi
**Abandoned** wharf by R. Vickrey
**ABBE, Mrs S. B.**
Voyageur              MoSLH
Rathbone
**ABBEY, Edwin Austin,** 1852-1911
King Lear's daughters       MM
  MM. 100 Amer ptrs
Mrs Edwin Austin Abbey     CtY
  CtY. Portrait index
**Abbey, Mary Gertrude (Mead)** 1851-1931
Abbey, E. A. Mrs Edwin Austin Abbey
**ABBOT, Agnes Anne,** 1897-
To the yacht races          MB
  MB. Ptgs in water color
**Abeel, Maria.** See Duyckinck, Maria (Abeel)
**Abeel, Garret,** 1734-1799
Kilburn, L. Garret Abeel
**Abeel, Mary (Byvanck)** 1742-1795
Kilburn, L. Mrs Garret Abeel
**Abelard** the drowned, master of the Phantom by M. Hartley
**ABERCROMBIE, Gertrude,** 1909-
Message for mercy
  IU. Contemp Amer ptg, 1951
The **abiding**—Summer and sea by N. Sandgren
**Above** the earth by M. Tobey
**Above** the excavation by N. Spencer
**Above** the river by E. Fiene
**Abraham** by B. Newman
**ABRAMS, Mary Tatum,** 1925-
Paradise tree
  VR. Amer ptg, 1958
**ABRAMS, Ross,** 1920-
Landscape
  VR. Amer ptg, 1958
**Absence** by J. Ernst
**Absolom** by J. W. Treiman
**Abstract** by G. Cavallon
**Abstract** by L. Schanker
**Abstract** composition by C. Barnes
**Abstract** landscape by K. Knaths
**Abstract** landscape by C. S. Price
**Abstract** portrait of Savadsky by K. S. Dreier
**Abstraction** by R. Armer
**Abstraction** by J. Berlandina
**Abstraction** by I. Bolotowsky
**Abstraction** by H. G. Burckhardt
**Abstraction** by K. Callahan
**Abstraction** by G. Cavallon

**Abstraction** by C. L. Cicero
**Abstraction** by B. Connelly
**Abstraction** by A. G. Dove
**Abstraction** by S. Francis
**Abstraction** by P. Ghikas
**Abstraction** by M. Hartley
**Abstraction** by K. Khosrovi
**Abstraction** by R. McChesney
**Abstraction** by G. J. McNeil
**Abstraction** by G. O'Keeffe
**Abstraction** by C. S. Price
**Abstraction** by M. L. Schamberg
**Abstraction** by B. W. Tomlin
**Abstraction** by J. Van Everen
**Abstraction**—storm by B. Greene
**Abstraction**—white iris by G. O'Keeffe
**Abstraction**—white rose by G. O'Keeffe
**Abstraction** with flowers by M. Hartley
**L'académicien** by R. Lindner
**Academy** of music, Philadelphia, Sketch for curtain by R. Smith
**Acadia** by M. B. Prendergast
**Accent** grave by F. J. Kline
**Access** by L. Bunce
**Accra** beach by S. M. Etnier
**Acheson, Alice (Stanley)**
James, A. Mrs Dean Acheson
**Acrobats**
Beckmann, M. Acrobat on trapeze
Beckmann, M. Acrobats
Curry, J. S. The passing leap
De Kooning, W. Acrobat
Demuth, C. H. Acrobats
Demuth, C. H. Female acrobats
Demuth, C. H. Two acrobats
Hirsch, J. Triumph
Kuhn, W. Acrobat in green
Kuhn, W. Acrobat in white
Kuhn, W. Acrobat in white and blue
Pickens, A. Acrobat, 1947
Weber, M. Acrobats
**Acropolis**—night by E. Ewing
**Across** four pines by W. A. Kienbusch
**Across** Penobscot bay by W. A. Kienbusch
**Across** the harbor by A. B. Davies
**Across** the road by A. G. Dove
**Across** the tracks by R. Gwathmey
**Action** by W. T. Murch
**Actor** by P. Guston
**Actor** and his family by A. Pickens
**Actors** by M. Beckmann
**Actors'** duel by C. R. Leslie
**Actress** by T. Eakins

An **actress**, Portrait of by W. M. Chase
**Adam** by K. Knaths
**Adam** by B. Newman
**Adam** and Eve by R. Cowles
**Adam** and Eve by S. G. Reinhardt
**Adam** and Eve by Unidentified artist
The **Adam** Lemp brewery by C. Wimar
**Adams, Abigail.** See Belcher, Abigail (Adams)
**ADAMS, Cassilly,** b 1843
  Custer's last fight
    McCracken. Portrait of the old west (col)
**Adams, John, president U.S.** 1735-1826
  Brown, M. John Adams
  Copley, J. S. John Adams
  Peale, C. W. John Adams
  Stuart, G. John Adams
  Trumbull, J. John Adams
**Adams, John Quincy, president U.S.** 1767-1848
  Bingham, G. C. John Quincy Adams
  Copley, J. S. John Quincy Adams
  Healy, G. P. A. John Quincy Adams
**Adams, Samuel,** 1722-1803
  Copley, J. S. Samuel Adams
**ADAMS, Wayman,** 1883-1959
  Alexander Ernestinoff        InIJ
    InIJ. 105 ptgs
  Musicos ambulantes
    PPC. International ex, 1950
**Adams family,** c1850
  Unidentified artist. Adams family
**Adams'** house by E. Hopper
**Addicks, Stanley**
  Eakins, T. The pianist (Stanley Addicks)
**Addicks, Weda (Cook)**
  Eakins, T. Concert singer (Weda Cook)
**Addie** by T. Eakins
**Addison E. Andrews (paddle steamship)**
  Bard, J. Paddle steamship Addison E. Andrews
**Adirondack** guide by W. Homer
**Adirondack** lake by W. Homer
**Adirondack** woods, guide and dog by W. Homer
**Adirondacks** by W. Homer
**Adirondacks** along Ausable river by J. Marin
**Adit** by S. Davis
**Adler, Felix,** 1851-1933
  Zerbe, K. Felix Adler
**ADLER, Samuel M.** 1898-
  Breakwater
    IU. Contemp Amer ptg & sculp, 1959
  Fortune teller
    IU. Contemp Amer ptg, 1950
  Invocation        WMAA
    IU. Contemp Amer ptg & sculp, 1953 (col)
  Pierson
    Pousette-Dart. Amer ptg
  Juxtaposition II
    IU. Contemp Amer ptg & sculp, 1961
  The lottery
    PA. Annual ex, 1951
  Mauve still life        IU
    IU. Contemp Amer ptg, 1952
    IU. 20th century

  The offering
    Pearson. Mod renaissance
  To thine own self
    IU. Contemp Amer ptg, 1951
  White still life
    IU. Contemp Amer ptg & sculp, 1955
**Admiration** of the orchestrelle for the cinematograph by M. Ray
**Adobe** houses by C. S. Price
**Adolescence** by G. Wood
**ADOLPHE, Albert Jean,** 1865-1940
  Self-portrait
    Chew. 250 years of art
**Adoration** of the Magi by D. Aronson
**Adoration** of the moon by M. Weber
**Adoration** of the mother by C. W. Hawthorne
**Adoring** angels by J. La Farge
**Adrenalin** hour by B. L. Culwell
**Advancing** sea by M. Avery
**Adventure** by A. B. Davies
The **advocate** by J. C. Wayne
**Aegina** from the Acropolis, Athens by H. B. Warren
**Aerial** gyrations by C. Sheeler
**Aerograph** by M. Ray
**Affection** by E. Cortor
**Affluent** surface by I. R. Pereira
**African** thistle by H. G. Keller
**Aft** deck no 2 by Z. L. Sepeshy
**After** all . . . , 1933 by C. H. Demuth
**After** an ambush by B. Perlin
**After** an ice storm by M. Weber
**After** night's study by J. F. Peto
**After** rain by E. Lawson
**After** rain by M. Sterne
**After** Sir Christopher Wren by C. H. Demuth
**After** sundown by R. A. Blakelock
**After** the bath by M. Cassatt
**After** the bath by Raphaelle Peale
**After** the fire by W. Thon
**After** the hunt by J. D. Chalfant
**After** the hunt by W. M. Harnett
**After** the hunt by W. Homer
**After** the questioning by G. Grosz
**After** the rain by M. Sterne
**After** the show by C. Prendergast
**After** the shower by J. E. Swinnerton
**After** the storm by T. H. Benton
**After** the storm by S. Browne
**After** the storm by W. M. Hart
**After** the storm by A. L. Ripley
**After** the storm by M. Sterne
**After** the tornado, Bahamas by W. Homer
**After** Titian by B. Shahn
**Afterglow** by G. R. Beal
**Afterglow** by W. Homer
**Afterglow,** Tautira river valley, Tahiti by J. La Farge
**Afternoon** by A. N. Wyeth
**Afternoon** at Tony's by M. J. Tolegian

Afternoon in August by Y. Johnston
Afternoon light by C. S. Hopkinson
Afternoon mail by W. Manning
Afternoon, Pincian hill, Rome by M. B. Prendergast
Afternoon sun by G. Prestopino
Afternoon wind by L. M. Eilshemius
Agate heights by E. Poe
Age of anxiety by B. Shahn
Age of reason by K. L. Seligmann
Aggressive by H. Hofmann
The aggressor by F. Ruvolo
Aggressors by W. Utley
Aggressors' retribution by W. Gropper
Agincourt by F. Roth
Aging actress by M. Siporin
Aging harlequin by K. Zerbe
The agitator by G. Grosz
Agnew clinic by T. Eakins
Agony by A. Gorky
Agrarian dishabille by W. W. Quirt
Agriculture and logging by T. H. Benton
Agrippina and her children mourning over the ashes of Germanicus by B. West
Agrippina landing at Brundisium with the ashes of Germanicus by B. West
Ahab and Abigail by K. L. Callahan
Ahko, Portrait of by A. Gorky
AHLAS, Lambro
  Jump rope
    NAD. Annual ex, 1957
Ainlee by J. D. Brooks
Ainslie, Eva Rosanna
  Theus, J. Mrs Theus (traditionally known as Eva Rosanna Ainslie)
Air raid by J. Hirsch
Air raid by V. Spagna
Aircraft factory by R. Crawford
Airplane synchromy in yellow and orange by S. MacDonald-Wright
Airplane synchromy in yellow-orange by S. Macdonald-Wright
Ajax by E. Melcarth
Aladjálov, Constantin. See Alajálov, Constantin
ALAJÁLOV, Constantin, 1900-
  Harlequin and woman                         CtY
    CtY. Soc Anonyme
Alameda shore by J. Lee
Alaska by H. Sterne
Albany, New York
  Eights, J. East side Market street (now Broadway) Albany, 1805
  Eights, J. Number 1 north side of State street, Albany, 1806
  Eights, J. State street in 1805
The Albany boat by G. R. Beal
Albany Schoharie stagecoach by F. Stucker
ALBEE, Percy Frederick, 1883-1959
  The bridge
    NAD. Annual ex, 1951
ALBERS, Josef, 1888-
  b and p (B+P)                               NNSG
    NNSG. Handbook
  City
    Rathbun

Dark
  CSFP. Annual ex, 1950/51
  MMA. Abstract
Facade
  ICA. Annual ex, 1947/48
The gate                                      CtY
  CtY. Soc Anoyme
  Pierson
Homage to the square
  Pousette-Dart. Amer ptg
Homage to the square: Ascending
                                              WMAA
  Goodrich. Amer art (col)
  Mendelowitz
  Pierson
Homage to the square: Dedicated
                                              NBuA
  NBuA. Acquisitions 1954-57 (col front)
Homage to the square: Legendary pasture
  Time. 300 years (col)
Homage to the square: Precinct (Homage to the square—early yellow)
  IU. Contemp Amer ptg, 1952
  MnMW. Classic tradition
Homage to the square: Ritardando
  Ponente. Mod ptg, 1960 (col)
Homage to the square: Yes
  DC. 25 biennial ex, 1957
Inside and out                                CtHW
  CoS. New accessions USA, 1954
Layered
  Rathbun (col)
Lowers
  Pearson. Mod renaissance
Red wall
  McCurdy
Study for an early diary
  Seiberling (col)
Study for painting, mirage A of 1940
  Read. Concise history
View
  Pearson. Mod renaissance
White front                                   MiA
  NUM. Art across America
Albert IV the Wise, count of Hapsburg, d 1239
  Walker, C. H. Albert IV the Wise
Albert bridge, London by M. Lichtenberg
Albert's son by A. N. Wyeth
ALBRIGHT, Ivan Le Lorraine, 1897-
  And God created man in his own image. See Room 203
  And man created God in his own image. See Room 203
  Fleeting time, thou hast left me old   MM
    Barker. From realism
    Mendelowitz
  Harbor of dreams                            OYB
    OYB. Catalogue 1951
  Heavy the oar to him who is tired, Heavy the coat, heavy the sea   ICA
    CoS. New accessions USA, 1950
    Gruskin (col)
  Hole in the wall gang
    NAD. Annual ex, 1954
  Hopscotch                                   MMA
    Barr. Masters p 160
  Into the world there came a soul called Ida   ICA
    Baur. New art
    Canaday
    CoS. New accessions USA, 1948
    Pierson

**ALBRIGHT, I. L.**—*Continued*
Maker of dreams (Man with a mallet)
                            CtHW
  CtHW.  Handbook
Maker of images
  Baur.  New art
Man with a mallet. See Maker of dreams
The picture of Dorian Gray
  ICA.  Annual ex, 1944/46
  Pearson, Mod renaissance
Poor room—There is no time, no end, no
    today, no yesterday, no tomorrow,
    only the forever, and forever, and
    forever, without end
  Baur.  New Art (col)
  Eliot.  Art of our time (col)
  ICA.  Amer artist paints the city
  Time.  300 years (col)
The purist
  PPC.  International ex, 1950
Roaring Fork, Wyoming
  WiMiA.  Amer ptg 1760-1960
Room 203 (And man created God in his
    own image; And God created man in
    his own image)                ICA
  Baur.  New art
  Flexner.  Amer ptg
  Flexner.  Short history
  McCurdy
  WMAA.  Julianna Force
Self-portrait, 1935
  Baur.  Revolution
Temptation of St Anthony
  MnMW.  Expressionism 1900-1955
  NBuA.  Expressionism
That which I should have done I did not
    do                            ICA
  Baur.  New art
  Newmeyer
  Pearson.  Mod renaissance
  Pearson.  Mod renaissance (detail)
  Pierson
  Richardson.  Ptg in America
There is man in God
  PA.  Annual ex, 1956
There were no flowers tonight
  DC.  20 biennial ex, 1947
  WiMiA.  Amer ptg 1760-1960
Tin
  DC.  24 biennial ex, 1955
Wherefore now ariseth the illusion of a
    third dimension
  MM.  Amer ptg today
The wild bunch                        MMA
  Pearson.  Mod renaissance
  Pousette-Dart.  Amer ptg
  WiMiA.  Amer ptg 1760-1960
Woman                                MMA
  Barr.  Masters
  MMA.  Masters
Yesterday
  NAD.  Annual ex, 1961

### Portrait of the artist

Bohrod, A.  Ivan Albright
**ALBRIGHT, Malvin Marr,** known as
  **Zsissly, 1897-**
Boothbay harbor, Maine
  PPC.  International ex, 1950
Dinner table                          GAtM
  GAtM.  Holbrook collection
Incoming tide, Maine                    OT
  OT.  Contemp Amer ptgs

Summer in Maine
  PPC.  Ptg in the U.S. 1949
Victoria
  Gruskin (col)
Yaquima bay, Oregon
  NAD.  Annual ex, 1948
**ALBRO, Maxine, 1903-**
Skipping                              ATU
  ATU.  Coll of Amer art
**ALCALAY, Albert, 1917-**
Earth
  MBIC.  View 1960
East end in New York
  IU.  Contemp Amer ptg & sculp, 1955
Heavy industry
  WMAA.  Contemp Amer ptg, 1955
Urban labyrinth
  IU.  Contemp Amer ptg & sculp, 1957
Vanishing city
  IU.  Contemp Amer ptg & sculp, 1959
**Alden, Hannah,** b 1798
  Unidentified artist.  Hannah Alden
**Alden, Sarah,** b 1796
  Unidentified artist.  Sarah Alden
The **alders** by C. Hassam
**ALDRICH, William Truman, 1880-**
Boathouse                              MB
  MB.  Ptgs in water color
Gasometer                              MB
  MB.  Ptgs in water color
A giant                                MB
  MB.  Ptgs in water color
Machine shop                          MB
  MB.  Ptgs in water color
Woodland scene                        MB
  MB.  Ptgs in water color
**Alexander, Cicely**
  Whistler, J. A. M. Cicely Alexander
**ALEXANDER, Cosmo John,** c 1724-1772
  Alexander Grant
    Pierson
  Charles Dudley
    DC.  Privately owned
  Mrs Charles Dudley
    DC.  Privately owned
**ALEXANDER, Francesca, 1837-1917**
  Lina Pistolesi
    MiD.  Travelers in Arcadia
**ALEXANDER, Francis, 1800-1880?**
  James Gates Percival              CtY
    CtY.  Portrait index
  Lydia Huntley Sigourney          NJMo
    NJMo.  Forty years
  Mrs Jared Sparks                  MCH
    Pierson
    Richardson.  Ptg in America
**ALEXANDER, Fred, 1914-**
  Interurban                        OYB
    OYB.  Catalogue 1951
**ALEXANDER, Henry, 1862-1895**
  Laboratory of Thomas Price
    Frankenstein.  After the hunt
**ALEXANDER, John White, 1856-1915**
  John Ferguson Weir                CtY
    CtY.  Portrait index
    Weir.  Recollections
  Phyllis                          InTH
    InTH.  Catalogue
  Study in black and green          MM
    MM.  100 Amer ptrs
  Thomas Nast
    Chew.  250 years of art

**Alfir's** delight by A. G. Dove

**Algerian** scene by J. Whorf

**Algerian** scene: the bridge by J. Whorf

**Algerian** soldiers by J. Teyral

**Algerian** street scene by J. Whorf

**Alice** by W. M. Chase

**Alice** in grey by L. Lucioni

**Alice** in the Shinnecock studio by W. M. Chase

**Alice** with wolfhound by W. M. Chase

**All** soundings are referred to high water by K. Sage

**All** things are changing, nothing dies by P. Mangravite

**ALLAN, Bill,** 1936-
Blind fish approaching summer
PPC. International ex, 1958

**Allée** by S. Davis

**Allegheny mountains**
Harvey, G. Amongst the Allegheny mountains

**Allegorical themes.** See Symbolical and allegorical themes

**Allegro** by M. Tobey

**ALLEN, Agnes**
J. Somers Smith
PA. Annual ex, 1947

**Allen, Ann (Crawford)** 1759-1808
Malbone, E. G. Mrs Zachariah Allen

**Allen, Beulah.** See Clarke, Beulah (Allen)

**ALLEN, Charles Curtis,** 1886-
Westwood hillside      MB
MB. Ptgs in water color

**Allen, Clara (Walker)** fl 1750
Hesselius, J. Mrs William Allen
Wollaston, J. Mrs William Allen

**Allen, Elizabeth.** See Deas, Elizabeth (Allen)

**ALLEN, Junius,** 1898-
North inlet
NAD. Annual ex, 1961

**Allen, Lydia,** b 1784
Malbone, E. G. Lydia Allen

**Allen, Samuel,** fl 1795
Peale, J. Samuel Allen of Philadelphia

**Allen, Solomon,** 1751-1821
Ames, E. Solomon Allen

**ALLEN, Thomas,** 1849-1924
Portal of the mission of San José, Texas
     MB
MB. Ptgs in water color

**Allen, William,** 1841-1849
Prior, W. M. William Allen

**Allen, Mrs William.** See Allen, Clara (Walker)

**Allen, Mrs Zachariah.** See Allen, Ann (Crawford)

**Alligators**
Sargent, J. S. Muddy alligators

**Allium** Sativum by G. Palazzola

**Allouard-Jouan, Madame**
Sargent, J. S. Madame Allouard-Jouan

The **all**-seeing eye by Unidentified artist

**All's** well by W. Homer

**Allston, Ann (Channing)** See Channing, Ann

**Allston, Rachel Moore.** See Flagg, Rachel Moore Allston

**ALLSTON, Washington,** 1779-1843
American scenery: Time, afternoon with a southwest haze      MB
Canaday
Richardson. Washington Allston
Angel releasing St Peter from prison MB
Richardson. Washington Allston
Artist's mother, Mrs Henry Collins Flagg
Richardson. Washington Allston
Beatrice
Richardson. Washington Allston
Belshazzar's feast      MB
Barker. Amer ptg
Flexner. Light of distant skies
Larkin
Larkin rev ed
NBuA. Expressionism
Richardson. Washington Allston
Roos
Benjamin West      MB
Richardson. Washington Allston
Buck's progress, no 1: Introduction of a country lad to a click of town bucks
Richardson. Washington Allston
The buck's progress, no 3: Midnight fray with a watchman
Flexner. Light of distant skies
Christ healing the sick, first study
Richardson. Washington Allston
Coast scene on the Mediterranean
NUM. Art across America
Richardson. Washington Allston
David playing before Saul      SCCG
Richardson. Washington Allston
The dead man revived by touching the bones of the prophet Elisha      PA
Canaday
Flexner. Light of distant skies
Richardson. Ptg in America
Richardson. Washington Allston
Death of King John
Richardson. Washington Allston (unfinished)
The deluge      MM
Baur. Amer ptg
Bazin
Flexner. Light of distant skies
Larkin (detail)
Larkin rev ed (detail)
Mendelowitz
Pierson
Richardson. Washington Allston
Walker. Ptgs from America
Diana in the chase      MCH
Pierson
Richardson. Washington Allston
Donna Mencia in the robbers' cavern MB
MB. Karolik coll
Richardson. Washington Allston
Elijah fed by the ravens (Elijah in the desert)      MB
Flexner. Light of distant skies
Larkin rev ed (col)
Lee. Art then and now
Pierson
Richardson. Washington Allston
Evening hymn
Richardson. Washington Allston
WiMiA. Amer ptg 1760-1960

**ALLSTON, Washington**—*Continued*

Flight of Florimell      MiD
  MiD. Treasures
  Pierson
  Richardson. Ptg in America (col detail)
  Richardson. Washington Allston (col)
Francis Dana Channing
  Richardson. Washington Allston
Head of a Jew      MB
  Richardson. Washington Allston
Isaac of York      MBA
  Richardson. Washington Allston
Italian landscape      MAP
  Canaday
  Larkin
  Larkin rev ed
  PPC. Amer classics
  Richardson. Washington Allston
Italian landscape      MiD
  MiD. Travelers in Arcadia
  Richardson. Washington Allston
  Roos
Italian landscape      OT
  MiD. Travelers in Arcadia
Italian shepherd boy      MiD
  Richardson. Washington Allston
Jacob's dream
  Richardson. Washington Allston
Jason returning to demand his **father's**
  kingdom
  Canaday
  Richardson. Washington Allston
Jeremiah dictating his prophecy of the
  destruction of Jerusalem      CtY
  Flexner. Light of distant skies
  Richardson. Washington Allston
Landscape      MCoL
  Richardson. Washington Allston
Landscape, American scenery. See Amer-
  ican scenery
Landscape, evening
  Richardson. Washington Allston
Landscape with a lake      MB
  MB. Karolik coll
  Richardson. Washington Allston
Lorenzo and Jessica
  Richardson. Washington Allston
Man in chains      MAP
  Richardson. Washington Allston
Mrs William Channing
  Richardson. Washington Allston
Moonlit landscape      MB
  Barker. Amer ptg
  Born
  Canaday
  Flexner. Amer ptg
  Flexner. Light of distant skies
  Flexner. Short history
  Mendelowitz
  MiD. Ptg in America
  Pierson
  Richardson. Ptg in America
  Richardson. Washington Allston
  Robb. Harper history
  Roos
  Time. 300 years (col)
Mother watching her sleeping child
  Richardson. Washington Allston
The poor author and the rich bookseller      MB
  Flexner. Light of distant skies
  ICA. From colony to nation
  Richardson. Washington Allston

Rebecca at the well
  Richardson. Washington Allston
Rising of a thunderstorm at sea      MB
  Pierson
  Richardson. Ptg in America
  Richardson. Washington Allston
Robert Rogers      RNR
  Richardson. Washington
Rosalie
  Flexner. Light of distant skies
  Richardson. Washington Allston
St Peter in prison, Study for head of
  Richardson. Washington Allston
Samuel Taylor Coleridge      ELNP
  Richardson. Washington Allston
Samuel Taylor Coleridge (Dana coll)
  Richardson. Washington Allston (un-
  finished
Samuel Williams
  MiD. Coll in progress
  Richardson. Washington Allston
  WiMiA. Amer ptg 1760-1960
Saul and the witch of Endor      MAC
  Richardson. Washington Allston
Self-portrait      MB
  Flexner. Light of distant skies
  MB. Great Americans
  Pierson
  Richardson. Washington Allston
The sisters
  Richardson. Washington Allston
Uriel in the sun
  Richardson. Washington Allston
The valentine
  Richardson. Washington Allston
William Ellery Channing      MB
  MB. Great Americans
  Richardson. Washington Allston

#### Portrait of the artist

Malbone, E. G. Washington Allston

**Allston, Mrs Washington.** See Channing,
  Ann

**Almost** airtight compartments by J. Berlandina

**Almost** silence by J. Ernst

**Alms** by C. Booth

**Almy, James G.** fl 1798
  Malbone, E. G. James G. Almy

**Alone** by J. Ernst

**Alone** by P. Evergood

**Alone** by M. Weber

**Along** the Arno by O. M. Pleissner

**Along** the Borgo pass by C. L. Cicero

**Along** the boulevard, Paris by M. B.
  Prendergast

**Along** the coast by M. B. Prendergast

**Along** the coast by P. Riba

**Along** the Erie canal by A. B. Davies

**Along** the North shore by S. W. Woodward

**Along** the path by S. Laufman

**Along** the river by P. Dickinson

**Along** the road, Cordoba, Mexico by D.
  Macknight

**Along** the Susquehanna by J. Kane

**Along** the waterfront by R. Marsh

**Alpine** district, New Jersey by J. Marin

The **Alps** by H. G. Keller

**ALSTON, Charles Henry,** 1907-
Painting
  MM. Amer ptg today
**Altar** boys by G. S. Ratkai
**Altar** of silence by Kim Chung
**Altitude** 2000 by J. de Diego
**Altoon** by J. Brooks
**Amalfi** by R. D. Gauley
**Amalfi** by E. Isenberger
**Amalia** by A. Brook
The **amateur** by J. Farnsworth
**AMATO, Samuel,** 1924-
  Garden frieze
    IU. Contemp Amer ptg & sculp, 1959
  Sleep and revelry
    WMAA. Contemp Amer ptg, 1959/60
  Still life
    IU. Contemp Amer ptg & sculp, 1961
**Amazing** juggler by Y. Kuniyoshi
**Amazon** by W. A. Baziotes
**Ambassador** of good will by G. Grosz
The **ambry** by H. E. Niese
**Ambush** by A. Bierstadt
**Ambush** by H. Hofmann
**America** (yacht)
  Butterworth, J. E. The yacht America
    leaving Boston harbor for England
**America** today by T. H. Benton
**American** academy by M. Pratt
The **American** boy by J. Koch
**American** errant by T. Cavanaugh
**American** farm by J. J. Jones
**American** frolic by H. Major
**American** frontier life by A. F. Tait
**American** fur company caravan en route to
    Wyoming, 1837 by A. J. Miller
**American** Gothic by G. Wood
**American** harvest by Unidentified artist
    (probably a copy after Cropsey)
**American** interior by C. Sheeler
**American** lake scene by T. Cole
**American** landscape by C. Sheeler
**American** landscape by J. Stella
**American** landscape by L. Whitney
**American** madonna and child by Unidenti-
    fied artist
**American** radiator building by G. O'Keeffe
**American** school by M. Pratt
**American** sea captains carousing in Surinam
    by J. Greenwood
**American** shrimp girl by P. Evergood
**American** telephone building, New York
    city by J. Marin
**American** tragedy by P. Evergood
**Americana** by E. Cortor
**Americana** by C. Sheeler
**Americans** in Paris by G. P. Du Bois
**Ames.** See also Emes
**Ames, Angelo,** 1803-1886
  Ames, E. Angelo Ames c 1818
  Ames, E. Angelo Ames c 1827
**AMES, Ezra,** 1768-1836
  Aaron Thorp
    Bolton. Ezra Ames

Absolom Townsend
  Bolton. Ezra Ames
Alexander Hamilton
  Bolton. Ezra Ames
Ambrose Latting Jordan          NCHA
  Bolton. Ezra Ames
Ambrose Spencer
  Bolton. Ezra Ames
Angelo Ames c 1818
  Bolton. Ezra Ames
Angelo Ames, c 1827          NAI
  Bolton. Ezra Ames
Ann Walsh
  Bolton. Ezra Ames
Benjamin Tallmadge
  Bolton. Ezra Ames
Children of Gov Daniel D. Tompkins
  Bolton. Ezra Ames
Clarkson Crolius          NNHS
  Bolton. Ezra Ames
Cornelius Egberts          NAI
  Cortelyou. Ezra Ames supp
Daniel D. Tompkins          NAI
  Bolton. Ezra Ames
Dewitt Clinton          NAI
  Bolton. Ezra Ames
Dolly Madison          NNHS
  Flexner. Light of distant skies
Edmond Charles Genet          NAI
  Bolton. Ezra Ames
Eleazer Burnham
  Bolton. Ezra Ames
Elias Mather          MNS
  Bolton. Ezra Ames
Elihu Phinney
  Bolton. Ezra Ames
Eliphalet Nott
  Bolton. Ezra Ames
Elkanah Watson
  Bolton. Ezra Ames
Elkanah Watson (after Copley)          NAI
  Bolton. Ezra Ames
Enos T. Throop          NAI
  Bolton. Ezra Ames
The Fondey family          NAI
  Bolton. Ezra Ames
Francis Bloodgood
  Bolton. Ezra Ames
George Clinton          NAS
  Bolton. Ezra Ames
  Frankenstein. Two journeyman ptrs
George Clinton          NNHS
  Bolton. Ezra Ames
  Larkin rev ed (detail)
George Clinton (Andrews coll)
  Bolton. Ezra Ames
George Provost
  Bolton. Ezra Ames
George Tibbits
  Bolton. Ezra Ames
George Washington          NAS
  Bolton. Ezra Ames
George Washington Clinton
  Bolton. Ezra Ames
Goldsbrow Banyar          NNHS
  Vail. Stuyvesant ports
Gouverneur Morris          NNHS
  Bolton. Ezra Ames
Harmanus Bleecker
  Bolton. Ezra Ames
Henry Emes
  Bolton. Ezra Ames
Henry Jones aged 20 years          NNHS
  Bolton. Ezra Ames

AMES, Ezra—*Continued*
Henry Newman
  Bolton. Ezra Ames
James Kent              NAI
  Bolton. Ezra Ames
James Rivington (after Stuart)  NNHS
  Bolton. Ezra Ames
James Wade
  Bolton. Ezra Ames
Jesse Emes, c 1790        NAI
  Bolton. Ezra Ames
Jesse Emes, 1819         NAI
  Bolton. Ezra Ames
Jesse Hawley            NNHS
  Bolton. Ezra Ames
John Jay (after Stuart)      NAI
  Bolton. Ezra Ames
John Kane
  Bolton. Ezra Ames
John Keyes Paige
  Bolton. Ezra Ames
John Lansing, jr
  Cortelyou. Ezra Ames supp
John Meads
  Bolton. Ezra Ames
John Taylor
  Bolton. Ezra Ames
Joseph Brant, Thayendanegea  NCHA
  Bolton. Ezra Ames
Joseph C. Yates           NAI
  Bolton. Ezra Ames
Julius Rubens Ames
  Bolton. Ezra Ames
Katharine Barber James (?)
  Bolton. Ezra Ames
Leonard Bleecker
  Bolton. Ezra Ames
Marcia L. Ames
  Bolton. Ezra Ames
Marcus T. Reynolds
  Bolton. Ezra Ames
Martin Van Buren         NAI
  Bolton. Ezra Ames
Matthias Burnett Tallmadge    CtY
  Bolton. Ezra Ames
  CtY. Portrait index
Mrs Aaron Thorp
  Bolton. Ezra Ames
Mrs Allan Melville
  Bolton. Ezra Ames
Mrs Benjamin Tallmadge
  Bolton. Ezra Ames
Mrs Daniel D. Tompkins     NNHS
  Bolton. Ezra Ames
Mrs Dewitt Clinton
  Bolton. Ezra Ames
Mrs Eleazer Burnham
  Bolton. Ezra Ames
Mrs Ezekiel Mulford
  Bolton. Ezra Ames
Mrs Ezra Ames
  Bolton. Ezra Ames
Mrs George Tibbits
  Bolton. Ezra Ames
Mrs Henry Sutliff          NAI
  Cortelyou. Ezra Ames supp
Mrs Jacob Jennings Brown
  Bolton. Ezra Ames
Mrs James King
  Bolton. Ezra Ames
Mrs Jesse Emes
  Bolton. Ezra Ames

Mrs John Hills
  Bolton. Ezra Ames
Mrs John Keyes Paige
  Bolton. Ezra Ames
Mrs John Meads
  Bolton. Ezra Ames
Mrs Jonathan Walton
  Bolton. Ezra Ames
Mrs Matthias Burnett Tallmadge  CtY
  Bolton. Ezra Ames
Mrs Peter Gansevoort      NAI
  Bolton. Ezra Ames
Mrs Philo Ruggles        NNCU
  Bolton. Ezra Ames
Mrs Pierre Van Cortlandt II   NNHS
  Cortelyou. Ezra Ames supp
Mrs Robert Hudson
  Bolton. Ezra Ames
Mrs Spencer Stafford
  Bolton. Ezra Ames
Mrs Stephen Reynolds
  Bolton. Ezra Ames
Mrs Thomas Humphrey Cushing
  Bolton. Ezra Ames
Mrs William Annesley (?)
  Bolton. Ezra Ames
Mrs William Clarke
  Cortelyou. Ezra Ames supp
Mrs William James
  Bolton. Ezra Ames
Perspective painting of Lake George [with
  the fort]
  Bolton. Ezra Ames
Philip Van Cortlandt        MM
  Bolton. Ezra Ames
Philo Ruggles
  Bolton. Ezra Ames
Pierre Van Cortlandt II
  Bolton. Ezra Ames
Richard Fenimore Cooper
  Courtelyou. Ezra Ames supp
Robert Hudson
  Bolton. Ezra Ames
Romantic landscape        NAI
  Bolton. Ezra Ames
Samuel Stevenson Fowler
  Bolton. Ezra Ames
Self-portrait c1790
  Bolton. Ezra Ames
Self-portrait c1800        NAI
  Bolton. Ezra Ames
  Courtelyou. Ezra Ames supp
Self-portrait c1800 (Edwards coll)
  Bolton. Ezra Ames
Self-portrait c1810
  Bolton. Ezra Ames
Self-portrait c1814
  Bolton. Ezra Ames
Solomon Allen            NNMC
  Bolton. Ezra Ames
Solomon Van Rensselaer
  Bolton. Ezra Ames
Spencer Stafford
  Bolton. Ezra Ames
Stephen Van Rensselaer     NCHA
  Bolton. Ezra Ames
Theodore Dwight
  Bolton. Ezra Ames
Theodore Strong
  Bolton. Ezra Ames
Thomas Hillhouse
  Bolton. Ezra Ames
Thomas Humphrey Cushing
  Bolton. Ezra Ames

Unidentified boy
  Courtelyou. Ezra Ames supp
Unidentified man
  Cortelyou. Ezra Ames supp
A view of Lake George and Caldwell
  village [without fort]
  Bolton. Ezra Ames
William Annesley (?)
  Bolton. Ezra Ames
William James
  Bolton. Ezra Ames
William Tully                              CtY
  Bolton. Ezra Ames
Ames, Julius Rubens, 1801-1850
  Ames, E. Julius Rubens Ames
Ames, Marcia Lucretia, 1797/98-1886
  Ames, E. Marcia L. Ames
Ames, Zipporah (Wood) 1775-1836
  Ames, E. Mrs Ezra Ames
AMFT, Robert, 1916-
  Landscape                               OYB
  OYB. Annual 1958
  OYB. Suplement 1959
Amidon, Mary, fl 1830
  Stock, J. W. (attributed works) Mary
    Amidon
Among the led horses by F. Remington
Amory, Elizabeth (Bowen) 1777-1857
  Malbone, E. G. Mrs Thomas Amory
Amory, Georgina Margaret. See Lowell,
    Georgia Margaret (Amory)
Amory, Katherine (Greene) 1731-1777
  Copley, J. S. Mrs John Amory
Amory, Thomas, 1722-1784
  Copley, J. S. Thomas Amory jr
Amory, Mrs Thomas. See Amory, Elizabeth
    (Bowen)
L'amour, toujours l'amour by H. Franken-
    thaler
The amulet by C. Howard
ANA by S. Davis
Anahita, the flight of night by W. M. Hunt
Anatomical man by B. Shahn
The anatomist by H. Bloom
Anatomy by J. McGarrell
Ancestor by E. Friedensohn
Anchor by I. R. Pereira
Ancient facade by P. Sarkisian
The ancient form by B. Greene
Ancient valley by R. Gleitsmann
And God created man in his own image by
    I. L. Albright
And man created God in his own image by
    I. L. Albright
". . . and the home of the brave" by C. H.
    Demuth
Andalusian garden by H. G. Keller
ANDERSEN, Andreas S. 1908-
  Susan                                   ATU
  ATU. Coll of Amer art
ANDERSEN, Leif
  Siesta
  NAD. Annual ex, 1957
Anderson, Miss
  Jarvis, J. W. Miss Anderson
Anderson, Alexander, 1775-1870
  Jarvis, J. W. Alexander Anderson
Anderson, Edward A. 1923-
  Delta Queen and Packet Whisper   OYB
  OYB. Annual 1955
  OYB. Supplement 1959

Anderson, Ellen Amory. See Curtis, Ellen
    Amory (Anderson)
ANDERSON, Guy, 1906-
  Sharp sea                               WaS
  OrPA. Ptgs & sculptures
ANDERSON, John, 1923-
  Creation of Eve
  IU. Contemp Amer ptg & sculp, 1953
  Pousette-Dart. Amer ptg
Anderson children by O. Frazer
Andes by F. J. Kline
André, John, 1751-1780
  Durand, A. B. Capture of Major André
  Toole, J. Capture of Major André
André-Michel, Mme Robert. See Ormond,
    Rose Marie
ANDREWS, Ambrose, fl 1824-1859
  Schuyler family                        NNHS
  Jones. Rediscovered ptrs
ANDREWS, Sperry, 1917-
  Mill race
  NAD. Annual ex, 1953
Anemones by James McLaughlin
Angel by K. Okada
Angel by F. C. Watkins
Angel battling demons by P. Mangravite
Angel posed by F. C. Watkins
Angel releasing St Peter from prison by
    W. Allston
Angel square by D. Kingman
The angel will turn a page in the book by
    F. C. Watkins
Angel with book by D. Aronson
Los angelitos by E. Berman
Angell, James Rowland, 1869-1949
  Johansen, J. C. James Rowland Angell
Angelo's place by G. O. Coleman
Angels administering to Christ by T. Cole
Angels at the cross by D. Aronson
Angels representing adoration, praise, thanks-
    giving and love by J. La Farge
Anglers. See Fishermen and fishing
Anglers' heaven by R. M. Mason
Angora goat by E. F. Spruce
Anguish by B. Greene
Animal and mineral by J. Ernst
Animal and young by D. Hayes
Animals
  See also Cattle, Horses, Sheep, etc.
  Curry, J. S. Sanctuary
  Field, E. S. Garden of Eden
  Hicks, E. Grave of William Penn
  Hicks, E. Noah's ark
  Hicks, E. The peaceable kingdom
  Hicks, E. The peaceable kingdom of the
    branch
  Hicks, E. Residence of David Twining
  Hidley, J. H. (attributed works) Noah's
    ark
  Keller, H. G. Returning from the Feria
  Pippin, H. The holy
  Pippin, H. Holy mountain
  Remington, F. Navajo raid
  Tait, A. F. Barnyard
  Unidentified artist. Creation scene
  Woodside, J. A. Country fair
  Zeliff, A. E. Barnyard

ANLIKER, Roger William, 1924?-
Any moment
DC. 22 biennial ex, 1951
ICA. Annual ex, 1951
Caerulea
Chew. 250 years of art
Remembering
IU. Contemp Amer ptg, 1952
Ann by G. Bellows
Ann by A. Brook
Anna by R. Lebrun
Anna's garden by H. G. Keller
Anne by H. V. Poor
Anne in purple wrap by G. W. Bellows
Anne in white by G. W. Bellows
Annesley, Margaret (La Casse) 1800-1832
Ames, E. Mrs William Annesley (?)
Annesley, William, 1793-1862
Ames, E. William Annesley (?)
Annette by E. G. Malbone
Annis, Sarah. See Sully, Sarah (Annis)
Anonymous by A. G. Dove
Another expulsion by G. P. Du Bois
Another Sunday by C. F. McCall
ANSHUTZ, Thomas Pollock, 1851-1912
Aunt Hannah
MiD. Coll in progress
Becky Sharp                                    PA
PA. Annual ex, 1955
Steamboats on the Ohio
Chew. 250 years of art
Steelworkers' noontime
Chew. 250 years of art
Davidson v 1
PA. Annual ex, 1955
Pierson
Richardson. Ptg in America
U.S. National Capital sesquicentennial
com
WiMiA. Amer ptg 1760-1960
The Tanagra                                    PA
PA. Annual ex, 1955
The answer is no by K. Sage
Antelao by L. C. Scarborough
Antelope
Audubon, J. W. Prong-horned antelope
Miller, A. J. Herd of antelope
Miller, A. J. Pawnee Indian shooting
antelope
Miller, A. J. Rock of Independence
O'Keeffe, G. Antelope
Antelope mountain by E. F. Spruce
Anthony, May. See Dyer, May (Anthony)
Antietam, Condition at by F. D. Duncan
Antinomes no 1, 1959 by W. Pachner
The antique by M. Weber
The antique cast by A. Gorky
Antiques by A. Bohrod
Antiquity by R. Courtright
ANTREASIAN, Garo Zareh, 1922-
Early spring—South side
IU. Contemp Amer ptg, 1948
ANUSZKIEWICZ, Richard, 1930-
Brightness as a third dimension
IU. Contemp Amer ptg & sculp, 1961
Any moment by R. W. Anliker

Apache village on Lake Ahrocum by G. Catlin
Apaches are coming by F. Remington
Apaches listening by F. Remington
Apartment house by M. Frary
Apartment no 2 by K. Zerbe
Apartment tower by N. Spencer
The Apennines by A. B. Davies
Aperitif by H. L. McFee
Apocalypse by G. Peterdi
Apocalyptic landscape by G. Grosz
The apostle by W. W. Quirt
Apotheosis by B. Shahn
Apotheosis of Marie-Henri Beyle by J. Wilde
Apotheosis of Mexican baroque by E. Berman
The apotheosis of Nelson by B. West
Apparition by H. Hofmann
The apparition by A. Revington
Apparition of danger by H. Bloom
The appeal of Coriolanus by B. West
Apple blossoms by M. J. Heade
Apple blossoms by J. La Farge
Apple blossoms by D. Macknight
Apple country by Joe Jones
Apple gatherers by Unidentified artist
Apple hill, Cooperstown, New York. View from by S. F. B. Morse
Apple of discord by T. H. Benton
Apple orchard by G. Inness
Apple trees in December by D. J. McCosh
APPLEBY, Theodore, 1923-
Esperance
PPC. International ex, 1958
Appleford, Thomas, fl 1736-1767
Wollaston, J. Thomas Appleford
Apples by A. Dasburg
Apples by W. Sommer
Apples by W. Whittredge
Apples and jug by S. Davis
Apples in a basket by J. F. Francis
Apples in the hay by W. Kuhn
Appleton, Margaret (Gibbs) 1701-1771
Copley, J. S. Mrs Nathaniel Appleton
The appointment by M. R. Barnes
Apprentice by W. M. Chase
Approaching a city by E. Hopper
Approaching night by M. Sokole
Approaching storm by L. M. Eilshemius
Approaching storm by G. Grosz
Approaching storm by C. W. Rain
Approaching storm: beach near Newport by M. J. Heade
Approaching storm from Alban hills by G. Inness
April cat by W. Sommer
April day by D. Lutz
April 1, 1957 by J. Levee
An April mood by C. E. Burchfield
April showers by A. Rattner
April snow by H. G. Keller

**April** snow by M. B. Prendergast
**Apsaras** by E. A. Donati
**Apteka** by J. Levine
**Apthorp, Charles,** 1698?-1758
  Feke, R. Charles Apthorp
**Apthorp, Grizzel.** See Trecothick, Grizzel (Apthorp)
**Apthorp, Hannah.** See Bulfinch, Hannah (Apthorp)
**Apthorp, Sarah Wentworth.** See Morton, Sarah Wentworth (Apthorp)
**Apthorp, Susan.** See Bulfinch, Susan (Apthorp)
**Aquarelle** by G. Grosz
**Aquarelle:** collage by Tseng Yo-ho
**Aqueduct** by J. De Martini
The **aqueduct,** Pittsburgh by R. Smith
**Aquitaine** by J. Youngerman
**Arabesque** by J. Pollock
**Arabesque** with bull by F. Martin
**Arachne** by J. Sloan
**Arapahos** by A. J. Miller
**ARBOGAST, Valentine**
  Mountain goats
    NSP. Sportscapes
**Arboretum** by flashbulb by S. Davis
**Arbuckle, James,** fl 1766
  Peale, C. W. James Arbuckle
**Arbuckle, Tabitha Scarborough (Custis)** fl 1776
  Peale, C. W. Mrs James Arbuckle and son Edward
**Arc** de Triomphe, Paris by E. D. Boit
**Arcadia** II by F. Dzubas
An **Arcadian** by T. Eakins
**Arch** hotel by S. Davis
**Arch** of Octavius by A. Bierstadt
**Arch** of silence by L. Gatch
**Arch** of Titus, Rome by G. P. A. Healy
**Arch** of Triumph by B. Shahn
**Archaeological** treasure by H. Bloom
**Archaic** idol by M. Rothko
**Archaic** landscape by J. Gregoropoulos
**Archaic** rock by S. Sarkisian
**Archaic** tree by L. Gatch
**Archangel** Gabriel by B. West
**Archbold, Anne**
  MacMonnies, F. W. Mrs Anne Archbold
**ARCHER, Edmund,** 1904-
  Howard Patterson of the Harlem Yankees
    WMAA
  Goodrich. Amer art
**Archer, William S.** 1789-1855
  Healy, G. P. A. William S. Archer
**Architect's** dream by T. Cole
**Architectural** cadences by C. Sheeler
**Architecture** by C. H. Demuth
**Arctic** cabin by J. Hultberg
The **arena** by H. Weston
**Arena** of civilization by M. Tobey
**Arethusa** by A. B. Davies
**Arezzo,** Street in by E. D. Boit
**Argali**—mountain sheep by A. J. Miller
**Arguing** angels by J. W. Treiman
**Argula** by A. Gorky

**Ariadne.** See Mythological themes—Ariadne
**Aricara** female by A. J. Miller
**L'Ariccia** by R. Smith
**Arid** land by S. Sherman
**Arizona**
  Eilshemius, L. M. Yuma, Arizona
  Macknight, D. Purple abyss, Grand Canyon, Arizona
  Moran, T. Arizona sunset near the Grand Canyon
**Ark** of the covenant by E. S. Field
The **Arkansa** near the Rocky mountains, View on by S. Seymour
**Arkansas (ship)**
  Hashagen, A. Ship Arkansas leaving Havana
**Arkansas** landscape by E. F. Spruce
**ARKUSH, Jacob**
  Leona
    NAD. Annual ex, 1948
**Armchair** strategists by W. Gropper
**Armenian** girl by W. J. Glackens
**ARMER, Ruth,** 1896-
  Abstraction, no 270                    CSFM
    CSFP. Annual ex, 1948/49
    Pousette-Dart. Amer ptg
  Twilight hush
    CSFP. Anual ex, 1948/49
**Armistead, George,** 1780-1818
  Peale, Rembrandt. Col George Armistead
**Armistice** night by G. B. Luks
The **armoire** of Proteus by Y. Tanguy
**Armor** must change by B. W. Tomlin
**ARMS, John Taylor,** 1887-1953
  Mont St Michel
  Roos
**Armstrong, Hannah**
  Robinson, B. Hannah Armstrong
**Army** of the Potomac by J. Hope
**Army** officer by F. Remington
**ARNEST, Bernard Patrick,** 1917-
  Man in orange
    PPC. International ex, 1952
  Portrait of D                          CoS
    CoS. New accessions USA, 1958
  Underpass
    WMAA. Contemp Amer ptg, 1953
  View of the city through signs      MnMW
    CoS. New accessions USA, 1952
The **Arno** by O. M. Pleissner
**Arnold, Miss,** fl 1830
  Unidentified artist. Miss Arnold knitting
**Arnold, Mrs,** fl 1830
  Unidentified artist. Mrs Arnold holding an apple
**ARNOLD, Edward,** c 1824-1866
  Battle of Port Hudson, 1863            DNC
    U.S. National Capital sesquicentennial com
**Arnold** by B. Nordberg
**ARONSON, David,** 1923-
  Adoration of the Magi
    Genauer
  Angel with book
    VR. Amer ptg, 1954
  Angels at the cross
    ICA. Annual ex, 1954
  Christ before Pilate
    WMAA. Contemp Amer ptg, 1949

**ARONSON, David**—*Continued*
Coronation of the Virgin                VR
  Baur. Revolution
  MMA. Fourteen
  Pierson
Joseph and the Ishmaelites no 1        IU
  IU. Contemp Amer ptg & sculp, 1957
  IU. 20th century
Joseph and the Ishmaelites no 2
  IU. Contemp Amer ptg & sculp, 1959
Last supper                            ICA
  MMA. Fourteen
Madonna and Child with saints
  MMA. Fourteen
The magician
  IU. Contemp Amer ptg & sculp, 1961
Presentation of the Virgin
  IU. Contemp Amer ptg, 1952
Resurrection
  MMA. Fourteen
  NBuA. Expressionism
Trinity
  IU. Contemp Amer ptg, 1949
  MMA. Fourteen
Young Christ
  MMA. Fourteen
Young Joseph
  IU. Contemp Amer ptg & sculp, 1955
**Around** painting by W. Hedrick
**Arrangement** by A. B. Carles
**Arrangement** by A. H. Maurer
**Arrangement** by M. A. Sprague
**Arrangement** by B. W. Tomlin
**Arrangement** in black and brown by J. A. M. Whistler
**Arrangement** in flesh-color and black by J. A. M. Whistler
**Arrangement** in grey and black (Artist's mother) by J. A. M. Whistler
**Arrangement** in grey and black (Thomas Carlyle) by J. A. M. Whistler
**Arrangement** in pink and purple by J. A. M. Whistler
**Arrangement** on a blue table by J. Jarvaise
**Arranging** the tulips by G. Melchers
**Arrest** of Monmouth before James II by J. S. Copley
The **arrival** by C. di Marca-Relli
**Arrival**-departure by W. Pachner
**Arrival** of Nike at Panmunjom by R. L. Grilley
**Art** dealer Fleischmann by W. M. Chase
**Art** of building by T. H. Benton
**Art** of painting by A. Bohrod
**Art** on the beach by P. Evergood
**Art** versus law by D. G. Blythe
**Arthur, Chester Alan, president U.S.** 1830-1886
  Healy, G. P. A. Chester A. Arthur
**ARTHUR, Revington,** 1909-
  Circus family
    IU. Contemp Amer ptg, 1950
  Green pool
    Gruskin
  The last supper
    PPC. Ptg in the U.S. 1949
An **artist**, Portrait of by X. Gonzales
**Artist** and his model by M. Hirshfield
**Artist** and his mother by A. Gorky

An **artist** as a young man by P. Evergood
**Artist** in his studio by P. Tilyard
**Artist** in summer by H. V. Poor
**Artist** looks at nature by C. Sheeler
**Artist** showing his picture of a scene from "Hamlet" to his parents by W. Dunlap
The **artist** sketching his friends by P. Weber
**Artist's** card rack by W. M. Harnett
**Artist's** daughter by W. M. Chase
**Artist's** daughter by G. Tooker
**Artist's** dream by G. H. Comegys
**Artist's** fantasy by P. Evergood
**Artist's** mother by M. Beckmann
**Artist's** mother by W. M. Chase
**Artist's** mother by W. H. Cotton
**Artist's** mother by J. A. M. Whistler
**Artists** sketching by W. Homer
The **artist's** son by W. Zorach
**Artist's** studio by W. M. Chase
**Artist's** studio by R. A. Mintz
**Artist's** studio by J. F. Weir
**Artist's** studio in an afternoon fog by W. Homer
**Artist's** wife by A. James
**Artist's** window, View from by W. M. Harnett
The **arts** of life by T. H. Benton
**Arts** of the west by T. H. Benton
**Arundel** castle by F. Stella
**As** the sunlight bursts by H. Spiers
**Ascendant** by V. Candell
**Ascension** by J. S. Copley
**Ascension** by S. Goodman
**Ascension** by J. La Farge
The **Ascension** of our Saviour by B. West
**Ascensions** by C. Schucker
**Ascutney** mountain from Claremont, N. H. by A. Bierstadt
**Ash** can by L. MacIver
**Ashburton, Alexander Baring, baron,** 1774-1848
  Healy, G. P. A. Lord Ashburton
**Ashby, Anne.** See Manigault, Anne (Ashby)
**Ashen** gods by L. Dodd
**Asheville** by W. De Kooning
**Ashley, Elizabeth Billings,** 1745-1826
  Field, E. S. Elizabeth Billings Ashley
**Asleep** on the path by W. Sommer
**Aspects** of the harbor by L. Manso
**Aspiration** by A. V. Tack
**Aspiring** by L. Dodd
**ASPLUND, Henry Martin,** 1909-
  Nude
    NAD. Annual ex, autumn 1949
**ASPLUND, Tore,** 1903-
  Rue de Rivoli, Paris
    NAD. Special ex, 1956
  Town of Jim Thorpe, Pennsylvania
    NAD. Annual ex, 1959
**Assignation** by A. Salemme
**Assiniboin** encampment on the upper Missouri by J. M. Stanley

L'Assommoir, Illustration for by C. H. Demuth

Assorted prints by J. G. Bruff

Astle, Thomas
West, B. Thomas Astle

Astor place by F. Criss

Astoria boulevard by M. Sievan

Astral assemblage by E. W. Day

Astral image by M. Rothko

Astronomical blessings are in order by A. Salemme

At a house in Harley street by C. H. Demuth

At Barrytown, Hudson river by D. Johnson

At close quarters by C. M. Russell

At dawn by G. D. Brush

At Golgotha by R. Breinin

At Maxie Ford's by S. E. Dickinson

At nature's mirror by R. A. Blakelock

At night by K. Zerbe

At the beach by M. Beckmann

At the beach by W. J. Glackens

At the beach by M. B. Prendergast

At the beach by L. L. Ribak

At the chestnut root by A. B. Davies

At the crossing by G. Martino

At the end of the rope by C. M. Russell

At the fair by Y. Tanguy

At the fishing grounds by F. H. Lane

At the inn by D. Burliuk

At the lake by M. Weber

At the mill by M. Weber

At the opera by M. Cassatt

At the piano by J. A. M. Whistler

At the shore by A. H. Maurer

At the shore by M. B. Prendergast

At the table by H. Baumbach

Athens by J. La Farge

Athens, U.S., View of by L. Dodd

ATHERTON, John C. 1900-1952
Christmas eve                          MMA
Pierson
Construction: Shaftsbury, Vermont
CSFP. Annual ex, 1952
Fisherman's chest
ICA. Annual ex, 1951
IU. Contemp Amer ptg, 1950
Icy shore
IU. Contemp Amer ptg & sculp, 1953
Low tide monument
CSFP. Annual ex, 1948/49
Nets, boats and sea
IU. Contemp Amer ptg, 1952
Rocky farmyard
NBuA. Contemporary ptgs
Pousette-Dart. Amer ptg
WMAA. Annual ex, 1952
Spirals
SCFP. Annual ex, 1947/48
Three towers
IU. Contemp Amer ptg, 1951
Villa Rotunda                          NBuA
NBuA. Contemporary ptgs
Winter Hudson
MM. Amer ptg today

Athlete and landscape by J. Glasco

Atkins, Martha. See Barnes, Martha (Atkins)

Atkinson, Frances Deering (Wentworth) See Wentworth, Frances Deering (Wentworth) lady

Atkinson, Hannah (Wentworth) 1700-1760
Blackburn, J. Mrs Theodore Atkinson

Atkinson, Theodore, 1698-1779
Blackburn, J. Col Theodore Atkinson

Atkinson, Theodore, 1736-1769
Blackburn. J. Theodore Atkinson jr

Atlantic by E. Kelly

Atlantic by H. E. Mattson

Atlantic by T. Yerxa

Atlantic cable
Dudley, R. Splicing the cable

Atlas and Hesperides by J. S. Sargent

Atmospheric conditions by H. Bayer

Atmospheric mood by F. Ruvolo

Attack by Crow Indians by A. J. Miller

Attack on an emigrant train by C. Wimar

Attack on the supply train by F. Remington

Attacked by the stickmen by G. Grosz

Attar by P. Guston

Attic by W. De Kooning

Attic dormer by J. W. McCoy

Attic windows by R. B. Tague

Attraction by B. Connelly

Attraction by F. Ruvolo

Atwater, Edward Elias, 1816-1887
Jocelyn, N. Edward Elias Atwater

Atwood's cove by C. F. Gaertner

Aubade by E. Kelly

Aucassin and Nicoletta by C. H. Demuth

Auction day by J. Kempsmith

Aude, Mme A. F. fl 1899
Cassatt, M. Mme A. F. Aude and her two daughters

Audition by C. A. Morris

AUDUBON, John James, 1785-1851
American porcupine                     NNAM
Pierson
Murphy. John James Audubon
Black-billed cuckoo                    NNHS
NYG. Fine art
Pierson
Black-tailed hare or jack-rabbit       MoSL
Rathbone
Blue grosbeak
NYG. Fine art
Blue jay
NYG. Fine art
Bobwhite (called Virginian partridge by the artist)                     NNHS
Time. 300 years (col)
Brown pelican                          NNHS
Larkin
Larkin rev ed
California condor
Murphy. John James Audubon
Carolina parrot
NYG. Fine art
Carolina parroquet                     NNHS
Mendelowitz
Carolina turtle-dove
NYG. Fine art

**AUDUBON, J. J.**—*Continued*

Chuck-Will's widow      NNHS
     Craven. Treasury 1952 ed
Common crossbill
     NYG. Fine art
Egret. See Snowy heron
European cormorant      NNHS
     Murphy. John James Audubon
Fisher or marten
     Rathbone
Fox and goose      OYB
     Chew. 250 years of art
     OYB. Catalogue 1951
Golden plover      NNHS
     Murphy. John James Audubon
Great black-backed gull      NNHS
     Murphy. John James Audubon
Green heron      MCH
     Rathbone
Gyrfalcon      NNHS
     Pierson
Head of a buffalo calf
     Rathbone
Ivory-billed woodpecker      MCH
     Rathbone
Mockingbird (with rattlesnake robbing nest)      NNHS
     Murphy. John James Audubon
Natchez, Mississippi in 1822
     Pierson
Osprey and the otter and the salmon      ATeS
     ATeS. Collection
     NUM. Art across America
Passenger pigeon      NNHS
     Murphy. John James Audubon
Pileated woodpecker
     NYG. Fine art
Portrait of a girl
     NYG. Fine art
Purple grackle      NNHS
     Larkin rev ed (col)
     Pierson
     Richardson. Ptg in America
Red-breasted merganser
     NYG. Fine art
Red-tailed hawk      MCH
     Rathbone
Richardson's Columbian squirrel
     CtY. Yale alumni
Roseate spoonbill      NNHS
     Murphy. John James Audubon
Ruby-throated hummingbird
     NYG. Fine art
Say's or western fox squirrel      MoSLB
     Rathbone
Sea eagle (so called)      NNHS
     Murphy. John James Audubon
Shoveller duck
     NYG. Fine art
Snowy heron or white egret
     Craven. Rainbow book (col)
     Craven. Treasury 1952 ed (col)
     Murphy. John James Audubon
Snowy owl      NNHS
     Craven. Treasury 1952 ed
Snowy owl      DN
     Walker. Ptgs from America
Trumpeter swan      NNHS
     Flexner. Light of distant skies
Turkey buzzard      NNHS
     Murphy. John James Audubon

Victor Gifford Audubon
     CtY. Yale alumni
Virginia deer      NBM
     Pierson
     Roos
Wild turkey      NNHS
     Lee. Art then and now
     Murphy. John James Audubon
     NYG. Fine art
     Time. 300 years (col)
Wolverene      NNNH
     Rathbone
Woodpeckers      NNHS
     Craven. Rainbow book
     Flexner. Amer ptg
     Flexner. Short history
     Taylor. Fifty centuries, 1954 ed (col)
Yellow-breasted chat
     NYG. Fine art

### Attributed works

A girl      DN
     NYG. Fine art

### Portrait of the artist

Audubon, V. G. and Audubon, J. W. John James Audubon
Inman, H. John James Audubon

**AUDUBON, John Woodhouse, 1812-1862**

Common American deer      NNNH
     Rathbone
A Forty-niner
     U.S. National Capital sesquicentennial com
Gray wolf or white American wolf      NNNH
     Rathbone
Hare
     CtY. Yale alumni
Prairie wolf or coyote      NNNH
     Rathbone
Prong-horned antelope      NNNH
     Rathbone

**AUDUBON, John Woodhouse, 1812-1862 and AUDUBON, Victor Gifford, 1809-1860**

John James Audubon      NNAM
     Murphy. John James Audubon

**AUDUBON, Victor Gifford, 1809-1860**

### Attributed works

Hudson river view      MB
     MB. Karolik coll

### Portrait of the artist

Audubon, J. J. Victor Gifford Audubon

**AUDUBON, Victor Gifford, 1809-1860 and AUDUBON, John Woodhouse, 1812-1862**

John James Audubon      NNAM
     Murphy. John James Audubon

**AUERBACH-LEVY, William, 1889-**

Vanity
     NAD. Annual ex, 1952

**August** by L. Gatch
**August** afternoon by C. E. Burchfield
**August** evening by C. E. Burchfield
**August** in the city by E. Hopper
**August** serenity by L. Kroll
**Augusta,** Maine by Unidentified artist
**Auguste** and his horse by A. J. Miller
**Augustin, Robert,** fl 1876
     Herff, C. A. Hanging of Bob Augustin

**Aull, Mrs Robert,** fl 1837
  Bingham, G. C. Mrs Robert Aull
**AULT, George C.** 1891-1948
  Brooklyn ice house                    NJN
    Brown. Amer ptg
  Factory chimney                       PPhM
    CoS. New accessions USA, 1950
  Sullivan street abstraction
    MnMW. Precisionist view
**Aunt** Fanny by G. W. Bellows
**Aunt** Hannah by T. P. Anshutz
**Aunt** Thankful's farm by W. Thon
**Aura** of a pond by A. Okamura
**Aurangabad** market by L. Dodd
**Auratum** lily by E. W. Motley
**Aurelia** by J. Farnsworth
**Aurora** by Unidentified artist
**AUSTIN, Darrel,** 1907-
  Beast enchanted
    Gruskin (col)
  Beautiful beast
    PPC. Ptg in the U.S. 1949
  Catamount                             MMA
    Pierson
    Read. Art now, 1948 ed
  Europa and the bull                   MiD
    Cheney. Story 1958 ed
  The garden
    Cheney. Expressionism 1948 ed
  Lady in the greenwood
    IU. Contemp Amer ptg & sculp, 1953
  Moon song
    Baur. Revolution
  Sorceress
    PA. Annual ex, 1950
  The tiger
    Newmeyer
  The tightrope                         MM
    MM. 100 Amer ptrs
  Tigress with three cubs
    IU. Contemp Amer ptg & sculp, 1955
  Vixen
    Bazin
  White catamount
    CSFP. Annual ex, 1948/49
**Austin, Elizabeth (Waldo)** fl 1747
  Greenwood, J. Mrs Benjamin Austin
**Austin, Warren Robinson,** 1877-
  Finck, F. J. The Hon. Warren Robinson
    Austin, chief of the United States mis-
    sion to the United Nations
**AUSTIN, Winnifred**
  Mandarin duck
    NSP. Sportscapes
**Autobiography** by J. E. Levi
**Autocrats** by B. W. Tomlin
**Automobiles**
  Burchfield, C. E. Promenade
  Lee, D. E. Country wedding
  Moses, A. M. R. The old automobile
  Taylor, W. L. Electric automobile, Boston,
    1892
  Whorf, J. Winter, North end, Boston
**Autumn** by M. Hartley
**Autumn** by M. Hewes
**Autumn** by W. Homer
**Autumn** by W. Plate
**Autumn** convocation by W. Bailey

**Autumn** dance by K. L. Callahan
**Autumn** desert by A. Dasburg
**Autumn** festival by M. B. Prendergast
**Autumn** fruit by A. Dasburg
**Autumn** fruit by H. V. Poor
**Autumn** fruits by H. G. Keller
**Autumn** glory by K. Matthew
**Autumn** in New England, cider making by
    G. H. Durrie
**Autumn** in the Catskills by W. M. Hart
**Autumn** landscape by A. Blanch
**Autumn** landscape by E. Spruce
**Autumn** landscape by N. Takehita
**Autumn** leaves by K. Knaths
**Autumn** migration by C. A. Morris
**Autumn** no 3 by C. A. Morris
**Autumn** oaks by G. Inness
**Autumn** on the road to Deblois by J. Marin
**Autumn** outing by C. M. Williamson
**Autumn** piece, Maine by J. Marin
**Autumn** pleasures by C. C. Ross
**Autumn**—Ranchos de Taos by A. Dasburg
**Autumn** rain by D. Macknight
**Autumn** recollections by F. C. Watkins
**Autumn** rhythm by J. Pollock
**Autumn** scene by G. Inness
**Autumn** still life by W. M. Chase
**Autumnal** by A. M. Duca
**Autumnal** fantasy by C. E. Burchfield
**Avalar** by B. Hopkins
**Ave** by B. Shahn
**Avegno, Judith.** See Madame X
**Avenue** of martyrs by W. Pachner
**Avenue** of trees by M. Weber
**AVERY, Milton,** 1893-
  Advancing sea
    Breeskin. Milton Avery
  Bicycle rider by the Loire
    Breeskin. Milton Avery
  Birds over sea
    IU. Contemp Amer ptg & sculp, 1959
  Boats on Gaspé bay                    GatM
    GatM. Holbrook collection
  Breaking sea                          MdBM
    Breeskin. Milton Avery
  Brook bathers
    Breeskin. Milton Avery
  Brown hat
    Bazin
    Breeskin. Milton Avery
    Wight. Milton Avery (col)
  Bucolic landscape                     NBuA
    CoS. New accessions USA, 1948
    NBuA. Contemporary ptgs
  Burlesque
    Breeskin. Milton Avery
  Cello player
    Breeskin. Milton Avery
  The circus
    Breeskin. Milton Avery
  Clear cut landscape                   CSFM
    Breeskin. Milton Avery
    CoS. New accessions USA, 1956
    Time. 300 years (col)
  Conversation in studio
    Breeskin. Milton Avery

**AVERY, Milton**—*Continued*
Dark forest
  Breeskin. Milton Avery
Eilshemius
  Breeskin. Milton Avery
Flower vendor
  PPC. Ptg in the U.S. 1949
Gaspé landscape
  Pierson
  Wight. Milton Avery (col)
Gaspé-pink sky
  Breeskin. Milton Avery
  Wight. Milton Avery (col)
Harbor at night            DP
  DP. Catalogue
Interior with flowers      MdBM
  Wight. Milton Avery (col)
The letter
  Rathbun
March in brown
  Breeskin. Milton Avery
Morning sea
  Breeskin. Milton Avery
Mother and child (Cohen coll)
  Wight. Milton Avery (col)
Mother and child (Karlis coll)
  Beeskin. Milton Avery (col)
Music lesson
  Wight. Milton Avery (col)
Music maker
  Wight. Milestones (col)
My wife. See Woman with green face
Offshore island          NeL
  CoS. New accessions USA, 1960
Orange vase
  IU. Contemp Amer ptg, 1952
Ox on hillside           AP
  NUM. Art across America
Pink cock
  Breeskin. Milton Avery
Pink tablecloth         NUM
  Breeskin. Milton Avery
Poetry after breakfast
  Pousette-Dart. Amer ptg
Red sun
  Breeskin. Milton Avery
Reflections
  Breeskin. Milton Avery
Riders in the park
  Breeskin. Milton Avery
Rocky landscape
  IU. Contemp Amer ptg, 1950
Rooster's domain
  Breeskin. Milton Avery
Sand, sea and sky
  Breeskin. Milton Avery
Sea and dunes
  Breeskin. Milton Avery
Seascape
  WMAA. Museum and its friends, 1958
The Seine          WMAA
  Goodrich. Amer art
  WMAA. Contemp Amer ptg, 1953
Self-portrait
  Wight. Milton Avery (col)
Sheep
  Breeskin. Milton Avery
Spring in France
  IU. Contemp Amer ptg & sculp, 1955
Spring orchard
  IU. Contemp Amer ptg & sculp, 1961
Still life          PPhM
  CoS. New accessions USA, 1946

Still life with derby
  Wight. Milton Avery (col)
Sunset           NBM
  Breeskin. Milton Avery
Sunset on a quiet sea
  Breeskin. Milton Avery
Swimmers and sunbathers     MM
  Breeskin. Milton Avery
Tangerine moon and wine dark sea
  Breeskin. Milton Avery (col)
Three cows on hillside
  CSFP. Annual ex, 1947/48
Three friends
  MnMW. Contemporary
Trees           OYB
  OYB. Catalogue 1951
Two figures at dusk
  Pierson
  Wight. Milton Avery (col)
  WMAA. Neuberger collection (col)
Upper pasture
  Breeskin. Milton Avery
White moon
  Breeskin. Milton Avery
Woman with green face (My wife)
  Breeskin. Milton Avery
  Wight. Milton Avery (col)
Yellow jacket
  Breeskin. Milton Avery
Yellow meadow
  Breeskin. Milton Avery
  IU. Contemp Amer ptg & sculp, 1957
Yellow sky
  Breeskin. Milton Avery
**AVERY, Ralph H.** 1906-
Downtown fantasy
  NAD. Annual ex, 1959
The **aviary** by H. G. Keller
The **Avignon** Pieta no 2, Variation on by
  W. J. Pachner
**Avocados** by A. Dasburg
**Avxentieff.** See Pregel, Alexandra
**Awakening** by D. Newman
**Awakening** night by M. Tobey
**Awalk** poplars by A. G. Dove
**Axtell, Margaret (De Peyster)** 1728-1781
  Unidentified artist. Mrs William Axtell
  (possibly Mrs Abraham De Peyster
  jr)
  Wollaston, J. Mrs William Axtell?
**Ayers, Harriet Hubbard,** fl 1878
  Chase, W. M. Harriet Hubbard Ayers
**Azalea** tropical trails (Florida) by K.
  Matthew
**Azilum,** Site of by J. O. Montalant
**Azoic** fugue by B. Browne
The **Azores** by R. D. Gauley
**Aztec** III by J. Youngerman

# B

**b** and **p** by J. Albers
**Babbling** brook by A. B. Durand
**Babcock, Adam,** 1740-1817
  Pelham, H. Adam Babcock
**Babcock, Alice (Wyer)** See Wyer, Alice

Babcock, Mrs Francis Adam. See Wyer, Alice

Babcock, Henry, 1784-1826?
  Malbone, E. G. Henry Babcock

Babcock, Martha Hubbard. See Higginson, Martha Hubbard (Babcock)

Babette by E. E. Speicher

Baby at play by T. Eakins

Baby in blue cradle by Unidentified artist

Baby in pink and white by Unidentified artist

Baby in red chair by Unidentified artist

Baby in wicker basket by J. W. Stock

Baby reclining by Unidentified artist

Baby with doll by S. J. Hambein (attributed works)

Baby with fruit by Unidentified artist

Baby's curse by A. Leslie

Bacchanalian revel by G. Hesselius

Bacchus and Ariadne by G. Hesselius

Bach by K. Knaths

Bach orchestra by M. Weber

BACHELDER, John B. fl 1865 and CHAPPEL, Alonzo, 1828-1887
  Death of Abraham Lincoln          RPB
    U.S. National Capital sesquicentennial com

Bachelor's drawer by J. Haberle

Bachelor's friend by W. M. Harnett (attributed works)

Back of a fisherman's shop by W. M. Chase

Back of Bear mountain by J. Marin

Back of beyond V by R. Ruben

Back porches by A. Janjigian

Backdrop of East Lynne by C. H. Demuth

Backrush by W. Homer

Backstage by W. Gropper

Backus, Eunice. See Trumbull, Eunice (Backus)

A backwater, Chalcot by J. S. Sargent

Backyard on Tenth street by W. De Kooning

Backyard, winter, Maine no 2 by W. A. Kienbusch

Backyards, Greenwich village by J. Sloan

Backyards in snow by C. E. Burchfield

Backyards in spring by C. E. Burchfield

Bacon, Asa, 1771-1857
  Dickinson, A. Asa Bacon

BACON, Henry, 1839-1912
  American boats in Venice harbor          MB
    MB. Ptgs in water color
  My camels resting          MB
    MB. Ptgs in water color
  Scene on the Nile          MB
    MB. Ptgs in water color
  Tomorrow we'll be sober          MB
    MB. Ptgs in water color
  Venice lacemakers          MB
    MB. Ptgs in water color

Bacon, Mrs John. See Goldthwait, Elizabeth

Bacon, Leonard, 1802-1881
  Weir, J. F. The Theological of Yale university

Bacon, Letitia Wilson Jordan, fl 1888
  Eakins, T. Letitia Wilson Jordan Bacon

BACON, Peggy, 1895-
  Blessed damosel          WMAA
  Brown. Amer ptg
  Nobody's pet
    NYG. Fine art
  Nosegay
    NYG. Fine art
  Untilled field          WMAA
    Pierson
  Wanderlust          ATU
    ATU. Coll of Amer art

**Portrait of the artist**
  Brook, A. Peggy Bacon and Metaphysics

Badger, James, 1757-1817
  Badger, J. James Badger

BADGER, Joseph, 1708-1765
  Cornelius Waldo          MWM
    Baker. Amer ptg
    Belknap
    NNHS. Waldron Phoenix Belknap coll
  Daniel Rea          OYB
    OYB. Catalogue 1951
  Elizabeth Greenleaf          VWR
    Kallir. Amer primitive ptgs
    VWR. Folk art (col)
  Hannah Upham Haskins          NBM
    Pierson
  James Badger          MM
    Flexner. First flowers
    Pierson
  James Bowdoin          MiD
    Belknap
    MiD. Ports of the Pitts family
  Jeremiah Belknap          OCl
    Larkin
    Larkin rev ed
  John Larrabee          MWM
    Pierson
  John Pitts (after Smibert)          MiD
    MiD. Ports of the Pitts family
  Jonathan Edwards sr          CtY
    CtY. Portrait index
    Flexner. Copley
    U.S. National Capital sesquicentennial com
  Mrs Cassius Hunt          NNHS
    Belknap
  Mrs Cornelius Waldo          MWM
    Belknap
  Mrs Isaac Foster          DN
    DN. Amer primitive ptgs, pt 2
  Mrs John Edwards          MB
    Flexner. First flowers
    Pierson
    Richardson. Ptg in America
  Still life          MeC
    NUM. Art across America
  Thomas Cushing          MSE
    Belknap
  Two children          VWR
    NUM. Art across America

**Attributed works**
  A man, Portrait of          DN
    Belknap

Badgers
  La Farge, J. Uncanny badger

BAER, Howard
  Cribbage players
    PPC. Ptg in the U.S. 1949
  Fortune hunters
    DC. 21 biennial ex, 1947

Bagnell dam on the Osage river by F. Martin

Bagshot heath, Surrey by B. West (attributed works)
The Bahamas
  Hart, G. O. The Bahamas
  Homer, W. Glass windows, Bahamas
Baigneuse by A. Katz
Les baigneuses by D. Park
Bailey, Benjamin, d 1832
  Jarvis, J. W. Benjamin Bailey
Bailey, Mrs Francis
  Peale, C. W. Mrs Francis Bailey
BAILEY, Vernon Howe, 1874-
  Metropolis
    NYG. Fine art
BAILEY, William. 1930-
  Autumn convocation
    MBIC. View 1960
  Figures in landscape
    IU. Contemp Amer ptg & sculp, 1961
Bailey's beach by C. Hassam
Bailleul: tents by J. S. Sargent
Bainbridge, William, 1774-1833
  Jarvis, J. W. Commodore William Bainbridge
BAKER, George Augustus, 1821-1880

### Attributed works

Augustus Van Horne Stuyvesant, sr
                                        NNHS
  Vail. Stuyvesant ports
Mrs A. V. H. Stuyvesant        NNHS
  Vail. Stuyvesant ports
Baker, Jim, fl 1850
  Love, W. Jim Baker, a dressed-up portrait wearing a costume made by a Sioux squaw
BAKER, Roger
  Three fishermen
    NAD. Annual ex, 1960
Baking day by W. R. Leigh
Le bal Bullier by A. H. Maurer
Bal Martinique by W. J. Glackens
Bal Tabarin by E. Shinn
Balancing rock, Gloucester harbor by J. Sloan
Balcony I by K. L. Seligmann
Balcony view by L. M. Eilshemius
Bald boy by W. Sommer
Baldwin, Lucy. See Durand, Lucy (Baldwin)
BALDWIN, William, fl 1844
  Merry raftsmen
  Rathbone
Bali bazaar by M. Sterne
Baling cotton by B. Shahn
BALIS, C. fl 1850
  George and Emma Eastman        MoKN
  Jones. Rediscovered ptrs
Ball, Miss
  Jarvis, J. W. Miss Ball
Ball, Eleanor, 1731-1770
  Theus, J. Eleanor Ball
Ball, Elias, c 1675-1751
  Theus, J. Elias Ball
Ball-play of the Choctaws by G. Catlin
Ballerina and the black cat by B. Lintot
Ballet dancer by E. Shinn
Ballet girl in pink by W. J. Glackens

BALLIN, Hugo, 1879-1956
  Journey's end
    NAD. Annual ex, autumn 1949
  Reflections
    NAD. Annual ex, 1947, 2d half
  Sister Rebecca Cleaden
    NAD. Annual ex, 1949, 1st half
The balloon by M. B. Prendergast
Balloon ascension at Baltimore, 1834 by N. V. Calyo
Balsam apple and vegetable by J. Peale
Balsam apples and turnips by Raphaelle Peale
Baltic—a recollection by L. Feininger
Baltimore, Maryland
  Calyo, N. V. Balloon ascension at Baltimore, 1834
  Calyo, N. V. Baltimore in 1837
  Doughty, T. Baltimore from Beech hill, View of
  Doughty, T. Baltimore from the seat of R. Gilmor
  Guy, F. Baltimore in 1802
  Guy, F. Baltimore, 1803
  Latrobe, B. H. Roman Catholic church, Baltimore, c 1805
  Maril, H. Baltimore waterfront
  Smith, R. Old Holliday street theatre, Baltimore
  Unidentified artist. View of Baltimore, c 1840
Bamboo by W. T. Murch
Banana plant and squash by H. L. McFee
Bananas by H. Giese
Bananas and blue grapes by K. Knaths
Bananas for the attorney general by W. Homer
Bancker, Anna (Boelen) 1733-1790
  Durand, J. Mrs Adriaan Bancker
Bancker, Richard, 1728-1775
  Durand, J. Richard Bancker
Bancker, Sarah (Duyckinck) b 1732
  Durand, J. Mrs Richard Bancker
Band, Hilde. See Kayn, Hilde (Band)
Banjo lesson by H. O. Tanner
Banjo player by W. S. Mount
BANKS, Virginia, 1920-
  Basket of line and bait
    PPC. Ptg in the U.S. 1949
Banks fisherman by W. Homer
Bannister, Christian (Stelle) fl 1774
  Stuart, G. Mrs John Bannister and her son
Bannock Indian by A. J. Miller
The banquet by J. Levine
Banyar, Elizabeth (Naden) c 1739-1808
  Blackburn, J. Mrs Goldsbrow Banyar
Banyar, Goldsbrow, 1724-1815
  Ames, E. Goldsbrow Banyar
  Dickinson, A. Goldsbrow Banyar, 1808
  Trumbull, J. Goldsbrow Banyar
Banyar, Mrs Goldsbrow. See Banyar, Elizabeth (Naden)
Baptisam of our Savour by A. Johnson
Baptising at Three Wells by P. Hurd
Baptism in Kansas by J. S. Curry
Baptismal scene by M. Rothko
Bar by G. P. Du Bois
Bar and grill by M. Roberts

Bar Italia by P. Cadmus

**Barber shops**
Davis, S. Barber shop
Hicks, T. Barber shop, the musicale
Sample, P. S. Barber shop

**BARBIER, D.**

### Attributed works

Chouteau's pond, St Louis     MoSLH
  Born (here as Unidentified artist)
  Ford. Pictorial folk art

Barbizon nymph by R. H. Colescott

**Barbour, William Macleod,** 1827-1899
Weir, J. F. The Theological of Yale
  university

Barcelona market II by Martyl

Barclay children by Unidentified artist

**Bard, Isabella MacDonald (MacNichol)**
  c 1785- c 1875
Stuart, G. Mrs James Bard

**BARD, James,** 1815-1897
Hudson river steamboat Daniel Drew
  Lipman. Primitive ptrs
Hudson river steamboat Rip Van Winkle
                    MB
  MB. Karolik coll
  Pierson
  Richardson. Ptg in America
Paddle steamship Addison E. Andrews
                    MeC
  Jetté. Amer heritage collection
The Robert L. Stevens breaking ice in the
  Hudson river
  Lipman. Primitive ptrs
Tugboat O. M. Pettit       NNHS
  Lipman. Primitive ptrs

**Bard, Mrs James.** See Bard, Isabella Mac-
  Donald (MacNichol)

Bare knuckles by G. A. Hayes

Bareback rider, Paris by M. B. Prendergast

Bareback riders by W. H. Brown

Barfüsserkirche in Erfurt by L. Feininger

Bargain hunters by K. H. Miller

Bargaining for a horse by W. S. Mount

**BARKER, Walter**
Calle Paradiso         MCH
  Pulitzer v2
Stormy sky, Venice       MB
  CoS. New accessions USA, 1960
View in Forest park     MCH
  Pulitzer v2

The barker by R. Vickrey

Barker's booth by H. Koerner

**Barksdale, Thomas,** 1780-1850
Malbone, E. G. Thomas Barksdale

Barn by C. E. Burchfield

Barn Bluff, Red Wing, Minnesota by Unidentified artist

Barn by the pool by W. S. Mount

Barn chair by A. Brook

Barn interior by K. Knaths

Barn reds by C. Sheeler

Barn variation by C. Sheeler

**BARNARD, S.** fl 1831
Charleston, South Carolina     CtY
  Davidson v 1

**Barnes, Abraham,** fl 1753
Wollaston, J. Col Abraham Barnes

**Barnes, Mrs Albert C.**
Glackens, W. J. Mrs Barnes and Grover

**BARNES, Charles,** 1915-
Abstract composition     CtY
  CtY. Soc Anonyme

**Barnes, Mrs Jabez.** See Barnes, Martha
  (Atkins)

**BARNES, Lucius,** fl 1834
Martha Atkins Barnes     VWR
  VWR. Folk art (col)

**Barnes, Martha (Atkins)** 1739-1834
Barnes, L. Mrs Martha Atkins Barnes

**BARNES, Matthew Rackham,** 1880-1951
The appointment      CSFM
  CoS. New accessions USA, 1952
High peak         MMA
  Baur. Revolution

**BARNES, Robert**
James Joyce
  ICA. Annual ex, 1961

**BARNET, Will,** 1911-
Creation
  WMAA. Annual ex, 1957
Multiple images I
  DC. 27 biennial ex, 1961
Old man's afternoon
  MoSL. Contemporary Amer ptg

**BARNETT, Herbert Phillip,** 1910-
County fair        ATU
  ATU. Coll of Amer art
Gray ruin and stone house   OCiM
  CoS. New accessions USA, 1956
Lime quarry
  DC. 20 biennial ex, 1947

**BARNETT, Rita Wolpé**
To the earth
  PA. Annual ex, 1951

**Barns.** See Farmyards and farm buildings

**Barnstable,** View of by Unidentified artist

**Barnwell, Mary H.** See Means, Mary H.
  (Barnwell)

**Barnyards.** See Farmyards and farm buildings

Barometer falling by H. M. Mayer

**Baron, Alexander,** b 1777
Malbone, E. G. Dr Alexander Baron jr

**Baron, Isabelle.** See Barron, Isabel

Baroque landscape by T. Chambers (attributed works)

Barracks by H. Pippin

**Barrell, Joseph,** fl 1765
Copley, J. S. Joseph Barrell

Barrels of money by V. Dubreuil

**BARRETT, Neil,** 1915-
Chicago image
  IU. Contemp Amer ptg & sculp, 1961
Compression
  ICA. Annual ex, 1959/60
Conquered king
  IU. Contemp Amer ptg & sculp, 1959

**Barrett, Mrs Roger.** See Barrett, Neil

The barrier by F. Martin

Barriers by C. Plochmann

**Barron, Isabel,** fl 1801
Malbone, E. G. Isabel Barron

**Barrooms**
Clonney, J. G. Politicians in a country bar
Knaths, K. Barroom
Sloan, J. McSorley's back room
Sloan, J. McSorley's bar
Sloan, J. McSorley's cats

**BARTLETT, Gray,** 1885-1951
Bart's place
Carlson. Gallery (col)
Hidden spring
Carlson. Gallery (col)
Indian camp
Carlson. Gallery (col)
Indian police
Carlson. Gallery (col)
Night herd
Carlson. Gallery (col)
Ox train
Carlson. Gallery (col)
Saddled for the first time
Carlson. Gallery (col)
**BARTLETT, John Russell,** fl 1850

### Attributed works
Crossing the quicksand
Davidson v 1
**Bartlett, Lydia.** See Reynolds, Lydia (Bartlett)
**Bartlett, Paul Wayland,** 1865-1929
Hamilton, J. M. Paul Wayland Bartlett in his Paris studio
**BARTLETT, William Henry,** 1809-1894
Faneuil hall from the water
Sears. Highlights
Mt Vernon                              MdBM
NYG. Fine art
Washington's tomb, Mt Vernon    MdBM
NYG. Fine art
**Bartol, Barnabas,** fl 1826
Cole, J. G. Capt Barnabas Bartol
**BARTOLL, William Thompson,** 1817-1859
Girl and cat                           VWR
VWR. Folk art (col)
**Barton, Samuel,** 1767-1795
Gullager, C. Samuel Barton
**Bart's** place by G. Bartlett
**BASCOM, Ruth (Henshaw) Miles,** 1772-1848
Edwin Davis                            MSt
Little. Country art
Eliza Jane Gay                         NCHA
Jones. New-found folk art
Horatio Gates Henshaw of Leicester, Massachusetts                 NCHA
Jones. New-found folk art
John White
Lipman. Primitive ptrs
Lady in a sheer white cap (possibly Mrs H. G. Henshaw)            NCHA
Jones. New-found folk art
Mr and Mrs Otis Jones of Athol, Mass.
Lipman. Primitive ptrs
Mrs H. G. Henshaw (?) See Lady in a sheer white cap
Profile of a boy                       VWR
VWR. Folk art (col)
Profile of baby in orange              NCHA
Jones. New-found folk art
Self-portrait
Ford. Pictorial folk art
Lipman. Primitive ptrs
**Baseball.** See Games and sports—Baseball
**Basement** room by C. Sheeler
**Bash-Bish** falls, South Egremont, Massachusetts by J. F. Kensett
**Basic** by G. Cox
**Basket** bouquet by K. Knaths

**Basket** of clams by W. Homer
**Basket** of fruit by M. Bradley
**Basket** of fruit by Rubens Peale
**Basket** of fruit with parrot by A. M. Randall
**Basket** of line and bait by V. Banks
**Basque** fishing boats, Pasajes-Ancho by M. J. Patterson
**Bass**
Homer, W. Bass
Homer, W. Life-size black bass
**Bass** boats by M. Logan
**Bass** Rocks by S. Davis
**BASSFORD, Wallace,** 1900-
Gull a'winging
IU. Contemp Amer ptg, 1950
Motif de fête
IU. Contemp Amer ptg, 1951
**Bastille** day by M. B. Prendergast
**Bateman, Margaret Creighton**
Chase, W. M. Mrs Margaret Creighton Bateman
**Bates, Isaac**
Harding, C. Isaac Bates
**Bath, Maine**
Unidentified artist. Burning of Old South church, Bath, Maine
The **bath** by M. Cassatt
The **bath** by H. Katzman
**Bather** by E. N. Bischoff
**Bather** by I. Bishop
**Bather** by R. Haines
**Bather** by N. J. Oliveira
**Bather** by R. Reid
**Bathers** by C. Browning
**Bathers** by J. Charlot
**Bathers** by E. Cortor
**Bathers** by C. H. Demuth
**Bathers** by L. Feininger
**Bathers** by W. M. Hunt
**Bathers** by B. Karfiol
**Bathers** by J. McGarrell
**Bathers** by M. B. Prendergast
**Bathers** by P. Tchelitchew
**Bathers** by A. Toney
**Bathers** by M. Weber
**Bathers** in a grotto by A. Ozenfant
**Bathers** on rocks by J. Marin
**Bathers,** the cove, La Jolla by H. G. Keller
**Bathers:** eight foreground figures by Walkowitz
**Bathers:** four foreground figures by A. Walkowitz
**Bathers:** three foreground figures by A. Walkowitz
**Bathing** at Bellport by W. J. Glackens
**Bathing,** Marblehead by M. B. Prendergast
**Bathing** party in New York by W. P. Chappel
**Bathing** pool by C. Codman
**Battell, Joseph,** 1806-1874
Hovenden, T. Joseph Battell
**Battell, Mrs Philip,** fl 1831
Mason, B. F. Mrs Philip Battell
**Battersea** Reach by J. A. M. Whistler

Battery Bee by C. W. Chapman

Battery belles by R. Marsh

Battery park, New York, in winter by G. W. Bellows

Battle at sunset with the God of the maize by A. Gorky

Battle front by J. S. Sargent

Battle of lights, Coney island by J. Stella

Battle of the elks by C. M. Russell

Battle of the gods by K. L. Callahan

**BAUM, Don,** 1922-
  Portrait
    ICA. Annual ex, 1957

**BAUM, Walter Emerson,** 1884-1956
  Winter's end            OT
    OT. Contemp Amer ptgs

**BAUMAN, Leila T.** fl 1850
  Geese in flight           DN
    DN. Amer primitive ptgs, pt 2
  U.S. mail boat         DN
    DN. Amer primitive ptgs, pt 2

**BAUMBACH, Harold,** 1903-
  At the table
    IU. Contemp Amer ptg, 1952
  New England landscape    ATU
    ATU. Coll of Amer art

**BAUMGARDEN, George**
  Telephone habit
    Davidson v2

**BAUMGARTNER, Warren W.** 1894-
  Cascade waters
    NAD. Annual ex, 1960
  La push
    NAD. Annual ex, 1955
  Stonehenge
    NAD. Annual ex, 1949, 2d half

The bay by W. Farndon

The bay beyond by A. Brook

Bay bottom by L. Bunce

Bay mare and colt and a couple of others by C. S. Price

Bay of Panama by M. J. Heade

Bayard, Anna Maria. See Jay, Anna Maria (Bayard)

Bayard, Mary (Beekman) See Beekman, Mary

Bayard, Mrs Stephen N. See Beekman, Mary

Bayard, Pierre du Terrail, seigneur de, 1474?-1524
  West, B. Death of the Chevalier Bayard

**BAYER, Herbert,** 1900-
  Atmospheric conditions
    Rathbun
  Linear structure
    CoS. New accessions USA, 1960
  Verdure           MNS
    CoS. New accessions USA, 1952

**BAYNE, Walter M. S.** fl 1853
  Landscape (painted in style of Doughty)
    Sears. Highlights

Bazaar with coconut palms, Bali by M. Sterne

**BAZIOTES, William A.** 1912-
  Amazon
    OCl. Some contemporary works
  The beach         WMAA
    Baur. Nature
    Cheney. Story 1958 ed
    Goodrich. Amer art

Black night           PPC
  CoS. New accessions USA, 1956
  IU. Contemp Amer ptg & sculp, 1955

Black on white        NUM
  NUM. Root bequest

Black silhouette
  CSFP. Annual ex, 1950/51

Blue mirror
  McCurdy
  MMA. Abstract (col)

Cat
  MMA. Fifteen

Congo
  ICA. Annual ex, 1954

Desert landscape
  IU. Contemp Amer ptg & sculp, 1953

Dragon           MM
  Baur. New art
  Brussels. Exposition
  MM. 100 Amer ptrs
  Taylor. Fifty centuries, 1954 ed (col)

Dusk           NNSG
  NNSG. Handbook

Dusk           PPC
  Read. Concise history

The dwarf         MMA
  Baur. New art
  Baur. Revolution
  MMA. Contemp ptrs
  MMA. New Amer ptg (col)
  Pierson

Egyptian
  MnU. 40 Amer ptrs

Flame           NNSG
  Chew. 250 years of art
  Mendelowitz
  IU. Contemp Amer ptg & sculp, 1957
  NNSG. Younger Amer ptrs

Flesh eaters
  PPC. International ex, 1952

The fountain
  Hess. Abstract ptg

Green night
  MnMW. 60 Amer ptrs

Jungle
  Baur. New art (col)
  MMA. Fifteen
  Pousette-Dart. Amer ptg

Moby Dick
  WMAA. Contemp Amer ptg, 1955
  WMAA. Museum and its friends, 1958

Moon animal        IU
  IU. Contemp Amer ptg, 1951
  IU. 20th century
  OCl. Some contemporary works

Moon fantasy
  WMAA. New decade

Moon forms
  Baur. New art
  CSFP. Annual ex, 1948/49
  WMAA. New decade

Mummy
  Hess. Abstract ptg

Night mirror
  MMA. Fifteen

Pompeii           MMA
  Art since 1945
  MMA. New Amer ptg
  Pierson
  Time. 300 years (col)

Primeval landscape     PPhM
  MMA. New Amer ptg
  WMAA. Contemp Amer ptg, 1953

**BAZIOTES, W. A.**—*Continued*
Red landscape      MnMI
  Hunter. Mod Amer ptg
The sea
  Ponente. Mod ptg, 1960 (col)
  WMAA. Contemp Amer ptg, 1959/60
Sleepwalker
  Blesh
  IU. Contemp Amer ptg, 1950
Still life, 1945
  MnU. 40 Amer ptrs
Toy in the sun      CLA
  CoS. New accessions USA, 1952
Toy world
  MMA. Fifteen
Trance
  MnMW. Reality and fantasy
  WMAA. New decade
White bird      NBuA
  NBuA. Acquisitions 1957-58
  WMAA. Annual ex, 1957
The **beach** by W. A. Baziotes
The **beach** by R. Frame
The **beach** by H. Koerner
The **beach** by W. Pachner
The **beach** by E. F. Spruce
**Beach** at Annisquam by W. J. Glackens
**Beach** at Dieppe by W. J. Glackens
**Beach** at Gloucester by M. B. Prendergast
**Beach** at Miramar by C. G. Farr
**Beach** at St Ives, Cornwall, England by H. Lever
**Beach** at St Jean de Luz by W. J. Glackens
**Beach** at Sestri Levante, Italy by E. D. Boit
**Beach** grass by H. Durfee
**Beach** hat by R. Henri
**Beach** patterns by H. G. Keller
**Beach** patterns by C. A. Morris
**Beach** scene near New London by W. J. Glackens
**Beach** scene with a newspaper by H. Sterner
**Beach** scene with figures by M. B. Prendergast
**Beach** with blue tree by M. B. Prendergast
**Beachcomber** by J. E. Levi
**Beachmont** by M. B. Prendergast
**Beacon-on-the-Hudson** by Unidentified artist
**BEAL, Gifford Reynolds, 1879-1956**
Afterglow      ATeS
  ATeS. Collection
The Albany boat      MM
  MM. 100 Amer ptrs
  Pierson
Circus at the Hippodrome
  McCurdy
Circus parade
  NAD. Annual ex, 1956
Circus ponies      DP
  DP. Catalogue
Columbus avenue, snowy day
  NAD. Annual ex, 1947, 2d half
Dock square
  NAD. Annual ex, 1951
Dublin pool
  NAD. Annual ex, 1948
Freight yards      NSyE
  Brown. Amer ptg

Hunter, winter
  NSP. Sportscapes
Impression from Life with father      DP
  DP. Catalogue
Sunday morning
  CSB. Impressionism
Terrace, Central park
  Gruskin
The **bear** dance by G. Catlin
**BEARD, James Henry, 1814-1893**
Land speculator
  U.S. National Capital sesquicentennial com
The long bill      OCiM
  Barker. Amer ptg
  U.S. National Capital sesquicentennial com
**BEARDEN, Romare, 1912-**
Christ driving the money changers from the Temple
  Rathbun
**Bearers** of gifts by K. M. Martin
**Bears**
  Miller, A. J. Grizzly bear
  Miller, A. J. Hunting the bear
  Russell, C. M. Capturing the grizzly
  Russell, C. M. A disputed trail
  Russell, C. M. Roping a grizzly
**Bear's** Paw by J. M. Stanley
The **beast** by W. Millarc
**Beast** enchanted by D. Austin
The **beast** in the jungle, Illustrations for by C. H. Demuth
**Beating** a retreat by A. J. Miller
**Beatrice** by W. Allston
**Beatrice** standing by W. J. Glackens
**BEATTIE, George**
Pisa      OCl
  Pousette-Dart. Amer ptg
**BEAUCHAMP, John W. 1906-**
Painting      WMAA
  Pousette-Dart. Amer ptg
**BEAUCHAMP, Robert, 1923-**
Two sisters
  PPC. International ex, 1961/62
**BEAUGUREAU, Francis H.**
Seoul, 1952
  NAD. Annual ex, 1959
**Beaulieu** by M. Beckmann
**Beauregard, Pierre Gustave Toutant, 1818-1893**
  Healy, G. P. A. General P. G. T. Beauregard
**Beautification** by M. Weber
**Beautiful** beast by D. Austin
The **beauty** by G. P. Du Bois
**Beauty** is where you find it by A. A. Dehn
**Beauty** parlor by C. M. Russell
**BEAUX, Cecilia, 1863-1942**
The dreamer      OYB
  OYB. Catalogue 1951
Fanny Travis Cochran. See A little girl—Fanny Travis Cochran
A little girl—Fanny Travis Cochran    PA
  Chew. 250 years of art
Man in white (Dr Henry S. Drinker)   DN
  Pierson
Les **beaux** by L. MacIver

**Beaver** lake, Lost river region by M. Hartley
**Beaver** Meadow by P. S. Sample
BECK, Leonard
  Mahu
    IU. Contemp Amer ptg, 1948
  Memory
    IU. Contemp Amer ptg, 1948
BECK, Margit, 1915-
  Rockport harbor
    NAD. Annual ex, 1955
  Rocks and pines
    ICA. Annual ex, 1961
BECK, Rosemarie, 1923-
  House of the moon, II, 1956
    Baur. Nature
  Number 2, 1955
    WMAA. Young America 1957
  Number 3, 1954      WMAA
    Pierson
    WMAA. Young America 1957
Becker, Mrs Alfred L.
  Hawthorne, C. W. Mrs Alfred L. Becker
BECKER, Joseph, 1841-1910
  First train on the Central Pacific railroad, 1869
    U.S. National Capital sesquicentennial com
BECKETT, Charles E. 1814-1866?
  Furbish's dash to Montreal    NCHA
    Jones. New-found folk art
Beckett, Marianne, fl 1829
  Peale, A. C. Marianne Beckett
BECKMANN, Max, 1884-1950
  Acrobat on trapeze
    MoSL. Beckmann
  Acrobats
    MMA. Contemp ptrs
  Actors
    MoSL. Beckmann
    Pearson. Mod renaissance
  Artist's mother
    MoSL. Beckmann
  At the beach
    Cheney. Expressionism 1948 ed
  Beaulieu
    IU. Contemp Amer ptg, 1950 (col)
  Begin the beguine    MiA
    MoSL. Beckmann
  Black lilies
    UNESCO. 1860-1955
  Blindman's buff
    MoSL. Beckmann
  The boat
    PA. Annual ex, 1951
  Boat on the Riviera
    MoSL. Beckmann
  Cabana
    MoSL. Beckmann
  Café
    MoSL. Beckmann
  Cattle in barn
    MoSL. Beckmann
  Christ and the woman taken in adultery
    MoSL. Beckmann
  Christ in Limbo
    MoSL. Beckmann
  Circus caravan
    Read. Concise history (col)
  Dancer with tambourine
    MoSL. Beckmann

Departure    MMA
  Barr. What is mod ptg
  Canaday
  50 years of mod art
  Janson. Key monuments
  Janson. Picture history (col)
  McCurdy
  MMA. Ptg and sculpture
  MoSL. Beckmann
  Myers. Art
  Newmeyer
  Robb. Harper history
Descent from the cross    MMA
  McCurdy
Double portrait
  MoSL. Beckmann
The dream
  Janson. Key monuments
  MoSL. Beckmann
Eternity
  MoSL. Beckmann
Euretta
  MoSL. Beckmann
Family picture    MMA
  MoSL. Beckmann
Fisherwomen
  MnMW. Expressionism 1900-1955
  PPC. Ptg in the U.S. 1949
  Time. 300 years (col)
Four men around a table    MoSLW
  McCurdy
  MMA. Contemp ptrs
  MoSL. Beckmann
Galleria Umberto
  MoSL. Beckmann
Genius
  MoSL. Beckmann
Girl with parrot
  MoSL. Beckmann
Hotel lobby    NBuA
  CoS. New accessions USA, 1950
  NBuA. Expressionism
  PPC. International ex, 1950
Ice floes
  Cheney. Expressionism 1948 ed
The king
  MoSL. Beckmann
Laboratory
  CSFP. Annual ex, 1948/49
Landscape with factory
  MoSL. Beckmann
Louise Pulitzer    MCH
  Pulitzer v2
Man and woman
  MoSL. Beckmann
Man with fish
  Read. Concise history
Masquerade    MCH
  Pulitzer v2
The mill
  MoSL. Beckmann
Mirror
  MoSL. Beckmann
The night
  Myers
Nude
  Read. Art now, 1948 ed
Pau de St Jannes
  MoSL. Beckmann
Portrait of the artist with a saxophone
  50 years of mod art
The prodigal son among swine    MMA
  MoSL. Beckmann

BECKMANN, Max—*Continued*
Quappi in turban
  MoSL. Beckmann
The rainbow
  UNESCO. 1860-1955
Reclining woman with mandolin
  Moderns and their world (col)
Removal of the Sphinxes
  MoSL. Beckmann
Robbery of Europe
  Moderns and their world
Self-portrait, 1912
  MoSL. Beckmann
Self-portrait, 1950
  Pearson. Mod renaissance
Self-portrait with a cigarette, 1923    MMA
  McCurdy
  MoSL. Beckmann
The shore
  UNESCO. 1860-1955
Skaters
  MoSL. Beckmann
Soldier's dream
  MoSL. Beckmann
Souvenir of Chicago    MCH
  Pulizter v 1
Still life with fish and pinwheel
  MoSL. Beckmann
Still life with flowers
  MoSL. Beckmann
The street
  MoSL. Beckmann
  Pearson. Mod renaissance
Studio corner
  CSFP. Annual ex, 1950/51
  MoSL. Beckmann
Summer day
  UNESCO. 1860-1955
Tightrope dancer
  IU. Contemp Amer ptg, 1949
Tulips
  UNESCO. 1860-1955
Two women
  50 years of mod art (col)
Young men by the sea, 1905
  MoSL. Beckmann
Young men by the sea, 1943    MoSL
  MoSL. Beckmann
  MoSL. Handbook 1953
Zeretelli    MCH
  MoSL. Beckmann
  Pulitzer v 1
BECKWITH, James Carroll, 1852-1917
Henry Parks Wright    CtY
  CtY. Portrait index
William H. Brewer    CtY
  CtY. Portrait index
Becky Sharp by T. P. Anshutz
Bedrooms
  Benson, F. W. Fisherman's bedroom,
    Eastham, Massachusetts
  De Martini, J. Interior with three figures
  Pittman, H. Nine P. M.
Bee hunter by A. J. Miller
Bee keeper by E. F. Spruce
The beech by L. Gatch
Beecher, Lyman, 1775-1863
  Harding, C. Lyman Beecher
BEECHER, William Ward
  Collector's cabinet
    CSFP. Annual ex, 1952

Beeches by A. B. Durand
Beechwood boulevard, Pittsburgh by J. Kane
Beekman, Catharina (De Boogh) fl 1720
  Unidentified artist. Lady of the Beekman
    family (Mrs William Beekman?)
Beekman, Catherine, 1762-1839
  Durand, J. Catherine Beekman
Beekman, Catherine Peters (De Lanoy)
    1691-1765
  Duyckinck, E. (attributed works) Mrs
    William Beekman
Beekman, Cornelia, 1708-1786
  Duyckinck, E. Cornelia Beekman
Beekman, Gerardus, 1684-1770
  Duyckinck, G. (attributed works)    Col
    Gerardus Beekman
Beekman, Henry
  Unidentified artist. Henry Beekman
Beekman, James, fl 1761
  Kilburn, L. James Beekman
Beekman, Mrs James. See Beekman, Jane
    (Keteltas)
Beekman, Jane (Keteltas)
  Kilburn, L. Mrs James Beekman
Beekman, Magdalen
  Unidentified artist. Magdalen Beekman
Beekman, Mary, 1765-1831
  Durand, J. Mary Beekman
Beekman, William, 1623-1707
  Unidentified artist. Gentleman of the
    Beekman family (William Beekman?)
Beekman, William, 1653-1728
  Duyckinck, G. (attributed works) Dr Wil-
    liam Beekman
Beekman, William, 1684-1770
  Duyckinck, E. (attributed works) Dr Wil-
    liam Beekman
Beekman, Mrs William, 1691-1765. See
    Beekman, Catherine Peters (De
    Lanoy)
Beekman, Mrs William, fl 1720. See Beek-
    man, Catharina (De Boogh)
Beers, Sally. See Leffingwell, Sally (Beers)
Beers, Timothy Phelps, 1789-1858
  Jocelyn, N. Timothy Phelps Beers
Beetle with red markings by C. Culver
Before the white man came by C. M. Russell
The beggars' dance of Teton Sioux by G.
    Catlin
Beggar's joys by P. Guston
Begin the beguine by M. Beckmann
Beginning by A. Osver
Beginning of a snowstorm by C. E. Burch-
    field
Begonias by E. E. Speicher
Behold by L. P. Smith
Behold . . . man by U. Romano
Belated wayfarers by G. C. Bingham
Belcher, Abigail (Adams) 1727-1771
  Copley, J. S. Mrs Jonathan Belcher
Belcher, Jonathan, 1710-1776
  Copley, J. S. Jonathan Belcher jr
Belfield by Rubens Peale (original by C. W.
    Peale)
Belgian melon by W. M. Chase
Belinda standing by A. Brook
Belisarius and the boy by B. West
Belknap, Aaron, 1789-1847
  Durand, A. B. Aaron Belknap

Belknap, Aaron Betts, 1816-1880
  Durand, A. B. Aaron Betts Belknap
Belknap, Jeremiah, b 1752
  Badger, J. Jeremiah Belknap
Belknap, Mary Josepha Lydia Stearns (Belknap) 1771-1862
  Durand, A. B. Mrs Aaron Belknap
BELKNAP, Zebakiah, 1781-1858
  Mrs Thomas Belknap                    VWR
    VWR. Folk art (col)
  Thomas Harrison                       VWR
    VWR. Folk art (col)
Bella Venezia by E. Berman
The Belle Creole at New Orleans by Unidentified artist
Belles of the Battery by R. Marsh
BELLOWS, Albert Fitch, 1829-1883
  Wayside inn                           MB
    MB. Ptgs in water color
Bellows, Anna (Smith)
  Bellows, G. W. My mother
Bellows, Anne
  Bellows, G. W. Anne in purple wrap
  Bellows, G. W. Anne in white
Bellows, Emma Louise Story
  For portraits of Mrs Bellows see entries under Bellows, G. W. beginning with titles "Emma"
Bellows, George, fl 1906
  Bellows, G. W. My father
Bellows, Mrs George. See Bellows, Anna (Smith)
BELLOWS, George Wesley, 1882-1925
  Ann                                   ATeS
    ATeS. Collection
  Anne in black                         MAC
    NUM. Art across America
  Anne in purple wrap                   MAP
    DN. Bellows
  Anne in white                         PPC
    DN. Bellows
  Aunt Fanny                            IaDM
    Baur, Revolution
    DN. Bellows
    Time. 300 years (col)
  Battery park, New York, in winter. See Blue snow, the Battery
  Beach at Coney island
    DN. Bellows
  Big dory                              CtNB
    DN. Bellows
  Blue morning
    DN. Bellows
  Blue snow, the Battery (Battery park, New York)
    DN. Bellows
    OCo. George Bellows
  Both members of this club             DN
    Baur. New art (col)
    Baur. Revolution
    DN. Bellows
    McCurdy
    NYG. Fine art
    Pierson
    Seiberling
    UNESCO. 1860-1949
    UNESCO. 1860-1955
    Walker. Ptgs from America
  A boy                                 InIJ
    InIJ. 105 ptgs

Chester Dale                            DN
  DN. Bellows
Children on the porch (On the porch)    OCo
  DN. Bellows
  Time. 300 years (col)
The circus                              MAP
  DN. Bellows
  Lee. Art then and now
  OCo. George Bellows
Cliff dwellers                          CLA
  CLA. 35 ptgs
  Craven. Treasury 1952 ed
  DN. Bellows
  Pierson
Club night
  DN. Bellows
  WMAA. Museum and its friends, 1958
Cornfield and harvest                   OCo
  DN. Bellows
Crowd, polo game. See Polo scene
Crucifixion                             ICA
  Brown. Amer ptg
  Cheney. Expressionism 1948 ed
Dawn of peace                           OCiM
  Brown. Amer ptg
Day in June                             MiD
  DN. Bellows
  MiD. Treasures
Dempsey and Firpo                       WMAA
  DN. Bellows
  Goodrich. Amer art
  Larkin
  Larkin rev ed
  Mendelowitz
  NYG. Fine art
  OCo. George Bellows
  Roos
  Upjohn
Edith Cavell                            MSM
  DN. Bellows
  MSM. Handbook
  OCo. George Bellows
Elinor, Jean and Anna                   NBuA
  Baur. New art
  Canaday
  DN. Bellows
  Lewisohn
  NAD. Amer tradition
  NBuA. Catalogue of the ptgs
  Pierson
  Roos
Emma and her children                   MB
  DC. 25 biennial ex, 1957
Emma in black (Emma at a window) DP
  DN. Bellows
  DP. Catalogue
Emma in purple dress                    TxD
  DN. Bellows
Fisherman
  DN. Bellows
Fisherman's family
  DN. Bellows
Fishermen's huts
  DN. Bellows
Floating ice                            WMAA
  DN. Bellows
  Goodrich. Amer art (col)
Fog breakers-sea spume                  GAtM
  GAtM. Holbrook collection

BELTON, Francis S. fl 1817-34
  Rochester, New York, c1820
    WiMiA. Amer ptg 1760-1960
BEMELMANS, Ludwig, 1898-1962
  Sketch for Parsley: The end
    NSP. Sportscapes
  Sketch for Parsley: The hunter's fall
    NSP. Sportscapes
Ben Cruachan by R. Smith
Benares by M. Sterne
Benares on the Ganges by M. Sterne
BENBRIDGE, Henry, 1744-1812
  Gatling children
    Chew. 250 years of art
  Hartley family group
    Pierson
Bend at Newton Hook by C. F. Gaertner
Bend in Storm King by C. F. Gaertner
Bender, Horace, pseud. See Greenough,
  Horatio
Benham, Jonathan, fl 1710
  Unidentified artist. Jonathan Benham
BENJAMIN, Max, 1928-
  Peninsula
    OrPA. Ptgs & sculptures
Benjamin Reber's farm, View of by C. Hof-
  mann
Benjamin's house by A. N. Wyeth
BENN, Ben, 1884-
  Mother and child                    WMAA
    Baur. Revolution
    Pierson
  Sea gulls
    PA. Annual ex, 1952
BENNET, F. R. fl 1875
  Dance on a Sequoia swamp           NCHA
    Jones. New-found folk art
Bennett, F. R. See Bennet, F. R.
BENNETT, Rainey, 1907-
  Blue mist
    IU. Contemp Amer ptg & sculp, 1959
  Composition
    IU. Contemp Amer ptg & sculp, 1961
  Evening light
    IU. Contemp Amer ptg, 1951
  Red studio
    IU. Contemp Amer ptg & sculp, 1957
BENNETT, William James, 1787-1844
  Broadway from Bowling Green, c 1826
    Davidson v2
  Detroit, 1836
    Davidson v2
  Packet Row, South street, New York
                                      NNPL
    Davidson v 1
BENRIMO, Thomas Duncan, 1887-1958
  Biaxial
    NNSG. Younger Amer ptrs
  Fetish
    ICA. Annual ex, 1951
  Figure in space
    WMAA. Contemp Amer ptg, 1952
  Goat song
    IU. Contemp Amer ptg & sculp, 1955
  Lute player
    IU. Contemp Amer ptg, 1951
  Mirage                               OCiM
    CoS. New accessions USA, 1954
  Nostalgic migration
    ICA. Annual ex, 1947/48

Pastorale
  IU. Contemp Amer ptg, 1952
Quiescent space
  IU. Contemp Amer ptg & sculp, 1953
Reflections
  Pousette-Dart. Amer ptg
Ring around the moon
  IU. Contemp Amer ptg & sculp, 1957
BENSON, Frank Weston, 1862-1951
  The bowsprit                         MB
    MB. Ptgs in water color
  Currituck marshes, North Carolina    MB
    MB. Ptgs in water color
  Danvers river, Massachusetts         MB
    MB. Ptgs in water color
  Fisherman's bedroom, Eastham, Massa-
    chusetts                           MB
    MB. Ptgs in water color
  Lower reservoir, Tihonet             MB
    MB. Ptgs in water color
  Meadows in winter                    MB
    MB. Ptgs in water color
  My daughters                         MWM
    Roos
  Rainy day                            ICA
    NYG. Fine art
  Red and gold                         OYB
    OYB. Catalogue 1951
  Redhead ducks                        MB
    MB. Ptgs in water color
  Still life                           DC
    NYG. Fine art
Benson, Robert, 1739-1823
  Trumbull, J. Robert Benson
BENTLEY, Claude Ronald, 1915-
  Colima
    IU. Contemp Amer ptg & sculp, 1957
  Separated
    IU. Contemp Amer ptg, 1949
  Smoking mirror
    DC. 27 biennial ex, 1961
  White sands
    IU. Contemp Amer ptg, 1951
BENTLEY, Lester
  George Wyckoff jr
    PPC. Ptg in the U.S. 1949
BENTON, Thomas Hart, 1889-
  Aaron                                PA
    Benton
    Craven. Treasury 1952 ed
  After the storm
    KLU. Benton
  Agriculture and logging (mural)
    Larkin (detail)
    Larkin rev ed (detail)
  America today                        NNSR
    Lewisohn
  Apple of discord
    KLU. Benton
  Art of building                      NNSR
    Roos
  Arts of life                         CtNB
    Cheney. Story 1958 ed
  Arts of the west                     CtNB
    Craven. Rainbow book
    Mendelowitz
    Pierson
  Arts of the west                     WMAA
    Craven. Treasury 1952 ed
    Myers
    Upjohn

**BENTON, T. H.**—*Continued*

Boomtown, 1928                                    NR
    Baur. New art
    Pierson
Carl Ruggles. See Sun treader
Catalytic crackers
    Benton
Cattle loading, West Texas                       MAP
    Wight. Milestones
Chilmark                                         OYB
    Baur. Revolution
    OYB. Catalogue 1951
Cradling wheat                                   MoSL
    KLU. Benton
    MoSL. Handbook 1953
Custer's last stand
    KLU. Benton
First crop                                       IBM
    Bazin
Hailstorm                                        NeO
    Baur. New art
    CoS. New accessions USA, 1952
Harzfeld's mural
    Benton
History of the early United States
    KLU. Benton
Hollywood
    KLU. Benton
Homestead                                        MMA
    Newmeyer
Jealous lover of Lone Green valley
    McCurdy
    Roos
Jessie, 17 years old
    KLU. Benton
July hay                                         MM
    Baur. New art (col)
    Flexner. Amer ptg
    Flexner. Short history
    Pierson
    Time. 300 years (col)
June hay                                         MM
    Benton
Little brown jug
    IaDa. Wood
Lord heal the child
    KLU. Benton
The Lord is my shepherd                          WMAA
    Goodrich. Amer art
    KLU. Benton
Louisiana rice fields                            NBM
    Baur. Revolution
    Canaday
    NYG. Fine art
The meal                                         WMAA
    Lee. Art then and now
Missouri mural
    Benton
Negro soldier
    Benton
    KLU. Benton
New England editor                               MB
    CoS. New accessions USA, 1948
Persephone
    Benton
    KLU. Benton
Photographing the bull
    KLU. Benton
Political, business and intellectual ballyhoo
    (Ceiling panel no 6)                         CtNB
    Brown. Amer ptg
Preparing the bill
    Baur. New art

Roasting ears                                    MM
    Craven. Rainbow book (col)
    Craven. Treasury 1952 ed (col)
    MM. 100 Amer ptrs (col)
    Taylor. Fifty centuries, 1954 ed (col)
Self-portrait
    Benton
    KLU. Benton
Silver vase
    KLU. Benton
Soldier's joy
    Benton
Sun treader—Portrait of Carl Ruggles,
    1934                                         MoKN
    Baur. New art
    KLU. Benton
Susanna and the elders                           CSFP
    Benton
    CSFP. Handbook
Three figures
    Brown. Amer ptg
    WMAA. Pioneers
Threshing wheat                                  InTH
    InTH. Catalogue
    KLU. Benton
    UNESCO. 1860-1955
Weighing cotton
    Gruskin (col)
White horse
    KLU. Benton

**BEN-ZION,** 1899-
De profundis
    Pearson. Mod renaissance
Handwriting on the wall
    IU. Contemp Amer ptg, 1952
Large thistles
    IU. Contemp Amer ptg & sculp, 1955
Moses
    Pierson
Orchard with yellow sky
    IU. Contemp Amer ptg & sculp, 1953
The poet and the saint
    Pearson. Mod renaissance
Symbols of our time
    Pearson. Mod renaissance
Three dancers
    ICA. Annual ex, 1947/48
White pitcher with field flowers
    IU. Contemp Amer ptg, 1950

**Berezov, Mrs Maurice.** See Fine, Perle
**Berg, Alban,** 1885-1935
    Rederer, F. J. Alban Berg, Portrait of
**Bergamo, Italy** by J. L. Smith
**BERGER, Jason,** 1924-
    Marilyn at the table
        MBIC. View 1960
**BERGHOFF, Jack**
    Nardin park                                  OYB
        OYB. Annual 1953
**BERGMANN, Franz,** 1898-
    Circus
        CSFP. Annual ex, 1946
**Berkeley, George,** bp, 1685-1753
    Smibert, J. Bishop Berkeley and his fam-
        ily
**Berkeley, Philippa Frances (Culpeper) Lady,**
    1635-1690?
    Unidentified artist. Lady Berkeley
**Berkeley 54,** 1955 by R. Diebenkorn
**Berkeley no 2** by R. Diebenkorn

Berkeley no 16 by R. Diebenkorn
Berkeley no 38 by R. Diebenkorn
Berks county almshouse, Views of the sur-
    roundings of by C. Hofman
Berkshire mountains
    Durand, A. B. Monument mountain, Berk-
        shires
BERLANDINA, Jane, 1898-
    Abstraction, 1945                    MCH
        Pulitzer v2
    Almost airtight compartments         MCH
        Pulitzer v2
    Figures in space
        IU. Contemp Amer ptg & sculp, 1955
    The garden                           MCH
        Pulitzer v2
    Let's search our souls               MCH
        Pulitzer v2
    Passage a travers                    MoSL
        CoS. New accessions USA, 1954
    Three clowns                         CSFD
        CoS. New accessions USA, 1948
BERLIN, Bernard, 1918-
    Dance hall
        ICA. Annual ex, 1959/60
Berlin, May 3, 1945 by J. Groth
BERMAN, Eugene, 1899-
    Los angelitos
        CSFP. Annual ex, 1948/49
    Apotheosis of\ Mexican baroque
        CSFP. Annual ex, 1950/51
    Bella Venezia
        ICA. Annual ex, 1947/48
    Bridges of Paris                     PPhM
        Canaday
    The cart                             MMA
        MMA. Soby collection
    Courtyard                            DP
        DP. Catalogue
    Dark muse
        Pearson. Mod renaissance
    Daybreak                             DP
        DP. Catalogue
    Dead life, sea lion skull, driftwood and
        coral
        CSFP. Annual ex, 1947/48
    Devil's holiday                      MMA
        MMA. Masters
    Evening in Venice
        Read. Art now, 1948 ed
    Gates of the city, nightfall         MMA
        CSFP. Illusionism
        McCurdy
        Pierson
    Hat seller                           CtHW
        CtHW. Handbook (col)
    Magic circle, Venice
        Myers
    Mélancholie
        CtY. Yale alumni
    Memory of Ischia                     MMA
        MMA. Soby collection
    Mexican pyramid—the living and the dead
                                         CSFP
        CoS. New accessions USA, 1960
    Muse of the western world           MM
        MM. 100 Amer ptrs
        Pierson
    Napolitana
        Bazin
        IU. Contemp Amer ptg & sculp, 1955

Obelisks
    Pearson. Mod renaissance
Ophelia
    PPC. Ptg in the U.S. 1949
Paludes
    Wight. Milestones (col)
Panel for a mural decoration
    CSFP. Illusionism
    Janson. Picture history
Perspective Mexican hill town
    DC. 22 biennial ex, 1951
Proserpine (Persephone)               MoSL
    Genauer
    MoSL. Handbook 1953
Rico Lebrun, Portrait of              IU
    IU. Contemp Amer ptg, 1948
    IU. 20th century
    Pearson. Mod renaissance
Steep bridge
    NAD. Annual ex, 1949, 1st half
Steep bridge no 3
    WMAA. Contemp Amer ptg, 1949
Summer still life
    IU. Contemp Amer ptg, 1950
Temptation of St Anthony
    Pearson. Mod renaissance
Through the marshes
    CtY. Yale alumni
Viva Mexico
    NAD. Annual ex, spring 1950
Wall of spikes
    IU. Contemp Amer ptg, 1949
BERMAN, Fred, 1926-
    Falling sun VI
        WMAA. Young America 1960
    Floating white city
        WMAA. Contemp Amer ptg, 1959/60
    Unfinished painting
        WMAA. Young America 1960
Berman, Leonid. See Leonid
Bermuda
    Demuth, C. H. Bermuda, 1917
    Demuth, C. H. Bermuda no 2
    Homer, W. Rocky shore
Bermuda group by J. Smibert
Bermuda window in a semitropical character
    by M. Hartley
Bernard by L. Karp
Berry boy by J. G. Brown
Berry pickers by W. Homer
Bertagna, Carmela, fl 1884
    Sargent, J. S. Carmela Bertagna
BERTOIA, Harry, 1915-
    Quadrilaterals                       NUM
        NUM. Root bequest
The Bessie of New York by A. G. Dove
Bethel (ship)
    Unidentified artist. Letter of marque ship
        Bethel of Boston
Bethlehem by L. Ford
Bethlehem, Pennsylvania by J. W. Hill
Bethlehem, Pennsylvania by Unidentified
    artist
Bethune, George, 1769-1859
    Malbone, E. G. George Bethune
Betrothal by A. Gorky
Betrothal I by A. Gorky
Betrothal II, 1947 by A. Gorky
BETSBERG, Ernestine, 1908-
    Roman shop
        IU. Contemp Amer ptg & sculp, 1959

**BETTS, Edward Howard,** 1920-
  Coastal landscape         OYB
    NAD. Annual ex, 1957
    OYB. Supplement 1959
  Driftwood         IaDa
    IaDa. Silver jubilee
  Rocky landscape
    NAD. Annual ex, 1953
  Storm tide         OYB
    OYB. Annual 1953
    OYB. Supplement
**Betts, Eliza.** See Rathbone, Eliza (Betts)
**BETTS, Louis,** 1873-
  Albert Arnold Sprague      CtY
    CtY. Portrait index
  Booth Tarkington      InIJ
    InIJ. 105 ptgs
  Frances and Judy      OYB
    OYB. Catalogue 1951
  Mary Julien Glover
    NAD. Annual ex, spring 1950
  Self-portrait      InTH
    InTH. Catalogue
**Between** acts by H. C. Pitz
**Between** Ceppo Morelli and Ponte Grande
  by F. E. Church
**Between** rounds by T. Eakins
**Beyle,** Marie-Henri, Apotheosis of by J.
  Wilde
**Beyond** the truth by S. Chun
**Beyond** white by J. Xcéron
**Bianca** by R. W. Weir
La **Biancheria** by J. S. Sargent
**Biarritz:** big sea by E. D. Boit
**Biaxial** by T. D. Benrimo
**Bibb, Mary Lucy Pocahontas,** 1818-1844
  Bush, J. H. Mary Lucy Pocahontas Bibb
**Biblical and religious themes**
  Allston, W. Belshazzar's feast
  Allston, W. Christ healing the sick, first
    study
  Allston, W. David playing before Saul
  Allston, W. Dead man revived by touch-
    ing the bones of the prophet Elijah
  Allston, W. Elijah fed by the ravens
  Allston, W. Jacob's dream
  Allston, W. Jeremiah dictating his proph-
    ecy
  Allston, W. Rebecca at the well
  Allston, W. Saul and the witch of Endor
  Aronson, D. Adoration of the Magi
  Aronson, D. Christ before Pilate
  Aronson, D. Coronation of the Virgin
  Aronson, D. Joseph and the Ishmaelites
  Aronson, D. Last supper
  Aronson, D. Resurrection
  Aronson, D. Young Christ
  Arthur, R. The last supper
  Bearden, R. Christ driving the money
    changers from the Temple
  Beckmann, M. Christ and the woman
    taken in adultery
  Beckmann, M. Christ in Limbo
  Beckmann, M. Descent from the cross
  Beckmann, M. The prodigal son among
    swine
  Bellows, G. W. Crucifixion
  Benton, T. H. Susanna and the elders
  Berman, E. Temptation of St Anthony
  Brewton, J. Suicide of Judas

  Church, F. E. Finding of Moses
  Cole, T. Angels administering to Christ
  Cole, T. Dead Abel
  Cole, T. Expulsion from the Garden of
    Eden
  Cole, T. John the Baptist in the wilder-
    ness
  Copley, J. S. The ascension
  Cowles, R. Adam and Eve
  Curry, J. S. Baptism in Kansas
  Devoll, R. The prodigal son
  Doolittle, A. Prodigal son reclaimed
  Eakins, T. Crucifixion
  Field, E. S. Garden of Eden
  Franck, F. S. Lazarus resurrected
  Greene, S. Cain and Abel
  Haidt, J. V. Christ before Pilate
  Haidt, J. V. Crucifixion
  Hesselius, G. The last supper
  Hicks, E. Peaceable kingdom
  Hidley, J. H. (attributed works) Noah's
    ark
  Hurd, P. Baptising at Three Wells
  Johnson, A. Baptisam of our Savour spok
  Kamihira, B. Lowering from the cross
  La Farge, J. Adoring angels
  La Farge, J. Ascension
  La Farge, J. The centurion: study for a
    window in Judson memorial church,
    New York
  La Farge, J. Christ and Nicodemus
  La Farge, J. Christ and the psalmist
  La Farge, J. Good Samaritan: design for
    a window, Trinity church, Buffalo
  La Farge, J. Good shepherd
  La Farge, J. St Paul: Study for a memo-
    rial window
  Land, J. Passover supper
  Laning, E. Moses with the tablets of the
    law
  Lathrop, B. B. Japhthah's return
  Lebrun, R. The centurion's horse
  Lebrun, R. The Magdalene
  Lebrun, R. Woman of the Crucifixion
  Motherwell, R. B. Decalogue, Jacob's lad-
    der and burning bush
  Nagler, F. The passion according to St
    Matthew
  Oakley, V. Christ and the woman of
    Samaria
  Page, W. Flight into Egypt
  Philipp, R. Raising the cross
  Pippin, H. Temptation of St Anthony
  Pippin, H. The woman taken in adultery
  Porter, R. Sacrifice of Isaac
  Quirt, W. W. Descent from the cross
  Reinhardt, S. G. Raising of Lazarus
  Ronson, D. Marriage at Cana
  Ryder, A. P. Christ appearing to Mary
  Ryder, A. P. Resurrection
  Ryder, A. P. Story of the cross
  Shirlaw, W. Susannah and the elders
  Snow, J. E. Belshazzar's feast
  Terry, L. Jacob's dream
  Unidentified artist. Abraham and Isaac
  Unidentified artist. Adam and Eve
  Unidentified artist. Adoration of the Magi
  Unidentified artist. Belshazzar's feast
  Unidentified artist. Christ and the woman
    of Samaria
  Unidentified artist. Christ at Emmaus
  Unidentified artist. Christ on the road to
    Emmaus

Unidentified artist. Creation scene
Unidentified artist. Crowning of **King** Jereboam
Unidentified artist. Crucifixion
Unidentified artist. Finding of Moses
Unidentified artist. Flight into Egypt
Unidentified artist. The four apostles writing the gospels
Unidentified artist. Good Samaritan
Unidentified artist. Isaac blessing Jacob
Unidentified artist. Joseph and his brethren
Unidentified artist. Joseph interpreting Pharaoh's dream
Unidentified artist. Marriage at **Cana**
Unidentified artist. Moses in the bulrushes
Unidentified artist. Prodigal son gambling
Unidentified artist. The prodigal son in misery
Unidentified artist. The prodigal son receiving his patrimony
Unidentified artist. The prodigal son reclaimed
Unidentified artist. The prodigal son reveling with harlots
Unidentified artist. Rebecca at the well
Unidentified artist. Ruth and Naomi
Van Duzer, C. E. Pieta
Vincent, T. Crucifixion
Watkins, F. C. Crucifixion
West, B. The angel of the Lord announcing the resurrection to the Marys at the sepulchre
West, B. The archangel Gabriel
West, B. The ascension of our Saviour
West, B. Christ healing the sick in the temple
West, B. Christ on the Mount of Olives
West, B. Christ rejected by the Jews
West, B. The conversion of St Paul
West, B. The destruction of the beast and the false prophets
West, B. Elijah convincing the false prophets of Baol
West, B. Hagar and Ishmael
West, B. Peter denying Christ
West, B. Raising of Lazarus
West, B. Return of Jephthah
West, B. St Paul persecuting the Christians
West, B. St Paul shaking off the viper
West, B. St Paul's restoration to sight by Ananias
West, B. Saul and the witch of Endor
Willson M. A. Prodigal son reclaimed by his father
**Bidart,** French Pyrenees by E. D. Boit
**BIDDLE, George,** 1885-
Cannibalism of war     MexS
    Biddle. Yes and no
    Pearson. Mod renaissance
Frankie Loper
    Gruskin
His first crossing
    Cheney. Expressionism 1948 ed
Kuniyoshi, Portrait of
    Pearson. Mod renaissance
Marguerite Zorach. See Woman with a letter
My neighbor, Al
    Pearson. Mod renaissance

Negro spiritual: Ride on, conquering king
    PPC. Ptg in the U. S. 1949
Not even he may rest
    Pearson. Mod renaissance
Raphael Soyer and his models
    Biddle. Yes and no
Tenement
    Robb. Harper history
Two Negroes
    Pearson. Mod renaissance
William Gropper
    Larkin
    Larkin rev ed
Woman with a letter (Marguerite Zorach)     MM
    MM. 100 Amer ptrs
    Pierson

**Portrait of the artist**
Brook, A. George Biddle playing the flute
**Biddle, John,** 1789?-1859
Sully, T. Major John Biddle
**Biddle, Mary,** 1781-1850
Malbone, E. G. Mary Biddle
**Biddle, Rebecca Cornell,** fl 1824
Sully, T. Rebecca Cornell Biddle
**Biddle, Thomas,** 1790-1831
Sully, T. Major Thomas Biddle (PA)
Sully, T. and Sully, T. W. Major Thomas Biddle (DN)

**BIDNER, Robert**
Rufescent idlers
    OYB. Annual 1952
**BIERSTADT, Albert,** 1830-1902
Ambush     MB
    MB. Karolik coll
Arch of Octavius     MBA
    MiD. Travelers in Arcadia
Ascutney mountain from Claremont, New Hampshire
    Sears. Highlights
Bison with coyotes
    McCracken. Portrait of the old west
Black horse     MB
    MB. Karolik coll
Bombardment of Fort Sumter     PPhU
    Born
    Pierson
    U. S. National Capital sesquicentennial com
Buffalo bull     NJN
    Rathbone
Buffalo trail     MB
    MB. Karolik coll
Burning ship
    Pierson
Couple driving
    Born
Fishing boats at Capri     MB
    MB. Karolik coll
Geyser, Yellowstone park     MB
    MB. Karolik coll
Giant redwood trees of California     MPB
    Davidson v 1
    NUM. Art across America
Grove of trees     MB
    MB. Karolik coll
Guerrilla warfare     NNCe
    Walker. Ptgs from America
Halt in the Rocky mountains
    McCracken. Portrait of the old west

**BIERSTADT, Albert**—*Continued*
In the Yosemite valley                CtHW
  CtHW. Handbook
Indian camp                           MB
  MB. Karolik coll
Indians near Fort Laramie             MB
  MB. Karolik coll
Jenny lake, Wyoming
  Rathbone
Lake Tahoe, California                MB
  MB. Karolik coll
Last of the buffalo                   DC
  Barker. Amer ptg
  DC. Masterpieces
  McCracken. Portrait of the old west
    (col)
  Pierson
  Rathbone (col)
Marina Grande in Capri                NBuA
  MiD. Travelers in Arcadia
  NBuA. Catalogue of the ptgs
Merced river, Yosemite valley         MM
  Bazin
  Canaday
  Larkin
  Larkin rev ed
Moose hunters' camp, Nova Scotia      MB
  MB. Karolik coll
Mount Corcoran                        DC
  McCracken. Portrait of the old west
    (col)
Mount Whitney                         MnMI
  Born
Mountain lake                         TxH
  Rathbone
Nooning on the Platte                 MoSL
  Rathbone
Oregon trail                          OYB
  OYB. Catalogue 1951
  Rathbone
Palm trees with a domed church        MB
  MB. Karolik coll
Rainbow over Jenny lake
  Time. 300 years (col)
Rocky mountains                       MM
  Davidson v 1
  Mendelowitz
  Pierson
Rocky mountains                       IBM
  McCracken. Portrait of the old west
Rocky mountains, Colorado             MB
  MB. Karolik coll
St Lawrence river from the citadel,
  Quebec                         MB
  MB. Karolik coll
  Pierson
San Rafael, California
  Sears. Highlights
Seal rocks, Farallones                MB
  MB. Karolik coll
Snow scene with buffaloes             MB
  MB. Karolik coll
Starr King mountain, California       OCl
  Roos
Storm in the mountains                MB
  MB. Karolik coll
Surveyor's wagon in the Rockies       MoSL
  Rathbone
Thunderstorm in the Rocky mountains
                     MB
  MiD. Ptg in America
  NYG. Fine art
  Pierson
  Rathbone
  Richardson. Ptg in America

Valley of the Yosemite                MB
  MB. Karolik coll
View from the Wind river mountains,
  Wyoming                        MB
  MB. Karolik coll
Western sunset
  Rathbone
Wind river country, Wyoming           CtNB
  Rathbone
**Big** apple tree by J. Sloan
**Big** Bend by E. F. Spruce
**Big** black by J. Youngerman
**Big** Bowl (a Crow chief) by A. J. Miller
**Big** business by C. Singer
**Big** dory by G. W. Bellows
**Big** horse by W. Sommer
The **big** noise by P. Evergood
**Big** nose George by C. M. Russell
**Big** red by S. Francis
**Big** Rock pool by H. E. Mattson
**Big** Sandy river, Scene on the by A. J.
  Miller
**Big** tree by K. E. Fortess
**Bigelow, William Sturgis**
  Chadwick, F. B. William Sturgis Bigelow
**BIGGS, Walter**, 1886-
  Night spot
    NAD. Annual ex, 1951
  Studio
    NAD. Annual ex, 1961
**BIGLER, Mary Jane**
  Planes in the sunflowers
    OYB. Annual 1952
**Bike** race by J. De Martini
**Billboard** by G. Hartigan
**BILLINGS, Henry**, 1901-
  Discovery
    Gruskin
**Billings, Mabel**
  Jennys, W. Mabel Billings
**BINFORD, Julien**, 1908-
  Crap shooter
    Gruskin (col)
  Red chair with straw flowers
    IaDa. 30th anniversary
    IU. Contemp Amer ptg & sculp, 1953
  Table with cyclamens
    IU. Contemp Amer ptg, 1952
  Woman with a purple hat
    Gruskin (col)
**BINGHAM, George Caleb**, 1811-1879
  Belated wayfarers
    McDermott. G. C. Bingham
    Rathbone
  Benoist Troost                   MoKN
    McDermott. G. C. Bingham
  Boatmen on the Missouri (copy of origi-
    nal)                         DeWin
    McDermott. G. C. Bingham
  Canvassing for a vote             MoKN
    McDermott. G. C. Bingham
    MoKN. Handbook
    OCiM. Rediscoveries
  Captured by Indians
    McDermott. G. C. Bingham
    Rathbone
  Checker players                   MiD
    McDermott. G. C. Bingham

**BINGHAM, G. C.**—*Continued*

Raftsmen playing cards      MoSL
  Barker. Amer ptg
  DC. De gustibus
  McDermott. G. C. Bingham
  MoSL. 50 masterworks
  MoSL. Handbook 1953
  PPC. Amer classics
  Richardson. Ptg in America
  Roos
  UNESCO. Prior to 1860
  UNESCO. Prior to 1860 3d ed
  UNESCO. Prior to 1860 5th ed
  Raftsmen playing cards no 2. See In a
    quandary
Sallie Ann Camden
  McDermott. G. C. Bingham
Samuel Bullitt Churchill
  McDermott. G. C. Bingham
Scene on the Ohio      MoSLH
  McDermott. G. C. Bingham
Self-portrait 1835      MoSL
  DC. Amer ptrs of the South
  McDermott. G. C. Bingham
  MoSL. Handbook 1953
  PA. Annual ex, 1955
Self-portrait, 1877?
  McDermott. G. C. Bingham
Shooting for the beef      NBM
  Flexner. Amer ptg
  Flexner. Short history
  McDermott. G. C. Bingham
  Mendelowitz
  Pierson
  Rathbone
The squatters
  McDermott. G. C. Bingham
The storm      CtHW
  CtHW. Handbook
  McDermott. G. C. Bingham
  Rathbone
Stump speaking      MoSLB
  Craven. Rainbow book
  Craven. Treasury 1952 ed (col)
  McDermott. G. C. Bingham
  Rathbone
  U.S. National Capital sesquicentennial
    com
Susan Howard Hockaday and her daughter
    Susan
  McDermott. G. C. Bingham
The thread of life
  McDermott. G. C. Bingham
Trappers' return      MiD
  Baur. Amer ptg
  McDermott. G. C. Bingham
  MiD. Ptg in America (col cover)
  MiD. Treasures
  Pierson
  Richardson. Ptg in America (col detail)
Two citizens engaged in a conversation
    MoSLM
  Roos
Verdict of the people      MoSLB
  Barker. Amer ptg
  Davidson v2
  McDermott. G. C. Bingham
  Mendelowitz
  Rathbone
The verdict of the people no 2, 1878  DN
  McDermott. G. C. Bingham
View of a lake in the mountains
  McDermott. G. C. Bingham

Washington crossing the Delaware
  McDermott. G. C. Bingham
Watching the cargo      MoSLH
  McDermott. G. C. Bingham
The wood boat      MoSL
  Canaday
  McDermott. G. C. Bingham
  MoSL. Handbook 1953
  OCiM. Rediscoveries
  Rathbone
  Time. 300 years (col)
Wood-boatmen on a river      MB
  MB. Karolik coll

**Birch, Mrs James T.** fl 1877
  Bingham, G. C. Mrs James T. Birch

**BIRCH, Thomas,** 1779-1851

Brig in a storm      MoSL
  MoSL. Handbook 1953
City of Philadelphia from the treaty elm.
  See Penn's treaty tree
The Constitution and the Guerrière  MAP
  Larkin
  Larkin rev ed
The Constitution and the Guerriere  MdAn
  U.S. National Capital sesquicentennial
    com
Edward Hunt
  WiMiA. Amer ptg 1760-1960
Fairmount water works      PA
  Pierson
  U.S National Capital sesquicentennial
    com
Landing of William Penn      MB
  MB. Karolik coll
Late summer
  Chew. 250 years of art
Marine view with ships
  Chew. 250 years of art
Milford, North Wales, Pennsylvania  MB
  MB. Karolik coll
New York harbor      MB
  MB. Karolik coll
Off the Maine coast
  Sears. Highlights
Penn's treaty tree (City of Philadelphia
  from the treaty elm)
  Born
  Flexner. Light of distant skies
  PA. Annual ex, 1955
  Pierson
Philadelphia from Petty Island c 1825
  MB. Karolik coll
Seascape      MB
  MB. Karolik coll
  Sears. Highlights
Seascape      MeC
  MeC. Inaugural ex
Shipwreck      NBM
  Born
  PA. Annual ex, 1955
Skating      MB
  MB. Karolik coll
Sleigh ride in the country      MB
  MB. Karolik coll
The United States and the Macedonian,
  1812      PH
  Davidson v 1
  Pierson
  Richardson. Ptg in America
Upper Hudson
  Sears. Highlights

The Wasp and the Frolic        MB
    MB. Karolik coll
Winter        PR
    NUM. Art across America
    PR. Catalogue
Winter scene outside of Bristol, Pennsylvania
    Chew. 250 years of art
**Birches** by J. Whorf
**Birckhead, Catharine A. (McEvers)** 1795-
    1868
    Peale, S. M. Mrs Hugh McC Birckhead
**Bird** and ball by R. Ruben
**Bird** and roses by P. W. Roberts
**Bird** bath by A. Rattner
**Bird** cloud by L. Feininger
**Bird** effort by J. Pollock
**Bird,** fish, fruit by S. Provan
**Bird** harbor, Maine by A. P. Chase
**Bird** in the heart by J. Carroll
**Bird** in the spirit by M. Graves
**Bird** in the sun no 2 by J. Zajac
**Bird** Key bay by S. Solomon
**Bird** mountain, Castleton, Vermont **by**
    J. Hope
**Bird** rock, California by H. G. Keller
The **birdcage** by K. Zerbe
**Birdie** with straw hat by L. Rivers
**Birds**
    *See also* names of individual birds, e.g.
        Cuckoos; Woodpecker
    Avery, M. Birds over sea
    Baziotes, W. A. White bird
    Blanch, A. Woman feeding birds
    Bohrod, A. Bird and gauntlet
    Graves, M. Bird in the mist
    Graves, M. Bird in the moonlight
    Graves, M. Bird in the spirit
    Graves, M. Bird maddened by the long
        winter
    Graves, M. Bird singing in the moonlight
    Graves, M. Blind bird
    Graves, M. Guardian
    Graves, M. In the air
    Graves, M. Little-known bird of the inner
        eye
    Graves, M. Masked bird fishing in the
        golden stream
    Graves, M. Message
    Graves, M. Pink bird
    Graves, M. Shore birds
    Graves, M. Spirit bird
    Graves, M. Surf birds
    Hartley, M. Birds of the Bagaduce
    Hartley, M. Give us this day
    Homer, W. Right and left
    Keller, H. G. Birds, rocks, and the sea
    Kriesberg, I. Birds alighting
    Ludens, E. Rare birds
    Norfeldt, B. J. O. Flight of birds
    Pollock, J. Bird
    Price, C. S. Bird by the sea
    Price, C. S. Black bird
    Price, C. S. Young birds
    Runquist, Arthur. Bird
    Siegriest, L. Birds at rest
    Thon, W. Seabirds
    Woellfer, E. Birds and orange sky
    Wyeth, A. N. Soaring

**Bird's-eye** view of the Mandan village by
    G. Catlin
**Birds** flying by C. Chen
**Bird's** nest by C. Sheeler
**Birmingham** meeting house I, 1940 by **H.**
    Pippin
**Birmington** from the top of Coal hill opposite Pittsburgh, 1834 by R. Smith
**Birth** by J. Pollock
**Birth** of Cephalopods by M. Rothko
**Birth** of spring by F. C. Watkins
**Birth** of Taurus by H. Hofmann
**Birth** of the atom (Atomic series) by **J.**
    De Diego
**Birthday** cake by R. H. Wilt
**Birthday** party by E. Giobbi
**Birthplace** by W. Pachner
**BISCHOFF, Elmer Nelson,** 1916-
    Bather
        WMAA. Contemp Amer ptg, 1959/60
    Figures in garden
        IU. Contemp Amer ptg & sculp, 1959
    Seated figure in garden        WMAA
        Goodrich. Amer art
    White flower
        IU. Contemp Amer ptg & scupl, 1961
**BISHOP, Isabel,** 1902-
    Bather        ATU
        ATU. Coll of Amer art
    Blowing rings
        Gruskin
    Girls waiting
        NAD. Annual ex, 1957
    Homeward
        Pierson
    Interlude
        PA. Annual ex, 1953
    The kid
        NYG. Fine art
    Lunch hour
        Gruskin
    Mending        WMAA
        WMAA. Sara Roby
    Nude        WMAA
        Goodrich. Amer art
    Snack bar        OCo
        McCurdy
    Subway scene
        WMAA. Annual ex, 1958
    Two girls        MM
        Mendelowitz
        MM. 100 Amer ptrs
    Waiting        NJN
        Baur. Revolution
        Pierson
**Bismarck, Otto Eduard Leopold, prince von,**
    1815-1898
    Healy, G.P.A. Otto von Bismarck
**Bison** with coyotes by A. Bierstadt
The **bistro** by A. Blatas
**BISTTRAM, Emil,** 1895-
    Bulldogging
        Pearson. Mod renaissance
    The fleet
        Pearson. Mod renaissance
    Koshares (New Mexico Indian dance
        series)
        Pearson. Mod renaissance
    Marine patterns
        Pearson. Mod renaissance
A **bit** of the Cape by F. J. Waugh

BLACK, Frederick E. 1924-
Untitled
IU. Contemp Amer ptg & sculp, 1959
WMAA. Contemp Amer ptg, 1959/60
Black abstraction by G. O'Keeffe
The black and the white by M. Rothko
Black & 3 whites by E. A. Donati
Black and white by C. Booth
Black and white by W. De Kooning
Black and white by A. D. F. Reinhardt
Black and white by J. De J. Smith
Black and white and read all over by H. Frankenthaler
Black and white no 5, 1952 by J. Pollock
Black and white painting by J. Pollock
Black angels by B. Greene
Black Ball liner by R. W. Salmon (attributed works)
Black-billed cuckoo by J. J. Audubon
Black bird by C. S. Price
Black bottle by H. Lotterman
Black bush, autumn, Dogtown by W. A. Kienbusch
Black city by W. G. Congdon
Black control by I. R. Pereira
Black cross by G. O'Keeffe
Black cross with red sky by G. O'Keeffe
Black dahlia by P. Jennins
Black demon by H. Hofmann
Black-eyed susans by S. Serisawa
Black freighter by J. Levine
Black Friday by W. De Kooning
Black harbor, grey moon by E. Wedin
Black hat by H. G. Dearth
Black Hawk (Sauk chief) 1767-1838
Catlin, G. Black Hawk
Black herd by H. Nichols
Black Hills by A. J. Miller
Black horse by A. Bierstadt
Black horse by M. O. Sheets
Black horse by W. Sommer
Black horses by A. M. R. Moses
Black houses by C. E. Burchfield
Black in red by S. Francis
Black interior by R. B. Motherwell
Black iris by G. O'Keeffe
Black iron by C. E. Burchfield
Black landscape by B. J. Gardner
Black landscape by Y. Tanguy
Black lilies by M. Beckmann
Black lion by B. Browne
Black movements by L. Dodd
Black night by W. A. Baziotes
Black no 8 by Y. Ohashi
Black on white by W. A. Baziotes
Black over reds by M. Rothko
Black palace with red courtyard by Y. Johnston
Black patio door by G. O'Keeffe
Black place green by G. O'Keeffe
Black place III by G. O'Keeffe
Black rocks, kelp and sea by W. Brice

Black roses by G. L. K. Morris
Black silhouette by W. A. Baziotes
Black still life by R. B. Motherwell
Black sun by J. Marin
Black table by N. Vasilieff
Black target by J. Johns
Black tree in bright light by K. Schrag
Black waves by M. Graves
Black, white and grey by J. Pollock
Black widow by M. Ray
Black wires by R. Koppe
Black yawl by L. Feininger
Blackberry picker by A. N. Wyeth
A blackbird with snow-covered red hills by G. O'Keeffe
The blackboard by K. Davies
The blackboard by C. Marca-Relli
BLACKBURN, Joseph, c 1700-1765
Elizabeth and James Bowdoin       MeB
  Pierson
Isaac Winslow and his family. See Winslow family
James Pitts                        MiD
  MiD. Ports of the Pitts family
  MiD. Treasures
John Erving jr
  Belknap
Mary (Polly) Warner               NHP
  NUM. Art across America
  Richardson. Ptg in America
Mary Sylvester Dering             NM
  Flexner. Copley
Mrs Goldsbrow Banyar              NNHS
  Vail. Stuyvesant ports
Mrs James Otis jr                 NBM
  Flexner. First flowers
Mrs James Pitts                   MiD
  Belknap
  MiD. Ptg in America
  MiD. Ports of the Pitts family
  MiD. Treasures
Mrs Jonathan Warner
  ICA. From colony to nation
Mrs Theodore Atkinson             OCl
  OCl. Handbook
  Pierson
Theodore Atkinson                 MWM
  Larkin (detail)
  Larkin rev ed (detail)
  Pierson
Theodore Atkinson jr              RPS
  Belknap
Winslow family (Isaac Winslow and his family)     MB
  Barker. Amer ptg
  Flexner. First flowers
  ICA. From colony to nation
  Larkin
  Larkin rev ed
  Mendelowitz
  Pierson
BLACKBURN, Morris Atkinson, 1902-
Blue door                         PPhM
  CoS. New accessions USA, 1952
Nets and boats                    OYB
  OYB. Annual 1953
  OYB. Supplement
Blackened monument by G. L. Mueller
The Blackfeet by A. J. Miller

Blackfoot doctor in his mystery dress endeavoring to cure his dying patient by G. Catlin
Blackfoot medicine man by G. Catlin
Blacksmith shop by E. Johnson
Blacksmiths
  Brown, J. G. The blacksmith
  Hunt, W. M. The forge
  Johnson, E. Blacksmith shop
  Mayer, F. B. Leisure and labor
  Neagle, J. Pat Lyon at the forge
  Neagle, J. Pat Lyon, blacksmith
Black-tailed hare or jack-rabbit by J. J. Audubon
BLAGDEN, Thomas P. 1911-
  Offshore wind
    CtY. Yale alumni
Blai, Boris, 1893-
  Watkins, F. C. Boris Blai
Blaine, James Gillespie, 1830-1893
  Healy, G. P. A. James G. Blaine
Blair, Frank P.
  Bingham, G. C. Gen Nathaniel Lyon and Gen Frank P. Blair starting from the Arsenal gate in St Louis to capture Camp Jackson
BLAIR, Jeanette
  Spring
    OYB. Annual 1954
BLAIR, Robert N. 1912-
  Light and shade                          OYB
    OYB. Annual 1953
    OYB. Supplement
BLAIR, Streeter, 1888-
  Downing house, Chester county, Pennsylvania
    Kallir. Amer primitive ptgs
Blair family by D. Blythe
Blake, Eliza (Izard)
  Wollaston, J. Mrs Daniel Blake
Blakelock, Cora Rebecca (Bailey) b 1836?
  Blakelock, R. A. Mrs Blakelock, Portrait of
BLAKELOCK, Ralph Albert, 1847-1919
  After sundown                            MAP
    WMAA. Blakelock
  At nature's mirror                       DNC
    NAD. Amer tradition
    WMAA. Blakelock
  Brook by moonlight                       OT
    Barker. Amer ptg
  The chase                                MWM
    McCracken. Portrait of the old west
    WMAA. Blakelock
  Evening silhouettes
    CtY. Yale alumni
    WMAA. Blakelock
  Golden autumn                            GAtM
    GAtM. Holbrook collection
  Indian encampment                        MM
    Pierson
    WMAA. Blakelock
  Indian madonna
    WMAA. Blakelock
  Landscape                                MM
    MM. 100 Amer ptrs
  Mrs Blakelock, Portrait of
    WMAA. Blakelock
  Moonlight                                NBM
    Baur. Amer ptg
    Mendelowitz
    Pierson
    Time. 300 years (col)
    WMAA. Blakelock

Moonlight                                  PPC
    WMAA. Blakelock
Moonlight, Indian encampment               DNC
    DNC. Gellatly coll, 1954
    Larkin
    Larkin rev ed
    McCracken. Portrait of the old west (col)
Moonlight landscape                        DP
    Born
Moonlight sonata                           MB
    WMAA. Blakelock
Nymphs
    WMAA. Blakelock
Old New York: northwest corner 55th street and Seventh avenue, c 1868 (Lemle coll)
    WMAA. Blakelock
Old New York, shanties at 55th street and Seventh avenue                        WiMiA
    NJN. Early N.J. artists
    PPC. Amer classics
Peace among the nations
    WMAA. Blakelock
Pink roses
    WMAA. Blakelock
Pipe dance                                 MM
    McCracken. Portrait of the old west
Rising moon                                ATeS
    ATeS. Collection
Rocky mountains                            MPB
    McCracken. Portrait of the old west
    Rathbone
Sunrise                                    NoCR
    NoCR. Catalogue
    WMAA. Blakelock
Three trees
    WMAA. Blakelock
Twilight                                   OYB
    OYB. Catalogue 1951
Vision of life                             ICA
    Pierson
Woods at sunset                            NJMo
    NJMo. Forty years
BLANCH, Arnold, 1896-
  Autumn landscape
    IU. Contemp Amer ptg, 1952
  Bull
    MnU. Arnold Blanch
  Cathedral
    MnU. Arnold Blanch
  Circus girl
    MnU. Arnold Blanch
  Flowermakers
    MnU. Arnold Blanch
  Forevermore
    MnU. Arnold Blanch
  Four ships                               WMAA
    Pierson
  Garden
    MnU. Arnold Blanch
  Georgia landscape                        MM
    MnU. Arnold Blanch
  Girl with cornflower
    MnU. Arnold Blanch
  Hooked rug
    MnU. Arnold Blanch
  In Colorado
    MnU. Arnold Blanch
  Music before winter
    MnU. Arnold Blanch
  New England
    NYG. Fine art

**BLANCH, Arnold**—*Continued*
Painter of birds
  MnU. 40 Amer ptrs
Pleasures of spring
  MnU. Arnold Blanch
Rodeo in the Rockies                    ATU
  ATU. Coll of Amer art
Snap shot
  MnU. Arnold Blanch
Swamp country                           NBM
  MnU. Arnold Blanch
Swamp folk                              NBM
  Gruskin
  Pierson
Table
  MnU. Arnold Blanch
Tampa fair
  IU. Contemp Amer ptg, 1951
Upright trees
  IU. Contemp ptg & sculp, 1955
The village
  MnU. 40 Amer ptrs
Woman feeding birds
  MnU. Arnold Blanch
**Blanch, Mrs Arnold.** See Lee, Doris
  (Emrick)
**BLANCH, Lucille,** 1895-
Outdoor circus
  NYG. Fine art
Still life in white                     ATU
  ATU. Coll of Amer art
**BLANCHARD, Carol,** 1919?-
Beachcomber
  IU. Contemp Amer ptg, 1951
Family portrait
  IU. Contemp Amer ptg, 1950
Family portrait
  IU Contemp Amer ptg & sculp, 1957
Late again                               IU
  CoS. New accessions USA, 1952
**Bland, Sarah (Fitzhugh)** See Fitzhugh,
  Sarah
**Bland, Mrs Theodorick.** See Fitzhugh,
  Sarah
**BLANEY, William,** 1865-1944
Old fish house                          MB
  MB. Ptgs in water color
**BLASHFIELD, Edwin Howland,** 1848-1936
Carry on                                MM
  Brown. Amer ptg
Power of the law
  Pierson

Portrait of the artist

Lockman, D. M. Edwin Howland Blashfield

**Blast** furnace by N. Spencer
**Blast** II by A. Gottlieb
**BLATAS, Arbit,** 1908-
The bistro
  IU. Contemp Amer ptg, 1951
Dinner still life
  Genauer (col)
Four figures in a bistro
  PPC. International ex, 1952
Pont Neuf
  IU. Contemp Amer ptg & sculp, 1955
Still life with black bottle
  IU. Contemp Amer ptg & sculp, 1957
**BLAUSTEIN, Alfred,** 1924?-
**Buffet supper**
  NBuA. Expressionism

Galleria, Naples
  IU. Contemp Amer ptg & sculp, 1957
Trussed sheep
  IU. Contemp Amer ptg & sculp, 1959
**Bleak** weather by A. Winter
**Bleecker, Frances (Wade)** 1787-1856
  Malbone, E. G. Annette (probably Mrs
    Alexander Bleecker)
  Malbone, E. G. Mrs Alexander Bleecker
**Bleecker, Harmanus,** 1779-1849
  Ames, E. Harmanus Bleecker
**Bleecker, Mrs Jan Jansen**
  Unidentified artist. Mrs Jan Jansen Bleeck-
    er
**Bleecker, Leonard,** 1755-1844
  Ames, E. Leonard Bleecker
**Bleecker** street Saturday night by J. Sloan
**Blessed** damosel by P. Bacon
**Blessing** of the fleet by L. Bosa
**Blind** accordion player by B. Shahn
**Blind** beggars by J. Lawrence
**Blind** botanist by B. Shahn
**Blind** fish approaching summer by B. Allan
The **blind** one by B. Greene
**Blind** Spanish singer by R. Henri
**Blindman's** buff by M. Beckmann
**Blizzard** by D. Macknight
**BLOCH, Albert,** 1882-
Portrait
  Cheney. Primer 1958 ed
**BLOCK, Laurens,** fl 1650
New Amsterdam                           NNHS
  Flexner. First flowers
**Block** Island by E. Kelly
**Blockade** of Boston, View of the by C.
  Remick
**Blocks** by W.T. Murch
**Blonde** model by J. S. Sargent
**Bloodgood, Francis,** 1768-1840
  Ames, E. Francis Bloodgood
**BLOOM, Cynthia,** 1933-
Lowlands
  MBCI. View 1960
**BLOOM, Donald S.**
Pool room
  OYB. Annual 1959
**BLOOM, Hyman,** 1913-
The anatomist                           WMAA
  Barker. From realism
  Baur. New art (col)
  Goodrich. Amer art (col)
  Larkin rev ed (col)
  Pierson
Apparition of danger
  Wight. Hyman Bloom (col)
Archaeological treasure
  Baur. New art
  Hess. Abstract ptg (col)
  MMA. Contemp ptrs
The bride
  WMAA. Neuberger collection (col)
Buried treasure
  Baur. Revolution
  CSFP. Annual ex, 1950/51
  IU. Contemp Amer ptg, 1952 (col)
  Wight. Hyman Bloom (col)
  Wight. Milestones (col)
Cadaver on a table
  ICA. Annual ex, 1954

Chandelier 1
  ICA. Annual ex, 1951
Chandelier II, 1945
  NBuA. Expressionism
  Wight. Hyman Bloom
Conquest
  NNSG. Younger Amer ptrs
Corpse of an elderly female
  Pierson
  Pousette-Dart. Amer ptg
Female corpse, back view
  Baur. New art
Female leg
  IU. Contemp Amer ptg & sculp, 1957
The harpies
  Wight. Hyman Bloom
The medium
  Wight. Hyman Bloom
Slaughtered animal            CLAU
  Time. 300 years (col)
  Wight. Hyman Bloom
The stone
  Hess. Abstract ptg
The synagogue                 MMA
  Baur. New art
  Pierson
  Wight. Hyman Bloom
Torso and limbs
  MnMW. Expressionism 1900-1955
Treasure map                  MAP
  Pierson
Blowing leaves by J. Gernand
Blowing rings by I. Bishop
Blue abstraction by A. B. Carles
Blue amorphous by R. Pousette-Dart
Blue and black by S. Francis
Blue and black by K. R. Morris
Blue and green music by G. O'Keeffe
The blue and the strawberry roan by
  M. B. Watkins
Blue at night by A. Gottlieb
Blue at noon by A. Gottlieb
Blue-black by S. Francis
Blue boat by W. Homer
Blue bowl by E. W. Motley
The blue boy by E. S. Field
The blue boy by W. Pachner
Blue brook water fall by J. H. Twachtman
Blue building by D. Stoltenberg
Blue canyon by C. A. Morris
Blue chair by G. Grosz
Blue chair by W. Sommer
Blue chair by F. C. Watkins
Blue chimney by A. Osver
Blue cloud by L. Feininger
Blue clown by W. Kuhn
Blue clown by P. Tchelitchew
Blue coast by L. Feininger
Blue cradle by J. Tworkov
Blue depths by J. Guerrero
Blue Devils marching down Fifth avenue
  by G. B. Luks
Blue doll by A. Pickens
Blue door by M. A. Blackburn
Blue evolution by C. K. Sibley

Blue eyes by Unidentified artist
Blue finch by F. E. Conway
Blue gable by G. Münter
Blue garden by Y. Johnston
Blue glasses by C. Brown
The blue gown by W. M. Chase
Blue grosbeak by J. J. Audubon
Blue hands by H. Warshaw
Blue hole on the Little Miami river by
  R. S. Duncanson
Blue horizon by P. Ghikas
Blue horse by M. Chagall
Blue horse by W. Sommer
Blue interior by D. L. Demboski
Blue is for bass by J. Lechay
Blue jay by J. J. Audubon
Blue juggler by W. Kuhn
Blue kimono by W. M. Chase
Blue landscape by L. Calcagno
Blue lines by R. Scarlett
Blue marine by L. Feininger
Blue marine by A. P. Ryder
Blue Medicine by G. Catlin
Blue mirror by W. A. Baziotes
Blue mist by R. Bennett
Blue moon by D. Kingman
Blue morning by G. W. Bellows
Blue mountain near Taos by J. Marin
Blue necklace by E. E. Speicher
Blue New York by M. Weber
Blue night by H. E. Mattson
Blue poles by J. Pollock
Blue rectangles by I. Bolotowsky
Blue rhythm by H. Hofmann
Blue rocks by M. Kahn
Blue sea, Crotch island by J. Marin
Blue shadows by D. Macknight
The blue shawl by R. Soyer
Blue sky by G. Grosz
Blue snow, the Battery by G. W. Bellows
Blue space by B. Greene
Blue spruce by W. A. Kienbusch
Blue table by J. Jarvaise
Blue table by M. Yektai
Blue territory by H. Frankenthaler
Blue tiger by H. Pippin
Blue II by G. O'Keeffe
The blue unconscious by J. Pollock
Blue vase by W. Sommer
Blue waterfall by V. Candell
Blue, white and grey by R. L. Knipschild
Blue with china ink . . . Homage to John
  Cage by R. B. Motherwell
The bluebird by P. Evergood
BLUEMNER, Oscar Florianus, 1867-1938
  Moonshine fantasy
    Baur. Revolution
  Old canal port                WMAA
    Goodrich. Amer art
    Pierson

BLUEMNER, O. F.—*Continued*
  Radiant night                    MAP
    Pierson
  Silktown on the Passaic
    Brown. Amer ptg
    Pierson
    WMAA. Pioneers
The **blues** singer by S. Menkès
**Bluff** house by H. M. Gasser
**Blum, Robert Frederick,** 1857-1903
  Chase, W. M. Robert Frederick Blum
**BLUMBERG, Yuli,** 1894-
  A man, Portrait of
    PPC. Ptg in the U.S. 1949
**BLUME, Peter,** 1906-
  The boat                         MMA
    Lewisohn
    NYG. Fine art
    UNESCO. 1860-1955
  The bridge
    Brown. Amer ptg
    MnMW. Precisionist view
  Buoy
    MMA. Contemp ptrs
  Crucifixion
    IU. Contemp Amer ptg & sculp, 1953
    Pousette-Dart. Amer ptg
    Roos (detail)
  Eternal city                     MMA
    Barr. What is mod ptg
    Baur. New art (col)
    Larkin
    Larkin rev ed
    MMA. Masters (col)
    Pearson. Mod renaissance
    Pierson
    Robb. Harper history
    WMAA. Juliana Force
  Excavation
    CSFP. Annual ex, 1947/48
    MMA. Contemp ptrs
  Half-way house
    Chew. 250 years of art
    WiMiA. Amer ptg 1760-1960
  Home for Christmas               OCo
    Brown. Amer ptg
  Key West beach                   MMA
    Baur. Revolution
    MMA. Soby collection
  Landscape with poppies           MMA
    CSB. Illusion
    Gruskin
  Light of the world               WMAA
    Baur. New art
    Goodrich. Am art
    Mendelowitz
    MnMW. Reality and fantasy
  Lilies                           MB
    MB. Ptgs in water color
  Maine coast
    Baur. New art
  Man of sorrows                   WMAA
    Goodrich. Amer art
    Pierson
  Parade                           MMA
    Baur. New art
    MMA. Ptg and sculpture
    McCurdy
    Pierson
  Passage to Etna                  MCH
    Pierson

The rock                           ICA
  Baur. New art
  Baur. Revolution
  Pearson. Mod renaissance
  Pierson
  PPC. International ex, 1950
The shrine
  Pearson. Mod renaissance
South of Scranton                  MM
  Baur. New art
  Biddle. Yes and no
  MM. 100 Amer ptrs
  Pearson. Mod renaissance
  Taylor. Fifty centuries, 1954 ed (col)
  Time. 300 years (col)
  Wight. Milestones
Underpass
  WMAA. Contemp Amer ptgs, 1953
White factory                      NeL
  Barker. From realism
  Pierson
**BLUMENSCHEIN, Ernest Leonard,** 1874-
  1960
  Enchanted forest
    NAD. Annual ex, 1947, 2d half
  The pass                         ATeS
    ATeS. Collection
**BLUNT, John S.** 1800?-1835
  Boston harbor                    MB
    MB. Karolik coll
  Topsail schooner in sheltered waters
    Flexner. Light of distant skies
  Winter scene                     MB
    MB, Karolik coll
**Blunt, Martha (Garsed)** 1803-1885
  R, M. Mrs George William Blunt
**BLYTH, Benjamin,** fl 1746-1787
  Samuel Curwen                    MSE
    Pierson

**Attributed works**
Samuel McIntire                    MSE
  MSE. Cat of ports, 1950
**BLYTHE, David Gilmor,** 1815-1865
Art versus law                     NBM
  Mendelowitz
  Miller, D. David G. Blythe
  Pierson
  Richardson. Ptg in America
Blair family
  Miller, D. David G. Blythe
Courtroom scene
  Miller, D. David G. Blythe
Dry goods and notions              PPD
  Miller, D. David G. Blythe
  OCiM. Rediscoveries
  PPC. Amer classics
Farm scene
  Chew. 250 years of art
Gen Doubleday watching his troops cross
  the Potomac                      NCB
  Miller, D. David G. Blythe
  Pierson
  U.S. National Capital sesquicentennial
  com
Gouty fisherman                    ATeS
  ATeS. Collection
Hideout
  Miller, D. David G. Blythe
In the Pittsburgh post office      MB
  MB. Karolik coll
James McDonald                     OYB
  OYB. Catalogue 1951

Libby prison                              MB
  MB. Karolik coll
  Miller, D. David G. Blythe
Lincoln crushing the dragon of rebellion
                                          MB
  MB. Karolik coll
Mrs Jeremiah Webber and son
  Miller, D. David G. Blythe
On the sly
  Miller, D. David G. Blythe
Pittsburgh horsemarket
  Miller, D. David G. Blythe
Post office                               PPG
  Barker. Amer ptg
  Miller, D. David G. Blythe
  OYB. Blythe
President Lincoln writing the Emancipa-
  tion proclamation
  Miller, D. David G. Blythe
Prospecting
  Miller, D. David G. Blythe
Recruits wanted
  Miller, D. David G. Blythe
The runaway                               PPD
  OCiM. Rediscoveries
Shoremen
  Miller, D. David G. Blythe
Silas Gault
  OYB. Blythe
Stagecoach                                PPD
  Miller, D. David G. Blythe
Street urchins                            OYB
  OYB. Blythe
  OYB. Catalogue 1951
Thomas Coburn
  Miller, D. David G. Blythe
Tramps hideout
  OYB. Blythe
Trial scene                               NR
  Miller, D. David G. Blythe
Whoa, Emma
  Larkin
  Larkin rev ed
  Miller, D. David G. Blythe
Young musician                            PW
  Chew. 250 years of art
  NUM. Art across America
BMT, Fourteenth street by R. Marsh
Boardley, Elizabeth Beale, 1777-1862
  Stuart, G. Elizabeth Boardley
Boardman, Daniel Sherman, 1768-1864
  Earl, R. Daniel Boardman
Boardman, Elijah, 1760-1823
  Earl, R. Elijah Boardman
Boardwalk in moonlight by L. Jackson
The boat by M. Beckmann
The boat by P. Blume
The boat by Y. Tanguy
Boat and grain elevator #2 by R. Crawford
Boat and grain elevators by R. Crawford
Boat dock on the Riviera by M. Beckmann
Boat fantasy, Deer isle, Maine series, no 30
  by J. Marin
Boat landing by M. B. Prendergast
Boat landing, Dinard by M. B. Prendergast
Boat off Deer isle by J. Marin
Boat race, Boston harbor by A. A. Law-
  rence
Boat, sky and sea, Small Point, Maine by
  J. Marin

Boat with blue by J. Marin
Boathouse by W. T. Aldrich
Boathouse, winter, Harlem river by E.
  Lawson
Boating party by A. Pickens
Boating party in Central park by W. Whit-
  tredge
Boating party on the Thames by G. P. A.
  Healy
Boats by J. E. Heliker
Boats at anchor by J. S. Sargent
Boats drying their sails, Sestri Levante, Italy
  by E. D. Boit
Boats off the coast of Devonshire by W.
  Homer
Boats on Gaspé bay by M. Avery
Boats, sea and rocks by J. Marin
Boca by S. Solomon
BOCCIA, Edward E. 1921-
  Lyric yellow
    IU. Contemp Amer ptg & sculp, 1957
  Suspended forms                         MoSL
    CoS. New accessions USA, 1954
BODMER, Karl, 1809-1893
  Buffalo coming to drink in the upper
    Missouri
    Morgan
  Buffalo dance of the Mandan
    Morgan (col)
  Crow Indians
    Morgan
  Fort Clark
    Morgan
  Fort Pierre
    Morgan
  Funeral scaffold of a Sioux chief
    Morgan (col)
  Indian bull boats on the Missouri
    Morgan (detail)
  Interior of the hut of a Mandan chief
    Morgan (col)
  A Mandan village
    Morgan (col)
  Mato-topé, with the marks of his exploits
    Morgan (col)
  The Minnetaree scalp dance
    Morgan
  Noapeh, an Assiniboin Indian; Psihdja-
    sahpa, a Yanktonai Indian
    Morgan (col)
  Travelers meeting Minnetaree Indians
    Morgan
  The Yellowstone and Missouri rivers
    Morgan
Boelen, Anna. See Bancker, Anna (Boelen)
BOESE, Henry, 1744-1860
  Delaware Water Gap
    McClintock
  Stage coach seventy-six of the Knicker-
    bocker line                           NNMC
  U.S. National Capital sesquicentennial
    com
Boeuf by K. Knaths
Bogardus, Magdalena
  Unidentified artist. Magdalena Bogardus
Bogart, Joseph Outen, fl 1820
  Peale, Rembrandt. Lt Col Joseph Outen
    Bogart
BOGGS, Frank, 1855-1926
  Le Havre
    CSB. Impressionism

Boheme girl by R. Soyer
The Bohemian by T. Eakins
BOHROD, Aaron, 1907-
Antiques
  PPC. Ptg in the U.S. 1949
The art of painting. See Self-portrait
Bird and gauntlet
  OYB. Annual 1957
Human comedy
  IU. Contemp Amer ptg & sculp, 1959
Ivan Albright (Through a glass darkly)
  WiMiA. Amer ptg 1760-1960
Landscape near Chicago          WMAA
  Baur. Revolution
  McCurdy
  NYG. Fine art
  Pierson
  Wight. Milestones
Merry-go-round                  IaDa
  IaDa Silver jubilee
  IaDa. 30th anniversary
Military necessity
  Time. 300 years (col)
Oak street platform             MB
  Larkin
  Larkin rev ed
Paper storm                     ATU
  ATU. Coll of Amer art
Pillar
  MnMW. Reality and fantasy
Rainy night
  Gruskin (col)
Sacred and profane
  IU. Contemp Amer ptg & sculp, 1957
Self-portrait (The art of painting)
  WiMiA. Amer ptg 1760-1960
Street in Peoria                OYB
  OYB. Catalogue 1951
Through a glass darkly. See Ivan Al-
    bright
West park, Pittsburgh
  IU. Contemp Amer ptg, 1948
Boiler synthesis by R. Crawford
Bois de Sioux river by J. M. Stanley
BOIT, Edward Darley, 1840-1915
Arc de Triomphe                 MB
  MB. Ptgs in water color
Beach at Sestri Levante, Italy  MB
  MB. Ptgs in water color
Biarritz, a big sea             MB
  MB. Ptgs in water color
Bidart, French Pyrenees         MB
  MB. Ptgs in water color
Boats drying their sails, Sestri Levante,
    Italy                       MB
  MB. Ptgs in water color
Bologna: A bright morning       MB
  MB. Ptgs in water color
Bordighera, Italy               MB
  MB. Ptgs in water color
The Capitol, Washington         MB
  MB. Ptgs in water color
East river, New York            MB
  MB. Ptgs in water color
Florence                        MB
  MB. Ptgs in water color
Florence from San Miniato       MB
  MB. Ptgs in water color
Genoa: A hillside               MB
  MB. Ptgs in water color
Genoa: The port                 MB
  MB. Ptgs in water color

Lake Orta, Italy                MB
  MB. Ptgs in water color
Lake Maggiore, Italy            MB
  MB. Ptgs in water color
London: A bend of the Thames at Chelsea
                                MB
  MB. Ptgs in water color
Morning at Gargagno, Lake of Garda
                                MB
  MB. Ptgs in water color
Morning at Rive, Lake of Garda  MB
  MB. Ptgs in water color
Morning near Paris              MB
  MB. Ptgs in water color
Old mill near St Enogat, Britanny  MB
  MB. Ptgs in water color
On the Consuma pass, Tuscany    MB
  MB. Ptgs in water color
Ouchy, Lake Geneva, Switzerland MB
  MB. Ptgs in water color
Park avenue, New York           MB
  MB. Ptgs in water color
Piccadilly, London              MB
  MB. Ptgs in water color
Place de l'Opéra, Paris         MB
  MB. Ptgs in water color
Place du Carrousel, Paris, 1911 MB
  MB. Ptgs in water color
Poppi in the Casentino, Tuscany MB
  MB. Ptgs in water color
Rio di San Barnaba, Venice      MB
  MB. Ptgs in water color
Rio di San Lorenzo, Venice      MB
  MB. Ptgs in water color
Rough sea at Portofino, Italy   MB
  MB. Ptgs in water color
St Malo from Dinard, low tide, Brittany
                                MB
  MB. Ptgs in water color
St Peter's, Rome                MB
  MB. Ptgs in water color
Street in Arezzo                MB
  MB. Ptgs in water color
Venice: Afternoon on the Campo San
    Trovaso                     MB
  MB. Ptgs in water color
Venice: Afternoon on the Grand canal
                                MB
  MB. Ptgs in water color
Venice: Fisherman's quarter on the Giu-
    decca                       MB
  MB. Ptgs in water color
Venice: Looking toward the Giudecca
                                MB
  MB. Ptgs in water color
Venice: Morning on the Grand canal
                                MB
  MB. Ptgs in water color
Venice: Off San Giorgio         MB
  MB. Ptgs in water color
Venice: Showery morning on the Zattere
                                MB
  MB. Ptgs in water color
Boit, Mary Louise (Cushing) fl 1888
  Sargent, J. S. Mrs Edward D. Boit
Boit children
  Sargent, J. S. Daughters of Edward D.
    Boit
Bolling, Mary (Randolph) 1775?-1845
  Hubard, W. J. Mrs William Bolling
Bologna: A bright morning by E. D. Boit

**BOLOTOWSKY, Ilya,** 1907-
  Abstraction, 1939      CtY
    CtY. Soc Anonyme
  Blue rectangles      WMAA
    Pierson
  Diamond shaped
    CSEP. Annual ex, 1950/51
  Large vertical      WMAA
    Goodrich. Amer art
  Sombre vertical with lines
    VR. Amer ptg 1958
The **bolter** by C. M. Russell

Bolton by F. Guy
Bolton landing by W. De Kooning
**BOMAR, Bill,** 1919-
  Lilacs and glasses
    IU. Contemp Amer ptg & sculp, 1955
  Melon      TxF
    CoS. New accessions USA, 1952
Bombardment of Fort Sumter by A. Bierstadt
Bombardment of Tripoli under Commodore Preble, 1804 by M. F. Corné
Bomber by R. Crawford
Bond, Gorham
  Goodridge, E. Gorham Bond
Bondsville fair by A. M. R. Moses
Bone, Richard
  Robinson, B. Richard Bone
Bone player by W. S. Mount
Bonfire by R. Cowles
**BONHAM, Horace,** 1835-1892
  Nearing the issue at the cockpit, 1870  DC
    Davidson v2
    Mendelowitz
Bonjean, Mme
  Tchelitchew, P. Madame Bonjean
The **book** by W. M. Chase
Book, beerstein and corncob pipe by J. F. Peto
Book of life by L. Pershing
Book, shell and ship by K. Knaths
**BOOKATZ, Samuel,** 1910-
  Gate watch      OYB
    OYB. Annual 1958
    OYB. Supplement 1959
  Steel town madonna
    IU. Contemp Amer ptg & sculp, 1953
The **bookcase** by K. Davies
Books by J. F. Peto
Books on a shelf by J. F. Peto
Boomtown by T. H. Benton
Boon by J. D. Brooks
Boon companions by E. H. Garrett
Boone, Daniel, 1735-1820
  Bingham, G. C. Daniel Boone escorting a band of pioneers into western country
  Cole, T. Daniel Boone and cabin on Great Osage lake
  Harding, C. Daniel Boone
  Harding, C. (attributed works) Daniel Boone
The **bootblack** by G. H. Yewell
**BOOTH, Cameron,** 1892-
  Alms
    ICA. Annual ex, 1951

Black and white      MnMW
  MnMW. 60 Amer ptrs
Clam bay farm
  Cheney. Expressionism 1948 ed
Evening
  Pousette-Dart. Amer ptg
Painting, 1951
  MnU. 40 Amer ptrs
Regal personages
  MnU. 40 Amer ptrs
Street in Stillwater      DP
  DP. Catalogue
The winters passed
  MnMW. Classic tradition
Boothbay harbor, Maine by M. M. Albright
Boots by M. Hartley
**BORDER limner,** fl 1815
  Alice Slade      DN
    DN. Amer primitive ptgs, pt 1
    Jones. Rediscovered ptrs
  Harriet Leavens
    ICA. From colony to nation
    Jones. Rediscovered ptrs
  Joseph Slade      DN
    DN. Amer primitive ptgs, pt 1
    Jones. Rediscovered ptrs
  Philip Slade      DN
    DN. Amer primitive ptgs, pt 2
  Robert Lockridge Dorr      VWR
    Ford. Pictorial folk art
Bordighera, Italy by E. D. Boit
Bordley, John Beale, 1727-1804
  Peale, C. W. John Beale Bordley
Bordley, Sarah Fishbourne, fl 1782
  Peale, C. W. Sarah Fishbourne Bordley
**BORDUAS, Paul Émil,** 1905-
  Morning candelabra      MMA
    Art since 1945
**BORIE, Adolphe,** 1877-1934
  Betty Campbell Madeira
    Chew. 250 years of art
**BORIS, Bessie**
  Old man with umbrella
    PA. Annual ex, 1961
Borland, Francis, 1691-1763
  Copley, J. S. Francis Borland
**BORTIN, Dora**
  Russian tea service
    PA. Annual ex, 1954
**BOSA, Louis,** 1905-
  Blessing of the fleet
    NAD. Annual ex, 1947, 1st half
  Carnival on ice
    DC. 22 biennial ex, 1951
    MM. Amer ptg today
  End of the festival      IU
    IU. Contemp Amer ptg, 1949
    IU. 20th century
  Fish story
    IU. Contemp Amer ptg, 1951
  Golden palace
    NAD. Annual ex, 1952
  Hallowe'en      MWM
    CoS. New accessions USA, 1950
    IU. Contemp Amer ptg, 1950
  Monks fishing, Venice      OYB
    OYB. Annual 1960
  Monks of Burano
    IU. Contemp Amer ptg & sculp, 1959
  My family reunion      WMAA
    Pierson
  Ponte Vecchio, Florence
    OYB. Annual 1956

**BOSA, Louis**—*Continued*
Procession of the Savior
IU. Contemp Amer ptg & sculp, 1953
San Barnaba
NAD. Annual ex, 1954
Spring on Ninth avenue
Gruskin
Welcome home
IU. Contemp Amer ptg, 1948
Boston, Massachusetts
Brown, G. L. Public gardens, Boston
Chambers, T. Boston harbor, c 1840
Fransioli, T. A. Louisburg square
Hardy, P. Tremont street, Boston
Harvey, G. Reaping on Boston Common, 1835-1840
Harvey, G. State House and Boston Common, 1830
Harvey, G. Tremont house, Boston
Hassam, C. Boston Common at twilight
Hassam, C. Columbus avenue, Boston: rainy day
Hassam, C. Rainy day
Hubbard, C. The National Lancers with the reviewing officers on Boston Common
Marston, J. B. State street and old State House, Boston, 1801
Paine, L. G. Copley square
Prendergast, M. B. South Boston
Prendergast, M. B. Street scene, Boston
Prendergast, M. B. Tremont street, Boston
Prendergast, M. B. West church, Boston
Ricci, J. Louisburg square, winter
Salmon, R. W. Boston harbor from Constitution wharf
Salmon, R. W. Boston harbor: Long and Central wharves, 1832
Savory, T. C. National Lancers on Boston Common
Sharp, W. Railroad jubilee on Boston Common
Zerbe, K. Park street, Boston
**Boston** daily by K. Zerbe
**Boston** harbor by J. S. Blunt
**BOSWORTH, Sala**
Jonathan Sprague                          OCoA
Ford. Pictorial folk art
Melissa Sprague                           OCoA
Ford. Pictorial folk art
**Botafogo** by R. S. Du Casse
**Botafogo** bay, Rio de Janeiro by J. Lavalle
**Both** members of this club by G. W. Bellows
**BOTHWELL, Dorr,** 1902-
Idea and forms
CSFP. Annual ex, 1947/48
Keepsake from Mallorca
CSFP. Annual ex, 1952
**BOTKIN, Henry Albert,** 1896-
The ceremony                              MB
CoS. New accessions USA, 1956
IU. Contemp Amer ptg, 1951
Performer
Gruskin
**Botsford, Polly,** 1754-1813
Unidentified artist. Mourning picture—
Polly Botsford and her children
**BOTT, Emil,** fl 1849-1880
Scene on the Monongahela
Chew. 250 years of art

**BOTTON, Jean de,** 1898-
The four horsemen of the Apocalypse
PPC. Ptg in the U.S. 1949
**BOUCHÉ, Louis,** 1896-
County home
WiMiA. Amer ptg 1760-1960
Fire
IU. Contemp Amer ptg, 1949
High street bus barn
Pousette-Dart. Amer ptg
Long Island sound
Gruskin (col)
Mural assistant                           CLA
Time. 300 years (col)
New Lebanon railroad station
PPC. Ptg in the U.S. 1949
Peppercombe porch
PPC. International ex, 1950
Piermont, New York
NAD. Annual ex, 1959
Self-portrait
WiMiA. Amer ptg 1760-1960
Stamford harbor                           WMAA
Goodrich. Amer art
NYG. Fine art
Ten cents a ride                          MM
MM. 100 Amer ptrs
Pierson
Unpainted horses                          ATeS
ATeS. Collection
**BOUCHÉ, René**
Saul Steinberg
IU. Contemp Amer ptg & sculp, 1957
**Boudé, Samuel,** fl 1755
West, B. Samuel Boudé
**Boudé, Mrs Samuel,** fl 1755
West, B. Mrs Samuel Boudé
**Boudoir** by W. De Kooning
**BOUDRO(U), Alexandr,** fl 1851
A. Dickson entering Bristol in 1819 VWR
VWR. Amer folk art
VWR. Folk art (col)
**Bounetheau's** aunt by E. G. Malbone
The **bountiful** board by Unidentified artist
**Bouquet** by H. Hofmann
**Bouquet** by R. Philipp
**Bouquet** by S. Serisawa
**Bouquet** abstraction by A. B. Carles
**Bouquet** in blue vase by A. B. Carles
**Bouquet** in Quimper pitcher by W. J. Glackens
**Bouquet** of flowers by H. G. Keller
**Bourgouis** W—r and his squaw by A. J. Miller
**Bourne, Mercy (Gorham)** 1695-1782
Copley, J. S. Mrs Sylvanus Bourne
**Bours, Peter,** 1783-1860
Malbone, E. G. Peter Bours
**BOUTELLE, De Witt Clinton,** 1820-1884
Indian surveying a landscape              MB
MB. Karolik coll
**Bovard, Mrs James M.**
Trebilcock, P. Mrs James M. Bovard
**BOVÉ, Richard John,** 1920-
Classic still life
NAD. Annual ex, 1954
New York scene
NAD. Annual ex, spring 1950
Steeplechase horses
NAD. Annual ex, 1956

**BOWDEN, H.**
View of the bay
CSFP. Annual ex, 1948/49
**Bowditch, Nathaniel, 1773-1838**
Stuart, G. Nathaniel Bowditch
**Bowdoin, Elizabeth, fl 1760**
Blackburn, J. Elizabeth and James Bowdoin
**Bowdoin, Elizabeth, 1750-1809. See Temple,**
Elizabeth (Bowdoin) lady
**Bowdoin, Elizabeth, fl 1754-1762. See Pitts,**
Elizabeth (Bowdoin)
**Bowdoin, Elizabeth (Erving) 1731-1803**
Feke, R. Mrs James Bowdoin
Malbone, E. G. Mrs James Bowdoin
**Bowdoin, James, 1676-1747**
Badger, J. James Bowdoin
**Bowdoin, James, 1726-1790**
Feke, R. James Bowdoin II
**Bowdoin, James, 1752-1811**
Malbone, E. G. Hon James Bowdoin
**Bowdoin, James, fl 1760**
Blackburn, J. Elizabeth and James Bowdoin
**Bowdoin, Mrs James. See Bowdoin, Elizabeth (Erving)**
**Bowdoin, Phoebe (Murdock) d 1772**
Feke, R. Mrs William Bowdoin
**Bowdoin, William, fl 1748**
Feke, R. William Bowdoin
**Bowdoin, Mrs William. See Bowdoin, Phoebe (Murdock)**
**Bowen, Elizabeth. See Amory, Elizabeth (Bowen)**
**Bowen, Lydia. See Clark, Lydia (Bowen)**
**BOWER, John, fl 1809-1819**
View of bombardment of Fort McHenry
ICH
U. S. National Capital sesquicentennial com
**BOWERS, Edward, fl 1855-1867**
Fruit and wine      MB
MB. Karolik coll
**Bowers, Mrs Jerathmael. See Bowers, Mary (Sherburne)**
**Bowers, Mary (Sherburne) 1735-1799**
Copley, J. S. Mrs Jerathmael Bowers
The **Bowery** by R. Marsh
The **Bowery** at night by W. L. Sonntag
**Bowery** at Pell street by R. Marsh
**Bowery** drunks by R. Marsh
The **bowl** by R. Marsh
**Bowl** of apples by W. Sommer
**Bowl** of fruit by Unidentified artist
**Bowl** of wild roses by J. La Farge
**Bowne, Walter, 1770-1846**
Malbone, E. G. Walter Bowne
The **bowsprit** by F. W. Benson
**Box** of tricks by C. H. Demuth
**Box** party by K. H. Miller
**Boxers and wrestlers**
Bellows, G. W. Both members of this club
Bellows, G. W. Club night
Bellows, G. W. Dempsey and Firpo
Bellows, G. W. Ringside seats
Eakins, T. Between rounds
Eakins, T. Wrestlers
Hayes, G. A. Bare knuckles

Luks, G. B. Wrestlers
Martin, F. The glory
Martin, F. Lullaby
Martin, F. The undefeated
**Boy** by G. W. Bellows
**Boy** by B. Karfiol
**Boy** by M. B. Prendergast
**Boy** by B. Shahn
**Boy** and girl by R. Soyer
**Boy** bathers by B. Karfiol
**Boy** carrying deer by W. Homer
**Boy** eating an apple by W. M. Chase
**Boy** feeding a cockatoo by W. M. Chase
**Boy** fishing by W. Homer
**Boy** from Stalingrad by P. Evergood
**Boy** from the plains by P. Hurd
**Boy** holding dog by J. Bradley (attributed works)
**Boy** holding lamb's head by W. Stein
**Boy** in beaver hat by A. M. Von Phul
**Boy** in blue coat by Unidentified artist
**Boy** in Mexico by C. L. Casebier
**Boy** in plaid by Unidentified artist
**Boy** in the grass by B. Perlin
**Boy** on stenciled carpet by E. S. Field (attributed works)
**Boy** picking apples by W. Homer
**Boy** picking flowers by F. Martin
**Boy** smoking by W. M. Chase
**Boy** stealing fruit by Y. Kuniyoshi
**Boy** with a cigar by W. M. Chase
**Boy** with a toy drum by Unidentified artist
**Boy** with birds by D. Jameson
**Boy** with chalice by C. A. Morris
**Boy** with cow by Y. Kuniyoshi
**Boy** with doves by S. Menkès
**Boy** with finch by Unidentified artist
**Boy** with guitar by H. Lotterman
**Boy** with hammer and iron pot by Unidentified artist
**Boy** with machine by R. Lindner
**Boy** with squirrel by J. S. Copley
**Boy** with still life by S. Roesen
**Boy** with the anchor by W. Homer
**Boy** with whip by Unidentified artist
**Boylston, Nicholas, 1716-1771**
Copley, J. S. Nicholas Boylston
**Boylston, Sarah (Morecock) 1696-1774**
Copley, J. S. Mrs Thomas Boylston
**Boynton, Emeline, b 1813?**
Walton, H. Emeline Boynton, age 32
**Boynton, Harriet Elizabeth, b 1843?**
Walton, H. Harriet Elizabeth Boynton, age 2 years
**Boynton, Henry, b 1806?**
Walton, H. Henry Boynton, age 39
**BOYNTON, James W. 1929?**
Bright stalk
WMAA. Young America 1957
Cove
NNSG. Younger Amer ptrs
Image and space
WMAA. Young America 1957

**BOYNTON, J. W.**—*Continued*
Limestone Edge                                        TxD
  Pierson
Sun trap                                              OYB
  Brussels. Exposition
Boys bathing by W. Homer
Boys beaching a dory by W. Homer
Boys caught napping in a field by **W. S.**
  Mount
Boys fishing by J. Kane
Boys in a pasture by W. Homer
Boys on the beach by J. S. Sargent
Boys skating by G. H. Durrie
Boys wading by W. Homer
Brace's rock, Eastern point, Gloucester by
  F. H. Lane
Brackett, Albert Gallatin, 1829-1896
  Healy, G. P. A. Albert G. Brackett
**BRACKMAN, Robert, 1898-**
Junior
  NAD. Annual ex, 1949, 1st half
Lighthouse keeper
  NAD. Annual ex, 1947, 2d half
  NAD. Annual ex, 1961
Peter Freuchen
  PA. Annual ex, 1958
  PPC. International ex, 1950
Portrait in studio light
  NAD. Annual ex, 1959
Sailor's holiday                                      MM
  MM. 100 Amer ptrs
Self-portrait
  NAD. Annual ex, 1953
Still life in gray
  IU. Contemp Amer ptg, 1952
Still life with figure                                IaDa
  Gruskin
  IaDa. Silver jubilee
Unmasked
  PPC. Ptg in the U.S. 1949
Young woman with bird
  NAD. Annual ex, spring 1950
**BRADFORD, Howard, 1919-**
Hanging bird
  ICA. Annual ex, 1957
**BRADFORD, William, 1823-1892**
Ship Dashing Wave off Boston **Light**
                                                      MSP
  NUM. Art across America
Bradley, Mr, fl 1835
  Philips (attributed works) Mr Bradley
Bradley, Mrs, fl 1835
  Phillips (attributed works). Mrs Bradley
**BRADLEY, I. J. H.** fl 1830-1855
The cellist                                           DP
  Barker. Amer ptg
  Baur. Amer ptg
  DP. Catalogue
  Pierson
**BRADLEY, J. C.**
Still life with red plush and thistle
  CSFP. Annual ex, 1946
**BRADLEY, John,** fl 1836-1847
Emma Homan                                            DN
  DN. Amer primitive ptgs, pt 2
Little girl in lavender                               DN
  DN. Amer primitive ptgs, pt 1
    **Attributed works**
Boy holding dog                                       VWR
  VWR. Folk art (col)

Girl with flower basket                               VWR
  VWR. Folk art (col)
Bradley, Lucy
  Earl. R. Lucy Bradley
**BRADLEY, Mary,** fl 1830
Basket of fruit                                       VWR
  Pierson
  VWR. Amer folk art (col)
**BRADSHAW, Glenn R.**
Factory no 1
  NAD. Annual ex, 1957
**BRADSHAW, J. W.**
An Indian                                             DN
  DN. Amer primitive ptgs, pt 2
Brailsford, Dr, fl 1802
  Malbone, E. G. Dr Brailsford
Brailsford, Samuel, b 1729
  Theus, J. Col Samuel Brailsford
Branch bank of the United States by **R.**
  Smith
Brandegee, Mary Bryant (Pratt)
  Sargent, J. S. Mrs Edward D. Brandegee
Brandywine by W. Sommer
Brandywine landscape by W. Sommer
The Brandywine, View on by J. Peale
Branford, William, 1756-1776
  Theus, J. Young William Branford
Brant, Joseph (Thayendanegea) 1742-1807
  Ames, E. Joseph Brant, Thayendanegea
**BRANTZ, Lewis**
Pittsburgh, 1790                                      PPC
  Davidson v2
Brasher, Miss, fl 1804
  Malbone, E. G. Miss Brasher
**Brass, Catherine.** See Yates, Catherine
  (Brass)
Brass band by J. Covert
Brattle, William, 1702-1776
  Copley, J. S. William Brattle
The bravado by A. J. Miller
The brave's return by C. M. Russell
Bread and circuses by R. Gwathmey
The breadline by G. B. Luks
Breadmakers by M. Sterne
Breaker by P. Busa
The breaker boy by G. B. Luks
Breakers by L. B. La Farge
Breakers, Maine coast by J. Marin
Breakfast at sunrise by A. J. Miller
The breakfast table by J. S. Sargent
Breaking down the wild horse by G. Catlin
Breaking sea by M. Avery
Breaking the home ties by T. Hovenden
Breaking up camp at sunrise by A. J. Miller
Breaking up the ice in spring by F. Reming-
  ton
Breaking wave by W. Homer
Breakwater by S. M. Adler
Breakwater by Y. Johnston
Breakwater by J. Kaplan
Breakwater, Tynemouth by W. Homer
**Breathitt, Jane.** See Sappington, **Jane**
  (Breathitt)
**BRECKNER, George, 1914-**
Mill entrance                                         OYB
  OYB. Annual 1954
  OYB. Supplement

**Breeches** buoy by A. Winter
**Breezing** up by W. Homer
**BREININ, Raymond,** 1908-
  At Golgotha              OYB
    OYB. Supplement
  City view
    CSFP. Annual ex, 1952
  He walks alone
    Gruskin
  In a garden of ancient loves
    IU. Contemp Amer ptg, 1948
  Jean Piccard
    Genauer
    PA. Annual ex, 1948
  The magicians
    NAD. Annual ex, 1947, 1st half
  The night            MB
    MB. Ptgs in water color
    Pierson
  They guard the night
    Baur. Revolution
  White house         MMA
    Cheney. Primer 1958 ed
**Breintall, Mary.** See Peters, Mary (Breintall)
**BREREWOOD, Francis,** fl 1730
  Benedict Leonard Calvert, Governor of
    Maryland        MdBW
    DC. Amer ptrs of the South
**BRETT, Dorothy Eugenie,** 1883-
  Women's dance
    IU. Contemp Amer ptg & sculp, 1953

      **Portrait of the artist**
Ray, R. D. The Honorable Dorothy
  Eugenie Brett
**Brewer, Nicholas**
  Peale, C. W. Nicholas Brewer I
**Brewer, William Henry,** 1828-1910
  Beckwith, J. C. William H. Brewer
**BREWSTER, Anna Richards,** 1870-1952
  Clovelly street, Devon     OYB
    OYB. Supplement
**BREWSTER, John,** 1766-1854?
  Child with a peach       MB
    MB. Karolik coll
  Francis O. Watts with bird  NCHA
    Jones. New-found folk art
  One shoe off         NCHA
    Jones. New-found folk art

      **Attributed works**
Eliphaz Thayer and his wife, Deliverance
                   NCHA
  Jones. New-found folk art
Gentleman in a landscape    NCHA
  Jones. New-found folk art
Lady in a landscape      NCHA
  Jones. New-found folk art
**BREWTON, James**
  Suicide of Judas
    PA. Annual ex, 1959-60
**Brewton, Rebecca.** See Motte, Rebecca
  (Brewton)
The **briarwood** pipe by W. Homer
**BRICE, William,** 1921-
  Black rocks, kelp and sea
    IU. Contemp Amer ptg & sculp, 1955
  Fragments of roses
    IU. Contemp Amer ptg & sculp, 1953

**Ocean** and cliffs          CLA
  CoS. New accessions USA, 1956
  ICA. Annual ex, 1957
Ocean and rocks
  PPC. International ex, 1955
Rose picture            MCH
  Pulitzer v2
Rose sequence
  Pousette-Dart. Amer ptg
Roses
  NBuA. Expressionism
Young woman with gloves
  PPC. Ptg in the U.S. 1949
**Bridal** veil and El Capitan, Yosemite valley
  by T. Hill
The **bride** by H. Bloom
The **bride** by A. Rattner
The **bride** by F. Robbins
**Bride** and owl by G. Hartigan
The **bridge** by C. Schucker
**Bridge** and steps, Venice by M. B. Prendergast
**Bridge** for fishing by L. M. Eilshemius
**Bridge** sign by E. Hicks
**BRIDGES, Charles,** fl 1725-1750
  Anne Byrd            VWR
    NUM. Art across America
  Maria Taylor Byrd of Westover, Virginia
                   MM
    Belknap
    Mendelowitz
    Pierson
    Richardson. Ptg in America
  Mrs William Byrd (?) (Stewart coll)
    Flexner. First flowers
  Wilhelmina Byrd (?)
    Belknap

      **Attributed works**
Mann Page the second (?)    VWC
  Barker. Amer ptg
**Bridges**
Albee, P. F. The bridge
Berman, E. Bridges of Paris
Blatas, A. Pont Neuf
Blume, P. The bridge
Bosa, L. Ponte Vecchio, Florence
Burliuk, D. Harlem river bridge
Cook, H. N. The bridge
Crawford, R. Whitestone bridge
Crimi, A. D. Brooklyn bridge
Davis, S. Bridge at Courbevoie
Dickinson, P. Bridge
Dickinson, P. Harlem
Dove, A. G. Holbrook's bridge, northwest,
  1938
Duveneck, F. The bridges, Florence
Drumlevitch, S. Bronx bridge
Feininger, L. Bridge
Glackens, W. J. La Villette
Goodwin, A. C. High bridge, New York
Guglielmi, L. The bridge
Halpert, S. Brooklyn bridge
Hill, J. W. Hudson river bridge near
  Waterford
Howard, W. Le Pont Neuf
Kane, J. Juniata river
Katzman, H. Brooklyn bridge
Koch, J. The bridge
Koerner, H. The bridge
Lawson, E. High bridge

Bridges—*Continued*
  Lawson, E. Spring night, Harlem river
  Lichtenberg, M. Albert bridge, London
  Moses, A. M. R. Sunday (The covered
    bridge)
  Prendergast, M. B. Bridge in Venice
  Prendergast, M. B. Ponte della Paglia
  Pucci, A. J. Ponte Vecchio
  Ranger, H. W. High bridge
  Rufty, E. M. Bridge over Dock street
  Schucker, C. The bridge
  Sheeler, C. Golden Gate
  Smith, R. Monongahela bridge after the
    freshet in 1832
  Smith, W. H. Hell Gate bridge
  Spencer, N. Two bridges
  Stella, J. The bridge
  Stella, J. Brooklyn bridge
  Stuempfig, W. The railroad bridge
  Toney, A. Bridge
  Unidentified artist. Town bridge
  Watson, R. The bridge
  Whistler, J. A. M. Last of old West-
    minster
  Whistler, J. A. M. Old Battersea bridge
Bridle path, Tahiti by J. La Farge
Bridle path, White mountains by W. Homer
Bridlington quay by W. Homer
Brig Antelope in Boston harbor by F. H.
  Lane
Brig Charles of Boston by M. F. Corné
Brig in a storm by T. Birch
Briggs, Mr, fl 1840
  Unidentified artist. Mr Briggs
Briggs, Mrs, fl 1840
  Unidentified artist. Mrs Briggs
BRIGGS, Ernest, 1923-
  Painting, 1954
    MMA. 12 Americans
  Painting, 1955 [1]
    MMA. 12 Americans
  Painting, 1955 [2]
    MMA. 12 Americans
  Painting, 1955 [3]
    MMA. 12 Americans
  Painting, 1955 [4]
    MMA. 12 Americans
  Painting, 1956
    MMA. 12 Americans (col)
Briggs, Mary, fl 1840
  Unidentified artist. Mary Briggs
Brigham's yard, Kingston by E. E. Speicher
Bright beyond by I. R. Pereira
Bright stalk by J. W. Boynton
Brightening Seine by J. Whorf
Brightness as a third dimension by R.
  Anuszkiewicz
Brighton, England by R. Smith
Brine, Augustus, 1770-1840
  Copley, J. S. Midshipman Augustus Brine
Bringing home the cattle—coast of Florida
  by T. Moran
Bringing home the moose by T. Eakins
Bringing home the new cook by F. Reming-
  ton
Bringing home the scalp by C. M. Russell
Bringing in the Christmas tree by A. M. R.
  Moses
Brinton, John H. 1832-1907
  Eakins, T. Dr John H. Brinton

Bristol mills by B. Miller
British fleet forcing the Hudson river pas-
  sage, 1776 by D. Serres
British privateers with French prizes in New
  York harbor by Unidentified artist
British troops at Concord by R. Earl
Broadway, night by J. Marin
Broadway, 1936 by M. Tobey
Broadway restaurant by G. Hartigan
BRODERSON, Morris, 1928-
  Chicken market
    WMAA. Young America 1960
  Sound of flowers
    WMAA. Young America 1960
BRODIE, Gandy, 1925-
  Momentous vision of spring
    WMAA. Annual ex, 1957
Brodnax, Edward, d 1746
  Unidentified artist. Edward Brodnax
Broe and McDonald listen in by K. Schmidt
Broken life by A. Refregier
Broken pot with blue vase by H. L. McFee
Broken tree by M. Weber
A bronc to breakfast by C. M. Russell
Bronson, Catherine. See Townsend, Cath-
  erine
Bronx bridge by S. Drumlevitch
Bronx light by B. Weiner
BROOK, Alexander, 1898-
  Amalia                                    OT
    OT. Contemp Amer ptgs
  Ann                                       MM
    Lewisohn
    MM. 100 Amer ptrs
  Barn chair
    PPC. Ptg in the U.S. 1949
  The bay beyond
    ICA. Annual ex, 1951
  Belinda standing                          MoSL
    MoSL. Handbook 1953
  Clifford Tallulah Maddox
    IU. Contemp Amer ptg, 1949
  Frogtown lady
    IU. Contemp Amer ptg, 1948
  George Biddle playing the flute           MMA
    Brown. Amer ptg
  Georgia jungle                            PPC
    Gruskin (col)
    Time. 300 years (col)
  Introspection
    CSFP. Annual ex, 1948/49
  The intruder
    WMAA. Juliana Force
  Mood                                      WMAA
    Goodrich. Amer art
  Mother and daughter
    NAD. Annual ex, 1957
  My wife                                   DC
    NYG. Fine art
  Peggy Bacon and metaphysics               NeL
    Gruskin
    Pierson
  Remnants                                  ATeS
    ATeS. Collection
    Pousette-Dart. Amer ptg
    PPC. International ex, 1950
  Rosa Maria
    NAD. Annual ex, 1959
  The sentinels                             WMAA
    Goodrich. Amer art (col)
    NYG. Fine art
    Pierson

Serafina
  NAD. Annual ex, 1956
The shore
  NAD. Annual ex, 1952
Sleeping girl
  Brown. Amer ptg
Southern belle
  DC. 22 biennial ex, 1951
  NAD. Annual ex, 1948
Summer wind
  Baur. Revolution
Which way to Sunbury?
  DC. 20 biennial ex, 1947
The yellow fan                            NUM
  NUM. Root bequest
Young pianist
  NAD. Annual ex, spring 1950
  PA. Annual ex, 1948

Brook, Mrs Alexander. See Knee, Gina
Brook, Gina (Knee) See Knee, Gina
Brook among rocks by J. S. Sargent
Brook bathers by M. Avery
Brook by moonlight by R. A. Blakelock
Brook in Vermont by G. H. Hallowell
Brook, Montclair by G. Inness
Brook Watson and the shark by J. S. Copley
BROOKES, Samuel Marsden, b 1816
  Salmon trout and smelt               CSFD
  Frankenstein. After the hunt
Brooklyn, New York
  Guy, F. Brooklyn, 1816-1820
  Unidentified artist. Street in Brooklyn
    c 1840-1860
Brooklyn bridge by A. D. Crimi
Brooklyn bridge by S. Halpert
Brooklyn bridge by H. Katzman
Brooklyn bridge by J. Stella
Brooklyn bridge—Variation on an old theme
    by J. Stella
Brooklyn ice house by G. Ault
Brooklyn Navy yard by J. W. Martens
BROOKS, James D. 1906-
  Ainlee                                  MM
    Art since 1945
    Pierson
  Altoon
    MMA. 12 Americans (col)
  Boon
    WMAA. Annual ex, 1958
  Cauthunda
    Seiberling
  Denain
    IU. Contemp Amer ptg & sculp, 1961
  Dolamen                               NNSG
    NNSG. Handbook
  E—1953
    WMAA. New decade
  Flight
    MnU. 40 Amer ptrs
  Gant                                   NBuA
    MMA. 12 Americans
    NBuA. Acquisitions 1954-57
  Gordian
    Hunter. Mod Amer ptg
  Holdan
    MMA. 12 Americans
  Jackson
    MMA. New Amer ptg
  Jondol
    PPC. International ex, 1961/62

Karrig                                   MnMW
  Art since 1945 (col)
  MMA. New Amer ptg (col)
  MnMW. 60 Amer ptrs (col)
Larpolo
  ICA. Annual ex, 1961
Loring
  Ponente. Mod ptg, 1960 (col)
M—1951
  PPC. International ex, 1952
M—1953
  NNSG. Younger Amer ptrs
Number 18, 1949
  Hess. Abstract ptg
Number 27, 1950                          WMAA
  Cheney. New world history
  Cheney. Story 1958 ed
  Hess. Abstract ptg
  McCurdy
  MMA. Abstract
  WMAA. New decade
Number 38, 1951
  MnU. 40 Amer ptrs
Number 44
  IU. Contemp Amer ptg, 1952
  Pousette-Dart. Amer ptg
Q—1952
  IU. Contemp Amer ptg & sculp, 1955
Qualm                                    MMA
  MMA. New Amer ptg
  MMA. 12 Americans
Quatic
  MMA. 12 Americans
R—1953
  Eliot. Art of our time (col)
  MMA. 12 Americans
  Time. 300 years (col)
Rasalus                                  WMAA
  Goodrich. Amer art (col)
S—1951
  IU. Contemp Amer ptg & sculp, 1953
T—1954
  WMAA. New decade
BROOKS, Nicholas A. fl 1880-1904
  Still life with playbill                OOb
  Frankenstein. After the hunt
Brother and sister sharing a book by W. M.
    Prior (manner of)
Brothers by A. G. Dove
Brothers by B. Shahn
BROUDY, Miriam
  Douarnenez
    NAD. Annual ex, 1961
Broughton, Mrs Alexander. See Ravenel,
    Elizabeth Damaris
Broughton, Anne, d 1755?
  Johnston, H. Anne Broughton (Mrs John
    Gibbes)
Broughton, Charlotte. See Izard, Charlotte
    (Broughton)
Broughton, Nicholson
  Unidentified artist. Captain Nicholson
    Broughton
Brower, Catherine, fl 1791
  MacKay. Catherine Brower
BROWERE, Alburtis Del Orient, 1814-1887
  Catskills                               NBM
    Born
  Crossing the Isthmus, c 1852
    U.S. National Capital sesquicentennial
    com
  Falls of San Joaquin, California        ICA
    Born

BROWERE, A. D.—*Continued*
Mrs McCormick's general store, Catskill, N.Y.                                              NCHA
    Davidson v2
    Jones. Rediscovered ptrs
Stockton, California, 1856                      CSFD
    Born

**Attributed works**
Hudson river landing                            NAI
    Jones, Rediscovered ptrs
Brown, Mrs Abiah, fl 1804
    Malbone, E. G. Mrs Abiah Brown
BROWN, Carlyle, 1919-
    Blue glasses
        DC. 27 biennial ex, 1961
    Red cabinet                                 WMAA
        Goodrich. Amer art
        McCurdy
        Pierson
        WMAA. New decade
    Red still life
        IU. Contemp Amer ptg & sculp, 1957
    The round table
        PPC. International ex, 1952
    Round table with fiasco and landscape
        ICA. Annual ex, 1954
        WMAA. New decade
    Shelf still life
        ICA. Annual ex, 1957
    Still life with bottles
        WMAA. Annual ex, 1954
    Still life with glasses and roses           IU
        Pierson
    Still life with landscape
        IU. Contemp Amer ptg & sculp, 1953
    Table with fish and scales
        ICA. Annual ex, 1951
    Table with glasses and napkin
        CSFP. Annual ex, 1952
        WMAA. Contemp Amer ptg, 1951
    Table with glasses and roses                IU
        IU. Contemp Amer ptg, 1952
        IU. 20th century
        Pousette-Dart. Amer ptg
BROWN, Douglas, 1899-
    Haunted house (Suburban development, Mexico city)                              MB
        MB. Ptgs in water color
BROWN, Douglas Edwin, 1904-
    Decadence in Guatemala                      CtY
        CtY. Soc Anonyme
Brown, Elizabeth (Byles) 1737-1763
    Copley, J. S. Mrs Gawen Brown
BROWN, George Loring, 1814-1889
    Castello Dell'ovo, Bay of Naples            MB
        MB. Karolik coll
    Leatherstocking kills the panther           MB
        MB. Karolik coll
    Medford marshes                             MB
        MB. Karolik coll
    Olneyville, Rhode Island
        Sears. Highlights
    Public gardens, Boston                      MB
        MB. Karolik coll
    View of Norwalk island                      MAP
        Born
BROWN, J. fl 1808
    Laura Hall                                  NCHA
        Jones. Rediscovered ptrs
        NUM. Art across America
    Mrs Calvin Hall                             VWR
        Jones. Rediscovered ptrs

**Attributed works**
Clarissa Partridge Childs                       VWR
    VWR. Amer folk art (col)
Brown, Jacob Jennings, 1775-1827
    Jarvis, J. W. General Jacob Jennings Brown
Brown, Mrs Jacob Jennings. See Brown, Pamela (Williams)
BROWN, Joan, 1938-
    Steam room at Boyes Hot Springs
        IU. Contemp Amer ptg & sculp, 1961
    The sun blew up in Salinas
        WMAA. Young America 1960
    Things and mess in classroom
        WMAA. Young America 1960
Brown, John, 1800-1859
    Hovenden, T. Last moments of John Brown
    Pippin, H. John Brown going to his hanging
    Pippin, H. John Brown reading his Bible
    Pippin, H. Trial of John Brown
Brown, Mrs John Ball. See Brown, Rebecca (Warren)
BROWN, John George, 1831-1913
    Berry boy                                   MSG
        Larkin
        Larkin rev ed
    The blacksmith                              NoCR
        NoCR. Catalogue
    County gallants                             OT
        Pierson
    Longshoremen's noon                         DC
        Davidson v 1
BROWN, Mather, 1761-1831
    Charles Bulfinch                            MCH
        Pierson
    John Adams                                  MBA
        ICA. From colony to nation
    Self-portrait                               MWA
        MWA. Checklist of portraits
    William Van Murray                          DN
        DN. Mellon coll
Brown, Nicholas(?) 1769-1841
    Malbone, E. G. Nicholas(?) Brown
Brown, Pamela (Williams) 1785-1878
    Ames, E. Mrs Jacob Jennings Brown
Brown, Rebecca (Warren)
    Harding, C. Mrs John Ball Brown
BROWN, Roy Henry, 1879-1956
    Early autumn snow
        NAD. Annual ex, 1947, 2d half
    Harbinger of spring
        NYG. Fine art
Brown, Sarah, 1773-1846
    Malbone, E. G. Sarah Brown
BROWN, W. H. fl 1886
    Bareback riders                             DN
        DN. Amer primitive ptgs, pt 2
Brown and black on plum by M. Rothko
Brown and white by W. De Kooning
Brown figure by R. B. Motherwell
Brown hat by M. Avery
Brown painting by C. A. Morris
Brown pelican by J. J. Audubon
Brown sweater by R. Soyer
Brown Swiss by A. N. Wyeth
BROWNE, Byron, 1907-
    Azoic fugue
        Pousette-Dart. Amer ptg

Black lion
ICA. Annual ex, 1947/48
The dancers
IU. Contemp Amer ptg, 1950
Still life in primary colors
Larkin
Summer night IU
IU. Contemp Amer ptg, 1951
IU. 20th century
Two figures
IU. Contemp Amer ptg
Variations on a still life
MMA. Abstract
Woman with bird WMAA
Pierson

Browne, Jane. See Livermore, Jane
(Browne)

Browne, Katherine (Winthrop) 1711-1781
Unidentified artist. Mrs Samuel Browne
jr

BROWNE, Syd, 1907-
After the storm
NAD. Annual ex, 1952

BROWNELL, Charles De Wolf, 1822-1901
The Charter Oak CtHW
CtHW. Handbook

BROWNING, Colleen, 1923-
The bathers
NAD. Annual ex, 1957
Film studio OYB
OYB. Annual 1954
OYB. Supplement
Fire escape
MnMW. Reality and fantasy
Holiday
PPC. International ex, 1952
Iberian landscape
IU. Contemp Amer ptg & sculp, 1953
Out CSFP
CSB. Illusion
Telephones
IU. Contemp Amer ptg & sculp, 1955
OYB. Annual 1955
OYB. Supplement 1959
The window
IU. Contemp Amer ptg & sculp, 1959

BRUCE, Edward, 1879-1943
Landscape of Provence
Baur. Revolution
Tuscan landscape
Lewisohn

BRUCE, Patrick Henry, 1880-1937
Composition II CtY
Baur. Revolution
Brown. Amer ptg
CtY. Soc Anonyme
McCurdy
MMA. Abstract
Pierson
Painting WMAA
Goodrich. Amer art
Pierson

Bruce, William, 1779-1845
Malbone, E. G. William Bruce

BRUCKMAN, Lodewÿk Karel, 1903-
Memories
IU. Contemp Amer ptg, 1952

BRUFF, Joseph Goldsborough, 1804-1889
Assorted prints
CSFP. Illusionism
The rack
Hess. Abstract ptg

BRUSH, George De Forest, 1855-1941
At dawn
McCracken. Portrait of the old west
In the garden MM
MM. 100 Amer ptrs
Pierson
Mother and child MB
Larkin
Larkin rev ed
Roos
Silence broken
McCracken. Portrait of the old west
Thea OYB
OYB. Catalogue 1951

Brushy hillside by E. F. Spruce

Bruyn, Severyn
Vanderlyn, J. Severyn Bruyn

Bryan, Jennie Byrd
Healy, G. P. A. Jennie Bryan

Bryan, Thomas B. fl 1857
Healy, G. P. A. The Bryan family

Bryant, William Cullen, 1794-1878
Gray, H. P. William Cullen Bryant
Morse, S. F. B. William Cullen Bryant

Bryant square by J. Marin

Buchanan, James, president U.S. 1791-1868
Healy, G. P .A. James Buchanan

Buchanan, Mildred. See Knowles, Mildred
(Buchanan)

Buchenwald cart by R. Lebrun

BUCK, Bennett, 1900-
Circus scene ATU
ATU. Coll of Amer art

BUCK, Claude, 1890-
Leslie InTH
InTH. Catalogue

BUCK, Lewis
Iotrio
Pousette-Dart. Amer ptg

Bucking bronco by C. M. Russell

Buckland, William, 1734-1774
Peale, C. W. William Buckland

Bucklin, Amelia. See Cornwall, Amelia
(Bucklin)

Bucks county barn by C. Sheeler

The buck's progress by W. Allston

Bucolic landscape by M. Avery

Budd children, fl 1825
Unidentified artist. Five children of the
Budd family

BUDINGTON, Jonathan, fl 1800-1812
Father and son DN
DN. Amer primitive ptgs, pt 2

BUDNICK, Sidney J. 1921-
Number 23
ICA. Annual ex, 1947/48

Buehr, Mrs George Frederick. See Hoff,
Margo

Buen Retiro, Madrid by W. J. Glackens

Buffalo, New York
Sellstedt, L. G. Buffalo harbor from the
foot of Porter avenue
Walsh, E. Fort Erie from Buffalo creek,
site of the city of Buffalo, c 1810

Buffalo Bill's traps by G. Cope

Buffalo dance of the Mandan by K. Bodmer

Buffalo hunting in summer by P. Rindisbacher

Buffalo newsboy by T. Le Clear

**Buffaloes**
Audubon, J. J. Head of a buffalo calf
Bierstadt, A. Buffalo bull
Bierstadt, A. Buffalo trail
Bierstadt, A. Last of the buffalo
Bierstadt, A. Snow scene with buffaloes
Bodmer, K. Buffalo coming to drink in the upper Missouri
Catlin, G. Buffalo chase
Catlin, G. Buffalo chase of the Sioux
Catlin, G. Buffalo chase, upper Missouri
Catlin, G. Buffalo crossing Yellowstone in winter
Catlin, G. Buffalo hunt on snow shoes
Catlin, G. Buffalo hunt, under the wolf mask
Catlin, G. Buffalo stampede
Catlin, G. Catlin hunting buffalo
Catlin, G. Sioux Indians hunting buffalo
Darley, F. O. C. Hunting buffaloes
Eastman, S. Hunting buffalo in winter
Miller, A. J. Approaching buffalo
Miller, A. J. The bravado
Miller, A. J. Buffalo at bay
Miller, A. J. Buffalo chase—by a female
Miller, A. J. Buffalo hunting near Independent rock
Miller, A. J. Buffalo turning on his pursuers
Miller, A. J. Buffaloes drinking and bathing at night
Miller, A. J. Hunting buffalo
Miller, A. J. Killing buffalo with the lance
Miller, A. J. Pawnee running buffalo
Miller, A. J. Running buffalo
Miller, A. J. Surround of buffalo by Indians
Miller, A. J. Wounded buffalo
Miller, A. J. Yell of triumph
Pippin, H. Buffalo hunt
Remington, F. Recruit from civilization
Rindisbacher, P. Buffaloes in winter
Rindisbacher, P. Indians hunting buffalo
Russell, C. M. Buffalo crossing the Missouri
Russell, C. M. The buffalo drive
Russell, C. M. Buffalo hunt
Russell, C. M. Wild man's meat
Russell, C. M. Wounded buffalo
Stanley, J. M. Buffalo hunt on the southern plains
Tait, A. F. Buffalo hunt
Trotter, N. H. Held up by buffalo
Unidentified artist. Buffalo hunter
Wimar, C. Buffalo dance
Wimar, C. Buffalo hunt
Wimar, C. Buffaloes crossing the Yellowstone
**Buffet** supper by A. Blaustein
**Bugbee** family by B. F. Mason
**BUHALIS, Nicholas**
Horse
PA. Annual ex, 1959-60
**Building** a dam, Shetucket by J. A. Weir
**Building** in a park by A. Ozenfant
**Buildings** at night by B. Currie
**Buildings,** Lancaster by C. H. Demuth
**Buildings** of Lebanon by C. Sheeler
The **bulb** by W. T. Murch

**Bulfinch, Charles,** 1763-1844
Brown, M. Charles Bulfinch
Dunkerley, J. (attributed works) Charles Bulfinch
**Bulfinch, Hannah (Apthorp)** fl 1787
Dunkerley, J. (attributed works) Mrs Charles Bulfinch
**Bulfinch, Susan (Apthorp)** 1734-1815
Smibert, J. Mrs Thomas Bulfinch
**Bulkley, Ellen.** See Ruggles, Ellen (Buckley)
**Bull-boating** by A. J. Miller
**Bull** dance of the Mandans by G. Catlin
**Bull** Durham by S. Davis
The **bull** ring by R. Lebrun
**Bulldogging** by E. Bisttram
**BULLER, Audrey,** 1902-
Comedy
NYG. Fine art
Nude in doorway
Baur. Revolution
**Bullfights and bullfighters**
Keller, H. G. Impressions of a bull fight
Marco-Relli, C. di. Bull fight
Martin, F. Killer in costume
Martin, F. The toss
Ulbricht, J. La Veronica
**Bullard, Robert Lee,** 1861-1947
Lockman, D. M. Lt Gen Robert Lee Bullard
**Bulls**
*See also* Cattle
Austin, D. Europa and the bull
Benton, T. H. Photographing the bull
Blanch, A. Bull
Corbino, J. Stampeding bulls
Nelson, R. A. Soldier and bull
Poor, H. V. The bull
Stevens, E. J. Mad bull
Tchelitchew, P. Bull fight
**Buloz, Christine Blaze de Bury,** fl 1879
Sargent, J. S. Mme Buloz
**BULTMAN, Fritz,** 1919-
Sleeper    WMAA
Pousette-Dart. Amer ptg
Sleeper no 2
WMAA. Contemp Amer ptg, 1952
Via Porta Romana II
IU. Contemp Amer ptg & sculp, 1953
**Bulwer-Lytton, Edward Robert, 1st earl of Lytton.** See Lytton, Edward Robert Bulwer-Lytton, 1st earl of
**BUMPAS, Rosemary Harley,** 1922-
Lumber for the Argo
VR. Amer ptg, 1958
**BUNCE, Louis,** 1907-
Access
OrPA. Ptgs & sculpture (col)
Bay bottom no 1    WaS
CoS. New accessions USA, 1952
**BUNDY, Horace,** 1814-1883
Vermont lawyer    DN
DN. Amer primitive ptgs, pt 1
**Bunker, Anna Hardaway**
Harding, C. Anna Hardaway Bunker
**Bunker Hill, Battle of,** 1775
Trumbull, J. Battle of Bunker's Hill
**Bunkerhill (steamboat)**
Huge, J. F. Steamboat Bunkerhill
**BUNTING, J. D.**
Darby, Pennsylvania, after the burning of Lord's mill
Baur. Amer ptg (detail)
Pierson

**Buoy** by P. Blume
**BURBANK, Elbridge Ayer,** 1858-1949
Hopi snake dance                     OYB
  OYB. Catalogue 1951
**BURCHFIELD, Charles Ephraim,** 1893-
An April mood                        WMAA
  Baur. Charles Burchfield (col)
  Baur. New art (col)
  Goodrich. Amer art (col)
  Larkin rev ed (col)
  Pierson
April woods
  OYB. Catalogue 1951
August afternoon                     MM
  NYG. Fine art
August evening
  IU. Contemp Amer ptg & sculp, 1959
Autumnal fantasy
  Flexner. Amer ptg
  Flexner. Short history
Backyards in snow                    ATeS
  ATeS. Collection
Backyards in spring                  PPhM
  Canaday
Barn                                 DP
  DP. Catalogue
Beginning of a snowstorm             WMAA
  Myers
Black houses
  Baur. Charles Burchfield
Black iron
  Baur. Charles Burchfield
  MiD. Coll in progress
  Pierson
  WiMiA. Amer ptg 1760-1960
  WMAA. Museum and its friends, 1958
Church bells ringing, rainy winter night
                            OCl
  Baur. Charles Burchfield (col)
  Baur. New art
  Cos. New accession USA, 1950
  Craven. Treasury 1952 ed
  MMA. Contemp ptrs
  OCl. Handbook
  Pierson
The cicada
  Baur. Charles Burchfield
Clatter of crows in spring woods
  Baur. Charles Burchfield
  Baur. Revolution
Coming of spring                     MM
  Baur. Charles Burchfield
  Baur. New art
  MM. 100 Amer ptrs
Cricket chorus in the arbor
  Baur. Charles Burchfield (col)
Dandelion seed balls and trees       MM
  Baur. Charles Burchfield
  WMAA. Pioneers
Day in midwinter                     NJMo
  NJMo. Forty years
Dusty road in July
  WMAA. Annual ex, 1958
Edge of town                         MoKN
  Baur. Charles Burchfield
End of day                           PA
  Baur. Charles Burchfield
Evening                              NJN
  Baur. Charles Burchfield
  Larkin
  Larkin rev ed

Evening peace
  CanO. Hirshhorn coll
February thaw                        NBM
  Brown. Amer ptg
First hepaticas                      MMA
  Larkin
  Larkin rev ed
The four seasons
  IU. Contemp Amer ptg & sculp, 1961
Freight cars
  MMA. Contemp ptrs
Freight cars under a bridge          MiD
  MiD. Treasures
Garden of memories                   MMA
  Baur. Charles Burchfield
Ghost plants
  Baur. Charles Burchfield
Glory of spring
  Baur. Charles Burchfield
Great elm                            PPC
  Bazin
Haunted evening
  Baur. Charles Burchfield
Hot September wind
  Baur. Charles Burchfield (col)
  MiD. Coll in progress (col)
House of mystery                     ICA
  Baur. Charles Burchfield
  Baur. Revolution
  Brown. Amer ptg
  Pierson
Hush before the storm                KW
  Baur. Charles Burchfield
Ice glare                            WMAA
  Goodrich. Amer art
  Lee. Art then and now
  Mendelowitz
  NYG. Fine art
In May                               MB
  MB. Ptgs in water color
Insects at twilight                  MMA
  Baur. Charles Burchfield
  Pierson
Interurban line                      MMA
  Newmeyer
July clouds
  Baur. Charles Burchfield
June radiance
  PA. Annual ex, 1958
Lace gables                          NUM
  MiA. Root coll
  NUM. Root bequest
Lavender and old lace                CtNB
  Baur. Charles Burchfield
March
  Cheney. Story 1958 ed
March sunlight                       MCH
  Baur. Charles Burchfield
March wind                           OCl
  Baur. Charles Burchfield
  Craven. Treasury 1952 ed
Mid-June                             NBuA
  NBuA. Contemporary ptgs
Moonflowers at dusk
  Baur. Charles Burchfield (col)
Mysterious bird                      DeW
  Baur. Charles Burchfield
Night of the equinox
  Baur. Charles Burchfield
  WMAA. Sara Roby

**BURCHFIELD, C. E.**—*Continued*

Night wind
  Barr. What is mod ptg
  Baur. Charles Burchfield
  Baur. New art
  Baur. Revolution
  Brown. Amer ptg
  McCurdy
  Rathbun
Noonday heat
  Baur. Charles Burchfield
Noontide in late May      WMAA
  Goodrich. Amer art (col)
November evening      MM
  Baur. Charles Burchfield
  Craven. Rainbow book
  Craven. Treasury 1952 ed (col)
  Wight. Milestones
October      OCo
  Brown. Amer ptg
Old house by creek      WMMA
  Baur. Charles Burchfield
  Bazin. History of art (col)
  Goodrich. Amer art
Old meetinghouse and locust trees
  Baur. Charles Burchfield
Oncoming spring
  PPC. International ex, 1955
  Time. 300 years (col)
The parade
  Baur. Charles Burchfield
  MiD. Coll in progress
Pippin house, East Liverpool, Ohio MMA
  MMA. Masters
Poplar trees
  Baur. Charles Burchfield
Poplars in June
  Baur. Charles Burchfield
Portrait study in a doorway      DP
  Baur. Charles Burchfield
Promenade
  Baur. New art
  Brown. Amer ptg
  Lewisohn
  McCurdy
  NYG. Fine art
Quiet pond      ATU
  ATU. Coll of Amer art
Radiant springtime
  IU. Contemp Amer ptg & sculp, 1957
Railroad in spring
  WiMiA. Amer ptg 1760-1960
Rainy night      CSD
  Baur. Charles Burchfield
  Gruskin
Red barn
  CtY. Yale alumni
Road in early spring      InIJ
  InIJ. 105 ptgs
Rogues' gallery      MMA
  Baur. Charles Burchfield
September wind and rain      OYB
  OYB. Annual 1953
  OYB. Supplement
Six o'clock      NSyE
  Baur. Charles Burchfield
  Baur. New art
  Time. 300 years
Song in the rain      CtHW
  CtHW. Handbook
  Pierson

Song of the katydids
  Baur. Charles Burchfield
  WiMiA. Amer ptg 1760-1960
Song of the marsh
  Baur. Charles Burchfield
  VR. Amer ptg, 1954
Song of the telegraph
  Baur. Charles Burchfield
The sphinx and the Milky way      NUM
  Baur. Charles Burchfield
  NUM. Art across America
  Pierson
  Richardson. Ptg in America
The star
  PPC. Ptg in the U.S. 1949
  WiMiA. Amer ptg 1760-1960
Still life in winter
  PPC. International ex, 1952
Sulphurous evening      MoSL
  Baur. Charles Burchfield
  MoSL. Handbook 1953
Summer afternoon
  Baur. Charles Burchfield
  Time. 300 years (col)
  WMAA. Annual ex, 1949
Sun and rocks      NBuA
  Baur. Charles Burchfield
  CoS. New accessions USA, 1954
  Mendelowitz
  NBuA. Expressionism
  Pierson
  Pousette-Dart. Amer ptg
  PPC. International ex, 1950
  Time. 300 years (col)
Sun setting through the catalpas      OCl
  Baur. Charles Burchfield
Three days of rain      DP
  DP. Catalogue
Three trees
  Baur. Charles Burchfield
Thunderclap
  Baur. Charles Burchfield
White violets and abandoned coal mine
         NBuA
  NBuA. Acquisitions 1954-57
White violets and coal mine      OCl
  Baur. Charles Burchfield
Window by the alley
  Baur. Charles Burchfield
Winter bouquet      MB
  Baur. Charles Burchfield
  MB. Ptgs in water color
Winter moonlight      KW
  Baur. Charles Burchfield
  Eliot. Art of our time (col)
Winter solstice      OCo
  Roos
Winter twilight      WMAA
  Roos
Wires down      PPC
  Baur. Charles Burchfield
Woman in doorway      DP
  DP. Catalogue

**Burckhardt, Rudolph**
  De Kooning, W. Rudolph Burckhardt
    (unfinished painting and detail)

The **Burden** family enjoying the Hudson
  river near Troy by J. M. Hart and
  A. F. Tait (attributed works)

**BURG, Copeland Charles,** 1895-
Flowers in the city
IU. Contemp Amer ptg, 1952
Mexican landscape
CSFP. Annual ex, 1946
**Burgoyne, John,** 1722-1792
Trumbull, J. Surrender of Gen Burgoyne at Saratoga
**Burial** by H. G. Burkhardt
**Burial** by S. Greene
**Burial** by B. W. Tomlin
**Burial** of a young man by R. Kent
**Burial** of an acrobat by M. Beckmann
**Burial** of the Queen of Sheba by P. Evergood
**Buried** treasure by H. Bloom
**BURKHARDT, Hans Gustave,** 1904-
Abstraction
WMAA. Annual ex, 1958
Burial
IU. Contemp Amer ptg, 1951
One monent of silence
ICA. Annual ex, 1951
Studio of G.
WMAA. Contemp Amer ptg, 1951
**BURKHART, Emerson,** 1905-
Dead duck
OYB. Annual 1952
Spiritual decadence
MnMW. Reality and fantasy
Spiritual decay                          OYB
OYB. Catalogue 1951
**Burlesque** by M. Avery
**BURLIN, Paul,** 1886-
Calypso
IU. Contemp Amer ptg & sculp, 1953
Composition
MnU. 40 Amer ptrs
Corridors of time
VR. Biennial ex, 1948
Ephiphany of a hero
NBuA. Expressionism
Homunculus
Pierson
In the shadow of a mystery
MnU. 49 Amer ptrs
The magnificence
Pousette-Dart. Amer ptg
New England landscape            WMAA
Pearson. Mod renaissance
WMAA. Pioneers
Nude figure
Myers. Art
Pool player
MoSL. Contemporary Amer ptg
Red, red, not the same           WMAA
Goodrich. Amer art
Red theme
Pearson. Mod renaissance
Soda jerker
Pearson. Mod renaissance
Street scene
NYG. Fine art
Wandering Jew
Myers
Witness the whatless
Genauer (col)
Young man alone with his face
Pearson. Mod renaissance
**BURLIUK, David,** 1882-
At the inn                               DP
DP. Catalogue

Harlem river bridge                      CtY
Pierson
White cow                               WMAA
Pierson
**Portrait of the artist**
Soyer, M. David Burliuk in his studio
**Burned** over by M. Tobey
**Burnet, William,** 1688-1729
Watson, J. Gov William Burnet
**Burnham, Caroline Matilda (Wood)** d 1832
Ames, E. Mrs Eleazer Burnham
**Burnham, Eleazer,** b 1780
Ames, E. Eleazer Burnham
**Burnham, Mrs Eleazer.** See Burnham, Caroline Matilda (Wood )
**Burnham, T. O. H. P.** See Burnham, Thomas Mickell
**BURNHAM, Thomas Mickell,** 1818-1866
First state election in Detroit, Michigan, 1837                                 MiD
U.S. National Capital sesquicentennial com
First state election in Michigan
Pierson
**Burning** of Charles Town by Unidentified artist
**Burning** of Old South church, Bath, Maine by Unidentified artist
**Burning** of the hearts by L. Siegriest
**Burning** of the Tombs, New York city by Unidentified artist
**Burning** ship by A. Bierstadt
The **Burnish** sisters by W. M. Prior
**Burnt** man by L. A. Golub
**Burnt** spinner by R. Lebrun
**BURPEE, Sophia,** fl 1806
**Attributed works**
Morning                                  VWR
VWR. Folk art (col)
**Portrait of the artist**
Unidentified artist. Sophia Burpee
**Burr, Thaddeus,** 1735-1801
Copley, J. S. Thaddeus Burr
**Burr, Theodosia,** 1783-1812?
Vanderlyn, J. Theodosia Burr
**Burrill, James,** 1772-1820
Malbone, E. G. James Burrill jr
**BURROUGHS, Bryson,** 1869-1934
The consolation of Ariadne              MM
MM. 100 Amer ptrs
**Burroughs** family by H. Dawkins
**Burst** by A. Gottlieb
**Burst** into life by H. Hofmann
**Bursting** flowers by W. Reiss
**Burtis, Betsy,** d 1813
Jarvis, J. W. Betsey Burtis
**BURTON, Charles,** fl 1820-1832
The Capitol, Washington, 1824          MM
Davidson v2
U.S. National Capital sesquicentennial com
Governor's room, City hall, New York, c 1830
Dickson. John Wesley Jarvis
**Bus** stop by S. Shawkey
**Bus** view by G. O. Coleman
**BUSA, Peter,** 1915-
Breaker
WMAA. Contemp Amer ptg, 1959/60

Bush, Hannah(?) c 1767-1807
  MacKay. Mrs John Bush
Bush, John, 1755-1816
  MacKay. John Bush
  Pratt, M. John Bush
Bush, Mrs John. See Bush, Hannah(?)
BUSH, Joseph H. 1794-1865
  Mary Lucy Pocahontas Bibb          KyLS
    KyLS. Kentucky port gall
The Bushkill, View on by T. Doughty
Business by C. H. Demuth
Bussey, Eliza. See Davis, Eliza (Bussey)
Buswell, Mrs Leslie
  Hailman, J. K. W.  Mrs Leslie Buswell
Butcher boy by G. B. Luks
Butcher shop by C. Semser
Butler, Edward, 1762-1803
  Malbone, E. G. Capt Edward Butler
Butler, Henry Audubon, 1872-1934
  Olinsky, I. G. Henry Audubon Butler
Butler, Joseph Green, 1840-1927
  Olinsky, I. G. Joseph Green Butler jr
  Watkins, F. C. Joseph C. Butler
Butler, Nicholas Murray, 1862-1947
  Lockman, D. M.  Dr Nicholas Murray
    Butler
Butler, Sara Grace Heath
  Speicher, E. E. Sara Grace Heath Butler
Butte, Utah by A. A. Dehn
Butterflies
  Peale, T. R.  Still life with flowers and
    insects
Buttersworth, James E.  See Butterworth,
  James E.
BUTTERWORTH, James E. 1817-1894
  Defense of America's cup, 1870
    Davidson v2
  Hudson river sloop Phillip R. Paulding
    DC.  Privately owned
  The yacht America leaving Boston harbor
    for England                        RPS
  U.S. National Capital sesquicentennial
    com
Buttes on the Missouri by C. Wimar
Button falls by H. E. Schnakenberg
Buttonwood farm by N. C. Wyeth
Buzzards
  Audubon, J. J. Turkey buzzards
  Phillips, M. A. Landscape: Buzzard
By the fireside by Unidentified artist
By the sea by R. Haines
By the sea by W. H. Holmes
By the shore by W. Homer
By the tomb of the prophet by A. P. Ryder
BYFIELD, Nathaniel, b 1676?
  Richard Middlecott
    Belknap

          Portrait of the artist
  Smibert, J. Nathaniel Byfield
BYGRAVE, William
  American clipper bark Zephyr in Messina
    harbor, Sicily
    Davidson v 1
Byles, Elizabeth.  See Brown, Elizabeth
  (Byles)
Byles, Mather, 1706-1788
  Pelham, P. Mather Byles

Byrd, Anne, fl 1735
  Bridges, C. Anne Byrd
Byrd, Maria (Taylor) 1674-1744
  Bridges, C. Maria Taylor Byrd of West-
    over, Virginia
  Bridges, C. Mrs William Byrd (?)
Byrd, Wilhelmina, d 1716
  Bridges, C. Wilhelmina Byrd (?)
Byrd, Mrs William.  See Byrd, Maria (Tay-
  lor)
BYRUM, Ruthven H.
  Grand view
    NYG.  Fine art
  Newfound gap (Smoky mountains)
    NYG.  Fine art
  Peaceful valley (Blue Ridge mountains)
    NYG.  Fine art
Byvanck, Mary.  See Abeel, Mary (Byvanck)
BYWATERS, Jerry, 1906-
  On the ranch                          TxD
    Gruskin


                    C

Cabana by M. Beckmann
Cabbage head by P. Tchelitchew
Cabell, Agnes S. B. (Gamble) 1783-1863
  Jarvis, J. W. Mrs William Henry Cabell
Cabell, William Henry, 1772-1853
  Jarvis, J. W. William Henry Cabell II
Cabin in the cotton I by H. Pippin
Cabin in the cotton III, by H. Pippin
Cabot, Mary (Fitch) 1723?-1756
  Greenwood, John. Mrs Francis Cabot
CABRAL, Flavio, 1918-
  Quiet day, Lisbon
    IU.  Contemp Amer ptg & sculp, 1961
Cabs for hire by L. M. Eilshemius
Cactus by C. Sheeler
Cactus and sundry by J. W. Treiman
Cadaver on a table by H. Bloom
The cadium sound by A. Gottlieb
Cadiz at dusk by D. W. Ellis
CADMUS, Paul, 1904-
  Bar Italia
    Pierson
  Fantasia on a theme by Dr S.        WMAA
    Goodrich.  Amer art (col)
    Gruskin
  The nap
    CSB.  Illusion
  Night in Bologna                     WMAA
    WMAA. Sara Roby (col)
  Playground
    Baur.  Revolution
    McCurdy
    Pierson
  Point o' view
    Gruskin
  Reflections
    ICA.  Annual ex, 1945/46
  The shower
    Bazin
  Sunday sun
    WMAA.  Contemp Amer ptg, 1959/60
Cadwalader, George
  Sully, T. Gen George Cadwalader

Cadwalader, John, 1742-1787
  Peale, C. W. Gen John Cadwalader
Cadwalader, Thomas, 1779-1841
  Malbone, E. G. Gen Thomas Cadwalader
Cadwalader, Mrs Thomas. See Biddle, Mary
CADY, Walter H.
  In old Kentucky
    NYG. Fine art
Caerulea by R. W. Anliker
Café by Y. Kuniyoshi
Café by J. Mitchell
Café de la Paix by W. J. Glackens
Café Florian, Venice by M. B. Prendergast
Café Lafayette by W. J. Glackens
Café on Riva degli Schiavoni, Venice by J. S.
    Sargent
Café, Place des Vosges by S. Davis
Café scene by J. Lawrence
CAFFERTY, James H. 1819-1869 and
    ROSENBERG, Charles D. fl 1858
  Wall street, half past 2 o'clock, Oct. 13,
    1857                                NNMC
    Davidson v2
    U.S. National Capital sesquicentennial
      com
Cain and Abel by S. Greene
CALCAGNO, Lawrence, 1916-
  Blue landscape
    Baur. Nature
  Earth legend VII
    PPC. International ex, 1958
  Pacific series, no IX—Sierra          NBuA
    NBuA. Acquisitions 1954-57
  Sapaque
    PPC. International ex, 1955
  Sapaque II                            WMAA
    Brussels. Exposition
  Vertical black
    VR. Amer ptg, 1958
  White painting no 3, 1958
    MnMW. 60 Amer ptrs
  White painting no 11, 1958
    IU. Contemp Amer ptg & sculp, 1959
Calcutta by W. A. Smith
CALDER, Alexander, 1898-
  Octopus
    Read. Art now, 1948 ed
  Spiny
    MMA. Abstract
  Untitled                                IU
    IU. 20th century
  Untitled                               MMA
    MMA. Soby collection
Calendars by A. Gorky
Calhoun, John Caldwell, 1782-1850
  Healy, G. P. A. John C. Calhoun
  Hubard, W. J. John C. Calhoun
  Trumbull, J. John C. Calhoun
CALIFANO, Frank
  Evening usualty
    Baur. Revolution
California condor by J. J. Audubon
California farm by L. H. Lebduska
California landscape by J. F. Cole
California mission by J. F. Cole
Call of the law by C. M. Russell
Call of the west wind by C. H. Davis
Calla with roses by G. O'Keeffe

CALLAHAN, Kenneth L. 1907-
  Abstraction I, 1950
    MMA. Abstract
  Ahab and Abigail. See Autumn dance
  Autumn dance (Ahab and Abigail)
    OrPA. Ptgs & sculptures
  Battle of the gods                      KW
    Cheney. Story 1958 ed
    ICA. Annual ex, 1957
  Challenge and response               WaSU
    CoS. New accessions USA, 1950
  Conversation                           NBM
    Baur. Revolution
  Fiery night
    Time. 300 years (col)
  Interwoven thread
    PPC. Ptg in the U. S. 1949
  Northwest landscape
    Cheney. Story 1958 ed
  Rock landscape no 2
    IU. Contemp Amer ptg & sculp, 1959
  The search
    DC. 22 biennial ex, 1951
  The seed was in itself                 WaS
    CoS. New accessions USA, 1954
  Shadows on the rock                    WaS
    Pousette-Dart. Amer ptg
  Transition                            WMAA
    Pierson
  The trapped
    WMAA. Contemp Amer ptg, 1952
  Vital storm
    Cheney. Expressionism 1948 ed
Callahan, Rose
  Sharrer, H. Rose Callahan and child
Callender, John, 1706-1748
  Feke, R. Rev John Callender
Calligraphic by M. Tobey
Calligraphy of rhythms by P. Fine
Calling of St Matthew by G. H. Hallowell
Calling the moose by P. R. Goodwin
Calm horizon by C. A. Morris
Cal-Sag by E. Lanyon
Calvert, Benedict Leonard, fl 1727
  Brerewood, F. Benedict Leonard Calvert,
    Governor of Maryland
Calvert, Charles, 1756-1777
  Hesselius, J. Charles Calvert and his
    Negro slave
Calvert, Elizabeth
  Hesselius, J. Elizabeth Calvert
CALVIN, Perry, 1924-
  Hucksters                              OYB
    OYB. Annual 1950
    OYB. Catalogue 1951
CALYO, Nicolino Vicomte, 1799-1884
  Balloon ascension at Baltimore, 1834
    Davidson v2
  Baltimore in 1837                     MdBH
    DC. Amer ptrs of the South
  The great fire in New York, 1835
    U.S. National Capital sesquicentennial
      com
  Hot corn girl
    Davidson v2
  Ice cart, c 1840
    Davidson v2
  Milk man, c 1840
    Davidson v2
  Soap-locks or Bowery boys, New York,
    c 1840
    Davidson v2

**CALYO, N. V.**—*Continued*
View of New York city, c 1835
 WiMiA. Amer ptg 1760-1960
View of the Merchants' exchange and
 Girard's bank, Philadelphia
 WiMiA. Amer ptg 1760-1960
The volante at Habana                VWR
 VWR. Folk Art (col)

### Attributed works

New York—Hoboken ferry, c 1838
 Davidson v2
**Calypso** by P. Burlin
**Calypso** by K. Martin
**Cambridge,** New York by A. M. R. Moses
**Cambridge** valley by A. M. R. Moses
**Camden, Sallie Ann,** fl 1840
 Bingham, G. C. Sallie Ann Camden
**Camden** hills from Baker's island, Penobscot
 bay by M. Hartley
**Camels**
 Bacon, H. My camels resting
**Camel's** Hump by E. Hopper
**Camp** Butler, Maryland, 1861 by Unidenti-
 fied artist
**Camp** fire, preparing the evening meal by
 A. J. Miller
**Camp** meeting by W. Whittredge
**Camp** receiving a supply of meat by A. J.
 Miller
**Camp** scene (Sioux) by A. J. Miller
**Campo** Santa Maria Formosa, Venice by
 M. B. Prendergast
**Canadian** Mounted Police with prisoners by
 C. M. Russell
**Canal** street no 2 by K. Zerbe
**Canals**
 Delbos, J. Canal
 Harvey, G. Afternoon, dead calm: View
  on the Erie Canal near Pittsford, New
  York
 Hill, J. W. Scene on the Erie canal
 Pickett, J. Lehigh canal, sunset, New
  Hope, Pennsylvania
 Ryder, A. P. The canal
 Smith, R. Aqueduct in the Pennsylvania
  canal over the Juniata
 Tobey, M. Canals
 Woodbury, C. H. Canal scene, Holland
**Canandaigua, New York**
 Jeffrey, A. Main street, Canandaigua, N.Y.
  1830-40
**CANDELL, Victor,** 1903-
 Ascendant                         WMAA
  Pierson
  WMAA. Contemp Amer ptg, 1952
 Blue waterfall
  PPC. International ex, 1952
 Contact
  IU. Contemp Amer ptg & sculp, 1955
 Conversation piece
  IU. Contemp Amer ptg & sculp, 1957
 Percussion
  DC. 26 biennial ex, 1959
 Summer
  DC. 27 biennial ex, 1961
 Village dog
  IU. Contemp Amer ptg & sculp, 1953
 Yule log
  IU. Contemp Amer ptg, 1952

**Candide** by A. James
**Canfield, Ithamar,** 1764-1848
 Jennys, R. Ithamar Canfield
**Canfield, Richard**
 Whistler, J. A. M. Richard Canfield
**Cannabin** by X. Gonzalez
**Cannibalism** of war by G. Biddle
**Cannon, Mrs Daniel.** See Trusler, Mary
**Canoes and canoeing**
 Brush, G. De F. At dawn
 Brush, G. De F. Silence broken
 Catlin, G. Down the Mississippi in a
  birch-bark canoe
 Catlin, G. Excavating a canoe, British
  Columbia
 Homer, W. Canoe in rapids
 Homer, W. Canoeing in the Adirondacks
 Homer, W. Entering the first rapid
 Homer, W. Guide fishing
 Homer, W. Under the falls, grand dis-
  charge
 Koerner, W. H. D. City man's vacation
**Cantey, Margaret.** See Sinkler, Margaret
 (Cantey)
**Canticle** by M. Tobey
**Canton** street by G. Martino
**Canvassing** for a vote by G. C. Bingham
The **canyon** by G. C. Delano
**Canyon** mosaic by C. A. Morris
**Cape** Ann by M. B. Prendergast
**Cape** Ann landscape by S. Davis
**Cape** Cod dunes by G. Grosz
**Cape** Cod evening by E. Hopper
**Cape** Cod marsh and sky by D. Macknight
**Cape** Cod morning by E. Hopper
**Cape** fog by R. G. Hamilton
**Cape** landscape by R. G. Hamilton
**Cape** May wharf by F. Yost
**Cape** Nedick by H. Strater
**Cape** Porpoise harbor by E. O'Hara
**Cape** still life by H. Maril
**Cape** Trinity, Saguenay river by W. Homer
**Cape** Trinity, Saguenay river, moonlight by
 W. Homer
El **Capitan** by T. Hill
The **Capitol,** Washington by E. D. Boit
**Capitol** reflections by K. Matthew
**Capri,** A corner in by E. Vedder
**Capri** cliffs by F. Crowninshield
**Capri** girl by J. S. Sargent
**Capriccioso** by H. Hofmann
**Captain** and crew by K. Knaths
**Captain** of the fishing fleet by W. M. Chase
The **captive** by H. F. Farny
**Captive** charger by C. Wimar
The **captive** Gaul by F. Remington
The **captives** by P. Trevigno
**Capture** of Major André by J. Toole
**Capture** of the Hessians at Trenton by J.
 Trumbull
**Capture** of wild horses by Indians by A. J.
 Miller
**Captured** by Indians by G. C. Rathbone
**Capturing** the grizzly by C. M. Russell

Car with dark top by E. Ewing
Caravan en route by A. J. Miller
Caravan on the Platte by A. J. Miller
Caravan on the prairies by W. T. Ranney
Caravan taking to the water by A. J. Miller
Caravan theater minstrels by J. De Martini
Caravan: trappers crossing the river by
    A. J. Miller
CARBONE, Francesco, 1923-
  War among the arthropods
    MBIC. View 1960
Carcass by J. Hirsch
Carcass by T. Roszak
Card players by J. Levine
Card players by R. C. Woodville
Card rack with oval photograph of Abraham
    Lincoln by J. F. Peto
Cardinal by F. J. Kline
A cardinal, Portrait of by T. B. Read
The cardinal's portrait by T. E. Rosenthal
Caresse enfantine by M. Cassatt
Cargo by C. di Marca-Relli
Caribbean cornucopia by A. A. Dehn
Caribbean moon by S. M. Etnier
CARLES, Arthur Becker, 1882-1952
  Arrangement             ICA
    PA. Annual ex, 1955
    PA. Carles (cover)
    Pierson
  Blue abstraction
    PA. Carles
  Bouquet abstraction       WMAA
    Goodrich. Amer art
    Pierson
  Bouquet in blue vase       PPhM
    Chew. 250 years of art
  Composition III, 1931-32     MMA
    McCurdy
    MMA. Abstract
  Composition no 6, 1936
    PA. Annual ex, 1955
    PA. Carles
  Flower piece
    PA. Annual ex, 1955
  French village church
    PA. Carles
  Glass and flowers
    Cheney. Primer 1958 ed
  Painting, 1935-40
    Hess. Abstract ptg
  Summer flowers
    PA. Carles
  Turkey              PPhM
    Hess. Abstract ptg
    PA. Carles
  White callas
    PA. Carles
  White nude with apple
    PA. Annual ex, 1955
CARLIN, A. B. fl 1871
  Sherman's march through Georgia, 1864
    U.S. National Capital sesquicentennial
    com
CARLIN, John, 1813-1891
  Sparking
    Chew. 250 years of art

CARLSEN, Emil 1853-1932
  Entrance to the harbor of St Thomas
                           PR
    PR. Catalogue
  The surf               OYB
    OYB. Catalogue 1951
Carlton, Linda Dietz
  Chase, W. M. Linda Dietz Carlton
Carlyle, Thomas, 1795-1881
  Whistler, J. A. M. Thomas Carlyle
CARMEN, Cicero, 1926-
  Near Tibidabo
    ICA. Annual ex, 1959/60
Carmencita, by W. M. Chase
Carmencita by J. S. Sargent
Carmer, Rachel. See Lenox, Rachel (Car-
  mer)
Carmick, Stephen, fl 1760
  West, B. Stephen Carmick
Carmine theater by J. Sloan
Carnation Lily, Lily Rose, Sketch for by
  J. S. Sargent
Carnes, Captain of Salem
  Unidentified artist. Capt Carnes of Salem
Carnival of autumn by M. Hartley
Carnival time by J. Kempsmith
Carnivals. See Fairs and festivals
The carob tree by A. M. Duca
Carol I, king of Rumania, 1839-1914
  Healy, G. P. A. Charles I
Carolina parroquet by J. J. Audubon
Carolina parrot by J. J. Audubon
Carolina turtle-dove by J. J. Audubon
Caroline Augusta by H. R. Rittenberg
Carolus-Duran (Charles Émile Auguste
  Durand) 1838-1917
  Sargent, J. S. Carolus Duran
CARONE, Nicolas, 1917-
  Member of a city cast no 9
    ICA. Amer artists paint the city
  Monk in white
    IU. Contemp Amer ptg & sculp, 1955
  Reflecting poet
    ICA. Annual ex, 1951
  Reverse image
    IU. Contemp Amer ptg & sculp, 1957
  St Francis of Assisi
    IU. Contemp Amer ptg & sculp, 1953
  Satyr
    MnMW. 60 Amer ptrs
  Self-portrait: head
    PPC. International ex, 1952
  Sound of blue light
    Brussels. Exposition
  Untitled
    IU. Contemp Amer ptg & sculp, 1961
Carousel, by A. H. Maurer
Carousel by M. B. Prendergast
Carousel by the sea by C. H. Carter
Carpenter, Mr, fl 1810
  Unidentified artist. Mr Carpenter
CARPENTER, Francis Bicknell, 1830-1900
              Attributed works
  A. Lincoln reception at the White house,
    1863
    U.S. National Capital sesquicentennial
    com
Carpenter, William, 1767-1823
  Earl, R. William Carpenter

**CARR, Lyell**
Remington's studio
McCracken. Remington
**CARR, William, fl 1833**
Harbor scene with fish market near Philadelphia
U.S. National Capital sesquicentennial com
Carrara: a little quarry by J. S. Sargent
Carrara: a quarry by J. S. Sargent
Carrara: in a quarry by J. S. Sargent
Carrara: Lizzatori I by J. S. Sargent
Carrara: Lizzatori II by J. S. Sargent
Carrara: M. Derville's quarry by J. S. Sargent
Carrara: marmo statuario by J. S. Sargent
Carrara: quarry I by J. S. Sargent
Carrara: quarry II by J. S. Sargent
Carrara: Trajan's quarry by J. S. Sargent
Carrara: wet quarries by J. S. Sargent
Carrara: workmen by J. S. Sargent
Carroll, Charles, 1737-1832
Harding, C. Charles Carroll of Carrollton
**Carroll, Mrs Charles.** See Chew, Harriet
**Carroll, Mrs Daniel.** See Darnall, Eleanor
**CARROLL, Edward**
Fairfield Osborn                          MM
CoS. New accessions USA, 1960
**CARROLL, John, 1892-1959**
Bird in her heart
IU. Contemp Amer ptg, 1948
Claire Luce as Camille
NAD. Annual ex, 1948
Evening                                    MiD
Cheney. Story 1958 ed
Jean
Gruskin (col)
Little sheep
CSFP. Annual ex, 1948/49
Lois
OYB. Annual 1953
Mrs Carroll
NAD. Annual ex, 1947, 1st half
Red roses
PPC. Ptg in the U.S. 1949
Sleeping
NYG. Fine art
Spring bonnet
Bazin
IU. Contemp Amer ptg, 1950
Truth is upward
NAD. Annual ex, 1960
White flower
IU. Contemp Amer ptg, 1951
Roos
White lace                                 OT
Baur. Revolution
Cheney. Story 1958 ed
Pierson
Young girl
Cheney. Expressionism 1948 ed
**Carroll, Mrs John**
Carroll, J. Mrs Carroll
**CARROLL, Leon, 1887-1937**
Three gold diggers                         CtY
CtY. Soc Anonyme

**Carry** on by E. H. Blashfield
**Cars** in sleet storm by A. G. Dove
**Carson's** men by C. M. Russell
The **cart** by E. Berman
**CARTER, Clarence Holbrook, 1904-**
Carousel by the sea
Gruskin
Jane Reed and Dora Hunt                    MMA
McCurdy
Pierson
Stew                                       OT
ICA. Annual ex, 1945/46
OT. Contemp Amer ptgs
Tide water
IU. Contemp Amer ptg, 1948
Yellow blinds                              OYB
OYB. Catalogue 1951
Carter, Mrs James Otis, b 1780
Malbone, E. G. Mrs James Otis Carter
**CARTER, Mrs Robert, fl 1833**
Napoleon's army crossing the Alps          MB
MB. Karolik coll
**CARTNEY, Mary Elizabeth, fl 1840**
Court house and Centre square, Easton
McClintock
Court house. Easton
McClintock
**CARTON, Norman, 1908-**
Ocean brilliance
IU. Contemp Amer ptg & sculp, 1961
**CARY, Samuel, 1742-1812**
Copley, J.S. Samuel Cary
Cary, Sarah (Gray) 1742-1825
Copley, J. S. Mrs Samuel Cary
La **casa** de Dios by S. Raffo
**Cascade** in the forest by J. F. Kensett
**Cascade** waters by W. W. Baumgartner
**CASEBIER, Cecil Lang, 1922-**
Boy in Mexico                              TxD
CoS. New accessions USA, 1956
Casey, Mrs John, fl 1840
Unidentified artist. Mrs John Casey and daughter
**Cashmere** shawl by J. S. Sargent
**CASILEAR, John William, 1811-1893**
Moonlight
Sears. Highlights
Reminiscence of the Genesee river
Sears. Highlights
Cass, Lewis, 1782-1866
Tuthill, A. G. D. Lewis Cass
**Cassatt, Alexander**
Cassatt, M. Alexander Cassatt and his son
Cassatt, Lydia, fl 1881
Cassatt, M. Lydia Cassatt reading
**CASSATT, Mary, 1845-1926**
After the bath (La sortie du bain)         OCl
OCl. Handbook
Pierson
Sweet
Alexander Cassatt and his son
PA. Annual ex, 1955
At the opera                               MB
Cheney. Story 1958 ed
Rewald. History of impressionism
The bath                                   FPP
Sweet

The bath (La toilette) ICA
  Flexner. Amer ptg
  Flexner. Short history
  Mendelowitz
  MiD. Ptg in America
  Newmeyer
  PA. Annual ex, 1955
  Pierson
  Riley. Your art heritage
  Sweet
Caresse enfantine DNC
  DC. 25 biennial ex, 1957
Child holding a dog CtHW
  CtHW. Handbook
Child with red hat MWiS
  MWiS. Ex 4 and 7
A cup of tea MB
  Bazin
  Sweet
  Time. 300 years (col)
The cup of tea MM
  McKinney
  Sweet
In the box
  Sweet
In the garden MdBM
  Sweet
In the loge DN
  Lee. Art then and now
Lady at the tea table MM
  McCurdy
  Sweet
La loge (Midy coll)
  Sweet
  Time. 300 years (col)
The loge (The opera box) DN
  Rewald. History of impressionism
  UNESCO. 1860-1955
Lydia Cassatt reading NEO
  CSB. Impressionism
Mme A. F. Aude and her two daughters
  Sweet
Mrs Havemeyer and her daughter
  Sweet
Mrs John Howard Whittemore. See Portrait of a grand lady
Mrs Peter Frelinghuysen
  DC. Privately owned
Morning toilet DN
  Rewald. History of impressionism
  Walker. Ptgs from America (col)
Mother and child PPhM
  Canaday
Mother and child OYB
  Chew. 250 years of art
  OYB. Catalogue 1951
Mother and child OCiM
  OCiM. Guide
Mother and child KW
  Pierson
  Sweet (col front)
  Time. 300 years (col)
Mother and child MWM
  Roos
Mother and child FPL
  UNESCO. 1860-1955
Mother and children MCH
  PPC. Amer classics
Mother holding child
  Sweet
On the balcony PPhM
  Sweet

The opera box. See The loge (DN)
Portrait of a grand lady (Mrs John Howard Whittemore)
  Sweet
Reading Le Figaro
  Sweet
Self-portrait
  Sweet
La sortie du bain. See After the bath
La toilette. See The bath
Torero and young girl MWiS
  MWiS. Ex 4 and 7
Under the horse-chestnut tree MMA
  MMA. Masters
Woman and child driving PPhM
  Pierson
  Sweet (col)
  Taylor. Fifty centuries, 1954 ed (col)
  Walker. Ptgs from America
Woman arranging her veil PPhM
  Canaday
  Pierson
  Sweet
Woman in black MoSL
  MoSL. Handbook 1953
  MoSL. Masterworks
Woman reclining
  NUM. Art across America
Woman with a dog DC
  DC. Masterpieces (col)
Women admiring a child MiD
  MiD. Treasures
Women picking fruit (Young women picking fruit) PPC
  Pierson
  Richardson. Ptg in America
A young girl MM
  MM. 100 Amer ptrs
Young girl in green bonnet DNC
  DNC. Gellatly col, 1954
Young girls InIJ
  InIJ. 105 ptgs
Young woman reading (Woman reading) MB
  Rewald. History of impressionism
  Sweet
Young women picking fruit. See Women picking fruit

**CASSILL, R. V.**
Small town evening IaDa
  IaDa. Silver jubilee
Castel Gandolfo by G. Innes
Castello Dell'ovo, Bay of Naples by G. L. Brown
**CASTELLÓN, Federico, 1914-**
Dark figure WMAA
  Baur. Revolution
  Goodrich. Amer Art
  Pierson
Return of the prodigal
  ICA. Annual ex, 1947/48
Supplication ATU
  ATU. Coll of Amer Art
Casting in the falls by W. Homer
Casting the fly by W. Homer
The castle by R. Eshoo
Castle Garden, New York
  Ulrich, C. F. In the land of promise: Castle Garden
A castle in England or Ireland by T. Doughty

Cat boats, Newport by C. Hassam
Cataclysm by H. Hofmann
Catalyst by H. Hofmann
Catalytic crackers by T. H. Benton
Catamount by D. Austin
Catching the Thanksgiving turkey by
A. M. R. Moses
Catching up by A. J. Miller
Catfish row by J. Lawrence
Cathedral entrance by D. W. Ellis
Cathedral in the woods by J. Lam
Cathedrals
Blanch, A. Cathedrals
Chavez, E. A. Cathedral
Feininger, L. Cathedral, Cammin
Feininger, L. The east choir of Halle
cathedral
Freibert, J. Urban cathedral
Halpert, S. Cathedral interior
Halpert, S. Notre Dame, Paris
Lewis, N. Cathedral
Pach, W. Cathedral
Pollock, J. Cathedral
Prendergast, M. P. Notre Dame, Paris
Sargent, J. S. Cordova: interior of the
cathedral
Catlin, Clara Bartlett (Gregory) 1808?-1845
Catlin, G. Mrs George Catlin
CATLIN, George, 1796-1872
Ah-mou-a, The Whale, Kee-o-kuk warrior
DNC
McCracken. George Catlin (col)
Apache village on Lake Ahrocum NNAM
Bazin
Archery of the Mandans or game of the
arrow
Morgan (col)
Ba-da-ah-chon-du, a Crow chief    NNAM
McCracken. George Catlin (col)
Ball-play of the Choctaws          DNC
Davidson v 1
McCracken. George Catlin
The bear dance                     DNC
McCracken. George Catlin
Morgan (col)
The beggars' dance of Teton Sioux DNC
McCracken. George Catlin
Bi-eets-ee-cure, The Very Sweet Man,
Crow warrior                   DNC
McCracken. George Catlin
Morgan
Bird's eye view of the Mandan village
DNC
Mendelowitz
Time. 300 years (col)
Black Hawk                         DNC
Rathbone
Blackfoot doctor in his mystery dress
endeavoring to cure his dying patient
NNAM
Flexner. Amer ptg
Flexner. Short history
Blackfoot medicine man             DNC
McCracken. George Catlin (col)
Blue Medicine
Rathbone
Breaking down the wild horse    PPhUn
Chew. 250 years of art

Buffalo chase                      NNAM
McCracken. Portrait of the old west
(col)
Rathbone
Buffalo chase in snowdirft         DNC
Pierson
Buffalo chase of the Sioux         DNC
McCracken. George Catlin
Buffalo chase, upper Missouri      DNC
McCracken. George Catlin (col)
Buffalo crossing Yellowstone in winter
McCracken. George Catlin
Buffalo hunt on snow shoes
Larkin rev ed
Buffalo hunt, under the wolf mask  DNC
Rathbone
Time. 300 years (col)
Buffalo stampede
McCracken. George Catlin
Bull dance of the Mandans          NNAM
McCracken. Portrait of the old west
Catlin hunting buffalo for food
McCracken. George Catlin
Catlin painting the Four Bears     NNAM
McCracken. George Catlin (col)
Champion Choctaw ball-player       DNC
McCracken. George Catlin
Chin-cah-pee, The Fire Bug         DNC
McCracken. George Catlin
Clara Gregory Catlin               DNC
McCracken. George Catlin
Clermont, first chief of the Osages DNC
McCracken. George Catlin
Time. 300 years (col)
Col-lee, chief of the Cherokees    DNC
McCracken. George Catlin
Comanche feats of horsemanship     DNC
McCracken. George Catlin
Comanche village in Texas          DNC
McCracken. George Catlin
Comanche war party meeting dragoons
DNC
McCracken. George Catlin (col)
Crow chief at his toilet           NNAM
McCracken. George Catlin (col)
A Crow tepee                       DNC
McCracken. George Catlin
Crow warriors bathing in Yellowstone
NNAM
McCracken. George Catlin (col)
Crow woman                         DNC
McCracken. George Catlin
Dance of the berdash of the Sauk and
Fox Morgan
DeWitt Clinton                     NNHS
McCracken. George Catlin
The Double Walker, Nom-ba-mon-nee, a
brave of the Omaha tribe
Morgan
Down the Mississippi in a birch-bark
canoe                          DNC
McCracken. George Catlin
Ee-ah-sa-pa, The Black Rock, a Sioux
chief                          DNC
McCracken. George Catlin
Encounter with buffalo on Missouri DNC
McCracken. George Catlin
The evil spirit, O-ke-pa
McCracken. George Catlin
Excavating a canoe, British Columbia
NNAM
McCracken. George Catlin (col)

Fort Pierre with Sioux camped around
DNC
McCracken. George Catlin
Fort Snelling on the upper Mississippi
OkTT
McCracken. George Catlin
Fort Union, mouth of the Yellowstone
DNC
McCracken. George Catlin
Ha-na-ta-nu-maik, The Wolf Chief, head
of the Mandans DNC
McCracken. George Catlin
The handsome dance, Venezuela, South
America NNAM
McCracken. George Catlin (col)
Haw-che-ke-sug-ga, chief of the Missouris
DNC
McCracken. George Catlin
Ha-won-je-tah, The One Horn, first chief
of the Sioux DNC
McCracken. George Catlin
Roos
He who drinks the juice of the stone
DNC
Rathbone
Hill of death, upper Missouri DNC
McCracken. George Catlin (col)
His-oo-san-chees, The Little Spaniard,
Comanche warrior DNC
McCracken. George Catlin
Indian boy MoKN
MoKN. Handbook
Indians atacking grizzly bears NNHS
McCracken. George Catlin
Kee-mo-ra-nia, a beau of the Peorias DNC
McCracken. George Catlin
Kee-o-kuk on horseback DNC
McCracken. George Catlin (col)
Morgan
Kee-o-kuk, the Running Fox DNC
McCracken. George Catlin (col)
Kiowa girl and boy DNC
McCracken. George Catlin
Konza warriors, woman and child NNAM
McCracken. George Catlin (col)
La-doo-ke-a, the Buffalo Bull, Grand
Pawnee warrior DNC
McCracken. George Catlin (col)
Lay-law-she-kaw, chief of the Shawnees
DNC
McCracken. George Catlin
Mah-to-he-ha, The Old Bear DNC
Morgan
Time. 300 years (col)
Mandan medicine man DNC
McCracken. George Catlin (col)
Mandan O-kee-pa, the bull dance DNC
McCracken. George Catlin (col)
Mandan torture ceremony NNAM
McCracken. George Catlin (col)
Mandan village DNC
McCracken. George Catlin
Morgan
The medicine bag dance of the Sauk and
Fox
Morgan
Mow-hew-she-kaw, The White Cloud,
chief of the Ioways
McCracken. George Catlin (col)
Minnetaree village DNC
McCracken. George Catlin

Mix-ke-móte-skin-na, The Iron Horn,
Blackfoot warrior DNC
McCracken. George Catlin
Moving camp DNC
McCracken. George Catlin
Muk-a-tah-mish-o-kah-kiak, The Black
Hawk DNC
McCracken. George Catlin (col)
Notch-ee-ming-a, No Heart, chief of the
Iowas DNC
McCracken. George Catlin
Morgan
No-way-ke-sug-gah, an Oto warrior DNC
McCracken. George Catlin (col)
Ojibway (Chippewa) woman and baby
DNC
McCracken. George Catlin
Oliver Wolcott
McCracken. George Catlin
Om-pah-ton-ga, Big Elk, Chief of the
Omahas DNC
McCracken. George Catlin (col)
One Horn, a Dakota (Sioux) chief ICH
Pierson
Richardson. Ptg in America
Osceola
McCracken. George Catlin
Osceola NNAM
Roos
Osceola, The Black Drink DNC
McCracken. George Catlin
Prairie bluffs burning, upper Missouri
DNC
McCracken, George Catlin (col)
Prairie fire DNC
Rathbone
Pshan-shaw, Arikara girl DNC
McCracken. George Catlin
The sacred red pipe—stone quarry OkTT
McCracken. George Catlin
Sah-ko-ka, The Mint Mandan girl DNC
McCracken. George Catlin
St Louis, 1836 DNC
Davidson v 1
Sam Houston
McCracken. George Catlin
Sam Perryman DNC
Rathbone
The Sauk and Fox slave dance
Morgan
Scalp dance of the Sioux DNC
McCracken. Portrait of the old west
(col)
Rathbone
Seehk-hee-da, The White Eyebrows, Man-
dan man DNC
McCracken. George Catlin
Self-portrait OkTT
McCracken. George Catlin
Se-non-ti-yak, The Blistered Foot, Ioway
medicine man NNAM
McCracken. George Catlin (col)
Sioux beggars' dance
Morgan
Sioux Indians hunting buffalo DNC
McCracken. George Catlin
Sioux Indians pursuing a stag in their
canoes DNC
Time. 300 years (col)
A Sioux village NNAM
McCracken. Portrait of the old west
(col)

**CATLIN, George**—*Continued*
Sky-se-ro-ka. a chief of the Pawnee Picks
DNC
McCracken. George Catlin
Snowshoe dance of the Chippewas  DNC
McCracken. George Catlin
Snowshoe dance of the Ojibbeway
DNC
Rathbone
Steamboat Yellowstone leaving St Louis
DNC
McCracken. George Catlin
Stee-tcha-ko-me-co, The Great King, chief
of the Creeks                    DNC
McCracken. George Catlin
Stu-mick-o-sucks,  The  Buffalo's  Back
Fat, chief of the Blackfeet      DNC
McCracken. George Catlin (col)
The sun dance
Morgan
Tah-teck-a-da-hair, The Steep Wind, a
Sioux warrior                    DNC
McCracken. George Catlin (col)
Tal-lee, Osage warrior               DNC
McCracken. George Catlin (col)
Ta-wah-que-nah, The Mountain of Rocks,
Comanche chief                   DNC
McCracken. George Catlin
Tcha-aes-ka-ding, Barefoot Boy       DNC
McCracken. George Catlin
Tcha-kauks-o-ko-maugh, The Great Chief
DNC
McCracken. George Catlin
Tchan-dee,  Tobacco,  second  chief  of
Oglala Sioux                     DNC
McCracken. George Catlin
Ten-squat-a-way, Shawnee prophet  DNC
McCracken. George Catlin
Morgan
Tis-se-woo-na-tis, wife of a Cheyenne chief
DNC
McCracken. George Catlin (col)
Toh-to-wah-kon-da-pee, The Blue Medi-
cine                             DNC
McCracken. George Catlin
Ud-je-jock, the Pelican              DNC
Baur. Amer ptg
United States Military Academy, West
Point, N.Y.                      CtY
Davidson v2
Upper Missouri: the grand detour  NNAM
Pierson
U.S.  National Capital sesquicentennial
com
Uruguay medicine man, South America
NNAM
McCracken. George Catlin (col)
View on the upper Missouri           DNC
Rathbone
Time. 300 years (col)
Village of the dead                  OkTT
McCracken. George Catlin
Virginia constitutional convention of 1829-
30                               NNHS
Davidson v2
McCracken. George Catlin
U.S. National Capital sesquicentennial
com
Wah-pa-ko-las-kuk,  The  Bear's  Track
DNC
McCracken. George Catlin
Wah-pe-kee-suck, The White Cloud  DNC
McCracken. George Catlin (col)

Wa-nah-de-tunk-ah, The Black Dog, East-
ern Sioux                        DNC
McCracken. George Catlin
Wee-ta-ra-sha-ro, chief of Pawnee Picks
DNC
McCracken. George Catlin
Wife of Kee-o-kuk                    DNC
McCracken. George Catlin
Wi-jun-jon, The Pigeon's Egg Head  DNC
McCracken. George Catlin (col)
William Clark
McCracken. George Catlin
Winter hunting on upper Missouri  DNC
McCracken. George Catlin
Wun-nee-tow, the White Buffalo, Black-
foot medicine man
McCracken. George Catlin
**Portrait of the artist**
Fisk, W. H. George Catlin
**Catlin, John Mortimer, 1801-1881**
Inman, H. John M. Catlin
**Catlin, Mrs George.** See Catlin, Clara Bart-
lett (Gregory)
**Catlin, Nicholas**
Walters, S. Memorial to Nicholas Catlin
**Cats**
Abercrombie, G. Message for mercy
Bacon, P. Nobody's pet
Bacon, P. Wanderlust
Bartoll, W. T. Girl and cat
Brook, A. Peggy Bacon and Metaphysics
Clemens, P.L. Ruth with cat
Cortor, E. Affection
De Diego, J. Guilty cats
Fransioli, T. A. The cat
Koch, J. Nude with cat
Lindner, R. Paul Verlaine [with cat]
Lintot, B. Ballerina
Luks, G. B. Cat and kittens
Luks, G. B. Woman with black cat
Philipp, R. Xmas morning
Pickens, A. Card players
Schnakenberg, H. E. Cat and kittens
Sloan, J. Backyards, Greenwich Village
Sloan, J. McSorley's cats
Tomlin, B. W. Outward preoccupation
Toole, J. Nannie Toole (with cat)
Unidentified artist. The cat
Unidentified artist. Cat and kittens
Unidentified artist. Caught in the act
Unidentified artist. Lydia and Tabitha
Unidentified artist. Picking flowers
Vasilieff, N. Girl with cat
**Cat's cradle** by J. Kearns
**Cat's cradle in blue** by B. Shahn
**Catskill Clove** by A. B. Durand
**Catskill mountains**
Browere, A. D. Catskills
Church, F. E. Catskill mountains, 1852
Cole, T. Catskill mountains
Cole, T. In the Catskills
Cole, T. Prometheus bound
Cole, T. River in the Catskills
Doughty, T. In the Catskills
Durand, A. B. Catskill mountains near
Shandaken
Hart, J. M. Catskill creek, New York
Hart, W. M. Autumn in the Catskills
A **Catskill** stream by A. B. Durand
**Cattel, Mary (Ladson)** fl 1801
Malbone, E. G. Mrs William Cattel

**Cattle**
*See also* Bulls
Avert, M. Three cows on a hillside
Beckmann, M. Cattle in barn
Bingham, G. C. Landscape with cattle
Burliuk, D. White cows
Casilaer, J. W. Reminiscence of the Gene-
see river
Dove, A. G. Cows in pasture
Fisher, A. The watering place
Hart, W. M. Cattle in a stream
Hicks, E. Cornell farm
Hinckley, T. H. Cows and sheep in pas-
ture
Hinckley, T. H. Great Blue hill and
Neponset river
Hinckley, T. H. Noon
Homer, W. Weaning the calf
Innis, G. Landscape with cattle
Nichols, H. Black herd
Palmer, W. C. Cows in the corn
Price, C. S. Cattle
Price, C. S. Cattle by the river
Price, C. S. Cow with calf
Price, C. S. Cows going to pasture
Price, C. S. The dream
Russell, C. M. The bolter
Russell, C. M. Heads or tails
Russell, C. M. Heeling a bad one
Russell, C. M. Jerked down
Russell, C. M. A loose cinch
Russell, C. M. Roping a wild one
Russell, C. M. The roundup
Russell, C. M. A serious predicament
Russell, C. M. Waiting for a chinook
Ryder, A. P. Evening glow—the old red
cow
Ryder, A. P. Pastoral study
Ryder, A. P. The pasture
Ryder, A. P. Summer's faithful pasture
Sommer, W. Cows
Sommer, W. Cows resting
Sommer, W. Pink cow
Spruce, E. F. White cow
West, B. Landscape with cow
**Cattle** loading, West Texas by T. H.
Benton
**Caucus** by W. Kuhn
**Caught** in net by M. Freedman
**Caught** in the equinox by A. Salemme
**Cavalcade** by A. J. Miller
**CAVALLON, Giorgio, 1904-**
Abstract no 6, 1952
Pousette-Dart. Amer ptg
Abstraction, 1950
McCurdy
MMA. Abstract
Untitled                                    NBuA
NBuA. Acquisitions 1959-1961
ICA. Annual ex, 1959/60
**Cavalry** charge on the western plain by
F. Remington
**CAVANAUGH, Tom**
American errant                             NeO
CoS. New accessions USA, 1954
**CAVAT, Irma, 1928-**
White morning
IU. Contemp Amer ptg & sculp, 1959
**Cavell, Edith Louise, 1865-1915**
Bellows, G. W. Edith Cavell
**Cayambe** by F. E. Church
**Celebration** by S. Magada

**Celebration** by F. Martin
**Celestral** by J. Grillo
The **'cellist** by I. J. H. Bradley
**Cello** player by E. W. Dickinson
**Cemeteries**
Chambers, S. Mount Auburn cemetery,
Cambridge
Cloar, C. Gibson bayou anthology
Herron, D. St Louis cemetery, New
Orleans
**Centaur** by J. Kinigstein
**Centaurs** by S. Sherman
**Central** park by G. Grosz
**Central** park by M. B. Prendergast
**Central** park at night by G. Grosz
**Central** park, winter by W. J. Glackens
**Centurion** by J. Corbino
**Centurion** by J. La Farge
**Centurion's** horse by R. Lebrun
**Century** plant by E. F. Spruce
**Ceracchi, Giuseppe, 1751-1802**
Trumbull, J. Giuseppe Ceracchi
**Ceremonial** bronze taking the form of a
bird by M. Graves
**Ceremony** by H. A. Botkin
**Ceremony** by P. Guston
**Cerulean** sea and isle by J. Marin
**CHADWICK, fl 1854**
Placer mining, 1854
Davidson v 1
**CHADWICK, Francis Brooks, 1850-1943**
William Sturgis Bigelow          MB
MB. Ptgs in water color

**Portrait of the artist**
Sargent, J. S. Francis Brooks Chadwick
**CHAET, Bernard, 1924-**
Pastoral
MBIC. View 1960
Remains II
IU. Contemp Amer ptg & sculp, 1961
White table
IU. Contemp Amer ptg & sculp, 1953
**CHAIKEN, William, 1921-**
Dusk
IU. Contemp Amer ptg & sculp, 1957
Vase with flowers
IU. Contemp Amer ptg & sculp, 1959
**Chair** by R. D'Arista
**Chair** by M. Goldberg
**Chair** with apples by W. Kuhn
La **Chaise-longue** by W. Gay
**Chakwa** tea plantation by W. Gropper
**CHALFANT, Jefferson David, 1856-1931**
After the hunt
Frankenstein. After the hunt
Old flintlock
Frankenstein. After the hunt
Old violin
Frankenstein. After the hunt
Which is which?
CSFP. Illusionism
Frankenstein. After the hunt
**Chalice** by M. Graves
**Chalice** and lyre by M. Graves
The **challenge** by C. M. Russell
**Challenge** and response by K. L. Callahan

Chalmers, Lionel, 1715-1777
  Theus, J. Dr Lionel Chalmers
Chalmers, Martha (Logan) (?) 1721-1765
  Theus, J. Mrs Lionel Chalmers
Chama running red by J. Sloan
Chamber music by J. De Botton
Chambered nautilus by A. N. Wyeth
CHAMBERLAIN, Elwyn, 1928-
  Icarus
    MnMW. Reality and fantasy
Chamberlayne, Mrs Thomas. See Byrd, Wilhelmina
Chamberlayne, Wilhelmina (Byrd). See Byrd, Wilhelmina
CHAMBERS, Thomas, b 1808?
  Boston harbor                              DN
    DN. Amer primitive ptgs, pt 1
  Connecticut river valley                   DN
    DN. Amer primitive ptgs, pt 1
  Hudson river valley, sunset                DN
    DN. Amer primitive ptgs, pt 2
  Mount Auburn cemetery, Cambridge  DN
    DN. Amer primitive ptgs, pt 2
  Old Sleepy Hollow church                   DN
    DN. Amer primitive ptgs, pt 2

                Attributed works
  Baroque landscape                        NCHA
    Jones. New-found folk art
CHAMBERS, Thomas, 1815-1866?
  Capture of H. B. M. frigate Macedonian
    by U.S. frigate United States. See
    The United States and the
    Macedonian
  Delaware Water Gap                       NCHA
    Jones. Rediscovered ptrs
  Hudson river landscape
    Lipman. Primitive ptrs
  Hudson river scene                        RPS
    Ford. Pictorial folk art
  Looking north to Kingston (View of
    Kingston, New York)                     MNS
    Barker. Amer ptg
    Larkin (detail)
    Larkin rev ed
  Niagara Falls                             CtHW
    Brussels. Exposition
    Ford. Pictorial folk art
  River scene
    Lipman. Primitive ptrs
  Under Cliff, seat of Gen G. P. Morris
                                            RPS
    Born
  The United States and the Macedonian
    Ford. Pictorial folk art
    Lipman. Primitive ptrs
  View of Kingston, New York. See Looking north to Kingston
  View of West Point                        MnMI
    Ford. Pictorial folk art
  View of the Hudson river at West Point
                                            NR
    Jones. Rediscovered ptrs

                Attributed works
  Landscape—probably a Hudson river
    scene                                   MeC
    Jetté. Amer heritage collection
Champion Choctaw ball-player by G. Catlin
Champs-Elysées by M. B. Prendergast

Chandelier 1 by H. Bloom
Chandler, Elizabeth. See Plummer, Elizabeth (Chandler)
CHANDLER, Joseph G. fl 1850
  Charles H. Sisson                          DN
    DN. Amer primitive ptgs, pt 1
Chandler, Samuel, fl 1780
  Chandler, W. Capt Samuel Chandler
Chandler, Mrs Samuel, fl 1780
  Chandler, W. Mrs Samuel Chandler
CHANDLER, Winthrop, 1747-1790
  Ebenezer and Samuel Crafts
    Lipman. Primitive ptrs
  Ebenezer Devotion
    Davidson v 1
    Larkin
    Larkin rev ed
    Pierson
  Mrs Ebenezer Devotion
    Pierson
  Mrs Gleason and Bethia                    OCoA
    Ford. Pictorial folk art
  Mrs Samuel Chandler                        DN
    Brussels. Exposition
    DN. Amer primitive ptgs, pt 2
    Richardson. Ptg in America
  Samuel Chandler                            DN
    DN. Amer primitive ptgs, pt 2
    Larkin (detail)
    Larkin rev ed (detail)
  View of a city
    Flexner. Light of distant skies
  William Glysson (William Gleason)
                                            OCoA
    Davidson v 1
    Flexner. Light of distant skies
    Ford. Pictorial folk art
Changes of time by J. Haberle
Changing seasons by T. Ochikubo
Chanler, Elizabeth
  Sargent, J. S. Miss Elizabeth Chanler
Channing, Ann, 1778-1815
  Malbone, E. G. Ann Channing
Channing, Francis Dana, b 1775
  Allston, W. Francis Dana Channing
Channing, Lucy Ellery, 1752-1834
  Allston, W. Mrs William Channing
Channing, William Ellery, 1780-1842
  Allston, W. William Channing
  Stuart, G. William Ellery Channing
The chant by J. Ernst
Chantet lane by A. Dasburg
CHAPIN, Francis, 1899-
  Harbor at Edgartown
    IU. Contemp Amer ptg, 1950
    PPC. Ptg in the U.S. 1949
  House of the dogs
    IU. Contemp Amer ptg, 1952
  Oak creek canyon, Arizona
    IU. Contemp Amer ptg & sculp, 1957
  Regatta at Edgartown
    DC. 23 biennial ex, 1952
CHAPIN, James, 1887-
  Ruby Green singing                         FaW
  Time. 300 years (col)
CHAPIN, Joshua Bicknell, 1814-1881
  Old mill, Hanover, N.H.                    MB
    MB. Ptgs in water color
  Young woman
    OYB. Annual 1954

**CHAPIN, Moses Thompson,** 1814-1836
Stone cottage, Hanover, New Hampshire
                                MB
  MB. Ptgs in water color
**CHAPMAN, Charles Shepard,** 1879-
Last parable
  NYG. Fine art
White water ahead
  NAD. Annual ex, 1947, 2d half
**CHAPMAN, Conrad Wise,** 1842-1913
Battery Bee              VRCM
  U.S. National Capital sesquicentennial
  com
Confederate submarine torpedo boat H. L.
  Hunley                 VRCM
  Pierson
  U.S. National Capital sesquicentennial
  com
Fort Sumter, December 8, 1863
  Pierson
Lady on a balcony in Rome      VRV
  MiD. Travelers in Arcadia
Panorama: the valley of Mexico   VRV
  Born
  Pierson
**CHAPMAN, F. A.** fl 1875
The day we celebrate, the fourth of July
                               CtY
  Davidson v2
**Chapman, George,** fl 1850
  Mason, B. F. George Chapman
**Chapman, Mrs George,** fl 1850
  Mason, B. F. Mrs George Chapman
**CHAPMAN, John Gadsby,** 1808-1889
Drawing a bead on a woodchuck   OYB
  OYB. Catalogue 1951
Landing of Columbus
  Ford. Edward Hicks
Looking for good scenery       VRV
  MiD. Travelers in Arcadia
Pines in the Villa Barberini     MB
  MB. Karolik coll
Scenery found                VRV
  MiD. Travelers in Arcadia
**Chapman, Mrs John Jay.** See Chanler,
  Elizabeth
**CHAPPEL, Alonzo,** 1828-1887
Surrender at Appomattox, 1865
  U.S. National Capital sesquicentennial
  com
**CHAPPEL, Alonzo,** 1828-1887 and **BACH-
ELDER, John B.** fl 1865
Death of Abraham Lincoln
  U.S. National Capital sesquicentennial
  com
**CHAPPEL, William P.** fl 1807-1810
Bathing party in New York
  Davidson v2
Citizens supplying a fire engine with water
  from a pump, New York, c 1809
  Davidson v2
City watchman and his watch box, New
  York, 1809
  Davidson v2
Lamp lighter
  Davidson v2 (detail)
Old tea water pump and cart, New York,
  1807
  Davidson v2
Raising a house, New York, 1810
  Davidson v2 (detail)

**Charash, Mrs Jack.** See Rosenthal, Doris
**Charge** of the Rough Riders at San Juan
  hill by F. Remington
**Charles I, king of Great Britain,** 1600-1649
  Copley, J.S. Charles I demanding im-
  peachment of five members of House
  of Commons
**Charles II, king of Great Britain,** 1620-1685
  West, B. Gen Monk receiving Charles II
  on the beach of Dover
**Charles of Boston (brig)**
  Corné, M. F. The Brig Charles of Boston
**Charleston, South Carolina**
  Barnard, S. Charleston, South Carolina,
  1831
  Elliott, P. C. Charleston, South Carolina
  Roberts, B. Charleston, View of
  Walker, W.A. Charleston harbor from the
  Battery during the bombardment of
  Fort Sumter, April 13, 1861
  Zerbe, K. St Philip's, Charleston
**Charlestown, Massachusetts**
  Unidentified artist. Burning of Charles
  Town
**CHARLOT, Jean,** 1898-
Bathers                        PPhM
  CoS. New accessions USA, 1958
**Charlotte W. White** (sailing vessel)
  Sanborn, P. Ship Charlotte W. White
**Charred** beloved by A. Gorky
The **Charter** Oak by C. D. Brownell
**Chartiers** creek near Pittsburgh, 1840 by
  R. Smith
**Chartiers** creek on the Ohio river, 1872 by
  R. Smith
**CHASE, A. P.** fl 1850
Bird harbor, Maine           MeC
  Jetté. Amer heritage collection
**Chase, Alice**
  Chase, W. M. Alice in the mirror
  Chase, W. M. Alice in the Shinnecock
  studio
  Chase, W. M. Alice with wolfhound
  Chase, W. M. My daughter Alice
**Chase, Alice (Gerson)**
  Chase, W. M. Mrs Chase and Cosy
  Chase, W. M. Mrs Chase as a Spanish
  girl
  Chase, W. M. Mrs Chase in Prospect
  park
**Chase, David H.**
  Chase, W. M. My father (David H.
  Chase)
**Chase, Dieudonnée**
  Chase, W. M. Dieudonnée (Dieudonnée
  Chase)
  Chase, W. M. Feather boa (Dieudonnée
  Chase)
**Chase, Dorothy**
  Chase, W. M. Dorothy Chase
  Chase, W. M. My little daughter Dorothy
  Chase, W. M. Sketch of a child (Dorothy
  Chase)
**Chase, Dorothy Bremond**
  Chase, W. M. Girl in a red embroidered
  jacket
**Chase, Eliza Grover,** fl 1852
  Mason, B. F. Eliza Grover Chase
**Chase, Harry Woodburn,** 1883-1955
  Lockman, D. M. Chancellor Harry Wood-
  burn Chase

**CHASE, W. M.**—*Continued*

Still life     InBU
  NSP. William Merritt Chase
Still life     OkT
  NSP. William Merritt Chase
Still life     TxD
  NSP. William Merritt Chase
Still life     PA
  PA. Annual ex, 1955
Still life, fruit and pottery     OCiM
  NSP. William Merritt Chase
Still life—Striped bass     MoKN
  NSP. William Merritt Chase
Still life with brushes and pottery OCiM
  NSP. William Merritt Chase
Still life with cockatoo (White cockatoo) NSP
  NSP. William Merritt Chase
Still life with fish     MoSL
  NSP. William Merritt Chase
Still life with fish     NSP
  NSP. William Merritt Chase
Still life with fish     OkT
  NSP. William Merritt Chase
Still life with fish     VCU
  NSP. William Merritt Chase
Still life with fish (A skate)     PA
  InIJ. Chase centennial
  NSP. William Merritt Chase
Still life with fish, brass kettle, lemon and onions
  NSP. William Merritt Chase (col)
Study in curves. See Reclining nude
Study of an old woman
  NSP. William Merritt Chase
Summertime
  NSP. William Merritt Chase
Sunlight and shadow
  NSP. William Merritt Chase
Tea time     MiM
  NSP. William Merritt Chase
The Tenth street studio     PPC
  InIJ. Chase centennial
The Tenth street studio     MoSL
  MoSL. Handbook 1953
  NSP. William Merritt Chase
Thomas Dewing     NAD
  NSP. William Merritt Chase
Turkish page (Boy feeding a cockatoo) OCiM
  InIJ. Chase centennial
  NSP. William Merritt Chase
Unknown Dane     PPhM
  NSP. William Merritt Chase
View of Fiesole     MNS
  NSP. William Merritt Chase
View of Venice     RPS
  NSP. William Merritt Chase
Whistling boy     MiD
  NSP. William Merritt Chase
White bench     NSP
  NSP. William Merritt Chase
White cockatoo. See Still life with cockatoo
William A. Clark     DC
  InIJ. Chase centennial
  NSP. William Merritt Chase
William Clyde Fitch     MAC
  NSP. William Merritt Chase
William Gutley Munson
  InIJ. Chase centennial
William Rockhill Nelson     MoKN
  MoKN. Handbook

William Worthington Scranton     NAD
  NSP. William Merritt Chase
A woman     CtHW
  NSP. William Merritt Chase
Woman in black     MNS
  NSP. William Merritt Chase
Woman in white     NUM
  PPC. Amer classics
Yellow roses     NSP
  NSP. William Merritt Chase

**Chase, Mrs. William Merritt.** See Chase, Alice (Gerson)

**Chase** homestead by W. M. Chase

A **Chase** student by W. M. Chase

The **chase** by R. A. Blakelock

**Chasm** of the Colorado by T. Moran

**Chassidic** dance by M. Weber

**Chateau** Argol, Environment of by K. L. Seligmann

**Chateau-Thierry** by W. J. Glackens

**Chatham, William Pitt, 1st earl of.** See Pitt, William, 1st earl of Chatham

**CHAVEZ, Edward Arcenio,** 1917-
Cathedral
  IU. Contemp Amer ptg & sculp, 1955
Mirage
  WMAA. Annual ex, 1957
Processional
  IU. Contemp Amer ptg, 1952
Taxidermist's window
  IU. Contemp Amer ptg, 1949
  NBuA. Expressionism

The **checkered** house by A. M. R. Moses

**Checkers.** See Games and sports—Checkers

**Cheese** factory by Unidentified artist

**Cheever's** mill on the St Croix by H. Lewis

**Chelsea, Massachusetts**
  Unidentified artist. Marine hospital, Chelsea

**Chelsea** girl by J. A. M. Whistler

**Chelsea** lady and Bouvardia by R. P. R. Neilson

**Chelsea** shop by J. A. M. Whistler

**CHEN, Chi,** 1912-
Birds flying     OYB
  OYB. Annual 1955
  OYB. Supplement 1959
Chuang tze
  PA. Annual ex, 1961
The good earth
  NAD. Annual ex, 1960
River flowing . . . flowing
  IU. Contemp Amer ptg & sculp, 1957

**Cheney family,** fl 1795
  Unidentified artist. Cheney family

**Cherbourg,** Port of by M. Jamieson

**CHERMAYEFF, Serge,** 1900-
Conference of great powers
  IU. Contemp Amer ptg, 1950
Emerging figure
  IU. Contemp Amer ptg, 1951
Yellow, plus and minus
  IU. Contemp Amer ptg, 1949

**CHERNEY, Marvin,** 1925-
Classical nude
  PA. Annual ex, 1959-60

**Cherry** orchard by J. Marin

**Cherry** twice by F. Martin

**Cherubs** and children by B. Shahn
**CHESNEY, Lee,** 1920-
Night sea no 2
OYB. Annual 1959
OYB. Supplement 1959
**Chess.** See Games and sports—Chess
**Chestnut-sided** warbler on barberry by C. E. Heil
**Chestnut** stallion, Discovery by V. Flannery
**Cheves, Mary Elizabeth (Dulles)** See Dulles, Mary Elizabeth
**Cheves, Mrs Langdon.** See Dulles, Mary Elizabeth
**Chew, Harriet,** 1775-1861
Trumbull, J. Harriet Chew
**Chew, Samuel Lloyd,** b 1737?
Hesselius, J. Samuel Lloyd Chew
**Chew** house by R. Smith
**Chez** le fleuriste by C. Hassam
**Chez** Mouquin by W. J. Glackens
**Chicago, Illinois**
Cuthbert, V. I. Environs of Chicago
Shahn, B. Chicago
**Chicago** image by N. Barrett
**Chicago** space no 7, 1941 by L. Moholy-Nagy
**Chicken** market by M. Broderson
The **chief** by F. J. Kline
**Child, Elizabeth (Jarvis)** 1782-1854
Jarvis, J. W. Mrs Lewis Child
A **child** by M. B. Prendergast
**Child** acrobats by L. P. Harmon
**Child** of an Idumean night by A. Gorky
**Children**
Ames, E. Children of Gov Daniel D. Tomkins
Balis, C. George and Emma Eastman
Bascom, R. H. M. Profile of baby in orange
Benbridge, H. Gatling children
Blanchard, C. Late again
Brewster, J. Child with a peach
Cassatt, M. Child holding a dog
Christopher, W. The child
Clonney, J. G. Sleigh ride
Copley, J. S. Child of the Greenleaf family
Copley, J. S. Children of George III
Corbino, J. A child
Durand, J. Rapalje children
Eakins, T. Baby at play
Ellsworth, J. S. Children
Emery, E. Child in sitting room of Matthew Cushing house
Evergood, P. The future belongs to them
Goodwin, E. W. Christmas presents
Grant, J. Two children
Gwathmey, R. Children dancing
Harmon, L. P. Nursery school
Herzog, H. Grandfather's lesson
Homer, W. Children on a fence
Homer, W. Children playing under a Gloucester wharf
Johnston, J. Edward and Sarah Rutter
Karfiol, B. Child holding apple
Mason limner. David, Joanna, and Abigail Mason
Myers, J. Playground pleasures
Paul, J. Four children playing in a courtyard
Peale, J. Jane and James Peale jr

Prendergast, M. B. Children playing on the beach
Prendergast, M. B. Fishing party
Prior, W. M. (attributed works) Two children with dog
Prior, W. M. (manner of) Brother and sister sharing a book
Quirk, T. C. Vigil at the beach
Ruellan, A. Children's mardi gras
Sachs, L. The Herbert children
Sargent, J. S. The Pailleron children
Sloan, J. Dust storm, Fifth avenue
Stearns, J. B. Children fishing
Stock, J. W. Child in a wicker basket
Stock, J. W. Wilcox children
Toole, J. Toole children
Tuthill, A. G. D Jackson, Solon, Elizabeth and Anna Miretta Vail
Tuthill, A. G. D. Sylvester, Julia, Jane and Catherine Larned
Unidentified artist. Angeline Eliza Shepard and her brother, Elisha Henry Shepard
Unidentified artist. Baby in blue cradle
Unidentified artist. Baby in pink and white
Unidentified artist. Baby in red chair
Unidentified artist. Baby reclining
Unidentified artist. Baby with fruit
Unidentified artist. Barclay children
Unidentified artist. Boy and girl
Unidentified artist. Child and doll
Unidentified artist. Child in blue
Unidentified artist. Child with rocking horse
Unidentified artist. Child with wheelbarrow
Unidentified artist. Children of Jacob Franks
Unidentified artist. Dover baby
Unidentified artist. Five children of the Budd family
Unidentified artist. George and Jane Bigelow
Unidentified artist. Hobby horse
Unidentified artist. Innocence
Unidentified artist. Mary and David Dalzell of South Egremont, Massachusetts
Unidentified artist. Raymond children
Unidentified artist. That's my doll!
Unidentified artist. Two children with a deer
Unidentified artist. Woodward children
Wollaston, J. Children of Warner Lewis
Woodside, J. A. Children in a courtyard
**Boys**
Allston, W. Italian shepherd boy
Badger, J. His son James
Badger, J. Jeremiah Belknap
Bascom, R. H. Profile of a boy
Bellows, G. B. Forty-two kids
Bingham, G. C. The mill boy
Blythe, D. G. On the sly
Blythe, D. G. Silas Gault
Blythe, D. G. Street urchins
Blythe, D. G. Young musician
Border limner. Robert Lockridge Dorr
Bradley, J. (attributed works) Boy holding dog
Brewster, J. Francis O. Watts with bird
Brackman, R. Junior
Brown, J. G. Berry boy
Casebier, C. L. Boy in Mexico

**Children—Boys—***Continued*
Catlin, G. Indian boy
Chandler, J. G. Charles H. Sisson
Chase, W. M. Boy eating an apple
Chase, W. M. Master Roland Dana Chase
Chase, W. M. Turkish page
Chase, W. M. Whistling boy
Cook, N. Little dandy
Copley, J. S. Jonathan Mountfort
Davis, G. R. Sea sounds
Davis, G. R. Study
Dinnerstein, S. Magnolia
Durrie, G. H. William J. Conover as a boy
Duveneck, F. A boy
Duveneck, F. Whistling boy
Field, E. S. Boy on stenciled carpet
Francis, J. F. Three children
Frazer, O. Anderson children
Freake limner. Henry Gibbs
Freake limner. Robert Gibbs
Goodridge, E. Gorham Bond
Goodridge, E. Stephen Salisbury
Greene, S. Ischia
Henri, R. Dutch Joe
Henri, R. Laughing child
Hesselius, J. Charles Calvert and his Negro slave
Homer, W. Boy picking apples
Homer, W. Boys bathing
Homer, W. Boys wading
Homer, W. Children on the beach
Homer, W. The seesaw
Homer, W. Snap the whip
Hubard, W. J. William A. Shafer
Inman, H. The newsboy
Inman, H. Young fishermen
James, A. Danny
Jameson, D. Boy with kite
Jamieson, M. Children of Rome
Johnston, J. The Westwood children
Kane, J. Boys fishing
Karfiol, B. Boy bathers
Knight, F. Portrait of a young artist
Kuniyoshi, Y. Boy stealing fruit
Kuniyoshi, Y. Little Joe with cow
Le Clear, T. Buffalo newsboy
Luks, G. B. Butcher boy
Luks, G. B. Flyweight champ of Jumel place
Luks, G. B. The gamin
Luks, G. B. Sulking boy
Malbone, E. G. James McPherson
Malbone, E. G. Jeremiah Kahler
Mason, B. F. Rufus and Gardner Wainwright
Matson, G. W. City child
Otis, B. Seated boy
Perlin, B. Orthodox boys
Phillips, J. C. Future admiral
Pickering, H. D. Some grow up
Prendergast, J. D. Young American artist
Prior, W. M. William Allen
Reeder, D. Walter Martin
Refregier, A. Boy drawing
Ruellan, A. Boy and gull
Sargent, J. S. Boys on the beach
Sargent, J. S. Gordon Fairchild holding a guinea-pig
Sargent, J. S. Peter Augustus Jay at the age of three
Sheffield, I. James Francis Smith
Sommer, W. Bald boy
Sommer, W. A boy
Sommer, W. One of the Dominskies
Sommer, W. Pensive boy

Sommer, W. Pompous boy
Sommer, W. Ray
Sommer, W. Seated boy in lavender overalls
Speicher, E. E. Greek boy
Stock, J. W. Horace Wilson Eddy
Stock, J. W. William Howard Smith
Stock, J. W. Young hammerer
Sully, T. Torn hat
Theus, J. Charles Burnham Cochran
Theus, J. Hutchinson boy
Theus, J. Maurice Keating
Tilyard, P. Charles Slade Tilyard
Toole, J. George Toole
Unidentified artist. Abraham Clark and his children
Unidentified artist. Boy in blue coat
Unidentified artist. Boy in plaid
Unidentified artist. Boy of the De Peyster family
Unidentified artist. Boy with a toy drum
Unidentified artist. Boy with finch
Unidentified artist. Boy with hammer and iron pot
Unidentified artist. Boy with whip
Unidentified artist. De Peyster boy with deer
Unidentified artist. Henry Gibbs
Unidentified artist. Henry Wells
Unidentified artist. John Van Cortlandt
Unidentified artist. John Whorf with bow and arrow
Unidentified artist. Little boy in red
Unidentified artist. Master Willoughby
Unidentified artist. Mrs Starke's brother of Troy
Unidentified artist. Negro child
Unidentified artist. Rhode Island choir boy
Unidentified artist. Schoolmaster and boys
Unidentified artist. Two boys in green tunics
Unidentified artist. Warren Crosby
Unidentified artist. Young man in a gray linen suit
Vanderlyn, J. Severyn Bruyn
Von Phul, A. M. Boy in beaver hat
Walton, H. De Mott Smith, aged 8
Zorach, W. The artist's son

**Girls**
Albro, M. Skipping
Ames, E. Ann Walsh
Ames, E. Katharine Barber James (?)
Bartoll, W. T. Girl and cat
Bellows, G. W. Children on the porch
Bellows, G. W. Emma and her children
Bellows, G. W. Jean with blue book and apple
Bellows, G. W. Lady Jean
Betts, L. Frances and Judy
Bingham, G. C. Little Red Riding Hood
Bingham, G. C. Sallie Ann Camden
Bradley, J. Emma Homan
Bradley, J. Little girl in lavender
Brewster, J. One shoe off
Brook, A. Belinda standing
Cassatt, M. Child holding a dog
Cassatt, M. Child with red hat
Cassatt, M. Young girl in green bonnet
Cassatt, M. Young girls
Chase, W. M. Dorothy Chase
Chase, W. M. Girl with doll
Chase, W. M. Helen Chase

Chase, W. M. My little daughter Dorothy
Chase, W. M. Sketch of a child (Dorothy Chase)
Copley, J. S. Mary Elizabeth Martin
Copley, J. S. Mary Warner
Copley, J. S. Three princesses
Darling, R. Child in a yellow chair
Dasburg, A. Ramoncita
Davis, G. R. Deborah and Nietzsche
De Peyster manner. Eva and Katherine De Peyster
Durand, J. Mary Beekman
Earl, R. Nathaniel Shaw Woodbridge and his daughter Mary
Earl, R. Stryker sisters
Eichholtz, J. Margaret Adelia Leman
Eichholtz, J. The Ragan sisters
Evergood, P. Girl with sunflowers
Fadden, M. French child on train
Farnsworth, J. The amateur
Field, E. S. Ellen Virtue Field
Field, E. S. Girl holding rattle
Field, E. S. Girl in yellow with a red doll
Glackens, W. J. Artist's daughter in Chinese costume
Hamblin, S. J. (attributed works) Baby with doll
Hesselius, J. Elizabeth Calvert
Hubard, W. J. Elizabeth and Anna Deans
Janicki, H. Weavers of a spell
Johnson, J. Letitia McCurdy
Karfiol, B. Child holding apple
Kühn, J. E. Eleanor Darnall
Lasker, J. Little match girl
Lewin, C. L. Girl with bird
Luks, G. B. The spielers
MacKay. Catherine Brower
Malbone, E. G. Perkins children
Malbone, E. G. Sarah Reeve Ladson
Mason, B. F. Julia, Ann and Harriet Tilden
Mason limner. Alice Mason
Morse, S. F. B. Little Miss Hone
Nura. News and soda pop
Paul, J. Children at play
Peckham, R. Memorial portrait of Mary L. Edgell
Prendergast, M. B. A child
Prendergast, M. B. Evening on a pleasure boat, Boston
Prendergast, M. B. Girl in blue
Prior, W. M. The Burnish sisters
Prior, W. M. Little child with big dog
Prior, W. M. Three sisters of the Coplan family
Prior, W. M. (attributed works) Girl seated on bench
Prior, W. M. (attributed works) Little girl holding apple
Prior, W. M. (manner of) Three children
Rosenthal, D. Girl and bananas
Sargent, J. S. Daughters of Edward D. Boit
Sommer, W. June
Sommer, W. Little girl with apple
Sommer, W. Tess
Stock, J. W. Mary Jane Smith
Stuart, G. Henrietta Elizabeth Frederica Vane
Theus, J. Col Jones' grandchild (Sarah Jones)
Theus, J. Elizabeth Damaris Ravenel and her sister
Theus, J. Little Alice Hayne
Thompson, C. Girl with dove
Toole, J. Jennie Toole
Unidentified artist. Abigail Hall
Unidentified artist. Catalinja Post
Unidentified artist. Charlotte Marsteller
Unidentified artist. Child holding eyeglasses
Unidentified artist. Child in blue dress
Unidentified artist. Child in red dress
Unidentified artist. Child with dog
Unidentified artist. Curls and scallops
Unidentified artist. Eva and Catherina De Peyster
Unidentified artist. Girl by the waterfall
Unidentified artist. Girl in black pinafore
Unidentified artist. Girl in green
Unidentified artist. Girl of the Ten Eyck family
Unidentified artist. Girl on balcony
Unidentified artist. Girl with hoop
Unidentified artist. Henrietta Frances Cuthbert
Unidentified artist. Jean Macdonald Lee Myers
Unidentified artist. Little girl and the cat
Unidentified artist. Little girl of the Schuyler family
Unidentified artist. Little girl with a flower book
Unidentified artist. Little girl with a snowberry
Unidentified artist. Lydia and Tabitha
Unidentified artist. Margaret Gibbs
Unidentified artist. Mary Briggs
Unidentified artist. Picking flowers
Unidentified artist. The Pool sisters
Unidentified artist. Sisters in red
Unidentified artist. Twin sisters
Unidentified artist. Two little girls in blue
Unidentified artist. Walking the puppy
Unidentified artist. Young girl in white
Walton, H. Harriet Elizabeth Boynton
Walton, H. Sarah Louisa Spencer
Watkins, F. C. Fanciful meeting long ago
Watkins, F. C. Prudence
Wetherby, I. A. Mary Eliza Jenkins
Whistler, J. A. M. The Chelsea girl
Whistler, J. A. M. Cicely Alexander
Whistler, J. A. M. Little Rose of Lyme Regis
Wood, G. Susan Angevine Shaffer
Children of Frejus by S. Gechtoff
Children on the porch by G. W. Bellows
Children's mardi gras by A. Ruellan
Children's prison by W. Pachner
Children's theatre by J. Myers
Childs, Mrs Asa. See Childs, Clarissa (Partridge)
Childs, Clarissa (Partridge) fl 1810
Brown, J. (attributed works) Clarissa Partridge Childs
Child's skull by H. Warshaw
Child's toy by D. Richardson
Chilmark by T. H. Benton
Chimborazo by F. E. Church
Chimera by H. Hofmann
Chimney rock by A. J. Miller
Chimneys by B. Wigfall
Chimneys and buildings by A. Osver
China Town no 1 by K. Zerbe

**Chinatown,** Maw Wah by J. Lechay
**Chinese** restaurant by J. Sloan
**Chinese** restaurant by M. Weber
**Chinook** burial grounds by J. M. Stanley
**Chinook** Indian by A. J. Miller
**CHIPMAN,** fl 1840
  Melons and grapes           DN
    DN. Amer primitive ptgs, pt 2
**Chittenden, Russell Henry,** 1856-1943
  Weir, J. F. Russell H. Chittenden
**Choate, Sarah.** See Sears, Sarah Choate
**Chocorua's** curse by T. Cole
The **choice** of Hercules by B. West
**Cholmondeley, Lady**
  Sargent, J. S. Lady Cholmondeley
**Choose** your partner by A. James
**Chop** suey by E. Hopper
**Chouteau's** Point, St Louis, Missouri by
  D. Barbier (attributed works)
**Christ** by H. Pippin
**Christ** and the psalmist by J. La Farge
**Christ** and the woman of Samaria by V.
  Oakley
**Christ** and the woman of Samaria by Un-
  identified artist
**Christ** and the woman taken in adultery by
  M. Beckmann
**Christ** at Emmaus by Unidentified artist
**Christ** before Pilate by D. Aronson
**Christ** before Pilate by J. V. Haidt
**Christ** driving the money changers from the
  Temple by R. Bearden
**Christ** healing the sick, first study by W.
  Allston
**Christ** in Limbo by M. Beckmann
**Christ** in thorns by J. Probst
**Christ** on the road to Emmaus by Unidenti-
  fied artist
**Christ** rejected by B. West
**Christening** by A. De Leon
**Christianbury** crags, Scotland, from the road
  to Langholm by A. Pope
**CHRISTIE, E. A.** fl 1870
  Wyoming valley
    McClintock
**Christie, Gabriel,** 1722-1799
  Earl, R. Gen Gabriel Christie
**Christina's** world by A. N. Wyeth
**Christmas** at the line camp by C. M. Russell
**Christmas** eve by J. C. Atherton
**Christmas** eve by G. Inness
**Christmas** eve by A. M. R. Moses
**Christmas** morning breakfast by H. Pippin
**Christmas** party by Unidentified artist
**Christmas** presents by E. W. Goodwin
**Christmas** tree by E. D. Lewandowski
**CHRISTOPHER, William,** 1924-
  The child
    MBIC. View 1960
**Christy, Samuel Cartmill,** fl 1821
  Harding, C. Samuel Cartmill Christy
**Chrysanthemums** by W. M. Chase
**Chuang** tze by Chi Chen
**Chuck-Will's-widow** by J. J. Audubon

**CHUN, Sungwoo,** 1935-
  Beyond the truth
    IU. Contemp Amer ptg & sculp, 1961
  Hyang-to (Homeland) no 2
    WMAA. Young America 1960
  Spring harvest
    WMAA. Young America 1960
**CHUNG, Kim,** 1930-
  Altar of silence
    IU. Contemp Amer ptg & sculp, 1961
**CHURCH, Frederick Edwin,** 1826-1900
  Between Ceppo Morelli and Ponte Grande
                        NNCo
    MiD. Travelers in Arcadia
  Catskill mountains          MnMW
    Barker. Amer ptg
    NYG. Fine art
  Cayambe                 MB
    MB. Karolik coll
  Chimborazo
    Born
  Cotopaxi, Ecuador           PR
    Born
    NUM. Art across America
    PR. Catalogue
  Finding of Moses           MB
    MB. Karolik coll
  Grand Manan, sunrise off the Maine coast
                         CtHW
    Pierson
  Harp of the winds           MB
    MB. Karolik coll
  Heart of the Andes          MM
    Bazin
    Flexner. Amer ptg
    Flexner. Short history (detail)
  Hooker's party coming to Hartford CtHW
    Baur. Amer ptg
    CtHW. Handbook
    Pierson
  Housetop in Ecuador        NNCo
    Richardson. Ptg in America
  The iceberg
    Larkin
    Larkin rev ed
  Mountains of Ecuador        CtHW
    Pierson
  Niagara Falls             DC
    DC. De gustibus
    Pierson
    Richardson. Ptg in America
    Time. 300 years (col)
  The Parthenon            MM
    Mendelowitz
  Scene in the Catskills        MNS
    Pierson
  Scene on the Magdalene      NAD
    NAD. Amer tradition
  Sunset                NUM
    NYG. Fine art
  Tropical sunset
    Sears. Highlights
  View of Cotopaxi          ICA
    Pierson
**Church** bells ringing, rainy weather night by
  C. E. Burchfield
**Church** street el by C. Sheeler
**Churches**
  Carles, A. B. French village church
  Chambers, T. Old Sleepy Hollow church
  Cole, J. F. California mission
  Crane, S. W. Church at Willow

Crowninshield, F.  Church in Rome
Dreier, D.  New York: the Little church around the corner
Feininger, L.  The church
Feininger, L.  Church in Halle
Feininger, L.  Church of the Minorites, II, 1926
Feininger, L.  Church on the hill
Feininger, L.  Village church (Nieder-Reissen)
Fletcher, A.  Communion service, First Presbyterian church
Fransioli, T. A.  St Andrew's church, Roanoke
Garber, D.  Old church, Carversville
Halpert, S.  Church interior
Hassam, C.  Church at Old Lyme, Connecticut
Harvey, G.  St Thomas church, Broadway, New York
Hicks, E.  Grave of William Penn
Hirsch, S.  Nuremberg
Kingman, D.  Old mission, San Diego
Kramer, P. S.  St Thomas church
Latrobe, B. H.  Roman Catholic church, Baltimore, c 1805
Lee, D. E.  Country wedding
Lutz, D.  Mountain church, San Cristobal
Middleton, T.  Interior of the Second street church, Charleston, South Carolina
Moses, A. M. R.  Going to church
Moses, A. M. R.  Picnic
Moses, A. M. R.  The Whiteside church
O'Keeffe, G.  Ranchos church
Perlin, B.  Santa Maria della Salute
Pippin, H.  Birmingham meetinghouse I, 1940
Prendergast, M. B.  St Mark's, Venice
Prendergast, M. B.  Santa Maria Formosa, Venice
Prendergast, M. B.  West church, Boston
Rosenthal, D.  Mexican church
Santo, P.  A ray of hope
Spencer, N.  Pike county church
Unidentified artist.  Burning of Old South church, Maine
Unidentified artist.  Twenty-two houses and a church
Whitaker, F.  Pro Deo, pro populo
Wyeth, A. N.  Tolling bell
Zerbe, K.  St Philip's, Charleston
Zerbe, K.  Terror
**Churchill, Samuel Bullitt,** fl 1837
Bingham, G. C.  Samuel Bullitt Churchill
The **cicada** by C. E. Burchfield
**CICERO, Carmen L.** 1926-
Abstraction                                    NJN
  WMAA.  Young America 1957
Along the Borgo Pass
  WMAA.  Contemp Amer ptg, 1959/60
Courtship
  DC.  26 biennial ex, 1959
The fall                                       NeL
  CoS.  New accessions USA, 1958
Leonardo
  ICA.  Annual ex, 1961
The mandarin
  WMAA.  Young America 1957
Odradek                                        NNSG
  NNSG.  Handbook
**Cider** making by W. M. Davis
**Cigar** box by K. Knaths

**Cigarette** papers by S. Davis
**CIKOVSKY, Nicolai,** 1894-
Flowers in a garden
  NAD.  Annual ex, 1958
Fruit, vase and mandolin
  Gruskin
Girl in bue
  IU.  Contemp Amer ptg, 1948
Landscape with sunflower
  IU.  Contemp Amer ptg, 1950
Spring melody                                  DC
  DC.  21 biennial ex, 1949
Wisconsin landscape                            ATU
  ATU.  Coll of Amer art
**Cin** Zin by K. Knaths
The **cinch** ring by C. M. Russell
**Cincinnati,** 1835 by J. C. Wild
**Cincinnati** Enquirer by W. M. Harnett
**Cinerarias** and fruit by M. B. Prendergast
**Circa** 1880 by J. A. Oneto
The **circle** by W. T. Murch
**Circle** image by L. Schanker
**Circle** painting, 4 by W. Hedrick
**Circles** in rectangles by L. Schanker
**Circular** forms by P. Strand
**Circus**
  *See also* Clowns and jesters
Avery, M.  The circus
Beal, G. R.  Circus at the Hippodrome
Beal, G. R.  **Circus parade**
Beal, G. R.  **Circus ponies**
Bellows, G. W.  The circus
Bennett, B.  Circus scene
Bergmann, F.  Circus
Blanch, L.  Outdoor circus
Brown, W. H.  Bareback riders
Demuth, C. H.  The circus
Kamihira, B.  Circus performers
Keller, H. G.  Circus folk
Keller, H. G.  First show at two
Kingman, D.  Circus and the lady
Kopman, B.  Circus
Logan, A.  The circus
Marin, J.  Circus forms
Marin, J.  Circus horses
Marin, J.  In the ring
Prendergast, M. B.  Bareback rider
Prendergast, M. B.  Nouveau cirque
Schwartz, L. O.  Circus fantasy
Shinn, E.  Saturday night, Sarasota, Florida
Shinn, E.  Trapeze, Winter garden, New York
Stahl, Ben.  Rehearsal under the big top
Wilt, R.  Circus triptych
**Circus** caravan by M. Beckmann
**Circus** elephants by J. Marin
**Circus** family by A. Revington
**Circus** girl by A. Blanch
**Circus** horses by A. De Knight
**Circus** is coming by C. C. Ward
**Circus** mirror by J. Corbino
**Citta** della torre by R. O. Pozzatti
The **city** by J. Albers
The **city** by X. Gonzales
The **city** by H. Hofmann
The **city** by E. Hopper
The **city** by L. MacIver

The **city** by C. di Marca-Relli
**City** at night by L. Feininger
**City** builders by M. Hoff
**City** child by G. W. Matson
**City** child by T. Yerxa
**City** construction by J. Marin
**City** evening by A. Jones
The **city** from Greenwich village by J. Sloan
**City** interior by C. Sheeler
**City** life by G. Hartigan
**City** man's vacation by W. H. D. Koerner
**City** moon by A. G. Dove
**City** movement, downtown Manhattan by J. Marin
**City** National bank by D. Nichols
The **city**—no 2 by R. Gleitsmann
**City** of dreadful night by B. Shahn
A **city** of fantasy by Unidentified artist
**City** of spires by R. Gleitsmann
**City** people in the country by P. Mangravite
**City Point, Virginia**
  Henry, E. L. City Point, Virginia, headquarters of General Grant
**City** radiance by M. Tobey
**City** scene by J. Gannam
**City**-shape by L. Lozowick
**City** shapes by N. Spencer
**City** still life by A. Rattner
**City** sunlight by E. Hopper
**City** view by R. Breinin
**City** walls by N. Spencer
**City** watchman and his watch box, New York by W. P. Chappel
**Ciudad** de Dos Corazones by R. S. Neuman
**Civic** center, San Francisco by F. J. Rederer
**Civil war, United States.** See Historical themes—United States—Civil war
**Civilization** by W. Gropper
**Civita** Vecchia by R. Smith
**Clam** bay farm by C. Booth
**Clam-diggers** by K. Knaths
**Clam-diggers**, Provincetown by K. Knaths
**Clark, Abraham**, fl 1820
  Unidentified artist. Abraham Clark and his children
**Clark, Agnes**
  Speicher, E. E. Agnes Clark
**CLARK, Eliot Candee**, 1883-
  Tuscany
    NAD. Annual ex, 1958
**Clark, Emily J.**
  Chase, W. M. The opera cloak (Miss Emily J. Clark)
**Clark, Mrs Innes.** See Clark, Lydia (Bowen)
**Clark, Jane**, b 1723
  Smibert, J. (attributed works) Jane Clark
**Clark, Mrs Joseph S.**
  Watkins, F. C. Mrs Joseph S. Clark jr
**Clark, Lucy.** See Croghan, Lucy (Clark)
**Clark, Lydia (Bowen)** 1752-1831?
  Malbone, E. G. Mrs Innes Clark
**Clark, Margo.** See Veres
**Clark, Mary Rebecca**, b 1843
  Heade, M. J. Mary Rebecca Clark

**Clark, Sheldon**, 1785-1840
  Morse, S. F. B. Sheldon Clark
**Clark, William**, 1770-1838
  Catlin, G. Gen William Clark
  Russell, C. M. Lewis and Clark meeting Flathead Indians
  Russell, C. M. Lewis and Clark meeting Mandans
**Clark, William Andrews**, 1839-1928
  Chase, W. M. Senator William A. Clark
**Clarke, Anne (Furneaux)** 1715-1784
  Greenwood, J. Anne Furneaux Clarke
**Clarke, Beulah (Allen)** c 1787-1827
  Ames, E. Mrs William Clarke
**Clarke, John**, 1702-1764
  Greenwood, J. John Clarke
**Clarke, Mrs William.** See Clarke, Beulah (Allen)
**Classic** and romantic art by J .S. Singer
**Classic** landscape by C. Sheeler
**Classic** male by W. De Kooning
**Classic** still life by R. J. Bové
**Classical** nude by M. Cherney
**Classical** still life by B. Greene
**Classical** still life by J. Jarvaise
**Clatter** of crows in spring woods by C. E. Burchfield
**Clay, Henry**, 1777-1852
  Healy, G. P. A. Henry Clay
  Hubard, W. J. Henry Clay
  Inman, H. Henry Clay
  Jarvis, J. W. Henry Clay
  Neagle, J. Henry Clay
  Peale, C. W. Henry Clay
**Clayton's** pasture by S. Laufman
**Clear** cut landscape by M. Avery
**Clearing** by R. Gwathmey
**Clearing** up by G. Inness
**CLEARY, Joseph S.**
  Prior to
    CSFP. Annual ex, 1950/51
**Clematis** henryi by W. C. Palmer
**CLEMENS, Paul Lewis**, 1911-
  Ruth with cat
  Gruskin (col)
**Clemens, Samuel Langhorne**, 1835-1910
  Shinn, E. Mark Twain
**Cleombrotus II, king of Sparta**, 212-240, B.C.
  West, B. Cleombrotus ordered into banishment by Leonidas II, king of Sparta
**Cleophas**, master of the Gilda Gray by M. Hartley
**Clermont**, first chief of the Osages, by G. Catlin
**Cleveland, Arthur**
  Wyeth, A. N. Arthur Cleveland
**Cleveland, Ohio**
  Heine, S. Southwest portion of the public square, Cleveland
**Cliché** by S. Davis
The **cliff** by E. F. Spruce
**Cliff** at Montauk by B. Greene
**Cliff** dwellers by G. W. Bellows
**Cliff** dwellings by R. Jonson
**Cliff** rock, Appledore by C. Hassam
**Cliffs** and the sea by L. Dodd
**Cliffs** at Manayunk by F. Speight

**Cliffs** at Newport, Rhode island by J. F. Kensett

**Cliffs** beyond Abiquiu, dry waterfall by G. O'Keeffe

**Cliffs** of red sandstone near the Rocky mountains by S. Seymour

**Cliffs** of the Green river, Wyoming by T. Moran

**Cliffs** of the Upper Colorado river by T. Moran

**Cliffs**, Soames sound by J. Heliker

**Clinton, Catherine (Jones)** 1783-1855
  Ames, E. Mrs DeWitt Clinton

**Clinton, DeWitt,** 1769-1828
  Ames, E. Dewitt Clinton, 1818
  Catlin, G. DeWitt Clinton
  Jarvis, J. W. De Witt Clinton

**Clinton, Mrs DeWitt.** See Clinton, Catherine (Jones)

**Clinton, Elizabeth.** See Tallmadge, Elizabeth (Clinton)

**Clinton, George,** 1739-1812
  Ames, E. Governor George Clinton

**Clinton, George Washington,** 1778-1818
  Ames, E. George W. Clinton

**Clinton** square, Syracuse, N.Y. by J. M. Culverhouse

**CLOAR, Carroll,** 1913-
  Forbidden thicket      OYB
    OYB. Annual 1956
    OYB. Supplement 1959
  Gibson bayou anthology
    IU. Contemp Amer ptg & sculp, 1957
  Promenade
    PPC. International ex, 1955
  Sun sinking in Tyrzona
    CanO. Hirshhorn coll (col)
  Where will you spend eternity
    IU. Contemp Amer ptg & sculp, 1959
  Wrecked building
    ICA. Annual ex, 1961

**Clock** by P. Guston

**Clock** by J. Haberle

**Clock** by J. D. McClusky

**Clock** by W. T. Murch

**Clock** and bottle by K. Knaths

**Clock** II, 1957 by P. Guston

The **cloister** by A. N. Wyeth

**Cloistered** island by L. O. Schwartz

The **Cloisters** by W. M. Chase

The **Cloisters** by A. N. Wyeth

**CLONNEY, James Goodwyn,** 1812-1867
  Happy moment      MB
    MB. Karolik coll
  Pierson
  In the cornfield      MB
    MB. Karolik coll
  In the woodshed      MB
    MB. Karolik coll
  Interior
    Jones. Rediscovered ptrs
  Politicians in a country bar    NCHA
    Jones. Rediscovered ptrs
  Sleigh ride      MB
    MB. Karolik coll
    Time. 300 years (col)
  Waking up      MB
    MB. Karolik coll
  What a catch!      MB
    Jones. Rediscovered ptrs
    MB. Karolik coll

**Closed** sea, wide world by Y. Tanguy

**Closet** door by J. F. Peto

**Closing** days by Y. Tanguy

**CLOSSON, William Baxter Palmer,** 1848-1929
  Pine tree and snow storm    MB
    MB. Ptgs in water color

**Clothesline** by G. F. Pucci

**Cloud** study by R. Smith

**Clouded** sun by G. Inness

**Cloudy** day, Rhode Island by M. J. Heade

**Clovelly** street, Devon by A. R. Brewster

**Clowns and jesters**
  *See also* Circus
  Bennett, B. Circus scene
  Brackman, R. Unmasked
  Chase, W. M. Jester
  Chase, W. M. The king's jester
  Berlandina, J. Three clowns
  Evergood, P. The jester
  Hensel, H. Clown with rooster
  Kuhn, W. Blue clown
  Kuhn, W. Clown in his dressing room
  Kuhn, W. Young clown
  Kuniyoshi, Y. The clown
  Lockman, D. M. Coco the clown
  Luks, G. B. The clown
  Martin, F. Clown act
  Moller, H. Clown
  Parshall, D. E. Clowns
  Rattner, A. Clowns and kings
  Romano, U. Green clown
  Shahn, B. Clown
  Sloan, J. Old clown making up
  Tchelitchew, P. Blue clown
  Tschacbasov, N. Clown

**Club** night by G. W. Bellows

**Clump** of trees, Study of a by J. F. Cropsey

**Coaching** through New Jersey by M. Klepper

**Coal** carrier by A. G. Dove

**Coal** mine by H. B. McCarter

**Coast** guard station by E. Hopper

**Coast** in winter by W. Homer

**Coast** of Brittany: alone with the tide by J. A. M. Whistler

**Coast** of Cornwall by G. Inness

**Coast** of Crete by R. D. Gauley

The **coast** of fog by R. Tam

**Coast** of Maine by F. J. Waugh

**Coast** of nevermore by L. Feininger

**Coast** of Sardinia by R. D. Gauley

**Coast** scene by J. H. Twachtman

**Coast** scene on the Mediterranean by W. Allston

**Coast** town by M. Frary

**Coastal** landscape by E. H. Betts

**Coastal** scene by J. F. Kensett

**Coastline** by C. S. Price

**Coates, Samuel,** 1748-1830
  Sully, T. Samuel Coates

**Coats, David**
  Gullager, C. Capt David Coats

**COBB, Darius,** 1834-1919
  Mary Abigail Dodge (known as Gail Hamilton)    MSE
    MSE. Cat of ports, 1950

**Cobblers** by M. Jules

**Cobb's** house by E. Hopper

**Coburn, Thomas,** fl 1853
Blythe, D. G. Thomas Coburn

**COCCO, Francesco di,** 1900-
Composition
CSFP. Annual ex, 1946

**Cochran, Charles Burnham,** 1766-1833
Malbone, E. G. Charles B. Cochran
Theus, J. Charles Burnham Cochran

**Cochran, Fanny Travis**
Beaux, C. A little girl—Fanny Travis
Cochran

**Cochran, William,** 1754?-1833
Trumbull, J. Rev William Cochran

The **cock** by Unidentified artist

**Cock** and glove by K. Knaths

**Cock** fight by H. Moller

**Cockatoos**
Chase, W. M. Still life with cockatoo
Chase, W. M. Turkish page

**Cocke, John Hartwell,** 1780-1866
Hubard, W. J. Gen John H. Cocke, of
Bremo

**Cockfight,** Mexico by G. O. Hart

**Coco** the clown by D. M. Lockman

**CODMAN, Charles,** 1800-1842
Bathing pool                          MB
MB. Karolik coll
Encampment and entertainment of the
Boston rifle company by the Portland
rifle company, 1830
U.S. National Capital sesquicentennial
com
The hayfield
Sears. Highlights
View near Portland, Maine
Sears. Highlights
Wounded deer
Sears. Highlights

**Codwise, James,** b 1772
Trumbull, J. Capt James Codwise

**Codwise, Rebecca (Rodgers)** fl 1797
Trumbull, J. Mrs James Codwise

**COE, Elias V.** fl 1837
Mrs Phebe Houston                     DN
DN. Amer primitive ptgs, pt 2

**Coenties** slip by J. Youngerman

**Coeymans, Ariaantje.** See Verplanck,
Ariaantje (Coeymans)

**Coffee** line by J. Sloan

**Coffin, Sir Isaac,** 1759-1852
Stuart, G. Admiral Sir Isaac Coffin

**Coffin, Martha.** See Derby, Martha (Coffin)

**COGGESHALL, Calvert,** 1907-
Landscape
NYG. Fine art
Nightscape
MMA. Abstract

**Cohen, Mendes**
Peale, R. Col Mendes Cohen

**COHOON, Hannah,** fl 1854
Tree of life
Pierson

**COLBURN, Francis Peabody,** 1909-
Lonely places
CSFP. Annual ex, 1946

**Cold** day by D. Macknight

**Cold** day by E. F. Spruce

**Cold** gray day by D. Macknight

**COLDEN, Cadwallader,** 1688-1776
Pratt, M. Cadwallader Colden and Warren
de Lancey

**Colden, Cadwallader David,** 1769-1834
Jarvis, J. W. Cadwallader D. Colden

**Colden family,** c 1780
Unidentified artist. Cadwallader Colden
family

**COLE, Joseph Foxcroft,** 1837-1892
A brook, Montecito, California         MB
MB. Ptgs in water color
California landscape                    MB
MB. Ptgs in water color
California mission                      MB
MB. Ptgs in water color
Mystic lake, Massachusetts             MB
MB. Ptgs in water color

**COLE, Joseph Greenleaf,** 1803-1858
Barnabas Bartol
Frankenstein. Two journeyman ptrs
Clement Storer
Frankenstein. Two journeyman ptrs

### Attributed works
Samuel Mountfort Pitts sr (possibly by
L. E. Cole)                          MiD
MiD. Ports of the Pitts family

**COLE, Thomas,** 1801-1848
American lake scene                    MiD
MiD. Treasures
Angels administering to Christ
CtHW. Thomas Cole
Architect's dream                      OT
CtHW. Thomas Cole
MiD. Travelers in Arcadia
Pierson
Richardson. Ptg in America (col detail)
Catskill mountains                     OCl
OCl. Handbook
Pierson
Time. 300 years (col)
Chocorua's curse
CtHW. Thomas Cole
Consummation                           NNHS
Larkin
Larkin rev ed
Daniel Boone and cabin on Great Osage
lake                                 MAC
CtHW. Thomas Cole
Dead Abel                              NAI
MiD. Travelers in Arcadia
The departure                          DC
DC. Masterpieces
Destruction of empire (Course of empire)
NNHS
Born
Pierson
Roos
Distant view of the Falls of Niagara
CtHW. Thomas Cole
Dream of Arcadia                       NNHS
Cowdrey v2
CtHW. Thomas Cole
Dream of Arcadia                       MoSL
CtHW. Thomas Cole
MoSL. Handbook 1953
Dream of Arcadia                       OT
Myers. Art
Evening in Arcady                      CtHW
CtHW. Thomas Cole
MiD. Travelers in Arcadia

Expulsion from the Garden of Eden   MB
  Barker. Amer ptg
  Larkin rev ed (col)
  MB. Karolik coll
  Mendelowitz
  Pierson
Expulsion from the Garden of Eden   MiD
  CtHW. Thomas Cole
Garden of Eden   MiD
  CtHW. Thomas Cole
Hartford, Connecticut
  CtHW. Thomas Cole
Head waters of Juniata
  CtHW. Thomas Cole
In the Catskills   MM
  Pierson
  Richardson. Ptg in America
Italian landscape   OYB
  CtHW. Thomas Cole
  OYB. Catalogue 1951
Italian scenery
  CtHW. Thomas Cole
John the Baptist in the wilderness   CtHW
  CtHW. Handbook
Landscape
  Chew. 250 years of art
Landscape with tree trunks   RPS
  Born
  Pierson
Last of the Mohicans   CtHW
  Robb. Harper history
Maid of the mist
  Born
Monte Video, summer home of Daniel
  Wadsworth   CtHW
  CtHW. Handbook
  CtHW. Thomas Cole
Mount Aetna from Taormina, Sicily
                    CtNL
  CtHW. Thomas Cole
Mountain ford
  Sears. Highlights
Mountain landscape with waterfall   RPS
  Born
  Pierson
Notch of the White mountains
  CtHW. Thomas Cole
Old mill at sunset   NBM
  CtHW. Thomas Cole
Oxbow of the Connecticut   MM
  Born
  Canaday
  Flexner. Amer ptg
  Flexner. Short history
  Larkin
  Larkin rev ed
  Mendelowitz
  Pierson
  Time. 300 years (col)
Prometheus bound
  NUM. Art across America
The return   DC
  DC. De gustibus
River in the Catskills   MB
  MB. Karolik coll
Roman aqueduct   MM
  MiD. Travelers in Arcadia
The Roman Campagna   CtHW
  MiD. Travelers in Arcadia
Romantic landscape   NoCR
  NoCR. Catalogue
Salvator Rosa sketching banditti
  CtHW. Thomas Cole

Sunny morning on the Hudson river MB
  MB. Karolik coll
Temple of Segesta with the artist sketch-
  ing   MB
  MB. Karolik coll
Titan's goblet   MM
  Baur. Amer ptg
  Bazin
  CtHW. Thomas Cole
The tornado   DC
  CtHW. Thomas Cole
Tree sketch from nature   NNHS
  CtHW. Thomas Cole
View near Conway, New Hampshire
  CtHW. Thomas Cole
View near Tamworth; In the White moun-
  tains   MiD
  CtHW. Thomas Cole
View near Ticonderoga or Mount Defiance
  CtHW. Thomas Cole
View of the White mountains   CtHW
  CtHW. Thomas Cole
Voyage of life: Childhood   NNSL
  CtHW. Thomas Cole
  Pierson
Voyage of life: Manhood   NUM
  Canaday
  Pierson
  Richardson. Ptg in America
Voyage of life: Old age   NUM
  Pierson
Voyage of life: Youth   NNSL
  Canaday
  CtHW. Thomas Cole
Voyage of life: Youth   NUM
  Pierson

### Portrait of the artist
Cummings, T. S. Thomas Cole
**Coleman, Constance.** See Richardson, Con-
  stance (Coleman)
**COLEMAN, Glenn O.** 1887-1932
Angelo's place   MMA
  Pierson
Bus view
  Brown. Amer ptg
Downtown street   WMAA
  Brown. Amer ptg
  Goodrich. Amer art
  McCurdy
  Pierson
Fort Lee ferry   NBM
  Pierson
**COLEMAN, Loring W.**
Rural pattern   OYB
  OYB. Annual 1959
  OYB. Supplement 1959
Shelter of longing
  NAD. Annual ex, 1961
Warmth of memory
  NAD. Annual ex, 1956
**Coleridge, Samuel Taylor,** 1772-1834
  Allston, W. Samuel Taylor Coleridge
**Coles, Hannah.** See Neilson, Hannah (Coles)
**COLESCOTT, Robert H.** 1925-
Barbizon nymph
  OrPA. Ptgs & sculptures
**Colford, Eleanor.** See Jones, Eleanor (Col-
  ford)
**Colima** by C. R. Bentley
The **collect** or fresh water pond by A. Rob-
  ertson (attributed works)

A **collection** of things by R. Koppe

**Collection** X, no 2 by K. Zerbe

**Collector's** cabinet by W. W. Beecher

**College** on the hill by W. Lester

**Colles, Christopher,** 1738-1816
Jarvis, J. W. Christopher Colles

**Colleti, Kathleen**
Speicher, E. E. Kathleen Colleti

**Collins, Edward,** 1704-1753
Pierpont limner. Edward Collins

**Collins, Henry,** fl 1729
Feke, R. Henry Collins (formerly called Gershom Flagg III)
Smibert, J. Henry Collins

**COLLINS, John,** fl 1846
Mauch Chunk
McClintock

**Colman, Benjamin**
Pelham, P. Rev Benjamin Colman

**Colman, Benjamin,** 1673-1747
Smibert, J. Benjamin Colman

**COLMAN, Samuel,** 1832-1920
Covered wagons crossing Medicine Bow creek (Emigrant train fording Medicine Bow creek)
Davidson v 1 (col front)
Rathbone
U.S. National Capital sesquicentennial com
Emigrant train fording Medicine Bow creek. See Covered wagons crossing Medicine Bow creek
Ships of the plains                    NNU
Pierson
Rathbone

**COLOMB, Christophe,** fl 1790
White Hall plantation, Louisiana c 1790
U.S. National Capital sesquicentennial com

**Colonial** cubism by S. Davis

**Color** analogy by M. Hartley

**Color** isolation by J. Ernst

**Color** poem by H. Hofmann

**Color** symphony by A. Walkowitz

**Colorado** river
Moran, T. Chasm of the Colorado

**Colossal** bust at low water mark, used as metre by the aborigines by J. J. Egan

**Colossal** head by L. A. Golub

**Colossal** luck by W. M. Harnett

**Colossal** owls and eagles of the inner eye by M. Graves

**Colosseum** by B. Perlin

**Colosseum** no 2 by W. G. Congdon

**Colts** at Soda Springs by H. Strater

**Columbia** by Unidentified artist

**Columbus, Christopher,** 1446?-1506
Chapman, J. G. Landing of Columbus
Hicks, E. Columbus
Kemmelmeyer, F. First landing of Christopher Columbus

**Columbus** avenue, Boston: rainy day by C. Hassam

**Columbus** avenue, snowy day by G. R. Beal

**Columbus** circle by D. Kingman

**Columbus** circle, New York by M. B. Prendergast

**COLYER, Vincent,** 1825-1888
Fort Arbuckle, Oklahoma territory
Rathbone

**Comanche** feats of horsemanship by G. Catlin

**Comanche** village in Texas by G. Catlin

**Comanche** war party meeting dragoons by G. Catlin

The **comb** by M. Weber

**Combination** concrete no 2 by S. Davis

**Combing** the ridges by W. R. Leigh

**Comedy** by A. Buller

**COMEGYS, George H.** fl 1838
Artist's dream
Cowdrey v 1

**Comer, Sarah.** See Dolbeare, Sarah (Comer)

**Coming** into port by L. J. Liberté

**Coming** of spring by C. E. Burchfield

**Coming** storm by W. Homer

**Coming** storm by G. Inness

**Coming** storm by Unidentified artist

**Coming** to the point by W. S. Mount

**Common** crossbill by J. J. Audubon

**Communion** by R. Gikow

**Communion** service, First Presbyterian church by A. Fletcher

**Company** for supper by D. Nichols

**Competitor** (ship)
Wales, G. C. Clipper ship Competitor

**Composed** from my window by J. Marin

**Composite** harbor scene with volcano by Unidentified artist

**Composition** by K. L. Seligmann

**Composition** around red by C. Sheeler

**Composition,** Cape Split, Maine, 1933 by J. Marin

**Composition**—Farmscape no 3, 1955 by A. Rattner

**Composition,** head and flowers by A. Rattner

**Composition** in an oval by T. Roszak

**Composition** in black and ochre by A. Yunkers

**Composition** in blue by B. Parker

**Composition** in red, yellow and blue by A. Leepa

**Composition** in white by I. R. Pereira

**Composition** in white by T. J. Roszak

**Composition** on green by H. Ferren

**Composition:** the storm by B. Greene

**Composition**—three figures by M. Weber

**Composition,** tree branch by R. Conover

**Composition** with clarinet and tin horn by B. Shahn

**Composition** with fried egg by W. Sanderson

**Composition** with head by A. Gorky

**Composition** with old shoes by A. Rattner

**Composition** with still life by E. W. Dickinson

**Composition** with three figures by A. Rattner

**Composition** with three figures by M. Weber

**Composition** with violet by B. Gonzales

**Compression** by N. Barrett

**CONANT, Lucy Scarborough,** 1867-1921
  Antelao                  MB
    MB. Ptgs in water color
**Concealed** enemy by G. C. Bingham
**Concentrated** pine top by M. Graves
**Conception** by S. MacDonald-Wright
**Conception** synchromy by S. MacDonald-
    Wright
**Concert** singer by T. Eakins
**Concord** by B. Newman
**Concord, Massachusetts**
  Earl, R. View of the town of Concord,
    Massachusetts, c 1775
**Concord, Battle of,** 1775
  Earl, R. Battle of Concord
**Concretion** by G. L. K. Morris
A **condition** of New England by F. D. Dun-
    can
**Condors**
  Audubon, J. J. California condor
**CONDUIT (Contoit), Louis**
  Pointer and quail
    NSP. Sportscapes
**CONE, Marvin,** 1891-
  Habitation
    ICA. Annual ex, 1945/46
  Silent watcher
    IU. Contemp Amer ptg & sculp, 1957
  Three doorways
    ICA. Annual ex, 1951
**Coney Island, New York**
  Bellows, G. W. Beach at Coney Island,
    N.Y.
  Davis, N. Coney Island: summer laby-
    rinth
  Marsh, R. Coney Island
  Marsh, R. Coney Island beach
  Stella, J. Battle of lights, Coney Island
**Confederate** submarine torpedo boat H. L.
    Hunley by C. W. Chapman
**Conference** at night by E. Hopper
**Conference** of great powers by S. Chermayeff
**Conference** of the treaty of peace with Eng-
    land by B. West
**Confidants** by G. Gluckman
The **confidence** by J. Hirsch
**Conflagration** at the museum by M. Siporin
**Conflict** by T. Egri
**CONGDON, William Grosvenor,** 1912-
  Black city
    WMAA. New decade
  Colosseum no 2
    IU. Contemp Amer ptg & sculp, 1953
  Istanbul no 6, 1953
    MnMW. Expressionism 1900-1955
  Notre Dame
    IU. Contemp Amer ptg & sculp, 1957
  Orvieto
    NBuA. Expressionism
  Piazza Navona             NUM
    MiA. Root coll
  Piazza San Marco
    CtY. Yale alumni
    IU. Contemp Amer ptg & sculp, 1959
    WMAA. Contemp Amer ptg, 1953
  Piazza, Venice
    DC. 23 biennial ex, 1952

  St Germaine             WMAA
    McCurdy
    Pierson
    WMAA. New decade
  Taj Mahal no 3
    IU. Contemp Amer ptg & sculp, 1955
  Venice no 1             MoSL
    Faulkner. Art today, 1956
    MoSL. Handbook 1953
    Pousette-Dart. Amer ptg
    WMAA. New decade
  Venice no 2
    PA. Annual ex, 1951
**Conglomeration** by J. Haberle
**Congo** by W. A. Baziotes
**Congregation** by Z. Sepeshy
**Congress** voting independence by R. E. Pine
    and E. Savage
**Conjurer** by J. Kirschenbaum
**Connecticut** clock by K. Knaths
**Connecticut** farm by M. Varga
**Connecticut** farm buildings by C. Sheeler
**Connecticut** field by W. Kienbusch
**Connecticut** river by A. G. Dove
**Connecticut** river valley by T. Chambers
**Connecticut** rocks by R. Cowles
**Connecticut** sea captain by I. Sheffield
**Connecticut** stream by R. Cowles
**Connecticut** woods by H. W. Ranger
**CONNELLY, Brian,** 1926-
  Abstraction             ICA
    ICA. Annual ex, 1951
    Pousette-Dart. Amer ptg
  Rosa gallica             NSyE
    CoS. New accessions USA, 1956
  The spectrum, a painting in four acts
    PPC. International ex, 1952
  Window with flowers
    MnMW. Reality and fantasy
**Connelly, John,** fl 1813
  Sully, T. John Connelly
**Conner's** rock, Cape Eliza, Maine by G. B.
    Luks
**Conover, Rebecca (Crawford)** fl 1842
  Durrie, G. H. Mrs Tunis V. Conover
**CONOVER, Robert,** 1920-
  Composition, 1951
    MnMW. Classic tradition
  Composition, tree branch
    Baur. Nature
  Gray abstraction
    MMA. Abstract
**Conover, Tunis V.** fl 1842
  Durie, G. H. Tunis V. Conover
**Conover, William J.** fl 1842
  Durrie, G. H. William J. Conover as a
    boy
**Conquered** king by N. Barrett
**Conquest** by H. Bloom
The **consolation** of Ariadne by B. Bryson
**Constance** by A. P. Ryder
**Constant** by E. W. Dickinson
**Constellation** by M. Tobey
The **Constitution (frigate)**
  Birch, T. The Constitution and the Guer-
    rière

The **Constitution (frigate)**—*Continued*
Corné, M. F. The Constitution and the Guerrière
Salmon, R. W. The Constitution in Boston harbor
**Construction** by B. Diller
**Construction** by N. Gabo
**Construction** by H. Hofmann
**Construction** by R. B. Motherwell
**Construction** in blue by P. Gaulois
**Construction** no 2 by G. Steele
**Construction:** Shaftsbury, Vermont by J. C. Atherton
**Constructions** by V. I. Cuthbert
**Consuela** by E. E. Speicher
**Consummation** by T. Cole
**Contact** by V. Candell
**Contemplation** by C. M. Russell
**Contemporary** American sculpture by B. Shahn
**Contentment** by L. Eilshemius
**Continence** of Scipio (copy of Poussin) by J. Smibert
**Continuum** number 16 by E. M. Smith
**Contrada** by F. J. Kline
**Convention** by B. Shahn
**Convergence** by J. Pollock
**Converging** disks by G. L. K. Morris
**Conversation** by K. L. Callahan
**Conversation** by J. Floch
**Conversation** by H. Pittman
**Conversation** by H. E. Schnakenberg
**Conversation** by Y. Tanguy
**Conversation** by R. Vickrey
**Conversation** by M. Weber
**Conversation** in studio by M. Avery
**Conversation** piece by V. Candell
**Conversation** piece by W. Williams
**Conversations** by B. Shahn
**Conversing** by signs by A. J. Miller
The **conversion** of St Paul by B. West
**CONWAY, Frederick E.** 1900-
Blue finch
IU. Contemp Amer ptg & sculp, 1955
Dancer
IU. Contemp Amer ptg, 1949
Green bird                                    MoSL
MoSL. Handbook 1953
Mystery
IU. Contemp Amer ptg, 1948
IU. Contemp Amer ptg, 1951
Red object
IU. Contemp Amer ptg & sculp, 1957
Witchery                                        DC
DC. 21 biennial ex, 1949
**Conway,** New Hampshire, View near by T. Cole
**Conway** castle, North Wales by B. West (attributed works)
**Cook, Alvah,** fl 1825
Unidentified artist. Dr Alvah Cook
**COOK, Howard Norton,** 1901-
The bridge no 1                               PPhM
Pousette-Dart. Amer ptg

Magical city
IU. Contemp Amer ptg & sculp, 1957
White structures
IU. Contemp Amer ptg, 1952
**Cook, James W.** fl 1810
Jarvis, J. W. James W. Cook
**Cook, Maud**
Eakins, T. Maud Cook (Young woman in pink dress)
**COOK, Nelson.** fl 1840
Little dandy                                    VtMS
NUM. Art across America
**Cook, Weda.** See Addicks, Weda (Cook)
**Cooke, Elisha**
Pollard limner (attributed works) Elisha Cooke
**Cooke, Sir George,** bart
Copley, J. S. Sir George Cooke, bart
**COOKE, L. M.** fl 1875
Salute to Gen Washington in New York harbor                                       DN
DN. Amer primitive ptgs, pt 1
**Cool** doll in pool by P. Evergood
**Coolidge, Calvin, president U.S.** 1872-1933
Lockman, D. M. President Calvin Coolidge
Salisbury, F. O. Calvin Coolidge
**Coolidge, Cornelius,** fl 1804
Malbone, E. G. Cornelius Coolidge
**Coolidge, Joseph,** 1747-1821
Stuart, G. Joseph Coolidge
**Coon** hunt by Unidentified artist
**COOPER, Colin Campbell,** 1856-1937
Lotus pool, El Encanto, Santa Barbara                                          PR
PR. Catalogue
**Cooper, Elizabeth (Fenimore)** fl 1816
Freeman, Mr. Mrs William Cooper
Unidentified artist. Elizabeth Fenimore Cooper
**COOPER, J.** fl 1714
Allegorical figures                             CtNL
Flexner. First flowers
Eighteenth-century gentleman                    NNHS
Barker. Amer ptg
Gentleman with violin                           NNHS
NNHS. Waldron Phoenix Belknap coll
**Cooper, James Fenimore,** 1789-1851
Jarvis, J. W. James Fenimore Cooper
**COOPER, Mario Ruben,** 1905-
East river dock
NAD. Annual ex, 1954
Peace memorial, Hiroshima                       OYB
OYB. Supplement 1959
**COOPER, Peter,** fl 1720
Southeast prospect of the city of Philadelphia, c 1720                          PPhL
U.S. National Capital sesquicentennial com
**Cooper, Richard Fenimore,** 1776-1813
Ames, E. Richard Fenimore Cooper
**COOPER, W. B.** fl 1840?
Mrs John Cornwall                               KyLS
KyLS. Kentucky port gall
**Cooper, William,** 1754-1809
Stuart, G. William Cooper of Cooperstown
**Cooper, Mrs William.** See Cooper, Elizabeth (Fenimore)
**Cooperstown, New York**
Morse, S. F. B. View from Apple hill, Cooperstown, New York
**Coot** hunter by A. N. Wyeth

**COPE, George,** 1855-1929
  Buffalo Bill's traps
    Frankenstein. After the hunt
  Fisherman's accoutrements    OYB
    OYB. Supplement 1959
  Hunter's equipment
    Chew. 250 years of art
  Professor Hunter Worrell's pipe
    Frankenstein. After the hunt
  Still life, 1902
    Frankenstein. After the hunt
  Still life, 1911
    Frankenstein. After the hunt

**Coplan sisters**
  Prior, W. M. Three sisters of the Coplan
    family

**COPLEY, John Singleton,** 1737-1815
  Ann Tyng    MB
    Flexner. Copley
    Larkin
    Larkin rev ed
    Pierson
  Arrest of Monmouth before James II
        MCH
    Pierson
  The ascension    MB
    Flexner. Copley
  Augustus Brine    MM
    Flexner. Copley
  Benjamin Pickman
    Flexner. Copley
  Boy with squirrel (Henry Pelham)
    Barker. Amer ptg
    Flexner. Copley (col front)
    Flexner. First flowers
    Mendelowitz
    Pierson
    Walker. Ptgs from America
  Brook Watson    InIJ
    InIJ. 105 ptgs
  Brook Watson and the shark. See Watson
    and the shark
  Brother and sisters of Christopher Gore
    (The Gore children)
    Flexner. Copley
    Pierson
  Charles I demanding impeachment of five
    members of House of Commons
        MCH
    Pierson
  Child of the Greenleaf family
    Belknap
  Children of George III
    Walker. Ptgs from America (col)
  Colonels Hugo and Schleppengull  MCH
    Flexner. Copley
  Copley family    DN
    Barker. Amer ptg
    Flexner. Copley
    Larkin
    Larkin rev ed
    Walker. Ptgs from America
  Death of Chatham    ELT
    Flexner. Copley
    Flexner. Light of distant skies
  Death of Major Pierson    ELN
    Flexner. Copley
  Deborah Scollay    MWM
    Flexner. Copley
    MB. New England miniatures
    Pierson

  Elizabeth Allen Stevens    NJMo
    NJMo. Your Montclair art museum
  Elizabeth Pitts    MiD
    MiD. Ports of the Pitts family
  Elizabeth Ross    MB
    Flexner. Copley
  Elkanah Watson    NJP
    Bolton. Ezra Ames
  An engraver, known as Henry Pelham
    Flexner. First flowers
  Epes Sargent    DN
    Flexner. Copley
    Flexner. Copley (detail)
    ICA. From colony to nation
    Pierson
    Walker. Ptgs from America
  Ezekiel Goldthwait    MB
    Pierson
    Richardson. Ptg in America
  Francis Borland
    MB. New England miniatures
  Galatea    MB
    Pierson
  George Green    MB
    MB. New England miniatures
  The Gore children. See Brother and sis-
    ters of Christopher Gore
  Isaac Smith    CtY
    CtY. Portrait index
    Pierson
  Jacob Fowle    DC
    Barker. Amer ptg
    DC. Masterpieces
    U.S. National Capital sesquicentennial
    com
  James Otis
    Flexner. Copley
  James Tilley, New England merchant
    Davidson v 1
  James Warren    MB
    MB. Great Americans
  Jane Browne    DN
    Flexner. First flowers
  Jeremiah Lee    CtHW
    Pierson (detail)
  Jeremiah Lee (Lee coll)
    Upjohn
  John Adams    MCH
    Roos
  John Gray    MiD
    MiD. Treasures
  John Greene    NHMC
    NUM. Art across America
  John Hancock    MB
    Craven. Rainbow book
    Flexner. Short history (col)
    MB. Great Americans
    Roos
  John Montresor (William? Montresor)
        MiD
    MiD. Treasures
    Richardson. Ptg in America
  John Quincy Adams    MB
    MB. Great Americans
    Roos
  John Winthrop    MCH
    Flexner. Copley
  Jonathan Belcher
    Belknap
    NNHS. Waldron Phoenix Belknap coll
  Jonathan Jackson
    MB. New England miniatures

**COPLEY, J. S.**—*Continued*

Jonathan Mountfort    MiD
   MiD. Ports of the Pitts family
Joseph Barrell    MWM
   Pierson
Joseph Mann    MB
   Flexner. First flowers
Joseph Sherburne    MM
   Flexner. First flowers
Joseph Warren    MB
   MB. Great Americans
Joshua Henshaw    CSFP
   CSFP. Handbook
Joshua Winslow
   Belknap
Lady Frances Wentworth    NNPL
   UNESCO. Prior to 1860
   UNESCO. Prior to 1860 3d ed
   UNESCO. Prior to 1860 5th ed
Mars, Venus, and Vulcan
   Flexner. First flowers
Mary and Elizabeth Royall    MB
   Richardson. Ptg in America
Mary Elizabeth Martin    MAP
   Flexner. Light of distant skies
Mary Warner
   Flexner. Copley
   Flexner. First flowers
   MiD. Ptg in America
Mr and Mrs Isaac Winslow    MB
   Flexner. First flowers
   Larkin
   Larkin rev ed
Mr and Mrs Ralph Izard    MB
   Flexner. Copley
Mr and Mrs Thomas Mifflin    PH
   Flexner. Copley
   Flexner. First flowers (col)
   Pierson
   Richardson. Ptg in America (col)
   Robb. Harper history
   Roos
Mrs Benjamin Pickman
   CtY. Yale alumni
   Flexner. Copley
Mrs Daniel Rea and child    OYB
   OYB. Catalogue 1951
Mrs Ezekiel Goldthwait    MB
   Flexner. Copley
   Pierson
Mrs Gawen Brown    CtY
   CtY. Portrait index
Mrs Gawen Brown (pastel, Lockwood
   coll)
   Flexner. First flowers
Mrs George Watson    CtY
   MB. New England miniatures
Mrs Isaac Smith    CtY
   CtY. Portrait index
   Pierson
Mrs James Warren    MB
   MB. Great Americans
Mrs Jerathmael Bowers    MM
   Belknap
   Flexner. First flowers
   Pierson
Mrs Jeremiah Lee    CtHW
   Pierson
Mrs John Amory    MB
   Flexner. First flowers

Mrs John Bacon    NBM
   NYG. Fine art
   UNESCO. Prior to 1860
   UNESCO. Prior to 1860 3d ed
   UNESCO. Prior to 1860 5th ed
Mrs John Greene    OCl
   Belknap
   OCl. Handbook
Mrs John Winthrop    MM
   Flexner. First flowers
Mrs Jonathan Belcher
   Belknap
Mrs Joseph Mann    MB
   Belknap
   Flexner. Copley
   Flexner. First flowers
   NNHS. Waldron Phoenix Belknap coll
Mrs Michael Gill
   Flexner. First flowers
Mrs Nathaniel Appleton    MCH
   Flexner. Copley
   Flexner. First flowers
Mrs Paul Richard
   Flexner. Copley
   Flexner. First flowers
Mrs Roger Morris
   MiD. Coll in progress
   WiMiA. Amer ptg 1760-1960
Mrs Samuel Cary
   Flexner. Copley
   MB. New England miniatures (col)
Mrs Samuel Waldo    CtY
   MB. New England miniatures
Mrs Seymour Fort    CtHW
   Craven. Treasury 1952 ed (col)
   CtHW. Handbook
   Janson. Picture history
   Lee. Art then and **now**
   MoSL. 40 masterpieces
   Pierson
   Robb. Art 1953 ed
   Time. 300 years (col)
Mrs Sylvanus Bourne    MM
   Richardson. Ptg in America
Mrs Thomas Boylston    MCH
   Barker. Amer ptg
   Bazin. History of art
   Gardner 1959 ed
   ICA. From colony to nation
   Janson. Key monuments
   Mendelowitz
   Walker. Ptgs from America
Mrs Thomas Greene
   WiMiA. Amer ptg 1760-1960
Mrs William Whipple
   Belknap
Nathaniel Hurd    OCl
   Barker. Amer ptg
   Larkin rev ed (col detail)
   Myers. Art
   OCl. Handbook
   Pierson
Nathaniel Hurd (miniature)
   Flexner. Copley
Nathaniel Hurd (unfinished)    NR
   Flexner. First flowers
Nathaniel Sparhawk
   Flexner. First flowers
Nicholas Boylston    MB
   Roos
   Time. 300 years (col)

Paul Revere                                    MB
  Flexner. First flowers
  MB. Great Americans
  McKinney
  Pierson
  Time. 300 years (col)
Richard, Earl Howe                             DN
  DN. Mellon coll
Samuel Adams                                   MB
  Flexner. First flowers
  Larkin
  Larkin rev ed
  MB. Great Americans
Samuel Cary
  Flexner. Copley
  MB. New England miniatures (col)
Samuel Fayerweather                            CtY
  CtY. Portrait index
  MB. New England miniatures
Samuel Pitts                                   MiD
  MiD. Ports of the Pitts family
Samuel Verplanck                               MM
  Davidson v 1
Self-portrait (Du Pont coll)
  Flexner. Copley
  Pierson
Self-portrait (Greene coll)
  Craven. Treasury 1952 ed
  Flexner. Copley
  MB. New England miniatures (col)
  Time. 300 years (col)
Self-portrait (Hammond coll)
  Flexner. Copley
Sir George Cooke, bart                         MoKN
  MoKN. Handbook (col)
Sir William Pepperrell and his family
                                               NoCR
  NoCR. Catalogue
Sketch for the Knatchbull family
  Flexner. Copley
Thaddeus Burr                                  MoSL
  MoSL. 50 masterworks
  MoSL. Handbook 1953
Thomas Amory jr
  Flexner. Copley
Thomas Hancock                                 MCH
  Flexner. Copley
Thomas Mifflin and Mrs Mifflin                 PH
  ICA. From colony to nation
Three princesses
  Flexner. Copley
  Flexner. Light of distant skies
Watson and the shark (Brook Watson
  and the shark)                               MB
  Barker. Amer ptg
  Craven. Treasury 1952 ed
  Flexner. Amer ptg
  Flexner. Copley
  Flexner. Light of distant skies
  Flexner. Short history
  Janson. Key monuments
  Janson. Picture history
  Mendelowitz
  MiD. Treasures
  Pierson
  Richardson. Ptg in America
  Roos
  Time. 300 years (col)
William Brattle
  Flexner. Copley
William Welsteed                               CtY
  Flexner. First flowers

Attributed works
Daniel D. Rogers
  MB. New England miniatures (col)
Henry Pelham (?)                               MB
  MB. New England miniatures (col)
Peter Oliver jr
  MB. New England miniatures
Whitehead Hicks                                NNMC
  Belknap

Portrait of the artist
Copley, J. S. Self-portrait
Copley family by J. S. Copley
Copley square by L. G. Paine
Copper kettle by K. Knaths
Copper light by I. R. Pereira
Coppet (Lake Geneva) by W. S. Haseltine
Copyist by C. Locke
Coq d'Or by K. Knaths
Coral necklace by T. Eakins
Corazziere by E. Martinelli
CORBETT, Edward, 1919-
  New Mexico number 34
    IU. Contemp Amer ptg & sculp, 1955
  Newcomb college                             NBuA
    NBuA. Acquisitions 1957-58
  Number 15                                   MMA
    Pierson
  Provincetown II
    ICA. Annual ex, 1959-60
  Provincetown no 6                           NJN
    CoS. New accessions USA, 1960
CORBINO, Jon, 1905-
  Centurion
    MM. Amer ptg today
  A child
    IU. Contemp Amer ptg, 1949
  Circus mirror
    NAD. Annual ex, 1957
    PPC. Ptg in the U.S. 1949
  Crucifixion
    PPC. International ex, 1950
  Equestrian sunrise
    NAD. Annual ex, 1961
  Eve
    IU. Contemp Amer ptg, 1951
  Family
    Gruskin
  Flood refugees                              MM
    MM. 100 Amer ptrs
    Pierson
  Flowers                                     MAP
    Rathbun
  The meeting                                 MoKN
    CoS. New accessions USA, 1946
  Moonlight
    Genauer (col)
  Race track                                  NJMo
    NJMo. Forty years
  Stampeding bulls                            OT
    Pierson
  Summer holiday
    NAD. Annual ex, 1948
  Three horsemen
    IU. Contemp Amer ptg, 1948
Corcoran, William Wilson, 1798-1888
  Healy, G. P. A. William W. Corcoran
Corder, Rose
  Whistler, J. A. M. Rose Corder

**Cordova:** interior of the cathedral by J. S. Sargent
**Coren, Susan.** See Towers, Mrs Susan (Coren)
**Corfu**
  Sargent, J. S. Corfu: cypresses
  Sargent, J. S. Corfu: lights and shadows
  Sargent, J. S. Corfu: the terrace
**Corinth** no 3, 1959 by T. Stamos
**Cormorants**
  Audubon, J. J. European cormorant
**Corn** belt city by E. Hopper
**Corn** dance, New Mexico by J. Marin
**Corn,** dark by G. O'Keeffe
**Corn** field by D. Macknight
**Corn** husking by W. Homer
**Corn** husking by E. Johnson
**Corn** husking at Nantucket by E. Johnson
**CORNÉ, Michele Felice,** 1752-1832
  Bombardment of Tripoli, 1804    RPHS
    Davidson v 1
    ICA. From colony to nation
    U.S. National Capital sesquicentennial com
  Brig Charles of Boston    MB
    MB. Ptgs in water color
  Constitution and the Guerrière    CtNH
    Davidson v 1
  Letter-of-Marque ship Mount Vernon of Salem
    Davidson v 1
  Ship America hand lining on the Grand Bank    MSP
    Davidson v 1
**Cornee, William,** fl 1836
  Peckham, R. William Cornee with flute
**Cornee, Mrs William,** fl 1836
  Peckham, R. Mrs William Cornee with music
**Cornelia** street by J. Sloan
**CORNELL, John V.** fl 1830
  Iron witch    NNHS
    Davidson v 2
  View of the Highlands from Ruggles house, Newburgh, New York  NNHS
    NNHS. Waldron Phoenix Belknap coll
**CORNELL, Joseph,** 1903-
  Pavilion
    Hunter. Mod Amer ptg
**Cornell, Katharine,** 1898-
  Speicher, E. E. Katharine Cornell as Candida, 1926
**Cornell** family, A gentleman of by J. W. Jarvis
**Cornell** farm by E. Hicks
**Corner** café by S. Davis
**Corner** of a pasture by E. Glannon
**Corner** saloon by E. Hopper
**Cornfield** and harvest by G. W. Bellows
**Cornwall, Amelia (Bucklin)** 1825-1891
  Cooper, W. B. Mrs John Cornwall
**Coronation** by J. Levine
**Coronation** of the Virgin by D. Aronson
**Corporation** shed by N. Spencer
**Corpse** of elderly female by H. Bloom
**Corpus** Christi, Santa Fe by J. Sloan
**Corpus** delicti by G. Grosz
**Corridors** by M. B. Prendergast

**Corridors** of time by P. Burlin
**Corroded** implement by D. W. Ellis
**Cortlandt, Mrs Pierre.** See Van Cortlandt, Anne (Stevenson)
**CORTOR, Eldzier,** 1915-
  Affection
    Pearson. Mod renaissance
  Americana
    IU. Contemp Amer ptg, 1948
  The bathers
    ICA. Annual ex, 1945/46
  Room number VI
    IU. Contemp Amer ptg, 1951
    Pearson. Mod renaissance
  Southern souvenir
    Pearson. Mod renaissance
  Two nudes
    Pearson. Mod renaissance
**CORWINE, Aaron Houghton,** 1802-1830
  Samuel Hildreth
    OCiM. Rediscoveries
  Thomas J. Matthews
    OCiM. Rediscoveries
**Coryell's** ferry by J. Pickett
**Cos Cob** by G. O'Keeffe
**Cosmic** synchromy by M. Russell
**COSTIGAN, John Edward,** 1888-
  Springtime    NJMo
    NJMo. Forty years
**Costume** figure with mask by A. Rattner
The **cot** by J. Sloan
**Cotopaxi,** View of by F. E. Church
**Cotopaxi,** Ecuador by F. E. Church
**Cottage,** Cape Cod by E. Hopper
**Cottage** landscape, Hawarden, Wales by M. B. Prendergast
**Cotter, Joanna.** See Somerby, Joanna (Cotter)
The **cotters'** Saturday night by E. G. H. Pinney
**Cotton, Mrs Leslie,** fl 1888
  Chase, W. M. Lady in black (Mrs Leslie Cotton)
**COTTON, William Henry,** 1880-
  Artist's mother
    NAD. Annual ex, 1958
**Cotton** from field to mill by P. Evergood
**Cotton** picker by R. Gwathmey
**Cotton** pickers by W. Homer
**Cotton** picker's home by W. A. Walker
**Cotton** plantation by C. Giroux
**Cottonwoods** on the Missouri by C. Wimar
The **couch** by B. Kamihira
**Cougars**
  Miller, A. J. Shooting a cougar
**Counterpoint** by T. Ochikubo
**Country** dance by M. E. Ferrill
**Country** dance by F. Martin
**Country** dance by W. S. Mount
**Country** fair by H. Sharrer
**Country** fair by J. A. Woodside
**Country** fair in Pennsylvania, 1824 by J. A. Woodside
**Country** flowers by E. Isenberger
**Country** gallants by J. G. Brown
**Country** girl by A. P. Ryder

Country horse show by P. S. Sample
A country house by W. S. Mason
Country in winter by D. Macknight
Country lass by G. Fuller
Country road by W. D. Fausett
Country school by W. Homer
Country wedding by J. L. Krimmel
Country wedding by D. E. Lee
County election by G. C. Bingham
County fair by H. P. Barnett
County fair by W. Peirce
County home by L. Bouché
The couple by G. Grosz
The couple by J. Hirsch
Couple driving by A. Bierstadt
Courbet at Trouville, Harmony in blue and
    silver by J. A. M. Whistler
Course of empire by E. Leutze
Court of death by Rembrandt Peale
The courtesan by S. Post
COURTRIGHT, Robert
    Antiquity                              OCo
    CoS. New accessions USA, 1960
Courtroom scenes
    Bingham, G. C. The puzzled witness
    Blythe, D. G. Courtroom scene
    Blythe, D. G. Trial scene
    Levine, J. Courtroom study
    Matteson, T. H. Justice's court in the
        backwoods
    Pippin, H. Trial of John Brown
    Wighe, A. Rural court scene, 1849
Courtship by C. L. Cicero
Courtyard by E. Berman
Courtyard, Tetuan by J. S. Sargent
COUSE, Eanger Irving, 1866-1936
    Making medicine
    OYB. Catalogue 1951
COUTURIER, Hendrick, fl 1660

Attributed works

    Governor Stuyvesant                   NNHS
    Mendelowitz
The cove by J. W. Boynton
The cove by W. Farndon
The cove by L. Kester
The cove by J. Marin
The cove by M. B. Prendergast
Cove at sunset by E. Isenburger
The covered bridge by A. M. R. Moses
Covered wagons
    Bartlett, G. Ox train
    Bierstadt, A. Nooning on the Platte
    Colman, S. Covered wagons crossing
        Medicine Bow creek
    Colman, S. Ships of the plains
    Eastman, S. Emigrants attacked by the
        Comanches
    Remington, F. Attack on the supply train
    Ranney, W. T. Pioneers
    Russell, C. M. Covered wagons
    Russell, C. M. The jerk line
    Russell, C. M. Wagon boss
    Scott, J. W. A. Old covered wagon
    Unidentified artist. Pennsylvania mill with
        conestoga wagon

COVERT, John, 1882-
    Brass band                             CtY
        Baur. Revolution
        Brown. Amer ptg
        CtY. Soc Anonyme
        Hunter. Mod Amer ptg
        McCurdy
        MMA. Abstract
        Pierson
        Rathbun
    Temptation of St Anthony               CtY
        MMA. Abstract
        Pierson
    Vocalization                           CtY
        Blesh
The covey by T. Hill
CORVILLE, H. E.
    Ye Boston baked beans                  NNHS
        Ford. Pictorial folk art
Cow and bird II by N. D. Daly
Cow and calf by N. Daly
Cow at play by A. G. Dove
Cow I, 1935 by A. G. Dove
Cowboys
    Bartlett, G. Night herd
    Dasburg, A. Portrait of a cowboy
    Dixon, M. Cowboy and packhorse
    Eakins, T. Cowboys in the Bad Lands
    Hurd, P. José Herrera
    Megargee, L. Cowboy and his lady
    Price, C. S. Cowboys at moonlight
    Russell, C. M. At the end of the rope
    Russell, C. M. Cowboy life
    Russell, C. M. Heads or tails
    Russell, C. M. A serious predicament
    Russell, C. M. The strenuous life
    Russell, C. M. Tight dally and loose latigo
Cowgirl by Y. Kuniyoshi
COWLES, Russell, 1887-
    Adam and Eve
        IU. Contemp Amer ptg, 1949
    Bonfire
        VR. Amer ptg, 1954
    Connecticut rocks
        Gruskin
    Connecticut stream
        DC. 22 biennial ex, 1951
    Forest boundary
        Pearson. Mod renaissance
    Parade                                 InTH
        Pearson. Mod renaissance
    Prodigal son
        Pearson. Mod renaissance
Cows. See Cattle
Cow's skull: red, white, and blue by G.
    O'Keeffe
Cow's skull with calico roses by G. O'Keeffe
Cox, David
    Peale, Rembrandt. David Cox
COX, Gardner, 1906-
    Basic
        IU. Contemp Amer ptg, 1950
    Basic no 2
        ICA. Annual ex, 1947-48
    Basic no 12                            MB
        CoS. New accessions USA, 1952
        IU. Contemp Amer ptg, 1951
    Maine study
        MMA. Amer ptg today

**COX, Jan,** 1919-
Maenades, Study for
MBIC. View 1960
**COX, Joe**
Room interior no 1
IU. Contemp Amer ptg, 1948
**COX, John Rogers,** 1915-
Gray and gold       OCl
CSB. Illusion
UNESCO. 1860-1949
UNESCO. 1860-1955
The meadow       OYB
CSFP. Annual ex, 1947/48
OYB. Annual 1956
OYB. Supplement 1959
White cloud
Gruskin (col)
**COX, Kenyon,** 1856-1919
Augustus Saint-Gaudens       MM
MM. 100 Amer ptrs
Pierson
The light of learning
Pierson
**Coxe, Sara (Cox)** fl 1813
Sully, T. Mrs John Redman Coxe
**Coyotes**
Audubon, J. W. Prairie wolf or coyote
Price, C. S. Coyotes
**Cradle** by J. Tworkov
**Cradling** wheat by T. H. Benton
**CRAFFT, R. B.** fl 1836
The merchant       VWR
VWR. Folk art (col)
**CRAFTS, Ebenezer,** fl 1781
Chandler, W. Col Ebenezer and Col Samuel Crafts
**CRAIG, Nancy Ellen,** 1928-
Study in brown
NAD. Annual ex, 1957
**CRAMER, Konrad,** 1888-
Improvisation no 1
Brown. Amer ptg
Improvisation no 2
Pierson
WMAA. Pioneers
**Cranberry** bogs: bright weather by R. W. Gray
**Cranberry** bogs: gray skies by R. W. Gray
**Cranberry** pickers by E. Johnson
**Cranberry** pickers in Nantucket by E. Johnson
**CRANE, Bruce,** 1857-1937
Winter idyl
NYG. Fine art
**Crane, Kent**
Sloan, J. Kent Crane
**Crane, Louisa.** See Meads, Louisa (Crane)
**CRANE, Stanley W.** 1905-
Church at Willow
IU. Contemp Amer ptg, 1950
Handel still life
PPC. Ptg in the U.S. 1949
**Cranes** by A. Osver
**Crap** shooter by J. Binford
**Crary, Albert,** fl 1825
Unidentified artist. Capt Albert Crary
**Crawford, Ann.** See Allen, Ann (Crawford)
**CRAWFORD, John S.** 1838-1876
Gov David Tod       OYB
OYB. Catalogue 1951

**CRAWFORD, Ralston,** 1906-
Aircraft factory (Aircraft plant)    OCiM
CoS. New accessions USA, 1950
WiMiA. Crawford
Boat and grain elevator #2, 1941-42   DP
WiMiA. Crawford
Boat and grain elevators       DP
DP. Catalogue
Boiler synthesis
MnMW. Precisionist view
Bomber
IU. Contemp Amer ptg, 1949
Bomber, 1944
WiMiA. Crawford
Elevated with black and white
WiMiA. Crawford
Fishing boats #2, 1955
WiMiA. Crawford
Fishing boats #3, 1955-56
WiMiA. Crawford
Freight cars, Minneapolis, 1949
WiMiA. Crawford
From the bridge
McCurdy
MMA. Abstract
Rathbun
The glass, 1954
WiMiA. Crawford
Grain elevator from the bridge
WiMiA. Crawford
Grain elevators, Minneapolis     MnMW
WiMiA. Crawford
Havana harbor
CSFP. Annual ex, 1948/49
Havana harbor #3, 1948
WiMiA. Crawford
Maitland bridge no 2
MnU. 40 Amer ptrs
Minneapolis grain elevators
ICA. Annual ex, 1951
MnMW. Classic tradition
Mountain bird maru       OT
CoS. New accessions USA, 1952
Nacelles, 1945
WiMiA. Crawford
Nacelles under construction
CSFP. Annual ex, 1947/48
Net, 1955
WiMiA. Crawford
Nets with blue, 1955-56
WiMiA. Crawford
New Orleans #2
WiMiA. Crawford
New Orleans #4
WiMiA. Crawford
New Orleans #5       NeL
WiMiA. Crawford
New Orleans still life
MnU. 40 Amer ptrs
Red barge #1, 1942
WiMiA. Crawford
S. S. Del Sud, 1954
WiMiA. Crawford
Sails #2, 1955
WiMiA. Crawford
Shaw's propellers no 2, 1960
MnMW. Precisionist view
Test-able       GAtM
GAtM. Holbrook collection
Third avenue el, 1949       MnMW
MnMW. Precisionist view
WiMiA. Crawford

Tour of inspection
  ICA. Annual ex, 1947/48
U.S.S. Pensacola, 1946
  WiMiA. Crawford
Whitestone bridge                              NR
  Larkin
  Larkin rev ed
  Pierson
Crawford, Rebecca. See Conover, Rebecca
  (Crawford)
Crazy Nora by W. E. Winner
Creation by W. Burnet
Creation of Eve by J. Anderson
Creation scene by Unidentified artist
Crécy, Battle of, 1346
  West, B. The battle of Crécy
The creeks: interior by G. Hartigan
Cremorne gardens by J. A. M. Whistler
Crenshaw, Alfred Valentine, fl 1850
  Hubard, W. J. Alfred V. Crenshaw
Creole child by Unidentified artist
Crescendo by A. B. Davies
Crest by J. Tworkov
Cret, Paul Philippe, 1876-1945
  Watkins, F. C. Paul P. Cret
Cribbage players by H. Baer
Cricket chorus in the arbor by C. E. Burch-
  field
CRIMI, Alfred Di Giorgio, 1900-
  Brooklyn bridge
  NAD. Annual ex, 1955
The crimson gown by F. Duveneck
CRISS, Frances, 1901-
  Astor place, 1932                            WMAA
  CSB. Illusion
The critic by J. Tester
Critics: San Giorgio degli Schiavoni, Venice
  by J. L. Smith
Crocky, Davy Emmet. See Kelly, Emmett
Croghan, George, 1791-1849
  Jarvis, J. W. Col George Croghan
Croghan, Lucy (Clark) 1765-1838
  Jarvis, J. W. Mrs William Croghan
Croghan, William, 1752-1822
  Jarvis, J. W. Major William Croghan
Croghan, Mrs William. See Croghan, Lucy
  (Clark)
Crolius, Clarkson, 1773-1843
  Ames, E. Clarkson Crolius
Crooke, Kitty. See Dudley, Kitty (Crooke)
CROOME, William, 1790-1860
  Crystal valley farm, a view of the Hudson
    river at the Overslaugh                    NAI
  Jones. Rediscovered ptrs
CROPSEY, Jasper Francis, 1823-1900
  Clump of trees, Study of                     MB
  MB. Karolik coll
  Eagle cliff, Franconia Notch, New Hamp-
    shire                                      NoCR
  NoCR. Catalogue
  Eagle cliff, New Hampshire                   MB
  MB. Karolik coll
  Pierson
  Hasting-on-the-Hudson, going fishing
  NSP. Sportscapes
  The Isle of Capri
  MiD. Travelers in Arcadia

Italian landscape                              MB
  MB. Karolik coll
Lake of Nemi                                   NAD
  NAD. Amer tradition
Mountain lakes
  NYG. Fine art (col)
Niagara Falls                                  NBM
  Born
Niagara Falls from the foot of Goat island
                                               MB
  MB. Karolik coll
Schatacook mountain, Housatonic valley,
    Connecticut                                MB
  MB. Karolik coll
Starrucca viaduct, Susquehanna valley OT
  Pierson
Upper Hudson
  Sears. Highlights
View of the Kaaterskill house                  MnMI
  Barker. Amer ptg
  Born
  Pierson
White mountains in autumn                      GAtM
  GAtM. Holbrook collection
Winter scene on the Hudson                     CtHW
  CtHW. Handbook
  Jones. Rediscovered ptrs
Woodland stream
  NYG. Fine art
Wyoming valley                                 MM
  McClintock
Youle's shot tower, East river shore
                                               NNHS
  Born
Croquet. See Games and sports—Croquet
Crosby, Warren
  Unidentified artist. Warren Crosby
CROSS, Bernice, 1912-
  Stone angel                                  DP
  DP. Catalogue
CROSS, Henry H. 1837-1918
  Geronimo                                     OkPP
  Time. 300 years (col)
  Red Cloud and Burning Heart                  OkPP
  Time. 300 years (col)
Cross by S. Francis
Cross-section, plant life by C. Seliger
Crossbills
  Audubon, J. J. Common crossbill
Crossing the Divide by A. J. Miller
Crossing the ford by H. G. Keller
Crossing the ford, Platte river, Colorado by
  W. Whittredge
Crossing the Kansas by A. J. Miller
Crossing the North fork of the Platte by
  A. J. Miller
Crossing the pasture by W. Homer
Crossing the river: moonlight by A. J.
  Miller
Crossing the river—trapper trying its depth
  by A. J. Miller
Crotch island derricks by J. De Martini
CROTEAU, Wilfred, 1930-
  Composition no 136, 1960
  MBIC. View 1960
Crouching figure by B. Greene
Crow chief at his toilet by G. Catlin
Crow encampment by A. J. Miller
A crow flew by by A. N. Wyeth

Crow Indian on the lookout by A. J. Miller
Crow Indians by K. Bodmer
Crow scouts in winter by C. M. Russell
A Crow teepee by G. Catlin
Crow warriors bathing in Yellowstone by G. Catlin
Crow woman by G. Catlin
Crowd, polo scene by G. W. Bellows
Crowell, Edward Payson, 1830-1911
    Unidentified artist. Edward P. Crowell
CROWLEY, Harry
    Illuminations
        IU. Contemp Amer ptg, 1952
Crown of thorns by H. Moller
CROWINSHIELD, Frederic, 1845-1918
    Capri cliff                                   MB
        MB. Ptgs in water color
    Church in Rome                                MB
        MB. Ptgs in water color
    From my studio                                MB
        MB. Ptgs in water color
    Mt Etna from Taormina                         MB
        MB. Ptgs in water color
    St Peter's, Rome, from the Palatine           MB
        MB. Ptgs in water color
    Spring blossoms                               MB
        MB. Ptgs in water color
    A street, Perugia                             MB
        MB. Ptgs in water color
    Taormina                                      MB
        MB. Ptgs in water color
Crowninshield's wharf, Salem by G. Ropes
Crows
    Burchfield, C. E. Clatter of crows in spring woods
    Graves, M. Moon and crow in surf
    Heil, C. E. Young crow
    Keller, H. G. Crows in winter
    McFee, H. L. Crow with peaches
Crow's nest by W. Whittredge
Crow's nest from Bull hill, Hudson river by Unidentified artist
Crucifixion by P. Blume
Crucifixion by J. Corbino
Crucifixion by T. Eakins
Crucifixion by J. V. Haidt
Crucifixion by R. Lebrun
Crucifixion by H. Pippin
Crucifixion by L. Schanker
Crucifixion by Unidentified artist
Crucifixion by T. Vincent
Crucifixion by J. Wolfe
Crucifixion, Sketch for by Z. L. Sepeshy
Crucifixion, Study for by T. Eakins
Crucifixion in yellow by A. Rattner
Crucifixion triptych by R. Lebrun
Cruger, Anna, fl 1740
    Unidentified artist. Anna Cruger
Cruger, John, 1677-1744
    Unidentified artist. John Cruger
Cruger, Mrs John Church, fl 1842
    Healy, G. P. Mrs John Church Cruger
Crumbs of comfort by J. F. Peto
Crystal valley farm, a view of the Hudson river at the Overslaugh by W. Croome

CSOKA, Stephen, 1897-
    Sorrow
        NAD. Special ex, 1956
El cuadro de los Abanicos by E. Francés
Cuautla, Mexico by D. Macknight
"Cuba Si" by J. Youngerman
Cuban nude by B. Karfiol
Cuckoos
    Audubon, J. J. Black-billed cuckoo
Cuernavaca by W. D. Fausett
Culpeper, Philippa Frances. See Berkeley, Philippa Frances (Culpeper) lady
CULVER, Charles, 1908-
    Beetle with red markings                     OYB
        OYB. Annual 1957
        OYB. Supplement 1959
CULVERHOUSE, Johann Mongels, fl 1849-1891
    Clinton square, Syracuse, N.Y.
        Jones. Rediscovered ptrs
CULWELL, Ben L. 1918-
    Adrenalin hour
        MMA. Fourteen
    Death by burning
        MMA. Fourteen
    Figment of erotic torture
        MMA. Fourteen
    Me and the battle of Tassafaronga, Guadalcanal
        MMA. Fourteen
    Men fighting and stars in the Solomons
        MMA. Fourteen
    Where sun and rain mate: landscape near Pali, Oahu, Hawaii
        MMA. Fourteen
Cumming, Mrs Alexander. See Goldthwait, Elizabeth
CUMMINGS, Thomas Seir, 1804-1894
    Thomas Cole                                   CtY
        CtY. Portrait index
Cunningham, Mrs Nathaniel. See Cunningham, Sarah (Kilby)
Cunningham, Ruth. See Otis, Ruth (Cunningham)
Cunningham, Sarah (Kilby) 1732-1759
    Greenwood, J. Sarah Kilby
    Smibert, J. Mrs Nathaniel Cunningham
A cup of tea by P. Evergood
Cup of tea by M. Cassatt
Cup of tea by M. Weber
Cupid. See Mythological themes—Cupid
Curfew by R. Rauschenberg
Curfew hour by A. P. Ryder
Curls and scallops by Unidentified artist
CURRAN, Charles Courtney, 1861-1942
    Dewdrops and roses
        NYG. Fine art
Currants by G. Wood
CURRIE, Bruce, 1911-
    Buildings at night                           OYB
        OYB. Annual 1954
        OYB. Supplement
    Girl drying her hair
        IU. Contemp Amer ptg & sculp, 1959
    Girl in yellow skirt                         OYB
        OYB. Annual 1958
        OYB. Supplement 1959

Seated woman
  IU. Contemp Amer ptg & sculp, 1961
Woman watering plant
  NAD. Annual ex, 1960
**CURRIER, Frank,** 1843-1909
  Whistling boy InIJ
  InIJ. 105 ptgs
**Currituck** marshes, North Carolina by F. W.
  Benson
**CURRY, John Steuart,** 1897-1946
  Baptism in Kansas WMAA
    Baur. Revolution
    Canaday
    DC. 25 biennial ex, 1957
    Goodrich. Amer art (col)
    Larkin
    Larkin rev ed
    McCurdy
    Wight. Milestones
  Flying Codonas WMAA
    NYG. Fine art
  Hog killing a rattlesnake
    Craven. Treasury 1952 ed
  Hogs killing a snake ATU
    ATU. Coll of Amer art
  Hogs killing rattlesnakes ICA
    Baur. Revolution
    Pierson
    Time. 300 years (col)
  John Brown MM
    MM. 100 Amer ptrs
  Line storm
    Craven. Treasury 1952 ed (col)
  The Mississippi MoSL
    Gruskin (col)
  The passing leap
    IaDa. Wood
  Sanctuary OYB
    OYB. Catalogue 1951
  The tornado MiM
    DC. De gustibus
    Pierson
    Roos
    WMAA. Juliana Force
  Wisconsin landscape MM
    Craven. Rainbow book
    Time. 300 years (col)
**Curse** of gold by Unidentified artist
**Curtain** call by E. Shinn
**Curtis, Ariana (Wormeley)** fl 1882
  Sargent, J. S. Mrs Daniel Sargent Curtis
**Curtis, Ellen Amory (Anderson)** fl 1903
  Sargent, J. S. Mrs Charles Pelham Curtis
**Curtis, Mrs Daniel Sargent.** See Curtis,
  Ariana (Wormeley)
**Curtis, Ralph Wormeley,** 1854-1922
  Sargent, J. S. Ralph Curtis on the beach
    at Scheveningen, Holland
**Curved** composition in yellow, red and blue
  by A. Leepa
**Curwen, Joseph,** 1778-1848
  Malbone, E. G. Joseph Curwen
**Curwen, Mrs Joseph.** See Curwen, Selina
  Fenwick (Gadsden)
**Curwen, Samuel,** 1715-1802
  Blyth, B. Samuel Curwen
**Curwen, Selina Fenwick (Gadsden)** d 1819
  Malbone, E. G. Mrs Joseph Curwen
**Curwin, George,** 1610-1685
  Unidentified artist. Capt George Curwin

**Cushing, Alice,** fl 1878
  Emery, E. Alice Cushing in the west par-
    lor of Peter Cushing house, Hingham,
    Massachusetts
**Cushing, Frank Hamilton,** 1857-1900
  Eakins, T. Frank Hamilton Cushing
**Cushing, Mrs Frank Hamilton**
  Eakins, T. Mrs Frank Hamilton Cushing
**Cushing, Margaret Eleanor (Norwood)**
  fl 1815
  Ames, E. Mrs Thomas Humphrey Cush-
    ing
**Cushing, Mary Louise.** See Boit, Mary
  Louise (Cushing)
**Cushing, Thomas,** 1696-1746
  Badger, J. Thomas Cushing
**Cushing, Thomas Humphrey,** 1755-1822
  Ames, E. Thomas Humphrey Cushing
**Cushing, Mrs Thomas Humphrey.** See Cush-
  ing, Margaret Eleanor (Norwood)
**Cushing** house. Child in sitting room of by
  E. Emery
**Custance, John,** fl 1778
  West, B. Mr and Mrs John Custance
**Custance, Mrs John,** fl 1778
  West, B. Mr and Mrs John Custance
**Custer's** last fight by C. Adams
**Custer's** last stand by T. H. Benton
**Custer's** last stand by C. M. Russell
**Custis, Eleanor Parke,** 1779-1852
  Trumbull, J. Eleanor Parke Custis, 1792
**Custis, Frances Parke,** b 1709
  Unidentified artist. Frances Parke Custis
**Custis, Tabitha Scarborough.** See Arbuckle,
  Tabitha Scarborough (Custis)
**Custom** house, Santiago de Cuba by W.
  Homer
**Cut-out** by J. Pollock
**Cuthbert, Henrietta Frances,** 1813-1889
  Unidentified artist. Henrietta Frances
    Cuthbert
**Cuthbert, James Alexander Ross,** 1767-1849
  Malbone, E. G. James Alexander Ross
    Cuthbert
**CUTHBERT, Virginia Isobel,** 1908-
  Alex Fletcher PW
    Chew. 250 years of art
  Environs of Chicago
    DC. 22 biennial ex, 1951
  Factory no 1, 1953
    VR. Amer ptg, 1954
  Office building NBuA
    NBuA. Contemporary ptgs
  Our classic heritage
    CSFP. Annual ex, 1950-51
  Talpa graveyard
    IU. Contemp Amer ptg, 1950
**Cutt, Catherine.** See Moffatt, Catherine
  (Cutt)
**Cut-Taa-Tas-Tia,** a Fox chief by J. O. Lewis
**Cutts, Rose Adèle.** See Williams, Rose
  Adèle (Cutts) Douglas
**Cuyler, Anna (Wendell),** fl 1780
  Unidentified artist. Anna Wendell Cuyler
**Cuyler, Catalina (Schuyler)** 1705-1759
  Unidentified artist. Catalina Schuyler
**Cuyler, Mrs Cornelius,** 1705-1759. See Cuy-
  ler, Catalina (Schuyler)
**Cuyler, Mrs Cornelius,** fl 1780. See Cuyler,
  Anna (Wendell)

Cybernetics by B. Shahn
Cycladic light by D. Lund
The cycle by M. Tobey
The cyclists by L. Feininger
Cylinder and orange by W. T. Murch
Cypresses by J. S. Sargent
Cyrus liberating the family of Astyges by
  B. West

# D

DABO, Leon, 1868-1960
  Rhythms                              InTH
    InTH. Catalogue
Dachau chamber, Study for by R. Lebrun
Dad's coming by W. Homer
Daggett, Miss, c 1785
  Unidentified artist. Miss Daggett
Daggett, David, 1764-1851
  Tenney, U. D. David Daggett
Daggett, Mrs Henry
  Bellows, G. W. Aunt Fanny
Dague, Paul B.
  Pippin, H. Paul B. Dague, deputy sheriff
    Chester county
Daily news by Y. Kuniyoshi
Daisies by C. H. Demuth
Daisies by G. B. Klitgaard
Daisies by M. Graves
Dakota encampment by S. Eastman
A Dakota village by S. Eastman
Dale, Chester, 1883-1962
  Bellows, G. W. Chester Dale
Dale, Maud (Murray)
  Bellows, G. W. Mrs Chester Dale
A Dallas night by G. Grosz
Dally, Christiana. See De Peyster, Chris-
    tiana (Dally)
DALY, Norman David, 1911-
  Cow and bird II
    IU. Contemp Amer ptg, 1950
  Cow and calf
    IU. Contemp Amer ptg & sculp, 1953
Dalzell children, fl 1845
  Unidentified artist. Mary and David Dal-
    zell of South Egremont, Massachu-
    setts
Damaged man by L. A. Golub
Dame à l'absence by Y. Tanguy
Der dampfer Odin by L. Feininger
Danaïdes by J. S. Sargent
The dance by J. Hirsch
The dance by S. Rosenberg
Dance hall by B. Perlin
Dance marathon by P. Evergood
Dance of the haymakers by W. S. Mount
Dance of the San Domingo Indians by J.
    Marin
Dance rhythm by E. Geller
Dancer by F. E. Conway
Dancer by G. Dante
Dancer by M. Soyer

Dancer dressing by F. Martin
Dancer in white by E. Shinn
Dancer with tambourine by M. Beckmann
Dancers by A. B. Davies
Dancers by the clock by M. Siporin
Dancers resting by M. Greenwood
Dancing dryads by A. P. Ryder
Dancing nuns by H. V. Olson
Dancing tree by A. G. Dove
Dandelion seed balls and trees by C. E.
    Burchfield
The dandy by Unidentified artist
Dangerous territory by C. M. Russell
DANIEL, Lewis C. 1901-1952
  Prayer makers
    IU. Contemp Amer ptg, 1950
Daniel Drew (steamboat)
  Bard, J. Hudson river steamboat Daniel
    Drew
Daniel in the lion's den by M. Hirshfield
DANIELL, George
  Oregon rocks
    PA. Annual ex, 1947
Daniell, Sarah Proctor. See Wilson, Sarah
    Proctor (Daniell)
Daniels, Josephus, 1862-1948
  Lockman, D. M. Josephus Daniels
Danny by A. James
DANTE, Giglio, 1916-
  The dancer                          MSM
    CoS. New accessions USA, 1946
DANTON, F. fl 1894
  Time is money                       CtHW
  Frankenstein. After the hunt
Danvers river, Massachusetts by F. W. Ben-
    son
Danville by G. E. Doudera
Daphne by J. De Feo
Daphne by J. McLarty
Daphne by J. S. Sargent
DAPHNIS, Nassos, 1914-
  Forward but beyond
    PPC. International ex, 1955
  3-61-MT
    NBuA. Acquisitions 1959-1961
Dappled with damson by O. E. L. Graves
Darby, Mrs John, fl 1852
  Bingham, G. C. Mrs John Darby
Darby, Pennsylvania, after the burning of
    Lord's mill by J. D. Bunting
D'ARISTA, Robert, 1929-
  The chair
    NNSG. Younger Amer ptrs
  Kitchen table                       OT
    CoS. New accessions USA, 1956
  Still life with coffee pot
    IU. Contemp Amer ptg & sculp, 1955
  Table with bottles and cheese
    PPC. International ex, 1955
Dark by J. Albers
Dark and light by F. Hillsmith
Dark anonymity by J. G. Haley
Dark figure by F. Castellón
Dark forest by M. Avery
Dark green painting by A. Gorky
Dark harbor by L. J. Liberté

Dark hills and white horses by E. J. Kosa
Dark in the forest by J. Kirschenbaum
Dark mountain by M. Hartley
Dark muse by E. Pearson
Dark night by A. A. Dehn
Dark pond by W. De Kooning
Dark rain by A. Rattner
Dark red leaves on white by G. O'Keeffe
Dark river by E. Magafan
Dark sky—dark water by J. Lechay
Dark stretch by H. Weber
Dark trees and sunny meadow by K. Schrag
Dark wave by R. Tam
Darkly, soft darts by A. Okamura
Darkness and light by B. Greene
**DARLEY, Felix Octavius Carr,** 1822-1888
   Emigrants crossing the plains
     McCracken. Portrait of the old west
     (col)
   Hunting buffaloes
     McCracken. Portrait of the old west
**Darley, Francis Thomas Sully**
   Sully, T. Mother and child (Mrs William
     H. W. Darley and Francis Thomas
     Sully Darley)
**Darley, Jane Cooper (Sully)** 1807-1877
   Sully, T. Mother and child (Mrs William
     H. W. Darley and Francis Thomas
     Sully Darley)
**DARLING, Robert,** fl 1835
   Child in a yellow chair      NCHA
     Jones. New-found folk art
**Darnall, Eleanor,** 1704-1796
   Kühn, J. E. Eleanor Darnall
**Darnall, Henry,** 1702-1788?
   Kuhn, J. E. Henry Darnall III
**Darrah, Mrs Robert K.** See Darrah, Sophia
   Towne
**DARRAH, Sophia Towne,** 1830?-1881
   Seascape      MB
     MB. Ptgs in water color
**DASBURG, Andrew,** 1887-
   Apples      WMAA
     Bywaters. Andrew Dasburg
     Pierson
   Autumn desert
     Bywaters. Andrew Dasburg (col)
   Autumn fruit
     Bywaters. Andrew Dasburg
     Pierson
   Autumn—Ranchos de Taos
     Bywaters. Andrew Dasburg
   Avocados
     Bywaters. Andrew Dasburg
   Chantet lane      CoD
     Bywaters. Andrew Dasburg (col)
   Ducks      MM
     Bywaters. Andrew Dasburg
   Fields of Llano      TxD
     Bywaters. Andrew Dasburg
   Gothic
     Bywaters. Andrew Dasburg
   Improvisation to form
     Brown. Amer ptg
     McCurdy
   Jo Bakos
     Bywaters. Andrew Dasburg

Judson Smith      TxD
   Bywaters. Andrew Dasburg
Landscape
   Larkin
   Larkin rev ed
   WMAA. Pioneers
Llano Quemado
   Bywaters. Andrew Dasburg
New Mexican landscape
   Bywaters. Andrew Dasburg
New Mexican village      NMS
   Bywaters. Andrew Dasburg
November, New Mexico      TxD
   Bywaters. Andrew Dasburg
Portrait of a cowboy
   Bywaters. Andrew Dasburg
Portrait of Ida
   Bywaters. Andrew Dasburg
Ramoncita      OCiM
   Bywaters. Andrew Dasburg
Road into Ranchos de Taos
   Bywaters. Andrew Dasburg
Road to Lamy      MM
   Bywaters. Andrew Dasburg
Sermon on the Mount
   Brown. Amer ptg
Still life, 1918
   Brown. Amer ptg
   Bywaters. Andrew Dasburg
Still life, 1924
   Bywaters. Andrew Dasburg
Talpa
   Bywaters. Andrew Dasburg
Taos plaza
   Bywaters. Andrew Dasburg
Tulips (1)
   Bywaters. Andrew Dasburg
Tulips (2)      CLA
   Bywaters. Andrew Dasburg
White morning
   Bywaters. Andrew Dasburg
**DAUGHERTY, James Henry,** 1889-
Mural decoration      CtY
   CtY. Soc Anonyme
**Daughter** of the mines by G. B. Luks
**Daughters** of revolution by G. Wood
**Dauntless** bird by M. Weber
**Davenport, John,** 1597-1669?
   Foster, J. (attributed works) John Daven-
     port
**Davenport, Iowa**
   Wild, J. C. View of Davenport, Iowa and
     the Mississippi
**DAVEY, Randall,** 1887-
   Girl in a hunting cap
     NAD. Annual ex, 1951
   Harness horse stables—Cape Girardeau
     PPC. Ptg in the U.S. 1949
   Jockey in red silk
     NAD. Annual ex, 1961
**David, Jean Terford,** 1792-1839
   Sully, T. Capt Jean T. David
**David, Mrs Jean Terford.** See David, Mary
   (Sicard)
**David, Mary (Sicard)** fl 1813
   Sully, T. Mary Sicard David
**David** playing before Saul by W. Allston
**David** playing to King Saul by P. Evergood
**David** the king by M. Schwartz

DAVIES, Arthur Bowen, 1862-1928
Across the harbor                    InIJ
  InIJ. 105 ptgs
Adventure                            MM
  Brown. Amer ptg
Along the Erie canal                 DP
  Born
  DP. Catalogue
  Richardson. Ptg in America
The Apennines                        NUM
  NUM. Art across America
Arethusa                             OYB
  OYB. Catalogue 1951
At the chestnut root                 NSyE
  NSyE. The eight
Crescendo                            WMAA
  Baur. Revolution
  Goodrich. Amer art
  Larkin (detail)
  Larkin rev ed (detail)
  NBuA. Fifty ptgs
Dancers                              MiD
  Brown. Amer ptg
  Pierson
Day of good fortune
  WMAA. Museum and its friends, 1958
The dream                            MM
  Mendelowitz
  Pierson
Evensong                             DNC
  DNC. Gellatly coll, 1954
Every Saturday                       NBM
  McCurdy
Facade
  Cheney. Primer 1958 ed
The flood                            DP
  DP. Catalogue
  Pierson
Inland tempest                       NUM
  NUM. Root bequest
Interior                             MnMI
  Cheney. Expressionism 1948 ed
Italian landscape, the Apennines
  NYG. Fine art
Maya, mirror of illusions            ICA
  Roos
Mother of dawn                       ATeS
  ATeS. Collection
Passing of dreams                    MB
  MB. Ptgs in water color
Springtime of delight                DP
  Born
  DP. Catalogue
Twilight travelling
  Lewisohn
Unicorns                             MM
  Cheney. Story 1958 ed
  MM. 100 Amer ptrs
  Pierson
DAVIES, Kenneth, 1925-
The blackboard
  Frankenstein. After the hunt
  IU. Contemp Amer ptg, 1952
The bookcase                         CtHW
  CoS. New accessions USA, 1952
Pocusmania                           MSM
  CoS. New accessions USA, 1952
  IU. Contemp Amer ptg, 1951 (col)
  MSM. Handbook (col)
The sword                            MiD
  MiD. Treasures

DAVIES, Thomas, 1737?-1812
View of Green Bush on the Hudson's river
  near Albany                     MiD
  Jones. Rediscovered ptrs
Davis, Charles, 1772-1821
  Stuart, G. Charles Davis
Davis, Mrs Charles. See Davis, Eliza (Bus-
  sey)
DAVIS, Charles Harold, 1856-1933
Call of the west wind                OYB
  OYB. Catalogue 1951
Northwest wind                       ICA
  NYG. Fine art
DAVIS, Eben Parsons, 1818-1902
Eben Davis' horse                    VWR
  VWR. Folk art (col)
Mr and Mrs Eben P. Davis             VWR
  VWR. Folk art (col)
Davis, Mrs Eben Parsons. See Davis, Rhoda
  Ann (Thatcher)
Davis, Mrs Edward Livingston. See Davis,
  Maria Louisa (Robbins)
Davis, Edwin, fl 1838
  Bascom, R. H. M. Edwin Davis
Davis, Eliza (Bussey) 1783-1825
  Stuart, G. Mrs Charles Davis
DAVIS, Gladys Rockmore, 1901-
Deborah and Nietzsche
  Gruskin (col)
  NYG. Fine art
End of summer                        OT
  OT. Contemp Amer ptgs
Pink tights                          IaDa
  IaDa. 30th anniversary
Sea sounds
  NAD. Annual ex, autumn 1949
Study                                ATU
  ATU. Coll of Amer art
Study of an old woman
  PA. Annual ex, 1952
Les sylphides
  Gruskin (col)
Davis, Isaac P. 1771-1855
  Malbone, E. G. Isaac P. Davis
DAVIS, Jerrold, 1926-
Figure before a field
  PPC. International ex, 1958
Painting of the ocean no 8
  IU. Contemp Amer ptg & sculp, 1961
Standing figure
  IU. Contemp Amer ptg & sculp, 1959
DAVIS, Joseph Hilliard, fl 1820-1837
Bartholomew Van Dame
  Lipman. Primitive ptrs
Esther Tuttle                        NNHS
  Lipman. Primitive ptrs
Henry Laurens Roberts
  Lipman. Primitive ptrs
James and Sarah Tuttle               NNHS
  Ford. Pictorial folk art
  Mendelowitz
  Pierson
Joseph and Sarah Ann Emery
  Lipman. Primitive ptrs
Levi B. Tasker                       MSt
  Little. Country art
A man and a lady
  Ford. Pictorial folk art
Separate tables                      NCHA
  Jones. New-found folk art

Tilton family                                VWR
  Flexner. Light of distant skies
  VWR. Folk art (col)
York family                                  MMA
  Baur. Amer ptg
            **Attributed works**
Frugal housewife                             VWR
  VWR. Folk art (col)
Hannah Goodwin Whitehouse Moulton
                                             MeC
  Jetté. Amer heritage collection
James Roberts Moulton                        MeC
  Jetté. Amer heritage collection
Mrs Tuttle
  Ford. Pictorial folk art
**DAVIS, Lew E.** 1910-
  Market                                     ATeS
  ATeS. Collection
**Davis, Livingston,** fl 1890
  Sargent, J. S. Mrs Edward Livingston
    Davis and her son Livingston Davis
**Davis, Maria Louisa (Robbins)** fl 1890
  Sargent, J. S. Mrs Edward Livingston
    Davis and her son Livingston
**DAVIS, Noel**
  Coney Island: summer labyrinth
  OYB. Annual 1959
**Davis, Rhoda Ann (Thatcher)** 1819-1877
  Davis, E. P. Mr and Mrs Eben P. Davis
**DAVIS, Stuart,** 1894-1964
  Adit no 2, 1928
    Goossen. Stuart Davis
  Alleé
    MnMW. Stuart Davis (col)
  ANA                                        MiC
    NUM. Art across America
  Apples and jug                             MLL
    Goossen. Stuart Davis
  Arboretum by flashbulb
    Blesh. Stuart Davis
    Cheney. Primer 1958 ed
    Goossen. Stuart Davis
  Arch hotel                                 NeL
    Barker. From realism
    CoS. New accessions USA, 1948
  Bass Rocks no 1                            KW
    Goossen. Stuart Davis (col)
    Pierson
  Bass Rocks no 2                            KW
    MnMW. Stuart Davis
  Barber shop
    MnMW. Contemporary
    WMAA. Neuberger collection
  Bridge at Courbevoie
    Goossen. Stuart Davis
  Bull Durham
    WMAA. Pioneers
  Café, Place des Vosges
    Goossen. Stuart Davis
    MnMW. Stuart Davis
  Cape Ann landscape
    Larkin
    Larkin rev ed
  Cigarette papers, 1921
    Goossen. Stuart Davis
  Cigarette papers, 1933 (Cahill coll)
    Goossen. Stuart Davis
  Cliché                                     NNSG
    Goossen. Stuart Davis
    NNSG. Handbook
    Read. Concise history

Cliché, Detail study for
  MnMW. Stuart Davis
Colonial cubism                              MnMW
  Goossen. Stuart Davis (col)
  PA. Annual ex, 1956
  Rosenblum (col)
  WMAA. Annual ex, 1955
Combination concrete, 1957
  Blesh. Stuart Davis (col)
Combination concrete no 2, 1958
  Goossen. Stuart Davis (col)
  WMAA. Museum and its friends, 1959
Corner café                                  DP
  DP. Catalogue
Deuce                                        CSFM
  Blesh. Stuart Davis
  Goossen. Stuart Davis
  IU. Contemp Amer ptg & sculp, 1955
  MnMW. Stuart Davis
Eggbeater no 1, 1927                         DP
  Blesh. Stuart Davis
  Brown. Amer ptg
  Pierson
Eggbeater no 2, 1927                         WMAA
  Blesh. Stuart Davis (col)
  Goodrich. Amer art
  MnMW. Stuart Davis
Eggbeater no 3, 1927                         MLL
  Blesh. Stuart Davis
  Goossen. Stuart Davis
  Time. 300 years (col)
Eggbeater no 4, 1927
  Blesh. Stuart Davis
Eggbeater no 5, 1930                         MMA
  CoS. New accessions USA, 1946
  Goossen. Stuart Davis
  MMA. Ptg and sculpture
Eye level                                    MLL
  Goossen. Stuart Davis
  MnMW. Stuart Davis
Famous firsts                                NBM
  Goossen. Stuart Davis
Feasible no 2, 1952                          MoSL
  Goossen. Stuart Davis
  MnMW. Stuart Davis
Flying carpet                                MMA
  Biddle. Yes and no
  MnMW. Stuart Davis
For internal use only
  Genauer (col)
  Goossen. Stuart Davis (col)
  MMA. Abstract (col)
  MnMW. Stuart Davis
Garage lights                                NR
  Blesh. Stuart Davis
  Richardson. Ptg in America
Gloucester street                            MLL
  Blesh. Stuart Davis
  Goossen. Stuart Davis
Gloucester sunset
  MnMW. Stuart Davis
Havana plaza
  Goossen. Stuart Davis
History of communication
  Blesh. Stuart Davis
Hot stillscape
  Munsterberg
Hot stillscape for six colors
  Cheney. Story 1958 ed
  DC. Halpert collection
  Goossen. Stuart Davis (col)

**DAVIS, Stuart—**_Continued_
Hotel de France
  Blesh. Stuart Davis
House and street        WMAA
  Blesh. Stuart Davis
  Brown. Amer ptg
  Goossen. Stuart Davis
  Lee. Art then and now
  MnMW. Stuart Davis
House, tree shapes
  Blesh. Stuart Davis
Industry             ATU
  ATU. Coll of Amer art
Interior
  Goossen. Stuart Davis
Iris                MM
  MM. 100 Amer ptrs
Itlksez           MLL
  Goossen. Stuart Davis
Landscape
  Goossen. Stuart Davis
Landscape with drying **sails**
  Blesh. Stuart Davis
Lawn and sky
  Blesh. Stuart Davis
Leroy's shift
  MnMW. Stuart Davis
Lesson I, 1956
  Goossen. Stuart Davis
  PPC. International ex, 1958
Little giant still life    VR
  CoS. New accessions USA, 1950
  Goossen. Stuart Davis
  MnMW. Classic tradition
  MnMW. Stuart Davis
  MnU. 40 Amer ptrs
Lobby wall
  DC. 27 biennial ex, 1961
Lucky strike        MMA
  Baur. New art
  Blesh. Stuart Davis
  Goossen. Stuart Davis (col)
  McCurdy
  MMA. Abstract
  Pierson
A man            MLL
  Goossen. Stuart Davis
Matches no 2, 1927
  Blesh. Stuart Davis
Max no 1, 1949
  MnMW. Stuart Davis
Max no 2, 1949
  Goossen. Stuart Davis
Medium still life
  Blesh. Stuart Davis
  Goossen. Stuart Davis
  MnMW. Stuart Davis
Mellow pad
  Blesh. Stuart Davis (col)
  Goossen. Stuart Davis
  MnMW. Stuart Davis
Memo           WMAA
  MnMW. Stuart Davis (col)
  WMAA. Sara Roby
Men without women
  Blesh. Stuart Davis
Midi             CtHW
  CtHW. Handbook
  Goossen. Stuart Davis
  ICA. Annual ex, 1954
  MnMW. Stuart Davis

Multiple views
  Blesh. Stuart Davis
  Goossen. Stuart Davis
Mural, Drake university
  Pierson
Music hall
  Blesh. Stuart Davis
Myopic vista       MLL
  Goossen. Stuart Davis
New Mexican landscape  WMAA
  Goossen. Stuart Davis
New York mural
  MnMW. Stuart Davis
New York, 1932
  MnU. 40 Amer ptrs
New York-Paris no 1, 1931  IaIU
  Blesh. Stuart Davis
  Goossen. Stuart Davis
New York-Paris no 2, 1931  OrPA
  MnMW. Stuart Davis
New York-Paris no 3, 1931
  Blesh. Stuart Davis
  Goossen. Stuart Davis
New York under gaslight
  Flexner. Amer ptg
  Flexner. Short history
  Goossen. Stuart Davis
New York waterfront    NBuA
  Bazin
  NBuA. Contemporary ptgs
Nu
  Goossen. Stuart Davis
The outside
  Goossen. Stuart Davis
  MnMW. Stuart Davis
Owh! in San Paó     WMAA
  Art since 1945
  Baur. New art (col)
  Blesh. Stuart Davis (col)
  Goodrich. Amer art (col)
  IU. Contemp Amer ptg, 1952 (col)
  MnMW. Stuart Davis (col)
  Pierson
  WMAA. Contemp Amer ptg, 1951
Package deal
  Goossen. Stuart Davis
Pad no 1, 1946       HaH
  Goossen. Stuart Davis
  MnMW. Stuart Davis
Pad no 4, 1947
  MnMW. Stuart Davis
Pajarite
  Goossen. Stuart Davis
The Paris bit       WMAA
  Goodrich. Amer art (col)
Percolator         MM
  Blesh. Stuart Davis
Place des Vosges no 1, 1928  NJN
  Goossen. Stuart Davis
Place des Vosges no 2, 1928
  Blesh. Stuart Davis (col)
  Goossen. Stuart Davis
Place Pasdeloup     WMAA
  Baur. New art
  Goodrich. Amer art (col)
  Goossen. Stuart Davis (col)
  Pierson
  WMAA. Juliana Force

Pochade
  Chew. 250 years of art
  Eliot. Art of our time (col)
  Goossen. Stuart Davis
  ICA. Annual ex, 1961
  WMAA. Annual ex, 1958
Première                                    CLA
  Blesh. Stuart Davis (col)
  DC. 26 biennial ex, 1959
The President
  Hess. Abstract ptg
Radio tubes                                 ATeS
  ATeS. Collection
Rapt at Rappaport's
  IU. Contemp Amer ptg & sculp, 1953
Rapt at Rappaport's (Hirshhorn coll)
  Goossen. Stuart Davis
Rapt at Rappaport's (Wolf coll)
  MnMW. Stuart Davis (col)
Ready-to-wear                               ICA
  Blesh. Stuart Davis (col)
  Goossen. Stuart Davis
  PPC. International ex, 1955
Ready to wear, Study for
  MnMW. Stuart Davis
Red cart                                    MAP
  Robb. Harper history
Roos
  Wight. Milestones (col)
Report from Rockport
  Baur. New art
  Blesh. Stuart Davis
  Gardner 1959 ed
  Goossen. Stuart Davis
  Gruskin (col)
  Hess. Abstract ptg
  Pierson
  Rosenblum
Rockport beach
  Blesh. Stuart Davis
  Goossen. Stuart Davis (col)
Rocky neck, Gloucester
  Blesh. Stuart Davis
Rue de L'Echaude
  Blesh. Stuart Davis
  Goossen. Stuart Davis (col)
Rue des Rats no 2, 1929
  Goossen. Stuart Davis
Rue Vercingetorix
  Goossen. Stuart Davis
Sail loft
  Blesh. Stuart Davis
  MnMW. Stuart Davis
Salt shaker                                 MMA
  Baur. New art
  Goossen. Stuart Davis (col)
  McCurdy
  Rosenblum
Salt shaker (Halpert coll)
  MMA. Abstract
  Read. Art now, 1948 ed
Semé
  Blesh. Stuart Davis (col)
  Goossen. Stuart Davis
  Pearson. Mod renaissance
Shapes of landscape space
  Goossen. Stuart Davis
Smith's cove
  Goossen. Stuart Davis

Snow on the mountain                        GAtM
  GAtM. Holbrook collection
Something on the eight ball                 PPhM
  Blesh. Stuart Davis (col)
  Goossen. Stuart Davis (col)
  ICA. Amer artists paint the city (col)
  Mendelowitz
  Myers. Art
  Pierson
Standard with still life
  IU. Contemp Amer ptg & sculp, 1959
Stele
  MnMW. Stuart Davis
  WMAA. Museum and its friends, 1958
Still life—three objects                    CtHW
  Blesh. Stuart Davis
  Goossen. Stuart Davis
Still life with flowers
  Pearson. Mod renaissance
Still life with saw                         DP
  Goossen. Stuart Davis
Street and bridge
  Myers
Summer landscape                            MMA
  Barr. What is mod ptg
  Baur. Revolution
  Blesh. Stuart Davis
  Goossen. Stuart Davis
  UNESCO. 1860-1955
Summer landscape no 2, 1940 (Alan coll)
  Goossen. Stuart Davis
Summer twilight
  Goossen. Stuart Davis
  MiD. Coll in progress
  WiMiA. Amer ptg 1760-1960
Sunrise
  Blesh. Stuart Davis
  Goossen. Stuart Davis (col)
Super table
  Goossen. Stuart Davis
  MnMW. Stuart Davis
Swing landscape                             InBu
  Blesh. Stuart Davis
  Goossen. Stuart Davis
Television
  Goossen. Stuart Davis
The terminal
  Goossen. Stuart Davis
  MnMW. Stuart Davis
Tournos                                     NUM
  Goossen. Stuart Davis (col)
  MnMW. Stuart Davis
  Pousette-Dart. Amer ptg
Town square                                 NJN
  Blesh. Stuart Davis
Triatic
  MnMW. Stuart Davis
Tropes de teens
  Blesh. Stuart Davis (col)
  IU. Contemp Amer ptg & sculp 1957
Ultra marine                                PA
  Baur. Revolution
  Blesh. Stuart Davis
  Goossen. Stuart Davis
  MnMW. Stuart Davis
U.N. conference room 3, 1956, Study for
  Goossen. Stuart Davis
  MnMW. Stuart Davis
Underpass no 2, 1955
  MnMW. Stuart Davis

**DAVIS, Stuart**—*Continued*
Ursine park
Baur. Nature (col)      IBM
Blesh. Stuart Davis (col)
Goossen. Stuart Davis (col)
Hunter. Mod Amer ptg (col)
Pearson. Mod renaissance
Visa      MMA
Baur. New art
Blesh. Stuart Davis (col)
Goossen. Stuart Davis (col)
MMA. Masters (col)
MnMW. Stuart Davis
PPC. International ex, 1952
Ways and means
IU. Contemp Amer ptg & sculp, 1961
Yellow hills
Goossen. Stuart Davis
**DAVIS, William M.** 1836?-1927
Cider making      NCHA
Davidson v 1
**D'Avouille, Camille**
Whistler, J. A. M. Mme Camille D'Avouille
**DAWKINS, Henry,** fl 1754-1776
Burroughs family
Flexner. First flowers
Ford. Pictorial folk art
**Dawn** by P. Evergood
**Dawn** by M. J. Heade
**Dawn** by H. Mattson
**Dawn** by J. Sloan
**Dawn** by M. Tobey
**Dawn** by R. S. Turner
**Dawn** at Culebra by J. Lie
**Dawn** II by A. G. Dove
**Dawn** III by A. G. Dove
**Dawn** in Pennsylvania by E. Hopper
**Dawn** light by H. E. Mattson
**Dawn** of peace by G. W. Bellows
**Dawn** over Fordham by A. Mosca
**Dawson, Matilda Washington**
Neagle, J. Matilda Washington Dawson
**Day, George Edward,** 1815-1905
Weir, J. F. The Theological of Yale university
**Day, Jeremiah,** 1773-1867
Morse, S. F. B. Jeremiah Day
**Day, Philo,** fl 1810
Unidentified artist. Mourning picture—Philo Day
**DAY, Worden,** 1916-
Astral assemblage
IU. Contemp Amer ptg, 1950
Prima Materia
MMA. Abstract
The wanderer
ICA. Annual ex, 1951
**Day family,** fl 1823
Goldsmith, D. Mr and Mrs Lyman Day and daughter, Cornelia
A **day** at the race by R. Diebenkorn
**Day** in bed by P. S. Sample
**Day** in June by G. W. Bellows
**Day** in June by L. Kroll
**Day** in midwinter by C. E. Burchfield
**Day** in the country by M. B. Prendergast
**Day** of good fortune by A. B. Davies

**Day** of mountain flowers by T. Meehan
**Daybreak** by E. Berman
**Daybreak** by E. Magafan
**Daymare** by C. W. Rain
A **day's** catch by S. A. Mount
**Day's** end by W. R. Derrick
**Day's** end by S. Menkès
**Day's** end by W. W. Quirt
**De** mains pâles aux cieux lassés by Y. Tanguy
**De** profundis by Ben-Zion
**De** profundis by W. S. Schwartz
**Dead** Abel by T. Cole
**Dead** bird by A. P. Ryder
**Dead** cottonwood tree by G. O'Keeffe
**Dead** duck by E. Burkhart
**Dead** end by D. Kingman
**Dead** leaves by E. K. Schwabacher
**Dead** life, sea lion skull, driftwood and coral by E. Berman
**Dead** man by J. Kinigstein
**Dead** man revived by touching the bones of the prophet Elijah by W. Allston
**Dead** men by F. Remington
**Dead** opossum by J. S. Eisenstat
**Dead** plover by M. Hartley
**Deadline** on the range by C. M. Russell
**Dean, Barbara**
Unidentified artist. Barbara Dean
**Deans, Anna Maria**
Hubard, W. J. Elizabeth and Anna Deans
**Deans, Elizabeth Patterson**
Hubard, W. J. Elizabeth and Anna Deans
**DEARTH, Henry Golden,** 1864-1918
Black hat      InIJ
InIJ. 105 ptgs
**Deas, Anne (Izard)** 1779-1863
Malbone, E. G. Mrs William Allen Deas
**DEAS, Charles,** 1818-1867
The death struggle
Pierson
The devil and Tom Walker
DC. Privately owned
Long Jakes. See The trapper
Prairie fire      NBM
Baur. Amer ptg
McCracken. Portrait of the old west (col)
Pierson
The trapper (Long Jakes)      CtY
Davidson v 1
McCracken. Portrait of the old west
Rathbone
Voyageurs      MB
Davidson v 1
MB. Karolik coll
**Deas, Elizabeth (Allen)** 1742-1803
Theus, J. Elizabeth Allen
**Deas, Mrs John.** See Deas, Elizabeth (Allen)
**Deas, Mary (Somers)** fl 1801
Malbone, E. G. Mrs David Deas
**Deas, Mrs William Allen.** See Deas, Anne (Izard)
**Death** by F. C. Watkins
**Death,** Study for by F. C. Watkins
**Death** by burning by B. L. Culwell

Death cry by B. W. Tomlin
Death in the orchard by F. C. Watkins
Death of a man by W. De Kooning
Death of a miner by B. Shahn
Death of Chatham by J. S. Copley
Death of Europe by E. F. Savage
Death of General Montgomery at Quebec
    by J. Trumbull
Death of Jane McCrea by J. Vanderlyn
Death of King John by W. Allston
Death of Major Pierson by J. S. Copley
Death of Socrates by B. West
Death of the general by F. Dzubas
Death on a pale horse by A. P. Ryder
Death on a pale horse by B. West
Death on the beach by B. Shahn
The death struggle by C. Deas
Death wish by J. De Feo
Death whoop by S. Eastman
Deathrose by J. De Feo
De Boogh, Catharina. See Beekman, Catharina (De Boogh)
Deborah and Nietzsche by G. R. Davis
DE BOTTON, Jean
    Chamber music
        NAD. Annual ex, 1948
Debris of summer by P. Perkins
Debuke, Jemima. See Winslow, Jemima
    (Debuke)
Decadence in Guatemala by D. E. Brown
Decalogue, Jacob's ladder and burning bush
    by R. B. Motherwell
Decatur, Stephen, 1779-1820
    Unidentified artist. Commodore Stephen
        Decatur
Decay and resurrection by K. Merrild
December by P. Horiuchi
Deciduous circumstance by R. Ruben
DECKER, Joseph, b 1853?
    Hard lot
        Frankenstein. After the hunt
Declaration of Independence by E. Hicks
Declaration of Independence by J. Trumbull
DECOMBES, Emilie, d 1906
    Surf at Ogunquit, Maine                MB
        MB. Ptgs in water color
    Swiss mountains                        MB
        MB. Ptgs in water color
    Young girl                             MB
        MB. Ptgs in water color
Decoration with cloud by M. Weber
DE DIEGO, Julio, 1900-
    Altitude 2000
        IU. Contemp Amer ptg, 1951
    Birth of the atom (Atomic series)
        Pearson. Mod renaissance
    Elements of reconstruction
        Gruskin (col)
    Forces against violent attack
        Rathbun
    Guilty cats                            IBM
        Genauer
    Heroic figures
        Pearson. Mod renaissance

Italy: historical town
    IU. Contemp Amer ptg & sculp, 1953
Perplexity of what to do
    Pearson. Mod renaissance
Phantom boat                               NJMo
    NJMo. Forty years
Prodigious industrial phenomenon
    VR. Biennial ex, 1948
They shall sail the seven seas
    Larkin
    Larkin rev ed
Trojan horse
    IU. Contemp Amer ptg, 1949
Unexpected encounter
    IU. Contemp Amer ptg, 1948
What are they going to do next (Disasters
    of the soul series)
    Pearson. Mod renaissance
The deep by J. Pollock
Deep orange on black by S. Francis
Deep river by J. Lie
Deep-sea trawlers, Maine by J. Marin
Deep vision by I. R. Pereira
Deer
    Audubon, J. W. Common American deer
    Audubon, J. J. Virginia deer
    Codman, C. Wounded deer
    Homer, W. Deer drinking
    Homer, W. Fallen deer
    Knaths, K. Deer at sunset
    Knaths, K. Frightened deer in moonlight
    Morse, H. D. Deer in a thicket
    Price, C. S. Mule deer
    Rungius, C. Moose
    Russell, C. M. Battle of the elks
    Russell, C. M. White tails
    Ryder, A. P. Stag and two does
    Ryder, A. P. Stag drinking
    Sample, P. S. Winter visitor
    Tait, A. F. Saved—a hard chase
    Tait, A. F. Young buck and doe
    Tait, A. F. and Gay, E. Deer at the lake
    Unidentified artist. Deer hunt
    Unidentified artist. De Peyster boy with
        deer
    Unidentified artist. Two children with a
        deer
    Whittredge, W. Deer, Mount Storm park,
        Cincinnati
Deer hunter by R. Huck
Deer island, Maine: Stonington waterfront
    by J. Marin
Deer isle, boats, and pertaining thereto by
    J. Marin
Deer isle islets, Maine by J. Marin
Deer isle, Maine, series no 30—Boat fantasy
    by J. Marin
Deer isle, Stonington, Maine by J. Marin
Deer Tongue lane by S. Laufman
DE ERDELY, Francis, 1904-
    Red sweater                            CoD
        CoS. New accessions USA, 1946
    Sevastopol
        ICA. Annual ex, 1945/46
Deer's skull with pedernal by G. O'Keeffe
DEEZIK, Val, 1914-
    V. J. day                              OYB
        OYB. Annual 1948
        OYB. Catalogue 1951

Defaced portrait by B. Shahn
The defendants by B. Shahn
Defending the stockade by C. Schreyvogel
Defense of America's cup, 1870 by J. E. Butterworth
DE FEO, Jay, 1929-
  Daphne
    MMA. Sixteen
  Death wish
    MMA. Sixteen
  Deathrose
    MMA. Sixteen
  Origin
    MMA. Sixteen
  The Veronica
    MMA. Sixteen
Defiance: Inviting a shot before Petersburg, Virginia by W. Homer
Defiant culprit by C. M. Russell
De Forest, David Curtis, 1774-1825
  Morse, S. F. B. David C. De Forest
DE GRAILLY, Victor
  View of Niagara Falls
    Sears. Highlights
  Washington's headquarters, Newburgh-on-the-Hudson
    Sears. Highlights
DE GRAILLY, Walter
  View from West Point
    Sears. Highlights
  Washington's tomb at Mount Vernon
    Sears. Highlights
De Haas, John Philip
  Peale, C. W. John Philip de Haas
DEHN, Adolph Arthur, 1895-
  Beauty is where you find it    WMAA
    Pierson
  Butte, Utah    MMA
    Gruskin
  Caribbean cornucopia
    IU. Contemp Amer ptg, 1952
  Dark night
    Pearson. Mod renaissance
  Garden of the gods
    Pearson. Mod renaissance
  Haitian heaven
    Pousette-Dart. Amer ptg
    PPC. International ex, 1952
  Haitian Mardi Gras    IaDa
    IaDa. Silver jubilee
  Jimmy Savo and rope    WMAA
    Goodrich. Amer art
    Pierson
  Jungle in Venezuela
    Pearson. Mod renaissance
  Market, Port-au-Prince, Haiti    ATeS
    ATeS. Collection
  Minnesota in August
    NYG. Fine art
  Sentinels of the west    ATU
    ATU. Coll of Amer art (col)
  Shower in Colorado    MB
    MB. Ptgs in water color
  The sisters    WMAA
    Brown. Amer ptg
  Spring in Central park    MM
    MM. 100 Amer ptrs
  Sunday painters
    Pearson. Mod renaissance
DeKay, Sidney G. 1880-1949
  Lockman, D. M. Col Sidney G. DeKay

DE KNIGHT, Avel
  Circus horses
    NAD. Annual ex, 1954
DE KOONING, Willem, 1904-
  Acrobat
    Hess. Willem De Kooning
    Janis. De Kooning
  Asheville    DP
    Baur. New art
    DP. Catalogue
    Hess. Abstract ptg (col)
    Hess. Willem De Kooning (col)
    Janis. De Kooning
    Larkin rev ed
    Pierson
  Attic
    Hess. Willem De Kooning
    Janis. De Kooning
  Backdrop for a dance recital, Study for
    Hess. Willem De Kooning
  Backyard on Tenth street    MdBM
    Hess. Willem De Kooning
  Black and white
    CSFP. Annual ex, 1950/51
  Black Friday, 1949 no 1 (Lloyd coll)
    Hess. Willem De Kooning
  Black Friday, 1949 no 2 (Lloyd coll)
    Hess. Willem De Kooning
  Bolton landing
    Hess. Willem De Kooning
  Boudoir    MoKN
    Hess. Willem De Kooning
  Boudoir (Tishler coll)
    Hess. Willem De Kooning
  Brown and white
    Hess. Willem De Kooning
  Classic male. See Seated figure
  Composition    NNSG
    Hunter. Mod Amer ptg (col)
    NNSG. Handbook
    Read. Concise history
  Dark pond
    WMAA. New decade
  Death of a man
    Hess. Willem De Kooning (detail)
  Detour
    Canaday
  Door to the river    WMAA
    Goodrich. Amer art (col)
  Duck pond
    Hess. Willem De Kooning
  Easter Monday    MM
    Art since 1945
    Hess. Willem De Kooning
    Janis. De Kooning (col)
  Elegy
    Hess. Willem De Kooning (col)
  Excavation    ICA
    Baur. New art
    CoS. New accessions USA, 1952
    Hess. Willem De Kooning (col)
    Janis. De Kooning (col)
    MMA. Abstract
    Pousette-Dart. Amer ptg
  February
    Baur. Nature
    Eliot. Art of our time (col)
    Hess. Willem De Kooning (col)
    Hess. Willem De Kooning (detail)
    Janis. De Kooning (col)
    Janis. De Kooning (detail)
    MMA. New Amer ptg

Figure, 1949
  Hess. Abstract ptg
Figure in landscape no 2
  Selz. New images
Fire Island
  Hess. Willem De Kooning
First of January
  Hess. Willem De Kooning
Forest of Zogbaum
  Hess. Willem De Kooning
  Janis. De Kooning
Gansevoort street
  Hess. Willem De Kooning
Glazier
  Hess. Willem De Kooning (col)
Gotham news                              NBuA
  50 years of mod art (col)
  Hess. Willem De Kooning
  ICA. Amer artists paint the city
  Janis. De Kooning (col)
  NBuA. Acquisitions 1954-57 (col)
  Ponente. Mod ptg, 1960 (col)
  Time. 300 years (col)
Interchanged
  Hess. Willem De Kooning (col)
  Janis. De Kooning
  WMAA. Museum and its friends, 1959
Jack Greenbaum
  Hess. Willem De Kooning (col)
January
  Hess. Willem De Kooning
July
  Hess. Willem De Kooning
Leaves in Weehawken
  Hess. Willem De Kooning
Light in August
  Hess. Willem De Kooning
Lisbeth's painting
  Janis. De Kooning
Little attic
  Hess. Willem De Kooning
Man
  Hess. Willem De Kooning (col)
Marilyn Monroe
  Selz. New images
The marshes
  Hess. Willem De Kooning
Matchbook. See Untitled painting (Match-
    book) c 1942
Max Margulis
  Hess. Willem De Kooning
Merritt parkway
  Janis. De Kooning (col)
  Ponente. Mod ptg, 1960 (col)
Montauk highway
  Hess. Willem De Kooning
The Netherlands
  Hess. Willem De Kooning
Night square
  NBuA. Expressionism
Noon
  Hess. Willem De Kooning
  Janis. De Kooning
Painting, 1948                           MMA
  Baur. New art
  Baur. Revolution
  Janis. De Kooning
  MMA. Abstract
  MMA. New Amer ptg
Painting, 1959
  Hess. Willem De Kooning (col)

Park Rosenberg
  Janis. De Kooning (col)
Pink angels
  Hess. Willem De Kooning (col)
  Janis. De Kooning
Pink lady, c 1944 (Porter coll)
  Hess. Willem De Kooning (col)
Pink lady, c 1948 (Blinken coll)
  Hess. Willem De Kooning
Police gazette                           NBuA
  Hess. Willem De Kooning
Rudolph Burckhardt
  Hess. Willem De Kooning (unfinished
    ptg and detail)
Ruth's zowie
  Janis. De Kooning (col)
Sagamore
  Hess. Willem De Kooning
Sailcloth
  Hess. Willem De Kooning
Saturday night                           MoSLW
  Hess. Willem De Kooning
  Janis. De Kooning
Seated figure (Classic male)
  Hess. Willem De Kooning
Seated man, c 1938
  Hess. Willem De Kooning
Seated man, c 1939
  Hess. Willem De Kooning
Seated woman, c 1940 (Greenfield coll)
  Hess. Willem De Kooning
  Janis. De Kooning
Seated woman, c 1942 (artist's coll)
  Hess. Willem De Kooning
September morn
  Janis. De Kooning
Spike's folly
  PPC. International ex, 1961/62
Standing male
  Hess. Willem De Kooning
Stenographer
  Hess. Willem De Kooning
Street corner incident
  Hess. Willem De Kooning
  Janis. De Kooning
Still life, c 1929 (artist's coll)
  Hess. Willem De Kooning
Still life, c 1929 (Robertson coll)
  Hess. Willem De Kooning
Suburb in Havana
  Janis. De Kooning (col)
The time of fire
  Hess. Willem De Kooning
Two men standing
  Hess. Willem De Kooning
Two standing women
  Hess. Willem De Kooning
Two women
  MnMW. Expressionism 1900-1955
Two women, 1953 (Townsend coll)
  Hess. Willem De Kooning
Two women on a wharf
  Hess. Willem De Kooning
Two women: Summer                        ICA
  Hess. Willem De Kooning (col)
Two women with still life
  Janis. De Kooning
Two women's torsos                       ICA
  Selz. New images
Unfinished painting, c 1940 (Denby-
    Rudolph Burckhardt coll)
  Hess. Willem De Kooning

**DE KOONING, Willem**—*Continued*
Untitled abstraction, c 1928
  Hess. Willem De Kooning
Untitled abstraction, c 1931
  Hess. Willem De Kooning
Untitled abstraction, 1940-41
  Janis. De Kooning
Untitled abstraction, 1955     NNSG
  Hess. Willem De Kooning (col)
Untitled painting, c 1931
  Hess. Willem De Kooning
Untitled painting, c 1934 (Becker coll)
  Hess. Willem De Kooning
Untitled painting, 1937 (artist's coll)
  Hess. Willem De Kooning
Untitled painting, c 1937 (Denby-Rudolph
  Burckhardt coll)
  Hess. Willem De Kooning
Untitled painting, c 1938 (Auerbach coll)
  Hess. Willem De Kooning
Untitled painting, c 1938 (Brustlein coll)
  Hess. Willem De Kooning
Untitled painting, 1938 (Denby-Rudolph
  Burckhardt coll)
  Hess. Willem De Kooning
Untitled painting, c 1939
  Hess. Willem De Kooning
Untitled painting, 1940
  Hess. Willem De Kooning
Untitled painting, c 1943 (Bing coll)
  Hess. Willem De Kooning
Untitled painting, c 1943 (Denby-Rudolph
  Burckhardt coll)
  Hess. Willem De Kooning
Untitled painting, c 1943 (O'Hara coll)
  Hess. Willem De Kooning
Untitled painting, c 1944 (Porter coll)
  Hess. Willem De Kooning
Untitled painting, 1946 (Brustlein coll)
  Hess. Willem De Kooning
Untitled painting, c 1946 (Goldowsky coll)
  Hess. Willem De Kooning
Untitled painting, 1947 (Poindexter coll)
  Hess. Willem De Kooning
Untitled painting, 1947, no 1 (Lazar coll)
  Hess. Willem De Kooning
Untitled painting, 1947, no 2 (Lazar coll)
  Hess. Willem De Kooning
Untitled painting, 1948
  CtY. Yale alumni
Untitled painting, c 1948     NPV
  Hess. Willem De Kooning
Untitled painting, 1948 (Lazar coll)
  Hess. Willem De Kooning
Untitled painting, c 1948, no 1
  Hess. Willem De Kooning
Untitled painting, c 1948, no 2
  Hess. Willem De Kooning
Untitled painting, 1949 (Rosenberg coll)
  Hess. Willem De Kooning
Untitled painting, 1959
  Hess. Willem De Kooning
Untitled painting (Matchbook) c 1942
  Hess. Willem De Kooning
Untitled woman, c 1947
  Hess. Willem De Kooning
Untitled woman, c 1948 (Poindexter coll)
  Hess. Willem De Kooning
Warehouse mannequins
  Hess. Willem De Kooning
The wave
  Hess. Willem De Kooning

Woman (1)
  ICA. Annual ex, 1954
Woman (2)
  IU. Contemp Amer ptg, 1952
Woman, 1942
  Hess. Willem De Kooning
Woman, c 1943
  Hess. Willem De Kooning
Woman, c 1949     NoCG
  Hess. Willem De Kooning
  Janis. De Kooning
  Selz. New images
Woman, c 1949 (Leavitt coll)
  Hess. Willem De Kooning
  Janis. De Kooning
Woman, 1953-54     NBM
  Hess. Willem De Kooning
Woman, 1954     NeL
  Hess. Willem De Kooning
Woman I, 1950-52     MMA
  Baur. New art (col)
  Blesh
  Hess. Willem De Kooning (col)
  Janis. De Kooning (col)
  Janis. De Kooning (detail)
  Mendelowitz
  MMA. Masters (col)
  MMA. New Amer ptg (col)
  Newmeyer
  Pierson
  Seiberling
  Selz. New images
  Time. 300 years (col)
Woman I, stage 1. Summer, 1950
  Hess. Willem De Kooning
Woman I, stage 2
  Hess. Willem De Kooning
Woman I, stage 3, 1951
  Hess. Willem De Kooning
Woman I, stage 4, 1951
  Hess. Willem De Kooning
Woman I, stage 5, 1951-52
  Hess. Willem De Kooning
Woman I, stage 6, 1951-52
  Hess. Willem De Kooning
Woman II, 1952-53     MMA
  Art since 1945 (col)
  Hess. Willem De Kooning
  Read. Concise history (col)
Woman III, 1952     MMA
  Janis. De Kooning
Woman III, 1952-53 (Pernas coll)
  Hess. Willem De Kooning
Woman IV, 1952-53     MoKN
  Hess. Willem De Kooning
  Janis. De Kooning
  MoKN. Handbook
  NNSG. Younger Amer ptrs
Woman V, 1952-53
  Hess. Willem De Kooning
  Janis. De Kooning (col)
Woman VI, 1953     PPC
  Hess. Willem De Kooning
  Hess. Willem De Kooning (col detail)
Woman and bicycle     WMAA
  Cheney. Story 1958 ed
  Goodrich. Amer art (col)
  Hess. Willem De Kooning
  Janis. De Kooning (col)
  McCurdy
  Selz. New images (col)
  WMAA. New decade

Woman as landscape
  Hess. Willem De Kooning
Woman in landscape I
  Janis. De Kooning
Woman (Green)
  Hess. Willem De Kooning
Woman (Ocher)
  Hess. Willem De Kooning
Woman sitting
  Hess. Willem De Kooning
Yellow river
  MnMW. 60 Amer ptrs
Delancey, Alice. See Izard, Alice (Delancey)
De Lancey, Mrs Oliver. See De Lancey, Phila (Franks)
De Lancey, Phila (Franks) 1722-1811
  Duyckinck, G. (attributed works) Children of Jacob Franks
  Duyckinck, G. (attributed works) Phila Franks
De Lancey, Warren, fl 1775
  Pratt, M. Cadwallader Colden and Warren de Lancey
DELANEY, Joseph, 1904-
  His last address                            ATU
    ATU. Coll of Amer art
  Innocence                                   ATU
    ATU. Coll of Amer art
DELANO, Gerard Curtis, 1890-
  The canyon
    Carlson. Gallery (col)
  Desert thunderhead
    Carlson. Gallery (col)
  Moonlight stampede
    Carlson. Gallery (col)
  Navajo
    Carlson. Gallery (col)
  Navajo boy
    Carlson. Gallery (col)
  Sheep on the desert
    Carlson. Gallery (col)
  Vermillion cliffs
    Carlson. Gallery (col)
DELANOY, Abraham, 1742-1795
  Benjamin West                               NNHS
  Pierson
De Lanoy, Catherine Peters. See Beekman, Catherine Peters (De Lanoy)
Delaware meadows by G. Inness
Delaware river and valley
  Chambers, T. Delaware Water Gap
  Eakins, T. On the Delaware
  Inness, G. Delaware valley
  Inness, G. Delaware Water Gap
  Inness, G. View on the Delaware, Water Gap in the distance
  McIlvaine, W. Delaware Water Gap
Delaware (river) country, Pennsylvania by J. Marin
Delaware Water Gap village by L. M. Eilshemius
DELBOS, Julius, 1879-
  Canal                                       InTH
    InTH. Catalogue
  Haiti
    NAD. Annual ex, 1953
  Martha's Vineyard
    NAD. Annual ex, 1947, 2d half
DE LEON, Amanda, 1908-
  Christening                                 OYB
    OYB. Supplement

Delfina by J. Youngerman
Delicate board by S. Provan
Delight by H. Hofmann
Delirium is our best deceiver by P. S. Sample
Deliverance by Y. Kuniyoshi
Delmores, Aimée
  Lockman, D. M. Aimée Delmores
De Long, Mehitabel Preston, fl 1865
  Mason, B. F. Mehitabel Preston de Long
Delta Queen and the packet Whisper by E. A. Anderson
The deluge by W. Allston
A demand of estimation by K. Nack
De Mare, Agnes (Healy) b 1842
  Healy, G. P. A. Agnes de Mare and her son
De Mare, Jeanne, fl 1889
  Healy, G. P. A. Jeanne de Mare
De Mare, Marie, fl 1882
  Healy, G. P. A. Marie de Mare
DE MARTINI, Joseph, 1896-
  Aqueduct
    PA. Annual ex, 1952
  Bike race no 2
    NAD. Annual ex, 1952
  Caravan theater minstrels                   ATU
    ATU. Coll of Amer art
  Crotch Island derricks                      MnMW
    Pierson
  Foggy night
    Genauer
  Interior with three figures
    CSFP. Annual ex, 1948/49
    IU. Contemp Amer ptg, 1949
  Lighthouse point                            NeL
    Gruskin
  Moonlight                                   ICA
    NYG. Fine art
  Mountain village
    IU. Contemp Amer ptg, 1950
  The promontory                              IU
    IU. Contemp Amer ptg, 1948
    IU. 20th century
  Quarry pool                                 MAP
    Cheney. Expressionism 1948 ed
    Cheney. Story 1958 ed
    Rathbun
  Self-portrait
    Cheney. Expressionism 1948 ed
  The wreck of the St Christopher             MM
    MM. 100 Amer ptrs
DEMBOSKI, Dorothy L.
  Blue interior                               OYB
    OYB. Annual 1960
Democracies fear peace offensive by B. Shahn
Demonstration in Paris by B. Shahn
Dempsey and Firpo by G. W. Bellows
DEMUTH, Charles Henry, 1883-1935
  Acrobats, 1916                              PMB
    MMA. Demuth
  Acrobats, 1918
    MMA. Demuth
  Acrobats, 1919                              MMA
    Baur. New art
    Biddle. Yes and no
    Larkin (detail)
    Larkin rev ed (detail)
    MM. Contemp ptrs

**DEMUTH, C. H.**—*Continued*
  MMA. Demuth (col)
  MMA. Masters (col)
  Pierson
  Richardson. Ptg in America
After all . . . , 1933            FaW
  MMA. Demuth
  MnMW. Precisionist view
  WMAA. Juliana Force
After Sir Christopher Wren
  Brown. Amer ptg
  MMA. Demuth
. . . and the home of the brave     ICA
  MMA. Demuth
  Rosenblum
Architecture
  MiD. Coll in progress
  WiMiA. Amer ptg 1760-1960
L'Assommoir, Illustration for     PPhM
  MMA. Demuth
At a house in Harley street      MMA
  MMA. Demuth
  PA. Annual ex, 1955
  Pierson
Aucassin and Nicoletta         OCo
  Moderns and their world
Backdrop of East Lynne        NeL
  MMA. Demuth
Bathers
  Chew. 250 years of art
The beast in the jungle, Illustrations for
  MMA. Demuth
Bermuda, 1917              PPhM
  PPhM. Arensberg coll
Bermuda no 2 (The schooner)     MMA
  MMA. Demuth
Box of tricks              PPhM
  Chew. 250 years of art
Buildings, Lancaster         WMAA
  Goodrich. Amer art
Business                ICA
  Hunter. Mod Amer ptg
  MMA. Demuth
The circus               OCo
  MMA. Demuth
  Pierson
Daisies                WMAA
  MMA. Demuth
Dunes                 OCo
  MMA. Demuth
Early houses, Provincetown      MMA
  MMA. Demuth
Eggplant                DP
  Bazin
  DP. Catalogue
Eggplant and plums          ICA
  Mendelowitz
  PA. Annual ex, 1955
Eggplant and summer squash     CtHW
  CtHW. Handbook
Eggplant and tomatoes
  MMA. Demuth
End of the parade: Coatsville, Pennsyl-
  vania
  Baur. New art (col)
  MMA. Demuth
Erdgeist, Illustration for
  MMA. Demuth
Factory
  CtY. Yale alumni

Female acrobats             MMA
  MMA. Soby collection
Flower piece
  MMA. Demuth
Flower study              OCl
  MMA. Demuth
Flower study no 1           ICA
  NYG. Fine art
Flower study no 4
  NYG. Fine art
Flowers                MB
  MB. Ptgs in water color
Flowers (Fleischman coll)
  MiD. Coll in progress
  MMA. Demuth
  WiMiA. Amer ptg 1760-1960
Flowers, cyclamen          ICA
  MMA. Demuth
Gloucester              RPS
  MMA. Demuth
Golden Swan (Hell Hole)
  MMA. Demuth
The governess first sees the ghost of
  Peter Quint
  PA. Annual ex, 1955
Grapes and turnips
  Chew. 250 years of art
Green dancer
  MMA. Demuth
Green pears
  MMA. Demuth
Hell Hole. See Golden Swan
Houses                 OCo
  MMA. Contemp ptrs
I saw the figure 5 in gold      MM
  Baur. New art
  MM. 100 Amer ptrs (col)
  MMA. Demuth (col)
  Pierson
  Taylor. Fifty centuries, 1954 ed (col)
In vaudeville            PPhM
  PPhM. Gallatin coll
In vaudeville (White coll)
  Baur. New art
  MMA. Contemp ptrs
Incense of a new church       OCo
  Brown. Amer ptg
  WMAA. Pioneers
Kiss-me-over-the-fence
  MiD. Coll in progress
  WiMiA. Amer ptg 1760-1960
Lancaster              PPhM
  PPhM. Arensberg coll
Lancaster, Pennsylvania, View of    NBuA
  MMA. Demuth
  Sewall. History of western art
Man and woman
  MMA. Demuth
Many brave hearts are asleep in the deep
  MMA. Demuth
Miles and the governess
  PA. Annual ex, 1955
Modern conveniences        OCo
  DC. De gustibus
  Roos
My Egypt              WMAA
  Gardner 1959 ed
  Goodrich. Amer art (col)
  Janson. Picture history
  Mendelowitz

MMA. Demuth
MnMW. Precisionist view (col)
PA. Annual ex, 1955
Pierson
Roos
Time. 300 years (col)
Wight. Milestones (col)
Nana, Illustrations for          MMA
MMA. Demuth
Nana, Illustrations for          PMB
MMA. Demuth
New Hope, Pennsylvania
MMA. Demuth
Nospmas M. Egiap, Lancaster, Pennsyl-
vania
Chew. 250 years of art
On stage
MiD. Coll in progress
WiMiA. Amer ptg 1760-1960
Pandora's box, Illustration for          PMB
MMA. Demuth
Pansies
MMA. Demuth
Paquebot, Paris          OCo
Baur. Revolution
Brown. Amer ptg
MMA. Demuth
Pierson
Poe's The masque of the red death, Illus-
tration for          PMB
MMA. Demuth
Poppies          NUM
NUM. Root bequest
Poppies (Halpert coll)
Baur. New art
MMA. Demuth
Pierson
Poster portrait of O'Keeffe
MnMW. Precisionist view
Purple pup
Baur. New art
Red chimneys          DP
Born
DP. Catalogue
Rue du Singe qui Pêche
MMA. Demuth
MnMW. Classic tradition
Sails          CSB
MMA. Demuth
The schooner. See Bermuda no 2
Sky after El Greco          ATeS
ATeS. Collection
Stairs, Provincetown          MMA
MMA. Demuth
MnMW. Precisionist view
Rosenblum
Still life          PPhM
Robb. Harper history
Still life, no 2, 1922          OCo
MMA. Demuth
Strolling          MMA
MMA. Demuth
Studio interior
MMA. Demuth
The tower          OCo
McCurdy
Trees          OCo
Brown. Amer ptg
Trees and barns, Bermuda          KLU
MMA. Demuth
Pierson

Tuberoses          MWiC
MMA. Demuth
The turn of the screw, Illustration for
Baur. Revolution
Lewisohn
MMA. Demuth
Two acrobats
MMA. Demuth
Vaudeville
MMA. Demuth
Vaudeville musicians          MMA
MMA. Demuth
Waiting          ICA
MMA. Demuth
PA. Annual ex, 1955
White architecture          MLL
MnMW. Precisionist view
Woman with walking stick
MMA. Demuth
Zinnias, larkspur and daisies
MMA. Demuth
The den by H. Pippin
Denain by J. D. Brooks
The denial by R. O. Pozzatti
Denison, Mr. c 1785
Unidentified artist. Mr Denison
Denison, Mrs. c 1785
Unidentified artist. Mrs Denison
Denison, Edward, 1778-1845
Peale, Rembrandt. Edward Denison
Denison, Eunice. See Hatch, Eunice (Deni-
son)
Denning family, fl 1772
Williams, W. The Denning family
Dennis, Aaron Chase, fl 1803
Malbone, E. G. Aaron Chase Dennis
DENNISON, Dorothy D.
Professional painters
OYB. Annual 1949
Dennison, Miss, fl 1775
Unidentified artist. Miss Dennison
Dennison hill, Southbridge, Massachusetts
by Unidentified artist
Departing boat by Z. Sepeshy
Departing guests by W. Thompson
Departure by M. Beckmann
Departure by T. Cole
Departure by J. Hirsch
Departure of Regulus by B. West
De Peyster, Abraham B. 1763-1801
Peale, C. W. Abraham B. De Peyster
De Peyster, Catherine, 1771-1799
Vanderlyn, P. (attributed works) Cath-
erine De Peyster
De Peyster, Christiana (Dally) 1748-1813
Peale, C. W. Mrs William De Peyster jr
De Peyster, Elizabeth, 1765-1804. See Peale,
Elizabeth (De Peyster)
De Peyster, Elizabeth, 1787-1826. See Rem-
sen, Elizabeth (De Peyster)
De Peyster, Elizabeth (Haring) 1743-1821
Peale, C. W. Mrs John De Peyster
De Peyster, Gerard, 1776-1824
Unidentified artist. Gerard De Peyster
De Peyster, Isaac, 1662-1728
Unidentified artist. Isaac De Peyster
De Peyster, James A. fl 1720
Unidentified artist. James A. De Peys-
ter (?)

De Peyster, James W. 1745-1812
  Peale, C. W. James W. De Peyster
De Peyster, Johannes, 1694-1789
  Unidentified artist. Johannes De Peyster III
De Peyster, John, 1731-1807
  Peale, C. W. John De Peyster
De Peyster, Mrs John. See De Peyster, Elizabeth (Haring)
De Peyster, John B. 1765-1846?
  Peale, C. W. John B. De Peyster
De Peyster, Margaret, 1728-1781. See Axtell, Margaret (De Peyster)
De Peyster, Margaret (De Peyster) 1774-1815
  Peale, C. W. Mrs Gerard De Peyster
De Peyster, William, 1709-1780?
  Peale, C. W. William De Peyster (copy after John Durand)
De Peyster, William, 1735-1803
  Peale, C. W. William De Peyster jr
De Peyster, Mrs William jr. See De Peyster, Christiana (Dally)
De Peyster children, 1730?
  Unidentified artist. Eva and Catherina De Peyster
De Peyster family, Member of
  Unidentified artist. Boy of the De Peyster family
  Unidentified artist. De Peyster boy with deer
  Unidentified artist. De Peyster girl with lamb (Margaret or Catherine)
Deposition by S. Greene
Deposition by W. Pachner
Depression by J. Lawrence
Derby, John, 1762-1831
  Malbone, E. G. John Derby
Derby, Martha (Coffin) fl 1802
  Malbone, E. G. Mrs Richard C. Derby
Derby hill theme: Hiawatha by P. Tchelitchew
Derby view by W. D. Fausett
The derelict by M. Roberts
Derelicts by F. Gill
Dering, Mary Sylvester, 1725-1794
  Blackburn, J. Mary Sylvester Dering
DERRICK, William Rowell, b 1857
Day's end
  NSP. Sportscapes
Duckblind
  NSP. Sportscapes
Descension by M. C. Morgan
Descent by F. C. Watkins
Descent from the cross by M. Beckmann
Descent from the cross by W. Quirt
Desdemona by A. P. Ryder
The desert by E. F. Spruce
Desert at night by E. F. Spruce
Desert domain by P. Grimm
Desert landscape by W. A. Baziotes
Desert landscape by L. Siegriest
Desert ranges by M. Dixon
Desert song by L. Megargee
Desert sun by R. F. Gates
Desert thunderhead by G. C. Delano
Desert twilight by L. Goldin

Deserted farm by M. Hartley
Deserted farm by M. Weber
Deserted Navajo home by J. E. Swinnerton
Deserted Navajo trading post by J. E. Swinnerton
Design for color by L. Lucioni
Design for the memory by A. Rattner
Desire by M. Jules
The desk by N. Spencer
Desperate stand by C. M. Russell
Destination unknown by T. Egri
The destruction of the beast and the false prophets by B. West
Destruction of the empire by T. Cole
Detour by W. De Kooning
Detour by K. Sage
Detroit, Michigan
  Bennett, W. J. Detroit, 1836
  Burnham, T. O. H. P. First state election in Detroit, Michigan
  H., E. Detroit, 1794
DÉTRÉ, Roland, 1903-
Nude in grisaille
  IU. Contemp Amer ptg & sculp, 1959
Deuce by S. Davis
DEUTSCH, Boris, 1892-
What atomic war will do to you
  IU. Contemp Amer ptg, 1949
Deutsche presse by W. M. Harnett
Deux personnages by G. Vass
The devil and Tom Walker by C. Deas
The devil and Tom Walker by J. Quidor
Devil's gate by A. J. Miller
Devil's holiday by E. Berman
DEVLAN, Francis Daniel, 1835-1870
Gibraltar forge                           PR
  PR. Catalogue
DEVOLL, Ruby, fl 1830
The prodigal son                         VWR
  VWR. Folk art (col)
Devotion, Ebenezer, 1684-1771
  Chandler, W. Rev Ebenezer Devotion
De Wandelaer, Catherine. See Gansevoort, Catherine (De Wandelaer)
De Wandelaer, Pau, fl 1725
  Gansevoort limner. Pau de Wandelaer
Dewdrops and roses by C. C. Curran
Dewees, William Potts, 1768-1841
  Neagle, J. Dr William Potts Dewees
Dewey, Thomas Edmund, 1902-
  Shahn, B. Dewey, Vandenberg and Taft
DEWING, Thomas Wilmer, 1851-1938
Lady in yellow                           MBI
  Richardson. Ptg in America
The letter                               MM
  MM. 100 Amer ptrs
Music
  DC. Privately owned
Orange and rose
  WiMiA. Amer ptg 1760-1960
The recitation                           MiD
  Pierson
The spinet                               DNC
  DNC. Gellatly coll, 1954
  Pierson

**Portrait of the artist**
Chase, W. M. Thomas Dewing

**Dexter, Franklin Bowditch,** 1842-1920
  Thomas, P. M. Franklin Bowditch **Dexter**
**Dial** by P. Guston
**Dialogue** 1 by A. Gottlieb
**Diamond** shaped by I. Bolotowsky
**Diamond** shoal by W. Homer
**Diana** by A. P. Ryder
**Diana** and Callisto by A. Russell
**Diana** in the chase, or Swiss scenery by W.
  Allston
**Diary** of a seducer by A. Gorky
**Dice** players by K. F. Roesch
**DICKINSON, Anson,** 1779-1852
  Asa Bacon                                CtY
    CtY. Portrait index
  Goldsbrow Banyar                         NNHS
    Vail. Stuyvesant ports
  Goldsbrow Banyar (replica)
    Vail. Stuyvesant ports
  Man with a harelip                       OCl
    OCl. Portrait miniatures

          Attributed works
  Sarah Pierce
    MB. New England miniatures
**DICKINSON, Edwin Walter,** 1891-
  Cello player                             WMAA
    WMAA. Sara Roby
  Composition with still life, 1933-37 MMA
    Baur. New art
  Constant
    NAD. Annual ex, 1952
    PPC. Ptg in the U.S. 1949
  Finger lakes
    MMA. Fifteen
  Fossil hunters                           WMAA
    Goodrich. Amer art (col)
  Ruin at Daphne                           MM
    Baur. New art
    McCurdy
    Pousette-Dart. Amer ptg
  Self-portrait
    Baur. New art
    MMA. Fifteen
  Surf, Point Lookout
    IU. Contemp Amer ptg & sculp, 1955
  Unfinished composition
    MMA. Fifteen
  View from window, Paris
    NAD. Annual ex, 1958
  Villa la Mouette                         MM
    MM. 100 Amer ptrs
  Windows, Paris
    ICA. Annual ex, 1954
  Woodland scene                           NIC
    Baur. New art
    MMA. Fifteen
    Pierson
**DICKINSON, Eleanor C.**
  My father                                OYB
    OYB. Annual 1960
**DICKINSON, Preston,** 1891-1930
  Along the river                          DP
    DP. Catalogue
  Bridge                                   NJN
    Larkin
    Larkin rev ed
    Mendelowitz

  The factory                              MB
    Baur. Revolution
    McCurdy
  The factory                              OCo
    Precisionist view
  Harlem river                             WMAA
    Born
    NYG. Fine art
  High bridge                              OCl
    Brown. Amer ptg
  Industry                                 WMAA
    Goodrich. Amer art
    Pierson
    Roos
  Mountain farm
    WMAA. Pioneers
  Old quarter, Quebec                      DP
    Wight. Milestones
  Quebec                                   OCiM
    Born
  The ramparts—Quebec                      MM
    MM. 100 Amer ptrs
  Still life                               OCl
    OCl. Handbook
  Still life with yellow green chair       OCo
    Brown. Amer ptg
    MnMW. Precisionist view
    NYG. Fine art
    Pierson
**DICKINSON, Sidney Edward,** 1890-
  At Maxie Ford's
    NAD. Annual ex, autumn 1949
  Mary                                     IaDa
    IaDa. 30th anniversary
    NAD. Annual ex, 1956
  Our son, Thorn
    NAD. Annual ex, 1949, 1st half
    PPC. Ptg in the U.S. 1949
  Peter Juley and son
    NAD. Annual ex, 1951
  Raphael Soyer
    NAD. Annual ex, 1961
  The search
    PPC. International ex, 1950
**Dickinson, Thorn**
  Dickinson, S. E. Our son, Thorn
**Di Cocco, Francesco.** See Cocco, Frances-
  co di
**DIEBENKORN, Richard,** 1922-
  Berkeley no 2, 1953
    NNSG. Younger Amer ptrs
    Read. Concise history
  Berkeley no 7, 1953                      MCH
    Pulitzer v2
  Berkeley no 16
    IU. Contemp Amer ptg & sculp, 1955
  Berkeley no 38
    PPC. International ex, 1955
  Berkeley no 54, 1955
    VR. Amer ptg, 1958
  A day at the race                        PPC
    CoS. New accessions USA, 1954
  Girl on a terrace
    Brussels. Exposition
    Selz. New images (col)
  Girl with three coffee cups (Girl with
    cups)
    MnMW. Eighty works
    Selz. New images
  Man and woman in a large room
    Selz. New images

DIEBENKORN, Richard—*Continued*
Man and woman seated
  Selz. New images
  Number 4, 1951
    Pulitzer v 1
  Pouring coffee
    PPC. International ex, 1958
  Two nudes
    PPC. International ex, 1961/62
  Woman and checkerboard          CSB
    NUM. Art across America
  Woman in a window               NBuA
    NBuA. Acquisitions 1957-58
  Yellow seascape
    IU. Contemp Amer ptg & sculp, 1961
Dieppe by M. B. Prendergast
Dies, Jane (Goelet) See Goelet, Jane
DIETZ, fl 1830
  Milford, North Wales, Pennsylvania   MB
    MB. Karolik coll
Digger by J. Hirsch
DI GIOIA, Frank, 1900-
  Fish market                      ATU
    ATU. Coll of Amer art
      Gruskin (col)
DIKE, Philip Latimer, 1906-
  Echo from the sea               OYB
    OYB. Annual 1959
    OYB. Supplement 1959
  Flags and fishes
    IU. Contemp Amer ptg, 1951
  Golden light
    NAD. Special ex, 1956
  Orchards and hills
    IU. Contemp Amer ptg, 1948
  Shore tapestry
    NAD. Annual ex, 1955
  Valley ranch                    ATeS
    ATeS. Collection
  Victorian tapestry
    IU. Contemp Amer ptg, 1950
  View of Los Angeles
    ICA. Annual ex, 1945/46
Dilemma by W. W. Quirt
DILLER, Burgoyne A. 1906-
  Composition
    McCurdy
    MMA. Abstract
  Construction                    CtY
    CtY. Soc Anonyme
  Number 10
    CSFP. Annual ex, 1950/51
Dimock, Edith. See Glackens, Edith (Di-
    mock)
Dinard by M. B. Prendergast
Dining rooms
  Clonney, J. G. Interior
  Koch, J. Interior—dining room
  Sargent, J. S. The breakfast table
  Sargent, H. Dinner party
Dinner still life by A. Blatas
Dinner table by M. M. Albright
DINNERSTEIN, Harvey
  Magnolia
    NAD. Annual ex, 1954
  Noah-Wolf
    PA. Annual ex, 1950
Diomed and his horses stopped by the light-
    ning of Jupiter by B. West

Diptych by E. M. Smith
Directional multiplicity by R. O. Preusser
Directions yellow by I. R. Pereira
Dirigo island by W. Kienbusch
Discarded treasures by W. M. Harnett (at-
    tributed works)
Discharge of cargo at pier by R. Marsh
Discovery by H. Billings
Discovery by G. Faddis
Dish of blackberries by Raphaelle Peale
Disintegrated and reanimated by M. Graves
Dismissal of school on an October afternoon
    by H. Inman
Dismounted: 4th troopers moving by F.
    Remington
Disorder by R. Soyer
A disputed trail by C. M. Russell
Disrobing figure by L. Johnson
Distant sail by K. Knaths
Distant view of lake by A. J. Miller
Distant view of the Rocky mountains by J. J.
    Egan
Distraction by A. G. Dove
Distributing goods to the Gros Ventres by
    J. M. Stanley
DI VALENTIN, Louis, 1908-
  Neither yet have you faith
    Genauer
    NAD. Annual ex, 1947, 1st half
Divisibilité indéfinie by Y. Tanguy
DIXON, James Budd
  Untitled
    CSFP. Annual ex, 1948/49
DIXON, Maynard, 1875-1946
  Cowboy and packhorse
    Carlson. Gallery (col)
  Desert ranges
    Carlson. Gallery (col)
  Drought and downpour
    Carlson. Gallery (col)
  Katchinamaker
    Carlson. Gallery (col)
  Lonesome road
    Carlson. Gallery (col)
  Peace in October
    Carlson. Gallery (col)
  Red gateway
    Carlson. Gallery (col)
  The wise men
    Carlson. Gallery (col)
Dobbin, Mrs George W. See Pue, Rebecca
Dock by C. A. Morris
Dock square by G. R. Beals
Docks, East Boston by M. B. Prendergast
Doctrine of the Trinity by J. S. Sargent
DODD, Lamar, 1909-
  Ashen gods
    DC. 21 biennial ex, 1949
  Aspiring
    IU. Contemp Amer ptg & sculp, 1955
  Athens [U.S.] View of             IBM
    Gruskin
  Aurangabad market
    IU. Contemp Amer ptg & sculp, 1961
  Black movements
    IU. Contemp Amer ptg, 1950

Cliffs and the sea
  IU. Contemp Amer ptg, 1951
  MM. Amer ptg today
Crucifixion no 2
  NAD. Annual ex, 1956
Granite city                                NAD
  Cheney. Story 1958 ed
Italian sunlight
  IU. Contemp Amer ptg & sculp, 1959
Madonnas of the rain
  IU. Contemp Amer ptg, 1948
Monhegan theme                              MM
  Pierson
  Pousette-Dart. Amer ptg
Objects on table
  IU. Contemp Amer ptg, 1949
A rainy ride                                GAtM
  GAtM. Holbrook collection
Savannah                                    NJMo
  NJMo. Forty years
Sicily
  NAD. Annual ex, 1960
Winter road
  VR. Biennial ex, 1948
**Dodd, William Lamar.** See Dodd, Lamar
**Dodge, Mrs James Mapes**
  Eakins, T. Portrait of a lady (Mrs James
    Mapes Dodge)
**Dodge, Mary Abigail,** 1833-1896
  Cobb, D. Mary Abigail Dodge (known as
    Gail Hamilton)
**Dodging** an arrow by A. J. Miller
**Dog** dance of the Dakotahs by S. Eastman
**Dog** dance of the Kansas Indians by S. Sey-
    mour
**Dogs**
  Bradley, J. (attributed works) Boy hold-
    ing dog
  Cassatt, M. Woman with a dog
  Chase, W. M. Alice with wolfhound
  Chase, W. M. Girl with dog
  Clonney, J. G. Sleigh ride
  Conduit, L. Pointer and quail
  Copley, J. S. Mary Warner [with dog]
  Eakins, T. Lady with a setter dog
  Evergood, P. Juju and her dog Copelia
  Glackens, W. J. Lenna and Imp
  Homer, W. Hunting dog among dead
    trees
  Homer, W. Huntsman and dogs
  Marsden, T. On a point
  Miller, A. J. Indians watching a canoe
  Osthaus, E. H. On the points
  Poore, H. R. Hound
  Prior, W. M. Little child with big dog
  Tracy, J. M. Grouse shooting
  Tracy, J. M. Pointers
  Unidentified artist. Two brown and white
    puppies
  Unidentified artist. Walking the puppy
  Woolworth, C. A. Little dog
  Wyeth, A. N. Raccoon
  Zorach, M. T. Hound
**Dolamen** by J. D. Brooks
**Dolbeare, Sarah (Comer)**
  Pollard limner. Mrs John Dolbeare
The **doll** by M. Siporin
The **doll** and the monster by G. P. Du Bois
**Dollar** bill and playbill by W. M. Harnett
    (attributed works)

**Dollarfish** and sheepshead by W. A. Walker
**Dolores** in blue costume by H. A. Sawyer
**Domain** by C. A. Hall
The **domino** girl by Unidentified artist
**Dominoes.** *See* Games and sports—Dominoes
**DONAGHY, John,** 1838-1931
  Three balls for five cents
    Chew. 250 years of art
**Donaldson, Althea (Lenox)** 1807-1878
  Thibault, A. Althea Lenox (?)
**DONATI, Enrico A.** 1909-
  Apsaras
    IU. Contemp Amer ptg & sculp, 1959
  Black & 3 whites
    NNSG. Younger Amer ptrs
  Ego et l'aurore
    IU. Contemp Amer ptg, 1948
  Electric eye
    IU. Contemp Amer ptg, 1951
  Gore et mandra                            WMAA
    Goodrich. Amer art
  Guirson
    IU. Contemp Amer ptg & sculp, 1961
  Habbaku dancers                           NBuA
    NBuA. Acquisitions 1959-1961
  Meteorite
    WMAA. Contemp Amer ptg, 1951
  Moss agate
    IU. Contemp Amer ptg, 1950
  Naram-Sin
    MnMW. 60 Amer ptrs
**Donkeys**
  Megargee, L. Donkey business
  Weir, J. A. Visiting neighbors
**Donna** Mencia in the robbers' cave by W.
    Allston
**DONNELLY, Thomas,** 1893-
  Valhalla bridge                           WMAA
    NYG. Fine art
**Don** Pasquale by D. Rosenthal
**Don Quixote**
  Folinsbee, J. F. Don Quixote
  Gonzalez, X. Don Quixote
  Meeker, D. J. Don Quixote
  Rattner, A. Composition: Don Quixote
**Don't** cry, little mother by P. Evergood
**DOOLITTLE, Amos,** 1754-1832
  Prodigal son reclaimed                    VWR
    Ford. Pictorial folk art
    **Portrait of the artist**
  Earl, R. Amos Doolittle
**Doomsday** by K. Knaths
**Door** to the river by W. De Kooning
**Doorway** by R. Vickrey
**Doorway,** Venice by J. A. M. Whistler
**Doreau, Clara C.**
  Lockman, M. D. Mrs Clara C. Doreau
**Dorian** Gray, Picture of by I. L. Albright
**Dorr, Henrietta,** fl 1818
  Unidentified artist. Henrietta **Dorr,**
    Chatham Center, New York
**Dorr, Robert Lockridge,** 1810-1815
  Border limner. Robert Lockridge Dorr
The **dory** by W. Homer
**Douarnenez** by M. Broudy
**Double** disparate by R. Lebrun
**Double** feature by R. Rauschenberg
**Double** indemnity by W. W. Quirt

**Double** portrait by M. Beckmann
**Double** portrait by C. S. Hopkinson
**Double** portrait of Berdie by L. Rivers
**Doubleday, Abner,** 1819-1893
  Blythe, D. G. Gen Doubleday watching
    his troops cross the Potomac
**Doubt** by W. W. Quirt
The **doubter** by Y. Tanguy
A **doubtful** guest by C. M. Russell
**DOUDERA, Gerard E.** 1932-
  Danville                 OYB
    OYB. Annual 1958
    OYB. Supplement 1959
**Doughboy's** equipment by C. A. Meurer
**Doughty, Mrs Thomas.** See Trusler, Mary
**DOUGHTY, Thomas,** 1793-1856
  Anglers
    NSP. Sportscapes
  Baltimore from Beech hill, View of   MB
    MB. Karolik coll
  Baltimore from the seat of R. Gilmor
                            MdBM
    MdBMu. Rendezvous
  A castle in England or Ireland
    Sears. Highlights
  Echo lake                 GAtM
    GAtM. Holbrook collection
  Fishing by a waterfall         MB
    MB. Karolik coll
  Fishing pool
    Sears. Highlights
  A home on the Hudson
    Sears. Highlights
  Ideal landscape           ATeS
    ATeS. Collection
  In nature's wonderland      MiD
    MiD. Treasures
    Pierson
    Richardson. Ptg in America
    Roos
  In the Catskills          MAP
    Canaday
    Larkin
    Larkin rev ed
    Pierson
  Landscape              MM
    Bazin
  Landscape, house on cliff above pool  PA
    Pierson
  Landscape, the ferry      MoKN
    MoKN. Handbook
  Landscape with fisherman     MB
    MB. Karolik coll
  Landscape with fisherman and sailboat
    WiMiA. Amer ptg 1760-1960
  Mountain torrent
    Sears. Highlights
  Naval home, Gray's ferry, Philadelphia
    MB. Karolik coll
  On the banks of the Susquehanna
    Born
  The raft              RPS
    Barker. Amer ptg
    Born
  Summer in the Catskills
    Sears. Highlights
  View from Stacey hill, Stoddard, New
    Hampshire          MB
    MB. Karolik coll

  View on the Bushkill
    Chew. 250 years of art
  Winter landscape         MB
    MB. Karolik coll
**Douglas, Mrs Stephen Arnold.** See Williams,
  Rose Adèle (Cutts) Douglas
**DOUGLASS, Lucy,** fl 1810
  Royal psalmist
    Flexner. Light of distant skies
**Douw, Magdalena**
  Unidentified artist. Magdalena Douw
**DOVE, Arthur G.** 1880-1946
  A. S. 1925, Portrait of       MMA
    Wight. Arthur G. Dove
  Abstraction, 1941
    NIC. Arthur G. Dove
    Wight. Arthur G. Dove
  Abstraction no 1, 1910
    NIC. Arthur G. Dove
  Abstraction no 1-6, 1910
    Wight. Arthur G. Dove
  Abstraction no 2, 1910
    NIC. Arthur G. Dove
    Time. 300 years (col)
    Wight. Arthur G. Dove (col)
  Across the road
    Wight. Arthur G. Dove
  Alfir's delight
    NIC. Arthur G. Dove
    Wight. Arthur G. Dove
    WMAA. Museum and its friends, 1958
  Anonymous, 1942          MM
    Wight. Arthur G. Dove (col)
  Awalk poplars
    Wight. Arthur G. Dove (col)
  The Bessie of New York     MdBM
    Wight. Arthur G. Dove (col)
  Brothers
    Hess. Abstract ptg
  Cars in sleet storm
    NIC. Arthur G. Dove
  City moon
    Wight. Arthur G. Dove
  Coal carrier           DP
    Wight. Arthur G. Dove (col)
  Connecticut river
    Wight. Arthur G. Dove
  Cow I, 1935
    Wight. Arthur G. Dove
  Cow at play          IBM
    Baur. New art
  Cows in pasture         DP
    DP. Catalogue
    NIC. Arthur G. Dove
    Wight. Arthur G. Dove (col)
  Dancing tree
    Wight. Arthur G. Dove
  Dawn II
    NIC. Arthur G. Dove
  Dawn III
    NIC. Arthur G. Dove
    Wight. Arthur G. Dove
  Distraction          WMAA
    Mendelowitz
  Electric peach orchard      DP
    DP. Catalogue
  Ferry boat wreck       WMAA
    Goodrich. Amer art (col)
    Wight. Arthur G. Dove (col)
  Fields of grain as seen from train  NBuA
    NBuA. Acquisitions 1957-58
    Wight. Arthur G. Dove

Flour mill II, 1938 (Flour mill abstraction)
                                   DP
  Baur. Revolution
  DP. Catalogue
  NIC. Arthur G. Dove
  Wight. Arthur G. Dove (col)
Fog horns                                    CoS
  Baur. New art
  NUM. Art across America
  Pierson
  Rathbun
  Wight. Arthur G. Dove
Frank Dusenberg, Portrait of
  Read. Art now, 1948 ed
George Gershwin's Rhaposody in blue
  part I, 1927
  Wight. Arthur G. Dove
Goat                                          MM
  Wight. Arthur G. Dove (col)
Gold, green and brown                         DP
  Baur. Revolution
Golden storm                                  DP
  DP. Catalogue
Graphite and blue
  NIC. Arthur G. Dove
Green, gold and brown                         DP
  NIC. Arthur G. Dove
  Pierson
Hand sewing machine, 1927                     MM
  MM. 100 Amer ptrs
  Wight. Arthur G. Dove
Hand sewing machine, 1941
  NIC. Arthur G. Dove
Hardware store
  Wight. Arthur G. Dove
High noon                                     KW
  Wight. Arthur G. Dove (col)
Holbrook's bridge, northwest, 1938
  Wight. Arthur G. Dove (col)
Huntington harbor                             DP
  DP. Catalogue
Huntington harbor no 2
  Wight. Arthur G. Dove
The inn
  Wight. Arthur G. Dove (col)
Landscape, c 1908
  NIC. Arthur G. Dove
Landscape, 1908-09
  NIC. Arthur G. Dove
Landscape in five flats
  NIC. Arthur G. Dove
Life goes by                                  DP
  DP. Catalogue
The lobster
  Wight. Arthur G. Dove
Long Island (oil)
  Wight. Arthur G. Dove
Long Island (water color)
  Wight. Arthur G. Dove
Mars, orange and green
  NYG. Fine art
  UNESCO. 1860-1949
  UNESCO. 1860-1955
Moon, 1935 (Zurier coll)
  Baur. New art (col)
  NBuA. Expressionism
  Wight. Arthur G. Dove
Moon, 1940 (Solinger coll)
  NIC. Arthur G. Dove
Naples yellow morning
  NIC. Arthur G. Dove

Nature symbolized, no 2, 1911                 ICA
  Baur. Nature
  Baur. Revolution
  Pierson
  Wight. Arthur G. Dove
No feather pillow                             NUM
  Wight. Arthur G. Dove (col)
October, 1935
  Wight. Arthur G. Dove
Out over the Sound
  NIC. Arthur G. Dove
Pagan philosophy
  WMAA. Pioneers
Parabola
  NIC. Arthur G. Dove
  Wight. Arthur G. Dove
Pieces of red, green & blue                   MLL
  Wight. Arthur G. Dove (col)
Plant forms                                   WMAA
  Goodrich. Amer art
  Hunter. Mod Amer ptg
  Wight. Arthur G. Dove (col)
Pozzuoli red                                  DP
  NIC. Arthur G. Dove
Rain or snow                                  DP
  DP. Catalogue
  NIC. Arthur G. Dove
  Pierson
  Wight. Arthur G. Dove
Reaching waves                                MM
  Brown. Amer ptg
Rise of the full moon                         DP
  DP. Catalogue
  NIC. Arthur G. Dove
  Read. Concise history
Rising moon
  Wight. Arthur G. Dove (col)
Rising tide
  McCurdy
  MMA. Abstract
  Wight. Arthur G. Dove
Rooftops                                      MLL
  NIC. Arthur G. Dove
  Wight. Arthur G. Dove (col)
Sails
  Wight. Arthur G. Dove
Sand barge                                    DP
  MMA. Abstract
  Wight. Arthur G. Dove (col)
  Wight. Milestones (col)
Silver tanks and moon                         PPhM
  Wight. Arthur G. Dove
Snow thaw                                     DP
  Larkin
  Larkin rev ed
  NIC. Arthur G. Dove
Square on the pond                            MLL
  Wight. Arthur G. Dove
Storm clouds in silver
  Cheney. Primer 1958
Summer, 1935                                  MLL
  Wight. Arthur G. Dove (col)
Summer orchard                                NUM
  NUM. Root bequest
Sunrise I, 1937                               MLL
  Baur. Nature (col)
  Wight. Arthur G. Dove (col)
Sunrise II, 1937
  Wight. Arthur G. Dove
Sunset III, 1937                              CtY
  CtY. Soc Anonyme
  Wight. Arthur G. Dove

**DOVE, A. G.**—*Continued*
Tanks                                          MLL
  Wight. Arthur G. Dove (col)
Team of horses
  Baur. New art
That red one                                   MLL
  NIC. Arthur G. Dove
  Wight. Arthur G. Dove (col)
Team of horses
  Wight. Arthur G. Dove
Telegraph pole                                 ICA
  Wight. Arthur G. Dove
Through a frosty moon
  DC. Privately owned
Waterfall                                      DP
  Wight. Arthur G. Dove (col)
Weather vane
  NIC. Arthur G. Dove
Willow tree                                    FaW
  Wight. Arthur G. Dove
Wind, clouds and water
  Cheney. Expressionism 1948 ed
Woodpecker                                     DP
  DP. Catalogue
**Dove** love by C. Howard
**Dove** of the inner eye by M. Graves
**Dover** baby by Unidentified artist
**Doves**
  Audubon, J. J. Carolina turtle-dove
  Thompson, C. Girl with dove
  Unidentified artist. Venus drawn by doves
**Dowager** in a wheelchair by P. Evergood
**Dowdall, Eliza Hopkins (Nicoll)** fl 1809
  Jarvis, J. W. Mrs George Robert Dowdall
**Dowdall, George Robert.** 1783-1820
  Jarvis, J. W. George Robert Dowdall
**Down** the ways by J. Schoener
**Down** to earth by A. James
**Down** the Mississippi in a birch-bark canoe
  by G. Catlin
**Downing** house, Chester county, Pennsylvania by S. Blair
**Downing** the nigh leader by F. Remington
**Downtown** fantasy by R. H. Avery
**Downtown** street by G. O. Coleman
**Dowse, Relief.** See Gill, Relief (Dowse)
**Doyer** by P. Guston
**DOZIER, Otis,** 1904-
  Fishermen
    MM. Amer ptg today
  Passage to the sea                      TxF
    Pousette-Dart. Amer ptg
  Pelicans
    IU. Contemp Amer ptg, 1952
  Summer                                   TxD
    Pierson
**Drachenfels** by W. Whittredge
**Dragon** by W. A. Baziotes
**Dragonwyck,** Costumes for by D. E. Lee
**Dramatis** personae by J. Levine
**Drapeau** by M. Weber
**Draped** head by M. Weber
**Drawing** a bead on a woodchuck by J. G. Chapman
**Drayton, Charlotte.** See Manigault, Charlotte (Drayton)
**Drayton, Maria Miles (Heyward)** See Heyward, Maria Miles

**Drayton, Mrs William.** See Heyward, Maria Miles
The **dream** by M. Beckmann
The **dream** by A. B. Davies
The **dream** by C. S. Price
**Dream** catch by P. Evergood
**Dream** of a good life by M. Siporin
**Dream** of Arcadia by T. Cole
**Dream** of Columbus by W. J. Hubard
**Dream** of flying by M. Hoff
**Dream** ride by W. J. Glackens
The **dreamer** by C. Beaux
**DREIER, Dorothea A.** 1870-1923
  Flower market at Geneva                 CtY
    CtY. Soc Anonyme
  New York: the Little church around the
    corner                               CtY
    CtY. Soc Anonyme
      **Portrait of the artist**
  Shirlaw, W. Dorothea A. Dreier
**DREIER, Katherine Sophie,** 1877-
  Abstract portrait of Marcel Duchamp
                 MMA
    MMA. Abstract
  Abstract portrait of Savadsky
    Cheney. Expressionism 1948 ed
  Explosion                               CtY
    CtY. Soc Anonyme

      **Portrait of the artist**
  Goldthwaite, A. Katherine S. Dreier
**Dress** rehearsal by M. B. Prendergast
**Dressing** room by W. Kuhn
**Dressmaker's** shop by R. Soyer
**DREWES, Werner,** 1899-
  Night fantasy                           CtY
    CtY. Soc Anonyme
  Re-awakening                            WMAA
    CoS. New accessions USA, 1948
  Still life, New York                    IBM
    Bazin (col)
**Drift** for summer by M. Tobey
**Driftwood** by E. H. Betts
**Driftwood** by W. Homer
**Driftwood** by F. James
**Driftwood** by Z. L. Sepeshy
**Driftwood,** Monegan by E. Fiene
**Driftwood,** North Pacific by B. J. O. Nordfeldt
**DRIGGS, Elsie,** 1898-
  Pittsburgh, 1927                        WMAA
    MnMW. Precisionist view
The **drive,** Central Park by W. J. Glackens
**Drought** and downpour by M. Dixon
**Drought**-stricken area by A. Hogue
**Drowsy** company by H. G. Keller
**Drugstore** by S. Wilson
**DRUMLEVITCH, Seymour,** 1923-
  Bronx bridge                            NBuA
    CoS. New accessions USA, 1952
  Roman aqueduct                          OYB
    OYB. Annual 1954
    OYB. Supplement
  Ruins
    WMAA. Annual ex, 1955
  Synagogue
    CanO. Hirshhorn coll (col)

**Drums,** Indian and word of God by M. Tobey

**Dry** goods and notions by D. G. Blythe

**Dry** nets by L. W. Quanchi

**Drying** codfish in Brittany by Leonid

**Duane, Anthony,** fl 1725
Unidentified artist. Anthony Duane

**DU BACK, Charles Steven**
Summer
WMAA. Contemp Amer ptg, 1959/60

**DUBIN, Ralph,** 1918-
Plaster
VR. Amer ptg, 1954

**Dublin** by G. Hartigan

**Dublin** and environs by L. MacIver

**Dublin** pool by G. R. Beal

**Dubocq, Mme,** fl 1807
Peale, J. Mme Dubocq and her four children

**DU BOIS, Guy Pène,** 1884-1958
Americans in Paris                    MMA
Lewisohn
Another expulsion
NAD. Annual ex, spring 1950
Bar
Brown. Amer ptg
The beauty
PPC. Ptg in the U. S. 1949
The doll and the monster              MM
MM. 100 Amer ptrs
Pierson
WMAA. Juliana Force
Glitter
OYB. Annual 1954
Morning, Paris cafe                   WMAA
NYG. Fine art
Pierson
Opera box                             WMAA
Larkin rev ed
Restaurant
Gruskin
Shovel hats                           WMAA
WMAA. Sara Roby
Waiter
Cheney. Story 1958 ed
Window in the Union club
Baur. Revolution
Woman with cigarette                  WMAA
Goodrich. Amer art

**Du Bosc, Mary.** See Wragg, Mary (du Bosc)

**DUBREUIL, V.**
Barrels of money
Frankenstein. After the hunt

**Dubuque,** Iowa by J. C. Wild

**DUCA, Alfred Milton,** 1920-
Autumnal
IU. Contemp Amer ptg, 1951
The carob tree
IU. Contemp Amer ptg & sculp, 1953

**DU CASSE, Ralph Saule,** 1916-
Botafogo
IU. Contemp Amer Ptg & sculp, 1957
The grandest of Noo
IU. Contemp Amer ptg & sculp, 1961
The kiss
IU. Contemp Amer ptg & sculp, 1953
St George and the calla lillies
VR. Amer ptg, 1958

San Francisco bay
IU. Contemp Amer ptg & sculp, **1955**
Strahmutchi                           NNSG
NNSG. Handbook
NNSG. Younger Amer ptrs

**Duchamp, Marcel,** 1887-
Dreier, K. S. Abstract portrait of Marcel Duchamp

**Duché, Jacob,** 1737?-1798
Duché, T. S. Rev Jacob Duché and Thomas Spence Duché

**DUCHÉ, Thomas Spence,** 1763-1790
Jacob and Thomas Spence Duché    PH
Chew. 250 years of art

**Duck** decoy by K. Knaths

**Duck** hunters on the Hoboken marshes by W. T. Ranney

**Duck** pond by W. De Kooning

**Duck** shooting by E. Moran

**Duck** shooting by A. F. Tait

**Duckblind** by W. R. Derrick

**Ducks**
Audubon, J. J. Red-breasted merganser
Audubon, J. J. Shoveller duck
Austin, W. Mandarin duck
Benson, F. W. Currituck marshes, North Carolina
Benson, F. W. Redhead ducks
Dasburg, A. Ducks
Derrick, W. R. Duckblind
Earle, L. C. Escape
Graves, M. Wounded scoter
Hartley, M. Labrador ducks
Knap, N. D. The flight
Knaths, K. Duck flight
Scott, P. M. Pintails

**Duclair** on Seine by H. D. Martin

**Dudley, Charles,** 1737-1797
Alexander, C. J. Charles Dudley

**Dudley, Kitty (Crooke)**
Alexander, C. J. Mrs Charles Dudley

**DUDLEY, Robert,** fl 1866
Awaiting the reply over the trans-Atlantic cable                                 MM
Davidson v 1
Splicing the cable                    MM
U.S. National Capital sesquicentennial com

**Duel** and pantomime by L. Michael

**Duel** of the entomologist by F. Ruvolo

**DUGMORE, Edward,** 1915-
Number six
PPC. International ex, 1955
Painting 1960-D                       NBuA
NBuA. Acquisitions 1959-1961

**Dull** lecture by G. S. Newton

**Dull** story by G. C. Bingham

**Dulles, Mary Elizabeth,** fl 1806
Malbone, E. G. Mary Elizabeth Dulles

**Dummy** by D. W. Ellis

**Dummy** by C. Maringer

**DU MOND, Frank Vincent,** 1865-1951
Fishing companions
NSP. Sportscapes

**DUNCAN, Frank Davenport,** 1915-
Condition at Antietam
PPC. International ex, 1950
A condition of New England
PPC. Ptg in the U.S. 1949

**DUNCAN, F. D.**—*Continued*
Le Faou
 IU. Contemp Amer ptg & sculp, 1955
Mallorca III
 PA. Annual ex, 1954
Through the window
 IU. Contemp Amer ptg, 1952
Through to the sea
 IU. Contemp Amer ptg, 1948
Within autumn
 Pousette-Dart. Amer ptg
**Duncan, Isadora,** 1877-1927
 Walkowitz, A. Three dance abstractions:
 Isadora Duncan
**DUNCANSON, Robert S.** 1821-1871
Blue hole on the Little Miami river
 OCiM
 OCiM. Rediscoveries
 Pierson
Uncle Tom and Little Eva MiD
 OCiM. Rediscoveries
**Dunes** by C. H. Demuth
**Dunes** and breakwaters by L. Feininger
**Dunes** and marshes by D. Macknight
**Dunes** at Marshfield by W. Homer
**Dunes,** Baltic by L. Feininger
**Dunes** with ray of light II by L. Feininger
**DUNKERLEY, Joseph,** fl 1783-1787
Ebenezer Storer (possibly after Copley)
 CtY
 CtY. Portrait index

**Attributed works**

Charles Bulfinch MB
 MB. New England miniatures
Mrs Charles Bulfinch MB
 MB. New England miniatures
**DUNLAP, William,** 1766-1839
Artist showing his picture of a scene from
 "Hamlet" to his parents NNHS
 Richardson. Ptg in America
David Van Horne MiD
 Pierson
Dunlap family NNHS
 ICA. From colony to nation
 Pierson
Samuel Griffin DN
 DN. Amer primitive ptgs, pt 1
Scene from the dramatization of James
 Fenimore Cooper's novel "The Spy"
 NCHA
 Davidson v2
Self-portrait CtY
 CtY. Portrait index
**Dunlap family,** fl 1788
 Dunlap, W. Dunlap family
**Dunn, Mary.** See Thorp, Mary (Dunn)
**DUNN, Robert,** 1932-
Figures and still life
 IU. Contemp Amer ptg & sculp, 1959
**Duo** I by J. Tworkov
**Duograph** by I. R. Pereira
**Duran, Carolus.** See Carolus-Duran
**DURAND, Asher Brown,** 1796-1886
Aaron Belknap NNHS
 NNHS. Waldron Phoenix Belknap coll
Aaron Betts Belknap NNHS
 NNHS. Waldron Phoenix Belknap coll

Andrew Jackson NNHS
 U.S. National Capital sesquicentennial
 com
Babbling brook MB
 MB. Karolik coll
Beeches MM
 Bazin
Capture of Major André MWM
 Cowdrey v 1
 Pierson
Catskill Clove NNCe
 Pierson
Catskill mountains near Shandaken
 NYG. Fine art
A Catskill stream NBM
 Mendelowitz
Early morning, Cold Spring, New York
 NJMo
 NJMo. Forty years
 NJMo. Your Montclair art museum
Hudson at Rhinebeck GAtM
 GAtM. Holbrook collection
Hunter ATeS
 ATeS. Collection
In the woods MAC
 NUM. Art across America
In the woods MM
 Upjohn
Kindred spirits NNPL
 Barker. Amer ptg
 Born
 Canaday
 Craven. Rainbow book
 CtHW. Thomas Cole
 Flexner. Amer ptg
 Flexner. Short history
 Larkin
 Larkin rev ed
 Pierson
 Richardson. Ptg in America
 Roos
 Time. 300 years (col)
 Walker. Ptgs from America
Lake George, New York MB
 MB. Karolik coll
Landscape InIJ
 InIJ. 105 ptgs
Landscape NJN
 NJN. Early N. J. artists
Mrs Aaron Belknap NNHS
 NNHS. Waldron Phoenix Belknap coll
Mrs Durand and her sister NJN
 Pierson
Mrs Nicholas William Stuyvesant NNHS
 Vail. Stuyvesant ports
Monument mountain, Berkshires MiD
 NYG. Fine art
 UNESCO. Prior to 1860
 UNESCO. Prior to 1860 3d ed
Morning of life NAD
 NAD. Amer tradition
Mountain valley
 Sears. Highlights
North Mountain reservation, South Orange,
 New Jersey
 Sears. Highlights
The old oak NNHS
 Pierson
Roman head NNHS
 MiD. Travelers in Arcadia
Sunday morning NNHS
 Born
 NYG. Fine art (col)

View of Rutland, Vermont          MiD
  MiD. Treasures
Yankee peddler at work          NCHA
  Davidson v 1

### Portrait of the artist
Healy, G. P. A. Asher B. Durand (?)

**Durand, Mrs Asher Brown.** See Durand, Lucy (Baldwin)

**Durand, Charles Émile Auguste.** See Carolus-Duran

**DURAND, John,** fl 1767-1782
Catherine Beekman
  Belknap
John Lothrop          DN
  DN. Amer primitive ptgs, pt 2
Mary Beekman
  Belknap
Mrs Abraham Jarvis          DeWin
  Belknap
Mrs Adriaan Bancker          NNHS
  Flexner. First flowers
  ICA. From colony to nation
Mrs Benjamin Peck          DeWin
  Belknap
Mrs John Lothrop          DN
  DN. Amer primitive ptgs, pt 2
Mrs Richard Bancker
  Belknap
Rapalje children          NNHS
  Davidson v 1
  ICA. From colony to nation
  Larkin
  Larkin rev ed
  Lipman. Primitive ptrs
  Pierson
  Richardson. Ptg in America
Richard Bancker
  Belknap

**Durand, Lucy (Baldwin)** d 1830
Durand, A. B. Mrs Durand and her sister

**Duret, Théodore,** 1838-1927
Whistler, J. A. M. Théodore Duret: Arrangement in flesh-colour and black

**DURFEE, Hazard,** 1915-
Beach grass
  IU. Contemp Amer ptg & sculp, 1955
Seascape no II
  IU. Contemp Amer ptg, 1952
Shore flowers II
  PPC. International ex, 1952

**DURRIE, George Henry,** 1820-1863
Autumn in New England, cider making
  CtHW. Durrie
Boys skating
  CtHW. Durrie
East rock
  CtHW. Durrie
East rock from the south          CtNH
  CtHW. Durrie
East rock, New Haven          CtNH
  CtHW. Durrie
East rock, New Haven (English real estate trust)
  CtHW. Durrie
Farm scene, summer
  CtHW. Durrie
Farmstead in winter
  CtHW. Durrie
Farmyard in winter
  CtHW. Durrie

Farmyard in winter, selling corn
  CtHW. Durrie
Farmyard, winter          NNHS
  CtHW. Durrie
  Pierson
Going to church
  CtHW. Durrie
  Davidson v2
John Durrie
  MB. New England miniatures
Jones' inn
  CtHW. Durrie
Landscape with cattle
  CtHW. Durrie
Mrs Tunis V. Conover          NJF
  CtHW. Durrie
New England farm scene, c 1860
  Davidson v 1
New England winter scene, 1858
  CtHW. Durrie
New England winter scene, c 1862
  CtHW. Durrie
Old mill, winter          NNHS
  CtHW. Durrie
Red schoolhouse
  CtHW. Durrie
Returning to the farm          NNHS
  CtHW. Durrie
  Larkin
  Larkin rev ed
Self-portrait, 1843
  CtHW. Durrie
Self-portrait, 1860
  CtHW. Durrie
Seven miles to Farmington
  CtHW. Durrie
Summer landscape (Freylinghausen coll)
  CtHW. Durrie
Summer landscape          MB
  MB. Karolik coll
Sunday in the country
  CtHW. Durrie
Sunset Mount Carmel, Connecticut
  CtHW. Durrie
Ten miles to Salem
  CtHW. Durrie
Tunis V. Conover          NJF
  CtHW. Durrie
View of New Haven, winter
  CtHW. Durrie
West rock, New Haven (Brinton coll)
  CtHW. Durrie
William J. Conover as a boy          NJF
  CtHW. Durrie
Winter farm scene
  CtHW. Durrie
Winter in the country, a cold morning, 1861
  CtHW. Durrie
Winter in the country, a cold morning, 1862
  CtHW. Durrie
Winter in the country, distant hills
  CtHW. Durrie
Winter in the country, getting ice
  CtHW. Durrie
Winter in the country, the old grist mill
  CtHW. Durrie
Winter landscape          CtY
  CtHW. Durrie

**DURRIE, G. H.**—*Continued*
Winter landscape; gathering wood     MB
  MB. Karolik coll
  Mendelowitz
Winter scene (Fleischman coll)
  WiMiA. Amer ptg 1760-1960
Winter scene (Hoppin coll)
  CtHW. Durrie
Winter scene in New England     CtY
  CtHW. Durrie
Winter scene, Jones' inn
  CtHW. Durrie
Wood for winter     NNHS
  Born
  CtHW. Durrie
  Pierson
Woodsman in winter
  CtHW. Durrie

**Durrie, John,** 1792-1857
  Durrie, G. H. John Durrie

**Dusenberg, Frank**
  Dove, A. G. Frank Dusenberg

**Dusk** by W. A. Baziotes

**Dusk** by W. Chaiken

**Dusk** by K. Knaths

**Dusk** at Fuji by P. Evergood

**Dust** bowl by A. Hogue

**Dust,** drought and destruction by W. C. Palmer

**Dust** storm, Fifth avenue by J. Sloan

**Dusty** road in July by C. E. Burchfield

**Dutch** girl in white by R. Henri

**Dutch** Joe by R. Henri

**Dutch** lunch by S. Rosen

**DUVENECK, Frank,** 1848-1919
  A boy     OYB
    OYB. Catalogue 1951
  The bridges, Florence     MoSL
    MoSL. Handbook 1953
  The crimson gown (Mrs Mary Goddard
    Williams     NoCR
    NoCR. Catalogue
  Georg von Hoesslin     MiD
    Canaday
  Head of an old man     DNC
    DNC. Gellatly coll, 1954
  Henry James
    NAD. Amer tradition
  Mary Cabot Wheelwright     NBM
    Pierson
  Mrs Mary Goddard Williams. See The
    crimson gown
  Music master
    Baur. Revolution
  Old town brook, Polling, Bavaria     OCiM
    Born
  Turkish page     PA
    Pierson
    Richardson. Ptg in America
  Venetian girl     OCl
    OCl. Handbook
  Whistling boy     OCiM
    Bauer. Amer ptg
    Brown. Amer ptg
    DC. De gustibus
    OCiM. Guide
    Pierson
    Roos

Woman with forget-me-nots     OCiM
  Pierson
Young man     NBM
  Mendelowitz
Young man (Nichols coll)
  Larkin

### Portrait of the artist
Chase, W. M. Duvenek in the studio
Chase, W. M. Duveneck painting the
  Turkish page

**Duyckinck, Anna (Rapalje)** 1733-1811
  Kilburn, L. Mrs Gerardus Duyckinck II

**DUYCKINCK, Evert,** 1667-1724?
  Mrs Gerardus Beekman (Magdalen
    Abeel) (1)
    Belknap

### Attributed works
Cornelia Beekman
  Belknap
Mrs Gerardus Beekman (Magdalen
  Beekman) (2)
  Belknap
Mrs William Beekman (1)
  Belknap
Mrs William Beekman (2)
  Belknap
William Beekman
  Belknap

**DUYCKINCK, Gerardus,** 1695-1745?

### Attributed works
Children of Jacob Franks (Phila and
  David Franks)     NNAJ
  Belknap
Flexner. First flowers (here as De
  Peyster manner)
Elizabeth Van Brugh     NNHS
Flexner. First flowers (here as De
  Peyster manner)
Gerardus Beekman
  Belknap
Joseph(?) Hallett     NNHS
  Belknap
Mrs Henry Van Rensselaer     NNHS
  Belknap
Mrs Jacob Franks     NNAJ
  Belknap
Mrs Joseph(?) Hallett     NNHS
  Belknap
Mrs Moses Levy     NNMC
  Belknap
Phila Franks     NNAJ
  Belknap
William Beekman
  Belknap

### Portrait of the artist
Kilburn, L. Gerardus Duyckinck II

**Duyckinck, Mrs Gerardus.** See Duyckinck,
  Anna (Rapalje)

**DUYCKINCK, Gerrit,** 1660-c 1710
  Mrs Augustus Jay     NNHS
    Belknap
    Vail. Stuyvesant ports
  Mrs Gerrit Duyckinck     NNHS
    Barker. Amer ptg
    Belknap
    Flexner. First flowers
    Larkin
    Larkin rev ed
    Mendelowitz
    Pierson

**DUYCKINCK, Gerrit**—*Continued*
Self-portrait                NNHS
  Belknap
  Flexner. First flowers
  Pierson
          **Attributed works**
Young lady                DN
  Belknap
  DN. Amer primitive ptgs, pt 1
**Duyckinck, Maria (Abeel)** 1666-1738
  Duyckinck, Gerrit. Mrs Gerrit Duyckinck
**Duyckinck, Sarah.** See Bancker, Sarah
  (Duyckinck)
**Dwarf** by W. A. Baziotes
**Dwelling** by C. A. Morris
**Dwight, Christiana (Broughton)** fl 1747
  Theus, J. Christiana Broughton (copy of
    pastel by Henrietta Johnston)
**Dwight, Mrs Daniel.** See Dwight, Christiana
  (Broughton)
**Dwight, Theodore,** 1764-1846
  Ames, E. Theodore Dwight
**Dwight, Timothy,** 1752-1817
  Trumbull, J. Timothy Dwight
**Dwight, Timothy,** 1828-1916
  Tarbell, E. C. Timothy Dwight
  Weir, J. F. The Theological of Yale uni-
    versity
**DYER, Briggs,** 1911-
Tabletop                ATU
  ATU. Coll of Amer art
**Dyer, Mrs Charles Gifford.** See Dyer, May
  (Anthony)
**Dyer, May (Anthony)** 1850-1914
  Sargent, J. S. Mrs Charles Gifford Dyer
**Dying** Hercules by S. F. B. Morse
**Dying** steer by R. Lebrun
**Dynasty** by K. Okada
**Dysart, Winifred**
  Fuller, G. Winifred Dysart
**DZUBAS, Friedelbald,** 1915-
Arcadia II
  WMAA. Annual ex, 1958
Death of the general          CtY
  CtY. Soc Anonyme

# E

**E,** 1915 by M. Hartley
**E**—1953 by J. D. Brooks
**E** pluribus unum by M. Tobey
**EADES, Luis,** 1923-
War prisoners             OYB
  OYB. Annual 1958
  OYB. Supplement 1959
**Eagle** cliff, Franconia Notch, New Hamp-
  shire by J. Cropsey
**Eagle** cliff, New Hampshire by J. F.
  Cropsey
**Eagle** in the rock by M. Graves
**Eagles**
  Audubon, J. J. Sea eagle (so called)
  Graves, M. Eagle
  Unidentified artist. Eagle and snake
  Unidentified artist. Screaming eagle

**Eakins, Benjamin,** 1818-1899?
  Eakins, T. Benjamin Eakins
**Eakins, Susan Hannah (MacDowell)** 1852-
  1938
  Eakins, T. Lady with a setter dog
**EAKINS, Thomas,** 1844-1916
A. W. Lee
  Porter. Thomas Eakins
  WiMiA. Amer ptg 1760-1960
The actress             PPhM
  Bazin (col detail)
Addie                PPhM
  Baur. Amer ptg
  Baur. Revolution
Agnew clinic           PPhUn
  Barker. Amer ptg
  Canaday
  Canaday (detail)
  Craven. Rainbow book
  Craven. Treasury 1952 ed
  Flexner. Amer ptg
  Flexner. Short history
  PA. Annual ex, 1955
  Pierson
  Porter. Thomas Eakins
  Robb. Harper history
  Roos
  U.S. National Capital sesquicentennial
    com
An Arcadian
  Porter. Thomas Eakins
Arthur B. Frost          PPhM
  Robb. Art 1953 ed
Baby at play
  CtY. Yale alumni
  Porter. Thomas Eakins
Baseball players, 1875       RPS
  Davidson v2
  NYG. Fine art
  Porter. Thomas Eakins
  U.S. National Capital sesquicentennial
    com
Beatrice Fenton. See Coral necklace
Benjamin Eakins          PPhM
  Cheney. Story 1958 ed
  Porter. Thomas Eakins
Benjamin Howard Rand     PPhJ
  Porter. Thomas Eakins
Between rounds         PPhM
  Pierson
  Porter. Thomas Eakins (col)
  Robb. Art 1953 ed
  Taylor. Fifty centuries, 1954 ed (col)
  Time. 300 years (col)
  U.S. National Capital sesquicentennial
    com
The Bohemian (Franklin Schenk)  PPhM
  Porter. Thomas Eakins
Bringing home the moose
  NSP. Sportscapes
Cardinal Martinelli
  Porter. Thomas Eakins
Cello player             PA
  PA. Annual ex, 1955
Charles Haseltine        NJMo
  NJMo. Forty years
  NJMo. Your Montclair art museum
Charles Lewis Fussel       PR
  PR. Catalogue
Charles Linford, the artist    IBM
  Porter. Thomas Eakins

**EAKINS, Thomas**—*Continued*

Chess players    MM
  Pierson
  Porter. Thomas Eakins
Concert singer (Weda Cook)    PPhM
  Craven. Treasury 1952 ed (col)
  DC. 25 biennial ex, 1957
  Larkin (detail)
  Larkin rev ed
  PA. Annual ex, 1955
  Pierson
  Porter. Thomas Eakins
  Time. 300 years (col)
Coral necklace (Beatrice Fenton)    OYB
  OYB. Accessions
  OYB. Supplement 1959
Cowboys in the Bad Lands
  Rathbone
  U.S. National Capital sesquicentennial
    com
Crucifixion    PPhM
  Porter. Thomas Eakins
Crucifixion, Study for
  Chew. 250 years of art
Elinor S. F. Pue    VR
  Porter. Thomas Eakins
Elizabeth at the piano    MAP
  Porter. Thomas Eakins
Ernest Lee Parker
  Porter. Thomas Eakins
Fairman Rogers four-in-hand    PPhM
  Porter. Thomas Eakins (col)
  Time. 300 years (col)
  U.S. National Capital sesquicentennial
    com
Frank Hamilton Cushing    OkTT
  Porter. Thomas Eakins
Frank Jay St John
  WiMiA. Amer ptg 1760-1960
Franklin Schenk. See The Bohemian
George Cadwalader    OYB
  OYB. Catalogue 1951
Gross clinic    PPhJ
  Canaday
  Janson. Key monuments
  Janson. Picture history
  Larkin
  Larkin rev ed
  Myers. Art
  PA. Annual ex, 1955
  Pierson
  Porter. Thomas Eakins
  Richardson. Ptg in America
Gross clinic, Sketch for    PPhM
  Chew. 250 years of art
  Porter. Thomas Eakins
Harrison S. Morris
  PA. Annual ex, 1953
Head of young woman
  Porter. Thomas Eakins
Henry A. Rowland    MAP
  Pierson
  Porter. Thomas Eakins
Home scene    NBM
  Porter. Thomas Eakins
Horatio C. Wood    MiD
  Porter. Thomas Eakins
Hunting
  MiD. Coll in progress
  WiMiA. Amer ptg 1760-1960

John Biglen in a single scull    CtY
  NYG. Fine art
  Robb. Harper history (col)
John Biglen in a single scull    MM
  Davidson v2
  McCurdy
  Porter. Thomas Eakins
John H. Brinton
  Porter. Thomas Eakins
John McClure Hamilton    CtHW
  CtHW. Handbook
John McClure Hamilton    GAtM
  GAtM. Holbrook collection
Joseph Leidy jr. See Man with red necktie
Katherine
  Porter. Thomas Eakins
Lady with a setter dog (Mrs Eakins)    MM
  Lee. Art then and now
  Pierson
  Porter. Thomas Eakins
Letitia Wilson Jordan Bacon    NBM
  MoSL. 40 masterpieces
  PA. Annual ex, 1955
  Pierson
  Porter. Thomas Eakins
Louis N. Kenton. See The thinker
Man with red necktie (Dr Joseph Leidy
  jr)    NJN
  Porter. Thomas Eakins
Margaret
  Porter. Thomas Eakins
Marguerite in skating costume    PPhM
  Porter. Thomas Eakins
Maud Cook (Young woman in pink dress)
  Porter. Thomas Eakins
Max Schmitt in a single scull    MM
  Barker. Amer ptg
  Canaday
  Lewisohn
  Mendelowitz
  NBuA. Expressionism
  PA. Annual ex, 1955
  Pierson
  Porter. Thomas Eakins (col)
  Roos
  Taylor. Fifty centuries, 1954 ed (col)
  Time. 300 years (col)
Maybelle
  Porter. Thomas Eakins (col)
Mending the net    PPhM
  Canaday
  Canaday (detail)
Miss Parker. See Old-fashioned dress
Miss Van Buren    DP
  Canaday (col)
  DP. Catalogue
  Pierson
  Porter. Thomas Eakins
  Walker. Ptgs from America (col)
Mrs Anna M. Kershaw
  Porter. Thomas Eakins
Mrs Eakins. See Lady with a setter dog
Mrs Edith Mahon    MNS
  Larkin
  Larkin rev ed
Mrs Frank Hamilton Cushing    PPhM
  Porter. Thomas Eakins
Mrs Gilbert Parker    MB
  Porter. Thomas Eakins

Mrs M. S. Stokes                      NCa
    Porter. Thomas Eakins
Mrs S                                 NCa
    NUM. Art across America
Mrs Thomas Eakins
    PA. Annual ex, 1955
Mrs William D. Frishmuth              PPhM
    Canaday
    Craven. Treasury 1952 ed
Mrs William Shaw Word
    Porter. Thomas Eakins
Monsignor Diomede Falconio            DN
    Porter. Thomas Eakins (col)
Music                                 NBuA
    Porter. Thomas Eakins
    PPC. Amer classics
Musicians rehearsing                  PPhM
    Canaday
Nude back
    Porter. Thomas Eakins
Oarsmen                               PPhM
    Chew. 250 years of art
    Porter. Thomas Eakins
Oarsmen on the Schuylkill             NBM
    Porter. Thomas Eakins
Oboe player (Benjamin Sharp)          PPhM
    Chew. 250 years of art
Old-fashioned dress (Miss Parker)
                                      PPhM
    Porter. Thomas Eakins
On the Delaware
    Porter. Thomas Eakins
Pathetic song                         DC
    Barker. Amer ptg
    DC. De gustibus
    DC. Masterpieces
    Gardner 1959 ed
    Mendelowitz
    MiD. Ptg in America
    Pierson
    Richardson. Ptg in America
The pianist (Stanley Addicks)         InIJ
    InIJ. 105 ptgs
Portrait of a lady (Mrs James Mapes
    Dodge)                            PPhM
    Porter. Thomas Eakins
Professionals at rehearsal            PPhM
    Porter. Thomas Eakins
Pushing for rail                      MM
    NYG. Fine art
Rail shooting. See Will Schuster and
    black man going shooting for rail
Riter Fitzgerald, Sketch for portrait
    (Fleischman coll)
    MiD. Coll in progress
    WiMiA. Amer ptg 1760-1960
Robert M. Lindsay, the print collector
                                      MiD
    MiD. Treasures
    Porter. Thomas Eakins
Robert M. Lindsay, Sketch for portrait
                                      MiD
    Porter. Thomas Eakins
Sailboats racing on the Delaware      PPhM
    Porter. Thomas Eakins
Sailing                               PPhM
    Craven. Treasury 1952 ed
    NYG. Fine art

Sailing boats                         PPhM
    Richardson. Ptg in America
Salutat                               MAP
    Canaday
    Hunter. Mod Amer ptg
    Porter. Thomas Eakins (col)
    Roos
Samuel Murray
    Porter. Thomas Eakins
Self-portrait, c 1902                 NAD
    NAD. Amer tradition
    PA. Annual ex, 1955
    Porter. Thomas Eakins
Signora Gomez d'Arza                  MM
    McKinney
    MM. 100 Amer ptrs
    Porter. Thomas Eakins (col)
Stanley Addicks. See The pianist
Starting out after rail               MB
    PA. Annual ex, 1955
Starting out after rail               KW
    Pierson
    Porter. Thomas Eakins (col)
Street scene in Seville
    Porter. Thomas Eakins
Study of a girl's head
    Porter. Thomas Eakins              PPhM
The swimming hole                     TxF
    PA. Annual ex, 1955
    Pierson
    Porter. Thomas Eakins (col)
    Time. 300 years (col)
Taking the count                      CtY
    Seiberling
Taking the count, Study for head of
    referee
    Porter. Thomas Eakins (col)
The thinker (Louis N. Kenton)         MM
    Myers. Art
    PA. Annual ex, 1955
    Pierson
Thomas Sharp. See Oboe player
Turning the stake boat                OCl
    OCl. Handbook
    Pierson
    Porter. Thomas Eakins
    Walker. Ptgs from America
The violinist
    Porter. Thomas Eakins
Walt Whitman                          PA
    Craven. Rainbow book
    Craven. Treasury 1952 ed
    Mendelowitz
    Pierson
    Porter. Thomas Eakins (col)
    Robb. Harper history
    Roos
    Time. 300 Years (col)
Weda Cook. See Concert singer
Will Schuster and black man going shoot-
    ing for rail (Rail shooting)
    Craven. Treasury 1952 ed (col)
    CtY. Yale alumni
    Porter. Thomas Eakins
    UNESCO. 1860-1949
    UNESCO. 1860-1955
William McDowell
    Porter. Thomas Eakins
William Rush and his model            HaH
    Porter. Thomas Eakins

**EAKINS, Thomas**—*Continued*
William Rush carving his allegorical figure
   of the Schuylkill river          NBM
   Bazin
   CtY. Yale alumni
   NBuA. Fifty ptgs
   Pierson
   Porter. Thomas Eakins (col)
William Rush carving his allegorical figure
   of the Schuylkill river          PPhM
   Larkin rev ed (col detail)
   Pierson
   Porter. Thomas Eakins (col)
   Time. 300 years (col)
   Walker. Ptgs from America
William Smith Forbes              PPhJ
   Porter. Thomas Eakins
A woman                           ATeS
   ATeS. Collection
Wrestlers, 1889                   NAD
   Porter. Thomas Eakins
Wrestlers, 1898                   PPhM
   Chew. 250 years of art
Wrestlers, Sketch for             PPhM
   Porter. Thomas Eakins
Young man                         PPhM
   Porter. Thomas Eakins
Young woman in pink dress. See Maud
   Cook
Youth playing fife
   Porter. Thomas Eakins
**Eakins, Mrs Thomas.** See Eakins, Susan
   Hannah (MacDowell)
**EARL, Ralph, 1751-1801**
Amos Doolittle                    CtNL
   NUM. Art across America
Andrew Jackson                    CtY
   Larkin (detail)
Baron von Steuben                 CtY
   Pierson
   Roos
Battle of Concord                 NNPL
   Davidson v 1
Battles of Lexington and Concord. See
   British troops at Concord
Benjamin Tallmadge and his son William
                                  CtLH
   Pierson
British troops at Concord (Battles of Lex-
   ington and Concord)
   Flexner. Light of distant skies
   Ford. Pictorial folk art
Daniel Boardman                   DN
   Flexner. Light of distant skies
Elijah Boardman
   Larkin
   Larkin rev ed
Gabriel Christie                  MoKN
   MoKN. Handbook
Lady Williams and child           MM
   Flexner. Light of distant skies
Looking east from Denny hill
   Barker. Amer ptg
   Pierson
Lucy Bradley                      MiD
   MiD. Treasures
Mrs Benjamin Tallmadge and son and
   daughter                       CtLH
   ICA. From colony to nation
   Pierson

Mrs Moses Seymour and her son Epaphro-
   ditus                          MoSL
   MoSL. 50 masterworks
   MoSL. Handbook 1953
Mrs William Moseley and her son Charles
                                  CtY
   Larkin
   Larkin rev ed
   Pierson
Mrs William Taylor and child      NBuA
   NBuA. Catalogue of the ptgs
   Pierson
   OCiM. Rediscoveries
Nathaniel Shaw Woodbridge and his
   daughter Mary
   CtY. Yale alumni
Oliver Ellsworth and his wife     CtHW
   CtHW. Handbook (col)
   Pierson
   Robb. Harper history
Roger Sherman                     CtY
   Barker. Amer ptg
   Canaday
   CtY. Portrait index
   Davidson v2
   Flexner. Amer ptg
   Flexner. Light of distant skies
   Flexner. Short history
   ICA. From colony to nation
   Mendelowitz
   MoSL. 40 masterpieces
   Pierson
   Richardson. Ptg in America
   Time. 300 years (col)
Stryker sisters                   OYB
   OYB. Catalogue 1951
View of the town of Concord, Massa-
   chusetts, c 1775
   Lipman. Primitive ptrs
William Austin                    CtY
   Roos
William Carpenter                 MWM
   NYG. Fine art
   Pierson
William Taylor                    NBuA
   Barker. Amer ptg
   Born
   ICA. From colony to nation
   NBuA. Catalogue of the ptgs
   OCiM. Rediscoveries
   Pierson
**EARL, Ralph Eleasar Whitesides,** 1788-
   1837
Andrew Jackson (Lee coll)
   DC. Privately owned
Andrew Jackson                    PH
   Ford. Edward Hicks
Andrew Jackson                    CtY
   Larkin rev ed
Andrew Jackson                    NoCR
   NoCR. Catalogue
Family portrait                   DN
   DN. Amer primitive ptgs, pt 1
**EARLE, Lawrence Carmichael,** 1845-1921
Escape
   NSP. Sportscape
**Earle, Ralph.** See Earl, Ralph
**Early** by L. MacIver
**Early** American abstract by M. Weber
**Early** autumn by M. Peck

Early autumn snow by R. H. Brown
Early evening by M. B. Prendergast
Early houses, Provincetown by C. H. Demuth
Early Italy by H. B. McCarter
Early morning after a storm at sea by W. Homer
Early morning, Cold Spring, New York by A. B. Durand
Early morning, Paris by O. M. Pleissner
Early morning, Paris by E. Shinn
Early spring by E. Lawson
Early spring by T. C. Steele
Early spring—South side by G. Z. Antreasian
Early spring tree by G. O'Keeffe
Early springtime on the farm by A. M. R. Moses
Early summer by M. B. Prendergast
Early summer, Vermont by E. Lawson
Early Sunday morning by E. Hopper
Early thaw by A. Obrosey
Earth by A. Alcalay
Earth and green by M. Rothko
Earth glow by K. Okada
Earth legend by L. Calcagno
Earth machines by F. Martin
Earth rhythms by R. Jonson
The easel by R. B. Motherwell
East barrier by J. Tworkov
East Charleston school by P. S. Sample
East field by T. Stamos
East Hampton, Long Island by W. Homer
East New York by H. Rose
East of Easter by R. Ruben
East of Lexington by K. Zerbe
East of the Bowery by J. Myers
East Riding of Yorkshire yeomanry disembarking from H. M. S. Cressy by R. A. Parker
East river by E. D. Boit
East river by J. E. Heliker
East river by J. Marin
East river by M. B. Prendergast
East river dock by M. R. Cooper
East river from Brooklyn by W. J. Glackens
East river nocturne by G. L. K. Morris
East river rooftops by G. A. Picken
East river, snow by R. Henri
East rock from the south by G. H. Durrie
East rock, New Haven by G. H. Durrie
East Sandwich marshes by D. Macknight
East Tenth street jungle by R. Marsh
East Twelfth street by B. Shahn
East wind by S. Wilson
East wind over Weehawken by E. Hopper
Easter and the totem by J. Pollock
Easter bonnet by G. Layton
Easter morning by W. De Kooning
Easter morning on Eye street by R. F. Lahey

Eastern elegy by M. Greenwood
Eastern memory by M. Greenwood
Eastern point, Prout's neck by W. Homer
Eastern tranquillity by C. C. Ross
Eastern twilight by R. Iwamoto
Eastman, Constance
    Lockman, D. M. Constance Eastman
EASTMAN, Seth, 1808-1875
    Dakota encampment                          MnSJ
        Rathbone
    Dakota village                             MnSJ
        Morgan
        Rathbone
    Death whoop
        McCracken. Portrait of the old west
    Dog dance of the Dakotahs
        McCracken. Portrait of the old west
    Emigrants attacked by the Comanches        MnSJ
        Rathbone
    Falls of St Anthony                        MnSJ
        Rathbone
    Hunting buffalo in winter
        McCracken. Portrait of the old west
    Indian attack                              MM
        Davidson v 1
    Indian sugar camp                          MnSJ
        Rathbone
    Indians traveling                          MnSJ
        Morgan
        Rathbone
    Lacrosse playing among the Sioux Indians   DC
        DC. Masterpieces
        McCracken. Portrait of the old west (col)
        Pierson
        Rathbone (col)
    Laughing waters                            MnSJ
        Rathbone
    Mourning for the dead
        Pierson
    Sioux Indians breaking up camp             MB
        MB. Karolik coll
        Pierson
    Squaws playing ball on the prairie         MCH
        Pierson
    View of Fort Snelling                      MnMI
        Born
        Davidson v 1
        U.S. National Capital sesquicentennial com
    Wenona's leap                              MnSJ
        Rathbone
EASTMAN, William
    Studio table                               OCl
        OCl. Handbook
Eastman children, fl 1850
    Balis, C. George and Emma Eastman
Easton, Pennsylvania
    Cartney, M. E. M. Court house and Centre square, Easton
    Cartney, M. E. M. Court house, Easton
    Unidentified artist. Easton
    Weygandt, C. E. Easton
Easy by L. Lewitin
Eaton family memorial by S. Jordan
L'eau nue by Y. Tanguy
Eau Sucre river by A. J. Miller

Ebsworth, Elizabeth. See Swinton, Elizabeth (Ebsworth)

Ecce Homo by U. Romano

Echo by J. Pollock

Echo by T. Stamos

Echo from the sea by P. L. Dike

Echo lake by T. Doughty

Echo of a dream by A. Salemme

Ecke, Mrs Gustav. See Tseng Yu-ho

Ecstasy by P. Mangravite

Ecstatic gander by M. Graves

Ecuador
Church, F. E. Cotopaxi, Ecuador
Church, F. E. Housetop in Ecuador

Eddy, Arthur Jerome, 1859-1920
Whistler, J. A. M. Arthur Jerome Eddy

Eddy, Horace Wilson, 1840-1850
Stock, J. W. Horace Wilson Eddy

EDDY, Oliver Tarbell, 1799-1868
Four youngest children of William Rankin and Abigail Ogden Rankin    NJN
NJN. Early N. J. artists

Eden by H. Frankenthaler

Edgartown, Massachusetts
Chapin, F. Harbor at Edgartown

Edge of August by M. Tobey

Edge of evening by N. Meitzler

Edge of the east water by J. Whorf

Edge of the field by A. N. Wyeth

Edge of the grove by M. B. Prendergast

Edge of town by C. E. Burchfield

Edgehill by R. Smith

Edgehill road, Philadelphia by R. Smith

Edgell, Mary L. fl 1830
Peckham, R. Memorial portrait of Mary L. Edgell

EDIE, Stuart Carson, 1908-
Still life    ATU
ATU. Coll of Amer art

Editorial by J. Hirsch

EDMONDS, Francis William 1806-1863
New scholar
Cowdrey v 1
Real estate agent offering valuable lots
Davidson v2
Sparking
Cowdrey v 1

EDMONDSON, Leonard, 1916-
Equivalent restraint
IU. Contemp Amer ptg & sculp, 1953
Experience of meaning
WMAA. Annual ex, 1952
External dictation
IU. Contemp Amer ptg & sculp, 1955
Fashion and purport
NNSG. Younger Amer ptrs
Passage    VR
CoS. New accessions USA, 1958
VR. Amer ptg, 1958

Edwards, Abigail (Fowles)
Badgar, J. Mrs John Edwards

EDWARDS, Ethel
Landscape in ivory
IU. Contemp Amer ptg & sculp, 1955

Edwards, Mrs John. See Edwards, Abigail (Fowle)

Edwards, John Cummings, fl 1844
Bingham, G. C. John Cummings Edwards

Edwards, Jonathan, 1703-1758
Badger, J. Jonathan Edwards

EDWARDS, Thomas, fl 1822-1856

### Attributed works

Franklin Haven    MB
MB. New England miniatures

Eel spearing at Setauket by W. S. Mount

Eeling by K. Knaths

Effervescence by K. L. Seligmann

Effort at speech between two people by E. Friedensohn

EGAN, John J. 19th cent
Colossal bust at low water mark, used as metre by the aborigines    PPhUn
Born (panorama detail)
Distant view of the Rocky mountains    PPhUn
Born (panorama detail)
Lake Concordia and aboriginal tumuli    PPhUn
Born (panorama detail)
Terraced mound in a snow storm at sunset    PPhUn
Born (panorama detail)

Egberts, Cornelius, fl 1826
Ames, E. Cornelius Egberts

Egg and rock by W. T. Murch

Egg salad by Unidentified artist

Eggbeater no 1 by S. Davis

Eggbeater no 2 by S. Davis

Eggbeater no 3 by S. Davis

Eggbeater no 4 by S. Davis

Eggbeater no 5 by S. Davis

Eggington, Elizabeth, b 1656
Unidentified artist. Elizabeth Eggington

Eggplant by C. H. Demuth

Eggplant and plums by C. H. Demuth

Eggplant and summer squash by C. H. Demuth

Eggplant and tomatoes by C. H. Demuth

Eggplants by C. H. Demuth

Eggs and carafe by M. Sterne

Ego et l'aurore by E. A. Donati

EGRI, Ted, 1913-
Bicycle riders
IU. Contemp Amer ptg, 1952
Conflict
IU. Contemp Amer ptg & sculp, 1953
Destination unknown
IU. Contemp Amer ptg & sculp, 1955

Egyptian by W. A. Baziotes

Egyptian girl by J. S. Sargent

EHNINGER. John Whetton, 1827-1889
October
Davidson v 1
Turkey shoot    MB
Davidson v2
MB. Karolik coll
Yankee peddler    NJN
Larkin
Larkin rev ed

**EICHHOLTZ, Jacob, 1776-1842**
An incident of the Revolution    MB
   MB. Karolik coll
Man in a yellow waistcoat    MB
   MB. Karolik coll
Margaret Adelia Leman    DN
   DN. Amer primitive ptgs, pt 1
Mr Kline    DN
   DN. Amer primitive ptgs, pt 1
Mrs Christopher B. Mayer    PR
   PR. Catalogue
The Ragan sisters    DN
   DC. Amer ptrs of the South
Rebecca Trissler Eichholtz
   Chew. 250 years of art
Self-portait
   Pierson
   Richardson. Ptg in America
**Eichholtz, Rebecca Trissler, fl 1841**
   Eichholtz, J. Rebecca Trissler Eichholtz
**Eiger** from Mürren by J. S. Sargent
**Eight** allegories of fate by C. Von Wiegand
**Eight** bathers by M. B. Prendergast
**Eight** bells by W. Homer
**Eight** bells' folly: memorial for Hart Crane
   by M. Hartley
**Eight** figures by M. Weber
**Eight** girls by the sea by M. B. Prendergast
**Eighteenth-century** gentleman by J. Cooper
**EIGHTS, James, 1798-1882**
   East side market (now Broadway) Al-
     bany    NAI
   Jones. Rediscovered ptrs
   Number 1 north side of State street, Al-
     bany, 1806    NAI
   Jones. Rediscovered ptrs
   State street, Albany, 1805    NAI
   Bolton. Ezra Ames
**EILSHEMIUS, Louis Michel, 1864-1943**
   Afternoon wind    MMA
   Baur. New art (col)
   Baur. Revolution
   Pierson
   Approaching storm    DP
   Larkin rev ed
   Loring
   Balcony view    DP
   DP. Catalogue
   Bridge for fishing    DP
   Baur. New art
   Born
   DP. Catalogue
   Pierson
   Cabs for hire    DP
   Bazin
   DP. Catalogue
   Contentment
   Wight. Milestones
   Delaware Water Gap village    MM
   MM. 100 Amer ptrs
   Don Quixote
   Baur. New art
   Falls
   CanO. Hirshhorn coll
   Figures in landscape    WMAA
   Goodrich. Amer art
   Flying Dutchman    WMAA
   McCurdy

Haunted house    MM
   Cheney. Story 1958 ed
   Walker. Ptgs from America
Jealousy
   Baur. New art
Madge in the morning    DP
   DP. Catalogue
Niagara Falls    MiD
   Richardson. Ptg in America
The pool    CtY
   CtY. Soc Anonyme
Rejected suitor    DP
   DP. Catalogue
Skater    ATeS
   ATeS. Collection
Tragedy or Found drowned    MM
   Baur. New art
   Pierson
Tranquility    MB
   MB. Ptgs in water color
Two bathers    OYB
   OYB. Catalogue 1951
West Point, New York
   NYG. Fine art
Yuma, Arizona    DP
   DP. Catalogue
       **Portrait of the artist**
   Avery, M. Eilshemius
**EISENSTAT, Jane Sperry**
   Dead opossum
   PA. Annual ex, 1958
The **el** and the snow by D. Kingman
**Eldorado** by R. Marsh
**Election** day at the State House by J. L.
   Krimmel
An **election** day bonfire, Fifth and Chestnut
   streets, Philadelphia by B. Uhle
**Election** night by J. Levine
**Election** scene, Catonsville, Baltimore county
   by A. J. Miller
**Election** scene during the Harrison—Van
   Buren campaign, 1840 by F. H. Schell
**Electric** automobile, Boston, 1892 by W. L.
   Taylor
**Electric** eye by E. A. Donati
**Electric** peach orchard by A. G. Dove
**Elegy** by H. Hofmann
**Elegy** by M. Kawabata
**Elegy** to the Spanish republic XXXIV by
   R. B. Motherwell
**Elegy** to the Spanish republic LVIII by
   R. B. Motherwell
**Elements** of reconstruction by J. De Diego
**Elements** of structure by C. A. Morris
**Elephants**
   Marin, J. Circus elephants
**Elevated** railway, Berlin by H. Post
**Elevated** with black and white by R. Craw-
   ford
**Eleventh** street by G. Vass
**Eli** Whitney gun factory by W. G. Munson
**Elijah** convincing the false prophets of Baol
   by B. West
**Elijah** fed by the ravens by W. Allston
**Elijah** in the desert by W. Allston
**Elinor,** Jean and Anna by G. W. Bellows
**Eliphaz** by K. Knaths

Elizabeth, consort of Albert I of Austria, king of Germany, fl 1300
Walker, C. H. Elizabeth of Tirol
Elizabeth, queen of Rumania, 1843-1916
Healy, G. P. A. Elizabeth, queen of Rumania
Elizabeth by F. J. Kline
Elizabeth at the piano by T. Eakins
Elizabeth, New Jersey
Opper, E. Fire engine, Elizabeth, New Jersey, c 1880
Elk
Miller, A. J. Elk swimming the Platte
Miller, A. J. Hunting elk
Miller, A. J. Hunting elk among the Black hills
Elle viendra by Y. Tanguy
Elliott, Barnard, 1740-1778
Theus, J. Col Barnard Elliott jr
ELLIOTT, Charles Loring, 1812-1868
Daniel Stanton		NNHS
Cowdrey v 1
John Wakefield Francis		NNHS
Cowdrey v 1
Mrs Thomas Goulding (Mary Anne Goulding)		NAD
Larkin
Larkin rev ed
NAD. Amer tradition
NJN. Early N. J. artists
Pierson
Prosper M. Wetmore		NNHS
Cowdrey v 1
Sanford Thayer		MB
MB. Karolik coll
Elliott, Mary Bellinger (Elliott) d 1774
Theus, J. Mrs Barnard Elliott jr
ELLIOTT, Philip Clarkson, 1903-
Charleston, South Carolina		NBuA
NBuA. Acquisitions 1954-57
Shelocta, Pennsylvania		NBuA
NBuA. Contemporary ptgs
Elliott, Mrs Philip Clarkson. See Cuthbert, Virginia Isobel
ELLIS, A. fl 1830
Gentleman with high collar		NCHA
Jones. New-found folk art
Lady with a nosegay
Jones. New-found folk art
ELLIS, Dean W. 1922?-
Cadiz at dusk
NAD. Annual ex, 1956
Cathedral entrance		MSM
CoS. New accessions USA, 1952
Corroded implement
OYB. Annual 1952
The dummy		OCl
CoS. New accessions USA, 1948
Fortifications of Elba
NAD. Annual ex, 1960
Fragments from yesterday
IU. Contemp Amer ptg, 1950
Intimate conversation		OYB
OYB. Annual 1949
OYB. Catalogue 1951
Scrap		OCI
Pousette-Dart. Amer ptg
Ellis, Maria (Wilcocks) b 1871
Jarvis, J. W. Mrs John French Ellis
Ellison, Thomas, 1773-1820
Jarvis, J. W. Col Thomas Ellison

Elliston, Mary (Perot) 1687-1775
Unidentified artist. Mrs Robert Elliston
Ellsworth, Abigail (Wolcott) 1756-1818
Earl, R. Oliver Ellsworth and his wife
ELLSWORTH, James Sanford, 1802-1874
Children
Lipman. Primitive ptrs
Couple
Lipman. Primitive ptrs
Mrs Jennie Post
Lipman. Primitive ptrs
Red-haired gentleman and his wife
Lipman. Primitive ptrs
Unidentified boy
Lipman. Primitive ptrs
Ellsworth, Oliver, 1745-1807
Earl, R. Chief Justice Oliver Ellsworth and his wife
Trumbull, J. Oliver Ellsworth
Ellsworth, Mrs Oliver. See Ellsworth, Abigail (Wolcott)
Elm fruit by L. McIver
ELMER, Edwin Romanzo, 1850-1923
A lady of Baptist Corner, Ashfield, Massachusetts
U.S. National Capital sesquicentennial com
Magic glass
Frankenstein. After the hunt
Mourning picture		MNS
Baur. Amer ptg
ELSHIN, Jacob, 1892-
Iconostas
MoSL. Contemporary Amer ptg
Emancipation proclamation by A. A. Lamb
Embarkation by C. A. Morris
Embattled farmer by A. James
Ember tree by J. H. Fitzgerald
Emblem of peace by Unidentified artist
Emblems of peace by W. M. Harnett
Embrace by H. Hofmann
The embryo by I. R. Pereira
Emerald by H. Moller
Emerald pool by J. H. Twachtman
Emergency by H. S. Gillette
Emerging figure by S. Chermayeff
Emerging forms by C. A. Morris
EMERY, Ella, fl 1870
Alice Cushing in the west parlor of Peter Cushing house, Hingham, Massachusetts
Pierson
Child in the sitting room of Matthew Cushing house
Ford. Pictorial folk art
Emery, Joseph, fl 1834
Davis, J. H. Joseph and Sarah Ann Emery
Emery, Sarah Ann, fl 1834
Davis, J. H. Joseph and Sarah Ann Emery
Emes. See also Ames
Emes, Fanny, fl 1819
Ames, E. Mrs Jesse Emes
Emes, Henry, 1783-1833
Ames, E. Henry Emes
Emes, Jesse, 1739-1839
Ames, E. Jesse Emes
Emigrant train fording Medicine Bow creek, Rocky mountains by S. Colman

Emigrants attacked by the Comanches by S. Eastman

Emigrants crossing the plains by F. O. C. Darley

The emigration of Daniel Boone by G. C. Bingham

Emma and her children by G. W. Bellows

Emma at a window by G. W. Bellows

Emma in black by G. W. Bellows

Emma in purple dress by G. W. Bellows

Emmet, Elizabeth. See Leroy, Elizabeth (Emmet)

**EMMONS, Alexander Hamilton**
Nathaniel William Taylor                    CtY
CtY. Portrait index

**EMMONS, Nathaniel, 1703-1740**
Andrew Oliver
  Belknap
  Flexner. First flowers
  NNHS. Waldron Phoenix Belknap coll
Samuel Sewall                               MBH
  Belknap

The emperor by A. Rattner

Emperor ploughs the fields by T. Stamos

Emperor's garden by C. R. Holty

Employment agency by I. Soyer

Emporium of Indian curiosities by J. F. Richardt

The empress by G. W. McLaughlin

Empty mansion by E. O'Hara

Empty town in desert by Y. Kuniyoshi

Encampment by A. J. Miller

Encampment and entertainment of the Boston rifle company by the Portland rifle company, 1830 by C. Codman

Encampment of Indians by A. J. Miller

Enchanted forest by E. L. Blumenschein

End of an era by M. Siporin

End of day by C. E. Burchfield

End of day by R. Gwathmey

End of day by Z. L. Sepeshy

End of day by W. Stuempfig

The end of Dover Beach by R. B. Motherwell

End of Fourteenth street crosstown line by R. Marsh

End of summer by G. R. Davis

End of summer by M. Tobey

End of the act by H. G. Keller

End of the day by H. G. Keller

End of the day by F. Remington

End of the day by V. P. Solomon

End of the festival by L. Bosa

End of the game by A. Salemme

End of the hunt by D. Nichols

End of the parade: Coatesville, Pa., 1920 by C. H. Demuth

End of the street by J. Myers

End of the war: starting home by H. Pippin

End of the world by G. Grosz

End of winter by J. H. Twachtman

Endeavor II and Ranger by **J. W. Golinkin**

**ENDERS, Cleade**
Subway
  NAD. Annual ex, 1955

**Endicott, Ellen (Peabody) 1833-1927**
Sargent, J. S. Mrs William Crowninshield Endicott

**ENGEL, Harry, 1901-**
Theatre
  IU. Contemp Amer ptg & sculp, 1955

**ENGEL, Irma**
Landscape
  CSFP. Annual ex, 1948/49

Engineer Heartfield by G. Grosz

**English, James Edward, 1812-1890**
Flagg, J. B, James Edward English

English cod by W. M. Chase

English cottage by S. P. R. Triscott

An English gentleman by B. West

English landscape by W. Groombridge

Enigma of the collective American soul by P. Evergood

Enigmatic combat by A. Gorky

Enigmatical section by A. Nepote

**ENNIS, George Pearse, 1884-1936**
Tapping a furnace                           OYB
  OYB. Supplement

Ennui and tranquillity by Y. Tanguy

**Ensor, James, baron, 1860-1949**
Katzman, H. Ensor seated before The Entry of Christ into Brussels

Entering the first rapid by W. Homer

The entertainers III by R. Markman

The entombment by J. Foote

The entombment by M. Rothko

Entrance by K. E. Fortess

Entrance by R. Gleitsmann

Entrance by D. Thrall

Entrance to a coal mine near Wheeling, Virginia by G. Harvey

Entrance to the harbor of St Thomas by E. Carlsen

Entretat, le Cabestan Capstan by Leonid

Envelopment (Rubezahl) by K. L. Seligmann

**Epaminondas, d 326 B. C.**
West, B. Death of Epaminondas

Ephiphany of a hero by P. Burlin

Epoch by T. George

Epoch by B. Shahn

Equestrian by C. R. Holty

Equestrian sunrise by J. Corbino

Equestrians by J. Marin

Equestrienne by J. Marin

Equinox by J. McGarrell

Equinox by C. W. Rain

Equivalent restraint by L. Edmondson

Erdgeist, Illustration for by C. H. Demuth

Erewhon by R. J. Wolff

**ERICKSON, John, 1919-**
The wall
  NNSG. Younger Amer ptrs

**Erie Canal**
Harvey, G. Afternoon, dead calm: View on the Erie canal near Pittsford, New York
Hill, J. W. Scene on the Erie Canal

Erie Canal—*Continued*
  Imbert, A. Erie canal celebration, New
    York, 1825
  Keys, M. Lockport on the Erie canal
Erie street boys by C. F. Gaertner
Erie underpass by N. Spencer
Ernestinoff, Alexander
  Adams, W. Alexander Ernestinoff
ERNST, Jimmy, 1920-
  Absence
    ICA. Amer artists paint the city
  Almost silence                            MM
    CoS. New accessions USA, 1954
  Alone                                    NNSG
    Mendelowitz
    NNSG. Handbook
    NNSG. Younger Amer ptrs
  Animal and mineral
    IU. Contemp Amer ptg & sculp, 1953
  The chant                               NBuA
    NBuA. Acquisitions 1954-57
    PPC. International ex, 1955
  Color isolation
    IU. Contemp Amer ptg, 1952
  Flying Dutchman                           MMA
    Read. Art now, 1948 ed
  Laboratory report
    PPC. Ptg in the U.S. 1949
  Narrative
    IU. Contemp Amer ptg & sculp, 1957
  Night flight
    WMAA. Annual ex, 1951
  Personal appearance
    Pousette-Dart. Amer ptg
  Personal history                         WMAA
    Goodrich. Amer art
    McCurdy
    Pierson
    WMAA. New decade
  Polar space                               NUM
    NUM. Root bequest
  Rock painting
    IU. Contemp Amer ptg & sculp, 1961
  Speculation                               NBM
    CoS. New accessions USA, 1952
  Stillness
    Brussels. Exposition
  Time for fear                             MMA
    MMA. Abstract
    Read. Concise history
  Timescape                                WMAA
    Pierson
    WMAA. Sara Roby
  Tomorrow morning
    VR. Amer ptg, 1958
  Tropic
    WMAA. Museum and its friends, 1958
    WMAA. New decade
Ernst, Mrs Max. See Tanning, Dorothea
Erving, Elizabeth. See Bowdoin, Elizabeth
    (Erving)
Erving, John, 1728-1816
  Blackburn, J. John Erving jr
Erving, Mrs John, fl 1732
  Smibert, J. Mrs John Erving
Escape by L. C. Earle
Escape by P. Evergood
Escape by X. Gonzales
Escape by J. W. Treiman
Escape from Blackfeet by A. J. Miller

Escudier, Mme Paul (Le Fevre) fl 1885
  Sargent, J. S. Mme Paul Escudier
ESHOO, Robert, 1926-
  The castle
    IU. Contemp Amer ptg & sculp, 1957
  Evolution of a day
    WMAA. Young America 1957
  Herkimer
    WMAA. Young America 1957
  Summer day
    MBIC. View 1960
  Verdant rise
    IU. Contemp Amer ptg & sculp, 1959
Esperance by T. Appleby
Essex market by G. Hartigan
Eternal city by P. Blume
Eternal dictation by L. Edmondson
Eternal pageant by W. W. Quirt
Eternal world by F. Puma
Eternity by M. Beckmann
ETHEROVICH, Anthony, 1916-
  Merry bench                               OYB
    OYB. Catalogue 1951
  The merry table                           OYB
    OYB. Annual 1951
Ethiopia saluting the colors by B. Robinson
Etna, Mount
  Crowninshield, F. Mt Etna from Taormina
  Silsbee, M. Taormina and Mt Aetna
Etnier, Mrs C. E.
  Watkins, F. C. Mrs C. E. Etnier
ETNIER, Stephen Morgan, 1903-
  Accra beach                               OYB
    OYB. Annual 1953
    OYB. Supplement
  Caribbean moon
    NAD. Annual ex, 1955
  Jamaica noon
    NAD. Annual ex, 1953
  Lighthouse service dock, Nassau
    NAD. Annual ex, 1958
  Port of call
    IU. Contemp Amer ptg & sculp, 1957
  Sea cross
    Gruskin
  The seiner
    NSP. Sportscapes
Etretat by G. Innes
ETTING, Emlen Pope, 1905-
  Spring song
    Gruskin (col)
Etting, Solomon, 1764-1847
  Jarvis, J. W. Solomon Etting
Etting, Mrs Solomon, 1764-1831
  Jarvis, J. W. Mrs Solomon Etting
Euclid avenue by J. Levine
Euretta by M. Beckmann
Europa and the bull by D. Austin
European cormorant by J. J. Audubon
EVANS, J. G. fl 1840-1859
  Commodore Perry carrying the gospel of
    God to the heathen, 1853         ICH
  U.S. National Capital sesquicentennial
    com
EVANS, James, fl 1825-1854
  The white squall                           DN
    DN. Amer primitive ptg, pt 2

EVANS, John T. fl 1815
### Attributed works
Man with a whip        MeC
  Jetté. Amer heritage collection
Evans, William T.
  Rouland, O. William T. Evans
Evaporating night by I. R. Pereira
Evarts, William Maxwell, 1818-1901
  Hunt, W. M. William Maxwell Evarts
Eve by J. Corbino
Evening by C. Booth
Evening by C. E. Burchfield
Evening by J. Carroll
Evening by K. Schrag
Evening by J. Schueler
Evening garden by A. Rattner
Evening glow—the old red cow by A. P. Ryder
Evening hymn by W. Allston
Evening image by K. R. Morris
Evening in Arcady by T. Cole
Evening in Keene valley by W. M. Hart
Evening in the country by D. Nichols
Evening in Venice by E. Berman
Evening landscape by R. Frame
Evening light by R. Bennett
Evening, Montauk by K. R. Morris
Evening on a pleasure boat, Boston by M. B. Prendergast
Evening on the road to Granada by H. G. Keller
Evening peace by C. E. Burchfield
Evening radiance by K. Schrag
Evening reading by P. Evergood
Evening shower, Paris by M. B. Prendergast
Evening silhouettes by R. A. Blakelock
Evening sky by K. Schrag
Evening song by W. Allston
Evening star by J. Jones
Evening storm. Schoodic, Maine by M. Hartley
Evening usualty by F. Califano
Evensong by A. B. Davies
Eventide by M. Friedman
Eventide by R. Haines
Eventide by H. E. Mattson
Everett, Edward, 1794-1865
  Healy, G. P. A. Edward Everett
Everett, Hannah (Vincent)
  Jarvis, J. W. Mrs James Everett
Everett, James
  Jarvis, J. W. Rev James Everett
EVERGOOD, Philip, 1901-
Alone        MNM
  Baur. Philip Evergood
American shrimp girl
  Baur. Philip Evergood
  Time. 300 years (col)
American tragedy
  Baur. Philip Evergood
  Time. 300 years (col)
Art on the beach
  Baur. Philip Evergood

An artist as a young man
  Baur. Philip Evergood
Artist's fantasy
  Baur. Philip Evergood (col)
The big noise
  Baur. Philip Evergood
The bluebird
  Baur. Philip Evergood
Boy from Stalingrad
  Baur. Philip Evergood
Burial of the Queen of Sheba
  Baur. Philip Evergood
Cool doll in pool
  Baur. Philip Evergood
Cotton from field to mill
  Baur. Philip Evergood
A cup of tea
  Baur. Philp Evergood
Dance marathon
  Baur. Philip Evergood
David playing to King Saul
  Baur. Philip Evergood
Dawn
  Baur. Philip Evergood
Don't cry, mother        MMA
  Biddle. Yes and no
  Mendelowitz
  Myers
  Riley. Your art heritage
Dowager in a wheelchair        WMAA
  Baur. Philip Evergood
  ICA. Annual ex, 1954
  PPC. International ex, 1955
  WMAA. Sara Roby
Dream catch
  Baur. New art
  Baur. Philip Evergood
  CanO. Hirshhorn coll
  Genauer
  Pierson
Dusk at Fuji
  Baur. Philip Evergood
Enigma of the collective American soul
  Baur. Philip Evergood (col)
Escape
  IU. Contemp Amer ptg & sculp, 1961
Evening reading
  Baur. Philip Evergood
Everybody wants to live        CLA
  CLA. 35 ptgs
Farmer's daughter
  Baur. Philip Evergood
Fascist company
  Baur. Philip Evergood
Flight of fancy        MdBM
  Baur. Philip Evergood
Flowers by the lake
  Baur. Philip Evergood
The forgotten man
  Baur. Philip Evergood
The future
  IU. Contemp Amer ptg & sculp, 1955
The future belongs to them
  Baur. Philip Evergood
Garden of Betty Mae
  Baur. Philip Evergood
Girl with sunflowers
  Baur. Philip Evergood (col)
Happy entrance
  Baur. Philip Evergood

**EVERGOOD, Philip**—*Continued*

Her world                       MM
    MM. 100 Amer ptrs
    PA. Annual ex, 1949
The hidden apple
    Baur. Philip Evergood (col)
The hunters
    Pousette-Dart. Amer ptg
Jester
    Baur. New art
    Baur. Philip Evergood (col)
    PPC. International ex, 1950
Juggler of doom
    Baur. Philip Evergood
Juju and her dog Copelia
    Baur. Philip Evergood
Juju as a wave
    Baur. Philip Evergood (col)
Julia
    Baur. Philip Evergood
Kleinholz family
    Baur. Philip Evergood
Laughing worker
    Baur. Philip Evergood
Leave it to the experts             ATU
    ATU. Coll of Amer art
Leda in high places
    Baur. Philip Evergood
    PPC. Ptg in the U. S. 1949
Lily and the sparrows             WMAA
    Baur. Philip Evergood (col)
    Baur. Revolution
    Goodrich. Amer art (col)
    McCurdy
    MnU. 40 Amer ptrs
    Pierson
The little captain
    Baur. Philip Evergood (col)
Lure of the waters
    IU. Contemp Amer ptg, 1948
M. T. Florinsky, D. S. Mirsky and the
    pidget
    Baur. Philip Evergood
The McConney flats
    Baur. Philip Evergood
Madonna of the mines
    Baur. Philip Evergood
Men and mountain
    Baur. Philip Evergood
Mine disaster
    Baur. Philip Evergood
Modern inquisitor
    Cheney. Expressionism 1948 ed
Mom's cathedral
    Baur. Philip Evergood
    NAD. Annual ex, 1952
Moon maiden
    Baur. Philip Evergood (col)
    MnU. 40 Amer ptrs
Mother and child               OYB
    OYB. Catalogue 1951
Music
    Baur. Philip Evergood
My forebears were pioneers
    Baur. New art
    Baur. Philip Evergood
    Larkin
    Larkin rev ed
My mother
    Baur. Philip Evergood
Nature without man
    Baur. Philip Evergood

New death
    Baur. Philip Evergood
The new Lazarus             WMAA
    Baur. New art (col)
    Baur. Philip Evergood (col)
    Goodrich. Amer art (col)
    Pierson
New York city Susannah
    IU. Contemp Amer ptg, 1950
Nude by the el
    Baur. Philip Evergood (col)
Nude with violin
    Baur. Philip Evergood (col)
Passing show
    Baur. Philip Evergood
The pink dismissal slip          NIC
    Baur. Philip Evergood
Proposal on horseback
    IU. Contemp Amer ptg & sculp, 1953
The quarantined citadel
    Baur. Philip Evergood
Railroad men
    Baur. New art
Renunciation
    Baur. Philip Evergood
    IU. Contemp Amer ptg, 1949
Resort beach
    Baur. Philip Evergood
Samson and the lion
    Baur. Philip Evergood
Satisfaction in New Jersey
    Baur. Philip Evergood (col)
Seeking a future
    Baur. Philip Evergood
Self-portrait, 1943
    Baur. Philip Evergood
Self-portrait with divining rod, c 1954
    Baur. Philip Evergood (col)
Self-portrait with nude
    Baur. Philip Evergood
The siding (Kaufman coll)
    Baur. Philip Evergood
The siding (Kleinholz coll)
    Gruskin
Snow city
    Baur. Philip Evergood
Snug harbor
    Baur. Philip Evergood
    WMAA. Annual ex, 1957
Solomon at the court of Sheba
    Baur. Philip Evergood
Still life, 1944
    Baur. Philip Evergood
The story of Richmond hill
    Baur. Philip Evergood
Street corner
    Baur. Philip Evergood
Sunny side of the street          DC
    Baur. Philip Evergood
    CoS. New accessions USA, 1952
    DC. Masterpieces
    DC. 22 biennial ex, 1951
Surprised wader
    Baur. Philip Evergood
Threshold to success            PA
    Baur. Philip Evergood
    PA. Annual ex, 1958
Through the mill             WMAA
    Baur. Philip Evergood
    McCurdy
Toiling hands
    Baur. Philip Evergood (col)

Treadmill
  Baur. Philip Evergood
Turmoil
  Baur. Philip Evergood
Twilight landscape
  Baur. Philip Evergood
Vase and flowers
  Baur. Philip Evergood
Virginia in the grotto          WMAA
  Baur. Philip Evergood
  Goodrich. Amer art
Wheels of victory
  Baur. Philip Evergood
Woman at piano
  Baur. Philip Evergood
Woman of Iowa
  Baur. Philip Evergood (col)
Worker's victory
  Baur. Philip Evergood
**Every** Saturday by A. B. Davies
**Everybody** wants to live by P. Evergood
**Everyday** sovereign by C. Howard
**Everyman** by B. Shahn
**EVETT, Kenneth,** 1913-
  Rodeo                         ATU
    ATU. Coll of Amer Art
  Trio                          NJMo
    IU. Contemp Amer ptg, 1951
    NJMo. Your Montclair art museum
The **evil** of drink by W. W. Quirt
**Evil** omen by A. Gottlieb
**Evolution** of a day by R. Eshoo
**Evora,** Portugal by J. S. Sargent
**Evocation** by J. Ferren
**EWING, Edgar,** 1913-
  Acropolis—night
    IU. Contemp Amer ptg & sculp, 1961
  Car with dark top
    ICA. Annual ex, 1951
  Parabolic San Francisco
    IU. Contemp Amer ptg & sculp, 1957
  St Cyr
    ICA. Annual ex, 1959/60
    IU. Contemp Amer ptg & sculp, 1959
  The sergeant's coat
    ICA. Annual ex, 1957
  View of Mt Wilson
    PPC. Ptg in the U. S. 1949
**Excavating** a canoe, British Columbia by
  G. Catlin
**Excavation** by P. Blume
**Excavation** by W. De Kooning
**Exclamation** by A. Gottlieb
**Execution** by J. Strombotne
**Exhibition** by B. Greene
**Exhuming** the mastodon by C. W. Peale
**Exit** by Y. Kuniyoshi
**Exit** in color by F. Martin
**Expanding** elements by C. A. Morris
**Expanse** of sky 1 by L. Feininger
**Expedition** to capture wild horses—Sioux by
  A. J. Miller
**Experience** of meaning by L. Edmondson
**Experience** of tragedy yet to come by W.
  W. Quirt
**Explosion** by K. S. Dreier
**Expression** of an impression by M. Sterne

**Expulsion** from the Garden of Eden by
  T. Cole
**Expulsion** of possessions in a danger of
  being gained by K. Nack
**Extinction** of the species by Y. Tanguy
**Extinction** of useless lights by Y. Tanguy
**Exuberance** by H. Hofmann
**Exultation** by S. Reinhardt
**Eye** level by S. Davis
**Eye** witness by C. E. Pickhardt
The **eyes** have it by W. W. Quirt
**Eyes** in the heat by J. Pollock
**Eyes** tested by R. Marsh

# F

The **fabulous** crustacean by L. E. Kupfer-
  man
**Facade** by J. Albers
**Facade** by A. B. Davies
**Facade** by H. Frankenthaler
**Face** of a rabbi by W. Pachner
**Factory** by G. R. Bradshaw
**Factory** by V. I. Cuthbert
**Factory** by C. H. Demuth
**Factory** by P. Dickinson
**Factory** by G. McConnell
**Factory** chimney by G. C. Ault
**Factory** window in Manhattan by L. Fein-
  inger
**FADDEN, Marie-Celeste**
  French child on train
    PA. Annual ex, 1950
**FADDIS, George,** 1920-
  Discovery                     OYB
    OYB. Supplement 1959
**Fading** light by H. Holt
**FAGNANI, Giuseppe,** 1819-1873
  Mrs A. V. H. Stuyvesant
    Vail. Stuyvesant ports
Die **fahne** hoch! by F. Stella
A **fair** wind by W. Homer
**Fairchild, Gordon,** 1822-1832
  Sargent, J. S. Gordon Fairchild holding
    a guinea pig
**Fairchild, Sally,** fl 1885
  Sargent, J. S. Lady with a blue veil
**Fairman** Rogers four-in-hand by T. Eakins
**Fairmont** water works by T. Birch
**Fairmount** and Schuylkill river by W.
  Groombridge
**Fairport** harbor by C. F. Gaertner
**Fairs and festivals**
  Barnett, H. County fair
  Bosa, L. Carnival on the ice
  Garrett, A. W. Western festival
  Hallowell, G. H. Italian fiesta, night
  Harrison, B. J. Fair of the American
    institute of New York, held at Niblo's
    garden, c 1845
  Higgins, V. Fiesta day
  Holty, C. R. Carousel
  Homer, W. The carnival

**Fairs and festivals**—*Continued*
Kempsmith, J. Carnival time
Kuniyoshi, Y. Carnival
Moses, A. M. R. Bondsville fair
Peirce, W. County fair
Pickens, A. Carnival
Prendergast, M. B. Autumn festival
Prendergast, M. B. Carnival
Prendergast, M. B. Festival day, Venice
Prendergast, M. B. Festival night, Venice
Prendergast, M. B. May day, Central park
Sample, P. S. Country horse show
Sawyer, H. A. Carnival
Shahn, B. Carnival
Sharrer, H. Country fair
Siporin, M. Fiesta in Trastevere
Sloan, J. Corpus Christi, Santa Fe
Varga, M. Country carnival
Wilson, S. Fisherman's festival
Woodside, J. A. Country fair in Pennsylvania, 1824

**Fairy** tale by H. Hofmann

**Faith,** hope and charity by W. Sommer

The **faithful** Colt by W. M. Harnett

**Fakirs** by Y. Kuniyoshi

**Falcon** by S. W. Hayter

**Falcon** by E. Kelly

**Falconio, Diomede,** 1842-1917
Eakins, T. Monsignor Diomede Falconio

**Falcons**
Audubon, J. J. Gyrfalcon

The **fall** by C. L. Cicero

**Fall** of old houses by E. Fiene

**Fallen** angels by K. L. Seligmann

**Fallen** deer by W. Homer

**Fallen** pine, Camp island by W. A. Kienbusch

**Fallen** rider by P. Tchelitchew

**Falling** rocket by J. A. M. Whistler

**Falling** sun VI by F. Berman

**Fallout** red by R. G. Hamilton

**Falls** by L. Eilshemius

**Falls** of Niagara taken from the road two miles below Chippawa by J. Trumbull

**Falls** of St Anthony by S. Eastman

**Falls** of San Joaquin, California by A. D. Browere

**Falls** of the Ohio and Louisville by A. H. Wyant

**Family** burying ground by Unidentified artist

**Family groups**
Ames, E. The Fondey family
Andrews, A. Schuyler family
Beckmann, M. Family picture
Bellows, G. W. Fisherman's family
Benbridge, H. Hartley family group
Blackburn, J. Winslow family
Blanchard, C. Family portrait
Bosa, L. My family reunion
Cassatt, M. Mme. A. F. Aude and her two daughters
Copley, J. S. Copley family
Copley, J. S. Sir William Pepperrell and his family

Copley, J. S. Sketch for the Knatchbull family
Corbino, J. Family
Davis, J. H. Separate tables
Davis, J. H. Tilton family
Dawkins, H. Burroughs family
Dunlap, W. Dunlap family
Earl, R. E. W. Family portrait
Evergood, P. Kleinholz family
Feke, R. Isaac Royall and his family
Field, E. S. Joseph Moore and his family
Glackens, W. J. Family group: Irene Dimock, Edith Glackens, Ira Glackens, Grace Dwight Morgan
Goldsmith, D. Mr and Mrs Lyman Day and daughter Cornelia
Goldsmith, D. Talcott family
Greene, S. Family portrait
Greenwood, J. Greenwood and Lee families
Healy, G. P. A. Bryan family
Johnson, E. Family group (Hatch family)
Johnston, J. The James McCormick family of Baltimore, c 1804
Kuniyoshi, Y. Maine family
Morse, S. F. B. Morse family
Peale, C. W. Peale family
Peale, J. James Peale and his family
Peale, J. Mme Dubocq and her four children
Peale, J. Self-portrait with his family
Pickens, A. Henry Hope and family
Rockmore, N. Family group
Rogoway, A. The family
Savage, E. The Washington family
Smibert, J. Bishop Berkeley and his family
Stettheimer, F. Family portrait
Stock, J. W. Parsons family
Trumbull, J. John Vernet and his family
Trumbull, J. Jonathan Trumbull jr and his family
Unidentified artist. Adams family
Unidentified artist. Cheney family
Unidentified artist. George Washington family
Unidentified artist. Gerard Stuyvesant family group
Unidentified artist. Hunter family of Germantown, Pennsylvania
Unidentified artist. Maryland family
Unidentified artist. Nathan Hawley and family
Unidentified artist. New England family group
Unidentified artist. Sargent family
Unidentified artist. Victorian family
Unidentified artist. Walker family
Walkowitz, A. Family group
Weber, M. Family reunion
West, B. The Adrian Hope family group
Williams, W. John Wiley, his mother and sisters
Williams, W. William Denning family
Wright, J. Self-portrait of the artist with his family

**Family rooms.** See Living rooms

**Family** tree by G. Palazzola

**Famous** firsts by S. Davis

**Fanciful** meeting long ago by F. C. Watkins

**Fancy** picture. Fishing with waterfall by Unidentified artist

The **fandango** by C. C. Nahl

Faneuil, Peter, 1700-1743
    Smibert, J. Peter Faneuil
Faneuil hall from the water by W. H. Bartlett
Fantasia on a theme by Dr S. by P. Cadmus
Fantasy by M. Golubov
Le Faou by F. D. Duncan
Far country—Synchromy by S. MacDonald-Wright
Faraway by C. W. Rain
The farewell by B. Perlin
Farewell to Pisa by E. Laning
Farewell to Union square by M. Kantor
Farley, Eben, 1775-1826
    Malbone, E. G. Eben Farley
Farm composition by A. Rattner
Farm machine by R. Lebrun
Farm machinery by C. Peake
Farm news by E. E. Speicher
Farm road by M. A. Phillips
Farm scene by Unidentified artist
Farm still life by A. Rattner
Farmer, Hannah. See Peck, Hannah (Farmer)
Farmer by B. Shahn
Farmer by E. E. Speicher
Farmer's daughter by P. Evergood
Farmers nooning by W. S. Mount
Farmer's wife by R. Gwathmey
Farmhouse in Mahantango valley by Unidentified artist
Farming
    Benton, T. H. Cradling wheat
    Benton, T. H. First crop
    Benton, T. H. June hay
    Benton, T. H. July hay
    Benton, T. H. Louisiana rice fields
    Benton, T. H. Threshing wheat
    Benton, T. H. Weighing cotton
    Codman, C. The hayfield
    Homer, W. Corn husking
    Homer, W. Harvest scene
    Homer, W. Haymaking
    Homer, W. Springtime in Virginia
    Homer, W. Veteran in a new field
    Johnson, E. Corn husking
    Jones, J. Harvest
    Jones, J. Wheat farmers
    Krans, O. Planting corn
    Krans, O. Sowing grain at Bishop hill
    Martin, F. Rural family
    Moses, A. M. R. Haying time
    Mount, W. S. Farmers nooning
    Nichols, D. Summer bounty
    Pleissner, O. M. Stacking alfalfa
    Price, C. S. Plowing
    Sterne, M. Reapers
    Thompson, J. B. Harvest in Vermont
    Unidentified artist. Haymakers
    Unidentified artist. Making hay
    Williams, V. Winnowing grain in California
    Wood, G. Iowa cornfield
Farmyards and farm buildings
    Blythe, D. G. Farm scene
    Burchfield, C. E. Barn
    Burchfield, C. E. Red barn

Durrie, G. H. Farm scene, summer
Durrie, G. H. Farmstead in winter
Durrie, G. H. Farmyard, winter
Durrie, G. H. Farmyard in winter, selling corn
Durrie, G. H. New England farm scene
Durrie, G. H. New England winter scene
Durrie, G. H. Returning to the farm
Durrie, G. H. Sunday in the country
Durrie, G. H. Winter farm scene
Durrie, G. H. Winter in the country, a cold morning
Hartley, M. Deserted farm
Hewes, M. Hollow hill pastoral
Hicks, E. Hillborn farm
Hofmann, C. View of Benjamin Reber's farm
Kroll, L. Farm in Maine
Lebduska, L. H. California farm
Moses, A. M. R. Bringing in the Christmas tree
Moses, A. M. R. Early springtime on the farm
Moses, A. M. R. Grandma goes to the city
Moses, A. M. R. Haying time
Moses, A. M. R. Home of Hezekiah King
Moses, A. M. R. In the springtime
Moses, A. M. R. McDonell farm
Moses, A. M. R. Mount Nebo in winter
Moses, A. M. R. The old oaken bucket
Moses, A. M. R. Our barn
Moses, A. M. R. Over the river to grandma's house
Moses, A. M. R. Wash day
Moses, A. M. R. A winter's day
Mount, W. S. Long Island farmhouse
O'Keeffe, G. Lake George barns
O'Keeffe, G. Stables
O'Keeffe, G. White Canadian barn
Palmer, F. F. American farm scene
Park, L. Flax-scutching, 1847
Richardson, C. C. French Canadian barn
Ryder, A. P. Barnyard
Sample, P. S. Maple sugaring in Vermont
Seigert, P. Wisconsin farm scene
Sepeshy, Z. L. January, Michigan farm
Sheeler, C. Barn variation
Sheeler, C. Bucks county barn
Sheeler, C. Connecticut farm buildings
Spangler, C. D. Old Hager farm
Tait, A. F. Barnyard
Thon, W. Aunt Thankful's farm
Unidentified artist. Farmhouse in Mahantango valley
Unidentified artist. New England farm in winter
Unidentified artist. Thrifty farm
Unidentified artist. A valley farm
Unidentified artist. Victorian dairy farm, study in green
Varga, M. Connecticut farm
Wheat, J. September harvest
Woodwell, J. R. Farmhouse at Scalp Level
Wyeth, A. N. McVey's barn
Zeliff, A. E. Barnyard
Farnam, Henry, 1803-1888
    Healy, G. P. A. Henry Farnam
FARNDON, Walter, 1876-
The bay
    NAD. Annual ex, 1949, 1st half

FARNDON, Walter—*Continued*
The cove
NAD. Annual ex, autumn 1949
The inlet
NAD. Annual ex, 1947, 2d half
Farnham, Captain, fl 1850
Unidentified artist. Capt Farnham of Farnham, Maine
FARNSWORTH, Jerry, 1895-
The amateur                                    OT
OT. Contemp Amer ptgs
Aurelia
IU. Contemp Amer ptg, 1949
NAD. Annual ex, spring 1950
Naked in the city
IU. Contemp Amer ptg, 1948
Standing with reluctant feet where brook and river meet
NAD. Annual ex, 1952
Young man from Arkansas
MM. Amer ptg today
Farnsworth, Mrs Jerry. See Sawyer, Helen Alton
FARNY, Henry F. 1847-1916
The captive                                   OCiM
McCracken. Portrait of the old west (col)
Song of the talking wire                      OCiT
McCracken. Portrait of the old west
FARR, Charles Griffin, 1908-
Beach at Miramar
CSFP. Annual ex, 1952
Figures in a hallway
CSFP. Annual ex, 1948/49
Street in Knoxville                           CSFM
Pousette-Dart. Amer ptg
Farr, Elizabeth, d 1813
Unidentified artist. Mourning picture— Elizabeth Farr
Farrington, Peter, fl 1781
Unidentified artist. Peter Farrington
FARRUGGIO, Remo M. 1906-
Monhegan
MM. Amer ptg today
Renaldo and the enchanted garden
IU. Contemp Amer ptg & sculp, 1957
Fascist company by P. Evergood
Fashion and purport by L. Edmondson
The fat and the thin by G. Grosz
Father and child by B. Shahn
Father and son by J. Budington
Fatma by P. Tchelitchew
FAULKNER, Barry, 1881-
Young Daniel Webster and the Constitution
NAD. Annual ex, 1946, 2d half
Fauré, Gabriel Urbain, 1845-1924
Sargent, J. S. Gabriel Fauré
FAUSETT, William Dean, 1913-
Country road
NYG. Fine art
Cuernavaca                                    ATU
ATU. Coll of Amer art (col)
Derby view                                    MMA
Barr. What is mod ptg
The lake
NYG. Fine art
A favorite by J. Haberle

Fay, Samuel Prescott Phillips, fl 1834
Mason, B. F. Judge Samuel Prescott Phillips Fay
Fay, Mrs Samuel Prescott Phillips, fl 1834
Mason, B. F. Mrs S. P. P. Fay
Fayerweather, Hannah. See Winthrop, Hannah Fayerweather
Fayerweather, Samuel, 1724-1781
Copley, J. S. Samuel Fayerweather
Fear by Y. Tanguy
Fear by R. Vickrey
FEARING, Kelly, 1918-
The place of the angel and Tobias
IU. Contemp Amer ptg & sculp, 1957
Saint Rose
IU. Contemp Amer ptg & sculp, 1955
Feasible by S. Davis
Feast of pure reason by J. Levine
Feather boa by W. M. Chase
February by W. De Kooning
February by L. Goldin
February thaw by C. E. Burchfield
February's sun by F. J. Mulhaupt
Fedalma by G. Fuller
Feeding the hungry by A. Refregier
Feeding the pigeons by W. M. Chase
FEININGER, Lyonel, 1871-1956
Baltic—a recollection                         OT
OCl. Feininger
Barfüsserkirche in Erfurt
Rosenblum
Bathers
MBIC. Villon and Feininger
Bicycle riders
Rosenblum
Bird cloud                                    MCH
OCl. Feininger
Black yawl                                    MCH
Pulitzer v 1
Blue cloud
MBIC. Villon and Feininger
Blue coast                                    OCo
IU. Contemp Amer ptg, 1950
UNESCO. 1860-1955
Blue marine                                   NUM
UNESCO. 1860-1955
Bridge no 3
McCurdy
Bridge V, 1919                                PPhM
Baur. New art
MM. Abstract
OCl. Feininger
Cathedral, Cammin, 1942
MBIC. Villon and Feininger
The church                                    MM
Gruskin (col)
MM. 100 Amer ptrs (col)
Church (Wuppertal)
UNESCO. 1860-1955
Church in Halle
Moderns and their world (col)
Church of the Minorites II, 1926  MnMW
Baur. New art
McCurdy
Pierson
UNESCO. 1860-1955
Church on the hill
MBIC. Villon and Feininger

City at night, 1941
  Baur. New art
  Pierson
Coast of nevermore
  IU. Contemp Amer ptg, 1951
  OCl. Feininger
The cyclists
  Moderns and their world
Der dampfer Odin                         GAtM
  GAtM. Holbrook collection
Dunes and breakwaters
  MBIC. Villon and Feininger
Dunes, Baltic                            MCH
  Pulitzer v2
Dunes with ray of light II, 1944         NBuA
  MBIC. Villon and Feininger
  NBuA. Contemporary ptgs
  Rathbun
  Rosenblum
East choir of Halle cathedral
  50 years of mod art
  Read. Concise history (col)
Expanse of sky 1                         NBuA
  NBuA. Acquisitions 1954-57
Factory windows in Manhattan
  CSFP. Annual ex, 1950/51
  ICA. Amer artists paint the city
  ICA. Annual ex, 1951
  MnU. 40 Amer ptrs
Fisher off the coast
  Bazin
Gaberndorf II                            MoKN
  MoKN. Handbook p 149
Gables I, 1925
  MBIC. Villon and Feininger
  OCl. Feininger
Gables IV
  OCl. Feininger
Gateway and tower I, 1924-26
  Raynal. History v3 (col)
Gelmeroda, 1927                          NNSG
  NNSG. Handbook
Gelmeroda IV, 1915                       NNSG
  NNSG. Handbook
  Time. 300 years (col)
Gelmeroda VIII, 1921                     WMAA
  Baur. New art (col)
  Goodrich. Amer art (col)
Gelmeroda XIII, 1936                     MM
  OCl. Feininger
The glorious victory of the sloop Maria
                                         MoSL
  Gruskin
  MoSL. Handbook 1953
  OCl. Feininger
  Pierson
  Rosenblum
  Sewall. History of western art
  Wight. Milestones (col)
Gothic spire
  UNESCO. 1860-1949
  UNESCO. 1860-1955
Her majesty the Barque II                 OCl
  OCl. Feininger
High houses
  MnMW. Contemporary
  WMAA. Neuberger collection
Houses by the river
  Baur. New art
  PPC. International ex, 1950
Jagged clouds                            CtHW
  CtHW. Handbook

Locomotive
  OCl. Feininger
Locomotive with big wheel
  Baur. New art
Lonesome shores                          CSFL
  OCl. Feininger
Longeuil, Normandy
  OCl. Feininger
Luminosity
  OCl. Feininger
Lunar web
  Baur. Nature (col)
  Cheney. Story 1958 ed
  Pousette-Dart. Amer ptg
Lüneburg II                              NNSG
  NNSG. Handbook
Manhattan architecture
  Munsterberg
Manhattan canyon                         MdBM
  OCl. Feininger
Manhattan, dawn
  OCl. Feininger
Manhattan, dusk
  MM. Amer ptg today
Manhattan, moonwake
  MBIC. Villon and Feininger
Manhattan, night 1941
  MBIC. Villon and Feininger
Marine, 1927
  MBIC. Villon and Feininger
Marine II, 1925
  OCl. Feininger
Old American locomotive
  MBIC. Villon and Feininger
On the Baltic I, 1941
  MBIC. Villon and Feininger
Portentous sunset
  MBIC. Villon and Feininger
Quimper at night
  OCl. Feininger
Racing skerry cruisers (Yacht race)
  OCl. Feininger
The river                                MWM
  OCl. Feininger
  Pierson
Side wheeler                             MiD
  Baur. Revolution
  Lee. Art then and now
  MiD. Treasures
  NBuA. Fifty ptgs
  OCl. Feininger
  Pierson
Spell
  PPC. International ex, 1952
Steamer Odin II, 1927                    MMA
  Canaday
  MMA. Masters (col)
  OCl. Feininger
  Read. Art now, 1948 ed
  Roos
Storm brewing
  MBIC. Villon and Feininger
Street in Paris
  Baur. Revolution
  McCurdy
Study in space V                         ATeS
  ATeS. Collection
Sunset                                   MB
  OCl. Feininger
Sunset fires
  PPC. International ex, 1955

**FEININGER, Lyonel**—*Continued*
Town gate tower II, 1925
  OCl. Feininger
Town hall (Zottelstedt)
  MBIC. Villon and Feininger
Town hall of Cammin
  OCl. Feininger
Trumpeter in the village
  MnMW. Expressionism 1900-1955
Tug                                    NNSG
  Mendelowitz
Umpferstedt II                          PPhM
  PPhM. Arensberg coll
Village                                   DP
  Read. Concise history
Village church, 1937
  MnU. 40 Amer ptrs
Village church (Nieder-Reissen) 1924
  MBIC. Villon and Feininger
Vita nova
  MMA. Abstract
Vollersroda
  Cheney. Primer 1958 ed
The voyage
  UNESCO. 1860-1955
Western roadstead
  MBIC. Villon and Feininger
Western sea                             MSM
  OCl. Feininger
Windclouds at sundown
  Baur. Revolution
Yacht
  Pierson
Yacht race. See Racing skerry cruisers
Zirchow V                               NBM
  CoS. New accessions USA, 1954
Zirchow VII
  MMA. Abstract
**FEININGER, Theodore Luke,** 1910-
Ghosts of engines                       MMA
  Baur. Revolution
  CoS. New accessions USA, 1948
**FEITELSON, Lorser,** 1898-
Genesis, first version                  CSFM
  Baur. Revolution
  Pierson
Magical forms
  IU. Contemp Amer ptg, 1950
Mirabilia
  IU. Contemp Amer ptg, 1951
Painting
  IU. Contemp Amer ptg, 1949
**FEKE, Robert,** c 1705-1760
Charles Apthorp                         OCL
  Belknap
  Flexner. First flowers
  OCl. Handbook
Henry Collins (formerly called Gershom
    Flagg III)
  Belknap
Isaac Royall and family                 MCH
  Flexner. First flowers
  ICA. From colony to nation
  Mendelowitz
  Pierson
Isaac Winslow                            MB
  Flexner. First flowers
  **Pierson**
James Bowdoin II                        MeB
  Flexner. First flowers
  MiD. Ptg in America
  Pierson
  Roos

John Callender                          RPHS
  Flexner. First flowers
Mary McCall                               PA
  OCiM. Rediscoveries
Mrs Barlow Trecothick                     KW
  Belknap
  NNHS. Waldron Phoenix Belknap coll
Mrs Charles Willing
  Flexner. First flowers
Mrs Gershom Flagg IV
  Flexner. First flowers
Mrs James Bowdoin                        MeB
  Belknap
  Flexner. Copley
  Pierson
Mrs John Vinal (?) See Unknown lady
    (Mrs John Vinal?)
Mrs Josiah Martin                        MiD
  Belknap
  Flexner. First flowers
  MiD. Treasures
Mrs William Bowdoin                      MeB
  Belknap
  Pierson
Mrs William Peters                        PH
  Flexner. First flowers
Samuel Waldo                             MeB
  Barker. Amer ptg
  Flexner. First flowers
  NUM. Art across America
  Pierson
  Richardson. Ptg in America
  Roos
Self-portrait, c 1750                    RPHS
  Mendelowitz
  Pierson
Self-portrait, 1730 (Foote coll)
  Flexner. First flowers
  Pierson
Thomas Hiscox
  Flexner. First flowers
  Pierson
  Time. 300 years (col)
Unknown lady (Mrs John Vinal?) NBM
  Flexner. Amer ptg
  Flexner. Short history
  ICA. From colony to nation
  Larkin
  Larkin rev ed
  Pierson
  Robb. Harper history
William Bowdoin                          MeB
  Flexner. Light of distant skies
Young colonial                           ATeS
  ATeS. Collection
Young girl in flower                     NBM
  Flexner. First flowers (col)

**Attributed works**

Mrs Ralph Inman (also attributed to
    Blackburn)
  Belknap
**FELDMAN, Walter,** 1925-
Once upon the past
  MBIC. View 1960

**Female** corpse, back view by H. Bloom
**Female** figure by R. Soyer
**Female** figure with turban by H. C. Peale
**Female** leg by H. Bloom
**Female** of the species by W. R. Leigh

Femme avec fourrures by J. S. Sargent
Fence builders by E. F. Spruce
Fence on the hill by W. S. Mount
Fencing master by G. Melchers
Fenno, Eliza, d 1817
  Malbone, E. G. Eliza Fenno
Fenton, Beatrice, 1887-
  Eakins, T. Coral necklace
FENTON, P. fl 1815
  Miranda E. Lord from Connecticut  MeC
  Jetté. Amer heritage collection
FERBER, Herbert, 1906-
  Number 1, 1959
  WMAA. Contemp Amer ptg, 1959/60
Ferguson, James
  Peale, Raphaelle. Major James Ferguson
Fernandez, Alice
  Chase, W. M. Alice Fernandez
FERREN, Herbert, 1906-
  Composition on green
  MMA. Abstract
FERREN, John, 1905-
  Evocation
  MnU. 40 Amer ptrs
  Figuration
  MnU. 40 Amer ptrs
  Fire vase
  Cheney. Story 1958 ed
  The garden                          WMAA
  Baur. Nature (col)
  CSFP. Annual ex, 1952
  Goodrich. Amer art (col)
  Pierson
  WMAA. Contemp Amer ptg, 1951
  WMAA. Contemp Amer ptg, 1955
  Medianus
  IU. Contemp Amer ptg & sculp, 1957
  Mojave no 1
  PPC. International ex, 1955
  Painting, 1950
  McCurdy
  MMA. Abstract
  Red and blue                         NeL
  CoS. New accessions USA, 1956
  Eliot. Art of our time (col)
  Time. 300 years (col)
FERRILL, M. E. fl 1869-1883
  Country dance
  Jones. Rediscovered ptrs
  Sleighing scene, Lansingburgh       MiD
  Jones. Rediscovered ptrs
  Pierson
Ferry boat wreck by A. G. Dove
Festa della regatta, Palazzo Barbaro by J. S.
  Sargent
Festivals. See Fairs and festivals
Fête champêtre by S. Sherman
Fête champêtre by D. Tanning
Fête du Suquet by W. J. Glackens
Fetish by T. Benrimo
FEUERHERM, Kurt Karl, 1926-
  Golden tree
  ICA. Annual ex, 1957
  Mexican meat market
  MM. Amer ptg today
  NBuA. Expressionism
Field, Eliza Willing Spring (Peters) 1820-
  1902
  Sargent, J. S. Mr and Mrs John W. Field

Field, Ellen Virtue, 1835-1916
  Field, E. S. Ellen Virtue Field
FIELD, Erastus Salisbury, 1805-1900
  Ark of the covenant                  DN
  DN. Amer primitive ptgs, pt 1
  The blue boy                         VWR
  Flexner. Amer ptg
  Flexner. Short history
  Boy on stenciled carpet              VWR
  VWR. Folk art (col)
  Elizabeth Billings Ashley            MSM
  Lipman. Primitive ptrs
  Ellen Virtue Field                   MSM
  Lipman. Primitive ptrs
  Garden of Eden                       MB
  Barker. Amer ptg
  Baur. Amer ptg
  Ford. Pictorial folk art
  Lipman. Primitive ptrs
  MB. Karolik coll
  Pierson
  Girl holding rattle                  VWR
  Pierson
  Historical monument of the American re-
  public                               MSM
  Ford. Pictorial folk art
  Larkin
  Larkin rev ed
  Lipman. Primitive ptrs
  Mendelowitz
  MSM. Handbook (col)
  Pierson
  Roos
  Time. 300 years (col)
  Joseph Moore and his family          MB
  Pierson
  A lady                               DN
  DN. Amer primitive ptgs, pt 1
  A man                                DN
  DN. Amer primitive ptgs, pt 1
  Mr Pearce (?)                        VWR
  Brussels. Exposition
  Ford. Pictorial folk art
  VWR. Folk art (col)
  Mrs Joseph Moore
  Pierson
  Mrs Pearce ? (A woman)               VWR
  Brussels. Exposition
  Ford. Pictorial folk art
  Larkin
  Larkin rev ed
  VWR. Folk art (col)
  The Taj Mahal                        DN
  DN. Amer primitive ptgs, pt 2
            Attributed works
  Girl in yellow with a red doll      NCHA
  Jones. New-found folk art
Field, Hannah (Gladding) 1768-1848
  Malbone, E. G. Mrs John Field
Field, Mrs John. See Field, Hannah (Glad-
  ding)
Field, John White, fl 1882
  Sargent, J. S. Mr and Mrs John W. Field
Field, Mrs John White. See Field, Eliza
  Willing Spring (Peters)
Field II by T. Stamos
Field III, 1954 by T. Stamos
Field flowers by S. Menkès
Fields of grain as seen from train by A. G.
  Dove
Fields of Llano by A. Dasburg

**FIENE, Alicia**
Sleep
    NAD. Annual ex, 1958
**FIENE, Ernest, 1894-**
Above the river          ATeS
    ATeS. Collection
Driftwood, Monegan
    NAD. Annual ex, 1952
Fall of old houses         DP
    NYG. Fine art
Hudson navigation boat    WMAA
    Pierson
Lobsterman's gear no 2
    IU. Contemp Amer ptg, 1951
Razing old post office, New York
    Gruskin
Second variation
    IU. Contemp Amer ptg, 1950
Self-portrait
    Larkin
    Larkin rev ed
Variations on a theme: the wreck no 2, 1948    WMAA
    Goodrich. Amer art
    Pierson
**Fiery** night by K. L. Callahan
**Fiesole,** View of by W. M. Chase
**Fiestas.** See Fairs and festivals
**Fifth** avenue by J. Sloan
**Fifth** avenue and Forty-second street by J. Marin
**Fifth** avenue nocturne by C. Hassam
**Fifth** vision of Queen Vaidehi by R. Gorchov
**Fifty-seventh** street by R. Henri
**Fight** for the waterhole by F. Remington
**Figment** of erotic torture by B. L. Culwell
**Figural** composition by W. Pachner
**Figuration** by J. Ferren
**Figure** by C. di Marca-Relli
**Figure** by R. B. Motherwell
**Figure** and mask by A. Rattner
**Figure** before a field by J. Davis
**Figure** in blue by R. Soyer
**Figure** in landscape by W. De Kooning
**Figure** in pictorial space by S. Menkès
**Figure** in pink and green by R. B. Motherwell
**Figure** in prayer by W. Pachner
**Figure** in space by T. D. Benrimo
**Figure** in the rain by R. Lebrun
**Figure** lost in the light by B. Greene
**Figure** study by J. S. Sargent
**Figure** study by F. Taubes
**Figure** study by M. Weber
**Figure** with bird by M. Weber
**Figure** with wings and mask by A. Rattner
**Figures** and still life by R. Dunn
**Figures** in a hallway by C. G. Farr
**Figures** in a park by M. B. Prendergast
**Figures** in garden by E. N. Bischoff
**Figures** in landscape by W. Bailey
**Figures** in landscape by L. M. Eilshemius

**Figures** in landscape by J. Glasco
**Figures** in space by J. Berlandina
**Figures** on the cross with lantern by R. Leburn
**Figures** waiting by A. Rattner
**Figures** with mobiles by H. J. Teyral
**Fillmore, Millard, president U.S.** 1800-1874
    Healy, G. P. A. Millard Fillmore
**Film** studio by C. Browning
**FILMUS, Tully, 1903-**
Gladys            WMAA
    CSB. Illusion
The **final** veteran by L. Rivers
**FINCH, Keith, 1920?-**
Locomotive         CLA
    Pousette-Dart. Amer ptg
Locust
    ICA. Annual ex, 1951
Standing figure
    PPC. International ex, 1955
Suburban figure
    IU. Contemp Amer ptg & sculp, 1959
**FINCK, Furman Joseph, 1900-**
I've got nothing to wear    OT
    OT. Contemp Amer ptgs
Warren Robinson Austin
    PPC. Ptg in the U. S. 1949
**Finding** of Moses by F. E. Church
**Finding** of Moses by M. Schwartz
**Finding** of Moses by Unidentified artist
**Finding** of Queen Zenobia by A. Russell
**FINE, Perle, 1908-**
Calligraphy of rhythms
    IU. Contemp Amer ptg, 1951
In the beginning
    Rathbun
Pink harlequin
    VR. Biennial ex, 1948
Storm departs
    Baur. Nature
Tolling bell
    WMAA. Annual ex, 1955
**Finger** lakes by E. W. Dickinson
**FINK, Don**
The wild one
    ICA. Annual ex, 1961
**FINKELSTEIN, Louis**
Green, green, I love you green
    WMAA. Contemp Amer ptg, 1959/60
**FIORE, Joseph, 1925-**
Poland Spring, Maine    WMAA
    IU. Contemp Amer ptg & sculp, 1961
**Fir** tree, Deer Isle, Maine by J. Marin
**Fire** by A. Refregier
**Fire** eater by F. C. Watkins
**Fire** engine by E. Opper
**Fire** engine, Elizabeth, New Jersey by E. Opper
**Fire** escape by C. Browning
**Fire** in the woods by A. M. R. Moses
**Fire** Island by W. De Kooning
**Fire** Island landing by B. Mitchell
**Fire** of the warehouse of Henry Webb and company, Baltimore, 1827 by Unidentified artist
**Fire** vase by J. Ferren
**Fire** wheel by J. A. M. Whistler

Firecrackers sold here by W. T. Wiley
Fireflies by H. G. Keller
Fireman by W. M. Prior (manner of)
Fireworks by G. O. Hart
FIRKS, Henry, fl 1849
  San Francisco, 1849                    RNH
    Davidson v 1
First branch of the White river, Vermont
  by E. Hopper
First child by L. P. Harmon
First crop by T. H. Benton
First envoy from Santo Domingo by P.
  Tilyard
First frost by K. Knaths
First hepaticas by C. E. Burchfield
The first hypothesis by C. Howard
First landing of Christopher Columbus by
  F. Kemmelmeyer
First of January by W. De Kooning
First row, orchestra by E. Hopper
First show at two by H. G. Keller
The first skating by A. M. R. Moses
First snow by D. Macknight
First step by R. C. Woodville
First Texas Central railroad by C. M.
  Williamson
Fish, Hamilton, 1808-1893
  Hicks, T. Hamilton Fish
Fish, Nicholas, 1758-1833
  Malbone, E. G. Nicholas Fish
Fish by W. M. Chase
Fish by J. D. McClusky
Fish and birds by E. F. Spruce
Fish and lobsters by W. M. Chase
The fish and the man by C. W. Hawthorne
Fish bowl by P. Tchelitchew
Fish cleaner by V. Vytlacil
Fish composition by V. Vytlacil
Fish forms by V. Schreckengost
Fish house door by J. F. Peto
Fish house, New England by M. Hartley
Fish houses, Newfoundland by D. Macknight
Fish in bottle by M. H. Visser't Hooft
Fish in sea and stars by M. Graves
The fish is on the other side by Unidentified
  artist
Fish kite by Y. Kuniyoshi
Fish market by F. Di Gioia
Fish market by L. Gatch
Fish reflected upon outer and mental space
  by M. Graves
Fish: Study for glass by J. La Farge
Fish weir, Maine by Leonid
Fish weir near Sprucehead by Leonid
Fisher, Alexander Metcalf, 1794-1822
  Morse, A. F. B. Alexander Metcalf Fisher
FISHER, Alvan, 1792-1863
  The Hudson pool
    Sears. Highlights
  Niagara
    Pierson
  Sugar loaf mountain                    MB
    MB. Karolik coll

  The watering place
    Sears. Highlights
  White mountains
    Sears. Highlights

### Attributed works
  Lakes and mountains                    MB
    MB. Karolik coll

### Portrait of the artist
  Fraser, C. Alvan Fisher
Fisher, James, fl 1802
  Malbone, E. G. James Fisher
FISHER, Jonathan, 1768-1847
  Building at Harvard college, c 1810  MeC
    Jetté. Amer heritage collection
  Self-portrait
    Larkin
    Larkin rev ed
Fisher, Samuel, 1814-1899
  Weir, J. F. The Theological of Yale uni-
    versity
Fisher off the coast by L. Feininger
Fisher or marten by J. J. Audubon
Fisherfolk in a boat by W. Homer
Fisherfolk on the beach at Tynemouth by
  W. Homer
Fisherman and the djinn by J. La Farge
Fisherman's accoutrements by G. Cope
Fisherman's bedroom, Eastham, Massachu-
  setts by F. W. Benson
Fisherman's bride by T. Roszak
Fisherman's chest by J. C. Atherton
A fisherman's day by W. Homer
Fisherman's family by G. W. Bellows
Fisherman's morning by Z. L. Sepeshy
Fisherman's still life by J. B. Stearns
Fishermen and fishing
  Baker, R. Three fishermen
  Bellows, G. W. Fisherman
  Cropsey, J. F. Hasting-on-the Hudson,
    going fishing
  Doughty, T. Anglers
  Dozier, O. Fishermen
  Etnier, S. M. The seiner
  Goodwin, P. R. Trout fishing
  Hartley, M. Nova Scotia fishermen
  Hassam, C. Montauk fisherman
  Homer, W. Boy fishing
  Homer, W. Casting the fly
  Homer, W. The dory
  Homer, W. Fisherfolk in a boat
  Homer, W. A fisherman's day
  Homer, W. Fishing
  Homer, W. Guide fishing
  Homer, W. Herring net
  Homer, W. Ouananiche fishing: Lake St
    John, Quebec
  Homer, W. Shark fishing
  Homer, W. Sunrise fishing in the
    Adirondacks
  Homer, W. Trout fishing, Lake St John,
    Quebec
  Luks, G. Conner's rock, Cape Eliza, Maine
  Marin, J. Fishermen and boats
  Mason, R. M. Anglers heaven
  Mason, R. M. Fishing at the Spillway
  Michelson, L. Fishermen on the Seine

Fishermen and fishing—*Continued*
  Price, C. S. Fisherman
  Price, C. S. Fishermen
  Rattner, A. Fisherman
  Sample, P. S. Iceland fishermen
  Sample, P. S. Two trout fishermen
  Spruce, E. F. Fisherman
  Spruce, E. F. Surf fisherman
  Stock, J. W. Fisherman with his dog
  Sword, J. B. The strike—trout fishing
  Tait, A. F. Striped-bass fishing
  Terrell, E. Fisherman
  Wertz, H. Fisherman in red hat and shirt
  Whorf, J. Edge of the east water
  Zajac, J. Anglers
Fishermen on shore by W. Homer
Fishermen's festival by S. Wilson
Fishermen's huts by G. W. Bellows
Fishermen's huts by A. P. Ryder
Fishermen's last supper by M. Hartley
The fisherwoman by Leonid
Fisherwomen by M. Beckmann
Fishes with red stripes by R. B. Motherwell
Fishing at the spillway by R. M. Mason
Fishing boat by J. Marin
Fishing boat and white sun by M. Kahn
Fishing boats by R. Crawford
Fishing boats at Capri by A. Bierstadt
Fishing by a waterfall by T. Doughty
Fishing companions by F. V. Du Mond
Fishing on the Mississippi by G. C. Bingham
Fishing party by M. B. Prendergast
Fishing party in the mountains by T. Hill
Fishing pool by T. Doughty
Fishing shrimps at Boulogne by Leonid
Fishing village by F. Martin
Fishing village by C. S. Price
Fishkill, New York, View from by W. G. Wall
FISK, William H.
  George Catlin                                DN
    McCracken. George Catlin (col)
    Morgan
Fitch, Eleazer Thompson, 1791-1871
  Stone, W. O. Eleazer Thompson Fitch
Fitch, John, fl 1725
  Unidentified artist. John Fitch
Fitch, Mary. See Cabot, Mary (Fitch)
Fitch, William Clyde
  Chase, W. M. William Clyde Fitch
The fitting room by K. H. Miller
FitzGerald, Charles
  Glackens, W. J. Charles FitzGerald
FITZGERALD, James Herbert, 1910-
  Ember tree
    OrPA. Ptgs & sculptures
  The witness tree                             WaS
    ICA. Annual ex, 1951
Fitzgerald, Riter, d 1911
  Eakins, T. Riter Fitzgerald, Sketch for portrait of
Fitzhugh, Sarah, 1746-1793
  Hesselius, J. Sarah Fitzhugh
Fitzwilliam by A. James
Five in the afternoon by R. B. Motherwell

Five islands, Maine by W. Zorach
Five-master by Unidentified artist
Five strangers by Y. Tanguy
Flag carried at the Siege of Louisburg by Unidentified artist
The flagellants by S. Fogel
Flagellation by S. Greene
The flagellators by S. Greene
FLAGG, George Whiting, 1816-1897
  Rebecca                                      NNHS
    MiD. Travelers in Arcadia
Flagg, Mrs Gershom IV. See Flagg, Hannah (Pitson)
Flagg, Hannah (Pitson) 1711-1784
  Feke, R. Mrs Gershom Flagg IV
FLAGG, Jared Bradley, 1820-1899
  James Edward English                         CtY
    CtY. Portrait index
  Samuel Johnson Hitchcock                     CtY
    CtY. Portrait index
  Seth Perkins Staples (after S. L. Waldo and William Jewett)                    CtY
    CtY. Portrait index
Flagg, Rachel Moore Allston
  Allston, W. Artist's mother, Mrs Henry Collins Flagg
Flagging antelope by C. M. Russell
Flags and fishes by P. Dike
Le flambeau by C. R. Holty
Flame by W. A. Baziotes
Flame by L. Gatch
Flame by J. Pollock
Flame and winter tree by K. Schrag
FLANNERY, Vaughn, 1898-
  Chestnut stallion, Discovery
    PPC. International ex, 1950
  The governor's cup                           DP
    DP. Catalogue
  Swan island                                  OT
    OT. Contemp Amer ptgs
Flatboatmen by night by G. C. Bingham
Flax-scutching bee by L. Park
Flayed arm by H. Tovish
Flayed hills by D. V. Schlegell
Fleecing the priest by C. M. Russell
Fleeting time, thou hast left me old by I. L. Albright
Flesh eaters by W. A. Baziotes
FLETCHER, Alex, 1866-1952
  Communion service, First Presbyterian church                                PW
    Chew. 250 years of art

  **Portrait of the artist**
  Cuthbert, V. I. Alex Fletcher
Fletcher, Levi
  Sully, T. Levi Fletcher
Flight by J. D. Brooks
Flight by E. Harris
Flight by R. D. King
Flight by N. D. Knap
Flight into Egypt by W. Page
Flight into Egypt by Unidentified artist
Flight into morning by J. Gelb
Flight of birds by B. J. O. Nordfeldt
Flight of fancy by P. Evergood

Flight of Florimell by W. Allston
Flight of night by W. M. Hunt
Flight of plover by M. Graves
Flight of the clowns by E. Shinn
Flintlock by S. Martin
Float at low tide, Revere beach by M. B. Prendergast
Float on the Schuylkill by W. Stuempfig
Floating ice by G. W. Bellows
Floating island by G. G. Russell
Floating white city by F. Berman
Floats and markers by S. Wilson
FLOCH, Joseph, 1894-
  Conversation
    NAD. Annual ex, 1947, 1st half
  Girl looking out of window          NJMo
    NJMo. Forty years
  Near the sea
    NAD. Annual ex, 1960
  Still life with nude
    NAD. Annual ex, 1958
  Terrace
    NAD. Annual ex, 1954
Flock of sheep by W. Homer
Flood by A. B. Davies
Flood by B. J. O. Nordfeldt
Flood refugees by J. Corbino
Floral composition by H. Hofmann
Florence by T. Roszak
Florence, Italy
  Boit, E. D. Florence
  Boit, E. D. Florence from San Miniato
  Bosa, L. Ponte Vecchio, Florence
  Duveneck, F. The bridges, Florence
  Pucci, A. J. Ponte Vecchio
  Sargent, J. S. Florence: Boboli gardens
  Sargent, J. S. Florence: Torre Galli
Florence protecting the arts by A. H. Thayer
Florentines by A. H. Maurer
Florida
  Harvey, G. White pelicans in Florida
  Heade, M. J. On the Sebastian river, Florida
  Homer, W. Homosassa river
  Homer, W. Indian in Florida swamps
  Homer, W. Thornhill bar, Florida
  Martin, F. Florida landscape
  Matthew, K. Azalea tropical trails, Florida
  Pleissner, O. M. Florida landscape
Florinsky, Michael T.
  Evergood, P. M. T. Florinsky, D. S. Mirsky and the pidget
Florist's window by J. Lawrence
FLORSHEIM, Richard Aberle, 1916-
  Night city
    Time. 300 years (col)
  Wharves                              MiD
    CoS. New accessions, USA, 1960
Flounder by R. Tam
Flour mill by A. G. Dove
Flower abstraction by M. Hartley
Flower eruption by T. Stamos
Flower forms by C. Sheeler
Flower market at Geneva by D. A. Dreier
Flower piece by A. B. Carles

Flower piece by C. H. Demuth
Flower piece by M. Weber
Flower still life by N. Tschacbasov
Flower study by C. H. Demuth
Flower study by N. L. Murphy
Flower vendor by M. Avery
Flower vendor by R. Soyer
Flower vendors by R. Gwathmey
Flower women by I. Rose
Flowered hat by H. V. Poor
Flowering branch by H. Hofmann
Flowering white by J. Tworkov
Flowermakers by A. Blanch
Flowers by J. Corbino
Flowers by C. H. Demuth
Flowers by A. H. Maurer
Flowers by F. J. Rederer
Flowers and fruit by Unidentified artist
Flowers, butterfly, and book by Unidentified artist
Flowers by the lake by P. Evergood
Flowers, cyclamen by C. H. Demuth
Flowers from Claire Spencer's garden by M. Hartley
Flowers from my garden by B. Klonis
Flowers in a garden by N. Cikovsky
Flowers in Pennsylvania Dutch teapot by F. C. Watkins
Flowers in the city by C. C. Burg
Flowers in vase by F. Papsdorf
Flowers on a window ledge by J. La Farge
Flowers with four doilies by H. Pippin
Flowers with hat and cane by H. Pippin
Floyd, Mary. See Tallmadge, Mary (Floyd)
Flutes. See Musicians and musical instruments—Flutes
Fluttering fowl by R. Koppe
Fluttering pendant by K. R. Morris
Flying box by J. Hultberg
Flying carpet by S. Davis
Flying Codonas by J. S. Curry
Flying Dutchman by L. M. Eilshemius
Flying Dutchman by J. Ernst
Flying Dutchman by A. P. Ryder
Flying horses by M. B. Prendergast
Flying kites, Montmartre by W. J. Glackens
Flying trapeze by A. Rattner
Flyweight champ of Jumel place by G. B. Luks
Fog horns by A. G. Dove
Fog lifts by J. Marin
Fog warning by W. Homer
FOGEL, Seymour, 1911-
  Driftwood structure
    Pearson. Mod renaissance
  The flagellants
    Pearson. Mod renaissance
  Genesis
    Pearson. Mod renaissance
  Icarian flight                       TxF
    Pousette-Dart. Amer ptg
  Labyrinth
    Pearson. Mod renaissance

**Foggy** night by J. De Martini

**Foggy** pasture by D. W. Gorsline

**Foissin, Elizabeth.** See Trapier, Elizabeth (Foissin)

**Folding** chair by A. Katz

**FOLINSBEE, John Fulton,** 1892-
Don Quixote
  NAD. Annual ex, 1953
Night
  NAD. Annual ex, spring 1950
Quarry pool
  NAD. Annual ex, 1955

**FOLLETT, Jean,** 1917-
Untitled, 1950
  NNSG. Younger Amer ptrs

**Fondey family,** fl 1803
Ames, E. The Fondey family

**Football.** See Games and sports—Ball

**Footbridge** at Bridgeport by J. H. Twackman

**FOOTE, John,** 1921-
The entombment
  IU. Contemp Amer ptg, 1951

**For** God must have loved them by E. Melcarth

**For** internal use only by S. Davis

**For** service rendered by W. Hedrick

**For** Thanksgiving by H. G. Keller

**FORBES, Donald,** 1905-
Landscape with bird's nest    ATU
  ATU. Coll of Amer art

**FORBES, Hannah Lucinda,** fl 1820
Mourning piece
  Ford. Pictorial folk art

**Forbes, William Smith,** 1831-1905
Eakins, T. Professor William Smith Forbes

**Forbidden** blossom by W. Pachner

**Forbidden** fruit by Y. Kuniyoshi

**Forbidden** thicket by C. Cloar

**Force** in space by C. G. Shaw

**Forces** against violent attack by J. De Diego

**FORD, Lauren,** 1891-
Bethlehem    InIJ
  InIJ. 105 ptgs
Nativity
  PC. Ptg in the U.S. 1949

The **ford** by H. G. Keller

**Foreboding** by H. M. Mayer

**Forest** by W. Homer

**Forest** by E. Magafan

**Forest** by S. Sherman

**Forest** by V. Vytlacil

**Forest** by M. Weber

**Forest** boundary by R. Cowles

**Forest** city by A. Friedman

**Forest** hill—the Nelson homestead near Boonville by G. C. Bingham

**Forest** of Arden by A. P. Ryder

**Forest** of Zogbaum by W. De Kooning

**Forest** park, View in by W. Barker

**Forest** stream, a study from nature by A. H. Wyant

**Forevermore** by A. Blanch

The **forge** by W. M. Hunt

**Forget** it by L. Lewitin

**Forging** the shaft, replica by J. F. Weir

**Forgotten** cabin by A. James

The **forgotten** man by P. Evergood

**Forlorn** one by R. S. Neuman

**FORMAN, Alice,** 1931-
Untitled landscape no 6, 1960
  WMAA. Young America 1960
Untitled landscape no 11, 1959
  WMAA. Young America 1960

**Forman, David**
Peale, C. W. Gen David Forman

**Formation** of rock by A. J. Miller

**Forms** by A. E. Gallatin

**Forms** abstracted by M. Hartley

**Forms** follow man by M. Tobey

**FORST, Miles,** 1923-
Cell
  NNSG. Younger Amer ptrs

**Forsythias** by H. Moller

**Fort, Mrs Seymour,** fl 1776
Copley, J. S. Mrs Seymour Fort

**Fort** Arbuckle, Oklahoma territory by V. Colyer

**Fort** Clark by K. Bodmer

**Fort** Harker, Kansas by H. Stieffel

**Fort** Keough, Montana by H. Stieffel

**Fort** Laramie by A. J. Miller

**Fort** Laramie, Interior of by A. J. Miller

**Fort** Lee ferry by G. O. Coleman

**Fort** McHenry, Star Spangled Banner over by Unidentified artist

**Fort** Montgomery, View near by W. G. Wall

**Fort** Pierre by K. Bodmer

**Fort** Pierre with Sioux camped around by G. Catlin

**Fort** Plain, New York by J. H. Hidley

**Fort** St Jean, Marseilles by R. Smith

**Fort** Snelling by Unidentified artist

**Fort** Snelling by J. C. Wild

**Fort** Snelling on the upper Mississippi by G. Catlin

**Fort** Snelling, View of by S. Eastman

**Fort** Sumter by C. W. Chapman

**Fort** Ticonderoga, Ruins of by R. Smith

**Fort** Union, mouth of the Yellowstone by G. Catlin

**Fort** Vancouver by H. J. Warre

**FORTESS, Karl Eugene,** 1907-
Big tree
  Pearson. Mod renaissance
Entrance
  Pearson. Mod renaissance
Group of trees
  Pearson. Mod renaissance
Landscape
  NYG. Fine art
Portrait
  IU. Contemp Amer ptg, 1949
Rockhill special    ATU
  ATU. Coll of Amer art
Upright 3
  IU. Contemp Amer ptg & sculp, 1955

**Fortifications** of Elba by D. W. Ellis

**Fortune** hunters by H. Baer

**Fortune** seller by K. Zerbe

Fortune teller by S. M. Adler
Fortune teller by W. J. Gordon
A Forty-niner by J. W. Audubon
Forty-second street by T. Roszak
Forty-two kids by G. W. Bellows
Forward but beyond by N. Daphnis
FOSBURGH, James Whitney, 1910-
  The kite
    CSFP. Annual ex, 1952
FOSS, Oliver, 1920-
  Paris under snow
    IU. Contemp Amer ptg, 1952
  Relaxation
    MoSL. Contemporary Amer ptg
Fossil hunters by E. W. Dickinson
Fossils by M. Tobey
Foster, Mrs Isaac, fl 1755
  Badger, J. Mrs Isaac Foster
FOSTER, John, 1648-1681
  John Wheelwright (?)                MBS
    Barker. Amer ptg

**Attributed works**

John Davenport                       CtY
    CtY. Portrait index
    Flexner. First flowers
    Ford. Pictorial folk art
    Pierson
Foul weather, Percé by H. G. Keller
FOUNTAIN, Albert J. 1862-1936
  Celebration of the Gadsden purchase
    NUM. Art across America
The fountain by W. A. Baziotes
The fountain by W. Thon
Fountains at night, World's Columbian exposition, Chicago by W. Homer
Fountains of Europe by M. Tobey
Four and a half out of every five by B. Shahn
The four apostles writing the Gospels by Unidentified artist
Four children playing in a street by J. Paul
Four dancers by M. Soyer
Four figures in a bistro by A. Blatas
Four girls in meadow by M. B. Prendergast
The four horsemen of the Apocalypse by J. de Botton
Four houses by A. P. Martino
Four-master off the Cape by J. Marin
Four men by D. Park
Four men around a table by M. Beckmann
Four o'clock in summer: hope by T. Tanguy
Four o'clock on the Seine by J. Marin
Four opposites by J. Pollock
Four-panel green by A. Leslie
Four part synchromy, no 7, 1914-15 by M. Russell
Four piece orchestra by B. Shahn
The four seasons by C. E. Burchfield
4 September 1960 by K. R. Morris
Fourcaud, Louis de, 1851-1914
  Sargent, J. S. Louis de Fourcaud
Fourteenth street by R. Marsh
Fourteenth street by K. H. Miller

Fourteenth street promenade by G. L. K. Morris
Fourth dimension by P. Sullivan
Fourth of July by L. Guglielmi
Fourth of July by C. W. Hare
Fourth of July celebration in Centre square, Philadelphia, 1819 by J. L. Krimmel
Fourth of July in Centre square, Philadelphia, c 1810 by J. L. Krimmel
Fourth of July orator by B. Shahn
Fourth of July picnic by S. Merrett
Fourth Pennsylvania Cavalry by Unidentified artist
Fowle, Jacob, 1704-1778?
  Copley, J. S. Jacob Fowle
Fowler, Samuel Stevenson, 1799-1850
  Ames, E. Samuel Stevenson Fowler
Fowles, Abigail. See Edwards, Abigail (Fowles)
FOWLER, O. R. fl 1838
  A gentleman                         MeC
    Jetté. Amer heritage collection
  A lady                              MeC
    Jetté. Amer heritage collection
Fox island, Maine by M. Hartley
Fox hunter by K. Knaths
Foxes
  Audubon, J. J. Fox and goose
  Darrel, A. Vixen
  Graves, M. Fox with phoenix wing
  Hazel, S. M. Fox
  Hinkley, T. Fox in West Virginia
  Homer, W. Fox hunt
  Hope, J. Winter scene: the red fox
  Pippin, H. The getaway
Fragment of an empire by F. Roth
Fragment of peace by M. Tobey
Fragment: three heads by H. J. Teyral
Fragment: two figures by H. J. Teyral
Fragments and reconstruction by U. Romano
Fragments from yesterday by D. W. Ellis
Fragments of elegance by W. Lockwood
Fragments of roses by W. Brice
Fragrance of fear by M. Tomkins
Fragrance of grasses by K. Schrag
FRAME, Robert, 1924-
  Beach no 1
    IU. Contemp Amer ptg & sculp, 1961
  Evening landscape
    IU. Contemp Amer ptg & sculp, 1957
FRANCES, Esteban, 1914-
  El cuadro de los Abanicos
    IU. Contemp Amer ptg, 1952
  Salto mortal
    CSP. Annual ex, 1947/48
Frances and Judy by L. Betts
Francis, John, 1763-1796
  Malbone, E. G. John Francis
FRANCIS, John F. 1810-1885
  Apples in a basket
    Chew. 250 years of art
    WiMiA. Amer ptg 1760-1960
  Grapes in a bowl
    CSFP. Illusionism
  Iris and snowballs
    Frankenstein. After the hunt

FRANCIS, J. F.—*Continued*
Still life                                    NJP
  Barker. Amer ptg
Still life, 1867                              MB
  Frankenstein. After the hunt
Still life with apples and chestnuts, 1859
                                              MB
  MB. Karolik coll
Still life with wine bottles and basket of
  fruit                                       MB
  MB. Karolik coll
Three children                               MB
  MB. Karolik coll
Francis, John Wakefield, 1810-1885
  Elliott, C. L. John Wakefield Francis
FRANCIS, Sam, 1923?-
Abstraction                                  WaS
  CoS. New accessions USA, 1958
Big red                                      MMA
  MMA. New Amer ptg (col)
  MMA. 12 Americans (col)
Black in red                                 MMA
  MMA. New Amer ptg
  MMA. 12 Americans
Blue and black (Power coll)
  MMA. New Amer ptg
  Ponente. Mod ptg, 1960 (col )
Blue—black                                   NBuA
  MMA. 12 Americans
  NBuA. Acquisitions 1954-57
Cross
  PPC. International ex, 1961/62
Deep orange on black
  MMA. 12 Americans
Gray
  MMA. 12 Americans
Red and black                                NNSG
  NNSG. Handbook
  PPC. International ex, 1955
Red in red, 1955
  McCurdy
  MMA. 12 Americans
Summer no 1
  50 years of mod art
  Read. Concise history (col)
Summer no II
  Art since 1945
Two worlds
  MnMW. 60 Amer ptrs
Watercolour
  Read. Concise history
The white line
  WMAA. Contemp Amer ptg, 1959/60
FRANCK, Frederick Sigfred, 1909-
From my attic
  NBuA. Expressionism
Lazarus resurrected
  IU. Contemp Amer ptg, 1949
New York from Hoboken
  IU. Contemp Amer ptg, 1950 (col)
New York with roller coaster
  IU. Contemp Amer ptg & sculp, 1953
The soothsayer
  IU. Contemp Amer ptg, 1952
Still life enters death
  IU. Contemp Amer ptg, 1951
Franconia range—mist and rain by J. Marin
FRANK, Eugene C. d 1914
Wyalusing
  McClintock
Frankenberg, Mrs Lloyd. See MacIver,
  Loren

FRANKENSTEIN, John Peter, 1816-1881
The artist in his studio
  Chew. 250 years of art
  WiMiA. Amer ptg 1760-1960
FRANKENTHALER, Helen, 1928-
L'amour, toujours l'amour
  IU. Contemp Amer ptg & sculp, 1959
Black and white and read all over
  ICA. Annual ex, 1961
Blue territory                               WMAA
  Goodrich. Amer art
  WMAA. Young America 1957
Eden
  Hunter. Mod Amer ptg (col)
The facade
  PPC. International ex, 1955
Italian beach
  PPC. International ex, 1961/62
Loreli
  Baur. Nature (col)
Las Mayas
  MnMW. 60 Amer ptrs
Round trip                                   NBuA
  NBuA. Acquisitions 1957-58
Trojan gates                                 MMA
  Cheney. Story 1958 ed
FRANKFURTER, Jack, 1929-
Reconstruction
  VR. Amer ptg, 1958
Franklin, Benjamin, 1706-1790
  Healy, G. P. A. Benjamin Franklin at the
    court of Louis XVI
  Peale, C. W. Benjamin Franklin
  West, B. Benjamin Franklin drawing
    electricity from the sky
  Wright, J. (attributed works) Benjamin
    Franklin
Franklin, Maud
  Whistler, J. A. M. Arrangement in black
    and white (The young American,
    Maud Franklin)
Franklin park, Boston by M. B. Prendergast
Franks, Bilhah Abigail (Levy)
  Duyckinck, G. (attributed works) Mrs
    Jacob Franks
Franks, David, 1720-1793
  Duyckinck, G. (attributed works) Chil-
    dren of Jacob Franks
Franks, Jacob, 1688-1769
  Unidentified artist. Jacob Franks
Franks, Mrs Jacob. See Franks, Bilhah
  Abigail (Levy)
Franks, Phila. See De Lancey, Phila
  (Franks)
FRANKS, Seymour, 1916-
Kaleidoscopic journey
  ICA. Annual ex, 1947/48
Vibration
  IU. Contemp Amer ptg, 1952
FRANSIOLI, Thomas Adrian, 1906-
The cat
  PPC. International ex, 1952
Interior number 2
  IU. Contemp Amer ptg & sculp, 1957
Louisburg square
  IU. Contemp Amer ptg, 1951
St Andrew's church, Roanoke
  IU. Contemp Amer ptg, 1952
Way to Penobscot
  IU. Contemp Amer ptg, 1950

FRARY, Michael, 1918-
  Apartment house                              TxD
    Pousette-Dart. Amer ptg
  Coast town                                   OYB
    OYB. Annual 1959
  Oil construction on the beach                OYB
    OYB. Annual 1955
    OYB. Supplement 1959
  Still life with thistles
    IU. Contemp Amer ptg & sculp, 1953
FRASCONI, Antonio, 1919-
  Warwick mine, exit no 1
    WMAA. Annual ex, 1956
Fraser, Alexander, 1722-1791
  Theus, J. Alexander Fraser
FRASER, Charles, 1782-1860
  Alvan Fisher                                 MM
    MM. New England miniatures (col)
  Rice Hope                                    SCCG
    Davidson v 1
The fratellini by L. MacIver
FRAZER, Oliver, 1808-1864
  Anderson children                          KyLS
    KyLS. Kentucky port gall
Freake, Elizabeth (Clarke) 1642-1713
  Freake limner. Mrs Freake and baby
    Mary
FREAKE limner, fl 1668-1723
  Henry Gibbs
    Flexner. First flowers
    Ford. Pictorial folk art (col)
    ICA. From colony to nation
    Larkin rev ed
  Margaret Gibbs
    Barker. Amer ptg
    Flexner. Amer ptg
    Flexner. First flowers
    Flexner. Short history
    Mendelowitz
    Time. 300 years (col)
  Mrs Freake and baby Mary                     MWM
    NYG. Fine art p211
    Richardson. Ptg in America
    Robb. Art 1953 ed
    Robb. Harper history
  Robert Gibbs
    Flexner. First flowers
    Pierson
FREDENTHAL, David, 1914-
  The immigrant
    WMAA. Annual ex, 1956
  The people                                   ATU
    ATU. Coll of Amer art
  Requiem
    Genauer
  Veni, vidi, vici
    IU. Contemp Amer ptg, 1949
The free trader by C. M. Russell
Free trappers in trouble by A. J. Miller
FREEDMAN, Maurice, 1904-
  Caught in net
    PPC. Ptg in the U. S. 1949
  Pemaquid lobster
    Gruskin (col)
  Squall off Christmas cove
    Cheney. Primer 1958 ed
FREEMAN, Mr. fl 1816
  Mrs William Cooper (Elizabeth Feni-
    more Cooper)                             NCHA
    Jones. Rediscovered ptrs
    Pierson

Peter Volo                                     NCHA
    Jones. New-found folk art
    **Attributed works**
  Catherine A. Russell
    Jones. Rediscoverd ptrs
  Rensselaer W. Russell (in his thirteenth
    year)
    Jones. Rediscovered ptrs
FREEMAN, Don, 1908-
  Carl Sandburg                                ATU
    ATU. Coll of Amer art
Freeman, Mrs Joseph. See Von Wiegand,
  Charmion
Freight cars by C. E. Burchfield
Freight cars in desert by P. S. Sample
Freight cars, Minneapolis by R. Crawford
Freight cars under a bridge by C. E. Burch-
  field
Freight yards by G. R. Beal
Frelinghuysen, Mrs Peter
  Cassatt, M. Mrs Peter Frelinghuysen
FRENCH, Jared, 1905-
  The rope                                     WMAA
    Goodrich. Amer art
    MnMW. Reality and fantasy
    Pierson
    WMAA. Contemp Amer ptg, 1955
French Canadian barn by C. C. Richardson
French child on train by M. Fadden
French village church by A. B. Carles
Fresh water cove from Dolliver's neck,
  Gloucester by F. H. Lane
Freuchen, Peter, 1886-
  Brackman, R. Peter Freuchen
FRIEBERT, Joseph, 1908-
  Synagogue                                    ICA
    Pousette-Dart. Amer ptg
  Urban cathedral
    ICA. Amer artists paint the city
FRIED, Theodore, 1902-
  Nursing mother
    PPC. Ptg in the U.S. 1949
FRIEDENSOHN, Elias, 1924-
  Ancestor
    IU. Contemp Amer ptg & sculp, 1961
  Effort at speech between two people
    WMAA. Young America 1957
  Jeune fille en fleur                         IU
    IU. Contemp Amer ptg & sculp, 1957
    IU. 20th century
  Prometheus
    IU. Contemp Amer ptg & sculp, 1959
  Secret
    WMAA. Young America 1957
FRIEDMAN, Arnold, 1873-1946
  Forest city
    Baur. Revolution
  Unemployable                                 MM
    Cheney. Story 1958 ed
FRIEDMAN, Martin, 1896-
  Eventide
    IU. Contemp Amer ptg, 1948
  The grotto
    PPC. Ptg in the U.S. 1949
  Metropolitan nocturne
    IU. Contemp Amer ptg & sculp, 1953
  Pink flower
    IU. Contemp Amer ptg & sculp, 1955

FRIEDMAN, Martin—*Continued*
The quarry    ATU
  ATU. Coll of Amer art
Sawtooth Falls    MMA
  Pierson
A friendly call by W. M. Chase
Friends or enemies by C. M. Russell
Friendship by M. Weber
FRIESEKE, Frederick Carl, 1874-1939
Yellow room    InIJ
  InIJ. 105 ptgs
Frieze by J. Pollock
Frightened deer in moonlight by K. Knaths
FRINCK, O. E. S. fl 1845
Landscape
  Sears. Highlights
Frishmuth, Mrs William D.
  Eakins, T. Mrs William D. Frishmuth
Frog monster by B. Shahn
Frogman by J. Pollock
Frogtown lady by A. Brook
From a cathedral by B. Margo
From afar by F. Nagler
From an ivory tower by J. L. Lasker
From Arkansas by G. Schreiber
From Avenue A by H. Rose
From Cranberry isle by J. F. Heliker
From elements of evening by B. Margo
From February by B. Margo
From my attic by F. S. Franck
From my studio by F. Crowninshield
From my studio window by J. Kane
From my window by C. C. Ross
From nature in the garden by Rubens Peale
From one night to the other by Y. Tanguy
From seeing Cape Split by J. Marin
From shipwrecks by B. Margo
From that day on by B. Shahn
From the bridge by R. Crawford
From the bridge, New York city by J. Marin
From the pelvis series by G. O'Keeffe
From the plain by G. O'Keeffe
From the plains no 1, 1953 by G. O'Keeffe
From the terrace by S. Laufman
From the town beyond the river by G. Grosz
From the upper terrace by J. H. Twachtman
From Weehawken heights by J. Marin
From Williamsburg bridge by E. Hopper
The fronfroneur by K. J. Priebe
Front face by W. M. Harnett
Front porch by R. Gwathmey
Front street by C. S. Price
Frontier by K. M. Martin
Frontiersman, Head of a by F. Remington
FROST, Arthur Burdett, 1851-1928
Hunting deer    MB
  MB. Ptgs in water color
Hunting the moose
  NSP. Sportscapes

Portrait of the artist
Eakins, T. Arthur B. Frost

FROST, John O. J.
Marblehead harbor
  Lipman. Primitive ptrs
Frothingham, Abby Langdon. See Wales,
  Abby Langdon (Frothingham)
Frowning cliff, Watkins glen, New York
  by J. Hope
Frozen sounds by A. Gottlieb
Frozen station by J. Hultberg
Frugal housewife by J. H. Davis (attribu-
  ted works)
Fruit by J. Peale
Fruit by H. V. Poor
Fruit and daisies by A. Pregel
Fruit and flowers by M. B. Prendergast
Fruit and flowers by Unidentified artist
Fruit and goldfinch by Wagguno
Fruit and melon by Unidentified artist
Fruit and table by K. Knaths
Fruit and wine by E. Bowers
Fruit bowl by H. Hofmann
Fruit bowl by W. Sommer
Fruit bowl with mirror by S. Menkès
Fruit in a white bowl by B. A. Sawyer
Fruit in yellow bowl by M. R. Wilson
Fruit on table by S. Roesen
Fruit, vase and mandolin by N. Cikovsky
Fruit with striped pottery by W. J.
  Glackens
Fruits of autumn by J. Peale
Fruits of Belfield by C. W. Peale
Fry, Catherine, 1780-1858
  Malbone, E. G. Catherine Fry
Full fathom five by J. Pollock
Full moon by H. B. Schleeter
Full white by L. P. Smith
FULLER, Augustus, 1812-1873
Fanny Negus Fuller and twins
  Ford. Pictorial folk art
A gentleman    MeC
  Jetté. Amer heritage collection
A lady    MeC
  Jetté. Amer heritage collection
Lady wearing a red pompon    MSM
  Ford. Pictorial folk art
  MSM. Handbook
FULLER, C. Sue, 1914-
String construction no 30
  IU. Contemp Amer ptg, 1952
String composition no 50
  IU. Contemp Amer ptg & sculp, 1955
Fuller, Fanny Negus, fl 1840
  Fuller, A. Mrs Fanny Negus Fuller and
    twins
FULLER, George, 1822-1884
Country lass    MNS
  Larkin
  Larkin rev ed
Fedalma    DNC
  DNC. Gellatly coll, 1954
Gold and old lace    OYB
  OYB. Catalogue 1951
Ideal head    DP
  DP. Catalogue
  Pierson
Mrs Weatherbee. See Old age (Mrs
  Weatherbee)

Nydia MM
NAD. Amer tradition
Old age (Mrs Weatherbee) MoSL
MoSL. Handbook 1953
The quadroon MM
Barker. Amer ptg
Tomato patch MiD
Pierson
Richardson. Ptg in America
Winifred Dysart MWM
Pierson
Fuller, Margaret. See Ossoli, Sarah Margaret (Fuller) marchesa d'
Fuller, Sue. See Fuller, C. Sue
Fully developed escutcheon by C. Howard
FULTON, Robert, 1765-1815
Mrs Oliver H. Perry
MB. New England miniatures (col)

**Portrait of the artist**
Leroy, E. E. Robert Fulton
Peale, Rembrandt. Robert Fulton
Fulton and Nostrand by J. Lawrence
Fulton street, New York by S. Pierson
La fumée d'ambre-gris by J. S. Sargent
Fun by W. W. Quirt
Funeral coach by B. Kamihira
Funeral of the poet Panizza by G. Grosz
Funeral scaffold of a Sioux chief by K. Bodmer
The fur jacket by J. A. M. Whistler
Fur traders descending the Misouri by G. C. Bingham
Fur trappers' rendezvous by A. J. Miller
Furbish, Dependence H.
Beckett, C. E. Furbish's dash to Montreal
Furling the foresail by C. R. Patterson
Furlough by G. Grosz
Furneaux, Anne. See Clarke, Anne (Furneaux)
FURNESS, John Mason, 1763-1804
John Vinal NBM
Flexner. Light of distant skies
Pierson
The furniture of time by Y. Tanguy
Furniture shop and warehouse of Duncan Phyfe, Fulton street, New York by Unidentified artist
Further festivities at the Contessa Sanseverini's by J. Wilde
Fury by H. Hofmann
Fusion by W. Kamys
Fussel, Charles Lewis, 1840-1909
Eakins, T. Charles Lewis Fussel
The future by P. Evergood
Future admiral by J. C. Phillips
The future belongs to them by P. Evergood

**G**

G-5, 1923-26 by L. Moholy-Nagy
Gaberndorf II by L. Feininger
Gables I, 1925 by L. Feininger
Gables IV by L. Feininger

GABO, Naum, 1890-
Blue construction in space—kinetic CtHW
CtHW. Handbook
Construction
Read. Art now, 1948 ed
Linear construction no 2, variation no 1, 1950 MAP
MnMW. Classic tradition
Gabriel by F. C. Watkins
Gabrielle by A. H. Maurer
Gadsden, Selina Fenwick. See Curwen, Selina Fenwick (Gadsden)
Gadsden purchase, Celebration of by A. J. Fountain
GAERTNER, Carl Frederick, 1898-1952
Atwood's cove
IU. Contemp Amer ptg, 1950
PPC. Ptg in the U. S. 1949
Bend at Newton hook OYB
OYB. Supplement
Bend in Storm King OCl
Pousette-Dart. Amer ptg
Erie street boys
NAD. Annual ex, spring 1950
Fairport harbor
MM. Amer ptg today
Lands end road
IU. Contemp Amer ptg, 1949
Pidge, Blink and the sea IaDa
IaDa. Silver jubilee
IaDa. 30th anniversary
Population—3000
VR. Biennial ex, 1948
River view and the plaza
IU. Contemp Amer ptg, 1948
The St Clair fire OCl
OCl. Handbook
Wharf players, moonlight
CSFP. Annual ex, 1952
Galatea by J. S. Copley
Gallagher, Mary
Henri, R. Mary Gallagher
GALLAGHER, Sears, b 1869
Landscape with a farmhouse MB
MB. Ptgs in water color
GALLATIN, Albert Eugene, 1881-1952
Composition, 1942 PPhM
PPhM. Gallatin coll
Forms
McCurdy
MMA. Abstract
Galleria, Naples by A. Blaustein
Galleria Umberto by M. Beckmann
Gallery of the Louvre by S. F. B. Morse
Gallond, Almira. See Moore, Almira (Gallond)
GALLOWAY, 1940-
Sea coming into the land
MBIC. View 1960
Galloway, Jane, 1745-1801
West, B. Jane Galloway
Galloway, Mrs Richard
Hesselius, J. Mrs Richard Galloway jr of Cedar Park, Maryland
Gambetta, Léon, 1838-1882
Healy, G. P. A. Léon Gambetta
Gamble, Agnes S. B. See Cabell, Agnes S. B. (Gamble)
The gamblers by E. Higgins
The game by B. Kamihira

The **game** by M. Schapiro
**Game** of chance by G. Ortman
**Game** of pretend by A. Pickens
**Games and sports**
    *See also* Boxers and wrestlers; Fisher-
    men and fishing; Hunters and hunting
Bosa, L. Hallowe'en
Cadmus, P. Playground
Kirschenbaum, J. Playground
Unidentified artist. Winter sports on the
    farm
### Archery
Catlin, G. Archery of the Mandans or
    game of the arrow
### Badminton
Lee, D. E. Badminton
### Ball
    *See also* other ball games below, e.g.
    Croquet; Pool; Tennis
Catlin, G. Ball-play of the Choctaws
Catlin, G. Champion Choctaw ball-player
Eakins, T. Baseball players
Eastman, S. Lacrosse playing among the
    Sioux
Phillips, M. A. Night baseball
Schanker, L. Football
Shahn, B. Handball
Warren, F. E, Night baseball game
    Cardinals vs. Dodgers
### Bicycling
Avery, M. Bicycle rider
De Martini, J. Bike race no 2
Egri, T. Bicycle riders
Egri, T. Destination unknown
Feininger, L. Bicycle riders
Wyeth, A. N. Young America
### Cards
Baer, H. Cribbage players
Bingham, G. C. In a quandary
Higgins, E. The gamblers
Johnson, E. Card playing at Fryeburg,
    Maine
Levine, J. Card players
Pickens, A. Card players
Stanley, J. M. Indians playing cards
Watkins, F. C. Solitaire
Woodville, R. C. Card players
### Checkers
Bingham, G. C. Checker players
### Chess
Eakins, T. Chess players
Lawrence, J. Chess on Broadway
Moller, H. Chess players
Poor, H. V. Chess game
Tooker, G. Chess game
### Croquet
Homer, W. Croquet match
Homer, W. Croquet players
Sample, P. S. Roque
### Dice
Binford, J. Crap shooter
### Dominoes
Pippin, H. Domino players
Unidentified artist. The domino girl

### Hopscotch
Albright, I. L. Hopscotch
MacIver, L. Hopscotch
Vickrey, R. Hopscotch
### Kite flying
Glackens, W. J. Flying kites, Montmartre
Kester, L. Kite fliers
### Polo
Bellows, G. W. Polo at Lakewood
Bellows, G. W. Polo scene
Hurd, P. Landscape with polo players
### Pool
Bloom, D. S. Pool room
Burlin, P. Pool player
### Quoits
Homer, W. Pitching quoits
### Rowing
Eakins, T. John Biglen in a single scull
Eakins, T. Oarsmen
### Skating
Beckmann, M. Skaters
Birch, T. Skating
Bosa, L. Carnival on the ice
Durrie, G. H. Boys skating
Eilshemius, L. Skater
Gignoux, F. R. (attributed works) Winter
    landscape with skaters
Glackens, W. J. Roller skating rink
Homer, W. Skating at Central park
Kuniyoshi, Y. Skating
Maril, H. Skaters
Moses, A. M. R. The first skating
Moses, A. M. R. The trappers II
Pepper, C. H. Skating
Schuessele, C. and Weber, P. Skating at
    Kelley's dam, Germantown
Smith, M. Skating at the wide waters
    on the canal
Stuart, G. The skater
Toole, J. Skating scene
### Skiing
Evergood, P. Men and mountain
Pike, J. Kids skiing
### Skipping rope
Ahlas, L. Jump rope
Albro, M. Skipping
Prendergast, M. B. Skipping rope
### Swimming
Bellows, G. W. Forty-two kids
### Tennis
Bellows, G. W. Tennis tournament
The **gamin** by G. B. Luks
**Gangster** funeral by J. Levine
**GANNAM, John**
    City scene
        NAD. Annual ex, 1952
**GANSEVOORT limner**
    Leonard Gansevoort
        Flexner. First flowers
    Mrs Leonard Gansevoort
        Flexner. First flowers

Pau De Wandelaer                              NAI
    Belknap
    Flexner. First flowers (col)
    Jones. Rediscovered ptrs
    NAI. Hudson valley
Gansevoort, Catherine (De Wandelaer)
    Gansevoort limner. Mrs Leonard Ganse-
        voort
Gansevoort, Catherine (Van Schaick) 1752-
    1830
    Ames, E. Mrs Peter Gansevoort
Gansevoort, Leonard, 1751-1810
    Gansevoort limner. Leonard Gansevoort
Gansevoort street by W. De Kooning
GANSO, Emil, 1895-1941
    Village church
    NYG. Fine art
Gant by J. Brooks
Garage lights by S. Davis
GARBER, Daniel, 1880-1958
    Old church, Carversville
    NAD. Annual ex, 1959
Pioneer's house                               InIJ
    InIJ. 105 ptgs
Garden by D. Austin
Garden by J. Berlandina
Garden by A. Blanch
Garden by J. Ferren
Garden by J. E. Levi
Garden frieze by S. Amato
Garden in Sochi by A. Gorky
Garden in Sochi motif by A. Gorky
A garden is a sea of flowers by R. S. Turner
Garden of Betty Mae by P. Evergood
Garden of Eden by T. Cole
Garden of Eden by E. S. Field
Garden of memories by C. E. Burchfield
Garden of the Generalife, Granada by R. D.
    Gauley
Garden of the gods by A. A. Dehn
Garden wall by M. Kahn
Garden wall by J. S. Sargent
Gardiner, Emma Jane (Tudor) 1785-1865
    Malbone, E. G. Mrs Robert Hallowell
        Gardiner
Gardiner, Robert Hallowell, 1782-1864
    Malbone, E. G. Robert H. Gardiner
GARDNER, Byron J. 1930-
    Black landscape
    OrPA. Ptgs & sculptures
Gardner, Isabella (Stewart) 1840-1924
    Sargent, J. S. Mrs John Lowell Gardner
Gargoyles no 5, Paris by A. Rattner
Gargoyles of Notre Dame by W. Homer
Garland, Elizabeth. See Richard, Elizabeth
    (Garland)
Garlics by P. Ruta
Garmisch-Partenkirchen by M. Hartley
GARNERAY, Ambroise Louis, 1783-1857
    Lake Erie, Battle of                       ICH
    U.S. National Capital sesquicentennial
        com
GARRETT, Adams Wirt, 1908-
    Western festival
    ICA. Annual ex, 1945/46

GARRETT, Edmund Henry, 1853-1929
    Boon companions                            MB
    MB. Ptgs in water color
GARVER, Walter R. 1927-
    Half a man
    NAD. Annual ex, 1956
Symbols                                        OYB
    OYB. Annual 1955
    OYB. Supplement 1959
Gas by E. Hopper
Gas tank by J. Stella
Gasometer by W. T. Aldrich
Gaspé fishermen by J. Lonergan
Gaspé landscape by M. Avery
Gaspé-pink sky by M. Avery
GASSER, Henry Martin, 1909-
    Bluff house
    NAD. Annual ex, 1949, 2d half
    Michel's house
    NAD. Annual ex, 1947, 1st half
    Pennsylvania
    NAD. Annual ex, autumn 1949
GATCH, Lee, 1902-
    Arch of silence
    ICA. Annual ex, 1959/60
    Archaic tree
    IU. Contemp Amer ptg & sculp, 1961
August                                         NeL
    Hess. Abstract ptg
    The beech
    DC. 27 biennial ex, 1961
    Fish market
    PA. Annual ex, 1959-60
The flame                                      MAP
    Hess. Abstract ptg (col)
    ICA. Annual ex, 1954
    IU. Contemp Amer ptg, 1951
    Pousette-Dart. Amer ptg
    Ghost club
    CSFP. Annual ex, 1950/51
Gothic night                                   MB
    OCl. Some contemporary works
    Pierson
    Greenhouse
    Baur. Nature (col)
    Pierson
    PPC. International ex, 1950
    WMAA. Neuberger collection
High tension tower                             NUM
    NUM. Root bequest
    OCl. Some contemporary works
Industrial night                              DP
    DP. Catalogue
    ICA. Amer artists paint the city
    Time. 300 years (col)
Jumping joy                                    WMAA
    Goodrich. Amer art
    McCurdy
    The lamb
    PPC. International ex, 1955
    Lambertville pietà
    ICA. Annual ex, 1959/60
Marching Highlanders                           DP
    DP. Catalogue
Night fishing                                  DP
    OCl. Some contemporary works
Pennsylvania farm                             MoSL
    MoSL. Handbook 1953
    Pierson
Pleasure garden
    CSFP. Annual ex, 1952

GATCH, Lee—*Continued*
Steeplechase
  MnU. 40 Amer ptrs
Studio tapestry
  PPC. International ex, 1961/62
Three candidates for election          DP
  DP. Catalogue
Winter wood
  IU. Contemp Amer ptg & sculp, 1959
Yaddo gardens
  MnU. 40 Amer ptrs
The **gate** by J. Albers
The **gate** by W. Pachner
**Gate** watch by S. Bookatz
**Gates, Horatio,** 1728-1806
  Stuart, G. Horatio Gates
**GATES, Robert Franklin,** 1906-
Desert sun                           MdBM
  CoS. New accessions, USA, 1960
Kitty Hawk                            DC
  CoS. New accessions USA, 1954
South window
  IU. Contemp Amer ptg & sculp, 1961
Sunflower                             DP
  DP. Catalogue
Sunflowers and goldfinches
  MM. Amer ptg today
**Gates** of the city, nightfall by E. Berman
**Gateway** and tower I by L. Feininger
**Gatfield,** Elizabeth. See Rogers, Elizabeth
  (Gatfield)
The **gathering** by W. Pachner
**Gatling children,** fl 1870
  Benbridge, H. Gatling children
**GAULEY, Robert David,** 1875-1943
Amalfi                                MB
  MB. Ptgs in water color
The Azores                            MB
  MB. Ptgs in water color
Coast of Crete                        MB
  MB. Ptgs in water color
Coast of Sardinia                     MB
  MB. Ptgs in water color
Garden of the Generalife, Granada     MB
  MB. Ptgs in water color
Mediterranean coast                   MB
  MB. Ptgs in water color
Mt Vesuvius from the bay of Naples
                                      MB
  MB. Ptgs in water color
Naples                                MB
  MB. Ptgs in water color
**GAULOIS, Paul,** 1901-1943
Construction in blue                  CtY
  CtY. Soc Anonyme
**Gault, Silas**
  Blythe, D. G. Silas Gault
**Gautier, Judith,** 1846-1917
  Sargent, J. S. Judith Gautier
**Gautreau, Mme**
  Sargent, J. S. Madame X (Madame
    Gautreau)
**GAW, William A.** 1895-
Surviving trace of something
  CSFP. Annual ex, 1952
**GAY, Edward,** 1837-1928 and **TAIT, Arthur
  Fitzwilliam,** 1819-1905
Deer at the lake
  NSP. Sportscapes

**Gay, Eliza Jane,** fl 1840
  Bascom, R. H. M. Eliza Jane Gay
**GAY, Walter,** 1865-1937
La chaise-longue                      MB
  MB. Ptgs in water color
Statue at Vaux-le-Vicomte             MB
  MB. Ptgs in water color
**Gay** head by A. P. Ryder
**Gay** philosopher—why worry by H. Major
**Gay** table cloth by J. M. Hanson
**GEAR, J.**
Cook enrag'd at the steerage passengers
  being late with their breakfast    ICH
  Davidson v 1
**Gear** by K. Knaths
**GECHTOFF, Sonia,** 1926-
Children of Frejus
  WMAA. Young America 1960
Love at high noon
  Brussels. Exposition
Untitled, 1953
  NNSG. Younger Amer ptrs
**Geese**
  Bauman, L. T. Geese in flight
  Bellows, G. W. Geese and stormy sky
  Graves, M. Ecstatic gander
  Graves, M. Young gander ready for flight
  Homer, W. Wild geese
  Hunt, L. B. Northeaster—Canada geese
  Wilson, B. Ross snow geese
**GELB, Jan,** 1906-
Flight into morning
  Baur. Nature
**Gellatly, John,** 1853-1931
  Wiles, I. R. John Gellatly
**GELLER, Esther,** 1921-
Dance rhythm                          MAP
  Rathbun
Lady with slouched hat
  IU. Contemp Amer ptg, 1951
Mountain landscape                    MB
  MB. Ptgs in water color
**Gelmeroda** by L. Feininger
**Gelmeroda** IV by L. Feininger
**Gelmeroda** VIII, 1921 by L. Feininger
**Gelmeroda** XIII by L. Feininger
**Gelston, David,** 1744-1828
  Jarvis, J. W. David Gelston
**General** Knox mansion by A. N. Wyeth
**Genesee river and valley**
  Casilear, J. W. Reminiscence of the
    Genesee river
**Genesis** by S. Fogel
**Genesis** by L. E. Kupferman
**Genesis** by Y. Tanguy
**Genesis** by M. Tobey
**Genesis** by M. Tomkins
**Genesis** by J. Xcéron
**Genesis,** first version by L. Feitelson
**Genet, Edmond Charles,** 1763-1834
  Ames, E. Edmond Charles Genet
**Genie** by M. Resnick
**Genius** by M. Beckmann
The **genius** of America encouraging the
  emancipation of the blacks by S.
  Jennings

Genoa, Italy
  Boit, E. D. Genoa: A hillside
  Boit, E. D. Genoa: The port
  Sargent, J. S. Genoa: the university
Gentleman farmer by Unidentified artist
Gentleman hunter by S. Steinberg
Gentleman in a landscape by J. Brewster
  (attributed works)
Gentleman with high collar by A. Ellis
George, Captain, fl 1820
  Unidentified artist. Capt George of Haver-
  hill, Massachusetts
George, Mrs, fl 1820
  Unidentified artist. Wife of Capt George,
  Haverhill, Massachusetts
GEORGE, Thomas, 1918-
  Epoch                              NBuA
    NBuA. Acquisitions 1959-1961
George Fryer's still life by W. M. Harnett
George Gershwin's Rhaposody in blue part I,
  1927 by A. G. Dove
George Tilyou's steeplechase by R. Marsh
George went swimming at Barnes hole, but
  it got too cold by J. Mitchell
Georgia jungle by A. Brook
Georgia landscape by A. Blanch
Geraniums
  Knaths, K. Geraniums in night window
  Peale, Rembrandt. Rubens Peale with the
  first geranium brought to America
  Weber, M. Geranium
GERARD, Joseph
  High tide                          DP
    DP. Catalogue
GERARDIA, Helen, 1913-
  Third avenue el
    IU. Contemp Amer ptg & sculp, 1959
GERASSI, Fernando, 1900?-
  Magic mountains
  Time. 300 years (col )
Germain by W. G. Congdon
German girl, Head of by W. M. Harnett
German officer, 1914 by M. Hartley
German train by W. Pachner
Germania by H. Hofmann
GERNAND, John, 1913-
  Blowing leaves                     DP
    DP. Catalogue
Geronimo by H. H. Cross
Gerrish, Abigail, fl 1750
  Greenwood, J. Abigail Gerrish and her
  grandmother
GERRY, Peggy
  Whelan's pier, Roslyn
    NSP. Sportscapes
GERRY, Samuel, 1813-1891
  Mount Washington, New Hampshire
                                     NoCR
    NoCR. Catalogue
Gerson, Alice. See Chase, Alice (Gerson)
Gertrude II by B. Greene
Gertrude III by B. Greene
Gesture by M. Weber
Gesturing figures by M. Russo
The getaway by H. Pippin
Getting ready by Martyl

Gettysburg, Battle of, 1863
  Richards, J. Battle of Gettysburg, 1863
Geyser, Yellowstone park by A. Bierstadt
GHIKAS, Panos, 1919-
  Abstraction no 1
    ICA. Annual ex, 1947/48
  Blue horizon
    MBIC. View 1960
Ghost club by L. Gatch
Ghosts of engines by T. L. Feininger
Ghost plants by C. E. Burchfield
Ghost stories by F. Remington
GIACOMETTI, Alberto, 1901-
  The studio                         PPC
    CoS. New accessions USA, 1958
A giant by W. T. Aldrich
Giant blue spring, Yellowstone region by
  T. Moran
Giant redwood trees of California by A.
  Bierstadt
Gibbes, Mrs John. See Broughton, Anne
Gibbes, Robert Morgan, 1796-1864
  Hubard, W. H. Robert Morgan Gibbes
Gibbs, George, 1776-1833
  Malbone, E. G. George Gibbs III
Gibbs, Henry, 1668-1723
  Freake limner. Henry Gibbs
GIBBS, Howard, 1904-
  Hearthstone
    MBIC. View 1960
Gibbs, Margaret, fl 1670
  Freake limner. Margaret Gibbs
Gibbs, Margaret, 1701-1771. See Appleton,
  Margaret (Gibbs)
Gibbs, Robert, 1665-1702
  Freake limner. Robert Gibbs
Gibraltar forge by F. D. Devlan
GIBRAN, Kahlil, 1881-1931
  Nude figure kneeling among clouds   MB
    MB. Ptgs in water color
Gibson bayou anthology by C. Cloar
GIESE, Harold
  Bananas                            DP
    DP. Catalogue
GIFFORD, Robert S. 1840-1905
  Island of Mount Desert from the mainland
    NUM. Art across America
GIFFORD, Sanford Robinson, 1823-1880
  In the wilderness                  OT
    Pierson
    Richardson. Ptg in America
  Kaaterskill Falls                  MM
    Pierson
  Tivoli                             MM
    MiD. Travelers in Arcadia
Gift bearer by M. O. Sheets
Gifts from the sea by B. J. O. Nordfeldt
Gignilliat, Jane Elizabeth. See Heyward,
  Jane Elizabeth (Gignilliat)
GIGNOUX, François Régis, 1816-1882
  Mountain valley
    Sears. Highlights
  Winter scene in New Jersey          MB
    MB. Karolik coll
  Winter sports
    Born
              Attributed works
  Winter landscape with skaters
    Sears. Highlights

Gignoux, Régis François. See Gignoux, François Régis
GIKOW, Ruth, 1914-
Communion
  IU. Contemp Amer ptg, 1950
Golden canopy
  IU. Contemp Amer ptg, 1949
Muted city
  IU. Contemp Amer ptg & sculp, 1957
Roman street scene
  WMAA. Annual ex, 1948
Teenagers
  IU. Contemp Amer ptg & Sculp, 1955
Gila river
  Pratt, H. C. Rio Gila, View on the
GILL, Frederick
Derelicts
  NAD. Annual ex, 1961
Gill, Relief (Dowse) 1676-1759
  Copley, J. S. Mrs Michael Gill
GILLETTE, Henry S.
Emergency
  NAD. Annual ex, 1949, 2d half
Gilmor, Robert, 1774-1848
  Hubard, W. J. Robert Gilmor II
  Jarvis, J. W. Robert Gilmor II
  Woodville, R. C. Robert Gilmor II
Gilmor, Mrs Robert. See Ladson, Sarah Reeve
Gilmor, Sarah Reeve (Ladson) See Ladson, Sarah Reeve
GIOBBI, Edward, 1926-
Birthday party
  IU. Contemp Amer ptg & sculp, 1957
Kitchen still life
  WMAA. Young America 1960
The voyage
  WMAA. Young America 1960
Giorgione book by K. Knaths
Giotto's tower by H. Katzman
Gipsies' camp by J. W. Jarvis (after Morland)
Girard by D. Lord
A girl by J. J. Audubon (attributed works)
A girl by J. Levine
A girl by W. M. Prior (attributed works)
Girl against a tree by B. Karfiol
Girl and bananas by D. Rosenthal
Girl and cat by W. T. Bartoll
Girl at the piano by T. Robinson
Girl at the Tuileries by J. Phillips
Girl by the waterfall by Unidentified artist
Girl crocheting by E. C. Tarbell
Girl drying her hair by B. Currie
Girl holding a dog by S. Menkès
Girl holding rattle by E. S. Field
Girl in a hunting cap by R. Davey
Girl in a mirror by M. Hirschfield
Girl in a red embroidered jacket by W. M. Chase
Girl in a white blouse by R. Soyer
Girl in black and white by W. J. Glackens
Girl in black pinafore by Unidentified artist
Girl in blue by N. Civosky
Girl in blue by M. B. Prendergast
Girl in blue dress by M. Sterne

Girl in blue dress by Unidentified artist
Girl in blue kimono by W. M. Chase
Girl in fur hat by J. Sloan
Girl in green and rose by J. Pascin
Girl in orange sweater by M. Soyer
Girl in white and silver by W. Kuhn
Girl in window by J. Sloan
Girl in yellow jacket by C. Ruthenberg
Girl in yellow skirt by B. Currie
Girl in yellow with a red doll by E. S. Field
Girl jumping rope by B. Shahn
Girl looking out of window by J. Floch
Girl of the Ten Eyck family by Unidentified artist
Girl on a terrace by R. Diebenkorn
Girl on balcony by Unidentified artist
Girl on sofa by Y. Kuniyoshi
Girl playing a pe-pa by S. Moy
Girl resting by M. S. Wilkes
Girl seated on bench by W. M. Prior (attributed works)
Girl waiting by Y. Kuniyoshi
Girl with a cat by W. Sutton (attributed works)
Girl with a hand mirror by W. M. Paxton
Girl with a letter by W. Homer
Girl with bird by C. L. Lewin
Girl with bird by L. Rossbach
Girl with cornflower by A. Blanch
Girl with cups by R. Diebenkorn
Girl with dog by W. M. Chase
Girl with doll by W. M. Chase
Girl with dove by C. Thompson
Girl with flower basket by J. Bradley (attributed works)
Girl with fruit bowl by S. Menkès
Girl with hoop by Unidentified artist
Girl with laurel by W. Homer
Girl with parrot by M. Beckmann
Girl with pigeons by M. Hirshfield
Girl with red hair by Y. Tanguy
Girl with pitchfork by W. Homer
Girl with sunflowers by P. Evergood
Girl with the red shoes (Magdalena Douw) by Unidentified artist
Girl with three coffee cups by R. Diebenkorn
Girls and bananas by D. Rosenthal
Girls from Fleugel street by J. Levine
Girls on a cliff by W. Homer
Girls on esplanade by M. B. Prendergast
Girls playing on the beach by W. M. Chase
Girls preparing kava, Samoa by J. La Farge
Girls waiting by I. Bishop
Girls with lobster by W. Homer
Girod, Mme. See Poirson, Suzanne
GIROUX, C. fl 1850
Cotton plantation                          MB
  Davidson v 1
  MB. Karolik coll

**GISH, Peter M.**
Toledo I
NAD. Annual ex, 1959
**Gist, Mordecai,** 1743-1792
Peale, C. W. Mordecai Gist
**Give** us this day by M. Hartley
**GIVLER, William H.** 1908-
Interior
OrPA. Ptgs & sculptures
**Glacier** streams—the Simplon by J. S.
Sargent
**GLACKENS, Edith (Dimock)** 1876-1955
The Sunday walk                          PMB
Glackens

### Portrait of the artist
Glackens, W. J. Artist's wife
Glackens, W. J. Artist's wife and son
**GLACKENS, Lenna**
William and Imp
Glackens

### Portrait of the artist
Glackens, W. J. Artist's daughter in
Chinese costume
Glackens, W. J. Lenna and Imp
**GLACKENS, William James,** 1870-1938
Armenian girl                            PMB
Glackens
Artist's daughter in Chinese costume
Glackens
Artist's wife                            CtHW
CtHW. Handbook
Glackens
NAD. Amer tradition
Artist's wife and son
Glackens
At the beach                             PA
Glackens
Bal Martinique
Glackens
Ballet girl in pink
Glackens
Bathing at Bellport
Glackens
Beach at Dieppe                          PMB
Glackens
Beach at Annisquam
NYG. Fine art
Beach at St Jean de Luz
Glackens
Beach scene near New London              OCo
Glackens
Beatrice standing
Glackens
Bouquet in Quimper pitcher
PA. Annual ex, 1955
Buen Retiro, Madrid
Glackens
WMAA. Juliana Force
Café de la Paix
Glackens
Café Lafayette
Glackens
Central park, winter                     MM
Bauer. New art
Glackens
Charles FitzGerald
Glackens
Chateau-Thierry
Glackens

Chez Mouquin                             ICA
Baur. New art
Brown. Amer ptg
Glackens (col)
Hunter. Mod Amer ptg
NBuA. Fifty ptgs
PA. Annual ex, 1955
Pierson
Richardson. Ptg in America
Roos
Walker. Ptgs from America
Dream ride
NYG. Fine art
The drive, Central park                  OCl
Glackens
OCl. Handbook
PA. Annual ex, 1955
East river from Brooklyn
Glackens
Family group: Irene Dimock, Edith
Glackens, Ira Glackens, Grace Dwight
Morgan
Glackens (col)
Ferdinand Sinzig
Glackens
Fête du Suquet                           WMAA
Glackens
Flying kites, Montmartre                 MB
CSB. Impressionism
Glackens
Fruit with striped pottery               ATeS
ATeS. Collection
Girl in black and white                  WMAA
Chew. 250 years of art
Green car                                MM
Bazin
Glackens (col)
MM. 100 Amer ptrs
George B. Luks
Glackens
Hammerstein's roof garden                WMAA
Baur. New art
Glackens
Goodrich. Amer art
McCurdy
Pierson
A holiday in the park. See Washington
square
Jetties at Bellport                      NBuA
NBuA. Catalogue of the ptgs
Lenna and Imp
Glackens
Luxembourg gardens                       DC
DC. Masterpieces
Glackens
Mahone bay                               NeL
Born
NSyE. The eight
March day, Washington square
Glackens (col)
WMAA. Museum and its friends, 1958
(col)
Mrs Barnes and Grover
Glackens
Night after San Juan
Brown. Amer ptg
U.S. National Capital sesquicentennial
com
Nude dressing hair
NUM. Art across America

**GLACKENS, W. J.**—*Continued*

Nude with apple    NBM
  Glackens (col)
  PA. Annual ex, 1955
  Time. 300 years (col)
Outside the Guttenburg race track
  Glackens
Park by the river    NBM
  Baur. Revolution
  Glackens (col)
  Time. 300 years (col)
Pony ballet    PMB
  Glackens
Race track    PMB
  Glackens
Roller skating rink
  Glackens
  Larkin
  Larkin rev ed
Shoppers (Mrs L. E. Travis, Edith
    Glackens, Florence Scovel Shinn)
  Glackens
  PA. Annual ex, 1955
Soda fountain    PA
  Baur. New art (col)
  Glackens
  Pierson
Still life—Crabapples in blue bowl
  CtY. Yale alumni
Still life with three glasses    OYB
  OYB. Accessions
  OYB. Supplement 1959
The swing
  Brown. Amer ptg
Temple gold medal nude
  Glackens
La Villette    PPC
  Glackens
Washington square (A holiday in the
    park)    MMA
  Brown. Amer ptg
West Hartford
  Glackens
Woman on sofa
  Glackens

### Portrait of the artist
Henri, R. William Glackens, 1904
**Glackens, Mrs William James.** See Glack-
  ens, Edith (Dimock)
**Gladding, Hannah.** See Field, Hannah
  (Gladding)
**Gladiators** by P. Guston
**Gladys** by T. Filmus
The **glance** of amber by Y. Tanguy
**GLANNON, Edward,** 1911-
  Corner of a pasture
    NYG. Fine art
**GLARNER, Fritz,** 1899-
  Composition, 1942
    MnU. 40 Amer ptrs
  Relational painting, 1943    CtY
    CtY. Soc Anonyme
  Relational painting, 1947-48    MMA
    Biddle. Yes and no
    MMA. Abstract (col)
    MMA. 12 Americans (col)
    Read. Concise history

Relational painting, 1949-51    WMAA
  Baur. New art (col)
  Goodrich. Amer art (col)
  MMA. 12 Americans
  Pierson
  WMAA. Contemp Amer ptg, 1951
Relational painting, 1950
  CSFP. Annual ex, 1950/51
Relational painting 53, 1950
  MMA. 12 Americans
Relational painting 55, 1951
  MMA. 12 Americans
Relational painting 61, 1953
  Baur. New art
Relational painting 64, 1953
  MMA. 12 Americans
Relational painting 67, 1953
  NNSG. Younger Amer ptrs
Relational painting 68, 1954
  McCurdy
Relational painting 79, 1956
  DC. 25 biennial ex, 1957
  VR. Amer ptg, 1958
Relational painting, tondo 6, 1948
  MMA. 12 Americans
Relational painting—tondo 18
  MnU. 40 Amer ptrs
  Pousette-Dart. Amer ptg
Relational painting, tondo 20, 1951-54
  Baur. New art
Relational painting, tondo 40, 1956
    MnMW
  CoS. New accessions USA, 1958
  MMA. 12 Americans
Tondo no 15    MdBM
  Pierson
Tondo no 21
  IU. Contemp Amer ptg, 1952
**GLASCO, Joseph,** 1925-
Athlete and landscape
  MMA. Fifteen
Figures in landscape
  Mendelowitz
  NNSG. Younger Amer ptrs
  WMAA. New decade
Head
  NBuA. Expressionism
Interior with standing man
  IU. Contemp Amer ptg & sculp, 1959
Male head
  IU. Contemp Amer ptg, 1952
Marvello
  WMAA. Contemp Amer ptg, 1953
  WMAA. New decade
Portrait of a poet    WMAA
  Goodrich. Amer art
  Pierson
Salome
  Pierson
  WMAA. New decade
Sleepers
  MMA. Fifteen
Sleeping figure
  Pierson
Sun bath
  CanO. Hirshhorn coll
  IU. Contemp Amer ptg, 1951
Two figures    MMA
  MMA. Fifteen
The **glass** by R. Crawford
**Glass** and flowers by A. B. Carles

Glass house lake by J. H. Hidley
Glass windows, Bahamas by W. Homer
Glazier by W. De Kooning
Gleason, Bethia, fl 1785
    Chandler, W. Mrs Gleason and Bethia
Gleason, William. See Glysson, William
GLEITSMANN, Raphael, 1910-
    Ancient valley
      IU. Contemp Amer ptg, 1949
    The city—no 2
      PPC. International ex, 1950
    City of spires
      PPC. Ptg in the U. S. 1949
    An entrance
      IU. Contemp Amer ptg, 1950 (col)
    Green wall               OYB
      OYB. Annual 1950
      OYB. Catalogue 1951
    The wall              IaDa
      IaDa. Silver jubilee
    Winter trees
      NAD. Annual ex, 1949, 1st half
Glen, Mrs John. See Jones, Sarah
Glimpse of Lake George by J. F. Kensett
Glitter by G. P. Du Bois
Glitter by G. Prestopino
Glittering moonlight by F. K. M. Rehn
The glorious victory of the sloop Maria by
    L. Feininger
The glory by F. Martin
Glory of spring by C. E. Burchfield
Gloucester, Massachusetts
    Davis, S. Gloucester street
    Demuth, C. H. Gloucester
    Lane, F. H. Gloucester from Brookbank
    Lane, F. H. View of Gloucester from
      Rocky Neck
    Prendergast, M. B. Gloucester
    Sloan, J. Balancing rock, Gloucester har-
      bor
    Sloan, J. Hill, Main street, Gloucester
    Zerbe, K. Gloucester alley
Gloucester boats by K. Matthew
Gloucester docks by E. Horter
Gloucester farm by W. Homer
Gloucester schooners and sloop by W.
    Homer
Gloucester sunset by S. Davis
Gloucester trolley by J. Sloan
Glover, Mary Julien
    Betts, L. Miss Mary Julien Glover
GLUCKMAN, Grigory, 1898-
    Confidants
      DC. 21 biennial ex, 1949
    Nu
      PPC. Ptg in the U. S. 1949
Glysson, William, fl 1780
    Chandler, W. Dr William Glysson
Goat song by T. D. Benrimo
Goats
    Arbogast, V. Mountain goats
    Dove, A. G. Goat
    Keller, H. G. Goats among the peaks
    Spruce, E. F. Angora goat
    Spruce, E. F. Goat
The goblet by W. Sommer
The goblet by B. W. Tomlin

GODDELL, J. G. fl 1830
    Attributed works
    Young lady of the Nathaniel Johnson
      family              MeC
      Jetté. Amer heritage collection
Godfrey of Bouillon, 1061?-1100
    Walker, C. H. Godfrey of Bouillon
God's day by C. F. McCall
GOEDIKE, Shirl, 1923-
    Race in the sun
      IU. Contemp Amer ptg & sculp, 1961
Goelet, Jane, 1720-1799
    Unidentified artist. Jane Goelet
Going through the thoroughfare by J.
    Marin
Going to church by G. H. Durrie
Going to church by A. M. R. Moses
Going to town by P. S. Sample
Going up by A. Osver
GOLD, Albert, 1906-
    Nicetown
      PA. Annual ex, 1950
Gold and old lace by G. Fuller
Gold, green and brown by A. G. Dove
Gold scab by J. A. M. Whistler
GOLDBERG, Michael, 1924-
    Chair               MnMW
      MnMW. 60 Amer ptrs
    Old Zip Coon
      PPC. International ex, 1961/62
    Still life
      WMAA. Young America 1957
    Still life with onion rolls
      WMAA. Young America 1957
    Summer house        NBuA
      NBuA. Acquisitions 1957-58
Golden afternoon, Oregon by C. Hassam
Golden autumn by R. A. Blakelock
Golden canopy by R. Gikow
Golden carnival by W. L. Metcalf
Golden dawn by R. Pousette-Dart
Golden gardens by M. Tobey
Golden Gate by C. Sheeler
Golden hat by K. Zerbe
The golden lady by W. M. Chase
Golden leaves by H. L. McFee
Golden light by P. L. Dike
Golden palace by L. Bosa
Golden plover by J. J. Audubon
Golden reverie by R. Pousette-Dart
Golden screen: caprice in purple and gold
    no 2, 1865 by J. A. M. Whistler
Golden splendor by H. Hofmann
Golden storm by A. G. Dove
Golden Swan by C. H. Demuth
Golden tree by K. K. Feuerherm
GOLDIN, Leon, 1923-
    Desert twilight
      IU. Contemp Amer ptg & sculp, 1957
    February
      IU. Contemp Amer ptg & sculp, 1961
    Gray beach
      PA. Annual ex, 1959-60
    Hill town
      IU. Contemp Amer ptg & sculp, 1959

**GOLDRING, Milton,** 1919?-
Morning hour
WMAA. Annual ex, 1957

**Goldsborough, Henrietta Maria (Tilghman)**
1707-1771
Unidentified artist. Mrs William Goldsborough and grandson

**GOLDSMITH, Deborah,** 1808-1836
George Addison Throop
Lipman. Primitive ptrs
Lady and gentleman          NCHA
Jones. Rediscovered ptrs
Mr and Mrs Lyman Day and daughter,
Cornelia
Jones. Rediscovered ptrs
Self-portrait
Lipman. Primitive ptrs
Talcott family          VWR
Lipman. Primitive ptrs
VWR. Amer folk art

**Goldthwait, Elizabeth,** 1733-1861
Copley, J. S. Mrs John Bacon

**Goldthwait, Elizabeth (Lewis)** 1714-1794
Copley, J. S. Mrs Ezekial Goldthwait

**Goldthwait, Ezekial,** 1710-1782
Copley, J. S. Ezekial Goldthwait

**GOLDTHWAITE, Anne,** 1873-1944
Katherine S. Dreier          CtY
CtY. Soc Anonyme

**Golf** course, East Gloucester by M. B.
Prendergast

**GOLINKIN, Joseph Webster,** 1896-
Endeavor II and Ranger
NYG. Fine art
The Hambletonian
NYG. Fine art

**GOLUB, Leon Albert,** 1922-
Burnt man
NNSG. Younger Amer ptrs
Colossal head
Selz. New images
Damaged man
Selz. New images
Head XXVI
IU. Contemp Amer ptg & sculp, 1961
Horseman
Selz. New images
Orestes
Selz. New images (col)
Parturition
IU. Contemp Amer ptg & sculp, 1957
Reclining youth
Selz. New images

**GOLUBOV, Maurice,** 1905-
Fantasy
MMA. Abstract

**Gomez d'Arza, Signora**
Eakins, T. Signora d'Arza

**Gondolas,** Venice by M. B. Prendergast

**Gondolier** by J. S. Sargent

**GONZALES, Boyer,** 1909-
Composition with violet
OrPA. Ptgs & sculptures

**GONZALEZ, Xavier,** 1899-
Cannabin
PPC. International ex, 1952
The city
ICA. Amer artists paint the city
Don Quixote
NAD. Annual ex, 1958

Escape
IU. Contemp Amer ptg, 1949
PPC. Ptg in the U.S. 1949
Landscape
Pousette-Dart. Amer ptg
Landscape no 9          WMAA
Pierson
WMAA. Annual ex, 1951
Landscape in construction
DC. 22 biennial ex, 1951
Landscape in grey
IU. Contemp Amer ptg & sculp, 1955
The offering
Pearson. Mod renaissance
Portrait of an artist
Pearson. Mod renaissance
Ram's head
IU. Contemp Amer ptg, 1950
Pearson. Mod renaissance
Terminal
ICA. Annual ex, 1954
Zen Buddist
NAD. Annual ex, 1960

**Gonzales, Mrs Xavier.** See Edwards, Ethel

**Good** angel tenanted by K. Zerbe

A **good** day's work—return from duck
hunt by J. B. Sword

The **good** earth by C. Chen

**Good** Friday by K. Zerbe

**Good** intent by J. Peters

**Good** keeper C. R. Holty

**Good** news by M. Weber

**Good** Samaritan by Unidentified artist

**Good** Samaritan: Design for a window,
Trinity church, Buffalo by J. La
Farge

**Good** shepherd by J. La Farge

**Good** time by A. Salemme

**Goodman, Mrs Nelson.** See Sturgis, Katharine

**GOODMAN, Sidney**
Ascension
PA. Annual ex, 1961

**GOODNOUGH, Robert,** 1917-
Movement of horses II
PPC. International ex, 1961/62
Seated figure with gray          WMAA
Goodrich. Amer art
The struggle          NBuA
NBuA. Acquisitions 1957-58
Tree in the field
Baur. Nature

**Goodrich, Mr,** fl 1818
Unidentified artist. Mr Goodrich, Hancock, Massachusetts

**Goodrich, Chauncey Allen,** 1790-1800
Jocelyn, N. Chauncey Allen Goodrich

**GOODRIDGE, E.**
Gorham Bond
MB. New England miniatures
Stephen Salisbury
MB. New England miniatures

**GOODRIDGE, Sarah,** 1788-1853
Gilbert Stuart          MB
MB. New England miniatures
John Lowell jr
MB. New England miniatures
Mrs Abel Peirson
MB. New England miniatures
Mrs John Lowell jr
MB. New England miniatures (col)

Mrs Thomas B. Wales
  MB. New England miniatures
Mrs Timothy Pickering (after Stuart)
  MB. New England miniatures
Timothy Pickering
  MB. New England miniatures
GOODWIN, Arthur Clifton, 1866-1929
  High bridge, New York
    Born
  Landscape with brook
    Born
GOODWIN, Edwin Weyburn, 1800-1845
  Christmas presents
    Jones. Rediscovered ptrs
GOODWIN, Philip R. 1882-1935
  Calling the moose
    NSP. Sportscapes
  Rainbow trout
    NSP. Sportscapes
  Trout fishing
    NSP. Sportscapes
GOODWIN, Richard LaBarre, 1840-1910
  Hunter's cabin door          MSM
    Frankenstein. After the hunt
  Kitchen piece
    Frankenstein. After the hunt
  Theodore Roosevelt's cabin door  MSM
    Frankenstein. After the hunt
    MSM. Handbook
Goodyear, Anson Conger, 1877-
  Speicher, E. E. A. Conger Goodyear,
    1942
Goodyear, Charles, 1800-1860
  Healy, G. P. A. Charles Goodyear
Goose river, by A. N. Wyeth
GORCHOV, Ron, 1930-
  Fifth vision of Queen Vaidehi
    WMAA. Young America 1960
  Sorcerer's gear
    WMAA. Young America 1960
Gordian by J. Brooks
GORDON, Maxwell, 1910-
  Parade
    IU. Contemp Amer ptg, 1952
  Pose downtown
    IU. Contemp Amer ptg, 1951
GORDON, William J.
  Fortune tellers
    IU. Contemp Amer ptg, 1948
Gore, Christopher, 1785-1827
  Trumbull, J. Christopher Gore
Gore children
  Copley, J. S. Brother and sisters of Chris-
    topher Gore
Gore et mandra by E. A. Donati
Gorge of the St Croix river by H. Lewis
Gorham, Mercy. See Bourne, Mercy (Gor-
    ham)
GORKY, Arshile, 1904-1948
  Agony          MMA
    Art since 1945 (col)
    Barr. What is mod ptg
    Baur. New art
    Baur. Revolution
    CoS. New accessions USA, 1950
    McCurdy
    MMA. Abstract (col)
    MMA. Masters (col)
    MMA. New Amer ptg (col)
    Pierson
    Read. Concise history (col)
    Schwabacher. Arshile Gorky (col)

Ahko, Portrait of
  Schwabacher. Arshile Gorky
The antique cast
  Schwabacher. Arshile Gorky
Argula          MMA
  Schwabacher. Arshile Gorky
Artist and his mother          WMAA
  Baur. New art
  Goodrich. Amer art (col)
  Schwabacher. Arshile Gorky (col)
Battle at sunset with the god of the maize
  Schwabacher. Arshile Gorky
Betrothal I
  OCl. Some contemporary works
  Schwabacher. Arshile Gorky
Betrothal II, 1947          WMAA
  Baur. New Art
  50 years of mod art
  Goodrich. Amer art (col)
  Hess. Abstract ptg (col)
  MnMW. 60 Amer ptrs
  Pierson
  Pousette-Dart. Amer ptg
  Read. Concise history
  Schwabacher. Arshile Gorky (col)
The calendars          WMAA
  MMA. New Amer ptg
  Schwabacher. Arshile Gorky (col)
  WMAA. Juliana Force
Charred beloved
  Blesh
  Schwabacher. Arshile Gorky
Child of an Idumean night
  Schwabacher. Arshile Gorky
Composition, 1932-33
  MMA. Abstract
Composition with head, c 1935
  Schwabacher. Arshile Gorky
Dark green painting
  MMA. New Amer ptg
  Ponente. Mod ptg, 1960 (col)
  Schwabacher. Arshile Gorky
Diary of a seducer
  Hess. Abstract ptg
  Janson. Key monuments
  Janson. Picture history
  MMA. Fourteen
  Schwabacher. Arshile Gorky
Enigmatic combat          CSFM
  Pierson
  Schwabacher. Arshile Gorky
Garden in Sochi, c 1938-41
  Schwabacher. Arshile Gorky
Garden in Sochi, 1941 (1)          MMA
  MMA. Fourteen
  Schwabacher. Arshile Gorky
  Time. 300 years (col)
Garden in Sochi, c 1941 (2)
  Schwabacher. Arshile Gorky
Garden in Sochi motif
  Schwabacher. Arshile Gorky
How my mother's embroidered apron un-
    folds in my life
  Schwabacher. Arshile Gorky
Image in Xhorkom          MMA
  Hess. Abstract ptg
  Schwabacher. Arshile Gorky
Image in Xhorkom (Raynal coll)
  Schwabacher. Arshile Gorky
Impatience
  Read. Art now, 1948 ed

**GORKY, Arshile**—*Continued*
Landscape table
  MMA. Fourteen
  Ponente. Mod ptg, 1960 (col)
  Schwabacher. Arshile Gorky
Last painting, 1948
  Schwabacher. Arshile Gorky
The leaf of the artichoke is an owl
  Schwabacher. Arshile Gorky
The limit
  Schwabacher. Arshile Gorky (col)
Liver is the cock's comb            NBuA
  Baur. New art (col)
  Jean. Surrealist ptg
  Larkin rev ed (col)
  NBuA. Acquisitions 1954-57
  OCl. Some contemporary works
  Pierson
  Schwabacher. Arshile Gorky
Myself and my imaginary wife, Portrait of
  Schwabacher. Arshile Gorky
Newark airport murals, Panel of
  Schwabacher. Arshile Gorky
Nighttime enigma and nostalgia
  NBuA. Expressionism
  Schwabacher. Arshile Gorky
Nude, 1946
  Schwabacher. Arshile Gorky
The orators
  Schwabacher. Arshile Gorky
Organization
  Schwabacher. Arshile Gorky
Painting, 1936-37                   WMAA
  Goodrich. Amer art
  Schwabacher. Arshile Gorky
The pirate II
  Schwabacher. Arshile Gorky
The plow and the song               OOb
  OCl. Some contemporary works
  Schwabacher. Arshile Gorky
The plow and the song (Gordon coll)
  Schwabacher. Arshile Gorky (col)
  WMAA. Museum and its friends, 1958
    (col)
Portrait
  Schwabacher. Arshile Gorky
Self-portrait, c 1937
  Schwabacher. Arshile Gorky
Soft night
  Schwabacher. Arshile Gorky
Still life, 1929
  Schwabacher. Arshile Gorky
Still life with palette
  Schwabacher. Arshile Gorky
Still life with skull
  Schwabacher. Arshile Gorky
Three roses
  Schwabacher. Arshile Gorky
The unattainable
  MMA. Fourteen
  Schwabacher. Arshile Gorky
Vartoosh, Portrait of
  Schwabacher. Arshile Gorky
Water of the flowery mill           MM
  Cheney. Story 1958 ed
  Schwabacher. Arshile Gorky
Waterfall
  Baur. Nature (col)
  Hess. Abstract ptg
  Hunter. Mod Amer ptg (col)
  Schwabacher. Arshile Gorky (col)

**GORSLINE, Douglas Warner**, 1913-
Foggy pasture
  NAD. Annual ex, 1949
Thomas Wolfe
  Gruskin
**GORSON, Aaron Harry**, 1872-1933
Steel mill at night
  Chew. 250 years of art
**Gosier** II by A. Yunkers
**Gosman** family, A gentleman of by J. W.
  Jarvis
**Gosse, Sir Edmund William**, 1849-1928
  Sargent, J. S. Sir Edmund Gosse
The **gossips** by H. Pittman
**Gotham** news by W. De Kooning
**Gothic** by A. Dasburg
**Gothic** by J. Pollock
**Gothic** by M. Tobey
**Gothic** enflamed by A. Rattner
**Gothic** light by L. Gatch
**Gothic** sentinels by P. Trivigno
**Gothic** spire by L. Feininger
**Gothic** woods and nymph by G. Grosz
**GOTO, Joseph**, 1916-
Landscape
  IU. Contemp Amer ptg & sculp, 1957
**GOTTLIEB, Adolph**, 1903-
Blast II
  PPC. International ex, 1958
  Read. Concise history
Blue at night
  VR. Amer ptg, 1958
Blue at noon
  Eliot. Art of our time (col)
  Time. 300 years (col)
Burst
  MMA. New Amer ptg (col)
The cadium sound
  IU. Contemp Amer ptg & sculp, 1955
Dialogue 1                          NBuA
  NBuA. Acquisitions 1959-1961
Evil omen
  MnMW. Contemporary
  Pierson
  WMAA. Neuberger collection
Exclamation
  MnMW. 60 Amer ptrs (col)
Frozen sounds no 1, 1951            WMAA
  Goodrich. Amer art (col)
  IU. Contemp Amer ptg & sculp, 1953
  Pierson
  Pousette-Dart. Amer ptg
Frozen sounds no 2, 1952            NBuA
  Hunter. Mod Amer ptg
  NBuA. Acquisitions 1954-57
Hot horizon
  Pierson
Labyrinth
  WMAA. New decade
Links of memory
  CSFP. Annual ex, 1947/48
Man and arrow
  MnU. 40 Amer ptrs
Man looking at woman
  CSFP. Annual ex, 1950/51
Pictograph                          CLA
  CoS. New accessions USA, 1960
  CSFP. Annual ex, 1948/49
  IU. Contemp Amer ptg, 1950
  Wight. Milestones (col)

Red sky
 Baur. Nature
Romanesque façade
 Hess. Abstract ptg (col)
 IU. Contemp Amer ptg, 1951 (col)
Sea and tide
 WMAA. New decade
The seer                                      DP
 DP. Catalogue
 Larkin rev ed
Side pull
 MMA. New Amer ptg
Souvenirs of the sea
 MnU. 40 Amer ptrs
Spectre of the sea
 IU. Contemp Amer ptg, 1948
 Roos
T
 ICA. Annual ex, 1951
 Hess. Abstract ptg
Tournament
 IU. Contemp Amer ptg, 1952
 MMA. New Amer ptg
Transfiguration no 2
 Pierson
Voyager's return                             MMA
 Art since 1945
 MMA. Contemp ptrs
W. 1954                                      NNSG
 NNSG. Handbook
 NNSG. Younger Amer ptrs
Waiting
 PPC. International ex, 1952
Watching
 NUM. Art across America
GOTTLIEB, Harry, 1895-
 Their only roof, 1930                       ATU
 ATU. Coll of Amer art
Gould, James, 1770-1838
 Waldo, S. L. James Gould
GOULD, L. A.
 Niagara seen with different eyes (after
  a print by Lumley)                         NCHA
 Jones. New-found folk art
Goulding, Mary Anne, fl 1858
 Elliott, C. L. Mrs Thomas Goulding
Gourds by J. S. Sargent
Gouty fisherman by D. G. Blythe
Gouverneur, Abram, 1671-1740
 Unidentified artist. Abram Gouverneur
Gouverneur, Mary (Leisler) d 1747
 Unidentified artist. Mrs Abram Gouver-
  neur
Gouverneur, Mrs Samuel, fl 1750
 Wollaston, J. Mrs Samuel Gouverneur
Government bureau by G. Tooker
Government house, Bowling Green, New
 York, 1797 by C. Milbourne
Governess and children by Unidentified
 artist
Governor II by W. T. Murch
The governor's cup by V. Flannery
Governor's room, City hall, New York,
 c 1830 by C. Burton
Goyescas, Study for by B. Shahn
GRABACH, John R. 1886-
 Pedestrians in village
 NAD. Annual ex, spring 1950
Grackles
 Audubon, J. J. Purple grackle

GRAHAM, Elwood
 Spanish lace                                CSFM
 Pousette-Dart. Amer ptg
Graham, Frances (Wickham) fl 1857
 Healy, G. P. A. Mrs James Graham
Graham, Mrs James Duncan. See Graham,
 Frances (Wickham)
GRAHAM, John D. 1888-
 Vox humana                                  CtY
 CtY. Soc Anonyme
GRAHAM, Robert M.
 New Guinea beer party
 IU. Contemp Amer ptg, 1948
Grain elevator from the bridge by R. Craw-
 ford
Grain elevators, Minneapolis by R. Craw-
 ford
GRAMATKY, Hardie, 1907-
 Throughway
 NAD. Special ex, 1956
Gramercy park by G. W. Bellows
Gramercy park by F. W. Howell
Granada by R. B. Motherwell
Granada gardens by V. Vytlacil
Grand Canyon by J. E. Swinnerton
Grand Canyon, Arizona by P. Wenck
Grand Canyon of the Yellowstone river by
 T. Moran
Grand central terminal by M. Weber
Grand finale by L. Pitts
Grand Manan, sunrise off the Maine coast
 by F. E. Church
Grand street brides by G. Hartigan
Grand view by R. H. Byrum
Granda flora by H. G. Keller
The grandest of Noo by R. S. Du Casse
Grandfather by H. Sterne
Grandfather's lesson by H. Herzog
Grandma goes to the big city by A. M. R.
 Moses
Grandma's hearthstone by J. Haberle
Granite city by L. Dodd
Granny Ames' house by G. W. Bellows
GRANT, Catharine Harley, 1897-
 Villa Maria
 PA. Annual ex, 1949
GRANT, Gordon, 1875-
 Harbor traffic
 NYG. Fine art
Grant, Ida M. (Honoré) fl 1874
 Healy, G. P. A. Mrs Frederick Dent
  Grant
GRANT, J. fl 1843
 Two children                                MB
 MB. Karolik coll
Grant, Ulysses Simpson, president U.S. 1822-
 1885
 Healy, G. P. A. Ulysses Simpson Grant
 Lambdin, J. R. Gen Ulysses S. Grant
Grape hill, Manayunk by G. Martino
Grapes and turnips by C. H. Demuth
Grapes in a bowl by J. F. Francis
Graphite and blue by A. G. Dove
Grass path in spring by M. A. Phillips
Gratz, Rachel, 1783-1823
 Malbone, E. G. Rachel Gratz

**Gratz, Rebecca,** 1781-1869
Malbone, E. G. Rebecca Gratz
**Grave** of William Penn by E. Hicks
**Gravel** by R. Vickrey
**Gravel** bar, White river by E. Hopper
**Gravel** pit by W. T. Turman
**Graves, Henry,** 1806-1892
Whistler, J. A. M. Henry Graves, the printseller
**GRAVES, Morris,** 1910-
Bird in the mist
Wight. Morris Graves
Bird in the moonlight (Ross coll)
Wight. Morris Graves
Bird in the spirit                     WMAA
Goodrich. Amer art (col)
MM. 100 Amer ptrs
Bird maddened by the long winter
IU. Contemp Amer ptg & sculp, 1953
Pierson
Bird singing in the moonlight    MMA
Baur. Revolution
Faulkner. Art today, 1956
McCurdy
MMA. Contemp ptrs
Pierson
Black waves                          NBuA
ICA. Annual ex, 1947/48
NBuA. Contemporary ptgs
Blind bird                           MMA
Baur. New art
Hunter. Mod Amer ptg (col)
Larkin
Larkin rev ed
MMA. Masters (col)
Rodman. Portrait of the artist
Wight. Morris Graves (col)
Blind bird no 2, 1940 (Markson coll)
Wight. Morris Graves (col)
Ceremonial bronze taking the form of a
bird                                  WaS
Wight. Morris Graves
Chalice                               DP
DP. Catalogue
Wight. Morris Graves
Chalice and lyre
Wight. Morris Graves
Colossal owls and eagles of the inner eye
NBuA. Expressionism
Concentrated pine top
Wight. Morris Graves
Daisies
Wight. Morris Graves (col)
Disintegrated and reanimated
Wight. Morris Graves
Dove of the inner eye
Wight. Morris Graves
Eagle                                 DP
DP. Catalogue
Wight. Morris Graves
Eagle in the rock
Wight. Morris Graves
Ecstatic gander
Wight. Morris Graves
Fish in sea and stars                 WaS
50 years of mod art
Fish reflected upon outer and mental space
Wight. Morris Graves (col)
Flight of plover                      WMAA
Goodrich. Amer art
Pierson
Wight. Morris Graves

Fox with phoenix wing                 PPhM
CoS. New accessions USA, 1956
Guardian                              IU
Canaday
IU. Contemp Amer ptg & sculp, 1955
IU. 20th century
Larkin rev ed (col)
Wight. Morris Graves (col)
WMAA. Museum and its friends, 1959
Guardian (Willis coll)
OrPA. Ptgs & sculptures
In the air
Wight. Morris Graves
Individual state of the world         MMA
Wight. Morris Graves (col)
Journey                               WaS
CoS. New accessions USA, 1948
Journey                               WMAA
Baur. New art
WMAA. Juliana Force
Journey no 2, 1943                    WMAA
Wight. Morris Graves
Journey (Baldwin coll)
Wight. Milestones
Joyous young pine                     MMA
Baur. New art
IU. Contemp Amer ptg, 1951
MMA. Contemp ptrs
Joyous young pine                     CSB
CoS. New accessions USA, 1958
Joyous young pine (Ludington coll)
CtY. Yale alumni
Joyous young pine (Wolf coll)
Wight. Morris Graves (col)
Little bird alone
Cheney. Story 1958 ed
Little-known bird of the inner eye MMA
Baur. New Art (col)
Cheney. Primer 1958 ed
Flexner. Amer ptg
Flexner. Short history
Read. Art now, 1948 ed
Wight. Morris Graves (col)
Masked bird fishing in the golden stream
Cheney. Story 1958 ed
Wight. Morris Graves
Message
Wight. Morris Graves
Moon and crow in the surf
Wight. Morris Graves
Moor swan                             WaS
Wight. Morris Graves
Pink bird
Wight. Morris Graves (col)
Preening sparrows                     WaS
Pousette-Dart. Amer ptgs
Time. 300 years (col)
Purification series
Wight. Morris Graves
Ritual vessel-mirror
Wight. Morris Graves
Sea and the morning redness           ICA
Wight. Morris Graves
Sea, fish, and constellation          WaS
Time. 300 years
Wight. Morris Graves
Shore birds no 1, c 1940
Wight. Morris Graves
Shore birds no 2, 1940
Baur. New art
Wight. Morris Graves
Shore birds submerged in moonlight
Wight. Morris Graves

Snake and moon MMA
  Barr. What is mod ptg
Spirit bird no 6, 1953
  Wight. Morris Graves
Spring WaS
  Read. Concise history
Surf birds MiD
  Wight. Morris Graves
Surf birds (Laughton coll)
  Wight. Morris Graves
Surf reflected upon higher space NUM
  NUM. Root bequest
Time of change
  UNESCO. 1860-1949
Trout in a stream
  MiD. Coll in progress
  Wight. Morris Graves
  WiMiA. Amer ptg 1760-1960
Woodpeckers WaS
  UNESCO. 1860-1957
  Wight. Morris Graves
Wounded gull DP
  Cheney. New world history
  DP. Catalogue
  Wight. Morris Graves
Wounded gull (Newberry coll)
  Munsterberg
Wounded gull (Tannahill coll)
  Baur. New art
  UNESCO. 1860-1949
  UNESCO. 1860-1955
Wounded ibis
  MnU. 40 Amer ptrs
Wounded scoter OCl
  OCl. Handbook
  Wight. Morris Graves (col)
Wounded sea gull
  MnMW. Expressionism 1900-1955
Young forest pine tree in bloom DP
  MnU. 40 Amer ptrs
  Wight. Morris Graves
Young gander ready for flight DP
  NNSG. Younger Amer ptrs
  Wight
Young owl and moth CoS
  NUM. Art across America
GRAVES, O. E. L. 1897-
Dappled with damson OYB
  OYB. Supplement 1959
GRAY, Cleve, 1918-
Hipparchus IU
  IU. Contemp Amer ptg, 1951
  IU. 20th century
Man and the northern lights MAP
  CoS. New accessions USA, 1952
Mosque, Cordova: no 2, 1959 WMAA
  Goodrich. Amer art
The wool winder
  ICA. Annual ex, 1961
GRAY, Henry Peters, 1819-1877
William Cullen Bryant NNHS
  Cowdrey v 1
Gray, John, 1713-1782
  Copley, J. S. John Gray
GRAY, Ralph Weld, 1880-1944
Cranberry bogs: bright weather MB
  MB. Ptgs in water color
Cranberry bogs: gray skies MB
  MB. Ptgs in water color
Home camp in March MB
  MB. Ptgs in water color
Gray, Sarah. See Cary, Sarah (Gray)

Gray by S. Francis
Gray abstraction by R. Conover
Gray and gold by J. R. Cox
Gray beach by L. Goldin
Gray day on the lagoon by W. M. Chase
Gray desert by G. Peirce
The gray man dances by G. Grosz
Gray rocks and gray trees by M. Kantor
Gray ruin and stone house by H. P. Barnett
Graziana by E. E. Speicher
Grazing horse by A. P. Ryder
The great barrier by E. Magafan
Great black-backed gull by J. J. Audubon
Great Blue hill and Neponset river by T. H.
  Hinckley
Great elm by C. E. Burchfield
The Great Goot by M. Wilson
The great mystery 11 by A. J. Jensen
Great seas by F. J. Waugh
The great waters by K. L. Seligmann
Great Western (steamship)
  Walter, J. Arrival of the Great Western
GREBENAK, Louis
Wall
  MM. Amer ptg today
Greek boy by E. E. Speicher
Greek island by T. Stamos
Greek love token by J. La Farge
Greek orison by T. Stamos
Green, George, 1742-1814
  Copley, J. S. George Green
Green, Rebecca (Spooner) 1743-1806
  Unidentified artist. Mrs Timothy Green
Green, Ruby
  Chapin, J. Ruby Green singing
GREEN, Samuel M. 1909-
Woodshed interior MNS
  Time. 300 years (col)
Green by B. W. Tomlin
Green and lavender horse by W. W. Quirt
Green apples by W. Homer
Green apples and scoop by W. Kuhn
Green ballet by E. Shinn
Green bird by F. E. Conway
The green bodice by J. A. Weir
Green bottle by H. Hofmann
Green burst by K. R. Morris
Green car by W. J. Glackens
Green composition by B. Greene
Green dancer by C. H. Demuth
Green depth by I. R. Miller
Green depth by I. R. Pereira
Green dory by W. Homer
Green, gold and brown by A. G. Dove
Green, green, I love you green by L. Finkel-
  stein
Green hat by E. E. Speicher
Green Head, Deer Isle, Maine by J. Marin
Green heron by J. J. Audubon
Green landscape by J. Tworkov
The green lion by P. Tchelitchew
Green night by W. A. Baziotes

Green on blue by M. Rothko
The green one by W. P. Morehouse
Green patio door by G. O'Keeffe
Green pears by C. H. Demuth
Green peppers by J. Wilde
Green pool by R. Arthur
Green premonitions by A. Lunak
Green river, Oregon by A. J. Miller
Green sea by H. E. Mattson
Green shore by M. B. Prendergast
Green silver by J. Pollock
Green squash by K. Knaths
Green striped bowl by A. H. Maurer
Green table by N. Spencer
Green target by J. Johns
Green wall by R. Gleitsmann
Green woods by B. J. O. Nordfeldt

Greene, Mr., fl 1810
  Jarvis, J. W. Mr Greene
Greene, Mrs, fl 1810
  Jarvis, J. W. Mrs Greene
GREENE, Balcomb, 1904-
  Abstraction—Storm
    Baur. Balcomb Greene
  Ancient form             MMA
    Baur. Balcomb Greene
    Baur. Revolution
    Pierson
    Read. Concise history
  Anguish
    Baur. Balcomb Greene
    Selz. New images
  Black angels
    Baur. Balcomb Greene
    Leepa
  The blind one
    IU. Contemp Amer ptg, 1952
  Blue space
    MMA. Abstract
  Classical still life
    ICA. Annual ex, 1961
  Cliff at Montauk
    Baur. Balcomb Greene
  Composition, 1940       NNSG
    Baur. Balcomb Greene
  Composition, 1958
    Baur. Balcomb Greene
    WMAA. Annual ex, 1958
  Composition: the storm    WMAA
    Baur. Nature (col)
    Goodrich. Amer art (col)
    Pierson
    Time. 300 years (col)
  Crouching figure
    Baur. Balcomb Greene
  Darkness and light
    Baur. Balcomb Greene
  Exhibition
    Baur. Balcomb Greene
  Figure lost in the light
    Baur. Balcomb Greene
    WMAA. Museum and its friends, 1958
  Gertrude II
    Selz. New images (col)
  Gertrude III
    Baur. Balcomb Greene
  Green composition
    Baur. Balcomb Greene

The heirloom man
  Baur. Balcomb Greene
Interior
  Baur. Balcomb Greene
Joan by the sea
  Baur. Balcomb Greene
The magistrate
  Baur. Balcomb Greene
Monument to light
  Baur. Balcomb Greene
The necklace
  Baur. Balcomb Greene (col)
Nude in yellow ochre
  Pousette-Dart. Amer ptg
  PPC. International ex, 1952
Olympia
  Baur. Balcomb Greene
Portrait, 1955-56
  Baur. Balcomb Greene
The sea
  Baur. Balcomb Greene
Seated figure
  Baur. Balcomb Greene
Seated woman
  Selz. New images
The studio
  Baur. Balcomb Greene
This architectural world    WMAA
  Baur. Balcomb Greene
  Read. Art now, 1948 ed
Three women
  Baur. Balcomb Greene
Tragic actor
  Baur. Balcomb Greene
Two heads
  Baur. Balcomb Greene
Two men
  Baur. Balcomb Greene
Two women
  Baur. Balcomb Greene (col)
Waiting figure
  Hess. Abstract ptg
  ICA. Annual ex, 1951
The white space
  ICA. Annual ex, 1947/48
Youth
  Baur. Balcomb Greene
Woman and man
  Baur. Balcomb Greene
Woman dressing
  Baur. Balcomb Greene
Woman with folded arms
  Baur. Balcomb Greene
The wreck, no 2, 1958
  Baur. Balcomb Greene
Yvanka
  IU. Contemp Amer ptg & sculp, 1959
Greene, Catherine (Greene) 1735-1785
  Copley, J. S. Mrs John Greene
GREENE, Gertrude, 1911-
  Monumentality
    MMA. Abstract
Greene, John, fl 1770
  Copley, J. S. John Greene
Greene, Mrs John. See Greene, Catherine
  (Greene)
Greene, Katherine. See Amory, Katherine
  (Greene)
Greene, Martha (Coit) 1706-1784
  Sargent, J. S. Mrs Thomas Greene
Greene, Martha Washington. See Night-
  ingale, Martha Washington (Greene)
Greene, Ray, 1765-1849
  Malbone, E. G. Hon Ray Greene

GREENE, Stephen, 1917-
  The burial          WMAA
    Bazin
    CSFP. Annual ex, 1948/49
    Goodrich. Amer art
    IU. Contemp Amer ptg, 1950
  Cain and Abel
    IU. Contemp Amer ptg & sculp, 1957
  The deposition        WMAA
    Genauer
    Mendelowitz
    WMAA. New decade
    MMA. Contemp ptrs
    Pierson
  Deposition from the cross    MCH
    Pulitzer v2
  Family portrait        MiD
    WMAA. Juliana Force
  Flagellation        MoKN
    CoS. New accessions USA, 1952
  The flagellators        MoSL
    CoS. New accessions USA, 1948
    MoSL. Handbook 1953
  Howl
    IU. Contemp Amer ptg & sculp, 1961
  Ischia
    CSFP. Annual ex, 1950/51
  Limbo
    CSFP. Annual ex, 1947/48
  The performance
    WMAA. New decade
  The sentinel
    VR. Amer ptg, 1954
  The studio
    IU. Contemp Amer ptg & sculp, 1955
  Tulips        MCH
    Pulitzer v2
Greene, Mrs Thomas. See Greene, Martha
  (Coit)
Greenhouse by L. Gatch
GREENLEAF, Benjamin
  Anna Hammond Pope      MSt
    Little. Country art
Greenleaf, Elizabeth, b 1748
  Badger, J. Elizabeth Greenleaf
Greenleaf, Stephen, 1652-1743
  Unidentified artist. Stephen Greenleaf jr
Greenleaf family, Child of by J. S. Copley
Greenough, Horatio, 1805-1852
  Hubard, W. J. Horatio Greenough, the
    American sculptor, in his studio in
    Florence
Greenville, South Carolina
  Tucker, J. South east view of Greenville,
    South Carolina, 1825
Greenville, Treaty of, 1795
  Unidentified artist. The Indian treaty of
    Greenville, 1795
GREENWOOD, Ethan Allen, 1779-1856
  Isaiah Thomas        MWA
    MWA. Checklist of portraits
  Rebecca Tufts Whittemore    MSt
    Little. Country art
GREENWOOD, John, 1727-1792
  Abigail Gerrish and her grandmother
                MSE
    NUM. Art across America
  Alice Furneaux Clarke      MSE
    MSE. Catalogue of ports, 1950
  American sea captains carousing at Suri-
    nam. See Sea captains carousing at
    Surinam

  Elizabeth Moffatt
    Belknap
  Greenwood and Lee families
    Flexner. First flowers
    Pierson
  John Clarke          MSE
    MSE. Catalogue of ports, 1950
  John Moffatt
    Belknap
  Judith Pickman        NNHS
    Belknap
  Lois (Pickering) Orne      MSE
    MSE. Catalogue of ports, 1950
  Mrs Benjamin Austin     DeWin
    Belknap
  Mrs Francis Cabot
    Flexner. Copley
  Mrs John Moffatt
    Belknap
  Sarah Kilby
    Belknap
  Sea captains carousing at Surinam (Amer-
    ican sea captains carousing at Suri-
    nam)            MoSL
    Davidson v 1
    Flexner. First flowers
    ICA. From colony to nation
    Mendelowitz
    MoSL. 50 masterworks
    MoSL. Handbook 1953
    Pierson
    Richardson. Ptg in America
    Robb. Harper history
    Time. 300 years (col)
    U. S. National Capital sesquicentennial
    com
GREENWOOD, Marion, 1909-
  Dancers resting
    Gruskin
    Pearson. Mod renaissance
  Eastern elegy         OYB
    OYB. Annual 1956
    OYB. Supplement 1959
  Eastern memory
    Pearson. Mod renaissance
  Invocation
    NAD. Annual ex, 1951
    PA. Annual ex, 1951
  Mississippi girl
    Pearson. Mod renaissance
  Rice line
    Pearson. Mod renaissance
  Simple confession       ATU
    ATU. Coll of Amer art
Greenwood and Lee families by J. Green-
  wood
The greeting by A. J. Miller
Greeting the trappers by A. J. Miller
GREGOROPOULOS, John, 1921-
  Archaic landscape
    MBIC. View 1960
GREGORY, A. V.
  The ship Ringleader      MSP
    Davidson v 1
Gregory, Clara Bartlett. See Catlin, Clara
  Bartlett (Gregory)
Gregory, Dudley Sanford
  Linen, G. Margaret Henderson Gregory
    and Dudley Sanford Gregory
Gregory, Margaret Henderson
  Linen, G. Margaret Henderson Gregory
    and Dudley Sanford Gregory

Grey and gold by J. R. Cox
Grey and green by G. J. Vander Sluis
Grey and silver, Battersea reach by J. A. M.
  Whistler
Grey day, Goochland by G. Inness
Grey day in Adirondacks by J. N. Rosen-
  berg
Grey hills by G. O'Keeffe
Grey note—mouth of the Thames by J. A.
  M. Whistler
Grey numbers by J. Johns
Grey on blue and brown by H. H. Holbrook
Grey rose by C. W. Hare
Grey sea by J. Marin
Greyed rainbow by J. Pollock
Griffin, Samuel, fl 1809
  Dunlap, W. Samuel Griffin
GRIFFITH, E. N. fl 1894
  Still life, 1894
    Frankenstein. After the hunt
GRILLEY, Robert L. 1920-
  Arrival of Nike at Panmunjom        IU
    IU. Contemp Amer ptg & sculp, 1953
    IU. 20th century
GRILLO, John, 1917-
  Celestral                         MnMW
    MnMW. 60 Amer ptrs
Grimball, Mary Magdalen (Prioleau) 1742-
  1813
    Theus, J. Mrs Thomas Grimball
Grimball, Thomas, 1745-1783
    Theus, J. Col Thomas Grimball
GRIMM, Paul
  Desert domain
    NYG. Fine art
  Pleasant retreat
    NYG. Fine art
Griswold, Eunice. See Pinney, Eunice
  (Griswold) Holcombe
Griswold family
  Johnson, Mr. Mr and Mrs Sherman
    Griswold and their three favorite
    sheep
Grizzly bear by A. J. Miller
GRODE, Shearly Mae, 1925-
  Two musicians                      LaN
    CoS. New accessions USA, 1956
GROOMBRIDGE, William, 1748-1811
  English landscape                 MdBH
    Flexner. Light of distant skies
  Fairmount and Schuylkill river     PH
    ICA. From colony to nation
    Pierson
  Woodlands, seat of William Hamilton,
    near Philadelphia
    Chew. 250 years of art
GROPPER, William, 1897-
  Aggressors' retribution            OYB
    OYB. Catalogue 1951
  Armchair strategists
    CanO. Hirshhorn coll
  Backstage
    PPC. Ptg in the U.S. 1949
  Chakwa tea plantation
    IU. Contemp Amer ptg, 1952
  Civilization
    Rathbun
  Headless horseman
    CSFP. Annual ex, 1947/48

Homeless                            MM
  MM. 100 Amer ptrs
  Pierson
Horseman                            ATU
  ATU. Coll of Amer art
Incumbent
  Cheney. Expressionism 1948 ed
Isolationist
  Wight. Milestones
Joe Magarac
  Bazin
Migration                           ATeS
  ATeS. Collection
  Mendelowitz
The opposition
  Larkin
  Larkin rev ed
The Senate                          MMA
  Barr. What is mod ptg
  Baur. Revolution
  Cheney. Story 1958 ed
  McCurdy
  NYG. Fine art
  Pierson
  Robb. Harper history
  UNESCO. 1860-1949
The speaker                         ATU
  ATU. Coll of Amer art
Talmudic student
  IU. Contemp Amer ptg & sculp, 1955
Time
  IU. Contemp Amer ptg, 1949
  Roos
Upper House                         PA
  Gruskin

**Portrait of the artist**
  Biddle, G. William Gropper
Grosbeak
  Audubon, J. J. Blue grosbeak
GROSS, Sidney, 1921-
  Industrial variations no 1
    PPC. Ptg in the U.S. 1949
  El motif
    NAD. Annual ex, 1948
  Untitled no 6
    DC. 27 biennial ex, 1961
Gross clinic by T. Eakins
Gross clinic, Sketch for by T. Eakins
GROSZ, George, 1893-1959
  After the questioning
    Baur. George Grosz
    Craven. Treasury 1952 ed
  The agitator
    Biddle. Yes and no
  The ambassador of good will         MM
    Baur. George Grosz
    MM. 100 Amer ptrs
  Apocalyptic landscape               IU
    IU. 20th century
  Approaching storm                  WMAA
    Baur. George Grosz (col)
    Gruskin (col)
  Aquarelle
    UNESCO. 1860-1955
    UNESCO. 1860-1959
  Attacked by the stickmen
    Baur. George Grosz
  Blue chair                          KW
    Baur. George Grosz
  Blue sky
    CanO. Hirshhorn coll

Cape Cod dunes
  Baur. George Grosz
Central park
  NYG. Fine art
Central park at night ICA
  Baur. George Grosz
Corpus delicti
  Baur. George Grosz
Couple WMAA
  Baur. George Grosz
  Baur. New art
  Goodrich. Amer art
  Mendelowitz
  Pierson
A Dallas night
  Pousette-Dart. Amer ptg
Dr Neisse. See Max Hermann-Neisse
End of the world
  Baur. George Grosz
Engineer Heartfield MMA
  Baur. George Grosz
  MMA. Masters
The fat and the thin
  Baur. George Grosz
From the town beyond the river
  PPC. Ptg in the U.S. 1949
Funeral of the poet Panizza
  McCurdy
Furlough
  Baur. George Grosz
Gothic woods and nymph
  VR. Biennial ex, 1948
The gray man dances
  Baur. George Grosz
  Newmeyer
Homage to Oskar Panizza (Nightmare)
  50 years of mod art
I am glad I came back ATeS
  ATeS. Collection
  Baur. George Grosz
I was always present MiC
  Baur. George Grosz
I woke one night and saw a burning
  house
  ICA. Annual ex, 1947/48
  Pearson. Mod renaissance
Landscape, Bornholm
  Baur. George Grosz
Little murderer
  Baur. George Grosz
  MnMW. Expressionism 1900-1955
Maid arranging hair of corpulent woman
PPhM
  Canaday
  Canaday (detail)
A man of opinion
  Craven. Treasury 1952 ed ,col)
Manhattan harbour
  UNESCO. 1860-1959
Max Hermann-Neisse (Dr Neisse) MMA
  Baur. George Grosz
  Cheney. Story 1958 ed
  Craven. Rainbow book
  Craven. Treasury 1952 ed
  McCurdy
Metropolis MMA
  McCurdy
  Myers
  Read. Concise history
Model in the studio
  Pearson. Mod renaissance
Night club whoopee GAtM
  GAtM. Holbrook collection

Nightmare. See Homage to Oskar Pa-
  nizza
No let up
  Wight. Milestones
Nude with bath towel
  Baur. George Grosz
Painter of the hole
  Baur. George Grosz
  Pearson. Mod renaissance
Peace II, 1946 WMAA
  Baur. George Grosz
  Goodrich. Amer art (col)
  WMAA. Juliana Force
A piece of my world no 1, c 1938 NJN
  Baur. New art (col)
  Genauer
  Pearson. Mod renaissance
A piece of my world no 2, c 1938
  Baur. George Grosz
The pit KW
  Baur. George Grosz (col)
  Baur. New art
  Baur. Revolution
  Cheney. Story 1958 ed
  Pierson
Punishment MMA
  Gruskin
Rainbow fiend
  IU. Contemp Amer ptg, 1949
  NBuA. Expressionism
Republican automatons MMA
  McCurdy
Self-portrait, 1938
  Baur. George Grosz
Shoeshine MB
  MB. Ptgs in water color
Street scene
  Baur. George Grosz
  Baur. Revolution
The survivor PPC
  Baur. George Grosz
  Pearson. Mod renaissance
  Pierson
Table-talk
  Read. Art now, 1948 ed
Theatrical dummy in Iwan Goll's Me-
  thusalem, design for
  Baur. George Grosz
The tortured ham
  Baur. George Grosz
Waiting for a job ATU
  ATU. Coll of Amer art
Waving the flag WMAA
  Baur. George Grosz
  Baur. New art
  Goodrich. Amer art
  Pierson

GROTH, John, 1908-
Berlin, May 3, 1945
  NAD. Annual ex, spring 1950
The grotto by M. Friedman
Ground-air control by D. L. Weismann
Ground swell by E. Hopper
The group by J. Strombotne
Group of artists by R. Soyer
Group of figures by M. Weber
Grouse
  Peale, Rubens. Two grouse in under-
    brush of laurel
Grouse shooting by J. M. Tracy
Grove by P. Guston
Grove by E. Ludins

Grove of trees by A. Bierstadt
Grove of trees by S. Laufman
Growth by M. Kantor
Growth by E. Vicente
The grudge by R. Thompson
GRUNEWALD, Gustavus, 1805-1878
  Wyoming valley (1)
    McClintock
  Wyoming valley (2)
    McClintock
Grymes, Alice. See Page, Alice (Grymes)
Guard room in the palace of Fontainebleau
  by W. P. P. Longfellow
Guardian by M. Graves
Guardian by R. Watson
Guardians of the secret by J. Pollock
Guerrilla warfare by A. Bierstadt
GUERIN, Jean
  Water waltz
    PPC. Ptg in the U.S. 1949
GUERIN, John William, 1921?-
  Meadow
    IU. Contemp Amer ptg & sculp, 1957
  Ship channel
    IU. Contemp Amer ptg & sculp, 1959
GUERRERO, José, 1914-
  Blue depths
    PPC. International ex, 1961/62
  Presence of black no 1    NBuA
    NBuA. Acquisitions 1959-1961
  Signs and portents    NNSG
    NNSG. Handbook
  Three blues
    NNSG. Younger Amer ptrs
GUGLIELMI, Louis, 1906-1956
  The bridge
    Gruskin
  Fourth of July
    CSFP. Annual ex, 1952
  Job's tears
    IU. Contemp Amer ptg, 1948
  Mental geography
    McCurdy
  A muted street
    MnMW. Precisionist view
  New York 21
    IU. Contemp Amer ptg, 1950
    MM. Amer ptg today
    PA. Annual ex, 1952
  Night windows
    IU. Contemp Amer ptg, 1951
  An odyssey for moderns
    Larkin
  Rampart street
    ICA. Annual ex, 1951
  The river    ICA
    Pierson
  Solitudes
    CSFP. Annual ex, 1948/49
  The temptation of St Anthony
    Genauer
    IU. Contemp Amer ptg, 1949
  Terror in Brooklyn    WMAA
    Baur. Revolution
    Cheney. Primer 1958 ed
    Goodrich. Amer art (col)
    Pierson
Guide and mountains and sky by W. Homer
Guide carrying deer by W. Homer

Guide fishing by W. Homer
Guide to Croaghan by R. Henri
Guilty cats by J. De Diego
Guinan, Texas, 1886-1956
  Marsh, R. Texas Guinan and her gang
Guirson by E. A. Donati
The guitar by G. B. Luks
Guitar player by M. Weber
Guizot, François Pierre Guillaume, 1787-1874
  Healy, G. P. A. François Pierre Guillaume
    Guizot
Gulch mine, Central city, Colorado by E.
  Leutze
Gulf coast shipyard by E. D. Lewandowski
Gulf stream by W. Homer
Gull a'winging by W. Bassford
GULLAGER, Christian, 1762-1826
  David Coats    MoSL
    MoSL. Handbook 1953
  John May    MWA
    Larkin
    Larkin rev ed
    MWA. Checklist of portraits
  Samuel Barton
    ICA. From colony to nation
Gulls
  Audubon, J. J. Great black-backed gull
  Benn, B. Sea gulls
  Evergood, P. American shrimp girl
  Graves, M. Wounded gull
  Graves, M. Wounded sea gull
  Keller, H. G. Gulls feeding
  Marin, J. Gulls, Cape Split, Maine
  Marin, J. Sea and gulls
  Marin, J. Sea gulls
  Mattson, H. E. Gulls and sea
  Ruellan, A. Boy and gull
  Spruce, E. F. Gull
  Spruce, E. F. Sea gulls
Gun foundry, Cold Spring, New York by
  J. F. Weir
GUSTON, Philip, 1912-
  Actor
    Ashton. Philip Guston
  Attar
    Ashton. Philip Guston (col)
  Beggar's joys
    Ashton. Philip Guston (col)
    MMA. New Amer ptg (col)
    MMA. 12 Americans (col)
  Ceremony
    Genauer
    MnU. Philip Guston
  The clock    MMA
    Ashton. Philip Guston (col)
    Hunter. Mod Amer ptg (col)
    MMA. New Amer ptg
  Clock II, 1957
    Ashton. Philip Guston
  Dial    WMAA
    Ashton. Philip Guston (col)
    Goodrich. Amer art (col)
  Doyer II, 1958
    Ashton. Philip Guston
  Fable, 1956    MoSLW
    Ashton. Philip Guston
  Fable II, 1957
    Ashton. Philip Guston (col)
  Gladiators
    MnU. Philip Guston
  Gouache
    Ashton. Philip Guston

Grove
  Ashton. Philip Guston (col)
Holiday
  NAD. Annual ex, 1947, 1st half
If this be not I                    MoSLW
  Gruskin (col)
  MnU. Philip Guston
Martial memory                      MoSL
  Larkin
  Larkin rev ed
  MnU. Philip Guston
  Pierson
  Roos
The mirror
  Art since 1945 (col)
  Read. Concise history
Musa Mckim
  MnU. Philip Guston
Native's return                     DP
  Ashton. Philip Guston
Night children
  Bazin
  MnU. Philip Guston
Nile
  WMAA. Museum and its friends, 1959
Number 5, 1952
  Ashton. Philip Guston
Number 6, 1952
  Ashton. Philip Guston
Painter's city
  Ashton. Philip Guston (col)
  Canaday
Painting, 1950
  Ashton. Philip Guston
Painting, 1952
  Ashton. Philip Guston (col)
  MMA. 12 Americans
Painting, 1954                      MMA
  McCurdy
  MMA. New Amer ptg
  MMA. 12 Americans
  NNSG. Younger Amer ptrs
Performers                          MM
  MM. 100 Amer ptrs
  MnU. Philip Guston
Poet
  Ashton. Philip Guston (col)
The porch no 1                      IU
  IU. Contemp Amer ptg, 1948
  IU. 20th century
Porch no 2, 1946-47                 NUM
  Ashton. Philip Guston
  MnU. Philip Guston
  NBuA. Expressionism
Review, 1948-49
  Ashton. Philip Guston
Review, 1950
  MnU. 40 Amer ptrs
The room
  Ashton. Philip Guston
  MMA. 12 Americans
  MnMW. 60 Amer ptrs
Sanctuary
  IU. Contemp Amer ptg, 1949
  MnU. Philip Guston
The sculptor                        VR
  CoS. New accessions USA, 1946
Sentimental moment
  Gruskin (col)
Shanah
  MnU. 40 Amer ptrs
  MnU. Philip Guston

Sleeper
  Ashton. Philip Guston
The street
  Pierson
Summer
  Eliot. Art of our time (col)
  Time. 300 years (col)
To B. W. T. 1951-52
  MMA. 12 **Americans**
To Fellini
  Ashton. Philip Guston
  Ponente. Mod ptg, 1960 (col)
The tormentors
  Ashton. Philip Guston
  PPC. International ex, 1950
Untitled painting, 1955-56
  Ashton. Philip Guston
  Baur. Nature (col)
Untitled painting, 1958
  Ashton. Philip Guston (col)
The visit
  MMA. 12 Americans
Voyage                              NBuA
  Ashton. Philip Guston (col)
  NBuA. Acquisitions 1954-57
White painting
  Ashton. Philip Guston
Zone
  Art since 1945
  Ashton. Philip Guston (col)
  WMAA. Museum and its friends, 1958
**GUTMANN, Gerrie**
The uninvited
  CSFP. Annual ex, 1952
**GUY, Francis, c 1760-1820**
Baltimore, 1803                     NBM
  Davidson v2
  DC. Amer ptrs of the South
Bolton
  Flexner. Light of distant skies
Brooklyn, 1816-1820 (Winter scene in
  Brooklyn)                         NBM
  Born
  Davidson v2
  Flexner. Light of distant skies
  Mendelowitz
  Pierson
Pennington mills, Baltimore, view down-
  stream                            MdBP
  Barker. Amer ptg
Pennington mills, Baltimore, view up-
  stream                            MdBP
  Davidson v 1
Tontine coffee house, New York c 1798
                                    NNHS
  Davidson v2
  Larkin
  Larkin rev ed
  Pierson
View of Baltimore, basin and Federal hill
  MdBMu. Rendezvous
Washington's tomb                   MdBH
  ICA. From colony to nation
Winter scene in Brooklyn. See Brooklyn,
  1816-1820
**GUY, James**
Composition no 6—50
  MM. Amer ptg today
**GUYOL DE GUIRAN, François-Marie,**
  fl 1815
Marie Elise Provenchere             MoSLH
  Pierson

**GWATHMEY, Robert,** 1903-
Across the tracks
  Larkin
  Larkin rev ed
Bread and circuses                    MSM
  Pierson
Children dancing                      OYB
  OYB. Catalogue 1951
Clearing
  DC. 25 biennial ex, 1957
Cotton picker
  IU. Contemp Amer ptg, 1951
End of day                            IBM
  Mendelowitz
Farmer's wife
  CanO. Hirshhorn coll
  IU. Contemp Amer ptg & sculp, 1953
Flower vendors
  CSFP. Annual ex, 1950/51
Front porch
  PPC. International ex, 1950
Hoeing                                PPC
  Bazin
  Gruskin (col)
  McCurdy
Hoeing tobacco                        GAtM
  GAtM. Holbrook collection
Painting of a smile                   NeL
  CoS. New accessions USA, 1954
  Pierson
Pick 'till the rain hits
  ICA. Annual ex, 1954
Poll tax country
  DC. 20 biennial ex, 1947
Singing and mending
  CSFP. Annual ex, 1948/49
Southern community
  IU. Contemp Amer ptg, 1950
Southern scene
  MM. Amer ptg today
Sowing                                WMAA
  Goodrich. Amer art
Vacationist
  Pierson
Winter's playground
  Pousette-Dart. Amer ptg
The **gypsy** by G. Tooker
**Gypsy** with a cigarette by R. Henri
**Gypsy's** house by M. Hoff
**Gyrfalcon** by J. J. Audubon

# H

**H., E.**
  Detroit, 1794 (Detroit public library)
    Davidson v2
**H. L. Hunley (submarine)**
  Chapman, C. W. Confederate submarine
    torpedo boat H. L. Hunley, 1863
**Habbaku** dancers by E. A. Donati
**HABERLE, John,** 1856-1933
  Bachelor's drawer
    Frankenstein. After the hunt
  Changes of time
    CSFP. Illusionism
    Frankenstein. After the hunt
  Clock
    Frankenstein. After the hunt

Conglomeration
  Frankenstein. After the hunt
A favorite                            MSM
  Frankenstein. After the hunt
Grandma's hearthstone                 MiD
  Frankenstein. After the hunt
  Pierson
  Richardson. Ptg in America
Time and eternity                     CtNB
  Frankenstein. After the hunt
  Pierson
Torn in transit
  CSFP. Illusionism
  Frankenstein. After the hunt
**Habersham, James,** 1712-1775
  Theus, J. Gov James Habersham
**Habitation** by M. Cone
**HACKER, Gerte F.**
  White pitcher
    OYB. Annual 1951
**HADDOCA, A.** fl 1830
  Red Jacket                          DN
    DN. Amer primitive ptgs, pt 1
**Hadley, Arthur Twining,** 1856-1930
  Kendall, W. S. Arthur Twining Hadley
**Hagar** and Ishmael by B. West
**HAHN, Walter H.** 1927-
  Satan
    IU. Contemp Amer ptg & sculp, 1953
**HAHN, William,** 1840?-1890?
  Yosemite valley
    U.S. National Capital sesquicentennial
      com
**HAIDT, John Valentin,** 1700-1780
  Christ before Pilate
    ICA. From colony to nation
  Crucifixion
    ICA. From colony to nation
  Timothy Horsfield jr
    Chew. 250 years of art
**HAILMAN, Johanna Knowles (Woodwell)**
  1871-
  Happy morning
    PPC. International ex, 1950
  Mrs Leslie Buswell
    PPC. Ptg in the U.S. 1949
  My house                            PPC
    Chew. 250 years of art
**Hailstorm** by T. H. Benton
**Haines, Charles Richard.** See Haines, Rich-
  ard
**HAINES, Richard,** 1906-
  The bather
    IU. Contemp Amer ptg & sculp, 1961
  By the sea
    MM. Amer ptg today
  Eventide
    IU. Contemp Amer ptg, 1950
  Mesa Verde
    IU. Contemp Amer ptg, 1951
  Morning sea                         MoKN
    CoS. New accessions USA, 1952
  Night of return
    CSFP. Annual ex, 1952
    Pousette-Dart. Amer ptg
  The prodigal son                    DC
    CoS. New accessions USA, 1952
    DC. 22 biennial ex, 1951
    PPC. Ptg in the U.S. 1949
  Town meeting                        ATeS
    ATeS. Collection
**Hairdresser's** window by J. Sloan
**Haiti** by J. Delbos

Haitian heaven by A. A. Dehn
Haitian Mardi Gras by A. A. Dehn
HAKLHUBER, F. fl 1860
  Herndon hotel, Omaha, Nebraska MoSLH
    Rathbone
Hale, Edward Everett, 1822-1909
  Chase, W. M. Edward Everett Hale
  Hale, P. L. Edward Everett Hale
HALE, Philip Leslie, 1865-1931
  Edward Everett Hale
    Larkin
    Larkin rev ed
HALEY, John Charles, 1905-
  Dark anonymity
    IU. Contemp Amer ptg & sculp, 1953
  Myriad
    IU. Contemp Amer ptg, 1952
  Monument valley
    IU. Contemp Amer ptg, 1951
HALEY, Sally, 1908-
  Red chair
    OrPA. Ptgs and sculptures (col)
  Robed figures in ambulatory
    MnMW. Reality and fantasy
Half a man by W. R. Garver
Halfway house by D. G. Blythe
Halibut fishing by W. Homer
Hall, Abigail, 1795-1878
  Unidentified artist. Abigail Hall
Hall, Mrs Calvin. See Hall, Mercy (Barnes)
HALL, Carl A. 1921-
  The dance
    IU. Contemp Amer ptg, 1948
  Domain
    PPC. Ptg in the U.S. 1949
  Junction
    OrPA. Ptgs & sculptures
  Vagrants
    IU. Contemp Amer ptg, 1951
Hall, David, fl 1775
  Williams, W. David Hall
Hall, Deborah, fl 1776
  Williams, W. Deborah Hall
Hall, Laura, fl 1808
  Brown, J. Laura Hall
Hall, Mercy (Barnes) fl 1808
  Brown, J. Mrs Calvin Hall
Hall, William
  Williams, W. William Hall
Hall at Shinnecock by W. M. Chase
Halle cathedral, East choir by L. Feininger
Les halles by W. A. Smith
Hallett, Joseph, 1678-1750
  Duyckinck, G. (attributed works)
    Joseph(?) Hallett
  Unidentified artist. Gentleman of the Hal-
    lett family (probably Joseph Hallett)
Hallett, Mrs Joseph. See Hallett, Mary
    (Lawrence) Greenoak
Hallett, Maria. See Tallmadge, Maria (Hal-
    lett)
Hallett, Mary (Lawrence) Greenoak, fl 1728
  Duyckinck, G. Mrs Joseph(?) Hallett
  Unidentified artist. Lady of the Hallett
    family (probably Mrs Joseph Hallett)
Hallett family, Member of
  Unidentified artist. Boy of the Hallett
    family
  Unidentified artist. Son of Capt Samuel
    Hallett
Hallowe'en by L. Bosa

Hallowe'en mask by R. Vickrey
HALLOWELL, George Hawley, 1871-1926
  Brook in Vermont                         MB
    MB. Ptgs in water color
  Calling of St Matthew (copy after Car-
    paccio)                                MB
    MB. Ptgs in water color
  Italian fiesta, night                    MSM
    MSM. Handbook
  Mountains in Dalmatia                    MB
    MB. Ptgs in water color
  Snow drapery                             MB
    MB. Ptgs in water color
  The tree                                 MB
    MB. Ptgs in water color
  Trees in winter                          MB
    MB. Ptgs in water color
HALPERT, Samuel, 1884-1930
  Brooklyn bridge                          WMAA
    Goodrich. Amer art
    Pierson
  Cathedral interior
    WMAA. Pioneers
  Church interior
    Brown. Amer ptg
  Notre Dame, Paris                        MM
    Brown. Amer ptg
HALSEY, William Melton, 1915-
  The onlookers
    Pousette-Dart. Amer ptg
Halt—dismount by F. Remington
Halt in the Rocky mountains by A. Bier-
    stadt
Halt of the wise men by J. LaFarge
HAMBLEN, Sturtevant J. fl 1856

                Attributed works

  Baby with doll                          VWR
    VWR. Folk art (col)
  Unknown woman                           MSt
    Little. Country art
The Hambletonian by J. W. Golinkin
Hamblin, Sturtevant J. See Hamblen, Sturte-
    vant J.
Hamilton, Alexander, 1757-1804
  Ames, E. Alexander Hamilton
  Peale, C. W. Alexander Hamilton
  Trumbull, J. Alexander Hamilton
Hamilton, Gail. See Dodge, Mary Abigail
HAMILTON, James, 1819-1878
  Monitor and Merrimac                    PH
    Chew. 250 years of art
HAMILTON, John McLure
  Paul Wayland Bartlett in his Paris studio
    Chew. 250 years of art
HAMILTON, Robert G. 1920?-
  Cape fog
    IU. Contemp Amer ptg & sculp, 1959
  Cape landscape
    NUM. Art across America
  Fallout red
    MBIC. View 1960
  Landscape with a mirror
    PPC. International ex, 1958
  Mayflower
    IU. Contemp Amer ptg & sculp, 1961
Hamlet and Horatio by J. Miller
HAMMER, John J. 1842-1906
  Peaceful day in the Mohawk valley MB
    MB. Karolik coll
  Sculptor's studio                       MB
    MB. Karolik coll

**Hammersley, Mrs Hugh**
  Sargent, J. S. Mrs Hugh Hammersley
**Hammerstein's** roof garden by W. J.
  Glackens
**Hammond, Anna.** See Pope, Anna (Hammond)
**Hancock, John,** 1737-1793
  Copley, J. S. John Hancock
**HANCOCK, Nathaniel,** fl 1805
  Jedidiah Morse                           CtY
    CtY. Portrait index
  Self-portrait                            CtY
    CtY. Portrait index
**Hancock, Thomas,** 1703-1764
  Copley, J. S. Thomas Hancock
**Hand** sewing machine by A. G. Dove
**Handball** by B. Shahn
**Handel** still life by S. W. Crane
**Handkerchief** point by M. B. Prendergast
The **handsome** dance, Venezuela, South
  America by G. Catlin
**Handwriting** on the wall by Ben-Zion
**Handy, John,** 1756?-1828
  Malbone, E. G. Major John Handy
**Hanging** bird by H. Bradford
**Hanging** clothes by J. Koch
**Hanging** of Bob Augustin by C. A. Herff
**HANSON, Joseph Mellor,** 1900-
  Composition
    Pousette-Dart. Amer ptg
  Gay table cloth
    WMAA. Contemp Amer ptg, 1950
  Red dominant
    CSFP. Annual ex, 1952
**Happy** entrance by P. Evergood
**Happy** family in Virginia by W. Homer
**Happy** moment by J. G. Clonney
**Happy** morning by J. K. W. Hailman
**HARARI, Hananiah,** 1912-
  Man's boudoir no 1 (realism)          ATU
    ATU. Coll of Amer art
  Man's boudoir no 2 (abstraction)      ATU
    ATU. Coll of Amer art
  Old valentine
    CSFP. Illusionism
**Harbinger** of spring by R. Brown
**Harbor** by M. B. Prendergast
**Harbor** by J. W. Schulein
**Harbor** by P. Wescott
**Harbor** at Edgartown by F. Chapin
**Harbor** at night by M. Avery
**Harbor** at night by M. Jackson
**Harbor** festivity by J. G. F. Von Wicht
**Harbor** of dreams by I. L. Albright
**Harbor** scene with fish market near Philadelphia by W. Carr
**Harbor** traffic by G. Grant
**Harbor** with red for Mary Lou by J. Lechay
**Hard** lot by J. Decker
**HARDING, Chester,** 1792-1866
  Amos Lawrence                            DN
    Mendelowitz
    Pierson
  Andrew Jackson
    DC. Privately owned

  Anna Hardaway Bunker                    InIJ
    Barker. Amer ptg
    InIJ. 105 ptgs
  Benjamin Pickman                         MB
    MB. Karolik coll
  Charles Carroll of Carrollton            DN
    DC. Amer ptrs of the South
  Chester Harding Krum                    MoSL
    MoSL. Handbook 1953
  Daniel Boone                           MoSLH
    Davidson v 1
  Isaac Bates
    Larkin
    Larkin rev ed
  John Marshall                            MBA
    Time. 300 years (col)
  John Randolph of Roanoke                 CtY
    CtY. Portrait index
  John Randolph of Roanoke                 DN
    DN. Mellon coll
  Lyman Beecher                            CtY
    CtY. Portrait index
  Mrs John Ball Brown                      MB
    Pierson
  Samuel Cartmill Christy
    Flexner. Light of distant skies
    **Attributed works**
  Daniel Boone (Filson club, Louisville)
    Ford. Pictorial folk art
**Hardware** store by A. G. Dove
**Hardy, Catherine Sears (Wheeler)** 1806-1876
  Hardy, J. P. Catherine Wheeler Hardy
    and her daughter
**HARDY, Jeremiah Pearson,** 1800-1888
  Catherine Wheeler Hardy and her daughter                                      MB
    MB. Karolik coll
    Pierson
    Richardson. Ptg in America
  Mary Ann Hardy                           MB
    MB. Karolik coll
  New England picnic, 1855                  MB
    Davidson v2
  Pic Nic, Camden, Maine                    MB
    MB. Karolik coll
**Hardy, Mrs Jeremiah Pearson.** See Hardy,
  Catherine Sears (Wheeler)
**Hardy, Mary Ann,** 1809-1887
  Hardy, J. P. Mary Ann Hardy
**HARDY, Philip,** fl 1843-1847
  Tremont street, Boston                    MB
    MB. Karolik coll
**HARE, Channing Weir,** 1899-
  Fourth of July
    IU. Contemp Amer ptg, 1950
  The grey rose                            IaDa
    IaDa. 30th anniversary
  John Horton
    PPC. Ptg in the U.S. 1949
  Passementerie
    IU. Contemp Amer ptg, 1952
  Young hunter
    NAD. Annual ex, 1948
**HARE, David,** 1917-
  Two
    Read. Art now, 1948 ed
The **harem** by M. Weber
**Hares**
  Audubon, J. J. Black-tailed hare or jack-rabbit
  Audubon, J. W. Hare

**Haring, Elizabeth.** See De Peyster, Elizabeth (Haring)

**Harkness** tower (Yale) by K. Matthew

**Harlem** by K. Zerbe

**Harlem** river by P. Dickinson

**Harlem** river by E. Lawson

**Harlem** river bridge by D. Burliuk

**Harlequin** by W. Kuhn

**Harlequin** by K. Zerbe

**Harlequin** and woman by C. Alajálov

**HARMON, Lily (Perelmutter)** 1913-
Child acrobats
    IU. Contemp Amer ptg & sculp, 1955
First child
    PPC. Ptg in the U.S. 1949
Nursery school
    IU. Contemp Amer ptg, 1952
Pink dunes
    IU. Contemp Amer ptg & sculp, 1957
Provincetown
    IU. Contemp Amer ptg & sculp, 1959
Sunset and white trees
    CanO. Hirshhorn coll

**Harmony** in blue and silver by J. A. M. Whistler

**Harmony** in grey and green by J. A. M. Whistler

**Harmony** in red: Lamplight by J. A. M. Whistler

**Harness** horse stables—Cape Girardeau by R. Davey

**HARNETT, William Michael,** 1848-1892
After the hunt                    CSFP
    CSFP. Handbook (col)
    CSFP. Illusionism
    Faulkner. Art today, 1956
    Flexner. Amer ptg
    Flexner. Short history
    Frankenstein. After the hunt (col)
    McCurdy
    Mendelowitz
    Pierson
    Richardson. Ptg in America (col)
    Time. 300 years (col)
After the hunt                    OCo
    Frankenstein. After the hunt
    PA. Annual ex, 1955
After the hunt                    OYB
    OYB. Supplement
Artist's card rack
    Frankenstein. After the hunt
    WiMiA. Amer ptg 1760-1960 (col)
Artist's window, View from
    Frankenstein. After the hunt
Cincinnati Enquirer
    Frankenstein. After the hunt
Colossal luck
    DC. Halpert coll
    Frankenstein. After the hunt
Deutsche presse
    Frankenstein. After the hunt
Emblems of peace                    MSM
    Baur. Revolution
    CSFP. Illusionism
    MSM. Handbook
    PA. Annual ex, 1955
    Pierson
The faithful Colt                    CtHW
    CtHW. Handbook
    Frankenstein. After the hunt
    Pierson

Front face
    Frankenstein. After the hunt
George Fryer's still life
    Frankenstein. After the hunt
German girl, Head of a                    MCH
    Frankenstein. After the hunt
Head of Minerva
    Frankenstein. After the hunt
Job lot, cheap
    Frankenstein. After the hunt
London Times
    Frankenstein. After the hunt
Meerschaum pipe
    Frankenstein. After the hunt
Merganser duck
    OYB. Catalogue 1951
Mortality and immortality
    Frankenstein. After the hunt
Music and good luck
    Frankenstein. After the hunt
Music and literature                    NBuA
    Frankenstein. After the hunt
    NBuA. Catalogue of the ptgs
    UNESCO. 1860-1955
    UNESCO. 1860-1959
Oil sketch, 1874
    Frankenstein. After the hunt
Old Cremona                    MM
    Bazin
Old cupboard door
    Frankenstein. After the hunt
Old models                    MB
    Baur. Amer ptg
    CSFP. Illusionism
    Frankenstein. After the hunt
    Janson. Picture history
    Larkin
    Larkin rev ed
    OCiM. Rediscoveries
    Pierson
    Roos
    Walker. Ptgs from America
Old North Carolina
    OCiM. Rediscoveries
The old refrain
    UNESCO. 1860-1955
    UNESCO. 1860-1959
Old violin                    OCiM
    Barker. Amer ptg
    CSFP. Illusionism
    Frankenstein. After the hunt
    PA. Annual ex, 1955
    Pierson
Searching the Scriptures
    Frankenstein. After the hunt
The secretary's table
    Chew. 250 years of art
Social club
    Frankenstein. After the hunt
Solace
    CSFP. Illusionism
Still life, 1877
    Frankenstein. After the hunt
Still life, 1887
    Frankenstein. After the hunt
Still life, 1888
    Frankenstein. After the hunt
Still life: salt glaze pot, pipe and Le Figaro
    Chew. 250 years of art
Still life with bric-a-brac                    MCH
    Frankenstein. After the hunt

**HARNETT, W. M.**—*Continued*
Still life with letter to Thomas B. Clarke
    MAP
  Frankenstein. After the hunt
Still life with tankard
  Frankenstein. After the hunt
Study table        NUM
  Frankenstein. After the hunt
  NUM. Art across America
Thieves in the pantry
  Frankenstein. After the hunt
Toledo blade
  Frankenstein. After the hunt
With the Staatszeitung    MoSL
  MoSL. Handbook 1953
Wooden box of catawba grapes
  Frankenstein. After the hunt
Ye knights of old
  Frankenstein. After the hunt

**Attributed works**

Bachelor's friend    MAP
  Frankenstein. After the hunt
Discarded treasures    MNS
  Frankenstein. After the hunt
Dollar bill and playbill
  Frankenstein. After the hunt
Old friends
  Frankenstein. After the hunt
Old reminiscences    DP
  Frankenstein. After the hunt
Old scraps    MMA
  Frankenstein. After the hunt
Old souvenirs
  Frankenstein. After the hunt
Protection
  Frankenstein. After the hunt
Still life with violin    OYB
  OYB. Catalogue 1951
To Edwin Booth
  Frankenstein. After the hunt
**Harp** of the winds by F. E. Church
**Harp** of the winds by H. D. Martin
**Harpie** by B. Shahn
The **harpies** by H. Bloom
**Harris, Charles,** b 1784
  Malbone, E. G. Charles Harris
**HARRIS, Eleanor,** 1899-
  Flight
    ICA. Annual ex, 1947/48
**Harris, Mrs Lebdeus,** fl 1831
  Mason, B. F. Mrs Lebdeus Harris
**Harris, Richard D.** b 1780
  Malbone, E. G. Richard D. Harris
**Harris, Samuel,** 1814-1899
  Weir, J. F. The Theological of Yale university
**HARRISON, B. J.**
  Fair of the American institute of New York, held at Niblo's garden, c 1845
    Davidson v 1
**Harrison, John** fl 1823
  Mayhew, N. John Harrison
**Harrison, Mrs John,** fl 1823
  Mayhew, N. Mrs John Harrison and her daughter Maria
**Harrison, Thomas,** fl 1815
  Belknap, Z. Capt Thomas Harrison
**Harrison, Mrs Thomas,** fl 1815
  Belknap, Z. Mrs Thomas Harrison

**HART, George Overbury,** 1868-1933
The Bahamas    WMAA
  NYG. Fine art
  Pierson
Cockfight, Mexico    NJN
  Pierson
Fireworks    OCl
  OCl. Handbook
Palisade amusement park    MB
  MB. Ptgs in water color
Sultan's tomb, Fez, Morocco    MB
  MB. Ptgs in water color
**HART, James MacDougal,** 1828-1901
Catskill creek, New York    NBuA
  NBuA. Catalogue of the ptgs
On the lake shore    MB
  MB. Karolik coll
Picnic on the Hudson    NBM
  Born
View on the Hudson    NCHA
  NYG. Fine art
**HART, James McDougal,** 1828-1901 **and Tait, Arthur Fitzwilliam,** 1819-1905

**Attributed works**

The Burden family enjoying the Hudson river near Troy    NAI
  Jones. Rediscovered ptrs
**Hart, John,** fl 1795
  Polk, C. P. John Hart
**Hart, Mrs John,** fl 1795
  Polk, C. P. Mrs John Hart and her daughter
**Hart, Pop.** See Hart, George Overbury
**Hart, Samuel,** fl 1806
  Unidentified artist. Dr Samuel Hart
**HART, William M.** 1823-1894
After the storm    MB
  Jones. Rediscovered ptrs
  MB. Karolik coll
Autumn in the Catskills
  Sears. Highlights
Cattle in a stream
  Sears. Highlights
Evening in Keene valley, Adirondacks
  Sears. Highlights
**Hartford, Connecticut**
  Cole, T. Hartford, Connecticut
**Hartford (steamship)**
  Smith, J. B. Steamer Hartford, 1849
**HARTIGAN, Grace,** 1922-
Billboard    MnMI
  Art since 1945
  Hunter. Mod Amer ptg (col)
Bride and owl
  MMA. 12 Americans
Broadway restaurant    MoKN
  Brussels. Exposition
  Eliot. Art of our time (col)
City life
  MMA. New Amer ptg
  MMA. 12 Americans
The creeks: interior
  Read. Concise history
Dublin
  MnMW. 60 Amer ptrs
Essex market
  MMA. New Amer ptg
Grand street brides
  Goodrich. Amer art
  Pierson
Interior—the creeks
  MMA. New Amer ptg (col)

New England, October NBuA
NBuA. Acquisitions 1957-58
Ocean bathers
MMA. 12 Americans
Persian jacket MMA
MMA. 12 Americans
River bathers MMA
McCurdy
MMA. 12 Americans (col)
St Valentine
PPC. International ex, 1961/62
Shinnecock canal MMA
MMA. Soby collection
The showcase
WMAA. Contemp Amer ptg, 1955
HARTL, Leon, 1889-
Still life with red fish CtHW
CoS. New accessions USA, 1960
HARTLEY, Marsden, 1877-1943
Abelard the drowned, master of the Phantom
McCausland. Marsden Hartley
Abstraction, 1911
McCausland. Marsden Hartley
Abstraction, 1916 MnU
MMA. Abstract
Abstraction with flowers
McCausland. Marsden Hartley
McCurdy
Albert Pinkham Ryder
Baur. New art
Cheney. Story 1958 ed
Riley. Your art heritage
Autumn
McCausland. Marsden Hartley
Beaver lake, Lost river region
McCausland. Marsden Hartley
Bermuda window in a semitropical character
McCausland. Marsden Hartley
Birds of the Bagaduce OYB
OYB. Accessions
OYB. Supplement 1959
Boots MMA
MMA. Masters
Camden hills from Baker's island, Penobscot bay
McCausland. Marsden Hartley
Carnival of autumn
McCausland. Marsden Hartley
Cleophas, master of the Gilda Gray
McCausland. Marsden Hartley
Color analogy OCo
Brown. Amer ptg
Dark mountain ICA
Brown. Amer ptg
Dead plover
McCausland. Marsden Hartley
Deserted farm
McCausland. Marsden Hartley
"E," 1915
Hunter. Mod Amer ptg (col)
McCurdy
Read. Concise history
Eight bells' folly: memorial for Hart Crane
McCausland. Marsden Hartley
Evening storm, Schoodic, Maine, MMA
McCurdy
Read. Concise history

Fishhouse, New England
NYG. Fine art
UNESCO. 1860-1949
UNESCO. 1860-1955
UNESCO. 1860-1959
Fishermen's last supper
Baur. New art
DC. De gustibus
Flexner. Amer ptg
Flexner. Short history
McCausland. Marsden Hartley
MnMW. Contemporary
MnMW. Expressionism 1900-1955
Pierson
WMAA. Neuberger collection
Flower abstraction
UNESCO. 1860-1955
UNESCO. 1860-1959
Flowers from Claire Spencer's garden NBuA
NBuA. Contemporary ptgs
Time. 300 years (col)
Forms abstracted
Larkin
Larkin rev ed
Fox island, Maine MAP
Cheney. Story 1958 ed
Wight. Milestones (col)
Garmisch-Partenkirchen
McCausland. Marsden Hartley
A German officer 1914 MM
Baur. New art (col)
Baur. Revolution
Pierson
Time. 300 years (col)
Give us this day
McCausland. Marsden Hartley
WMAA. Museum and its friends, 1958
Himmel MoKN
MoKN. Handbook p 149
Hurricane island, Vinal Haven, Maine PPhM
Canaday
In the moraine, Dogtown common, Cape Ann
McCausland. Marsden Hartley
Labrador ducks
McCausland. Marsden Hartley
Landscape no 29, 1907?
McCausland. Marsden Hartley
Landscape, no 32, 1911
McCausland. Marsden Hartley
Landscape no 56, 1909
McCausland. Marsden Hartley
Landscape, New Mexico OCl
OCl. Handbook
Landscape, Venice
McCausland. Marsden Hartley
Last of New England—the beginning of New Mexico ICA
Baur. Revolution
Lighthouse
Baur. Revolution
Lincoln, Portrait of
CtY. Yale alumni
Lobster buoys and nets
McCausland. Marsden Hartley
Lobster fishermen MM
MM. 100 Amer ptrs
Taylor. Fifty centuries, 1954 ed (col)
Lobster pots and buoy
NUM. Art across America

**HARTLEY, Marsden**—*Continued*
Log jam, Penobscot bay                MiD
  Mendelowitz
  MiD. Treasures
  Richardson. Ptg in America
Maine landscape, autumn               TNF
  Brown. Amer ptg
Maine snowstorm
  McCausland. Marsden Hartley
Marie St Esprit
  McCausland. Marsden **Hartley**
Military
  McCausland. Marsden Hartley
Mount Katahdin
  CanO. Hirshhorn coll
  McCausland. Marsden Hartley
Mount Katahdin, autumn no 1           NeL
  Barker. From realism (col)
  Baur. New art
  Pierson
  Roos
Mount Katahdin, Maine (Lowenthal coll)
  NBuA. Expressionism
Movement
  Cheney. Primer 1958 ed
Movement no 9, 1916
  McCausland. Marsden Hartley
Movements, 1915                       ICA
  Brown. Amer ptg
New England fishhouse. See Fishhouse,
  New England
New Mexico
  Cheney. Primer 1958 ed
New Mexico: landscape
  McCausland. Marsden Hartley
New Mexico recollections              OCo
  Brown. Amer ptg
Nova Scotia fishermen                 IBM
  Bazin (col)
  WMAA. Juliana Force
Number 48                             NBuA
  NBuA. Fifty ptgs
Off to the Banks                      DP
  DP. Catalogue
Old bars, Dogtown                     WMAA
  Goodrich. Amer art
  Munsterberg
Painting no 5, 1914-15                WMAA
  Goodrich. Amer art (col)
  Pierson
Paysage
  McCausland. Marsden Hartley
Pears
  McCausland. Marsden Hartley
Peasants' paradise
  McCausland. Marsden Hartley
Portrait
  McCausland. Marsden Hartley
Red cross
  WMAA. Pioneers
Robin Hood cove, Georgetown, Maine
  McCausland. Marsden Hartley
  Time. 300 years (col)
Roses
  McCausland. Marsden Hartley
Rubber plant                          CtY
  CtY. Soc Anonyme
Smelt brook falls                     MoSL
  Born
  Gruskin (col)
  Larkin
  Larkin rev ed
  MoSL. Handbook 1953

Still life, 1912
  McCausland. Marsden Hartley
Still life, 1923
  McCausland. Marsden Hartley
Still life, 1929                      ATeS
  ATeS. Collection
Still life no 3, 1916
  McCausland. Marsden Hartley
Still life no 12, 1910
  McCausland. Marsden Hartley
Still life: fruit
  McCausland. Marsden Hartley
Storm clouds, Maine
  McCausland. Marsden Hartley
Waterfall, Morse pond
  McCausland. Marsden Hartley
The wave                              MWM
  Baur. New art
  Pierson
Wild roses                            DP
  Baur. New art
  DP. Catalogue
  UNESCO. 1860-1955
  UNESCO. 1860-1959
Young worshipper of the truth
  McCausland. Marsden Hartley
**Hartley family**
  Benbridge, H. Hartley family group
**Harvard college**
  Fisher, J. Building at Harvard college,
    c 1810
**Harvest** by J. Jones
**Harvest** by K. Knaths
**Harvest** by J. Penney
**Harvest** by M. Tobey
**Harvest** in Vermont by J. B. Thompson
**Harvest** scene by W. Homer
**HARVEY, George,** fl 1840-1878
  Afternoon, dead calm: View on the Erie
    canal near Pittsford, New York (Late
    afternoon—Calm on the Erie canal)
  Jones. Rediscovered ptrs
  U.S. National Capital sesquicentennial
    com
  Amongst the Allegheny mountains    NBM
  Born
  Entrance to a coal mine near Wheeling,
    **Virginia**
  U.S. National Capital sesquicentennial
    com
  Extra-curricular activity under the Apostle
    oak, 1841
  Davidson v2
  Hastings landing—Palisade rocks in shad-
    ow                               NNHS
  Jones. Rediscovered ptrs
  Houses on a tobacco plantation     NNHS
  Davidson v 1
  Late afternoon—Calm on the Erie canal.
    See Afternoon, dead calm: View on
    the Erie canal near Pittsford, New
    York
  Portland pier, Lake Erie           NNHS
  Davidson v2
  Reaping on Boston common, 1835-1840
    (Blair coll)
  Davidson v2
  St Thomas church, Broadway, New York,
    c1835
  Davidson v2

Spring: burning up fallen trees, a girdled clearing, Canada          NBM
  Pierson
State House and Boston Common, 1830
  Tolman
Tremont house, Boston          MBA
  Larkin
View on the Hudson          MB
  MB. Karolik coll
White pelicans in Florida          MB
  MB. Karolik coll
Winter: an impediment in travelling          MB
  MB. Ptgs in water color
HARVEY, James V. 1929-
  Helmund II
    WMAA. Young America 1960
  Yaddo
    DC. 27 biennial ex, 1961
Harvey, Rachel. See Montgomery, Rachel (Harvey)
HARVEY, Sarah E. fl 1877
  Winstead, Connecticut          NJP
    NJP. Amer folk art
The Harvey breaker, West Nanticoke by T. Hill
Harwood, Adeline, fl 1820
  Unidentified artist. Adeline Harwood
Harwood, Margaret (Strachan) fl 1772
  Peale, C. W. Mrs Thomas Harwood
Harzfeld's mural by T. H. Benton
Haseltine, Charles F. 1840-1915
  Eakins, T. Charles Haseltine
HASELTINE, William Stanley, 1835-1900
  Coppet (Lake Geneva)          OYB
    OYB. Supplement
  Seascape
    Chew. 250 years of art
HASEN, Burton, 1921-
  Night watch, New Guinea
    IU. Contemp Amer ptg & sculp, 1961
Hasey, Susanna. See Lindall, Susanna (Hasey)
HASHAGEN, A. fl 1847
  Ship Arkansas leaving Havana          DN
    DN. Amer primitive ptgs, pt 1
Hasidic dance by M. Weber
Haskell's house by E. Hopper
Haskins, Hannah Upham, fl 1759
  Badger, J. Hannah Upham Haskins
HASSAM, Childe, 1859-1935
  The alders
    NAD. Amer tradition
  Bailey's beach          ICA
    NYG. Fine art
  Boston Common at twilight          MB
    McCurdy
  Canterbury, 1889          MB
    MB. Ptgs in water color
  Cat boats, Newport          PA
    CSB. Impressionism
  Chez la fleuriste
    PPC. Amer classics
  Church at Old Lyme          NBuA
    NBuA. Catalogue of the ptgs
    NBuA. Expressionism
    NBuA. Fifty ptgs
    Roos
  Church at Old Lyme, Connecticut          NSP
    Time. 300 years (col)
  Cliff rock, Appledore          InIJ
    InIJ. 105 ptgs

Columbus avenue, Boston: rainy day          MWM
  Pierson
Fifth avenue nocturne          OCl
  OCl. Handbook
Golden afternoon, Oregon          MM
  NYG. Fine art
July 14, Rue Daunou          MM
  MM. 100 Amer ptrs
Laurel in the ledges          ATeS
  ATeS. Collection
Little cobbler's shop          MAP
  Pierson
Melting snow, Fifth avenue, 1905          OYB
  OYB. Catalogue 1951
Montauk fisherman
  NSP. Sportscapes
New York window          DC
  DC. 25 biennial ex, 1957
Rainy day, Boston          OT
  Pierson
Southwest wind          MWM
  Pierson
  Richardson. Ptg in America
Street scene in winter          MM
  Mendelowitz
Sunny blue sea          DNC
  Born
  DNC. Gellatly coll, 1954
Union square in spring          MNS
  Larkin
  Larkin rev ed
Washington arch, spring          DP
  Bazin
  DP. Catalogue
Winter nightfall in the city
  NYG. Fine art
Hassam, Frederick Childe. See Hassam, Childe
Hastings landing—Palisade rocks in shadow by G. Harvey
Hastings-on-the-Hudson, going fishing by J. F. Cropsey
Hat display by R. Marsh
Hat seller by E. Berman
Hat, umbrella and bag by J. F. Peto
Hatch, Eunice (Denison)
  Jennys, W. Mrs Reuben Hatch
Hatch, Reuben
  Jennys, W. Major Reuben Hatch
Hatch family
  Johnson, E. Family group (Hatch family)
HATHAWAY, Rufus, 1770-1822
  Joseph Robertson Tolman          DN
    DN. Amer primitive ptgs, pt 2
Hauling in the gill net by F. Remington
Haunted evening by C. E. Burchfield
Haunted house by D. Brown
Haunted house by L. M. Eilshemius
Haunted house by M. Kantor
Haunted house by W. Peirce
Havana bandana by K. Knaths
Havana harbor by R. Crawford
Havana plaza by S. Davis
HAVELL, Robert, 1793-1878
  Pendennis castle, Falmouth, Cornwall          MB
    MB. Ptgs in water color
  Sing Sing, 1856          NScU
    NYG. Fine art

HAVELL, Robert—*Continued*
  View of the Hudson river from Horton's
    road near Croton            MnMI
  Born
            **Attributed works**
  Mohawk valley                 NCHA
    Jones. Rediscovered ptrs
    U.S. National Capital sesquicentennial
      com
Havemeyer, Louisine (Waldron)
  Cassatt, M. Mrs Havemeyer and her
    daughter
Haven, Franklin, fl 1830
  Edwards, T. (attributed works) Franklin
    Haven
HAVILAND, Matilda A. fl 1825
  Tilted bowl                   VWR
    VWR. Folk art (col)
Hawaii
  Culwell, B. L. Where sun and rain mate:
    landscape near Pali, Oahu, Hawaii
Hawks
  Audubon, J. J. Red-tailed hawk
  Spruce, E. F. The hawk
  Wilson, B. Hawk and quail
Hawley, Jesse, 1773-1842
  Ames, E. Jesse Hawley
Hawley family, fl 1801
  Unidentified artist. Nathan Hawley and
    family
Ha-won-je-tah, The One Horn, first chief of
  the Sioux by G. Catlin
HAWTHORNE, Charles Webster, 1872-
  1930
  Adoration of the mother       OYB
    OYB. Accessions
    OYB. Supplement 1959
  The fish and the man          TxD
    CoS. New accessions USA, 1948
  Mrs Alfred L. Becker          InIJ
    InIJ. 105 ptgs
Hawthorne, New York by G. A. Picken
Hay ledge by A. N. Wyeth
Hay wagon by C. S. Price
HAYES, David, 1931-
  Animal and young              NNSG
    NNSG. Handbook
HAYES, George A. fl 1860
  Bare knuckles                 DN
    DN. Amer primitive ptgs, pt 1
    Time. 300 years (col)
Hayes, Patrick, abp, 1867-1938
  Lockman, D. M. Patrick Cardinal Hayes
HAYES, William Jacob, 1830-1875
  Wapiti
    Rathbone
The hayfield by C. Codman
Haying time by A. M. R. Moses
Haymakers by Unidentified artist
Haymaking by W. Homer
Hayne, Alice, fl 1750
  Theus, J. Little Alice Hayne
HAYS, William Jacob, 1872-1934
  Westchester hills
    NYG. Fine art
Haystack: Belle-île, Brittany by D. Mac-
  knight
HAYTER, Stanley William, 1901-
  Falcon
    DC. 20 biennial ex, 1947

Leaping figure
  ICA. Annual ex, 1947/48
Red figure                      MoSL
  CoS. New accessions USA, 1960
Seated witness
  Read. Art now, 1948 ed
Victim                          MoSL
  CoS. New accessions USA, 1950
Hayter, William. See Hayter, Stanley Wil-
  liam
Hazard, Mrs Benjamin. See Lyman, Har-
  riet
Hazard, Harriet (Lyman) See Lyman, Har-
  riet
HAZELL, S. M. fl 1890
  Fox
    NSP. Sportscapes
Hazeltine, William Stanley. See Haseltine,
  William Stanley
Hazy sunrise at sea by M. J. Heade
He did what he wanted by Y. Tanguy
He walks alone by R. Breinin
He who drinks the juice of the stone by G.
  Catlin
HEAD, Josef, 1921-
  Impressions of Milan
    IU. Contemp Amer ptg & sculp, 1953
Head by J. Glasco
Head by A. H. Maurer
Head by W. Pachner
Head by C. S. Price
Head in landscape by A. H. Maurer
Head in motion by A. H. Maurer
Head of a cretin by B. Shahn
Head of an old man by F. Duveneck
Head of Stevie by L. Rivers
Head of winter by P. Tchelitchew
Head XXVI by L. A. Golub
Head waters of Juniata by T. Cole
Head with yellow ground by K. Khosrovi
HEADE, Martin Johnson, 1819-1904
  Apple blossoms
    WiMiA. Amer ptg 1760-1960
  Approaching storm: beach near Newport
                                MB
    MB. Karolik coll
  Pierson
    Time. 300 years (col)
  Bay of Panama                 MB
    MB. Karolik coll
  Cloudy day, Rhode Island      MB
    MB. Karolik coll
  Dawn                          MB
    MB. Karolik coll
  Hazy sunrise at sea           VtMS
    NUM. Art across America
  High tide on the marshes      OCl
    OCl. Handbook
  Hummingbirds and gold and purple or-
    chids
    Chew. 250 years of art
  Hummingbirds and orchids      MiD
    Pierson
    Richardson. Ptg in America
  Hunters resting               MB
    MB. Karolik coll
  Lake George
    Baur. Amer ptg

Magnolia grandiflora                     MB
  MB. Karolik coll
Magnolias                                MB
  MB. Karolik coll
Mary Rebecca Clark                       MB
  MB. Karolik coll
Off shore: after the storm               MB
  MB. Karolik coll
On the Sebastian river, Florida
  Born
Orchids and hummingbird                  MB
  Larkin
  Larkin rev ed
  MB. Karolik coll
Orchids and spray orchids with humming-
  birds                                  MB
  MB. Karolik coll
Passion flowers and hummingbirds         MB
  MB. Karolik coll
Rocks in New England                     MB
  MB. Karolik coll
Rocky shore                              MB
  MB. Karolik coll
Roses on a palette                       MB
  MB. Karolik coll
Salt marshes, Newport, Rhode Island MB
  MB. Karolik coll
South American river                     MB
  MB. Karolik coll
  Pierson
Spring shower, Connecticut valley MB
  Baur. Revolution
  MB. Karolik coll
  Pierson
Storm approaching Narragansett bay
  Mendelowitz
Storm over Narragansett bay              OYB
  OYB. Supplement 1959
Stranded boat                            MB
  MB. Karolik coll
Sunset                                   MiD
  MiD. Treasures
Sunset, Black rock, Connecticut          MB
  MB. Karolik coll
Sunset: Lake Champlain                   MB
  MB. Karolik coll
Sunset on Long beach                     MB
  MB. Karolik coll
Sunset over the marshes                  MB
  MB. Karolik coll
Sunset: tropical marshes                 MB
  MB. Karolik coll
Tropical landscape
  Born
Vase of mixed flowers                    MB
  MB. Karolik coll
Water lily                               MB
  MB. Karolik coll
Headed for Boston by J. Marin
Headland by H. E. Mattson
Headless horse who wants to jump by Y.
  Kuniyoshi
Headless horseman by W. Gropper
Heads by A. Rattner
Heads by M. Weber
Heads or tails by C. M. Russell
Healy, Agnes
  Healy, G. P. A. Agnes and Mary Healy
Healy Edith, b 1848?
  Healy, G. P. A. Mrs Healy and Edith:
    The Healy garden in Paris

HEALY, George Peter Alexander, 1813-
  1894                                   DC
Abraham Lincoln                          DC
  DC. Masterpieces
  Time. 300 years (col)
Abraham Lincoln                          DN
  U.S. National Capital sesquicentennial
    com
  VR. Healy's sitters
Agnes and Mary Healy                     KyLS
  VR. Healy's sitters
Albert G. Brackett                       DN
  VR. Healy's sitters
Albert J. Myer                           DNC
  VR. Healy's sitters
Alice Tyler
  VR. Healy's sitters
Andrew Jackson                           DC
  VR. Healy's sitters
Arch of Titus                            NJN
  Larkin
  Larkin rev ed
  MiD. Travelers in Arcadia
  Pierson (Here as by Church, Healy
    and McEntee)
  U.S. National Capital sesquicentennial
    com
  VR. Healy's sitters
Asher, B. Durand (?)                     NNHS
  VR. Healy's sitters
Ave de Pennedegie
  VR. Healy's sitters
Benjamin Franklin at the court of Louis
  XVI                                    PPhA
  VR. Healy's sitters
Boating party on the Thames, excursion
  of the Healy and Whitehouse families
  VR. Healy's sitters
Bryan family                             VR
  VR. Healy's sitters
Cardinal McCloskey                       ICN
  Barker. Amer ptg
  VR. Healy's sitters
Charles I, king of Roumania              ICN
  De Mare. G. P. A. Healy
  VR. Healy's sitters
Charles Goodyear
  VR. Healy's sitters
Chester A. Arthur                        DC
  VR. Healy's sitters
Daniel Webster                           VR
  De Mare. G. P. A. Healy
  VR. Healy's sitters
Edward Everett                           ICN
  VR. Healy's sitters
Elizabeth, queen of Roumania             ICN
  De Mare. G. P. A. Healy
  VR. Healy's sitters
Emma Thrusby                             NNHS
  VR. Healy's sitters
Ferdinand de Lesseps                     ICN
  VR. Healy's sitters
François Pierre Guillaume Guizot         DNC
  De Mare. G. P. A. Healy
  VR. Healy's sitters
Franklin Pierce                          MB
  MB. Karolik coll
Franklin Pierce                          DC
  VR. Healy's sitters
Franz Liszt                              ICN
  De Mare. G. P. A. Healy
  VR. Healy's sitters

**HEATH, James,** 1757-1834
George Washington (after G. Stuart)
Frankenstein. Two journeyman ptrs

Portrait of the artist
Stuart, G. James Heath
**Heathcote, Caleb,** 1666-1721
Unidentified artist. Caleb Heathcote
**HEATON, William,** 1918-
Heraldic hedge
IU. Contemp Amer ptg & sculp, 1959
The **heavens** by R. Tamayo
**Heavy,** heavy by R. Kent
**Heavy** industry by A. Alcalay
**Heavy** sea, Manchester by M. R. Sturgis
**Heavy** the oar to him who is tired, heavy
the coat, heavy the sea by I. L. Al-
bright
**Hebrew** books, holy day books by B. Shahn
**Hector** parting with his wife and child at
the Scæan gate by B. West
**HEDRICK, Wally,** 1928-
Around painting
MMA. Sixteen
Circle painting, 4
MMA. Sixteen
For service rendered
MMA. Sixteen
Heroic image
MMA. Sixteen
Spirit
MMA. Sixteen
**Heeling** a bad one by C. M. Russell
**HEGELHEIMER, William,** 1928-
Landscape
MBIC. View 1960
**HEIDEL, Frederick,** 1915-
OrPA. Ptgs & sculptures              OrPA
**Height** by K. Okada
**HEIL, Charles Emile,** 1870-
Bay-breasted warbler on apple blossom
MB
MB. Ptgs in water color
Chestnut-sided warbler on barberry   MB
MB. Ptgs in water color
Field sparrow on blackberry          MB
MB. Ptgs in water color
Lotus                                MB
MB. Ptgs in water color
Ovenbird and pink lady's slipper     MB
MB. Ptgs in water color
Young crow                           MB
MB. Ptgs in water color
**HEINE, Sebastian**
Southwest portion of the public square,
Cleveland
Barker. Amer ptg
**Heir** to the future by A. Refregier
The **heirloom** man by B. Greene
**HEITLAND, Wilmot Emerton,** 1893-
Road to Bonao                        ICA
NYG. Fine art
Sheepshead shore
NAD. Annual ex, spring 1950
**Held** up by N. H. Trotter
**Helen** by J. Sloan
**Heliker, Edward.** See Heliker, John Edward
**HELIKER, Jacob,** 1917-
Cliffs, Soames sound
WMAA. Annual ex, 1960

**HELIKER, John Edward,** 1909-
Boats                                ATeS
ATeS. Collection
East river
Cheney. Story 1958 ed
WMAA. New decade
From Cranberry isle                  WMAA
Goodrich. Amer art
Imaginary landscape                  IU
IU. Contemp Amer ptg, 1949
IU. 20th century
Maine coast
Gruskin
IU. Contemp Amer ptg & sculp, 1955
Maine rocks
CSFP. Annual ex, 1948/49
Mediterranean landscape              NeL
CoS. New accessions USA, 1950
Monreale                             PPhM
IU. Contemp Amer ptg, 1951
Pierson
WMAA. New decade
Nova Scotia landscape                OCl
CoS. New accessions USA, 1958
Of Maine                             WMAA
Baur. Nature
Old factory                          ATU
ATU. Coll of Amer art
Palazzo
Pousette-Dart. Amer ptg
Perilous night
NAD. Annual ex, 1948
Scava
MMA. Abstract
Self-portrait, 1957
VR. Amer ptg, 1958
Self-portrait, 1958
WiMiA. Amer ptg 1760-1960
Spring
IU. Contemp Amer ptg & sculp, 1961
Tarquinia
IU. Contemp Amer ptg, 1950
Viterbo
IU. Contemp Amer ptg & sculp, 1953
White rocks, Nova Scotia             WMAA
Pierson
WMAA. Sara Roby (col)
**Helios** in the lead by H. G. Keller
**Hell** Gate bridge by W. H. Smith
**Hell** Gate tie by G. Vass
**Hell** hole by C. H. Demuth
**Helleu, Paul César,** 1859-1927
Sargent, J. S. Paul Helleu
Sargent, J. S. Paul Helleu sketching and
his wife
**Helmund** II by J. V. Harvey
**Hemenway, Harriet (Lawrence)** fl 1890
Sargent, J. S. Mrs Augustus Hemenway
**Hemlock** by J. Mitchell
**Hemlock** pool by J. H. Twachtman
**Henderson, John,** 1747-1785
Stuart, G. John Henderson
**Hendrickson, Catharine,** fl 1770
Unidentified artist. Catharine Hendrick-
son
**Henka.** See Sawyer, Helen Alton
**HENNESSEY, Timothy**
Madonna enthroned                    MCH
Pulitzer v2

HENRI, Robert, 1865-1929
Beach hat                          MiD
  PA. Annual ex, 1955
Blind Spanish singer
  NBuA. Fifty ptgs
Dutch girl in white                MM
  MM. 100 Amer ptrs
Dutch Joe                          WiMi
  Roos
East river, snow
  Brown. Amer ptg
  PA. Annual ex, 1955
Eva Green                          KW
  PA. Annual ex, 1955
  Pierson
Fifty-seventh street. See West 57th street
  in 1902
George Luks                        CanO
  PA. Annual ex, 1955
  Pierson
Guide to Croaghan
  PA. Annual ex, 1955
Gypsy with a cigarette             IBM
  Bazin
Herself                            ICA
  NYG. Fine art
Himself                            ICA
  NYG. Fine art
Indian girl                        InIJ
  InIJ. 105 ptgs
Irish girl                         ATeS
  ATeS. Collection
Jimmie O'D                         NJMo
  NJMo. Forty years
John Sloan, 1906
  Brooks. John Sloan
Laughing child                     WMAA
  Chew. 250 years of art
Little dancer                      OYB
  OYB. Catalogue 1951
La Madrilenita                     GST
  NUM. Art across America
Mary                               MAP
  Larkin
  Larkin rev ed
Mary Gallagher                     NJN
  Mendelowitz
Moira
  NSyE. The eight
New York street in winter
  Walker. Ptgs from America
Old model and her daughter
  Time. 300 years (col)
Picnic at Menhoppen, Pennsylvania, July
  4, 1902                          PW
  Chew. 250 years of art
Sea and cliffs
  McKinney
Sissy                              GAtM
  GAtM. Holbrook collection
Storm tide
  Goodrich. Amer art
West 57th street in 1902 (Fifty-seventh
  street)                          CtY
  Brown. Amer ptg
  PA. Annual ex, 1955
  Pierson
William Glackens, 1904
  Glackens
Willie Gee                         NJN
  Brown. Amer ptg

Young woman in white               DN
  McCurdy
  PA. Annual ex, 1955
  Robb. Harper history
Zenka of Bohemia
  NAD. Amer tradition
HENRIKSEN, Mae
Abandoned
  NAD. Special ex, 1956
HENRY, Edward Lamson, 1841-1919
City point, Virginia, headquarters of Gen-
  eral Grant                       MAP
  U.S. National Capital sesquicentennial
  com
The 9:45 accommodation, Stratford, Conn.,
  1867                             MM
  Barker. Amer ptg
  Davidson v2
  Pierson
The old Westover mansion           DC
  U.S. National Capital sesquicentennial
  com
Henry, William, fl 1755
  West, B. William Henry
HENSEL, Hopkins, 1921-
Clown with rooster                 MB
  CoS. New accessions USA, 1946
Drummers
  IU. Contemp Amer ptg, 1948
Ice cream parlor                   OT
  PPC. Ptg in the U.S. 1949
The widow
  IU. Contemp Amer ptg, 1949
Henshaw, Horatio Gates, fl 1839
  Bascom, R. H. M. Horatio Gates Hen-
  shaw
Henshaw, Mrs Horatio Gates (?) fl 1839
  Bascom, R. H. M. Lady in a sheer white
  cap (possibly Mrs Horatio Gates Hen-
  shaw)
Henshaw, Joshua, 1703-1777
  Copley, J. S. Joshua Henshaw
Henshaw, Ruth. See Bascom, Ruth (Hen-
  shaw) Miles
Her majesty the Barque II by L. Feininger
Her world by P. Evergood
Heraldic ground by J. Muller
Heraldic hedge by W. Heaton
Herbert, George Hubert, 1872-1949
  Lockman, D. M. Coco the clown
Herbert, Jane. See Vanderveer, Jane (Her-
  bert)
The Herbert children by L. Sachs
Hercules (ship)
  Unidentified artist. Ship Hercules of Sa-
  lem, 1809
Hérédité des caractères by Y. Tanguy
HERFF, Charles Adelbert, 1853-1943
  Hanging of Bob Augustin
  Ford. Pictorial folk art
HERFORD, Oliver, 1863-1935
Spider's nightmare                 MB
  MB. Ptgs in water color
HERING, Harry, 1887-
Woodstock art conference
  PPC. Ptg in the U.S. 1949
HERIOT, George
The Capitol after the British assault on
  Washington, 1815                 NNHS
  Davidson v 1

Herkimer by R. Eshoo
**Hermann-Neisse, Max**
  Grosz, G. Max Hermann-Neisse (Dr Neisse)
**Hermitage,** Talavera by H. G. Keller
**Herndon** hotel, Omaha, Nebraska by F. Haklhuber
**Hero** by K. Okada
**Heroic** figures by J. De Diego
**Heroic** image by W. Hedrick
**Herons**
  Audubon, J. J. Green heron
  Audubon, J. J. Snowy heron or white egret
**Herrera, José**
  Hurd, P. José Herrera
**Herreshoff, Carl Frederick, 1763-1819**
  Malbone, E. G. Carl F. Herreshoff
**Herreshoff, Sarah (Brown)** See Brown, Sarah
**Herring** net by W. Homer
**Herriot, Mary (Ouldfield)** fl 1761
  Theus, J. Polly Ouldfield of Winyah
**Herriot, Mrs Robert.** See Herriot, Mary (Ouldfield)
**HERRON, Davis, 1908-**
  St Louis cemetery, New Orleans          ATU
  ATU. Coll of Amer art
**HERSCH, Lee, 1896-**
  Number 3G
  ICA. Annual ex, 1947/48
**Herself** by R. Henri
**HERZOG, Hermann, 1832-**
  Grandfather's lesson
  NSP. Sportscapes
**HESS, J. N.**
  Rail shooting
  NSP. Sportscapes
**HESS, James,** fl 1879
  University of Kansas, c 1879          KLU
  U.S. National Capital sesquicentennial com
**HESS, Leta English**
  Still life
  DC. 26 biennial ex, 1959
**HESSELIUS, Gustavus, 1682-1755**
  Bacchanalian revel
    Flexner. First flowers
  Bacchus and Ariadne          MiD
    MiD. Ptg in America
    MiD. Treasures
    Pierson
    Richardson. Ptg in America
  Lapowinsa          PH
    Flexner. Amer ptg
    Flexner. First flowers
    Flexner. Short history
    Mendelowitz
    Pierson
    Roos
  The last supper
    Flexner. First flowers
  Mrs Lydia Hesselius          PH
    Pierson
  Self-portrait          PH
    Flexner. First flowers
    Pierson
    Roos

Tishcohan
  Barker. Amer ptg
  Flexner. First flowers
  U.S. National Capital sesquicentennial com
**Hesselius, Mrs Gustavus.** See Hesselius, Lydia (Addison)
**HESSELIUS, John, 1728-1778**
  Abraham Keteltas
    Pierson
  Charles Calvert and his Negro slave          MdBM
    Barker. Amer ptg
    Flexner. First flowers
    ICA. From colony to nation (col cover detail)
    NYG. Fine art
    Pierson
    Roos
    Time. 300 years (col)
    UNESCO. Prior to 1860
    UNESCO. Prior to 1860 3d ed
  Elizabeth Calvert          MdBM
    Larkin
    Larkin rev ed
  Margaret Robins          DN
    DN. Amer primitive ptgs, pt 2
  Mrs Abraham Keteltas
    Pierson
  Mrs Richard Galloway jr of Cedar Park, Maryland          MM
    Mendelowitz
    Pierson
    Roos
  Mrs William Allen          MiD
    Belknap
  Samuel Lloyd Chew
    Chew. 250 years of art
  Sarah Fitzhugh          MdBH
    Belknap
**Hesselius, Lydia (Addison)** d 1745?
  Hesselius, G. Mrs Lydia Hesselius
**HETZEL, George, 1826-1899**
  Sunshine and shadow
    Chew. 250 years of art
**HEWES, Madeline, 1910-**
  Autumn
    VR. Amer ptg, 1954
  Hollow hill pastoral
    PPC. Ptg in the U.S. 1949
  The outing
    PPC. International ex, 1952
**Hewitt, Mr**
  Jennys, W. Mr Hewitt
**Hewitt, Mrs**
  Jennys, W. Mrs Hewitt
**Heyward, Daniel, 1720-1778**
  Theus, J. Col Daniel Heyward
**Heyward, Mrs Daniel.** See Heyward, Jane Elizabeth (Gignilliat)
**Heyward, Elizabeth (Savage)** 1770-1833
  Malbone, E. G. Mrs Thomas Heyward jr
**Heyward, Hannah Miles, 1773-1867**
  Malbone, E. G. Hannah Miles Hayward
**Heyward, Jane Elizabeth (Gignilliat)**
  Theus, J. Mrs Daniel Heyward
**Heyward, Maria Miles, 1784-1862**
  Malbone, E. G. Maria Miles Heyward
**Hialeah** by A. Leslie
**HICKS, Edward, 1780-1849**
  Bridge sign
    Ford. Edward Hicks

**HICKS, Edward**—*Continued*
Columbus
  Ford. Edward Hicks
Cornell farm                                    DN
  Brussels. Exposition
  DN. Amer primitive ptgs, pt 2
  Lipman. Primitive ptrs
Cornell farm (Lee coll)
  Ford. Edward Hicks (col)
Declaration of Independence                     DN
  DN. Amer primitive ptgs, pt 2
  Ford. Edward Hicks
Declaration of Independence (Lipman
  coll)
  Lipman. Primitive ptrs
Falls of Niagara
  Ford. Edward Hicks
  Lipman. Primitive ptrs
Grave of William Penn                           VWR
  VWR. Folk art (col)
Grave of William Penn (Garbisch coll)
  Ford. Edward Hicks pl 26
Grave of William Penn (Hicks coll)
  Ford. Edward Hicks
Hillborn farm
  Ford. Edward Hicks
Innocence, meekness, liberty
  Ford. Edward Hicks
Landscape
  Ford. Edward Hicks pl 33
Noah's ark                                      PPhM
  Ford. Edward Hicks (col)
  Ford. Pictorial folk art
Peaceable kingdom                               NBuA
  Baur. Amer ptg
  Ford. Edward Hicks
  Ford. Edward Hicks pl 34
  NBuA. Catalogue of the ptgs
Peaceable kingdom                               PPhM
  Canaday
  Canaday (detail)
  Ford. Edward Hicks
Peaceable kingdom                               DP
  DP. Catalogue
Peaceable kingdom                               MWM
  Flexner. Light of distant skies
  Ford. Edward Hicks pl 21
  Janson. Picture history
Peaceable kingdom                               NCHA
  Ford. Edward Hicks (col)
  Taylor. Fifty centuries, 1954 ed (col)
  Time. 300 years (col)
Peaceable kingdom                               NNHS
  Ford. Edward Hicks
  OCiM. Rediscoveries
Peaceable kingdom                               NBM
  Ford. Pictorial folk art
  Larkin
  Larkin rev ed
  Newmeyer
  NYG. Fine art
  Riley. Your art heritage
Peaceable kingdom                               OCl
  OCl. Handbook
Peaceable kingdom                               MMA
  UNESCO. Prior to 1860 3d ed
  UNESCO. Prior to 1860 5th ed
  UNESCO. 1860-1949
  Walker. Ptgs from America
Peaceable kingdom                               VWR
  VWR. Amer folk art (col)
  VWR. Folk art (col)

Peaceable kingdom (Cahill coll)
  Flexner. Short history (col detail)
  Ford. Edward Hicks pl 24
  Lipman. Primitive ptrs (col)
  Pierson
  Richardson. Ptg in America (col)
  Robb. Harper history (col)
Peaceable kingdom (Carle coll)
  Ford. Edward Hicks pl 1
  Ford. Edward Hicks pl 3
The peaceable kingdom (Carlen coll)
  Ford. Edward Hicks pl 35
Peaceable kingdom (Grossman coll)
  Ford. Edward Hicks
Peaceable kingdom (Halpert coll)
  Chew. 250 years of art
  DC. Halpert collection
The peaceable kingdom (Kirk coll)
  Ford. Edward Hicks pl 23
Peaceful kingdom                                DN
  DN. Amer primitive ptgs, pt 1
Penn's treaty with the Indians                  DN
  DN. Amer primitive ptgs, pt 1
Penn's treaty with the Indians (1)
  Ford. Edward Hicks
Penn's treaty with the Indians (2)
  OCiM. Rediscoveries
Penn's treaty with the Indians (Carle coll)
  Flexner. Light of distant skies
Residence of David Twining                      MMA
  Barker. Amer ptg
  Davidson v 1
  Ford. Edward Hicks
  Ford. Pictorial folk art
Residence of David Twining                      VWR
  Larkin rev ed (col)
  Pierson
  VWR. Folk art (col)
Washington crossing the Delaware
  Lipman. Primitive ptrs

**Attributed works**
The lion family
  Ford. Pictorial folk art
**Portrait of the artist**
Hicks, T. Edward Hicks
**HICKS, Thomas,** 1823-1890
Barber shop, the musicale                       NoCR
  NoCR. Catalogue
Edward Hicks
  Ford. Edward Hicks
Gerard Stuyvesant                               NNHS
  Vail. Stuyvesant ports
Hamilton Fish                                   NNCH
  Barker. Amer ptg
  Larkin
  Larkin rev ed
Sarah Margaret Fuller, Marchioness Ossoli
  MiD. Travelers in Arcadia
**Hicks, Whitehead,** 1728-1770
  Copley, J. S. (attributed works) White-
    head Hicks
**Hicks, Zechariah,** 1755-1842
  Pelham, H. (attributed works) Zechariah
    Hicks (?)
The **hidden** apple by P. Evergood
**Hidden** spring by G. Bartlett
**Hide-and-seek** by W. M. Chase
**Hide-and-seek** by P. Tchelitchew
**Hideout** by D. G. Blythe
**HIDLEY, Joseph H.** 1830-1872
Fort Plain, New York, c 1865
  Lipman. Primitive ptrs

Glass house lake
  Lipman. Primitive ptrs
Poestenkill, New York          NCHA
  Born
  Ford. Pictorial folk art
  Jones. Rediscovered ptrs
Poestenkill, New York, summer
  Lipman. Primitive ptrs
Poestenkill, New York, winter
  Lipman. Primitive ptrs
West Sand lake
  Lipman. Primitive ptrs

**Attributed works**

Noah's ark          VWR
  VR. Amer folk art
**Higby, J.** fl 1800
  Malbone, E. G. J. Higby
**HIGGINS, Eugene,** 1874-1958
  The gamblers          MM
    Pierson
  Les pauvres
    Brown. Amer ptg
  Share croppers
    NAD. Annual ex, autumn 1949
  Weary
    Baur. Revolution
**HIGGINS, Victor,** 1884-1949
  Fiesta day          OYB
    OYB. Catalogue 1951
  Holy week procession          InIJ
    InIJ. 105 ptgs
  Indian fields          MB
    MB. Ptgs in water color
**Higgins** pier by M. Sterne
**Higginson, Mrs George.** See Higginson,
  Martha Hubbard (Babcock)
**Higginson, Henry Lee,** 1834-1919
  Sargent, J. S. Maj Henry Lee Higginson
**Higginson, Martha Hubbard (Babcock)**
  1781-1863
  Malbone, E. G. Mrs George Higginson
**High** bridge by P. Dickinson
**High** bridge by E. Lawson
**High** bridge by H. W. Ranger
**High** bridge, New York by A. C. Goodwin
**High** cliff, coast of Maine by W. Homer
**High** houses by L. Feininger
**High** noon by A. G. Dove
**High** noon by E. Hopper
**High** peak by M. R. Barnes
**High** priest by K. L. Seligman
**High** snow—low sun by T. Stamos
**High** street bus barn by L. Bouché
**High** tension tower by L. Gatch
**High** tide by J. Gerard
**High** tide (detail) by W. Homer
**High** tide on the marshes by M. J. Heade
**High** water in the Bayou country by Un-
  identified artist
**High** yaller by R. Marsh
**Highland** light by M. Kantor
**Highland** light by J. Kaplan
The **Highlands** from West Point, View of
  by J. F. Weir
**Highway** by G. Tooker
**Hilda** by B. Karfiol

**HILDEBRANDT, Lily**
  Horses          CtY
    Rathbun
**Hildreth, Samuel**
  Corwine, A. H. Dr Samuel Hildreth
**HILL, John William,** 1812-1897
  Bethlehem, Pennsylvania          NNPL
    McClintock
  Hudson river bridge near Waterford
                                      NNHS
    Jones. Rediscovered ptrs
  Scene on the Erie canal
    Davidson v2
    WiMiA. Amer ptg 1760-1960
  Schenectady, N.Y.          NNHS
    Jones. Rediscovered ptrs
**HILL, Thomas,** 1829-1908
  Bridal veil and El Capitan, Yosemite val-
    ley
    Sears. Highlights
  El Capitan, Yosemite valley near Mirror
    lake
    Born
  The covey
    NSP. Sportscapes
  Fishing party in the mountains          CSFD
    Born
  The Harvey breaker, West Nanticoke
    McClintock
  Wyoming valley (1)
    McClintock
  Wyoming valley (2)
    McClintock
**Hill** beyond the bridge by P. S. Sample
**Hill** in winter by D. Macknight
**Hill,** Main street, Gloucester by J. Sloan
**Hill** of death, upper Missouri by G. Catlin
**Hill** town by L. Goldin
**Hill** town by C. Prendergast
**Hill** town in Campania by R. Morgan
**Hillborn** farm by E. Hicks
**Hillside** by J. S. Sargent
**Hillhouse, James,** 1754-1832
  Vanderlyn, J. James Hillhouse
**Hillhouse, James Abraham,** 1789-1841
  Jocelyn, N. James Abraham Hillhouse
**Hillhouse, Thomas,** 1766-1834
  Ames, E. Thomas Hillhouse
**Hills, Huldah (Mulford)** 1806-1878
  Ames, E. Mrs John Hills
**Hills** by B. Karfiol
**Hills** of the Trap formation by S. Seymour
**Hills,** South Truro by E. Hopper
**HILLSMITH, Fannie,** 1911-
  Dark and light
    IU. Contemp Amer ptg & sculp, 1959
  The house
    ICA. Annual ex, 1947/48
  Interior at Honfleur
    IU. Contemp Amer ptg & sculp, 1961
  Midnight
    IU. Contemp Amer ptg & sculp, 1955
  Queen's gambit
    PPC. International ex, 1955
  Signs of the city
    NNSG. Younger Amer ptrs
  Town house
    IU. Contemp Amer ptg & sculp, 1957
**HILTON, Roy,** 1892-
  Ivory tower
    IU. Contemp Amer ptg, 1952

Himmel by M. Hartley
Himself by R. Henri
HINCHEY, William J. 1829-1893
  Dedication of the Eads bridge at St
    Louis, Missouri, 1874
  U.S. National Capital sesquicentennial
    com
HINCKLEY, Thomas Hewes, 1813-1896
  Cows and sheep in pasture
    Sears. Highlights
  Great Blue hill and Neponset river
    Sears. Highlights
  Noon
    Sears. Highlights
  Rotherham, Yorkshire, England    **MB**
    MB. Karolik coll
HINKLE, Clarence K. 1880-
  Spring landscape
    CSFP. Annual ex, 1952
HINKLEY, Thomas, 1879-
  Fox in West Virginia
    NSP. Sportscapes
Hipparchus by C. Gray
Hiroshima by E. Reindel
HIRSCH, Joseph, 1910-
  Air raid    **MM**
    MM. 100 Amer ptrs
  Carcass
    IU. Contemp Amer ptg, 1952
    NAD. Annual ex, 1954
  The confidence
    Baur. Revolution
  The couple    **MSM**
    CoS. New accessions USA, 1958
    WMAA. Contemp Amer ptg, 1955
  Dance
    ICA. Annual ex, 1959/60
  Departure
    PPC. International ex, 1950
  Digger
    Genauer (col)
  Editorial    **ATU**
    ATU. Coll of Amer art
  The iceman
    NAD. Annual ex, 1947, 1st half
  Memorial
    NAD. Annual ex, 1957
  Nine men
    MM. Amer ptg today
    PPC. Ptg in the U.S. 1949
  An old man    **MB**
    Wight. Milestones
  Politicians    **WMAA**
    Larkin
  Prisoner    **WMAA**
    CSB. Illusion
  The senator    **WMAA**
    Larkin rev ed
    Pierson
  Singing man
    CSFP. Annual ex, 1947/48
  Triumph
    IU. Contemp Amer ptg, 1950
HIRSCH, Stefan, 1899-
  Lower Manhattan (New York, Lower
    Manhattan    **DP**
    Brown. Amer ptg
    Cheney. Story 1958 ed
    MnMW. Precisionist view
  Nurenberg
    Genauer
  Pic of Orizaba    **WMAA**
    Pierson

HIRSHFIELD, Morris, 1872-1946
  Artist and his model
  50 years of mod art
  Daniel in the lion's den
    Read. Art now 1948
  Girl in a mirror    **MMA**
    Pierson
  Girl with pigeons
    Rathbun
  Nude at window
    Read. Art now 1948
    Wight. Milestones
  Tiger    **MMA**
    Baur. Revolution
    Lipman. Primitive ptrs
    McCurdy
  Two women in front of a mirror
    Jean. Surrealist ptg
HIRST, Claude Raguet, d 1942
  An interesting book
    Frankenstein. After the hunt
His first crossing by G. Biddle
Hiscox, Thomas, 1686-1773
  Feke, R. Rev Thomas Hiscox
Historical monument of the American re-
  public by E. S. Field
Historical themes

### Great Britain
*14th century*
West, B. King Edward III entertain-
  ing his prisoners after the battle of
  Calais
West, B. Queen Philippa interceding for
  the burgesses of Calais
*17th century*
West, B. General Monk receiving
  Charles II on the beach at Dover
*18th century*
Trumbull, J. Sortie from Gibraltar

### Rome
West, B. Agrippina and her children
  mourning the ashes of Germanicus
West, B. Agrippina landing at Brundi-
  sium with the ashes of Germanicus
West, B. The appeal of Coriolanus

### Sparta
West, B. Cleombrotus ordered into ban-
  ishment by Leonidas II, king of
  Sparta

### United States
*See also* Indians of North America—
  Wars
*Colonial period*
Hicks, E. Penn's treaty with the Indians
Pine, R. E. and Savage, E. Congress
  voting independence, July, 1776
West, B. Penn's treaty with the Indians
*Revolutionary period*
*See also* names of battles, e.g. Bunker
  Hill, Battle of; Concord, Battle of;
  Princeton, Battle of
Bingham, G. C. Washington crossing the
  Delaware
Earl, R. British troops at Concord
Hicks, E. Declaration of independence
Kemmelmeyer, F. George Washington
  reviewing the western army at Fort
  Cumberland

Leutze, E. Washington crossing the Delaware
Peale, J. Washington and his generals at Yorktown
Pine, R. E. and Savage, E. Congress voting independence, July, 1776
Reed, R. L. Washington and Lafayette at the battle of Yorktown
Remick, C. Blockade of Boston, View of
Rivers, L. Washington crossing the Delaware
Serres, D. British fleet forcing the Hudson river passage, 1776
Toole, J. Capture of Major André
Trumbull, J. Attack on Quebec
Trumbull, J. Capture of the Hessians at Trenton
Trumbull, J. Death of General Mercer at the battle of Princeton
Trumbull, J. Declaration of Independence
Trumbull, J. Resignation of General Washington at Annapolis
Trumbull, J. Signing the Declaration of Independence
Trumbull, J. Surrender of General Burgoyne at Saratoga
Trumbull, J. Surrender of Lord Cornwallis at Yorktown
Tucker, A. Washington crossing the Delaware
West, B. Conference of the treaty of peace with England
White, J. B. Gen Marion in his swamp encampment inviting a British officer to dinner

*1800-1860*

Birch, T. The Constitution and the Guerrière
Catlin, G. Virginia constitutional convention of 1829-30
Corné, M. F. Bombardment of Tripoli under Commodore Preble, 1804
Corné, M. F. The Constitution and the Guerrière
Myers, W. H. Battle of the plains of Mesa, 1847
Unidentified artist. Privateer schooner Surprise of Baltimore capturing the British ship Star, 1815

*Civil war*

Bierstadt, A. Bombardment of Fort Sumter
Bingham, G. C. Gen Nathaniel Lyon and Gen Frank P. Blair starting from the Arsenal gate in St Louis to capture Camp Jackson
Bingham, G. C. Order no 11, 1869
Carlin, A. B. Sherman's march through Georgia
Chapman, C. W. Fort Sumter, December 8, 1863
Chappel, A. Surrender at Appomattox
Hamilton, J. Monitor and Merrimac
Homer, W. Defiance: Inviting a shot before Petersburg, Virginia, 1864
Homer, W. Prisoners from the front
Homer, W. Skirmish in The Wilderness
Hopper, E. Light battery at Gettysburg
O'Neil, M. Civil war encampment
Siporan, M. Order No 11

Unidentified artist. Attack of the rebel ram Manassas on the U.S.S. Pensacola
Unidentified artist. Camp Butler, Maryland, 1861
Unidentified artist. Civil war battle scene
Unidentified artist. Civil war—Symbolic panorama
Unidentified artist. Fourth Pennsylvania cavalry

*Spanish-American war*

Glackens, W. J. The night after San Juan: tending the wounded
Remington, F. Charge of the Rough Riders at San Juan Hill
Remington, F. The scream of shrapnel at San Juan hill, Cuba, July 1, 1898
Zogbaum, R. F. Admiral Dewey at Manila bay, 1898

History of communication by S. Davis
History of the early United States by T. H. Benton
Hitchcock, Samuel Johnson, 1786-1845
Flagg, J. B. Samuel Johnson Hitchcock
Hite, Mrs Isaac, fl 1790
Polk, C. P. Mrs Isaac Hite and James Madison Hite
Hnizdovsky, Jacques. See Hnizdovsky, Yakiv
HNIZDOVSKY, Yakiv, 1915-
New housing
   IU. Contemp Amer ptg & sculp, 1961
New York subway                    OYB
   OYB. Annual 1960
Passage Denfert
   IU. Contemp Amer ptg & sculp, 1959
Hobbs, Sarah, fl 1830
Unidentified artist. Sarah Hobbs
Hobby horse by Unidentified artist
Hockaday, Susan Howard, fl 1859
Bingham, G. C. Susan Howard Hockaday and her daughter Susan
Hoeing by R. Gwathmey
Hoeing tobacco by R. Gwathmey
HOENER, Arthur, 1929-
Seated figure, Yakshi
   MBIC. View 1960
HOFF, Margo
City builders
   IU. Contemp Amer ptg & sculp, 1959
Dream of flying
   IU. Contemp Amer ptg, 1951
Gypsy's house
   IU. Contemp Amer ptg, 1950
Mosque
   IU. Contemp Amer ptg & sculp, 1955
Surprise party
   IU. Contemp Amer ptg & sculp, 1953
Wind rose
   IU. Contemp Amer ptg & sculp, 1961
Woman in a white room
   IU. Contemp Amer ptg & sculp, 1957
Hoffman, Eliza, 1779-1857
Hubard, W. J. Eliza Hoffman
Hoffman, Harriet Emily, 1815-1892
Hubard, W. J. Jeremiah Hoffman and daughter
Hoffman, Jeremiah, 1777-1845
Hubard, W. J. Jeremiah Hoffman and his daughter
Hoffman, John, 1772-1837
Hubard, W. J. John Hoffman

**Hoffman, William Henry,** 1813-1865
  Sully, T. William Henry Hoffman
    (replica)
**Hoffman's** slough by A. N. Wyeth
**HOFMANN, Charles,** fl 1872-78
  View of Benjamin Reber's farm    DN
    DN. Amer primitive ptgs, pt 1
    Time. 300 years (col)
  View of the Schuylkill county almshouse
    property, Pennsylvania, 1876    DN
    DN. Amer primitive ptgs, pt 2
  Views of the buildings and surroundings
    of the Berks county almshouse, 1878
                       DN
    U.S. National Capital sesquicentennial
    com
**HOFMANN, Hans,** 1880-1957
  Aggressive
    Wight. Hans Hofmann
  Ambush                   MMA
    Biddle. Yes and no
  Apparition
    IU. Contemp Amer ptg, 1950
  Birth of Taurus
    Wight. Hans Hofmann (col)
  Black demon              MAP
    CoS. New accessions USA, 1948
  Blue enchantment
    IU. Contemp Amer ptg, 1952
    Pousette-Dart. Amer ptg
  Blue rhythm              ICA
    CoS. New accessions USA, 1954
  Bouquet
    Wight. Hans Hofmann (col)
  Burst into life
    IU. Contemp Amer ptg & sculp, 1953
    (col)
    Wight. Hans Hofmann (col)
  Capriccioso
    IU. Contemp Amer ptg & sculp, 1957
  Cataclysm
    Rathbun
  Catalyst
    IU. Contemp Amer ptg, 1949
  Chimera
    IU. Contemp Amer ptg & sculp, 1961
  The city
    ICA. Annual ex, 1959/60 (col cover)
  Color poem
    Hess. Abstract ptg
  Composition no I, 1951
    MnMW. Classic tradition
  Construction           WMAA
    Mendelowitz
    WMAA. Annual ex, 1950
  Delight                MMA
    Wight. Hans Hofmann (col)
  Elegy               MnMW
    MnMW. 60 Amer ptrs
    Wight. Hans Hofmann
  Embrace             MLL
    Wight. Hans Hofmann (col)
  Exuberance         NBuA
    Art since 1945 (col)
    Hunter. Mod Amer ptg
    NBuA. Acquisitions 1954-57 (col)
    Read. Concise history
    Wight. Hans Hofmann (col)
  Fairy tale
    Hess. Abstract ptg
  Floral composition
    Wight. Hans Hofmann (col)

Flowering branch
  Wight. Hans Hofmann (col)
Fruit bowl             NeL
  Barker. From realism
  CoS. New accessions USA, 1952
Fruit bowl, 1950 (Neuberger coll)
  Wight. Hans Hofmann (col)
Fury no 1
  ICA. Annual ex, 1947/48
Germania, 1951         MdBM
  Wight. Hans Hofmann
Germania: version 6
  CSFP. Annual ex, 1952
Golden splendor
  IU. Contemp Amer ptg & sculp, 1959
Green bottle           MLL
  Wight. Hans Hofmann
Idolatress, 1944
  Wight. Hans Hofmann
Idolatress, 1949
  MnU. 40 Amer ptrs
Interior
  Wight. Hans Hofmann (col)
Joy
  CSFP. Annual ex, 1950/51
Libration
  Wight. Hans Hofmann
Magenta and blue       WMAA
  Cheney. Story 1958 ed
  CoS. New accessions USA, 1952
  Goodrich. Amer art (col)
  Pierson
  Wight. Hans Hofmann (col)
The magician
  Ponente. Mod ptg, 1960 (col)
Mrs Hans Hofmann
  Wight. Hans Hofmann
Morning mist
  DC. 27 biennial ex, 1961
Mosaics, 1956 (Northeast corner,  711
  Third avenue, New York)
  Wight. Hans Hofmann (col)
Mosaics, 1956 (Southwest corner,  711
  Third avenue, New York)
  Wight. Hans Hofmann (col)
Orange vase
  Wight. Hans Hofmann (col)
Orchestral dominance in yellow
  Wight. Hans Hofmann (col)
Phoenix
  Blesh
The pond
  ICA. Annual ex, 1959/60
  MnMW. Eighty works
Provincetown wharves
  Wight. Hans Hofmann
Push and pull no 3
  ICA. Annual ex, 1951
Radiant space
  Baur. Nature (col)
The ravine
  WMAA. Museum and its friends, 1958
The red cap
  PA. Annual ex, 1954
Red lift
  PPC. International ex, 1952
Red trickle
  Time 300 years (col)
  Wight. Hans Hofmann (col)
Reminiscence
  IU. Contemp Amer ptg, 1951
Rising sun
  Ponente. **Mod ptg, 1960 (col)**

Scotch and Burgundy
  Wight. Hans Hofmann (col)
Seated girl
  MnU. 40 Amer ptrs
Self-portrait, 1902
  Wight. Hans Hofmann
Serpentine
  Cheney. Story 1958 ed
Sommernachtstraum                        NBuA
  NBuA. Acquisitions 1957-58
Studio number 1, in grey
  IU. Contemp Amer ptg & sculp, 1955
Submerged
  Wight. Hans Hofmann
The third hand
  IU. Contemp Amer ptg, 1948
Visione nobilissima
  NBuA. Expressioniam
Voices of spring
  ICA. Annual ex, 1961
The window                                  MM
  McCurdy
  MMA. Abstract
X—1955
  Wight. Hans Hofmann (col)
**Hofmann, Mrs Hans**
  Hofmann, H. Mrs Hans Hofmann
Hogs killing a snake by J. S. Curry
Hogs killing rattlesnake by J. S. Curry
**HOGUE, Alexander,** 1898-
  Drought-stricken area                      TxD
  Pierson
  Dust bowl                                  IBM
  Baur. Revolution
**HOLBROOK, Hollis Howard,** 1909-
  Grey on blue and brown
  IU. Contemp Amer ptg & sculp, 1961
Holbrook's bridge, northwest by A. G.
  Dove
Holcombe, Eunice (Griswold) See Pinney,
  Eunice (Griswold) Holcombe
Holding up the payroll by F. Remington
Holding up the sheriff by C. M. Russell
Holding up the stage by C. M. Russell
Hole in the wall gang by I. L. Albright
Holiday by C. Browning
Holiday by C. K. Sibley
Holiday in the park by W. J. Glackens
Holiday on the Hudson by G. B. Luks
Holidays by M. B. Prendergast
Hollingsworth, Anna Maria. See Morris,
  Anna Maria (Hollingsworth)
Hollingsworth, Mary. See Morris, Mary
  (Hollingsworth)
Hollow hill pastoral by M. Hewes
Holly house, Cos Cob, Connecticut by J. H.
  Twachtman
Hollyhocks by E. Johnson
Hollywood by T. H. Benton
Holme, Isaac, 1702-1751
  Theus, J. Hon Isaac Holme
**HOLMEAD (Holmead Phillips)** 1889-
  St George and the dragon               CtY
  CtY. Soc Anonyme
Holmes, Abiel, 1763-1837
  Savage, E. Abiel Holmes
Holmes, Oliver Wendell, 1841-1935
  Hopkinson, C. S. Oliver Wendell Holmes

**HOLMES, William Henry,** 1864-1933
  By the sea
    Born
  Maryland landscape
    Born
**HOLT, Henry,** 1889-1941
  Fading light, Stowe valley               MB
    MB. Ptgs in water color
**HOLTY, Carl Robert,** 1900-
  Carousel
    Pierson
  Emperor's garden
    VR. Amer ptg, 1958
  Equestrian
    MMA. Abstract
  Le flambeau                               IU
    IU. Contemp Amer ptg, 1948
    IU. 20th century
  Good keeper
    Rathbun
  Still life
    IU. Contemp Amer ptg, 1950
  Suspension of forms
    Baur. Revolution
**HOLTZMAN, Harry,** 1912-
  Sculpture                                 CtY
    CtY. Soc Anonyme
The holy by H. Pippin
Holy mountain I, 1944 by H. Pippin
Holy mountain II, 1944 by H. Pippin
Holy mountain IV, 1946 by H. Pippin
Holy Name mission by R. Marsh
Holy week procession by V. Higgins
Holyoke, Edward, 1689-1769
  Pelham, H. (after Copley) Edward Holy-
  oke
Holyoke, Mrs Edward Augustus. See Pick-
  man, Judith
Holyoke, Judith (Pickman) See Pickman,
  Judith
Homage to Boston by J. Levine
Homage to John Cage by R. B. Motherwell
Homage to Rome by E. Isenburger
Homage to the square: Ascending by J.
  Albers
Homage to the square: Precinct by J. Al-
  bers
Homage to the square: Yes by J. Albers
Homan, Emma, fl 1843
  Bradley, J. Emma Homan
Home at Montclair by G. Inness
Home by the sea by W. Whittredge
Home camp in March by R. W. Gray
Home for Christmas by P. Blume
Home for Thanksgiving by A. M. R.
  Moses
Home of Hezekiah King by A. M. R.
  Moses
Home of the heron by G. Inness
A home on the Hudson by T. Doughty
Home on the ranch by L. Megargee
Home scene by T. Eakins
Home, sweet home by W. Homer
Home, sweet home by W. R. Leigh
Home, sweet home by C. Sheeler
Homeless by W. Gropper

**HOMER, Winslow,** 1836-1910
  Adirondack guide                     MB
    Goodrich. Winslow Homer (col)
    MB. Ptgs in water color
    Pierson
  Adirondack lake                      MB
    MB. Ptgs in water color
  Adirondack woods, guide and dog
    CtY. Yale alumni
    DN. Homer
  Adirondacks                          MCH
    Goodrich. Winslow Homer (col)
    Pierson
    Robb. Art 1953 ed
  After the hunt                       CLA
    DN. Homer
  After the tornado, Bahamas (After the
      hurricane, Bahamas)              ICA
    Barker. Amer ptg
    Goodrich. Winslow Homer (col)
    Larkin rev ed (col detail)
    Pierson
  Afterglow (Boats off the coast of Devon-
      shire)                           MB
    MB. Ptgs in water color
  Afternoon fog                        NR
    Goodrich. Winslow Homer
  All's well. See The lookout—All's well
  Artists sketching
    Goodrich. Winslow Homer
  Artist's studio in an afternoon fog  NR
    DN. Homer
  Autumn
    Goodrich. Winslow Homer
  Backrush
    Goodrich. Winslow Homer
  Bananas for the attorney general
    DN. Homer
  Banks fishermen. See Herring net
  A basket of clams
    Goodrich. Winslow Homer
  Bass                                 ATeS
    ATeS. Collection
    Craven. Treasury 1952 ed
  Berry pickers                        MeC
    Goodrich. Winslow Homer
    MNS. Homer
  Blue boat                            MB
    MB. Ptgs in water color
  Boats off the coast of Devonshire. See
      Afterglow
  Boy carrying deer
    CtY. Yale alumni
  Boy fishing
    DN. Homer
    Goodrich. Winslow Homer
  Boy picking apples
    MiD. Coll in progress
    WiMiA. Amer ptg 1760-1960
  Boy with the anchor                  OCl
    OCl. Handbook
  Boys bathing                         MWiC
    Goodrich. Winslow Homer
  Boys beaching a dory                 OT
    Goodrich. Winslow Homer
  Boys in a pasture                    MB
    Goodrich. Winslow Homer
  Boys wading                          MeC
    Goodrich. Winslow Homer
    MeC. Inaugural ex
  Breaking wave                        MB
    Goodrich. Winslow Homer
    MB. Ptgs in water color

  Breakwater, Tynemouth
    DN. Homer
  Breezing up (A fair wind)            DN
    DN. Homer (col cover)
    Goodrich. Winslow Homer
    Janson. Picture history
    MoSL. 40 masterpieces
    Roos
    Walker. Ptgs from America (col)
  The briarwood pipe                   OCl
    OCl. Handbook
  Bridle path, White mountains         MWiS
    Goodrich. Winslow Homer
    Larkin (detail)
    Larkin rev ed
    MWiS. Ex 4 and 7
    Pierson
  Bridlington quay                     MB
    MB. Ptgs in water color
  By the shore
    DN. Homer
  Canoe in rapids                      MCH
    Pierson
  Canoeing in the Adirondacks
    MiD. Coll in progress
    WiMiA. Amer ptg 1760-1960
  Cape Trinity, Saguenay river
    DN. Homer
  Cape Trinity, Saguenay river, moonlight
    Goodrich. Winslow Homer
  The carnival                         MM
    Goodrich. Winslow Homer (col)
  Casting in the falls
    Goodrich. Winslow Homer
  Casting the fly
    DN. Homer
  Children on a fence                  KLU
    Pierson
  Children on the beach
    Goodrich. Winslow Homer
  Children playing under a Gloucester wharf
                                       MB
    DN. Homer
    MB. Ptgs in water color
  Coast in winter                      MWM
    Walker. Ptgs from America
  Coming storm                         NBM
    DN. Homer
    Goodrich. Winslow Homer (col)
    NYG. Fine art
  Corn husking                         ATeS
    ATeS. Collection
  Cotton pickers
    DN. Homer
    Goodrich. Winslow Homer
    U.S. National Capital sesquicentennial
      com
  Country school                       MoSL
    Davidson v2
    MoSL. 50 masterworks
    MoSL. Handbook 1953
    Pierson
    Richardson. Ptg in America (col de-
      tail)
    U.S. National Capital sesquicentennial
      com
  Croquet match
    Barr. What is mod ptg
    DN. Homer
    Goodrich. Winslow Homer
    MNS. Homer

Croquet players                    NBuA
  NBuA. Catalogue of the ptgs
Croquet scene                       ICA
  Davidson v 2
  Goodrich. Winslow Homer
  Pierson
  UNESCO. 1860-1949
  UNESCO. 1860-1955
  UNESCO. 1860-1959
Crossing the pasture
  DN. Homer
  Goodrich. Winslow Homer
Custom house, Santiago de Cuba
  Goodrich. Winslow Homer
Dad's coming
  Goodrich. Winslow Homer
Deer drinking
  DN. Homer
  Goodrich. Winslow Homer
Defiance: Inviting a shot before Peters-
    burg, Virginia, 1864            MiD
  MiD. Treasures
Diamond shoal                       IBM
  Baur. Amer ptg
The dinner horn                     MiD
  MiD. Treasures
The dory                             MB
  MB. Ptgs in water color
Driftwood
  DN. Homer
  NBuA. Fifty ptgs
Dunes at Marshfield. See Sand dune
Early morning after a storm at sea  OCl
  Baur. Amer ptg
  Baur. Revolution
  Goodrich. Winslow Homer
  OCl. Handbook
East Hampton, Long Island
  DN. Homer
Eastern point, Prout's neck         MWiS
  MWiS. Ex 4 and 7
Eight bells                         MAP
  Goodrich. Winslow Homer (col)
  Larkin
  Larkin rev ed
  Pierson
  Time. 300 years (col)
Entering the first rapid
  Goodrich. Winslow Homer
A fair wind. See Breezing up
Fallen deer                          MB
  Larkin (detail)
  Larkin rev ed (detail)
  MB. Ptgs in water color
Fisherfolk in a boat                MCH
  Goodrich. Winslow Homer
Fisherfolk on the beach at Tynemouth
                                     DP
  Goodrich. Winslow Homer
A fisherman's day                    DF
  Born
Fishing
  NSP. Sportscapes
Flock of sheep, Houghton farm
  Goodrich. Winslow Homer
Fog warning (Halibut fishing)        MB
  Bazin. History of art
  Goodrich. Winslow Homer
The forest. See Hunting dog among dead
    trees

Fox hunt                             PA
  DC. De gustibus
  DN. Homer
  Goodrich. Winslow Homer (col)
  McCurdy
  Pierson
  Robb. Harper history
Gargoyles of Notre Dame
  Goodrich. Winslow Homer
Girl with a letter
  Goodrich. Winslow Homer
Girl with laurel                    MiD
  DN. Homer
Girl with pitchfork                  DP
  DN. Homer
Girls on a cliff                     MB
  MB. Ptgs in water color
Girls with lobster                  OCl
  DN. Homer
  MNS. Homer
Glass windows, Bahamas              NBM
  DN. Homer
Gloucester farm                    PPhM
  Canaday
Gloucester schooners and sloop     PPhM
  DN. Homer
Green apples
  MNS. Homer
Green dory                           MB
  MB. Ptgs in water color
  Pierson
Guide and mountains and sky. See Woods-
    man and fallen tree
Guide carrying deer
  Lewisohn
Guide fishing                       InIJ
  InIJ. 105 ptgs
Gulf stream                          MM
  Craven. Rainbow book (col)
  Craven. Treasury 1952 ed (col)
  Flexner. Amer ptg (col)
  Flexner. Short history (col)
  Goodrich. Winslow Homer (col)
  MM. 100 Amer ptrs
  MM. 100 Amer ptrs (col detail)
  NYG. Fine art
  Pierson
  Taylor. Fifty centuries, 1954 ed (col)
  Time. 300 years (col)
  UNESCO. 1860-1949
  UNESCO. 1860-1955
  UNESCO. 1860-1959
Halibut fishing. See Fog warning
Harvest scene                       NCa
  DN. Homer
Haymaking                           OCo
  Goodrich. Winslow Homer
Herring net (Banks fishermen)       ICA
  Lee. Art then and now
  McKinney
  NYG. Fine art
  Roos
  U.S. National Capital sesquicentennial
    com
High cliff, coast of Maine          DNC
  Goodrich. Winslow Homer
High tide                            MM
  Bazin (col detail)
  Goodrich. Winslow Homer
Home, sweet home
  DN. Homer
  Goodrich. Winslow Homer

**HOMER, Winslow**—*Continued*

Homosassa river                    NBM
  NYG. Fine art
Hound and hunter                   DN
  DN. Homer
The Houses of Parliament
  DN. Homer
Hudson river (River scene, lumberman,
  and logs in river)              MB
  Goodrich. Winslow Homer
  MB. Ptgs in water color
Hudson river, logging              DC
  DC. Masterpieces
  DN. Homer
  NYG. Fine art (col)
The hunter                         PPhM
  Canaday
Hunting dog among dead trees (On the
  track; The forest)              MB
  MB. Ptgs in water color
Huntsman and dogs                  PPhM
  DN. Homer
  Goodrich. Winslow Homer (col)
  Mendelowitz
  MiD. Ptg in America
  Pierson
  Richardson. Ptg in America
Hurricane, Bahamas
  Taylor. Fifty centuries, 1954 ed (col)
In charge of the baby
  Goodrich. Winslow Homer
In the mountains                   NBM
  Goodrich. Winslow Homer
Indian camp                        MB
  MB. Ptgs in water color
Indian hunter in the Everglades (Indian
  **in Florida** swamps; Young hunter in
  woods)                          MB
  MB. Ptgs in water color
Indian woman at oven. See Native wom-
  **an cooking**
The initials
  DN. Homer
  Goodrich. Winslow Homer
  MiD. Coll in progress
  WiMiA. Amer ptg 1760-1960
Inland water, Bermuda
  Goodrich. Winslow Homer
Inside the bar, Tynemouth          MM
  DN. Homer
  Pierson
Kissing the moon                   MAP
  DN. Homer
  Goodrich. Winslow Homer
Leaping trout                      MB
  DN. Homer
  Goodrich. Winslow Homer
  MB. Ptgs in water color
The life line                      PPhM
  Canaday
  Goodrich. Winslow Homer
  Pierson
Life-size black bass
  Goodrich. Winslow Homer
Light on the sea                   DC
  DC. Masterpieces
Long Branch, New Jersey            MB
  Barker. Amer ptg
  Goodrich. Winslow Homer (col)
  Pierson
  Richardson. Ptg in America
The lookout                        MCH
  Robb. Harper history

The lookout—All's well             MB
  Craven. Rainbow book
  Craven. Treasury 1952 ed
  DN. Homer
  Goodrich. Winslow Homer
  Mendelowitz
  Roos
Lost on the Grand Banks            CLA
  DN. Homer
Maine coast
  Rosenblum
Milking time
  DN. Homer
  Goodrich. Winslow Homer
The morning bell at a New England fac-
  tory (Clark coll)
  CtY. Yale alumni
  Davidson v 1
  DN. Homer
  Goodrich. Winslow Homer
  Janson. Key monuments
  MNS. Homer
Morning-glories
  DN. Homer
Mussel gatherers                   MdBM
  DN. Homer
Nassau                             MM
  DN. Homer
Nassau, woman at campfire. See Native
  woman cooking
Native woman cooking (Negro woman
  cooking; Indian woman at oven; Nas-
  sau, woman at campfire)         MB
  MB. Ptgs in water color
Negro woman cooking. See Native woman
  cooking
The new novel                      MSM
  DN. Homer
The nooning                        CtHW
  CtHW. Handbook
  Goodrich. Winslow Homer
Northeaster                        MM
  Canaday
  NAD. Amer tradition
  NYG. Fine art
  Pierson
  Upjohn
Old friends                        MWM
  DN. Homer
Old settlers, Adirondacks          MB
  DN. Homer
  MB. Ptgs in water color
On a lee shore                     RPS
  Born
  DN. Homer
  Goodrich. Winslow Homer (col)
On guard
  Goodrich. Winslow Homer
On the beach                       NCa
  DN. Homer
On the beach at Marshfield
  MNS. Homer
On the stile                       MeC
  Goodrich. Winslow Homer
On the track. See Hunting dog among
  dead trees
Orange tree and gate, Nassau
  MiD. Coll in progress
Ouananiche fishing: Lake St John, Quebec
                                   MB
  MB. Ptgs in water color
Palm tree
  CanO. Hirshhorn coll

Palm tree, Nassau          MM
  Bazin. History of art (coll)
  DN. Homer (col)
  NYG. Fine art
  Time. 300 years (col)
  UNESCO. 1860-1959
Palm trees, Florida          MB
  DN. Homer
  Goodrich. Winslow Homer
Pitching quoits          MCH
  U.S. National Capital sesquicentennial
    com
Playing old soldier          MB
  U.S. National Capital sesquicentennial
    com
The portage
  NYG. Fine art
Prisoners from the front          MM
  Canaday
  Pierson
  Richardson. Ptg in America
  Time. 300 years (col)
Promenade on the beach          MSM
  MSM. Handbook
Prospect rock, Essex county, N.Y.   DNC
  DNC. Gellatly coll, 1954
  Goodrich. Winslow Homer
Prout's Neck, breakers          ICA
  DN. Homer
The rapids, Hudson river, Adirondacks
                                   ICA
  NYG. Fine art
Reading in the sun
  Goodrich. Winslow Homer
Return of the gleaner
  Goodrich. Winslow Homer
Right and left          PPhM
  Bazin
Right and left          DN
  DN. Homer
  Goodrich. Winslow Homer
Right and left (Morgan coll)
  Walker. Ptgs from America
River scene, lumberman, and logs in river.
  See Hudson river
Rocky coast          CtHW
  DN. Homer
Rocky shore, Bermuda          MB
  MB. Ptgs in water color
Rowing home          DP
  DP. Catalogue
Royal palm trees
  DN. Homer
Rum cay          MWM
  Goodrich. Winslow Homer
The rustics
  Goodrich. Winslow Homer
Saguenay river, lower rapids          MWM
  Goodrich. Winslow Homer
  Richardson. Ptg in America
Sailing a dory
  DN. Homer
Sailing boats in a watering trough
  MNS. Homer
Sailing the catboat
  DN. Homer
Sand dune (Dunes at Marshfield)
  DN. Homer
Santiago de Cuba
  DN. Homer
Schooners at anchor, Key West
  DN. Homer

Searchlight, harbor entrance, Santiago de
  Cuba          MM
  DN. Homer
  Goodrich. Winslow Homer
  Pierson
The seesaw          NCa
  MNS. Homer
Shark fishing
  DN. Homer
  Goodrich. Winslow Homer
The shell heap          NBM
  DN. Homer
  NYG. Fine art
Shepherdess of Houghton farm
  MiD. Coll in progress
Ship unfurling sails          PPhM
  Canaday
Shipbuilding at Gloucester          MNS
  MNS. Homer
Shooting the rapids, Saguenay river   MM
  Goodrich. Winslow Homer
Shore and surf, Nassau          MM
  DN. Homer
The sick chicken          MeC
  DN. Homer
  Goodrich. Winslow Homer
Skating at Central park
  NYG. Fine art
Skating in Central park, New York, 1860
                                   MoSL
  Davidson v2
  MoSL. Handbook 1953
Sketch in Florida. See Thornhill bar,
  Florida
Skirmish in The Wilderness          CtNB
  DN. Homer
  U.S. National Capital sesquicentennial
    com
Sloop, Bermuda          MM
  Mendelowitz
  NYG. Fine art
  Roos
Snap-the-whip          OYB
  Goodrich. Winslow Homer (col)
  MNS. Homer
  OYB. Catalogue 1951
  Pierson
  Time. 300 years (col)
Sponge diver          MB
  MB. Ptgs in water color
Sponge fishermen, Bahamas
  DN. Homer
Spring
  DN. Homer
Spring blossoms
  MNS. Homer
Springtime in Virginia
  Richardson. Ptg in America
Startled
  MiD. Coll in progress
  WiMiA. Amer ptg 1760-1960
Storm in the Bahamas          MM
  Myers. Art
  Riley. Your art heritage
Stowing sails, Bermuda          ICA
  DN. Homer
  NYG. Fine art
Summer night
  DN. Homer
  Goodrich. Winslow Homer (col)

**HOMER, Winslow**—*Continued*

Summer squall      MWiS
    Goodrich. Winslow Homer
    MWiS. Ex 4 and 7
    Time. 300 years (col)
Sunday morning in Virginia      OCiM
    DN. Homer
Sunlight on the coast      OT
    DN. Homer
Sunrise fishing in the Adirondacks
    DN. Homer
Sunset, Saco bay      MWiS
    MWiS. Ex 4 and 7
Taking sunflower to teacher      GAtM
    GAtM. Holbrook collection
Thornhill bar, Florida (Sketch in Florida)
                                MB
    MB. Ptgs in water color
Three boys on the shore
    Goodrich. Winslow Homer
Three men in a canoe
    Goodrich. Winslow Homer
To the rescue      DP
    DP. Catalogue
Trout fishing, Lake St John, Quebec   MB
    MB. Ptgs in water color
The turtle pound (Turtle pond)      NBM
    Goodrich. Winslow Homer (col)
    Pierson
Two boats
    DN. Homer
Two guides      MWiS
    Goodrich. Winslow Homer (col)
    MWiS. Ex 4 and 7
    Pierson
Two trout      IBM
    DN. Homer
Tynemouth sands      MB
    MB. Ptgs in water color
Under the coco palm      MCH
    DN. Homer
    Goodrich. Winslow Homer
Under the falls, grand discharge
    Goodrich. Winslow Homer
Undertow      MWiS
    Goodrich. Winslow Homer
    MWiS. Ex 4 and 7
Unruly calf
    DN. Homer
    MiD. Coll in progress
Veteran in a new field
    DN. Homer
A voice from the cliffs
    DN. Homer
Water fan
    Goodrich. Winslow Homer
Weaning the calf      NoCR
    Goodrich. Winslow Homer
    NoCR. Catalogue
    UNESCO. 1860-1959
Weary
    DN. Homer
Weatherbeaten, or Stormbeaten
    CtY. Yale alumni
    Goodrich. Winslow Homer
West point, Prout's neck      MWiS
    Goodrich. Winslow Homer (col)
    MWiS. Ex 4 and 7
    Pierson
The west wind      MAP
    Goodrich. Winslow Homer
Wild geese
    DN. Homer

Winter coast
    Barker. Amer ptg
    DN. Homer
    Goodrich. Winslow Homer
Woman driving geese      AP
    NUM. Art across America
Woman sewing      DC
    DC. Masterpieces
Woman with flower
    DN. Homer
The woodchopper
    Born
The woodcutter
    DN. Homer
    Goodrich. Winslow Homer
Woodsman and fallen tree (Guide and
    mountains and sky)      MB
    MB. Ptgs in water color
World's Columbian exposition—the foun-
    tains at night      MeB
    DN. Homer
    U.S. National Capital sesquicentennial
    com
The wreck      PPC
    Goodrich. Winslow Homer
    PPC. Amer classics
The wreck of the Iron Crown
    DN. Homer
    Goodrich. Winslow Homer
The wreck, or girl with red stockings MB
    Goodrich. Winslow Homer
The wrecked schooner      MoSL
    MoSL. Handbook 1953
Young hunter in woods. See Indian hunter
    in the Everglades
**Homeric** struggle by B. Shahn
**Homestead** by T. H. Benton
**Homestead** by J. Kane
**Homestead** mill near Pittsburgh by W. C.
    Wall
**Homeward** by I. Bishop
**Homeward** bound by A. P. Ryder
**Hommage** à Albert Camus by F. Roth
**Hommage** à Andrés Segovia by R. J. Stein
**Homosassa** river by W. Homer
**Homunculus** by P. Burlin
**Hooft, Martha Visser 't.** See Visser 't Hooft,
    Martha
**Hooked** rug by A. Blanch
**Hooker, Mary.** See Pierpont, Mary (Hooker)
**Hooker, Thomas,** 1586?-1647
    Church, F. E. Thomas Hooker's party
    coming to Hartford
**Hoosick** Falls in winter by A. M. R. Moses
**HOPE, James,** 1818?-1892
    Army of the Potomac      MB
    MB. Karolik coll
    Bird mountain, Castleton, Vermont   MB
    MB. Karolik coll
    Frowning cliff, Watkins glen, New York
                                MB
    MB. Karolik coll
    Winter scene: the red fox      MB
    MB. Karolik coll
**Hope family**
    West, B. The Adrian Hope family group
**Hopi** snake dance by E. A. Burbank
**HOPKINS, Budd,** 1931-
    Avalar
    WMAA. Young America 1960
    Number 1
    WMAA. Young America 1960

Hopkins, Eliza. See Page, Eliza (Hopkins)
**HOPKINSON, Charles Sydney, 1869-**
  Afternoon light     MB
    MB. Ptgs in water color
    Pierson
  Double portrait
    PPC. Ptg in the U.S. 1949
  Oliver Wendell Holmes
    Time. 300 years (col)
  Rocks and sea     MB
    MB. Ptgs in water color
**HOPKINSON, Francis, 1737-1791**
  Self-portrait     MdBH
    MdBMu. Rendezvous
**HOPPER, Edward, 1882-**
  Adams' house
    Goodrich. Edward Hopper (col)
  Approaching a city     DP
    DP. Catalogue
    Goodrich. Edward Hopper
  August in the city     FaW
    Goodrich. Edward Hopper (col)
    ICA. Annual ex, 1951
  Camel's Hump     NUM
    Goodrich. Edward Hopper (col)
    NUM. Root bequest
  Cape Cod evening
    Baur. New art
    Goodrich. Edward Hopper (col)
  Cape Cod morning     WMAA
    Time. 300 years (col)
    WMAA. Sara Roby (col)
  Chop suey
    Goodrich. Edward Hopper
  The city     ATU
    ATU. Coll of Amer art
    Larkin
    Larkin rev ed
    NUM. Art across America
  City sunlight
    PPC. International ex, 1955
  Coast Guard station     NJMo
    NJMo. Forty years
    NJMo. Your Montclair art museum
  Cobb's house     MWM
    Goodrich. Edward Hopper
  Conference at night
    MnU. 40 Amer ptrs
    PPC. Ptg in the U.S. 1949
  Cornbelt city
    MMA. Contemp ptrs
  Corner saloon     MMA
    Goodrich. Edward Hopper (col)
    Pierson
    WMAA. Juliana Force
  Cottage, Cape Cod     ATeS
    ATeS. Collection
  Cottages at Wellfleet
    MiD. Coll in progress
  Dawn in Pennsylvania
    Baur. Revolution
    Goodrich. Edward Hopper (col)
    Wight. Milestones
  Early Sunday morning     WMAA
    Baur. New art
    Brown. Amer ptg
    Canaday
    DC. De gustibus
    Faulkner. Art today, 1956
    Gardner 1959 ed
    Goodrich. Amer art (col)

  Goodrich. Edward Hopper (col)
  Hunter. Mod Amer ptg (col)
  ICA. Amer artists paint the city
  Mendelowitz
  MiD. Ptg in America
  Pierson
  Richardson. Ptg in America
  Time. 300 years (col)
East wind over Weehawken
  Goodrich. Edward Hopper
First branch of the White river, Vermont     MB
  MB. Ptgs in water color
First row, orchestra
  CanO. Hirshhorn coll
  WMAA. Contemp Amer ptg, 1951
From Williamsburg bridge     MM
  MM. 100 Amer ptrs
Gas     MMA
  Baur. New art
  Goodrich. Edward Hopper (col)
  MMA. Contemp ptrs
  Pierson
Gravel bar, White river
  Goodrich. Edward Hopper (col)
Ground swell     DC
  Goodrich. Edward Hopper
  NYG. Fine art
Haskell's house
  Goodrich. Edward Hopper
High noon
  PPC. International ex, 1950
Hills, South Truro     OCl
  OCl. Handbook
Hotel lobby
  ICA. Annual ex, 1945/46
Hotel room     MMA
  Seiberling
House by the railroad     MMA
  Barr. What is mod ptg
  Brown. Amer ptg
  MMA. Masters (col)
  Goodrich. Edward Hopper (col)
  Pierson
  Seiberling
House of the foghorn no 3
  CtY. Yale alumni
House on Pamet river     WMAA
  Goodrich. Amer art
  Goodrich. Edward Hopper
  NYG. Fine art
  Pierson
  UNESCO. 1860-1949
Lee shore     WMAA
  CSB. Illusion
Light battery at Gettysburg     MoKN
  CoS. New accessions USA, 1948
Lighthouse
  Upjohn
Lighthouse at Two Lights
  Baur. New art
  Goodrich. Edward Hopper (col)
  Taylor. Fifty centuries, 1954 ed (col)
  WiMiA. Amer ptg 1760-1960
Manhattan bridge and Lily apartments
  Goodrich. Edward Hopper
  MiD. Coll in progress
  WiMiA. Amer ptg 1760-1960
Manhattan bridge loop     MAP
  Goodrich. Edward Hopper
  Rathbun
  Time. 300 years (col)

**HOPPER, Edward**—*Continued*
  Methodist church, Provincetown    CtHW
    CtHW.  Handbook
  Morning in a city
    Goodrich.  Edward Hopper
    WMAA.  Museum and its friends, 1958
  New York movie                    MMA
    50 years of mod art
    Goodrich.  Edward Hopper (col)
    Mendelowitz
    Newmeyer
  New York, New Haven and Hartford
                                     InIJ
    InIJ.  105 ptgs
  New York pavements
    MiD.  Coll in progress
  Night windows                     MMA
    Goodrich.  Edward Hopper
  Nighthawks                        ICA
    Baur.  New art (col)
    Baur.  Revolution
    Craven.  Rainbow book
    Flexner.  Amer ptg
    Flexner.  Short history
    Goodrich.  Edward Hopper
    McCurdy
    Pierson
    Time.  300 years (col)
  Office at night                   MnMW
    Goodrich.  Edward Hopper
  Pennsylvania coal town            OYB
    DC.  21 biennial ex, 1949
    Larkin rev ed (col)
    OYB.  Catalogue 1951
    Pierson
  Room in Brooklyn                  MB
    Goodrich.  Edward Hopper
  Room in New York                  NeL
    Goodrich.  Edward Hopper
  Room on the sea
    Eliot.  Art of our time (col)
    Time.  300 years (col)
    WMAA.  Museum and its friends
  Rooms by the sea
    Pousette-Dart.  Amer ptg
  Rooms for tourists
    Goodrich.  Edward Hopper (col)
  Route 6, Eastham                  InTH
    Goodrich.  Edward Hopper
  Saltillo rooftops
    Goodrich.  Edward Hopper (col)
  Second-story sunlight             WMAA
    Goodrich.  Amer art
  Seven A. M. 1948                  WMAA
    CSFP.  Annual ex, 1952
    Goodrich.  Amer art (col)
    MnU.  40 Amer ptrs
  Sheridan theatre                  NJN
    Gruskin (col)
  Shoshone cliffs                   OYB
    OYB.  Annual 1954
    OYB.  Supplement
  Sierra Madre at Saltillo
    WiMiA.  Amer ptg 1760-1960
  Skylights
    Baur.  New art
    Goodrich.  Edward Hopper (col)
  Sunday                            DP
    Bazin
    Cheney.  Primer 1958 ed
    Cheney.  Story 1958 ed
  Sunlight on brownstones
    Time.  300 years (col)

  Tony's house                      NBuA
    NBuA.  Acquisitions 1954-57
  Two on the aisle                  OT
    Brown.  Amer ptg
  White river at Sharon             WMAA
    Pierson
    WMAA.  Sara Roby
**Hopscotch.**  See Games and sports—Hop-
  scotch
**Horace** Tuttle's livery stable by Unidentified
  artist
**HORIUCHI, Paul,** 1906-
  December no 1
    OrPA.  Ptgs & sculptures
**Horizon** conditions by R. Tam
**Horizontal** arrangement by C. W. Smith
**Horizontal** illusion by I. R. Pereira
**Horn** pipe by M. Tobey
**Horner, William Edmonds,** fl 1836
  Sully, T.  Dr William Edmonds Horner
    (detail)
**Horry, Daniel,** d 1785?
  Theus, J.  Col Daniel Horry
**Horse** mackerel by K. Knaths
**Horse** power by R. Strang
**Horseman** by L. A. Golub
**Horseman** by W. Gropper
**Horseneck** brook, winter by J. H. Twacht-
  man
**Horses**
  Bartlett, G.  Hidden spring
  Bartlett, G.  Indian police
  Bartlett, G.  Night herd
  Bartlett, G.  Saddled for the first time
  Beal, G. R.  Circus ponies
  Bellows, G. W.  Polo at Lakewood
  Bellows, G. W.  Sand team
  Bellows, G. W.  White horse
  Bennett, B.  Circus scene
  Benton, T. H.  White horse
  Bierstadt, A.  Black horse
  Bingham, G. C.  The mill boy
  Blythe, D. G.  Pittsburgh horsemarket
  Blythe, D. G.  The runaway
  Boudro(u), A. A.  Dickson entering Bris-
    tol in 1819
  Buhalis, N.  Horse
  Catlin, G.  Breaking down wild horses
  Catlin, G.  Comanche feats of horseman-
    ship
  Catlin, G.  Keokuk on horseback
  Davis, E. P.  Eben Davis' horse
  De Knight, A.  Circus horses
  Delano, G. C.  Moonlight stampede
  Delano, G. C.  Navajo
  Dixon, M.  Cowboy and packhorse
  Dixon, M.  Peace in October
  Dixon, M.  Red gateway
  Eakins, T.  Fairman Rogers four-in-hand
  Evett, K.  Rodeo
  Flannery, V.  Chestnut stallion, Discovery
  Flannery, V.  The governor's cup
  Freeman.  Peter Volo
  Gropper, W.  Horseman
  Hewes, M.  Hollow hill pastoral
  Hildebrandt, L.  Horses
  Homer, W.  Bridle path, White mountains
  Johnson, F. T.  Mountain trail
  Keller, H. G.  End of the act
  Keller, H. G.  Storm-frightened animals

Keyes, C. A. Geo. S. Howe driving Rough and Ready
Kosa, E. J. Dark hills and white horses
Lebrun, R. Centurion's horse
Leigh, W. R. Combing the ridges
Leigh, W. R. Female of the species
Leigh, W. R. A lowdown trick
Leigh, W. R. The rescue
Miller, A. J. Approaching buffalo
Miller, A. J. Arapahos
Miller, A. J. Auguste and his horse
Miller, A. J. Beating a retreat
Miller, A. J. The Blackfeet
Miller, A. J. Camp scene (Sioux)
Miller, A. J. Capture of wild horses by Indians
Miller, A. J. Crow encampment
Miller, A. J. Crow Indian on the lookout
Miller, A. J. Dodging an arrow
Miller, A. J. Escape from Blackfeet
Miller, A. J. Indian certificate
Miller, A. J. Indian girls racing
Miller, A. J. Indian oracle
Miller, A. J. Indian woman on horseback in the vicinity of the Cut rocks
Miller, A. J. Indians in a storm: night scene
Miller, A. J. Indians returning to camp with game
Miller, A. J. Pawnee running buffalo
Miller, A. J. Picketing horses
Miller, A. J. Shoshone female catching a horse
Miller, A. J. Shoshone Indian and his pet horse
Miller, A. J. Snake Indians
Miller, A. J. Stampede of wild horses
Miller, A. J. Wild horses
Palmer, W. C. Horses in landscape
Prendergast, M. B. Bareback rider, Paris
Prendergast, M. B. Dress rehearsal
Prendergast, M. B. Horse and wagon
Prendergast, M. B. The rider
Price, C. S. Bay mare and colt and a couple of others
Price, C. S. Horses
Price, C. S. Horses in a barnyard
Price, C. S. Mare and foal
Price, C. S. Mare with colt
Price, C. S. White mare with foal
Quidor, J. Tom Walker's flight
Quirt, W. W. Horses and man
Ranney, W. T. The lasso
Ray, R. Survivors
Remington, F. Among the led horses
Remington, F. Apaches are coming
Remington, F. Apaches listening
Remington, F. Dismounted: 4th troopers moving
Remington, F. Downing the nigh leader
Remington, F. End of the day
Remington, F. General Leonard A. Wood on horseback
Remington, F. Halt—dismount
Remington, F. The last march
Remington, F. An old time plains fight
Remington, F. On the southern plains in 1860
Remington, F. Pioneer and the Indian
Remington, F. The scout: friends or enemies?
Remington, F. The snow trail
Remington, F. Snowbound on the overland stage
Remington, F. United States cavalry defending a position
Russell, C. M. The bolter
Russell, C. M. Bucking bronco
Russell, C. M. Capturing the grizzly
Russell, C. M. Caught with the goods
Russell, C. M. The challenge
Russell, C. M. The cinch ring
Russell, C. M. Cowboy life
Russell, C. M. A dangerous cripple
Russell, C. M. The free trader
Russell, C. M. Heeling a bad one
Russell, C. M. Holding up the sheriff
Russell, C. M. In without knocking
Russell, C. M. Jerked down
Russell, C. M. A loose cinch
Russell, C. M. Roping a grizzly
Russell, C. M. Sagebrush sport
Russell, C. M. The scout
Russell, C. M. Smoke of a .45
Russell, C. M. Smoking them out
Russell, C. M. Stampeded
Russell, C. M. Surprise attack
Russell, C. M. An unscheduled stop
Russell, C. M. When law dulls the edge of chance
Russell, C. M. When Sioux and Blackfeet meet
Russell, C. M. Wild horse hunters
Russell, C. M. Wild men's meat
Ryder, A. P. Grazing horse
Ryder, A. P. Hunter's rest
Ryder, A. P. In the stable
Ryder, A. P. Lone scout
Ryder, A. P. Racetrack
Ryder, A. P. Roadside meeting
Ryder, A. P. White horse
Saalburg, A. R. Wild horses
Sample, P. S. Going to town
Schreyvogel, C. My bunkie
Sheets, M. O. Black horse
Simkhovitch, S. Two horses
Sommer, W. Big horse
Sommer, W. Black horse
Sommer, W. Blue horse
Sommer, W. Horses in the snow
Sommer, W. Languid leisure
Sommer, W. Three horses in alarm
Sommer, W. Two yellow horses
Strang, R. Horse power
Strang, R. Slow poke
Strang, R. Spring
Strang, R. Water
Strater, H. Colts at Soda Springs
Troye, E. Edward Troye and an unidentified boy
Troye, E. Richard Singleton
Unidentified artist. Buffalo hunter
Unidentified artist. General Washington on white charger
Unidentified artist. Horses in a stream
Unidentified artist. Lady Suffolk
Unidentified artist. Runaway horse
Unidentified artist. Start of the hunt
Unidentified artist. The trotter
Unidentified artist. War horses
Van Zandt, T. K. Judge Van Arbam in his sleigh
Watkins, M. B. The blue and the strawberry roan
Wimar, C. Captive charger

Horse's skull on blue by G. O'Keeffe
**Horsfield, Timothy**
 Haidt, J. V. Timothy Horsfield jr
**HORTER, Earl, 1881-1940**
 Gloucester docks
  NYG. Fine art
**Horton, John**
 Hare, C. W. John Horton
**Hortus** occlusus by G. Kepes
The **host** by G. W. McLauchlin
**Hostiles** by C. M. Russell
**Hot** corn girl by N. V. Calyo
**Hot** horizon by A. Gottlieb
**Hot** house by W. Plate
**Hot** September wind by C. E. Burchfield
**Hot** springs near the Yellowstone by T. Moran
**Hot** stillscape by S. Davis
**Hot** stillscape for six colors by S. Davis
**HOTCHKISS, Thomas Hiram,** c 1834-1869
 Old aqueduct                          MB
  MB. Ptgs in water color
 Taormina, the island of Sicily        NNHS
  MiD. Travelers in Arcadia
**Hotel** corridor by R. B. Motherwell
**Hotel** corridor by D. Rosenthal
**Hotel** lobby by M. Beckmann
**Hotel** lobby by E. Hopper
**Hotel** lobby by H. C. Pitz
**Hotels, restaurants, etc**
 Bellows, A. F. Wayside inn
 Boudro(u), A. A. Dickson entering Bristol
 Cropsey, J. F. View of Kaaterskill house
 Davis, S. Hotel de France
 Du Bosi, G. P. Restaurant
 Durrie, G. H. Jones' inn
 Durrie, G. H. Winter scene, Jones' inn
 Guy, F. Tontine coffee house, New York
 Haklhuber, F. Herndon hotel, Omaha, Nebraska
 Harvey, G. Tremont house, Boston
 Krimmel, J. L. Interior of an American inn
 Lawrence, J. Cafe scene
 Sloan, J. Chinese restaurant
 Sloan, J. Lafayette hotel
 Sloan, J. Renganeschi's, Saturday night
 Sloan, J. Soula's Rathskeller
 Sloan, J. Yeats at Petitpas
 Unidentified artist. Fashionable inn, New York
 Unidentified artist. Judd's hotel, Philadelphia
**HOUMÈRE, Walter,** 1895-
 Lute, flute and dance
  Robb. Art 1953 ed
**Hound** by H. R. Poore
**Hound** by M. T. Zorach
**Hound** and hunter by W. Homer
The **hours** by E. G. Malbone (copy of miniature by Samuel Shelley)
The **house** by F. Hillsmith
The **house** by E. Laning
**House** and street by S. Davis
**House** by the railroad by E. Hopper
**House** in the pines by S. Laufman

**House** in the woods by S. Laufman
**House** maid by W. M. Paxton
**House** of cards by S. Serisawa
**House** of mystery by C. E. Burchfield
**House** of the dogs by F. Chapin
**House** of the foghorn by E. Hopper
**House** of the moon by R. Beck
**House** on Pamet river by E. Hopper
**House** on Teel's island by A. N. Wyeth
**House** on the sea by W. Whittredge
**House,** tree shapes by S. Davis
**Houseman, Jacob,** fl 1809
 Jarvis, J. W. Jacob Houseman
**Houses** by C. H. Demuth
**Houses** by the river by L. Feininger
The **Houses** of Parliament by W. Homer
**Housetop** in Ecuador by F. E. Church
**Houston, Henry W.** fl 1837
 Coe, E. V. Henry W. Houston
**Houston, Phebe,** fl 1837
 Coe, E. V. Mrs Phebe Houston
**Houston, Samuel,** 1793-1863
 Catlin, G. Gen Sam Houston
 Unidentified artist. Samuel Houston as Marius
**HOVENDEN, Thomas,** 1840-1895
 Breaking the home ties               PPhM
  Chew. 250 years of art
  DC. De gustibus
 Joseph Battell                       CtY
  CtY. Portrait index
 Last moments of John Brown           MM
  Davidson v2
  U.S. National Capital sesquicentennial com
 Old version
  WiMiA. Amer ptg 1760-1960
 Self-portrait
  Chew. 250 years of art
**How** my mother's embroidered apron unfolds in my life by A. Gorky
**How** order no 6 came through by F. Remington
**HOWARD, Charles,** 1899-
 The amulet
  Read. Concise history
 California
  Genauer (col)
 Dove love
  CSFP. Annual ex, 1946
 Everyday sovereign
  CSFP. Annual ex, 1950/51
 The first hypothesis
  CSFP. Annual ex, 1947/48
  IU. Contemp Amer ptg, 1949
 Fully-developed escutcheon
  IU. Contemp Amer ptg, 1950
 The matement
  PPC. International ex, 1952
 Prescience                           MM
  MM. 100 Amer ptrs
  Pierson
 The progenitors
  CSFP. Annual ex, 1948/49
 Rumour
  Read. Art no, 1948 ed

Trinity                                    ICA
  ICA. Anual ex, 1945/46
  McCurdy
  MMA. Abstract
Howard, Mrs Henry. See Berlandina, Jane
Howard, John Eager, 1752-1827
  Peale, C. W. Gov John Eager Howard
    (after Rembrandt Peale)
HOWARD, John Langley
  Spring cleaning
    ICA. Annual ex, 1951
  Storm coming
    CSFP. Annual ex, 1952
Howard, Mrs Robert Boardman. See Kent,
  Adaline
HOWARD, Wing
  Le Pont Neuf
    NAD. Annual ex, 1947, 1st half
Howarden, Margaret. See Livingston, Mar-
  garet (Howarden)
Howe, George S. fl 1860
  Keys, C. A. Geo. S. Howe driving Rough
    and Ready
Howe, Richard, 1st earl, 1726-1799
  Copley, J. S. Richard, Earl Howe
HOWELL, Felicie Waldo, 1897-
  Gramercy park                            InIJ
    InIJ. 105 ptgs
Howl by S. Greene
Howl of the weather by F. Remington
Hubard, Maria Mason (Tabb) 1813-1888
  Hubard, W. J. Mrs 'William James Hub-
    ard
HUBARD, William James, 1807-1862
  Alfred V. Crenshaw                       VRV
    VRV. William James Hubard
  Dream of Columbus                        VRV
    VRV. William James Hubard
  Eliza Hoffman
    VRV. William James Hubard
  Elizabeth and Anna Deans
    VRV. William James Hubard
  Henry Clay                               VCU
    VRV. William James Hubard
  Horatio Greenough in his studio in Flor-
    ence                                   VRV
    MiD. Travelers in Arcadia
    Pierson
    Richardson. Ptg in America
    VRV. William James Hubard
  Jeremiah Hoffman and daughter
    VRV. William James Hubard
  John C. Calhoun                          DC
    Time. 300 years (col)
    VRV. William James Hubard
  John H. Cocke, of Bremo                  VCU
    VRV. William James Hubard
  John Hoffman
    VRV. William James Hubard
  John Marshall
    VRV. William James Hubard
  Mann S. Valentine                        VRV
    VRV. William James Valentine
  Mann S. Valentine, 2nd, and the artist
                                           VRV
    MiD. Travelers in Arcadia
    VRV. 'William James Hubard
  Milk man and the maid
    VRV. 'William James Hubard
  Mrs Henry Wythe Tabb
    VRV. William James Hubard
  Mrs John C. Rutherfoord
    VRV. William James Hubard

Mrs John Tabb
    VRV. William James Hubard
  Mrs William Bolling
    VRV. William James Hubard
  Mrs William James Hubard
    VRV. William Jamès Hubard
  Mrs William James Hubard
    VRV. William James Hubard
  Rebecca Pue
    VRV. William James Hubard
  Robert Gilmor II                         MdBM
    DC. Amer ptrs of the South
  Robert Morgan Gibbes                     MdBH
    VRV. William James Hubbard
  Self-portrait
    VRV. William James Hubard
  Thomas Williamson
    VRV. William James Hubard
  William A. Shafer
    VRV. William James Hubard
Hubbard, Bradford
  Moulthrop, R. Bradford Hubbard
HUBBARD, Charles, fl 1837
  The National Lancers with the reviewing
    officers on Boston Common             MB
    MB. Lane
Hubbard, Elbert Green, 1856-1915
  Chase, W. M. Elbert Hubbard
Hubbard, Henry, 1769-1844
  Malone, E. G. Henry Hubbard
Hubbell, Anna Gibbon (Johnson) 1809-1895
  Neagle, J. Anna Gibbon Johnson
HUCK, Robert, 1923-
  Deer hunter
    OrPA. Ptgs & sculptures
Huckleberry pickers by C. S. Price
The hucksters by P. Calvin
HUDSON, Charles William, 1871-1943
  Spruce tree in a landscape              MB
    MB. Ptgs in water color
Hudson, Eliza, fl 1820
  Ames, E. Mrs Robert Hudson
HUDSON, John Bradley, 1832-1903
  View in Maine                           MB
    MB. Karolik coll
Hudson, Maria (Mackie) 1795-1862
  Sully, T. Mrs Edward Hudson
Hudson, Robert, c 1785-1825
  Ames, E. Robert Hudson
HUDSON, William, fl 1850
  Political debate between two Irishmen
    Davidson v2
Hudson autumn by B. Mitchell
Hudson Bay fur company by R. Marsh
Hudson burlesk chorus by R. Marsh
Hudson burlesk, Union City, New Jersey
  by R. Marsh
Hudson navigation boat by E. Fiene
Hudson river and valley
  Audubon, V. G. (attributed works) Hud-
    son river view
  Bellows, G. 'W. Floating ice [Hudson
    river] 1910
  Bellows, G. W. Morning snow [The
    Hudson from Riverside park]
  Bellows, G. W. Rain on the river [Hud-
    son river from Riverside drive, 1908]
  Bellows, G. W. Up the Hudson
  Birch, T. Upper Hudson
  Browere, A. D. (attributed works) Hud-
    son river landing
  Chambers, T. Hudson river landscape
  Chambers, T. Hudson river scene
  Chambers, T. Hudson river valley, sunset

**Hudson river and valley**—*Continued*
Chambers, T. View of the Hudson river at West Point
Chambers, T. (attributed works) Landscape—probably a Hudson river scene
Cornell, J. V. View of the Highlands from Ruggles house, Newburgh, New York
Croome, W. Crystal valley farm, a view of the Hudson river at the Overslaugh
Cropsey, J. F. Upper Hudson
Cropsey, J. F. Winter scene on the Hudson
Davies, T. View of Green Bush on the Hudson's river near Albany
De Grailly, W. View from West Point
Durand, A. B. Hudson at Rhinebeck
Fisher, A. The Hudson pool
Hart, J. M. View on the Hudson
Hart, J. M. and Tait. A. F. (attributed works) The Burden family enjoying the Hudson river near Troy
Harvey, G. View on the Hudson
Havell, R. View of the Hudson river from Horton's road near Croton
Hill, J. W. Hudson river bridge near Waterford
Homer, W. Hudson river
Homer, W. Hudson river logging
Homer, W. The rapids, Hudson river, Adirondacks
Johnson. D. At Barrytown, Hudson river
Lechay, J. Hudson river
Mitchell, B. Hudson autumn
Moore, C. H. Down the Hudson to West Point
Porter, R. Hudson river highlands
Unidentified artist. Beacon-on-the Hudson
Unidentified artist. Crow's nest, from Bull hill, Hudson river looking toward West Point
Unidentified artist. Hudson river landscape
Unidentified artist. Hudson river landscape with sailboats
Unidentified artist. Hudson river view
Unidentified artist. Outing on the Hudson
Unidentified artist. Palisades
Unidentified artist. Sunset by the river
Wall, W. G. Hudson river from West Point
Wall, W. G. View near Fishkill, N.Y.
Wall, W. G. View near Fort Montgomery
Weir, J. F. View of the Highlands from West Point
Wheelock, M. G. On the Hudson
Wyant, A. H. On the upper Hudson
**Hudson** river bridge near Waterford by J. W. Hill
**Hudson** river school series, 30 by J. Jarvaise
**Hudson** river school series, 59 by J. Jarvaise
**Hudson** river school series, 86 by J. Jarvaise
**Hudson** river schooner Robert Knapp by J. Bard
**Hudson** river sloop Phillip R. Paulding by J. E. Butterworth
**Hudson** river steamboat Rip Van Winkle by J. Bard
**HUGE, J. Frederick**
Steamboat Bunkerhill
Ford. Pictorial folk art

**Huger, Daniel Elliott,** 1779-1854
Malbone, E. G. Judge Daniel E. Huger
**Hughes, John,** abp, 1797-1865
Healy, G. P. A. Archbishop John Hughes
**Hugo, Colonel**
Copley, J. S. Colonels Hugo and Schleppengull
**Hull, Isaac,** 1773-1843
Jarvis, J. W. Commodore Isaac Hull
**HULTBERG, John,** 1922-
Arctic cabin                                    IU
  CoS. New accessions USA, 1958
  IU. Contemp Amer ptg & sculp, 1957
  IU. 20th century
Flying box                                      MM
  CoS. New accessions USA, 1956
Frozen station
  IU. Contemp Amer ptg & sculp, 1959
Italian journey                               NBuA
  NBuA. Acquisitions 1954-57
  PPC. International ex, 1955
The lake
  VR. Amer ptg, 1958
Night still life                               WMAA
  Pierson
  WMAA. Annual ex, 1955
Number 1, 1960
  IU. Contemp Amer ptg & sculp, 1961
Tilted horizon                                  NeL
  NUM. Art across America
Yellow sky                                       DC
  DC. Masterpieces
  DC. 24 biennial ex, 1955
**Human** comedy by A. Bohrod
The **human** fold—flowering by J. W. Treiman
**Human** pool tables by R. Marsh
**Hummingbirds**
Audubon, J. J. Ruby-throated hummingbird
Heade, M. J. Hummingbirds and gold and purple orchids
Heade, M. J. Hummingbirds and orchids
Heade, M. J. Orchids and hummingbird
Heade, M. J. Orchids and spray orchids with hummingbirds
Heade, M. J. Passion flowers and hummingbirds
**Humphreys, David,** 1752-1818
Stuart, G. David Humphreys
**Hunger** by B. Shahn
**Hunt, Mrs Cassius,** fl 1760
Badger, J. Mrs Cassius Hunt
**Hunt, Edward,** fl 1810
Birch, T. Edward Hunt
**HUNT, H. P.** fl 1848
Lady holding a book                             MeC
  Jetté. Amer heritage collection
**HUNT, Lynn Bogue**
Northeaster—Canada geese
  NSP. Sportscapes
**Hunt, Mrs Richard Morris**
Hunt, W. M. Mrs Richard Morris Hunt and child
**HUNT, William Morris,** 1824-1879
Anahita, the flight of night                    MB
  Pierson
Bathers                                         MWM
  DC. De gustibus
  Roos

Flight of night                              PA
  Barker. Amer ptg
  Larkin rev ed
  Pierson
  Richardson. Ptg in America
  Roos
Flight of night (mural)
  Larkin
The forge                                    OYB
  OYB. Supplement
Gloucester harbor                            MB
  Pierson
Ida Mason                                    MB
  Pierson
Ideal head                                   InIJ
  InIJ. 105 ptgs
Lemuel Shaw
  Larkin rev ed (col detail)
  Pierson
Marguerite                                   MB
  Pierson
Mrs Richard Morris Hunt and child
  Pierson
Self-portrait                                MB
  Larkin
  Larkin rev ed
  Mendelowitz
  Pierson
William Maxwell Evarts                       CtY
  CtY. Portrait index
The **hunt** by W. W. Quirt
**Hunted** sky by Y. Tanguy
**Hunter, Mary (Smyth)**
  Sargent, J. S. Mrs Charles Hunter
**Hunter family, fl 1835**
  Unidentified artist. Hunter family of Ger-
    mantown, Pennsylvania
**Hunter** in the hills by L. Kroll
**Hunters and hunting**
  Beal, G. R. Hunter, winter
  Bingham, G. B. Shooting for the beef
  Catlin, G. Buffalo chase
  Catlin, G. Buffalo chase of the Sioux
  Catlin, G. Buffalo chase, upper Missouri
  Catlin, G. Winter hunting on upper Mis-
    souri
  Chapman, J. G. Drawing a bead on a
    woodchuck
  Darley, F. O. C. Hunting buffaloes
  Durant, A. B. Hunter
  Eakins, T. Hunting
  Eakins, T. Pushing for rail
  Eakins, T. Will Schuster and black man
    going shooting (Rail shooting)
  Eastman, S. Hunting buffalo in winter
  Evergood, P. The hunters
  Frost, A. B. Hunting deer
  Frost, A. B. Hunting the moose
  Goodwin, P. R. Calling the moose
  Hess, J. N. Rail shooting
  Homer, W. Hound and hunter
  Homer, W. Huntsman and dogs
  Homer, W. Indian hunter in the Ever-
    glades
  Kuhn, R. Wounded wolves
  Mason, R. M. The moment that makes
    duck hunting
  Miller, A. J. Argali—mountain sheep
  Miller, A. J. Buffalo at bay
  Miller, A. J. Buffalo hunting near Inde-
    pendence rock
  Miller, A. J. Grizzly bear
  Miller, A. J. Head of antelope
  Miller, A. J. Hunters in search of game
  Miller, A. J. Hunting buffalo
  Miller, A. J. Hunting elk
  Miller, A. J. Hunting the bear
  Miller, A. J. Killing buffalo with the
    lance
  Miller, A. J. Running buffalo
  Miller, A. J. Shooting a cougar
  Miller, A. J. Trappers starting for the
    beaver hunt
  Miller, A. J. Trapping beaver
  Miller, A. J. Wounded buffalo
  Miller, A. J. Yell of triumph
  Moran, E. Duck shooting
  Osthaus, E. H. On the points
  Ranney, W. T. Duck hunters on the
    Hoboken marshes
  Russell, C. M. When meat was plentiful
  Russell, C. M. When tracks spell meat
  Russell, C. M. Wild horse hunters
  Ryder, A. P. Hunter's rest
  Stanley, J. M. Buffalo hunt on the south-
    ern plains
  Sword, J. B. A good day's work—return
    from duck hunt
  Tait, A. F. Buffalo hunt
  Tait, A. F. Duck shooting
  Tracy, J. M. Grouse shooting
  Tracy, J. M. Hunter and two dogs
  Tracy, J. M. Pointers
  Unidentified artist. Buffalo hunter
  Unidentified artist. Coon hunt
  Unidentified artist. End of the hunt
  Unidentified artist. Hunting scene
  Unidentified artist. Start of the hunt
  Williamson, C. M. Night hunters
  Wyeth, A. C. Coot hunter
**Hunter's** cabin door by R. L. Goodwin
**Hunter's** equipment by G. Cole
**Hunter's** rest by A. P. Goodrich
**Hunters** resting by M. J. Heade
**Hunting** dog among dead trees by W.
  Homer
**HUNTINGTON, Daniel, 1816-1906**
  George Peabody                             CtY
    CtY. Portrait index
  Martha Washington's reception
    NYG. Fine art
**HUNTINGTON, Daniel, 1816-1906, and
  KENSETT, John Frederick, 1816-
  1872**
  Seascape, Newport
    MB. Karolik coll
**Huntington, Jabez, 1719-1786**
  Trumbull, J. Major General Jabez Hunt-
    ington
**Huntington, Jabez, 1767-1848**
  Trumbull, J. Jabez Huntington
**Huntington** harbor by A. G. Dove
**Hurd, Nathaniel, 1730-1777**
  Copley, J. S. Nathaniel Hurd
**HURD, Peter, 1904-**
  Baptising at Three Wells                   GAtM
    GAtM. Holbrook collection
  Boy from the plains
    McCurdy
    Pierson
  Gerald Marr                                CoS
    CoS. New accessions USA, 1954

HURD, Peter—*Continued*
José Herrera                      MoKN
　Eliot. Art of our time (col)
　MoKN. Handbook
　Time. 300 years (col)
Landscape with polo players
　Gruskin (col)
Rainy season                     NBM
　Baur. Revolution
Hurdy-gurdy by G. S. Ratkai
Hurricane, Bahamas by W. Homer
Hurricane island by W. A. Kienbusch
Hurricane island, Vinal Haven, Maine by
　M. Hartley
Husband and wife in a landscape by W.
　Williams
Hush before the storm by C. E. Burchfield
Hutchinson, Edwin, fl 1846
　Mason, B. F. Edwin Hutchinson
Hutchinson, Sally. See Oliver, Sally (Hutch-
　inson)
Hutchinson boy by J. Theus
Huts, Newfoundland by D. Macknight
Hutson, Mary (Woodward) 1717-1785
　Theus, J. Mrs William Hutson
Hutson, Richard, 1747-1793
　Earl, J. (attributed works) Richard Hut-
　son
Hyacinth by L. MacIver
Hyang-to (Homeland) by S. Chun
Hybrid by F. Ruvolo
Hyde, Richard, 1783-1854
　Malbone, E. G. Richard Hyde
Hydrant water conveyed through wooden
　pipes, 1816, York, Pennsylvania by
　L. Miller

# I

I.R.T. by G. L. K. Morris
I am glad I came back by G. Grosz
I bear the children of tomorrow by U.
　Romano
I got a harp by D. Lutz
I looked into a dream by J. Thecla
I, my own keeper by N. Tschacbasov
I saw the letter 5 in gold by C. H. Demuth
I think so by Y. Kuniyoshi
I was always present by G. Grosz
I woke up one night and saw a house burn-
　ing by G. Grosz
Iberia by P. Trivigno
Iberian landscape by C. Browning
Icarian flight by S. Fogel
Icarus by E. Chamberlain
Icarus by J. Molzahn
Icarus descended by R. Lytle
Ice cart, c 1840 by N. V. Calyo
Ice cream parlor by H. Hensel
Ice cream vendor by C. W. Rain
Ice floes by M. Beckmann
Ice glare by C. E. Burchfield

Iceberg by F. E. Church
Iceland fishermen by P. S. Sample
The iceman by J. Hirsch
Ices by J. Lawrence
Ichabod Crane at a ball at the Van Tassel
　mansion by J. Quidor
Ichabod Crane pursued by the Headless
　Horseman by J. Quidor
Iconostas by J. Elshin
Icy shore by J. Atherton
Ida, Portrait of by A. Dasburg
Ide, Mrs Gregory. See Childs, Clarissa
　(Partridge)
Idea and forms by D. Bothwell
Ideal head by G. Fuller
Ideal head by W. M. Hunt
Ideal head by E. Vedder
Ideal landscape by T. Doughty
The ides by P. Jenkins
Idolatress by H. Hoffman
The idols by C. Wells
If this be not I by P. Guston
Ikon no 386 by J. Xceron
île de la cité by R. Kuntz
I'll take the high road by E. J. Kosa
Illimited sequences by Y. Tanguy
Illumination by R. Pousette-Dart
Illuminations by H. Crowley
Ilsley, Silas, fl 1834
　Unidentified artist. Rev Silas Ilsley
I'm glad I came back by G. Grosz
I'm tired by Y. Kuniyoshi
Image and space by J. W. Boynton
Image in Xhorkom by A. Gorky
Images of Pompeii by V. Vytlacil
Imaginary landscape by J. E. Heliker
Imagined music by K. F. Roesch
IMBERT, Anthony, fl 1824-1836
　Erie canal celebration, New York, 1825
　　　　　　　　　　　　　　　NNMC
　Davidson v2
　U.S. National Capital sesquicentennial
　com
The immigrant by D. Fredenthal
Immigrants' arrival at New York, 1847 by S.
　B. Waugh
Impatience by A. Gorky
Imploring dead by R. Lebrun
Impressionism by C. Sheeler
Imprisoned force by C. A. Morris
Improvisation no 1 by K. Cramer
Improvisation no 2 by K. Cramer
Improvisation in a Greek key by J. Levine
Improvisation on a mill town by C. Sheeler
Improvisation to form by A. Dasburg
In a garden of ancient loves by R. Breinin
In a quandary by G. C. Bingham
In biege with sand by R. B. Motherwell
In charge of the baby by W. Homer
In Colorado by A. Blanch
In Fairmont by N. Spencer
In May by C. E. Burchfield

In my own time by W. Pachner
In nature's wonderland by T. Doughty
In old Kentucky by W. H. Cady
In the air by M. Graves
In the beginning by P. Fine
In the beginning by M. Morgan
In the box by M. Cassatt
In the cabin by N. Spencer
In the Catskills by J. F. Kensett
In the cornfield by J. G. Clonney
In the fields by E. Johnson
In the forest by R. Pousette-Dart
In the garden by G. D. Brush
In the garden by M. Cassatt
In the garden by L. Kester
In the Generalife by J. S. Sargent
In the hollow of the hill by D. Macknight
In the library by M. B. Prendergast
In the loge by M. Cassatt
In the Luxembourg gardens by M. B. Prendergast
In the Luxembourg gardens by J. S. Sargent
In the moraine, Dogtown common, Cape Ann by M. Hartley
In the mountains by W. Homer
In the park by A. M. R. Moses
In the park by M. B. Prendergast
In the parlor by H. Sharrer
In the patio by G. O'Keeffe
In the ring by J. Marin
In the Rockies by W. Whittredge
In the shadow of a mystery by P. Burlin
In the springtime by A. M. R. Moses
In the stable by A. P. Ryder
In the studio by J. Ricci
In the studio by R. Soyer
In the summerhouse by G. Tooker
In the swamp opposite Bayou Sara by J. R. Meeker
In the third sleep by K. Sage
In the valley by D. Macknight
In the wake of the buffalo hunters by C. M. Russell
In the wake of the ferry by J. Sloan
In the wilderness by S. R. Gifford
In the woods by A. B. Durand
In the woodshed by J. G. Clonney
In vaudeville by C. H. Demuth
In without knocking by C. M. Russell
Inauguration by J. Levine
Incantation by C. Sheeler
Incantation no 2 by G. Johanson
Incense of a new church by C. H. Demuth
Inches, Louise (Pomeroy) fl 1887
    Sargent, J. S. Mrs Charles Edward Inches
An incident of the Revolution by J. Eichholtz
Incoming tide by M. M. Albright
Incumbent by W. Gropper
Indefinite divisibility by Y. Tanguy

Independence, Missouri
    Warren, F. E. Town square, Independence
Independence hall, Philadelphia by K. Matthew
Independence hall, Philadelphia by E. Shinn
India by B. Shahn
Indian blanket by K. Knaths
Indian bull boats on the Missouri by K. Bodmer
Indian camp by G. Bartlett
Indian camp by A. Bierstadt
Indian camp by W. Homer
Indian campfire by C. Wimar
Indian encampment by G. C. Bingham
Indian encampment by R. A. Blakelock
Indian encampment by Unidentified artist
Indian fields by V. Higgins
Indian penny by W. W. Quirt
Indian sugar camp by S. Eastman
Indian telegraph by J. M. Stanley
Indian village of Alpuyeca by E. Isenburger
Indians of North America
    See also Medicine man; Tepees; also names of Indian chiefs, e.g., Black Hawk (Sauk chief), Red Jacket (Sagoyewatha) (Seneca Indian chief)
    Bartlett, G. Indian camp
    Bartlett, G. Indian police
    Bierstadt, A. Indians near Fort Laramie
    Bingham, G. C. Concealed enemy
    Birch. T. Landing of William Penn
    Blakelock, R. A. Indian madonna
    Bodmer, K. Crow Indians
    Bodmer, K. Interior of the hut of a Mandan chief
    Bodmer, K. Mato-topé with the marks of his exploits
    Bodmer, K. Noapeh, an Assiniboin Indian; Psihdja-Sahpa, a Yanktonai Indian
    Boutelle, D. C. Indian surveying a landscape
    Bradshaw, J. W. An Indian
    Brush, G. D. At dawn
    Brush, G. D. Silence broken
    Catlin, G. See titles under name of artist
    Couse, E. I. Making medicine
    Cross, H. H. Red Cloud and Burning Heart
    Delano, G. C. Navajo
    Delano, G. C. Navajo boy
    Dixon, M. Katchinamaker
    Eastman, S. Death whoop
    Eastman, S. Indian attack
    Eastman, S. Indians travelling
    Eastman, S. Lacrosse playing among the Sioux
    Eastman, S. Sioux Indians breaking up camp
    Eastman, S. Squaws playing ball on the prairie
    Farny, H. F. Song of the talking wire
    Henri, R. Indian girl
    Hesselius, G. Tishcohan
    Hesselius, G. Lapowinsa
    Hicks, E. Penn's treaty with the Indians
    Homer, W. Indian camp
    Homer, W. Indian hunter in the Everglades

**Indians of North America**—*Continued*
Homer, W. Indian woman at oven
King, C. B. No Heart—Ioway
King, C. B. Shaumonekusse, chief of the Otoes
King, C. B. Young Omahaw, War Eagle, Little Missouri and Pawnees
King, G. B. No-way-ke-sug-ga, an Oto
King, G. B. Tah-ro-hon, an Iowa warrior
King, G. B. (attributed works) Le Soldat du Chêne, an Osage chief
Krans, O. Indians
Krieghof, C. Indians portaging furs
Leigh, W. R. Baking day
Leigh, W. R. The mystic
Lewis, J. O. Cut-Taa-Tas-Tia, a Fox chief
Lewis, J. O. Me-no-quet, a Pottawattomie chief
Lewis, J. O. Nabu-Naa-Kee-Shick, a Chippewa chief
Lewis, J. O. Pe-che-co, a Pottawattomie chief
Lewis, J. O. Sun-a-get, a Pottawattomie chief
Lewis, J. O. Tens-qua-ta-wa, the Shawnee prophet
Lewis, J. O. Waa-Na-Taa, chief of the Sioux
Mathies, J. L. D. Seneca veterans of the war of 1812
Miller, A. J. See titles under name of artist
Neagle, J. Indian heads
Neagle, J. Knife Chief of the Pawnee Loups
Remington, F. Apaches listening
Remington, F. The outlier
Remington, F. Pioneer and the Indian
Rindisbacher, P. Indians hunting buffalo
Rindisbacher, P. Indians returning from war
Russell, C. M. See titles under name of artist
Schreyvogel, C. The silenced war whoop
Seymour, S. Indians
Seymour, S. Oto council
Seymour, S. Pawnee council
Sharp, J. H. Young chief's mission
Shaw, J. Indians sighting a ship
Stanley, J. M. Indians playing cards
Stanley, J. M. Ko-kak-koo-kiss, a Towoc-cono warrior
Stevens, J. Sioux Indians attacking a Minnesota farm
Unidentified artist. Buffalo hunter
Unidentified artist. Indian chief
Unidentified artist. Murder of Jane Mc-Crea
Vanderlyn, J. Death of Jane McCrea
West, B. William Penn's treaty with the Indians
Wilgus, W. J. Ut-Ha-Wah (Capt Cole)
Wimar, C. Attack on an emigrant train, 1856
Wimar, C. Buffalo hunt
Wimar, C. Captive charger
Wimar, C. Indians approaching Fort Benton
Wimar, C. On the warpath

**Dancers and dancing**
Bodmer, K. Buffalo dance of the Mandan
Bodmer, K. The Minnetaree scalp dance
Burbank, E. A. Hopi snake dance
Catlin, G. The bear dance
Catlin, G. The beggars' dance of Teton Sioux
Catlin, G. Bull dance of the Mandans
Catlin, G. Dance of the berdash of the Sauk and Fox
Catlin, G. Mandan O-kee-pa, the bull dance
Catlin, G. The medicine bag dance of the Sauk and Fox
Catlin, G. The Sauk and Fox slave dance
Catlin, G. Scalp dance of the Sioux
Catlin, G. Sioux beggar's dance
Catlin, G. Snowshoe dance of the Chippewas
Catlin, G. Snowshoe dance of the Ojibbeway
Catlin, G. The sun dance
Eastman, S. Dog dance of the Dakotahs
Marin, J. Corn dance, New Mexico
Marin, J. Dance of the San Domingo Indians
Rindisbacher, P. Indian dance
Rindisbacher, P. War dance of the Sauks and Foxes
Seymour, S. Dog dance of the Kansas Indians
Stanley, J. M. Osage scalp dance
Wimar, C. Buffalo dance

**Wars**
Adams, C. Custer's last fight
Catlin, G. Comanche war party meeting dragoons
Mathies, J. L. D. Seneca veterans of the war of 1812
Miller, A. J. Threatened attack
Remington, F. Cavalry charge on the southern plains
Russell, C. M. Custer's last stand
Russell, C. M. Desperate stand
Russell, C. M. Indian warfare
Schreyvogel, C. Defending the stockade
Schreyvogel, C. The silenced war whoop

**Indians of South America**
Catlin, G. The handsome dance, Venezuela, South America
Catlin, G. Uruguay medicine man, South America

**Individual** state of the world by M. Graves
**Industrial** by R. L. Ochs
**Industrial** composition by E. D. Lewandowski
**Industrial** façade by C. A. Morris
**Industrial** landscape by G. L. K. Morris
**Industrial** night by L. Gatch
**Industrial** scene by H. D. Sharrer
**Industrial** town by A. Rattner
**Industrial** variations by S. Gross
**Industrial** worker by B. Shahn
**Industry** by S. Davis
**Industry** by P. Dickinson
An **infanta** (Souvenir of Velásquez) by W. M. Chase
**Infernal** machine at dawn by J. W. McCullough

**Infinite** divisibility by Y. Tanguy
**Inflation** means depression by B. Shahn
The **informer** by F. Ruvolo
**Ingersoll, R. Sturgis,** 1891-
 Watkins, F. C. R. Sturgis Ingersoll
**INGHAM, Charles Cromwell,** 1796-1863
 Katherine Sedgwick
 MB. New England miniatures
**Ingraham, Solomon,** d 1806?
 Verstille, W. Capt Solomon Ingraham
**Ingram** mansion, Pittsburgh by J. Kane
**Initial** by F. J. Kline
**Initials** by W. Homer
**Inland** pool by L. Kroll
**Inland** tempest by A. B. Davies
**Inland** water, Bermuda by W. Homer
The **inlet** by W. Farndon
**INMAN, Henry,** 1801-1846
 David Sproat Kennedy               NNHS
 NNHS. Waldron Phoenix Belknap coll
 Dismissal of school on an October after-
  noon                             MB
 MB. Karolik coll
 Georgianna Buckham and her mother MB
 Larkin (detail)
 Larkin rev ed (detail)
 Pierson
 Henry Clay
 Time. 300 years (col)
 John James Audubon
 CtY. Yale alumni
 John M. Catlin                     CtY
 CtY. Portrait index
 John Marshall
 MB. Great Americans
 John Wesley Jarvis                 MCH
 Dickson. John Wesley Jarvis
 Mrs Robert Lenox                   NNHS
 NNHS. Waldron Phoenix Belknap coll
 The newsboy                        MAP
 NJN. Early N.J. artists
 Picnic in the Catskills            NBM
 Born
 Pierson
 Richard Varick                     NHMC
 NUM. Art across America
 Rural happiness
 NYG. Fine art
 Samuel Jones                       CtY
 CtY. Portrait index
 Self-portrait                      PA
 Richardson. Ptg in America
 Young fishermen                    MM
 Bazin
**Inman, Mrs Ralph,** 1725-1761
 Feke, R. (attributed works) Mrs Ralph
  Inman (also attributed to Blackburn)
The **inn** by A. G. Dove
**INNESS, George,** 1825-1894
 Apple orchard                      MiD
 MiD. Treasures
 Approaching storm from Alban hills OCl
 OCl. Handbook
 Autumn oaks                        MM
 Barker. Amer ptg
 NYG. Fine art
 Pierson
 Taylor. Fifty centuries, 1954 ed (col)
 Upjohn

 Autumn scene                       GAtM
 GAtM. Holbrook collection
 Brook, Montclair                   PR
 PR. Catalogue
 Castel Gandolfo                    OrPA
 PPC. Amer classics
 Christmas eve                      NJMo
 NJMo. Forty years
 Clearing up                        MSG
 Baur. Amer ptg
 Clouded sun                        PPC
 Pierson
 Coast of Cornwall
 Cheney. Story 1958 ed
 Coming storm, 1878                 NBuA
 Larkin
 Larkin rev ed
 NBuA. Catalague of the ptgs
 Coming storm, 1880                 MAP
 Larkin rev ed (col)
 Pierson
 Time. 300 years (col)
 Delaware meadows                   MnMW
 Larkin
 Delaware valley                    MM
 McClintock
 Robb. Harper history
 Delaware Water Gap                 MM
 Born
 Flexner. Amer ptg
 Flexner. Short history
 McClintock
 Pierson
 Delaware Water Gap                 NJMo
 McClintock
 NJMo. Your Montclair art museum
 Time. 300 years (col)
 Etretat                            CtHW
 CtHW. Handbook
 Evening at Medfield                MM
 Cheney. New world history
 Grey day, Goochland                DP
 Pierson
 Richardson. Ptg in America
 Harvest scene in the Delaware valley
                                    MnMW
 Larkin rev ed
 Home at Montclair                  MWiS
 MWiS. Ex 4 and 7
 Home of the heron                  ICA
 Gardner 1959 ed
 Lee. Art then and now
 Mendelowitz
 Pierson
 June                               NBM
 Mendelowitz
 Pierson
 Time. 300 years (col)
 Lackawanna valley                  DN
 Born
 McClintock
 Pierson
 U.S. National Capital sesquicentennial
  com
 Walker. Ptgs from America
 Lake Albano                        DP
 DP. Catalogue
 Late afternoon, Montclair, New Jersey
                                    ATeS
 ATeS. Collection
 March of the crusaders
 Sears. Highlights

**INNESS, George**—*Continued*
The monk                                      MAP
  NUM. Art across America
  Pierson
Moonlight on Passamaquoddy bay    ICA
  McKinney
Moonlight, Tarpon Springs             DP
  DP. Catalogue
Near the village, October            OCiM
  OCiM. Guide
Old mill                              ICA
  Barker. Amer ptg
Painting at Montclair                InTH
  InTH. Catalogue
Passing shower
  NYG. Fine art
Peace and plenty                      MM
  NYG. Fine art
  Pierson
  Richardson. Ptg in America
  Roos
The rainbow                           InIJ
  InIJ. 105 ptgs
Roman Campagna                       MoSL
  Born
  MoSL. Handbook 1953
Sacred grove near Rome
  MiD. Travelers in Arcadia
Tiber below Perugia                   OT
  MiD. Travelers in Arcadia
Under the greenwood
  NAD. Amer tradition
Venice: S. Giorgio Maggiore          KLU
  Pierson
View on the Delaware, Water Gap in the
  distance
  McClintock
Woodgatherers: autumn afternoon MWiS
  MWiS. Ex 4 and 7
Woodland vista                        MB
  MB. Karolik coll

     **Portrait of the artist**
Chase, W. M. George Inness
**INNESS, George,** 1853-1926
Landscape with cattle               NJMo
  NJMo. Forty years
**Innocence** by J. Delaney
**Innocence,** meekness, liberty by E. Hicks
The **innocents** by C. L. Martin
**Inns.** See Hotels, restaurants, etc.
**Inquisition** by A. Salemme
**Insects** at twilight by C. E. Burchfield
**Inside** and out by J. Albers
**Inside** looking out by B. Shahn
**Inside** of an Indian tent by P. Rindisbacher
**Inside**—outside by I. R. Pereira
**Inside** the bar by W. Homer
**Interchange** by W. De Kooning
An **interesting** book by C. R. Hirst
**Interior** by A. B. Davies
**Interior** by S. Davis
**Interior** by W. H. Givler
**Interior** by B. Greene
**Interior** by H. Hofmann
**Interior** by L. Kroll
**Interior** by T. McKibben

**Interior** by R. M. Pollack
**Interior** by M. Ray
**Interior** by C. Sheeler
**Interior** by B. Swan
**Interior** by R. Watson
**Interior** and bay by J. C. Lewis
**Interior** and exterior by W. Zorach
**Interior** at Honfleur by F. Hillsmith
**Interior** of Fort Laramie by A. J. Miller
**Interior** of the fourth dimension by M.
  Weber
**Interior**—the creeks by G. Hartigan
**Interior** with figure by R. Soyer
**Interior** with figures by M. Weber
**Interior** with flowers by M. Avery
**Interior** with men by M. Weber
**Interior** with standing figure by J. Glasco
**Interior** with three figures by J. Martini
**Interlude** by I. Bishop
**Interlude** by Z. L. Sepeshy
**Interlunar** sea by C. Wells
**Intersection** by M. Tobey
**Interurban** by F. Alexander
**Interurban** line by C. E. Burchfield
**Interwoven** thread by K. Callahan
**Intimate** conversation by D. W. Ellis
**Into** Dogtown, autumn by W. Kienbusch
**Into** the world there came a soul called Ida
  by I. L. Albright
**Introspection** by A. Brook
The **intruder** by A. Brook
The **intruder** by H. Janicki
**Invasion** by B. Kopman
**Invasion** by E. Millman
**Invention**—dance by M. Ray
**Invention** on a microscopic theme by L. E.
  Kupferman
The **inventor** by K. Zerbe
**Invitation** by G. J. McNeil
**Invocation** by S. M. Adler
**Invocation** by M. Greenwood
**Ionian** sea by C. Oscar
**Iotrio** by L. Buck
**Iowa (battleship)**
  Aldrich, W. T. A giant
**Iowa** cornfield by G. Wood
**IPPOLITO, Angelo,** 1922-
  Morning
    WMAA. Young America 1957
  Storm                              WMAA
    Baur. Nature (col)
    Goodrich. Amer art (col)
    WMAA. Young America 1957
  West
    WMAA. Annual ex, 1958
**Ipswich** bay by F. H. Lane
**Ipswich** sand dunes by A. T. Roberts
**Iris** by K. Schrag
**Iris,** Study of by J. La Farge
**Iris** and snowballs by J. E. Francis
**Irish** girl by R. Henri
**Irish** landscape by L. McIver

The **Iron Crown (ship)**
    Homer, W. Wreck of the Iron Crown
**Iron** dragon by J. E. Levi
**Iron** witch by J. V. Cornell
The **ironers** by Unidentified artist
**Iroquois** Indian by A. J. Miller
**Irving, Washington,** 1783-1859
    Jarvis, J. W. Washington Irving
**Isaac** blessing Jacob by Unidentified artist
**Isaac** of York by W. Allston
**Ischia** by S. Greene
**Iselin, Eleanora (O'Donnell)** 1821-1897
    Sargent, J. S. Mrs Adrian Iselin
**ISENBURGER, Eric,** 1902-
    Amalfi
        IU. Contemp Amer ptg, 1951
    Country flowers
        VR. Biennial ex, 1948
    Cove at sunset
        IU. Contemp Amer ptg, 1948
    Homage to Rome
        NAD. Annual ex, 1951
    Indian village of Alpuyeca
        IU. Contemp Amer ptg & sculp, 1959
    Jimmy Savo
        NAD. Annual ex, 1960
    Roar of the wooden horse
        PPC. Ptg in the U.S. 1949
    Romantic figure              DC
        DC. 21 biennial ex, 1949
    Sea and wharf at Provincetown
        NAD. Annual ex, 1957
    Self-portrait
        ICA. Annual ex, 1945/46
    Still life
        NAD. Annual ex, 1956
**Island** of happiness by Y. Kuniyoshi
**Island** of Mount Desert from the mainland
    by R. S. Gifford
**Island,** Small point, Maine by J. Marin
The **Isle** of Capri by J. F. Cropsey
**Isle** of the gods by E. J. Stevens
**Isolationist** by W. Gropper
**Isotopes** by W. T. Murch
**Israel** by W. Pachner
**Israel** by S. Rosenberg
**Istanbul** by W. G. Congdon
**It** was blue and green by G. O'Keeffe
**It** will soon be here by O. Kraus
**Italian** beach by H. Frankenthaler
**Italian** farmyard by G. Wood
**Italian** fiesta, night by G. H. Hallowell
**Italian** flower market by M. B. Prendergast
**Italian** girl by M. B. Prendergast
**Italian** head by J. S. Sargent
**Italian** journey by J. Hultberg
**Italian** shepherd boy by W. Allston
**Italian** sunlight by L. Dodd
**Italy**
    *See also* Florence; Rome; Venice
    Allston, W. Italian landscape
    Bierstadt, A. Marina Grande in Capri
    Boit, E. D. See titles under name of artist
    Bruce, E. Tuscan landscape

    Church, F. E. Between Ceppo Morelli and
        Ponte Grande
    Cole, T. Italian landscape
    Cole, T. Italian scenery
    Cole, T. Roman aqueduct
    Cropsey, J. F. The Isle of Capri
    Cropsey, J. F. Italian landscape
    Cropsey, J. F. Lake of Nemi
    Davies, A. B. The Apennines
    Davies, A. B. Italian landscape, the Apen-
        nines
    De Diego, J. Italy: historical town
    McCarter, H. B. Early Italy
    Prendergast, M. B. Roman Campagna
    Shahn, B. Italian landscape
    Toole, J. Vesuvius
    Vedder, E. Bed of the Torrent Mugnone,
        near Florence
    Vedder, E. Italian landscape
    Weiss, H. Italian village
**Ithaca, New York**
    Walton, H. View of Ithaca, Tompkins
        county, N.Y. in November 1838
**Itlksez** by S. Davis
**I've** got nothing to wear by F. J. Furman
**Ives, Eli,** 1779-1861
    Jocelyn, N. Eli Ives
**IVEY, William,** 1919-
    White painting
        OrPA. Ptgs & sculptures (col)
**Ivory-billed** woodpecker by J. J. Audubon
**Ivory** tower by R. Hilton
**IWAMOTO, Ralph,** 1927-
    Eastern twilight           OYB
        OYB. Annual 1957
        OYB. Supplement 1959
**Izard, Alice (Delancey)**
    Copley, J. S. Mr and Mrs Ralph Izard
**Izard, Anne.** See Deas, Anne (Izard)
**Izard, Charlotte (Broughton)** c 1729-1801
    Theus, J. Mrs Henry Izard
**Izard, Eliza,** 1784-1862
    Malbone, E. G. Eliza Izard
**Izard, Eliza (Mrs Daniel Blake)** See Blake,
    Eliza (Izard)
**Izard, George,** 1776-1828
    Malbone, E. G. Capt George Izard
**Izard, Mrs Henry.** See Izard, Charlotte
    (Broughton)
**Izard, Margaret.** See Manigault, Margaret
    (Izard)
**Izard, Ralph,** 1742-1804
    Copley, J. S. Mr and Mrs Ralph Izard
    Malbone, E. G. Capt Ralph Izard
    Theus, J. Ralph Izard as a boy
    Turnbull, J. Ralph Izard
**Izard, Mrs Ralph.** See Izard, Alice (De-
    lancey)

# J

**J** by J. McGarrell
The **jacket** by B. Perlin
**Jack-in-the-pulpit** by G. O'Keeffe
**Jackman, Gracie Beardsley Jefferson,** fl 1835
    Unidentified artist. Gracie Beardsley Jef-
    ferson Jackman and her daughter

**Jackson, Andrew, president U.S.** 1767-1845
  Durand, A. B. Andrew Jackson
  Earl, R. Andrew Jackson
  Earl, R. E. W. Andrew Jackson
  Harding, C. Andrew Jackson
  Healy, G. P. A. Andrew Jackson
  Jarvis, J. W. Gen Andrew Jackson
  Peale, A. C. Andrew Jackson
  Peale, C. W. Andrew Jackson
  Sully, T. Andrew Jackson
  Waldo, S. L. Andrew Jackson
**Jackson, Jonathan,** 1743-1810
  Copley, J. S. Jonathan Jackson
**JACKSON, Lee,** 1909-
  Boardwalk in moonlight
    NAD. Annual ex, spring 1950
**JACKSON, Martin,** 1919-
  Harbor at night                              DC
    CoS. New accessions USA, 1950
    DC. 21 biennial ex, 1949
  Night fair
    NAD. Annual ex, 1952
  Tintype, 1948
    IU. Contemp Amer ptg, 1949
    NAD. Annual ex, 1948
  Toy battle                                   OYB
    OYB. Annual 1953
    OYB. Supplement
**Jackson** by J. D. Brooks
**JACOBI, Rudolf,** 1889-
  Landscape                                    CtY
    CtY. Soc Anonyme
**Jacob's** dream by W. Allston
**Jacob's** dream by L. Terry
**Jacquelin, Edward,** fl 1722
  Unidentified artist. Edward Jacquelin the
    second
**Jagged** clouds by L. Feininger
El **Jaleo** by J. S. Sargent
**Jamaica** noon by S. M. Etnier
**JAMES, Alexander,** 1890-1946
  Artist's wife                                KW
    NHMC. Alexander James
  Candide                                      MSM
    MSM. Handbook
  Choose your partner
    NHMC. Alexander James
  Danny
    NHMC. Alexander James
  Down to earth
    Gruskin (col)
  Embattled farmer
    NHMC. Alexander James
  Fitzwilliam
    NHMC. Alexander James
  Forgotten cabin
    NHMC. Alexander James
  Heart of darkness
    NHMC. Alexander James
  Joan
    NHMC. Alexander James
  John P. Marquand
    NHMC. Alexander James
  Luther Smith
    NHMC. Alexander James
  Mrs Dean Acheson
    NHMC. Alexander James
  Sandy                                        MoKN
    NHMC. Alexander James
  Selectmen
    NHMC. Alexander James

  Self-portrait, 1940
    NHMC. Alexander James
  A solitary
    NHMC. Alexander James
**James, Alexander Robertson**
  James, A. Sandy
**James, Catharine (Barber)** 1782-1859
  Ames, E. Mrs William James
**JAMES, Frederic**
  Driftwood
    NAD. Annual ex, 1949, 2d half
**James, Frederika**
  James, A. Artist's wife
**James, Henry,** 1843-1916
  Duveneck, F. Henry James, 1882
  Sargent, J. S. Henry James
**James, Katharine Barber,** 1834-1890
  Ames, E. Katharine Barber James (?)
**James, Marcia Lucretia (Ames)** See Ames,
    Marcia Lucretia
**James, William,** 1771-1782
  Ames, E. William James
**James, Mrs William,** 1782-1854. See James,
    Catharine (Barber)
**James, Mrs William,** 1797/98-1886.   See
    Ames, Marcia Lucretia
**JAMESON, Demetrios,** 1919-
  Boy with birds
    OrPA. Ptgs & sculptures
  Boy with kite
    NNSG. Younger Amer ptrs
**JAMIESON, Mitchell,** 1915-
  Children of Rome
    MM. Amer ptg today
  Convoy entering Mers-el-Kebir
    NYG. Fine art
  Maelstrom                                    WaS
    Pousette-Dart. Amer ptg
  Off Hatteras                                 TxF
    CoS. New accessions USA, 1956
  Port of Cherbourg
    PPC. Ptg in the U.S. 1949
**Jane** Reed and Dora Hunt by C. H. Carter
**JANICKI, Hazel,** 1918-
  The intruder
    IU. Contemp Amer ptg & sculp, 1953
  Weavers of a spell                           OYB
    OYB. Annual 1951
    OYB. Catalogue 1951
**Janitor's** holiday by P. S. Sample
**JANJIGIAN, Anahid**
  Back porches
    NAD. Annual ex, 1959
**January** by W. De Kooning
**January,** Michigan farm by Z. L. Sepeshy
**Japanese** peasants by J. La Farge
**Japanese** toy tiger and odd objects by Y.
    Kuniyoshi
**Japhthah's** return by B. B. Lathrop
**JARVAISE, James,** 1925-
  Arrangement on a blue table                  OYB
    OYB. Annual 1955
    OYB. Supplement 1959
  Blue table
    IU. Contemp Amer ptg & sculp, 1953
  Classical still life
    IU. Contemp Amer ptg & sculp, 1957

JARVIS, J. W.—*Continued*
Nathan Starr jr (of Middletown, Conn.)
    NNHS
  Dickson. John Wesley Jarvis
Oliver Hazard Perry    NNCH
  Dickson. John Wesley Jarvis
  Dickson. John Wesley Jarvis (detail)
  Larkin
  Larkin rev ed
  Pierson
Peter Scoyen    NJF
  Dickson. John Wesley Jarvis
The pirate Laffite    LaNM
  Dickson. John Wesley Jarvis
Robert Gilmor jr    PA
  Dickson. John Wesley Jarvis
Samuel Chester Reid    MnMI
  Dickson. John Wesley Jarvis
Self-portrait (Giskra coll)
  Dickson. John Wesley Jarvis
Self-portrait (Lambert coll)
  Dickson. John Wesley Jarvis
Self-portrait    MdBW
  MdBMu. Rendezvous
Solomon Etting    MdBH
  Dickson. John Wesley Jarvis
Thomas Ellison    NNHS
  Dickson. John Wesley Jarvis
Thomas Macdonough
  Dickson. John Wesley Jarvis
  Dickson. John Wesley Jarvis (detail)
Thomas Paine
  U.S. National Capital sesquicentennial
  com
Unknown man    MM
  Dickson. John Wesley Jarvis
Washington Irving    CtY
  CtY. Portrait index
Washington Irving (Sunnyside restoration
  coll)
  Dickson. John Wesley Jarvis
William Bainbridge    NNCH
  Dickson. John Wesley Jarvis
William Croghan
  Dickson. John Wesley Jarvis
William Henry Cabell II
  Dickson. John Wesley Jarvis
William Johnston    NNHS
  Dickson. John Wesley Jarvis
William Leffingwell    CtY
  CtY. Portrait index
  Dickson. John Wesley Jarvis
William Linn
  Dickson. John Wesley Jarvis
William Neilson
  Dickson. John Wesley Jarvis
William Samuel Johnson
  Dickson. John Wesley Jarvis
  Flexner. Light of distant skies
William W. Van Ness    NNHS
  Dickson. John Wesley Jarvis
Young boy
  WiMiA. Amer ptg 1760-1960

**Attributed works**

Sailor's head (reputed self-portrait of
  Jarvis)
  Dickson. John Wesley Jarvis

**Portrait of the artist**

Inman, H. John Wesley Jarvis
Otis, B. John Wesley Jarvis (after Jarvis'
  self-portrait)

Jarvis, Lydia (Liscome) 1799-1848
  Jarvis, J. W. Lydia Liscome
Jarvis, Mrs John Wesley, d 1813. See Burtis,
  Betsey
Jarvis, Mrs John Wesley, 1799-1848. See
  Jarvis, Lydia (Liscome)
Jason by R. Morrow
Jason returning to demand his father's king-
  dom by W. Allston
Jaudennes y Nebot, Joseph de, fl 1795
  Stuart, G. Joseph de Jaudennes y Nebot
Jaudenes y Nebot, Louise Carolina Matilde
  (Stoughton) de, 1778-1822?
  Stuart, G. Matilde de Jaudenes y Nebot
Jay, Anna Maria (Bayard) b 1670
  Duyckinck, Gerret. Mrs Augustus Jay
Jay, Augustus, 1665-1751
  Unidentified artist. Augustus Jay
Jay, John, 1745-1829
  Ames, E. John Jay (after Stuart)
Jay, Peter Augustus, 1877-1933
  Sargent, J. S. Peter Augustus Jay at the
  age of three
Jazz by M. Ray
Jazz band by B. Perlin
Je t'aime, II, 1955 by R. B. Motherwell
Jealous lover of Lone Green valley by T. H.
  Benton
Jealousy by L. M. Eilshemius
Jean by G. W. Bellows
Jean by J. Carroll
Jean, Anne and Joseph by G. W. Bellows
Jean in blue by E. E. Speicher
Jean with blue book and apple by G. W.
  Bellows
Jeanne by A. H. Maurer
Jeanne d'Arc, Saint, 1412-1431
  Ryder, A. P. Joan of Arc
Jefferson, Joseph, 1829-1905
  Leslie, C. R. Actors' duel: Mr Jefferson
  and Mr Blissett
Jefferson, Thomas, president U.S. 1743-1826
  Peale, C. W. Thomas Jefferson, c 1791
  Peale, Raphaelle. Thomas Jefferson
  Peale, Rembrandt. Thomas Jefferson
  Pyle, H. Thomas Jefferson
  Stuart, G. Thomas Jefferson
  Sully, T. Thomas Jefferson
  Trumbull, J. Thomas Jefferson, detail
  from the Declaration of Independence
JEFFREY, Agnes, 1806-1896
  Main street, Canandaigua
  Jones. Rediscovered ptrs
Jenkins, Mary Eliza
  Wetherby, I. A. Mary Eliza Jenkins
JENKINS, Paul, 1923-
  Black dahlia
  Baur. Nature
  The ides
    Cheney. Story 1958 ed
    WMAA. Young America 1957
  Phenomena—with nitrogen before
    IU. Contemp Amer ptg & sculp, 1961
  St George
    IU. Contemp Amer ptg & sculp, 1959
  To Queequeg
    Read. Concise history

**JENNINGS, Samuel,** fl 1789-1834
Liberty displaying the arts and sciences (The genius of America encouraging the emancipation of the blacks)
Davidson v2
ICA. From colony to nation
U.S. National Capital sesquicentennial com
**Jenny** lake, Wyoming by A. Bierstadt
**Jennys, J. William.** See Jennys, William
**JENNYS, Richard,** fl 1774-1832
Ithamar Canfield
Lipman. Primitive ptrs
**JENNYS, William,** fl 1802
Constant Storrs                    PA
Pierson
Eneas Munson                       CtY
CtY. Portrait index
Gentleman of the Brewer family (Man in the coonskin hat)
Pierson
Mabel Billings
Larkin
Larkin rev ed
Member of the Smith family of Suffield, Connecticut and Rutland, Vermont
Lipman. Primitive ptrs
Mr Hewitt                          MSM
MSM. Handbook
Mrs Constant Storrs                PA
Richardson. Ptg in America
Pierson
Mrs Hewitt                         MSM
MSM. Handbook
Mrs Reuben Hatch                   CtNL
Pierson
Reuben Hatch                       CtNL
Pierson
William Stoddard Williams
ICA. From colony to nation
Woman with a fan                   DC
DC. Masterpieces

**Attributed works**
Young girl                         MeR
NUM. Art across America
**Jensen, Alfred Julio,** 1903-
The great mystery 11               NBuA
NBuA. Acquisitions 1959-1961
**Jereboam, King**
Unidentified artist. Crowning of King Jereboam
**Jeremiah** dictating his prophecy by W. Allston
The **jerk** line by C. M. Russell
**Jerked** down by C. M. Russell
**Jersey** hills by J. Marin
**Jersey** shore by J. J. Jones
**Jersey** turnpike, View from by R. A. Parker
**Jessie,** 17 years old by T. H. Benton
**JESSUP, Jared,** fl 1800-1810
Overmantel, Burk tavern, Bernardston
Flexner. Light of distant skies
**Jesters.** See Clowns and jesters
**Jesus** exalted in song by B. Shahn
**Jet** and turquoise by W. Lockwood
**Jetties** at Bellport by W. J. Glackens
**Jeune** fille en fleur by E. Friedensohn
A **Jew,** Head of by W. Allston

**JEWETT, William,** 1795-1873 and **WALDO, Samuel Lovett,** 1783-1861
Frederick Wolcott                  CtY
CtY. Portrait index
John Trumbull                      CtY
CtY. Portrait index
**Jimmie** O'D by Henri
**Jimmy** Savo and rope by A. Dehn
**Jo** by J. A. M. Whistler
**Jo** Bakos by A. Dasburg
**Joan** by A. James
**Joan** by the sea by B. Greene
**Joan of Arc.** See Jeanne d'Arc, Saint
**Job** lot, cheap by W. M. Harnett
**Job** no 2, 1958 by A. Rattner
**Job** no 9, 1959 by A. Rattner
**Job's** tears by L. Guglielmi
**JOCELYN, Nathaniel,** 1796-1881
Augustus Russell Street            CtY
CtY. Portrait index
Chauncey Allen Goodrich            CtY
CtY. Portrait index
Edward Elias Atwater               CtY
CtY. Portrait index
Eli Ives                           CtY
CtY. Portrait index
James Abraham Hillhouse            CtY
CtY. Portrait index
James Luce Kingsley                CtY
CtY. Portrait index
Jonathan Knight                    CtY
CtY. Portrait index
Timothy Phelps Beers               CtY
CtY. Portrait index

**Portrait of the artist**
Munger, G. Nathaniel Jocelyn
**Jockey** in red silk by R. Davey
**JOE, Dale,** 1928-
Pocket
WMAA. Young America 1960
Profile
WMAA. Young America 1960
**Joe** Magarac by W. Gropper
**Joel** by W. Meyerowitz
**Joel's** cave by M. Weber
**JOHANSEN, John Christen,** b 1876
James Rowland Angell               CtY
CtY. Portrait index
**JOHANSON, George,** 1928-
Incantation no 2
OrPA. Ptgs & sculptures
**John** Biglen in a single scull by T. Eakins
**John** street, New York by J. B. Smith
**John** the Baptist in the wilderness by T. Cole
**Johnny** Appleseed by K. Knaths
**JOHNS, Jasper,** 1930-
Black target
MMA. Sixteen
Green target                       MMA
MMA. Sixteen
Grey numbers
PPC. International ex, 1958
Large white flag
MMA. Sixteen
Numbers in color                   NBuA
MMA. Sixteen
NBuA. Acquisitions 1959-1961

**JOHNS, Jasper**—*Continued*
  Target with four faces                MMA
    MMA. Sixteen
  Tennyson
    MMA. Sixteen
  Two flags
    WMAA. Contemp Amer ptg, 1959-60
  White numbers                         MMA
    MMA. Sixteen
  White target                          MMA
    MMA. Soby collection
**JOHNSON, Mr.** fl 1825-1837
  Mr and Mrs Sherman Griswold and their
    three favorite sheep
    Jones. Rediscovered ptrs
**JOHNSON, Ann,** fl 1840
  Baptisam of our Savour                VWR
    VWR. Folk art (col)
**Johnson, Anna Gibbon.** See Hubbell, Anna
    Gibbon (Johnson)
**Johnson, Catharine Livingston Thorn,**
    fl 1796
  Sharples, J. Catharine Livingston Thorn
    Johnson
**JOHNSON, David,** 1827-1908
  At Barrytown, Hudson river
    DC. Privately owned
  Mount Marcy
    Born
  Old mill, West Milford, New Jersey
                                        NBM
    Born
**JOHNSON, Eastman,** 1824-1906
  Blacksmith shop                       NoCR
    NoCR. Catalogue
  Blacksmith shop                       NCHA
    U.S. National Capital sesquicentennial
      com
  Card playing at Fryeburg, Maine
    MiD. Coll in progress
    WiMiA. Amer ptg 1760-1960
  Corn husking                          NSyE
    Davidson v2
    Pierson
  Corn husking at Nantucket             MM
    Davidson v 1
  Cranberry pickers
    CSB. Impressionism
  Cranberry pickers in Nantucket        ATeS
    ATeS. Collection
  Family group (The Hatch family)       MM
    Mendelowitz
    Pierson
    Roos
  Hollyhocks                            CtNB
    NUM. Art across America
  In the fields                         MiD
    MiD. Treasures
    Pierson
    Richardson. Ptg in America
  Letter home                           MB
    MB. Karolik coll
  Maple sugar campfire, Fryeburg, Maine
                                        CtY
    Davidson v 1
  Measurement and contemplation         MB
    MB. Karolik coll
  Nantucket school of philosophy        MdBW
    Mendelowitz
  Noah Porter                           CtY
    CtY. Portrait index

  Not at home                           NBM
  Larkin
  Larkin rev ed
  Old Kentucky home, life in the South
                                        NNHS
    Cheney. Expressionism 1948 ed
    NAD. Amer tradition
    Pierson
    Roos
  The old stage coach                   WiMi
    Time. 300 years (col)
  The pension agent                     CSFP
    CSFP. Handbook
  A ride for liberty: the fugitive slave NBM
    U.S. National Capital sesquicentennial
      com
  Study in red—morning news at the camp
    Baur. Amer ptg
  Sugaring off                          OYB
    OYB. Catalogue 1951
  Two men (Samuel W. Rowse and Robert
    Rutherford)                         MM
    Barker. Amer ptg
    Pierson
    Richardson. Ptg in America
  Winnowing grain                       MB
    MB. Karolik coll
**Johnson, Edward,** 1767-1829
  Peale, Rembrandt. Mayor Edward John-
    son
**JOHNSON, Frank Tenney,** 1874-1939
  Mountain trail                        ATeS
    ATeS. Collection
  On Salt Lake trail                    IaDa
    IaDa. 30th anniversary
**Johnson, Guy,** 1740?-1788
  West, B. Col Guy Johnson
**Johnson, Jonathan Eastman,** See Johnson,
    Eastman
**JOHNSON, Larry,** 1935-
  Disrobing figure
    WMAA. Young America 1960
  Landscape with still life
    WMAA. Young America 1960
**JOHNSON, Lester,** 1919-
  Self-portrait in ochre
    PPC. International ex, 1961/62
**Johnson, Thomas,** 1732-1819
  Peale, C. W. Gov Thomas Johnson and
    family
**Johnson, Sir William, bart,** 1715-1774
  Wollaston, J. Sir William Johnson
**Johnson, William Samuel,** 1727-1819
  Jarvis, J. W. William Samuel Johnson
**Johnson family member,** c 1830
  Goddell, J. G. (attributed works) Young
    lady of the Nathaniel Johnson family
**JOHNSTON, David Claypoole,** 1799-1865
  Early New England schoolroom scene
                                        MWA
    Davidson v2
  Militia muster                        MWA
    Pierson
    Richardson. Ptg in America
  Ship smashing against rocks
    WiMiA. Amer ptg 1760-1960
  Sound asleep and wide awake
    WiMiA. Amer ptg 1760-1960
  Termination of a militia sham fight   MWA
    Pierson
  View near Milton, Massachusetts with Flat
    pond and buildings
    WiMiA. Amer ptg 1760-1960

**JOHNSTON, Henrietta,** fl 1707-1729
Anne Broughton                           CtY
  CtY. Portrait index
  Flexner. First flowers (detail)
Mrs Samuel Wragg                        SCCG
  Pierson
William Rhett                           SCCG
  Flexner. First flowers
  Pierson
**JOHNSTON, Joshua,** c 1770-1830
Edward and Sarah Rutter                   DN
  DN. Amer primitive ptgs, pt 2
The James McCormick family of Balti-
  more                                  MdBH
  Lipman. Primitive ptrs
Letitia McCurdy
  Larkin
  Larkin rev ed
Westwood children                         DN
  DN. Amer primitive ptgs, pt 2
**JOHNSTON, William,** 1732-1777
Thomas Mumford V                         NBM
  Mendelowitz
Johnston, William, 1769-1848
  Jarvis, J. W. William Johnson
**JOHNSTON, Ynez,** 1920-
Afternoon in August
  IU. Contemp Amer ptg & sculp, 1957
Black palace with red courtyard        CtHW
  Pousette-Dart. Amer ptg
Blue garden
  IU. Contemp Amer ptg, 1952
Breakwater                              WMAA
  Pierson
Reflections in a Roman river
  IU. Contemp Amer ptg & sculp, 1955
Steps to the lighthouse                   IU
  CoS. New accessions USA, 1954
  IU. Contemp Amer ptg & sculp, 1953
Summer storm
  WMAA. Annual ex, 1956
Jolly flatboatmen by G. C. Bingham
Jolly flatboatmen in port by G. C. Bingham
Jonah by A. P. Ryder
Jondol by J. Brooks
**JONES, Amy,** 1899-
City evening
  NAD. Annual ex, 1949, 2d half
Jones, Catherine. See Clinton, Catherine
  (Jones)
Jones, Mrs D. Blair. See Jones, Amy
Jones, Eleanor (Colford) 1755-1824
  Jarvis, J. W. Mrs John Jones III
Jones, Henry, b 1790
  Ames, E. Henry Jones aged 20 years
Jones, Mrs John. See Jones, Eleanor (Col-
  ford)
Jones, John Paul, 1747-1792
  Peale, C. W. John Paul Jones
**JONES, John Paul,** 1924-
The table                                CSB
  CoS. New accessions USA, 1960
Jones, Joe. See Jones, Joseph J.
**JONES, Joseph J.** 1909-
American farm                           WMAA
  Pierson
Apple country
  Gruskin
Evening Star                            NJMo
  NJMo. Your Montclair art museum
Harvest                                  ATU
  ATU. Coll of Amer art

Jersey shore
  CSFP. Annual ex, 1952
Landscape with houseboat
  IU. Contemp Amer ptg, 1951
Landscape with swans
  IU. Contemp Amer ptg, 1952
Regatta
  PPC. International ex, 1952
Rockport                                 MoKN
  UNESCO. 1860-1959
Wheat farmers
  Larkin
  Larkin rev ed
Jones, Mrs Otis, fl 1831
  Bascom, R. H. M. Mr and Mrs Otis Jones
  of Athol, Massachusetts
**JONES, Prescott Merrill M.** 1904-
Lubec, Maine                               MB
  MB. Ptgs in water color
Jones, Samuel, 1770-1853
  Inman, H. Samuel Jones
Jones, Sarah, fl 1775
  Theus, J. Col Jones' grandchild (Sarah
  Jones)
Jones, Thomas Pascal, 1774-1848
  Malbone, E. G. Dr Thomas Pascal Jones
Jones' inn by G. H. Durrie
**JONSON, Raymond,** 1891-
Cliff dwellings no 3
  Cheney. Primer 1958 ed
  Cheney. Story 1958 ed
Composition eleven
  Cheney. Expressionism 1948 ed
Earth rhythms no 9
  Cheney. Expressionism 1948 ed
Earth rhythms no 11
  Cheney. Primer 1958 ed
Jordan, Ambrose Latting, 1789-1865
  Ames, E. Ambrose Latting Jordan
**JORDAN, Samuel,** b 1804?
Eaton family memorial                      DN
  DN. Amer primitive ptgs, pt 1
Joseph and his brethren by Unidentified
  artist
Joseph and the Ishmaelites by D. Aronson
Joseph interpreting Pharaoh's dream by Un-
  identified artist
Josephine and Mercie by E. C. Tarbell
Joslin, Mrs Milton, fl 1840
  Peckham, R. (attributed works) Widow
  Milton Joslin
**JOUETT, Matthew Harris,** 1787-1827
Edward Shippen
  Flexner. Light of distant skies
Mrs Rufus Somerby                        KyLS
  KyLS. Kentucky port gall
Principal building of Transylvania univer-
  sity
  Davidson v2
Robert Llewellyn Todd                    KyLS
  KyLS. Kentucky port gall
Jourdain, Mlle
  Sargent, J. S. Mlle Jourdain
Journey by M. Graves
Journey in white by M. Tobey
Journey's end by H. Ballin
The joust by C. di Marca-Relli
Joy by H. Hofmann

**Joyce, James**
  Barnes, R.  James Joyce
**Joyce** by E. E. Speicher
**Joyous** landscape by A. P. Russo
**Joyous** young pine by M. Graves
**Juana,** called **La Loca, queen of Castile,** 1479-1555
  Walker, C. H.  Joanna of Castile, the mad
**JUDD, De Forrest**
  Maguey                                    TxD
    CoS.  New accessions USA, 1952
**Judd's** hotel, Philadelphia, c 1825 by Unidentified artist
**Judd's** house, Southold, Long Island by Unidentified artist
The **judge** by J. Levine
The **Judith** roundup by C. M. Russell
**Judson** Stoddard by R. Robinson
**Jugglers**
  Evergood, P.  Juggler of doom
  Kuhn, W.  Juggler
  Kuniyoshi, Y.  Amazing juggler
**Juju** and her dog Copelia by P. Evergood
**Juju** as a wave by P. Evergood
**Juke** box by D. Tanning
**JULES, Mervin,** 1912-
  Cobblers
    NYG.  Fine art
  Desire                                    ATU
    ATU.  Coll of Amer art
  Museum of Modern art
    Larkin
**Juley, Peter**
  Dickinson, S. E.  Peter Juley and son
**Julia** by P. Evergood
**Juliet** by F. Martin
**July** by W. De Kooning
**July** clouds by C. E. Burchfield
**July** 4th, 5th, and 6th by F. Martin
**July** 14, Rue Daunou by C. Hassam
**July** hay by T. H. Benton
**Jump** rope by L. Ahlas
**Jumping** joy by L. Gatch
**Junction** by C. A. Hall
**Junction** by J. W. McCoy
**June** by G. Inness
**June** by W. Sommer
**June** day by W. T. Richards
**June** hay by T. H. Benton
**June** night by H. Koerner
**June** radiance by C. E. Burchfield
**Jungle** by W. A. Baziotes
**Jungle** by E. J. Stevens
**Jungle** in Venezuela by A. A. Dehn
**Juniata** river by J. Kane
**Junior** by R. Brackman
**Junk** yard by H. Koerner
**Juno** receiving the cestus from Venus by B. West
**Justice's** court in the backwoods by T. H. Matteson
**Juxtaposition** by S. M. Adler

# K

**Kaaterskill** Falls by S. R. Gifford
**Kaaterskill** house, View of by J. F. Cropsey
**KABAK, Robert,** 1930-
  New York harbor
    IU.  Contemp Amer ptg & sculp, 1959
**KACHADOORIAN, Zubel,** 1924-
  Matriarch and the prodigal son
    IU.  Contemp Amer ptg & sculp, 1961
  Romanscape
    IU.  Contemp Amer ptg & sculp, 1959
**KACHMER, George,** 1911-
  Winter along the mills                    OYB
    OYB.  Annual 1956
    OYB.  Supplement 1959
**KAEP, Louis Joseph,** 1903-
  Men of Nazare
    NAD.  Annual ex, 1958
**Kahler, Jeremiah,** 1795-1881
  Malbone, E. G.  Jeremiah Kahler
**Kahler, Jeremiah J.** 1749-1830
  Malbone, E. G.  Jeremiah Kahler
**KAHN, Max,** 1903-
  Blue rocks
    PA.  Annual ex, 1959-60
  Fishing boat and white sun
    ICA.  Annual ex, 1961
  Garden wall
    IU.  Contemp Amer ptg & sculp, 1959
  Village in the mountains
    IU.  Contemp Amer ptg, 1952
  We gather together
    DC.  26 biennial ex, 1959
**KAHN, Wolf,** 1927-
  Large olive grove                         WMAA
    WMAA.  Young America 1960
  September light
    IU.  Contemp Amer ptg & sculp, 1959
  Silver sea
    WMAA.  Young America 1960
  Summer 1954
    IU.  Contemp Amer ptg & sculp, 1957
**Kalamazoo** cove by D. Lutz
**Kaleidoscopic** journey by S. Franks
**Kaleidoscopic** journey by F. Ruvolo
**KALF, Willem,** 1622-1693
  Still life                                MSM
    Rathbun
**KALLEM, Henry,** 1913?-
  Rococo table
    DC.  26 biennial ex, 1959
**KAMIHIRA, Ben,** 1925-
  Circus performers
    NAD.  Annual ex, 1954
  The couch                                 WMAA
    Goodrich.  Amer art
  Funeral coach
    WiMiA.  Amer ptg 1760-1960
    WMAA.  Young America 1960
  The game
    WMAA.  Annual ex, 1958
  Interior
    WMAA.  Young America 1960
  Lowering from the cross
    PA.  Annual ex, 1958
  Segment of Spain
    NAD.  Annual ex, 1959
  Wedding dress
    DC.  27 biennial ex, 1961

Kamperman, George
  Watkins, F. C. Dr George Kamperman
KAMROWSKI, Gerome, 1917-
  Open twist
    IU. Contemp Amer ptg, 1950
  Urgent hour
    IU. Contemp Amer ptg, 1952
    MMA. Abstract
KAMYS, Walter, 1917-
  Fusion
    MBIC. View 1960
  Seaquake                                CtY
    CtY. Soc Anonyme
Kane, John, 1734-1808
  Ames, E. John Kane
KANE, John, 1860-1934
  Along the Susquehanna
    Cheney. Story 1958 ed
  Beechwood boulevard, Pittsburgh
    Kallir. Amer primitive ptgs
  Boys fishing
    NSP. Sportscapes
  From my studio window
    Baur. New art (col)
  Homestead                               MM
    Cheney. Story 1958 ed
  Ingram mansion, Pittsburgh
    CtY. Yale alumni
  Juniata river                           NBuA
    NBuA. Contemporary ptgs
  Panther Hollow                          WMAA
    Goodrich. Amer art
  Prosperity's increase
    Wight. Milestones
  Scotch day at Kennywood                 MMA
    Baur. New art
    Pierson
  Self-portrait                           MMA
    Barr. What is mod ptg
    Baur. New art
    Baur. Revolution
    Lipman. Primitive ptrs
    McCurdy
    Mendelowitz
    MMA. Masters (col)
    Pierson
    Time. 300 years (col)
    Walker. Ptgs from America
  Through Coleman Hollow up the Alle-
    gheny valley                          MMA
    Chew. 250 years of art
  Turtle creek valley                     KW
    Baur. New art
    Pierson
Kane, John Kintzing, 1795-1858
  Neagle, J. John Kintzing Kane
Kansas, University of
  Hess, J. University of Kansas, c 1879
KANTOR, Morris, 1896-
  Farewell to Union square                NJN
    Brown. Amer ptg
    Wight. Milestones
  Gray rocks and gray trees
    ICA. Annual ex, 1947/48
  Growth                                  IU
    IU. Contemp Amer ptg, 1951
    IU. 20th century
  Haunted house                           ICA
    Pierson
  Highland light
    Lewisohn

On the beach                              MM
  MM. 100 Amer ptrs
Orchestra
  Brown. Amer ptg
Pines and fog                             ATU
  ATU. Coll of Amer art
Skyrocket                                 WMAA
  Goodrich. Amer art
Still life (1)
  Cheney. Expressionism 1948 ed
Still life (2)
  NYG. Fine art
Still life (Phillips coll)
  Gruskin
Storm                                     WMAA
  Pierson
Summertime
  Pousette-Dart. Amer ptg (col)
Tranquility
  IU. Contemp Amer ptg, 1950
Union square, night                       DP
  DP. Catalogue
KAPLAN, Joseph, 1900-
  Breakwater
    IU. Contemp Amer ptg, 1950
  Highland light
    IU. Contemp Amer ptg, 1951
  Interior
    IU. Contemp Amer ptg & sculp, 1953
KARFIOL, Bernard, 1886-1952
  Bathers
    Roos
  Boy                                     DP
    DP. Catalogue
    Wight. Milestones
  Boy bathers                             WMAA
    Baur. Revolution
    Goodrich. Amer art (col)
    Pierson
    WMAA. Pioneers
  Child holding apple
    Brown. Amer ptg
  Christina                               ICA
    Baur. Revolution
  Christina                               PPC
    Pierson
  Cuban nude                              MM
    Pierson
  Girl against a tree
    PPC. Ptg in the U.S. 1949
  Hilda
    Cheney. Expressionism 1948 ed
  Hills
    Cheney. Expressionism 1948 ed
  Laurent pony cart
    NYG. Fine art
  Nude on red couch
    IU. Contemp Amer ptg & sculp, 1953
  Repose
    Pousette-Dart. Amer ptg
  Seated nude                             MMA
    Brown. Amer ptg
  Standing nude                           WMAA
    Larkin
    Larkin rev ed
  Summer                                  DC
    DC. 25 biennial ex, 1957
  Two bathers
    Gruskin
  Two standing figures
    Brown. Amer ptg
Karl by A. Wyeth

**KARP, Leon,** 1903-1951
  Bernard
    VR. Biennial ex, 1948
  Spring flowers
    PPC. Ptg in the U.S. 1949
  Still life with banjo
    IU. Contemp Amer ptg, 1950
**Karrig** by J. D. Brooks
**Kasson, Mrs Ambrose.** See Hall, Laura
**Katchinamaker** by M. Dixon
**Katharine** by E. E. Speicher
**Katherine** by T. Eakins
**Kathryn** by J. L. King
**KATZ, Alex,** 1927-
  Baigneuse
    WMAA. Young America 1960
  Folding chair
    WMAA. Young America 1960
**KATZMAN, Herbert,** 1923-
  The bath
    PPC. International ex, 1952
  Brooklyn bridge
    ICA. Amer artists paint the city
    MMA. Fifteen
    MnMW. Expressionism 1900-1955
  Ensor seated before The Entry of Christ
    into Brussels
    IU. Contemp Amer ptg & sculp, 1959
  Giotto's tower
    MMA. Fifteen
  Horse butcher
    MMA. Fifteen
  New York skyline
    IU. Contemp Amer ptg & sculp, 1961
  Red coffee pot
    WMAA. New decade
  Two nudes before Japanese screen
                                      WMAA
    Goodrich. Amer art
    PA. Annual ex, 1953
    Pierson
  Woman drying her hair
    WMAA. New decade
  Zinnias                             KLU
    Pierson
**KAWABATA, Minoru,** 1911-
  Elegy
    PPC. International ex, 1961/62
**KAYN, Hilde (Band)** 1903-1950
  New moon                            OT
    OT. Contemp Amer ptgs
  Swingtime                           NJMo
    NJMo. Forty years
**KEANE, William,** fl 1880
  Still life
    Frankenstein. After the hunt
**KEARNS, James,** 1925?-
  Cat's cradle
    WMAA. Contemp Amer ptg, 1959/60
  Self-portrait
    WiMiA. Amer ptg 1760-1960
**Keating, Maurice,** b 1747?
  Theus, J. Maurice Keating
**KEEFE, W. Ranford,** fl 1850
  Tree of foreboding
    Born
**Kee-oh-mee** by C. M. Russell
**Kee-o-kuk, chief of the Sauk and Foxes,**
    fl 1790-1848
  Catlin, G. Kee-o-kuk on horseback
  Catlin, G. Kee-o-kuk, the Running Fox
  Lewis, J. O. Kee-o-kuk, chief of the Sauk
**Keeper** of the bell by J. Whorf
**Keepsake** from Mallorca by D. Bothwell
**Keith, Mrs. Boudinot.** See Wheeler, Dora
**KELLER, Henry George,** 1870-1949
  Abstract impressions of surf
    OCl. Keller
  African thistle
    OCl. Keller
  The Alps
    OCl. Keller
  Andalusian garden
    OCl. Keller
  Anna's garden
    OCl. Keller
  April snow                          OCl
    OCl. Keller
  Autumn fruits                       DP
    OCl. Keller
  The aviary                          OCl
    OCl. Keller
  Bathers, the cove, La Jolla
    OCl. Keller
  Beach patterns
    OCl. Keller
  Bird rock, California               WMAA
    OCl. Keller
  Birds, rocks, and the sea
    OCl. Keller
  Bouquet of flowers                  OCl
    OCl. Keller
  Circus folk
    OCl. Keller
  Crossing the ford
    OCl. Keller
  Crows in winter
    OCl. Keller
  Drowsy company
    OCl. Keller
  End of the act
    OCl. Keller
  End of the day
    OCl. Keller
  Evening on the road to Granada
    OCl. Keller
  Fireflies
    OCl. Keller
  First show at two                   OCl
    OCl. Keller
  Fog banks, Tyrol
    OCl. Keller
  For Thanksgiving
    OCl. Keller
  The ford                            OCl
    OCl. Keller
  Foul weather, Percé
    OCl. Keller
  Goats among the peaks
    OCl. Keller
  Granda flora
    OCl. Keller
  Gulls feeding                       OCl
    OCl. Keller
  Helios in the lead
    OCl. Keller
  Hermitage, Talavera                 OCl
    OCl. Keller
  Impressions of a bull fight
    OCl. Keller
  In the park
    OCl. Keller

In the path of the sun
  OCl. Keller
Kelp gatherers                                MAP
  OCl. Keller
Land's end, Golden gate, California
  OCl. Keller
Memories of Andalusia
  OCl. Keller
Morning, Upper Frazer river
  OCl. Keller
Mountains, Puget sound
  OCl. Keller
Peacock
  OCl. Keller
Percé rock, Gaspe
  OCl. Keller (col)
Pescaderia, Malaga
  OCl. Keller
Ranch life, western Texas
  OCl. Keller
Ready to clean the catch, Percé           OYB
  OYB. Catalogue 1951
Returning from the Feria
  OCl. Keller
Rhythms
  OCl. Keller
San Diego zoo
  OCl. Keller
Snails
  OCl. Keller
Spell of Italy
  OCl. Keller
Still life with fruit
  OCl. Keller
Still life with fruit and flowers          MB
  MB. Ptgs in water color
Storm-frightened animals                   OCl
  OCl. Handbook
  OCl. Keller
Storm-frightened horses                    MB
  MB. Ptgs in water color
Sudden windstorm over the Vega
  OCl. Keller
Sunday morning in Gordon park, Cleve-
    land
  OCl. Keller
Sunflower patterns
  OCl. Keller
Sunflowers
  OCl. Keller
Sun's path
  OCl. Keller
Torment, Puerto Rico
  OCl. Keller
White horses at the sand pit
  OCl. Keller
Winter landscape                           ICA
  OCl. Keller
Wisdom and destiny                         OCl
  OCl. Keller
KELLEY, Donald, 1928-
Old god
  MBIC. View 1960
KELLY, Ellsworth, 1923-
Atlantic
  WMAA. Young America 1957
Aubade
  PPC. International ex, 1958
Block Island no 2
  PPC. International ex, 1961/62
Falcon
  MMA. Sixteen

New York                                   NBuA
  Brussels. Exposition
  NBuA. Acquisitions 1959-1961
Rebound
  MMA. Sixteen
Slip
  MMA. Sixteen
Wave motif
  MMA. Sixteen
York
  MMA. Sixteen
Kelly, Emmett
  MacIver, L. Emmett Kelly
  Veres. Davy Emmet Crocky (Emmett
    Kelly)
KELLY, Marie Tuiccillo, 1916-
Parade
  Chew. 250 years of art
  PPC. International ex, 1952
Three kings no 11                          OYB
  OYB. Annual 1953
Kelp gatherers by H. G. Keller
Kemble, Fanny. See Kemble, Frances Anne
Kemble, Frances Anne, 1809-1893
  Sully, T. Fanny Kemble as Beatrice
  Sully, T. Fanny Kemble as Bianca
KEMMELMEYER, Frederick, fl 1790-1810
First landing of Christopher Columbus
                                           DN
  DN. Amer primitive ptgs, pt 2
George Washington reviewing the west-
    ern army at Fort Cumberland    DN
  DN. Amer primitive ptgs, pt 1
  Flexner. Light of distant skies
  U.S. National Capital sesquicentennial
    com
KEMPSMITH, Joan
Auction day
  OYB. Annual 1950
Carnival time                              OCl
  CoS. New accessions USA, 1952
Kempton, Caleb, fl 1830
  Unidentified artist. Capt Caleb Kempton
KENDALL, William Sergeant, 1869-1938
Arthur Twining Hadley                      CtY
  CtY. Portrait index
William Howard Taft                        CtY
  CtY. Portrait index
KENISTON, George A. 1850-1932
Table of fruit
  DN. Amer primitive ptgs, pt 2
KENNEDY, D. J. fl 1840
View of Broad and Cherry streets above
    Arch street
  Chew. 250 years of art
Kennedy, David Sproat, 1791-1853
  Inman, H. David Sproat Kennedy
Kennedy, John Pendleton, fl 1827
  Tilyard, P. John Pendleton Kennedy
KENNEDY, Terence J. 1820-1879?
Symbolical painting                        NCHA
  Jones. Rediscovered ptrs
KENSETT, John Frederick, 1816-1872
Bash-Bish Falls, South Egremont, Massa-
    chusetts                               MB
  MB. Karolik coll
Cascade in the forest                      MiD
  MiD. Treasures
  Pierson
Cliffs at Newport, Rhode Island            MB
  MB. Karolik coll
Coast scene with figures                   CtHW
  Pierson

**KENSETT, J. F.**—*Continued*

Coastal scene      CtHW
  Baur. Amer ptg
Glimpse of Lake George
  Sears. Highlights
In the Catskills
  Sears. Highlights
Lake George
  Taylor. Fifty centuries, 1954 ed (col)
Mountain stream      NAD
  NAD. Amer tradition
Newport harbor, Rhode Island (Kesler
  coll)
  Born
Newport harbor, Rhode Island (Sturges
  coll)
  DC. De gustibus
  Larkin
  Larkin rev ed
Niagara Falls and the rapids      MB
  MB. Karolik coll
Paradise rock, Newport      NJM
  Mendelowitz
River scene      MM
  Pierson
  Richardson. Ptg in America
  Time. 300 years (col)
Rydal Falls, England      MSG
  Barker. Amer ptg
Sea and rocky shore      MM
  Bazin
Third beach, Newport      ICA
  Pierson
Trenton Falls, New York      MB
  MB. Karolik coll
View near Newport      OCl
  OCl. Handbook

**KENSETT, John Frederick, 1816-1872, and HUNTINGTON, Daniel, 1816-1906**
Seascape, Newport      MB
  MB. Karolik coll

**KENT, Adaline, 1900-1957**
Untitled      CSFM
  CoS. New accessions USA, 1954

**Kent, James, 1763-1847**
Ames, E. James Kent
Jarvis, J. W. James Kent

**KENT, Rockwell, 1882-**
Burial of a young man      DP
  DP. Catalogue
Heavy, heavy
  PPC. Ptg in the U.S. 1949
Mount Equinox, winter      ICA
  Pierson
Road roller      DP
  Brown. Amer ptg
Shadows of evening      WMAA
  Goodrich. Amer art
  Pierson
Toilers of the sea      CtNB
  Baur. Revolution
The trapper      WMAA
  Cheney. Story 1958 ed
Winter      MM
  MM. 100 Amer ptrs
  NYG. Fine art

**Kenton, Louis N.**
Eakins, T. The thinker

**Keokuk.** See Kee-o-kuk, chief of the Sauk
  and Foxes

**KEPES, Gyorgy, 1906-**
Hortus occlusus
  IU. Contemp Amer ptg & sculp, 1961
Landscape number 3
  IU. Contemp Amer ptg & sculp, 1955
Random pattern
  MBIC. View 1960

**Kershaw, Anna M.**
Eakins, T. Mrs Anna M. Kershaw

**KESTER, Lenard, 1913-**
The cove
  NAD. Annual ex, 1952
In the garden
  IU. Contemp Amer ptg, 1949
Kite fliers
  MoSL. Contemporary Amer ptg
November 7th
  NAD. Annual ex, 1958
Picnickers
  IU. Contemp Amer ptg, 1948
Rehearsal
  IU. Contemp Amer ptg, 1950

**Keteltas, Abraham, fl 1758**
Hesselius, J. Rev Abraham Keteltas

**Keteltas, Jane.** See Beekman, Jane (Keteltas)

**Keteltas, Sarah (Smith) fl 1757**
Hesselius, J. Mrs Abraham Keteltas

**The key** by J. Pollock

**Key West** beach by P. Blume

**KEYES, Charles A. fl 1856**
Geo. S. Howe driving Rough and Ready
     NCHA
  Jones. New-found folk art

**KEYS, Mary, fl 1832**
Lockport on the Erie canal      NUM
  Jones. Rediscovered ptrs

**Keys** and feather by W. T. Murch

**KEYSER, Robert, 1924-**
Lyric piece
  IU. Contemp Amer ptg & sculp, 1961

**KHOSROVI, Karim, 1925-**
Abstraction
  IU. Contemp Amer ptg & sculp, 1955
Head with yellow ground
  NNSG. Younger Amer ptrs

**The kid** by I. Bishop

**Kids** skiing by J. Pike

**KIENBUSCH, William Austin, 1914-**
Across four pines (Hurricane island)
     WMAA
  WMAA. Sara Roby
Across Penobscot bay      TxH
  Eliot. Art of our time (col)
Backyard, winter, Maine no 2
  PPC. International ex, 1955
Barns and fences no 1      CtNB
  Pierson
Black bush, autumn, Dogtown
  Pierson
Blue spruce      TxF
  CoS. New accessions USA, 1952
Connecticut field
  WMAA. Annual ex, 1954
Dirigo island
  WMAA. New decade
Fallen pine, Camp island      NBuA
  NBuA. Acquisitions 1954-57
Hurricane island. See Across four pines
Into Dogtown, autumn
  VR. Amer ptg, 1958

Low tide                                 MMA
  McCurdy
  MMA. Abstract
New England stove
  WMAA. New decade
Red vine, autumn, Dogtown, 1954
  WMAA. New decade
Red vine, autumn, Dogtown, 1956
  Baur. Nature
  Goodrich. Amer art
Rocky field, Camp island, Maine
  NBuA. Expressionism
Through the pines, the ocean
  Brussels. Exposition
Twin pine                                WMAA
  Pousette-Dart. Amer ptg
The weir and the island                  MM
  Time. 300 years (col)
Winter, Dirigo island
  WMAA. Museum and its friends, 1958
**KILBURN, Lawrence,** fl 1761
Garret Abeel                             NNHS
  Belknap
Gerardus Duyckinck II                    NNHS
  Belknap
James Beekman
  Belknap
Mrs Garret Abeel                         NNHS
  Belknap
Mrs Gerardus Duyckinck II                NNHS
  Belknap
Mrs James Beekman
  Flexner. First flowers
**Kilby, Sarah.** See Cunningham, Sarah (Kil-
  by)
**Kildeer** by E. F. Spruce
**Killer** in costume by F. Martin
**Killing** buffalo with the lance by A. J.
  Miller
**Kindred** spirits by A. B. Durand
**Kine** no 1 by K. Okada
**KING, Charles Bird,** 1785-1862
No Heart—Ioway                           DNC
  Rathbone
The poor artist's cupboard               DC
  DC. Masterpieces
  Mendelowitz
Rope walk interior                       NCHA
  Jones. New-found folk art
Shaumonekusse, chief of the Otoes
  Rathbone
Vanity of an artist's dream              MCH
  Barker. Amer ptg
  Pierson
  Richardson. Ptg in America
Young Omahaw, War Eagle, Little Mis-
  souri and Pawnees                      DNC
  Pierson
  Rathbone
  U.S. National Capital sesquicentennial
  com
**King, Edith**
  Prendergast, M. B. La Rouge: Edith King
**King, Ellen (James)** 1800-1823
  Ames, E. Mrs James King
**King, Frederic Gore,** 1801-1829
  Morse, S. F. B. Dr Frederic Gore King
**KING, George Bird,** fl 1837
No-way-ke-sug-ga, an Oto
  Morgan (col)
Tah-ro-hon, an Iowa warrior
  Morgan (col)

**Attributed works**
Le Soldat du Chêne, an Osage chief
  Morgan (col)
**KING, Henrietta (Campbell)**
10:00 P.M.
  NYG. Fine art
**King, Mrs. James.** See King, Ellen (James)
**KING, John Lord,** 1909-
Kathryn
  PA. Annual ex, 1954
**King, Mrs Mitchell.** See King, Henrietta
  (Campbell)
**KING, Paul,** 1867-
Mystery of the East
  NYG. Fine art
**KING, Robert D.**
The flight
  OYB. Annual 1949
Landscape no 3
  OYB. Annual 1951
The **king** by M. Beckmann
The **king** by G. W. McLaughlin
**King** cock by K. Knaths
**King** Cophetua and the beggar maid by
  A. P. Ryder
**King** Lear by B. West
**King** Lear's daughters by E. A. Abbey
**King** of spades by J. Mitchell
**King** Saul by J. Levine
The **king** visits his paramour by S. Moy
**KINGMAN, Dong,** 1911-
Angel square
  IU. Contemp Amer ptg, 1952
  Time. 300 years (col)
Blue moon                                MB
  MB. Ptgs in water color
Circus and the lady
  IU. Contemp Amer ptg & sculp, 1953
Columbus circle
  Gruskin (col)
Dead end
  NAD. Annual ex, 1951
The el and snow                          WMAA
  Pierson
Lighthouse                               OYB
  OYB. Catalogue 1951
Mile drive, California
  NAD. Annual ex, 1954
Moon and locomotive
  Pousette-Dart. Amer ptg
Old Mission—San Diego                    IaDa
  IaDa. Silver jubilee
  IaDa. 30th anniversary
Washington square, New York
  NAD. Annual ex, 1961
**KINGMAN, Helen M.** fl 1845
Mississippi river landing                DN
  DN. Amer primitive ptgs, pt 2
The **king's** jester by W. M. Chase
**King's** joke by D. J. Meeker
**Kingsley, James Luce,** 1778-1852
  Jocelyn, N. James Luce Kingsley
**Kingston, New York**
  Chambers, T. Looking north to Kings-
  ton
**KINIGSTEIN, Jonah,** 1924-
The centaur                              OYB
  OYB. Annual 1954
  OYB. Supplement
Dead man
  IU. Contemp Amer ptg & sculp, 1959

**KINIGSTEIN, Jonah**—*Continued*
Old lady
  IU. Contemp Amer ptg & sculp, 1957
Old man
  WMAA. Young America 1957
Pastry window
  WMAA. Young America 1957
Piazza di Spagna
  MnMW. Expressionism 1900-1955
Sicilian altar
  IU. Contemp Amer ptg & sculp, 1955
**Kinlock, Mrs Frederick.** See Lowndes, Mary I'On
**Kinlock, Mary I'On (Lowndes)** See Lowndes, Mary I'On
**Kioto,** View of by J. La Farge
**Kiowa** encampment by S. Seymour
**KIRKLAND, Vance H.** 1904-
Phantasy
  IU. Contemp Amer ptg, 1952
**KIRSCHENBAUM, Jules,** 1929?-
Conjurer
  IU. Contemp Amer ptg & sculp, 1959
Dark in the forest
  NAD. Annual ex, 1955
Playground            OYB
  ICA. Annual ex, 1957
  OYB. Annual 1957
  OYB. Supplement 1959
Portrait of my father
  NAD. Annual ex, 1953
Still life with skulls
  ICA. Annual ex, 1959/60
Woman with fighting dogs
  NAD. Annual ex, 1961
The **kiss** by R. S. Du Casse
The **kiss** by C. Seliger
**Kiss-me-over-the-fence** by C. H. Demuth
**Kissing** the moon by W. Homer
**Kit** and kin by K. Knaths
**Kitchell, Harvey,** fl 1865
  Mason, B. F. Harvey Kitchell
**Kitchen** ball at White Sulphur Springs, Virginia, 1838 by C. Mayr
**Kitchen** piece by R. L. Goodwin
**Kitchen** table by R. D'Arista
**Kitchens**
  Edmonds, F. W. Real estate agent offering valuable lots
  Giobbi, E. Kitchen still life
  Lee, D. E. Thanksgiving
  Lee, D. E. Thanksgiving day
  Mintz, R. A. The kitchen
  Pippin, H. Christmas morning breakfast
  Pippin, H. Quaker mother and child
  Pippin, H. Saturday night bath
  Pippin, H. Saying prayers
  Pippin, H. Sunday morning breakfast
  Rosenfeld, E. Kitchen sink
  Sommer, W. Kitchen
The **kite** by J. W. Fosburgh
**Kite** fliers by L. Kester
**Kitty** Hawk by R. F. Gates
Eine **kleine** nachtmusik by D. Tanning
**KLEINHOLZ, Frank,** 1901-
Rendezvous
  IU. Contemp Amer ptg, 1952

Spring is in the air
  Cheney. Expressionism 1948 ed
**Kleinholz family**
  Evergood, P. Kleinholz family
**KLEPPER, Max**
Coaching through New Jersey, 1903    NNHS
  Davidson v2
**Kline, Mr.** fl 1825
  Eichholz, J. Mr Kline
**KLINE, Franz Josef,** 1910-
Accent grave
  MMA. New Amer ptg
  MMA. 12 Americans
  Read. Concise history
Andes
  WMAA. Annual ex, 1958
Cardinal
  Hess. Abstract ptg
  MMA. New Amer ptg
  MMA. 12 Americans
The Chief            MMA
  Biddle. Yes and no
  Hess. Abstract ptg
  McCurdy
  MMA. 12 Americans
  Newmeyer
  Pousette-Dart. Amer ptg
Contrada
  PPC. International ex, 1961-62
Cross-section
  Time. 300 years
Elizabeth
  Chew. 250 years of art
Initial
  Ponente. Mod ptg, 1960
Laureline
  Baur. Nature
Leda
  PPC. International ex, 1952
Mahoning            WMAA
  Goodrich. Amer art
  MnMW. 60 Amer ptrs
  Pierson
New Year wall: Night
  Ponente. Mod ptg, 1960 (col)
New York           NBuA
  ICA. Amer artists paint the city
  NBuA. Acquisitions 1954-57
Number 2, 1954
  Cheney. Story 1958 ed
Painting, 1951
  Blesh
Painting no 2, 1954
  WMAA. New decade
Painting no 7, 1952      NNSG
  NNSG. Handbook
  NNSG. Younger Amer ptrs
  Pierson
  Read. Concise history
  WMAA. New decade
Painting no 11, 1953
  PPC. International ex, 1955
Requiem
  NBuA. Acquisitions 1959-1961
Siegfried           PPC
  Mendelowitz
  PPC. International ex, 1958
  WMAA. Museum and its friends, 1959
Third avenue
  Hunter. Mod Amer ptg

Wanamaker block
    Art since 1945
    Eliot. Art of our time
    MMA. New Amer ptg
    MMA. 12 Americans
    MnMW. Eighty works
White forms
    50 years of mod art
    MMA. 12 Americans
**KLITGAARD, Georgina (Berrian) 1893-**
Daisies
    NYG. Fine art
**KLONIS, Bernard, 1906-1957**
Flowers from my garden        ATU
    ATU. Coll of Amer art
**KNAP, N. D.**
The flight
    NSP. Sportscapes
**Knatchbull family**
Copley, J. S. Sketch for the Knatchbull
    family
**KNATHS, Karl, 1891-**
Abstract landscape
    IU. Contemp Amer ptg, 1949
Adam
    PPC. Ptg in the U.S. 1949
Autumn leaves        NBM
    Mocsanyi. Karl Knaths
    Pierson
Bach
    Mocsanyi. Karl Knaths
Bananas and blue grapes        DP
    Mocsanyi. Karl Knaths
Barn interior
    Mocsanyi. Karl Knaths
    WMAA. Four Amer expressionists
Barroom        DP
    Mocsanyi. Karl Knaths
Basket bouquet
    MM. Amer ptg today
    Mocsanyi. Karl Knaths
Boeuf
    OCl. Some contemporary works
Book, shell and ship        IaDM
    CoS. New accessions USA, 1954
    Mocsanyi. Karl Knaths
Captain and crew
    IU. Contemp Amer ptg & sculp, 1961
Cigar box
    Mocsanyi. Karl Knaths
Cin Zin        DP
    Mocsanyi. Karl Knaths
    UNESCO. 1860-1959
Clam-diggers        DP
    DP. Catalogue
Clam-diggers, Provincetown        MM
    MM. 100 Amer ptrs
Clock and bottle        IU
    IU. Contemp Amer ptg, 1948
    IU. 20th century
Cock and glove        DP
    DP. Catalogue
    Mocsanyi. Karl Knaths
    Pierson
    Roos
Connecticut clock        DP
    DP. Catalogue
    Mocsanyi. Karl Knaths (col)
Copper kettle
    MnU. 40 Amer ptrs
Coq d'Or
    MnMW. Classic tradition

Deer at sunset        DP
    Mocsanyi. Karl Knaths (col)
Distant sail
    OCl. Some contemporary work
Doomsday        NBuA
    ICA. Annual ex, 1947/48
    NBuA. Acquisitions 1954-57
    WMAA. Four Amer expressionists
Duck decoy, 1951        DP
    Mocsanyi. Karl Knaths
Duck decoy, 1954        DP
    Mocsanyi. Karl Knaths (col)
Duck flight        WMAA
    Baur. Revolution
    Goodrich. Amer art (col)
    IU. Contemp Amer ptg, 1950
    Mocsanyi. Karl Knaths
    Pierson
    WMAA. Four Amer expressionists (col)
Dusk
    Mocsanyi. Karl Knaths
    WMAA. Museum and its friends, 1958
Eeling
    Mocsanyi. Karl Knaths
Eliphaz        PA
    Mocsanyi. Karl Knaths
First frost
    OCl. Some contemporary works
Fox hunter        MoSL
    MoSL. Handbook 1953
Frightened deer in moonlight        DP
    DP. Catalogue
    Mocsanyi. Karl Knaths
    WMAA. Four Amer expressionists
Fruit and table
    Leepa
Gear        InBu
    Mocsanyi. Karl Knaths
    NUM. Art across America
    WMAA. Four Amer expressionists
Geraniums in night window        DP
    Mocsanyi. Karl Knaths
Giorgione book        MMA
    Mocsanyi. Karl Knaths
Green squash        DP
    Mocsanyi. Karl Knaths
Harvest        DP
    Bazin
    DP. Catalogue
    MnU. 40 Amer ptrs
    Mocsanyi. Karl Knaths (col)
    Read. Concise history
Havana bandana        MdBM
    CoS. New accessions USA, 1956
Head of young woman        ATeS
    ATeS. Collection
Horse mackerel        MoSL
    Eliot. Art of our time (col)
    Time. 300 years (col)
Hunters        NHMC
    CoS. New accessions USA, 1960
Indian blanket        NeL
    DC. 21 biennial ex, 1949
    Mocsanyi. Karl Knaths
Johnny Appleseed
    Mocsanyi. Karl Knaths
King cock        DP
    Mocsanyi. Karl Knaths
Kit and kin        DP
    DP. Catalogue
    Mocsanyi. Karl Knaths

**KNATHS, Karl**—*Continued*
Lady
  WMAA. Four Amer expressionists
Lilacs                     DP
  Mocsanyi. Karl Knaths
Lilacs and books          NR
  Mocsanyi. **Karl Knaths**
Maritime              DP
  McCurdy
  MMA. Abstract
  Mocsanyi. Karl Knaths
  Wight. Milestones
Mexican platter       WMAA
  CoS. New accessions USA, 1958
  WMAA. Four Amer expressionists
Mexican platter       DP
  DC. De gustibus
  Mocsanyi. Karl Knaths
Moby Dick
  Mocsanyi. Karl Knaths
The moon           MWM
  CoS. New accessions USA, 1952
  CSFP. Annual ex, 1950/51
  Hess. Abstract ptg
  Mocsanyi. Karl Knaths
Moonlight, harbour town    DP
  Mocsanyi. Karl Knaths
The moors           DP
  Mocsanyi. Karl Knaths (col)
Net mender           DP
  Mocsanyi. Karl Knaths
  WMAA. Four Amer expressionists
Number seven—Saul
  WMAA. Four Amer expressionists
Number zero—Adam     NBuA
  CoS. New accessions USA, 1952
  Mocsanyi. Karl Knaths
  NBuA. Expressionism
Orarian              DP
  Mocsanyi. Karl Knaths
Overhauling the trawl     DP
  Mocsanyi. Karl Knaths (col)
Pennsylvania landscape    DP
  Mocsanyi. Karl Knaths
Picasso book
  IU. Contemp Amer ptg & sculp, 1957
Pine bough           MB
  Mocsanyi. Karl Knaths
Pine timber (Pine tree)    DP
  Mocsanyi. Karl Knaths (col)
  Richardson. Ptg in America
  WMAA. Four Amer expressionists
  (col)
Pink lustre
  Mocsanyi. Karl Knaths
Provincetown jamboree
  PCC. International ex, 1950
Queen of clubs
  CSFP. Annual ex, 1948/49
  Mocsanyi. Karl Knaths
Red clock
  OCl. Some contemporary works
  Mocsanyi. Karl Knaths
  Pousette-Dart. Amer ptg
  WMAA. Four Amer expressionists
Red table             DP
  Mocsanyi. Karl Knaths
Ruined wharf         NUM
  Mocsanyi. Karl Knaths
Rye bread
  Mocsanyi. Karl Knaths

Salt flats         MnMW
  CoS. New accessions USA, 1952
  Mocsanyi. Karl Knaths
Sculling
  DC. 27 biennial ex, 1961
Sou'easter interim
  Mocsanyi. Karl Knaths
Still life (1)
  Cheney. Expressionism 1948 ed
Still life (2)         PPhM
  Mocsanyi. Karl Knaths
Store and gear        ICA
  Mocsanyi. Karl Knaths
The sun             DP
  Mocsanyi. Karl Knaths (col)
  WMAA. Four Amer expressionists
  (col)
Sunflower
  Mocsanyi. Karl Knaths
Table top
  Mocsanyi. Karl Knaths
Time, tide and town
  Mocsanyi. Karl Knaths
Tired violin
  Mocsanyi. Karl Knaths
The tower
  ICA. Annual ex, 1951
Two fishermen
  WMAA. Four Amer expressionists
White vase
  IU. Contemp Amer ptg & sculp, 1955
Winter wharf
  Baur. Nature
  Mocsanyi. Karl Knaths
**KNEE, Gina,** 1898-
Saturday, again
  VR. Biennial ex, 1948
    **Portrait of the artist**
Brook, A. My wife
**Knife** Chief of the Pawnee Loups by J.
  Neagle
**KNIGHT, Frederic,** 1898-
Portrait of a young artist    ATU
  ATU. Coll of Amer art
**Knight, Jonathan,** 1789-1864
Jocelyn, N. Jonathan Knight
**KNIPSCHILD, Robert L.** 1927-
Blue, white and grey
  PPC. International ex, 1952
**Knockout** by L. Lewitin
**Knoedler's,** 34th street by E. Shinn
**KNOLL, Charles**

    **Attributed works**
Panic of 1869         MeC
  Jette. Amer heritage collection
**Knowles, Mildred (Buchanan)**
Sargent, J. S. Mrs Knowles and her
  children
**Knox, Henry,** 1750-1806
Stuart, G. Henry Knox
**Knoxville,** Street in by C. G. Farr
**KOCH, John,** 1909-
The American boy      GAtM
  GAtM. Holbrook collection
The bridge         CSFP
  CSFP. Annual ex, 1952
  Time. 300 years (col)
Hanging clothes
  NAD. Annual ex, 1951
Interior—dining room
  NAD. Annual ex, 1957

Manuscript
CSB. Illusion
The movers
NAD. Annual ex, 1955
Nude with cat
Gruskin
Stairway
NAD. Annual ex, 1948
10 A.M.
NAD. Annual ex, 1960
The visit
ICA. Annual ex, 1961
**KOCH, Samuel,** 1887-
Orchard street, New York city          ATU
ATU. Coll of Amer art
**KOERNER, Henry,** 1915-
Barker's booth
IU. Contemp Amer ptg, 1950
The beach
CSFP. Annual ex, 1948/49
The bridge
PPC. Ptg in the U.S. 1949
June night
Time. 300 years (col)
Junk yard
PA. Annual ex, 1949
Monkey bars
Baur. Revolution
The monument
DC. 21 biennial ex, 1949
Mountain top
DC. 22 biennial ex, 1951
My parents
Time. 300 years (col)
The prophet
IU. Contemp Amer ptg, 1949
Subway
NAD. Annual ex, 1949, 1st half
Vanity Fair          WMAA
Bazin
CoS. New accessions USA, 1948
Goodrich. Amer art
McCurdy
Pierson
WMAA. Juliana Force
Winter journey
Eliot. Art of our time (col)
**KOERNER, William Henry Dethlef,** 1878-1938
City man's vacation
NSP. Sportscapes
**KOESTER, Frederic,** 1924-
Street corner, Paris
IU. Contemp Amer ptg, 1952
**KOFFLER, Mary Mintz,** 1906-
Mementos
NAD. Annual ex, 1958
**Ko-kak-koo-kiss,** a Towoccono warrior by J. M. Stanley
**Konza** warriors, woman and child by G. Catlin
**KOPF, Maxim,** 1892-
The star
Genauer
**KOPMAN, Benjamin,** 1887-
Circus
Brown. Amer ptg
Invasion          ATU
ATU. Coll of Amer art
The lynching
Cheney. Expressionism 1948 ed

Meditation
Baur. Revolution
Portrait—Bear
Pierson
**KOPPE, Richard,** 1916-
Black wires
IU. Contemp Amer ptg, 1950
A collection of things
IU. Contemp Amer ptg, 1948
Roos
Fluttering fowl
IU. Contemp Amer ptg, 1951
Primitive dance
WMAA. Annual ex, 1953
Winged web
PPC. International ex, 1952
**Kormendi, Mrs Laszlo.** See Varga, Margit
**KOSA, Emil Jean,** 1903-
Dark hills and white horses
NAD. Annual ex, 1953
I'll take the high road          OT
OT. Contemp Amer ptgs
Stepping out
NAD. Annual ex, 1948
Summit of Antelope valley
ICA. Annual ex, 1945/46
**Kosciusko, Thaddeus,** 1746-1817
West, B. General Kosciusko
**Koshares** (New Mexico Indian dance series) by E. Bisttram
**KOSKI, Ray J.** 1910-
Performers          OYB
OYB. Catalogue 1951
**KOZLOW, Richard,** 1926-
Palermo          OYB
OYB. Annual 1951
OYB. Catalogue 1951
**KRAMER, Jack,** 1923-
Three figures
MBIC. View 1960
**KRAMER, Paul S.**
St Thomas church
NAD. Annual ex, 1953
The scullers
NAD. Annual ex, 1955
**Krans, Beta,** fl 1900
Krans, O. Mrs Beta Krans
**KRANS, Olof,** 1838-1916
Indians
Lipman. Primitive ptrs
It will soon be here
Ford. Pictorial folk art
Mrs Beta Krans
Lipman. Primitive ptrs
Planting corn
Ford. Pictorial folk art
Self-portrait, c 1900
Lipman. Primitive ptrs
Sowing grain at Bishop hill
Lipman. Primitive ptrs
U.S. National Capital sesquicentennial com
**KRAUSKOPF, Bruno,** 1892-
Sun on the lake
PPC. International ex, 1952
**KREIDER, Stanton,** 1922-
Plexus counterplexus
MoSL. Contemporary Amer ptg
**KRIEGHOF, Cornelius,** 1812-1872
Indians portaging furs
U.S. National Capital sesquicentennial com

**KRIESBERG, Irving,** 1919-
Birds alighting
MMA. Fifteen
Yellow sheep
MMA. Fifteen
**KRIMMEL, John Lewis,** 1787-1821
Country wedding      PA
Chew. 250 years of art
Flexner. Light of distant skies
Election day at the State house    NNHS
Pierson
Election scene in front of the State house
in Philadelphia (Independence hall)
about 1818      PH
Davidson v2
Fourth of July celebration in Centre
square, Philadelphia, 1819    PH
Pierson
Richardson. Ptg in America
U.S. National Capital sesquicentennial
com
Fourth of July in Centre square, Philadel-
phia, c 1810      PA
Davidson v2
Pierson
Interior of an American inn    OT
Pierson
Parade passing Independence hall, Phila-
delphia      MoSp
Chew. 250 years of art
U.S. National Capital sesquicentennial
com
Quilting party      DeWin
Pierson
**KROLL, Leon,** 1884-
Abandoned quarry
NAD. Annual ex, 1960
August serenity
PPC. International ex, 1950
The bridge
Brown. Amer ptg
Day in June
PPC. Ptg in the U.S. 1949
Farm in Maine      WMAA
Larkin
Larkin rev ed
Hunter in the hills
Gruskin (col)
In the country      MiD
Baur. Revolution
Pierson
Inland pool
NAD. Annual ex, 1956
Interior
NAD. Annual ex, autumn 1949
Naiad
NAD. Annual ex, 1947, 2d half
Nude      MM
MM. 100 Amer ptrs
Pierson
Nude in rocky background
IU. Contemp Amer ptg, 1952
Odalisque
NAD. Annual ex, 1958
Reverie
NAD. Annual ex, 1948
Road from the cove
Lewisohn
Time. 300 years (col)
Road through willows      WMAA
Goodrich. Amer art
McCurdy

**Krum, Chester Harding**
Harding, C. Chester Harding Krum
**KRUSE, Alexander Z.** 1890-
Mayor La Guardia as conductor    ATU
ATU. Coll of Amer art
**KÜHN, Justus Engelhardt,** fl 1708-1717
Eleanor Darnall      MdBH
Barker. Amer ptg
Flexner. First flowers
ICA. From colony to nation
Larkin
Larkin rev ed
Pierson
Robb. Harper history
Henry Darnall III      MdBH
Pierson
**KUHN, Robert**
Wounded wolf
NSP. Sportscapes
**KUHN, Walt,** 1880-1949
Acrobat in green      MAP
Brown. Amer ptg
Acrobat in white
Cheney. Expressionism 1948 ed
Cheney. Story 1958 ed
Acrobat in white and blue
CanO. Hirshhorn coll
Apples in the hay      MMA
Pierson
Blue clown      WMAA
Baur. Revolution
Goodrich. Amer art (col)
McCurdy
Pierson
Robb. Harper history
UNESCO. 1860-1955
UNESCO. 1860-1959
Wight. Milestones
Blue juggler      MoKN
Bazin
Caucus
Brown. Amer ptg
Chair with apples      NUM
NUM. Art across America
Clown in his dressing room    WMAA
Pierson
Dressing room      NBM
Pierson
Girl in white and silver      MM
MM. 100 Amer ptrs
Pierson
Green apples and scoop
CtY. Yale alumni
Harlequin
Brown. Amer ptg
Juggler      MoKN
MoKN. Handbook p 150
Man with ship model
WMAA. Pioneers
Peaches
IU. Contemp Amer ptg, 1948
Roberto
Genauer
Larkin
Larkin rev ed
Trio      CoS
Time. 300 years (col)
Tulip buds      DP
DP. Catalogue
Victoria
Brown. Amer ptg
White clown
Cheney. Primer 1958 ed

Young clown                              ATeS
  ATeS. Collection
  Mendelowitz
Young clown                              CoD
  Gruskin
KUNIYOSHI, Yasuo, 1893-1953
Abandoned treasures                      GAtM
  Goodrich. Yasuo Kuniyoshi
Amazing juggler                          IaDM
  Baur. New art
  IU. Contemp Amer ptg & sculp, 1953
  Pierson
  Pousette-Dart. Amer ptg
  Time. 300 years (col)
Bouquet and stove (Stove and bouquet)
                                  KW
  Goodrich. Yasuo Kuniyoshi
  Larkin
  Larkin rev ed
  Wight. Milestones
Bow with cow
  Lewisohn
Boy stealing fruit                       OCo
  Brown. Amer ptg
  Riley. Your art heritage
Café                                     WMAA
  Goodrich. Yasuo Kuniyoshi
Carnival
  CSFP. Annual ex, 1950/51
  IU. Contemp Amer ptg, 1950
  PPC. Ptg in the U. S. 1949
The clown                                OYB
  OYB. Catalogue 1951
Cowgirl                                  ATU
  ATU. Coll of Amer art
Daily news                               OCiM
  CoS. New accessions USA, 1960
  Goodrich. Yasuo Kuniyoshi
  Grushkin (col)
Deliverance                              WMAA
  Goodrich. Amer art (col)
  Goodrich. Yasuo Kuniyoshi (col)
  Myers
The dream
  Goodrich. Yasuo Kuniyoshi
Empty town in desert
  Goodrich. Yasuo Kuniyoshi
Exit                                     MM
  MM. 100 Amer ptrs (col)
Fakirs                                   WMAA
  CSFP. Annual ex, 1952
  NBuA. Expressionism
  WMAA. Sara Roby
Festivities ended
  Goodrich. Yasuo Kuniyoshi
Fish kite
  Baur. New art (col)
  MM. Amer ptg today
Forbidden fruit
  MnU. 40 Amer ptrs
  Pearson. Mod renaissance
  PPC. International ex, 1950
Girl on sofa                             ATeS
  ATeS. Collection
Girl waiting
  Cheney. Story 1958 ed
Headless horse who wants to jump  MiC
  Baur. New art
  ᴅaur. Revolution
  Goodrich. Yasuo Kuniyoshi
  ICA. Annual ex, 1945/46
  McCurdy
  NUM. Art across America
  Pierson

I think so                               NBuA
  NBuA. Contemporary ptgs
I'm tired                                WMAA
  Bazin
  Goodrich. Amer art (col)
  Goodrich. Yasuo Kuniyoshi
  NYG. Fine art
  Pierson
Island of happiness                      WMAA
  Baur. New art
  Goodrich. Yasuo Kuniyoshi
  Pearson. Mod renaissance
Japanese toy tiger and odd objects
  Goodrich. Yasuo Kuniˑˑoshi
  NYG. Fine art
Lay figure                               MnMW
  Goodrich. Yasuo Kuniyoshi
  MnU. 40 Amer ptrs
Little girl run for your life
  Goodrich. Yasuo Kuniyoshi
Little Joe with cow                      DC
  Baur. New art
  DC. Halpert collection
  Goodrich. Yasuo Kuniyoshi
  Pierson
Look, it flies
  CanO. Hirshhorn coll
  Goodrich. Yasuo Kuniyoshi
  Pierson
Lover's pike
  CSFP. Annual ex, 1947/48
  Goodrich. Yasuo Kuniyoshi
  IU. Contemp Amer ptg, 1948
Maine family                             DP
  DP. Catalogue
The mirror                               WMAA
  Goodrich. Yasuo Kuniyoshi
  Pearson. Mod renaissance
Mr Ace
  PPC. International ex, 1952
Mother and daughter                      PPC
  Goodrich. Yasuo Kuniyoshi
  MnMW. Expressionism 1900-1955
Nude
  Cheney. Primer 1958 ed
Revelation                               KW
  Pearson. Mod renaissance
  Pierson
Room 110                                 NeL
  Barker. From realism
  Goodrich. Yasuo Kuniyoshi
  Pearson. Mod renaissance
Rotting on the shore
  CSFP. Annual ex, 1948/49
  Goodrich. Yasuo Kuniyoshi
  IU. Contemp Amer ptg, 1949
Season ended
  Goodrich. Yasuo Kuniyoshi
Self-portrait as a golf player          MMA
  Goodrich. Yasuo Kuniyoshi
  Roos
She mourns                               GAtM
  GAtM. Holbrook collection
She walks among the ruins
  Genauer
  Goodrich. Yasuo Kuniyoshi
Skating
  Cheney. Expressionism 1948 ed
Somebody tore my poster
  Baur. New art
  Goodrich. Yasuo Kuniyoshi
  WMAA. Museum and its friends, 1958
  (col)

**KUNIYOSHI, Yasuo**—*Continued*
Squash
  Brown. Amer ptg
Stove and bouquet. See Bouquet and stove
Strong woman and child        WMAA
  Goodrich. Yasuo Kuniyoshi
  Pierson
  WMAA. Juliana Force
Summer storm        MiD
  Goodrich. Yasuo Kuniyoshi
This is my playground
  Goodrich. Yasuo Kuniyoshi
To the ball
  ICA. Annual ex, 1951
Upside down table and mask        MMA
  Goodrich. Yasuo Kuniyoshi
Weather vane and sofa        CSB
  Goodrich. Yasuo Kuniyoshi
  **Portrait of the artist**
  Biddle, G. Kuniyoshi, Portrait of, 1938
**KUNTZ, Roger,** 1927?-
Île de la Cité
  IU. Contemp Amer ptg & sculp, 1955
Los Angeles freeway
  IU. Contemp Amer ptg & sculp, 1957
**KUPFERMAN, Lawrence Edward,** 1909-
The fabulous crustacean        MB
  CoS. New accessions USA, 1950
Genesis
  IU. Contemp Amer ptg & sculp, 1961
Invention on a microscopic theme
  Baur. Revolution
Microscopic
  IU. Contemp Amer ptg, 1950
The tempest        IU
  IU. Contemp Amer ptg & sculp, 1953
  IU. 20th century
Walden pond
  Pousette-Dart. Amer ptg
Worship at Eleusis
  MBIC. View 1960
**KURZ, Friedrich,** b 1818
Minnetarees on Upper Missouri        MCH
  McCracken. Portrait of the old west
  (col)
**KUUSI, Helmi,** 1913-
Shepherd's eve
  UNESCO. 1860-1949
Kwaunon by J. La Farge

# L

**L., H. B.** fl 1861
Conflagration in a city on the eastern
  seaboard, 1861
  U.S. National Capital sesquicentennial
  com
Laboratory by M. Beckmann
Laboratory of Thomas Price by H. Alexander
Laboratory report by J. Ernst
Labrador ducks by M. Hartley
Labyrinth by S. Fogel
Labyrinth by A. Gottlieb
Labyrinth by J. O'Neil
Labyrinth by B. Shahn
Labyrinth by R. Vickrey
La Casse, Margaret. See Annesley, Margaret (La Casse)

Lace cap by S. F. B. Morse
Lace gables by C. E. Burchfield
**LACHOWICZ, William,** 1925?-
Signal        OYB
  OYB. Annual 1956
  OYB. Supplement 1959
Lackawanna valley by G. Inness
Lacrosse playing among the Sioux by S.
  Eastman
A lad from the fleet by F. Martin
The ladder by J. C. Wayne
Ladies in waiting by H. Mandel
Ladies of the evening by R. Philipp
The ladle by J. Marin
Ladson, James, 1753-1812
  Malbone, E. G. Major James Ladson
Ladson, Judith (Smith) 1762-1820
  Malbone, E. G. Mrs James Ladson
Ladson, Mary. See Cattel, Mary (Ladson)
Ladson, Sarah Reeve, 1790-1866
  Malbone, E. G. Sarah Reeve Ladson
Lady and gentleman by D. Goldsmith
Lady and her son by J. Vanderlyn
Lady at the tea table by M. Cassatt
Lady holding a book by H. P. Hunt
Lady in a dark blue dress by S. L. Waldo
  and W. Jewett
Lady in a fine scarf by W. M. Prior (manner of)
Lady in a landscape by J. Brewster (attributed works)
Lady in a sheer white cap by R. H. M.
  Bascom
Lady in black by W. M. Chase
Lady in pink skirt by M. B. Prendergast
Lady in purple by M. B. Prendergast
Lady in the greenwood by D. Austin
Lady in white bonnet by Unidentified artist
Lady in yellow by T. W. Dewing
Lady Jean by G. W. Bellows
Lady of eleven by Y. Tanguy
Lady of the lake by H. Pippin
Lady of the lake by Unidentified artist
Lady of the Lange Lijsen by J. A. M.
  Whistler
Lady on a balcony in Rome by C. W. Chapman
Lady on a wet day by M. B. Prendergast
Lady playing guitar by W. M. Chase
Lady wearing a red pompon by A. Fuller
Lady with a blue veil by J. S. Sargent
Lady with a harp by T. Sully
Lady with a nosegay by A. Ellis
Lady with a rose by Unidentified artist
Lady with a setter dog by T. Eakins
Lady with a white shawl by W. M. Chase
Lady with brown eyes by Unidentified artist
Lady with curls by Unidentified artist
Lady with fan by W. M. Chase
Lady with fan by N. Tschacbasov
Lady with lavender ribbons by Unidentified
  artist
Lady with plumed headdress by Unidentified
  artist

LA FARGE, John—*Continued*
Uncanny badger
  WiMiA. Amer ptg 1760-1960
View of Kioto                          MB
  MB. Ptgs in water color
LA FARGE, John, 1835-1910 and LOW,
  Will H., 1853-1932
Decorative panel                       MB
  MB. Ptgs in water color
LA FARGE, Louis Bancel, 1866-1938
Breakers                               MB
  MB. Ptgs in water color
Seashore                               MB
  MB. Ptgs in water color
Lafayette, Marie Joseph Paul Yves Roch
  Gilbert du Motier, marquis de, 1757-
  1834
Morse, S. F. B. Lafayette
Peale, C. W. Washington, Lafayette, and
  Tench Tilghman
Reed, R. L. Washington and Lafayette at
  the battle of Yorktown
Lafayette hotel by J. Sloan
Laffite, Jean, c 1780-c 1825
Jarvis, J. W. The pirate Laffite
The Lagoon, Venice by M. B. Prendergast
The Lagoon, Venice by J. A. M. Whistler
La Guardia, Fiorello Henry, 1882-1947
Kruse, A. Z. Mayor La Guardia as con-
  ductor
LAHEY, Richard Francis, 1893-
Easter morning on Eye street
  DC. 22 biennial ex, 1951
Paula
  NAD. Annual ex, 1947, 1st half
Ruth Ann
  PPC. Ptg in the U. S. 1949
Laight, Edward, fl 1802
Malbone, E. G. Edward Laight
Lair of the sea serpent by E. Vedder
The lake by W. D. Fausett
The lake by J. Hultberg
Lake Albano by G. Inness
Lake and mountain scene by A. J. Miller
Lake Concordia and aboriginal tumuli by
  J. J. Egan
Lake Erie, Battle of, 1812
Garneray, A. L. Battle of Lake Erie
Lake George by A. B. Durand
Lake George by M. J. Heade
Lake George by J. K. Kensett
Lake George by A. H. Wyant
Lake George and Caldwell village, A view
  by E. Ames
Lake George barns by G. O'Keeffe
Lake George, coat and red by G. O'Keeffe
Lake George near Caldwell, New York by
  R. Smith
Lake George, Perspective painting of by E.
  Ames
Lake George window by G. O'Keeffe
A lake in the mountains, View of by G. C.
  Bingham
Lake in wooded country: sunset by B. West
  (attributed works)
Lake landscape by A. Rattner
Lake Lure by J. Pike
Lake Maggiore, Italy by E. D. Boit

Lake of Nemi by J. F. Cropsey
Lake Orta, Italy by E. D. Boit
Lake Sanford in the Adirondacks by H. D.
  Martin
Lake scene—Mountains of the winds by A.
  J. Miller
Lake scene, Rocky mountains by A. J. Mil-
  ler
Lake scene, Wind river mountains by A. J.
  Miller
Lake Tahoe, California by A. Bierstadt
Lake, Tunk mountain by J. Marin
Lakes and mountains by A. Fisher (attrib-
  uted works)
LAM, Jennette, 1911-
Cathedral in the woods
  IU. Contemp Amer ptg & sculp, 1961
LAMB, A. A. fl 1865
Emancipation proclamation             DN
  DN. Amer primitive ptgs, pt 1
The lamb by L. Gatch
LAMBDIN, George Cochran, 1830-1896
The pruner                            MB
  Chew. 250 years of art
  MB. Karolik coll
LAMBDIN, James Reid, 1807-1889
John Penn (copy of ptg by Pine)       PH
  Chew. 250 years of art
Ulysses S. Grant                      PA
  Chew. 250 years of art
Lambertville pietà by L. Gatch
Laming, Benjamin
Peale, C. W. Benjamin Laming and wife
LA MORE, Chet, 1908-
Segment of the garden
  PPC. Ptg in the U. S. 1949
LAMOTTE, Bernard, 1903-
Nogent-le-Rotrou
  IU. Contemp Amer ptg, 1949
Rue de Crimée
  CSFP. Annual ex, 1947/48
Lamplight by R. Soyer
The lamplight portrait by C. W. Peale
Lamplighter, New York, 1806 by W. P.
  Chappel
LANCASTER, Robert L.
Staccato for dormers                  OYB
  OYB. Annual 1953
Lancaster by C. H. Demuth
LAND, Jerome
Passover supper
  OYB. Annual 1948
Land and seawater scape by Unidentified
  artist
Land of Evangeline by J. R. Meeker
Land of promise, Castle garden, New York
  by C. F. Ulrich
Land of the bright sun by R. Rosenborg
Land speculator by J. H. Beard
Landing the charettes by A. J. Miller
Lands End, Cornwall by W. T. Richards
Land's end, Golden gate, California by H.
  G. Keller
Lands end road by C. F. Gaertner
Landscape by R. Abrams
Landscape by R. Amft
Landscape by R. A. Blakelock
Landscape by W. M. Chase

Landscape by T. Cole
Landscape by A. Dasburg
Landscape by S. Davis
Landscape by T. Doughty
Landscape by A. G. Dove
Landscape by A. B. Durand
Landscape by I. Engel
Landscape by K. E. Fortess
Landscape by O. E. S. Frinck
Landscape by W. Hegelheimer
Landscape by E. Hicks
Landscape by R. Jacobi
Landscape by R. King
Landscape by H. E. Mattson
Landscape by A. H. Maurer
Landscape by W. Pachner
Landscape by C. Sheeler
Landscape by J. H. Twachtman
Landscape by M. Weber
Landscape, Bornholm by G. Grosz
Landscape, evening by W. Allston
Landscape for contemplation by L. Manso
Landscape forms by R. Rosenborg
Landscape from above by C. Wells
Landscape, house on cliff above pool by T. Doughty
Landscape in construction by S. Laufman
Landscape in five flats by A. G. Dove
Landscape in grey by X. Gonzáles
Landscape in ivory by E. Edwards
Landscape in Maine by J. Marin
Landscape near Chicago by A. Bohrod
Landscape, New Mexico by M. Hartley
Landscape no 29, 1907? by M. Hartley
Landscape no 32, 1911 by M. Hartley
Landscape no 36 by M. Hartley
Landscape of Provence by E. Bruce
Landscape of the absolute by I. R. Pereira
Landscape table by A. Gorky
Landscape, the ferry by T. Doughty
Landscape II, 1953 by P. Wonner
Landscape, Venice by M. Hartley
Landscape with a broken tree by K. H. Miller
Landscape with a farmhouse by S. Gallagher
Landscape with a lake by W. Allston
Landscape with a mirror by R. Hamilton
Landscape with bird's nest by D. Forbes
Landscape with blue-violet by W. Rakocy
Landscape with brook by A. C. Goodwin
Landscape with cattle by G. C. Bingham
Landscape with cattle by G. H. Durrie
Landscape with cattle by G. Inness jr
Landscape with cow by B. West
Landscape with drying sails by S. Davis
Landscape with factory by M. Beckmann
Landscape with farm by A. H. Maurer
Landscape with figures by R. L. Loftin
Landscape with figures by W. S. Mount

Landscape with fisherman and sailboat by T. Doughty
Landscape with fishermen by T. Doughty
Landscape with flowers by P. Blume
Landscape with houseboat by J. J. Jones
Landscape with houses by H. L. McFee
Landscape with letters by K. Zerbe
Landscape with mansion and white mantel by H. Pittman
Landscape with mountains by H. W. Rice
Landscape with polo players by P. Hunt
Landscape with poppies by P. Blume
Landscape with potted plant in foreground by Zalmar
Landscape with rider by J. Pollock
Landscape with scrap metal III by K. Zerbe
Landscape with still life by L. Johnson
Landscape with sunflowers by N. Cikovsky
Landscape with swans by J. Jones
Landscape with tree trunks by T. Cole
LANE, Fitz Hugh, 1804-1865
At the fishing grounds   MB
   MB. Lane
Brace's rock, Eastern point, Gloucester   MB
   MB. Karolik coll
   MB. Lane
Brig Antelope in Boston harbor   MB
   MB. Karolik coll
   MB. Lane
Fresh water cove from Dolliver's neck, Gloucester   MB
   MB. Karolik coll
   MB. Lane
   Pierson
Gloucester from Brookbank   MB
   MB. Karolik coll
   MB. Lane
Ipswich bay   MB
   MB. Lane
Maine inlet   MB
   MB. Karolik coll
   MB. Lane
   Pierson
New England coast shipping
   OCiM. Rediscoveries
New York harbor   MB
   MB. Karolik coll
   MB. Lane
Off Mount Desert island   NBM
   Baur. Amer ptg
Owl's head, Penobscot bay, Maine   MB
   MB. Karolik coll
   MB. Lane
   Time. 300 years (col)
Ships in ice off Ten Pound island, Gloucester   MB
   MB. Karolik coll
   MB. Lane
   Mendelowitz
   Pierson
View of Gloucester from Rocky Neck
   NUM. Art across America
Lang, Florence O. R.
   Seyffert, L. Florence O. R. Lang
Lang, Mrs Henry. See Lang, Florence O. R.

**Langhorne, Pennsylvania,** c 1845
  Hicks, E. Residence of David Twining, 1787
**Langsdorf, Mrs Alexander** jr. See Martyl
  (Suzanne Schweig)
**Languid** leisure by W. Sommer
**LANING, Edward,** 1906-
  Farewell to Pisa
    ICA. Annual ex, 1945/46
  The house
    WMAA. Contemp Amer ptg, 1952
  Learning to read                          NNPL
    Gruskin (col)
  Medieval scribe                           NNPL
    Gruskin (col)
  Moses with the tablets of the law NNPL
    Gruskin (col)
  Mural                                     NNPL
    NAD. Annual ex 1946, 2d half
**Lansing, John,** 1754-1829
  Ames, E. John Lansing jr
**LANYON, Ellen,** 1926-
  Cal-Sag
    IU. Contemp Amer ptg & sculp, 1957
  Terminal
    IU. Contemp Amer ptg & sculp, 1953
**Lapowinsa** by G. Hesselius
**Laramie,** Fort. See Fort Laramie
**Large** collage by R. B. Motherwell
**Large** encampment north of the Cut rocks
  by A. J. Miller
**Large** olive grove by W. Kahn
A **large** picture which is a landscape by
  Y. Tanguy
**Large** vertical by I. Bolotowsky
**Large** white flag by J. Johns
**Large** white nude by J. Sloan
**Larned, George,** fl 1825
  Tuthill, A. G. D. Col George Larned
**Larned** children, fl 1825
  Tuthill, A. G. D. Sylvester, Julia, Jane
    and Catherine Larned
**Larpolo** by J. D. Brooks
**Larrabee, John,** 1686-1762
  Badger, J. Capt John Larrabee
**Larry's** creek, West branch, Susquehanna
  by R. Smith
**Lasher, Caim**
  Speicher, E. E. Caim Lasher
**LASKER, Joseph L.** 1919-
  From an ivory tower
    IU. Contemp Amer ptg, 1952
  Little match girl
    IU. Contemp Amer ptg, 1951
  Naples                                    WMAA
    Goodrich. Amer art
  Sticks and stones
    CSFP. Annual ex, 1952
  Wallscape
    NAD. Annual ex, 1957
The **lasso** by W. T. Ranney
The **last** days by Y. Tanguy
The **last** Don Quixote by A. Rattner
The **last** king by J. Levine
**Last** of New England—beginning of New
  Mexico by M. Hartley
**Last** of old Westminster by J. A. M.
  Whistler
**Last** of the buffalo by A. Bierstadt

**Last** of the herd by C. M. Russell
**Last** of the lighthouse by J. E. Levi
**Last** of the Mohicans by T. Cole
**Last** parable by C. S. Chapman
**Last** snow by W. C. Palmer
**Last** stop by S. Wilson
The **last** supper by D. Aronson
The **last** supper by R. Arthur
The **last** supper by G. Hesselius
**Late** afternoon by R. Vickrey
**Late** afternoon—Calm on the Erie canal
  by G. Harvey
**Late** afternoon, Montclair, New Jersey by
  G. Inness
**Late** again by C. Blanchard
**Late** edition by C. Osver
**Late** summer by T. Birch
**Latest** news by M. Weber
**Lathom, Lady Wilma (Radnor) countess of,**
  1869-1931
  Sargent, J. S. The countess of Lathom
**LATHROP, Betsy B.** fl 1812
  Japhthah's return                         VWR
    VWR. Folk art (col)
**LATHROP, William Langson,** 1859-1938
  Muskrat hunter                            PR
    PR. Catalogue
**LATROBE, Benjamin Henry,** 1766-1820
  East front of the President's house, with
    the addition of the North and South
    porticos, 1807                          DLC
    Davidson v2
  Roman Catholic church, Baltimore, c 1805
    Davidson v2
**LAUFMAN, Sidney,** 1891-
  Along the path
    NAD. Annual ex, 1953
  Clayton's pasture
    IU. Contemp Amer ptg, 1948
  Deer Tongue lane                          InIJ
    InIJ. 105 ptgs
  From the terrace
    MM. Amer ptg today
  Grove of trees
    NAD. Annual ex, 1958
  House in the pines                        OT
    OT. Contemp Amer ptgs
  House in the woods
    DC. 22 biennial ex, 1951
  The path
    PA. Annual ex, 1951
  Pines                                     OYB
    OYB. Annual 1954
    OYB. Supplement
  Plowed field
    NYG. Fine art
  Spring landscape
    Gruskin
  Through the woods
    IU. Contemp Amer ptg & sculp, 1957
  Trees
    IU. Contemp Amer ptg, 1951
  Vernal
    NAD. Annual ex, 1960
  View from the terrace
    NAD. Annual ex, 1952
**Laughing** child by R. Henri
**Laughing** waters by S. Eastman
**Laughing** worker by P. Evergood

Laughton, Charles, 1899-1962
  Martin, F. Charles Laughton as Captain
    Kidd
Launching by G. W. Bellows
Laurel blossoms in vase by J. Marin
Laurel in the ledges by C. Hassam
Laurel run by E. W. Redfield
Laureline by F. J. Kline
Laurens, Eleanor (Ball) See Ball, Eleanor
Laurens, Mrs Henry. See Ball, Eleanor
Laurens, Tryntje. See Provost, Tryntje
  (Laurens)
LAURENT, John, 1921-
  From Mount Agamenticus—fall
    IU. Contemp Amer ptg & sculp, 1959
Laurent pony cart by B. Karfiol
LAVALLE, John, 1896-1940?
  Botafogo bay, Rio de Janeiro          MB
  MB. Ptgs in water color
Lavender and old lace by C. E. Burchfield
Lavender mist by J. Pollock
Law court by J. C. Wayne
LAWMAN, Jasper Holman, 1825-1906
  Snyder's Hollow          PPC
  Chew. 250 years of art
Lawn and sky by S. Davis
Lawrence, Mr, fl 1803
  Malbone, E. G. Mr Lawrence
LAWRENCE, A. A. fl 1852
  Boat race, Boston harbor (Boat race be-
    tween Harvard boat clubs in Boston
    harbor)          MB
  MB. Karolik coll
Lawrence, Amos, fl 1845
  Harding, C. Amos Lawrence
Lawrence, Harriet, 1793-1870. See Peirson,
  Harriet (Lawrence)
Lawrence, Harriet, fl 1890. See Hemenway,
  Harriet (Lawrence)
LAWRENCE, Jacob, 1917-
  Blind beggars          MM
  MM. 100 Amer ptrs
  Café scene          ATU
  ATU. Coll of Amer art
  Gruskin (col)
  Catfish row
  Pearson. Mod renaissance
  Chess on Broadway
  ICA. Amer artists paint the city
  Depression, 1950
  Baur. New art
  Florist's window
  IU. Contemp Amer ptg, 1952
  Fulton and Nostrand
  WMAA. Annual ex, 1958
  Ices
  IU. Contemp Amer ptg & sculp, 1961
  Magic man
  IU. Contemp Amer ptg & sculp, 1959
  Masks
  IU. Contemp Amer ptg & sculp, 1955
  Migration of the Negro          MMA
  McCurdy
  Most of the people are very poor
  Larkin
  Larkin rev ed
  Seamstress
  Baur. New art

Sedation          MMA
  Pierson
Shipping out          WMAA
  Goodrich. Amer art
Slums, 1951
  Baur. New art (col)
Tombstones          WMAA
  Baur. New art
  Bazin
  Pierson
Vaudeville
  Eliot. Art of our time (col)
  Pearson. Mod renaissance
  Time. 300 years (col)
War series: another patrol          WMAA
  Goodrich. Amer art
  Pierson
Woman at work (Migration of the Negro
  series)          DP
  DP. Catalogue
You can buy whiskey for twenty-five
  cents a quart
  Pearson. Mod renaissance
Lawrence, Rachel (Longfield) 1689-1768
  Unidentified artist. Mrs Thomas Lawrence
Lawrence, Thomas, 1689-1754
  Unidentified artist. Thomas Lawrence
Lawrence, William Augustus
  Morse, S. F. B. William Augustus Law-
    rence
LAWSON, Ernest, 1873-1939
  After rain          DP
  DP. Catalogue
  Glackens
  Boat house, winter, Harlem river          DC
  Larkin
  Larkin rev ed
  Early spring
  NSyE. The eight
  Early summer, Vermont          OCo
  Pierson
  Harlem river          NJN
  NBuA. Fifty ptgs
  High bridge          WMAA
  Bazin
  Goodrich. Amer art
  May in the mountains          DP
  DP. Catalogue
  Misty day in March          OYB
  OYB. Catalogue 1951
  Old mill          InIJ
  InIJ. 105 ptgs
  Spring night, Harlem river          DP
  Born
  CSB. Impressionism
  DP. Catalogue
  McCurdy
  Pierson
  Sunset, High bridge          DP
  Cheney. Story 1958 ed
  DP. Catalogue
  The valley          OCo
  Brown. Amer ptg
  Winter          MM
  MM. 100 Amer ptrs
  Winter, Central park, New York          ATeS
  ATeS. Collection
  Winter on the river          WMAA
  Pierson
Lay figure by Y. Kuniyoshi
Layered by J. Albers

**LAYTON, Gloria**
Easter bonnet
  NAD. Annual ex, 1954
The **leader** by W. M. Chase
The **leaf** of the artichoke is an owl by A. Gorky
**Leaning** figure by M. Weber
**Leaping** figure by S. W. Hayter
**Leaping** trout by W. Homer
**Learning** to read by E. Laning
**Leatherstocking** kills the panther (il for Cooper's Pioneers) by G. L. Brown
**Leave** it to the experts by P. Evergood
**Leavens, Harriet,** fl 1815
  Border limner. Harriet Leavens
**Leaves** in Weehawken by W. De Kooning
**Leaving** the manor house by Unidentified artist
**LEAVITT, Joseph Warren,** fl 1825
At Loudon, New Hampshire
  Ford. Pictorial folk art
House of Moses Morse, Loudon, New Hampshire
  Pierson
**Lebanon,** Buildings at by C. Sheeler
**LEBDUSKA, Lawrence H.** 1894-
California farm                              ATU
  ATU. Coll of Amer art (col)
**Lebrun, Federico.** See Lebrun, Rico
**LEBRUN, Rico,** 1900-1964
Anna
  NYG. Fine art
Buchenwald cart                              PA
  OCl. Some contemporary works
The bull ring                                MM
  MM. 100 Amer ptrs
Burnt spinner
  IU. Contemp Amer ptg, 1951
Centurion's horse
  MM. Amer ptg today
  Pearson. Mod renaissance
Crucifixion                                  NSyE
  IU. Contemp Amer ptg & sculp, 1957
  Mendelowitz
Crucifixion triptych
  Baur. New art
Dachau chamber, Study for
  Selz. New images (col)
Double disparate
  Selz. New images
Dying steer
  IU. Contemp Amer ptg & sculp, 1959
Farm machine no 1, 1947
  MnU. 40 Amer ptrs
Figure in the rain                           MMA
  Baur. New art (col)
Figures on the cross with lantern            CoD
  CoS. New accessions USA, 1958
  PA. Annual ex, 1953
Imploring dead
  IU. Contemp Amer ptg & sculp, 1961
The Magdalene
  Pearson. Mod renaissance
Migration to nowhere
  Baur. New art
Mocking soldier                              IU
  IU. Contemp Amer ptg, 1949
  IU. 20th century
Pilgrim with flowered hat
  PPC. International ex, 1955

Rooster on arm of the cross                  MoSL
  Baur. New art
  MnMW. Expressionism 1900-1955
  NBuA. Expressionism
  Pousette-Dart. Amer ptg
  PPC. International ex, 1952
  VR. Amer ptg, 1954
Shell of Mary
  Baur. Revolution
Still life, melons                           CSB
  CoS. New accessions USA, 1946
Study for a soldier                          CLA
  CoS. New accessions USA, 1950
Vertical composition
  Pearson. Mod renaissance
  Wight. Milestones
Woman of the crucifixion                     NeL
  Barker. From realism
  CoS. New accessions USA, 1952
  ICA. Annual ex, 1951
  MnU. 40 Amer ptgs
Wood of the holy cross                       WMAA
  Goodrich. Amer art
  Pierson

    Portrait of the artist
Berman, E. Rico Lebrun
**LECHAY, James,** 1907-
Blue is for bass
  CSFP. Annual ex, 1952
  IU. Contemp Amer ptg, 1951
Chinatown, Maw Wah
  WMAA. Annual ex, 1955
Dark sky—dark water
  VR. Biennial ex, 1948
Harbor with red for Mary Lou                 OCl
  CoS. New accessions USA, 1954
Hudson river                                 ATU
  ATU. Coll of Amer art
**LE CLEAR, Thomas,** 1818-1882
Buffalo newsboy                              NBuA
  Baur. Amer ptg
  NBuA. Catalogue of the ptgs
  NJN. Early N.J. artists
  Pierson
**Leda** by F. J. Kline
**Leda** in high places by P. Evergood
**Lee, A. W.**
  Eakins, T. A. W. Lee
**Lee, Anne (Theus)** b 1750
  Theus, J. Mrs William Lee
**LEE, Doris (Emrick)** 1905-
Badminton
  IU. Contemp Amer ptg, 1952
  Pearson. Mod renaissance
Costumes for Dragonwyck
  Pearson. Mod renaissance
Country wedding                              NBuA
  Gruskin (col)
  NBuA. Contemporary ptgs
The runaway                                  ATU
  ATU. Coll of Amer art (col)
Sappho
  IU. Contemp Amer ptg & sculp, 1955
Shelves
  PPC. International ex, 1952
Siesta                                       PPC
  Pearson. Mod renaissance
Summer                                       NBuA
  NBuA. Acquisitions 1957-58
Thanksgiving                                 ICA
  NYG. Fine art

Thanksgiving day
  Pearson. Mod renaissance
Winter in the Catskills
  NYG. Fine art
**Lee, Geraldine**
  Bellows, G. W. Geraldine Lee
**Lee, Jeremiah,** 1721-1775
  Copley, J. S. Jeremiah Lee
**Lee, Mrs Jeremiah,** fl 1769
  Copley, J. S. Mrs Jeremiah Lee
**LEE, Joseph,** fl 1870
  Alameda shore         CSFD
  Born
  Oak Knoll, Napa      CSFD
  Born
  Pierson
**Lee, Robert Edward,** 1807-1870
  Healy, G. P. A. Robert E. Lee
**LEE, Robert J.**
  Trombone player       MSM
    CoS. New accessions USA, 1956
**Lee, Vernon, pseud.** See Paget, Violet
**Lee, Mrs William.** See Lee, Anne (Theus)
**Lee** shore by E. Hopper
**Leeds, Lucy (Orcutt)** fl 1840
  Unidentified artist. Lucy Orcutt Leeds
    and her son
**LEEPA, Allen,** 1919-
  Composition in red, yellow and blue
    Leepa
  Curved composition in yellow, red and
    blue
    Leepa
  Nude
    Leepa
  Still life in green
    Leepa
  Still life in red, yellow, white and blue
    Leepa
  Tree
    Leepa
**LEE-SMITH, Hughie**
  Old man and youth
    NAD. Annual ex, 1959
**Leffingwell, Sally (Beers)** fl 1807
  Jarvis, J. W. Mrs William Leffingwell
**Leffingwell, William,** 1765-1834
  Jarvis, J. W. William Leffingwell
**Lefort, Henri,** b 1852
  Sargent, J. S. Henri Lefort
**Legareville,** South Carolina by P. A. Tren-
  holm
**Le Havre** by F. Boggs
**Lehigh** canal, sunset, New Hope, Pennsyl-
  vania by J. Pickett
**Leidy, Joseph,** 1866-1942
  Eakins, T. Man with red necktie (Dr
    Joseph Leidy jr)
**LEIGH, William Robinson,** 1866-1955
  Baking day
    Carlson. Gallery (col)
  Combing the ridges
    Carlson. Gallery (col)
  Female of the species
    Carlson. Gallery (col)
  Home sweet home
    Carlson. Gallery (col)
  A lowdown trick
    Time. 300 years (col)
  The mystic
    Carlson. Gallery (col)

The rescue
  Carlson. Gallery (col)
Voice of the desert
  Carlson. Gallery (col)
**Leila** by A. K. Stoddard
**Leisler, Hester.** See Rynders, Hester
  (Leisler)
**Leisler, Mary.** See Gouverneur, Mary
  (Leisler)
**Leisure** and labor by F. B. Mayer
**Leman, Margaret Adelia,** fl 1825
  Eichholtz, J. Margaret Adelia Leman
**Lemons** and sugar by Rubens Peale
**Lenna** and Imp by W. J. Glackens
**Lenox, Althea.** See Donaldson, Althea
  (Lenox)
**Lenox, Elizabeth Sproat.** See Maitland,
  Elizabeth Sproat (Lenox)
**Lenox, James,** 1772-1839
  Jarvis, J. W. James Lenox
**Lenox, James,** 1800-1880
  Unidentified artist. James Lenox
**Lenox, Rachel (Carmer)** 1763-1843
  Inman, H. Mrs Robert Lenox
  Trumbull, J. Mrs Robert Lenox
  Unidentified artist. Mrs Robert Lenox
  Unidentified artist. Mrs Robert Lenox
    (possibly a copy of Inman portrait)
**Lenox, Robert,** 1759-1839
  Thibault, A. Robert Lenox
  Trumbull, J. Robert Lenox
  Unidentified artist. Robert Lenox (after
    Jarvis)
**Lenox, Mrs Robert.** See Lenox, Rachel
  (Carmer)
**Lenox family, Member of**
  Thibault, A. Lady of the Lenox family
**Leona** by J. Arkush
**Leonardo** by C. L. Cicero
**LEONID (Leonid Berman)** 1896-
  Drying codfish in Brittany
    ICA. Annual ex, 1951
  Entretat, le Cabestan Capstan   CtHW
    Pierson
  Fish weir, Maine
    ICA. Annual ex, 1954
  Fish weir near Sprucehead
    WMAA. Contemp Amer ptg, 1953
  The fisherwoman          MMA
    MMA. Soby collection
  Fishing shrimps at Boulogne    NJN
    CoS. New accessions USA, 1956
  Malamocco             MMA
    McCurdy
    Pierson
  Mussel gatherers at high tide   MMA
    MMA. Soby collection
  Narragansett bay
    VR. Amer ptg, 1954
  Port Jefferson           MoKN
    MoKN. Handbook p 150
  Portuguese sea
    CSFP. Annual ex, 1948/49
  Provincetown
    IU. Contemp Amer ptg, 1952
    Pousette-Dart. Amer ptg
  Rice field near Milan
    WMAA. Annual ex, 1955
**LeRoy, Daniel,** 1761-1791
  Unidentified artist. Daniel LeRoy

**LEROY, Elizabeth (Emmet)** fl 1815-1830
  Robert Fulton           MWA
    MWA. Checklist of portraits
**Le Roy,** New York by Unidentified artist
**Leroy's** shift by S. Davis
**LESLIE, Alfred,** 1928-
  Baby's curse           MnMW
    MMA. Sixteen
    MnMW. 60 Amer ptrs
  Four-panel green
    MMA. Sixteen
  Hialeah           NBuA
    NBuA. Acquisitions 1959-1961
  Money
    PPC. International ex, 1961/62
  Number 25
    WMAA. Contemp Amer ptg, 1959/60
  The second two-panel horizontal
    MMA. Sixteen
  Soldier's medal         NBuA
    NBuA. Acquisitions 1959-1961
**LESLIE, Charles Robert,** 1794-1859
  Actors' duel: Mr Jefferson and Mr. Blissett
    Flexner. Light of distant skies
  Murder of Rutland       PA
    Flexner. Light of distant skies
  Personification of murder    MdBMu
    MdBMu. Rendezvous
  Sophia Western         PA
    Flexner. Light of distant skies
**Leslie** by C. Buck
**Lesseps, Ferdinand Marie, viscount de,** 1805-1894
  Healy, G .P. A. Ferdinand de Lesseps
**The lesson** by J. S. Sargent
**Lesson I,** 1956 by S. Davis
**LESTER, William,** 1910-
  College on the hill
    CSFP. Annual ex, 1952
  Old Fort Davis         TxF
    Pousette-Dart. Amer ptg
**Lesueur, Charles Alexandre**
  Peale, C. W. Charles Alexandre Lesueur
**Let us pray** by W. Pachner
**Let's** search our souls by J. Berlandina
**The letter** by M. Avery
**The letter** by T. W. Dewing
**The letter** by R. L. Newman
**Letter** home by E. Johnson
**Letter** rack with jack of hearts by J. F. Peto
**Letter** rack with Lerado postmark by J. F. Peto
**Letty** in leghorn by R. Philipp
**LEUTZE, Emanuel,** 1816-1868
  Course of empire
    Barker. Amer ptg
  Gulch mine, Central city, Colorado CoDP
    Rathbone
  Washington crossing the Delaware
    Davidson v 1
  Westward the course of empire takes its
    way           DN
    Pierson
**Levant** for E. W. R. by T. Stamos
**Levant** no 7 by T. **Stamos**
**LEVEE, John,** 1924-
  April 1, 1957
    Read. Concise history

  May 2, 1956
    WMAA. Young America 1957
  Painting
    PPC. International ex, 1955
  September 1, 1956
    WMAA. Young America 1957
**The levee** by J. W. Taylor
**LEVER, Hayley,** 1876-1958
  Beach at St Ives, Cornwall, England
                    NJMo
    NJMo. Forty years
  Still life
    NAD. Annual ex, 1959
**Lever, Richard Hayley.** See Lever, Hayley
**LEVI, Julian Edwin,** 1900-
  Autobiography
    CSFP. Annual ex, 1947/48
  Beachcomber
    Gruskin (col)
  The garden
    ICA. Annual ex, 1961
  Iron dragon
    IU. Contemp Amer ptg & sculp, 1955
    NAD. Annual ex, 1956
  Last of the lighthouse      NJN
    Pierson
  Margaret Boni playing the recorder NBuA
    NBuA. Contemporary ptgs
  Poseidon
    IU. Contemp Amer ptg & sculp, 1959
  Red pastoral          MiD
    CoS. New accessions USA, 1958
  Sand and sky
    PPC. Ptg in the U.S. 1949
  Ship graveyard
    Baur. Revolution
  Strata
    IU. Contemp Amer ptg & sculp, 1961
  Tarring nets          ATU
    ATU. Coll of Amer art
  Tidewater shapes
    IU. Contemp Amer ptg, 1948
  Weir
    IU. Contemp Amer ptg, 1951
  The widow
    IU. Contemp Amer ptg, 1949
**LEVINE, David,** 1927?-
  Preliminary examination
    ICA. Annual ex, 1961
**LEVINE, Jack,** 1915-
  Apteka
    DC. 20 biennial ex, 1947
    ICA. Amer artists paint the city
    MBIC. Jack Levine
    PA. Annual ex, 1948
  The banquet
    MBIC. Jack Levine
    WMAA. Neuberger collection
  Black freighter
    IU. Contemp Amer ptg & sculp, 1959
  Card players
    Lewisohn
  City lights
    MnU. 40 Amer ptrs
  Coronation
    MnU. 40 Amer ptrs
  Courtroom study
    IU. Contemp Amer ptg & sculp, 1955
  Dramatis personae        ATU
    ATU. Coll of Amer art

Election night                    MMA
  CoS. New accessions USA, 1956
  PPC. International ex, 1955
  Time. 300 years (col)
Euclid avenue
  WMAA. Contemp Amer ptg, 1950
Feast of pure reason              MMA
  Baur. New art
  Cheney. Story 1958 ed
  Larkin
  Larkin rev ed
  MBIC. Jack Levine
  McCurdy
  MMA. Masters
  Myers
  Read. Concise history
  Roos
  Seiberling
Gangster funeral                  WMAA
  Baur. New art
  Goodrich. Amer art (col)
  Larkin rev ed (col detail)
  Pierson
Gangster's funeral, Study for
  NUM. Art across America
A girl
  CanO. Hirshhorn coll
Girls from Fleugel street
  DC. 26 biennial ex, 1959
Homage to Boston
  IU. Contemp Amer ptg, 1951
  MBIC. Jack Levine
  PPC. International ex, 1950
Improvisation in a Greek key
  IU. Contemp Amer ptg, 1950
Inauguration                      WMAA
  WMAA. Sara Roby
The judge
  PA. Annual ex, 1956
King Josiah
  Munsterberg
King Saul
  Eliot. Art of our time (col)
  Time. 300 years (col)
The last king
  DC. 21 biennial ex, 1949
Love, oh careless love
  ICA. Annual ex, 1959/60
  OYB. Annual 1959
Magician
  CSFP. Annual ex, 1948/49
  IU. Contemp Amer ptg, 1948
Medicine show IV                  KW
  CoS. New accessions USA, 1960
Neighborhood physician            MnMW
  MnMW. Expressionism 1900-1955
The passing scene                 MMA
  MBIC. Jack Levine
Pawnshop
  MBIC. Jack Levine
Pensionnaire                      NeL
  Barker. From realism
  CoS. New accessions USA, 1946
Reception in Miami
  IU. Contemp Amer ptg, 1949
  MBIC. Jack Levine
Self-portrait with muse
  IU. Contemp Amer ptg & sculp, 1961
The street
  Pierson

String quartette                  MM
  Gruskin (col)
  MM. 100 Amer ptrs
  Taylor. Fifty centuries, 1954 ed (col)
  Wight. Milestones
Tombstone cutter
  MBIC. Jack Levine
  MiD. Coll in progress
  NBuA. Expressionism
  WiMiA. Amer ptg 1760-1960
The trial                         ICA
  Baur. New art (col)
  Pierson
  WMAA. Museum and its friends, 1959
The trial                         OCo
  CoS. New accessions USA, 1956
The turnkey
  IU. Contemp Amer ptg & sculp, 1957
Under the el                      DP
  Pousette-Dart. Amer ptg
Welcome home                      NBM
  Baur. New art
  Baur. Revolution
  CoS. New accessions USA, 1948
  Genauer
  MBIC. Jack Levine
  Mendelowitz
  MMA. Contemp ptrs
  Pierson
Woodstock pastorale               CSFP
  CoS. New accessions USA, 1952
  CSFP. Annual ex, 1952
  CSFP. Handbook
Levine, Mrs Jack. See Gikow, Ruth
LEVINSON, Abraham Frater, 1883-1946
  Mexican vase with flowers        MB
  MB. Ptgs in water color
Levy, Bilhah Abigail. See Franks, Bilhah
  Abigail
Levy, Grace (Mears)
  Duyckinck, G. (attributed works) Mrs
  Moses Levy
Levy, Moses, 1665?-1728
  Unidentified artist. Moses Levy
LEWANDOWSKI, Edmund D. 1914-
  Christmas tree
  ICA. Annual ex, 1951
  MMA. Abstract
  Gulf coast shipyard
  Pousette-Dart. Amer ptg
  Industrial composition           NBM
  Baur. Revolution
  Ore freighter                    WiMi
  MnMW. Precisionist view
  White sails
  WMAA. Annual ex, 1950
  Winter port                      MB
  MB. Ptgs in water color
LEWIN, C. L. fl 1850
  Girl with bird
  Ford. Pictorial folk art
LEWIS, Edmund Darch, 1837-1910
  Wyoming valley
  McClintock
Lewis, Eleanor Parke (Custis). See Custis,
  Eleanor Parke
Lewis, Elizabeth. See Goldthwait, Elizabeth
  (Lewis)
LEWIS, Henry, 1819-1904
  Cheever's mill on the St Croix, 1847
                           MnMI
  U.S. National Capital sesquicentennial
  com

LEWIS, Henry—*Continued*
Gorge of the St Croix river, 1847 MnMI
Davidson v2
A street in St Louis                MoSL
MoSL. Handbook 1953
**Attributed works**
St Louis after the great fire
Born
Lewis, Isaac, 1746-1840
Jarvis, J. W. Dr Isaac Lewis
LEWIS, James Otto, fl 1820-1835
Cut-Taa-Tas-Tia, a Fox chief
McCracken. Portrait of the old west
(col)
Kee-o-kuk, chief of the Sauk
McCracken. Portrait of the old west
(col)
Me-no-quet, a Pottawattomie chief
Morgan (col)
Nabu-Naa-Kee-Shick, a Chippewa chief
McCracken. Portrait of the old west
(col)
Pe-che-co, a Pottawattomie chief
Morgan (col)
Sun-a-get, a Pottawattomie chief
Morgan
Tens-qua-ta-wa, the Shawnee prophet
Morgan (col)
Waa-Na-Taa, chief of the Sioux
McCracken. Portrait of the old west
(col)
Lewis, Jane (Clark). See Clark, Jane
Lewis, Mrs John. See Clark, Jane
LEWIS, John Chapman, 1920-
Interior and bay                DC
CoS. New accessions USA, 1956
Penthesilean trawler
IU. Contemp Amer ptg, 1952
Lewis, John L.
Noxon, H. R. John L. Lewis
Lewis, Meriwether, 1774-1809
Russell, C. M. Lewis and Clark meeting
Flathead Indians
Russell, C. M. Lewis and Clark meeting
the Mandans
LEWIS, Norman, 1909-
Cathedral
ICA. Amer artists paint the city
Newer grounds
CSFP. Annual ex, 1952
Night walk
Baur. Nature
Urban
MMA. Abstract
Lewis, Rebecca
Wollaston, J. Warner Lewis II and
Rebecca
Lewis, Warner, fl 1756
Wollaston, J. Warner Lewis
Wollaston, J. Warner Lewis II and Re-
becca
Lewis, Mrs Warner, fl 1756
Wollaston, J. Mrs Warner Lewis
LEWIS, William A. 1918-
Winter's day                OYB
OYB. Annual 1958
OYB. Supplement 1959
Lewis children
Wollaston, J. Children of Warner Lewis
LEWITIN, Landès, 1892-
Easy
MMA. Sixteen

Forget it
MMA. Sixteen
Knockout
MMA. Sixteen
Think of me, dear
MMA. Sixteen
Lexington and Concord, Battles of, 1775
Earl, R. Battles of Lexington and Con-
cord
Lexington battle monument by Unidentified
artist
Leyland, Frederick R.
Whistler, J. A. M. Arrangement in black
LIBBY, William Charles, 1919-
Nonconformists                OYB
OYB. Catalogue 1951
Libby prison by D. G. Blythe
Liberation by B. Shahn
LIBERMAN, Alexander, 1912-
Two circles
NNSG. Younger Amer ptrs
Liberté, Jean. See Liberté, Lewis Jean
LIBERTÉ, Lewis Jean, 1895-
Coming into port                ATU
ATU. Coll of Amer art
Dark harbor
IU. Contemp Amer ptg, 1950
Lighthouse at night                GAtM
GAtM. Holbrook collection
Monhegan hill
Gruskin
Sunset, Gloucester
IU. Contemp Amer ptg, 1949
Libration by H. Hofmann
LICHTENBERG, Manes
Albert bridge, London
NAD. Annual ex, 1961
LIE, Jonas, 1880-1940
Dawn at Culebra
U.S. National Capital sesquicentennial
com
Deep river                WMAA
Larkin
Larkin rev ed
Old ships drawn to home again    NBM
Pierson
LIEBMAN, Marjorie
Number 9—1953
IU. Contemp Amer ptg & sculp, 1955
Lieutenant Bulkley's PT boats at Bataan
by G. A. Picken
Life goes by by A. G. Dove
The life line by W. Homer
Life-size black bass by W. Homer
Life with father, Impression from by G. R.
Beal
Lifting night by C. A. Morris
The light by W. T. Murch
Light and shade by R. N. Blair
Light battery at Gettysburg by E. Hopper
Light, earth and blue by M. Rothko
Light in August by W. De Kooning
Light in autumn by W. Thon
Light is gold by I. R. Pereira
The light of learning by K. Cox
Light of the world by P. Blume
Light on the sea by W. Homer
Light wells by A. Osver

**Lighter** relieving a steamboat aground by G. C. Bingham
**Lighthouse** keeper by R. Brackman
**Lighthouse** service dock, Nassau by S. M. Etnier
**Lighthouses**
  De Martini, J. Foggy night
  De Martini, J. Lighthouse point
  Hartley, M. Lighthouse
  Hopper, E. Lighthouse at Two Lights
  Kantor, M. Highland light
  Kaplan, J. Highland light
  Kingman, D. Lighthouse
  Liberté, L. J. Lighthouse at night
  Thon, W. The outpost
**Lightning** at sea by G. O'Keeffe
**Lights** by C. A. Morris
**Lilacs** by K. Knaths
**Lilacs** and books by K. Knaths
**Lilacs** and glasses by B. Bomar
**Lilies** by P. Blume
**Lilies** by H. Pippin
**Lily** and the sparrows by P. Evergood
**Lilya** by E. E. Speicher
**Limbo** by S. Greene
**Lime** quarry by H. P. Barnett
**Limestone** edge by J. W. Boynton
**Limestone** quarry by R. O. Pozzatti
The **limit** by A. Gorky
**Lincoln, Abraham, president U.S.** 1809-1865
  Bachelder, J. B. and Chappel, A. Death of Abraham Lincoln
  Blythe, D. G. Lincoln crushing the dragon of rebellion
  Blythe, D. G. President Lincoln writing the Emancipation proclamation
  Hartley, M. Portrait of Lincoln
  Healy, G. P. A. Abraham Lincoln
  Healy, G. P. A. The peacemakers
  Peto, J. F. Lincoln and the Pfleger stretcher
  Peto, J. F. Rack picture with portrait of Lincoln
  Pippin, H. Abe Lincoln, the great emancipator
  Pippin, H. Abraham Lincoln and his father building their cabin on Pigeon creek
  Unidentified artist. Lincoln and his Cabinet, c 1860
A **Lincoln** reception at the White house by F. B. Carpenter (attributed works)
**Lind, Jenny,** 1820-1887
  Healy, G. P. A. Jenny Lind
**Lindall, Elizabeth.** See Pitts, Elizabeth (Lindall)
**Lindall, Susanna (Hasey)** 1660-1733
  Smibert, J. Mrs James Lindall
**LINDNER, Richard,** 1901-
  L'académicien
    ICA. Annual ex, 1954
    IU. Contemp Amer ptg & sculp, 1955
  Boy with machine
    ICA. Annual ex, 1957
  Paul Verlaine
    MnMW. Reality and fantasy
**Lindsay, Robert M.** d 1908
  Eakins, T. Robert M. Lindsay
**Linear** pattern by W. Saltzman

**Linear** structure by H. Bayer
**LINEN, George,** 1802-1888
  Margaret Henderson Gregory and Dudley Sanford Gregory
    DC. Privately owned
**Linford, Charles,** 1846-1897
  Eakins, T. Charles Linford, the artist
**Links** of memory by A. Gottlieb
**Linn, William,** 1752-1808
  Jarvis, J. W. Dr William Linn
**LINTOT, Barbara**
  Ballerina and the black cat
    NAD. Annual ex, 1947, 1st half
**Lions**
  Browne, B. Black lion
  Hicks, E. (attributed works) The lion family
  Marin, J. The lions in the ring
**Lisbeth's** painting by W. De Kooning
**Liscome, Lydia.** See Jarvis, Lydia (Liscome)
**Listening** to the voice of stone by G. Mofchum
**Liszt, Franz,** 1811-1886
  Healy, G. P. A. Franz Liszt
**Litter** by E. Melcarth
**Little** attic by W. De Kooning
**Little Big Horn, Battle of,** 1876
  Benton, T. H. Custer's last stand
**Little** bird alone by M. Graves
**Little** bouquet by M. A. Phillips
**Little** boy in red by Unidentified artist
**Little** canyon by E. F. Spruce
**Little** captain by P. Evergood
**Little** child with big dog by W. M. Prior
**Little** coat and fur shop by K. H. Miller
**Little** cobbler's shop by C. Hassam
**Little** dancer by R. Henri
**Little** dandy by N. Cook
**Little** dog by C. A. Woolworth
**Little** Falls, New York by Unidentified artist
**Little** giant still life by S. Davis
**Little** girl and the cat by Unidentified artist
A **little** girl—Fanny Travis Cochran by C. Beaux
**Little** girl holding apple by W. M. Prior (attributed works)
**Little** girl in lavender by J. Bradley
**Little** girl run for your life by Y. Kuniyoshi
**Little** girl with a snowberry by Unidentified artist
**Little** girl with apple by W. Sommer
**Little** Joe with cow by Y. Kuniyoshi
**Little** king by J. Pollock
**Little-known** bird of the inner eye by M. Graves
**Little** madonna by G. B. Luks
**Little** maid of Arcady by A. P. Ryder
**Little** match girl by J. L. Lasker
**Little** Miss Hone by S. F. B. Morse
**Little** movie theater by J. Sloan
**Little** murderer by G. Grosz
**Little** Red Riding Hood by G. C. Bingham
**Little** Rose of Lyme Regis by J. A. M. Whistler

Little sailboat by J. Marin

Little Scheveningen: grey note by J. A. M. Whistler

Little Scotch girl by E. G. Malbone

Little sheep by J. Carroll

The little white girl by J. A. M. Whistler

Littleton, New Hampshire by Unidentified artist

The liver is the cock's comb by A. Gorky

Livermore, Jane (Browne) 1734-1803
  Copley, J. S. Jane Browne

Livermore, Mrs Samuel. See Livermore, Jane (Browne)

Living rooms
  Benson, F. W. Rainy day
  Carlin, J. Sparking
  Pippin, H. Victorian interior
  Pittman, H. Reflections
  Sargent, H. Tea party
  Sharrer, H. D. In the parlor

Livingston, Eliza, 1786-1860
  Malbone, E. G. Eliza Livingston

Livingston, Mrs Jasper H. See Livingston, Eliza

Livingston, John W. 1778-1860
  Malbone, E. G. John W. Livingston

Livingston, Margaret, 1681-1758. See Vetch, Margaret (Livingston)

Livingston, Margaret, 1738-1818. See Stuyvesant, Margaret (Livingston)

Livingston, Margaret (Howarden) fl 1717
  Unidentified artist. Mrs Robert Livingston

Livingston, Robert, 1654-1728
  Unidentified artist. Robert Livingston

Livingston, Robert R. 1746-1813
  Vanderlyn, J. Robert R. Livingston

Llano Quemado by A. Dasburg

Lloyd, Henry, 1685-1763
  Mare, J. Henry Lloyd I (copy after Wollaston)

Lobby wall by S. Davis

The lobster by A. G. Dove

Lobster boat by J. Marin

Lobster boat, Cape Split, Maine by J. Marin

Lobster buoys and nets by M. Hartley

Lobster fishermen by M. Hartley

Lobster pots and buoy by M. Hartley

Lobster traps by S. J. Twardowicz

Lobsterman's gear by E. Fiene

The lock by W. T. Murch

Lock Haven, Pennsylvania by Unidentified artist

LOCKE, Charles, 1899-
  Copyist
    NAD. Annual ex, 1949, 1st half

LOCKMAN, DeWitt McClellan, 1870-1957
  Aimée Delmores
    NNHS. Lockman
  Calvin Coolidge         NNHS
    NNHS. Lockman
  Clara C. Doreu
    NNHS. Lockman
  Coco the clown (George Hubert Herbert)
                           NNHS
    NNHS. Lockman
  Constance Eastman (1)
    NNHS. Lockman

Constance [Eastman] (2)
  NNHS. Lockman

Edwin Howland Blashfield    NNHS
  NNHS. Lockman

Harry Woodburn Chsae    NNHS
  NNHS. Lockman

I. N. Phelps Stokes    NNHS
  NNHS. Lockman

Josephus Daniels    NNHS
  NNHS. Lockman

Maxwell D. Taylor    NWP
  NNHS. Lockman

Mrs DeWitt M. Lockman. See The porphyry jar

Mrs George Perkins
  NAD. Annual ex, autumn 1949

Nicholas Murray Butler    NNHS
  NNHS. Lockman

Patrick Cardinal Hayes    NNHS
  NNHS. Lockman

The porphyry jar (Mrs DeWitt M. Lockman)
  NNHS. Lockman

Robert Lee Bullard    NNHS
  NNHS. Lockman

Samuel Montgomery Roosevelt
  NNHS. Lockman

Self-portrait
  NNHS. Lockman

Sidney G. DeKay
  NNHS. Lockman

William Sowden Sims    NNHS
  NNHS. Lockman

Lockman, Mrs DeWitt McClellan. See Lockman, Evelyn Clair Walker

Lockman, Evelyn Clair Walker
  Lockman, D. M. The porphyry jar

Lockport on the Erie canal by M. Keys

LOCKWOOD, Ward, 1894-
  Fragments of elegance
    MM. Amer ptg today
  Jet and turquoise
    IU. Contemp Amer ptg, 1952
  Restrained flow
    IU. Contemp Amer ptg & sculp, 1959
  Southwest no 4    WMAA
  Pierson
  Southwest no 9—riders
    IU. Contemp Amer ptg & sculp, 1955
  Valley below
    IU. Contemp Amer ptg, 1951

Locomotives
  Feininger, L. Locomotive with big wheel
  Feininger, L. Old American locomotive
  Feininger, T. L. Ghosts of engines
  Finch, K. Locomotives
  Marsh, R. Locomotives watering
  Sintzenich, E. Train leaving Auburn station at Rochester, New York
  Unidentified artist. Railroad engine, the Star

Locust by K. Finch

Loeffler, Charles Martin, 1861-1935
  Sargent, J. S. Charles M. Loeffler

Loftus, Edward
  Stuart, G. Edward Loftus

Log jam, Penobscot bay by M. Hartley

LOGAN, A. fl 1874
  The circus    DN
    DN. Amer primitive ptgs, pt 1

Logan, Martha. See Chalmers, Martha (Logan) (?)

LOGAN, Maurice, 1886-
  Bass boats
    NAD. Annual ex, 1955
La loge by M. Cassatt
Logging camp by H. D. Martin
Logs drifting by B. J. O. Nordfeldt
Lois by J. Carroll
The Loma, New Mexico by H. C. Smith
London, England
  Boit, E. D. London: a bend of the
    Thames at Chelsea
  Boit, E. D. Piccadilly, London
  Homer, W. The Houses of Parliament
London Hippodrome by E. Shinn
London Music Hall by E. Shinn
London omnibus by J. Marin
London Times by W. M. Harnett
Lone cowboy by W. W. Quirt
Lone fisherman by W. M. Chase
Lone horseman by A. P. Ryder
Lone scout by A. P. Ryder
Lone tenement by G. W. Bellows
Loneliness by H. Weston
Lonely places by F. P. Colburn
Lonely ways by H. Lundeberg
The loner by W. W. Quirt
LONERGAN, John, 1896-
  Gaspé fisherman          ATU
    ATU. Coll of Amer art
  Peggy's cove          ATU
    ATU. Coll of Amer art
Lonesome road by M. Dixon
Lonesome shores by L. Feininger
Lonesome valley by E. Magafan
The long bill by J. H. Beard
Long Branch, New Jersey by W. Homer
Long Island by A. G. Dove
Long Island farmhouses by W. S. Mount
Long Island scene by W. S. Mount
Long Island Sound by L. Bouché
Long Island sunset by G. O'Keeffe
Long Jakes by C. Deas
The long story by W. S. Mount
Longeuil, Normandy by L. Feininger
Longfellow, Henry Wadsworth, 1807-1882
  Healy, G. P. A. Henry W. Longfellow
LONGFELLOW, William Pitt Preble,
    1836-1913
  Guard room in the palace of Fontaine-
    bleau          MB
    MB. Ptgs in water color
  On the Normandy coast      MB
    MB. Ptgs in water color
  Sala del Collegio, Ducal palace, Venice
          MB
    MB. Ptgs in water color
Longfield, Rachel. See Lawrence, Rachel
  (Longfield)
Long's Peak, Colorado by W. Whittredge
Longshoremen's noon by J. G. Brown
Look homeward, America by D. Nichols
Look, it flies by Y. Kuniyoshi
Looking east from Denny hill by R. Earl

Looking for scenery by J. G. Chapman
Looking north to Kingston by T. Chambers
Looking out to Washington square by J.
  Sloan
Looking up the Monongahela river from
  Coal hill by R. Smith
The lookout by W. Homer
The lookout—All's well by W. Homer
The lookout, Vermont by A. M. R. Moses
A loose cinch by C. M. Russell
Loper, Frankie
  Biddle, G. Frankie Loper
LORAN, Erle, 1905-
  Navajo desert camp
    IU. Contemp Amer ptg, 1949
  Rock fluorescence
    IU. Contemp Amer ptg, 1952
  Sea depth
    IU. Contemp Amer ptg & sculp, 1953
  Under sea          CSFM
    Pousette-Dart. Amer ptg
LORD, Don, 1929-
  Girard          OYB
    OYB. Annual 1955
    OYB. Supplement 1959
  Tattle tale grey
    OYB. Annual 1948
  Tree house          OYB
    OYB. Annual 1960
Lord, Miranda E. fl 1815
  Fenton, P. Miranda E. Lord from Connec-
    ticut
Lord heal the child by T. H. Benton
The Lord is my shepherd by T. H. Benton
Lord Ullin's daughter by A. P. Ryder
The Lorelei by A. P. Ryder
Loreli by H. Frankenthaler
Lorenzo and Jessica by W. Allston
Loring by J. A. Brooks
Los Angeles, California
  Dike, P. L. View of Los Angeles
  Kuntz, R. E. Los Angeles Freeway
  Sicard, P. Night over Los Angeles
Lost greenhorn by A. J. Miller
The lost mind by E. Vedder
Lost on the Grand Banks by W. Homer
Lost warrior by F. Remington
Lothrop, John, fl 1770
  Durand, J. John Lothrop
LOTTERMAN, Hal, 1920-
  Black bottle
    PPC. International ex, 1952
  Boy with guitar
    NAD. Annual ex, 1954
The lottery by S. M. Adler
Lotus by C. E. Heil
Lotus pool, El Encanto, Santa Barbara by
  C. C. Cooper
Louis Philippe, king of the French, 1773-1850
  Healy, G. P. A. Louis Philippe, king of
    France
Louisburg square by T. A. Fransioli
Louisburg square, winter by J. Ricci
Louisiana
  *See also* New Orleans
  Benton, T. H. Louisiana rice fields

**Louisiana**—*Continued*
  Colomb, C. White Hall plantation, Louisiana, c 1790
  Meeker, J. R. Land of Evangeline
  Persac, A. Shadows-on-the-Teche
  Persac, A. Sugar mill on Bayou Teche, Oliver plantation
The **Louvre** by S. F. B. Morse
**LOVE, Waldo**
  Jim Baker, dressed-up portrait wearing a costume made by a Sioux squaw                CoDH
    Davidson v 1
**Love** at high noon by S. Gechtoff
**Love** note by H. Pippin
**Love,** oh careless love by J. Levine
The **lovers** by P. Mangravite
The **lovers** by B. Perlin
The **lovers** by A. P. Ryder
The **lovers** by Y. Tanguy
The **lovers'** boat by A. P. Ryder
**Lover's** pike by Y. Kuniyoshi
**Low, Mary Anne (Whittemore)** 1800-1867
  Unidentified artist. Mrs Henry Somes Low
**LOW, Will H.** 1853-1912, and **LA FARGE, John,** 1835-1910
  Decorative panel                        MB
    MB. Ptgs in water color
**Low** tide by W. A. Kienbusch
**Low** tide by H. Maril
**Low** tide by E. F. Spruce
**Low** tide, Beachmont by M. B. Prendergast
**Low** tide monument by J. C. Atherton
A **lowdown** trick by W. R. Leigh
**Lowell, Abbott Lawrence,** 1865-1943
  Sargent, J. S. A. Lawrence Lowell, president of Harvard
**Lowell, Georgina Margaret (Amory)** d 1830
  Goodridge, S. Mrs John Lowell jr
**Lowell, John,** 1799-1836
  Goodridge, S. John Lowell jr
The **Lowell** committee by Ben Shahn
**Lowell** house (Harvard university) by K. Matthew
**Lower** Manhattan by S. Hirsch
**Lower** Manhattan, 1920 by J. Marin
**Lower** Manhattan, 1922 by J. Marin
**Lower** Manhattan from Communipaw by T. Moran
**Lower** Manhattan from the river by J. Marin
**Lower** reservoir, Tihonet by F. W. Benson
**Lowering** from the cross by B. Kamihira
**Lowlands** by C. Bloom
**Lowndes, Mrs James,** fl 1801
  Malbone, E. G. Mrs James Lowndes
**Lowndes, Mary I'On,** fl 1802
  Malbone, E. G. Mary I'On Lowndes
**Lowndes, Sarah (Jones)** b 1757?
  Theus, J. Mrs Rawlins Lowndes
**Lowndes, Thomas,** 1765-1843
  Malbone, E. G. Thomas Lowndes
**LOWRIE, Agnes Potter (van Ryn)** 1892-
  To the dock, Tadoussac
    ICA. Annual ex, 1945/46

**Lowrie, Mrs Selden Gale.** See Lowrie, Agnes Potter (van Ryn)
**LOZOWICK, Louis,** 1892-
  City-shape                              CtY
    CtY. Soc Anonyme
  New York, 1926-27
    MnMW. Precisionist view
  Oklahoma
    Brown. Amer ptg
**Lubec,** Maine by P. M. M. Jones
**Luce, Claire,** 1905-
  Carroll, J. Claire Luce as Camille
**LUCIONI, Luigi,** 1900-
  Alice in grey
    MM. Amer ptg today
  Design for color                        OT
    CoS. New accessions USA, 1946
    OT. Contemp Amer ptgs
  Tracery of leaves
    NAD. Annual ex, 1951
    PPC. International ex, 1950
  Victorian still life                    WMAA
    CSB. Illusion
**Lucky** strike by S. Davis
**LUDINS, Eugene,** 1904-
  Grove
    IU. Contemp Amer ptg & sculp, 1957
  Maze
    PPC. International ex, 1955
  Rare birds
    VR. Amer ptg, 1954
  The valley
    PA. Annual ex, 1948
  Water front
    IU. Contemp Amer ptg, 1949
**LUKS, George Benjamin,** 1867-1933
  Armistice night                         WMAA
    Chew. 250 years of art
    Goodrich. Amer art
    Pierson
  Blue devils marching down Fifth avenue  DP
    Brown. Amer ptg
  The breadline
    U.S. National Capital sesquicentennial com
  The breaker boy
    NSyE. The eight
  Butcher boy
    Brown. Amer ptg
  Cat and kittens
    Chew. 250 years of art
  The clown                               MB
    PA. Annual ex, 1955
  Conner's rock, Cape Eliza, Maine
    NSP. Sportscapes
  Daughter of the mines                   NUM
    NUM. Root bequest
  Flyweight champ of Jumel place          OYB
    OYB. Supplement
  The gamin                               ATeS
    ATeS. Collection
  The guitar
    NYG. Fine art
  Hester street                           NBM
    Baur. Revolution
    McCurdy
  Holiday on the Hudson                   OCl
    OCl. Handbook
  Little madonna                          MAP
    Baur. Revolution
  Man with violin                         NJMo
    NJMo. Forty years

Mrs Gamley WMAA
  Goodrich. Amer art
  Mendelowitz
  PA. Annual ex, 1955
  Roos
  Walker. Ptgs from America
The old duchess MM
  MM. 100 Amer ptrs
  Pierson
Otis Skinner as Col Bridau DP
  Bazin
  Brown. Amer ptg
  DP. Catalogue
  PA. Anual ex, 1955
Roundhouses at High Bridge NUM
  NUM. Art across America
The spielers MAP
  Brown. Amer ptg
  Canaday
  Chew. 250 years of art
  Larkin
  Larkin rev ed
  NBuA. Fifty ptgs
  Pierson
  Roos
  Time. 300 years (col)
  Wight. Milestones
Sulking boy DP
  DP. Catalogue
Telling fortunes DP
  DP. Catalogue
West side docks
  Brown. Amer ptg
Widow Magee
  Glackens
Woman with black cat DC
  DC. 25 biennial ex, 1957
Wrestlers MB
  Brown. Amer ptg
  PA. Annual ex, 1955
  Pierson

**Portrait of the artist**
Glackens, W. J. George B. Luks, c 1899
**Lullaby** by F. Martin
**Lumber** for the Argo by R. H. Bumpas
**Luminosity** by L. Feininger
**Luminous** loot by L. Mullican
**LUNAK, Alan,** 1915-
  Green premonitions
  ICA. Annual ex, 1959-60
**Lunar** binge by A. Salemme
**Lunar** magic by F. E. Warren
**Lunar** voyage by A. Salemme
**Lunar** web by L. Feininger
**Lunch** hour by I. Bishop
**Luncheon** scene by R. Petersen
**LUND, David,** 1925-
  Cycladic light
  WMAA. Young America 1960
**LUNDEBERG, Helen,** 1908-
  Lonely ways
  IU. Contemp Amer ptg & sculp, 1959
  Micro-macrocosmic landscape
  ICA. Annual ex, 1947/48
The mirror CLA
  IU. Contemp Amer ptg, 1952
  Pousette-Dart. Amer ptg
Peaches
  IU. Contemp Amer ptg & sculp, 1957

Season of mists
  IU. Contemp Amer ptg, 1951
Spring
  IU. Contemp Amer ptg, 1950
Winter sun
  IU. Contemp Amer ptg & sculp, 1955
**Lüneburg** II by L. Feininger
**Lupton, Mrs Francis P.** fl 1803
  Malbone, E. G. Mrs Francis P. Lupton
**Lure** of the waters by P. Evergood
**Lute,** flute and dance by W. Houmère
**Lutes.** See Musicians and musical instruments—Lutes
**LUTZ, Dan,** 1906-
  April day ATeS
  ATeS. Collection
  I got a harp
  Gruskin
  Kalamazoo cove
  IU. Contemp Amer ptg, 1949
  Mountain church, San Cristobal
  IU. Contemp Amer ptg & sculp, 1957
  Sylvan episode
  IU. Contemp Amer ptg, 1950
**Luxembourg** gardens by W. J. Glackens
**Luxembourg** gardens at twilight by J. S. Sargent
**Lydia** and Tabitha by Unidentified artist
**Lyell, Fenwick,** fl 1807
  Jarvis, J. W. Fenwick Lyell
**Lyman, Harriet,** 1784-1875
  Malbone, E. G. Harriet Lyman
**Lynch, Mrs Scolley.** See Bibb, Mary Lucy
  Pocahontas
The **lynching** by B. Kopman
**Lyon, Nathaniel,** 1818-1861
  Bingham, G. C. Gen Nathaniel Lyon and Gen Frank P. Blair starting from the Arsenal gate in St Louis to capture Camp Jackson
**Lyon, Patrick,** 1779?-1829
  Neagle, J. Pat Lyon at his forge
**Lyons, Richard Bickerton Pemell Lyons, 1st earl,** 1817-1887
  Healy, G. P. A. Lord Richard Bickerton Pemell Lyons
**Lyric** by M. Tobey
**Lyric** piece by R. Keyser
**Lyric** yellow by E. E. Boccia
**LYTLE, Richard,** 1935-
  Icarus descended MMA
  MMA. Sixteen
  The possessed
  MMA. Sixteen
  Prometheus
  MMA. Sixteen
  Verge
  MMA. Sixteen
**Lytton, Edward Robert Bulwer-Lytton, 1st earl of,** 1831-1891
  Healy, G. P. A. Lord Lytton

# M

**M**—1951 by J. D. Brooks
**M.** R. D. by H. Sterne
**Ma** vie blanche et noire by Y. Tanguy

**Macbeth** and the witches by A. P. Ryder
**Macbraire, Robert**
  Unidentified artist. Robert Macbraire
**Macbraire, Mrs Robert**
  Unidentified artist. Mrs Robert Macbraire
**McCALL, Charles Ford**
  Another Sunday
    OYB. Annual 1950
  God's day
    PPC. Ptg in the U.S. 1949
**McCall, Mary.** See Plumsted, Mary (McCall)
**McCARTER, Henry Bainbridge,** 1864-1942
  Coal mine             PA
    PA. Annual ex, 1955
  Early Italy
    PA. Annual ex, 1955
  Still life
    PA. Annual ex, 1955
  Sunset in the fields
    PA. Annual ex, 1955
**McCHESNEY, Robert,** 1913-
  Abstraction 2A
    ICA. Annual ex, 1947/48
**McCloskey, John, cardinal,** 1810-1885
  Healy, G. P. A. John McCloskey
**McClurg, Elizabeth S.** See Wickham, Elizabeth S. (McClurg)
**McCLUSKY, John D.** 1914-
  Clock
    IU. Contemp Amer ptg & sculp, 1959
  Fish
    IU. Contemp Amer ptg & sculp, 1961
**McCONNELL, G.** fl 1871
  Factory             NCHA
    Jones. New-found folk art
The **McConney** flats by P. Evergood
**McCord, David,** 1797-1855
  Jarvis, J. W. David McCord
**McCormick, Leander James,** 1819-1900
  Healy, G. P. A. Leander James McCormick
**McCormick family**
  Johnston, J. The James McCormick family of Baltimore, c1804
**McCOSH, David J.** 1903-
  Apple trees in December
    OrPA. Ptgs & sculptures
**McCOY, John W.** 1910-
  Attic dormer
    NAD. Annual ex, 1954
  The junction
    NAD. Annual ex, 1946, 2d half
**McCrea, Jane,** fl 1846
  Unidentified artist. Murder of Jane McCrea
**McCULLOUGH, Joseph W.** 1922-
  Infernal machine at dawn
    IU. Contemp Amer ptg & sculp, 1957
**McCurdy, Letitia Grace,** 1797-1875
  Johnston, J. Letitia McCurdy
**McDonald, James,** fl 1855
  Blythe, D. G. Col James McDonald
**MacDONALD-WRIGHT, Stanton,** 1890-
  Airplane synchromy in yellow and orange
              PPhM
    Baur. New art
  Airplane synchromy in yellow-orange
              MM
    Baur. Revolution

Conception synchromy      WMAA
  Baur. New art
  Brown. Amer ptg
  Hunter. Mod Amer ptg
  McCurdy
  MMA. Abstract
  Pierson
Far country—Synchromy      MiD
  Larkin
  Larkin rev ed
Organization 5
  Cheney. Primer 1958 ed
Oriental: synchromy in blue-green
              WMAA
  Baur. New art (col)
  Goodrich. Amer art (col)
  Pierson
Sacrifice of the hair
  IU. Contemp Amer ptg, 1950
Synchromy (Shawan coll)
  Brown. Amer ptg
Synchromy, 1917-      MMA
  MMA. Abstract
  Read. Concise history
Synchromy in green and orange, 1916
  MnMW. Classic tradition
Synchromy no 3      PPhM
  WMAA. Pioneers
Two women      CP
  CoS. New accessions USA 1946
**McDonell** farm by A. M. R. Moses
**Macdonough, Thomas,** 1783-1825
  Jarvis, J. W. Capt Thomas Macdonough
  Stuart, G. Commodore Thomas Macdonough
**Macdougal** alley by C. Sheeler
**McDowell, William H.**
  Eakins, T. William McDowell
**McEvers, Catharine A.** See Birckhead, Catharine A. (McEvers)
**McFEE, Henry Lee,** 1886-1953
  Aperitif      InIJ
    InIJ. 105 ptgs
  Banana plant and squash
    PPC. International ex, 1950
  Broken pot with blue vase
    Pearson. Mod renaissance
  Crow with peaches      WMAA
    Pierson
  Golden leaves
    CSFP. Annual ex, 1947/48
  Landscape with houses
    Pearson. Mod renaissance
  Painting no 3—still life
    MM. Amer ptg today
  The skull      MM
    MM. 100 Amer ptrs
  Still life
    Brown. Amer ptg
  Still life      OCo
    Baur. Revolution
    WMAA. Pioneers
  Still life: apples
    NYG. Fine art
  Still life: oranges      WMAA
    Gruskin
    Larkin
    Larkin rev ed
  Still life with a green jar      FIPN
    Pearson. Mod renaissance
  Still life with decanter
    Baur. Revolution

Still life with ivy
    NAD. Annual ex, 1951
Still life with white cloth
    IU. Contemp Amer ptg, 1948
Things on a table
    Pousette-Dart. Amer ptg
Wild flowers and grasses          GAtM
    GAtM. Holbrook collection
Yellow pitcher
    CSFP. Annual ex, 1948/49
McGARRELL, James, 1930-
Anatomy          OrPA
    CoS. New accessions USA, 1960
    OrPA. Ptgs & sculptures
Bathers
    Selz. New images (col)
Equinox
    Selz. New images
J
    IU. Contemp Amer ptg & sculp, 1961
Reflection, self-portrait
    WMAA. Contemp Amer ptg, 1959-60
Rest in air
    IU. Contemp Amer ptg & sculp, 1959
    Selz. New images

Machias, Maine by J. Marin
Machine by G. W. McLaughlin
Machine by C. A. Morris
Machine by M. L. Schamberg
Machine oil by M. L. Schamberg
Machine shop by W. T. Aldrich
McIlhenny, Henry P.
    Watkins, F. C. Henry P. McIlhenny
McILVAINE, William, fl 1857
Delaware Water Gap
    McClintock
McILWORTH, Thomas, fl 1758-1769
Gerardus Stuyvesant          NNHS
    Vail. Stuyvesant ports
Nicholas William Stuyvesant          NNHS
    Vail. Stuyvesant ports
McIntire, Samuel, 1757-1811
    Blyth, B. (attributed works) Samuel Mc-
        Intire
MacIVER, Loren, 1909-
Ashcan
    MMA. Fourteen
    MnU. 40 Amer ptrs
Les beaux          ICA
    Baur. Nature
    Baur. New art
The city
    Baur. MacIver and Pereira
    MMA. Fourteen
Dublin and environs
    Baur. MacIver and Pereira
    IU. Contemp Amer ptg, 1951
Early
    Baur. MacIver and Pereira
Elm fruit
    WMAA. Annual ex, 1958
Emmett Kelly
    Baur. MacIver and Pereira
    Baur. New art
    MMA. Contemp ptrs
    Pierson
    WMAA. Neuberger collection
The fratellini          MWiC
    Baur. MacIver and Pereira
    NUM. Art across America

Hearth
    ICA. Annual ex, 1959-60
Hopscotch          MMA
    Barr. What is mod ptg
    Baur. MacIver and Pereira
    Baur. New art
    Baur. Revolution
    Mendelowitz
    MMA. Fourteen
    MMA. Masters
    Pierson
Hyacinth
    MnU. 40 Amer ptrs
Irish landscape
    IU. Contemp Amer ptg & sculp, 1957
Jimmy Savo
    Genauer
    MMA. Fourteen
Jimmy Savo's shoes
    Baur. MacIver and Pereira
Moonlight
    Baur. MacIver and Pereira
Mountain laurel
    MMA. Fourteen
Naples aquarium
    Baur. MacIver and Pereira
New York, 1952
    Baur. MacIver and Pereira
Night shadows          NBuA
    NBuA. Acquisitions 1959-1961
Oil splatters and leaves
    Baur. MacIver and Pereira
    Baur. New art (col)
Paris          MM
    MM. 100 Amer ptrs
Paris night meanders
    ICA. Annual ex, 1959/60
The poet
    Baur. MacIver and Pereira
Puddle
    Baur. MacIver and Pereira
Red votive lights          MMA
    Baur. MacIver and Pereira
    McCurdy
    MMA. Contemp ptrs
    MMA. Fourteen
    Read. Concise history
Rue Daguerre          NUM
    CoS. New accessions USA, 1956
Shack          MMA
    Myers
Sidewalk          MAP
    Rathbun
    Wight. Milestones
Skylight          MMA
    MMA. Soby collection
Snowscape
    Cheney. Story 1958 ed
Splatters and leaves
    Pousette-Dart. Amer ptg
The street          DC
    DC. 25 biennial ex, 1957
    Time. 300 years (col)
The street is young with spring
    PPC. International ex, 1952
Strunsky house
    Baur. MacIver and Pereira
Subway lights
    IU. Contemp Amer ptg & sculp, 1961
Taxi          CtHW
    Baur. MacIver and Pereira
    CtHW. Handbook

McLAUGHLIN, James
  Anemones                                      DP
    DP. Catalogue
McLAUGHLIN, John, 1898-
  Untitled, 1955
    VR. Amer ptg, 1958
Macmillan, Mrs Floyd. See Davis, Gladys
  (Rockmore)
MacMONNIES, Frederick William, 1863-
  1937
  Mrs Anne Archbold
    DC. Privately owned
McNEIL, George Joseph, 1909-
  Abstraction, 1949
    MMA. Abstract
  Abstraction, 1951
    PPC. International ex, 1952
  Invitation
    MnMW. 60 Amer ptrs
  Painting
    Pousette-Dart. Amer ptg
MacNUTT, Glenn Gordon, 1906-
  Scallop fleet
    NAD. Annual ex, 1958
Macomb, Mary Cornell (Pell). See Pell,
  Mary Cornell
Macomb, Robert, 1783-1832
  Malbone, E. G. Robert Macomb
Macomb, Mrs Robert. See Pell, Mary Cor-
  nell
Macphaedris, Mary. See Warner, Mary
  (Macphaedris)
McPherson, James, fl 1801
  Malbone, E. G. James McPherson
McPherson, John, fl 1801
  Malbone, E. G. Gen John McPherson
McSorley's back room by J. Sloan
McSorley's bar by J. Sloan
McSorley's cats by J. Sloan
McVey's barn by A. N. Wyeth
Mad bull by E. J. Stevens
Madam X by A. Salemme
Madame X (Madame Gautreau) by J. S.
  Sargent
Maddox, Clifford Tallulah
  Brook, A. Clifford Tallulah Maddox
Madeira, Betty Campbell
  Borie, A. Mrs Betty Campbell Madeira
Madge in the morning by L. M. Eilshemius
Madison, Dorothea (Payne) Todd, 1768-1849
  Ames, E. Dolly Madison
Madison, James, president U.S. 1751-1836
  Peale, C. W. James Madison
Madison, Mrs James. See Madison, Doro-
  thea (Payne) Todd
Madison square, New York by M. B. Pren-
  dergast
Madonna by G. Melchers
Madonna by W. W. Quirt
Madonna and child by R. L. Newman
Madonna and child with saints by D. Aron-
  son
Madonna enthroned by T. Hennessy
Madonna of the mines by P. Evergood
Madonnas of the rain by L. Dodd
Madrigal by J. Madson
La Madrilenita by R. Henri

MADSON, Jack, 1928-
  Madrigal
    WMAA. Young America 1957
  Pursuit no 3
    WMAA. Young America 1957
Maelstrom by M. Jamieson
Maenades, Study for by J. Cox
MAGADA, Stephen, 1925-
  Celebration                                   OYB
    OYB. Annual 1954
    OYB. Supplement
MAGAFAN, Ethel, 1916-
  Dark river
    IU. Contemp Amer ptg, 1952
  Daybreak
    NAD. Annual ex, 1953
  Forest
    NAD. Annual ex, 1956
  The great barrier
    NAD. Annual ax, 1959
  Lonesome valley
    MM. Amer ptg today
  Near the mountain
    IU. Contemp Amer ptg & sculp, 1961
  Summer
    NAD. Annual ex, 1960
The Magdalene by R. Lebrun
Magenta and blue by H. Hofmann
Magic circle, Venice by E. Berman
Magic glass by E. R. Elmer
Magic man by J. Lawrence
Magic mirror by J. Pollock
Magic mountains by F. Gerassi
Magical city by H. N. Cook
Magical forms by L. Feitelson
The magician by D. Aronson
The magician by H. Hofmann
The magician by J. Levine
The magician by R. Rauschenberg
The magicians by R. Breinin
The magistrate by B. Greene
Magnetic mountain by K. L. Seligmann
The magnificence by P. Burlin
The magnificent by R. Pousette-Dart
Magnolia by H. Dinnerstein
Magnolia grandiflora by M. J. Heade
Magnolia grandiflora by J. LaFarge
Magnolias by M. J. Heade
Maguey by D. Judd
Mahantango valley farm by Unidentified
  artist
Mahatmas of the lunar shore by A. Salemme
Mahon, Edith
  Eakins, T. Mrs Edith Mahon
Mahone bay by W. J. Glackens
Mahoning by F. J. Kline
Mah-to-he-ha, the old bear by G. Catlin
Mahu by L. Beck
Maid arranging hair of corpulent woman
  by G. Grosz
The maid of the grove by Unidentified artist
Maid of the mist by T. Cole
Mail coach by C. S. Price
Main street, Gloucester by J. Sloan

**Maine**
Albright, M. M. Boothbay harbor, Maine
Blume, P. Maine coast
Hartley, M. Hurricane island, Vinal Haven, Maine
Hartley, M. Maine landscape, autumn
Hartley, M. Mount Katahdin, Maine
Heliker, J. E. Maine coast
Heliker, J. E. Maine rocks
Homer, W. Maine coast
Hudson, J. B. View in Maine
Inness, G. Moonlight on Passamaquoddy bay
Kienbusch, W. A. Across Penobscot bay
Lane, F. H. Maine inlet
Marin, J. See titles under name of artist
Rosenberg, S. Maine
Spencer, N. The cove, Ogunquit
Sterne, M. Maine coast
Zorach, W. Popham beach no 1, Maine

**Maine** family by Y. Kuniyoshi
**Maine** night by C. L. Nelson
**Maine** snowstorm by M. Hartley
**Maine** study by G. Cox
**Maine** swimming hole by W. Peirce
**Maitland, Elizabeth Sproat (Lenox) 1785-1864**
Mooney, E. L. Mrs Robert Maitland
Thibault, A. Mrs Robert Maitland
**Maitland, Robert, 1768-1846**
Mooney, E. L. Robert Maitland
**Maitland** bridge no 2 by R. Crawford
**Majestic** tenement by A. Osver
**MAJOR, Henry, 1889-1948**
American frolic
   NYG. Fine art
Gay philosopher—why worry
   NYG. Fine art
Philosopher's heir
   NYG. Fine art
Philosopher's offspring
   NYG. Fine art
Philosopher's wife
   NYG. Fine art
**Major** Dean in jail by G. C. Bingham
**Maker** of dreams by I. L. Albright
**Maker** of images by I. L. Albright
**Mal** du pays by G. A. Walker
**Malamocco** by Leonid
**MALBONE, Edward Greene, 1777-1807**
Aaron C. Dennis             MB
Tolman
Alexander Baron jr
Tolman
Alexander von Pfister
Tolman
Alice Wyer
Tolman
Alicia Hopton Russell
Tolman
Ann Channing              MoSL
Tolman
Ann Elizabeth Ryan
Tolman
Anne-Louis de Tousard
Tolman
Annette (probably Mrs Alexander Bleecker)          MB
Tolman

Archibald Taylor           CtY
Tolman
Asher Marx               PA
Tolman
Augusta G. Temple
Tolman
Benjamin West
Tolman
Benjamin Winslow
Tolman
Bounetheau's aunt (Young lady in pink)         DNC
Tolman
Carl F. Herreshoff
Tolman
Catherine Fry            RNH
Tolman
Charles B. Cochran
Tolman
Charles C. Pinckney
Tolman
Charles Fenton Mercer
Tolman
Charles Harris
Tolman
Charles Sinkler (?)
Tolman
Cornelius Coolidge
Tolman
Daniel E. Huger
**Tolman**
David Moses
Tolman
Dr Brailsford
Tolman
Eben Farley           MWM
Tolman
Edward Butler
Tolman
Edward Laight
Tolman
Edward Martin
Tolman
Edward Perry
Tolman
Elisha Poinsett
Tolman
   WiMiA. Amer ptg 1760-1960
Eliza Fenno
Tolman
Eliza Izard, 1801        SCCG
Tolman
Eliza Izard, 1802 (Pinckney coll)
Tolman
Eliza Livingston
Tolman
Eliza Mason
Tolman
Eye of Maria Miles Heyward
Tolman
G. Patten
Tolman
George Bethune
Tolman
George Gibbs III, c 1796
Tolman
George Gibbs III, c 1804
Tolman
George Izard             MM
Tolman
Hannah Miles Heyward
Tolman

**MALBONE, E. G.**—*Continued*
Mrs John L. Sullivan
  Tolman
Mrs John Nightingale
  Tolman
Mrs Joseph Curwen
  Tolman
Mrs Joseph Manigault
  Tolman
Mrs Moses Poor
  Tolman
Mrs Richard C. Derby          MM
  Tolman
Mrs Richard Sullivan          CtY
  CtY. Portrait index
  Tolman
Mrs Robert H. Gardiner
  Tolman
Mrs Robert Means
  Tolman
Mrs Thomas Amory
  Tolman
Mrs Thomas Heyward jr
  Tolman
Mrs William Allen Deas
  Tolman
Mrs William Cattel
  Tolman
Mrs William Montgomery
  Tolman
Mrs Zachariah Allen          RPS
  Tolman
Nathaniel Pearce
  Tolman
Nicholas (?) Brown          NNHS
  Tolman
Nicholas Fish
  Tolman
Nicholas Power          RPAt
  Tolman
Perkins children          MBH
  Tolman
Peter Bours
  Tolman
Rachel Gratz (Hunter coll)
  Tolman
Ralph Izard II
  Tolman
Ray Greene
  Tolman
Rebecca Gratz (?) (Bortman coll)
  Tolman
Rebecca Gratz (Nathan coll)
  Tolman
Rebecca Power
  Tolman
Richard D. Harris
  Tolman
Richard Hyde
  Tolman
Robert H. Gardiner
  Tolman
Robert Mackay
  Tolman
Robert Macomb
  CtY. Yale alumni
  Time. 300 years (col)
  Tolman (col)
Samuel Wragg          MAC
  Tolman
Sarah Alicia Shubrick
  Tolman

Sarah Brown
  Tolman
Sarah Reeve Ladson          SCCG
  Tolman
Self-portrait          DC
  DC. Amer ptrs of the South (col)
  Tolman (col)
Self-portrait c 1800          RPAt
  Tolman
Shakespeare on the lap of the muse of
    inspiration
  Tolman
Solomon Moses
  Tolman
Susan Poinsett (formerly called Anna
    Frances Poinsett)
  Tolman
  WiMiA. Amer ptg 1760-1960
Thomas Barksdale
  Tolman
Thomas Cadwalader
  Tolman
Thomas L. Winthrop
  Tolman
Thomas Lowndes
  Tolman
Thomas Means
  Tolman
Thomas Pascal Jones
  Tolman
Thomas Pinckney
  Tolman
Thomas Pinckney jr          SCCG
  Tolman
Thomas Radcliffe          CtY
  Tolman
Thomas Russell c 1796          MBH
  Tolman
Thomas Russell (Fearing coll)
  MB. New England miniatures (col)
Unknown gentleman          DNC
  Tolman
Unknown gentleman          RPS
  Tolman
Unknown young lady          SCCG
  **Tolman**
Walter Bowne
  Tolman
Washington Allston          MB
  MB. New England miniatures
  Pierson
  Time. 300 years (col)
  Tolman
William Bruce
  Tolman
Young lady in pink. See Bounetheau's
    aunt
**Malbone, Francis,** d 1809
  Stuart, G. Francis and Saunders Malbone
**Malbone, Saunders,** d 1784
  Stuart, G. Francis and Saunders Malbone
**Male** and female by J. Pollock
**Male** head by J. Glasco
Le **malheur** adoucit les pierres by Y. Tanguy
**MALICOAT, Philip Cecil,** 1908-
  November gale
    NAD. Annual ex, 1954
The **Mall,** Central park by M. B. Prender-
    gast
**Mallarme's** swan by R. B. Motherwell
**Mallorca** III by F. D. Duncan
**Mama,** Papa is wounded by Y. Tanguy

**Mamout, Yarrow**
Peale, C. W. Yarrow Mamout
**Man Ray.** See Ray, Man
A **man** by W. M. Chase
A **man** by S. Davis
**Man** by W. De Kooning
A **man** by J. Peale
A **man** by W. M. Prior (attributed works)
A **man**, Portrait of by Y. Blumberg
A **man**, Portrait of by J. Van der Pool (attributed works)
A **man** and a lady by J. H. Davis
**Man** and arrow by A. Gottlieb
**Man** and fish by M. Beckmann
**Man** and machine by I. R. Pereira
**Man** and the northern lights by C. Gray
**Man** and woman by M. Beckmann
**Man** and woman in a large room by R. Diebenkorn
**Man** and woman seated by R. Diebenkorn
**Man** building bridge by C. Ruhtenburg
**Man** from Maine by A. N. Wyeth
**Man** in a blue coat by Unidentified artist
**Man** in a yellow waistcoat by J. Eichholtz
**Man** in black coat by N. Rogers
**Man** in chains by W. Allston
**Man** in gray coat by Raphaelle Peale
**Man** in orange by B. P. Arnest
**Man** in red by Unidentified artist
**Man** looking at woman by A. Gottlieb
**Man-made** man, bewildered by nature by C. A. Morris
**Man** meets woman, tips hat by W. W. Quirt
A **man** of opinion by G. Grosz
**Man** of sorrows by P. Blume
**Man** of sorrows by W. W. Quirt
**Man** reading by J. S. Sargent
**Man** walking by N. J. Oliveira
**Man** with a harelip by A. Dickinson
**Man** with a mallet by I. L. Albright
**Man** with a watch fob by S. L. Waldo
**Man** with a whip by J. T. Evans (attributed works)
**Man** with blue eyes by Unidentified artist
**Man** with red necktie by T. Eakins
**Man** with ship model by W. Kuhn
**Man** with the glove by W. M. Chase
**Man** with violin by G. B. Luks
**Man** with wild flowers by B. Shahn
**Manassas (ram)**
Unidentified artist. Attack of the rebel ram Manassas on the U.S.S. Pensacola, 1862
**Manayunk** winter by A. P. Martino
**MANCHESTER, M. M.** fl 1834
Conversation piece: a Yates family portrait    NR
Jones. Rediscovered ptrs
**Manchester** by C. Sheeler
**Manchester** valley by J. Pickett
**Mandan** medicine man by G. Catlin
**Mandan** O-kee-pa, the bull dance by G. Catlin
**Mandan** torture ceremony by G. Catlin

A **Mandan** village by K. Bodmer
A **Mandan** village by G. Catlin
The **mandarin** by C. L. Cicero
**Mandarin** duck by W. Austin
**MANDEL, Howard,** 1917-
Ladies in waiting
WMAA. Contemp Amer ptg, 1950
Midnight
Pearson. Mod renaissance
Saints deposed
Pearson. Mod renaissance
Walled village
NAD. Annual ex, 1956
**Maneuver** for position by B. W. Tomlin
**MANGRAVITE, Peppino,** 1896-
All things are changing, nothing dies
WMAA. Annual ex, 1953
Angel battling demons
MM. Amer ptg today
City people in the country    WMAA
Pierson
Ecstasy
Pearson. Mod renaissance
Incubus
IU. Contemp Amer ptg, 1952
The lovers
IU. Contemp Amer ptg, 1948
Mountain bouquet
Pearson. Mod renaissance
Of sin and error
Pearson. Mod renaissance
Passions and feverishness
Pearson. Mod renaissance
Recollections
Gruskin
Succubus
Pearson. Mod renaissance
Young couple drinking    NUM
NUM. Root bequest
Young lovers
IU. Contemp Amer ptg, 1950
**Manhattan** by S. Hirsch
**Manhattan** architecture by L. Feininger
**Manhattan** bridge and Lily apartments by E. Hopper
**Manhattan** bridge loop by E. Hopper
**Manhattan** canyon by L. Feininger
**Manhattan**, dawn by L. Feininger
**Manhattan**, dusk by L. Feininger
**Manhattan** harbour by G. Grosz
**Manhattan**, moonwake by L. Feininger
**Manhattan**, night 1941 by L. Feininger
**Manhattan**, St Paul's by J. Marin
**Manhattan** tops by H. Rose
**Manigault, Anne (Ashby)** d 1782
Theus, J. Mrs Gabriel Manigault
**Manigault, Charlotte (Drayton)** 1781-1855
Malbone, E. G. Mrs Joseph Manigault
**Manigault, Elizabeth (Wragg)** b 1736
Theus, J. Mrs Peter Manigault
**Manigault, Gabriel,** 1704-1781
Theus, J. Gabriel Manigault
**Manigault, Mrs Gabriel,** d 1782. See Manigault, Anne (Ashby)
**Manigault, Mrs Gabriel,** 1762-1824. See Manigault, Margaret (Izard)
**Manigault, Joseph,** 1763-1843
Malbone, E. G. Joseph Manigault
**Manigault, Mrs Joseph.** See Manigault, Charlotte (Drayton)

Manigault, Margaret (Izard) 1768-1824
 Malbone, E. G. Mrs Gabriel Manigault
MANIGAULT, Middleton, 1887-1922
 Procession    OCo
 Pierson
 Source
 Baur. Revolution
 Wooden Indian
 WMAA. Pioneers
Manigault, Mrs Peter. See Manigault, Elizabeth (Wragg)
Manila no 4 by F. Vidar
Mann, Bethia (Torrey) 1731-1798
 Copley, J. S. Mrs Joseph Mann
Mann, John P. fl 1850
 Toole, J. John Mann
Mann, Joseph, 1717?-1807
 Copley, J. S. Joseph Mann
Mann, Mrs Joseph. See Mann, Bethia (Torrey)
MANNING, Wray, 1898-
 Afternoon mail    OYB
 OYB. Annual 1950
 OYB. Catalogue 1951
Man's boudoir no 1 (realism) by H. Harari
Man's boudoir no 2 (abstraction) by H. Harari
Man's child by M. Peterson
Mansion doorway by P. F. Samuelson
MANSO, Leo, 1914-
 Aspects of the harbor
 IU. Contemp Amer ptg, 1951
 IU. 20th century
 Landscape for contemplation
 IU. Contemp Amer ptg & sculp, 1955
 Morning
 IU. Contemp Amer ptg & sculp, 1957
Mantel arrangement by H. Pittman
Manuscript by J. Koch
MANVILLE, Elsie, 1922-
 Yellow hat
 PA. Annual ex, 1953
Many brave hearts are asleep in the deep by C. H. Demuth
Maple sugar campfire, Fryeburg, Maine by E. Johnson
Maple sugaring in Vermont by P. S. Sample
Marblehead harbor by J. O. J. Frost
Marca-Relli, Conrad. See Marca-Relli, Corrado di
MARCA-RELLI, Corrado di, 1913-
 The arrival
 PPC. International ex, 1958
 The blackboard
 PPC. International ex, 1961/62
 Bull fight
 OCl. Some contemporary works
 Cargo
 WMAA. Contemp Amer ptg, 1959/60
 The city
 Cheney. Story 1958 ed
 Collage, 1954    ICA
 OCl. Some contemporary works
 Collage, 1955
 OCl. Some contemporary works
 Collage, 1957
 OCl. Some contemporary works
 Figure
 PA. Annual ex, 1958

The joust    MnMW
 MnMW. 60 Amer ptrs
New York City, 1953
 ICA. Amer artists paint the city
Ochre building
 IU. Contemp Amer ptg & sculp, 1955
Odalisque    NBuA
 NBuA. Acquisitions 1957-58
Sleeping figure    MMA
 Pierson
Strategist
 Brussels. Exposition
The tenant
 PPC. International ex, 1955
23 September 1959
 IU. Contemp Amer ptg & sculp, 1961
27 December 1959
 ICA. Annual ex, 1961
Warrior    NNSG
 NNSG. Handbook
March by C. E. Burchfield
March day, Washington square by W. J. Glackens
March in brown by M. Avery
March of the crusaders by G. Inness
March sunlight by C. E. Burchfield
March wind by C. E. Burchfield
March wind by C. F. Ryder
March woodlands by J. H. Twachtman
Marching Highlanders by L. Gatch
MARCUS, Marcia, 1928-
 Seated self-portrait
 WMAA. Young America 1960
 Still life with dead leaves
 WMAA. Young America 1960
MARE, John, 1739-1795?
 Henry Lloyd I (copy after Wollaston)
 DC. Privately owned
 John Keteltas
 Pierson
Mare, Tiburce de, 1840-1900
 Healy, G. P. A. Tiburce de Mare
Mare and foal by C. S. Price
Mare with colt by C. S. Price
Margaret by T. Eakins
Margaret Boni playing the recorder by J. E. Levi
MARGO, Boris, 1902-
 From a cathedral
 Pousette-Dart. Amer ptg
 From elements of evening    NBuA
 NBuA. Acquisitions 1957-58
 From February
 Baur. Nature
 From shipwrecks
 IU. Contemp Amer ptg, 1952
 Matrix of an unfathomable
 Rathbun
 Number 5
 IU. Contemp Amer ptg, 1950
 Number 7, 1945
 Baur. Revolution
 Pulsation of light
 IU. Contemp Amer ptg & sculp, 1961
 Reflections no 6
 IU. Contemp Amer ptg, 1951
Marguerite by W. M. Hunt
MARGULES, De Hirsh, 1899-
 Lower Fifth avenue    ATU
 ATU. Coll of Amer art

Painter in the landscape
  Cheney. Expressionism 1948 ed
Waterbury bridge: number one    MB
  MB. Ptgs in water color
**Margulis, Max**
  De Kooning, W. Max Margulis
**Maria** by R. B. Motherwell
**Maria** with dog under a tree by Unidentified
  artist
**Marianna** by E. E. Speicher
**Marie** St Esprit by M. Hartley
**Marietta** earth works by C. Sullivan
**MARIL, Herman,** 1908-
  Baltimore waterfront    DP
    DP. Catalogue
  Cape still life    MdBM
    CoS. New accessions USA, 1958
  Low tide    DC
    CoS. New accessions USA, 1960
  Rocks and water
    Cheney. Story 1958 ed
  Skaters
    OYB. Annual 1952
  3 A.M.
    NAD. Annual ex, 1960
**Marilyn** at the table by J. Berger
**MARIN, John,** 1870-1953
  Adironacks along Ausable river
    UNESCO. 1860-1955
    UNESCO. 1860-1959
  Alpine district, New Jersey
    MiD. Coll in progress
  American telephone building, New York
    city
    ICA. Amer artists paint the city
  Autumn on road to Deblois    TxH
    CoS. New accessions USA, 1954
  Autumn piece, Maine
    PA. Annual ex, 1955
  Back of Bear mountain    DP
    DP. Catalogue
    John Marin
  Bathers on rocks
    Helm. John Marin
  The black sun. See Movement no 2—re-
    lated to downtown New York
  Blue mountain near Taos
    Helm. John Marin
  Blue sea, Crotch island    MAP
    Rathbun (col)
  Boat fantasy, Deer isle
    Helm. John Marin
    John Marin
  Boat off Deer isle    PPhM
    Read. Concise history (col)
  Boat, sky, and sea, Small point, Maine
    Cheney. Story 1958 ed
  Boat with blue
    Helm. John Marin
  Boats, sea and rocks
    Helm. John Marin (col)
  Breakers, Maine coast    OCo
    Seiberling
  Broadway, night
    Helm. John Marin
  Bryant square    DP
    DP. Catalogue
  Cape Split, Maine    ICA
    NYG. Fine art
    UNESCO. 1860-1949
    UNESCO. 1860-1955
    UNESCO. 1860-1959

Cerulean sea and isle
  Lewisohn
Cherry orchard
  CtY. Yale alumni
Circus elephants    ICA
  John Marin
  UNESCO. 1860-1949
  UNESCO. 1860-1955
  UNESCO. 1860-1959
Circus forms
  Helm. John Marin (col)
Circus horses
  Helm. John Marin
City construction    NBuA
  Moderns and their world
City movement, downtown Manhattan
  no 2, 1936
  WiMiA. Amer ptg 1760-1960
Composed from my window    InIJ
  InIJ. 105 ptgs
Composition, Cape Split, Maine, no 2, 1933
  Baur. New art
  Helm. John Marin
  John Marin (col)
  WiMiA. Amer ptg 1760-1960
Corn dance, New Mexico    MM
  John Marin (col)
The cove    OCo
  Roos
Dance of the San Domingo Indians
  Helm. John Marin
Deep-sea trawlers, Maine
  Helm. John Marin
Deer island, Maine: Stonington waterfront
                   CtY
  CtY. Soc Anonyme
  Mendelowitz
Deer isle, boats, and pertaining thereto
  Wight. Milestones
Deer isle islets, Maine
  NYG. Fine art
  UNESCO. 1860-1949
  UNESCO. 1860-1955
  UNESCO. 1860-1959
Deer isle, Maine    MoSL
  MoSL. Handbook 1953
Deer isle, Maine series no 30—Boat fan-
  tasy
  MnU. 40 Amer ptrs
Deer isle, Stonington, Maine
  Helm. John Marin
Delaware (river) country, Pennsylvania
  Helm. John Marin
East river no 3, 1934
  Helm. John Marin
Equestrians
  UNESCO. 1860-1955
Equestrienne
  Helm. John Marin
Fifth avenue and Forty-second street DP
  Bazin
  DP. Catalogue
  PA. Annual ex, 1955
Fir tree, Deer isle, Maine    NJN
  Baur. New art
Fishermen and boats
  UNESCO. 1860-1955
  UNESCO. 1860-1959
Fishing boat no 2, 1933
  Helm. John Marin
Fog lifts
  John Marin (col)
  MMA. Abstract
  MnU. 40 Amer ptrs

**MARIN, John**—*Continued*

Four-master off the Cape      DP
  DP. Catalogue
Four o'clock on the Seine
  Helm. John Marin
Franconia range—mist and rain
  Cheney. Expressionism 1948 ed
From seeing Cape Split
  Helm. John Marin
From the bridge, New York city   CtHW
  CoS. New accessions USA, 1950
  CtHW. Handbook
  Pierson
From Weehawken heights
  Pearson. Mod renaissance
Going through the thoroughfare
  UNESCO. 1860-1955
  UNESCO. 1860-1959
Green Head, Deer isle, Maine
  CanO. Hirshhorn coll
Grey rock, blue-grey sea and boat
  Baur. Revolution
Grey sea      DP
  DP. Catalogue
  John Marin (col)
Gulls, Cape Split, Maine
  PA. Annual ex, 1955
Headed for Boston      ICA
  Helm. John Marin (col)
  Taylor. Fifty centuries, 1954 ed (col)
In the ring
  Helm. John Marin
Island, Small point, Maine      PPhM
  Born
Jersey hills
  PA. Annual ex, 1954
The ladle
  John Marin
Lake, Tunk mountain, Maine series no 12,
    1934
  Helm. John Marin
Landscape in Maine      ICA
  Cheney. Expressionism 1948 ed
Laurel blossoms in vase
  Helm. John Marin
Lions in the ring
  UNESCO. 1860-1955
  UNESCO. 1860-1959
Little sailboat
  John Marin
Lobster boat
  Helm. John Marin
  John Marin
Lobster boat, Cape Split, Maine
  John Marin (col)
London omnibus      MM
  Helm. John Marin
  John Marin
Looking up Fifth avenue from Thirtieth
  street
  Helm. John Marin
  Raynal. History v3 (col)
Lower Manhattan from the river   MM
  Helm. John Marin
  John Marin (col)
  UNESCO. 1860-1949
  UNESCO. 1860-1955
  UNESCO. 1860-1959
Lower Manhattan, 1920
  Barr. What is mod ptg
  Baur. New art
  Cheney. Primer 1958 ed
  Cheney. Story 1958 ed (col)
  Craven. Rainbow book

  Gruskin
  Janson. Picture history (col)
  John Marin (col)
  Robb. Art 1953 ed
Lower Manhattan, 1922      MMA
  Canaday
  Hunter. Mod Amer ptg (col)
  McCurdy
  MMA. Abstract
  MMA. Contemp ptrs
  MMA. Masters (col)
  MMA. Ptg and sculpture
  Pierson
  Read. Art now 1948
  Rosenblum
Lower New York
  Cheney. Expressionism 1948 ed
Machias, Maine, 1945
  Helm. John Marin
  John Marin (col)
Machias, Maine, 1952
  John Marin (col)
Maine coast
  Riley. Your art heritage
Maine islands      DP
  Baur. New art (col)
  Bazin. History of art
  Cheney. Story 1958 ed
  DP. Catalogue
  Faulkner. Art today, 1956
  Gardner 1959 ed
  John Marin
  MMA. Contemp ptrs
  NYG. Fine art
  Pierson
  Richardson. Ptg in America
  Robb. Harper history
  Roos
  Rosenblum
  UNESCO. 1860-1955
  UNESCO. 1860-1959
Maine, 1928
  Cheney. Expressionism 1948 ed
Maine—the sail boat
  Cheney. Primer 1958 ed
Manhattan, St Paul's
  WMAA. Pioneers
Marin island, Small point, Maine   PPhM
  Brown. Amer ptg
  Helm. John Marin
  Larkin
  Larkin rev ed
Mid-Manhattan II, 1932
  MnMW. Classic tradition
Midtown, New York, 1928
  Helm. John Marin
Mount Chocorua      OYB
  OYB. Supplement
Mountain top      OCl
  Larkin
  Larkin rev ed
  Myers
  OCl. Handbook
The mountain, Tyrol
  Helm. John Marin
Movement, boat and sea, Deer isle, Maine
  Helm. John Marin
Movement—boat and sea in grey
  John Marin
Movement, boat, sea, rocks and sky, Maine
                               WMAA
  PA. Annual ex, 1955
Movement—Fifth avenue      ICA
  John Marin
  Pierson

Movement—green, red and black
  PPC. Ptg in the U.S. 1949
Movement in grey, green and red no 2,
  1949
  John Marin
Movement in paint [1]
  Helm. John Marin
Movement in paint [2]
  Helm. John Marin
Movement in paint [3]
  Helm. John Marin
Movement in paint [4]
  Helm. John Marin
Movement no 2—related to downtown
  New York (The black sun)          MM
  50 years of mod art
  Helm. John Marin (col)
  John Marin
  WMAA. Juliana Force
Movement, sea and rocks, Cape Split,
  Maine
  PPC. International ex, 1952
Movement, sea and sky          MLL
  DC. 21 biennial ex, 1949
  John Marin (col)
  Pierson
  WMAA. Museum and its friends, 1958
    (col)
Movement—sea or mountain, as you will
  Baur. Nature
  IU. Contemp Amer ptg, 1949
Movement: Tunk mountains
  CSFP. Annual ex, 1952
My Hell raising sea
  John Marin
Near Great Barrington          DP
  DP. Catalogue
Near Santa Fe, New Mexico
  MiD. Coll in progress
  WiMiA. Amer ptg 1760-1960
New Mexico
  Cheney. Expressionism 1948 ed
New York at night no 3, 1950
  John Marin (col)
New York, downtown
  Helm. John Marin
New York, East river
  Helm. John Marin
New York harbor, 1920          MB
  MB. Ptgs in water color
Off Cape Split, Maine          MM
  Helm. John Marin
  Newmeyer
Off Stonington          OCo
  Munsterberg
Off York island, Maine          PPhM
  Canaday
  John Marin
The old salt          MM
  50 years of mod art
  Pearson. Mod renaissance
On Morse mountain, Maine
  Cheney. Expressionism 1948 ed
  Helm. John Marin (col)
On Morse mountain, Small point, Maine
  Helm. John Marin (col)
  John Marin
  Lee. Art then and now
Peach trees in blossom
  UNESCO. 1860-1955
  UNESCO. 1860-1959

Pertaining to Deer isle, the harbor    MM
  Brown. Amer ptg
  Helm. John Marin
  John Marin
Pertaining to Nassau street, New York
                                       NeL
  Barker. From realism
Pertaining to Stonington harbor, Maine,
  no 4                                 MM
  John Marin
  Pierson
Phippsburg, Maine
  Helm. John Marin (col)
Pine tree, Small point, Maine          ICA
  Pierson
  UNESCO. 1860-1959
Pont Alexandre
  Helm. John Marin
The Pont Neuf
  UNESCO. 1860-1955
Pueblo and mesa, Taos mountains
  Helm. John Marin
Quoddy Head, Maine coast               DP
  DP. Catalogue
Ramapo river near Suffern, New York
  UNESCO. 1860-1955
  UNESCO. 1860-1959
Red sun—Brooklyn bridge                ICA
  John Marin
Region of Brooklyn bridge fantasy
                                       WMAA
  Goodrich. Amer art (col)
  John Marin
  Pierson
Region Weehawken, New Jersey
  MiD. Coll in progress
River effect, Paris                    PPhM
  Cheney. Story 1958 ed
  PPhM. Gallatin coll
River movement—downtown
  John Marin
Rocks and sea, Small point, Maine    OCl
  Cheney. Primer 1958 ed
  Helm. John Marin
  OCl. Handbook
Sea after hurricane                    CSFM
  Cheney. Story 1958 ed
Sea and gulls                          MM
  Helm. John Marin
  MM. 100 Amer ptrs
Sea and rocks
  MnMW. Contemporary
  WMAA. Neuberger collection
Sea and sky
  IU. Contemp Amer ptg, 1948
Sea gulls
  Helm. John Marin
Sea horses—sea movement off Deer
  island, Maine                        WMAA
  McCurdy
Sea piece                              WMAA
  Cheney. Story 1958 ed
  Goodrich. Amer art (col)
  WMAA. Contemp Amer ptg, 1952
Sea piece (Fleischman coll)
  MiD. Coll in progress
  Richardson. Ptg in America
Sea piece—Boat fantasy
  Time. 300 years (col)
Sea piece, 1951 (Schulte coll)
  John Marin
Sea with red sky
  Helm. John Marin

**MARIN, John**—*Continued*

Seascape                              CLA
  CLA. 35 ptgs
Seascape fantasy, Maine
  Time. 300 years (col)
Ships
  Lewisohn
Singer building                      PPhM
  Canaday
A southwester
  Helm. John Marin
Speed—Lake Champlain                 NUM
  John Marin
Spring no 1                          DP
  Eliot. Art of our time (col)
  John Marin
  Time. 300 years (col)
Stock exchange, New York city
  John Marin (col)
Stonington and the harbor, Maine
  MiD. Coll in progress
  WiMiA. Amer ptg 1760-1960
Stonington harbor
  Helm. John Marin
Storm over Taos                      DN
  Helm.  John Marin  (col)
  John Marin
  Pierson
Street crossing, New York            DP
  Helm. John Marin
  John Marin
Street movement, abstraction, New York
  MiD. Coll in progress
A street seeing
  Helm. John Marin (col)
Sun, isles and sea                   MdB
  John Marin (col)
  Time. 300 years (col)
Sunset                               WMAA
  Goodrich. Amer art
  Mendelowitz
  NYG. Fine art
  UNESCO. 1860-1949
  UNESCO. 1860-1955
  UNESCO. 1860-1959
Sunset (Halpert coll)
  DC. Halpert collection
  John Marin (col)
  Pierson
  Pousette-Dart. Amer ptg (col)
Sunset, Casco bay
  Baur. Revolution
  Helm. John Marin
**Taos**
  Biddle. Yes and no
Taos landscape, New Mexico
  Helm. John Marin
The three-master
  UNESCO. 1860-1955
  UNESCO. 1860-1959
Three nudes
  Helm. John Marin
Tree and sea, Maine                  ICA
  Brown. Amer ptg
  PA. Annual ex, 1955
Tree, Cape Split
  CtY. Yale alumni
Tree forms
  MMA. Abstract
Tree no 1, Cape Split, Maine coast
  Helm. John Marin

Tunk mountains, autumn, Maine    DP
  Baur. New art (col)
  DP. Catalogue
  Larkin rev ed (col)
  Pierson
  UNESCO. 1860-1959
Tunk mountains, Maine
  NBuA. Expressionism
Two-master becalmed, Maine       MM
  Baur. New art
  Helm. John Marin
Tyrol at Kufstein, Tyrol series, no 3, 1910
  Helm. John Marin
Tyrolean mountains                OCo
  Brown. Amer ptg
Village, Maine
  Helm. John Marin
White mountain country            OCl
  John Marin
White mountain country, Dixville Notch
    no 1, 1927
  Cheney. Story 1958 ed
  John Marin
White mountain country, New Hampshire
                                   ATeS
  ATeS. Collection
White mountains, autumn
  Helm. John Marin
Wind on land and sea, Maine
  Cheney. New world history
  Cheney. Story 1958 ed
Women and sea
  UNESCO. 1860-1955
  UNESCO. 1860-1959
Women forms and sea
  Helm. John Marin
  John Marin
Woolworth building
  Baur. Revolution
  Flexner. Amer ptg
  Flexner. Short history
Woolworth building in construction
  NBuA. Fifty ptgs
Woolworth building no 31, 1912
  Baur. New art
  Brown. Amer ptg
  Helm. John Marin
  John Marin
  Rosenblum
Young man of the sea, Maine series no 10,
    1934                           MM
  Helm. John Marin
  John Marin
**Marin** island, Small point, Maine by J.
    Marin
**Marina** Grande in Capri by A. Bierstadt
**Marine** by L. Feininger
**Marine** by A. P. Ryder
**Marine** by J. A. M. Whistler
**Marine** hospital, Chelsea, Massachusetts,
    1835-40 by Unidentified artist
**Marine** Sampson by A. Polonsky
**Marine** view with ships by T. Birch
**Marine** with shipping by J. Peale jr
A **mariner** by Unidentified artist
**MARINGER, Carol**
  Dummy
    NAD. Annual ex, 1956
**MARIO, Alessandro,** fl 1858-1868
  Construction work in New York, 1868
                                   NNHS
    Davidson v2

Marion, Francis, 1732-1795
  White, J. B. Gen Marion in his swamp
    encampment inviting a British officer
    to dinner
MARISOL (Marisol Escobar) 1930?-
  Purgatorio
    IU. Contemp Amer ptg & sculp, 1959
Maritime by K. Knaths
MARK, George Washington, fl 1817-1879
  Mountains
    Ford. Pictorial folk art
Market basket, hat, and umbrella by J. F.
    Peto
Market place, Venice by M. B. Prendergast
Markets
  Davis, L E. The market
  Dehn, A. A. Market, Port-au-Prince
  Di Gioia, F. Fish market
  Prestopino, G. The market
MARKMAN, Ronald, 1931-
  The entertainers III
    WMAA. Young America 1960
  Parade figure
    WMAA. Young America 1960
Marlin by J. Mitchell
Marmaduke, Meredith M. fl 1834
  Bingham, G. C. Meredith M. Marmaduke
Maroon on blue by M. Rothko
Marquand, John Phillips, 1893-
  James, A. John P. Marquand
Marr, Gerald
  Hurd, P. Gerald Marr
Marriage by M. Tobey
Marriage at Cana by Unidentified artist
The marriage of Heaven and Hell, Study for
  by B. Shahn
Marriage of reason and squalor by F. Stella
Mars, orange and green by A. G. Dove
Mars, Venus, and Vulcan by J. S. Copley
MARSDEN, Thomas
  On a point
    NSP. Sportscapes
Marseilles, night by R. A. Parker
Marsh, Charles, fl 1846
  Mason, B. F. Charles Marsh
Marsh, Molly. See Seymour, Molly (Marsh)
MARSH, Reginald, 1898-1954
  Along the waterfront                   OYB
    OYB. Catalogue 1951
  Belles of the Battery (Battery belles)
                                         OYB
    OYB. Accessions
    OYB. Supplement 1959
    WMAA. Marsh
  BMT, Fourteenth street
    WMAA. Marsh
  The Bowery                             MM
    Brown. Amer ptg
    Craven. Rainbow book
    Larkin
    Larkin rev ed
    MM. 100 Amer ptrs
  Bowery at Pell street
    WMAA. Marsh
  Bowery drunks
    IU. Contemp Amer ptg, 1951
    WMAA. Marsh
  The bowl                               NBM
    Baur. Revolution
    Pierson
    WMAA. Marsh

Coney island beach                       CtHW
  CtHW. Handbook
Coney island beach, 1934
  WMAA. Marsh
Coney island beach, 1943                 WMAA
  Mendelowitz
Coney island beach, 1947
  WMAA. Marsh
Coney island beach, 1951                 WMAA
  WMAA. Marsh
  WMAA. Sara Roby
Coney island, 1939
  CtY. Yale alumni
Discharge of cargo at pier
  Pierson
East Tenth street jungle
  WMAA. Marsh
Eldorado
  WMAA. Marsh
End of Fourteenth street crosstown line
                                         PA
  WMAA. Marsh
Eyes tested
  WiMiA. Amer ptg 1760-1960
  WMAA. Marsh
Fourteenth street
  WMAA. Marsh
George Tilyou's steeplechase            PMB
  WMAA. Marsh
Hat display
  WMAA. Marsh
High yaller
  Craven. Treasury 1952 ed
  NYG. Fine art
  Roos
  WMAA. Marsh
Holy Name mission                        IBM
  ICA. Amer artists paint the city
Hudson Bay fur company
  WMAA. Marsh
Hudson burlesk chorus (Hudson bur-
    lesque chorus)
  NAD. Annual ex, 1955
  WMAA. Marsh
Hudson burlesk, Union City, New Jersey
  WMAA. Marsh
Human pool tables                        WMAA
  Goodrich. Amer art (col)
  WMAA. Marsh (col)
Locomotives watering
  WMAA. Marsh
Martial spirit
  Bazin
Matinee
  WMAA. Marsh (detail)
Memories of the Stork club
  WMAA. Marsh
Merry-go-round
  MM. Amer ptg today
  WMAA. Marsh
Mink and mannequin
  WMAA. Marsh (col)
Minsky's chorus
  WMAA. Marsh
Monarch of Bermuda                       ATeS
  ATeS. Collection
Monday night at the Metropolitan         ATU
  ATU. Coll of Amer art (col)
  WMAA. Marsh
Morning in May
  WMAA. Marsh
Naked over New York
  WMAA. Marsh

**MARSH, Reginald**—*Continued*
Negroes on Rockaway beach
   Time. 300 years (col)
   WMAA. Marsh
New dodgem                           WMAA
   WMAA. Marsh
No turns permitted
   WMAA. Marsh
Park bench                              NeL
   Barker. From realism
Pip and Flip
   WMAA. Marsh
Prometheus in Rockefeller center
   WMAA. Marsh
Pursuit                                  OT
   Gruskin
   OT. Contemp Amer ptgs
Steel structure                          MB
   MB. Ptgs in water color
Steeplechase park
   WMAA. Marsh
   WMAA. Museum and its friends, 1958
Street scene                            ATU
   ATU. Coll of Amer art
Strip tease
   WMAA. Marsh
Stripper
   WMAA. Marsh
Swimming off West Washington market
                                       NBuA
   NBuA. Contemporary ptgs
   Pierson
   WMAA. Marsh
Swinging chairs
   WMAA. Marsh
Tattoo and haircut                      ICA
   McCurdy
   Pierson
   WMAA. Marsh
Taxi dance hall
   WMAA. Marsh
Ten shots ten cents                    MoSL
   MoSL. Handbook 1953
Texas Guinan and her gang              NUM
   NUM. Root bequest
They pay to be seen                    PPhM
   Canaday
Twenty-cent movie                      WMAA
   WMAA. Marsh
Under the el                            MM
   Lewisohn
Why not use the el                     WMAA
   Craven. Treasury 1952 ed
   Goodrich. Amer art
   Robb. Harper history
   Time. 300 years (col)
   Wight. Milestones
   WMAA. Marsh
Wooden horses
   Craven. Treasury 1952 ed (col)
**Marsh** in winter by D. Macknight
**Marshall, John,** 1755-1835
   Harding, C. Chief Justice John Marshall
   Hubard, W. J. John Marshall
   Inman, H. John Marshall
   Jarvis, J. W. John Marshall
The marshes by W De Kooning
Marshland by D. Macknight
**Marsteller, Charlotte,** c 1790
   Unidentified artist. Charlotte Marsteller

**MARSTON, James B.**
State street and the old State House,
   Boston, 1801                        MBH
   Davidson v2
**MARTENS, J. W.**
Brooklyn Navy yard (Frigate USS United
   States)
   Pierson
**Martha** by Unidentified artist
**Martha** Washington's reception by D. Hunt-
   ington
**Martha's** Vineyard by J. Delbos
**Martial** memory by P. Guston
**Martial** spirit by R. Marsh
**MARTIN, Caroline Louise,** 1903-
The innocents
   CSFP. Annual ex, 1952
**Martin, Edward,** 1782-1860
   Malbone, E. G. Edward Martin
**MARTIN, Fletcher,** 1904-
Arabesque with bull
   Ebersole. Fletcher Martin
Bagnell dam on the Osage river
   Ebersole. Fletcher Martin
The barrier
   Ebersole. Fletcher Martin
Boy picking flowers
   Ebersole. Fletcher Martin
Celebration                            MoKN
   Ebersole. Fletcher Martin
Charles Laughton as Captain Kidd
   Ebersole. Fletcher Martin
Cherry twice                           WMAA
   Ebersole. Fletcher Martin
   NAD. Annual ex, 1949, 1st half
   Pierson
Clown act
   Ebersole. Fletcher Martin
Country dance
   Ebersole. Fletcher Martin
Dancer dressing
   Ebersole. Fletcher Martin
   PA. Annual ex, 1947
Earth machines
   Ebersole. Fletcher Martin
Exit in color
   Ebersole. Fletcher Martin
Fishing village
   Ebersole. Fletcher Martin
Florida landscape
   Ebersole. Fletcher Martin
The glory
   Ebersole. Fletcher Martin
Helen
   Ebersole. Fletcher Martin
Juliet                                  MM
   Ebersole. Fletcher Martin
**July 4th, 5th, and 6th**              IBM
   Ebersole. Fletcher Martin
Killer in costume
   Ebersole. Fletcher Martin
A lad from the fleet
   Ebersole. Fletcher Martin
Lullaby
   Ebersole. Fletcher Martin
   Gruskin (col)
Out at home
   Baur. Revolution
   Ebersole. Fletcher Martin
Picador
   Ebersole. Fletcher Martin

Quarry at night
  Ebersole. Fletcher Martin
Ruby
  Ebersole. Fletcher Martin
Rural family
  Ebersole. Fletcher Martin
Shooting gallery
  Cheney. Story 1958 ed
  Ebersole. Fletcher Martin
Still life with skull
  Ebersole. Fletcher Martin
Temptation in Tonopah
  Ebersole. Fletcher Martin
'Tis me O Lord
  Ebersole. Fletcher Martin
Tomorrow and tomorrow
  Ebersole. Fletcher Martin
The toss
  Ebersole. Fletcher Martin
Toy birds
  Ebersole. Fletcher Martin
Trouble in Frisco                              MMA
  Ebersole. Fletcher Martin
  Pierson
The undefeated
  Ebersole. Fletcher Martin
Urchin's game
  Ebersole. Fletcher Martin
Vacation
  Ebersole. Fletcher Martin
Weeping girl
  Ebersole. Fletcher Martin
Wonderful object
  Ebersole. Fletcher Martin
  IU. Contemp Amer ptg & sculp, 1953
MARTIN, Homer Dodge, 1836-1897
Duclair on Seine                               MB
  MB. Ptgs in water color
Harp of the winds (View of the Seine)
                                               MM
  NYG. Fine art
  Pierson
  Richardson. Ptg in America
  Roos
Lake Sanford in the Adirondacks    NNCe
  Larkin
  Larkin rev ed
  Pierson
Logging camp                                   MB
  Pierson
Newport landscape                              OYB
  OYB. Catalogue 1951
Preston ponds, Adirondacks         MnMI
  Born
Sand dune, Lake Ontario                        MM
  Pierson
View of the Seine. See Harp of the winds
Martin, Mrs Josiah. See Martin, Mary
  (Yeamans)
MARTIN, Keith Morrow, 1911-
Bearers of gifts
  WMAA. Contemp Amer ptg, 1955
Frontier                                       OYB
  OYB. Annual 1958
  OYB. Supplement 1959
MARTIN, Knox, 1923-
Calypso
  IU. Contemp Amer ptg & sculp, 1955
Martin, Mary Elizabeth, b 1763?
  Copley, J. S. Mary Elizabeth Martin
Martin, Mary (Yeamans) 1720-1805
  Feke, R. Mrs Josiah Martin

MARTIN, Silas, 1841-1906
Flintlock
  Frankenstein. After the hunt
Martin, Walter
  Reeder, D. Walter Martin
MARTINELLI, Ezio, 1912-
Corazziere
  ICA. Annual ex, 1947/48
Martinelli, Sebastiano, b 1848
  Eakins, T. His Eminence Cardinal Martinelli
MARTINO, Antonio Pietro, 1902-
Four houses
  NAD. Annual ex, 1951
Manayunk winter
  NAD. Annual ex, 1955
MARTINO, Giovanni, 1908-
At the crossing
  NAD. Annual ex, 1947, 1st half
Canton street
  OYB. Annual 1956
Grape hill, Manayunk                           OYB
  OYB. Supplement
MARTYL (Suzanne Schweig) 1918-
Barcelona market II
  IU. Contemp Amer ptg & sculp, 1957
Getting ready                                  ATU
  ATU. Coll of Amer art
Northern lights
  IU. Contemp Amer ptg & sculp, 1959
South of Taxco
  IU. Contemp Amer ptg, 1951
Sun valley                                     ATU
  ATU. Coll of Amer art
View of Oxford
  IU. Contemp Amer ptg & sculp, 1961
Martyr by A. Rattner
Marvello by J. Glasco
Marx, Asher, fl 1803
  Malbone, E. G. Asher Marx
Marx, Joseph, fl 1806
  Malbone, E. G. Joseph Marx
Mary by S. E. Dickinson
Mary by R. Henri
Mary by S. Serisawa
Maryland family
  Unidentified artist. Maryland family
Maryland, View into by M. Reinhardt
Maryland landscape by W. H. Holmes
Masked bird fishing in the golden stream
  by M. Graves
Masks by J. Lawrence
Mason, Alice, b 1668
  Mason limner. Alice Mason
Mason, Alice, fl 1885
  Sargent, J. S. Mrs Alice Mason
MASON, Alice Trumbull, 1904-
Staff, distaff and rod
  NNSG. Younger Amer ptrs
MASON, Benjamin Franklin, 1804-1871
Bugbee family
  Frankenstein. Two journeyman ptrs
Charles K. Williams
  Frankenstein. Two journeyman ptrs
Charles Marsh
  Frankenstein. Two journeyman ptrs
Edwin Hutchinson
  Frankenstein. Two journeyman ptrs
Eliza Grover Chase
  Frankenstein. Two journeyman ptrs

**MASON, B. F.—**_Continued_
Elizabeth de Long Rockwell
  Frankenstein. Two journeyman ptrs
George Chapman
  Frankenstein. Two journeyman ptrs
Halsey Wing
  Frankenstein. Two journeyman ptrs
Harvey Kitchell
  Frankenstein. Two journeyman ptrs
Horatio Seymour
  Frankenstein. Two journeyman ptrs
Ira Stewart
  Frankenstein. Two journeyman ptrs
John Godfrey Saxe
  Frankenstein. Two journeyman ptrs
Julia, Mary Ann and Harriet Tilden
  Frankenstein. Two journeyman ptrs
Mehitabel Preston de Long
  Frankenstein. Two journeyman ptrs
Mrs George Chapman
  Frankenstein. Two journeyman ptrs
Mrs Halsey Wing
  Frankenstein. Two journeyman ptrs
Mrs John Godfrey Saxe
  Frankenstein. Two journeyman ptrs
Mrs Lebdeus Harris      VtMS
  Frankenstein. Two journeyman ptrs
Mrs Philip Battell
  Frankenstein. Two journeyman ptrs
Mrs Rufus Wainwright
  Frankenstein. Two journeyman ptrs
Mrs Samuel P. P. Fay
  Frankenstein. Two journeyman ptrs
Mrs Simeon Rockwell
  Frankenstein. Two journeyman ptrs
Rufus and Gardner Wainwright
  Frankenstein. Two journeyman ptrs
Rufus Wainwright
  Frankenstein. Two journeyman ptrs
Samuel Prescott Phillips Fay
  Frankenstein. Two journeyman ptrs
Simeon Rockwell
  Frankenstein. Two journeyman ptrs
Thomas E. Powers
  Frankenstein. Two journeyman ptrs

### Attributed works

Norman Williams
  Frankenstein. Two journeyman ptrs
**Mason, Eliza, 1784-1826**
Malbone, E. G. Eliza Mason
**Mason, Elizabeth Champlin.** See Perry, Elizabeth Champlin (Mason)
**Mason, Elizabeth (Heltzhoover)**
Stuart, G. Mrs John Thompson Mason
**Mason, Ida**
Hunt, W. M. Miss Ida Mason
**Mason, Lowell, 1792-1872**
Unidentified artist. Lowell Mason
**MASON, Roy Martell, 1886-**
Anglers heaven
  NSP. Sportscapes
Fishing at the Spillway
  NSP. Sportscapes
The moment that makes duck hunting
  NSP. Sportscapes
**MASON, William Sanford, fl 1838-1865**
A country house      MB
  Chew. 250 years of art
  MB. Karolik coll
Venus and Cupid      MB
  MB. Karolik coll

**MASON limner, fl 1670**
Alice Mason
  Flexner. First flowers
  Ford. Pictorial folk art
  NUM. Art across America
Alice Mason      MQ
  Roos
David, Joanna, and Abigail Mason
  Flexner. First flowers
  Ford. Pictorial folk art
**Mason children**
Mason limner. David, Joanna, and Abigail Mason
**Masonic** memorial by E. G. H. Pinney
**Masqued** image by J. Pollock
**Masquerade** by M. Beckmann
**Master** Willoughby by Unidentified artist
**Masterpiece** by W. Williams
**Matau-Tathonca,** Bull Bear—an Ogillalah, Head of by A. J. Miller
**Matchbook** by W. De Kooning
**Matches** no 2, 1927 by S. Davis
The **matement** by C. Howard
**Maternità,** 1943 by W. Pachner
**Maternità,** 1954-55 by W. Pachner
**Maternità,** 1956 by W. Pachner
**Maternità** no 1, 1957 by W. Pachner
**Mather, Cotton, 1663-1728**
Pelham, P. Rev Cotton Mather
**Mather, Elias, 1776-1843**
Ames, E. Elias Mather
**Mather, Increase, 1639-1723**
Vanderspritt, J. Increase Mather
**MATHIES, John Lee Douglas, 1780-1834**
Jemima Wilkinson: the Publick Universal Friend
  Jones. Rediscovered ptrs
Red Jacket
  Jones. Rediscovered ptrs
Seneca veterans of the war of 1812
  Jones. Rediscovered ptrs
Wreck of the steamer Walk-in-the-water      MiD
  Jones. Rediscovered ptrs
**Matinee** by R. Marsh
**Matlack, Timothy, fl 1795**
Peale, C. W. Timothy Matlack
**Mato-tope** with the marks of his exploits by K. Bodmer
**Matriarch** and the prodigal son by Z. Kachadoorian
**Matriarchy** by M. Tomkins
**Matrix** by D. R. Stuart
**Matrix** of an unfathomable by B. Margo
**MATSON, Greta Wilhelmina, 1915-**
City child
  OYB. Annual 1948
**MATTERN, Karl, 1892-**
Winter shapes      IaDM
  CoS. New accessions USA, 1956
**MATTESON, Thompkins Harrison, 1813-1884**
Justice's court in the backwoods  NCHA
  Jones. Rediscovered ptrs
Sculptor's studio      NAI
  Larkin
  Larkin rev ed
Turkey shoot (from Cooper's The pioneer)  NCHA
  Jones. Rediscovered ptrs

**MATTHEW, K.**
Autumn glory
 NYG. Fine art
Azalea tropical trails, Florida
 NYG. Fine art
Capitol reflections
 NYG. Fine art
Charming New Orleans
 NYG. Fine art
Gloucester boats
 NYG. Fine art
Harkness tower (Yale)
 NYG. Fine art
Independence hall (Philadelphia)
 NYG. Fine art
Lowell house (Harvard university)
 NYG. Fine art
Nassau hall (Princeton university)
 NYG. Fine art
Rocky neck (Gloucester)
 NYG. Fine art
Skyline (New York)
 NYG. Fine art
Spring idyll
 NYG. Fine art
Summer vista
 NYG. Fine art
Tropical surf (Florida)
 NYG. Fine art
Waterfront (New York)
 NYG. Fine art
Winter's dreamland
 NYG. Fine art
**Matthews, Thomas J.**
Corwine, A. H. Thomas J. Matthews
**MATTSON, Henry Elis,** 1887-
Atlantic
 NAD. Annual ex, 1951
Big Rock pool OT
 OT. Contemp Amer ptgs
Blue night
 IU. Contemp Amer ptg 1948
Dawn
 IU. Contemp Amer ptg & sculp, 1961
Dawn light
 Cheney. Primer 1958 ed
Eventide WMAA
 Goodrich. Amer art
Green sea NBM
 Baur. Revolution
Gulls and sea ATeS
 ATeS. Collection
Headland
 Pousette-Dart. Amer ptg
Landscape MAP
 NYG. Fine art
Moonlit landscape WMAA
 Pierson
Self-portrait
 Cheney. Story 1938 ed
 PA. Annual ex, 1950
Spring WMAA
 Gruskin
Wings of the morning MM
 Cheney. New world history
 Cheney. Story 1958 ed
 Pierson
 Wight. Milestones
**Maua,** our boatman by J. LaFarge
**Mauch** Chunk, Pennsylvania by J. Collins
**Mauch** Chunk, Pennsylvania by B. Mitchell

**MAURER, Alfred Henry,** 1868-1932
Abstraction DP
 Larkin
 Larkin rev ed
An arrangement WMAA
 McCausland. A. H. Maurer
At the shore
 Brown. Amer ptg
Le bal Bullier MNS
 Baur. New art
Carousel NBM
 McCausland. A. H. Maurer
Florentines DP
 McCausland. A. H. Maurer
Flowers, c 1912 WMAA
 McCausland. A. H. Maurer
 McCurdy
Flowers, c 1925
 McCausland. A. H. Maurer
Gabrielle
 McCausland. A. H. Maurer
George Washington
 McCausland. A. H. Maurer
Green striped bowl
 McCausland. A. H. Maurer
Head in landscape
 MnMW. Contemporary
 WMAA. Neuberger collection
Head in motion
 Rathbun
Jeanne
 McCausland. A. H. Maurer
Landscape, c 1912
 Baur. Revolution
Landscape in the Vineyard
 Pierson
Landscape with farm
 Brown. Amer ptg
Nude
 McCausland. A. H. Maurer
Self-portrait, 1897
 McCausland. A. H. Maurer
Self-portrait with hat MnMW
 Baur. New art
 Baur. Revolution
 McCausland. A H. Maurer (col front)
 Pierson
Still life
 NBuA. Expressionism
Still life: pear
 UNESCO. 1860-1955
 UNESCO. 1860-1959
Still life with ashtray
 Brown. Amer ptg
Still life with doily DP
 Baur. New art (col)
 DP. Catalogue
 McCausland. A. H. Maurer
 Pierson
 UNESCO. 1860-1955
 UNESCO. 1860-1959
Still life with pears MAP
 Hess. Abstract ptg
 McCausland. A. H. Maurer
Twin heads WMAA
 Baur. New art
 Goodrich. Amer art
 McCausland. A. H. Maurer
 Pierson
Two girls
 WMAA. Pioneers
Two heads
 Brown. Amer ptg

**MAURER, A. H.**—*Continued*
Two heads (Godsoe and Knox coll)
McCausland. A. H. Maurer
Two heads (Neumann coll)
McCausland. A. H. Maurer
Two sisters
McCausland. A. H. Maurer
Young girl              MeC
MeC. Inaugural ex
**MAURICE, E. Ingersoll**, 1901-
Wood rose
OYB. Annual 1955
**Mauve** recession by G. L. K. Morris
**Mauve** still life by S. M. Adler
**Ma-wo-ma** by A. J. Miller
**Max** by S. Davis
**Max** Schmidt in a single scull by T. Eakins
**Maxon, Polly**, fl 1815
Unidentified artist. Polly Maxon of Ste-
phentown, New York
**MAXWELL, John**, 1905-
Winter forms         OYB
OYB. Annual 1957
OYB. Supplement 1959
**May, John**, 1748-1812
Gullager, C. Col John May
**May** day, Central park by M. B. Prendergast
**May** 5 by B. Shahn
**May** in the mountains by E. Lawson
**May**: making soap, washing sheep by A. M.
R. Moses
**May** night by W. L. Metcalf
**May** 2, 1956 by J. Levee
**Maya**, mirror of illusion by A. B. Davies
Las **Mayas** by H. Frankenthaler
**Maybank, Susannah**, b 1745
Theus, J. Susannah Maybank
**Maybelle** by T. Eakins
**Mayer, Mrs Christopher B.** 1761-1848
Eichholtz, J. Mrs Christopher B. Mayer
**MAYER, Frank Blackwell**, 1827-1899
Leisure and labor        DC
DC. Amer ptrs of the South
**MAYER, Henrik Martin**, 1908-
Barometer falling        OYB
OYB. Annual 1949
Foreboding
OYB. Annual 1952
**Mayer, Susan B.** See Mayer, Mrs Christo-
pher B.
**Mayflower** by R. G. Hamilton
**MAYHEW, Nathaniel**, fl 1823
John Harrison        DN
DN. Amer primitive ptgs, pt 2
Mrs John Harrison and her daughter
Marie        DN
DN. Amer primitive ptgs, pt 2
**MAYR, Christian**, 1805-1850
Kitchen ball at White Sulphur Springs,
Virginia, 1838        NoCR
Davidson v 1
NoCR. Catalogue
**Mazatlan** women by M. O. Sheets
**Maze** by E. Ludins
**Mazyck, Mary (Mazyck)**
Theus, J. Mrs William Mazyck
**Mazyck, Stephen**, 1718-1770
Theus, J. Stephen Mazyck

**Mazyck, Susanne (Ravenel)**
Theus, J. Mrs Stephen Mazyck
**Mazyck, William**, 1739-1775
Theus, J. William Mazyck
**Me** and the battle of Tassafaronga, Guadal-
canal by B. L. Culwell
**Mead, Mary Gertrude.** See Abbey, Mary
Gertrude (Mead)
**MEADOR, Joshua Lawrence**, 1911-
Remnants of an era
NAD. Annual ex, 1955
The **meadow** by J. R. Cox
The **meadow** by J. W. Guerin
**Meadow** and hills: sunset by B. West (at-
tributed works)
**Meadows** in winter by F. W. Benson
**Meads, John**, 1777-1859
Ames, E. John Meads
**Meads, Louisa (Crane)** b 1785
Ames, E. Mrs John Meads
The **meal** by T. H. Benton
**Means, Mary H. (Barnwell)** 1781-1849
Malbone, E. G. Mrs Robert Means
**Means, Thomas**, 1767-1828
Malbone, E. G. Thomas Means
**Mears, Grace.** See Levy, Grace (Mears)
**Measurement** and contemplation by E. John-
son
**Mechanical** abstraction by M. L. Schamberg
**MECHAU, Frank Albert**, 1904-1946
Tom Kenney comes home
Taylor. Fifty centuries, 1954 ed (col)
**Medfield**, Evening at by G. Inness
**Medford** marshes by G. L. Brown
**Medianus** by J. Ferren
**Medicine** bag by C. Wimar
**Medicine** bag dance of the Sauk and Fox by
G. Catlin
**Medicine** circles by A. J. Miller
**Medicine** man
Catlin, G. Blackfoot doctor in his mystery
dress endeavoring to cure his dying
patient
Catlin, G. Blackfoot medicine man
Catlin, G. Mandan medicine man
Catlin, G. Se-non-ti-yak, the Blistered
Foot, Ioway medicine man
Catlin, G. Uruguay medicine man, South
America
Catlin, G. Wun-nee-tow, the White Buf-
falo, Blackfoot medicine man
Russell, C. M. The medicine man
**Medicine** show IV by J. Levine
**Medieval** scribe by E. Laning
**Meditation** by B. Kopman
**Meditation** by C. M. Russell
**Meditation** by A. H. Thayer
**Meditation** by the sea by Unidentified artist
**Meditation** in space by W. Sommer
**Meditative** series no 9, 1954 by M. Tobey
**Mediterranean** coast by R. D. Gauley
**Mediterranean** landscape by J. E. Heliker
The **medium** by H. Bloom
**Medium** still life by S. Davis
**MEEHAN, Thomas**, 1923-
Day of mountain flowers        OYB
OYB. Annual 1953
OYB. Supplement

**MEEKER, Dean Jackson,** 1920-
Don Quixote
 IU. Contemp Amer ptg & sculp, 1953
King's joke                               WiMiA
 CoS. New accessions USA, 1956
**MEEKER, Joseph Rusling,** 1827-1889
In the swamp opposite Bayou Sara
 Rathbone
Land of Evangeline                        MoSL
 Baur. Amer ptg
 Born
 MoSL. Handbook 1953
 Pierson
Meerschaum pipe by W. M. Harnett
**MEERT, Joseph John Paul,** 1905-
Motif in pink
 IU. Contemp Amer ptg & sculp, 1955
Still life on a sewing machine
 PA. Annual ex, 1950
The meeting by J. Corbino
Meeting of the three by F. Ruvolo
**MEGARGEE, Lon,** 1886-
Cowboy and his lady
 NYG. Fine art
Desert song
 NYG. Fine art
Donkey business
 NYG. Fine art
Home on the ranch
 NYG. Fine art
Saturday night on the ranch
 NYG. Fine art
**MEIGS, Walter,** 1918-
Still life with milk bottle
 IU. Contemp Amer ptg & sculp, 1953
White mist to greens
 ICA. Annual ex, 1961
**MEITZLER, Neil,** 1930-
Edge of evening
 IU. Contemp Amer ptg & sculp, 1959
Time of change
 OrPA. Ptgs & sculptures
Melancholia by K. Zerbe
Mélancholie by E. Berman
**MELCARTH, Edward,** 1915-
Ajax
 ICA. Annual ex, 1945/46 (cover)
For God must have loved them
 Genauer
Litter
 PPC. Ptg in the U.S. 1949
The sleepers
 ICA. Annual ex, 1951
String of pearls
 PPC. International ex, 1952
Washerwomen
 WMAA. Contemp Amer ptg, 1952
**MELCHERS, Gari,** 1860-1932
Arranging the tulips                      DNC
 DNC. Gellatly coll, 1954
Fencing master                            MiD
 MiD. Treasures
 Pierson
In my garden                              OYB
 OYB. Catalogue 1951
Madonna                                   MM
 MM. 100 Amer ptrs
Mrs Samuel Mountfort Pitts                MiD
 MiD. Ports of the Pitts family
Mother and child                          ICA
 NYG. Fine art

Penelope                                  DC
 NYG. Fine art
Thomas Pitts                              MiD
 MiD. Ports of the Pitts family
Thomas Pitts, Head of                     MiD
 MiD. Ports of the Pitts family
Mellow pad by S. Davis
Melon by B. Bomar
Melon, peaches and grapes by Rubens Peale
Melons and grapes by Chipman
Melons and morning glories by Raphaelle
 Peale
Melons and other fruit by Unidentified
 artist
Melting horizon by I. R. Pereira
Melville, Deborah (Scollay). See Scollay,
 Deborah
Melville, Mrs John. See Scollay, Deborah
Melville, Maria (Gansevoort) 1791-1872
 Ames, E. Mrs Allan Melville
Member of a city cast no 9 by N. Carone
Mementos by M. M. Koffler
Memo by S. Davis
Memorial by J. Hirsch
Memorial day by A. N. Wyeth
Memories by L. K. Bruckman
Memories by K. Okada
Memories by W. Quirt
Memories of Andalusia by H. G. Keller
Memories of the Stork club by R. Marsh
Memory by L. Beck
Memory of Ischia by E. Berman
Men and mountain by P. Evergood
Men fighting and stars in the Solomons by
 B. L. Culwell
Men of progress: American inventors, 1861
 by J. Sartain (after Christian Schus-
 sele)
Men of the docks by G. W. Bellows
Men of the open range by C. M. Russell
Men without women by S. Davis
Men working by K. Sage
Mending by I. Bishop
Mending fence by E. F. Spruce
Mending the harness by A. P. Ryder
Mending the nets by A. P. Ryder
**MENG, John,** 1734-c 1754
Self-portrait                             PH
 Chew. 250 years of art
**MENKES, Sigmund,** 1896-
The blues singer
 NAD. Annual ex, 1953
Boy playing harmonica                     MMA
 Pousette-Dart. Amer ptg
Boy with doves no 3
 PPC. International ex, 1952
Day's end
 DC. 20 biennial ex, 1947
 IU. Contemp Amer ptg, 1948
 UNESCO. 1860-1949
 UNESCO. 1860-1955
Field flowers
 CSFP. Annual ex, 1948/49
Figure in pictorial space
 PPC. Ptg in the U.S. 1949

MENKÈS, Sigmund—*Continued*
  Fruit bowl with mirror
    IU. Contemp Amer ptg, 1949
  Girl holding a dog
    IU. Contemp Amer ptg & sculp, 1953
  Girl with fruit bowl                    MnMW
    CoS. New accessions USA, 1950
  The painter                             WMAA
    Pierson
  Repose
    Genauer (col)
  Self-portrait
    NAD. Annual ex, 1948
  Still life in gold and green
    CanO. Hirshhorn coll
  Still life with blue vase
    PA. Annual ex, 1956
  White lilac
    NAD. Annual ex, 1959
Menkès, Zygmund. See Menkès, Sigmund
Me-no-quet, a Pottawattomie chief by J. O.
    Lewis
Mental geography by L. Guglielmi
Merced river, Yosemite valley by A. Bier-
    stadt
Mercer, Charles Fenton, 1778-1858
  Malbone, E. G. Charles Fenton Mercer
Mercer, Hugh, c 1725-1777
  Trumbull, J. Death of Gen Mercer at the
    Battle of Princeton
MERCER, William, 1773?-1850?
  Battle of Princeton, 1777               NJP
    Davidson v 1
  Battle of Princeton, 1777               PH
    U.S. National Capital sesquicentennial
    com
The merchant by R. B. Crafft
Merchants' exchange and Girard's bank,
    Philadelphia, View of by N. V. Calyo
Merganser duck by W. M. Harnett
Mermaid by M. A. Willson
MERRETT, Susan, fl 1848
  Fourth of July picnic
    Born
    Ford. Pictorial folk art
MERRILD, Knud, 1894-1954
  Decay and resurrection
    IU. Contemp Amer ptg, 1952
MERRILL, Sarah, fl 1810
  Mourning picture
    Ford. Pictorial folk art
Merrill, Sarah, 1813-1896. See Pitts, Sarah
    (Merrill)
Merritt parkway by W. De Kooning
Merry bench by A. Etherovich
Merry-go-rounds
  Bohrod, A. Merry-go-round
  Carter, C. H. Carousel by the sea
  Marsh, R. Merry-go-round
  Prendergast, M. B. Flying horses
  Prendergast, M. B. Merry-go-round
Mesa Grande by H. Aach
Mesa Verde by R. Haines
Message by M. Graves
Message for mercy by G. Abercrombie
The messenger by R. Ray
The messenger by J. C. Wayne
Metamorphosis by F. Ruvolo
Metamorphosis by T. Takai

METCALF, Willard Leroy, 1858-1925
  Golden carnival                         NR
    NYG. Fine art
  May night                               DC
    DC. 25 biennial ex, 1957
  North country                           MM
    NYG. Fine art
  November mosaic                         CtNB
    NYG. Fine art
  October morning, Deerfield, Massachusetts
                                          DF
    Born
Meteorite by E. A. Donati
Methodist church, Provincetown by E.
    Hopper
Metope by C. Oscar
Metronome by W. T. Murch
Metropolis by G. Grosz
The Metropolitan museum in Fourteenth
    street, 1881 by F. Waller
Metropolitan nocturne by M. Friedman
MEURER, Charles Alfred, b 1865
  Doughboy's equipment
    Frankenstein. After the hunt
  The pen is mightier than the sword
    Frankenstein. After the hunt
Mexican meat market by K. F. Feuerherm
Mexican news by R. C. Woodville
Mexican platter by K. Knaths
Mexican ruin by H. Sternberg
Mexican vase with flowers by A. F. Levin-
    son
Mexico
  Berman, E. Apotheosis of Mexican ba-
    roque
  Berman, E. Mexican pyramid—the living
    and the dead
  Berman, E. Perspective of Mexican hill
    town
  Burg, C. C. Mexican landscape
  Chapman, C. W. Panorama; the valley of
    Mexico
  Fausett, W. D. Cuernavaca
  Hirsch, S. Pic of Orizaba
  Macknight, D. Along the road, Cordoba,
    Mexico
  Macknight, D. Cuautla, Mexico
  Macknight, D. Environs of Jalapa, Mexico
  Macknight, D. In the valley
  Ray, R. D. Manzanillo, Mexico
  Rosenthal, D. Mexican church
  Zerbe, K. Street in Tepoztlan, Mexico
Meyer de Schauensee sisters
  Watkins, F. C. Misses Maude and Maxine
    Meyer de Schauensee
MEYEROWITZ, William, 1893-
  Joel
    NAD. Annual ex, 1949, 1st half
MEYR, Christian
  Fire masters and officers of volunteer fire
    companies of Charleston, 1840
    Davidson v2
MICHAEL, Lily, 1912-
  Duel and pantomime
    IU. Contemp Amer ptg, 1952
Michel's house by H. M. Gasser
MICHELSON, Leo, 1887-
  Fishermen on the Seine
    NSP. Sportscapes
Michigan landscape by L. Ritman
Micro-macrocosmic landscape by H. Lunde-
    berg

**Microscopic** by L. E. Kuperman

**Middlecott, Richard,** fl 1713
Byfield, N. Richard Middlecott

**Middleton, Alicia Hopton (Russell)** See Russell, Alicia Hopton

**Middleton, Arthur,** fl 1771
West, B. Arthur Middleton, his wife and son

**Middleton, Mrs Arthur.** See Russell, Alicia Hopton

**MIDDLETON, John Izard,** 1785-1849
General view of the site of the ancient city of Norba          MCH
Richardson. Ptg in America

**MIDDLETON, Thomas,** 1797-1863
Interior of the Second street Philip's church, Charleston, South Carolina, 1836
U.S. National Capital sesquicentennial com

**Midi** by S. Davis

**Mid-June** by C. E. Burchfield

**Midnight** by F. Hillsmith

**Midnight** by H. Mandel

**Midnight** quarry by W. Thon

**Midnight** ride of Paul Revere by G. Wood

**Midsummer** phlox by H. Pittman

**Midtown,** New York by J. Marin

**Midwest** by C. Sheeler

**MIFFLIN, Lloyd,** 1846-1921
View of the Susquehanna, below Wrightsville, Pennsylvania
Chew. 250 years of art
View of the Susquehanna, Wrightsville, Pennsylvania
Chew. 250 years of art

**Mifflin, Sarah (Morris)** 1747?-1790
Copley, J. S. Mr and Mrs Thomas Mifflin

**Mifflin, Thomas,** 1744-1800
Copley, J. S. Mr and Mrs Thomas Mifflin
West, B. Thomas Mifflin

**Migration** by W. Gropper

**Migration** of the Negro by J. Lawrence

**Migration** to nowhere by R. Lebrun

**Mike** and the chart by W. Peirce

**Milan, Italy**
Heade, J. Impressions of Milan

**MILBOURNE, Charles,** fl 1790
Government house, Bowling Green, New York, 1797          NNHS
Dickson. John Wesley Jarvis

**Mile** drive, California by D. Kingman

**Mile** high by G. Peirce

**Miles, Ruth (Henshaw)** See Bascom, Ruth (Henshaw) Miles

**Miles** and the governess by C. H. Demuth

**Miles City,** Montana by H. Steiffel

**Milford,** North Wales, Pennsylvania by T. Birch

**Milford,** North Wales, Pennsylvania by Dietz

**Military** by M. Hartley

**Military** necessity by A. Bohrod

**Militia** muster by D. C. Johnston

**Milk** sledge by P. S. Sample

**Milking** time by W. Homer

**Milkman** by N. V. Calyo

**Milkman** and the maid by W. J. Hubard

**Milkman** of Goshen by H. Pippin

The **mill** by Unidentified artist

The **mill** boy by G. C. Bingham

**Mill** entrance by G. Breckner

**Mill** race by S. Andrews

**Mill** stream by W. L. Stevens

**Mill** wheel by L. Powell

**MILLARC, William,** 1920-
The beast
IU. Contemp Amer ptg, 1950

**MILLER, Alfred Jacob,** 1810-1874
American fur company caravan en route to Wyoming, 1837          MdBW
Davidson v 1
Antoine Clement          MdBW
Miller, A. J. The West
Approaching buffalo [1]          MdBW
Miller, A. J. The West
Approaching buffalo [2]          MdBW
Miller, A. J. The West
Arapahos          MdBW
Miller, A. J. The West
Argali—mountain sheep          MdBW
Miller, A. J. The West
Aricara female          MdBW
Miller, A. J. The West
Attack by Crow Indians          MdBW
Miller, A. J. The West
Auguste and his horse          MdBW
Miller, A. J. The West
Bannock, Indian          MdBW
Miller, A. J. The West
Beating a retreat          MB
MB. Karolik coll
Pierson
Beating a retreat          MdBW
Miller, A. J. The West
Bee hunter          MdBW
Miller, A. J. The West
Big Bowl (a Crow chief)          MdBW
Miller, A. J. The West
Black Hills          MdBW
Miller, A. J. The West
The Blackfeet          MdBW
Miller, A. J. The West
Bourgouis W---r and his squaw          MdBW
Miller, A. J. The West
The bravado          MdBW
Baum. Amer ptg
Miller, A. J. The West
Breakfast at sunrise          MdBW
Miller, A. J. The West
Breaking up camp at sunrise          MdBW
Miller, A. J. The West
Buffalo at bay          MdBW
Miller, A. J. The West
Buffalo chase—by a female          MdBW
Miller, A. J. The West
Buffalo hunting near Independence rock          MdBW
Miller, A. J. The West
Buffalo turning on his pursuers          MdBW
Miller, A. J. The West
Buffaloes drinking and bathing at night          MdBW
Miller, A. J. The West
Rathbone
Bull-boating          MdBW
Miller, A. J. The West
Rathbone

MILLER, Barse, 1904-
Bristol mills OYB
OYB. Catalogue 1951
Mud hook
NAD. Annual ex, 1958
Parish playground
NAD. Annual ex, autumn 1949
Waterfall
NAD. Annual ex, 1951
MILLER, Charles F. fl 1850
Seven Sisters mountain
Chew. 250 years of art
MILLER, Kenneth Hayes, 1876-1952
Albert P. Ryder DP
DP. Catalogue
Bargain hunters WMAA
WMAA. Sara Roby
Box party WMAA
McCurdy
Pierson
The fitting room MM
MM. 100 Amer ptrs
Pierson
Fourteenth street
Brown. Amer ptg
Landscape with a broken tree
NAD. Annual ex, 1948
Little coat and fur shop
NYG. Fine art
Reverie
ICA. Annual ex, 1945/46
Shopper WMAA
Goodrich. Amer art
Larkin
Larkin rev ed
Wight. Milestones
Show window no 2
Gruskin
MILLER, Lewis
Hydrant water conveyed through wooden
pipes, 1816, York, Pennsylvania
Davidson v2
MILLER, William R. fl 1853-1869
Old mill by waterfall
Sears. Highlights
MILLMAN, Edward, 1907-
Invasion
Pousette-Dart. Amer ptg
Night chant
MM. Amer ptg today
Mills
Boit, E. D. Old mill near St Enogat, Brittany
Breckner, G. Mill entrance
Chapin, J. B. Old mill, Hanover, New Hampshire
Cole, T. Old mill at sunset
Durrie, G. H. Old mill, winter
Durrie, G. H. Sunset, Mount Carmel, Connecticut
Durrie, G. H. Winter in the country, the old grist mill
Inness, G. Old mill
Johnson, D. Old mill, West Milford, New Jersey
Kachmer, G. Winter along the mills
Lawson, E. Old mill
Miller, B. Bristol mills
Miller, W. R. Old mill by waterfall
Moses, A. M. R. The red mill
Unidentified artist. Mill of C. J. Hill & Son

Unidentified artist. Old mill
Unidentified artist. Pennsylvania mill with Conestoga wagon
Unidentified artist. Red mill
Wall, W. C. Homestead mill near Pittsburgh
Mills residence, Ames, New York by Unidentified artist
MILNE, A. 19th cent
Smithtown, Long Island, c 1860 MSM
Davidson v 1
Milnor, Joseph Kirkbride, 1775-1828
Malbone, E. G. Joseph K. Milnor II
Milton, Massachusetts with Flat pond and buildings, View near by D. C. Johnston
Mime by M. Ray
Mine disaster by P. Evergood
Mine disaster by B. Shahn
Miners resting by P. S. Sample
Miners' wives by B. Shahn
Minerva, Head of by W. M. Harnett
MINGLE, fl 1878
Victorian building MeC
Jetté. Amer heritage collection
Mink and mannequin by R. Marsh
Minneapolis grain elevator by R. Crawford
Minnehaha, Death of by F. Remington
Minnesota in August by A. A. Dehn
The Minnetaree scalp dance by K. Bodmer
Minnetarees on the Upper Missouri by F. Kurz
Minot, Mrs Stephen, fl 1805
Trumbull, J. Mrs Stephen Minot
Minot, Mrs William. See Sedgwick, Katherine
Minsky's chorus by R. Marsh
Minstrel banjo player by D. Morrill
Minstrel show by C. Winter
Minthorne, Hannah. See Tomkins, Hannah (Minthorne)
MINTZ, Harry, 1907-
One day in spring
IU. Contemp Amer ptg, 1948
Self-portrait
CSFP. Annual ex, 1946
View of Toledo, Spain
IU. Contemp Amer ptg & sculp, 1961
MINTZ, Raymond August, 1925-
Artist's studio
CSFP. Annual ex, 1952
The kitchen
IU. Contemp Amer ptg, 1952
The sink
ICA. Annual ex, 1951
Window
IU. Contemp Amer ptg & sculp, 1959
MIRA, Alfred S. 1900-
Washington monument, Washington square, N.Y.
PPC. Ptg in the U.S. 1949
Mirabilia by L. Feitelson
The miracle by S. G. Reinhardt
Mirage by T. D. Benrimo
Mirage by E. A. Chavez
Mirage of time by Y. Tanguy
Mirage—ships at night by W. Zorach
The mirror by M. Beckmann

The **mirror** by W. M. Chase
The **mirror** by P. Guston
The **mirror** by Y. Kuniyoshi
The **mirror** by H. Lundeberg
The **mirror** by P. Tchelitchew
**Mirsky, D. S.**
    Evergood, P. M. T. Florinsky, D. S. Mirsky and the pidget
**Miss** C. Parsons as the Lady of the Lake by T. Sully
**Miss** Liberty by Unidentified artist
**Mississippi** girl by M. Greenwood
**Mississippi river and valley**
    Curry, J. S. The Mississippi
    Kingman, H. M. Mississippi river landing
    Palmer, F. F. Champions of the Mississippi
    Palmer, F. F. Wooding up on the Mississippi
    Sebron, V. V. Sugar levee, New Orleans
    Walker, W. A. Scene along the lower Mississippi
    Wild, J. C. Dubuque, Iowa
    Wild, J. C. View of Davenport, Iowa and the Mississippi
**Missouri** mural by T. H. Benton
**Missouri river and valley**
    Bingham, G. C. Fur traders descending the Missouri
    Bingham, G. C. Missouri landscape
    Catlin, G. Upper Missouri: grand detour
    Catlin, G. View on the upper Missouri—Riccaree village
**Mist** by D. Macknight
**Mist** in the Yellowstone by T. Moran
**Mr** Ace by Y. Kuniyoshi
**Mr** River's garden by A. N. Wyeth
**Mrs** Besant takes action by G. Russell
**Mrs** Gamley by G. B. Luks
**Mrs** McCormick's general store, Catskill, N.Y. by A. Del O. Browere
**Mrs** S by T. Eakins
**Mrs** Starke's brother of Troy by Unidentified artist
**Mrs** T in cream silk by G. W. Bellows
**Mrs** T in wine silk by G. W. Bellows
**Misty** day in March by E. Lawson
**Misty** ocean by G. Peterdi
**MITCHELL, Bruce,** 1908-1963
    Fire island landing      MM
      NYG. Fine art
    Hudson autumn      ATU
      ATU. Coll of Amer art
      Gruskin (col)
    Mauch Chunk, Pennsylvania      ATU
      ATU. Coll of Amer art
**MITCHELL, Fred,** 1923-
    White, black and red
      NNSG. Younger Amer ptrs
**MITCHELL, Joan,** 1926-
    Cafe
      OCl. Some contemporary works
    George went swimming at Barnes hole, but it got too cold      NBuA
      NBuA. Acquisitions 1957-58
    Hemlock
      Baur. Nature
    King of spades
      OCl. Some contemporary works

Marlin
    PPC. International ex, 1961/62
Painting, 1953      MnMW
    MnMW. 60 Amer ptrs
Ste Hilaire
    DC. 26 biennial ex, 1959
To the harbourmaster      PPC
    Read. Concise history
**Mitchell, Margaret.** See Sewall, Margaret (Mitchell)
**MITCHELL, Wallace,** 1911-
Processional
    MnMW. Classic tradition
**Mix, John,** fl 1788
    Unidentified artist. John Mix
**Mix, Ruth (Stanley)** b 1756
    Unidentified artist. Mrs Ruth Stanley Mix
**Moby** Dick by W. A. Baziotes
**Moby** Dick by K. Knaths
**Moby** Dick by B. Robinson
**Mocking** soldier by R. Lebrun
**Mockingbird** with rattlesnake robbing nest by J. J. Audubon
**MODEL, Evsa,** 1900-
    Uptown
      MMA. Abstract
The **model** by W. M. Chase
The **model** by I. Soyer
**Model** in dressing room by J. Sloan
**Model** in the studio by G. Grosz
**Modern** classic by C. Sheeler
**Modern** conveniences by C. H. Demuth
**Modern** inquisitor by P. Evergood
**MOFCHUM, Gerald**
    Listening to the voice of stone
      NAD. Annual ex, 1958
    Shadow and substance
      NAD. Annual ex, 1957
**Moffatt, Catherine (Cutt)** 1700-1769
    Greenwood, J. Mrs John Moffatt
**Moffatt, Elizabeth,** b 1725
    Greenwood, J. Elizabeth Moffatt
**Moffatt, John,** 1692-1786
    Greenwood, J. John Moffatt
**Moffatt, Mrs John.** See Moffatt, Catherine (Cutt)
**Mohawk valley**
    Hammer, J. J. Peaceful day in the Mohawk valley
    Havell, R. (attributed works) Mohawk valley
    Unidentified artist. Mohawk valley
    Wyant, A. H. Mohawk valley
**MOHOLY-NAGY, László,** 1895-1946
    Ch Beata 1, 1939      NNSG
      50 years of mod art
    Chicago space no 7, 1941      NNSG
      MnMW. Classic tradition
    G-5, 1923-26      CtY
      CtY. Soc Anonyme
    Space modulator      WMAA
      Goodrich. Amer art
      Pierson
**Mojave** by J. Ferren
**MOLLER, Hans,** 1905-
    Chess players
      Genauer (col)
    Clown
      DC. 22 biennial ex, 1951

Cock fight
  IU. Contemp Amer ptg, 1949
Composition
  IU. Contemp Amer ptg, 1952
Crown of thorns
  Pierson
  WMAA. Annual ex, 1958
Emerald
  IU. Contemp Amer ptg & sculp, 1957
Flutes
  IU. Contemp Amer ptg & sculp, 1953
Forsythias
  Baur. Nature (col)
Music
  IU. Contemp Amer ptg & sculp, 1955
Reflections
  NBuA. Expressionism
Station of the Cross
  IU. Contemp Amer ptg & sculp, 1959
Still life with hourglass
  DC. 20 biennial ex, 1947
Towards Monhegan
  DC. 27 biennial ex, 1961
Winter
  VR. Biennial ex, 1948
Woodpile
  IU. Contemp Amer ptg, 1950
**MOLZAHN, Johannes,** 1892-
  Icarus
    Rathbun
  Phenomena                                    CtY
    CtY. Soc Anonyme
**Moment** in time by S. Rosenberg
The **moment** that makes duck hunting by
  R. M. Mason
**Momentous** vision of spring by G. Brody
**MOMMER, Paul,** 1899-1963
  Studio interior no 2
    Pousette-Dart. Amer ptg
**Mom's** cathedral by P. Evergood
**Monarch** of Bermuda by R. Marsh
**Monday** night at the Metropolitan by R.
  Marsh
**Money** by A. Leslie
**Money** diggers by J. Quidor
**Monhegan** by R. M. Farruggio
**Monhegan** hill by L. J. Liberté
**Monhegan** theme by L. Dodd
**Monitor** and Merrimac by J. Hamilton
The **monk** by G. Inness
**Monk** in white by N. Carone
**Monkey** bars by H. Koerner
**Monkeys**
  Trivigno, P. Captives
  Tschacbasov, N. The monkey
  Watkins, F. C. Make the monkey jump
**Monks** fishing, Venice by L. Bosa
**Monks** of Burano by L. Bosa
**Monmouth, James Scott, duke of,** 1649-1685
  Copley, J. S. Arrest of Monmouth before
    James II
The **Monongahela,** Scene on by E. Bott
**Monongahela** bridge after the freshet in 1832
  by R. Smith
**Monongahela** river opposite Pittsburgh by
  R. Smith
**Monreale** by J. E. Heliker
**Monroe, James, president U.S.** 1758-1831
  Stuart, G. James Monroe

**Monroe, Marilyn,** 1926-1962
  De Kooning, W. Marilyn Monroe
**Mont** St Michel by J. T. Arms
**Montague,** Massachusetts, Gentleman from,
  by Unidentified artist
**Montague,** Massachusetts, Lady from, by
  Unidentified artist
**MONTALANT, Joseph O.** fl 1855
  Site of Azilum
    McClintock
  The Susquehanna
    McClintock
  Tioga point valley
    McClintock
  Wyalusing
    McClintock
**Montauk** fisherman by C. Hassam
**Montauk** highway by W. De Kooning
**Montauk** montage by R. B. Motherwell
**Monte** Video, summer home of Daniel Wads-
  worth by T. Cole
**Monte** Video, View of by T. Cole
**Montesquiou-Fezensac, Robert, Comte de,**
  1797-1850
  Whistler, J. A. M. Comte Robert de
    Montesquiou-Fezensac
**Montezuma** alarmed by evil signs by L. Sie-
  griest
**Montgomery, Mrs James**
  Sully, T. Mrs James Montgomery
**Montgomery, Mrs John,** fl 1800
  Peale, Raphaelle. Mrs John Montgomery
**Montgomery, Rachel (Harvey)** fl 1781
  Malbone, E. G. Mrs William Montgomery
**Montgomery, Richard,** 1736?-1775
  Trumbull, J. Death of Gen Montgomery
    at Quebec
**Montmartre** by O. M. Pleissner
**Montmartre** impasse by W. A. Smith
**Montparnasse,** Paris by M. B. Prendergast
**Montresor, John,** fl 1772
  Copley, J. S. Col John Montresor (Wil-
    liam? Montresor)
**Montserrat** by K. Schrag
The **monument** by H. Koerner
**Monument** in the plaza by J. Sloan
**Monument** mountain, Berkshires by A. B.
  Durand
**Monument** to light by B. Greene
**Monument** valley by J. C. Haley
**Monumentality** by G. Greene
**Mood** by A. Brook
**Mood** indigo by C. Seliger
The **mood** of now by Y. Tanguy
**Moon** by A. G. Dove
**Moon** by K. Knaths
**Moon** and locomotive by D. Kingman
**Moon** and shoals by R. Tam
**Moon** animal by W. A. Baziotes
**Moon** bathers by F. Puma
**Moon** fantasy by W. A. Baziotes
**Moon** forms by W. A. Baziotes
**Moon** mad crow in the surf by M. Graves
**Moon** maiden by P. Evergood
**Moon** song by D. Austin
**Moon** vibrations by J. Pollock
**Moon** woman cuts a circle by J. Pollock

**MOONEY, Edward Ludlow,** 1813-1887
Mrs Robert Maitland                NNHS
    NNHS. Waldron Phoenix Belknap coll
Robert Maitland                    NNHS
    NNHS. Waldron Phoenix Belknap coll
Mooney, Thomas J. Zechariah, 1885-1942
    Shahn, B. Rena and Tom Mooney
**Moonflowers** at dusk by C. E. Burchfield
**Moonlight** by R. A. Blakelock
**Moonlight** by J. W. Casilear
**Moonlight** by Corbino
**Moonlight** by J. De Martini
**Moonlight** by L. MacIver
**Moonlight** by A. P. Ryder
**Moonlight** at sea by A. P. Ryder
**Moonlight**—camp scene by A. J. Miller
**Moonlight,** harbour town by K. Knaths
**Moonlight,** Indian encampment by R. A.
    Blakelock
**Moonlight** landscape by R. A. Blakelock
**Moonlight** marine by A. P. Ryder
**Moonlight** on Passamaquoddy bay by G.
    Innes
**Moonlight** on the sea by A. P. Ryder
**Moonlight** on the waters by A. P. Ryder
**Moonlight** scene by G. C. Bingham
**Moonlight** sonata by R. A. Blakelock
**Moonlight** stampede by G. C. Delano
**Moonlight,** Tarpon Springs by G. Inness
**Moonlit** cove by A. P. Ryder
**Moonlit** landscape by W. Allston
**Moonlit** landscape by H. E. Mattson
**Moonrise,** marine by A. P. Ryder
**Moonrise**—northern Arizona by J. E. Swin-
    nerton
**Moonset** and sunrise by M. T. Zorach
**Moonshine** fantasy by O. F. Bluemner
**Moor** swan by M. Graves
Moore, Almira (Gallond) fl 1840
    Field, E. S. Mrs Joseph Moore
**MOORE, Charles Herbert,** 1840-1930
    Down the Hudson to West Point   NPV
    Born
    Old bridge                      NJP
    Baur. Revolution
    Born
Moore, Elizabeth (Vander Horst) 1737-1790
    Theus, J. Mrs John Moore
Moore, Hannah. See Peale, Hannah (Moore)
**MOORE, Harriet,** b 1812
    Richardson memorial            NCHA
    Time. 300 years (col)
Moore, Joseph, fl 1840
    Field, E. S. Joseph Moore and his family
Moore, Mrs John. See Moore, Elizabeth
    (Vander Horst)
Moore, Mrs Joseph. See Moore, Almira
    (Gallond)
**Moorland** landscape by B. West (attributed
    works)
The **moors** by K. Knaths
**Moose.** See Deer
**Moose** hunters' camp, Nova Scotia by A.
    Bierstadt

Mopp, Maximilian. See Oppenheimer, Max
**MORAN, Edward,** 1829-1901
    Duck shooting
    NSP. Sportscapes
    Unveiling the statue of Liberty, 1886
    U. S. National Capital sesquicentennial
    com
**MORAN, Thomas,** 1837-1926
    Arizona sunset near the Grand Canyon
                                    OYB
    OYB. Supplement 1959
    Bringing home the cattle—coast of Florida
                                    NBuA
    NBuA. Catalogue of the ptgs
    Chasm of the Colorado           DCap
    Born
    Cliffs of the Green river, Wyoming DNC
    Rathbone
    Cliffs of the Upper Colorado river, Wyo-
        ming territory              DNC
    Born
    Pierson
    Giant blue spring, Yellowstone region
    Rathbone
    Grand Canyon of the Yellowstone river
                                    DN
    Pierson
    Hot Springs near the Yellowstone
    Rathbone
    Lower Manhattan from Communipaw
                                    MdHW
    NJN. Early N. J. artists
    Mist in the Yellowstone
    McCracken. Portrait of the old west
        (col)
    Spirit of the Indian            OkT
    McCracken. Portrait of the old west
    Teton range                     MM
    Bazin
    Davidson v2
    Mendelowitz
    Myers. Art
    View of Venice                  DC
    Chew. 250 years of art
    Western landscape               CtNB
    Barker. Amer ptg
    Rathbone
**MORE, Hermon,** 1887-
    Rocky hillside                  WMAA
    Goodrich. Amer art
Morehouse, Henry A. b 1816
    Unidentified artist. Henry A. Morehouse
**MOREHOUSE, William P.** 1929-
    The green one
    WMAA. Contemp Amer ptg, 1959/60
    Number 509—blue
    IU. Contemp Amer ptg & sculp, 1961
    Vertical
    NNSG. Younger Amer ptrs
Morgan, Charles S. 1799-1859
    Unidentified artist. Morgan addressing his
        friends
Morgan, Daniel, c 1736-1802
    Trumbull, J. Daniel Morgan
**MORGAN, Maud (Cabot)** 1903-
    Descension
    IU. Contemp Amer ptg, 1951
    Pousette-Dart. Amer ptg
    In the beginning
    Rathbun
Morgan, Mrs Patrick Henry. See Morgan,
    Maud (Cabot)

**MORGAN, Randall,** 1920-
Hill town in Campania
  MnMW. Contemporary
  WMAA. Neuberger collection
Mediterranean night
  MMA. Abstract
Port at night                                        WMAA
  Pierson
Ravello
  WMAA. Contemp Amer ptg, 1949
Warehouse
  McCurdy
**Morning** by S. Burpee (attributed works)
**Morning** by A. Ippolito
**Morning** by L. Manso
**Morning** by E. K. Schwabacher
**Morning** by Z. L. Sepeshy
**Morning** by B. Shahn
**Morning** at Gargagno, Lake of Garda by E. D. Boit
**Morning** at Riva, Lake of Garda by E. D. Boit
**Morning** bell at a New England factory by W. Homer
**Morning** candelabra by P. É. Borduas
**Morning-glories** by W. Homer
**Morning** glow, autumn by W. Zorach
**Morning** hour by C. A. Morris
**Morning** in a city by E. Hopper
**Morning** in May by R. Marsh
**Morning** in the Blue Ridge mountains by W. L. Sonntag
**Morning** mist by H. Hofmann
**Morning** near Paris by E. D. Boit
**Morning** of life by A. B. Durand
**Morning** of November first by J. E. Wagner
**Morning,** Paris café by G. P. Du Bois
**Morning** sea by M. Avery
**Morning** snow by G. W. Bellows
**Morning** toilet by M. Cassatt
**Morning,** Upper Frazer river by H. G. Keller
**Morocco**
  Macknight, D. Outside the walls, Marrakech, Morocco
  Macknight, D. Palms with ripe dates, Morocco
  Macknight, D. White town, Azemmour, Morocco
**MORRILL, D.**
Minstrel banjo player                                CtHW
  Ford. Pictorial folk art
**Morris, Anna Maria** (Hollingsworth) 1783-1847
  Sully, T. Mrs John Boucher Morris
**MORRIS, Carl A.** 1911-
Audition
  Morley. Carl Morris
Autumn
  Pierson
Autumn migration
  IU. Contemp Amer ptg & sculp, 1959
Beach patterns
  Morley. Carl Morris
Blue canyon
  Morley. Carl Morris
Boy with chalice                                     CSFM
  Morley. **Carl Morris**

**Brown painting**                                   NNSG
  NNSG. Handbook
  NNSG. Younger Amer ptrs
  Read. Concise ptg
Calm horizon
  Morley. Carl Morris
Canyon mosaic
  Morley. Carl Morris
Dock
  Morley. Carl Morris
Dwelling
  ICA. Annual ex, 1951
Elements of structure
  Morley. Carl Morris
Embarkation
  Morley. Carl Morris
Emerging forms
  Morley. Carl Morris
Expanding elements no 1, 1958
  Morley. Carl Morris
Expanding elements no 2, 1958
  Morley. Carl Morris
Five panels
  WMAA. Annual ex, 1955
Imprisoned force
  Morley. Carl Morris
Industrial facade                                    MM
  Morley. Carl Morris
Lifting night
  Morley. Carl Morris
Lights
  WMAA. Annual ex, 1957
Machine no 2, 1951                                   CSFM
  Morley. Carl Morris
Man-made man, bewildered by nature
  Morley. Carl Morris
New shores
  Morley. Carl Morris
Night figures
  Morley. Carl Morris
Night image
  ICA. Annual ex, 1961
Night river                                          CSFP
  Morley. Carl Morris
Out of the Coulee                                    WaS
  Morley. Carl Morris
Quiet river
  Morley. Carl Morris
Red forest                                           WaS
  Morley. Carl Morris
Reflected verticals                                  CSB
  Morley. Carl Morris
Restless horizon
  Morley. Carl Morris
Riders no 10                                         WaS
  Pousette-Dart. Amer ptg
Rising city
  Morley. Carl Morris (col)
River night                                          CSFP
  CoS. New accessions USA, 1958
Rockbound forms
  Morley. Carl Morris
Seawall
  IU. Contemp Amer ptg & sculp, 1957
Seed
  WMAA. Contemp Amer ptg, 1949
Solids into blue
  Morley. Carl Morris (col)
Still harbor
  Morley. Carl Morris
Stone matrix                                         WMAA
  Morley. Carl Morris
Striated forest
  Morley. Carl Morris

**MORRIS, C. A.**—*Continued*
  Suede and tiger stripe no 2, 1957
    Morley. Carl Morris
  Time enclosure
    Morley. Carl Morris
  Tower
    Morley. Carl Morris
  Turbulent forest             NBuA
    Morley. Carl Morris
  Vertical
    Morley. Carl Morris
  The wave
    Morley. Carl Morris
  White tablet
    Morley. Carl Morris
  Written in stone            OrPa
    CoS. New accessions USA, 1956
    Morley. Carl Morris
  Yellow arc
    IU. Contemp Amer ptg & sculp, 1961
  Yellow light              IU
    Morley. Carl Morris
    OrPa. Ptgs & sculptures (col)
**MORRIS, George Lovett Kingsland,** 1905-
  Black roses
    CSFP. Annual ex, 1948/49
  Composition, 1940          PPhM
    PPhM. Gallatin coll
  Concretion
    McCurdy
    MMA. Abstract
  Converging disks
    MnMW. Classic tradition
  East river nocturne
    IU. Contemp Amer ptg & sculp, 1953
  Fourteenth street promenade
    ICA. Annual ex, 1954
  I.R.T.
    Pearson. Mod renaissance
  Industrial landscape
    Pousette-Dart. Amer ptg
  Mauve recession
    CtY. Yale alumni
  Nautical composition       WMAA
    Goodrich. Amer art
    Pierson
  Orvieto               IBM
    Pearson. Mod renaissance
  Percussion
    NNS. Younger Amer ptrs
  Precision bombing
    Read. Art now, 1948 ed
  Pursuit in depth
    IU. Contemp Amer ptg & sculp, 1959
  Recessional
    ICA. Annual ex, 1951
  Saks Fifth Avenue window
    Pearson. Mod renaissance
  String trio
    Rathbun
  Suspended discs
    Cheney. Story 158 ed
    MMA. Abstract
**Morris, Gouverneur,** 1752-1816
  Ames, E. Gouverneur Morris
**Morris, Harrison S.** 1856-1948
  Eakins, T. Harrison S. Morris
**Morris, Israel W.** 1778-1870
  Malbone, E. G. Israel W. Morris
**Morris, Mrs John Boucher.** See Morris,
  Anna Maria (Hollingsworth)

**MORRIS, Kyle R.** 1918-
  Blue and black         NNSG
    NNSG. Handbook
    NNSG. Younger Amer ptrs
  Evening image
    WMAA. Annual ex, 1958
  Evening, Montauk no 2, 1957
    Brussels. Exposition
  Fluttering pendant
    IU. Contemp Amer ptg & sculp, 1955
  4 September 1960
    IU. Contemp Amer ptg & sculp, 1961
  Green burst           NBuA
    NBuA. Acquisitions 1957-58
  Number 2, 1956
    Baur. Nature
  Number 5
    IU. Contemp Amer ptg & sculp, 1957
  Red flow
    MnMW. 60 Amer ptrs
**Morris, Lewis,** 1671-1746
  Watson, J. Gov Lewis Morris of New
    Jersey
**Morris, Lewis,** 1752-1824
  Malbone, E. G. Col Lewis Morris IV
**Morris, Mary (Hollingsworth)** 1776-1820
  Malbone, E. G. Mrs Israel W. Morris
**Morris, Mary (Philipse)** 1730-1825
  Copley, J. S. Mrs Roger Morris
**Morris, Sarah.** See Mifflin, Sarah (Morris)
**MORRISON, George,** 1919-
  Structural landscape       NeO
    CoS. New accessions USA, 1956
**MORROW, Robert,** 1917-
  Jason              OYB
    OYB. Annual 1950
    OYB. Catalogue 1951
**MORSE, Henry D.** 1826-1888
  Deer in a thicket
    NSP. Sportscapes
**Morse, Isaac Edward,** 1809-1866
  Jarvis, J. W. Isaac Edward Morse
**Morse, Jedidiah,** 1761-1826
  Hancock, N. Jedidiah Morse
**Morse, Lucretia Pickering (Walker)** d 1825
  Morse, S. F. B. Artist's family
**MORSE, Samuel Finley Breese,** 1791-1872
  Alexander Metcalf Fisher     CtY
    Baur. Amer ptg
  Allegorical landscape      NNHS
    Born
  Artist's family
    Flexner. Light of distant skies
  Benjamin Silliman         CtY
    CtY. Portrait index
  Congress hall. See Old House of Repre-
    sentatives
  David C. De Forest        CtY
    CtY. Portrait index
  Dying Hercules          CtY
    Flexner. Light of distant skies
  Eli Whitney            CtY
    CtY. Portrait index
  Frederic Gore King        NAD
    NAD. Amer tradition
  Gallery of the Louvre      NSU
    Barker. Amer ptg
    Larkin
    Larkin rev ed
    Pierson
    Roos
  Jeremiah Day            CtY
    CtY. Portrait index

Katherine Munro of Charleston, South Carolina GAtM
GAtM. Holbrook collection
Lace cap OYB
OYB. Catalogue 1951
Lafayette NNCH
Flexner. Amer ptg
Flexner. Short history
Larkin (detail)
Larkin rev ed
Pierson
Lafayette NNPL
Gardner 1959 ed
Little Miss Hone MB
MB. Karolik coll
Mrs David Mussey MNS
Larkin
Mrs Jane Robinson ATeS
AteS. Collection
Morse family DNC
Flexner. Light of distant skies
The muse, Susan Walker Morse MM
Mendelowitz
Pierson
Nathan Smith CtY
CtY. Portrait index
Niagara Falls from Table Rock MB
MB. Karolik coll
Pierson
Old House of Representatives, 1821-22 (Congress hall) DC
Davidson v2
DC. Masterpieces
Mendelowitz
Pierson
Richardson. Ptg in America (col)
Roos
Time. 300 years (col)
U.S. National Capital sesquicentennial com. 7 (col front)
Sheldon Clark CtY
Bazin
CtY. Portrait index
The shrine
MiD. Travelers in Arcadia
Susan Walker Morse. See The muse
Thomas Harvey Skinner MB
MB. Karolik coll
View from Apple hill, Cooperstown, N.Y.
Barker. Amer ptg
Born
CtY. Yale alumni
Pierson
William Augustus Lawrence NJMo
NJMo. Forty years
NUM. Art across America
William Cullen Bryant NAD
NAD. Annual ex. 1947, 1st half
PPC. Amer classics

Portrait of the artist
Stone, W. O. Samuel F. B. Morse
Morse, Mrs Samuel Finley Breese. See Morse, Lucretia Pickering (Walker)
Morse, Susan Walker, 1819-1885
Morse, S. F. B. The muse: Susan Walker Morse
Morse family by S. F. B. Morse
Mortality and immortality by W. M. Harnett
Morton, Sarah Wentworth (Apthorp) 1759-1846
Stuart, G. Mrs Perez Morton

Mosaics, 1956 (Northeast corner, 711 Third avenue, New York) by H. Hofmann
Mosaics, 1956 (Southwest corner, 711 Third avenue, New York) by H. Hofmann
MOSCA, August, 1909-
Dawn over Fordham
CSFP. Annual ex, 1946
Moseley, Laura (Wolcott) 1761-1814
Earl, R. Mrs William Moseley and her son Charles
MOSES, Anna Mary (Robertson) 1860-1961
Black horses
Moses
Bondsville fair
Moses
Bringing in the Christmas tree
Lipman. Primitive ptrs
Moses (col)
Bringing in the maple sugar
Moses
Cambridge, New York
Moses
Cambridge valley
Moses
Catching the Thanksgiving turkey
Cheney. Story 1958 ed
Moses
The checkered house
Moses (col)
Christmas at home
Time. 300 years (col)
Christmas eve
Moses
The covered bridge. See Sunday
Early springtime on the farm
Moses (col)
Fire in the woods
Moses
The first skating
Moses
Going to church
Moses
Grandma goes to the big city
Ford. Pictorial folk art (col)
Moses (col)
Haying time
Moses
Home for Thanksgiving
Moses
Home of Hezekiah King
Moses
Hoosick Falls in winter
Moses
In harvest time
Moses
In the park
Moses
In the springtime
Moses
The lookout, Vermont, 1777
Moses
McDonell farm DP
Born
Moses
May: making soap, washing sheep
Moses
Mount Nebo in winter
Moses
The old automobile
Moses
The old oaken bucket
Moses (col)
Our barn
Moses

**MOSES, A. M. R.**—*Continued*

Out for the Christmas tree
    Time. 300 years (col)
Over the bridge to grandma's house
    Cheney. Primer 1958 ed
Over the river
    Moses
Over the river to grandma's house
    Moses
Picnic
    Moses
The red mill
    Moses
Shenandoah valley
    Moses
Spring in the valley
    Ford. Pictorial folk art
Sugaring-off
    Moses (col)
Sugaring-off in maple orchard
    Moses
Sunday (The covered bridge)
    Moses
A tramp on Christmas day
    McCurdy
The trappers II
    Moses
Wash day
    Moses
Whiteside church
    Moses
Williamstown
    Kallir. Amer primitive ptgs
A winter's day
    Moses

**Moses, David,** 1776-1858
    Malbone, E. G. David Moses

**Moses, Grandma.** See Moses, Anna Mary
    (Robertson)

**Moses, Rachel (Gratz)** See Gratz, Rachel

**Moses, Solomon,** 1774-1857
    Malbone, E. G. Solomon Moses

**Moses, Mrs Solomon.** See Gratz, Rachel

**Moses** by Ben-Zion

**Moses** by A. Rattner

**Moses** in the bulrushes by Unidentified artist

**Moses,** the Baltimore news vendor by T. W.
    Wood

**Moses** with the tablets of the law by E.
    Laning

**Mosque** by M. Hoff

**Mosque,** Cordova by C. Gray

**Mosquito** net by J. S. Sargent

**Moss** agate by E. A. Donati

**Most** of the people are very poor by J.
    Lawrence

The **mother** by A. Vellanti

**Mother and child**

Allston, W. Mother watching her sleeping
    child
Avery, M. Mother and child
Bellows, G. W. Emma and her children
Benn, B. Mother and child
Bingham, G. C. Susan Howard Hockaday
    and her daughter Susan
Brush, G. D. Mother and child
Cassatt, M. Mrs Havemeyer and her
    daughter
Cassatt, M. Mother and child
Cassatt, M. Mother and children

Cassatt, M. Mother holding child
Catlin, G. Ojibway (Chippewa) woman
    and baby
Chase, W. M. Mother and child
Copley, J. S. Mrs Daniel Rea and child
Earl, R. Lady Williams and child
Earl, R. Mrs Moses Seymour and her
    son
Earl, R. Mrs William Moseley and her
    son Charles
Earl, R. Mrs William Taylor and child
Evergood, P. Mother and child
Freake limner. Mrs Freake and Baby
    Mary
Fried, T. Nursing mother
Glackens, W. J. Artist's wife and son
Hardy, J. P. Catherine Wheeler Hardy
    and her daughter
Harmon, L. P. First child
Hawthorne, C. Adoration of the mother
Hunt, W. M. Mrs Richard Morris Hunt
    and child
Jennys, W. Member of the Smith family
    of Suffield, Connecticut and Rutland,
    Vermont, c 1800
Kopf, M. The star
La Farge, J. Mother and child
Mayhew, N. Mrs John Harrison and her
    daughter Maria
Melchers, G. Mother and child
Newman, R. L. Mother and son
Palmer, C. B. R. Mother and child
Peale, C. W. Hannah Moore Peale and
    stepdaughter
Peale, C. W. Mrs James Arbuckle and
    son Edward
Peale, J. Mme Dubocq and her four chil-
    dren
Polk, C. P. Mrs Isaac Hite and James
    Madison Hite jr
Polk, C. P. Mrs John Hart and her
    daughter
Rattner, A. Mother and child
Sargent, J. S. Mrs Edward Livingston
    Davis and her son Livingston
Sargent, J. S. Mrs Fiske Warren and her
    daughter Rachel
Sargent, J. S. Mrs Knowles and her chil-
    dren
Sharrer, H. Rose Callahan and child
Sterne, M. Mother and child
Stuart, G. Mrs John Bannister and her son
Sully, T. Mother and son
Unidentified artist. American madonna
    and child
Unidentified artist. Aphia Salisbury Rich
    and baby Edward
Unidentified artist. Gracie Beardsley Jef-
    ferson Jackman and her daughter
Unidentified artist. Mrs John Casey and
    daughter
Unidentified artist. Mrs Mann Page II
    and baby John
Unidentified artist. Mother and child in
    white
Unidentified artist. Mother and child in
    Windsor chair
Vanderlyn, J. Mrs Marinus Willett and
    child
Vellanti, A. The mother
Weber, M. Mothers and children
West, B. Mrs West and her son Raphael
**Mother** and daughter by A. Brook

Mother and daughter by Y. Kuniyoshi
Mother Archie's church by A. N. Wyeth
Mother earth by B. Stahl
Mother of dawn by A. B. Davies
MOTHERWELL, Robert Burns, 1915-
  Black interior
    IU. Contemp Amer ptg, 1952
  Black still life
    WMAA. Contemp Amer ptg, 1951
  Blue with china ink (Homage to John
    Cage) Abstraction
    CtY. Yale alumni
    MnMW. Eighty works
  Brown figure
    IU. Contemp Amer ptg, 1949
  Construction
    MMA. Contemp ptrs
  Decalogue, Jacob's ladder and burning
    bush
    IU. Contemp Amer & sculp, 1953
  The easel
    IU. Contemp Amer ptg & sculp, 1955
  Elegy to the Spanish republic XXXIV
                                    NBuA
    MMA. New Amer ptg
    NBuA. Acquisitions 1954-57
    Pierson
    Ponente. Mod ptg, 1960 (col)
  Elegy to the Spanish republic LVIII
    PPC. International ex, 1961/62
  The end of Dover Beach
    PPC. International ex, 1958
  Figure
    Read. Art now, 1948 ed
  Figure in pink and green
    MMA. Fourteen
  Fishes with red stripe
    Baur. New art
    WMAA. New decade
  Five in the afternoon
    Baur. Revolution
  Granada
    Hess. Abstract ptg
    MoSL. Contemporary Amer ptg
  Homage to John Cage. See Blue with
    china ink
  Hotel corridor
    IU. Contemp Amer ptg, 1951
  In beige with sand              MCH
    Pulitzer v2
  Je t'aime II
    PPC. International ex, 1955
    WMAA. Museum and its friends, 1958
  Large collage
    MMA. Fourteen
  Mallarme's swan
    MnU. 40 Amer ptrs
  Maria
    MMA. Fourteen
  Montauk montage
    CSFP. Annual ex, 1948/49
  Mural fragment                  MnU
    MnMW. 60 Amer ptrs
  Orange personage
    MnU. 40 Amer ptrs
  Painting
    CSFP. Annual ex, 1950-51
  Pancho Villa, dead and alive, 1943  MMA
    Baur. New art
    MMA. Fourteen
    Read. Concise history

  Person with orange
    Leepa
  Personage with yellow ochre and white
                                    MMA
    MMA. New Amer ptg
  Red skirt                       WMAA
    Goodrich. Amer art
  La résistance
    IU. Contemp Amer ptg, 1950
  Room 8, Hotel Flora, Cannes
    ICA. Annual ex, 1951
    VR. Amer ptg, 1954
  Small personage
    MMA. Fourteen
  The voyage                      MMA
    Art since 1945 (col)
    Baur. New art (col)
    Hunter. Mod Amer ptg (col)
    MMA. New Amer ptg (col)
    Pierson
    WMAA. New decade
  Wall painting, 1950
    Mendelowitz
  Wall painting III
    Pousette-Dart. Amer ptg
  Wall painting IV, 1954
    Brussels. Exposition
    NNSG. Younger Amer ptrs
  Western air                     MMA
    Biddle. Yes and no
    McCurdy
    MMA. Abstract
    Time. 300 years (col)
El motif by S. Gross
Motif de fête by W. Bassford
Motif in pink by J. J. P. Meert
MOTLEY, Eleanor Warren, 1847-1942
  Auratum lily                    MB
    MB. Ptgs in water color
  Blue bowl                       MB
    MB. Ptgs in water color
  Purple petunias                 MB
    MB. Ptgs in water color
Motley, Mrs Thomas. See Motley, Eleanor
  Warren
The motor by W. T. Murch
Motorists by D. Richardson
Motte, Isaac, fl 1740
  Theus, J. Isaac Motte (?)
Motte, Mrs Jacob jr. See Motte, Rebecca
  (Brewton)
Motte, Rebecca (Brewton) 1729-1781
  Theus, J. Rebecca Motte
MOULTHROP, Reuben, 1763-1814
  Ammi Ruhamah Robbins            CtY
    Flexner. Light of distant skies
    Pierson
  Bradford Hubbard                CtNH
    Pierson
    Richardson. Ptg in America
  Elisha Williams                 CtY
    CtY. Portrait index
  Ezra Stiles                     CtY
    CtY. Portrait index
  Thomas Robbins                  CtHH
    ICA. From colony to nation
  Timothy Pitkin                  CtY
    CtY. Portrait index
Moulton, Hannah Goodwin (Whitehouse)
    fl 1838
  Davis, J. H. (attributed works) Hannah
    Goodwin (Whitehouse) Moulton

**Moulton, James Roberts,** fl 1838
  Davis, J. H. (attributed works) James
    Roberts Moulton
**Moulton, Mrs James Robert.** See Moulton,
    Hannah Goodwin (Whitehouse)
**Moultrie, William,** 1731-1805
  Fraser, C. William Moultrie
**MOUNT, Shepard Alonzo,** 1804-1868
  A day's catch
    NSP. Sportscapes
**MOUNT, William Sidney,** 1807-1868
  Banjo player                          MiD
    MiD. Treasures
    OCiM. Rediscoveries
    Pierson
    Roos
    Time. 300 years (col)
  Banjo player                          NStS
    NUM. Art across America
  Bargaining for a horse               NNHS
    Flexner. Amer ptg
    Flexner. Short history
    Mendelowitz
    Pierson
    UNESCO. Prior to 1860 3d ed
  Barn by the pool                       MB
    MB. Karolik coll
  Bone player                            MB
    MB. Karolik coll
  Boys caught napping in a field        NBM
    DC. De gustibus
    Pierson
  Coming to the point                   NNPL
    Davidson v2
  Country dance. See Rustic dance
  Dance of the haymakers. See Music is
    contagious
  Eel spearing at Setauket              NNHS
    Barker. Amer ptg
    Baur. Amer ptg
    Pierson
    Richardson. Ptg in America
  Farmers nooning                       NStS
    PPC. Amer classics (col front)
  Fence on the hill                      MB
    MB. Karolik coll
  Landscape with figures                 PA
    Pierson
  Long Island farmhouses                 MM
    Bazin
    Born
    OCiM. Rediscoveries
    Pierson
    UNESCO. Prior to 1860 3d ed
    Walker. Ptgs from America
  Long Island scene
    CtY. Yale alumni
  The long story                         DC
    DC. Masterpieces
    U.S. National Captial sesquicentennial
      com
  The Mount brothers' music stand       MStS
    CSFP. Illusionism
  Music is contagious (Dance of the hay-
    makers)                             NStS
    NAD. Amer tradition
  News from the gold diggings (Melville
    coll)
    Davidson v 1

Painter's triumph                        PA
  Larkin (detail)
  Larkin rev ed (detail)
  Pierson
  Richardson. Ptg in America
Power of music
  Larkin
  Larkin rev ed
  Larkin rev ed (col detail)
  Pierson
Ringing the pig                         NNHS
  PPC. Amer classics
Rustic dance (Rustic dance after a sleigh-
  ride; Country dance)                   MB
  Davidson v 1
  MB. Karolik Coll
**MOUNT, William Sidney,** 1807-1868 and
  **RANNEY, William Tylee,** 1813-1857
Pipe of friendship                       NJN
  NJN. Early N. J. artists
Mount Aetna from Taormina, Sicily by T.
  Cole
Mount Auburn cemetery, Cambridge by T.
  Chambers
The Mount brothers' music stand by W. S.
  Mount
Mount Chocorua by J. Marin
Mount Corcoran by A. Bierstadt
Mount Equinox. winter by R. Kent
Mount Katahdin, autumn by M. Hartley
Mount Katahdin, Maine by M. Hartley
Mount Lassen by L. Siegriest
Mount Marcy by D. Johnson
Mount Nebo in winter by A. M. R. Moses
Mount Overlook by F. J. Reilly
Mount Vernon
  Bartlett, W. H. Mt Vernon
  Bartlett, W. H. Washington's tomb, Mt
    Vernon
  Guy, F. Washington's tomb
  Prior, W. M. Washington's tomb at
    Mount Vernon
  Unidentified artist. Mount Vernon (after
    aquatint by Francis Jukes)
  Whitcomb, S. Mount Vernon
Mount Vesuvius from the bay of Naples
  by R. D. Gauley
Mount Washington, New Hampshire by S.
  Gerry
Mount Whitney by A. Bierstadt
Mount Wilson, View of by E. Ewing
The mountain by S. Serisawa
Mountain bird maru by R. Crawford
Mountain brook, Adirondacks by A. H.
  Wyant
Mountain church, San Cristobal by D. Lutz
Mountain farm by P. Dickinson
Mountain ford by T. Cole
Mountain goats by V. Arbogast
Mountain gorge by G. C. Bingham
Mountain gorge near Dambulla, Ceylon by
  J. La Farge
Mountain lake by A. Bierstadt
Mountain lakes by J. F. Cropsey
Mountain landscape by E. Geller
Mountain landscape with cattle by B. West
  (attributed works)
Mountain landscape with waterfall by T.
  Cole

Mountain laurel by L. MacIver
Mountain of the Winds by A. J. Miller
Mountain pores by A. Okamura
Mountain scene with deer by G. C. Bingham
Mountain scene with fisherman by G. C. Bingham
Mountain sea by R. Haines
Mountain stream by J. F. Kensett
Mountain top by H. Koerner
Mountain top by J. Marin
Mountain torrent by T. Doughty
Mountain torrent by A. J. Miller
Mountain trail by F. T. Johnson
The mountain, Tyrol by J. Marin
Mountain valley by A. B. Durand
Mountain valley by F. R. Gignoux
Mountain village by J. De Martini
The mountaineer by E. E. Speicher
A mountaineer and Kansas Indians, Group of by A. J. Miller
Mountains by G. W. Mark
Mountains and trees by K. Schrag
Mountains in Dalmatia by G. H. Hallowell
Mountains of Ecuador by F. E. Church
Mountains, Puget sound by H. G. Keller
The mountebanks by Y. Tanguy
Mountfort, Jonathan, 1746-1785
    Copley, J. S. Jonathan Mountfort
Mounting of the Guard by Unidentified artist
Mourning pictures
    Elmer, E. R. Mourning picture
    Jordan, S. Eaton family memorial
    Merrill, S. Mourning picture
    Unidentified artist. Mourning picture—Elizabeth Farr
    Unidentified artist. Mourning picture—left behind
    Unidentified artist. Mourning picture—Polly Botsford and her children
    Unidentified artist. Mourning picture—Philo Day
    Unidentified artist. Mourning picture sacred to the memory of Jerhusha Williams
    Unidentified artist. Mourning scene
    Unidentified artist. Smith memorial
    Unidentified artist. Tomb in memory of Richard Newhall
    Walters, S. Memorial to Nicholas Catlin
    Warner, C. T. Mourning picture—George Washington
Mourning piece by H. L. Forbes
Mourning the child by J. Schwarz
Movement by M. Hartley
Movement by B. J. O. Nordfeldt
Movement, boat and sea, Deer isle, Maine by J. Marin
Movement—boat and sea in grey by J. Marin
Movement—Fifth avenue by J. Marin
Movement in grey, green and red by J. Marin
Movement in paint by J. Marin
Movement no 9, 1916 by M. Hartley
Movement no 2, related to downtown New York by J. Marin
Movement of horses II by R. Goodnough

Movement, sea and rocks, Cape Split, Maine by J. Marin
Movement, sea and sky by J. Marin
Movement—sea or mountain—as you will by J. Marin
Movement: Tunk mountains by J. Marin
Movements, 1915 by M. Hartley
Movements and acts by Y. Tanguy
The movers by J. Koch
Moving camp by G. Catlin
Moving camp by A. J. Miller
MOY, Seong, 1921-
    Girl playing a pe-pa
        VR. Amer ptg, 1954
    The king visits his paramour
        IU. Contemp Amer ptg & sculp, 1953
        MM. Amer ptg today
    Recipe for bouillabaisse
        IU. Contemp Amer ptg & sculp, 1959
    Spring song
        IU. Contemp Amer ptg & sculp, 1955
Mud hook by B. Miller
Muddy alligators by J. S. Sargent
MUELLER, George Ludwig, 1929-
    Blackened monument
        IU. Contemp Amer ptg & sculp, 1955
    Night
        ICA. Amer artists paint the city
    Numena
        PPC. International ex, 1955
    Spad
        WMAA. Young America 1957
    Stage fragment: Faust                    NNSG
        NNSG. Handbook
        NNSG. Younger Amer artists
    The study                                WMAA
        Goodrich. Amer art
        Pierson
    Stuka
        Brussels. Exposition
    Wayout—side                              NJN
        WMAA. Young America 1957
Mug, pipe, and newspaper by J. F. Peto
Mulberry Bend park, New York by M. B. Prendergast
Mule deer by C. S. Price
Mulford, Betsy. See Sutliff, Betsy (Mulford)
Mulford, Huldah. See Hills, Huldah (Mulford)
Mulford, Sally (Emes) 1773-1861
    Ames, E. Mrs Ezekiel Mulford
MULHAUPT, Frederick John, 1871-1938
    February's sun                           PR
        PR. Catalogue
MULLER, Jan, 1923-1958
    Hamlet and Horatio
        Selz. New images
    Hanging piece
        Selz. New images
    Heraldic ground
        Selz. New images
    Of this time, of that place
        WMAA. Young America 1957
    Temptation of St Anthony
        Selz. New images (col)
    The virgins
        PPC. International ex, 1958
MULLICAN, Lee, 1919-
    Luminous loot
        IU. Contemp Amer ptg & sculp, 1953

MULLICAN, Lee—*Continued*
Salt fire
  Pousette-Dart. Amer ptg
Solstice rider
  IU. Contemp ptg & sculp, 1955
Weights of the Pacific
  IU. Contemp Amer ptg & sculp, 1957
Multiform by J. Xcéron
Multiple images I by W. Barnet
Multiple portrait by M. Weber
Multiple views by S. Davis
Multiplication of the arcs by Y. Tanguy
Mumford, Thomas, fl 1776
  Johnston, W. Thomas Mumford V
Mummy by W. A. Baziotes
MUNGER, George, 1781-1825
  Nathaniel Jocelyn         CtY
    CtY. Portrait index
Munich head. W. M. Chase
Munro, Katherine
  Morse, S. F. B. Katherine Munro of
    Charleston, South Carolina
Munson, Eneas, 1734-1826
  Jennys, W. Eneas Munson
Munson, Israel, 1764-1844
  Unidentified artist. Israel Munson
MUNSON, William Giles, fl 1826
  Eli Whitney's gun factory     CtY
    Davidson v 1
    U.S. National Capital sesquicentennial
    com
Munson, William Gurley, fl 1868
  Chase, W. M. William Gurley Munson
MÜNTER, Gabriele, 1877-
  Blue gable           IU
    IU. 20th century
Mural by J. Pollock
Mural assistant by L. Bouché
Mural decoration by J. H. Daugherty
Murals at Roosevelt, New Jersey, Community center by B. Shahn
MURCH, Walter Tandy, 1907-
Action
  CSFP. Annual ex, 1952
Bamboo
  IU. Contemp Amer ptg & sculp, 1961
Blocks
  Pousette-Dart. Amer ptg
The bulb           WMAA
  MoSL. Contemporary Amer ptg
  Pierson
The circle          NBM
  Baur. Revolution
The clock
  WMAA. New decade
Cylinder and orange
  WiMiA. Amer ptg 1760-1960
Egg and rock
  ICA. Annual ex, 1961
Governor II, 1952      WMAA
  Goodrich. Amer art
  Pierson
Isotopes
  IU. Contemp Amer ptg, 1951
Keys and feather
  ICA. Annual ex, 1947/48
The light          NBuA
  NBuA. Acquisitions 1959-1961
The lock
  IU. Contemp Amer ptg, 1949

Metronome
  MMA. Contemp ptrs
The motor          IU
  IU. Contemp Amer ptg, 1952
  IU. 20th century
Perspective
  CSB. Illusion
Sewing machine
  WMAA. New decade
Taking off         OT
  ICA. Annual ex, 1954
Time clock
  ICA. Amer artists paint the city
The wall
  WiMiA. Amer ptg 1760-1960
Murder of Jane McCrea by Unidentified
  artist
Murder of Rutland by C. R. Leslie
Murdock, Phoebe. See Bowdoin, Phoebe
  (Murdock)
MURPHY, Gerald
Watch
  Blesh
Murphy, Mrs H. Dudley. See Murphy, Nelly
  Littlehale
MURPHY, Nelly Littlehale, 1867-1941
Flower study         MB
  MB. Ptgs in water color
Peonies           MB
  MB. Ptgs in water color
Murray, Mr, fl 1820
  Unidentified artist. Mr Murray
Murray, Mrs, fl 1820
  Unidentified artist. Mrs Murray
MURRAY, Albert K. 1906-
  Chester W. Nimitz
  PPC. Ptg in the U.S. 1949
Murray, Samuel, b 1870
  Eakins, T. Samuel Murray
Murray, William Vans, 1762-1803
  Brown, M. William Vans Murray
Murray Bay landscape by E. E. Speicher
The muse: Susan Walker Morse by S. F. B.
  Morse
Muse of the western world by E. Berman
Muses by M. Weber
Muses of painting, poetry and music by W. E.
  West
Music by T. W. Dewing
Music by H. Moller
Music and good luck by W. M. Harnett
Music and literature by W. M. Harnett
Music before winter by A. Blanch
Music—black, blue and green by G. O'Keeffe
Music hall by S. Davis
Music lesson by M. Avery
Music maker by M. Avery
Music master by F. Duveneck
Music of the Orient by M. Weber
Music room by J. A. M. Whistler
Musical evening by M. Weber
Musicians and musical instruments
  Adams, W. Musicos ambulantes
  Allston, W. Evening hymn
  Blythe, D. G. Young musician
  Demuth, C. H. Vaudeville musicians
  Dewing, T. W. Music
  Eakins, T. Musicians rehearsing
  Eakins, T. Street scene in Seville

Evergood, P. Music
Evett, K. Trio
Grode, S. M. Two musicians
Harnett, W. M. Music and good luck
Harnett, W. M. Old models
Hicks, T. Barber shop, the musicale
Perlin, B. Jazz band
Philipp, R. Request number
Platt, G. W. Relics of a den
Sexton, F. Musical instruments
Shahn, B. Composition with clarinets and tin horn
Shahn, B. Four piece orchestra
Shahn, B. Portrait of myself when young
Unidentified artist. Musicians in the snow
Watkins, F. C. Musician
Weber, M. Bach orchestra
Weber, M. Music
Weber, M. Musical evening
Weber, M. Solo
Weber, M. String music
Weber, M. The trio
Weber, M. Two musicians
Weber, M. Wind orchestra

### Accordions
Shahn, B. Blind accordion player

### Bagpipes
Kane, J. Scotch day at Kennywood

### Banjos
Karp, L. Still life with banjo
Mount, W. S. Banjo player

### Cellos
Avery, M. Cello player
Bradley, I. J. H. The 'cellist
Dickinson, E. W. Cello player

### Clarinets
Crane, S. W. Handel still life
Shahn, B. Composition with clarinet and tin horn

### Drums
Hensel, H. Drummers

### Fifes
Eakins, T. Youth playing fife

### Flutes
Moller, H. Flutes
Peckham, R. William Cornee with flute
Weber, M. Flute soloist

### Guitars
Benton, T. H. Jessie, 17 years old
Brackman, R. Sailor's holiday
Chase, W. M. Lady playing guitar
Gwathmey, R. Singing and mending
Henri, R. Blind Spanish singer
Lotterman, H. Boy with guitar
Luks, G. B. The guitar
Roszak, T. Self-portrait
Sargent, J. S. El Jaleo
Shahn, B. The song
Tooker, G. Guitar
Weber, M. Guitar player

### Harmonicas
Menkès, S. Boy playing harmonica

### Harps
Douglass, L. Royal psalmist
La Farge, J. Harpist

Lutz, D. I got a harp
Sully, T. Lady with a harp: Eliza Ridgely

### Hurdy-gurdies
Myers, J. The tambourine

### Lutes
Benrimo, T. D. Lute player
Shahn, B. Lute no 2, 1957

### Mandolins
Cikovski, N. Fruit, vase and mandolin
Cikovsky, N. Spring melody
Lucioni, L. Design for color

### Oboes
Eakins, T. Oboe player (Benjamin Sharp)

### Organs
Sample, P. S. Sweet hour of prayer

### Pianos
Benton, T. H. Sun treader—Portrait of Carl Ruggles
Eakins, T. Elizabeth at the piano
Eakins, T. Home scene
Robinson, T. Girl at the piano
Sample, P. S. Spring song
Watkins, F. C. Rosemary Thompson
Whistler, J. A. M. At the piano
Whistler, J. A. M. Gold scab
Zorach, W. Leo Ornstein (Piano concert)

### Recorders
Levi, J. E. Margaret Boni playing the recorder

### Saxophones
Beckmann, M. Portrait of the artist with a saxophone

### Singers
Eakins, T. Concert singer
Eakins, T. Pathetic song

### Spinets
Dewing, T. W. The spinet

### Tambourines
Beckmann, M. Dancer with tambourine
Myers, J. The tambourine

### Trombones
Lee, R. J. Trombone

### Violins
Avery, M. Music maker
Chalfant, J. D. Old violin
Eakins, T. Music
Eakins, T. The violinist
Evergood, P. Nude with violin
Harnett, W. M. Old Cremona
Harnett, W. M. Old violin
Harnett, W. M. Still life, 1888
Harnett, W. M. (attributed works) Still life with violin
James, A. Choose your partner
Knaths, K. Tired violin
Levine, J. String quartette
Shahn, B. Violin player
Spruce, E. F. Fiddler
Von Wicht, J. G. F. Paganini

**Musidora** by B. West
**Muskrat** hunter by W. L. Lathrop

Mussel gatherers by W. Homer
Mussel gatherers at high tide by Leonid
Mussey, Mrs David
 Morse, S. F. B. Mrs David Mussey
Mutation by W. Quirt
Muted city by R. Gikow
A muted street by L. Guglielmi
My bunkie by C. Schreyvogel
My daughters by F. W. Benson
My Egypt by C. H. Demuth
My family reunion by L. Bosa
My father by G. W. Bellows
My father by W. M. Chase
My father by E. C. Dickinson
My forebears were pioneers by P. Evergood
My heart by G. O'Keeffe
My Hell raising sea by J. Marin
My house by J. K. W. Hailman
My life white and black by Y. Tanguy
My little daughter Dorothy by W. M. Chase
My mother by G. W. Bellows
My mother by P. Evergood
My mother by M. S. Parcell
My neighbor Al by G. Biddle
My parents by H. Koerner
My son is innocent by B. Shahn
My wife by M. Avery
Myer, Albert James, 1829-1880
 Healy, G. P. A. Albert J. Myer
Myers, Jacob, fl 1833
 Unidentified artist. Jacob Myers
Myers, Mrs Jacob, fl 1833
 Unidentified artist. Mrs Myers with baby
Myers, Jean Macdonald Lee, fl 1850
 Unidentified artist. Jean Macdonald Lee
  Myers
MYERS, Jerome, 1867-1940
 Children's theatre                           MiD
  Richardson. Ptg in America
 East of the Bowery                           NJMo
  NJMo. Forty years
 End of the street
  Pierson
 Night mission                                MM
  Brown. Amer ptg
 Playground pleasures                         DNC
  DNC. Gellatly coll, 1954
 Self-portrait
  WiMiA. Amer ptg 1760-1960
 Summer night, East side park                 WMAA
  Goodrich. Amer art
  Pierson
 The tambourine                               DP
  Brown. Amer ptg
  DP. Catalogue
  McCurdy
 Windy corner
  Baur. Revolution
Myers, John, d 1844
 Sully, T. John Myers
MYERS, William H. fl 1847
 Battle of the plains of Mesa, 1847
  U.S. National Capital sesquicentennial
  com
Myopic vista by S. Davis
Myriad by J. S. Haley

Myself and my imaginary wife, Portrait of
 by A. Gorky
Mysterious bird by C. E. Burchfield
Mystery by F. E. Conway
Mystery of the East by P. King
The mystic by W. R. Leigh
Mystic lake, Massachusetts by J. F. Cole
Mythological themes
 Austin, D. Europa and the bull
 Copley, J. S. Mars, Venus, and Vulcan
 Hesselius, G. Bacchus and Ariadne
 Mason, W. S. Venus and Cupid
 Morse, S. F. B. Dying Hercules
 Page, W. Cupid and Psyche
 Russell, A. Venus Anadyomene no 2
 Sargent, J. S. Atlas and the Hesperides
 Sargent, J. S. The Danaïdes
 Unidentified artist. Venus drawn by doves
 Vanderlyn, J. Ariadne
 West, B. The choice of Hercules
 West, B. Cupid and Psyche
 West, B. Diomed and his horses stopped
  by the lightning of Jupiter
 West, B. Hector parting with his wife and
  child at the Scæan gate
 West, B. Juno receiving the cestus from
  Venus
 West, B. Thetis bringing the armor to
  Achilles
 West, B. Una and the lion
 West, B. Venus lamenting the death of
  Adonis
Mythomania by K. Seligmann


# N

Nabu-Naa-Kee-Shick, a Chippewa chief by
 J. O. Lewis
Nacelles by R. Crawford
Nacelles under construction by R. Crawford
NACK, Kenneth, 1923-
 A demand of estimation
  IU. Contemp Amer ptg & sculp, 1955
 Expulsion of possessions in a danger of
  being gained
  NNSG. Younger Amer ptrs
Naden, Elizabeth. See Banyar, Elizabeth
 (Naden)
NAGLER, Fred, 1891-
 From afar
  NAD. Annual ex, 1952
NAHL, Charles Christian, 1818-1875
 The fandango                                 CSC
  Davidson v 1
 Passion according to St Matthew
  Gruskin (col)
 Sunday morning in the mines                  CSC
  Davidson v 1
  Mendelowitz
Naiad by L. Kroll
Naked in the city by J. Farnsworth
Naked over New York by R. Marsh
Nana by R. Ray
Nana, Illustrations for by C. H. Demuth
Nancy (ship)
 Thomas, J. The ship Nancy, homeward
  bound

Nancy by E. E. Speicher

**NANGERONI, Carlo,** 1922-
Picnic
    IU. Contemp Amer ptg & sculp, 1959

Nantucket school of philosophy by E. Johnson

The **nap** by P. Cadmus

**Naples** by R. D. Gauley

**Naples** by J. L. Lasker

**Naples** aquarium by L. MacIver

**Naples** yellow morning by A. G. Dove

Napoleon's army crossing the Alps by Mrs Robert Carter

**Napoli** forio by E. S. Woelffer

**Napolitana** by E. Berman

**Naram-Sin** by E. A. Donati

**Narcissus** by B. West

**Nardin** park by J. Berghoff

**Narragansett** bay by Leonid

**Narragansett** light from northeast by Capt "Phindoodle"

**Narrative** by J. Ernst

The **Narrows** from Fort Hamilton, New York Harbor by Unidentified artist

**Nassau**
    Homer, W. Nassau
    Homer, W. Scene in Nassau
    Homer, W. Shore and surf, Nassau

**Nassau** hall (Princeton university) by K. Matthew

**Nassau,** woman at campfire by W. Homer

**Nast, Thomas,** 1840-1902
    Alexander, J. W. Thomas Nast

**Natchez,** Mississippi in 1822 by J. J. Audubon

**National** Lancers on Boston Common by T. C. Savory

**National** Lancers with the reviewing officers on Boston Common by C. Hubbard

**Native** house by J. La Farge

**Native** woman cooking by W. Homer

**Natives** beaching a boat, Samoa by J. La Farge

**Natives** cooking poi, Tahiti by J. La Farge

**Native's** return by P. Guston

**Native's** return by R. Strang

**Nativity** by L. Ford

**NATKIN, Robert,** 1930-
Summer
    WMAA. Young America 1960

**Nature** symbolized by A. G. Dove

**Nature** without man by P. Evergood

**Nausicaa** by J. Tworkov

**Nautical** by L. Phillips

**Nautical** composition by G. L. K. Morris

**Navajo** by G. C. Delano

**Navajo** boy by G. C. Delano

**Navajo** desert camp by E. Loran

**Navajo** land by R. Ray

**Navajo** land by J. E. Swinnerton

**Navajo** raid by F. Remington

**Naval** home, Gray's ferry, Philadelphia by T. Doughty

The **navigator** by Unidentified artist

The **navigator's** wife by Unidentified artist

Naxos by J. Youngerman

**NEAGLE, John,** 1796-1865
    Anna Gibbon Johnson            PA
      PA. Annual ex, 1955
    George Peabody                MB
      MB. Great Americans
      MB. Karolik coll
    Gilbert Stuart                MB
      MB. Great Americans
      Pierson
    Henry Clay                  PPhU
      Pierson
    Indian heads                 PH
      Chew. 250 years of art
      PA. Annual ex, 1955
    John Kintzing Kane          NJP
      NUM. Art across America
    Joseph Tagert              OYB
      OYB. Supplement
    Knife Chief of the Pawnee Loups   PH
      MdBMu. Rendezvous
    Matilda Washington Dawson     PA
      Pierson
    Pat Lyon at the forge (Pat Lyon, blacksmith)                 MBA
      Davidson v 1
      Flexner. Light of distant skies
      Larkin
      Larkin rev ed
    Pat Lyon at the forge (Pat Lyon, blacksmith)                 PA
      PA. Annual ex, 1955
      Pierson
      Robb. Harper history
      Roos
      Time. 300 years ⟨col⟩
    Patrick Lyon at the forge, Study for  PH
      Chew. 250 years of art
    The Schuylkill, View on the       ICA
      Baur. Amer ptg
      Larkin
      Larkin rev ed
      Pierson
    William Potts Dewees        PPhUn
      PA. Annual ex, 1955
    William Strickland           CtY
      CtY. Portrait index
      Pierson

**Near** Avenue A by N. Spencer

**Near** Great Barrington by J. Marin

**Near** Manayunk by R. Smith

**Near** Paradise, Newport, Rhode island by W. T. Richards

**Near** the beach, Shinnecock by W. M. Chase

**Near** the mountain by E. Magafan

**Near** the sea by J. Floch

**Near** the village, October by G. Inness

**Near** Tibidabo by C. Carmen

**Nearing** the issue at the cock pit by H. Bonham

**Nearly** everybody reads the Bulletin by B. Shahn

**Nebraska** landscape by R. O. Pozzatti

The **necklace** by B. Greene

The **necklace** by J. Sloan

**Negro** Pietà by W. Pachner

**Negro** spiritual: Ride on conquering king by G. Biddle

Negroes
Anshutz, T. P. Aunt Hannah
Archer, E. Howard Patterson of the Harlem Yankees
Benton, T. H. Negro soldier
Biddle, G. Two Negroes
Brook, A. Frogtown lady
Brook, A. Southern belle
Carter, C. H. Stew
Chapin, J. Ruby Green singing
Clonney, J. G. In the cornfield
Clonney, J. G. In the woodshed
Clonney, J. G. Waking up
Curry, J. S. The Mississippi
Delaney, J. Innocence
Dinnerstein, H. Magnolia
Eakins, T. Will Shuster and black man going shooting
Evergood, P. Her world
Greenwood, M. Dancers resting
Greenwood, M. Invocation
Gwathmey, R. Hoeing
Harnett, W. M. Front face
Henri, R. Willie Gee
Hesselius, J. Charles Calvert and his Negro slave
Hirsch, J. Singing men
Homer, W. The carnival
Homer, W. Happy family in Virginia
Homer, W. Native woman cooking
Homer, W. Rum cay
Homer, W. Shark fishing
Homer, W. Sponge diver
Homer, W. Sunday morning in Virginia
Homer, W. Taking sunflowers to teacher
Homer, W. Under the coco palm
Homer, W. Unruly calf
James, A. Heart of darkness
Johnson, E. A ride for liberty: the fugitive slave
Lawrence, J. Migration of the Negro
Lawrence, J. Most of the people are very poor
Lawrence, J. Woman at work
Lawrence, J. You can buy whiskey for twenty-five cents a quart
Marsh, R. High yaller
Marsh, R. Negroes on Rockaway beach
Martin, F. Ruby
Martin, F. 'Tis me O Lord
Morrill, D. Minstrel banjo player
Mount, W. S. Bone player
Mount, W. S. Power of music
Pachner, W. Negro Pietà
Pippin, H. Sunday morning breakfast
Pippin, H. Uncle Tom
Prior, W. M. (manner of) Lady in a fine scarf
Prior, W. M. (manner of) William Whipper
Robinson, B. Ethiopia saluting the colors
Sepeshy, Z. L. Negro meeting
Shahn, B. Three men
Tanner, H. O. Banjo lesson
Turnbull, J. B. Son of a sharecropper
Unidentified artist. Enigmatic foursome
Unidentified artist. Negro child
Unidentified artist. The old plantation
Walker, G. A. Mal du pays
Watkins, F. C. Negro spiritual
Wood, T. W. Negress
Wyeth, A. N. A crow flew by

NEGUS, Caroline, fl 1837
Mrs James Page                           MB
MB. New England miniatures
Neighborhood physician by J. Levine
Neilson, Hannah (Coles) fl 1810
Jarvis, J. W. Mrs William Neilson
NEILSON, Raymond Perry Rodgers, 1881-
Chelsea lady and Bouvardia
NAD. Annual ex, spring 1950
Hayley Lever
NAD. Annual ex, 1947, 2d half
Hobart Nichols
NAD. Annual ex, 1949, 1st half
Neilson, William, 1774-1852
Jarvis, J. W. William Neilson
NEIMAN, LeRoy, 1921-
Toro
ICA. Annual ex, 1961
Neisse, Max Hermann-. See Hermann-Neisse, Max
Neither yet have you faith by L. Di Valentin
NELSON, Carl L.
Maine night no 2
Pousette-Dart. Amer ptg
Nelson, Elizabeth (Tailer) 1667-1734
Unidentified artist. Mrs John Nelson
Nelson, Horatio Nelson, viscount, 1758-1805
West, B. The apotheosis of Nelson
West, B. Death of Lord Nelson
West, B. Project for a monument. The apotheosis of Nelson
Nelson, Mrs John. See Nelson, Elizabeth (Tailer)
Nelson, Mary Gay (Wyan) fl 1862
Bingham, G. C. Mrs Thomas W. Nelson
Nelson, Mrs Merlin. See Craig, Nancy Ellen
NELSON, Robert A.
Soldier and bull
DC. 27 biennial ex, 1961
Nelson, Mrs Thomas W. See Nelson, Mary Gay (Wyan)
Nelson, William Rockhill, 1841-1915
Chase, W. M. William Rockhill Nelson
Nelson's island showing Monument hill and Allegheny waterfront by R. Smith
Neon thoroughfare by M. Tobey
Neponset bay by M. B. Prendergast
Neponset river, Milton by J. Wagner
NEPOTE, Alexander, 1913-
Enigmatical section
IU. Contemp Amer ptg, 1951
Ominous
IU. Contemp Amer ptg, 1952
Secluded                              CSFM
CoS. New accessions USA, 1950
A nervous woman by W. W. Quirt
The nest by J. Pollock
Nests of lightning by K. Sage
Net mender by K. Knaths
The Netherlands by W. De Kooning
Nets and boats by M. A. Blackburn
Nets, boats and sea by J. C. Atherton
Nets with blue by R. Crawford
Neue Weinsteige by R. S. Neuman
NEUMAN, Robert S. 1926-
Ciudad de Dos Corazones
MBIC. View 1960
Forlorn one
IU. Contemp Amer ptg, 1952

Neue Weinsteige
  PPC. International ex. 1961/62
The struggle
  IU. Contemp Amer ptg & sculp, 1953
Un vista
  IU. Contemp Amer ptg & sculp, 1961
New, 1955 by R. Crawford
New Amsterdam by L. Block
New Bedford in 1807 by W. A. Wall
New costume by M. Sawyer
New death by P. Evergood
New dodgem by R. Marsh
New England
  See also names of New England states,
    e.g., Maine; and of cities, e.g., Boston
  Baumbach, H. New England landscape
  Blanch, A. New England
  Burlin, P. New England landscape
  Durrie, G. H. Autumn in New England,
    cider making
  Durrie, G. H. New England winter scene
  Durrie, G. H. Winter scene in New Eng-
    land
  Hartigan, G. New England, October
  Heade, M. J. Rocks in New England
  Prendergast, M. B. New England village
  Unidentified artist. New England farm in
    winter
  Unidentified artist. New England hillside
  Unidentified artist. New England village
New England coast shipping by F. H. Lane
New England editor by T. H. Benton
New England faces: husband and wife by
    Unidentified artist
New England family group by Unidentified
    artist
New England goddess by Unidentified artist
New England picnic by J. P. Hardy
New England stove by W. A. Kienbusch
New Guinea beer party by R. M. Graham
New Hampshire
  Bierstadt, A. Ascutney mountain from
    Claremont, New Hampshire
  Cole, T. View near Conway, New Hamp-
    shire
  Cole, T. View near Tamworth; In the
    White mountains
  Cropsey, J. Eagle cliff, Franconia notch
  Gerry, S. Mount Washington, New Hamp-
    shire
  Leavitt, J. W. At Loudon, New Hamp-
    shire
  Macknight, D. Shelburne woods, New
    Hampshire
  Marin, J. Mountain top
  Unidentified artist. In the heart of New
    Hampshire
  Unidentified artist. Silver lake, New
    Hampshire
New Hope, Pennsylvania
  Demuth, C. H. New Hope, Pennsylvania
  Pickett, J. Lehigh canal, sunset, New
    Hope, Pennsylvania
New housing by Y. Hnizdovsky
New Jersey
  See also Delaware river and valley;
    Newark, New Jersey
  Durand, A. B. North mountain reserva-
    tion, Orange, New Jersey
Inness, G. Late afternoon, Montclair, New
    Jersey
Marin, J. Alpine district, New Jersey
The new Lazarus by P. Evergood
New Lebanon railroad station by L. Bouché
New life (Resurrection) by M. Tobey
New Mexico
  Dasburg, A. Autumn—Ranchos de Taos
  Dasburg, A. New Mexican landscape
  Dasburg, A. New Mexican village
  Dasburg, A. November, New Mexico
  Dasburg, A. Road into Ranchos de Taos
  Dasburg, A. Taos plaza
  Davis, S. New Mexican landscape
  Hartley, M. Landscape, New Mexico
  Hartley, M. New Mexico
  Hartley, M. New Mexico: landscape
  Marin, J. Blue mountain near Taos
  Marin, J. Near Santa Fe, New Mexico
  Marin, J. New Mexico
  Marin, J. Pueblo and mesa, Taos moun-
    tains
  Marin, J. Storm over Taos, New Mexico
  Marin, J. Taos
  Marin, J. Taos landscape, New Mexico
New Mexico number 34 by E. Corbett
New Mexico recollections by M. Hartley
New moon by H. B. Kayn
The new novel by W. Homer
New Orleans
  Crawford, R. New Orleans #2, 1953
  Crawford, R. New Orleans #4, 1953
  Crawford, R. New Orelans #5, 1954
  Herron, D. St Louis cemetery, New Or-
    leans
  Matthew, K. Charming New Orleans
  Philipp, R. Patio Royale, New Orleans
  Woiseri, L. J. B. de. New Orleans, 1803
New Orleans still life by R. Crawford
New scholar by F. W. Edmonds
New shores by C. A. Morris
New world a' coming by I. R. Pereira
New Year wall: Night by F. J. Kline
New York (city)
  Alcalay, A. East end in New York
  Beal, G. R. Terrace, Central park
  Bellows, G. W. Blue snow, the Battery
  Bellows, G. W. Cliff dwellers
  Bellows, G. W. Gramercy park
  Bellows, G. W. Men of the docks
  Bellows, G. W. Riverfront no 1
  Bellows, G. W. Summer night, Riverside
    drive
  Bennett, W. J. Broadway from Bowling
    Green, c 1826
  Bennett, W. J. Packet Row, South street,
    New York
  Birch, T. New York harbor
  Blakelock, R. A. Old New York: north-
    west corner 55th street and Seventh
    avenue, c 1868
  Blakelock, R. A. Old New York, shanties
    at 55th street and 7th avenue
  Block, L. New Amsterdam
  Boit, E. D. East river, New York
  Boit, E. D. Park avenue, New York
  Bové, R. J. New York scene
  Burton, C. Governor's room, City hall,
    New York, c 1830

**New York (city)**—*Continued*

Cafferty, J. H. and Rosenberg, C. D. Wall street half past 2 o'clock, Oct 13, 1857

Calyo, N. V. The great fire in New York, 1835

Calyo, N. V. View of New York city, c 1835

Chappel, W. P. Citizens supplying a fire engine with water from a pump, New York, 1809

Chappel, W. P. City watchman and his watch box, New York, 1809

Chappel, W. P. Old tea water pump and cart, New York, 1807

Criss, F. Astor place, 1932

Davis, S. New York, 1932

Davis, S. New York under gaslight

Davis, S. New York waterfront

Dehn, A. A. Spring in Central park

De Kooning, W. Gansevoort street

Dreier, D. A. New York: the Little church around the corner

Feininger, L. Factory windows in Manhattan

Feininger, L. Manhattan, dawn

Feininger, L. Manhattan, dusk

Feininger, L. Manhattan, moonwake

Feininger, L. Manhattan, night 1941

Fiene, E. Razing Old post office, New York

Franck, F. S. New York from Hoboken

Franck, F. S. New York with roller coaster

Glackens, W. J. Central park, winter

Glackens, W. J. The drive, Central park

Glackens, W. J. March day, Washington square

Grosz, G. Central park

Grosz, G. Central park at night

Grosz, G. Manhattan harbour

Guglielmi, L. New York 21

Guy, F. Tontine coffee house, New York, c 1798

Harvey, G. St Thomas church, Broadway, New York

Hassam, C. Fifth avenue nocturne

Hassam, C. Melting snow, Fifth avenue

Hassam, C. Union square in spring

Hassam, C. Washington arch, spring

Henri, R. Fifty-seventh street

Henri, R. New York street in winter

Henri, R. West 57th street in 1902

Hirsch, S. Lower Manhattan

Hirsch, S. Manhattan

Hnizdovsky, Y. New York subway

Hofmann, H. Mosaics, 1956 (Northeast corner, 711 Third avenue, New York)

Hofmann, H. Mosaics, 1956 (Southwest corner, 711 Third avenue, New York)

Homer, W. Skating in Central park, New York, 1860

Hopper, E. From Williamsburg bridge

Hopper, E. Manhattan bridge and Lily apartments

Hopper, E. New York pavements

Howell, F. W. Gramercy park

Imbert, A. Celebrating the opening of the Erie canal, New York harbor, Nov 4, 1825

Kabak, R. New York harbor

Kantor, M. Farewell to Union Square

Kantor, M. Union square, night

Kelly, E. New York

Kingman, D. Columbus circle

Kingman, D. Washington square, New York

Kline, F. J. New York

Koch, S. Orchard street, New York city

Lane, F. H. New York harbor

Lawson, E. Winter, Central park, New York

Lozowick, L. New York, 1926-27

Luks, G. B. Blue Devils marching down Fifth avenue

MacIver, L. New York

Marca-Relli, C. di. New York City

Margules, D. Lower Fifth avenue

Marin, J. American telephone building, New York City

Marin, J. Broadway night

Marin, J. Bryant square

Marin, J. Fifth avenue and Forty-second street

Marin, J. Looking up Fifth avenue from Thirtieth street

Marin, J. Lower Manhattan, 1920

Marin, J. Lower Manhattan, 1922

Marin, J. Lower Manhattan from the river

Marin, J. Manhattan, St Paul's

Marin, J. Mid-Manhattan II, 1932

Marin, J. Midtown, New York, 1928

Marin, J. Movement—Fifth avenue

Marin, J. New York at night

Marin, J. New York, downtown

Marin, J. New York, East river

Marin, J. New York harbor, 1920

Marin, J. Pertaining to Nassau street, New York

Marin, J. Singer building

Marin, J. Stock exchange, New York city

Marin, J. Street crossing, New York

Marin, J. Street movement, abstraction, New York

Marin, J. Woolworth building in construction

Marin, J. Woolworth building, no 31, 1912

Mario, A. Construction work in New York, 1868

Marsh, R. BMT, Fourteenth street

Marsh, R. The Bowery

Marsh, R. The Bowery at Pell street

Marsh, R. East Tenth street jungle

Marsh, R. End of Fourteenth street crosstown line

Marsh, R. Fourteenth street

Marsh, R. Monday night at the Metropolitan

Marsh, R. Naked over New York

Marsh, R. Prometheus in Rockefeller center

Marsh, R. Under the el

Matthew, K. Skyline (New York)

Matthew, K. Waterfront (New York)

Milbourne, C. Government house, Bowling Green, New York, 1797

Mira, A. S. Washington monument, Washington square, New York

Moran, T. Lower Manhattan from Communipaw

Myers, J. East of the Bowery

O'Keeffe, G. American Radiator building

O'Keeffe, G. New York, night

Pierson, S. Fulton street, New York, 1821

Pollard, C. Residence of Hendrick Remsen, c 1820

Prendergast, M. B. Central park in 1903
Prendergast, M. B. Columbus circle, New York
Prendergast, M. B. East river
Prendergast, M. B. Madison square, New York
Prendergast, M. B. The Mall, Central park
Prendergast, M. B. May day, Central park
Prendergast, M. B. Mulberry Bend park, New York
Robertson, A. New York city from North river
Rose, H. East New York
Rose, H. From Avenue A
Rose, H, Manhattan tops
**Roszak, T. Forty-second street**
Searle, J. Interior of Park theater, New York, 1822
Shahn, B. East Twelfth street
Shahn, B. New York
Shawkey, S. Saturday night in New York city
Sheeler, C. Macdougal alley
Shinn, E. Knoedler's, 34th street
Sloan, J. Backyards, Greenwich village
Sloan, J. Bleecker street Saturday night
Sloan, J. The city from Greenwich village, 1922
Sloan, J. Cornelia street
Sloan, J. Dust storm, Fifth avenue
Sloan, J. Fifth avenue
Sloan, J. Lafayette hotel
Sloan, J. Looking out on Washington square
Sloan, J. Roofs: 23rd street, sunset
Sloan, J. Sixth avenue and Third street
Sloan, J. Sixth avenue and Thirteenth street
Sloan, J. Sixth avenue and 30th street
Sloan, J. Sixth avenue elevated at Third street, 1928
Sloan, J. Sunday in Union square
Sloan, J. The White way
Smith, J. B. John street, c 1768
Sonntag, W. L. The Bowery at night, c 1895
Stella, J. American landscape
Tiffany, L. C. Old New York, c 1878
Tobey, M. Broadway, 1936
Tobey, M. New York
Unidentified artist. Burning of the Tombs
Unidentified artist. Fashionable inn, New York, c 1825
Unidentified artist. Five points, New York, c 1829
Unidentified artist. Furniture shop and warehouse of Duncan Phyfe, Fulton street
Unidentified artist. High bridge across the Harlem river, c 1840
Unidentified artist. Southeast prospect of the city of New York c 1850
Walkowitz, A. New York
Walkowitz, A. New York, improvisation, 1913
Waller, F. Interior of the Metropolitan museum of art, 1881
Waller, F. The Metropolitan Museum in Fourteenth street
Weber, M. Grand central terminal
Weber, M. New York
Weber, M. New York at night
Weber, M. Rush hour, New York, 1915

New York city Susannah by P. Evergood
New York—Hoboken ferry by N. V. Calyo
New York movie by E. Hopper
New York mural by S. Davis
New York, New Haven and Hartford by E. Hopper
New York-Paris no 1, 1931, by S. Davis
New York-Paris no 2, 1931 by S. Davis
New York-Paris no 3, 1931 by S. Davis
New York skyline by H. Katzman
New York subway by Y. Hinzdovsky
New York tablet by M. Tobey
New York 21 by L. Guglielmi
New York (state) Senate
    Unidentified artist. The Senate, Albany, 1850
New York window by C. Hassam
Newark, New Jersey
    Unidentified artist. David Alling house and shop
Newark airport murals, Panel of A. Gorky
Newcomb college by E. Corbett
Newer grounds by N. Lewis
Newfound gap (Smoky mountains) by R. H. Byrum
Newhall, Richard, fl 1829
    Unidentified artist. Tomb in memory of Richard Newhall
NEWMAN, Barnett, 1905-
Abraham
    MMA. New Amer ptg
Adam
    MMA. New Amer ptg
Concord
    MMA. New Amer ptg
Ulysses
    WMAA. Contemp Amer ptg, 1959/60
NEWMAN, Daniel, 1929-
Awakening
    WMAA. Young America 1960
Tempest
    WMAA. Young America 1960
Newman, Henry, 1780-1875
    Ames, E. Henry Newman
NEWMAN, Henry Roderick, 1833?-1918
Pont de Minimes, Chartres          MB
    MB. Ptgs in water color
Temple at Philae          MB
    MB. Ptgs in water color
Wild flowers          MB
    MB. Ptgs in water color
NEWMAN, Robert Loftin, 1827-1912
Landscape with figures          NBM
    Pierson
The letter          DP
    Larkin
    Larkin rev ed
Madonna and child
    Pierson
Mother and son          GAtM
    GAtM. Holbrook collection
Newport, Rhode Island
    Hassam, C. Bailey's beach
    Heade, M. J. Salt marshes, Newport, Rhode Island
    Kensett, J. F. Newport, View near
    Kensett, J. F. Newport harbor, Rhode Island

Newport Rhode Island—*Continued*
  Kensett, J. F. and Huntington, D. Seascape, Newport
  Martin, H. D. Newport landscape
  Richards, W. T. Near Paradise, Newport, Rhode Island
**News** and soda pop by Nura
**News** from the gold diggings by W. S. Mount
The **newsboy** by H. Inman
**Newsboys** by B. Riley
**NEWTON, Gilbert Stuart**, 1794-1835
  Dull lecture
    Flexner. Light of distant skies
**NEY, Lancelot**, 1900-
  Composition                                   MWM
    CoS. New accessions USA, 1958
**Nez-Percés** Indian by A. J. Miller
**Niagara Falls**
  Chambers, T. Niagara Falls
  Church, F. E. Niagara Falls
  Cole, T. Distant view of the Falls of Niagara
  Cropsey, J. F. Niagara Falls
  Cropsey, J. F. Niagara Falls from the foot of Goat island
  De Grailly, V. View of Niagara Falls
  Eilshemius, L. M. Niagara Falls
  Fisher, A. Niagara
  Hicks, E. Falls of Niagara, c 1825
  Gould, L. A. Niagara seen with different eyes (after a print by Lumley)
  Kensett, J. F. Niagara Falls and the rapids
  Morse, S. F. B. Niagara Falls from Table rock
  Trumbull, J. Panoramas of Niagara Falls
  Trumbull, J. View of Niagara from upper bank on British side
  Unidentified artist. Suspension bridge at Niagara
  Vanderlyn, J. Falls of Niagara
  Vanderlyn, J. Falls of Niagara taken from under the Table rock
  Vanderlyn, J. Niagara
**Nice** drums by J. Robinson
**Nicetown** by A. Gold
**Nicholas** by A. N. Wyeth
**Nicholl, Mr**, fl 1809
  Jarvis, J. W. Mr Nicholl
**NICHOLS, Dale**, 1904-
  City National bank                            ATU
    ATU. Coll of Amer art
  Company for supper
    NYG. Fine art
  End of the hunt                               MM
    NYG. Fine art
  Evening in the country
    NYG. Fine art (col)
  Look homeward, America
    NYG. Fine art
  Summer bounty
    NYG. Fine art (col)
**Nichols, Francis**
  Peale, C. W. Gen Francis Nichols
**NICHOLS, Hobart**, b 1869
  Black herd
    NAD. Annual ex, autumn 1949
  Northwest wind                                NJMo
    NJMo. Forty years
  Shifting shadows
    NAD. Annual ex, 1947, 2d half

**Portrait of the artist**
  Neilson, R. P. R. Hobart Nichols
**NICHOLS, Spencer Baird**, 1875-1950
  Tumbling waters
    NAD. Annual ex, 1947, 2d
**Nicoll, Eliza Hopkins.** See Dowdall, Eliza Hopkins (Nicoll)
**Nicot, Georges**
  O'Hara, E. Georges Nicot
**NIESE, Henry E.** 1924-
  The ambry                                     WMAA
    WMAA. Young America 1960
  The red room
    WMAA. Young America 1960
  The window
    DC. 24 biennial ex, 1955
**Night** by M. Beckmann
**Night** by R. Breinin
**Night** by J. F. Folinsbee
**Night** by G. L. Mueller
**Night** by C. S. Price
**Night** by A. J. Pucci
**Night** by K. Zerbe
**Night** after San Juan by W. J. Glackens
**Night** and clouds by A. P. Ryder
**Night** and prophecy by N. Rubington
**Night** baseball by M. A. Phillips
**Night** baseball game Cardinals vs. Dodgers by F. E. Warren
**Night** ceremony by J. Pollock
**Night** chant by E. Millman
**Night** children by P. Guston
**Night** city by R. A. Florsheim
**Night** clouds by A. P. Ryder
**Night** club whoopee by G. Grosz
**Night** event no 2, 1958 by W. Pachner
**Night** fair by M. Jackson
**Night** fantasy by W. Drewes
**Night** figures by C. A. Morris
**Night** fisherman by E. F. Spruce
**Night** fishing by L. Gatch
**Night** flight by J. Ernst
**Night** herd by G. Bartlett
**Night** hunters by C. M. Williamson
**Night** image by C. A. Morris
**Night** in Bologna by P. Cadmus
**Night** journey by C. Oscar
**Night** mirror by W. A. Baziotes
**Night** mission by J. Myers
**Night** music by G. Ratkai
**Night** of return by R. Haines
**Night** of the equinox by C. E. Burchfield
**Night** of the ritual by A. Salemme
**Night** over Buffalo by W. C. Palmer
**Night** passage by W. Thon
**Night** river by C. A. Morris
**Night** scene by W. Pachner
**Night** sea by L. Chesney
**Night** shadows by L. MacIver
**Night** sounds by J. Pollock
**Night** spot by W. Biggs
**Night** square by W. De Kooning
**Night** still life by J. Hultberg
**Night** study of flowers by M. B. Prendergast

Night walk by N. Lewis
Night watch, New Guinea by B. Hasen
Night wind by C. E. Burchfield
Night windows by L. Guglielmi
Night windows by E. Hopper
Night worker by J. Teyral
Nighthawks by E. Hopper
Nightingale, Martha Washington (Greene) fl 1796
    Malbone, E. G. Mrs John Nightingale
Nightmare by G. Grosz
Nightscape by C. Coggeshall
Nighttime, enigma and nostalgia by A. Gorky
Nile by P. Guston
Nile river, Egypt
    Bacon, H. Scene on the Nile
Nimitz, Chester William, 1885-
    Murray, A. K. Fleet Admiral Chester W. Nimitz, U.S.N.
The 9:45 accommodation by E. L. Henry
Nine men by J. Hirsch
Nine P. M. by H. Pittman
1951 by M. Tobey
Nisus and Scylla by J. W. Treiman
Nixon, John, 1733-1808
    Malbone, E. G. John Nixon
Nixtamal y postole by D. Rosenthal
No feather pillow by A. G. Dove
No Heart—Ioway by C. B. King
No let up by G. Grosz
No one heard the thunder by K. Sage
No passing by K. Sage
No turns permitted by R. Marsh
Noah-Wolf by H. Dinnerstein
Noah's ark by E. Hicks
Noah's ark by J. H. Hidley
Nobody's pet by P. Bacon
Nocturne by B. Shahn
Nocturne in black and gold by J. A. M. Whistler
Nocturne in blue and green by J. A. M. Whistler
Nocturne in blue and silver by J. A. M. Whistler
Nogent-le-Rotrou by B. Lamotte
Nolan, Daniel J. d 1920
    Sargent, J. S. Daniel J. Nolan
Noncomformist by W. C. Libby
Nooka sound, View of by J. Webber
Noon by W. De Kooning
Noon by T. H. Hinckley
Noon on the reef by R. Tam
Noonday heat by C. E. Burchfield
Noonday rest by A. J. Miller
The nooning by W. Homer
Nooning on the Platte by A. Bierstadt
Noontide in late May by C. E. Birchfield
Norba, General view of by J. I. Middleton
NORDBERG, Barbara
    Arnold
        NAD. Annual ex, 1954

NORDFELDT, Bror Julius Olsson, 1878-1955
    Driftwood, North Pacific
        IU. Contemp Amer ptg, 1949
    Flight of birds                              ATeS
        ATeS. Collection
    Flood                                        DC
        DC. 21 biennial ex, 1949
    Gifts from the sea
        ICA. Annual ex, 1945/46
    Green woods
        NBuA. Expressionism
    Logs drifting
        Cheney. Story 1958 ed
    Movement                                     MM
        MM. 100 Amer ptrs
    Pietà
        PPC. International ex, 1953
    Sea and rocks
        Cheney. Primer 1958 ed
        Cheney. Story 1958 ed
    Shore birds, Tomales Bay                     IaDM
        CoS. New accessions USA, 1958
    Willow-Swamp, Minnesota
        Gruskin
NORDFELDT, Iris E. 1913-
    Surf, ten mile
        VR. Amer ptg, 1954
Norma by I. G. Olinsky
NORMAN, Irving, 1910-
    Rush hour
        IU. Contemp Amer ptg & sculp, 1957
Normandie by O. M. Pleissner
NORRIS, Ben, 1910-
    The pali
        MM. Amer ptg today
North, William, 1755-1836
    Peale, C. W. Gen William North
North country by W. L. Metcalf
North inlet by J. Allen
North mountain reservation, South Orange, N.J. by A. B. Durand
North river by G. W. Bellows
North river shad by W. M. Chase
Northeaster by W. Homer
Northeaster—Canada geese by L. B. Hunt
Northern lights by Martyl
Northern point by A. N. Wyeth
Northern seascape by R. Rosenborg
Northwest landscape by K. L. Callahan
Northwest wind by C. H. Davis
Northwest wind by H. Nichols
Northwestern town by Unidentified artist
Northwood, New Hampshire
    Unidentified artist. New England village, possibly Northwood, New Hampshire
Norwalk island, View of by G. L. Brown
Norwood, Margaret Eleanor. See Cushing, Margaret Eleanor
Nosegay by P. Bacon
Nospmas M. Egiap, Lancaster, Pennsylvania by C. H. Demuth
Nostalgia migration by T. D. Benrimo
Nostalgic night by M. Sokole
Not at home by E. Johnson
Not even he may rest by G. Biddle
Notch of the White mountains by T. Cole

The **note** by C. Sebree
**Notre** Dame, Paris by W. G. Congdon
**Notre** Dame, Paris by S. Halpert
**Notre** Dame, Paris by M. B. Prendergast
**Nott, Eliphalet,** 1773-1866
  Ames, E. Eliphalet Nott
**Notte** Napolitana by A. Osver
**Nouveau** Cirque, Paris by M. B. Prender-
  gast
**Nova** Scotia fishermen by M. Hartley
**Nova** Scotia landscape by J. E. Heliker
**November** evening by C. E. Burchfield
**November** gale by P. C. Malicoat
**November** mosaic by W. L. Metcalf
**November,** New Mexico by A. Dasburg
**November** 1951 by C. E. Spohn
**November** 7th by L. Kester
**NOVOTNY, Elmer L.** 1909-
  Wingaersheek beach          OYB
    OYB. Annual 1958
    OYB. Supplement 1959
**Norwalk** island, View of by G. L. Brown
**No-way-ke-sug-ga,** an Oto by G. B. King
**NOXON, Herbert R.**
  John L. Lewis
    NAD. Annual ex, 1953
**Noyes, Sarah.** See Tibbits, Sarah (Noyes)
**NOYES, Wilbur Fiske,** 1897-
  Alden Perley White (copy)    MSE
    MSE. Catalogue ports, 1950
**Nu** by S. Davis
**Nu** by G. Gluckmann
**Nude** by H. M. Asplund
**Nude** by M. Beckmann
**Nude** by I. Bishop
**Nude** by L. Kroll
**Nude** by Y. Kuniyoshi
**Nude** by A. Leepa
**Nude** by A. H. Maurer
**Nude** by R. Philipp
**Nude** by J. A. M. Whistler
**Nude** and nine apples by J. Sloan
**Nude** at foot of stairs by J. Sloan
**Nude** at window by M. Hirshfield
**Nude** back by T. Eakins
**Nude** back by E. E. Speicher
**Nude** by the el by P. Evergood
**Nude** combing her hair by R. Philipp
**Nude** dressing hair by W. J. Glackens
**Nude** figure by P. Burlin
**Nude** figure kneeling among clouds by
  E. Geller
**Nude** image no 5 by N. Rubington
**Nude** in doorway by A. Buller
**Nude** in grisaille by R. Détré
**Nude** in profile by R. Soyer
**Nude** in rocky background by L. Kroll
**Nude** in yellow ocre by B. Greene
**Nude** on red couch B. Karfiol
**Nude** on the roof by J. Sloan
**Nude** reclining by B. Shahn
**Nude** with apple by W. J. Glackens

**Nude** with bath towel by G. Grosz
**Nude** with cat by J. Koch
**Nude** with fan by G. W. Bellows
**Nude** with flowers by D. Park
**Nude** with red hair by G. W. Bellows
**Nude** with violin by P. Evergood
**Number** zero—Adam by K. Knaths
**Numbers** in color by J. Johns
**Numena** by G. L. Mueller
**NURA (Nura [Woodson] Ulreich)** 1900?-
  1950
  News and soda pop
    PPC. Ptg in the U.S. 1949
**Nuremberg** by S. Hirsch
**Nursery** school by L. P. Harmon
**Nursing** mother by T. Fried
**Nydia** by G. Fuller
**Nymphs** by R. A. Blakelock

# O

**Oak** creek canyon, Arizona by F. Chapin
**Oak** Knoll, Napa by J. Lee
**Oak** street platform by A. Bohrod
**OAKLEY, Violet,** 1874-1960
  Christ and the woman of Samaria
    PA. Annual ex, 1948
The **oarsmen** by T. Eakins
**Oarsmen** on the Schuylkill by **T. Eakins**
**Obelisks** by E. Berman
**Objects** on table by L. Dodd
**Oblique** illusion by I. R. Pereira
**Oblique** progression by I. R. **Pereira**
**Oboe** player by T. Eakins
**OBROSEY, Arthur**
  Early thaw
    PA. Annual ex, 1959-60
**Occasion** by J. Stefanelle
**Ocean** and cliffs by W. Brice
**Ocean** and rocks by W. Brice
**Ocean** bathers by G. Hartigan
**Ocean** brilliance by N. Carton
**Ocean** greyness by J. Pollock
**OCHIKUBO, Tetsuo,** 1928-
  Changing seasons
    DC. 27 biennial ex, 1961
  Counterpoint             NBuA
    NBuA. Acquisitions 1957-58
**Ochre** building by C. di Marca-Relli
**OCHS, Robert L.**
  Industrial               OYB
    OYB. Annual 1952
**October** by C. E. Burchfield
**October** by J. W. Ehninger
**October,** 1935 by A. G. Dove
**October** morning, Deerfield, Massachusetts
  by W. L. Metcalf
**Octopus** by A. Calder
**Odalisk** by K. F. Roesch
**Odalisque** by L. Kroll
**Odalisque** by C. di Marca-Relli

O'Donnell, Eleanora. See Iselin, Eleanora (O'Donnell)
Odradek by C. L. Cicero
An odyssey for moderns by L. Guglielmi
Oedipus at Colonos by E. K. Schwabacher
OERTEL, Johannes Adam Simon, 1823-1909
  The Shed, Woodruff stables, Jerome avenue, the Bronx, 1848    NNMC
    NJN. Early N.J. artists
Of Maine by J. Heliker
Of sin and error by P. Mangravite
Of the resistance by A. Rattner
Of this time, of that place by J. Muller
Off Cape Split by J. Marin
Off Hatteras no 2 by M. Jamieson
Off Mount Desert island by F. H. Lane
Off Stonington by J. Marin
Off the Maine coast by T. Birch
Off to the Banks by M. Hartley
Off York island, Maine by J. Marin
The offering by S. M. Adler
The offering by X. Gonzales
The offering by N. Tschacbasov
Office at night by E. Hopper
Office board for Smith Brothers coal company by J. F. Peto
Office building by V. I. Cuthbert
Office girls by I. Soyer
Offices by C. Sheeler
Offshore island by M. Avery
Offshore wind by T. P. Blagden
Oganda by P. Wieghardt
OGDEN, Frederick, D.
  Silvery night
    NYG. Fine art
  Winter silence
    NYG. Fine art
Ogden, William Butler, 1805-1877
  Healy, G. P. A. William B. Ogden
Ogdensburg, New York
  Wall, W. G. View of Ogdensburg
Oglethorpe, James Edward, 1696-1785
  Verelst, W. Oglethorpe presenting Tomo-Chi-Chi and the Indians to the Lord Trustees of the colony of Georgia
O'HARA, Eliot, 1890-
  Cape Porpoise harbor    OYB
    OYB. Catalogue 1951
  Empty mansion
    NAD. Annual ex, autumn 1949
  Georges Nicot
    NAD. Annual ex, 1949, 2d half
OHASHI, Yutaka, 1923-
  Black no 8
    IU. Contemp Amer ptg & sculp, 1961
  Stone garden    NNSG
    NNSG. Handbook
  Stone garden IV
    VR. Amer ptg, 1958
  Untitled painting
    NUM. Art across America
Ohio evening by R. Roberts
Ohio magic by B. Shahn
Ohio river and valley
  Bingham, G. C. Scene on the Ohio
  Smith, R. Scene on the Ohio
Ohio skyline by B. Shahn
Oil construction on the beach by M. Frary

Oil splatters and leaves by L. MacIver
OKADA, Frank S. 1931-
  Taurus
    OrPA. Ptgs & sculptures
OKADA, Kenzo, 1902-
  Angel
    VR. Amer ptg, 1958
  Dynasty    NBuA
    NBuA. Acquisitions 1954-57
  Earth glow
    WMAA. Annual ex, 1958
  Height
    Ponente. Mod ptg, 1960 (col)
  Hero
    WMAA. Contemp Amer ptg, 1959/60
  Kine no 1    OCo
    NUM. Art across America
  Memories    WMAA
    Goodrich. Amer art (col)
  Painting on 23
    CtY. Yale alumni
  Silver
    MnMW. 60 Amer ptrs
  Snow mountain
    Baur. Nature
  Solstice    NNSG
    NNSG. Handbook
    NNSG. Younger Amer ptrs
    Read. Concise history
  Tanabata    MB
    Pierson
  White and gold    NBuA
    NBuA. Acquisitions 1959-1961
    PPC. International ex, 1961/62
OKAMURA, Arthur, 1932-
  Aura of a pond
    ICA. Annual ex, 1959-60
  Darkly, soft darts
    IU. Contemp Amer ptg & sculp, 1959
  Mountain pores
    IU. Contemp Amer ptg & sculp, 1961
O'KEEFFE, Georgia, 1887-
  Abstraction, 1926    WMAA
    Goodrich. Amer art
    MnMW. Precisionist view
  Abstraction—white iris
    Cheney. Expressionism 1948 ed
  Abstraction, White rose
    MWM. Georgia O'Keeffe
  American Radiator building    TNF
    Brown. Amer ptg
    Richardson. Ptg in America
  Antelope
    IU. Contemp Amer ptg & sculp, 1955
    MWM. Georgia O'Keeffe
  Black abstraction, 1927    MM
    Baur. New art
  Black cross    ICA
    McCurdy
  Black cross with red sky
    MWM. Georgia O'Keeffe
  Black iris    MM
    Baur. New art (col)
    Cheney. Story 1958 ed
    Pierson
  Black patio door
    IU. Contemp Amer ptg & sculp, 1959
    MWM. Georgia O'Keeffe
  Black place III
    MWM. Georgia O'Keeffe
  Black place green
    MWM. Georgia O'Keeffe

**O'KEEFFE, Georgia**—*Continued*
A blackbird with snow-covered red hills
  MWM. Georgia O'Keeffe
Blue II
  WMAA. Contemp Amer ptg, 1959/60
Blue and green music       ICA
  Brown. Amer ptg
  Pierson
Calla with roses
  Brown. Amer ptg
Cliffs beyond Abiquiu, dry waterfall
  MM. Georgia O'Keeffe
Corn, dark       MM
  Baur. Revolution
Cos Cob
  Cheney. Primer 1958 ed
Cow's skull
  Taylor. Fifty centuries, 1954 ed (col)
Cow's skull, red, white and blue  MM
  Baur. New art
  MM. 100 Amer ptrs (col)
  Pierson
Cow's skull with calico roses
  Gruskin
Dark red leaves on white      DP
  DP. Catalogue
Dead cottonwood tree      CSB
  CoS. New accessions USA, 1952
  MWM. Georgia O'Keeffe
Deer's skull with pedernal
  WMAA. Museum and its friends, 1958
    (col)
Early spring tree
  Pousette-Dart. Amer ptg
From the pelvis series
  MMA. Abstract
From the plains
  Baur. Nature (col)
  WMAA. Pioneers
From the plains no 1, 1953
  Time. 300 years (col)
Green patio door      NBuA
  NBuA. Acquisitions 1957-58
Grey hills      InIJ
  InIJ. 105 ptgs
Horse's skull on blue      ATeS
  ATeS. Collection
  Mendelowitz
In the patio no 1
  MWM. Georgia O'Keeffe
In the patio no 5
  CSFP. Annual ex, 1952
In the patio no 9, 1950      DC
  DC. Halpert collection
It was blue and green
  MWM. Georgia O'Keeffe
Jack-in-the-pulpit
  Cheney. Expressionism 1948 ed
Lake George barns      MnMW
  MnMW. Precisionist view
  MnMW. Reality and fantasy
Lake George, coat and red
  MnMW. Precisionist view
Lake George window      MMA
  Baur. New art
Lightning at sea      MLL
  MWM. Georgia O'Keeffe
Long island sunset      IBM
  Lee. Art then and now
Music—black, blue and green
  Cheney. Primer 1958 ed
My heart
  MWM. Georgia O'Keeffe

New York, night      NeL
  Barker. From realism
  ICA. Amer artists paint the city
  MnMW. Precisionist view (col)
  Time. 300 years (col)
Patio with black door      MLL
  WMAA. Museum and its friends, 1959
Patio with cloud      WiMi
  MnMW. Precisionist view
Pedernal form the ranch no 1
  DC. 27 biennial ex, 1961
Pelvis series, red and yellow
  MWM. Georgia O'Keeffe
Pelvis series, red with blue
  MnMW. Precisionist view
Pelvis with shadows and the moon
  MWM. Georgia O'Keeffe
Pelvis with the moon, New Mexico
  WMAA. Juliana Force
Pink vase and green leaves
  Cheney. Expressionism 1948 ed
Piñons with cedar
  IU. Contemp Amer ptg & sculp, 1957
Poppies      CtMS
  MWM. Georgia O'Keeffe
Ram's head, hollyhock, little hills
  Myers
Ram's head with pedernal
  Lewisohn
Ram's skull with brown leaves
  NUM. Art across America
Ranchos church      DP
  Cheney. Story 1958 ed
Ranchos church, front
  MWM. Georgia O'Keeffe
Seaweed
  MWM. Georgia O'Keeffe
Skunk cabbage      WMAA
  Larkin
  Larkin rev ed
Stables      MiD
  MiD. Treasures
  MnMW. Precisionist view
Summer days
  MWM. Georgia O'Keeffe
Wall with green door
  MWM. Georgia O'Keeffe
The wave      MAP
  Rathbun
White Canadian barn no 2, 1932  MMA
  Baur. New art
  UNESCO. 1860-1949
  UNESCO. 1860-1955
  UNESCO. 1860-1959
White flower      WMAA
  Goodrich. Amer art
White iris
  Cheney. Expressionism 1948 ed
The white place in shadow      DP
  DP. Catalogue
  Pierson
Winter cottonwoods east, V
  MWM. Georgia O'Keeffe

Portrait of the artist
Speicher, E. E. Georgia O'Keeffe
**OKIMOTO, Jerry, 1924-**
Study no 3      NBuA
  NBuA. Acquisitions 1957-58
**Old**ahoma by L. Lozowick
**Old** age by G. Fuller
**Old** American locomotive by L. Feininger
**Old** aqueduct by T. H. Hotchkiss

The old automobile by A. M. R. Moses
Old barn door by J. M. Shinn
Old bars, Dogtown by M. Hartley
Old Battersea bridge by J. A. M. Whistler
Old black pot by W. M. Chase
Old boats and beach by S. Wilson
Old bridge by C. H. Moore
Old canal port by O. F. Bluemner
Old church, Carversville by D. Garber
An old clearing by A. H. Wyant
Old clown making up by J. Sloan
Old companions by J. F. Peto
Old cottager by W. M. Chase
Old courthouse in Philadelphia, 1835 by R. Smith
Old Cremona by W. M. Harnett
Old cupboard door by W. M. Harnett
The old duchess by G. B. Luks
Old factory by J. E. Heliker
Old-fashioned girl by T. Eakins
Old fish house by W. Blaney
Old flintlock by J. D. Chalfant
Old Fort Davis by W. Lester
Old friends by W. M. Harnett (attributed works)
Old friends by W. Homer
Old god by D. Kelley
Old Holliday street theatre, Baltimore by R. Smith
Old homestead by the sea by W. Whittredge
Old horizon by Y. Tanguy
Old house by creek by C. E. Burchfield
Old House of Representatives by S. F. B. Morse
Old Kentucky home, life in the South by E. Johnson
Old lady with a Bible by Unidentified artist
Old lady with a plaid shawl by Unidentified artist
Old man and youth by H. Lee-Smith
Old man with umbrella by B. Boris
Old man's afternoon by W. Barnet
Old meetinghouse and locust trees by C. E. Burchfield
Old mill by G. Inness
Old mill by E. Lawson
Old mill by Unidentified artist
Old mill at sunset by T. Cole
Old mill by waterfall by W. R. Miller
Old mill, Hanover, New Hampshire by J. B. Chapin
Old mill near St Enogat, Brittany by E. D. Boit
Old mill, West Milford, New Jersey by D. Johnson
Old mill, winter by G. H. Durrie
Old mission, San Diego by D. Kingman
Old model and her daughter by R. Henri
Old models by W. M. Harnett
Old New York, c 1878 by L. C. Tiffany
Old North Carolina by W. M. Harnett
The old oaken bucket by A. M. R. Moses
The old order changeth by C. E. Heaney

The old plantation by Unidentified artist
Old quarter, Quebec by P. Dickinson
The old refrain by W. M. Harnett
Old reminiscences by W. M. Harnett (attributed works)
The old salt by J. Marin
Old scraps by W. M. Harnett (attributed works)
Old scraps by J. F. Peto
Old settlers by W. Homer
Old sexton's place by G. Wood
Old ships drawn to home again by J. Lie
Old shipyard by M. B. Prendergast
The old shop window by P. W. Roberts
Old Sleepy Hollow church by T. Chambers
Old South wharf by J. Sharp
Old souvenirs by W. M. Harnett (attributed works)
The old stage coach by E. Johnson
An old time plains fight by F. Remington
Old town brook, Polling, Bavaria by F. Duveneck
Old tree by E. F. Spruce
Old trees at Ormsby farm by R. Smith
Old valentine by H. Harari
Old version by T. Hovenden
Old violin by J. D. Chalfant
Old violin by W. M. Harnett
Old Walnut street prison, Philadelphia in 1835 by R. Smith
The old Westover mansion by E. L. Henry
Old woman, Paris by M. B. Prendergast
Old Zip Coon by M. Goldberg
Oldest house at foot of Coal hill, opposite Market street by R. Smith
OLINSKY, Ivan Gregorewitch, 1878-1962
Henry Audubon Butler                          OYB
   OYB. Supplement 1959
Joseph Green Butler jr                        OYB
   OYB. Catalogue 1951
Norma
   NAD. Annual ex, autumn 1949
Red ribbon
   NAD. Annual ex, 1961
Rosalind
   NAD. Annual ex, 1947, 2d half
Oliphant, Robert
Peale, Raphaelle. Robert Oliphant
OLIVEIRA, Nathan J. 1928-
Bather II
   IU. Contemp Amer ptg & sculp, 1961
Bridge
   IU. Contemp Amer ptg & sculp, 1957
Man walking
   Selz. New images
Seated man with object
   PPC. International ex, 1958
   Selz. New images
Standing man and stick                        MMA
   Selz. New images (col)
Standing woman
   ICA. Annual ex, 1959/60
Standing woman with hat
   Selz. New images
X-1000
   MnMW. Eighty works
Oliver, Andrew, 1707-1774
Emmons, N. Andrew Oliver

Oliver, Daniel, 1664-1732
  Smibert, J. Daniel Oliver
Oliver, Mrs Daniel, fl 1731
  Smibert, J. Mrs Daniel Oliver
Oliver, Elizabeth. See Watson, Elizabeth
  (Oliver)
Oliver, Griselda. See Waldo, Griselda
  (Oliver)
Oliver, Peter, 1741-1821
  Copley, J. S. (attributed works) Peter
    Oliver jr
Oliver, Sally (Hutchinson) fl 1773
  Pelham, H. (attributed works) Mrs Peter
    Oliver jr
Oliver family
  Smibert, J. Daniel, Peter and Andrew
    Oliver
Olmstead, Sarah Ingersoll. See Sanford,
  Sarah Ingersoll (Olmstead)
Olneyville, Rhode island by G. L. Brown
Olsen, Christina
  Wyeth, A. N. Christina Olsen
Olsen, Herb. See Olson, Herbert Vincent
Olsen, John
  Wyeth, A. N. John Olsen's funeral
OLSON, Herbert Vincent, 1905-
  Dancing nuns
    NAD. Annual ex, 1961
  Stella
    NAD. Annual ex, 1949, 2d half
Olson, Olof. See Krans, Olof
Olympia by B. Greene
Omaha, Nebraska
  Haklhuber, F. Herndon hotel, Omaha,
    Nebraska
Ominous by A. Nepote
Omnia vincit amor by B. West
On a lee shore by W. Homer
On a point by T. Marsden
On a Shaker theme by C. Sheeler
On day herd by C. M. Russell
On deck by Z. L. Sepeshy
On guard by W. Homer
On many levels by A. Osver
On Morse mountain, Maine by J. Marin
On Salt lake trail by F. T. Johnson
On stage by C. H. Demuth
On the Ammonoosuc river by H. C. Pratt
On the balcony by M. Cassatt
On the Baltic by L. Feininger
On the banks of the Susquehanna by T.
  Doughty
On the beach by W. M. Chase
On the beach by W. Homer
On the beach by M. Kantor
On the beach by M. B. Prendergast
On the beach by E. F. Spruce
On the Consuma pass, Tuscany by E. D.
  Boit
On the Corso, Rome by M. B. Prendergast
On the Hudson by M. G. Wheelock
On the lake shore by J. M. Hart
On the Normandy coast by W. P. P. Long-
  fellow
On the points by E. H. Osthaus
On the porch by G. W. Bellows

On the porch by N. Vasilieff
On the ranch by J. Bywaters
On the road by T. Otter
On the sly by D. G. Blythe
On the southern plains in 1860 by F. Rem-
  ington
On the stile by W. Homer
On the track by W. Homer
On the warpath by A. F. Tait
On the warpath by C. Wimar
Once upon the past by W. Feldman
Oncoming spring by C. E. Burchfield
One by J. Pollock
One day in spring by H. Mintz
One-eyed creature by K. L. Seligmann
One Horn, a Dakota (Sioux) chief by G.
  Catlin
One moment of silence by H. G. Burkhardt
One of the Dominskis by W. Sommer
One shoe off by J. Brewster
O'NEIL, John, 1915-
  Labyrinth
    IU. Contemp Amer ptg, 1948
O'NEIL, M.
  Civil war encampment                    DN
    DN. Amer primitive ptgs, pt 2
Oneness by H. Saslow
ONETO, Joseph Americus, 1911-
  Circa 1880
    CSFP. Annual ex, 1950/51
  White portico
    PPC. International ex, 1952
The onlookers by W. M. Halsey
ONSLOW-FORD, Gordon
  Untitled, 1960
    ICA. Annual ex, 1961
Open air breakfast by W. M. Chase
Open road by W. De Kooning
Open sea by F. J. Waugh
Open twist by G. Kamrowski
Opening of the wilderness by T. P. Rossiter
The opera box by M. Cassatt
The opera box by G. P. Du Bois
The opera cloak by W. M. Chase
Ophelia by E. Berman
OPPENHEIMER, Max, 1885-1954
  Symphony
    NYG. Fine art
OPPER, E. fl 1880
  Fire engine, Elizabeth, New Jersey, c 1880
                                            RPS
    Davidson v2
    NYG. Fine art
The opposition by W. Gropper
Opposition within a circle by T. Roszak
The oracle by A. Salemme
Orange and rose by T. W. Dewing
Orange and yellow by M. Rothko
Orange door by W. Sommer
Orange market by M. B. Prendergast
Orange over yellow by M. Rothko
Orange personage by R. B. Motherwell
Orange tree and gate, Nassau by W. Homer
Orange vase by M. Avery

Orange vase by H. Hofmann

Orange, wine glass and pansies by Maria Peale

Orarian by K. Knaths

The orators by A. Gorky

Orchard lane by R. Lane

Orchard lane road, Woodstock by J. Pike

Orchard scene by R. Porter

Orchard street, New York city by S. Koch

Orchard with yellow sky by Ben-Zion

Orchards and hills by P. L. Dike

Orchestra by M. Kantor

Orchestral dominance in yellow by H. Hofmann

Orchids and hummingbirds by M. J. Heade

Orchids and spray orchids with humming-birds by M. J. Heade

Order no 11 by M. Siporin

Order no 11, 1868 by G. C. Bingham

Ordinary objects in the artist's creative mind by J. F. Peto

Ore freighter by E. Lewandowski

OREAR, Lucinda Redmon, 1823-1852
  Permelia Redmon Wheeler    MoSL
    MoSL. Handbook 1953

Oregon rocks by G. Daniell

Oregon trail by A. Bierstadt

Orestes by L. A. Golub

Organization by A. Gorky

Organization 5 by S. MacDonald-Wright

Oriental beggar by T. Stamos

Oriental camp by A. P. Ryder

Oriental head by A. Walkowitz

Oriental simplicity by C. C. Ross

Oriental: synchromy in blue-green by S. MacDonald-Wright

Origin by J. De Feo

Origin of life by W. Quirt

Ormond, Mrs Francis. See Ormond, Violet (Sargent)

Ormond, Rose Marie, 1893-1918
  Sargent, J. S. Cashmere shawl (Rose Marie Ormond)
  Sargent, J. S. Nonchaloire (Sargent's niece, Rose Marie Ormond)

Ormond, Violet (Sargent) 1870-1955
  Sargent, J. S. The breakfast table: Sargent's sister Violet
  Sargent, J. S. Violet Sargent

Ornamatique by W. Sommer

Orne, Lois (Pickering) 1684-1753
  Greenwood, J. Lois Pickering Orne

Ornstein, Leo, 1895-
  Zorach, W. Leo Ornstein (Piano concert)

Oropesa by K. Schrag

Orpheus by M. Tobey

ORR, Elliot, 1904-
  Arrangement
    IU. Contemp Amer ptg, 1950
  Storm    NBM
    Baur. Revolution

Orthodox boys by B. Perlin

ORTMAN, George, 1926-
  Game of chance
    WMAA. Young America 1960
  Tales of love
    WMAA. Young America 1960

Orvieto by W. G. Congdon

Orvieto by G. L. K. Morris

Osage scalp dance by J. M. Stanley

Osborn, Fairfield
  Carroll, E. Fairfield Osborn

Osborn, Mrs James M.
  Schnakenberg, H. E. Mrs James M. Osborn

OSCAR, Charles, 1924?-
  Ionian sea
    WMAA. Annual ex, 1956
  Metope
    WMAA. Contemp Amer ptg, 1959/60
  Night journey
    IU. Contemp Amer ptg & sculp, 1955
    Pousette-Dart. Amer ptg

Osceola, Seminole chief, 1804-1838
  Catlin, G. Osceola

OSGOOD, Charles, 1809-1890
  Joseph Gilbert Waters    MSE
    MSE. Catalogue of ports, 1950

Osprey and the otter and the salmon by J. J. Audubon

Ossining, New York
  Havell, R. Sing Sing, 1856

Ossoli, Sarah Margaret (Fuller) marchesa d', 1810-1850
  Hicks, T. Sarah Margaret Fuller

OSTHAUS, Edmund H. 1858-1928
  On the points
    NSP. Sportscapes

OSVER, Arthur, 1912-
  Beginning
    IU. Contemp Amer ptg & sculp, 1959
  Blue chimney
    VR. Biennial ex, 1948
  Chimneys and buildings    IU
    IU. Contemp Amer ptg, 1949
    IU. 20th century
  Cranes
    MM. Amer ptg today
  Going up
    DC. 22 biennial ex, 1951
  Light wells
    CSFP. Annual ex, 1952
  Majestic tenement    PA
    Cheney. Expressionism 1948 ed
    Genauer
    PA. Annual ex, 1947
  Notte Napolitana
    Cheney. Story 1958 ed
  On many levels    NJMo
    NJMo. Your Montclair art museum
  The tall red
    IU. Contemp Amer ptg & sculp, 1961
  Two ventilators    MM
    IU. Contemp Amer ptg, 1950
    MM. 100 Amer ptrs
    Pierson
  Villa dei misteri
    IU. Contemp Amer ptg & sculp, 1955
  Winter rooftops
    ICA. Amer artists paint the city
  World of wires
    IU. Contemp Amer ptg, 1951

Osver, Mrs Arthur. See Betsberg, Ernestine

OSVER, Charles, 1923-
  Late edition
    ICA. Amer artists paint the city

OTIS, Bass, 1784-1861
  John Wesley Jarvis (after Jarvis' self-por-
    trait)                                    NNHS
    Dickson. John Wesley Jarvis
  Seated boy
    Chew. 250 years of art
Otis, James, 1702-1778
  Copley, J. S. James Otis
Otis, Mercy. See Warren, Mercy (Otis)
Otis, Ruth (Cunningham) 1728-1789
  Blackburn, J. Mrs James Otis jr
Oto council by S. Seymour
O'Toole, John. See Toole, John
OTTER, Thomas, fl 1860
  On the road                                MoKN
  Rathbone
Otters
  Audubon, J. J. Osprey and the otter and
    the salmon
Ouananiche fishing: Lake St John, Quebec
  by W. Homer
Ouchy, Lake of Geneva, Switzerland by
  E. D. Boit
Ouldfield, Polly. See Herriot, Mary (Ould-
  field)
Our barn by A. M. R. Moses
Our camp by A. J. Miller
Our classic heritage by V. I. Cuthbert
Our flag is there by Unidentified artist
Our son Thorn by S. E. Dickinson
Out at home by F. Martin
Out back by W. A. Smith
Out by C. Browning
Out for a drive by Unidentified artist
Out for the Christmas tree by A. M. R.
  Moses
Out of the Coulee by C. A. Morris
Out of the web by J. Pollock
Out over the Sound by A. G. Dove
Outdoor circus by L. Blanch
The outing by M. Hewes
The outlier by F. Remington
The outpost by W. Thon
Outside by S. Davis
Outside the Guttenberg race track by W. J.
  Glackens
Outside the walls, Marrakech, Morocco by
  D. Macknight
Outskirts of the forest by W. Whittredge
Outward bound by A. P. Ryder
Outward preoccupation by B. W. Tomlin
Ovenbird and pink lady's-slipper by C. E.
  Heil
Over the bridge to grandma's house by A.
  M. R. Moses
Over the river by A. M. R. Moses
Over the river to grandma's house by A. M.
  R. Moses
Overhauling the trawl by K. Knaths
Owh! in San Paó by S. Davis
Owls
  Audubon, J. J. Snowy owl
  Graves, M. Young owl and moth
  Parker, R. A. Some owls at night
  Price, C. S. Owl
Owl's head by W. Thon

Owl's head, Penobscot bay, Maine by F. H.
  Lane
The Oxbow by T. Cole
The Oxbow by Unidentified artist
Oxen
  Avery, M. Ox on hillside
  Bartlett, G. Ox train
  Ranney, W. T. Pioneers
Oxford, England
  Martyl. View of Oxford
Oyster gatherers of Cancale by J. S. Sar-
  gent
OZENFANT, Amédée, 1886-
  Bathers in a grotto
    Read. Art now 1948
  Building in a park
    Pousette-Dart. Amer ptg
  Still life (L'esprit nouveau II)           NNSG
    NNSG. Handbook
    Read. Concise history
  Theme and variations
    Rosenblum
  Vases                                       MMA
    McCurdy

# P

PACE, Stephen, 1918-
  Prophecy
    PPC. International ex, 1955
PACH, Walter, 1883-1958
  The cathedral
    WMAA. Pioneers
  St Patrick's at night
    MMA. Abstract
PACHNER, William, 1915-
  Antinomes no 1, 1959
    Donahue. William Pachner
  Arrival-departure
    Donahue. William Pachner
  Avenue of martyrs
    Donahue. William Pachner
  The beach
    Donahue. William Pachner
  The beach no 4. See Landscape
  Birthplace
    Donahue. William Pachner
  Blue boy
    Donahue. William Pachner
  Children's prison
    Donahue. William Pachner
  Deposition
    Donahue. William Pachner
  Face of a rabbi. See Head
  Figural composition
    Donahue. William Pachner
  Figure in prayer
    Donahue. William Pachner
  Forbidden blossom
    Donahue. William Pachner
  The gate
    Donahue. William Pachner
  The gathering
    Donahue. William Pachner
  German train
    Donahue. William Pachner
  Head (Face of a rabbi)
    Donahue. William Pachner
  In my own time
    Donahue. William Pachner

Israel
  Donahue. William Pachner
Landscape (The beach no 4)
  Donahue. William Pachner
Let us pray
  Donahue. William Pachner
Maternità, 1943
  Donahue. William Pachner
Maternità, 1954-55 (Theme of earth)
  Donahue. William Pachner
Maternità, 1956
  Donahue. William Pachner
Maternità no 1, 1957
  Donahue. William Pachner
Negro Pietà
  Donahue. William Pachner
Night event no 2, 1958
  Donahue. William Pachner
Night scene, 1958
  Donahue. William Pachner
Night scene, 1959
  Donahue. William Pachner
Rosh Hashana
  Donahue. William Pachner
Scholar
  Donahue. William Pachner
Space, time, embrace
  Donahue. William Pachner
Theme of earth. See Maternità, 1954-55
The truck
  Donahue. William Pachner (col)
Variation on the Avignon Pietà no 1, 1958
  Donahue. William Pachner (col)
Variation on the Avignon Pietà no 2, 1959
                                      OYB
  Donahue. William Pachner
  OYB. Annual 1959
  OYB. Supplement 1959
The **Pacific** by J. A. M. Whistler
**Pacific** circle by M. Tobey
**Pacific** landscape by B. Shahn
**Pacific** series, no 1X—Sierra by L. Calcagno
**Pacific** transition by M. Tobey
**Package** deal by S. Davis
**PACKMAN, Harry**
Sunday morning                        OYB
  OYB. Annual 1952
**Pad** by S. Davis
**Pa-da-he:** Wa-con-da—Elk Horn:—a Crow
  Indian by A. J. Miller
**Paddle** boats. See Side-wheelers
**Paddy, Elizabeth.** See Wensley, Elizabeth
  (Paddy)
**Padre** by G. W. Bellows
**Padre** island by E. F. Spruce
**Padre** Paolo of Pisa by W. Thon
**Padre** Sebastiano by J. S. Sargent
**Pagan** philosophy by A. G. Dove
**Paganini** by J. G. F. Von Wicht
**Page, Alice (Grymes)** fl 1744
  Unidentified artist. Mrs Mann Page II
  and baby John
**Page, Eliza (Hopkins)** fl 1837
  Negus, C. Mrs James Page
**Page, Harlan,** fl 1815
  Unidentified artist. Harlan Page
**Page, Mrs James.** See Page, Eliza (Hop-
  kins)

**Page, Mann**
  Bridges, C. (attributed works) Mann Page
  the second (?)
**Page, Mrs Mann II.** See Page, Alice
  (Grymes)
**Page, Sophie Candace (Stevens)** fl 1860
  Page, W. Portrait of his wife, Sophie
  Candace Stevens
**PAGE, William,** 1811-1885
  Cupid and Psyche
    MiD. Travelers in Arcadia
    Pierson
    Richardson. Ptg in America
    WiMiA. Amer ptg 1760-1960
  Flight into Egypt
    MiD. Travelers in Arcadia
  Portrait of his wife, Sophie  Candace
    Stevens                             MiD
    Baur. Amer ptg
    DC. De gustibus
    Mendelowitz
    MiD. Travelers in Arcadia
    Pierson
    Richardson. Ptg in America
  Self-portrait                         MiD
    MiD. Travelers in Arcadia
    MiD. Treasures
  Young merchants                       PA
    Barker. Amer ptg
    MiD. Travelers in Arcadia
    NJN. Early N.J. artists
    Pierson
**Page, Mrs. William.** See Page, Sophie Can-
  dace (Stevens)
**Page,** 1959 by M. Resnick
**Paget, Violet,** 1856-1935
  Sargent, J. S. Vernon Lee
**Paige, Helen Maria (Yates)** 1797-1829
  Ames, E. Mrs John Keyes Paige
**Paige, John Keyes,** 1788-1857
  Ames, E. John Keyes Paige
**Pailleron children,** fl 1880
  Sargent, J. S. Pailleron children
**PAINE, L. Gerard,** 1905-
  Copley square                         MB
    MB. Ptgs in water color
**Paine, Thomas,** 1737-1809
  Jarvis, J. W. Thomas Paine
The **painter** by S. Menkès
The **painter** by K. Schrag
A **painter,** Portrait of by F. Taubes
**Painter** in the landscape by De H. Margules
**Painter** of birds by A. Blanch
**Painter** of the hole by G. Grosz
**Painter's** triumph by W. S. Mount
**Painting** at Montclair by G. Inness
**Painting** of a smile by R. Gwathmey
**Painting** of the ocean by J. Davis
**Painting** with red letter S by R. Rauschen-
  berg
**Pajarito** by S. Davis
**Palace** of the windowed rocks by Y. Tanguy
**Palaestra** by D. Tanning
**Palazzo** by J. E. Heliker
**PALAZZOLA, Guy,** 1920?-
  Allium sativum                        MiD
    CoS. New accessions USA, 1950
    ICA. Annual ex, 1951

**PALAZZOLA, Guy—**_Continued_
Family tree            OYB
  OYB. Annual 1957
Prometheus rebound      OYB
  OYB. Annual 1958
  OYB. Supplement 1959
**Palermo** by R. Kozlow
The **pali** by B. Norris
**Palisade** amusement park by G. O. Hart
**Palisades** by Unidentified artist
The **palm** leaf shade by G. C. Bingham
**Palm** tree by W. Homer
**Palm** tree, Nassau by W. Homer
**Palm** trees, Florida by W. Homer
**Palm** trees with a domed church by A. Bierstadt
**PALMER, Charles B. R.** fl 1826
  Mother and child          VWR
  VWR. Folk art (col)
**Palmer, Elsie**
  Sargent, J. S. Miss Elsie Palmer
**PALMER, F. F.**
  American farm scene, 1853
    Davidson v 1
  Champions of the Mississippi, 1866
    Davidson v2
  Wooding up on the Mississippi, 1861
    Davidson v2
**PALMER, Walter Launt,** 1854-1932
  Woods in winter           MB
  MB. Ptgs in water color
**PALMER, William**
  Hovering twilight
    IaDa. 30th anniversary
**PALMER, William Charles,** 1906-
  Clematis henryi           NUM
    NUM. Root bequest
  Cows in the corn
    MoSL. Contemporary Amer ptg
  Dust, drought and destruction    WMAA
    Pierson
  Horses in landscape
    Gruskin
  Last snow           WMAA
    Pierson
  Night over Buffalo
    WMAA. Annual ex, 1957
**Palms** with ripe dates, Marrakech, Morocco by D. Macknight
**Paludes** by E. Berman
**Pan** and the wolf by J. A. Weir
**Panama, Isthmus of**
  Browere, A. Del O. Crossing the Isthmus
**Pancho** Villa, dead and alive by R. B. Motherwell
**Pancoast, Ella.** See Widener, Ella (Pancoast)
**Pandora's** box, Illustration for by C. H. Demuth
**Panic** of 1869 by C. Knoll (attributed works)
**Panizza, Oskar**
  Grosz, G. Homage to Oskar Panizza
**Panorama,** Penobscot bay islands by W. A. Kienbusch
**Panorama;** the valley of Mexico by C. W. Chapman
**Panoramic** view of the palace and gardens of Versailles by J. Vanderlyn
**Pansies** by C. H. Demuth
**Panther** Hollow by J. Kane

**Papa,** maman est blessée by Y. Tanguy
**Paper** flowers and paper by C. Vinson
**Paper** storm by A. Bohrod
**PAPSDORF, Frederick,** 1883-
  Flowers in vase          OYB
  OYB. Supplement
**Paquebot,** Paris by C. H. Demuth
The **parable** by B. Shahn
**Parabola** by A. G. Dove
**Parabolic** San Francisco by E. Ewing
**Parade** by P. Blume
**Parade** by C. E. Burchfield
**Parade** by R. Cowles
**Parade** by M. Gordon
**Parade** by W. T. Kelly
**Parade** figure by R. Markman
**Parade** for repeal with Jimmy Walker by B. Shahn
**Parade** passing Independence hall, Philadelphia by J. L. Krimmel
**PARADISE, John Wesley,** 1809-1862
  Mrs Elizabeth Oakes Smith
    NJN. Early N.J. artists
**Paradise** rock, Newport by J. F. Kensett
**Paradise** tree by M. T. Abrams
**Paradise** valley, Newport by J. La Farge
The **parallels** by Y. Tanguy
**Parcell, Emma (Minor)**
  Parcell, M. S. My mother
**PARCELL, Malcolm Stevens,** 1896-1921
  F. E. Richardson jr.
    PPC. Ptg in the U.S. 1949
  My mother           OYB
    OYB. Catalogue 1951
**PARELLA, Albert**
  Roof pattern
    OYB. Annual 1952
**Paris, France**
  Asplund, T. Rue de Rivoli, Paris
  Berman, E. Bridges of Paris
  Boit, E. D. Arc de Triomphe
  Boit, E. D. Place de l'Opera
  Boit, E. D. Place du Carrousel, 1911
  Foss, O. Paris under snow
  Glackens, W. J. Luxembourg gardens
  Hassam, C. July 14, rue Daunou
  Kuntz, R. Île de la Cité
  MacIver, L. Paris
  Morse, S. F. B. Gallery of the Louvre
  Pleissner, O. M. Early morning, Paris
  Prendergast, M. B. Montparnasse
  Prendergast, M. B. Notre Dame, Paris
  Prendergast, M. B. Paris boulevard in rain
  Prendergast, M. B. Sketch of Paris
  Prendergast, M. B. Tuileries gardens
  Sargent, J. S. In the Luxembourg gardens
  Sargent, J. S. Luxembourg gardens at twilight
  Shinn, E. Early morning, Paris
The **Paris** bit by S. Davis
**Paris** café, morning by G. P. Du Bois
**Paris** music hall by E. Shinn
**Paris** night meanders by L. MacIver
**Parish** playground by B. Miller
La **Parisienne** by M. Weber
**PARK, David,** 1911-1960
  Les baigneuses
    DC. 27 biennial ex, 1961

Four men                              WMAA
  Goodrich. Amer art (col)
Nude with flowers
  IU. Contemp Amer ptg & sculp, 1959
The patio
  VR. Amer ptg, 1958
Riverbank
  IU. Contemp Amer ptg & sculp, 1957
Standing couple
  IU. Contemp Amer ptg & sculp, 1961
Three bathers
  PA. Annual ex, 1959-60
PARK, Linton, 1826-1870?
  Flax-scutching bee                  DN
  Chew. 250 years of art
  Davidson v2
  DN. Amer primitive ptgs, pt 1
  Ford. Pictorial folk art
  U.S. National Capital sesquicentennial
    com
Park avenue, New York by E. D. Boit
Park bench by W. M. Chase
Park bench by R. Marsh
Park bench by H. Pippin
Park by the river by W. J. Glackens
Park by the sea by M. B. Prendergast
The park, Salem by M. B. Prendergast
Park Rosenberg by W. De Kooning
Park street, Boston by K. Zerbe
Park theater, Interior of, by J. Searle
Parke, Frances, d 1715
  Unidentified artist. Miss Parke (possibly
    Frances Parke)
PARKER, Bill, 1922-
  Composition in blue
  IU. Contemp Amer ptg & sculp, 1957
Parker, Eliza (Mason) See Mason, Eliza
Parker, Ernest Lee
  Eakins, T. Ernest Lee Parker
Parker, Helen, fl 1908
  Eakins, T. Old-fashioned dress (Miss
    Parker)
Parker, Mary A. (Cox)
  Eakins, T. Mrs Gilbert Lafayette Parker
PARKER, Raymond, 1922-
  Summer afternoon
  CoS. New accessions USA, 1960
  Untitled                            NBuA
  IU. Contemp Amer ptg & sculp, 1961
  MnMW. 60 Amer ptrs
  NBuA. Acquisitions 1959-1961
PARKER, Robert Andrew, 1927-
  East Riding of Yorkshire yeomanry dis-
    embarking from H.M.S. Cressy
  WMAA. Young America 1957
  Marseilles, night                   WMAA
  Pierson
  Red ship
  WMAA. Annual ex, 1956
  Some owls at night
  WMAA. Annual ex, 1958
  View from the Jersey turnpike, no 2
  WMAA. Young America 1957
Parker, Mrs Samuel Dunn. See Mason,
  Eliza
Parkland and trees by B. West (attributed
  works)
Parrish, Sarah Redwood
  Chase. W. M. Sarah Redwood Parrish

Parrots
  Audubon, J. J. Carolina parrot
  Beckmann, M. Girl with parrot
  Randall, A. M. Basket of fruit with par-
    rot
  Zerbe, K. The parrot and decanter
PARSHALL, Douglass Ewell, 1899-
  Clowns
  CSEP. Annual ex, 1952
Parsley, Sketch for by L. Bemelmans
Parson Weems' fable by G. Wood
PARSONS, Jackson
  Number 30, 1950
  MMA. Fifteen
Parsons family, fl 1850
  Stock, J. W. Parsons family
Parthenon
  Church, F. The Parthenon
  Walker, C. H. Section of the Parthenon
  Warren, H. B. Corner of the Parthenon,
    Athens
  Warren, H. B. The Parthenon, Athens
Partitions of the city by M. Tobey
Parturition by L. A. Golub
Pa's brainstorm by W. Sommer
PASCIN, Jules, 1885-1930
  Child with cat
  Cheney. Expressionism 1948 ed
  Girl in green and rose
  Brown. Amer ptg
  Reclining model                     MMA
  Pierson
Pasiphae by J. Pollock
The pass by E. L. Blumenschein
Passacaglia by A. V. Tack
Passage by L. Edmondson
Passage à travers by J. Berlandina
Passage of the Delaware by T. Sully
Passage to Etna by P. Blume
Passage to the sea by O. Dozier
Passementerie by C. W. Hare
Passenger pigeon by J. J. Audubon
The passing leap by J. S. Curry
Passing of dreams by A. B. Davies
The passing scene by J. Levine
Passing show by P. Evergood
Passing shower by G. Inness
Passion according to St Matthew by F.
  Nagler
Passion flowers and hummingbirds by M. J.
  Heade
Passion of Sacco and Vanzetti by B. Shahn
Passions and feverishness by P. Mangravite
Passover supper by J. Land
Pastor De Segovia by D. Pond
Pastoral by B. Chaet
Pastoral study by A. P. Ryder
Pastorale by T. D. Benrimo
Pastorale by A. Pickens
Pastorale by K. Zerbe
Pastry window by J. Kinigstein
The pasture by A. P. Ryder
Pat Lyon at his forge by J. Neagle
Patch picture for Dr Physick by Raphaelle
  Peale
Patchwork cows by W. Sommer

Paterson by B. Shahn
The path by S. Laufman
Path in motion by F. Ruvolo
Pathetic song by T. Eakins
The patio by D. Park
Patio Royale by R. Philipp
Patio with black door by G. O'Keeffe
Patio with cloud by G. O'Keeffe
The patriarch by S. Rosenberg
Patten, G. fl 1798
   Malbone. E. G. Dr G. Patten
Patterns by Z. Sepeshy
PATTERSON, Charles Robert, 1878-
   Furling the foresail
     NYG. Fine art
Patterson, Elizabeth De Peyster (Peale)
   fl 1818
   Peale, C. W. Elizabeth De Peyster Peale
    Patterson
Patterson, Howard
   Archer, E. Howard Patterson of the Har-
    lem Yankees
Patty by E. E. Speicher
Pau de St Jannes by M. Beckmann
PAUL, Jeremiah, fl 1791-1820
   Four children playing in a courtyard
    (Children at play)
   Flexner. Light of distant skies
   Richardson. Ptg in America
   WiMiA. Amer ptg 1760-1960
Paul and Virginia by Unidentified artist
Paula by R. F. Lahey
Les pauvres by E. Higgins
Pavilion by J. Cornell
Pawnee chief by C. M. Russell
Pawnee council by S. Seymour
Pawnee Indian shooting antelope by A. J.
   Miller
Pawnee Indians migrating by A. J. Miller
Pawnee Indians watching the caravan by
   A. J. Miller
Pawnee running buffalo by A. J. Miller
Pawnshop by J. Levine
PAXTON, William McGregor, 1869-1941
   Girl with a hand mirror    PR
    PR. Catalogue
   House maid    DC
    DC. De gustibus
   Sylvia    OYB
    OYB. Catalogue 1951
Payne, Dorothea. See Madison, Dorothea
   (Payne) Todd
Payne, Jennie (Bryan) See Bryan, Jennie
Payne, John Howard, 1792-1852
   Bingham, G. C. John Howard Payne
Payne, Mrs John Barton. See Bryan, Jennie
Paysage by M. Hartley
Peabody, Ellen. See Endicott, Ellen (Pea-
   body)
Peabody, George, 1795-1869
   Healy, G. P. A. George Peabody
   Huntington, D. George Peabody
   Neagle, J. George Peabody
Peabody, Mrs Stephen, fl 1809
   Stuart, G. Mrs Stephen Peabody
Peace II, 1946 by G. Grosz
Peace among the nations by R. A. Blakelock

Peace and plenty by G. Inness
Peace in October by M. Dixon
Peace memorial, Hiroshima by M. R. Cooper
The peace pipe by C. M. Russell
The peaceable kingdom by E. Hicks
Peaceable kingdom by W. T. Wiley
The peaceable kingdom of the branch by
   E. Hicks
Peaceful day in the Mohawk valley by J. J.
   Hammer
Peaceful valley (Blue ridge mountains) by
   R. H. Byrum
The peacemakers by G. P. A. Healy
Peach jacket by E. E. Speicher
Peach trees in blossom by J. Marin
Peaches by W. Kuhn
Peaches by H. Lundeberg
Peacocks
   Davis, J. H. (attributed works) Mrs Tuttle
    (with peacock)
   Keller, H. G. Peacock
   Roberts, P. W. Plumage
Peak of Maua Roa, Moorea, Society islands
   by J. La Farge
PEAKE, Channing, 1910-
   Farm machinery
    IU. Contemp Amer ptg & sculp, 1955
PEALE, Anna Claypoole, 1791-1878
   Andrew Jackson    CtY
    CtY. Portrait index
   Marianne Beckett    PH
    Chew. 250 years of art
   Rubens Peale
    WiMiA. Amer ptg 1760-1960
   Still life    MAC
    OCiM. Ptgs by the Peale family
   Still life with strawberries
    MdBMu. Rendezvous
Peale, Benjamin Franklin. See Peale, Frank-
   lin
Peale, Charles Linnaeus, 1794-1832
   Peale, C. W. Charles Linnaeus Peale
PEALE, Charles Willson, 1741-1827
   Abraham B. De Peyster
    Belknap
   Alexander and Angelica Robinson
    Sellers. C. W. Peale v2
   Alexander Hamilton    PPhI
    Time. 300 years (col)
   Andrew Jackson
    Sellers. C. W. Peale v2
   Artist in his museum (Self-portrait in his
    museum)    PA
    Mendelowitz
    OCiM. Ptgs by the Peale family
    PA. Annual ex, 1955
    Pierson
    Robb. Harper history
    Roos
    Sellers. C. W. Peale v2
   Benjamin Franklin    PA
    Lee. Art then and now
    Robb. Harper history
    Roos
   Benjamin Franklin    PH
    OCiM. Ptgs by the Peale family
    Pierson
    U.S. National Capital sesquicentennial
    com
   Benjamin Laming and wife
    OCiM. Ptgs by the Peale family

Benjamin Rush
  Flexner. Light of distant skies
Charles Alexandre Lesueur
  OCiM. Ptgs by the Peale family
Charles Linnaeus Peale            MdBH
  Sellers. C. W. Peale v2
Charles Waterton                  ELNP
  Sellers. C. W. Peale v2
Coleman Sellers
  Sellers. C. W. Peale v2
David Forman                      MPB
  NUM. Art across America
Elizabeth De Peyster Peale Patterson
  Sellers. C. W. Peale v2
Exhuming the mastodon             MdBMu
  Barker. Amer ptg
  Flexner. Amer ptg
  Flexner. Light of distant skies
  Flexner. Short history
  Larkin
  Larkin rev ed
  MdBMu. Rendezvous (detail)
  OCiM. Ptgs by the Peale family
  Pa. Annual ex, 1955
  Pierson
  Roos
  Sellers. C. W. Peale v2
  Time. 300 years (col)
  U.S. National Capital sesquicentennial
    com
Family group. See Peale family
Francis Bailey
  OCiM. Ptgs by the Peale family
Francis Nichols                   MoKN
  MoKN. Handbook
Fruits of Belfield
  Sellers. C. W. Peale v2
George Washington                 OCl
  Chew. 250 years of art
George Washington, 1776           NBM
  U.S. National Capital sesquicentennial
    com
George Washington, 1779           PA
  OCiM. Ptgs by the Peale family
  Pierson
  Roos
George Washington at the Battle of
    Princeton                     CtY
  CtY. Portrait index
Hannah Moore Peale and step-daughter
                                  MdBH
  Sellers. C. W. Peale v2
Henry Clay                        PH
  OCiM. Ptgs by the Peale family
  Sellers. C. W. Peale v2
James Arbuckle
  Flexner. First flowers
James Madison
  Time. 300 years (col)
James Peale (The lamplight portrait)
                                  MiD
  Flexner. Light of distant skies
  MiD. Treasures
  OCiM. Ptgs by the Peale family
  Pierson
  Richardson. Ptg in America
  Sellers. C. W. Peale v2
James Peale painting a miniature  MAC
  DC. Amer ptrs of the South
  OCiM. Ptgs by the Peale family
James W. De Peyster               NNHS
  Belknap

John Adams
  Time. 300 years (col)
John B. De Peyster                NNHS
  Belknap
John Beale Bordley                NNHS
  OCiM. Ptgs by the Peale family
John Cadwalader
  WiMiA. Amer ptg 1760-1960
John De Peyster                   NNHS
  Belknap
  Larkin
  Larkin rev ed
John Eager Howard (after Rembrandt
    Peale)
  MdBMu. Rendezvous
John Paul Jones                   PPhI
  Time. 300 years (col)
John Philip de Haas               DN
  DN. Mellon coll
The lamplight portrait. See James Peale
Mary Tilghman
  Sellers. C. W. Peale v2
Mrs Charles Willson Peale         NNHS
  Belknap
Mrs Elizabeth De Peyster Peale
  Sellers. C. W. Peale v2
Mrs Francis Bailey
  OCiM. Ptgs by the Peale family
Mrs Gerard De Peyster             NNHS
  Belknap
  NNHS. Waldron Phoenix Belknap coll
Mrs James Arbuckle and son Edward
  Flexner. First flowers
Mrs John De Peyster               NNHS
  Belknap
Mrs Thomas Harwood                MM
  PA. Annual ex, 1955
Mrs William De Peyster jr         NNHS
  Belknap
Mordecai Gist
  WiMiA. Amer ptg 1760-1960
Nicholas Brewer I
  OCiM. Ptgs by the Peale family
Peale family                      NNHS
  Larkin
  Larkin rev ed
  PA. Annual ex, 1955
  Pierson
  Richardson. Ptg in America
  Roos
Pleasure party by a mill
  MiD. Ptg in America
  WiMiA. Amer ptg 1760-1960
Rachel weeping
  Flexner. Light of distant skies
Richard Tilghman
  Sellers. C. W. Peale v2
Samuel B. Webb
  MB. New England miniatures
Sarah Fishbourne Bordley          NJMo
  NJMo. Your Montclair art museum
Self-portrait                     NNHS
  MdBMu. Rendezvous
Self-portrait                     PA
  Roos
  Sellers. C. W. Peale v2
Self-portrait in his museum. See The artist
    in his museum
Self-portrait in uniform
  OCiM. Ptgs by the Peale family
Sophonisba Peale Sellers
  Sellers. C. W. Peale v2

**PEALE, C. W.**—*Continued*
Staircase group                    PPhM
  Barker. Amer ptg
  ICA. From colony to nation
  Larkin
  Larkin rev ed (front)
  PA. Annual ex, 1955
  Pierson
  Richardson. Ptg in America
  Roos
  Sellers. C. W. Peale
  Taylor. Fifty centuries, 1954 ed (col)
  Time. 300 years (col)
  Walker. Ptgs from America
Thomas Jefferson                   PPhI
  Pierson
  U.S. National Capital sesquicentennial
    com
Thomas Johnson and family
  Flexner. Light of distant skies
Timothy Matlack                    DN
  Mendelowitz
Titian Ramsay Peale II: in the uniform of
    a naturalist                   MdBH
  Sellers. C. W. Peale v2
Washington, Lafayette and Tilghman at
    Yorktown
  ICA. From colony to nation
  Pierson
  Roos
  Time. 300 years (col)
William Buckland                   CtY
  CtY. Portrait index
  Pierson
William De Peyster (copy after John
    Durand)                        NNHS
  Belknap
William De Peyster jr              NNHS
  Belknap
  NNHS. Waldron Phoenix Belknap coll
William North                      MiD
  MiD. Treasures
William Smallwood
  MdBMu. Rendezvous
Worthy of liberty, Mr Pitt scorns to in-
    vade the liberties of other people  IU
  Roos
Yarrow Mamout                      PH
  Sellers. C. W. Peale v2

### Portrait of the artist
West, B. Charles Willson Peale
**PEALE, Charles Willson,** 1741-1827 and
  **PEALE, Rembrandt,** 1778-1870
Gilbert Stuart                     NNHS
  Sellers. C. W. Peale v2
**Peale, Mrs Charles Willson,** 1765-1804. See
  Peale, Elizabeth (De Peyster)
**Peale, Mrs Charles Willson,** d 1821. See
  Peale, Hannah (Moore)
**Peale, Elizabeth (De Peyster)** 1765-1804
  Peale, C. W. Mrs Charles Willson Peale
**Peale, Franklin,** 1795-1870
  Peale, Rembrandt. Franklin Peale
**Peale, Hannah (Moore)** d 1821
  Peale, C. W. Hannah Moore Peale
**PEALE, Harriet (Cany)** 1800-1869
  Female figure with turban
    Chew. 250 years of art
**PEALE, James,** 1749-1831
  Bailey Washington
    DC. Privately owned
  Balsam apple and vegetable       MM
    Mendelowitz

Edmond Rouvert
  Chew. 250 years of art
Fruit                              DC
  DC. Masterpieces
Fruits of autumn                   WMAA
  Barker. Amer ptg
James Peale and his family         PA
  Flexner. Light of distant skies
  OCiM. Ptgs by the Peale family
  Richardson. Ptg in America
Jane and James Peale jr
  MiD. Coll in progress
  WiMiA. Amer ptg 1760-1960
Jane Rouvert
  Chew. 250 years of art
Mme Dubocq and her four children
                                   KyLS
  OCiM. Ptgs by the Peale family
  KyLS. Kentucky port gall
A man                              MoKN
  MoKN. Handbook
Mrs Susan Coren Towers             OCl
  OCl. Portrait miniatures
Ramsay-Polk family at Carpenter's point,
    Maryland
  MiD. Coll in progress
  Pierson
  WiMiA. Amer ptg 1760-1960
Rembrandt Peale                    CtY
  CtY. Portrait index
  OCiM. Ptgs by the Peale family
  Seller. C. W. Peale v2
Samuel Allen of Philadelphia
  WiMiA. Amer ptg 1760-1960
Self-portrait with his family      PA
  Pierson
Still life                         ATeS
  ATeS. Collection
Still life                         MWM
  Flexner. Light of distant skies
Still life                         DeWin
  Pierson
Still life with fish bowl
  WiMiA. Amer ptg 1760-1960
Still life with fruit
  Chew. 250 years of art
Still life with grapes             OYB
  OYB. Catalogue 1951
Still life with watermelon
  DC. Privately owned
View on the Brandywine
  WiMiA. Amer ptg 1760-1960
Washington and his generals at Yorktown
                                   MdBH
  MdBMu. Rendezvous
  Pierson
  U.S. National Capital sesquicentennial
    com

### Attributed works
Watermelon and fruit               MB
  MB. Karolik coll

### Portrait of the artist
Peale, C. W. James Peale (the lamplight
    portrait)
Peale, C. W. James Peale painting a
    miniature
**PEALE, James,** 1789-1876
  Marine with shipping
    OCiM. Ptgs by the Peale family

### Portrait of the artist
Peale, J. James Peale jr
Peale, J. Jane and James Peale jr

**Peale, Jane**
Peale, J. Jane and James Peale jr
**PEALE, Margaretta Angelica,** 1795-1882
Still life
Chew. 250 years of art
Still life with cake, raisins and nuts
WiMiA. Amer ptg 1760-1960
Strawberries and cherries          PA
OCiM. Ptgs by the Peale family
**PEALE, Maria,** 1787-1866
Orange, wine glass and pansies
WiMiA. Amer ptg 1760-1960
Rubens Peale at his easel (Interior show-
ing Rubens Peale painting)
Chew. 250 years of art
WiMiA. Amer ptg 1760-1960
**PEALE, Mary Jane,** 1827-1902
Still life, fruit in a monogrammed bowl,
"R.P."
Chew. 250 years of art
**PEALE, Raphaelle,** 1774-1825
After the bath          MoKN
Janson. Picture history
Larkin
Larkin rev ed
Mendelowitz
MoKN. Handbook
OCiM. Ptgs by the Peale family
Pierson
Richardson. Ptg in America
Roos
Time. 300 years (col)
WiMiA. Raphaelle Peale
Balsam apples and turnips
WiMiA. Amer ptg 1760-1960
WiMiA. Raphaelle Peale
Dish of blackberries
OCiM. Ptgs by the Peale family
WiMiA. Raphaelle Peale
Fox grapes and peaches          PA
WiMiA. Raphaelle Peale
James Ferguson          MdBH
WiMiA. Raphaelle Peale
Man in gray coat          WiMiA
WiMiA. Raphaelle Peale
Melons and morning glories
WiMiA. Amer ptg 1760-1960
Mrs John Montgomery          MM
WiMiA. Raphaelle Peale
Nathan Towson          MdBH
MdBMu. Rendezvous
Otho Holland William
MdBMu. Rendezvous
Patch picture for Dr Physick
Frankenstein. After the hunt
OCiM. Ptgs by the Peale family
Robert Oliphant          DNC
WiMiA. Raphaelle Peale
Rubens Peale: mascot of the Macpher-
son's Blues          DNC
Sellers. C. W. Peale v2
WiMiA. Raphaelle Peale
Still life          CtHW
Baur. Amer ptg
Still life          MiD
Flexner. Light of distant skies
Still life          PH
Frankenstein. After the hunt
Still life c 1810          CtHW
WiMiA. Raphaelle Peale
Still life, 1813 (Stuempfig coll)
ICA. From colony to nation

Still life, 1815          PH
CSFP. Illusionism
Still life, 1818 (Graham coll)
OCiM. Ptgs by the Peale family
WiMiA. Raphaelle Peale
Still life, c 1820          OT
Larkin rev ed (col)
Pierson
WiMiA. Raphaelle Peale
Still life: balsam apples and turnips. See
Balsam apples and turnips
Still life—Fruit and nuts
CtY. Yale alumni
Still life with cake          NBM
Barker. Amer ptg
DC. Amer ptrs of the South (col)
Larkin
Larkin rev ed
Time. 300 years (col)
Still life with herring          PH
MdBMu. Rendezvous
WiMiA. Raphaelle Peale
Still life with peaches          NBM
WiMiA. Raphaelle Peale
Still life with raisin cake
WiMiA. Raphaelle Peale
Still life with steak          NUM
WiMiA. Raphaelle Peale
Still life with vegetables          CtHW
Roos
Still life with watermelon          MSM
Chew. 250 years of art
WiMiA. Raphaelle Peale
Still life with watermelon (Stralem coll)
WiMiA. Raphaelle Peale (col cover)
Thomas Jefferson
MdBMu. Rendezvous
Watermelon and fruit
CtY. Yale alumni
Young man          PPC
WiMiA. Raphaelle Peale
**PEALE, Rembrandt,** 1778-1860
Court of death          MiD
Barker. Amer ptg
Richardson. Ptg in America
Court of death (Sellers coll)
Larkin
Larkin rev ed
David Cox          InIJ
InIJ. 105 ptgs
Edward Denison
MdBMu. Rendezvous
Edward Johnson          MdBMu
MdBMu. Rendezvous
Franklin Peale
Sellers. C. W. Peale v2
George Armistead          MdBMu
MdBMu. Rendezvous
George Washington          MdBP
MdBMu. Rendezvous
George Washington (porthole portrait)
Chew. 250 years of art
PW
George Washington (porthole portrait)
OYB
OYB. Accessions
OYB. Supplement 1959
George Washington (porthole portrait)
PA
Pierson
Joseph Outen Bogart          DC
DC. Masterpieces

**PEALE, Rembrandt**—*Continued*
Mendes Cohen                              MoSL
  MoSL. Handbook 1953
Robert Fulton                             MiD
  MiD. Treasures
  Pierson
Rubens Peale with the first geranium
    brought to America, 1801
  MdBMu. Rendezvous
  Sellers. C. W. Peale
Samuel Smith                              MdBMu
  MdBMu. Rendezvous
  OCiM. Ptgs by the Peale family
Self-portrait                             MiD
  MiD. Treasures
  Pierson
Self-portrait                             PA
  OCiM. Ptgs by the Peale family
Self-portrait 1791, age 13
  Sellers. C. W. Peale v2
Thomas Jefferson                          NNHS
  Larkin
  Larkin rev ed
  Mendelowitz
  Pierson
  Roos
  Time. 300 years (col)

#### Portrait of the artist
Peale, J. Rembrandt Peale
**PEALE, Rembrandt, 1778-1870** and
  **PEALE, Charles Willson, 1741-1827**
Gilbert Stuart                            NNHS
  Sellers. C. W. Peale v2
**PEALE, Rubens, 1784-1865**
Basket of fruit                           MB
  Chew. 250 years of art
  MB. Karolik coll
Belfield (original by C. W. Peale)
  Sellers. C. W. Peale v2
From nature in the garden
  WiMiA. Amer ptg 1760-1960
Lemons and sugar                          PR
  PR. Catalogue
Melon, peaches and grapes
  WiMiA. Amer ptg, 1760-1960
Peale's museum
  OCiM. Ptgs by the Peale family
Still life 1860
  Larkin
  Larkin rev ed
Still life with fruit                     MAP
  Chew. 250 years of art
Two grouse in underbrush of laurel        MiD
  OCiM. Ptgs by the Peale family
  Pierson

#### Portrait of the artist
Peale, A. C. Rubens Peale
Peale, Maria. Rubens Peale at his easel
Peale, Raphaelle. Rubens Peale, mascot
    of the Macpherson's Blues
Peale, Rembrandt. Rubens Peale with
    the first geranium brought to Amer-
    ica, 1801
**PEALE, Sarah Miriam, 1800-1885**
Mrs Hugh McC Birckhead
  MdBMu. Rendezvous
Still life
  OCiM. Ptgs by the Peale family
Still life with melon and grapes
  MdBMu. Rendezvous

Peale, Sophonisba. See Sellers, Sophonisba
  Angusciola (Peale)
**PEALE, Titian Ramsay, 1799-1885**
Bright house, Rehoboth beach, Delaware
  WiMiA. Amer ptg 1760-1960
Still life with flower and insects
  Chew. 250 years of art
Peale, Titian Ramsay, d 1846
  Peale, C. W. Titian Ramsay Peale II:
    in the uniform of a naturalist
Peale family
  Peale, C. W. Peale family
Peale family (James Peale)
  Peale, J. James Peale and his family
Peale's museum by Rubens Peale
Pear tree in winter by D. Macknight
Pearce, Mr, fl 1835
  Field, E. S. Mr Pearce
Pearce, Mrs fl 1835
  Field, E. S. Mrs Pearce (?)
Pearce, Nathaniel, 1770-1851
  Malbone, E. G. Nathaniel Pearce
**PEARLSTEIN, Philip, 1924-**
Uprooted tree
  ICA. Annual ex, 1959/60
Peasant girl by M. Sterne
Peasant woman by T. Roszak
Peasants' paradise by M. Hartley
Pe-che-co, a Pottawattomie chief by J. O.
  Lewis
Peck, Mrs Benjamin. See Peck, Hannah
  (Farmer)
Peck, Hannah (Farmer) fl 1770
  Durand, J. Mrs Benjamin Peck
**PECK, Miriam, 1910-**
Early autumn                              OYB
  OYB. Annual 1951
  OYB. Catalogue 1951
**PECKHAM, Robert, 1785-1877**
Memorial portrait of Mary L. Edgell
                                          DN
  DN. Amer primitive ptgs, pt 2
Mrs William Cornee with music  NCHA
  Jones. New-found folk art
William Cornee with flute      NCHA
  Jones. New-found folk art

#### Attributed works
Widow Milton Joslin
  Ford. Pictorial folk art
Peddlers
  Ehninger, J. W. Yankee peddler
Pedernal form the ranch no 1 by G.
  O'Keeffe
Pedestrians in village by J. R. Grabach
Peel, Elizabeth, fl 1757
  West, B. Elizabeth Peel
Peep show by J. B. Thompson
Pegasus by D. Porter
Pegasus by A. P. Ryder
Peggy's cove by J. Lonergan
**PEIRCE, Gerry, 1900-**
Gray desert                               MB
  MB. Ptgs in water color
Mile high                                 ATU
  ATU. Coll of Amer art
Timber line, Estes park, Colorado   MB
  MB. Ptgs in water color

**PEIRCE, Waldo,** 1884-
County fair
   Gruskin (col)
Time. 200 years (col)
Haircut by the sea              MM
   Pierson
Halldis Prince                 ATU
   ATU. Coll of Amer art (col)
Haunted house               OYB
   OYB. Catalogue 1951
Maine swimming hole
   Bazin
Mike and the chart
   Gruskin (col)
Sun bathers
   PPC. Ptg in the U.S. 1949
**Peirson, Harriet Lawrence,** 1793-1870
Goodridge, S. Mrs Abel Lawrence Peirson

**PELHAM, Henry,** 1749-1806
Adam Babcock
   MB. New England miniatures
Edward Holyoke (after Copley)
   MB. New England miniatures

**Attributed works**

Mrs Peter Oliver jr            CtY
   MB. New England miniatures
Zechariah Hicks (?)
   MB. New England miniatures

**Portrait of the artist**

Copley, J. S. Boy with squirrel (Henry Pelham)
Copley, J. S. An engraver, known as Henry Pelham
Copley, J. S. (attributed works) Henry Pelham)

**PELHAM, Peter,** 1684-1751
Benjamin Colman            MB
   Larkin
   Larkin rev ed
Cotton Mather            MWA
   Flexner. Copley
   MWA. Checklist of portraits
   Pierson
Mather Byles            MWA
   Flexner. First flowers

**Pelicans**
Audubon, J. J. Brown pelican
Dozier, O. Pelicans
Willson, M. A. Pelican
**Pell, Mary Cornell,** 1785-1854
Malbone, E. G. Mary Cornell Pell
**PELLEW, John C.** 1903-
Wingaersheek marsh
   NAD. Special ex, 1956
**Pelvis** series, red and yellow by G. O'Keeffe
**Pelvis** series, red with blue by G. O'Keeffe
**Pelvis** with shadows and the moon by G. O'Keeffe
**Pelvis** with the moon, New Mexico by G. O'Keeffe
**Pemaquid** lobster by M. Freedman
The **pen** is mightier than the sword by C. A. Meurer
**Pendennis** castle, Falmouth, Cornwall by R. Havell
**Penelope** by G. Melchers
**Peninsula** by M. Benjamin
**Penitente** by C. Wells

**Penn, John,** 1760-1834
Lambdin, J. R. John Penn (copy of ptg by Pine )
**Penn, William,** 1621-1670
Birch, T. Landing of William Penn
Hicks, E. Grave of William Penn
Hicks, E. Penn's treaty with the Indians
West, B. Penn's treaty with the Indians
**PENNEY, James,** 1910-
Harvest
   IU. Contemp Amer ptg, 1951
Pines, night, 1956
   Baur. Nature
**Pennington** mills, Baltimore, view downstream by F. Guy
**Pennington** mills, Baltimore, view upstream by F. Guy
**Penn's** treaty tree by T. Birch
**Pennsylvania**
   *See also* Philadelphia; Pittsburgh; Susquehanna river; Wyoming valley
Birch, T. Milford, North Wales, Pennsylvania
Birch, T. Winter scene outside Bristol, Pennsylvania
Blair, S. Downing house, Chester county, Pennsylvania
Gasser, H. M. Pennsylvania
Gatch, L. Pennsylvania farm
Hopper, E. Pennsylvania coal town
Knaths, K. Pennsylvania landscape
Mitchell, B. Mauch Chunk, Pennsylvania
Pickett, J. Lehigh canal, sunset, New Hope, Pennsylvania
**Pennsylvania** Dutch lady by Unidentified artist
**Pennsylvania** excavation by G. W. Bellows
**Pennsylvania** hospital by Unidentified artist
The **pension** agent by E. Johnson
**Pensionnaire** by J. Levine
**Pensive** boy by W. Sommer
**Pensive** girl by R. Soyer
**Penthesilean** trawler by J. C. Lewis
The **people** by D. Fredenthal
**People** in the park by A. Walkowitz
**People** on 6th avenue by A. Rattner
**Peoria, Illinois**
Bohrod, A. Street in Peoria
**PEPPER, Charles Hovey,** 1864-
Skating            MB
   MB. Ptgs in water color
The statesman            MB
   MB. Ptgs in water color
**Peppercombe** porch by L. Bouché
**Pepperrell, Mary (Hirst) lady,** 1703-1789
Smibert, J. Lady Pepperrell
**Pepperrell, Sir William, 1st bart,** 1696-1759
Smibert, J. Sir William Pepperrell
**Pepperrell, Sir William, 2d bart,** originally **William Pepperrell Sparhawk,** b 1746?
Copley, J. S. Sir William Pepperrell and his family
**Percé** rock, Gaspe by H. G. Keller
**Percival, James Gates,** 1795-1856
Alexander, F. James Gates Percival
**Percolator** by S. Davis
**Percussion** by V. Candell
**Percussion** by G. L. K. Morris

**PEREIRA, Irene Rice,** 1907-
Affluent surface
  Baur. MacIver and Pereira
Anchor
  Baur. MacIver and Pereira
Black control                          MdBM
  CoS. New accessions USA, 1952
Bright beyond
  Baur. MacIver and Pereira
Composition in white                   NJN
  MMA. Abstract
  MMA. Fourteen
  Pearson. Mod renaissance
Copper light
  Baur. MacIver and Pereira
Deep vision
  WMAA. Neuberger collection
Direction yellow
  ICA. Annual ex, 1951
  Robb. Art 1953 ed
Duograph
  CSFP. Annual ex, 1948/49
  DC. 21 biennial ex, 1949
The embryo
  Pearson. Mod renaissance
Evaporating night                      TxD
  Baur. MacIver and Pereira
  Baur. New art
  CoS. New accessions USA, 1954
  Pearson. Mod renaissance
  Pierson
Green depth                            MM
  McCurdy
  Mendelowitz
  MM. 100 Amer ptrs
  MMA. Fourteen
  Wight. Milestones
Horizontal illusion
  Genauer
Inside—outside
  Baur. MacIver and Pereira
Inverted light
  MnU. 40 Amer ptrs
Landscape of the absolute              WMAA
  Cheney. Story 1958 ed
  Goodrich. Amer art
  Pierson
Light is gold                          WMAA
  Pearson. Mod renaissance
Man and machine
  Baur. MacIver and Pereira
Melting horizon
  Baur. MacIver and Pereira
New world a'coming
  Pearson. Mod renaissance
Oblique illusion                       ATeS
  ATeS. Collection
Oblique progression                    WMAA
  Baur. MacIver and Pereira (col)
  Goodrich. Amer art (col)
Projecting planes                      OT
  WMAA. Juliana Force
Quadrigraph
  MMA. Contemp ptrs
  MMA. Fourteen
Receding red
  Roos
Rectangles                             ATU
  ATU. Coll of Amer art
Red and blue
  Baur. MacIver and Pereira
Red, yellow and blue
  Baur. MacIver and Pereira
  IU. Contemp Amer ptg, 1948

Reflection
  MMA. Fourteen
The riddle
  Baur. MacIver and Pereira
Ruby flux
  Pousette-Dart. Amer ptg
Seven red squares
  Baur. MacIver and Pereira
Somewhere today
  Baur. MacIver and Pereira
Soul of space
  WMAA. Annual ex, 1958
Spirit of air
  Read. Concise history
Spring, twelve o'clock, 1952
  Baur. MacIver and Pereira
  Baur. Nature
  Baur. New art (col)
Transfluent lines
  Baur. New art
  Riley. Your art heritage
Transforming gold
  VR. Amer ptg, 1954
Transparent planes
  Baur. MacIver and Pereira
Transverse parallels
  Baur. MacIver and Pereira
Transversion                           DP
  Baur. Revolution
  DP. Catalogue
  MMA. Fourteen
Two up
  Baur. MacIver and Pereira
Undulating arrangement                 CtHW
  Larkin rev ed (col)
  Pierson
View, 1942
  MnU. 40 Amer ptrs
White lines                            MMA
  Baur. MacIver and Pereira
  Baur. New art
  MMA. Fourteen
  Pierson
  Read. Art now, 1948 ed
White rectangle no 1
  Baur. MacIver and Pereira
The wind of the sun
  IU. Contemp Amer ptg & sculp, 1955
Yellow lines
  CSFP. Annual ex, 1947/48
Yellow oblongs
  Larkin
  Larkin rev ed
The **performance** by S. Greene
**Performer** by H. A. Botkin
**Performers** by P. Guston
**Performers** by R. J. Koski
**Perfume** counter by W. Y. Stamper
**Perilous** night by J. E. Heliker
**Perkins, Mrs George**
  Lockman, D. M. Mrs George Perkins
**PERKINS, Philip**
  Debris of summer
  Genauer
**Perkins, Thomas Handasyd,** 1764-1854
  Sully, T. Col Thomas Handasyd Perkins
**Perkins children,** fl 1806
  Malbone, E. G. Perkins children
**PERLIN, Bernard,** 1918-
  After an ambush
  Time. 300 years (col)
  Boy in the grass
  CSB. Illusion

Colosseum
 IU. Contemp Amer ptg & sculp, 1955
 McCurdy
 WMAA. New decade
The farewell                                WMAA
 Pierson
 PPC. International ex, 1952
 WMAA. Sara Roby
The jacket                                  WMAA
 Faulkner. Art today, 1956
 Goodrich. Amer art
 IU. Contemp Amer ptg, 1952
 Pousette-Dart. Amer ptg
 WMAA. New decade
Jazz band
 ICA. Annual ex, 1959/60
The lovers                                   MMA
 Pierson
Orthodox boys                                 ELT
 ICA. Amer artists paint the city
 PPC. Ptg in the U. S. 1949
Potatoes and onions
 CSFP. Annual ex, 1952
Santa Maria della Salute
 Brussels. Exposition
The shore
 Mendelowitz
 WMAA. New decade
The street                                   MSM
 CoS. New accessions USA, 1950
 IU. Contemp Amer ptg, 1949
 MSM. Handbook
Street dance                                  VR
 CoS. New accessions USA, 1960
 IU. Contemp Amer ptg & sculp, 1959
Perot, Mary. See Elliston, Mary (Perot)
Perplexity of what to do by J. De Diego
Perrette by A. P. Ryder
Perrin, John, fl 1835
 Unidentified artist. Rev John Perrin
Perry, Edward, 1774-1800
 Malbone, E. G. Edward Perry
Perry, Elizabeth Champlin (Mason) fl 1811
 Fulton, R. Mrs Oliver Hazard Perry
Perry, Matthew Calbraith, 1794-1858
 Evans, J. G. Commodore Perry carrying
  the Gospel of God to the heathen
Perry, Oliver Hazard, 1785-1819
 Jarvis, J. W. Commodore Oliver Hazard
  Perry
 Wood, J. (attributed works) Commodore
  Oliver Hazard Perry
Perry, Mrs Oliver Hazard. See Perry,
 Elizabeth Champlin (Mason)
PERSAC, Adrien
 Shadows-on-the-Teche
 Larkin
 Larkin rev ed
 Sugar mill on Bayou Teche, Oliver planta-
  tion
 Davidson v 1
Persephone by T. H. Benton
Persephone by E. Berman
PERSHING, Louise, 1904-
 Book of life
 PPC. International ex, 1950
Person with orange by R. B. Motherwell
Personage with yellow ochre and white by
 R. B. Motherwell
Personal appearance by J. Ernst
Personal history by J. Ernst

Personification of murder by C. R. Leslie
Perspective by W. T. Murch
Perspective of Mexican hill town by E.
 Berman
Pertaining to Deer isle, the harbor by J.
 Marin
Pertaining to harbour by J. G. F. Von Wicht
Pertaining to Nassau street, New York by
 J. Marin
Pertaining to Stonington harbor, Maine by
 J. Marin
Pertaining to yachts and yachting by C.
 Sheeler
Pescaderia, Malaga by H. G. Keller
Pet rooster by R. Wilson
Peter, Saint
 Allston, W. Angel releasing St Peter from
  prison
 Allston, W. St Peter in prison, Study for
  head of
 West, B. Peter denying Christ
Peter and the wolf by B. Shahn
Peter Volo by Freeman
PETERDI, Gabor, 1915-
 Apocalypse
  ICA. Annual ex, 1954
 Misty ocean                                 NBM
  Pierson
 Summer IV
  PA. Annual ex, 1958
 Tidal                                      WMAA
  Baur. Nature (col)
  Goodrich. Amer ptg (col)
 White landscape                             MiA
  NUM. Art across America
PETERS, J. fl 1800
 Good intent
  Born
Peters, Mary (Breintall) d 1789?
 Feke, R. Mrs William Peters
PETERSEN, Martin, 1870-
 Stevedores in the hole                       MB
  MB. Ptgs in water color
PETERSEN, Roland, 1926-
 Luncheon scene
  IU. Contemp Amer ptg & sculp, 1961
PETERSON, Margaret, 1903-
 Man's child                                 CSFM
  Pousette-Dart. Amer ptg
 Sun King and merganser
  VR. Amer ptg, 1958
PETO, John Frederick, 1854-1907
 After night's study                         MiD
  Pierson
 Book, beerstein and corncob pipe
  PA. Annual ex, 1955
 Books
  Frankenstein. After the hunt
 Books on a shelf
  Frankenstein. After the hunt
 Card rack with oval photograph of
  Abraham Lincoln
  CSFP. Illusionism
 Closet door
  Frankenstein. After the hunt
 Crumbs of comfort
  OCiM. Rediscoveries
 Fish house door
  Frankenstein. After the hunt
 Hat, umbrella and bag
  PA. Annual ex, 1955

PETO, J. F.—*Continued*
  Letter rack with jack of hearts
    Frankenstein. After the hunt
  Letter rack with Lerado postmark
    Frankenstein. After the hunt
  Lincoln and the Pfleger stretcher
    Frankenstein. After the hunt
  Market basket, hat, and umbrella
    Frankenstein. After the hunt
  Mug, pipe, and newspaper
    Frankenstein. After the hunt
  Office board for Christian Faser
    Frankenstein. After the hunt
  Office board for Smith Brothers coal company
    Frankenstein. After the hunt
  Old companions
    PA. Annual ex, 1955
  Old scraps                                    MMA
    Barr. What is mod ptg
    OCiM. Redscoveries
    PA. Annual ex, 1955
  Ordinary objects in the artist's creative mind
    PA. Annual ex, 1955
  Pistol, gate latch, and powder horn
    Frankenstein. After the hunt
  Poor man's store                               MB
    Frankenstein. After the hunt
    Pierson
    Richardson. Ptg in America
  The rack                                      ATeS
    ATeS. Collection
  Rack picture with portrait of Lincoln
    Frankenstein. After the hunt
  Self-portrait with rack picture
    Frankenstein. After the hunt
  Still life: book, pipe, beer stein
    Chew. 250 years of art
  Still life: pipe, beer stein, book
    Chew. 250 years of art
  Still life with lanterns                       NBM
    Baur. Revolution
    Frankenstein. After the hunt
  Still life with portrait of the artist's daughter
    Frankenstein. After the hunt
PETROV, Dimitri
  Poet's pipe
    ICA. Annual ex, 1951
Phantasy by V. H. Kirkland
Phantom boat by J. De Diego
Pharmaceutic cabinet by B. Utter
Phelps, William Lyon, 1865-1943
  Wickwire, J. R. William Lyon Phelps
Phenomena by J. Molzahn
Phenomena—with nitrogen before by P. Jenkins
Philadelphia
  Birch, T. Penn's treaty tree
  Birch, T. Philadelphia from Petty island, c 1825
  Caly, N. V. View of the Merchants' exchange and Girard's bank, Philadelphia, c 1835
  Cooper, P. Southeast prospect of the city of Philadelphia, c 1720
  Doughty, T. Naval home, Gray's ferry, Philadelphia
  Kennedy, D. J. View of Broad and Cherry street above Arch street, 1842
  Krimmel, J. L. Election scene in front of the State house in Philadelphia

  Krimmel, J. L. Fourth of July in Centre Square, Philadelphia, c 1810
  Matthew, K. Independence hall
  Shinn, E. Independence hall
  Sloan, J. East entrance, City hall, Philadelphia, 1901
  Smith, R. Edgehill road, Philadelphia
  Smith, R. Old courthouse in Philadelphia
  Smith, R. Old Walnut street prison, Philadelphia in 1835
  Uhle, B. An election day bonfire, Fifth and Chestnut streets, Philadelphia
  Unidentified artist. Judd's hotel, Philadelphia, c 1825
  Unidentified artist. Pennsylvania hospital
  Unidentified artist (after William Henry Bartlett) View of the Schuylkill waterworks, Philadelphia
  Unidentified artist. Waterworks, Centre square, Philadelphia c 1810
Philemon and Baucis by K. L. Seligmann
Philip the Good, duke of Burgundy, 1396-1467
  Walker, C. H. Philip the Good
PHILIPP, Robert, 1895-
  Bouquet
    IU. Contemp Amer ptg, 1952
  Ladies of the evening
    PPC. International ex, 1950
  Letty in leghorn                               ATU
    ATU. Coll of Amer art
  Nude
    NAD. Annual ex, 1958
  Nude combing her hair
    IU. Contemp Amer ptg, 1948
  Patio Royale, New Orleans
    NAD. Annual ex, 1948
  Raising the cross
    Genauer
    NAD. Annual ex, 1947, 1st half
  Rendezvous                                     IaDa
    Gruskin
    IaDa. Silver jubilee
  Request number
    NAD. Anual ex, spring 1950
  Rochelle
    NAD. Annual ex, 1956
  Summer breezes
    NAD. Annual ex, 1961
  Xmas morning
    PPC. Ptg in the U. S. 1949
Philipse, Adolphus, 1665-1702
  Unidentified artist. Adolphus Philipse
Philipse, Philip
  Wollaston, J. Philip Philipse
Philipse manor at Yonkers, New York by Unidentified artist
PHILLIPS, fl 1835

Attributed works
  Mr Bradley                                      DN
    DN. Amer primitive ptgs, pt 2
  Mrs Bradley                                     DN
    DN. Amer primitive ptgs, pt 2
Phillips, Anna Lewis. See Phoenix, Anna Lewis (Phillips)
Phillips, Mrs Duncan. See Phillips, Marjorie (Acker)
Phillips, George, 1664-1739
  Unidentified artist. Rev George Phillips
Phillips, Holmead. See Holmead

PHILLIPS, J. Campbell, b 1873
Future admiral
NYG. Fine art
PHILLIPS, James, 1930?-
Girl at the Tuileries
WMAA. Young America 1957
Self-portrait, Versailles
WMAA. Young America 1957
Phillips, John, 1770-1823
Malbone, E. G. John Phillips
Phillips, John, fl 1793
Steward, J. John Phillips
PHILLIPS, Laughlin
Nautical                                          DP
DP. Catalogue
PHILLIPS, Marjorie (Acker) 1894-
Farm road                                         DP
DP. Catalogue
Grass path in spring
PPC. International ex, 1950
Landscape: buzzard                                CtY
CtY. Soc Anonyme
Little bouquet                                    DP
DP. Catalogue
Night baseball                                    DP
DP. Catalogue
Poppies                                           DP
DP. Catalogue
Sun after rain                                    DP
DP. Catalogue
The philosopher by E. Vedder
Philosopher's camp in the Adirondacks by
W. J. Stillman
Philosopher's heir by H. Major
Philosopher's offspring by H. Major
Philosopher's wife by H. Major
"PHINDOODLE," Captain
Narragansett light from northeast     CtNL
Ford. Pictorial folk art
Phinney, Elihu, 1756-1813
Ames, E. Elihu Phinney
Phipps, Mrs Ogden
Speicher, E. E. Mrs Ogden Phipps
Phippsburg, Maine by J. Marin
Phoenix, Anna Lewis (Phillips) 1765-1854
Unidentified artist. Mrs Daniel Phoenix
Phoenix by H. Hofmann
Phoenix by A. Urban
Photographing the bull by T. H. Benton
PHUL, Anna Maria
St Louis belle                               MoSLH
Rathbone
Phyllis by J. W. Alexander
The pianist by T. Eakins
Piano concert by W. Zorach
Piazza di San Marco, Venice by M. B.
Prendergast
Piazza di Spagna by J. Kinigstein
Piazza Navona by W. G. Congdon
Piazza Navona, Rome by J. S. Sargent
Piazza San Marco by W. G. Congdon
Pic of Orizaba by S. Hirsch
Pica Cotto by R. Scarlett
Picador by F. Martin
Picasso book by K. Knaths
Piccadilly, London by E. D. Boit
Piccard, Jean
Breinin, R. Dr Jean Piccard
Pick 'till the rain hits by R. Gwathmey

PICKEN, George Alexander, 1898-
East river rooftops
Pousette-Dart. Amer ptg
Hawthorne, New York
NYG. Fine art
Lieutenant Bulkley's PT boats at Bataan
ATU
ATU. Coll of Amer art
PICKENS, Alton, 1917-
Acrobat
Baur. New art
Baur. Revolution
MMA. Contemp ptrs
Actor and his family
MMA. Fourteen
WMAA. New decade
Blue doll                                          MMA
Baur. New art
MMA. Fourteen
Pierson
Boating party
IU. Contemp Amer ptg, 1951
Card players
ICA. Annual ex, 1945/46
Carnival                                           MMA
Baur. New art (col)
Flexner. Amer ptg
Flexner. Short history
Game of pretend
Miller. Fourteen
Henry Hope family
Baur. New art
ICA. Annual ex, 1954
WMAA. New decade
Pastorale
MMA. Fourteen
The send-off
ICA. Annual ex, 1951
WMAA. New decade
Under the river
MMA. Fourteen
PICKERING, H. Douglas, 1921-
Some grow up                                       OYB
OYB. Annual 1949
OYB. Catalogue 1951
Pickering, Lois. See Orne, Lois (Pickering)
Pickering, Rebecca (White) 1754-1828
Goodridge, S. (after Stuart) Mrs Timothy
Pickering
Pickering, Timothy, 1745-1829
Goodridge, S. (after Stuart) Timothy
Pickering
Picketing horses by A. J. Miller
PICKETT, Joseph, 1848-1918
Coryell's ferry, 1776                              WMAA
Baur. New art
Chew. 250 years of art
Ford. Pictorial folk art
Goodrich. Amer art (col)
Pierson
Lehigh canal, sunset, New Hope, Pennsyl-
vania
Born
Kallir. Amer primitive ptgs
Manchester valley                                  MMA
Baur. New art
Baur. Revolution
Ford. Pictorial folk art (col)
McCurdy
Mendelowitz

PICKETT, Joseph—*Continued*
  MMA. Masters (col)
  MMA. Ptg and sculpture
  Pierson
  Roos
  UNESCO. 1860-1949
  Washington under the council tree, Coryell's ferry, New Hope, Pennsylvania                                NJN
  Baur. New Art
  Pierson
PICKHARDT, Carl E. 1908-
  Eye witness
    IU. Contemp Amer ptg, 1951
Picking cotton by B. Shahn
Pickman, Benjamin, 1740-1819
  Copley, J. S. Benjamin Pickman
Pickman, Benjamin, 1763-1843
  Harding, C. Benjamin Pickman
Pickman. Judith, 1735-1756
  Greenwood, J. Judith Pickman
Pickman, Mary (Toppan) 1744-1818
  Copley, J. S. Mrs Benjamin Pickman
Picnic by G. W. Bellows
Picnic by G. C. Bingham
Picnic by A. M. R. Moses
Picnic by C. Nangeroni
Picnic by M. B. Prendergast
Picnic by F. C. Watkins
Picnic at Menhoppen, Pennsylvania by R. Henri
Picnic grounds by J. Sloan
Picnic grove by M. B. Prendergast
Picnic in the Catskills by H. Inman
Picnic on the Hudson by J. M. Hart
Picnic on the Hudson by T. P. Rossiter
Picnic on the ridge by J. Sloan
Picnic with red umbrella by M. B. Prendergast
Picnickers by L. Kester
Pictograph by A. A. Gottlieb
Picture hat by H. V. Poor
Picture of Dorian Gray by I. L. Albright
Picture of my young son by A. Refregier
Pidge, blink and the sea by C. F. Gaertner
A piece of my world by Grosz
Pieces of red, green & blue by A. G. Dove
The pier by S. Wilson
Pier composition by A. Rattner
Pierce, Franklin, president U. S. 1804-1869
  Healy, G. P. A. Franklin Pierce
Pierce, Sarah, 1767-1852
  Dickinson, A. (attributed works) Sarah Pierce
Piermont, New York by L. Bouché
Pierpont, James, fl 1711
  Pierpont limner. Rev James Pierpont
Pierpont, Mary (Hooker) fl 1711
  Pierpont limner. Mrs James Pierpont
PIERPONT limner
  Edward Collins                               NAI
    Belknap
    NAI. Hudson valley
  James Pierpont
    Flexner. First flowers
    Larkin
    Pierson

  Mrs James Pierpont
    Flexner. First flowers
    Pierson
Pierre by A. J. Miller
Pierson, Francis, d 1781
  Copley, J. S. Death of Major Pierson
PIERSON, Sarah, fl 1821
  Fulton street, New York, 1821
    U.S. National Capital sesquicentennial com
Pietà by J. O. Nordfeldt
Pietà by S. G. Reinhardt
Pietà by C. E. Van Duzer
Pigeon cove, Rockport, Massachusetts by K. Sturgis
Pigeons
  Audubon, J. J. Passenger pigeon
  Hirshfield, M. Girl with pigeons
  Sloan, J. Pigeons
  Spruce, E. F. Pigeons on a roof
Pigs
  Curry, J. S. Hogs killing a snake
  Mount, W. S. Ringing the pig
Pigtails by E. E. Speicher
PIKE, John, 1911-
  Kids skiing
    NAD. Annual ex, spring 1950
  Lake Lure
    NYG. Fine art
  Orchard lane road, Woodstock
    NAD. Annual ex, 1947, 2d half
Pike county church by N. Spencer
Pike's peak, View of by G. C. Bingham
Pileated woodpecker by J. J. Audubon
Pilgrim with flowered hat by R. Lebrun
Pillar by A. Bohrod
The pillow by W. Stein
Pincian hill, Rome by M. B. Prendergast
Pinckney, Charles Cotesworth, 1746-1825
  Malbone, E. G. Maj Gen Charles C. Pinckney
Pinckney, Eliza (Izard) See Izard, Eliza
Pinckney, Thomas, 1750-1828
  Malbone, E. G. Gen Thomas Pinckney
Pinckney, Thomas, 1780-1830
  Malbone, E. G. Thomas Pinckney jr
Pinckney, Mrs Thomas. See Izard, Eliza
PINE, Robert Edge, 1730-1788 and SAVAGE, Edward, 1761-1817
  Congress voting independence, July, 1776                                        PH
    Davidson v 1                             PH
    Pierson
    Richardson. Ptg in America
    U.S. National Capital sesquicentennial com
Pine bough by K. Knaths
Pine timber by K. Knaths
Pine tree by K. Knaths
Pine tree and snowstorm by W. B. P. Closson
Pine tree, Small point, Maine by J. Marin
Pine trees by K. Steinitz
Pineapple by Unidentified artist
Pines by S. Laufman
Pines and fog by M. Kantor
Pines in the Villa Barberini by J. G. Chapman

**Pines,** night by J. Penney
**Pink** angels by W. De Kooning
**Pink** bird by M. Graves
**Pink** cock by M. Avery
**Pink** cow by W. Sommer
The **pink** dismissal slip by P. Evergood
**Pink** dress by J. S. Sargent
**Pink** dunes by L. Harmon
**Pink** fan by F. Serger
**Pink** flower by M. Friedman
**Pink** harlequin by P. Fine
**Pink** lustre by K. Knaths
**Pink** masks by A. Ruellan
**Pink** Mississippi by J. Tworkov
**Pink** roses by R. A. Blakelock
**Pink** roses by Unidentified artist
**Pink** tablecloth by M. Avery
**Pink** tablecloth by H. V. Poor
**Pink** tablecloth by N. Vasilieff
**Pink** tights by G. R. Davis
**Pink** vase and green leaves by G. O'Keeffe
**PINNEY, Eunice (Griswold) Holcombe,**
    1770-1849
  The cotters' Saturday night
    Lipman. Primitive ptrs
  Masonic memorial
    Lipman. Primitive ptrs
  Plenty
    Lipman. Primitive ptrs
  Two women            NCHA
    Barker. Amer ptg
    Flexner. Light of distant skies
    Lipman. Primitive ptrs
    Pierson
  Undedicated memorial
    Lipman. Primitive ptrs
**Piñons** with cedar by G. O'Keeffe
**Pintails** by P. M. Scott
**Pioneer** and the Indian by F. Remington
**Pioneers** by W. T. Ranney
**Pioneers** by W. E. Russell
**Pioneer's** camp by Unidentified artist
**Pioneer's** house by D. Garber
**Pip** and Flip by R. Marsh
**Pipe** and bowl by P. W. Roberts
**Pipe** of friendship by W. T. Ranney and
    W. S. Mount
**Pipe** of peace by A. J. Miller
**Pipe** of peace by C. M. Russell
**PIPPIN, Horace,** 1888-1946
  Abe Lincoln, the great emancipator
    Rodman. Horace Pippin
  Abraham Lincoln and his father building
    their cabin on Pigeon creek    PMB
    Rodman. Horace Pippin
  After supper, Westchester
    Bazin
    McCurdy
  Artist's wife
    Rodman. Horace Pippin
  The barracks            DP
    DP. Catalogue
    Rodman. Horace Pippin
  The barracks, Sketch for
    Rodman. Horace Pippin

Birmingham meeting house I, 1940
    Rodman. Horace Pippin
Blue tiger
    Rodman. Horace Pippin
Buffalo hunt            WMAA
    Chew. 250 years of art
    Rodman. Horace Pippin
    Pierson
Cabin in the cotton I, 1935
    Rodman. Horace Pippin
Cabin in the cotton III, 1944
    Rodman. Horace Pippin
Christ
    Rodman. Horace Pippin
Christian Brinton          PPhM
    Rodman. Horace Pippin
Christmas morning breakfast
    Rodman. Horace Pippin
Crucifixion
    Rodman. Horace Pippin
The den
    Rodman. Horace Pippin
Domino players          DP
    DP. Catalogue
    Rodman. Horace Pippin (col)
End of the war: starting home    PPhM
    Ford. Pictorial folk art
    Rodman. Horace Pippin
Flowers with four doilies
    Rodman. Horace Pippin
Flowers with hat and cane
    Rodman. Horace Pippin
The getaway
    Rodman. Horace Pippin (col)
Harmonizing
    Rodman. Horace Pippin
The holy
    CanO. Hirshhorn coll
Holy mountain I, 1944
    Rodman. Horace Pippin
Holy mountain II, 1944
    Rodman. Horace Pippin (col)
    Wight. Milestones
Holy mountain IV, 1946
    Rodman. Horace Pippin
John Brown going to his hanging    PA
    Brussels. Exposition
    Rodman. Horace Pippin
    Time. 300 years (col)
John Brown reading his Bible
    Rodman. Horace Pippin
Lady of the lake
    Rodman. Horace Pippin
Lilies
    Rodman. Horace Pippin
Love note
    Rodman. Horace Pippin
Milkman of Goshen
    Rodman. Horace Pippin
Park bench
    Rodman. Horace Pippin
Paul B. Dague, deputy sheriff Chester
    county
    Rodman. Horace Pippin
Quaker mother and child    RPS
    Rodman. Horace Pippin
Red, yellow and white roses
    Rodman. Horace Pippin
Roses with red chair
    Rodman. Horace Pippin
Saturday night bath
    Rodman. Horace Pippin
Saying prayers
    Rodman. Horace Pippin

**PIPPIN, Horace**—*Continued*
Self-portrait I, 1941          NBuA
  NBuA. Contemporary ptgs
  Rodman. Horace Pippin
Shell holes and observation balloon
  Rodman. Horace Pippin
Summer flowers with two chairs
  Rodman. Horace Pippin
Sunday morning breakfast
  Rodman. Horace Pippin
Temptation of St Anthony
  Rodman. Horace Pippin
Trial of John Brown
  Larkin
  Larkin rev ed
  Rodman. Horace Pippin
Uncle Tom
  Rodman. Horace Pippin
Victorian interior I, 1945
  Rodman. Horace Pippin
Victorian interior II, 1945
  Rodman. Horace Pippin (col)
West Chester courthouse
  Rodman. Horace Pippin
West Chester, Pennsylvania      KW
  Rodman. Horace Pippin
Woman at Samaria            PMB
  Rodman. Horace Pippin
The woman taken in adultery
  Rodman. Horace Pippin

**Pippin, Mrs Horace**
  Pippin, H. Artist's wife

**Pippin** house, East Liverpool, Ohio by C. E.
  Burchfield

The **pirate** by A. Gorky

The **pirate** Laffite by J. W. Jarvis

**Pirates'** island by A. P. Ryder

**Pisa** by G. Beattie

**Pistol,** gate latch, and power horn by J. F.
  Peto

**Pistolesi, Lina,** fl 1878
  Alexander, F. Lina Pistolesi

The **pit** by G. Grosz

**Pitching** quoits by W. Homer

**Pitkin, Timothy,** 1726-1812
  Moulthrop, R. Timothy Pitkin

**Pitson, Hannah.** See Flagg, Hannah (Pitson)

**Pitt, William,** 1st earl of **Chatham,** 1708-
  1778
  Copley, J. S. Death of Chatham
  Peale, C. W. Worthy of liberty, Mr Pitt
    scorns to invade the liberties of other
    people

**PITTMAN, Hobson,** 1900-
The conversation
  DC. 20 biennial ex, 1947
The gossips
  Gruskin (col)
Landscape with mansion and white mantel
  CSFP. Annual ex, 1952
Mantel arrangement          OYB
  CSFP. Annual ex, 1947/48
  Genauer
  OYB. Annual 1955
  OYB. Supplement 1959
Midsummer phlox
  OYB. Annual 1950
Nine P.M.                 DP
  DP. Catalogue

Nine P.M.                 OYB
  OYB. Catalogue 1951
Reflection
  Chew. 250 years of art
  PPC. International ex, 1950
Spring festival
  PPC. Ptg in the U.S. 1949
Studio in Charleston
  NAD. Annual ex, 1954
Veiled bouquet
  DC. 23 biennial ex, 1953
The widow                 WMAA
  Baur. Revolution
Yellow chair
  IU. Contemp Am ptg. 1948
**Pitts, Elizabeth,** 1734-1810
  Copley, J. S. Elizabeth Pitts
**Pitts, Elizabeth (Bowdoin)** fl 1754-1762
  Blackburn, J. Mrs James Pitts
**Pitts, Elizabeth (Lendall)** 1680-1763
  Smibert, J. Mrs John Pitts
**PITTS, Elizabeth (McCord)** 1880-
  Maida in our Paris studio      MiD
    MiD. Ports of the Pitts family
    **Portrait of the artist**
  Roper, M. M. Elizabeth McCord
**Pitts, James,** 1710-1776
  Blackburn, J. James Pitts
**Pitts, Mrs James.** See Pitts, Elizabeth
  (Bowdoin)
**Pitts, John,** 1668-1731
  Badger, J. (after Smibert) John Pitts
**Pitts, Mrs John.** See Pitts, Elizabeth
  (Lendall)
**PITTS, Lendall,** 1875-1938
Grand finale                MiD
  MiD. Ports of the Pitts family
Source of the Romanche         MiD
  MiD. Ports of the Pitts family
    **Portrait of the artist**
  Shumacher, W. E. Lendall Pitts
**Pitts, Mrs Lendall.** See Pitts, Elizabeth
  (McCord)
**Pitts, Samuel,** 1745-1805
  Copley, J. S. Samuel Pitts
**Pitts, Samuel Mountfort,** b 1835?
  Unidentified artist (possibly J. G. or L. E.
    Cole) Samuel Mountford Pitts sr
**Pitts, Samuel Mountfort,** d 1868
  Stanley, J. M. Samuel Mountfort Pitts
    jr
**Pitts, Mrs Samuel Mountfort.** See Pitts,
  Sarah (Merrill)
**Pitts, Sarah (Merrill)** 1813-1896
  Melchers, G. Mrs Samuel Mountfort Pitts
**Pitts, Thomas,** 1841-1907
  Melchers, G. Thomas Pitts
  Melchers, G. Thomas Pitts, Head of
**Pittsburgh, Pennsylvania**
  Blythe, D. G. In the Pittsburgh post
    office
  Bohrod, A. West park, Pittsburgh
  Brantz, L. Pittsburgh, 1790
  Driggs, E. Pittsburgh, 1927
  Kane, J. Beechwood boulevard, Pittsburgh
  Smith, R. The aqueduct, Pittsburgh, 1829
  Smith, R. North avenue, Pittsburgh
  Smith, R. Oldest house at foot of Coal
    hill, opposite Market street
  Smith, R. Powder magazine, Fort Du-
    quesne, Pennsylvania
  Smith, R. View of Pittsburgh from the
    salt works on Saw mill run

Wall, W. G. Homestead mill near Pittsburgh
Wall, W. C. Pittsburgh after the fire of 1845
**Pittsburgh** horsemarket by D. G. Blythe
**PITZ, Henry Clarence,** 1895-
Between acts
  NAD. Special ex, 1956
Hotel lobby                                     OYB
  OYB. Annual ex, 1953
  OYB. Supplement
**Place** de l'Opéra, Paris by E. D. Boit
**Place** des Vosges, by S. Davis
**Place** du Carrousel, Paris by E. D. Boit
The **place** of the angel and Tobias by K. Fearing
**Place** Pasdeloup by S. Davis
A **place** to swim by H. E. Schnakenberg
**Placer** mining, 1854 by Chadwick
**Planes** in the sunflowers by M. J. Bigler
**Planning** the attack by C. M. Russell
**Plant** forms by A. G. Dove
The **plantation** by Unidentified artist
**Planting** corn by O. Krans
**Plaster** by R. Dubin
**PLATE, Walter,** 1925-
Autumn
  Baur. Nature
Hot house
  DC. 26 biennial ex, 1959
Interior no 1
  IU. Contemp Amer ptg & sculp, 1959
Salmon river
  PPC. International ex, 1955
Still life                                      WMAA
  WMAA. Young America 1957
Untitled
  WMAA. Young America 1957
**PLATT, George W.** 1839-1899
Quail
  Frankenstein. After the hunt
Relics of a den
  Frankenstein. After the hunt
Wild West
  Frankenstein. After the hunt
**Platt, Mrs Nathaniel,** fl 1820
  Tuthill, A. G. D. Mrs Nathaniel Platt
**Platte river**
  Whittredge, W. On the Platte
**Playfair, Edith Hammond (Russell) lady,** fl 1884
  Sargent, J. S. Lady Playfair
**Playground** by P. Cadmus
**Playground** by J. Kirschenbaum
**Playground** by B. Shahn
**Playground** pleasures by J. Meyers
**Playing** old soldier by W. Homer
**Pleasant** retreat by P. Grimm
**Pleasure** garden by L. Gatch
**Pleasure** party by a mill by C. W. Peale
**Pleasures** of spring by A. Blanch
**Pleasures** of summer by M. Weber
**PLEISSNER, Ogden Minton,** 1905-
Along the Arno                                  MM
  MM. 100 Amer ptrs
  Pierson

The Arno                                        OT
  CoS. New accessions USA, 1952
  IU. Contemp Amer ptg, 1950
  PPC. Ptg in the U. S. 1949
Early morning, Paris
  NAD. Annual ex, 1949, 1st half
Florida landscape                               IaDa
  IaDa. Silver jubilee
Montmartre                                      NJMo
  NAD. Annual ex, autumn 1949
  NJMo. Forty years
  NJMo. Your Montclair art museum
Normandie
  NAD. Annual ex, 1952
The portal
  MM. Amer ptg today
The Ramparts, St Malo                           MWM
  CoS. New accessions USA, 1952
Rue Gabrielle
  NAD. Annual ex, 1955
Stacking alfalfa
  Gruskin
The tower, Avallon
  Time. 300 years (col)
**Plenty** by E. G. H. Pinney
**Plexus** counterplexus by S. Kreider
**PLOCHMANN, Carolyn,** 1926-
Barriers                                        OYB
  OYB. Annual 1952
  OYB. Supplement
**Ploughland** and distant hills by B. West (attributed works)
**Plovers**
  Audubon, J. J. Golden plover
  Hartley, M. Dead plover
The **plow** and the song by A. Gorky
**Plowed** field by S. Laufman
**Plowing** by C. S. Price
**Plum** girl by M. Sterne
**Plumage** by P. W. Roberts
**PLUMMER, Edwin,** b 1802
  Mrs Elizabeth Chandler Plummer   VWR
  VWR. Folk art (col)
**Plummer, Elizabeth (Chandler)** 1760-1839
  Plummer, E. Mrs Elizabeth Chandler Plummer
**Plummer, Mrs Thomas.** See Plummer, Elizabeth (Chandler)
**Plumstead, Anna Helena Amelia (Ross)** 1776-1846
  Stuart, G. Mrs George Plumstead
**Plumstead, Mary (McCall)** b 1725
  Feke, R. Miss Mary McCall
**Plumstead, Mrs William.** See Plumstead, Mary (McCall)
**Plymouth** Sound, England by R. W. Salmon
**Pochade** by S. Davis
**Pocket** by D. Joe
**Pocusmania** by K. Davies
**POE, Elisabeth,** 1888-1947
Agate heights                                   DP
  DP. Catalogue
**Poem**—2 by M. D. Simpson
**Poestenkill,** New York by J. H. Hidley
The **poet** by P. Guston
The **poet** by L. MacIver
The **poet** on Pegasus entering the realm of the Muses (Pegasus) by A. P. Ryder

Poetry after breakfast by M. Avery

Poet's pipe by D. Petrov

Poinsett, Elisha, 1723-1804
Malbone, E. G. Dr Elisha Poinsett

Poinsett, Elizabeth. See Richardson, Elizabeth (Poinsett)

Poinsett, Joel Roberts, 1779-1851
Jarvis, J. W. Joel Roberts Poinsett
Malbone, E. G. Joel Roberts Poinsett

Poinsett, Susan, 1782-1804
Malbone, E. G. Susan Poinsett (formerly
called Anna Frances (Poinsett)

Point o' view by P. Cadmus

Pointer and quail by L. Conduit

Pointers by J. M. Tracy

Poirson, Suzanne, fl 1884
Sargent, J. S. Mlle Suzanne Poirson

Poland Spring, Maine by J. Fiore

Polar space by J. Ernst

Police gazette by W. De Kooning

Political, business and intellectual ballyhoo
(Ceiling panel no 6) by T. H. Benton

Political debate between two Irishmen by
W. Hudson

Political scene in early Bloomington by T. A.
Wylie

Politicians by J. Hirsch

Politicians in a country bar by J. G. Clonney

Politics in an oyster house by R. C. Woodville

POLK, Charles Peale, 1767-1822
John Hart                                    DN
DN. Amer primitive ptgs, pt 2
Mrs Isaac Hite and James Madison Hite
jr                                          MdBH
Flexner. Light of distant skies
Mrs John Hart and her daughter    DN
DN. Amer primitive ptgs, pt 2

Polk, James Knox, president U.S. 1795-1849
Healy, G. P. A. James K. Polk

Poll tax country by R. Gwathmey

POLLACK, Reginald Murray, 1924-
Interior I
WMAA. Annual ex, 1958
Still life I
IU. Contemp Amer ptg & sculp, 1957

Pollard, Ann, fl 1700
Pollard limner. Ann Pollard

POLLARD, Calvin, fl 1823-1843?
Residence of Hendrick Remsen    NNHS
NNHS. Waldron Phoenix Belknap coll

POLLARD limner
Ann Pollard                                 MBH
Barker. Amer ptg
Flexner. Amer ptg
Flexner. First flowers
Flexner. Short history
Ford. Pictorial folk art
Larkin
Larkin rev ed
Mendelowitz
Pierson
Time. 300 years (col)
Mrs John Dolbeare
Flexner. First flowers
Thomas Thatcher (?)
Flexner. First flowers
Pierson
            **Attributed works**
Elisha Cooke
Flexner. First flowers

POLLOCK, Jackson, 1912-1956
Arabesque
MnMW. Eighty works
Autumn rhythm                               M M
Mendelowitz
O'Hara. Jackson Pollock (col)
Pierson
Robertson. Jackson Pollock
Bird
Robertson. Jackson Pollock (col)
Bird effort
Hess. Abstract ptg
Birth
O'Hara. Jackson Pollock
Robertson. Jackson Pollock
Black and white no 5, 1952
O'Hara. Jackson Pollock
Robertson. Jackson Pollock
Black and white painting 1951-52
O'Hara. Jackson Pollock
Robertson. Jackson Pollock
Selz. New images
Black, white and grey
O'Hara. Jackson Pollock
Blue poles
Robertson. Jackson Pollock (col)
Blue poles (Heller coll)
O'Hara. Jackson Pollock (col )
Ponente. Mod ptg, 1960 (col)
Blue poles (Olsen coll)
Baur. New art (col)
WMAA. New decade
The blue unconscious
MMA. Jackson Pollock
O'Hara. Jackson Pollock (col)
Robertson. Jackson Pollock
Cathedral                                   TxD
Art since 1945 (col)
McCurdy
MMA. Jackson Pollock
O'Hara. Jackson Pollock
Robertson. Jackson Pollock (col)
Circumcision
Robertson. Jackson Pollock
Convergence                                 NBuA
ICA. Amer artists paint the city
Larkin rev ed (col)
NBuA. Acquisitions 1954-57
O'Hara. Jackson Pollock (col)
Pierson
Robertson. Jackson Pollock
Cut out
O'Hara. Jackson Pollock
Robertson. Jackson Pollock
The deep
O'Hara. Jackson Pollock (col)
Robertson. Jackson Pollock
WMAA. New decade
Drawing, c 1938
Robertson. Jackson Pollock
Drawing, c 1938-43
Robertson. Jackson Pollock
Drawing, 1943
O'Hara. Jackson Pollock
Drawing, c 1943-45
Robertson. Jackson Pollock (col)
Drawing c 1944
Robertson. Jackson Pollock
Drawing, 1945
Robertson. Jackson Pollock
Drawing, c 1946-49
Robertson. Jackson Pollock (col)
Drawing, 1950
O'Hara. Jackson Pollock

Easter and the totem
  O'Hara. Jackson Pollock
  PPC. International ex, 1955
  Robertson. Jackson Pollock (col)
Echo
  MMA. Jackson Pollock
  O'Hara. Jackson Pollock
  Robertson. Jackson Pollock
Eyes in the heat I, 1946
  Hess. Abstract ptg
  O'Hara. Jackson Pollock
  Robertson. Jackson Pollock (col)
Eyes in the heat II, 1947
  O'Hara. Jackson Pollock
The flame
  O'Hara. Jackson Pollock
  Robertson. Jackson Pollock (col)
Four opposites
  Art since 1945
  O'Hara. Jackson Pollock
  Robertson. Jackson Pollock (col)
Frieze
  Robertson. Jackson Pollock (col)
Frogman. See Number 32, 1951
Full fathom five                    MMA
  Biddle. Yes and no
  O'Hara. Jackson Pollock (col)
  Robertson. Jackson Pollock (col)
Gothic
  O'Hara. Jackson Pollock
  Robertson. Jackson Pollock (col)
Green silver
  O'Hara. Jackson Pollock
Greyed rainbow                      ICA
  O'Hara. Jackson Pollock
  Robertson. Jackson Pollock
Guardians of the secret             CSFM
  Baur. New art
  MMA. Jackson Pollock
  O'Hara. Jackson Pollock
  Robertson. Jackson Pollock (col)
The key
  ICA. Annual ex, 1947/48
  O'Hara. Jackson Pollock
  Robertson. Jackson Pollock (col)
Landscape with rider
  Robertson. Jackson Pollock
Lavender mist
  MMA. Jackson Pollock
  O'Hara. Jackson Pollock (col)
  Robertson. Jackson Pollock (col)
Little king
  Robertson. Jackson Pollock
Magic mirror
  O'Hara. Jackson Pollock
  Robertson. Jackson Pollock
Male and female
  O'Hara. Jackson Pollock (col)
  Robertson. Jackson Pollock (col)
Masqued image
  Robertson. Jackson Pollock
Mixed media, 1944
  Robertson. Jackson Pollock
Moon vibrations
  O'Hara. Jackson Pollock
  Robertson. Jackson Pollock
Moon woman cuts a circle
  O'Hara. Jackson Pollock
  Robertson. Jackson Pollock
Mural, 1943                         IaIU
  O'Hara. Jackson Pollock
  Robertson. Jackson Pollock

The nest
  Robertson. Jackson Pollock
Night ceremony
  O'Hara. Jackson Pollock
  Robertson. Jackson Pollock
Night sounds
  Robertson. Jackson Pollock
Number 1, 1948                      MMA
  Baur. New art
  Cheney. Story 1958 ed
  MMA. Abstract
  MMA. Jackson Pollock
  MMA. Masters (col)
  Newmeyer
  O'Hara. Jackson Pollock
  Pierson
  Robertson. Jackson Pollock
Number 1, 1949
  Cheney. Story 1958 ed (col)
  Hess. Abstract ptg (col)
  O'Hara. Jackson Pollock
  Robertson. Jackson Pollock (col)
Number 2, 1949                      NUM
  50 years of mod art
  MnMW. 60 Amer ptrs (col)
  O'Hara. Jackson Pollock
  Robertson. Jackson Pollock
Number 2, 1951
  WMAA. Contemp Amer ptg, 1951
  WMAA. New decade
Number 3, 1951
  Baur. New art
  ICA. Annual ex, 1951
  MMA. Fifteen
  Selz. New images
Number 3, 1952
  Robertson. Jackson Pollock
Number 4, 1949
  IU. Contemp Amer ptg, 1951
  O'Hara. Jackson Pollock
Number 4, 1952
  Robertson. Jackson Pollock
Number 5, 1948
  IU. Contemp Amer ptg & sculp, 1953
  O'Hara. Jackson Pollock
Number 5, 1950                      MMA
  Hess. Abstract ptg (col)
  Seiberling (col)
Number 5, 1951
  Robertson. Jackson Pollock
Number 6, 1949
  O'Hara. Jackson Pollock
Number 6, 1952
  O'Hara. Jackson Pollock
  Selz. New images
Number 7, 1950
  Barr. What is mod ptg
  MMA. Fifteen
  Robertson. Jackson Pollock
Number 7, 1952
  Robertson. Jackson Pollock
Number 8, 1949
  MMA. New Amer ptg
  O'Hara. Jackson Pollock
Number 8, 1950
  Cheney. Primer 1958 ed
  O'Hara. Jackson Pollock
  WMAA. Neuberger collection
Number 8, 1952                      CtHW
  Robertson. Jackson Pollock (col)
Number 10, 1949
  OHara. Jackson Pollock
  Robertson. Jackson Pollock

**POLLOCK, Jackson—*Continued***

Number 10, 1950
  Baur. Revolution
  Robertson. Jackson Pollock
Number 10, 1951
  Robertson. Jackson Pollock
Number 11, 1951
  IU. Contemp Amer ptg, 1950
  O'Hara. Jackson Pollock
  Robertson. Jackson Pollock
Number 12, 1949                              MMA
  Robertson. Jackson Pollock
Number 12, 1950
  MnU. 40 Amer ptrs
Number 12, 1952
  Cheney. Story 1948 ed
  Hunter. Mod Amer ptg (col)
  MMA. Jackson Pollock
  MMA. New Amer ptg (col)
  O'Hara. Jackson Pollock
  Pousette-Dart. Amer ptg
  Robertson. Jackson Pollock (col)
Number 14, 1948
  MMA. Jackson Pollock
  O'Hara. Jackson Pollock
  Robertson. Jackson Pollock
Number 14, 1951
  MMA. Jackson Pollock
  O'Hara. Jackson Pollock
  Robertson. Jackson Pollock
Number 16, 1950
  Robertson. Jackson Pollock
Number 17, 1949
  Robertson. Jackson Pollock
Number 22A, 1948
  MnU. 40 Amer ptrs
Number 23, 1949
  Time. 300 years (col)
Number 23, 1951
  Selz. New images
Number 24, 1948
  O'Hara. Jackson Pollock
  Robertson. Jackson Pollock
Number 26, 1951
  O'Hara. Jackson Pollock
Number 27, 1950                              WMAA
  Goodrich. Amer art (col)
  O'Hara. Jackson Pollock
Number 27, 1951
  MMA. New Amer ptg
  O'Hara. Jackson Pollock
  PPC. International ex, 1952
  Robertson. Jackson Pollock
Number 28, 1950
  O'Hara. Jackson Pollock
  Robertson. Jackson Pollock (col)
Number 28, 1951
  Robertson. Jackson Pollock
Number 29, 1950
  Gardner 1959 ed
  MMA. Jackson Pollock
  O'Hara. Jackson Pollock
  Robertson. Jackson Pollock
Number 32, 1950
  Janson. Key monuments
  MMA. Jackson Pollock
  O'Hara. Jackson Pollock
  Robertson. Jackson Pollock
Number 32 (Frogman) 1951
  O'Hara. Jackson Pollock
Number 34, 1949                              NUM
  Faulkner. Art today, 1956
  NUM. Root bequest

Ocean greyness                               NNSG
  Baur. Nature
  Baur. New art
  MMA. Jackson Pollock
  NNSG. Handbook
  NNSG. Younger Amer ptrs
  O'Hara. Jackson Pollock
  Robertson. Jackson Pollock
One
  MMA. Jackson Pollock (col)
  O'Hara. Jackson Pollock
  Ponente. Mod ptg, 1960 (col)
  Robertson. Jackson Pollock (col)
Out of the web
  MMA. Jackson Pollock
  O'Hara. Jackson Pollock (col)
  Robertson. Jackson Pollock (col)
Painting, 1933
  MMA. Jackson Pollock
Painting, c 1944
  Robertson. Jackson Pollock
Painting, 1946
  Robertson. Jackson Pollock
Painting, 1948
  O'Hara. Jackson Pollock
  Robertson. Jackson Pollock (col)
Painting, 1951 (1)
  MMA. Jackson Pollock
  Robertson. Jackson Pollock
Painting, 1951 (2)
  MMA. Jackson Pollock
  O'Hara. Jackson Pollock
  Robertson. Jackson Pollock
Painting, 1956
  Robertson. Jackson Pollock
Panel, c 1936
  Robertson. Jackson Pollock
Pasiphaë
  O'Hara. Jackson Pollock (col)
  Robertson. Jackson Pollock (col)
Phosphorescence                              MAP
  NUM. Art across America
Portrait and a dream
  O'Hara. Jackson Pollock
  Read. Concise history (col)
  Robertson. Jackson Pollock (col)
Ritual
  O'Hara. Jackson Pollock
Scent
  Eliot. Art of our time (col)
  O'Hara. Jackson Pollock
  O'Hara. Jackson Pollock (col detail)
  Robertson. Jackson Pollock (col)
  Time. 300 years (col)
Search
  O'Hara. Jackson Pollock (col)
  Robertson. Jackson Pollock
Seascape
  O'Hara. Jackson Pollock
  Robertson. Jackson Pollock (col)
Shadows
  Bazin
  Robertson. Jackson Pollock
The she-wolf                                 MMA
  MMA. Contemp ptrs
  O'Hara. Jackson Pollock
  Read. Concise history
  Robertson. Jackson Pollock (col)
Shimmering substance
  Art since 1945
  MMA. Jackson Pollock
  O'Hara. Jackson Pollock
  Robertson. Jackson Pollock

Silver square
  O'Hara. Jackson Pollock
Sleeping effort                       MoSLW
  O'Hara. Jackson Pollock
  Robertson. Jackson Pollock
Summertime
  O'Hara. Jackson Pollock
  Robertson. Jackson Pollock
There were seven in eight
  O'Hara. Jackson Pollock
  Robertson. Jackson Pollock
Three
  O'Hara. Jackson Pollock
Totem I, 1944
  MMA. Jackson Pollaok
  O'Hara. Jackson Pollock
  Robertson. Jackson Pollock
Totem II, 1945
  Leepa
  O'Hara. Jackson Pollock
Totem (lesson I) 1945
  Read. Art now, 1948 ed
Two
  Robertson. Jackson Pollock
Unformed figure
  O'Hara. Jackson Pollock
  Robertson. Jackson Pollock
Untitled
  CSFP. Annual ex, 1950/51
Untitled, c 1936
  O'Hara. Jackson Pollock
  Robertson. Jackson Pollock
Untitled, 1937
  O'Hara. Jackson Pollock
  Robertson. Jackson Pollock
Untitled, 1945 (Bareiss coll)
  Robertson. Jackson Pollock
Untitled, 1945 (Stuart coll)
  Robertson. Jackson Pollock
Untitled, 1950
  O'Hara. Jackson Pollock
  Robertson. Jackson Pollock
White cockatoo
  O'Hara. Jackson Pollock
  Robertson. Jackson Pollock (col)
White horizontal
  O'Hara. Jackson Pollock
White light
  O'Hara. Jackson Pollock
  Ponente. Mod ptg, 1960 (col)
  Robertson. Jackson Pollock
White on black I, 1949
  O'Hara. Jackson Pollock
White on black II, 1949
  Robertson. Jackson Pollock
Wounded beast (Wounded animal)
  CtY. Yale alumni
  O'Hara. Jackson Pollock
Polly by E. E. Speicher
Polo. See Games and sports—Polo
POLONSKY, Arthur, 1925-
  Marine Sampson
  MBIC. View 1960
Pomeroy, Asahel, 1749-1833
  Unidentified artist. Asahel Pomeroy
Pomeroy, Louise. See Inches, Louise (Pomeroy)
Pompeii by W. A. Baziotes
Pompous boy by W. Sommer
POND, Dana
  Pastor De Segovia
  NAD. Annual ex, 1956

The pond by H. Hofmann
The pond by A. P. Ryder
Pont Alexandre by J. Marin
Pont de Minimes, Chartres by H. R. Newman
Le Pont Neuf by A. Blatas
Le Pont Neuf by W. Howard
Ponte della Paglia by M. B. Prendergast
Ponte Margherita by J. Stefanelli
Ponte Vecchio by L. Bosa
Ponte Vecchio by A. J. Pucci
Pony ballet by W. J. Glackens
Pool sisters, fl 1845
  Unidentified artist. The Pool sisters
Pool. See Games and sports—Pool
The pool by L. Eilshemius
The pool by B. Shahn
Pool room by D. S. Bloom
Poor, Charlotte (White) 1782-1863
  Malbone, E. G. Mrs Moses Poor
POOR, Henry Varnum, 1888-
  Anne
    NYG. Fine art
  Artist in summer
    PA. Annual ex, 1951
  Autumn fruit                        WMAA
    Goodrich. Amer art
  The bull
    PPC. Ptg in the U.S. 1949
  Chess game
    Gruskin
  Flowered hat
    Genauer
  Fruit                               MM
    MM. 100 Amer ptrs
  Picture hat
    Genauer
  Pink tablecloth                     OCI
    Baur. Revolution
  Pierson
  Summer bouquet                      ATeS
    ATeS. Collection
  White cloud
    IU. Contemp Amer ptg, 1948
Poor, Mrs Moses. See Poor, Charlotte (White)
The poor artist's cupboard by C. B. King
The poor author and the rich bookseller by W. Allston
Poor man's store by J. F. Peto
Poor room—There is no time, no end, no today, no yesterday, no tomorrow, only the forever and forever and forever without end by I. L. Albright
POORE, Henry Rankin, 1859-1940
  Hound
    NSP. Sportscapes
POPE, Alexander, 1849-1924
  Pups in transit
    Frankenstein. After the hunt
  Sportman's still life
    Frankenstein. After the hunt
  Still life
    Frankenstein. After the hunt
Pope, Anna (Hammond) fl 1800
  Greenleaf, B. Mrs Anna Hammond Pope
POPE, Arthur, 1880-
  Christianbury crags, Scotland, from the road to Langholm              MB
    MB. Ptgs in water color

**Pope, Mrs Joseph.** See Pope, Anna (Hammond)

**Poperinghe:** two soldiers by J. S. Sargent

**Popham** beach, Maine by W. Zorach

**Poplar** trees by C. E. Burchfield

**Poppi** in the Casentino, Tuscany, E. D. Boit

**Poppies** by C. H. Demuth

**Poppies** by G. O'Keeffe

**Poppies** by M. A. Phillips

**Poppies** by M. Silverman

**Poppies** in blue vase by M. B. Prendergast

**Population**—3000 by C. F. Gaertner

The **porch** by P. Guston

**Porch** no 2 by J. W. Treiman

**Porch** no 2, 1946-47 by P. Guston

**Porcupine**
    Audubon, J. J. American porcupine

The **porphyry** jar by D. M. Lockman

**Port** at night by R. Morgan

The **port** from New York interpreted by
    J. Stella

**Port Hudson, Battle of,** 1863
    Arnold, E. Battle of Port Hudson, 1863

**Port** Jefferson by Leonid

**Port** of call by S. M. Etnier

The **portage** by W. Homer

The **portal** by O. M. Pleissner

**Port-au-Prince, Haiti**
    Dehn, A. A. Market, Port-au-Prince, Haiti

**Portentous** sunset by L. Feininger

**Porter, David,** 1780-1843
    Unidentified artist. Commodore David
    Porter

**PORTER, David,** 1912-
    Pegasus
      IU. Contemp Amer ptg & sculp, 1953
    Sunrise in the stratosphere
      IU. Contemp Amer ptg & sculp, 1961

**Porter, Noah,** 1811-1892
    Johnson, E. Noah Porter

**PORTER, Rufus,** 1792-1884
    Hudson river highlands
      Lipman. Primitive ptrs
    Orchard scene
      Lipman. Primitive ptrs
    Rural scene
      Lipman. Primitive ptrs
    Sacrifice of Isaac
      Lipman. Primitive ptrs

**Portland,** Maine, View near by C. Codman

**Portland** pier, Lake Erie by G. Harvey

**Portrait** and a dream by J. Pollock

**Portrait**—Bear by B. Kopman

**Portrait** in studio light by R. Brackman

**Portrait** of a grand lady by M. Cassatt

**Portrait** of a poet by J. Glasco

**Portrait** of A. S. 1925 by A. G. Dove

**Portrait** of myself when young by B. Shahn

**Portrait** study in a doorway by C. E. Burchfield

**Portuguese** sea by Leonid

**Pose** downtown by M. Gordon

**Poseidon** by J. E. Levi

The **possessed** by R. Lytle

**Post, Catalynje,** fl 1730
    Unidentified artist. Catalynje Post

**POST, Herman,** 1873?-1939
    Elevated railway, Berlin       CtY
      CtY. Soc Anonyme

**Post, Jennie,** fl 1835
    Ellsworth, J. S. Mrs Jennie Post

**POST, Shelly**
    The courtesan
      NAD. Annual ex, 1949, 1st half

**Post** office by D. G. Blythe

The **poster** by R. Vickrey

**Poster** portrait of O'Keeffe by C. H. Demuth

**Potatoes** and onions by B. Perlin

**Poultry** market by Walter Williams

**Pounding** surf by F. J. Waugh

**Pouring** coffee by R. Diebenkorn

**POUSETTE-DART, Nathaniel J.** 1886-
    Renaissance
      Pousette-Dart. Amer ptg

**POUSETTE-DART, Richard,** 1916-
    Blue amorphous
      WMAA. New decade
    Golden dawn
      Baur. Nature
    Golden reverie
      IU. Contemp Amer ptg, 1952
      NBuA. Expressionism
    Illumination
      PPC. International ex, 1958
    In the forest       NBuA
      NBuA. Acquisitions 1957-58
    The magnificent      WMAA
      Cheney. Story 1958 ed
      Goodrich. Amer art
      Pierson
      Pousette-Dart. Amer ptg
      WMAA. New decade
    Number 11: a presence      MMA
      MMA. Abstract
    Subterranean
      IU. Contemp Amer ptg, 1951
    White garden
      IU. Contemp Amer ptg & sculp, 1953
    White reverie
      WMAA. New decade

**Powder** magazine, Fort Duquesne, Pennsylvania by R. Smith

**POWELL, H. M. T.** fl 1849-1858
    J. M. Studebaker in his wagon tire shop
      at Hangtown, California, 1853    DN
      U.S. National Capital sesquicentennial
      com

**POWELL, Leslie,** 1906-
    Mill wheel      ATU
      ATU. Coll of Amer art

**Power, Nicholas,** 1771-1844
    Malbone, E. G. Nicholas Power

**Power, Rebecca,** fl 1803
    Malbone, E. G. Rebecca Power

**Power** line by C. F. Ryder

**Power** of music by W. S. Mount

**Power** of the law by E. H. Blashfield

**POWERS, Marilyn,** 1925-
    Still life
      MBIC. View 1960

**Powers, Thomas E.** fl 1858
    Mason, B. F. Dr Thomas E. Powers

**POZZATTI, Rudy O.** 1925-
    Citta della torre
      WMAA. Young America 1960
    The denial      OYB
      OYB. Annual 1952

Limestone quarry
WMAA. Annual ex, 1956
Nebraska landscape
IU. Contemp Amer ptg & sculp, 1957
Red rocks
WMAA. Young America 1960
Yesterday            OYB
OYB. Annual 1951
OYB. Catalogue 1951
**Pozzuoli** red by A. G. Dove
**Prairie** by A. J. Miller
**Prairie** bluffs burning, upper Missouri by G. Catlin
**Prairie** burial by W. T. Ranney
**Prairie** encampment by J. M. Stanley
**Prairie** fire by G. Catlin
**Prairie** fire by C. Deas
**Prairie** fire by W. T. Ranney
**Prairie** landscape by A. Rattner
**Prairie** on fire by A. J. Miller
**Prairie** scene: mirage by A. J. Miller
**Prairie** sky by A. Rattner
**PRATT, Henry Cheever,** 1803-1880
On the Ammonoosuc river     MB
MB. Karolik coll
View on the Rio Gila, 1855
U.S. National Capital sesquicentennial com
**Pratt, Hiram,** fl 1839
Tuthill, A. G. D. Hiram Pratt
**Pratt, Mary Bryant.** See Brandegee, Mary Bryant (Pratt)
**PRATT, Matthew,** 1734-1805
American school       MM
Barker. Amer ptg
Davidson v 1
ICA. From colony to nation
Pierson
Richardson. Ptg in America
Roos
Taylor. Fifty centuries, 1954 ed (col)
U.S. National Capital sesquicentennial com
Benjamin West       PA
Chew. 250 years of art
Pierson
Cadwallader Colden and Warren de Lancey
Flexner. Light of distant skies
John Bush       MWA
Larkin
Larkin rev ed
Mrs Benjamin West       PA
Pierson
**Prayer** makers by L. Daniel
**Precipice** by E. F. Spruce
**Precision** bombing by G. L. K. Morris
**Preening** sparrow by M. Graves
**PREGEL, Alexandra (Avxentieff)** 1907-
Fruit and daisies
NAD. Annual ex, 1947, 1st half
**Pregel, Mrs Boris.** See Pregel, Alexandra (Avxentieff)
**Prehistoric** construction by A. Russell
**Prehistoric** playground by M. Tobey
**Preliminary** examination by D. Levine
**Première** by S. Davis

**PRENDERGAST, Charles,** 1868-1948
After the show
CtY. Yale alumni
Hill town       MAP
Glackens
**PRENDERGAST, James Donald,** 1907-
Young American artist       ATU
ATU. Coll of Amer art
**PRENDERGAST, Maurice Brazil,** 1859-1924
Acadia       MMA
Hunter. Mod Amer ptg (col)
MMA. Masters (col)
Afternoon, Pincian hill, Rome       DP
Canaday
DP. Catalogue
Along the boulevard, Paris       NBuA
MB. Prendergast
NBuA. Contemporary ptgs
Along the coast
MB. Prendergast
April snow (DP). See Snow in April
April snow, Salem       MMA
MB. Prendergast (col)
Pierson
At the beach
Lewisohn
At the shore       MAP
Cheney. Story 1958 ed
Autumn festival       DP
Baur. New art (col)
DP. Catalogue
Pierson
The balloon       MAP
MB. Prendergast (col)
Bareback rider, Paris       OCl
MB. Prendergast
Bartol church. See West church, Boston
Bastille day (Le quatorze juillet) 1892       OCl
MB. Prendergast
The bathers
MB. Prendergast
Bathing, Marblehead       MB
MB. Ptgs in water color
Beach at Gloucester
MB. Prendergast
Beach late afternoon, Maine       MB
MB. Prendergast
Beach, St Malo
MB. Prendergast
Beach scene with figures
MB. Prendergast
Beach with blue tree
MB. Prendergast
Beachmont       CtNB
McKinney
Boat landing       CtHW
CtHW. Handbook
Boat landing, Dinard
MB. Prendergast
A boy       MoKN
MB. Prendergast
Bridge and steps, Venice       FaW
Baur. New art
Bridge in Venice       OCl
MB. Prendergast
Café Florian, Venice
MB. Prendergast
Campo Santa Maria Formosa, Venice
MB. Prendergast (col)
Cape Ann       MB
MB. Prendergast

**PRENDERGAST, M. B.**—*Continued*
Straw bridge                                    DP
 UNESCO.  1860-1955
 UNESCO.  1860-1959
Street scene, Boston
 MB.  Prendergast
Summer
 WMAA.  Museum and its friends, 1958
Summer day
 MB.  Prendergast
Summer in the park
 MB.  Prendergast (col)
Summer outing on the rocks
 MB.  Prendergast (col)
Sunday promenade
 MB.  Prendergast
Sunlight on the Piazzetta, Venice
 MB.  Prendergast (col)
Sunset
 MB.  Prendergast
Sunset and sea fog                              OYB
 MB.  Prendergast
 OYB.  Supplement 1959
 Pierson
 Time.  300 years (col)
The swans                                       MAP
 MB.  Prendergast
Tremont street, Boston                          MAP
 MB.  Prendergast
Tuileries gardens
 MB.  Prendergast
Two girls in New England woodland
 MB.  Prendergast
Umbrellas in the rain, Venice                   MB
 MB.  Prendergast (col)
Venice
 CtY.  Yale alumni
Via delle Corso, Rome. See On the Corso,
 Rome
Waterfall
 MB.  Prendergast
West church, Boston, 1909                       MB
 MB.  Prendergast (col)
West church, Boston (Bartol church)
 MB.  Prendergast
Wet day, Paris. See Paris boulevard in
 rain
Woman arranging her hair
 MB.  Prendergast
**Preparing** for a buffalo hunt by A. J.
 Miller
**Preparing** the bill by T. H. Benton
**Prescience** by C. Howard
**Prescott, Harry,** fl 1804
 Malbone, E. G.  Harry Prescott
**Presence** of black no 1 by J. Guerrero
The **present** by S. Rosenberg
**Presentation** of the Virgin by D. Aronson
**Presents** to Indians by A. J. Miller
The **President,** 1922 by S. Davis
**Preston, William C.** 1794-1860
 Healy, G. P. A.  William C. Preston
**Preston** ponds, Adirondacks by H. D. Mar-
 tin
**PRESTOPINO, Gregorio,** 1907-
 Afternoon sun                                OYB
  OYB.  Annual 1958
  OYB.  Supplement 1959
 Glitter no 3                                 WMAA
  Pierson

The market                                      IU
 IU.  Contemp Amer ptg, 1951
 IU.  20th century
Railroad center
 IU.  Contemp Amer ptg, 1959
Roots
 IU.  Contemp Amer ptg, 1952
 Pousette-Dart.  Amer ptg
Summer
 IU.  Contemp Amer ptg & sculp, 1955
Sunset
 IU.  Contemp Amer ptg & sculp, 1953
Trolley car
 Genauer
Winter                                          WMAA
 Gruskin
 Pierson
**Pretty** girl milking the cow by B. Shahn
**Pretty** ships by M. B. Prendergast
**PREUSSER, Robert Ormerod,** 1919-
 Directional multiplicity
  Pearson.  Mod renaissance
 Prismatic refractions
  Pearson.  Mod renaissance
 Twentieth century baroque
  Pearson.  Mod renaissance
**Priam** returning the body of Hector by J.
 Trumbull
**PRICE, Clayton S.** 1874-1950
 Abstract landscape
  OrPA.  C. S. Price (col)
 Abstraction, 1949
  OrPA.  C. S. Price
 Abstraction IV, 1943-45
  OrPA.  C. S. Price
 Adobe houses
  MMA.  Fourteen
  OrPA.  C. S. Price
 Bay mare and colt and a couple of
  others
  OrPA.  C. S. Price
 Bird by the sea                             MM
  MM.  100 Amer ptrs
  OrPA.  C. S. Price
 Black bird
  OrPA.  C. S. Price
 Cattle
  OrPA.  C. S. Price
 Cattle by the river
  OrPA.  C. S. Price
 Coastline
  OrPA.  C. S. Price
 Cow with calf
  OrPA.  C. S. Price
 Cowboys at moonlight
  OrPA.  C. S. Price
 Cows going to pasture
  OrPA.  C. S. Price
 Coyotes
  OrPA.  C. S. Price
 The dream
  MMA.  Fourteen
  OrPA.  C. S. Price (col)
 Fisherman                                   MiD
  Baur.  Revolution
  MMA.  Fourteen
  OrPA.  C. S. Price
  Pierson
 Fishing village
  OrPA.  C. S. Price
 Front street                                OrPA
  MMA.  Fourteen
  OrPA.  C. S. Price

Hay wagon
  OrPA. C. S. Price
Head
  OrPA. C. S. Price
Head (self-portrait)
  OrPA. C. S. Price
Horses                                          OrPA
  OrPA. C. S. Price
Horses in a barnyard
  OrPA. C. S. Price
Huckleberry pickers                             OrPA
  OrPA. C. S. Price
In the mountains
  OrPA. C. S. Price
Mail coach
  OrPA. C. S. Price
Mare and foal
  OrPA. C. S. Price
Mare with colt
  OrPA. C. S. Price
Mule deer
  OrPA. C. S. Price
Night
  OrPA. C. S. Price
Owl
  OrPA. C. S. Price (col)
Plowing                                         NUM
  OrPA. C. S. Price (col)
The river                                       OrPA
  CoS. New accession USA, 1950
Self-portrait. See Head
Two birds
  OrPA. C. S. Price
Two heads, c 1935
  OrPA. C. S. Price
Two heads, 1940-42
  OrPA. C. S. Price
Vase of flowers, 1943-45
  OrPA. C. S. Price
Vase of flowers, c 1948
  OrPA. C. S. Price
White mare and foal
  OrPA. C. S. Price
Wolves
  MMA. Fourteen
  OrPA. C. S. Price
Young birds
  OrPA. C. S. Price
PRIEBE, Karl John, 1914-
  Early immigrants
    IU. Contemp Amer ptg, 1950
  The fronfroneur
    IU. Contemp Amer ptg, 1948
  Roos
  The socialite
    IU. Contemp Amer ptg, 1949
Priestley, Flora, b 1859
  Sargent, J. S. Flora Priestley
Prima materia by W. Day
Primeval landscape by W. A. Baziotes
Primitive dance by R. Koppe
Prince, Halldis
  Peirce, W. Halldis Prince
La princesse du pays de la porcelaine by
  J. A. M. Whistler
Princeton, Battle of, 1777
  Mercer, W. Battle of Princeton, 1777
  Sanford, M. M. Washington at Princeton
  Trumbull, J. Death of General Mercer
    at the Battle of Princeton

PRINGLE, James, 1788-1847
  Smith and Dimon shipyard, New York,
    1833                                        NCHA
    U.S. National Capital sesquicentennial
      com
Prioleau, Mary Magdalen. See Grimball,
  Mary Magdalen (Prioleau)
PRIOR, William Matthew, 1806-1873
  The Burnish sisters                           DN
    DN. Amer primitive ptgs, pt 1
    Ford. Pictorial folk art (col)
  A gentleman                                   MeC
    Jetté. Amer heritage collection
  Little child with big dog                     NCHA
    Jones. New-found folk art
  Three sisters of the Coplan family   MB
    Lipman. Primitive ptrs
    MB. Karolik coll
  Unidentified portrait (of a man) c 1846
    Lipman. Primitive ptrs
  Washington's tomb at Mount Vernon
                                                VWR
    VWR. Folk art (col)
  William Allen with greyhounds       MB
    Lipman. Primitive ptrs
    MB. Karolik coll
  A young man
    Ford. Pictorial folk art

### Attributed works

  A girl                                        RPS
    Ford. Pictorial folk art
  Girl seated on bench                          VWR
    VWR. Folk art (col)
  Little girl holding apple                     DN
    DN. Amer primitive ptgs, pt 2
  A man                                         NJN
    Ford. Pictorial folk art
  Two children with their dog Minny   MSt
    Little. Country art
    NUM. Art across America
  Unknown woman                                 MSt
    Little. Country art
  A woman                                       NJN
    Ford. Pictorial folk art

### Manner of

  Brother and sister sharing a book
                                                NCHA
    Jones. New-found folk art
  Fireman                                       NCHA
    Jones. New-found folk art
  Lady in a fine scarf                          NCHA
    Jones. New-found folk art
  Three children                                NCHA
    Jones. New-found folk art
  William Whipper                               NCHA
    Jones. New-found folk art
Prior to by J. S. Cleary
Prize flowers by C. C. Ross
Prismatic refractions by R. O. Preusser
Prisoner by J. Hirsch
Prisoners from the front by W. Homer
Pro Deo, pro populo by F. Whitaker
PROBST, Joachim, 1913-
  Christ in thorns
    IU. Contemp Amer ptg & sculp, 1959
Procession by M. Manigault
Procession of the Savior by L. Bosa
Procession, Venice by M. B. Prendergast
Processional by E. A. Chavez

Processional by W. Mitchell

The processional by H. Saslow

Prodigal son by R. Cowles

Prodigal son by R. Devoll

Prodigal son by R. Haines

Prodigal son by B. West

The prodigal son among swine by M. Beckmann

The prodigal son gambling by Unidentified artist

The prodigal son in misery by Unidentified artist

The prodigal son receiving his patrimony by Unidentified artist

The prodigal son reclaimed by A. Doolittle

The prodigal son reclaimed by Unidentified artist

The prodigal son reclaimed by his father by M. A. Willson

The prodigal son reveling with harlots by Unidentified artist

Prodigious industrial phenomenon by J. De Diego

Profanation of the host by D. Tanning

Professional painters by D. D. Dennison

Professionals at rehearsal by T. Eakins

Professor Hunter Worrell's pipe by G. Cope

Profile by D. Joe

Profile of a boy by R. H. M. Bascom

Profile of baby in orange by R. H. M. Bascom

Profiles no 8 by N. Tschacbasov

The progenitors by C. Howard

PROHASKA, Ray, 1901-
  Space between
    IU. Contemp Amer ptg & sculp, 1953

Project for a monument: the apotheosis of Nelson by B. West

Projecting planes by I. R. Pereira

Promenade by C. E. Burchfield

Promenade by C. Cloar

Promenade by M. B. Prendergast

Promenade by M. Ray

Promenade, France by M. B. Prendergast

Promenade, Gloucester by M. B. Prendergast

Promenade on the beach by W. Homer

Promenade on the pier, Nantasket by M. B. Prendergast

Prometheus by E. Friedensohn

Prometheus by R. Lytle

Prometheus bound by T. Cole

Prometheus in Rockefeller center by R. Marsh

Prometheus rebound by G. Palazzola

Promise of immortality by J. La Farge

The promontory by J. De Martini

Prong-horned antelope by J. W. Audubon

Prophecy by S. Pace

The prophet by H. Koerner

Prophetic light by M. Tobey

The proposal by C. M. Russell

Proposal on horseback by P. Evergood

The Propylaea, Athens by H. B. Warren

Proserpina by E. Berman

Prospect park, Brooklyn by W. M. Chase

Prospect rock, Essex county, N.Y. by W. Homer

Prospecting by D. G. Blythe

Prospectors by Unidentified artist

Prosser, Evelina Matilda. See Tabb, Mrs John

Protection by W. M. Harnett (attributed works)

Proudfit, Alexander, 1770-1843
  Jarvis, J. W. Rev Alexander Proudfit

Proudfit, Susan (Williams) 1780-1852
  Jarvis, J. W. Mrs Alexander Proudfit

Prout's Neck, breakers by W. Homer

PROVAN, Sara, 1917-
  Bird, fish, fruit
    MM. Amer ptg today
  Delicate board
    IU. Contemp Amer ptg & sculp, 1953

Provincetown, Massachusetts
  Corbett, E. Provincetown no 2
  Corbett, E. Provincetown no 6
  Harmon, L. Provincetown
  Isenburger, E. Sea and wharf at Provincetown
  Knaths, K. Provincetown jamboree
  Leonid. Provincetown
  Sterne, M. Provincetown seascape

Provoost, David, 1642-1720?
  Unidentified artist. David Provoost (?)

Provoost, Margareta. See Van Brugh, Margareta (Provoost)

Provost, George, fl 1805
  Ames, E. Major George Provost

Provost, Tryntje (Laurens) b 1650
  Unidentified artist. Mrs David Provoost (?)

Prudence by F. C. Watkins

The pruner by G. C. Lambdin

The pseudolucànus reconsidered by J. Wilde

Public gardens, Boston by G. L. Brown

PUCCI, Albert John
  Night
    NAD. Annual ex, 1951
  Ponte Vecchio
    NAD. Annual ex, 1955

PUCCI, Gigi Ford
  Clothesline
    NAD. Annual ex, 1949, 1st half

Puddle by L. MacIver

Pue, Elinor S. F.
  Eakins, T. Miss Elinor S. F. Pue

Pue, Rebecca, 1812-1884
  Hubard, W. J. Rebecca Pue

Pueblo and mesa, Taos mountains by J. Marin

Pulitzer, Joseph, 1847-1911
  Sargent, J. S. Joseph Pulitzer

Pulitzer, Louise
  Beckmann, M. Louise Pulitzer

Pulsation of light by B. Margo

PUMA, Fernando, 1919-1955
  Eternal world
    IU. Contemp Amer ptg, 1952
  Moon bathers
    Cheney. Primer 1958 ed

Punishment by G. Grosz

Puppet and child by S. Serisawa

Puppets by G. S. Ratkai

Pups in transit by A. Pope
Purification series by M. Graves
The purist by I. L. Albright
Purlieu by J. Wolfe
Purple abyss, Grand canyon, Arizona by
   D. Macknight
Purple brook by D. Macknight
Purple grackle by J. J. Audubon
Purple petunias by E. W. Motley
Purple pup by C. H. Demuth
Pursuer and pursued by W. Rimmer
Pursuit by J. Madson
Pursuit by R. Marsh
Pursuit in depth by G. L. K. Morris
La push by W. W. Baumgartner
Push and pull by H. Hofmann
Pushing for rail by T. Eakins
PUSHMAN, Hovsep, 1877-
   When autumn is here         IU
     NYG. Fine art (col)
Putnam, Israel, 1718-1790
   Unidentified artist. General Putnam
   Unidentified artist. General Putnam's leap
Putnam, Rufus, 1738-1824
   Turnbull, J. Rufus Putnam
PUTNAM, Wallace B. 1899-
   Sheep in fog             CtY
     CtY. Soc Anonyme
The puzzled witness by G. C. Bingham
PYLE, Howard, 1853-1911
   Thomas Jefferson
     Larkin (detail)
PYTLAK, Leonard, 1910-
   Winter rhythm
     NAD. Annual ex 1946, 2d half

# Q

Q—1952 by J. D. Brooks
Quadrigraph by I. R. Pereira
Quadrilaterals by H. Bertoia
Quail
   Hill, T. The covey
   Platt, G. W. Quail
Quaker mother and child by H. Pippin
Qualm by J. D. Brooks
QUANCHI, Leon William, 1892-
   Dry nets
     IU. Contemp Amer ptg, 1951
Quappi in turban by M. Beckmann
The quarantined citadel by P. Evergood
The quarrel by F. Remington
The quarry by J. De Martini
The quarry by M. Friedman
Quarry pool by J. F. Folinsbee
Quarry pool by J. De Martini
Quatic by J. D. Brooks
Le quatorze juillet by M. B. Prendergast
Quebec by P. Dickinson

Quebec, Battle of, 1775
   Trumbull, J. Attack on Quebec
   Trumbull, J. Death of General Montgom-
     ery at Quebec
Queen of clubs by K. Knaths
Queen Philippa interceding for the burgesses
   of Calais by B. West
Queen's gambit by F. Hillsmith
QUIDOR, John, 1801-1881
   Battle scene from Knickerbocker's His-
     tory of New York         MB
     MB. Karolik coll
     Pierson
   The devil and Tom Walker
     MiD. Coll in progress
     Richardson. Ptg in America
     WiMiA. Amer ptg 1760-1960
   Ichabod Crane at a ball at the Van Tassel
     mansion
     NUM. Art across America
   Ichabod Crane pursued by the Headless
     Horseman            CtY
     Larkin
     Larkin rev ed
   Leatherstocking defies the law    NCHA
     Davidson v2
   Money diggers            NBM
     Baur. Amer ptg
     DC. De gustibus
     Pierson
   Paul Revere             ATeS
     AteS. Collection
   Return of Rip Van Winkle      DN
     Davidson v 1
     Mendelowitz
     OCiM. Rediscoveries
   Rip Van Winkle at Nicholas Vedder's
     tavern               MB
     MB. Karolik coll
     Time. 300 years (col)
   Tom Walker's flight
     MiD. Coll in progress
     WiMiA. Amer ptg 1760-1960
   Voyage to Hell Gate from Communipaw
                           KW
     Pierson
   Wolfert's will             NBM
     Barker. Amer ptg
     Flexner. Amer ptg
     Flexner. Short history
     Pierson
     Roos
Quiescent space by T. Benrimo
A quiet day in Utica by C. M. Russell
Quiet day, Lisbon, F. Cabral
Quiet pond by C. E. Burchfield
Quiet river by C. A. Morris
Quiet street by D. A. White
Quilting party by J. L. Krimmel
Quilting party by Unidentified artist
Quimper at night by L. Feininger
QUINCY, Edmond, 1903-
   View from my window       ATU
     ATU. Coll of Amer art
Quincy, Eliza Susan (Morton) 1775-1850
   Stuart, G. Mrs Josiah Quincy
Quincy, Josiah, 1772-1864
   Stuart, G. Josiah Quincy
QUIRK, Thomas Charles, 1922-
   Vigil at the beach        OYB
     OYB. Annual 1957
     OYB. Suppplement 1959

**RAFFO, Steve**
La casa de Dios
  PA. Annual ex, 1948
Vote for me
  PPC. Ptg in the U.S. 1949
The **raft** by T. Doughty
**Raft** on the river by Unidentified artist
**Raftsmen** at night by G. C. Bingham
**Raftsmen** playing cards by G. C. Bingham
The **Ragan** sisters by J. Eichholtz
**Rogers, Daniel Denison,** fl 1780
  Copley, J. S. (attributed works) Daniel
    D. Rogers
**Rail** shooting by T. Eakins
**Rail** shooting by J. N. Hess
The **railroad** bridge by W. Stuempfig
**Railroad** center by G. Prestopino
**Railroad** engine, the Star by Unidentified
  artist
**Railroad** jubilee on Boston common by W.
  Sharp
**Railroad** men by P. Evergood
**Railroads**
  Becker, J. First train on the Central
    Pacific railroad, 1869
  Burchfield, C. E. Railroad in spring
  Henry, E. L. The 9:45 accommodation,
    Stratford, Connecticut, 1867
  Moses, A. M. R. Hoosick falls in winter
  Pachner, W. German train
  Pickett, J. Manchester valley
  Russell, C. M. Trail of the iron horse
  Sample, P. S. Freight cars in desert
  Sintzenich, E. Train leaving Auburn sta-
    tion at Rochester, New York
  Williamson, C. M. First Texas Central
    railroad
**RAIN, Charles Wheldon,** 1911-
  Approaching storm
    IU. Contemp Amer ptg & sculp, 1957
  Daymare                                    ATeS
    ATeS. Collection
    IU. Contemp Amer ptg, 1951
  Equinox
    CSEP. Annual ex, 1948/49
    IU. Contemp Amer ptg, 1949
  Faraway
    IU. Contemp Amer ptg, 1950 (col)
  Ice cream vendor
    IU. Contemp Amer ptg & sculp, 1953
  Summer's end
    VR. Amer ptg, 1954
**Rain** on Park south by F. Wong
**Rain** on the river by G. W. Bellows
**Rain** or snow by A. G. Dove
**Rainbow** fiend by G. Grosz
**Rainbow** trout by P. R. Goodwin
**Rainbows**
  Beckmann, M. The rainbow
  Bierstadt, A. Jenny lake, Wyoming
  Bierstadt, A. Rainbow over Jenny lake
  Inness, G. The rainbow
**Rainsford's** island, Boston harbor by R. W.
  Salmon
**Rainstorm** by K. Schrag
**Rainstorm** on the moors by B. West (at-
  tributed works)
**Rainy** day by F. W. Benson
**Rainy** day, Boston by C. Hassam

**Rainy** morning by C. M. Russell
**Rainy** night by A. Bohrod
**Rainy** night by C. E. Burchfield
A **rainy** ride by L. Dodd
**Rainy** season by P. Hurd
**Raising** a house, New York by W. P.
  Chappel
**Raising** of Lazarus by S. G. Reinhardt
**Raising** of Lazarus by B. West
**Raising** the cross by R. Philipp
**RAKOCY, William,** 1914-
  Landscape with blue-violet
    OYB. Annual 1954
**Ram** by J. Youngerman
**Ramapo** river near Suffern, New York by
  J. Marin
**Ramoncita** by A. Dasburg
**Rampart** street by L. Guglielmi
The **ramparts** by J. W. Taylor
The **ramparts**—Quebec by P. Dickinson
The **ramparts,** St Malo by O. M. Pleissner
**Ram's** head by X. Gonzalez
**Ram's** head, hollyhock, little hills by G.
  O'Keeffe
**Ram's** skull with brown leaves by G.
  O'Keeffe
**Ramsay-Polk** family at Carpenter's Point,
  Maryland by J. Peale
**RAMSEY, Milne,** 1846-
  Still life, 1911
  Frankenstein. After the hunt
**Ranch** life, western Texas by H. G. Keller
**Ranchos** church by G. O'Keeffe
**Ranchos** church, front by G. O'Keeffe
**Rand, Benjamin Howard**
  Eakins, T. Benjamin Howard Rand
**Rand, Jasper Raymond,** fl 1845
  Stock, J. W. Jasper Raymond Rand
**RANDALL, A. M.** fl 1777
  Basket of fruit with parrot           DN
    DN. Amer primitive ptgs, pt 2
**Randolph, John,** 1773-1833
  Harding, C. John Randolph of Roanoke
  Jarvis, J. W. John Randolph
  Stuart, G. John Randolph
**Randolph, Mary.** See Bolling, Mary (Ran-
  dolph)
**Random** pattern by G. Kepes
**RANGER, Henry Ward,** 1858-1916
  Connecticut woods                      DNC
    Born
  High bridge                            MM
    Born
**Rankin children**
  Eddy, O. T. Four youngest children of
    William Rankin and Abigail Ogden
    Rankin
**RANNEY, William Tylee,** 1813-1857
  Caravan on the prairies
    Rathbone
  Duck hunters on the Hoboken marshes
                                          MB
    MB. Karolik coll
  The lasso
    Rathbone
  Pioneers
    Rathbone

RANNEY, W. T.—*Continued*
  Prairie burial
    Rathbone
  Prairie fire
    McCracken. Portrait of the old west
    Rathbone
  Retreat
    Rathbone
  Scouting party
    Rathbone
  Trappers
    Rathbone
RANNEY, William Tylee, 1813-1857 and
    MOUNT, William Sidney, 1807-1868
  Pipe of friendship         NJN
    NJN. Early N.J. artists
Rapalje, Anna. See Duyckinck, Anna (Ra-
  palje)
Rapalje children
  Durand, J. Children of Helena Nyse Ra-
    palje of New York city
Rapidity of sleep by Y. Tanguy
The rapids, Hudson river, Adirondacks by
  W. Homer
Rapt at Rappaport's by S. Davis
Rare birds by E. Ludens
Rasalus by J. D. Brooks
Rathbone, Elijah, 1792-1849
  Rowley, R. Elijah Rathbone
Rathbone, Eliza (Betts) 1803-1873
  Rowley, R. Eliza Betts Rathbone
Rathbone, Mrs Elijah. See Rathbone, Eliza
  (Betts)
The Rathskeller by J. Sloan
RATKAI, George Stephen, 1907-
  Altar boys
    IU. Contemp Amer ptg & sculp, 1957
  Hurdy-gurdy
    IU. Contemp Amer ptg, 1951
  Night music
    IU. Contemp Amer ptg & sculp, 1955
  Puppets
    PPC. Ptg in the U. S. 1949
  Revelers         OYB
    OYB. Annual 1956
    OYB. Supplement 1959
  Wise bird
    IU. Contemp Amer ptg & sculp, 1953
RATTNER, Abraham, 1895-
  April showers
    MnMW. Contemporary
    Pierson
    Riley. Your art heritage
    Wight. Milestones (col)
    WMAA. Four Amer expressionists
    WMAA. Neuberger collection
  Bird bath         NBuA
    NBuA. Contemporary ptgs
  The bride
    CanO. Hirshhorn coll
  City still life         MnMW
    Larkin
  Clowns and kings
    Genauer
    WMAA. Four Amer expressionists
  Composition
    Getlein. Abraham Rattner
  Composition: Don Quixote
    PPC. Ptg in the U. S. 1949
  Composition—Farmscape no 3, 1955
    Baur. Nature

Composition, head and flowers
  Getlein. Abraham Rattner
Composition with old shoes
  Getlein. Abraham Rattner
Composition with three figures
  Cheney. Story 1958 ed
  DC. 23 biennial ex, 1953
  Time. 300 years (col)
Costume figure with mask
  Getlein. Abraham Rattner
Crucifixion         IaDM
  CoS. New accessions USA, 1952
Crucifixion in yellow
  WMAA. Four Amer expressionists
Dark rain         NJN
  Getlein. Abraham Rattner
Design for the memory
  Getlein. Abraham Rattner
The emperor         WMAA
  Baur. Revolution
  Mendelowitz
  Myers
  Pierson
Evening garden
  MM. Amer ptg today
  MnU. 40 Amer ptrs
Farm composition no 1
  Pearson. Mod renaissance
  Pousette-Dart. Amer ptg
Farm still life
  Getlein. Abraham Rattner
Figure and mask         IU
  IU. Contemp Amer ptg, 1950 (col)
  Pierson
  WMAA. Four Amer expressionists
Figure with wings and mask
  PPC. International ex, 1950
Figures waiting
  UNESCO. 1860-1955
  UNESCO. 1860-1959
  WMAA. Four Amer expressionists
Fisherman
  Pearson. Mod renaissance
Flying trapeze
  Getlein. Abraham Rattner
Gargoyles no 5, Paris
  IU. Contemp Amer ptg & sculp, 1961
Gothic enflamed
  Getlein. Abraham Rattner
Heads
  Getlein. Abraham Rattner
Industrial town         ATeS
  ATeS. Collection
Job no 2, 1958
  Getlein. Abraham Rattner (col)
Job no 9, 1959
  Getlein. Abraham Rattner
Lake landscape
  WMAA. Four Amer expressionists (col)
The last Don Quixote
  WMAA. Four Amer expressionists
Martyr
  Getlein. Abraham Rattner
Moses
  Getlein. Abraham Rattner
  IU. Contemp Amer ptg & sculp, 1959
Mother and child         MMA
  Getlein. Abraham Rattner
Of the resistance
  Getlein. Abraham Rattner
People on 6th avenue
  Gruskin

Pier composition      MoKN
  CoS. New accessions USA, 1956
  IU. Contemp Amer ptg, 1951
Prairie landscape
  Getlein. Abraham Rattner
Prairie sky
  Getlein. Abraham Rattner
  IU. Contemp Amer ptg & sculp, 1955
  (col front)
  MiD. Coll in progress (col cover)
Prairie sky no 6      PPC
  PPC. International ex, 1955
  Read. Concise history
Red tapestry chair
  MnU. 40 Amer ptrs
Rome no 1, 1951-52
  Getlein. Abraham Rattner
Rome no 4, 1951
  IU. Contemp Amer ptg & sculp, 1953
  WMAA. Four Amer expressionists
Self-portrait, 1947
  Getlein. Abraham Rattner (col)
Self-portrait, 1957      MiD
  Getlein. Abraham Rattner
Song of Esther      WMAA
  Goodrich. Amer art (col)
  WMAA. Four Amer expressionists (col)
Still life with mirror
  Pearson. Mod renaissance
Still life with oysters
  UNESCO. 1860-1955
  UNESCO. 1860-1959
Storm composition no 4
  IU. Contemp Amer ptg & sculp, 1957
Temptation of St Anthony
  Getlein. Abraham Rattner
  IU. Contemp Amer ptg, 1949
Transcendence
  NBuA. Expressionism
Valley of dry bones—triptych
  WMAA. Four Amer expressionists
Window cleaner no 1, 1951
  WMAA. Four Amer expressionists
Window cleaner no 3, 1951
  Getlein. Abraham Rattner
Window cleaner, 1953
  UNESCO. 1860-1959
Window composition
  WMAA. Four Amer expressionists
  (col)
Woman cutting bread      MM
  CoS. New accessions USA, 1952
  MM. 100 Amer ptrs
Workman's lunch
  Getlein. Abraham Rattner
Yellow table      OkNU
  NUM. Art across America

RAUSCHENBERG, Robert, 1925-
Curfew
  IU. Contemp Amer ptg & sculp, 1959
  MMA. Sixteen
Double feature
  MMA. Sixteen
The magician
  MMA. Sixteen
Painting with red letter S      NBuA
  NBuA. Acquisitions 1959-1961
  PPC. International ex, 1958
Satellite
  MMA. Sixteen
Second time painting
  PPC. International ex, 1961/62
Summer storm
  MMA. Sixteen

Ravello by R. Morgan
Ravenel, Daniel, c 1734-1774
  Theus, J. Daniel Ravenel
Ravenel, Elizabeth Damaris
  Theus, J. Elizabeth Damaris Ravenel and
  her sister
Ravenel, Elizabeth Jane (Ravenel) 1734-1809
  Theus, J. Mrs Daniel Ravenel
Ravenel, Susanne. See Mazyck, Susanne
  (Ravenel)
The ravine by H. Hofmann
RAY, Man, 1890-
  Admiration of the orchestrelle for the
    cinematograph      MMA
  Pierson.
  Aerograph
    Baur. New art
    MMA. Abstract
  Black widow
    McCurdy
    MMA. Abstract
  Interior, 1915      PPhM
    PPhM. Gallatin coll
  Invention—dance
    Brown. Amer ptg
  Jazz      OCo
    Brown. Amer ptg
  Mime
    WMAA. Pioneers
  Promenade      CtY
    CtY. Soc Anonyme
  Rope dancer accompanies herself with her
    shadows      MMA
    Baur. New art (col)
    Hunter. Mod Amer ptg
    MMA. Abstract
    Pierson
  La rue Férou
    Jean. Surrealist ptg
  Taming of the shrew
    Baur. New art
  Through the Luxembourg
    Read. Concise history
RAY, Robert D. 1924-
  The Honorable Dorothy Eugenie Brett
    IU. Contemp Amer ptg & sculp, 1957
  Manzanillo, Mexico
    IU. Contemp Amer ptg & sculp, 1959
RAY, Ruth, 1919-
  The messenger
    NAD. Annual ex, 1960
  Nana
    NAD. Annual ex, 1955
  Navajo land
    NAD. Annual ex, 1948
  Survivors
    NAD. Annual ex, 1952
  What is man
    IU. Contemp Amer ptg & sculp, 1959
Ray by W. Sommer
A ray of hope by P. Santo
Raymond children, c 1840
  Unidentified artist. Joseph and Anna Ray-
  mond
Razing old Post office, New York by E.
  Fiene
Rea, Daniel, fl 1750
  Badger, J. Daniel Rea
Rea, Mrs Daniel
  Copley, J. S. Mrs Daniel Rea and child
Reaching waves by A. G. Dove

READ, Thomas Buchanan, 1822-1872
  Portrait of a cardinal          OCiM
  MiD. Travelers in Arcadia
Reade, Catharine Livingston. See Stuy-
  vesant, Catharine Livingston (Reade)
Reading by J. S. Sargent
Reading in the sun by W. Homer
Reading Le Figaro by M. Cassatt
Ready-to-wear by S. Davis
Ready-to-wear, Study for by S. Davis
Real estate agent offering valuable lots by
  F. W. Edmonds
Real numbers by Y. Tanguy
Reapers by M. Sterne
Reavey, Mrs George. See Pereira, Irene
  (Rice)
Re-awakening by W. Drewes
Rebecca by G. W. Flagg
Rebecca at the well by W. Allston
Rebecca at the well by Unidentified artist
Rebecca street by H. Scheuch
Rebound by E. Kelly
Receding red by I. R. Pereira
Reception in Miami by J. Levine
Recipe for bouillabaisse by S. Moy
The recitation by T. W. Dewing
Reclining figure by H. Warshaw
Reclining model by J. Pascin
Reclining nude by W. M. Chase
Reclining nude by E. L. Kirchner
Reclining woman with mandolin by M. Beck-
  mann
Reclining youth by L. A. Golub
Recollections by P. Mangravite
Reconstruction by J. Frankfurter
Reconstruction by B. Shahn
Recruit from civilization by F. Remington
Recruiting, Union square by J. Sloan
Recruits wanted by D. G. Blythe
Rectangles by I. R. Pereira
Red and black by S. Francis
Red and black by C. Still
Red and blue by J. Ferren
Red and blue by I. R. Pereira
Red and gold by F. W. Benson
Red and white parasols by M. B. Prender-
  gast
Red barge 1 by R. Crawford
Red barn by C. E. Burchfield
Red bird by E. J. Stevens
Red box by B. W. Tomlin
Red-breasted merganser by J. J. Audubon
Red-breasted warbler on apple blossom by
  C. E. Heil
Red bridge by J. A. Weir
Red, brown and black by M. Rothko
Red cabinet by C. Brown
Red Cap (pseud) See Ball, Elias
Red cap by H. Hofmann
Red cap by M. Weber
Red carpet by G. Tooker
Red cart by S. Davis

Red chair by S. Haley
Red chair with straw flowers by J. Binford
Red chimneys by C. H. Demuth
Red clock by K. Knaths
Red Cloud and Burning Heart by H. H.
  Cross
Red coffee pot by H. Katzman
Red cross by M. Hartley
Red dominant by J. M. Hanson
Red figure by S. W. Hayter
Red flow by K. R. Morris
Red forest by C. A. Morris
Red gateway by M. Dixon
Red-haired gentleman and his wife by J. S.
  Ellsworth
Red hand mirror by J. Sloan
Red house by H. Rose
Red in red by S. Francis
Red Jacket (Sagoyewatha) (Seneca Indian
  chief) 1751?-1830
  Haddoca, A. Red Jacket
  Mathies, J. L. D.  Red Jacket
  Weir, R. W. Red Jacket
Red kimono on the roof by J. Sloan
Red landscape by W. A. Baziotes
Red lift by H. Hofmann
Red man—white man—black man by M.
  Tobey
Red mill by A. M. R. Moses
Red mill by Unidentified artist
Red Molly by L. Rivers
Red mule by E. F. Spruce
Red object by F. E. Conway
Red paint mill by J. Sloan
Red pastoral by J. E. Levi
Red quarry by K. Schrag
Red, red, not the same by P. Burlin
Red ribbon by I. G. Olinsky
Red rocks by R. O. Pozzatti
The red room by H. E. Niese
Red roses by J. Carroll
Red schoolhouse by G. H. Durrie
Red Sea terrace no 1 by T. Stamos
Red ship by R. A. Parker
Red skirt by R. B. Motherwell
Red sky by A. Gottlieb
Red snapper and still life by W. M. Chase
Red stairway by B. Shahn
Red still life by C. Brown
Red studio by R. Bennett
Red sun by M. Avery
Red sun—Brooklyn bridge by J. Marin
Red sweater by F. De Erdely
Red table by K. Knaths
Red-tailed hawk by J. J. Audubon
Red tapestry chair by A. Rattner
Red theme by P. Burlin
Red torso by J. Strombotne
Red trickle by H. Hofmann
Red vine by G. W. Bellows

Red vine, autumn, Dogtown by W. A. Kien-
busch
Red votive lights by L. MacIver
Red, white and brown by M. Rothko
Red, yellow and blue by I. R. Pereira
Red, yellow and white roses by H. Pippin
REDERER, Franz Joseph, 1899-
Alban Berg, Portrait of
IU. Contemp Amer ptg, 1949
Civic center, San Francisco
CSFP. Annual ex, 1946
Flowers
IU. Contemp Amer ptg, 1952
REDFIELD, Edward Willis, 1869-
Laurel run                              OBY
Chew. 250 years of art
OYB. Catalogue 1951
Winter in the valley                    PR
PR. Catalogue
Redhead ducks by F. W. Benson
Redlake by J. Tworkov
Redwood, William, 1734-1784
Stuart, G. William Redwood
Reed, Hezekiah Hutchins, fl 1825
Tuthill, A. G. D. Hezekiah Hutchins
Reed
REED, Orrel P. 1921-
Untitled, 1954
NNSG. Younger Amer ptrs
REED, Reuben Law, 1841-1921
Washington and Lafayette at the battle
of Yorktown                          VWR
VWR. Amer folk art
VWR. Folk art (col)
Reed, Thomas, fl 1825
Tuthill, A. G. D. Thomas Reed
REEDER, Dickson
Walter Martin
OYB. Annual 1957
Reflected verticals by C. A. Morris
Reflection by I. R. Pereira
Reflection by H. Pittman
Reflection by W. W. Quirt
Reflection by R. Soyer
Reflection, self-portrait by J. McGarrell
Reflections by M. Avery
Reflections by H. Ballin
Reflections by T. D. Benrimo
Reflections by P. Cadmus
Reflections by H. Moller
Reflections by J. H. Twachtman
Reflections in a Roman river by Y. Johnston
Reflections number 6 by B. Margo
REFREGIER, Anton, 1905-
Boy drawing
PPC. Ptg in the U.S. 1949
Broken life                             ATU
ATU. Coll of Amer art (col)
Feeding the hungry
Gruskin
Fire: 1906
Mendelowitz
Heir to the future
Larkin
Larkin rev ed
Picture of my young son
IU. Contemp Amer ptg, 1951

Shipbuilding in the 18th century
Pierson
The staircase                           WMAA
Goodrich. Amer art
IU. Contemp Amer ptg, 1950
Pierson
Refugees by M. Siporin
Refugees by M. Weber
Regal lilies by S. C. Sears
Regal personages by C. Booth
Regatta by J. Jones
Regatta by M. Roberts
Regatta at Edgartown by F. S. Chapin
Region of Brooklyn bridge fantasy by J.
Marin
Region Weehawken, New Jersey by J. Marin
Regulus (Marcus Atilius Regulus) d 250
B.C.
West, B. Departure of Regulus
Rehearsal by L. Kester
Rehearsal of the Pas de Loup Orchestra
at the Cirque d'Hiver by J. S. Sargent
Rehearsal under the big top by B. Stahl
REHN, Frank Knox Morton, 1848-1914
Glittering moonlight                    DC
NYG. Fine art
Rehoboth beach, Delaware
Peale, T. R. Bright house, Rehoboth
beach, Delaware
REICH, Don, 1931-
Texas landscape no 3                    CSFP
IU. Contemp Amer ptg & sculp, 1961
REID, Robert, 1862-1929
The bather                              CtY
CtY. Soc Anonyme
Reid, Samuel Chester, 1818-1897
Jarvis, J. W. Capt Samuel Chester Reid
REILLY, Frank Joseph, 1906-
Mount Overlook
NAD. Annual ex, 1956
REILLY, John William
Old man, Portrait of an
NAD. Annual ex, 1957
Transients
NAD. Annual ex, 1959
REINDEL, Edna, 1900-
Hiroshima
ICA. Annual ex, 1947-48
REINHARDT, Adolph Frederick, 1913-
Black and white, 1950
MNU. 40 Amer ptrs
Number 1, 1959
MnMW. 60 Amer ptrs
Number 2
Pousette-Dart. Amer ptg
Number 7A, 1953
WMAA. New decade
Number 11, 1949
McCurdy
MMA. Abstract
Number 12, 1952
PPC. International ex, 1955
Number 14, 1948
MnU. 40 Amer ptrs
Number 15                               NBuA
NBuA. Acquisitions 1957-58
Number 18, 1948-49                      WMAA
Pierson
WMAA. New decade
Number 18, 1950
Hess. Abstract ptg

**REINHARDT, A. F.**—*Continued*
Number 19, 1953
  VR. Amer ptg, 1954
Number 24, 1954
  Pierson
  WMAA. New decade
Triptych
  Brussels. Exposition
Untitled painting, 1945
  Hess. Abstract ptg

**REINHARDT, Marnye**
View into Maryland            VR
  Pousette-Dart. Amer ptg

**REINHARDT, Siegfried G.** 1925-
Adam and Eve
  WMAA. Young America 1960
Exultation
  NAD. Annual ex, 1960
The miracle
  WMAA. Young America 1960
Pieta               MoSL
  CoS. New accessions USA, 1952
Raising of Lazarus
  MnMW. Reality and fantasy
Resistance
  IU. Contemp Amer ptg & sculp, 1957
Sentinel
  Pousette-Dart. Amer ptg
  WMAA. Contemp Amer ptg, 1951
Sentry
  MoSL. Contemporary Amer ptg

**REISS, Wallace,** 1926?-
Bursting flowers
  WMAA. Contemp Amer ptg, 1955

**Rejected** suitor by L. M. Eilshemius

**Relation** within space by F. Ruvolo

**Relational** painting by F. Glarner

**Relaxation** by O. Foss

**Relics** of a den by G. W. Platt

**Religious themes.** See Biblical and religious themes

**Remains** II by B. Chaet

**Remember** me by F. C. Watkins

**Remember** now the days of thy youth by P. S. Sample

**Remembering** by R. W. Anliker

**Remembrance** of things past by B. Ullrich

**REMICK, Christian,** b 1726
Blockade of Boston, View of the    MSE
  Flexner. First flowers

**REMINGTON, Frederic,** 1861-1909
Among the led horses
  Carlson. Gallery (col)
Apaches are coming          NOR
  McCracken. Remington
Apaches listening          NOR
  Carlson. Gallery (col)
  McCracken. Remington
Army officer             NOR
  McCracken. Remington
Attack on the supply train
  McCracken. Portrait of the old west (col)
Breaking up the ice in spring    NOR
  McCracken. Remington
Bringing home the new cook
  Carlson. Gallery (col)
The captive Gaul          NOR
  McCracken. Remington

Cavalry charge on the southern plains    MM
  McCracken. Remington
  MM. 100 Amer ptrs
Cavalry charge on the western plain   MM
  Mendelowitz
Charge of the Rough Riders at San Juan hill          NOR
  McCracken. Remington
Dead men
  McCracken. Remington
Death of Minnehaha
  McCracken. Portrait of the old west
Dismounted: 4th troopers moving   MWiS
  MWiS. Ex 4 and 7
Downing the nigh leader
  McCracken. Remington
End of the day           NOR
  McCracken. Remington
Fight for the water hole      TxH
  Time. 300 years (col)
General Leonard A. Wood on horseback          NOR
  McCracken. Remington
Ghost stories           NOR
  McCracken. Remington
Halt—dismount
  McCracken. Remington
Hauling in the gill net      NOR
  McCracken. Remington
Head of a frontiersman
  McCracken. Portrait of the old west (col)
Holding up the payroll
  Carlson. Gallery (col)
How order no 6 came through
  McCracken. Portrait of the old west
Howl of the weather        NOR
  McCracken. Remington
  Time. 300 year (col)
The last march          NOR
  McCracken. Remington (col)
Lost warrior
  McCracken. Remington
Navajo raid
  McCracken. Remington
An old time plains fight     NOR
  Carlson. Gallery (col)
  McCracken. Remington (col front)
On the southern plains in 1860
  Carlson. Gallery (col)
The outlier             NOR
  McCracken. Remington
Pioneer and the Indian      ATeS
  ATeS. Collection
The quarrel
  McCracken. Remington
Recruit from civilization
  McCracken. Portrait of the old west
The scout: friends or enemies?    MWiS
  McCracken. Portrait of the old west
  McCracken. Remington
  MWiS. Ex 4 and 7
  Rathbone
  Time. 300 years (col)
The scream of shrapnel at San Juan hill, Cuba          CtY
  U.S. National Capital sesquicentennial com
The sentinel           NOR
  Larkin
  Larkin rev ed
  McCracken. Remington
  NUM. Art across America

The snow trail                    NOR
  McCracken. Remington
Snowbound on the overland stage
  Carlson. Gallery (col)
Sun dance                         NOR
  McCracken. Remington
United States cavalry defending a posi-
  tion, 1895                      NOR
  McCracken. Remington
Visitation of the buffalo gun
  McCracken. Remington
Waiting in the moonlight          NOR
  McCracken. Remington
Remington's studio by L. Carr
Reminiscence by H. Hofmann
Reminiscence of the Genesee river by J. W.
  Casilear
Reminiscent Italia by P. Zimmerman
Remnants by A. Brook
Remnants of an era by J. L. Meador
Remote field by M. Tobey
Removal of the Sphinxes by M. Beckmann
Remsen, Elizabeth (De Peyster) 1787-1826
  Unidentified artist. Mrs Hendrick Rem-
    sen
Remsen, Hendrick, 1762-1843
  Pollard, C. Residence of Hendrick Rem-
    sen
  Unidentified artist. Hendrick Remsen
Remsen, Mrs Hendrick. See Remsen, Eliza-
  beth (De Peyster)
Renaissance by N. J. Pousette-Dart
Renaldo and the enchanted garden by R. M.
  Farruggio
Renascence by B. Shahn
Rendezvous by F. Kleinholz
Rendezvous by A. J. Miller
Rendezvous by R. Philipp
Rendezvous by M. Siporin
Rendezvous in the Wind river mountains by
  A. J. Miller
Renganeschi's Saturday night by J. Sloan
Renunciation by P. Evergood
Repair shack interior by S. Wilson
Report from Rockport by S. Davis
Repose by B. Karfiol
Repose by S. Menkès
Repose by J. S. Sargent
Repose no 2 by M. Weber
The reprimand by W. Stuempfig
Republican automatons by G. Grosz
Request number by R. Philipp
Requiem by D. Fredenthal
Requiem by F. J. Kline
The rescue by W. R. Leigh
Residence of David Twining by E. Hicks
La résistance by R. B. Motherwell
Resistance by S. G. Reinhardt
RESNICK, Milton, 1917-
  Genie                           WMAA
    Goodrich. Amer art (col)
  Page, 1959
    MnMW. 60 Amer ptrs
  Rubble
    Art since 1945
  Untitled painting, 1954
    CtY. Yale alumni

Resort beach by P. Evergood
Rest in air by J. McGarrell
Restaurants. See Hotels, restaurants, etc.
Resting by J. S. Sargent
Resting at the bazaar by M. Sterne
Restless horizon by C. A. Morris
Restrained flow by W. Lockwood
Resurrection by D. Aronson
Resurrection by A. P. Ryder
Resurrection by F. C. Watkins
Resurrection by J. Zajac
Retreat by W. T. Ranney
The return by F. C. Watkins
Return from Bohemia by G. Wood
Return of Jephthah by B. West
Return of Rip Van Winkle by J. Quidor
Return of the gleaner by W. Homer
Return of the prodigal by F. Castellon
Return of the warriors by C. M. Russell
Returning by R. Taylor
Returning from the Feria by H. G. Keller
Returning to the farm by G. H. Durrie
Revelation by Y. Kuniyoshi
Revelers by G. S. Ratkai
Revere, Paul, 1735-1818
  Copley, J. S. Paul Revere
  Quidor, J. Paul Revere
  Wood, G. Midnight ride of Paul Revere
Revere beach by M. B. Prendergast
Reverie by L. Kroll
Reverie by K. H. Miller
Reverse image by N. Carone
Review, 1948-49 by P. Guston
REVINGTON, Arthur
  The apparition
    Cheney. Expressionism 1948 ed
Revolving head by P. Tchelitchew
Revue by E. Shinn
The reward by T. Stamos
Reynolds, Lydia (Bartlett) 1770-1843
  Ames, E. Mrs Stephen Reynolds
Reynolds, Marcus Tullius, 1788-1864
  Ames, E. Marcus T. Reynolds
Reynolds, Sir Joshua, 1732-1792
  Stuart, G. Sir Joshua Reynolds
Rhett, William, b 1666
  Johnston, H. Col William Rhett
Rhode Island choir boy by Unidentified
  artist
Rhythms by L. Dabo
Rhythms by H. G. Keller
RIBA, Paul, 1912-
  Along the coast
    OYB. Annual 1952
  Sandpipers
    PPC. International ex, 1952
  Symbol of the sun and moon
    NAD. Annual ex, 1958
RIBAK, Louis Leon, 1903-
  At the beach                    ATU
    ATU. Coll of Amer art
  White city no 3
    IU. Contemp Amer ptg & sculp, 1959

The **ribbon** of extremes by Y. Tanguy
**Ricci, Geraldine.** See Ricci, Jerri
**RICCI, Jerri,** 1916-
In the studio
NAD. Annual ex, 1953
Louisburg square, winter
NAD. Special ex, 1956
**RICE, Henry Webster,** 1853-1934
Landscape with mountains     MB
MB. Ptgs in water color
Seascape     MB
MB. Ptgs in water color
Sunset in the mountains     MB
MB. Ptgs in water color
**Rice** field near Milan by Leonid
**Rice** Hope by C. Fraser
**Rice** line by M. Greenwood
**Rich, Aphia Salisbury,** fl 1833
Unidentified artist. Aphia Salisbury Rich
and baby Edward
**Richard, Elizabeth (Garland)** 1700-1774
Copley, J. S. Mrs Paul Richard
**RICHARDS, John,** 1831-1889
Battle of Gettysburg, 1863
U. S. National Capital sesquicentennial
com
**RICHARDS, William Trost,** 1833-1905
June day     OCl
Chew. 250 years of art
Lands End, Cornwall     OYB
OYB. Catalogue 1951
Near Paradise, Newport, Rhode island
    MB
MB. Ptgs in water color
**RICHARDSON, Constance (Coleman)**
1905-
French Canadian barn
WiMiA. Amer ptg 1760-1960
Wyoming desert
WiMiA. Amer ptg 1760-1960
**RICHARDSON, Dean,** 1931-
Child's toy
MBIC. View 1960
Motorists     WMAA
WMAA. Contemp Amer ptg, 1959/60
WMAA. Young America 1960
**Richardson, Mrs Edgar Preston.** See Richardson, Constance (Coleman)
**Richardson, Mrs Edward.** See Richardson, Elizabeth (Poinsett)
**Richardson, Elizabeth (Poinsett)** b c 1751
Theus, J. Mrs Edward Richardson
**Richardson, F. E.**
Parcell, M. S. F. E. Richardson jr
**Richardson, William,** 1743-1786
Theus, J. Col William Richardson
**Richardson** memorial by H. Moore
**Richardson's** Columbian squirrel by J. J. Audubon
**RICHARDT, Joachim Ferdinand,** 1819-1895
Emporium of Indian curiosities     NCHA
Jones. New-found folk art
**Richmond** Hill, Story of by P. Evergood
**Richmond,** Virginia by Unidentified artist
The **riddle** by I. R. Pereira
A **ride** for liberty: the fugitive slave by E. Johnson
The **rider** by M. B. Prendergast
**Rider** against blue hills by M. B. Prendergast

**Riders** by C. A. Morris
**Riders** in the hills by J. Sloan
**Riders** in the park by M. Avery
**Ridge** and forecast by R. Tam
**Ridgely, Eliza,** 1802-1867
Sully, T. Lady with a harp: Eliza Ridgely
**Ridgely, Mary (Middleton) Vining,** 1705-1761
Unidentified artist. Mrs Nicholas Ridgely
**Ridgeway** by J. Tworkov
**Rigging** by J. S. Sargent
**Right** and left by W. Homer
**Riker's** island prison, Study for mural at by B. Shahn
**RILEY, Bernard**
Newsboys
NAD. Annual ex, 1959
**Riley, James Whitcomb,** 1849-1916
Sargent, J. S. James Whitcomb Riley
**RIMMER, William,** 1816-1879
Flight and pursuit (Pursuer and pursued)
    MB
Mendelowitz
Pierson
Richardson. Ptg in America
**Rinaldo** and Armida by B. West
**RINDISBACHER, Peter,** 1806-1834
Buffalo hunting in summer     MCH
Rathbone
Buffaloes in winter     MCH
Rathbone
Indian dance
Rathbone
Indians hunting buffalo
Rathbone
Indians returning from war     MCH
Rathbone
Inside of an Indian tent     MCH
Rathbone
War dance of the Sauks and Foxes
McCracken. Portrait of the old west (col)
Rathbone
**Ring** around the moon by T. D. Benrimo
**Ringing** the pig by W. S. Mount
**Ringside** seats by G. W. Bellows
**Rio** di San Barnaba, Venice by E. D. Boit
**Rio** di San Lorenzo, Venice by E. D. Boit
**Rip Van Winkle (steamboat)**
Bard, J. Hudson river steamboat Rip Van Winkle
**Rip** Van Winkle at Nicholas Vedder's tavern by J. Quidor
**RIPLEY, Alden Lassell,** 1896-
After the storm     MB
MB. Ptg in water color
Winter morning
NAD. Annual ex, 1949, 2d half
**Rise** of the full moon by A. G. Dove
**Rishi** calling up a storm by J. La Farge
**Rising** city by C. A. Morris
**Rising** moon by R. A. Blakelock
**Rising** moon by A. G. Dove
**Rising** of a thunderstorm at sea by W. Allston
**Rising** sun by H. Hofmann
**Rising** tide by A. G. Dove
A **risk** in each hand by Y. Tanguy

RITMAN, Louis
  Michigan landscape
    NAD. Annual ex, 1959
RITTENBERG, Henry R. 1879-
  Caroline Augusta                    OYB
    OYB. Catalogue 1951
Ritual by J. Pollock
Ritual vessel-mirror by M. Graves
Riva San Biagio, Venice by M. B. Prender-
    gast
The river by L. Feininger
The river by L. Guglielmi
The river by C. S. Price
River bathers by G. Hartigan
River Eau Sucre by A. J. Miller
River effect, Paris by J. Marin
River flowing . . . flowing by Chen Chi
River front no 1, 1915 by G. W. Bellows
River in the Catskills by T. Cole
River men by J. Whorf
River movement—downtown by J. Marin
River night by C. A. Morris
River Rouge plant by C. Sheeler
River scene by T. Chambers
River scene by J. F. Kensett
River scene, lumberman, and logs in river
    by W. Homer
River scene, watering horses, by A. J. Mil-
    ler
River view from the plaza by C. F. Gaert-
    ner
River view with shepherd and animals by
    Unidentified artist
Riverbank by D. Park
Riverfront no 1 by G. W. Bellows
Rivers, Deborah. See Skaats, Deborah
    (Rivers)
RIVERS, Larry, 1923-
  Birdie with straw hat
    McCurdy
  Double portrait of Birdie          WMAA
    MMA. 12 Americans
    Pierson
  The final veteran
    NBuA. Acquisitions 1959-1961
  Head of Stevie
    MMA. 12 Americans
  Red Molly
    WMAA. Museum and its friends, 1958
  Saxophone player—Jay Cameron
    IU. Contemp Amer ptg & sculp, 1959
  Self figure                         DC
    DC. 24 biennial ex, 1955
    MMA. 12 Americans
  Washington crossing the Delaware   MMA
    MMA. 12 Americans (col)
  Water mill prospect
    MMA. 12 Americans
Riverton yacht club, New Jersey by A. B.
    Serwazi
Rivington, James, 1724-1802
  Ames, E. James Rivington (after Stuart)
The road between by G. Seibert
Road from the cove by L. Kroll
Road in early spring by C. E. Burchfield
Road in Midi by J. S. Sargent
Road into Ranchos de Taos by A. Dasburg

Road roller by R. Kent
Road through the willows by L. Kroll
Road through the woods by D. Macknight
Road to Alcumenar by C. Voorhies
Road to Bonao by W. E. Heitland
Road to Danbury by M. Varga
Road to friendship by A. N. Wyeth
Road to Golgotha by J. P. Wheat
Road to Lamy by A. Dasburg
Road to Sparta by T. Stamos
Road to the West by G. Tattersall
The road with no turn by W. W. Quirt
Roads no 6 by H. Sterne
Roadside meeting by A. P. Ryder
Roanoke, Virginia
  Fransioli, T. A. St Andrew's church,
    Roanoke
Roar of the wooden horse by E. Isenburger
Roasting ears by T. H. Benton
Roasting the hump rib by A. J. Miller
Robbery of Europe by M. Beckmann
Robbins, Ammi Ruhamah
  Moulthrop, R. Rev Ammi Ruhamah Rob-
    bins
ROBBINS, Franklin
  The bride
    NAD. Annual ex, 1956
Robbins, Maria Louisa. See Davis, Maria
    Louisa (Robbins)
Robbins, Thomas, 1777-1865
  Moulthrop, R. Thomas Robbins
Robert Knapp (schooner)
  Bard, J. Hudson river schooner Robert
    Knapp
The Robert L. Stevens breaking ice in the
    Hudson river by J. Bard
Roberto by W. Kuhn
ROBERTS, Alice T. 1876-
  Ipswich sand dunes no 2
    PA. Annual ex, 1952
ROBERTS, Bishop, fl 1735-1739
  Charleston before 1739
    Davidson v 1
    Flexner. First flowers (detail)
Roberts, Henry Laurens, fl 1831
  Davis, J. H. Henry Laurens Roberts
Roberts, Mary W. fl 1823
  Unidentified artist. Mrs Mary W. Roberts
ROBERTS, Morton, 1927-
  Bar and grill
    OYB. Annual 1956
  The derelict
    NAD. Annual ex, 1954
  Regatta
    NAD. Annual ex, 1957
Roberts, Owen Josephus, 1875-1955
  Watkins, F. C. Justice Owen J. Roberts
ROBERTS, Priscilla W. 1916-
  Bird and rose
    NAD. Annual ex, 1949, 1st half
  The old shop window
    IU. Contemp Amer ptg & sculp, 1961
  Pipe and bowl
    IU. Contemp Amer ptg, 1949
  Plumage
    IU. Contemp Amer ptg, 1950
    PPC. Ptg in the U. S. 1949

ROBERTS, P. W.—*Continued*
Self-portrait
  IU. Contemp Amer ptg, 1951
  NAD. Annual ex, 1947, 1st half
  PPC. International ex, 1950
ROBERTS, Richard
  Ohio evening                                    OYB
  OYB. Annual 1954
ROBERTSON, Archibald, 1765-1835
  New York city from North river, View of
                                                NNHS
  Larkin
  Larkin rev ed
  Tidal mill
  Davidson v 1

**Attributed works**

The collect or fresh water pond
  Flexner. Light of western skies
ROBERTSON, Thomas
  Composition no 30                               MAP
  Rathbun
Robeson mill at the mouth of the Wis-
  sahickon by R. Smith
Robin by G. W. Bellows
Robin Hood cove, Georgetown, Maine by
  M. Hartley
Robinhood marina by W. Zorach
Robins, Margaret, fl 1745
  Hesselius, J. Margaret Robins
Robinson, Alexander, fl 1795
  Peale, C. W. Alexander and Angelica
  Robinson
Robinson, Angelica, fl 1795
  Peale, C. W. Alexander and Angelica
  Robinson
Robinson, Annie, fl 1794
  Unidentified artist. Annie Robinson
ROBINSON, Boardman, 1876-1952
  The Dutch in the Baltic
  Larkin rev ed
  Ethiopia saluting the colors
  Genauer (col)
  Hannah Armstrong                               ATU
  ATU. Coll of Amer art
  Judson Stoddard                                ATU
  ATU. Coll of Amer art
  Moby Dick
  Cheney. Expressionism 1948 ed
  Richard Bone                                   ICA
  Pierson
  Stubb and Starbuck                             GAtM
  GAtM. Holbrook collection
  Wintry park
  Gruskin
Robinson, Faith. See Trumbull, Faith
  (Robinson)
ROBINSON, Florence Vincent, 1860?-1930
  Versailles                                      MB
  MB. Ptgs in water color
Robinson, Mrs Henry
  Sully, T. Mrs Henry Robinson
ROBINSON, J. C. fl 1848
  An old lady                                     DN
  DN. Amer primitive ptgs, pt 1
  An old man                                      DN
  DN. Amer primitive ptgs, pt 1
Robinson, Jane, fl 1826
  Morse, S. F. B. Mrs Jane Robinson
ROBINSON, Jay, 1915-
  Nice drums
  PPC. Ptg in the U. S. 1949

ROBINSON, Theodore, 1852-1896
  Girl at the piano                               OT
    Richardson. Ptg in America
  Spring in Giverney
    CSB. Impressionism
    NUM. Art across America
  Val d'Arconville                                ICA
    Born
    Pierson
  Watering pots                                  NBM
    Pierson
  Willows                                        NBM
    Mendelowitz
Robinson, Tony
  Speicher, E. E. Tony Robinson
Rochelle by R. Philipp
Rochester, New York
  Belton, F. S. Rochester, New York
  Unidentified artist. Mill of C. J. Hill &
    Son, Rochester, New York
The rock by P. Blume
Rock fluorescence by E. Loran
Rock formations by A. J. Miller
Rock landscape by K. L. Callahan
Rock of Independence by A. J. Miller
Rock painting by J. Ernst
Rock vista by G. W. Bellows
Rockbound forms by C. A. Morris
Rockefeller, John Davidson, 1839-1937
  Sargent, J. S. John D. Rockefeller
Rockhill special by K. E. Fortess
ROCKMORE, Noel
  Family group
  OYB. Annual 1953
Rockport by J. J. Jones
Rockport beach by S. Davis
Rockport harbor by M. Beck
Rockport window by J. Teyral
Rocks and pines by M. Beck
Rocks and rubble by W. Schock
Rocks and sea by C. S. Hopkinson
Rocks and sea, Small point, Maine by J.
  Marin
Rocks and water by H. Maril
Rocks in New England by M. J. Heade
Rocks in the sea by H. Wentz
Rockwell, Elizabeth de Long, fl 1865
  Mason, B. F. Elizabeth de Long Rock-
    well
Rockwell, Simeon, fl 1867
  Mason, B. F. Simeon Rockwell
Rockwell, Mrs Simeon, fl 1867
  Mason, B. F. Mrs Simeon Rockwell
Rocky cliffs—Yosemite valley by W. Zorach
Rocky coast by W. Homer
Rocky coast by A. Walkowitz
Rocky farmyard by J. C. Atherton
Rocky field, Camp island, Maine by W. A.
  Kienbusch
Rocky hillside by H. More
Rocky landscape by E. H. Betts
Rocky moorland by B. West (attributed
  works)
Rocky mountains
  Bierstadt, A. Rocky mountains
  Blakelock, R. A. Rocky mountains

Egan, J. J. Distant view of the Rocky
  mountains
Miller, A. J. Lake scene, Rocky moun-
  tains
Miller, A. J. Wild scenery
Seymour, S. View near the base of the
  Rocky mountains
Seymour, S. View of the Rocky moun-
  tains on the Platte
Wenck, P. Rockies from Bear lake
Whittredge, W. In the Rockies
**Rocky** neck, Gloucester by S. Davis
**Rocky** neck (Gloucester) by K. Matthew
**Rocky** place by E. F. Spruce
**Rocky** shore by M. J. Heade
**Rocky** shore by W. Homer
**Rococo** table by H. Kallem
**Rodeo** by K. Evett
**Rodeo** in the Rockies by A. Blanch
**Rodgers, Rebecca.** See Codwise, Rebecca
  (Rodgers)
**Rodin, Auguste,** 1840-1917
  Sargent, J. S. Auguste Rodin
**Rodman, Mr,** fl 1800
  Malbone, E. G. Mr Rodman
**ROESCH, Kurt Ferdinand,** 1905-
  Dice players
    IU. Contemp Amer ptg, 1951
  Imagined music                    NBuA
    NBuA. Acquisitions 1957-58
  Odalisk
    IU. Contemp Amer ptg, 1952
  Walk in town                        PA
    Pousette-Dart. Amer ptg
**ROESEN, Severin,** c 1815-1871
  Boy with still life                OYB
    OYB. Supplement 1959
  Dutch lunch
    Frankenstein. After the hunt
  Fruit on table
    NUM. Art across America
  Still life with fruit and flowers
    Chew. 250 years of art
**Rogers, Elizabeth (Gatfield)** fl 1780
  Unidentified artist. Mrs Leonard Rogers
**Rogers, Helen**
  Speicher, E. E. Helen Rogers
**ROGERS, Nathaniel,** 1788-1844
  Man in black coat
    OCl. Portrait miniatures
**Rogers, Robert,** 1758-1835
  Allston, W. Robert Rogers
**ROGOWAY, Alfred,** 1905-
  The family
    IU. Contemp Amer ptg & sculp, 1955
  Summer
    IU. Contemp Amer ptg & sculp, 1953
**Rogues'** gallery by C. E. Burchfield
**Roller** skating rink by W. J. Glackens
**Rolling** power by C. Sheeler
**Rollins, James S.** fl 1871
  Bingham, G. C. James S. Rollins, Study
    for portrait
**Rolph, James,** 1869-1934
  Shahn, B. Gov James Rolph jr of Cali-
    fornia
**Roman** aqueduct by S. Drumlevitch
The **Roman** Campagna by T. Cole
The **Roman** Campagna by G. Inness

**Roman** Campagna by M. B. Prendergast
**Roman** head by A. B. Durand
**Roman** shop by E. Betsberg
**Romanesque** facade by A. Gottlieb
**Romanscape** by Z. Kachadoorian
**ROMANO, Umberto,** 1905-
  Behold . . . man
    IU. Contemp Amer ptg, 1949 (col)
  Ecce Homo
    Genauer (col)
  Fragments and reconstruction
    NAD. Annual ex, 1956
  Green clown
    IU. Contemp Amer ptg, 1950
  I bear the children of tomorrow
    NAD. Annual ex, 1961
**Romantic** figure by E. Isenburger
**Romantic** landscape by E. Ames
**Romantic** landscape by T. Cole
**Rome, Italy**
  Bierstadt, A. Arch of Octavius
  Blume, P. Eternal city
  Boit, E. D. St Peter's Rome
  Gikow, R. Roman street scene
  Healy, G. P. A. Arch of Titus
  Pelin, B. Colosseum
  Prendergast, M. B. Afternoon, Pincian
    hill, Rome
  Prendergast, M. B. On the Corso, Rome
  Prendergast, M. B. Pincian hill, Rome
  Prendergast, M. B. Spanish steps, Rome
  Rattner, A. Rome no 1, 1951-52
  Rattner, A. Rome no 4
  Sargent, J. S. Piazza Navona, Rome
  Vanderlyn, J. View in Rome
  Vedder, E. Rome
**Rome—St** Augustine by K. Zerbe
**Romeyn, Harriet.** See Stafford, Harriet
  (Romeyn)
**RONALD, William,** 1927?-
  Seventy-seven                      MnMW
    MnMW. 60 Amer ptrs
  The visitor
    MnMW. Eighty works
**RONDEL, Frederic,** 1826-1892
  Self-portrait
    WiMiA. Amer ptg 1760-1960
**RONSON, David,** 1923-
  Marriage at Cana
    Pearson. Mod renaissance
**Roof** gossips by J. Sloan
**Roof** pattern by A. Parella
The **roof** playground by W. Zorach
**Roofs:** 23rd street, sunset by J. Sloan
**Rooftops** by A. G. Dove
The **room** by P. Guston
**Room** 8—hotel Flora, Cannes by R. B.
  Motherwell
**Room** in Brooklyn by E. Hopper
**Room** in New York by E. Hopper
**Room** interior no 1 by J. Cox
**Room** number VI by E. Cortor
**Room** 110 by Y. Kuniyoshi
**Room** 203 by I. L. Albright
**Rooms** by the sea by E. Hopper
**Rooms** for tourists by E. Hopper

Roosevelt, Franklin **Delano**, president **U.S.**
1882-1945
  Salisbury, F. O. Franklin D. Roosevelt
  Woolf, S. J. Franklin D. Roosevelt
  Woolf, S. J. Franklin D. Roosevelt—
    beginning of his office
Roosevelt, **Samuel Montgomery**, 1864-1920
  Lockman, D. M. Samuel Montgomery
    Roosevelt
Roosevelt, **Theodore**, president **U.S.** 1853-
1919
  Sargent, J. S. Theodore Roosevelt
**Roosters**
  Avery, M. Pink cock
  Avery, M. Rooster's domain
  Hensel, H. Clown with rooster
  Knaths, K. Cock and glove
  Knaths, K. King cock
  Lebrun, R. Rooster on arm of the cross
  Luks, G. B. Mrs Gamley [with rooster]
  Spruce, E. F. Yellow rooster
  Zerbe, K. Rooster
  Unidentified artist. The cock
  Wilson, R. Pet rooster
**Root-diggers** by A. J. Miller
**Roots** by G. Prestopino
The **rope** by J. French
**Rope** dancer accompanies herself with her
  shadows by M. Ray
**Rope** walk interior by C. B. King
**ROPES, George,** 1788-1819
  Crowninshield's wharf, Salem, 1806  MSP
    Davidson v 1
  Launching the ship Fame at Salem  MSP
    Davidson v 1
**Roping** a grizzly by C. M. Russell
**Roping** a wild one by C. M. Russell
**Roque** by P. S. Sample
**Rosa, Salvator,** 1615-1676
  Cole, T. Salvator Rosa sketching banditti
**Rosa** gallica by B. Connelly
**Rosa** Maria by A. Brook
**Rosalie** by W. Allston
**Rosalind** by I. G. Olinsky
**ROSE, Herman,** 1909-
  East New York
    MMA. Fifteen
  From Avenue A
    MMA. Fifteen
  Manhattan tops
    Pierson
  Red house
    MMA. Fifteen
**ROSE, Iver,** 1899-
  Flower women                              MAP
    Gruskin
  Sharp drummer
    Genauer (col)
  Take my picture, mister
    NAD. Annual ex, 1955
  Three slickers                            MSM
    CoS. New accessions USA, 1954
  A world I never made
    PPC. Ptg in the U.S. 1949
**Rose, Johannes,** 1694-1718
  Unidentified artist. Johannes Rose
**Rose** of the four winds by Y. Tanguy
**Rose** sequence by W. Brice
**Roseate** spoonville by J. J. Audubon

**ROSEN, Charles,** 1878-1950
  Two tugs                                   OT
    OT. Contemp Amer ptgs
**Rosen, Katherine**
  Bellows, G. W. Katherine Rosen
**ROSENBERG, Charles D,** fl 1858 and **CAF-**
**FERTY, James H.** 1819-1869
  Wall street, half past 2 o'clock, October
    13, 1857
    U.S. National Capital sesquicentennial
    com
**ROSENBERG, James N.** 1874-
  Grey day in Adirondacks                  GAtM
    GAtM. Holbrook collection
**ROSENBERG, Samuel,** 1896-
  Composition no 5, 1956
    PPC. International ex, 1958
  The dance                                  PGr
    Chew. 250 years of art
  Israel                                     PPC
    Gruskin
  Maine
    Chew. 250 years of art
  Moment in time
    IU. Contemp Amer ptg, 1952
  The patriarch                             OYB
    OYB. Catalogue 1951
  The present
    PPC. Ptg in the U.S. 1949
  The season's turning
    PPC. International ex, 1955
  Street by the mill
    Chew. 250 years of art
  Time echoes
    IU. Contemp Amer ptg & sculp
    PPC. International ex, 1952
**ROSENBORG, Ralph,** 1911-
  Land of the bright sun
    IU. Contemp Amer ptg & sculp, 1955
  Landscape forms
    IU. Contemp Amer ptg & sculp, 1961
  Northern seascape
    IU. Contemp Amer ptg & sculp, 1959
  Subjective landscape                      CtY
    CtY. Soc Anonyme
**ROSENFELD, Edward,** 1906-
  Kitchen sink                               DP
    DP. Catalogue
**ROSENTHAL, Doris**
  Don Pasquale                              IaDa
    IaDa. Silver jubilee
    Pearson. Mod renaissance
  Girl and bananas                           OT
    Gruskin (col)
    OT. Contemp Amer ptgs
    Pearson. Mod renaissance
  Hotel corridor
    IU. Contemp Amer ptg, 1948
    OYB. Annual 1953
  Mexican church                            ATU
    ATU. Coll of Amer art (col)
  Nixtamal y postole
    MM. Amer ptg today
  Tops                                      MMA
    Gruskin (col)
**ROSENTHAL, Toby Edward,** 1848-1917
  The cardinal's portrait                   CSFP
    CSFP. Handbook (col)
  Seine Madonna                             CSFP
    NYG. Fine art
**Roses** by W. Brice
**Roses** by M. Hartley

Roses on a palette by M. J. Heade
Roses with red chair by H. Pippin
Rosh Hashana by W. Pachner
Ross, Anna Helena Amelia. See Plumstead, Anna Helena Amelia (Ross)
ROSS, C. Chandler
    Autumn pleasures
      NYG. Fine art
    Eastern tranquillity
      NYG. Fine art (col)
    From my window
      NYG. Fine art
    Oriental simplicity
      NYG. Fine art (col)
    Prize flowers
      NYG. Fine art
    Tang horse
      NYG. Fine art
    Thoroughbreds
      NYG. Fine art
    Treasures from China
      NYG. Fine art
Ross, Elizabeth, 1751-1781. See Tyng, Elizabeth (Ross) 1751-1831
ROSS, Jamie, 1931-
    Uncompleted bridge         OYB
      OYB. Annual 1955
      OYB. Supplement 1959
Ross snow geese by B. Wilson
ROSSBACH, Lois, 1922
    Girl with bird         OCl
      CoS. New accessions USA, 1952
    Tired         OYB
      OYB. Annual 1955
      OYB. Supplement 1959
ROSSITER, Thomas Pritchard, 1817-1871
    Opening of the wilderness     MB
      MB. Karolik coll
    Picnic on the Hudson
      U.S. National Capital sesquicentennial com
ROSZAK, Theodore J. 1907-
    Carcass
      MnMW. Roszak
    Composition in an oval
      MnMW. Roszak
    Composition in white
      MMA. Abstract
    Fisherman's bride       WMAA
      MnMW. Roszak
    Florence
      MnMW. Roszak
    Forty-second street, 1936
      MNMW. Roszak
    Opposition within a circle
      MnMW. Roszak
    Peasant woman
      MnMW. Roszak
    Seated figure
      MnMW. Roszak
    Self-portrait
      MnMW. Roszak (col)
Rotating vision by F. Ruvolo
ROTH, Frank, 1936-
    Agincourt       NBuA
      NBuA. Acquisitions 1957-58
    Fragment of an empire     CSB
      WMAA. Young America 1960
    Hommage à Albert Camus
      WMAA. Young America 1960

ROTH, Jack, 1927-
    Untitled, 1954
      NNSG. Younger Amer ptrs
Rotherham, Yorkshire, England by T. H. Hinckley
ROTHKO, Mark, 1903-
    Archaic idol
      MMA. Contemp ptrs
    Astral image
      CSFP. Annual ex, 1947/48
    Baptismal scene       WMAA
      MMA. Rothko
    Birth of cephalopods
      Hess. Abstract ptg
    The black and the white
      MMA. New Amer ptg
      MMA. Rothko (col)
    Black over reds
      Art since 1945 (col)
      MMA. Rothko
      Read. Concise history
    Brown and black on plum
      Ponente. Mod ptg, 1960 (col)
    Earth and green
      Hunter. Mod Amer ptg (col)
    Entombment I, 1946     WMAA
      Goodrich. Amer art
    Green on blue       ATU
      NUM. Art across America
    Light, earth and blue
      MMA. Rothko
    Maroon on blue
      PPC. International ex, 1961/62
    Mural number 1, 1958, Sketch for
      MMA. Rothko (col)
    Mural number 6, 1958, Sketch for
      MMA. Rothko (col)
    Mural, section 3, 1959
      MMA. Rothko
    Mural, section 7, 1959
      MMA. Rothko
    Number 1, 1949
      MMA. Fifteen
    Number 2, 1954
      MMA. Rothko
    Number 4, 1948
      Hess. Abstract ptg
    Number 4A, 1947
      MnU. 40 Amer ptrs
    Number 7, 1960
      MMA. Rothko
    Number 8, 1952
      MMA. Rothko (col)
    Number 8, 1953
      MMA. Rothko
    Number 8, 1960
      MMA. Rothko
    Number 9, 1958
      MMA. Rothko
    Number 10, 1950       MMA
      Barr. What is mod ptg
      McCurdy
      MMA. Fifteen
      MMA. New Amer ptg (col)
      Newmeyer
      Pierson
      Read. Concise history (col)
    Number 12, 1948       DP
      MMA. Rothko
    Number 12, 1960
      MMA. Rothko

**ROTHKO, Mark**—*Continued*
Number 14, 1949
  Hess. Abstract ptg (col)
  MMA. Abstract
Number 14, 1960
  MMA. Rothko
Number 17, 1949
  MnU. 40 Amer ptrs
Number 18, 1948
  MMA. Rothko
Number 18, 1951
  MMA. Fifteen
Number 18, 1952
  MMA. Rothko (col)
Number 19
  IU. Contemp Amer ptg, 1951
Number 19, 1948     ICA
  MMA. Rothko
Number 19, 1958
  MMA. Rothko
Number 22, 1950
  MMA. Rothko
Number 24, 1947
  MMA. Rothko
Orange and yellow     NBuA
  Barker. From realism (col)
  Eliot. Art of our time
Orange over yellow
  Time. 300 years (col)
Painting     ICA
  Pierson
Red, brown and black     MMA
  MMA. Rothko
Red, white and brown     SwB
  Ponente. Mod ptg, 1960 (col)
Tan and black on red
  MMA. New Amer ptg
  MMA. Rothko
Three forms
  Cheney. Story 1958 ed
Untitled
  CSEP. Annual ex, 1948/49
Untitled, 1946
  MMA. Rothko
Vessels of magic     NBM
  Baur. Revolution
  Pierson

White and greens in blue
  MMA. Rothko (col)
  Ponente. Mod ptg, 1960 (col)
White center
  MnMW. 60 Amer ptrs
Yellow over purple
  Art since 1945
**Rothmaler, Elizabeth,** fl 1757
  Theus, J. Elizabeth Rothmaler
**Rotting** on the shore by Y. Kuniyoshi
**Rough** sea at Portofino, Italy by E. D. Boit
**ROULAND, Orlando,** 1871-1945
  William T. Evans     NJMo
  NJMo. Forty Years
  NJMo. Your Montclair art museum
**Round** table by C. Brown
**Round** table with fiasco and landscape by C. Brown
**Round** trip by H. Frankenthaler
**Roundhouses** at High Bridge by G. B. Luks
The **roundup** by C. M. Russell
**Route** 6, Eastham by E. Hopper
**Rouvert, Edmond**
  Peale, J. Edmond Rouvert

**Rouvert, Jane**
  Peale, J. Jane Rouvert
**ROWELL, A. J.**
  George Washngton (miniature)     OYB
  OYB. Catalogue 1951
**Rowing** home by W. Homer
**Rowland, Henry A.** 1848-1901
  Eakins, T. Professor Henry A. Rowland
**Roy, Ann.** See Rutherfoord, Ann (Roy)
**Royal** palm trees by W. Homer
**Royal** psalmist by L. Douglass
**Royall, Elizabeth,** 1747-1775
  Copley, J. S. Mary and Elizabeth Royall
**Royall, Sir Isaac,** 1719-1781
  Feke, R. Sir Isaac Royall and his family
**Royall, Mary Macintosh,** 1745-1786
  Copley, J. S. Mary and Elizabeth Royall
**ROWLEY, Reuben,** fl 1825-1835
  Elijah Rathbone
    Jones. Rediscovered ptrs
  Eliza Betts Rathbone
    Jones. Rediscovered ptrs
**Rubber** plant by M. Hartley
**Rubble** by M. Resnik
**RUBEN, Richard,** 1924-
  Back of beyond V     CP
    CoS. New accessions USA, 1956
  Bird and ball
    IU. Contemp Amer ptg, 1952
  Deciduous circumstance
    NNSG. Younger Amer ptrs
  East of Easter
    VR. Amer ptg, 1958
**RUBINGTON, Norman,** 1923?
  Night and prophecy
    IU. Contemp Amer ptg & sculp, 1955
  Nude image no 5
    IU. Contemp Amer ptg & sculp, 1959
**Ruby** by F. Martin
**Ruby** flux by I. R. Pereira
**Ruby-throated** hummingbird by J. J. Audubon
**Rudy:** midget by J. Teyral
**Rue** Daguerre by L. MacIver
**Rue** de Crimee by B. Lamotte
La **rue** de la Santé by Y. Tanguy
**Rue** de l'Echaude by S. Davis
La **rue** de Nevers by A. Russell
**Rue** de Rivoli, Paris by T. Asplund
**Rue** des Rats by S. Davis
**Rue** du Singe qui Pêche by C. H. Demuth
La **rue** Férou by M. Ray
**Rue** Gabrielle by O. M. Pleissner
**Rue** Saint Denis by A. Russell
**Rue** Vercingetorix by S. Davis
**RUELLAN, Andreé,** 1905-
  Boy and gull
    NAD. Annual ex, 1948
  Children's mardi gras
    MM. Amer ptg today
  Pink masks
    IU. Contemp Amer ptg, 1950
  White shell
    IU. Contemp Amer ptg & sculp, 1957
  Portrait of the artist
  Speicher, E. E. Andrée Ruellan
**Rufescent** idlers by R. Bidner

RUFTY, Eleanor M. 1936-
Bridge over Dock street
VR. Amer ptg, 1958
Ruggles, Carl, 1876-
Benton, T. H. Sun treader—Portrait of
Carl Ruggles
Ruggles, Ellen (Bulkley) 1779-1865
Ames, E. Mrs Philo Ruggles
Ruggles, Philo, 1765-1829
Ames, E. Philo Ruggles
RUHTENBERG, Cornelis, 1923-
Men building bridge
NAD. Annual ex, 1960
Staircase no 1, 1953
VR. Amer ptg, 1954
Ruin at Daphne by E. W. Dickinson
Ruined wharf by K. Knaths
Ruins by S. Drumlevitch
Ruins, Brantone by C. Zerbe
Rum cay by W. Homer
Rumour by C. Howard
The runaway by D. G. Blythe
The runaway by D. E. Lee
Runaway horse by Unidentified artist
RUNGIUS, Carl, 1869-1959
Moose
NSP. Sportscapes
Running buffalo by A. J. Miller
RUNQUIST, Arthur, 1891-
Bird                                          OrPA
OrPA. Ptgs & sculptures
Summer day
OrPA. Ptgs & sculptures
Rural family by F. Martin
Rural happiness by H. Inman
Rural pattern by L. W. Coleman
Rural scene by R. Porter
Rush, Benjamin, 1745-1813
Peale, C. W. Benjamin Rush
Rush, William, 1756-1833
Eakins, T. William Rush and his model
Eakins, T. William Rush carving his alle-
gorical figure of the Schuylkill river
Rush hour by I. Norman
Rush hour, New York, 1915 by M. Weber
Rush the wind by W. W. Quirt
RUSSELL, Alfred, 1920-
Diana and Callisto
WMAA. New decade
Finding of Queen Zenobia
WMAA. New decade
Painting no 24
IU. Contemp Amer ptg, 1952
Pousette-Dart. Amer ptg
Prehistoric construction
ICA. Annual ex, 1947/48
La rue de Nevers                            WMAA
WMAA. New decade
Rue Saint Denis
MMA. Abstract
Venus Anadyomene no 2
IU. Contemp Amer ptg & sculp, 1953
Russell, Alicia Hopton, 1791-1840
Malbone, E. G. Alicia Hopton Russell
Russell, Catherine A. b 1804
Freeman, Mr. (attributed works) Cather-
ine A. Russell (in her twelfth year)

RUSSELL, Charles Marion, 1864-1926
At close quarters
McCracken. Charles M. Russell (col)
At the end of the rope
Carlson. Gallery (col)
Battle of the elks
McCracken. Charles M. Russell
Beauty parlor
McCracken. Charles M. Russell
Before the white man came
McCracken. Charles M. Russell
Big nose George
McCracken. Charles M. Russell
The bolter
McCracken. Charles M. Russell (col)
The brave's return
McCracken. Charles M. Russell
Bringing home the scalp
McCracken. Charles M. Russell
A bronc to breakfast
McCracken. Charles M. Russell (col)
Bucking bronco                              ATeS
ATeS. Collection
Bucking bronco                              MonH
McCracken. Charles M. Russell
Buffalo crossing the Missouri
McCracken. Charles M. Russell
The buffalo drive
McCracken. Charles M. Russell
Buffalo hunt (1)
McCracken. Charles M. Russell
Buffalo hunt (2)
McCracken. Charles M. Russell (col)
Call of the law
McCracken. Charles M. Russell
Canadian Mounted Police with prisoners
McCracken. Charles M. Russell
Capturing the grizzly
McCracken. Charles M. Russell (col)
Carson's men
McCracken. Charles M. Russell (col)
Caught with the goods
McCracken. Charles M. Russell (col)
The challenge
Carlson. Gallery (col)
Charles Russell and his friends      MonH
McCracken. Charles M. Russell
Charles Russell on Red Bird
McCracken. Charles M. Russell
Christmas at the line camp
McCracken. Charles M. Russell
The cinch ring
McCracken. Charles M. Russell (col)
Contemplation
McCracken. Charles M. Russell
Cowboy life
McCracken. Charles M. Russell
Crow scouts in winter
McCracken. Charles M. Russell
Custer's last stand
McCracken. Charles M. Russell
A dangerous cripple
McCracken. Charles M. Russell (col)
Dangerous territory
McCracken. Charles M. Russell
Deadline on the range
McCracken. Charles M. Russell (col)
Defiant culprit
McCracken. Charles M. Russell
Desperate stand
McCracken. Charles M. Russell (col)

When shadows hint death
  McCracken. Charles M. Russell
When Sioux and Blackfeet meet
  McCracken. Charles M. Russell (col)
When the trail was long between camps
  Carlson. Gallery (col)
When tracks spell meat          OkTT
  McCracken. Charles M. Russell
When wagon trails were dim
  Carlson. Gallery (col)
When white men turn red
  McCracken. Charles M. Russell
White tails
  McCracken. Charles M. Russell
Wild horse hunters
  McCracken. Charles M. Russell (col)
Wild man's meat
  McCracken. Charles M. Russell
Wolf men
  McCracken. Charles M. Russell
Wounded buffalo
  McCracken. Charles M. Russell
York in the lodge of the Mandans
                              MonH
  McCracken. Charles M. Russell
Russell, Daniel
  Unidentified artist. Daniel Russell
Russell, Edith Hammond. See Playfair, Edith
  Hammond (Russell) lady
Russell, Elizabeth. See Sullivan, Elizabeth
  (Russell)
RUSSELL, Frank J. 1921-
  Star watchers
    IU. Contemp Amer ptg & sculp, 1953
Russell, George Gordon. See Russell, Gor-
  don
RUSSELL, Gordon, 1932-
  Floating island
    IU. Contemp Amer ptg & sculp, 1957
  Mrs Besant takes action
    IU. Contemp Amer ptg & sculp, 1961
Russell, Jane Henrietta, fl 1844
  Stock, J. W. Jane Henrietta Russell
RUSSELL, Morgan, 1886-1953
  Four part synchromy, no 7, 1914-15
                              WMAA
    Goodrich. Amer art
  Synchromie cosmique (Cosmic synchromy)
    Brown. Amer ptg
    Cheney. Primer 1958 ed
    WMAA. Pioneers
  Synchromy no 2 to light, 1912
    Read. Concise history
  Synchromy no 3, color counterpoint
                              MMA
    Pierson
  Synchromy no 5, 1914
    Baur. Revolution
  Synchromy to form          MnMW
    McCurdy
    MMA. Abstract
  To form synchromy no 4, 1914
    Hess. Abstract ptg
  Synchromy to form: orange     NBuA
    NBuA. Acquisitions 1957-58
Russell, Rensselaer W. b 1803
  Freeman, Mr. (attributed works) Rens-
    selaer W. Russell
Russell, Sarah. See Sullivan, Sarah (Rus-
  sell)
Russell, Thomas, 1740-1796
  Malbone, E. G. Thomas Russell c 1796
  Malbone, E. G. Thomas Russell (Fearing
    coll)

RUSSELL, Warren E.
  The pioneers
    NAD. Annual ex, 1959
Russian ballet by M. Weber
Russian tea service by D. Bortin
RUSSO, Alexander Peter, 1922-
  Joyous landscape
    IU. Contemp Amer ptg & sculp, 1957
RUSSO, Michele, 1909-
  Gesturing figures
    OrPA. Ptgs & sculptures
Rustic dance by W. S. Mount
Rustic dance after a sleigh ride by W. S.
  Mount
The rustics by W. Homer
RUTA, Peter
  Garlics
    ICA. Annual ex, 1951
Rutgers, Anthony, 1675-1746?
  Unidentified artist. Anthony Rutgers
Rutgers, Elsje. See Vas, Elsje (Rutgers)
  Schuyler
Ruth and Naomi by Unidentified artist
Ruth Ann by R. F. Lahey
Ruth with cat by P. C. Lewis
RUTHENBERG, Cornelis, 1923-
  Girl in yellow jacket
    DC. 21 biennial ex, 1949
Rutherfoord, Ann (Roy) 1831-1908
  Hubard, W. J. Mrs John C. Rutherfoord
Rutherford, Margaret. See White, Margaret
  (Rutherford)
Ruth's zowie by W. De Kooning
Rutland, Vermont, View of by A. B.
  Durand
Rutter children, fl 1805
  Johnston, J. Edward and Sarah Rutter
RUVOLO, Felix, 1912-
  The aggressor
    IU. Contemp Amer ptg, 1949
  Atmospheric mood
    IU. Contemp Amer ptg, 1952
  Attraction                  MnMW
    MnMW. 60 Amer ptrs
  Duel of the entomologist
    Genauer
  Hybrid
    IU. Contemp Amer ptg & sculp, 1961
  The informer
    CSFP. Annual ex, 1946
  Kaleidoscopic journey
    IU. Contemp Amer ptg, 1951
  Meeting of the three
    CSFP. Annual ex, 1952
  Metamorphosis
    ICA. Annual ex, 1947/48
  The monarch
    IU. Contemp Amer ptg, 1950
  Path in motion
    NBuA. Expressionism
  Relation within space
    IU. Contemp Amer ptg & sculp, 1953
  Rotating vision
    CSFP. Annual ex, 1950/51
  Transcendental                CSFM
    Pousette-Dart. Amer ptg
  Transcending motion
    ICA. Annual ex, 1951
  Undulating landscape
    MMA. Abstract

**Ryan, Ann Elizabeth,** fl 1803
  Malbone, E. G. Ann Elizabeth Ryan
**Rydal** falls, England by J. F. Kensett
**RYDER, Albert Pinkham,** 1847-1917
  The barnyard                                    NUM
    Goodrich. Ryder
  Blue marine
    Leepa
  By the tomb of the prophet
    Goodrich. Ryder
  The canal                                       ATeS
    ATeS. Collecton
    Goodrich. Ryder
  Christ appearing to Mary                        DN
    Goodrich. Ryder (col)
  Constance                                       MB
    DC. Ryder (col front)
    Goodrich. Ryder (col)
    Goodrich. Ryder (detail)
    Larkin rev ed (col )
    Pierson
    WMAA. Ryder
  Country girl
    Goodrich. Ryder
  Curfew hour                                     MM
    Goodrich. Ryder
  Dancing dryads                                  DN
    Goodrich. Ryder
  Dead bird
    Barker. Amer ptg
    DC. Ryder (col)
    DP. Catalogue
    Goodrich. Ryder (col)
    Pierson
    Walker. Ptgs from America
  Death on a pale horse. See Race track
  Desdemona                                       DP
    DC. Ryder
    DP. Catalogue
    Goodrich. Ryder
  Diana
    DC. Ryder
    Goodrich. Ryder
  Evening glow—the old red cow                    NBM
    Goodrich. Ryder
  Fishermen's huts                                DP
    Born
    DP. Catalogue
  Flying Dutchman                                 DNC
    Baur. Revolution
    Cheney. Story 1958 ed
    Goodrich. Ryder (col)
    Pierson
    Walker. Ptgs from America (col)
  Forest of Arden
    Baur. Revolution
    Craven. Rainbow book (col)
    Craven. Treasury 1952 ed (col)
    Goodrich. Ryder (col)
    Goodrich. Ryder (detail)
    Pierson
    WMAA. Ryder
  Gay Head
    DP. Catalogue
    Goodrich. Ryder
  Grazing horse                                   NBM
    Goodrich. Ryder
    Pierson
    Time. 300 years (col)
  Homeward bound                                  DP
    DP. Catalogue
    Goodrich. Ryder

  Hunter's rest
    DC. Ryder
    Goodrich. Ryder
    MiD. Coll in progress
    WiMiA. Amer ptg 1760-1960
  In the stable                                   DN
    Goodrich. Ryder
  Joan of Arc                                     MWM
    DC. Ryder
    Goodrich. Ryder
    MWAA. Ryder
  Jonah                                           DNC
    Barker. Amer ptg
    DNC. Gellatly coll, 1954
    Goodrich. Ryder (col)
    Lewisohn
    Pierson
  King Cophetua and the beggar maid               DN
    Goodrich. Ryder
  Landscape                                       MM
    DC. Ryder
  Little maid of Arcady
    DC. Ryder
  Lone horseman
    Goodrich. Ryder
  Lone scout
    Goodrich. Ryder
  Lord Ullin's daughter. See The sea
  The Lorelei
    DC. Ryder
    Goodrich. Ryder
  The lovers                                      NPV
    Goodrich. Ryder
  Lovers' boat (Moonlight on the waters)
    DC. Ryder
    Goodrich. Ryder
  Macbeth and the witches                         DP
    Cheney. Expressionism 1948 ed
    DC. Ryder (col)
    DP. Catalogue
    Goodrich. Ryder (col)
    Goodrich. Ryder (detail)
    Larkin
    Larkin rev ed
    Pierson
    WMAA. Ryder
  Marine
    DC. Ryder
    Goodrich. Ryder
  Mending the harness                             DN
    DC. Ryder
    DC. 25 biennial ex, 1957
    Goodrich. Ryder
    Lewisohn
    WMAA. Ryder
  Moonlight                                       DNC
    Goodrich. Ryder
  Moonlight                                       NBM
    Goodrich. Ryder
  Moonlight at sea                                DNC
    Cheney. Story 1958 ed
  Moonlight-marine                                MM
    Bazin. History of art
    Craven. Treasury 1952 ed
    Goodrich. Ryder (col)
    MM. 100 Amer ptrs
    MM. 100 Amer ptrs (col detail)
    Pierson
  Moonlight on the sea                            KW
    Goodrich. Ryder
    WMAA. Ryder
  Moonlight on the waters. See Lovers'
    boat

Moonlit cove      DP
    Cheney. Story 1958 ed
    DC. Ryder (col)
    DP. Catalogue
    Goodrich. Ryder
    NYG. Fine art
    Pierson
    UNESCO. 1860-1949
    UNESCO. 1860-1955
    UNESCO. 1860-1959
    WMAA. Ryder
Moonrise, marine
    Goodrich. Ryder
Night and clouds      MoSL
    MoSL. Handbook 1953
Night clouds      MoSL
    Cheney. Story 1958 ed
    Lewisohn

Noli me tangere. See Resurrection
Oriental camp      MAC
    DC. Ryder
    Goodrich. Ryder
Outward bound      DC
    Cheney. Expressionism 1948 ed
Passing song      DN
    Goodrich. Ryder
Pastoral study      DNC
    Barker. Amer ptg
    Goodrich. Ryder
    Pierson
The pasture      NoCR
    Goodrich. Ryder
    NoCR. Catalogue
Pegasus (The poet on Pegasus entering
    the realm of the Muses)      MWM
    Cheney. Expressionism 1948 ed
    DC. Ryder
    Goodrich. Ryder
    WMAA. Ryder
Perrette      MNS
    DC. Ryder
    Goodrich. Ryder
Pirates island      GAtM
    GAtM. Holbrook collection
    NUM. Art across America
    PPC. Amer classics
Poet on Pegasus entering the realm of the
    Muses. See Pegasus
The pond      MnMW
    Goodrich. Ryder
Race track (Death on a pale horse)   OCl
    Baur. Amer ptg
    Canaday
    Cheney. Expressionism 1948 ed
    Cheney. Story 1958 ed
    Craven. Rainbow book
    Craven. Treasury 1952 ed
    Goodrich. Ryder (col)
    Goodrich. Ryder (detail)
    Lee. Art then and now
    Lewisohn
    Myers. Art
    NAD. Amer tradition
    NBuA. Expressionism
    OCl. Handbook
    Pierson
    Riley. Your art heritage
    Robb. Art 1953 ed
    Roos
    Time. 300 years (col)
    WMAA. Ryder

Resurrection (Noli me tangere)    DP
    DP. Catalogue
    Goodrich. Ryder
    WMAA. Ryder
Roadside meeting      OYB
    Goodrich. Ryder (col)
    OYB. Catalogue 1951
    WMAA. Ryder
Sailing by moonlight
    Cheney. Story 1958 ed
The sea (Lord Ullin's daughter)    DN
    Goodrich. Ryder
Self-portrait
    DC. Ryder
    Goodrich. Ryder
    MiD. Coll in progress
    WiMiA. Amer ptg 1760-1960
Sentimental journey      NCa
    DC. Ryder
    Goodrich, Ryder
The sheepfold      NBM
    Goodrich, Ryder
The shepherdess      NBM
    Goodrich, Ryder
Shore scene      GAtM
    Goodrich, Ryder
Siegfried and the Rhine maidens    DN
    Barker. Amer ptg
    Bazin
    DC. Ryder
    DN. Mellon coll
    Goodrich. Ryder (col)
    Goodrich. Ryder (details)
    Mendelowitz
    MiD. Ptg in America
    Pierson
    Richardson. Ptg in America
    Roos
    Time. 300 years (col)
    Walker. Ptgs from America
    WMAA. Ryder
Smugglers' cove      MM
    Goodrich. Ryder
Spring      OT
    Goodrich. Ryder
Stag and two does (Stag drinking)
    CtY. Yale alumni
    Goodrich. Ryder
Story of the cross
    DC. Ryder (col)
    Goodrich. Ryder (col)
Summer's fruitful pasture      NBM
    Goodrich. Ryder
Sunset hour
    Goodrich. Ryder
The tempest      MiD
    DC. Ryder
    Goodrich. Ryder
    MiD. Treasures
    Pierson
    Richardson. Ptg in America (col)
Temple of the mind
    Cheney. Story 1958 ed
    DC. Ryder (col)
    Goodrich. Ryder (col)
    Goodrich. Ryder (detail)
    McCurdy
    NBuA. Catalogue of the ptgs
    Pierson
    WMAA. Ryder
Toilers of the sea      MAP
    Cheney. New world history
    Cheney. Story 1958 ed

**RYDER, A. P.**—*Continued*
Flexner. Amer ptg
Flexner. Short history
McKinney
NYG. Fine art
Rathbun (col)
Robb. Art 1953 ed
Robb. Harper history (col)
Roos
UNESCO. 1860-1949
UNESCO. 1860-1955
UNESCO. 1860-1959
Toilers of the sea                                                MM
Goodrich. Ryder (col)
Pierson
Time. 300 years (col)
WMAA. Ryder
Under a cloud
Cheney. Story 1958 ed
DC. Ryder
Goodrich. Ryder (col)
Time. 300 years (col)
WMAA. Ryder
Weir's orchard
DC. Ryder
Goodrich. Ryder
WMAA. Ryder
White horizon                                                    ATeS
ATeS. Collection
White horse                                                       NJP
Goodrich. Ryder
The windmill
Goodrich. Ryder
With sloping mast and dipping prow    DN
Goodrich. Ryder
Wood road
Goodrich. Ryder
**Portrait of the artist**
Hartley, M. Albert Pinkham Ryder
Miller, K. H. Albert P. Ryder
**RYDER, Chauncey Foster,** 1868-1949
March wind
NYG. Fine art
Power line
NAD. Annual ex, autumn 1949
Rye bread by K. Knaths
**Rynders, Barent,** d 1726
Unidentified artist. Barent Rynders
**Rynders, Hester (Leisler)** 1673-1757?
Unidentified artist. Mrs Barent Rynders

# S

S—1951 by J. D. Brooks
S.S. Del Sud, 1954 by R. Crawford
**SAALBURG, Allen Russell,** 1899-
Wild horses
NYG. Fine art
Sabbath by M. Weber
Sabbath phantoms by K. Seligmann
**Sacco, Nicola,** 1892-1927
Shahn, B. Sacco and Vanzetti in coffins
Sacco-Vanzetti series. See Shahn, B. The
Lowell committee; Passion of Sacco
and Vanzetti: Webster Thayer
**SACHS, L.** fl 1857
The Herbert children                                             DN
DN. Amer primitive ptgs, pt 1
Mendelowitz

Sacramento, California, View from water-
front by G. Tirrell
**Sacred** and profane by A. Bohrod
**Sacred** grove near Rome by G. Inness
The **sacred** red pipe—stone quarry by G.
Catlin
The **sacrifice** by A. Salemme
**Sacrifice** of Chronos by T. Stamos
**Sacrifice** of Isaac by R. Foster
**Sacrifice** of the hair by S. MacDonald-
Wright
The **sad** departure by Unidentified artist
**Sad** interior by M. Soyer
**Saddled** for the first time by G. Bartlett
**SAFFER, Saraga Philip**
Three queens
NAD. Annual ex, 1961
**Sagamore** by W. De Kooning
**SAGE, Kay,** 1898-
All soundings are referred to high water
CSFP. Annual ex, 1948/49
The answer is no
DC. 27 biennial ex, 1961
WMAA. Annual ex, 1958
Detour
ICA. Annual ex, 1959/60
In the third sleep
ICA. Annual ex, 1945/46
Man working
VR. Amer ptg, 1954
Nests of lightning
DC. 22 biennial ex, 1951
No one heard the thunder
Jean. Surrealist ptg
No passing                                                      WMAA
CoS. New accessions USA, 1956
Goodrich. Amer art
Pierson
Small portrait
Pearson. Mod renaissance
Starlings caravan
CSFP. Annual 1950/51
A stranger passed
ICA Annual ex, 1947/48
Suspension bridge for swallows
IU. Contemp Amer ptg & sculp, 1959
Three thousand miles to the point of be-
ginning
ICA. Annual ex, 1951
Tomorrow is never                                               MM
Jean. Surrealist ptg
Unicorns came down to the sea
IU. Contemp Amer ptg, 1949
Pierson
Unusual Thursday
Pearson. Mod renaissance
Watching the clock                                              MMA
MMA. Soby collection
**Sagebrush** sport by C. M. Russell
**Saguenay** river, lower rapids **by W. Homer**
**Sail** loft by S. Davis
**Sailboats** by J. Whorf
**Sailboats** racing on the Delaware by T.
Eakins
**Sailcloth** by W. De Kooning
**Sailing** by T. Eakins
**Sailing** a dory by W. Homer
**Sailing** boats by T. Eakins

Sailing boats in a watering trough by W. Homer
Sailing by moonlight by A. P. Ryder
Sailing by moonlight by W. Zorach
Sailing in the mist by J. H. Twachtman
Sailing the catboat by W. Homer
Sailing vessels
  Bard, J. Hudson river schooner Robert Knapp
  Birch, T. Brig in a storm
  Birch, T. Marine view with ships
  Birch, T. New York harbor
  Birch, T. Off the Maine coast
  Birch, T. Seascape
  Birch, T. The United States and the Macedonian
  Birch, T. The Wasp and the Frolic
  Blunt, J. S. Boston harbor
  Blunt, J. S. Topsail schooner in sheltered waters
  Bradford, W. Ship Dashing Wave off Boston Light
  Bygrave, W. American clipper bark Zephyr in Messina harbor, Sicily
  Chambers, T. Boston harbor
  Corné M. F. The brig Charles of Boston
  Corné, M. F. The Constitution and the Guèrriere
  Corné, M. F. Letter-of-marque ship Mount Vernon of Salem
  Corné, M. F. Ship America hand-lining on the Grand Bank
  Eilshemius, L. M. Flying Dutchman
  Evans, J. The white squall
  Garneray, A. L. Lake Erie, Battle of
  Grant, G. Harbor traffic
  Gregory, A. V. The ship Ringleader
  Hashagen, A. Ship Arkansas leaving Havana
  Homer, W. Breezing up
  Homer, W. Gloucester schooners and sloop
  Homer, W. The wreck of the Iron Crown
  Lane, F. H. At the fishing grounds
  Lane, F. H. Brig Antelope in Boston harbor
  Lane, F. H. New England coast shipping
  Lane, F. H. New York harbor
  Lane, F. H. Owl's Head, Penobscot, Maine
  Lane, F. H. Ships in the ice off Ten Pound island, Gloucester
  Marin, J. Deep-sea trawlers, Maine
  Marin, J. Four-master off the Cape
  Marin, J. Headed for Boston
  Marin, J. The three master
  Marin, J. Two master becalmed, Maine
  Patterson, C. R. Furling the foresail
  Prendergast, M. B. Pretty ships
  Salmon, R. W. Plymouth sound, England
  Salmon, R. W. South Sea whale fishing
  Salmon, R. W. Storm at sea
  Salmon, R. W. (attributed works) Black Ball liner, New York
  Sanborn, P. Ship Charlotte W. White
  Thomas, J. The ship Nancy, homeward bound
  Unidentified artist. Five master
  Unidentified artist. Letter of marque ship Bethel of Boston
  Unidentified artist. Privateer hermaphrodite brig Rambler of Medford
  Unidentified artist. Privateer schooner Surprise of Baltimore capturing the British ship Star, 1815
  Unidentified artist. Ship Bavaria
  Unidentified artist. Ship Hercules of Salem, 1809
  Unidentified artist. The Southern Belle
  Unidentified artist. Whaling scene
  Unidentified artist. Whaling scene—Triton of New Bedford
  Wales, G. C. Clipper ship Competitor
  Walter, J. Arrival of the Great Western at New York, 1838
  West, B. F. Whaling scene: Ship Julien and Bark Richard
  Wight, J. H. (attributed works) U. S. Ship Constellation
A sailor by Unidentified artist
Sailors by Unidentified artist
Sailor's holiday by R. Brackman
Sailor's wedding by R. C. Woodville
Sails by R. Crawford
Sails by C. H. Demuth
Sails by A. G. Dove
St Andrew's church, Roanoke by T. A. Fransioli
The St Clair fire by C. F. Gaertner
St Cyr by E. Ewing
St Francis of Assisi by N. Carone
Saint-Gaudens, Augustus, 1848-1907
  Cox, K. Augustus Saint-Gaudens
St George by P. Jenkins
St George by J. La Farge
St George and the calla lilies by R. S. Du Casse
St George and the dragon by Holmead
St George and the dragon by B. West
St Germaine by W. G. Congdon
St John, Frank Jay
  Eakins, T. Frank Jay St John
St Lawrence river from the citadel, Quebec by A. Bierstadt
St Louis, Missouri
  Catlin, G. St Louis, 1836
  Hinchey, W. J. Dedication of the Eads bridge at St Louis, 1874
  Lewis, H. A street in St Louis
  Lewis, H. (attributed works) St Louis after the great fire
  Unidentified artist. Chouteau's pond, St Louis
  Wild, J. C. View of St Louis, c 1841
St Louis belle by A. M. Von Phul
St Louis cemetery, New Orleans by D. Herron
St Louis drawing room by K. Zerbe
St Louis post office mural by M. Siporin
St Malo from Dinard, low tide, Brittany by E. D. Boit
St Mark's, Venice by M. B. Prendergast
St Martin's summer by J. S. Sargent
Saint-Méry, Moreau de, fl 1797
  Sharples, J. Moreau de Saint-Méry
St Patrick's at night by W. Pach

St Paul persecuting the Christians by B. West

St Paul's restoration to sight by Ananias by B. West

St Paul shaking off the viper by B. West

St Peter's, Rome by E. D. Boit

St Peter's, Rome from the Palatine by F. Crowninshield

St Philip's, Charleston by K. Zerbe

St Rose by K. Fearing

**St Thomas**
  Carlsen, E. Entrance to the harbor of St Thomas

St Thomas church by P. S. Kramer

St Valentine by G. Hartigan

Ste Hilaire by J. Mitchell

**Saints** deposed by H. Mandel

**Saks** Fifth avenue window by G. L. K. Morris

**Sala** del Collegio, Ducal palace, Venice by W. P. P. Longfellow

**Salem, Massachusetts**
  Ropes, G. Crowninshield's wharf, Salem, 1806

**Salem** willows by M. B. Prendergast

**SALEMME, Attilio,** 1911-1955
  Assignation
    McCurdy
  Astronomical blessings are in order
    MBIC. Salemme (col)
  Caught in the equinox                    MM
    Newmeyer
    Pierson
    WMAA. New decade
  Echo of a dream
    MBIC. Salemme (col)
  End of the game
    MBIC. Salemme (col)
  Good time
    MBIC. Salemme (col)
  Inquisition                              WMAA
    Goodrich. Amer art (col)
    MBIC. Salemme (col)
    Pierson
    WMAA. New decade
  Lunar voyage
    IU. Contemp Amer ptg & sculp, 1955
    MBIC. Salemme (col)
  Madam X
    WMAA. New decade
  Mahatmas of the lunar shore
    NNSG. Younger Amer ptrs
  Night of the ritual
    MM. Amer ptg today
  The oracle                               PPhM
    MBIC. Salemme (col)
  The sacrifice                            WMAA
    Pousette-Dart. Amer ptg
    WMAA. Contemp Amer ptg, 1952
  Vintage of uncertainties
    MBIC. Salemme (col)

**Salisbury, Elizabeth (Tuckerman)** 1768-1851
  Stuart, G. Mrs Stephen Salisbury I

**SALISBURY, Frank O.** 1874-
  Calvin Coolidge                          MWA
    MWA. Checklist of portraits
  Franklin D. Roosevelt
    NYG. Fine art

**Salisbury, Stephen**
  Goodridge, E. Stephen Salisbury

**Salisbury, Mrs Stephen, 1st.** See Salisbury, Elizabeth (Tuckerman)

**SALMON, Robert W.** fl 1800-1840
  Boston harbor from Constitution wharf
                                           MdAN
    Pierson
  Boston harbor: Long and Central wharves, 1832 (Dalton coll)
    Davidson v2
  The Constitution in Boston harbor
    Baur. Amer ptg (detail)
  Plymouth Sound, England                  MB
    MB. Karolik coll
  Rainsford's island, Boston harbor        MB
    MB. Karolik coll
  South Sea whale fishing                  MB
    Davidson v 1
    Pierson
  Storm at sea                             MB
    MB. Karolik coll

  **Attributed works**
  Black Ball liner, New York
    Davidson v 1

**Salmon**
  Audubon, J. J. Osprey and the otter and the salmon
  Homer, W. Ouananiche fishing: Lake St John, Quebec

**Salmon** river by W. Plate

**Salmon** trout and smelt by S. M. Brookes

**Salome** by J. Glasco

**Salt** fire by L. Mullican

**Salt** flats by K. Knaths

**Salt** marshes, Newport, Rhode Island by M. J. Heade

The **salt** sea by R. Tam

**Salt** shaker by S. Davis

**Saltillo** rooftops by E. Hopper

**Saltimbanques** by Y. Tanguy

**Salto** mortal by E. Frances

**Saltonstall, Gurdon,** 1666-1724
  Unidentified artist. Gurdon Saltonstall

**SALTZMAN, William,** 1916-
  Linear pattern
    CSFP. Annual ex, 1947/48

**Salutat** by T. Eakins

**Salute** to General Washington in New York harbor by L. M. Cooke

**Salute** to the robe trade by C. M. Russell

**Sam** Perryman by G. Catlin

**SAMANT, Manmohan,** 1926-
  Sun chariot
    PPC. International ex, 1961/62

**SAMPLE, Paul Starrett,** 1896-
  Barber shop
    Gruskin (col)
    NHMC. Paul Sample
  Beaver meadow                            NHD
    NHMC. Paul Sample
  Country horse show
    PPC. Ptg in the U. S. 1949
  Day in bed
    NHMC. Paul Sample
  Delirium is our best deceiver
    NAD. Annual ex, 1947, 2d half
  East Charleston school                   MWiC
    NHMC. Paul Starrett
  Freight cars in desert
    NHMC. Paul Sample

Going to town IBM
  NHMC. Paul Sample
Hill beyond the bridge
  NHMC. Paul Sample
Iceland fishermen
  NSP. Sportscapes
Janitor's holiday MM
  Pierson
Maple sugaring in Vermont
  Larkin
  Larkin rev ed
Milk sledge OYB
  OYB. Catalogue 1951
Miners resting NeL
  NHMC. Paul Sample
Real wealth MB
  MB. Ptgs in water color
Remember now the days of thy youth
  NAD. Annual ex, 1953
Roque NCa
  NHMC. Paul Sample
Spring song
  NHMC. Paul Sample
Sweet hour of prayer
  NHMC. Paul Sample
Two trout fishermen
  NSP. Sportscapes
Winter holiday
  NAD. Annual ex, spring 1950
Winter visitor
  NHMC. Paul Sample
Samson and the lion by P. Evergood
**SAMSTAG, Gordon,** 1906-
  Young man desiring position InTH
    InTH. Catalogue
**SAMUELSON, Paul F.** 1924-
  Mansion doorway OYB
    OYB. Annual 1949
    OYB. Catalogue 1951
San Barnaba by L. Bosa
San Diego zoo by H. G. Keller
**SANBORN, Percy,** fl 1860
  Ship Charlotte W. White MeC
    Jetté. Amer heritage collection
The sanctified by J. C. Wayne
Sanctuary by J. S. Curry
Sanctuary by P. Guston
Sand and sea by D. MacKnight
Sand and sky by J. E. Levi
Sand barge by A. G. Dove
Sand dune by W. Homer
Sand dunes by W. M. Chase
Sand, sea and sky by M. Avery
Sand team by G. W. Bellows
Sandburg, Carl, 1878-
  Freeman, D. Carl Sandburg
Sandcart by G. W. Bellows
Sanders, John, 1714-1783
  Unidentified artist. John Sanders
Sanders, Robert, 1705-1765
  Unidentified artist. Robert Sanders
Sanderson, Mrs Luther. See Hall, Abigail
**SANDERSON, William,** 1905-
  Composition with fried egg CoD
    CoS. New accessions USA, 1952
**SANDGREN, Nelson,** 1917-
  The abiding—summer and sea
    OrPA. Ptgs & sculptures

Sandpipers by P. Riba
Sandy by A. James
**SANFORD, M. M.**
  Washington at Princeton NCHA
    Time. 300 years (col)
Sanford, Sarah Ingersoll (Olmstead) 1774-
  1838
  Jarvis, J. W. Mrs Benjamin Sanford
San Francisco, California
  Du Casse, R. S. San Francisco bay
  Firks, H. San Francisco, 1849
  Rederer, F. J. Civic center, San Francisco
  Sheeler, C. San Francisco, 1956
  Tobey, M. San Francisco street
  Unidentified artist. Telegraph hill, San
    Francisco, c 1849
San José mission
  Allen, T. Portal of the mission of San
    José, Texas
San Rafael, California by A. Bierstadt
Santa Maria della Salute by B. Perlin
Santa Maria Formosa, Venice by M. B.
  Prendergast
Santiago de Compostela, Spain by J. S. Sar-
  gent
Santiago de Cuba by W. Homer
**SANTO, Patsy,** 1894-
  A ray of hope ATU
    ATU. Coll of Amer art (col)
Sapaque by L. Calcagno
Sappho by D. E. Lee
Sappington, Jane (Breathitt) b 1783?
  Bingham, G. C. Mrs John Sappington
Sappington, John, b 1775?
  Bingham, G. C. Dr John Sappington
Sarasate y Navascuez, Pablo Martín Meli-
  tón, 1844-1908
  Chase, W. M. Pablo de Sarasate
Sargasso sea by J. Skolle
Sargeant, Isabella. See Vallé, Isabella (Sar-
  geant)
Sargent, Emily, 1857-1936
  Sargent, J. S. Simplon pass: the lesson
Sargent, Epes, 1690-1762
  Copley, J. S. Epes Sargent senior
Sargent, FitzWilliam, 1768-1822
  Sargent, J. S. Dr FitzWilliam Sargent
**SARGENT, Henry,** 1770-1845
  Dinner party MB
    Baur. Amer ptg (detail)
    Pierson
    Richardson. Ptg in America
    U.S. National Capital sesquicentennial
      com
  Tea party MB
    Barker. Amer ptg
    Flexner. Light of distant skies
    Pierson
    Roos
**SARGENT, John Singer,** 1856-1925
  A. Lawrence Lowell MCH
    McKibbin. Sargent's Boston
  Asher Wertheimer ELT
    Craven. Treasury 1952 ed
    Mount. John Singer Sargent
  Atlas and Hesperides MB
    McKibbin. Sargent's Boston
  Auguste Rodin
    Mount. John Singer Sargent
  A backwater, Chalcot
    NSP. Sportscapes

SARGENT, J. S.—*Continued*
Bailleul: tents                                   MB
  MB. Ptgs in water color
Battle front
  Mount. John Singer Sargent
La biancheria                                     MB
  MB. Ptgs in water color
Blonde model                                      MWiS
  MWiS. Ex 4 and 7
Boats at anchor                                   MWM
  UNESCO. 1860-1949
  UNESCO. 1860-1955
  UNESCO. 1860-1959
Boys on the beach                                 MWiS
  MWiS. Ex 4 and 7
The breakfast table: Sargent's sister
  Violet                                          MCH
  McKibbin. Sargent's Boston
Brook among rocks                                 MB
  MB. Ptgs in water color
Café on Riva degli Schiavoni, Venice
  Sweet
Capri girl
  Sweet
Carmela Bertagna                                  OCo
  Sweet
Carmencita                                        FPL
  Mount. John Singer Sargent
Carnation Lily, Lily Rose, Sketch for
  Mount. John Singer Sargent
Carolus-Duran                                     MWiS
  MWiS. Ex 4 and 7
Carrara: a quarry                                 MB
  MB. Ptgs in water color
Carrara: in a quarry                              MB
  MB. Ptgs in water color
Carrara: little quarry                            MB
  MB. Ptgs in water color
Carrara: Lizzatori I                              MB
  MB. Ptgs in water color
Carrara: Lizzatori II                             MB
  MB. Ptgs in water color
Carrara: M Derville's quarry                      MB
  MB. Ptgs in water color
Carrara: marmo statuario                          MB
  MB. Ptgs in water color
Carrara: quarry I                                 MB
  MB. Ptgs in water color
Carrara: quarry II                                MB
  MB. Ptgs in water color
Carrara: Trajan's quarry                          MB
  MB. Ptgs in water color
Carrara: wet quarries                             MB
  MB. Ptgs in water color
Carrara: workmen                                  MB
  MB. Ptgs in water color
Cashmere shawl (Rose Marie Ormond)
                                                  MB
  MB. Ptgs in water color
  McKibbin. Sargent's Boston
  Mount. John Singer Sargent
Charles M. Loeffler                               MBI
  McKibbin. Sargent's Boston
Classic and romantic art (ceiling decora-
  tion)                                           MB
  McKibbin. Sargent's Boston
Cordova: interior of the cathedral                MB
  MB. Ptgs in water color
Corfu: a rainy day                                MB
  MB. Ptgs in water color
Corfu: cypresses                                  MB
  MB. Ptgs in water color

Corfu: lights and shadows                         MB
  MB. Ptgs in water color
Corfu: the terrace                                MB
  MB. Ptgs in water color
Corner of the church of St Staë, Venice
  Mount. John Singer Sargent
The countess of Lathom                            IBM
  Sweet
Courtyard, Tetuan
  Mount. John Singer Sargent
Cypresses
  Mount. John Singer Sargent
The Danaïdes (lunette)                            MB
  MB. Ptgs in water color
  McKibbin. Sargent's Boston
Daniel J. Nolan                                   DC
  Mount. John Singer Sargent
Daphne                                            MB
  MB. Ptgs in water color
Daughters of Asher Wertheimer               ELT
  Upjohn
Daughters of Edward D. Boit                       MB
  Larkin
  Larkin rev ed
  Larkin rev ed (col detail)
  McKibbin. Sargent's Boston (col)
  Mendelowitz
  Pierson
  Sweet
  Time. 300 years (col)
Decorations in the dome, Boston public
  library
  Pierson
Doctrine of the Trinity                           MBP
  Pierson
Edmund Gosse
  Mount. John Singer Sargent
Egyptian girl
  Sweet
  Time. 300 years (col)
Eiger from Mürren                                 MB
  MB. Ptgs in water color
Elizabeth Chanler
  NAD. Amer tradition
Elsie Palmer                                      NBuA
  NBuA. Catalogue of the ptgs
Elsie Swinton                                     ICA
  Mount. John Singer Sargent
En route pour la pêche. See Oyster
  gatherers of Cancale
Evora, Portugal                                   MB
  MB. Ptgs in water color
Femme avec fourrures                              MWiS
  MWiS. Ex 4 and 7
Festa della regatta, Palazzo Barbaro
  McKibbin. Sargent's Boston
Figure study
  Mount. John Singer Sargent
FitzWilliam Sargent
  McKibbin. Sargent's Boston
  Mount. John Singer Sargent
Flora Priestley
  Mount. John Singer Sargent
Florence: Boboli gardens                          MB
  MB. Ptgs in water color
Florence: Torre Galli                             MB
  MB. Ptgs in water color
Florence: Torre Galli, wine bags                  MB
  MB. Ptgs in water color
Francis Brooks Chadwick
  McKibbin. Sargent's Boston
Frederick Porter Vinton                           RPS
  McKibbin. Sargent's Boston

La fumée d'ambre-gris       MWiS
    MWiS. Ex 4 and 7
Gabriel Fauré
    Mount. John Singer Sargent
Garden wall       MB
    MB. Ptgs in water color
Genoa: the university       MB
    MB. Ptgs in water color
Glacier streams—the Simplon       MSM
    MSM. Handbook
Gondolier
    Mount. John Singer Sargent
Gondolier (Nicola d'Inverno)
    Mount. John Singer Sargent
Gordon Fairchild holding a guinea-pig
    McKibbin. Sargent's Boston
Gourds       NBM
    Mount. John Singer Sargent
    Sweet
Henri Lefort
    Mount. John Singer Sargent
Henry James       ELP
    Mount. John Singer Sargent
Henry Lee Higginson       MCH
    McKibbin. Sargent's Boston
Herbert M. Sears on his yacht Constella-
    tion
    McKibbin. Sargent's Boston
Hillside       MB
    MB. Ptgs in water color
In the Generalife       MM
    Sweet
In the Luxembourg gardens
    Born
Italian head       NCa
    NUM. Art across America
El Jaleo       MBI
    McKibbin. Sargent's Boston
    Pierson
    Time. 300 years (col)
    UNESCO. 1860-1949
    UNESCO. 1860-1955
    UNESCO. 1860-1959
James Whitcomb Riley       InIJ
    InIJ. 105 ptgs
    PPC. Amer classics
John D. Rockefeller
    Mount. John Singer Sargent
Joseph Pulitzer       MCH
    Pulitzer v2
    Sweet
Judith Gautier
    Mount. John Singer Sargent
Lady Cholmondeley
    Mount. John Singer Sargent
Lady Sassoon
    Sweet
Lady with a blue veil (Sally Fairchild)
    McKibbin. Sargent's Boston
Lady Playfair       MCH
    McKibbin. Sargent's Boston
    Sweet
The lesson. See Simplon pass: the lesson
Louis de Fourcaud
    Mount. John Singer Sargent
Luxembourg gardens at twilight       MnMI
    Pierson
    Sweet
Mme Allouard-Jouan
    Mount. John Singer Sargent
Mme Buloz
    Mount. John Singer Sargent

Mme Paul Escudier       MWiS
    CtY. Yale alumni
    MWiS. Ex 4 and 7
    Sweet
Madame X (Madame Gautreau)       MM
    Craven. Treasury 1952 ed
    Flexner. Amer ptg
    Flexner. Short history
    Lee. Art then and now
    McKibbin. Sargent's Boston
    Mendelowitz
    Mount. John Singer Sargent
    Pierson
    Sweet (col cover)
    Taylor. Fifty centuries, 1954 ed (col)
    Time. 300 years (col)
Mlle Jourdain       MWiS
    MWiS. Ex 4 and 7
Man reading       PR
    PR. Catalogue
Mr and Mrs Isaac Newton Phelps Stokes
       MM
    Pierson
    Sweet
Mr and Mrs John W. Field       PA
    Pierson
    Sweet
Mrs Adrian Iselin
    Sweet
Mrs Alice Mason
    Sweet
Mrs Asher Wertheimer       ELT
    Sweet
Mrs Augustus Hemenway
    McKibbin. Sargent's Boston
Mrs Charles Edward Inches
    McKibbin. Sargent's Boston
Mrs Charles Gifford Dyer       ICA
    Canaday
    Lewisohn
    Pierson
    Richardson. Ptg in America
    Sweet
Mrs Charles Hunter       ELT
    Mount. John Singer Sargent
Mrs Charles Pelham Curtis
    McKibbin. Sargent's Boston
Mrs Daniel Sargent Curtis
    McKibbin. Sargent's Boston
Mrs Edward D. Boit
    McKibbin. Sargent's Boston
Mrs Edward D. Brandegee
    McKibbin. Sargent's Boston
Mrs Edward Livingston Davis and her
    son Livingston
    McKibbin. Sargent's Boston
Mrs Fiske Warren and her daughter
    Rachel
    McKibbin. Sargent's Boston
Mrs George Swinton       ICA
    Canaday
Mrs Henry White       DC
    DC. De gustibus
Mrs Hugh Hammersley
    Sweet
Mrs J. Montgomery Sears
    McKibbin. Sargent's Boston
Mrs John Joseph Townsend
    Mount. John Singer Sargent
Mrs John Lowell Gardner       MBI
    McKibbin. Sargent's Boston
Mrs Joseph E. Widener
    Mount. John Singer Sargent

**SARGENT, J. S.**—*Continued*
Mrs Jules Vallé
  Mount. John Singer Sargent
Mrs Knowles and her children   OYB
  OYB. Catalogue 1951
Mrs William Crowninshield Endicott  DN
  McKibbin. Sargent's Boston
  Sweet
Mosquito net
  NBuA. Fifty ptgs
  Sweet
Muddy alligators      MWM
  Pierson
Nonchaloire (Sargent's niece, Rose Marie
  Ormond)        DN
  McKibbin. Sargent's Boston (col front)
Oyster gatherers of Cancale (En route
  pour la pêche)
  DC. Masterpieces
  McKibbin. Sargent's Boston (replica)
  NYG. Fine art (col)
  Sweet
Padre Sebastiano      MM
  Bazin
  Sweet
Pailleron children
  Sweet
Paul Helleu
  Mount. John Singer Sargent
Paul Helleu sketching and his wife  NBM
  Sweet
Peter Augustus Jay at the age of three
  DC. Privately owned
Piazza Navona, Rome
  Sweet
Pink dress
  Mount. John Singer Sargent
Poperinghe: two soldiers    MB
  MB. Ptgs in water color
Ralph Curtis on the beach at Scheven-
  ingen, Holland
  McKibbin. Sargent's Boston
Reading       MB
  MB. Ptgs in water color
Rehearsal of the Pas de Loup orchestra
  at the Cirque d'Hiver
  Sweet
Repose       DN
  Bazin
  Craven. Treasury 1952 ed
Resting      MWiS
  MWiS. Ex 4 and 7
Rigging      MBM
  Sweet
Road in Midi    MWiS
  MWiS. Ex 4 and 7
Robert Louis Stevenson    OCiT
  Craven. Rainbow book
  McKinney
  Roos
  Sweet
  Time. 300 years (col)
Robert Louis Stevenson (Whitney coll)
  Cheney. Story 1958 ed
  CtY. Yale alumni
  Richardson. Ptg in America
Rose Marie Ormond. See Nonchaloire
St Martin's summer
  Mount. John Singer Sargent
Sally Fairchild. See Lady with a blue
  veil
Santiago de Compostela, Spain   MB
  MB. Ptgs in water color

Scuola di San Rocco, Venice
  Sweet
Self-portrait at twenty-one
  McKibbin. Sargent's Boston
Self-portrait aged thirty-six
  McKibbin. Sargent's Boston
  Mount. John Singer Sargent
Señor Subercaseaux in a gondola in Venice
  Sweet
Shadowed stream    MB
  MB. Ptgs in water color
Shallows
  MB. Ptgs in water color
Simplon pass: at the top   MB
  MB. Ptgs in water color
Simplon pass: avalanche track  MB
  MB. Ptgs in water color
Simplon pass: chalets   MB
  MB. Ptgs in water color
Simplon pass: crags   MB
  MB. Ptgs in water color
Simplon pass: fresh snow  MB
  MB. Ptgs in water color
Simplon pass: mountain brook  MB
  MB. Ptgs in water color
Simplon pass: the foreground  MB
  MB. Ptgs in water color
Simplon pass: the green parasol  MB
  MB. Ptgs in water color
Simplon pass: the lesson (Emily Sargent,
  Rose Marie and Reine Ormond)  MB
  Canaday
  McKibbin. Sargent's Boston
  MB. Ptgs in water color
  Sweet
Simplon pass: the tease   MB
  MB. Ptgs in water color
Spanish boys at play. See Vianna do
  Castello, Portugal
Spanish soldiers    NBM
  Sweet
A staircase    MWiS
  MWiS. Ex 4 and 7
Street in Venice   MWiS
  MWiS. Ex 4 and 7
Suzanne Poirson
  Sweet
  Time. 300 years (col)
Tents at Lake O'Hara   CtHW
  CtHW. Handbook
Theodore Roosevelt
  Mount. John Singer Sargent
Thomar, Portugal   MB
  MB. Ptgs in water color
Tyrolese crucifixion
  Taylor. Fifty centuries, 1954 ed (col)
Val d'Aosta, stepping stones
  Mount. John Singer Sargent
Val d'Aosta, a stream over rocks
  Mount. John Singer Sargent
Venetian bead stringers  NBuA
  NBuA. Catalogue of the ptgs
Venetian interior   MWiS
  MWiS. Ex 4 and 7
  Sweet
Venice: I Gesuati   MB
  MB. Ptgs in water color
Venice: La Dogana   MB
  MB. Ptgs in water color
Venice: La Salute   MB
  MB. Ptgs in water color
Venice: Under the Rialto bridge  MB
  MB. Ptgs in water color

Vernon Lee     ELT
   Mount. John Singer Sargent
Sweet
   Walker. Ptgs from America (col)
Vianna do Castello, Portugal (Spanish
   boys at play)
   MB. Ptgs in water color
Villa di Marlia: a fountain     MB
   MB. Ptgs in water color
Villa di Marlia, Lucca     MB
   MB. Ptgs in water color
Villa di Marlia: the balustrade     MB
   MB. Ptgs in water color
Villa Falconiere     MB
   MB. Ptgs in water color
Vines and cypresses     MB
   MB. Ptgs in water color
Violet at seven
   Mount. John Singer Sargent
Violet Sargent     MBI
   McKibbin. Sargent's Boston
White ships     NBM
   NYG. Fine art
The winds I     MB
   MB. Ptgs in water color
The winds II     MB
   MB. Ptgs in water color
The Wyndham sisters     MM
   Gardner 1959 ed
   McCurdy
   MM. 100 Amer ptrs
Sargent, Violet. See Ormond, Violet (Sargent)
Sargent family
   Unidentified artist. Sargent family
SARKISIAN, Paul, 1928-
   Ancient facade     OYB
   OYB. Annual 1959
   OYB. Supplement 1959
SARKISIAN, Sarkis, 1909-
   Archaic rock     OYB
   OYB. Annual 1955
   OYB. Supplement 1959
Self-portrait
   WiMiA. Amer ptg 1760-1960
SARTAIN, John, 1808-1897
   Men of progress: American inventors,
     1861 (after Christian Schuessele)
   U.S. National Capital sesquicentennial
     com
SASLOW, Herbert, 1920-
   Oneness
   IU. Contemp Amer ptg & sculp, 1957
   The processional
   IU. Contemp Amer ptg & sculp, 1955
Sassoon, Aline Caroline (de Rothschild)
   lady, d 1909
   Sargent, J. S. Lady Sassoon
Satan by W. H. Hahn
Sa-tan-ti addressing the Peace commissioners by H. Stieffel
Satellite by R. Rauschenberg
Satisfaction in New Jersey by P. Evergood
SATO, Tadashi, 1923-
   Composition, 1953-54     NBuA
   NBuA. Acquisitions 1954-57
   NNSG. Younger Amer ptrs
   Composition no 10—three lines, 1957
       NBuA
   NBuA. Acquisitions 1957-58

Sea form no 4
   IU. Contemp Amer ptg & sculp, 1961
Untitled     NNSG
   NNSG. Handbook
Saturday afternoon by Z. L. Sepeshy
Saturday again by G. Knee
Saturday night by W. De Kooning
Saturday night bath by H. Pippin
Saturday night in New York city by S.
   Shawkey
Saturday night on the ranch by L. Megargee
Saturday night, Sarasota, Florida by E.
   Shinn
Satyr by N. Carone
The Sauk and Fox slave dance by G. Catlin
Saul and the witch of Endor by B. West
SAVAGE, Edward, 1761-1817
   Abiel Holmes
   DC. Privately owned
   Abraham Whipple
   Larkin
   Larkin rev ed
   Mrs Edward Savage     MWM
   MB. New England miniatures
   Self-portrait     MWM
   Dickson. John Wesley Jarvis
   The Washington family     DN
   DN. Mellon coll
   UNESCO. Prior to 1860
   UNESCO. Prior to 1860 3d ed
SAVAGE, Edward, 1761-1817, and PINE,
   Robert Edge, 1730-1788
   Congress voting independence     PH
   U.S. National Capital sesquicentennial
     com
Savage, Elizabeth. See Heyward, Elizabeth
   (Savage)
SAVAGE, Eugene Francis, 1883-
   Death of Europe
   NAD. Annual ex, 1949, 1st half
Savage, Sarah (Seaver) 1765-1861
   Savage, E. Mrs Edward Savage
Savage, Thomas, c 1606-1682
   Unidentified artist. Thomas Savage
Savannah by L. Dodd
Saved—a hard chase by A. F. Tait
Savo, Jimmy, 1896-1960
   Dehn, A. A. Jimmy Savo and rope
   Isenburger, E. Jimmy Savo
   MacIver, L. Jimmy Savo's shoes
   Miller, L. Jimmy Savo
SAVORY, Thomas C. fl 1837-1852
   National lancers on Boston Common, 1838
   U.S. National Capital sesquicentennial
     com
Sawtooth Falls by A. Friedman
SAWYER, Belinda A., fl 1820
   Fruit in a white bowl     VWR
   Ford. Pictorial folk art
SAWYER, Helen Alton, known as Henka,
   1900-
   Carnival
   IU. Contemp Amer ptg, 1948
   Dolores in blue costume
   NAD. Annual ex, 1949, 1st half
   Valentine still life     OT
   OT. Contemp Amer ptgs
Saxe, John Godfrey, 1816-1887
   Mason, B. F. John Godfrey Saxe

Saxe, Sophia Newell (Sollace) fl 1841-1875
  Mason, B. F. Mrs John Godfrey Saxe
Saxophone player—Jay Cameron by L.
  Rivers
Say, Thomas, 1787-1834
  Wood, J. Thomas Say
Saying prayers by H. Pippin
Say's or western fox squirrel by J. J.
  Audubon
Scallop fleet by G. G. MacNutt
Scalp dance by G. Catlin
The scalplock by A. J. Miller
SCARLETT, Rolph, 1890-
  Blue lines
    IU. Contemp Amer ptg & sculp, 1953
  Pica Cotto
    MM. Amer ptg today
  Yellow above
    IU. Contemp Amer ptg, 1951
Scava by J. Heliker
Scene at rendezvous by A. J. Miller
Scene in the Catskills by F. E. Church
Scene on the Magdalene by F. E. Church
Scenery found by J. G. Chapman
Scent by J. Pollock
Scenting the breeze by A. J. Miller
SCHAMBERG, Morton L. 1882-1918
  Abstraction
    MMA. Abstract
  A girl, Study of
    WMAA. Pioneers
  Landscape                              PPhM
    PPhM. Arensberg coll
  Machine                                CtY
    Baur. Revolution
    CtY. Soc Anonyme
    McCurdy
    MMA. Abstract
    Pierson
  Mechanical abstraction                 PPhM
    PPhM. Arensberg coll
  Still life, camera flashlight
    MnMW. Precisionist view
  Telephone                              OCo
    Brown. Amer ptg
    Pierson
SCHANKER, Louis, 1903-
  Abstract no 1                          NBM
    Pousette-Dart. Amer ptg
  Circle image
    NNSG. Younger Amer ptrs
  Circle image number 18
    IU. Contemp Amer ptg & sculp, 1955
  Circles in rectangles
    MnU. 40 Amer ptrs
  Crucifixion
    Rathbun
  Football
    MnU. 40 Amer ptrs
  Number 9, 1951
    PPC. International ex, 1952
  Sea grass
    IU. Contemp Amer ptg & sculp, 1957
SCHAPIRO, Miriam, 1923-
  The game
    IU. Contemp Amer ptg & sculp, 1961
  Summer's end
    WMAA. Annual ex, 1958
SCHARF, William, 1927-
  A share of fire
    IU. Contemp Amer ptg & sculp, 1961

Schatacook mountain, Housatonic valley,
  Connecticut by J. F. Crospey
SCHELL, F. Cresson
  Trolley-car excursion, 1896            DLC
    Davidson v2
SCHELL, Francis H.
  Election scene during the Harrison-Van
    Buren campaign, 1840
    Davidson v2
Schenectady, New York, 1832 by J. W. Hill
Schenk, Franklin L.
  Eakins, T. The Bohemian (Franklin
    Schenk)
SCHEUCH, Harry William, 1907-
  Rebecca street
    OYB. Annual 1952
  Soho portrait
    VR. Biennial ex, 1948
SCHLEETER, Howard B. 1903-
  Full moon
    NNSG. Younger Amer ptrs
Schleppengull, Colonel
  Copley, J. S. Colonels Hugo and Schlep-
    pengull
SCHMIDT, Katherine, 1898-
  Broe and McDonald listen in           WMAA
    Goodrich. Amer art
    Pierson
  Waiting for his turn                   ATU
    ATU. Coll of Amer art (col)
SCHNAKENBERG, Henry Ernest, 1892-
  Button falls
    Gruskin
  Cat and kittens
    NYG. Fine art
  Conversation                           WMAA
    Goodrich. Amer art
    Mrs James M. Osborn
    WMAA. Juliana Force
  A place to swim
    PPC. Ptg in the U.S. 1949
SCHOCK, William, 1913-
  Rocks and rubble
    IU. Contemp Amer ptg, 1950
Schock, Mrs William. See Janicki, Hazel
SCHOENER, Jason
  Down the ways
    OYB. Annual 1952
Scholar by W. Pachner
Schools and school teachers
  Durrie, G. H. Red schoolhouse
  Edmonds, F. W. New scholar
  Harvey, G. Extra-curricular activity under
    the Apostle oak, 1841
  Homer, W. Country school
  Johnston, D. C. Early New England
    schoolroom scene
  Pickett, J. Manchester valley
  Rosenthal, D. Don Pasquale
  Sample, P. S. East Charleston school
  Unidentified artist. Ceremonies at a young
    ladies' seminary, 1810-1820
  Unidentified artist. Schoolmaster and
    boys
  Unidentified artist. The schoolroom,
    c 1830
The schooner by C. H. Demuth
Schooner and scow by S. Wilson
Schooners at anchor, Key West by W.
  Homer

**SCHRAG, Karl,** 1912-
Black tree in bright light
  Gordon. Karl Schrag
Coast after sundown
  Gordon. Karl Schrag
Dark trees and sunny meadow
  Gordon. Karl Schrag
Edge of the town
  Gordon. Karl Schrag
Evening
  Gordon. Karl Schrag
Evening radiance
  Gordon. Karl Schrag
Evening sky
  Gordon. Karl Schrag
Flame and winter tree
  Gordon. Karl Schrag
Fragrance of grasses
  Gordon. Karl Schrag (col)
Heat wave
  Gordon. Karl Schrag
Iris
  Gordon. Karl Schrag
Montserrat          WMAA
  Gordon. Karl Schrag
Mountains and trees
  Gordon. Karl Schrag
Oropesa
  Gordon. Karl Schrag
The painter
  Gordon. Karl Schrag
Rainstorm
  Gordon. Karl Schrag
Red quarry
  Gordon. Karl Schrag
Self-portrait
  Gordon. Karl Schrag
Still life
  Gordon. Karl Schrag
Stillness and reflections
  Gordon. Karl Schrag
Summer thoughts in winter
  Gordon. Karl Schrag
Sun filled fields
  Gordon. Karl Schrag (col)
Sun sinking into the sea
  Gordon. Karl Schrag
Tree tops and veiled moon
  Gordon. Karl Schrag
Trees against the sky          NBM
  Gordon. Karl Schrag
Trees and sinking sun
  Gordon. Karl Schrag
Trees, light and movement
  Gordon. Karl Schrag
Waves of love and of the sea
  Gordon. Karl Schrag
Wild iris          CtHW
  Gordon. Karl Schrag
Wind, wave and tree
  Gordon. Karl Schrag
**SCHRECKENGOST, Viktor,** 1906-
Fish forms
  Pousette-Dart. Amer ptg
**SCHREIBER, Georges,** 1904-
From Arkansas          InTH
  InTH. Catalogue
**SCHREYVOGEL, Charles,** 1861-1912
My bunkie          MM
  McCracken. Portrait of the old west
  (col)
The silenced war whoop
  McCracken. Portrait of the old west
  (col)

**SCHUCKER, Charles,** 1908-
Ascensions
  WMAA. Contemp Amer ptg, 1955
The bridge          WMAA
  Goodrich. Amer art
  Pierson
Tree
  Baur. Nature
**SCHUELER, Jon,** 1916-
Evening
  Baur. Nature
Snow cloud and blue sky          WMAA
  Goodrich. Amer art
**SCHUESSELE, Christian,** 1824?-1879 and
  **WEBER, Paul,** 1823-1916
Skating at Kelly's dam, Germantown PH
  Chew. 250 years of art
**SCHULDT, H.**
Traffic halt, 1878          RPS
  Davidson v2
**SCHULEIN, Julius Wolfgang,** 1881-
Harbor
  IU. Contemp Amer ptg, 1952
Schuyler, Anne (Van Rensselaer). See Van
  Rensselaer, Anne
Schuyler, Ariaantje. See Van Rensselaer,
  Ariaantje (Schuyler)
Schuyler, Catharina, b 1703
  Unidentified artist. Catharina Schuyler
Schuyler, Catherine (Van Rensselaer) 1734-
  1803
  Unidentified artist. Mrs Philip Schuyler
Schuyler, David Davidse, 1669-1715
  Unidentified artist. David Davidse
  Schuyler
Schuyler, Elizabeth Staats (Wendell) d 1737
  Watson, J. (attributed works) Capt Jo-
  hannes Schuyler and his wife Eliza-
  beth Staats Wendell
Schuyler, Elsje (Rutgers) See Vas, Elsje
  (Rutgers) Schuyler
Schuyler, Johannes, 1668-1747
  Watson, J. (attributed works) Capt Jo-
  hannes Schuyler and his wife Eliza-
  beth Staats Wendell
Schuyler, Mrs Johannes. See Schuyler, Eliz-
  abeth Staats (Wendell)
Schuyler, Johannes, 1697-1741
  Unidentified artist. Johannes Schuyler
Schuyler, Mrs John. See Van Rensselaer,
  Anne
Schuyler, Philip, 1695-1745
  Unidentified artist. Col Philip Schuyler
Schuyler, Mrs Philip See Schuyler, Catherine
  (Van Rensselaer)
Schuyler, Pieter, 1657-1724
  Unidentified artist. Pieter Schuyler
Schuyler family, fl 1824
  Andrews, A. Schuyler family
Schuyler family, Member of
  Unidentified artist. Gentleman of the
  Schuyler family
  Unidentified artist. Little girl of the
  Schuyler family
The **Schuylkill,** View on the by J. Neagle
**Schuylkill** at Manayunk by F. Speight
**Schuylkill** county almshouse property, View
  of the by C. Hofmann

**SCHWABACHER, Ethel K.** 1903-
Dead leaves
Baur. Nature (col)
Morning                              NBuA
NBuA. Acquisitions 1959-1961
Oedipus at Colonos no 2, 1959  WMAA
Goodrich. Amer art
Shannon
WMAA. Annual ex, 1958
**SCHWARTZ, Lester O.** 1912-
Circus fantasy
IU. Contemp Amer ptg, 1950
Cloistered island
IU. Contemp Amer ptg, 1948
**SCHWARTZ, Manfred,** 1909-
David the king no 1
Genauer
David the king no 2
Genauer
Finding of Moses
WMAA. Annual ex, 1955
**SCHWARTZ, William Samuel,** 1896-
De Profundis
IU. Contemp Amer ptg, 1948
Through my cosmic eye
IU. Contemp Amer ptg, 1950
Time and space                      NJMo
NJMo. Forty years
NJMo. Your Montclair art museum
**SCHWARZ, Joseph**
Mourning the child                  OYB
OYB. Annual 1955
Schweig, Martyl. See Martyl
Schweig, Suzanne. See Martyl
Scobie, James, fl 1804
Malbone, E. G. James Scobie
Scollay, Deborah, 1737-1794
Copley, J. S. Deborah Scollay
Scotch and Burgundy by H. Hofmann
Scotch day at Kennywood by J. Kane
**SCOTT, John W. A.** 1815-1890
Old covered wagon
Sears. Highlights
**SCOTT, Peter Markham,** 1909-
Pintails
NSP. Sportscapes
Scott's Bluff by A. J. Miller
Scott's Run, West Virginia by B. Shahn
The scout by C. M. Russell
The scout: friends or enemies? by F. Rem-
ington
Scouting party by W. T. Ranney
Scoyen, Peter, d 1832
Jarvis, J. W. Peter Scoyen
Scranton, William Worthington
Chase, W. M. William Worthington
Scranton
Scrap by D. W. Ellis
The scream of shrapnel at San Juan Hill,
Cuba by F. Remington
Screaming eagle by Unidentified artist
The scullers by P. S. Kramer
Sculling by K. Knaths
Sculling by W. Stuempfig
The sculptor by P. Guston
Sculptor's studio by J. J. Hammer
Sculptor's studio by T. H. Matteson
Sculpture by H. Holtzman
Scuola di San Rocco, Venice by J. S.
Sargent

Sea captains carousing at Surinam by J.
Greenwood
Sea cross by S. Etnier
Sea depth by E. Loran
Sea eagle by J. J. Audubon
Sea form by T. Sato
Sea grass by L. Schanker
Sea gulls by B. Benn
Sea gulls by J. Marin
Sea gulls by E. F. Spruce
Sea gulls by M. Sterne
Sea gulls by W. Thon
Sea horses—sea movement off Deer island,
Maine by J. Marin
Sea nymph drawn by dolphins by J. La
Farge
Sea piece—Boat fantasy by J. Marin
Sea sounds by G. R. Davis
Sea wall by C. Morris
Seal rocks, Farallones by A. Bierstadt
Seamstress by J. Lawrence
Seamstress by R. Soyer
Seaquake by W. Kamys
The search by K. L. Callahan
The search by S. E. Dickinson
The search by J. Pollock
Searching the Scriptures by W. M. Harnett
Searchlight, harbor entrance, Santiago de
Cuba by W. Homer
Searle, John, fl 1822
Interior of the Park theater, New York,
1822                              NNHS
Davidson v2
U.S. National Capital sesquicentennial
com
Sears, Herbert Mason, 1867-1942
Sargent, J. S. Herbert M. Sears on his
yacht Constellation
Sears, Mrs Joshua Montgomery. See Sears,
Sarah (Choate)
**SEARS, Richard**
Towards integrating sculptural influence
CSFM
Pousette-Dart. Amer ptg
**SEARS, Sarah Choate,** 1858-1935
Regal lilies                        MB
MB. Ptgs in water color
**Portrait of the artist**
Sargent, J. S. Mrs Joshua Montgomery
Sears
Seascape
Avery, M. Advancing sea
Avery, M. Sand, sea and sky
Avery, M. Sea and dunes
Avery, M. Seascape
Avery, M. Sunset on a quiet sea
Baziotes, W. A. The sea
Bellows, G. W. Fog breakers—sea spume
Bellows, G. W. Seascape
Birch, T. Off the Maine coast
Birch, T. Seascape
Birch, T. Shipwreck
Carlsen, E. The surf
Chesney, L. Night sea
Darrah, S. T. Seascape
Davis, J. Painting of the ocean
Durfee, H. Seascape no II

Eilshemius, L. M.  Flying Dutchman
Evans, J.  The white squall
Galloway,  Sea coming into the land
Gottlieb, A.  Sea and tide
Graves, M.  Sea and the morning redness
Graves, M.  Sea, fish and constellation
Greene, B.  The sea
Haseltine, W. S.  Seascape
Hassam, C.  Sunny blue sea
Homer, W.  Backrush
Homer, W.  Coast in winter
Homer, W.  Early morning after a storm at sea
Homer, W.  Eastern point, Prout's neck
Homer, W.  Lost on the Grand Banks
Homer, W.  Northeaster
Homer, W.  On a lee shore
Homer, W.  Summer squall
Homer, W.  Sunlight on the coast
Homer, W.  Weatherbeaten
Homer, W.  Wreck of the Iron Crown
Jamieson, M.  Off Hatteras no 2
Johnston, D. C.  Ship smashing against rocks
Kensett, J. F.  Sea and rocky shore
Kensett, J. F. and Huntington, D.  Seascape, Newport
Marin, J.  Boats, sea and rocks
Marin, J.  Cape Split, Maine
Marin, J.  Movement, boat and sea, Deer isle, Maine
Marin, J.  My Hell raising sea
Marin, J.  Rocks and sea, Small point, Maine
Marin, J.  Sea after hurricane
Marin, J.  Sea and gulls
Marin, J.  Sea and rocks
Marin, J.  Sea and sky
Marin, J.  Sea piece
Marin, J.  Sea with red sky
Marin, J.  Seascape fantasy, Maine
Mattson, H. E.  Atlantic
Mattson, H. E.  Eventide
Nordfeldt, B. J. O.  Sea and rocks
Pollock, J.  Seascape
Remington, F.  Hauling in the gill net
Remington, F.  Howl of the weather
Rice, H. W.  Seascape
Ryder, A. P.  The sea
Singer, C.  Stormy weather
Sterne, M.  After the storm
Sterne, M.  Sea, sand and wind
Tam, R.  The salt sea
Unidentified artist.  Whaling
Waugh, F. J.  A bit of the Cape
Waugh, F. J.  Breakers at floodtide
Waugh, F. J.  Coast of Maine
Waugh, F. J.  Great seas
Waugh, F. J.  Open sea
Waugh, F. J.  Pounding surf
Waugh, F. J.  Surf under moonlight
Waugh, F. J.  Windward shore
West, B.  Seascape
Zajac, J.  Seacoast
Zajac, J.  Seascape
Seashore by L. B. La Farge
Seashore by M. B. Prendergast
Season ended by Y. Kuniyoshi
Season of mists by H. Lundeberg
The season's turning by S. Rosenberg
Seated boy by B. Otis

Seated boy in lavender overalls by W. Sommer
Seated figure by W. De Kooning
Seated figure by B. Greene
Seated figure by T. Roszak
Seated figure in garden by E. N. Bischoff
Seated figure of a young woman by W. M. Chase
Seated figure with gray by R. Goodnough
Seated figure, Yakshi by A. Hoener
Seated girl by H. Hofmann
Seated man by W. De Kooning
Seated man with object by N. J. Oliveira
Seated nude by B. Karfiol
Seated nude by K. S. Williams
Seated self-portrait by M. Marcus
Seated witness by S. W. Hayter
Seated woman by B. Currie
Seated woman by W. De Kooning
Seated woman by B. Greene
Seaver, Sarah. See Savage, Sarah (Seaver)
Seaweed by G. O'Keeffe
Sebastian, Saint, d 286
    Taubes, F.  Phantasy on the martyrdom of St Sebastian
Sebastian river, Florida by M. J. Heade
SEBREE, Charles, 1914-
    The note
        ICA. Annual ex, 1951
SEBRON, Victor Valentin
    Sugar levee, New Orleans, 1853
        Davidson v2
Secluded by A. Nepote
Second allegory by B. Shahn
Second floor front by K. Zerbe
Second spring by B. Shahn
Second-story sunlight by E. Hopper
Second time painting by R. Rauschenberg
The second two-panel horizontal by A. Leslie
Second variation by E. Fiene
Secret by E. Friedensohn
The secretary's table by W. M. Harnett
Security of the mother by C. Walker
Sedation by J. Lawrence
Sedgwick, Katherine, 1820-1880
    Ingham, C. C.  Katherine Sedgwick
Seed by C. A. Morris
Seed corn by A. N. Wyeth
The seed was in itself by K. L. Callahan
Seedling by T. Stamos
Seeking a future by P. Evergood
Seeking the trail by C. M. Russell
Seeking work by M. Weber
The seer by A. Gottlieb
The seesaw by W. Homer
Segment of Spain by B. Kamihira
Segment of the garden by C. La More
Segovia, Andrés, 1894-
    Stein, R. J.  Hommage à Andrés Segovia
SEIBERT, Garfield, 1881-
    The road between
        IU. Contemp Amer ptg & sculp, 1959

**SEIFERT, Paul A.,** 1840-1921
Jacob Bennett farm, Gotham, Wisconsin, c 1886
Lipman. Primitive ptrs
Residence of Lemuel Cooper, Plain, Wisconsin
Lipman. Primitive ptrs
Residence of Mr. E. R. Jones, Dodgeville, Wisconsin
Lipman. Primitive ptrs
Wisconsin farm scene      NCHA
Time. 300 years (col)
The **Seine** by M. Avery
The **Seine,** View of by H. D. Martin
**Seine** Madonna by T. E. Rosenthal
The **seiner** by S. M. Etnier
**SEKULA, Sonia,** 1918-
Succession of feelings
IU. Contemp Amer ptg & sculp, 1953
**Selectmen** by A. James
**Self** figure by L. Rivers
**Self-portraits**
Adolphe, A. J. Self-portrait
Albright, I. L. Self-portrait, 1935
Allston, W. Self-portait
Ames, E. Self-portrait
Avery, M. Self-portait
Bascom, R. H. M. Self-portrait
Beckmann, M. Portrait of the artist with a saxophone
Beckmann, M. Self-portrait, 1912
Beckmann, M. Self-portrait, 1950
Beckmann, M. Self-portrait with a cigarette
Bellows, G. W. Self-portrait
Benton, T. H. Self-portrait, 1925
Betts, L. Self-portrait
Bingham, G. C. Self-portrait, 1877?
Bohrod, A. Self-portrait
Bouché, L. Self-portrait
Brackman, R. Self-portrait
Brown, M. Self-portrait
Carone, N. Self-portrait: head
Cassatt, M. Self-portrait
Catlin, G. Self-portrait, 1824
Chapman, J. G. Looking for good scenery
Chapman, J. G. Scenery found
Chase, W.M. Self-portrait
Copley, J. S. Copley family
Copley, J. S. Self-portrait (Hammond coll)
Copley, J. S. Self-portrait (miniature, Green coll)
Copley, J. S. Self-portrait (pastel, Du Pont coll)
Davis, E. P. Mr and Mrs Eben P. Davis
De Martini, J. Self-portrait
Dickinson, E. W. Self-portrait, 1941
Douché, T. S. Dr Jacob and Thomas Spence Douché
Dunlap, W. Self-portrait
Durrie, G. H. Self-portrait
Duyckinck, Gerrit. Self-portrait
Eakins, T. Self-portrait
Eichholtz, J. Self-portrait
Evergood, P. Self-portrait, 1943
Evergood, P. Self-portrait with divining rod
Evergood, P. Self-portrait with nude

Feke, R. Self-portrait
Fiene, E. Self-portrait
Fisher, Jonathan. Self-portrait
Frankenstein, J. P. The artist in his studio
Goldsmith, D. Self-portrait
Gorky, A. Artist and his mother
Gorky, A. Self-portrait, c 1937
Grosz, G. Self-portrait, 1938
Hancock, N. Self-portrait
Heliker, J. E. Self-portrait
Hesselius, G. Self-portrait
Hofmann, H. Self-portrait
Hopkinson, F. Self-portrait
Hovenden, T. Self-portrait
Hubard, W. J. Mann S. Valentine, 2nd, and the artist
Hubard, W. J. Self-portrait
Hunt, W. M. Self-portrait
Inman, H. Self-portrait
Isenburger, E. Self-portrait
James, A. Self-portrait, 1940
Jarvis, J. W. Self-portrait
Johnson, L. Self-portrait in ochre
Kearns, J. Self-portrait
Krans, O. Self-portrait
Kuniyoshi, Y. Self-portrait as a golf player
La Farge, J. Self-portrait
Levine, J. Self-portrait with muse
Lockman, D. M. Self-portrait
McGarrell, J. Reflection, self-portrait
Malbone, E. G. Self-portrait
Marcus, M. Seated self-portrait
Mattson, H. E. Self-portrait
Maurer, A. H. Self-portrait, 1897
Maurer, A. H. Self-portrait with hat
Meng, J. Self-portrait
Menkès, S. Self-portrait
Mintz, H. Self-portrait
Myers, J. Self-portrait
Page, W. Self-portrait
Peale, C. W. The artist in his museum
Peale, C. W. Self-portrait
Peale, C. W. Self-portrait in uniform
Peale, J. Self-portrait with his family
Peale, Rembrandt. Self-portrait
Peale, Rembrandt. Self-portrait, 1791, age 13
Peto, J. F. Self-portrait with rack picture
Phillips, J. Self-portrait, Versailles
Pickens, A. Actor and his family
Pippin, H. Self-portrait
Price, C. S. Head
Rattner, A. Self-portrait, 1947
Rattner, A. Self-portrait, 1957
Roberts, P. W. Self-portrait
Rondel, F. Self-portrait
Roszak, T. Self-portrait
Russell, C. M. Charles Russell on Red Bird
Russell, C. M. Self-portrait
Ryder, A. P. Self-portrait, c 1880
Sargent, J. S. Self-portrait at thirty-six
Sargent, J. S. Self-portrait at twenty-one
Sarkisian, S. Self-portrait
Savage, E. Self-portrait

Schrag, K. Self-portrait
Shahn, B. Self-portrait among church-
  goers
Sloan, J. Self-portrait
Smibert, J. Self-portrait (detail from Ber-
  muda group)
Smith, R. Self-portrait, 1887
Smith, T. Self-portrait
Soyer, R. Self-portrait
Street, R. Likeness of himself
Sully, T. Self-portrait
Sully, T. Thomas Sully and Mrs Sully
Thayer, A. H. Self-portrait, c 1898
Tilyard, P. Artist in his studio
Tomlin, B. W. Self-portrait, 1932
Toole, J. Self-portrait
Troye, E. Edward Troye and an un-
  identified boy
Trumbull, J. Portrait of an artist, prob-
  ably self-portrait
Trumbull, J. Self-portrait at 18 years
Trumbull, J. Self-portrait at about 56
  years
Tuthill, A. G. D. Self-portrait
Vanderlyn, J. Self-portrait
Waldo, S. L. Self-portrait
Watkins, F. C. Self-portrait
Weir, R. W. Self-portrait
West, B'. Self-portrait
West, B. Self-portrait in miniature,
  c 1756-57
Whistler, J. A. M. Self-portrait, c 1858
Whistler, J. A. M. Self-portrait, 1867
Whittredge, W. Self-portrait: the artist
  at his easel
Wood, G. Return from Bohemia
Wood, G. Self-portrait
Wright, J. Self-portrait of the artist and
  family
Wyeth, A. N. Self-portrait
Ziroli, N. Self-portrait
SELIGER, Charles, 1926-
Cross-section, plant life          NUM
  NUM. Root bequest
Don Quixote
  Read. Art now, 1948 ed
The kiss
  Read. Concise history
Mood indigo
  ICA. Annual ex, 1947/48
Winterscape
  MMA. Abstract
SELIGMANN, Kurt L. 1900-1961
Age of reason
  Pearson. Mod renaissance
The balcony I, 1949-50          WMAA
  Goodrich. Amer Art
  Pierson
Composition.
  Read. Art now
Effervescence no 3
  Pousette-Dart. Amer ptg
Envelopment (Rubezahl)
  IU. Contemp Amer ptg & sculp, 1961
Environment of the Chateau Argol
  Pearson. Mod renaissance
Fallen angels
  DC. 22 biennial ex, 1951
  ICA. Annual ex, 1957
  Pierson
The great waters
  ICA. Annual ex, 1947/48

High priest                          IU
  IU. Contemp Amer ptg, 1951
  IU. 20th century
Magnetic mountain
  WMAA. Contemp Amer ptg, 1950
Mythomania
  IU. Contemp Amer ptg & sculp, 1957
One-eyed creature
  Pearson. Mod renaissance
Philemon and Baucis
  CSFP. Annual ex, 1948/49
  IU. Contemp Amer ptg, 1950
Sabbath phantoms                    MMA
  Read. Concise history
Sleepwalkers' meeting
  IU. Contemp Amer ptg, 1952
Souvenir of America                NBuA
  NBuA. Contemporary ptgs
Sellers, Coleman
  Peale. C. W. Coleman Sellers
Sellers, Mrs Coleman. See Sellers, Sophon-
  isba Angusciola (Peale)
Sellers, Sophonisba Angusciola (Peale)
  1786-1859
  Peale, C. W. Sophonisba Peale Sellers
SELLSTEDT, Lars Gustaf, 1819-1911
Buffalo harbor from the foot of Porter
  avenue                          NBuA
  NBuA. Catalogue of ptgs
  U.S. National Capital sesquicentennial
  com
Seme by S. Davis
SEMSER, Charles, 1922-
Butcher shop
  IU. Contemp Amer ptg & sculp, 1955
Semtua by N. Yamamoto
SENAT, Prosper Louis, 1852-1925
Street in Taormina                   MB
  MB. Ptgs in water color
The Senate by W. Gropper
The Senate, Albany, 1850 by Unidentified
  artist
The senator by J. Hirsch
Send-off by A. Pickens
Seneca veterans of the war of 1812 by
  J. L. D. Mathies
SENNHAUSER, John, 1907-
Collage, no 3 (watercolor)
  WMAA. Annual ex, 1956
Synchroformic no 4, staccato
  WMAA. Contemp Amer ptg, 1949
Synchroformic 27
  Pousette-Dart. Amer ptg
Synchroformic no 28, étude in yellows
  IU. Contemp Amer ptg & sculp, 1953
Sentimental journey by A. P. Ryder
Sentimental moment by P. Guston
The sentinel by S. Greene
Sentinel by S. G. Reinhardt
The sentinel by F. Remington
Sentinels by A. Brook
Sentinels of the West by A. Dehn
Sentry by S. Reinhardt
Seoul, 1952 by F. H. Beaugureau
Separate tables by J. H. Davis
Separate worlds by W. W. Quirt
Separated by C. R. Bentley

**SEPESHY, Zoltan L.** 1898-
Aft deck no 2
  NAD. Annual ex, 1949, 2d half
Congregation
  PPC. Ptg in the U.S. 1949
Crucifixion, Sketch for
  NAD. Annual ex, 1955
Departing boat           IaDa
  IaDa. 30th anniversary
Driftwood
  Baur. Revolution
End of day             ATU
  ATU. Coll of Amer art
Fisherman's morning
  Gruskin (col)
Interlude
  NAD. Annual ex, 1951
January, Michigan farm, 1937
  MiC. Zoltan Sepeshy
Morning, 1940          MoSL
  MiC. Zoltan Sepeshy
Negro meeting, 1933
  MiC. Zoltan Sepeshy
On deck
  Pierson
Patterns
  MM. Amer ptg today
  MiC. Zoltan Sepeshy
Saturday afternoon      NBuA
  NBuA. Contemporary ptgs
Siesta
  CSFP. Annual ex, 1948/49
Sunday afternoon
  Gruskin
They wait            MoKN
  CoS. New accessions USA, 1950
  IU. Contemp Amer ptg, 1948
Where are the people I knew
  IU. Contemp Amer ptg, 1949
**September** 1, 1956 by J. Levee
**September** harvest by J. Wheat
**September** light by W. Kahn
**September** morn by W. De Kooning
**September** wind and rain by C. E. Burchfield
**Serafina** by A. Brook
The **sergeant's** coat by E. Ewing
**SERGER, Frederick,** 1889-
Pink fan            OYB
  OYB. Supplement 1959
A **serious** predicament by C. M. Russell
**SERISAWA, Sueo,** 1910-
Black-eyed susans
  PPC. International ex, 1952
Bouquet            ATeS
  ATeS. Collection
Figure
  CSFP. Annual ex, 1952
House of cards
  IU. Contemp Amer ptg, 1952
Mary, 1948
  IU. Contemp Amer ptg, 1950
The mountain
  WMAA. Annual ex, 1958
Pierrot
  PA. Annual ex, 1947
Puppet and child
  MM. Amer ptg today
Summer afternoon
  IU. Contemp Amer ptg & sculp, 1953

**Sermon** on the Mount by A. Dasburg
**Serpentine** by H. Hoffmann
**SERRES, Dominique,** 1722-1793
British fleet forcing the Hudson river
  passage, 1776
  Davidson v 1
**SERWAZI, Albert B.**
Riverton yacht club, New Jersey
  NAD. Annual ex, 1954
Still life at Christmas
  PPC. Ptg in the U.S. 1949
**SESSLER, Alfred**
The year eleven         OYB
  OYB. Annual 1961
**Setting** out the decoys by J. Whorf
**Seurat's** lunch by B. Shahn
**Sevastopol** by F. de Erdély
**Seven** A. M. by E. Hopper
**Seven** miles to Farmington by G. H. Durrie
**Seven** red squares by I. R. Pereira
**Seven** Sisters mountain by C. F. Miller
**Seventy-seven** by W. Ronald
**Sewall, Margaret (Mitchell)** 1664-1736
Smibert, J. Mrs Stephen Sewall
**Sewall, Samuel,** 1652-1730
Emmons, N. Samuel Sewall
**Sewing** machine by W. T. Murch
**Sexton, Fred,** 1907?-
Musical instruments
  CSFP. Annual ex, 1947/48
The **sexton** by A. N. Wyeth
**SEYFFERT, Leopold,** 1884-1956
Florence O. R. Lang     NJMo
  NJMo. Forty years
  NJMo. Your Montclair art museum
**Seymour, Horatio,** fl 1846
Mason, B. F. Horatio Seymour
**Seymour, Molly (Marsh)** 1752-1826
Earl, R. Mrs Moses Seymour and her
  son Epaphroditus
**SEYMOUR, Samuel,** 1797-1882
Cliffs of red sandstone near the Rocky
  mountains           CtY
  McDermott. Samuel Seymour
  Rathbone
Dog dance of the Kansas Indians   CtY
  Rathbone
Hills of the Trap formation      CtY
  McDermott. Samuel Seymour
Indians             WMAA
  Ford. Pictorial folk art
  McDermott. Samuel Seymour
Kiowa encampment         CtY
  McDermott. Samuel Seymour
Oto council
  McCracken. Portrait of the old west
  McDermott. Samuel Seymour
Pawnee council           CtY
  McDermott. Samuel Seymour
  Rathbone
View near the base of the Rocky mountains           CtY
  McDermott. Samuel Seymour
View of the Rocky mountains on the
  Platte           NNPL
  McCracken. Portrait of the old west
  Rathbone
View on the Arkansa near the Rocky
  mountains           CtY
  McDermott. Samuel Seymour

View parallel to the base of the mountains at the head of the Platte CtY
McDermott. Samuel Seymour
War [dog] dance in the interior of a Konza lodge CtY
McDermott. Samuel Seymour

**Seymour, Thomas Youngs, 1757-1811**
Turnbull, J. Capt Thomas Youngs Seymour

**Shack** by L. MacIver

**Shackelford, Eliza (Pulliam)** fl 1839
Bingham, G. B. Mrs Eliza Pulliam Shackelford

**Shadow** and substance by G. Mofchum

**Shadow** country by Y. Tanguy

**Shadowed** stream by J. S. Sargent

**Shadows** by J. Pollock

**Shadows** of evening by R. Kent

**Shadows** on the rock by K. L. Callahan

**Shafer, William Anton**
Hubard, W. J. William A. Shafer

**Shaffer, Susan Angevine**
Wood, G. Susan Angevine Shaffer

**Shahah** by P. Guston

**SHAHN, Ben,** 1898-
After Titian WMAA
WMAA. Sara Roby
Age of anxiety
IU. Contemp Amer ptg & sculp, 1955
Allegory
Rodman. Portrait of the artist
Anatomical man
Rodman. Portrait of the artist
Anger
ICA. Annual ex, 1959-60
Apotheosis (Mooney series)
MMA. Shahn
Arch of Triumph
Rodman. Portrait of the artist
Ave CtHW
CoS. New accessions USA, 1952
Baur. New art (col)
50 years of mod art
ICA. Amer artists paint the city
MnU. 40 Amer ptrs
Pearson. Mod renaissance
Read. Concise history (col)
Baling cotton (detail of Bronx Post Office mural)
Soby. Ben Shahn
Bartolomeo Vanzetti (Sacco-Vanzetti series)
MMA. Shahn
Rodman. Portrait of the artist
Bartolomeo Vanzetti and Nicola Sacco. See Vanzetti and Sacco
Blind accordion player
MnMW. Contemporary
Rodman. Portrait of the artist
Soby. Ben Shahn (col)
WMAA. Neuberger collection
Blind botanist KW
Larkin rev ed (col)
Pierson
Boy MiA
Rodman. Portrait of the artist
Brothers
CanO. Hirshhorn coll
Rodman. Portrait of the artist

Carnival
Rodman. Portrait of the artist
Soby. Ben Shahn
Carpenters (detail of mural for Social Security building)
Rodman. Portrait of the artist
Cat's cradle in blue PA
CoS. New accessions USA, 1960
Cherubs and children WMAA
Rodman. Portrait of the artist
Soby. Ben Shahn
Chicago
PA. Annual ex, 1956
City of dreadful night
PPC. International ex, 1952
Clown
Shahn (col)
Composition with clarinets and tin horn MiD
Baur. New art
CoS. New accessions USA, 1952
MiD. Ptg in America
MiD. Treasures
Pousette-Dart. Amer ptg
Richardson. Ptg in America
WMAA. Museum and its friends, 1959
Contemporary American sculpture
MnU. 40 Amer ptrs
Convention
CSFP. Annual ex, 1950/51
Rodman. Portrait of the artist
Conversations WMAA
Goodrich. Amer art
Cybernetics
WMAA. Contemp Amer ptg, 1953
Death of a miner MM
MM. 100 Amer ptrs
Rodman. Portrait of the artist
Death on the beach
Soby. Ben Shahn (col)
Defaced portrait
PPC. International ex, 1958
Read. Concise history
The defendants (Mooney series)
MMA. Shahn
Democracies fear peace offensive. See Spring
Demonstration in Paris (Sacco-Vanzetti series)
MMA. Shahn
Dewey, Vandenberg and Taft
Rodman. Portrait of the artist
East Twelfth street
MMA. Shahn
Rodman. Portrait of the artist (col)
Epoch PPhM
Baur. New art
Canaday
Newmeyer
Everyman WMAA
Goodrich. Amer art (col)
Pierson
Farmer (detail of Bronx Post Office mural)
MMA. Shahn
Father and child MMA
Baur. Revolution
MMA. Shahn
MMA. Soby collection
Read. Art now, 1948 ed
Rodman. Portrait of the artist (col)
Shahn

**SHAHN, Ben**—*Continued*
Four and a half out of every five
  MiD. Coll in progress
Four piece orchestra
  Soby. Ben Shahn
Fourth of July orator
  MMA. Shahn
  Wight. Milestones
Frog monster
  Shahn
From that day on
  DC. 27 biennial ex, 1961
Girl jumping rope
  Rodman. Portrait of the artist
  Soby. Ben Shahn (col)
Handball                                    MMA
  Barr. What is mod ptg
  Baur. New art
  Faulkner. Art today, 1956
  Gardner 1959 ed
  Hunter. Mod Amer ptg (col)
  McCurdy
  Mendelowitz
  MMA. Masters (col)
  Robb. Art 1953 ed
  Rodman. Portrait of the artist
  Roos
  Soby. Ben Shahn (col)
Harpie
  Shahn (col)
Head (detail of Roosevelt mural)
  Rodman. Portrait of the artist
Head of a cretin
  Rodman. Portrait of the artist
Hebrew books, holy day books        MiD
  CoS. New accessions USA, 1956
Helix and crystal
  WMAA. Annual ex, 1957
Homeric struggle
  WMAA. Annual ex, 1952
Hunger
  Larkin
  Pearson. Mod renaissance
  Soby. Ben Shahn
India
  Rodman. Portrait of the artist
Industrial worker (detail of Bronx Post
    Office mural)
  MMA. Shahn
Inflation means depression            MMA
  Soby. Ben Shahn
Inside looking out                    OYB
  OYB. Supplement
Italian landscape I                   MnMW
  MMA. Shahn
  Rodman. Portrait of the artist
Italian landscape II
  MMA. Shahn
  Pearson. Mod renaissance
James Rolph jr of California (Mooney
    series)
  Soby. Ben Shahn
Jesus exalted in song
  MMA. Shahn
Labyrinth
  ICA. Annual ex, 1954
Labyrinth, detail no 2
  Pearson. Mod renaissance
**Liberation**
  Janson. Key monuments
  Janson. Picture history (col)
  Rodman. Portrait of the artist
  **Soby. Ben Shahn (col)**

The Lowell committee (Sacco-Vanzetti
    series)                            WMAA
  Rodman. Portrait of the artist
  Soby. Ben Shahn
Lullaby                                   CSB
  CoS. New accessions USA, 1954
Lute no 2, 1957
  Shahn (col)
Man with wild flowers
  IU. Contemp Amer ptg & sculp, 1957
May 5
  Rodman. Portrait of the artist
Mine disaster                            ICA
  PPC. Ptg in the U.S. 1949
Miners' wives                           PPhM
  Flexner. Amer ptg
  Flexner. Short history
  Rodman. Portrait of the artist
Morning                                   DP
  MMA. Shahn
Mural at Roosevelt, New Jersey, Com-
    munity center
  MMA. Shahn
  Rodman. Portrait of the artist
  Soby. Ben Shahn
My son is innocent (Mooney series)
  Soby. Ben Shahn
Nearly everybody reads the Bulletin
  Canaday
  MMA. Shahn
  Rodman. Portrait of the artist
New York
  IU. Contemp Amer ptg, 1949
  MMA. Shahn
  Rodman. Portrait of the artist
Nocturne
  Rodman. Portrait of the artist
Nude reclining
  Rodman. Portrait of the artist
Ohio magic                               CSFP
  CSFP. Annual ex, 1948/49
  CSFP. Handbook
  MMA. Shahn
Ohio skyline
  MMA. Shahn
Pacific landscape                        MMA
  Rodman. Portrait of the artist
  Soby. Ben Shahn
The parable                              NUM
  NUM. Art across America
Parade for repeal with Jimmy Walker
    (Prohibition series)
  MMA. Shahn
Passion of Sacco and Vanzetti (Sacco-
    Vanzetti series)                    WMAA
  Baur. New art
  Baur. Revolution
  Canaday
  Goodrich. Amer art (col)
  McCurdy
  MMA. Shahn
  Pearson. Mod renaissance
  Pierson
Paterson
  Rodman. Portrait of the artist
Peter and the wolf
  Soby. Ben Shahn (col)
Picking cotton (detail of Bronx Post
    Office mural)
  Soby. Ben Shahn
The playground
  MiD. Coll in progress
  WiMiA. Amer ptg 1760-1960

The pool
  CtY. Yale alumni
  Rodman. Portrait of the artist
Portrait of myself when young          MMA
  Rodman. Portrait of the artist
  Soby. Ben Shahn (col)
Pretty girl milking a cow
  Rodman. Portrait of the artist
  Soby. Ben Shahn (col)
Reconstruction                         WMAA
  Lewisohn
  Pierson
  Rodman. Portrait of the artist
  Soby. Ben Shahn
  WMAA. Juliana Force
Red stairway                           MoSL
  Gruskin (col)
  MMA. Contemp ptrs
  MoSL. Handbook 1953
  Myers. Art
  Pierson
  Riley. Your art heritage
  Rodman. Portrait of the artist
  Soby. Ben Shahn (col)
  Time. 300 years (col)
Rena and Tom Mooney
  Rodman. Portrait of the artist
Renascence
  MMA. Shahn
  Rodman. Portrait of the artist
Riker's island prison, Study for mural at
  MMA. Shahn
Sacco and Vanzetti in coffins (detail)
  Rodman. Portrait of the artist
Scotts Run, West Virginia             WMAA
  Goodrich. Amer art
  Mendelowitz
  Myers
  Soby. Ben Shahn (col)
Second allegory
  IU. Contemp Amer ptg & sculp, 1953
    (col)
Second spring
  PPC. International ex, 1955
Self-portrait among churchgoers
  Rodman. Portrait of the artist
  Soby. Ben Shahn
Seurat's lunch
  MMA. Shahn
Sing sorrow
  Rodman. Portrait of the artist
Six                                    MdBM
  MnMW. Expressionism 1900-1955
Social security murals (Federal Security
    building, Washington)
  MMA. Shahn
  Soby. Ben Shahn (detail)
The song
  CanO. Hirshhorn coll (col cover)
  DC. 22 biennial ex, 1951
Sound in the mulberry tree             MNS
  Baur. New art
  NBuA. Expressionism
  Rodman. Portrait of the artist
Speakeasy closed for violation (Prohibi-
    tion series)
  MMA. Shahn
Spring                                 NBuA
  MMA. Contemp ptrs
  MMA. Shahn
  Munsterberg
  NBuA. Contemporary ptgs
  Rodman. Portrait of the artist
  Time. 300 years (col)

Spring (Democracies fear peace offensive)
  MMA. Shahn
Spring on Morton street
  Rodman. Portrait of the artist
Still life
  IU. Contemp Amer ptg & sculp, 1959
Still music                            DP
  DP. Catalogue
Study for Goyescas
  Shahn (col)
Study for The Marriage of Heaven and
    Hell
  Shahn
Summertime                             MAP
  CoS. New accessions USA, 1950
  Rodman. Portrait of the artist
Sunday football
  MMA. Shahn
Sunday painting
  Soby. Ben Shahn
The Supreme Court of California
    (Mooney series)
  MMA. Shahn
Susanna and the elders
  Rodman. Portrait of the artist
Textile mill worker (Textile worker) de-
    tail of Bronx Post Office mural)
  MMA. Shahn
  Rodman. Portrait of the artist
Textile mills (detail of Bronx Post Office
    mural)
  Soby. Ben Shahn
Three doors
  Rodman. Portrait of the artist
Three men
  MiD. Coll in progress
  WiMiA. Amer ptg 1760-1960
Trouble
  MMA. Shahn
Two witnesses, Mellie and Sadie Edeau
    (Mooney series)                   MMA
  Rodman. Portrait of the artist
  Soby. Ben Shahn (col)
Vacant lot                            CtHW
  CtHW. Handbook
  Larkin
  Larkin rev ed
  Pierson
  Rodman. Portrait of the artist
  Soby. Ben Shahn
Vanzetti and Sacco                     MMA
  Cheney. Story 1958 ed
  Soby. Ben Shahn (col)
Violin player                          MMA
  Biddle. Yes and no
  MMA. Shahn
W.C.T.U. parade, 1933-34 (Prohibition
    series)
  Soby. Ben Shahn (col)
Walker greets Mooney (Mooney series)
  Rodman. Portrait of the artist
Walker greets mother of Mooney
    (Mooney series)
  MMA. Shahn
  Rodman. Portrait of the artist
Webster Thayer (Sacco-Vanzetti series)
  MMA. Shahn
The welders                            MMA
  Larkin
  Larkin rev ed
  Pierson
  Rodman. Portrait of the artist
  Soby. Ben Shahn (col)

**SHAHN, Ben**—*Continued*
Willis avenue bridge
    Rodman. Portrait of the artist
    Soby. Ben Shahn (col)
Woman in chair
    Rodman. Portrait of the artist
World's greatest comics
    DC. Halpert collection
    Rodman. Portrait of the artist
    WMAA. Museum and its friends, 1958
**Shakespeare** on the lap of the muse of inspiration by E. G. Malbone
**Shallows** by J. S. Sargent
**Shambattle** by R. Wilt
**Shanah** by P. Guston
**Shannon** by E. K. Schwabacher
**Shapes** of landscape space by S. Davis
**Shapiro, Mrs Harold.** See Geller, Esther
**Share** croppers by E. Higgins
A **share** of fire by W. Schraf
**Sharks**
    Copley, J. S. Watson and the shark
    Homer, W. Shark fishing
**SHARON, W. C.**
    Western landscape                          DN
    DN. Amer primitive ptgs, pt 2
**Sharp, Benjamin,** 1858-1915
    Eakins, T. Oboe player (Benjamin Sharp)
**SHARP, John,** 1911-
    Old South wharf
    IU. Contemp Amer ptg, 1952
    Thompson-Neely house
    PPC. Ptg in the U. S. 1949
**SHARP, Joseph Henry,** 1859-
    Young chief's mission                     OYB
    OYB. Catalogue 1951
**SHARP, William,** 1819?-1885?
    Railroad jubilee on Boston Common  MB
    MB. Karolik coll
    Time. 300 years (col)
**Sharp** drummer by I. Rose
**Sharp** sea by G. Anderson
**SHARPLES, James,** 1751?-1811
    Catharine Livingston Thorn Johnson
    WiMiA. Amer ptg 1760-1960
    Isaiah Thomas                            MWA
    Larkin
    Larkin rev ed
    Moreau de Saint-Méry                      MM
    Pierson
    Richardson. Ptg in America
**SHARRER, Honoré Desmond,** 1920?-
    Country fair
    CSFP. Annual ex, 1946
    MMA. Fourteen
    In the parlor
    MMA. Fourteen
    Industrial scene
    Baur. Revolution
    Rose Callahan and child
    WMAA. New decade
    Tribute to the American working people
                                            WMAA
    WMAA. New decade
    WMAA. Sara Roby
    Workers and paintings                     MMA
    MMA. Contemp ptrs
    MMA. Fourteen (col)
    Pierson

Workers and paintings (study)  MMA
    MMA. Fourteen
**Shaumonekusse,** chief of the Otoes by C. B. King
**SHAW, Charles Green,** 1892-
    Force in space
    MMA. Abstract
    Tonal rhapsody
    Pousette-Dart. Amer ptg
**SHAW, Joshua,** c 1777-1860
    Indians sighting a ship
    Chew. 250 years of art
    On the Susquehanna                         MB
    MB. Karolik coll
**Shaw, Lemuel,** 1781-1861
    Hunt, W. M. Chief Justice Lemuel Shaw
**SHAWKEY, Sigmund**
    Bus stop                                  OYB
    OYB. Annual 1960
    Saturday night in New York city
    OYB. Annual 1952
**Shaw's** propeller no 2, 1960 by R. Crawford
**She** mourns by Y. Kuniyoshi
**She** walks among the ruins by Y. Kuniyoshi
The **she-wolf** by J. Pollock
**SHEARER, Christopher High,** 1846-1926
    Smoky range, Allegheny mountains  PR
    PR. Catalogue
The **Shed,** Woodruff stables, Jerome avenue, the Bronx, 1848 by J. A. S. Oertel
**SHEELER, Charles,** 1883-
    Aerial gyrations
    WMAA. Museum and its friends, 1959
    American interior
    NYG. Fine art
    American landscape                        MMA
    Barr. What is mod ptg
    Cheney. Story 1958 ed
    Flexner. Amer ptg
    Flexner. Short history
    Gruskin (col)
    McCurdy
    Americana, 1931
    Baur. New art
    MnU. 40 Amer ptrs
    MnMW. Precisionist view
    Architectural cadences                   WMAA
    Baur. New art (col)
    Goodrich. Amer art (col)
    Larkin rev ed (col)
    Newmeyer
    Pierson
    Artist looks at nature                    ICA
    Born (col front)
    Time. 300 years (col)
    Barn abstraction                         PPhM
    Rosenblum
    Barn reds
    Barker. From realism
    Barn variation                           ATeS
    ATeS. Collection
    Basement room                             MiD
    CoS. New accessions USA, 1946
    Bird's nest
    CSFP. Annual ex, 1947/48
    Bucks county barn                         OCo
    Brown. Amer ptg
    Goodrich. Amer art
    MnMW. Precisionist view
    NYG. Fine art

Buildings at Lebanon
  CSFP. Annual ex, 1950/51
  ICA. Annual ex, 1951
Cactus                                    PPhM
  PPhM. Arensberg coll
Church street el, 1919                    MMA
  Baur. New art
  Baur. Revolution
  Brown. Amer ptg
  Larkin
  Larkin rev ed
City interior                            MWM
  Baur. New art
  Baur. Revolution
  Pierson
Classic landscape (Modern classic) (Ford
  coll)
  Baur. New art
  Born
  Hunter. Mod Amer ptg
  MiD. Ptg in America
  Pierson
  Richardson. Ptg in America
Classical landscape (Fleischman coll)
  MiD. Coll in progress
  WiMiA. Amer ptg 1760-1960
Composition around red
  IU. Contemp Amer ptg & sculp, 1959
  WMAA. Contemp Amer ptg, 1959/60
Connecticut farm buildings               NJN
  Born
Croton dam. See The web
Flower forms
  Cheney. Primer 1958 ed
Golden Gate                              MM
  Eliot. Art of our time (col)
  Time. 300 years (col)
Home, sweet home                         MiD
  MiD. Treasures
Impressionism (Lhasa)                    OCo
  WMAA. Pioneers
Improvisation on a mill town
  DC. 21 biennial ex, 1949
  MM. Amer ptg today
Incantation                              NBM
  Baur. Revolution
  CoS. New accessions USA, 1950
  Mendelowitz
  MnMW. Precisionist view
Interior                                 WMAA
  Chew. 250 years of art
  CSB. Illusion
  Roos
Landscape, 1915                          MLL
  MnMW. Precisionist view
Landscape, 1925                          PPhM
  PPhM. Arensberg coll
Macdougal alley
  NUM. Art across America
Manchester                               MdBM
  CSFP. Annual ex, 1952
  MnMW. Precisionist view
  MnU. 40 Amer ptrs
  Pousette-Dart. Amer ptg
  WMAA. Contemp Amer ptg, 1949
Midwest                                  MnMW
  IU. Contemp Amer ptg & sculp, 1955
  MnMW. Precisionist view (col detail)
Modern classic. See Classic landscape
Offices                                  DP
  Bazin
  DP. Catalogue

On a Shaker theme
  MnMW. Precisionist view
Pertaining to yachts and yachting
                                         WMAA
  Pierson
  Riley. Your art heritage
  WMAA. Juliana Force
River Rouge plant                        WMAA
  Brown. Amer ptg
  Goodrich. Amer art
Rolling power                            MNS
  MnMW. Precisionist view
San Francisco, 1956                      WMAA
  IU. Contemp Amer ptg & sculp, 1957
  WMAA. Sara Robie (col)
Skyline                                  KW
  MnMW. Classic tradition
Staircase, Doylestown
  McCurdy
Steam turbine                            OYB
  OYB. Catalogue 1951
Steel—Croton                             VR
  CoS. New accessions USA, 1954
  MnMW. Reality and fantasy
  VR. Amer ptg, 1954
Still life no I                          OCo
  Roos
Still life, pitcher
  Brown. Amer ptg
Upper deck                               MCH
  Baur. New art
  Baur. Revolution
  Brown. Amer ptg
  Larkin
  Larkin rev ed
  Mendelowitz
  Pierson
  Wight. Milestones
Water                                    MM
  ICA. Annual ex, 1945/46
  MM. 100 Amer ptrs
  Taylor. Fifty centuries, 1954 ed (col)
The web (Croton dam)
  ICA. Amer artists paint the city (col)
  WMAA. Museum and its friends, 1958
    (col)
Western industrial
  WMAA. Contemp Amer ptg, 1955
Wind, sea and sails
  DC. Halpert collection

**Sheep**
  Avery, M. Sheep
  Delano, G. C. Sheep on the desert
  Elmer, E. R. Mourning picture
  Hinckley, T. H. Cows and sheep in
    pasture
  Hinckley, T. H. Great Blue hill and
    Neponset river
  Hinckley, T. H. Noon
  Homer, W. Shepherdess of Houghton
    farm
  Moses, A. M. R. May: making soap,
    washing sheep
  Putnam, W. B. Sheep in fog
  Ryder, A. P. The shepherdess
  Unidentified artist. The shepherd and his
    flock
  Wall, A. B. Shepherd and his flock
The **sheepfold** by A. P. Ryder
**Sheepshead** shore by W. E. Heitland

SHEETS, Millard Owen, 1907-
  Black horse            WMAA
    Pierson
  Gift bearer
    Gruskin
  Mazatlan women        ATeS
    ATeS. Collection
  Tropical squall
    MM. Amer ptg today
SHEFFIELD, Isaac, 1798-1845
  Connecticut sea captain    DN
    DN. Amer primitive ptgs, pt 2
  James Francis Smith       CtNL
    NUM. Art across America
Shelburne woods, New Hampshire by D.
    Macknight
Sheldon, J. B. fl 1825
  Unidentified artist. J. B. Sheldon
Sheldon, Mrs J. B. fl 1825
  Unidentified artist. Mrs J. B. Sheldon of
    Unionville, Ohio
Shelf still life by C. Brown
The shell heap by W. Homer
Shell holes and observation balloon by H.
    Pippin
Shell of Mary by R. Lebrun
Shelocta, Pennsylvania by P. C. Elliott
Shelter of longing by L. W. Coleman
Shelves by D. E. Lee
Shenandoah valley by A. M. R. Moses
Shepard, Angeline Eliza, 1837-1919
  Unidentified artist. Angeline Eliza Shep-
    ard and her brother, Elisha Henry
    Shepard
Shepard, Elisha Henry, 1834-1852
  Unidentified artist. Angeline Eliza Shep-
    ard and her brother, Elisha Henry
    Shepard
The shepherd and his flock by Unidentified
    artist
The shepherd and his flock by A. B. Wall
The shepherdess by A. P. Ryder
Shepherdess of Houghton farm by W.
    Homer
Sherburne, Joseph, 1710-1779
  Copley, J. S. Joseph Sherburne
Sherburne, Mary. See Bowers, Mary (Sher-
    burne)
Sherburne, Mrs John. See Moffatt, Eliza-
    beth
Sherburne, Mrs Samuel. See Warner, Mary
Sheridan theatre by E. Hopper
Sherman, Ellen (Ewing)
  Healy, G. P. A. Mrs William T. Sherman
Sherman, Roger, 1721-1793
  Earl, R. Roger Sherman
SHERMAN, Sarai, 1922-
  Arid land
    IU. Contemp Amer ptg & sculp, 1955
  The centaurs
    WMAA. Contemp Amer ptg, 1959/60
  Fête champêtre
    IU. Contemp Amer ptg & sculp, 1961
  The forest
    IU. Contemp Amer ptg & sculp, 1959
  Voyage to Matera
    WMAA. Contemp Amer ptg, 1955
Sherman, William Tecumseh, 1820-1891
  Healy, G. P. A. William T. Sherman
Sherman's march through Georgia by A. B.
    Carlin

Sherwood, Elizabeth (Moffatt) See Moffatt,
    Elizabeth
Shewell, Elizabeth. See West, Elizabeth
    (Shewell)
Shifting shadows by H. Nichols
Shim-a-co-che, Crow chief by A. J. Miller
Shimmering substance by J. Pollock
SHINN, Everett, 1876-1953
  Bal Tabarin           WMAA
    McCurdy
  Ballet dancer          GAtM
    GAtM. Holbrook collection
  Curtain call
    Glackens
  Dancer in white        OYB
    OYB. Accessions
    OYB. Supplement 1959
  Early morning, Paris      ICA
    PA. Annual ex, 1955
    Pierson
  Flight of the clowns
    NAD. Annual ex, 1947, 2d half
  Green ballet          PW
    Chem. 250 years of art
    NUM. Art across America
  Independence hall, Philadelphia
    Chew. 250 years of art
  Knoedler's, 34th street
    PA. Annual ex, 1955
  London Hippodrome      ICA
    Brown. Amer ptg
    PA. Annual ex, 1955
    Pierson
  London Music Hall       MM
    MM. 100 Amer ptrs
  Mark Twain
    MiD. Coll in progress
  Paris Music Hall
    WiMiA. Amer ptg 1760-1960
  Revue             WMAA
    Goodrich. Amer art
    Larkin (detail)
    Larkin rev ed (detail)
  Saturday night, Sarasota, Florida
    NAD. Annual ex, spring 1950
  Sleeping clown
    NSyE. The eight
  Theatre
    PA. Annual ex, 1955
  Theatre box          NBuA
    NBuA. Fifty ptgs
  Trapeze, Winter garden, New York
    CtY. Yale alumni
    Time. 300 years (col)
  Trenton, New Jersey Commission cham-
    bers murals
    Brown. Amer ptg
  Winter scene         NJMo
    NJMo. Your Montclair art museum
SHINN, John Marion, 1849-1936
  Old barn door
    Frankenstein. After the hunt
Shinnecock canal by G. Hartigan
Shinnecock hills by W. M. Chase
Shinnecock hills landscape by W. M. Chase
Ship chandlers' row by R. Spencer
Ship channel by J. W. Guerin
Ship Dashing Wave off Boston Light by
    W. Bradford

**Ship** graveyard by J. E. Levi

**Ship** smashing against rocks by D. C. Johnston

**Ship** unfurling sails by W. Homer

**Shipbuilding** in the 18th century by A. Refregier

**Shippen, Anne.** See Willing, Anne (Shippen)

**Shippen, Edward,** 1729-1806
  Jouett, M.H. Edward Shippen
  Stuart, G. Chief Justice Edward Shippen of Pennsylvania

**Shippen, Jane (Galloway)** See Galloway, Jane

**Shippen, Mrs Joseph.** See Galloway, Jane

**Shipping** out by J. Lawrence

**Ships** by J. Marin

**Ships** in ice off Ten Pound island, Gloucester by F. H. Lane

**Ships** of the plains by S. Colman

**Shipwreck** by T. Birch

**Shipwreck** by W. Snelgrove

**Shipwreck** at sea by R. W. Weir (attributed works)

**Shipyard,** Singapore by D. Teague

**SHIRLAW, Walter,** 1838-1909
  Dorothea A. Dreier
    CtY. Soc Anonyme
  Susannah and the elders                    MB
    MB. Ptgs in water color

**Shoeshine** by G. Grosz

**Shooting** a cougar by A. J. Miller

**Shooting** birds by B. West (attributed works)

**Shooting** for the beef by G. C. Bingham

**Shooting** gallery by F. Martin

**Shooting** the rapids, Saguenay river by W. Homer

The **shopper** by K. H. Miller

**Shoppers** by W. J. Glackens

The **shore** by M. Beckmann

The **shore** by A. Brook

The **shore** by B. Perlin

**Shore** and surf, Nassau by W. Homer

**Shore** birds by M. Graves

**Shore** birds submerged in moonlight by M. Graves

**Shore** birds, Tomales bay by B. J. O. Nordfeldt

**Shore** flowers II by H. Durfee

**Shore** house by G. W. Bellows

**Shore** scene by A. P. Ryder

**Shore** scene by J. L. Smith

**Shore** tapestry by P. L. Dike

**Shoremen** by D. G. Blythe

**Shoshone** cliffs by E. Hopper

**Shoshone** female catching a horse by A. J. Miller

**Shoshone** Indian and his pet horse by A. J. Miller

**Shoshone** Indian preparing his meal by A. J. Miller

**Shoshone** Indian smoking by A. J. Miller

**Shoshone** Indians fording a river by A. J. Miller

**Shovel** hats by G. P. Du Bois

**Shoveller** duck by J. J. Audubon

**Show** window no 2 by K. H. Miller

The **showcase** by G. Hartigan

The **shower** by P. Cadmus

**Shower** in Colorado by A. A. Dehn

**Shrewsbury** river near Seabright, New Jersey by Unidentified artist

The **shrine** by P. Blume

The **shrine** by S. F. B. Morse

**Shubrick, Sarah Alicia,** fl 1801
  Malbone, E. G. Sarah Alicia Shubrick

**SHULKIN, Anatol,** 1899-1961
  Summer storm on Sunday afternoon
    Gruskin
  You can't come home again
    IU. Contemp Amer ptg, 1950

**SHUMACHER, William Emile,** 1870-1931
  Lendall Pitts                              MiD
    MiD. Ports of the Pitts family

**SIBLEY, Charles Kenneth,** 1921-
  Blue evolution
    VR. Amer ptg, 1958
  Holiday
    NAD. Annual ex, 1953

**SICARD, Pierre,** 1900-
  Night over Los Angeles
    IU. Contemp Amer ptg & sculp, 1957

**Sicilian** altar by J. Kinigstein

**Sicily** by L. Dodd

The **sick** chicken by W. Homer

**Side** pull by A. Gottlieb

The **sideboard** by F. C. Watkins

The **sidewalk** by L. MacIver

**Side-wheelers**
  Anderson, E. A. Delta Queen and Packet Whisper
  Baumann, L. T. U.S. mail boat
  Catlin, G. Steamboat Yellowstone leaving St Louis
  Feininger, L. Side-wheeler
  Palmer, F. F. Champions of the Mississippi
  Palmer, F. F. Wooding up on the Mississippi
  Sebron, V. V. Sugar levee, New Orleans
  Unidentified artist. Belle Creole at New Orleans

The **siding** by P. Evergood

**Siegfried** by F. J. Kline

**Siegfried** and the Rhine maidens by A. P. Ryder

**SIEGRIEST, Louis B.** 1899-
  Virginia City building
    CSFP. Annual ex, 1950/51

**SIEGRIEST, Lundy,** 1925-
  Birds at rest
    CSFP. Annual ex, 1952
  Burning of the hearts
    VR. Amer ptg, 1958
  Desert landscape
    IU. Contemp Amer ptg & sculp, 1955
  Montezuma alarmed by evil signs
    WMAA. Young America 1957
  Mount Lassen
    IU. Contemp Amer ptg & sculp, 1961

SIEGRIEST, Lundy—*Continued*
Temple fragment                                  CSB
CoS. New accessions USA, 1956
Tenochtitlan
WMAA. Young America
Under the pier
IU. Contemp Amer ptg & sculp, 1953
Village above the river
Brussels. Exposition
Siena by M. B. Prendergast
Sierra Madre at Saltillo by E. Hopper
Siesta by L. Andersen
Siesta by D. E. Lee
Siesta by Z. L. Sepeshy
SIEVAN, Maurice, 1898-
Astoria boulevard                                ATU
ATU. Coll of Amer art
Sifter of gold by Y. Tanguy
Sign of the sun by M. Tomkins
Signal by W. Lachowicz
Signal fire by C. M. Russell
Signing of the Declaration of Independence
by J. Trumbull
Signs and portents by J. Guerrero
Signs of the city by F. Hillsmith
Sigourney, Lydia Howard (Huntley) 1791-
1865
Alexander, F. Lydia Huntley Sigourney
Silence and evening light by G. Symonds
Silence broken by G. D. Brush
Silenced war whoop by C. Schreyvogel
Silent watcher by M. Cone
Silktown on the Passaic by O. F. Bluemner
Silliman, Benjamin, 1779-1864
Morse, S.F.B. Benjamin Silliman
SILSBEE, Martha, 1858-1929
Taormina and Mt Aetna                            MB
MB. Ptgs in water color
Silver by K. Okada
Silver lake, New Hampshire by Unidentified
artist
Silver sea by W. Kahn
Silver square by J. Pollock
Silver tanks by N. Spencer
Silver tanks and moon by A. G. Dove
Silver vase by T. H. Benton
SILVERMAN, Miles
Poppies
OYB. Annual 1948
Silvers, Herbert Ferber. See Ferber, Her-
bert
Silvery night by F. D. Ogden
SIMKHOVITCH, Simka, 1893-
Two horses
Gruskin (col)
Simple confession by M. Greenwood
Simplon pass: at the top by J. S. Sargent
Simplon pass: avalanche track by J. S.
Sargent
Simplon pass: chalets by J. S. Sargent
Simplon pass: crags by J. S. Sargent
Simplon pass: fresh snow by J. S. Sargent
Simplon pass: the foreground by J. S.
Sargent

Simplon pass: the green parasol by J. S.
Sargent
Simplon pass: the lesson by J. S. Sargent
Simplon pass: mountain brook by J. S.
Sargent
Simplon pass: the tease by J. S. Sargent
SIMPSON, Merton D. 1928-
Poem—2
NNSG. Younger Amer ptrs
Sims, William Sowden, 1858-1936
Lockman, D. M. Admiral William Sowden
Sims
Sing Sing, 1856 by R. Havell
Sing sorrow by B. Shahn
SINGER, Clyde, 1908-
Big business
OYB. Annual 1948
Selections from the permanent collection
OYB
OYB. Supplement
Stormy weather                                   OYB
OYB. Catalogue 1951
Singer building by J. Marin
Singing men by J. Hirsch
Single handed by C. M. Russell
The sink by R. A. Mintz
Sinkler, Charles, fl 1802
Malbone, E. G. Charles Sinkler (?)
Sinkler, Margaret (Cantey) 1763-1821
Malbone, E. G. Mrs James Sinkler
SINTZENICH, Eugene, 1792-1848
Train leaving Auburn station at Roches-
ter, New York
Jones. Rediscovered ptrs
Sinzig, Ferdinand
Glackens, W. J. Ferdinand Sinzig
A Sioux, Head of by A. J. Miller
Sioux beggar's dance by G. Catlin
Sioux Indian at a grave by A. J. Miller
Sioux Indian guard by A. J. Miller
Sioux Indians by A. J. Miller
Sioux Indians attacking a Minnesota farm
by J. Stevens
Sioux Indians breaking up camp by S. East-
man
Sioux Indians pursuing a stag in their
canoes by G. Catlin
Sioux reconnoitering by A. J. Miller
A Sioux village by G. Catlin
SIPORIN, Mitchell, 1910-
Aging actress
Pousette-Dart. Amer ptg
Conflagration at the museum                      OYB
OYB. Annual 1960
Dancers by the clock                             WMAA
CoS. New accessions USA, 1952
Goodrich. Amer art
Pierson
The doll
ICA. Annual ex, 1951
Dream of a good life
Wight. Milestones (col)
End of an era
Rathbun
Fiesta in Trastevere
CSFP. Annual ex, 1952
OYB. Annual 1953

Order No 11                           ATU
  ATU. Coll of Amer art
The refugees                          MMA
  Pierson
Rendezvous
  WMAA. Contemp Amer ptg, 1955
St Louis Post office mural
  Larkin
  Larkin rev ed
  Winter soldiers
  IU. Contemp Amer ptg, 1948
Sirens in voice by J. Tworkov
Si-roc-u-an-tua by A. J. Miller
Sisson, Charles H. fl 1850
  Chandler, J. G. Charles H. Sisson
SISSON, Laurence Philip, 1928-
  New England November
  IU. Contemp Amer ptg, 1952
Sissy by R. Henri
Sister Rebecca Cleaden by H. Ballin
The sisters by W. Allston
The sisters by A. Dehn
Sisters by W. Zorach
Sisters in red by Unidentified artist
Siva dance, Samoa by J. La Farge
Six by B. Shahn
Six o'clock by C. E. Burchfield
Six sketches of ladies by M. B. Prendergast
Sixth avenue and Thirteenth street by J.
  Sloan
Sixth avenue and Thirtieth street by J.
  Sloan
Sixth avenue elevated at Third street, 1928
  by J. Sloan
Skaats, Deborah (Rivers) fl 1794
  Trumbull, J. Mrs Bartholomew Skaats
Skating. See Games and sports—Skating
Sketch in Florida by W. Homer
Sketch of a child by W. M. Chase
SKINAS, John C. 1924-
  Composition I, 1953
  NNSG. Younger Amer ptrs
Skinner, Elizabeth (Van Cortlandt)
  Unidentified artist. Mrs William Skinner
Skinner, Otis, 1858-1942
  Luks, G. B. Otis Skinner as Colonel
  Bridau in The honor of the family
Skinner, Thomas Harvey, 1791-1871
  Morse, S. F. B. Rev Thomas Harvey
  Skinner
Skipping. See Games and sports—Skipping
  rope
Skirmish in The Wilderness by W. Homer
SKOLLE, John, 1903-
  Sargasso sea
  CSFP. Annual ex, 1946
The skull by H. L. McFee
Skunk cabbage by G. O'Keeffe
Sky after El Greco by C. H. Demuth
Sky and boats by V. Vytlacil
Sky festival by G. Wagner
Skylight by L. MacIver
Skylights by E. Hopper
Skyline by C. Sheeler
Skyline (New York) by K. Matthew
Skyrocket by M. Kantor

Skyscrapers (central panel of New York
  interpreted) by J. Stella
Slade, Alice, b 1767?
  Border limner. Alice Slade
Slade, Joseph, fl 1816
  Border limner. Joseph Slade
Slade, Philip, fl 1818
  Border limner. Philip Slade
Slaughtered animal by H. Bloom
Sleep by A. Fiene
Sleep and revelry by S. Amato
Sleeper by F. Bultman
Sleeper by P. Guston
Sleepers by J. Glasco
Sleepers by E. Melcarth
Sleeping by J. Carroll
Sleeping clown by E. Shinn
Sleeping effort by J. Pollock
Sleeping figure by J. Glasco
Sleeping figure by C. di Marca-Relli
Sleeping girl by Brook
Sleeping man by W. W. Quirt
Sleepwalker by W. A. Baziotes
Sleepwalkers' meeting by K. L. Seligmann
Sleighs
  Beckett, C. E. Furbish's dash to Montreal
  Birch, T. Sleigh ride in the country
  Clonney, J. G. Sleigh ride
  Ferrill, M. E. Sleighing scene, Lansing-
  burgh
  Keyes, C. A. Geo. S. Howe driving Rough
  and Ready
  Van Zandt, T. K. Judge Van Arnam in his
  sleigh
Sleight, Helena Jansen
  Vanderlyn, P. Helena Jansen Sleight
Sligo opposite Pittsburgh by R. Smith
Slip by E. Kelly
Sloan, Anna M. (Wall) d 1943
  Sloan, J. My wife in blue (Dolly)
SLOAN, John, 1871-1951
  Arachne                             PPhM
    Canaday
  Backyards, Greenwich village        WMAA
    Canaday
    Craven. Treasury 1952 ed
    Goodrich. Amer art (col)
    Goodrich. John Sloan
    Mendelowitz
    PA. Annual ex, 1955
    Pierson
  Balancing rock, Gloucester harbor
    NUM. Art across America
  Big apple tree
    Goodrich. John Sloan
  Bleecker street Saturday night
    Brooks. John Sloan
  Carmine theatre
    CanO. Hirshhorn coll
  The Chama running red
    Brooks. John Sloan
    Goodrich. John Sloan
  Chinese restaurant
    Brooks. John Sloan
  The city from Greenwich village, 1922
    Goodrich. John Sloan (col)
    Gruskin (col)

**SLOAN, John**—*Continued*
Coffee line
  Brown. Amer ptg
Cornelia street
  WiMiA. Amer ptg 1760-1960
Corpus Christi, Santa Fe
  Goodrich. John Sloan
The cot
  Brooks. John Sloan
Dawn                      ATU
  ATU. Coll of Amer art
Dust storm, Fifth avenue       MM
  MM. 100 Amer ptrs (col)
East entrance, City hall, Philadelphia, 1901
  Goodrich. John Sloan
Fifth avenue, 1909
  Goodrich. John Sloan
Girl in fur hat              CtNB
  Goodrich. John Sloan
Girl in window
  Goodrich. John Sloan
Gloucester trolley          NCa
  Goodrich. John Sloan
Hairdresser's window       CtHW
  Baur. New art (col)
  Baur. Revolution
  CtHW. Handbook
  DC. De gustibus
  Goodrich. John Sloan
Haymarket            NBM
  Baur. Revolution
  Brooks. John Sloan
  Brown. Amer ptg
  Goodrich. John Sloan
  Hunter. Mod Amer ptg (col)
  McCurdy
  WMAA. Juliana Force
Helen. See Tea for one
Hill, Main street, Gloucester
  MnU. 40 Amer ptrs
In the wake of the ferry     DP
  Cheney. Story 1958 ed
Kent Crane
  Brooks. John Sloan
Lafayette hotel, 1927       MM
  Brooks. John Sloan
  Time. 300 years (col)
Large white nude
  Goodrich. John Sloan
Little movie theater        OT
  Goodrich. John Sloan
Looking out on Washington square
  Goodrich. John Sloan
McSorley's back room
  Brooks. John Sloan
McSorley's bar          MiD
  Brooks. John Sloan
  Cheney. Story 1958 ed
  Craven. Treasury 1952 ed (col)
  Gruskin (col)
  MiD. Treasures
  NBuA. Fifty ptgs
  PA. Annual ex, 1955
  Robb. Harper history
  Wight. Milestones
McSorley's cats
  Goodrich. John Sloan
Main street, Gloucester
  Brooks. John Sloan

Model in dressing room
  Goodrich. John Sloan
  Time. 300 years (col)
Monument in the plaza
  Goodrich. John Sloan
My wife in blue (Dolly)
  Brooks. John Sloan
The necklace
  Goodrich. John Sloan
Nude and nine apples      WMAA
  Baur. New art
  Brooks. John Sloan
  Chew. 250 years of art
  Goodrich. Amer art (col)
  Goodrich. John Sloan (col)
  PA. Annual ex, 1955
Nude at foot of stairs
  Goodrich. John Sloan
Nude on the roof
  Brooks. John Sloan
Old clown making up      DP
  Bazin
  DP. Catalogue
  Lee. Art then and now
Picnic grounds         WMAA
  Brooks. John Sloan
  Goodrich. Amer art
  Goodrich. John Sloan
  Mendelowitz
  Pierson
Picnic on the ridge
  WiMiA. Amer ptg 1760-1960
Pigeons             MB
  Brooks. John Sloan
  Brown. Amer ptg
  Time. 300 years (col)
The Rathskeller (Soula's Rathskeller)   OCI
  Goodrich. John Sloan
  PA. Annual ex, 1955
Recruiting, Union square    OYB
  Chew. 250 years of art
  OYB. Supplement
Red hand mirror
  MnU. 40 Amer ptrs
Red kimono on the roof
  NSyE. The eight
Red paint mill
  Goodrich. John Sloan
Renganeschi's, Saturday night   ICA
  Goodrich. John Sloan
Riders in the hills       WMAA
  Goodrich. John Sloan
  Pousette-Dart. Amer ptg
Roof gossips          ATeS
  ATeS. Collections
Roofs: Twenty-third street, sunset
  CSFP. Annual ex, 1952
Savings bank
  Goodrich. John Sloan
Self-portrait           ATU
  ATU. Coll of Amer art
Self-portrait, 1924 (Fleischman coll)
  WiMiA. Amer ptg 1760-1960
Sixth avenue and Thirteenth street, 1907
  Brooks. John Sloan
  Brown. Amer ptg
  Goodrich. John Sloan
Sixth avenue elevated at Third street, 1928   WMMA
  Baur. New art
  Craven. Rainbow book
  Flexner. Amer ptg

Flexner. Short history
Goodrich. Amer art
Goodrich. **John Sloan**
Pierson
South Beach bathers        MnMW
Baur. New art
Goodrich. John Sloan
Pierson
Spring planting
**Goodrich. John Sloan**
WMAA. Museum and its friends, 1958
Sunday in Union square
Goodrich. John Sloan
Sunday, women drying their hair    MAP
Brown. Amer ptg
DC. 25 biennial ex, 1957
Goodrich. John Sloan
NYG. Fine art
Tea for one (Helen)
Brooks. John Sloan
Goodrich. John Sloan
Three A.M. 1909            PPhM
Baur. New Art
Goodrich. John Sloan (col)
Larkin rev ed (col detail)
Pierson
Wake of the ferry (Wake of the ferry
   boat II)                 DP
Brooks. John Sloan
Canaday
CSB. Impressionism
DP. Catalogue
Goodrich. John Sloan
Larkin
Larkin rev ed
MiD. Ptg in America
Myers. Art
NYG. Fine art
PA. Annual ex, 1955
**Pierson**
Richardson. Ptg in America
Time. 300 years
The White way           PPhM
Goodrich. John Sloan
Gruskin (col)
Woman's work
Brooks. John Sloan
Yeats at Petitpas'         DC
Brooks. John Sloan
Goodrich. John Sloan
Pierson

**Portrait of the artist**
Henri, R. John Sloan, 1906
**SLOANE, Marian Parkhurst**
Vermont hamlet         NJMo
NJMo. Forty years
The **sloop**—Bermuda by W. Homer
**Slow** poke by R. Strang
**Slowly** toward the north by Y. Tanguy
**Slums** by J. Lawrence
**Small** personage by R. B. Motherwell
**Small** pine and snow by F. Heidel
**Small** portrait by K. Sage
**Small** town evening by R. V. Cassill
**Smallwood, William,** b 1732
Peale, C. W. Gov William Smallwood
A **smart** turnout by unidentified artist
**Smelt, Ann (Tyng)** 1733-1756
Copley, J. S. Ann Tyng
**Smelt** brook falls by M. Hartley

**SMIBERT, John,** 1688-1751
Artist's wife           MBH
Flexner. First flowers
Benjamin Colman
Flexner. First flowers
Bishop Berkeley and his family (Berkeley
  family; Berkeley group; Bishop
  Berkeley and his entourage; The Ber-
  muda group)          CtY
CtY. Portrait index
Flexner. First flowers
Foote. John Smibert
Gardner 1959 ed
McKinney
Mendelowitz
Pierson
Richardson. Ptg in America
Robb. Harper history
Roos
U.S. National Capital sesquicentennial
  com
Continence of Scipio (copy of Poussin)
Flexner. First flowers
Daniel Oliver
Belknap
Foote. John Smibert
Daniel, Peter and Andrew Oliver    MB
Pierson
Ebenezer Turell
Foote. John Smibert
Henry Collins
Belknap
Jane Clark               MBH
Belknap
Flexner. First flowers
MiD. Ptg in America
Pierson
Joseph Wanton         RPHS
Time. 300 years (col)
Lady Pepperrell
Belknap
Mrs Daniel Oliver
Belknap
Mrs James Lindall        MiD
MiD. Ports of the Pitts family
MiD. Treasures
Mrs John Erving
Belknap
Mrs John Pitts           MiD
MiD. Ports of the Pitts family
Mrs Nathaniel Cunningham      OT
Belknap
Mrs Stephen Sewall       MSE
Foote. John Smibert
NUM. Art across America
Mrs Thomas Bulfinch       OCl
OCl. Handbook
Nathaniel Byfield         MM
Flexner. First flowers
Pierson
Roos
Peter Faneuil            DC
DC. Masterpieces
Peter Faneuil          MBH
ICA. From colony to nation
Self-portrait           NJMo
NUM. Art across America
Self-portrait (detail from Bishop Berkeley
  and his family)        CtY
Flexner. First flowers
Roos
Three gentlemen
Barker. Amer ptg

**SMIBERT, John**—*Continued*
Sir William Pepperrell      MSE
    Larkin
    Larkin rev ed
**Smibert, Mary (Williams)**
    Smibert, J. Artist's wife
**Smibert, Mrs John.** See Smibert, Mary
    (Williams)
**SMIBERT, Nathaniel,** 1734-1756
    Ezra Stiles      CtY
    CtY. Portrait index
    Foote. John Smibert
    Pierson
**SMITH, Arthur Hall**
    Wraith, wreath, and a final horn    VR
    CoS. New accessions USA, 1952
**Smith, Benjamin,** fl 1790
    Unidentified artist. Capt Benjamin Smith
**Smith, Betsy.** See Smith, Elizabeth Ann
**SMITH, Charles William,** 1893-
    Horizontal arrangement
    Read. Art now, 1948 ed
    Tall building
    Read. Art now, 1948 ed
**Smith, De Mott,** b 1839?
    Walton, H. De Mott Smith, aged 8
**SMITH, Edith M.** 1925-
    Continuum number 16
    IU. Contemp Amer ptg & sculp, 1955
    Diptych
    IU. Contemp Amer ptg & sculp, 1957
**Smith, Elizabeth Ann,** fl 1730
    Theus, J. Elizabeth Smith
**Smith, Elizabeth (Oakes)** fl 1845
    Paradise, J. W. Mrs Elizabeth Oakes
    Smith
**Smith, Elizabeth (Storer)** 1726-1788
    Copley, J. S. Mrs Isaac Smith
**SMITH, Francis Hopkinson,** 1838-1915
    Venice: canal scene I      MB
    MB. Ptgs in water color
    Venice: canal scene II      MB
    MB. Ptgs in water color
**SMITH, Hassel Wendell,** 1915-
    Number 4, 1960      NBuA
    NBuA. Acquisitions 1959-1961
**SMITH, Houghton Cranford**
    The Loma, New Mexico
    PPC. Ptg in the U.S. 1949
**Smith, Isaac,** 1719-1787
    Copley, J. S. Isaac Smith
**Smith, J. Somers**
    Allen, A. J. Somers Smith
**SMITH, Jacob Getlar,** 1895-
    Old blacksmith shop
    Gruskin
**Smith, James Francis,** b 1833?
    Sheffield, I. James Francis Smith
**Smith, Jesse Kittredge,** fl 1842
    Woolson, E. Jesse Kittredge Smith
**SMITH, Joseph B.**
    John street, New York, c 1768    NNMC
     Ford. Pictorial folk art
    Steamer Hartford, 1849 (Blair coll)
     Davidson v 1
**SMITH, Joseph Lindon,** 1863-1950
    Bergamo, Italy      MB
    MB. Ptgs in water color
    Critics: San Giorgio degli Schiavoni,
     Venice      MB
    MB. Ptgs in water color
    Shore scene      MB
    MB. Ptgs in water color

**Smith, Judith.** See Ladson, Judith (Smith)
**SMITH, Judson De Jonge,** 1880-
    Black and white
    WMAA. Contemp Amer ptg, 1953
    **Portrait of the artist**
    Dasburg, A. Judson Smith
**SMITH, Lawrence Beall,** 1902-
    Trio at the bar      ATU
    ATU. Coll of Amer art
**SMITH, Leon Polk,** 1906-
    Behold      ATU
    ATU. Coll of Amer art
    Full white
    PPC. International ex. 1961/62
**Smith, Luther**
    James, A. Luther Smith
**Smith, Maria Catherine,** fl 1693
    Smith, T. Maria Catherine Smith
**SMITH, Mary,** fl 1862
    Skating at the wide waters on the canal
    Jones. Rediscovered ptrs
**Smith, Mrs Isaac.** See Smith, Elizabeth
    (Storer)
**Smith, Mary Ann,** 1774-1825
    Malbone, E. G. Mary Ann Smith
**Smith, Mary Jane,** b 1836
    Stock, J. W. Mary Jane Smith
**Smith, Mrs Noah,** fl 1798
    Unidentified artist. Mrs Noah Smith and
    family
**Smith, Nathan,** 1762-1829
    Morse, S. F. B. Nathan Smith
**SMITH, Russell,** 1812-1896
    Academy of music, Philadelphia, Sketch
     for curtain
     Lewis, V. E. Russell Smith
    Aqueduct in the Pennsylvania canal over
     the Juniata, 1876
     Lewis, V. E. Russell Smith
    The aqueduct, Pittsburgh
     Lewis, V. E. Russell Smith
    L'Ariccia
     Lewis, V. E. Russell Smith
    Ben Cruachan
     Lewis, V. E. Russell Smith
    Birmingham from the top of Coal hill
     opposite Pittsburgh, 1834
     Lewis, V. E. Russell Smith
    Blockhouse as residence of Isaac Craig
     Lewis, V. E. Russell Smith
    Branch bank of the United States
     Lewis, V. E. Russell Smith
    Brighton, England
     Lewis, V. E. Russell Smith
    The Capitol from Mr Elliott's garden,
     1839
     Lewis, V. E. Russell Smith
    Chartiers creek near Pittsburgh, 1840
     Lewis, V. E. Russell Smith
    Chartiers creek on the Ohio river, 1872
     Lewis, V. E. Russell Smith
    Chew house      PA
     Lewis, V. E. Russell Smith
    Civita Vecchia
     Lewis, V. E. Russell Smith
    Cloud study
     Lewis, V. E. Russell Smith
    Curtain study for Edwin Booth: Dell
     scene from Boccaccio
     Lewis, V. E. Russell Smith
    Curtain study for the Brooklyn theatre:
     Francesca da Rimini
     Lewis, V. E. Russell Smith

Edgehill
Lewis, V. E. Russell Smith
Edgehill road, Philadelphia
Lewis, V. E. Russell Smith
Fort St Jean, Marseilles
Lewis, V. E. Russell Smith
Grave of John Keats and the pyramid of
Sestius
Lewis, V. E. Russell Smith
In the falls of the Saco, Crawford's notch
Lewis, V. E. Russell Smith
Lake George near Caldwell, New York
Lewis, V. E. Russell Smith
Larry's creek, Westbranch, Susquehanna
Lewis, V. E. Russell Smith
Looking up the Monongahela river from
Coal hill                                  PPC
Lewis, V. E. Russell Smith
Monongahela bridge after the freshet in
1832
Lewis, V. E. Russell Smith
Monongahela river opposite Pittsburgh,
1837
Lewis, V. E. Russell Smith
Near Manayunk
Lewis, V. E. Russell Smith
Nelson's island showing Monument hill
and Allegheny waterfront in 1840
PPC
Lewis, V. E. Russell Smith
North avenue, Pittsburgh
Lewis, V. E. Russell Smith
Old courthouse in Philadelphia, 1835
Lewis, V. E. Russell Smith
Old Holiday street theatre, Baltimore,
1839
Lewis, V. E. Russell Smith
Old trees at Ormsby farm            PPC
Lewis, V. E. Russell Smith
Old Walnut street prison, Philadelphia in
1835
Lewis, V. E. Russell Smith
Oldest house at foot of Coal hill, opposite
Market street                       PPC
Lewis, V. E. Russell Smith
Original tomb of Washington, 1836
Lewis, V. E. Russell Smith
Powder magazine, Fort Duquesne, Penn-
sylvania, 1832
Lewis, V. E. Russell Smith
Robeson mill at the mouth of the Wissa-
hickon
Lewis, V. E. Russell Smith
Ruins of Fort Ticonderoga, Lake Cham-
plain
Lewis, V. E. Russell Smith
Scene on the Ohio
Lewis, V. E. Russell Smith
Self-portrait, 1887
Lewis, V. E. Russell Smith
Sligo opposite Pittsburgh
Lewis, V. E. Russell Smith
Val Ticino, St Gothard route
Lewis, V. E. Russell Smith
View of Pittsburgh from the salt works on
Saw mill run
Chew. 250 years of art
Lewis, V. E. Russell Smith
Western university of Pennsylvania  PPC
Lewis, V. E. Russell Smith

Wingahocking at Shoemaker's lane, Ger-
mantown, 1836
Lewis, V. E. Russell Smith
Wissahickon
Lewis, V. E. Russell Smith
Smith, Samuel, 1752-1839
Peale, Rembrandt. Gen Samuel Smith
Smith, Sarah. See Keteltas, Sarah (Smith)
SMITH, Thomas, fl 1669-1693
Maria Catherine Smith            MWA
Flexner. First flowers
Mendelowitz
Self-portrait                    MWA
Barker. Amer ptg
Belknap
Flexner. First flowers (col)
ICA. From colony to nation
Larkin
Larkin rev ed
MWA. Checklist of portraits
Pierson
Richardson. Ptg in America
Time. 300 years (col)

**Attributed works**
Thomas Savage
Belknap (as Unidentified artist)
Davidson v 1
Flexner. First flowers
Pierson
SMITH, Wallace Henderson, 1901-
Hell gate bridge
NYG. Fine art
SMITH, William Arthur, 1918-
Calcutta
NAD. Annual ex, 1960
Les Halles
NAD. Annual ex, 1953
Montmartre impasse
NAD. Annual ex, 1951
Out back
NAD. Annual ex, 1949, 2d half
OYB. Annual 1953
Smith, William Howard, b 1832
Stock, J. W. William Howard Smith
Smith family, Member of
Jennys, W. Member of the Smith family
of Suffield, Connecticut and Rutland,
Vermont, c 1800
Smith and Dimon shipyard, New York by
J. Pringle
Smith memorial by Unidentified artist
Smith's cove by S. Davis
Smithtown, Long Island, c 1860 by A. Milne
Smoke of a .45 by C. M. Russell
Smoking mirror by C. R. Bentley
Smoking them out by C. M. Russell
Smoky range, Allegheny mountains by C. H.
Shearer
Smugglers' cove by A. P. Ryder
Smyth, Mary. See Hunter, Mary (Smyth)
Snack bar by I. Bishop
Snails by H. G. Keller
Snake Indian and his dog by A. J. Miller
Snake Indian camp by A. J. Miller
Snake Indian pursuing a Crow horse thief
by A. J. Miller
Snake Indians by A. J. Miller

**Snake** Indians fording a river by A. J. Miller
**Snake** Indians shooting elk by A. J. Miller
**Snake** Indians—testing bows by A. J. Miller
**Snakes**
    Audubon, J. J. Mockingbird (with rattlesnake robbing nest)
    Curry, J. S. Hog killing a rattlesnake
    Curry, J. S. Hogs killing a snake
    Graves, M. Snake and moon
**Snap** shot by A. Blanch
**Snap** the whip by W. Homer
**SNELGROVE, Walter,** 1924-
    Shipwreck
        CSFP. Annual ex, 1950/51
**SNOW, Jenny Emily,** fl 1850
    Belshazzar's feast
        Ford. Pictorial folk art
**Snow,** Cape Cod by D. Macknight
**Snow** city by P. Evergood
**Snow** cloud and blue sky by J. Schueler
**Snow** drapery by G. H. Hallowell
**Snow** horse by W. Sommer
**Snow** in April by M. B. Prendergast
**Snow** on the mountain by S. Davis
**Snow** scene by J. H. Twachtman
**Snow** thaw by A. G. Dove
The **snow** trail by F. Remington
**Snow,** White mountains by D. Macknight
**Snowbound** on the overland stage by F. Remington
**Snowscape** by L. MacIver
**Snowshoe** dance of the Ojibbeway by G. Catlin
**Snowy** heron or white egret by J. J. Audubon
**Snowy** owl by J. J. Audubon
**Snug** harbor by P. Evergood
**Snyder's** Hollow by J. H. Lawman
**Soap-locks** or Bowery boys, New York by N. V. Calyo
**Soaring** by A. N. Wyeth
**Social** club by W. M. Harnett
**Social** security murals by B. Shahn
The **socialite** by K. J. Priebe
**Soda** fountain by W. J. Glackens
**Soda** jerker by P. Burlin
**Soft** night by A. Gorky
**Softly** falling snow by D. Macknight
**Soho** portrait by H. W. Scheuch
**SOKOLE, Miron,** 1901-
    Approaching night
        Gruskin
    The aquarium
        IU. Contemp Amer ptg, 1950
    Nostalgic night
        IU. Contemp Amer ptg, 1949
    Within the confines of window frame
        IU. Contemp Amer ptg, 1948
**Solace** by W. M. Harnett
Le **Soldat** du Chêne, an Osage chief by G. B. King (attributed works)
**Soldier** and bull by R. A. Nelson
**Soldier's** dream by M. Beckmann
**Soldier's** joy by T. H. Benton

**Soldier's** medal by A. Leslie
**Solids** into blue by C. A. Morris
**Soliloquy** by F. C. Watkins
**Solitaire.** See Games and sports—Cards
A **solitary** by A. James
**Solitudes** by L. Guglielmi
**Solo** by M. Weber
**SOLOMON, Hyde,** 1911-
    Vermont autumn            WMAA
    Baur. Nature
**SOLOMON, Syd,** 1907-
    Bird Key bay            OYB
        OYB. Annual 1957
        OYB. Supplement 1959
    Boca
        Pousette-Dart. Amer ptg
**SOLOMON, Vita P.**
    End of the day
        NAD. Annual ex, 1959
**Solomon** at the court of Sheba by P. Evergood
**Solstice** by K. Okada
**Solstice** rider by L. Mullican
**Sombre** vertical with lines by I. Bolotowsky
**Some** grow up by H. D. Pickering
**Somebody** tore my poster by Y. Kuniyoshi
**Somerby, Joanna (Cotter)** 1805-1886
    Jouett, M. H. Mrs Rufus Somerby
**Somers, Mary.** See Deas, Mary (Somers)
**Something** on the eight ball by S. Davis
**Somewhere** today by I. R. Pereira
**SOMMER, William,** 1867-1949
    Apples
        OCl. Sommer
    April cat
        OCl. Sommer
    Asleep on the path
        OCl. Sommer
    Bald boy
        OCl. Sommer
    Big horse
        OCl. Sommer
    Black horse
        OCl. Sommer
    Blue chair
        OCl. Sommer
    Blue horse
        OCl. Sommer
    Blue vase
        OCl. Sommer
    Bowl of apples
        OCl. Sommer
    A boy            ICA
        OCl. Sommer
    Brandywine
        OCl. Sommer
    Brandywine landscape
        OCl. Sommer
    Cows
        OCl. Sommer
    Cows resting
        OCl. Sommer
    Faith, hope, and charity
        OCl. Sommer
    Fruit bowl
        OCl. Sommer
    The goblet
        OCl. Sommer

Horses in the snow
  OCl. Handbook
  OCl. Sommer
June
  OCl. Sommer
Kitchen
  OCl. Sommer
Languid leisure
  OCl. Sommer
Little girl with apple
  OCl. Sommer
Little Mozart
  OCl. Sommer
Marvin
  OCl. Sommer
Meditation in space
  OCl. Sommer
One of the Dominskis
  OCl. Sommer
Orange door
  OCl. Sommer
Ornamatique
  OCl. Sommer
Pa's brainstorm
  OCl. Sommer
Patchwork cows
  OCl. Sommer
Pensive boy
  OCl. Sommer
Pink cow
  OCl. Sommer
Pompous boy
  OCl. Sommer
Portrait
  OYB. Catalogue 1951
Ray
  OCl. Sommer
Rose montage
  OCl. Sommer
Seated boy in lavender overalls
  OCl. Sommer
Snow horse
  OCl. Sommer
Spinach tree
  OCl. Sommer
Still life: the blue vase
  OCl. Sommer
Tess
  OCl. Sommer
Three horses in alarm
  OCl. Sommer
Tree forms
  OCl. Sommer
Turreted pitcher
  OCl. Sommer
Two yellow horses
  OCl. Sommer
Waiting in Bethlehem
  OCl. Sommer
Winter landscape, 1923
  OCl. Sommer
Winter landscape, c 1934
  OCl. Sommer
**Sommernachtstraum** by H. **Hofmann**
**Son** of a sharecropper by J. B. **Turnbull**
The **song** by B. Shahn
**Song** in the rain by C. E. Burchfield

**OCl** Song of Esther by A. Rattner
Song of the guitar by W. W. Quirt
Song of the katydids by C. E. Burchfield
Song of the katydids on an August morning by C. E. Burchfield
Song of the marsh by C. E. Burchfield
Song of the talking wire by H. F. Farny
Song of the telegraph by C. E. Burchfield
**SONNTAG, William Louis,** 1869-1898
  The Bowery at night, c 1895       NNMC
  U.S. National Capital sesquicentennial com
    Morning in the Blue Ridge mountains
    Sears. Highlights
The **soothsayer** by F. S. Franck
**Sorcerer's** gear by R. Gorchov
**Sorceress** by D. Austin
**Sorrow** by S. Csoka
La **sortie** du bain by M. Cassatt
**Sortie** from Gibraltar by J. Trumbull
**Sortie** of the British garrison from Gibraltar by J. Trumbull
**Sou'easter** interim by K. Knaths
The **soul** leaving the body by W. W. Quirt
**Soul** of space by I. R. Pereira
**Soula's** Rathskeller by J. Sloan
**Soult, Nicolas Jean de Dieu, duke of Dalmatia,** 1769-1851
  Healy, G. P. A. Nicolas Jean de Dieu Soult, duke of Dalmatia, 1769-1851
**OYB** **Sound** asleep and wide awake by D. C. Johnston
**Sound** in the mulberry trees by B. Shahn
**Sound** of blue light by N. Carone
**Sound** of flowers by M. Broderson
**Sounds** in the rock by T. Stamos
**Source** by M. Manigault
**Source** of the Romanche by L. Pitts
**South** American river by M. J. Heade
**South** Beach bathers by J. Sloan
**South** Boston pier by M. B. Prendergast
**OCl** **South** of Scranton by P. Blume
**South** of Taxco by Martyl
**South** Sea whale fishing by R. W. Salmon
**South** window by R. F. Gates
**Southern** belle by A. Brook
The **Southern** Belle by Unidentified artist
**Southern** community by R. Gwathmey
**Southern** scene by R. Gwathmey
**Southern** souvenir by E. Cortor
**Southern** tier by M. H. Visser't Hooft
**OCl** **Southwest** no 4 by W. Lockwood
**Southwest** no 9—riders by W. Lockwood
**Southwest** wind by C. Hassam
A **southwester** by J. Marin
**Souvenir** of America by K. L. Seligmann
**Souvenir** of Chicago by M. Beckmann
**Souvenirs** of the sea by A. Gottlieb
**Sowing** by R. Gwathmey
**Sowing** grain at Bishop hill by O. Krans

**SOYER, Isaac,** 1907-
  Employment agency                    WMAA
    Baur. Revolution
    Goodrich. Amer art
    McCurdy
    Pierson
    WMAA. Juliana Force
  The model
    Gruskin (col)
  Office girls
    Bazin
**SOYER, Moses,** 1899-
  Dancer
    NAD. Annual ex, 1959
  Dancers
    NAD. Annual ex, 1961
  David Burliuk in his studio
    CSFP. Annual ex, 1948/49
  Four dancers
    OYB. Annual 1953
  Girl in orange sweater              WMAA
    Goodrich. Amer art
    Pierson
  New costume
    Gruskin (col)
  Sad interior
    Brown. Amer ptg
  Three dancers
    MM. Amer ptg today
**SOYER, Raphael,** 1899-
  The blue shawl
    CSFP. Annual ex, 1948/49
  Boheme girl
    CSFP. Annual ex, 1950/51
  Boy and girl
    NAD. Annual ex, spring 1950
  Brown sweater                        WMAA
    Goodrich. Amer art
    Pierson
  Disorder
    NAD. Annual ex, 1949, 1st half
  Dressmaker's shop
    NAD. Annual ex, 1954
  Female figure                        ATeS
    ATeS. Collection
  Figure in blue
    VR. Amer ptg, 1954
  Flower vendor
    NYG. Fine art
  Girl in a white blouse               MM
    MM. 100 Amer ptrs
  A group of artists
    NAD. Annual ex, 1956
  In the studio
    ICA. Annual ex, 1945/46
  Interior with figure
    IU. Contemp Amer ptg, 1949
  Lamplight
    Brown. Amer ptg
  Nude in profile
    WMAA. Contemp Amer ptg, 1950
  Office girls                         WMAA
    Baur. Revolution
    Goodrich. Amer art (col)
    Mendelowitz
    Pierson
  Pensive girl                         PPC
    CoS. New accessions USA, 1948
  Reflection
    WMAA. Museum and its friends, 1958
  Seamstress
    NAD. Annual ex, 1948
    WMAA. Annual ex, 1957

  Self-portrait                        ATU
    ATU. Coll of Amer art
  Still life
    NAD. Annual ex, 1957
  Subway platform
    Gruskin
  Two sisters
    NAD. Annual ex, 1947, 1st half
    VR. Biennal ex, 1948
  Waiting for the audition
    DC. 22 biennial ex, 1951
  Waiting room                         DC
    Larkin
    Larkin rev ed
    Pierson
  Young woman
    PPC. Ptg in the U.S. 1949

**Portrait of the artist**
  Biddle, G. Raphael Soyer and his model
  Dickinson, S. E. Raphael Soyer
**Space** intangibles by M. Tobey
**Space** modulator by L. Moholy-Nagy
**Space** ritual no 3 by M. Tobey
**Space,** time, embrace by W. Pachner
**Spad** by G. L. Mueller
**SPAGNA, Vincent,** 1898-
  Air raid
    Gruskin
**Spanish** boys at play (Vianna do Castello,
    Portugal) by J. S. Sargent
**Spanish** cavalier by W. M. Chase
**Spanish** lace by E. Graham
**Spanish** soldiers by J. S. Sargent
**Spanish** steps, Rome by M. B. Prendergast
**Sparhawk, Nathaniel,** 1715-1776
  Copley, J. S. Nathaniel Sparhawk
**Sparhawk, William Pepperrell.** See Pepper-
    rell, Sir William, 2d bart
**Sparking** by J. Carlin
**Sparking** by F. W. Edmonds
**Sparks, Mary Crowninshield (Silsbee)** 1809-
    1887
  Alexander, F. Mrs Jared Sparks
**Sparrows**
  Evergood, P. Lily and the sparrows
  Graves, M. Preening sparrows
  Heil, C. E. Field sparrow on blackberry
**Speakeasy** closed for violation by B. Shahn
The **speaker** by W. Gropper
**Spectator** by H. Warshaw
**Spectre** of the sea by A. Gottlieb
The **spectrum,** a painting in four acts by
    B. Connelly
**Speculation** by J. Ernst
**Speed**—Lake Champlain by J. Marin
**SPEICHER, Eugene Edward,** 1883-
  Agnes Clark
    NAD. Annual ex, 1948
  Andrée Ruellan                       ATeS
    ATeS. Collection
    CSFP. Annual ex, 1952
  A. Conger Goodyear, 1942             MMA
    NBuA. Eugene Speicher
  Babette, 1931                        PPC
    NBuA. Eugene Speicher
  Begonias, 1947
    NBuA. Eugene Speicher
  Blue necklace                        OT
    Larkin
    Larkin rev ed

Brigham's yard, Kingston　　　　　NUM
　NUM. Root bequest
Caim Lasher
　CSFP. Annual ex, 1947-48
Consuela
　NAD. Annual ex, 1947, 2d half
Farm news, 1944
　NBuA. Eugene Speicher
Farmer
　IU. Contemp Amer ptg, 1948
Flowers in pineapple pitcher, 1947
　NBuA. Eugene Speicher
Georgia O'Keeffe, 1908
　NBuA. Eugene Speicher
Graziana
　Bazin
Greek boy
　Baur. Revolution
　NBuA. Fifty ptgs
Green hat　　　　　　　　　　　FaW
　Lewisohn
Helen Rogers
　DC. 20 biennial ex, 1947
Henry Emerson Tuttle, 1945　　　　CtY
　CtY. Portrait index
　NBuA. Eugene Speicher
Jean Bellows, 1940　　　　　　　ICA
　NBuA. Eugene Speicher
Jean in blue
　Gruskin (col)
Joyce　　　　　　　　　　　　　InIJ
　InIJ. 105 ptgs
Katharine　　　　　　　　　　　MB
　NBuA. Eugene Speicher
　WMAA. Juliana Force
Katharine Cornell as Candida, 1926
　　　　　　　　　　　　　　NBuA
　NBuA. Eugene Speicher
　Pierson
Kathleen Colleti
　PPC. International ex, 1950
Lilya　　　　　　　　　　　　　OCiM
　Baur. Revolution
　NBuA. Eugene Speicher
Marianna　　　　　　　　　　　WMAA
　Goodrich. Amer art
　McCurdy
Mrs Ogden Phipps
　Time. 300 years (col)
The mountaineer
　NBuA. Eugene Speicher
　Pierson
Murray Bay landscape, 1933　　　WMAA
　NBuA. Eugene Speicher
Nancy, 1942
　NBuA. Eugene Speicher
Nude back　　　　　　　　　　　OCo
　CoS. New accessions USA, 1960
　NYG. Fine art
　WMAA. Museum and its friends, 1958
Patty
　NBuA. Eugene Speicher
Peach jacket　　　　　　　　　　VR
　NBuA. Eugene Speicher
Pigtails, 1939　　　　　　　　　MoKN
　NBuA. Eugene Speicher
Polly　　　　　　　　　　　　　MM
　MM. 100 Amer ptrs
Portrait of a girl　　　　　　　WMAA
　Roos
Sara Grace Heath Butler　　　　　OYB
　OYB. Catalogue 1951

Steve
　NAD. Annual ex, 1952
Tony Robinson
　IU. Contemp Amer ptg, 1949
Tulips in a white pitcher　　　　MoSL
　MoSL. Handbook 1953
Yvette von Kories
　PPC. Ptg in the U.S. 1949
SPEIGHT, Francis, 1896-
Cliffs at Manayunk
　NAD. Annual ex, 1952
End of the street　　　　　　　OYB
　OYB. Catalogue 1951
Schuylkill at Manayunk
　NAD. Annual ex, 1958
Spell by L. Feininger
Spell of Italy by H. G. Keller
Spencer, Ambrose, 1765-1848
　Ames, E. Ambrose Spencer, 1811
　Jarvis, J. W. Ambrose Spencer
SPENCER, Lilly Martin, 1822-1902
The war spirit at home, celebrating the
　victory of Vicksburg　　　　NJN
　NJN. Early N.J. artists
　U.S. National Capital sesquicentennial
　com
SPENCER, Niles, 1893-1952
Above the excavation
　MnMW. Classic tradition
Apartment tower　　　　　　　WMAA
　Goodrich. Amer art
Blast furnace
　MnU. 40 Amer ptrs
City shapes　　　　　　　　　　ATeS
　ATeS. Collection
City walls　　　　　　　　　　　MMA
　Baur. New art
　McCurdy
　MMA. Masters
　MnMW. Precisionist view
　Pierson
Corporation shed　　　　　　　OCo
　Brown. Amer ptg
The cove, Ogunquit　　　　　　NJN
　Baur. New art
The desk　　　　　　　　　　　CSFM
　DC. 22 biennial ex, 1951
　MnMW. Precisionist view
Erie underpass　　　　　　　　MM
　Baur. New art
　MM. 100 Amer ptrs
　MnU. 40 Amer ptrs
Green table　　　　　　　　　　WMAA
　Baur. New art
　Goodrich. Amer art
　Pierson
In Fairmont　　　　　　　　　MMA
　Baur. New art (col)
　IU. Contemp Amer ptg, 1952
　Pierson
　Pousette-Dart. Amer ptg
In the cabin
　ICA. Annual ex, 1951
Near Avenue A　　　　　　　　MMA
　Baur. Revolution
Pike county church
　VR. Biennial ex, 1948
Silver tanks
　PPC. Ptg in the U.S. 1949
Still life
　NYG. Fine art

**SPENCER, Niles**—*Continued*
  Two bridges
    Hunter. Mod Amer ptg (col)
    McCurdy
    MMA. Abstract (col)
    MnMW. Contemporary (col)
    WMAA. Neuberger collection (col)
  Wake of the hurricane                   MnMW
    MnMW. Precisionist view (col)
  Watch factory                              OYB
    OYB. Catalogue 1951
**SPENCER, Robert**, 1879-1931
  Ship chandlers' row                         DP
    DP. Catalogue
**Spencer, Sarah Louisa**, b 1841
  Walton, H. Sarah Louisa Spencer
The **sphinx** and the Milky way by C. E.
  Burchfield
The **sphinx** on the seashore by E. Vedder
**Spider's** nightmare by O. Herford
The **spielers** by G. B. Luks
**SPIERS, Harry,** 1870-1947
  As the sunlight bursts                      MB
    MB. Ptgs in water color
**Spike's** folly by W. De Kooning
**Spinach** tree by W. Sommer
**Spindrift** by A. N. Wyeth
The **spinet** by T. W. Dewing
**Spirals** by J. C. Atherton
**Spirit** bird by M. Graves
**Spirit** of air by I. R. Pereira
**Spirit** of the Indian by T. Moran
**Spirit** 3 by W. Hedrick
**Spiritual** decadence by E. Burkhart
**Spiritual** decay by E. Burkhart
**Splatters** and leaves by L. MacIver
**Splicing** the cable by R. Dudley
**SPOHN, Clay Edgar,** 1898-
  November 1951
    IU. Contemp Amer ptg & sculp, 1953
  Number 11-24-46
    CSFP. Annual ex, 1947/48
**Spong, Hilda**
  Chase, W. M. Hilda Spong
**Sponge** diver by W. Homer
**Sponge** fishermen, Bahamas by W. Homer
**Spoonbills**
  Audubon, J. J. Roseate spoonbill
**Spooner, Rebecca.** See Green, Rebecca
  (Spooner)
**Sports, Barent**
  Unidentified artist. Barent Sports of Al-
  bany
**Sports.** See Games and sports
**Sportsman's** still life by A. Pope
**Sprague, Albert Arnold,** 1835-1915
  Betts, L. Albert Arnold Sprague
**Sprague, Jonathan,** fl 1828
  Bosworth, S. Jonathan Sprague
**Sprague, Mrs Jonathan.** See Sprague,
  Melissa
**SPRAGUE, Mark A.**
  Arrangement
    ICA. Annual ex, 1951
**Sprague, Melissa,** fl 1828
  Bosworth, S. Melissa Sprague
**Spring** by J. Blair

**Spring** by M. Graves
**Spring** by J. E. Heliker
**Spring** by W. Homer
**Spring** by H. Lundeberg
**Spring** by H. E. Mattson
**Spring** by A. P. Ryder
**Spring** by B. Shahn
**Spring** by J. Stella
**Spring** by R. Strang
**Spring** by W. Zorach
**Spring** beauty by A. N. Wyeth
**Spring** blossoms by F. Crowninshield
**Spring** blossoms by W. Homer
**Spring** bonnet by J. Carroll
**Spring:** burning up fallen trees, a girdled
  clearing, Canada by G. Harvey
**Spring** cleaning by J. L. Howard
**Spring** festival by H. Pittman
**Spring** fishing by Unidentified artist
**Spring** flowers by L. Karp
**Spring** harvest by S. Chun
**Spring** idyll by K. Matthew
**Spring** in Central park by A. A. Dehn
**Spring** in France by M. Avery
**Spring** in Giverney by T. Robinson
**Spring** in the country by G. Wood
**Spring** in the valley by A. M. R. Moses
**Spring** in town by G. Wood
**Spring** is in the air by F. Kleinholz
**Spring** landscape by C. Hinkle
**Spring** landscape by S. Laufman
**Spring** landscape by G. Wood
**Spring** melody by N. Cikovsky
**Spring** mist by W. Thon
**Spring** night, Harlem river by E. Lawson
**Spring** no 1 by J. Marin
**Spring** no 1, 1913 by W. Zorach
**Spring** on Morton street by B. Shahn
**Spring** on Ninth avenue by L. Bosa
**Spring** orchard by M. Avery
**Spring** planting by J. Sloan
**Spring** shower, Connecticut valley by M. J.
  Heade
**Spring** song by E. P. Etting
**Spring** song by S. Moy
**Spring** song by P. S. Sample
**Spring** song by W. Stuempfig
**Spring,** twelve o'clock by I. R. Pereira
**Springtime** by J. E. Costigan
**Springtime** by H. B. Kayn
**Springtime** by D. Macknight
**Springtime** by D. W. Tryon
**Springtime** by F. C. Watkins
**Springtime** in Virginia by W. Homer
**Springtime** of delight by A. B. Davies
**Sproat, David,** 1734-1799
  Trumbull, J. David Sproat
**Sprouting** coconuts by R. Tam

SPRUANCE, Benton, 1904-
  Still life with horns
    PPC. Ptg in the U.S. 1949
SPRUCE, Everett Franklin, 1907-
  Angora goat
    Leeper. Everett Spruce
  Antelope mountain
    Leeper. Everett Spruce
  Arkansas landscape                          DP
    Leeper. Everett Spruce
  Autumn landscape                            TxD
    Leeper. Everett Spruce
  The beach                                   MdBM
    Leeper. Everett Spruce
  Bee keeper
    Leeper. Everett Spruce
  Big Bend
    Leeper. Everett Spruce
  Bird study
    Leeper. Everett Spruce
  Brushy hillside                             WMAA
    Goodrich. Amer art
    Leeper. Everett Spruce
  Century plant                               LaN
    DC. 21 biennial ex, 1949
    Leeper. Everett Spruce
  The cliff
    Leeper. Everett Spruce
  Cold day
    Leeper. Everett Spruce
  Dark mountains
    PA. Annual ex, 1947
  The desert                                  MiD
    Leeper. Everett Spruce
    PPC. Amer ptg in the U.S. 1949
  Desert at night
    CSFP. Annual ex, 1950/51
  Fence builders
    Leeper. Everett Spruce
  Fiddler
    Leeper. Everett Spruce
  Fish and birds                              MnU
    Leeper. Everett Spruce (col)
  Fisherman
    IU. Contemp Amer ptg, 1950
    NBuA. Expressionism
  Goat
    MM. Amer ptg today
  Gull
    Leeper. Everett Spruce
  The hawk                                    MMA
    Leeper. Everett Spruce
    Pierson
  Kildeer
    Leeper. Everett Spruce
  Little canyon
    VR. Biennial ex, 1948
  Low tide
    Leeper. Everett Spruce
  Mending fence
    Leeper. Everett Spruce
  Night fisherman
    Leeper. Everett Spruce (col)
  Old tree                                    MnMW
    Leeper. Everett Spruce
  On the beach
    Leeper. Everett Spruce
  Padre island
    Leeper. Everett Spruce
  Pigeons on a roof                           MM
    MM. 100 Amer ptrs

  Precipice
    Pousette-Dart. Amer ptg
  Red mule
    Leeper. Everett Spruce
  Rocky place
    IU. Contemp Amer ptg, 1952
  Sea gulls
    Leeper. Everett Spruce
  Surf fisherman
    Leeper. Everett Spruce
  The wave
    Leeper. Everett Spruce
  Wave breaking
    Leeper. Everett Spruce
  Waves
    Leeper. Everett Spruce
  Whippoorwill, sandpiper
    Leeper. Everett Spruce
  White cow
    Leeper. Everett Spruce
  White mountain
    Leeper. Everett Spruce
  Yellow rooster
    Leeper. Everett Spruce
Spruce tree in a landscape by C. W. Hudson
Squall off Christmas cove by M. Freedman
The square by P. W. Zimmerman
Square on the pond by A. G. Dove
Squash by Y. Kuniyoshi
The squatters by G. C. Bingham
Squirrels
  Audubon, J. J. Richardson's Columbian
    squirrel
  Audubon, J. J. Say's or western fox squir-
    rel
  Copley, J. S. Boy with squirrel (Henry
    Pelham)
Stables by G. O'Keeffe
Staccato for dormers by R. L. Lancaster
Stacey hill, Stoddard, New Hampshire,
    View from by T. Doughty
Stacking alfalfa by O. M. Pleissner
Staff, distaff and rod by A. T. Mason
Stafford, Harriet (Romeyn) 1792-1848
  Ames, E. Mrs Spencer Stafford
Stafford, Spencer, 1772-1844
  Ames, E. Spencer Stafford
Stag and two does by A. P. Ryder
Stag at Sharkey's by G. W. Bellows
Stag drinking by A. P. Ryder
Stage fragment, Faust by G. L. Mueller
Stagecoaches
  Blythe, D. G. Stagecoach
  Boese, H. Stagecoach seventy-six of the
    Knickerbocker line
  Johnson, E. The old stagecoach
  Johnson, F. T. On Salt lake trail
  Peters, J. Good intent
  Remington, F. Snowbound on the over-
    land stage
  Russell, C. M. Holding up the stage
  Shinn, E. Winter scene
  Stucker, F. Albany Schoharie stagecoach
  Tattersall, G. Road to the west
Stages of man by Unidentified artist
STAHL, Ben, 1910-
  Mother earth
    NAD. Annual ex, 1952
  Rehearsal under the big top
    NAD. Annual ex, 1948, 1st half

**STAIGG, Richard Morell,** 1817-1881
  Mrs Gerard Stuyvesant            NNHS
    Vail. Stuyvesant ports
The staircase by A. Refregier
Staircase by C. Ruhtenberg
A staircase by J. S. Sargent
Staircase, Doylestown by C. Sheeler
Staircase group by C. W. Peale
Stairs, Provincetown by C. H. Demuth
Stairway by J. Koch
Stamford harbor by L. Bouché
**STAMOS, Theodoros,** 1922-
  Corinth no 3, 1959
    MnMW. 60 Amer ptrs
  Death of the anarchist
    Pousette-Dart. Amer ptg
  East field
    PPC. International ex, 1961/62
  Echo
    MM. 100 Amer ptrs
  The emperor ploughs the fields    MiD
    MiD. Treasures
    WMAA. Contemp Amer ptg, 1950
  Field II
    CtY. Yale alumni
  Field III, 1954
    WMAA. New decade
  Flower eruption
    CSFP. Annual ex, 1950/51
    PPC. Ptg in the U.S. 1949
  Greek island
    NUM. Art across America
  Greek orisons                    WMAA
    Faulkner. Art today, 1956
    Mendelowitz
    Pierson
    WMAA. New decade
  Heart of Norway spruce            DC
    DC. Masterpieces
    Eliot. Art of our time (col)
    Time. 300 years (col)
  High snow, low sun, no 3, 1957
    MMA. New Amer ptg (col)
  High snow, low sun, no 11, 1957
    Baur. Nature (col)
    Goodrich. Amer art (col)
  Levant for E. W. R.              NBuA
    NBuA. Acquisitions 1957-58
  Levant no 7
    IU. Contemp Amer ptg & sculp, 1961
  Lupine                           DP
    Larkin rev ed
  Oriental beggar
    IU. Contemp Amer ptg & sculp, 1955
  Red Sea terrace no 1
    CoS. New accessions USA, 1960
  The reward                       NUM
    NUM. Root bequest
  Road to Sparta
    WMAA. New decade
  Sacrifice of Chronos no 2, 1948  DP
    McCurdy
    MMA. Abstract
  Seedling                         NUM
    MiA. Root coll
  Sounds in the rock               MMA
    Baur. Revolution
    MMA. Contemp ptrs
    Pierson

Sun games no 2, 1958
  MMA. New Amer ptg
Theatre
  IU. Contemp Amer ptg, 1950
A walk in the poppies
  Barker. From realism
White field no 2, 1957
  MMA. New Amer ptg
World tablet                       DP
  DP. Catalogue
Stampede of wild horses by A. J. Miller
Stampeded by C. M. Russell
Stampeding bulls by L. Corbino
**STAMPER, Willson Y.** 1910-
  Perfume counter
    NBuA. Expressionism
Standard with still life by S. Davis
Standing couple by D. Park
Standing figure by J. Davis
Standing figure by K. Finch
Standing in the need of prayer by C. M.
    Williamson
Standing male by W. De Kooning
Standing man and stick by N. J. Oliveira
Standing nude by B. Karfiol
Standing with reluctant feet where brook and
    river meet by J. Farnsworth
Standing woman by N. J. Oliveira
Standing woman with hat by N. J. Oliveira
Stanford, John, 1754-1834
  Jarvis, J. W. Rev John Stanford
**STANLEY, A. R.** fl 1840
  Eliza Wells                      DN
    DN. Amer primitive ptgs, pt 1
Stanley, Sir Henry Morton, 1841-1904
  Healy, G. P. A. Sir Henry M. Stanley
**STANLEY, John Mix,** 1814-1872
  Assiniboin encampment on the upper Mis-
    souri                         MiD
    Rathbone
  Bear's Paw
    WiMiA. Amer ptg 1760-1960
  Bois de Sioux river
    WiMiA. Amer ptg 1760-1960
  Buffalo hunt on the southern plains
                                   DNC
    McCracken. Portrait of the old west
    (col)
  Chinook burial grounds            MiD
    Rathbone
  Distributing goods to the Gros Ventres
    McCracken. Portrait of the old west
  Gov Stevens at Fort Benton
    McCracken. Portrait of the old west
  Indian telegraph                  MiD
    Rathbone
  Indians playing cards             MiD
    Pierson
  Ko-kak-koo-kiss, a Towoccono warrior
                                   DNC
    Roos
  Osage scalp dance                 DNC
    McCracken. Portrait of the old west
    (col)
    Rathbone
  Prairie encampment                MiD
    Rathbone
  Samuel Mountfort Pitts jr         MiD
    MiD. Ports of the Pitts family

Western landscape          MiD
  Larkin
  Larkin rev ed
  Rathbone
Stanley, Ruth.  See Mix, Ruth (Stanley)
Stanton, Daniel
  Elliott, C. L.  Daniel Stanton
Staples, Seth Perkins, 1776-1861
  Flagg, J. B.  Seth Perkins Staples (after
    Waldo and Jewett)
The star by C. E. Burchfield
The star by M. Kopf
Star watchers by F. J. Russell
Starlings caravan by K. Sage
Starr, Abigail.  See Taylor, Abigail (Starr)
Starr, Nathan, 1784-1852
  Jarvis, J. W.  Nathan Starr jr (of Middle-
    town, Connecticut)
Starr King mountain, California by A. Bier-
    stadt
Starrucca viaduct, Susquehanna valley by
    J. F. Cropsey
Start of the hunt by Unidentified artist
Starting out after rail by T. Eakins
Startled by W. Homer
STASACK, Edward, 1929-
  Undersea mountain
    IU.  Contemp Amer ptg & sculp, 1961
State street, Albany by J. Eights
The statesman by C. H. Pepper
Station of the Cross by H. Moller
Statue at Vaux-le-Vicomte by W. Gay
Statue of Liberty
  Moran, E.  Unveiling the statue of Lib-
    erty, 1886
Steam room at Bayes Hot Springs by J.
    Brown
Steam turbine by C. Sheeler
Steamboats on the Ohio by T. P. Anshutz
Steamship Odin by L. Feininger
STEARNS, Junius Brutus, 1810-1885
  Children fishing          OYB
    OYB.  Catalogue 1951
  Fisherman's still life          OT
    Pierson
Steel—Croton by C. Sheeler
Steel mill at night by A. H. Gorson
Steel structure by R. Marsh
Steel town madonna by S. Bookatz
STEELE, Gordon
  Construction no 2          OYB
    OYB.  Annual 1960
STEELE, Theodore Clement, 1847-1926
  Early spring          InTH
    InTH.  Catalogue
Steelworkers' noontime by T. P. Anshutz
Steep bridge by E. Berman
Steeplechase by L. Gatch
Steeplechase horses by R. J. Bové
Steeplechase park by R. Marsh
STEFANELLI, Joseph, 1921-
  Occasion
    WMAA.  Annual ex, 1957
  Ponte Margherita
    IU.  Contemp Amer ptg & sculp, 1961

Stein, Gertrude, 1874-1946
  Tomlin, B. W.  Number 9: in praise of
    Gertrude Stein
STEIN, Ronald Jay, 1930-
  Hommage à Andrés Segovia
    PPC.  International ex, 1958
STEIN, Walter, 1930-
  Boy holding lamb's head
    ICA.  Annual ex, 1957
  The pillow
    IU.  Contemp Amer ptg, 1952
STEINBERG, Saul, 1914-
  Gentleman hunter          NBuA
    NBuA.  Acquisitions 1954-57
    Portrait of the artist
  Bouché, R.  Saul Steinberg
Steinberg, Mrs Saul.  See Sterne, Hedda
STEINITZ, Kaethe, 1889-
  Pine trees          CtY
    CtY.  Soc Anonyme
Steinman, Mrs John F.
  Watkins, F. C.  Mrs John F. Steinman
Stele by S. Davis
STELLA, Frank, 1936-
  Arundel castle
    MMA.  Sixteen
  Die fahne hoch!
    MMA.  Sixteen
  Marriage of reason and squalor
    MMA.  Sixteen
  Tomlinson court park
    MMA.  Sixteen
STELLA, Joseph, 1880-1946
  American landscape
    Janson.  Picture history
  Battle of light, Coney island          CtY
    Baur.  New art
    Baur.  Revolution
    Brown.  Amer ptg
    CtY.  Soc Anonyme
    Hess.  Abstract ptg
    Hunter.  Mod Amer ptg (col)
    McCurdy
    MMA.  Abstract
    NUM.  Art across America
    Pierson
    WMAA.  Juliana Force
    WMAA.  Pioneers
  The bridge (Brooklyn bridge)          NJN
    Larkin (detail)
    Larkin rev ed
    Pierson
    Richardson.  Ptg in America
    Time.  300 years (col)
  Brooklyn bridge          CtY
    Baur.  Revolution
    Blesh
    Brown.  Amer ptg
    Cheney.  Primer 1958 ed
    Cheney.  Story 1958 ed
    CtY.  Soc Anonyme
    Gardner.  1959 ed
    Gruskin
    Janson.  Key monuments
    MMA.  Abstract
    Pierson
    Rosenblum
  Brooklyn bridge—Variation on an old
    theme
    Baur.  New art (col)
    Goodrich.  Amer art (col)
    ICA.  Amer artists paint the city

**STELLA, Joseph**—*Continued*
Gas tank
  WMAA. Neuberger collection
The port from New York interpreted NJN
  Baur. Revolution
  Brown. Amer ptg
Skyscrapers (central panel of New York interpreted) NJN
  Baur. New art
  Mendelowitz
Spring CtY
  Baur. Nature
  Baur. New art
  MMA. Abstract
  Pierson
Voice of the nightingale
  NYG. Fine art
**Stella** by H. V. Olson
**Stenographer** by W. De Kooning
**Stepping** out by E. J. Kosa
**Steps** to the lighthouse by Y. Johnston
**STERNBERG, Harry,** 1904-
Mexican ruin
  PPC. Ptg in the U.S. 1949
**STERNE, Hedda,** 1916-
Alaska 1 NBuA
  NBuA. Acquisitions 1957-58
Grandfather
  ICA. Annual ex, 1947/48
M. R. D.
  IU. Contemp Amer ptg & sculp, 1961
New York
  ICA. Amer artists paint the city (col)
Number 32, 1952
  Pousette-Dart. Amer ptg
Roads no 6
  PPC. International ex, 1958
**STERNE, Maurice,** 1878-1957
After rain DP
  DP. Catalogue
After the rain MMA
  Time. 300 years (col)
After the storm
  IU. Contemp Amer ptg, 1950
  PPC. Ptg in the U.S. 1949
Bali bazaar WMAA
  Goodrich. Amer art
  Pierson
Bazaar with coconut palms, Bali MM
  MM. 100 Amer ptrs
Benares DP
  DP. Catalogue
  WMAA. Pioneers
Benares on the Ganges
  NAD. Annual ex, 1957
Breadmakers MB
  Baur. Revolution
  Pierson
Eggs with carafe
  Lewisohn
Expression of an impression MM
  CoS. New accessions USA, 1952
  NAD. Annual ex, 1958
Girl in blue dress MMA
  Cheney. Story 1958 ed
Higgins pier
  IU. Contemp Amer ptg, 1948
Maine coast MB
  MB. Ptgs in water color
Mother and child DP
  DP. Catalogue

Peasant girl
  Cheney. Primer 1958 ed
Plum girl
  NYG. Fine art
Provincetown seascape
  Lewisohn
Reapers DP
  Cheney. Expressionism 1948 ed
  Cheney. Primer 1958 ed
Resting at the bazaar MMA
  Baur. Revolution
  Brown. Amer ptg
  Gruskin
  McCurdy
Sea gulls
  Genauer (col)
Sea, sand and wind
  PA. Annual ex, 1949
Still life MoSL
  MoSL. Handbook 1953
Summer shower
  IU. Contemp Amer ptg, 1949
Winding road
  Lewisohn
**STERNER, Harold,** 1895-
Beach scene with a newspaper MB
  MB. Ptgs in water color
**STETTHEIMER, Florine,** d 1944
Family portrait no 2 MMA
  MnMW. Reality and fantasy
  Pierson
**STETTINIUS, Samuel Enredy,** 1768-1815
    **Attributed works**
Jane L. Van Reid DN
  DN. Amer primitive ptgs
Mr and Mrs Wolfersberger
  Chew. 250 years of art
Wellington Van Reid DN
  DN. Amer primitive ptgs, pt 1
**Steuben, Friedrich Wilhelm Ludolf Gerhard Augustin, baron von,** 1730-1794
  Earl, R. Baron von Steuben
**Steve** by E. E. Speicher
**Stevedores** in the hole by M. Petersen
**Stevens, Ebenezer,** 1751-1823
  Turnbull, J. Ebenezer Stevens
**STEVENS, Edward John,** 1923-
Isle of the gods
  IU. Contemp Amer ptg & sculp, 1953
The jungle
  IU. Contemp Amer ptg & sculp, 1959
Mad bull
  ICA. Annual ex, 1947/48
Red bird
  Pousette-Dart. Amer ptg
Voyage of the gods
  IU. Contemp Amer ptg, 1952
**Stevens, Elizabeth (Allen)** 1713-1778
  Copley, J. S. Elizabeth Allen Stevens
**Stevens, Isaac Ingalls,** 1818-1862
  Stanley, J. M. Gov Stevens at Fort Benton
**STEVENS, John**
Sioux Indians attacking a Minnesota farm MnSH
  Ford. Pictorial folk art
**Stevens, Sophie Candace.** See Page, Sophie Candace (Stevens)
**Stevens, Mrs William.** See Stevens, Elizabeth (Allen)

STEVENS, William Lester, 1888-
  Mill stream
    NAD. Annual ex, 1947, 2d half
Stevenson, Mrs Andrew. See Stevenson,
    Sarah (Coles)
Stevenson, Robert Louis, 1850-1894
  Sargent, J. S. Robert Louis Stevenson
Stevenson, Sarah (Coles) fl 1841
  Healy, G. P. A. Mrs Andrew Stevenson
Stevenson memorial angel by A. H. Thayer

Stew by C. H. Carter
STEWARD, Joseph, 1750-1822
  John Phillips                          NHD
    Flexner. Light of distant skies
    ICA. From colony to nation
Stewart, Charles, 1778-1860
  Sully, T. Capt Charles Stewart
Stewart, Ira, fl 1846
  Mason, B. F. Ira Stewart
Stewart, Isabella. See Gardner, Isabella
    (Stewart)

Sticks and stones by J. L. Lasker
STIEFFEL, Hermann, b 1826
  Fort Harker, Kansas                    DNC
    Rathbone
  Fort Keough, Montana                   DNC
    Rathbone
  Miles city, Montana                    DNC
    Rathbone
  Sa-tan-ti addressing the Peace commis-
    sioners at Council Grove             DNC
    Rathbone
  Wichita mountains from the Medicine
    Bluffs                               DNC
    Rathbone
  Yellowstone river near Fort Keough
                                         DNC
    Rathbone
Stieglitz, Alfred, 1864-1946
  Chase, W. M. Alfred Stieglitz
Stieglitz, Mrs Alfred. See O'Keeffe, Georgia
Stiles, Ezra, 1727-1795
  Moulthrop, R. Ezra Stiles
  Smibert, N. Ezra Stiles
STILL, Clyfford E. 1904-
  1907—Y
    NBuA. Still
  1907-8—W
    NBuA. Still
  1938—N
    NBuA. Still
  1941—R
    NBuA. Still
  1943—J
    NBuA. Still
  1943—M
    NBuA. Still
  1944—A
    NBuA. Still
  1944—G
    NBuA. Still
  1944—N
    NBuA. Still
  1945—H
    NBuA. Still
  1945—R
    NBuA. Still
  1946—C
    NBuA. Still
  1946—E
    NBuA. Still

  1946—H
    NBuA. Still
  1946—L
    NBuA. Still
  1946—M
    NBuA. Still
  1946—T
    NBuA. Still (col)
  1947—F
    NBuA. Still
  1947—G
    NBuA. Still
  1947—H-No 1
    NBuA. Still
  1948—B
    NBuA. Still
  1948—D
    NBuA. Still
  1948—E
    NBuA. Still
  1948—S
    NBuA. Still
  1949—D
    NBuA. Still
  1950—A
    NBuA. Still (col)
  1950—B
    NBuA. Still
  1950—K
    NBuA. Still
  1950—M-No 1
    NBuA. Still (col)
  1951—D
    NBuA. Still
  1951—K
    NBuA. Still
  1954—S
    NBuA. Still
  1955—D
    NBuA. Still
  1955—H
    NBuA. Still (col)
  1956—H
    NBuA. Still
  1956—J
    NBuA. Still
  1957—D no 1
    NBuA. Acquisitions 1959-1961 (col)
  1957—G
    NBuA. Still
  1957—J
    NBuA. Still (col)
  Number 2, 1949
    Art since 1945 (col)
    Hunter. Mod Amer ptg (col)
    MMA. New Amer ptg (col)
  A painting
    CSFP. Annual ex, 1948/49
  Painting, 1947 (1)
    MMA. Fifteen
  Painting, 1947 (2)
    MMA. Fifteen
  Painting, 1949
    MnMW. 60 Amer ptrs
  Painting, 1951                         MMA
    McCurdy
    MMA. New Amer ptg
    Pierson
    Read. Concise history
  Red and black                          NBuA
    Eliot. Art of our time (col)
    NBuA. Acquisitions 1957-58 (col cover)

**STILL, C. E.**—*Continued*
Untitled
  CSFP. Annual ex, 1950/51
Untitled                                    SwB
  Ponente. Mod ptg, 1960
Still harbor by C. A. Morris
Still life by S. Amato
Still life by M. Avery
Still life by J. Badger
Still life by W. A. Baziotes
Still life by W. F. Benson
Still life by G. Cope
Still life by A. Dasburg
Still life by S. Davis
Still life by W. De Kooning
Still life by C. H. Demuth
Still life by P. Dickinson
Still life by S. C. Edie
Still life by P. Evergood
Still life by J. F. Francis
Still life by M. Goldberg
Still life by A. Gorky
Still life by E. N. Griffith
Still life by W. M. Harnett
Still life by M. Hartley
Still life by L. E. Hess
Still life by C. R. Holty
Still life by E. Isenburger
Still life by M. Kantor
Still life by W. Keane
Still life by H. Lever
Still life by H. B. McCarter
Still life by H. L. McFee
Still life by A. H. Maurer
Still life by A. Ozenfant
Still life by A. C. Peale
Still life by M. A. Peale
Still life by Raphaelle Peale
Still life by S. M. Peale
Still life by W. Plate
Still life by A. Pope
Still life by M. Powers
Still life by M. Ramsey
Still life by K. Schrag
Still life by C. Sheeler
Still life by R. Soyer
Still life by M. Sterne
Still life by D. Teague
Still life by B. W. Tomlin
Still life by F. C. Watkins
Still life by M. Weber
Still life by J. A. Weir
Still life by T. Yerxa
Still life: apples by H. L. McFee
Still life at Christmas by A. B. Serwazi
Still life: balsam apples and turnips by
  Raphaelle Peale
Still life: book, pipe, beer stein by J. F.
  Peto
Still life, bread and peppers by M. Weber

Still life, camera flashlight by M. L. Scham-
  berg
Still life—crabapples in blue bowl by W. J.
  Glackens
Still life—delphinium by P. W. Zimmerman
Still life, Egyptian pot by M. Weber
Still life: fruit by M. Hartley
Still life—fruit and nuts by Raphaelle Peale
Still life, fruit and pottery by W. M. Chase
Still life, fruit in a monogrammed bowl,
  "R. P." by M. J. Peale
Still life in gold and green by S. Menkès
Still life in gray by R. Brackman
Still life in green by A. Leepa
Still life in primary colors by B. Browne
Still life in red, yellow, white and blue by
  A. Leepa
Still life in white by L. Blanch
Still life in winter by C. E. Burchfield
Still life, melons by R. Lebrun
Still life, New York by W. Drewes
Still life on a sewing machine by J. J. P.
  Meert
Still life—oranges by H. L. McFee
Still life: pear by A. H. Maurer
Still life: pipe, beer stein, book by J. F.
  Peto
Still life, pitcher by C. Sheeler
Still life: salt glaze pot, pipe and Le Figaro
  by W. M. Harnett
Still life—striped bass by W. M. Chase
Still life: the blue vase by W. Sommer
Still life with a green jar by H. L. McFee
Still life with apples by M. B. Prendergast
Still life with apples and chestnuts by J. F.
  Francis
Still life with ashtray by A. H. Maurer
Still life with banjo by L. Karp
Still life with black bottle by A. Blatas
Still life with blue vase by S. Menkès
Still life with bottles by C. Brown
Still life with bric-a-brac by W. M. Harnett
Still life with brushes and pottery by W. M.
  Chase
Still life with cake by Raphaelle Peale
Still life with cake, raisins and nuts by
  M. A. Peale
Still life with Christmas candy by J. Wilde
Still life with cockatoo by W. M. Chase
Still life with coffee pot by R. D'Arista
Still life with currants by J. Wilde
Still life with dead leaves by M. Marcus
Still life with decanter by H. L. McFee
Still life with derby by M. Avery
Still life with doily by A. H. Maurer
Still life with figure by R. Brackman
Still life with fish by W. M. Chase
Still life with fish by N. Vasilieff
Still life with fish—a skate by W. M. Chase
Still life with fish and pinwheel by M.
  Beckmann
Still life with fish bowl by J. Peale
Still life with fish, brass kettle, lemon and
  onions by W. M. Chase

Still life with flower and insects by T. R. Peale

Still life with flowers by M. Beckmann

Still life with flowers by S. Davis

Still life with flowers by M. Weber

Still life with fruit by H. G. Keller

Still life with fruit by J. Peale

Still life with fruit by Rubens Peale

Still life with fruit and flowers by S. Roesen

Still life with glasses and roses by C. Brown

Still life with grapes by J. Peale

Still life with herring by Raphaelle Peale

Still life with horns by B. Spruance

Still life with hourglass by H. Muller

Still life with ivy by H. L. McFee

Still life with Johnson's dictionary by Unidentified artist

Still life with landscape by C. Brown

Still life with lanterns by J. F. Peto

Still life with letter to Thomas B. Clarke by W. M. Harnett

Still life with lobster by N. Vasilieff

Still life with melon and grapes by S. M. Peale

Still life with melons by Unidentified artist

Still life with melons by B. Wood

Still life with milk bottle by W. Meigs

Still life with mirror by A. Rattner

Still life with nude by J. Floch

Still life with onion rolls by M. Goldberg

Still life with oysters by A. Rattner

Still life with palette by A. Gorky

Still life with palette by M. Weber

Still life with peaches by Raphaelle Peale

Still life with pears by A. H. Maurer

Still life with playbill by N. A. Brooks

Still life with portrait of the artist's daughter by J. F. Peto

Still life with raisin cake by Raphaelle Peale

Still life with red fish by L. Hartl

Still life with red plush and thistle by J. C. Bradley

Still life with saw by S. Davis

Still life with skull by A. Gorky

Still life with skull by F. Martin

Still life with skulls by J. Kirschenbaum

Still life with steak by Raphaelle Peale

Still life with strawberries by A. C. Peale

Still life with tankard by W. M. Harnett

Still life with thistles by M. Frary

Still life with three glasses by W. Glackens

Still life with two tables by M. Weber

Still life with vegetables by Raphaelle Peale

Still life with violin by W. M. Harnett (attributed works)

Still life with watermelon by J. Peale

Still life with watermelon by Raphaelle Peale

Still life with watermelon by Unidentified artist

Still life with white cloth by H. L. McFee

Still life with wine bottles and basket of fruit by J. F. Francis

Still life with yellow-green chair by P. Dickinson

Still music by B. Shahn

STILLMAN, William James, 1828-1901
Philosophers' camp in the Adirondacks (unfinished sketch)                MCoL
Jones. Rediscovered ptrs

Stillman sisters by A. H. Thayer

Stillness by J. Ernst

Stillness and reflections by K. Schrag

STOCK, Joseph Whiting, 1815-1855
Child in wicker basket (Baby in wicker basket)                DN
DN. Amer primitive ptgs, pt 1
Ford. Pictorial folk art
Fisherman with his dog                MSM
Lipman. Primitive ptrs
MSM. Handbook
Horace Wilson Eddy                VWR
Ford. Pictorial folk art
Jane Henrietta Russell
Ford. Pictorial folk art
Lipman. Primitive ptrs
Jasper Raymond Rand                NJN
Pierson
Luther Stock
Lipman. Primitive ptrs
Mary Jane Smith                VWR
VWR. Amer folk art (col)
VWR. Folk art (col)
Parsons family
Ford. Pictorial folk art
Wilcox children                DN
DN. Amer primitive ptgs, pt 2
William Howard Smith                VWR
VWR. Amer folk art (col)
VWR. Folk art (col)
Young hammerer                NCHA
Jones. New-found folk art

Attributed works
Mary Amidon                MSM
Ford. Pictorial folk art

Stock, Luther, b 1811
Stock, J. W. Luther Stock

Stock exchange, New York city by J. Marin

Stockton, California by A. D. Browere

STODDARD, Alice Kent
Leila                PR
PR. Catalogue

Stokes, Edith (Minturn) d 1937
Sargent, J. S. Mr and Mrs Isaac Newton Phelps Stokes

Stokes, Isaac Newton Phelps, 1867-1944
Lockman, D. M. I. N. Phelps Stokes
Sargent, J. S. Mr and Mrs Isaac Newton Phelps Stokes

Stokes, Mrs Isaac Newton Phelps. See Stokes, Edith (Minturn)

STOKES, John Stogdell, 1870-1947
Wedding in the Big Smoky mountains
Davidson v2

Portrait of the artist
Watkins, F. C. J. Stogdell Stokes

Stokes, Mrs M. S.
Eakins, T. Mrs M. S. Stokes

STOLTENBERG, Donald, 1927-
Blue building
MBIC. View 1960
STONE, William Oliver, 1830-1875
Eleazer Thompson Fitch     CtY
CtY. Portrait index
Samuel F. B. Morse     CtY
CtY. Portrait index
The stone by H. Bloom
Stone angel by B. Cross
Stone city by G. Wood
Stone cottage, Hanover, New Hampshire by M. T. Chapin
Stone garden by Y. Ohashi
Stone in the tree by Y. Tanguy
Stone matrix by C. A. Morris
Stonehenge by W. W. Baumgartner
Stonington and the harbor, Maine by J. Marin
Stonington harbor by J. Marin
Stony beach, Ogunquit by M. B. Prendergast
Store and gear by K. Knaths
Storer, Clement, fl 1829
Cole, J. G. Clement Storer
Storer, Ebenezer, 1730-1807
Dunkerley, J. Ebenezer Storer (possibly after Copley)
Storer, Elizabeth. See Smith, Elizabeth (Storer)
Storm by G. C. Bingham
Storm by A. Ippolito
Storm by M. Kantor
Storm by A. V. Tack
Storm by Y. Tanguy
Storm approaching Narragansett bay by M. J. Heade
Storm at sea by R. W. Salmon
Storm at the Bahamas by W. Homer
Storm brewing by L. Feininger
Storm clouds in silver by A. G. Dove
Storm clouds, Maine by M. Hartley
Storm coming by J. L. Howard
Storm composition number 4 by A. Rattner
Storm departs by P. Fine
Storm-frightened animals by H. G. Keller
Storm-frightened horses by H. G. Keller
Storm in the mountains by A. Bierstadt
Storm over Narragansett bay by M. J. Heade
Storm over Taos by J. Marin
Storm tide by E. H. Betts
Storm tide by R. Henri
Storm: waiting for the caravan by A. J. Miller
Stormy sky, Venice by W. Barker
Stormy weather by W. H. Singer
Storrs, Constant, fl 1802
Jennys, W. Constant Storrs
Storrs, Mrs Constant, 1758-1839
Jennys, W. Mrs Constant Storrs
Story, Margaret
Bellows, G. W. Margarite
Story of the cross by A. P. Ryder

Stoughton, William, 1631-1701
Unidentified artist. William Stoughton
STOUT, Myron S. 1908-
Number 3, 1957
PPC. International ex, 1958
Stoutenburg, Jacobus, b 1696
Unidentified artist. Jacobus Stoutenburg
Stoutenburg, Margaret (Teller) b 1696
Unidentified artist. Mrs Jacobus Stoutenburg
Stoves
Kuniyoshi, Y. Stove and bouquet
Wood, G. Dinner for threshers
Stowing sails, Bermuda by W. Homer
Strachan, Margaret. See Harwood, Margaret (Strachan)
Strahmutchi by R. S. Du Casse
STRAND, Paul, 1890-
Circular forms
Brown. Amer ptg
Stranded boat by M. J. Heade
STRANG, Ray, 1893-
Horse power
Carlson. Gallery (col)
Native's return
Carlson. Gallery (col)
Slow poke
Carlson. Gallery (col)
Spring
Carlson. Gallery (col)
Waiting for the mail
Carlson. Gallery (col)
Water
Carlson. Gallery (col)
Wood gatherers
Carlson. Gallery (col)
Strange thing little Kiosai saw in the river by J. La Farge
A stranger passed by K. Sage
Strata by J. E. Levi
Strategist by C. di Marca-Relli
STRATER, Henry, 1896-
Cape Nedick     ATU
ATU. Coll of Amer art
Colts at Soda Springs
NYG. Fine art
Winter in the Verde valley
NYG. Fine art
Strathmere by W. Stuempfig
Stratton, Barnard, b 1796
Willson, Mr. Barnard Stratton of Amherst, New Hampshire
Straw bridge by M. B. Prendergast
Strawberries and cherries by M. A. Peale
Strawbridge, James, fl 1802
Malbone, E. G. James Strawbridge
Stream and distant hills by B. West (attributed works)
Street, Augustus Russell, 1791-1866
Jocelyn, N. Augustus Russell Street
STREET, Robert, 1796-1865
Likeness of himself     MB
MB. Karolik coll
The street by M. Beckmann
The street by P. Guston
The street by J. Levine
The street by L. MacIver
The street by B. Perlin

Street and bridge by S. Davis
Street by the mill by S. Rosenberg
Street corner by P. Evergood
Street corner incident by W. De Kooning
Street corner, Paris by F. Koester
Street crossing, New York by J. Marin
Street dance by B. Perlin
Street in Paris by L. Feininger
Street in Stillwater by C. Booth
Street in Tepoztlan, Mexico by K. Zerbe
The street is young with spring by L. Mac-
    Iver
Street movement, abstraction, New York by
    J. Marin
Street music by W. Stuempfig
A street, Perugia by F. Crowninshield
Street scene by P. Burlin
Street scene by G. Grosz
Street scene by R. Marsh
Street scene, Boston by M. B. Prendergast
Street scene in Seville by T. Eakins
Street scene in winter by C. Hassam
A street seeing by J. Marin
Street urchins by D. G. Blythe
The strenuous life by C. M. Russell
Striated forest by C. A. Morris
**STRICKLAND, William, 1787-1854**
    View on the Susquehanna
        McClintock

### Portrait of the artist

Neagle, J. William Strickland
The strike—trout fishing by J. B. Sword
String composition number 50 by C. S. Fuller
String construction by C. S. Fuller
String music by M. Weber
String of pearls by E. Melcarth
String quartette by J. Levine
String trio by G. L. K. Morris
Strings of amber by Tseng Yu-ho
Strip tease by R. Marsh
Stripper by R. Marsh
Strolling by C. H. Demuth
**STROMBOTNE, James, 1934-**
    Execution
        IU. Contemp Amer ptg & sculp, 1961
    The group
        WMAA. Young America 1960
    Red torso
        WMAA. Young America 1960
    Three bathers
        WMAA. Contemp Amer ptg, 1959-60
**Strong, Theodore, 1790-1869**
    Ames, E. Theodore Strong
Strong woman and child by Y. Kuniyoshi
Structure by M. Tobey
The struggle by R. Goodnough
The struggle by R. S. Neuman
Strunsky house by L. MacIver
Stryker sisters by R. Earl
**STUART, Duncan Robert, 1919-**
    Matrix
        Pousette-Dart. Amer ptg

**STUART, Gilbert, 1755-1828**
    Benjamin West                        ELNP
        Roos
    Caleb Whitefoord                     NJMo
        NJMo. Forty years
        NJMo. Your Montclair art museum
    Charles Davis                        NoCR
        NoCR. Catalogue
    David Humphreys                      CtY
        CtY. Portrait index
    Edward Loftus                        InIJ
        InIJ. 105 ptgs
    Edward Shippen of Pennsylvania       DC
        DC. Masterpieces
    Elizabeth Boardley                   PA
        Roos
    Francis and Saunders Malbone
        Flexner. Light of distant skies
    Gabriel Manigault                    NBuA
        NBuA. Catalogue of the ptgs
    George Washington                    MWiS
        MWiS. Ex 4 and 7
    George Washington
        Taylor. Fifty centuries, 1954 ed (col)
    George Washington (Allibone type) OCiM
        OCiM. Guide
    George Washington (Athenaeum type)
                                         MB
        Craven. Rainbow book
        Craven. Treasury 1952 ed (col)
        Flexner. Amer ptg
        Flexner. Light of distant skies
        Flexner. Short history
        MB. Great Americans
        Mendelowitz
        NYG. Fine art
        Pierson
        Roos
        UNESCO. Prior to 1860
        UNESCO. Prior to 1860 3d ed
        UNESCO. Prior to 1860 5th ed
    George Washington (Athenaeum type)
                                         MoSL
        MoSL. Handbook 1953
    George Washington (Gibbs-Channing-
        Avery type)                      MM
        NYG. Fine art
        Roos
        UNESCO. Prior to 1860
        UNESCO. Prior to 1860 3d ed
        UNESCO. Prior to 1860 5th ed
    George Washington (Lansdowne type) PA
        Flexner. Light of distant skies
        ICA. From colony to nation
        Pierson
        Time. 300 years (col)
    George Washington (Miller-Cake-J. Stew-
        art portrait)                    PR
        PR. Catalogue
    George Washington (Vaughan type) DN
        DN. Mellon coll
        Flexner. Light of distant skies
        Pierson
    George Washington (Vaughan-Sinclair
        type)                            DN
        DN. Mellon coll
    George Williams
        MdBMu. Rendezvous
    Henrietta Elizabeth Frederica Vane MNS
        NUM. Art across America
    Henry Knox                           MB
        MB. Great Americans

**STUART, Gilbert**—*Continued*
Horatio Gates
  Flexner. Light of distant skies
Isaac Coffin
  Barker. Amer ptg
Isaac de Abraham Touro          MSE
  MSE. Cat of ports, 1950
James Heath                  CtHW
  CtHW. Handbook
James Madison             MAC
  ICA. From colony to nation
James Monroe             MM
  ICA. From colony to nation
James Monroe             PA
  Time. 300 years (col)
James Ward               MnMi
  Roos
John Adams
  Larkin
  Larkin rev ed
  Pierson
John Henderson
  CLA. 35 ptgs
John Quincy Adams (finished by T. Sully)
                        MCH
  Time. 300 years (col)
John Randolph           DN
  DN. Mellon coll
John Young
  Chew. 250 years of art
Joseph Coolidge         DN
  DN. Mellon coll
Joseph de Jaudenes y Nebot    MM
  Pierson
Josiah Quincy            MB
  MB. Great Americans
Lawrence Yates          DN
  DN. Mellon coll
Martha Washington       MB
  MB. Great Americans
  NYG. Fine art
Mathilde de Jaudenes y Nebot   MM
  Larkin
  Larkin rev ed
  Pierson
Mrs Charles Davis         NoCR
  NoCR. Catalogue
Mrs Gabriel Manigault     NBuA
  NBuA. Catalogue of the ptgs
Mrs George Plumstead      PA
  Flexner. Light of distant skies
Mrs James Bard           NJMo
  NJMo. Forty years
Mrs John Bannister and her son   RNR
  Pierson
Mrs John Thompson Mason    OCl
  OCl. Handbook
Mrs John Wickham
  DC. Privately owned
Mrs Josiah Quincy
  DC. Privately owned
Mrs Maria Barclay Young
  Chew. 250 years of art
Mrs Perez Morton         MWM
  Larkin rev ed (col detail)
  Lee. Art then and now
  Pierson
  Robb. Art 1953 ed
  Robb. Harper history
  Roos
  Walker. Ptgs from America

Mrs Richard Yates          DN
  Barker. Amer ptg
  Craven. Treasury 1962 ed
  DN. Mellon Coll
  Gardner 1959 ed
  McKinney
  Mendelowitz
  MoSL. 40 masterpieces
  Pierson
  UNESCO. Prior to 1860
  UNESCO. Prior to 1860 3d ed
  UNESCO. Prior to 1860 5th ed
  Walker. Ptgs from America
Mrs Stephen Peabody      ATeS
  ATeS. Collection
Mrs Stephen Salisbury I     MWM
  ICA. From colony to nation
Nathaniel Bowditch
  Flexner. Light of distant skies
  CtY. Portrait index
Oliver Wolcott            CtY
  CtY. Portrait index
Petrus Stuyvesant       MNHS
  Vail. Stuyvestant ports
Richard Yates            DN
  DN. Mellon coll
Sir Joshua Reynolds       DN
  DN. Mellon coll
  Flexner. Light of distant skies
The skater              DN
  Craven. Treasury 1952 ed
  Pierson
  Time. 300 years (col)
  Walker. Ptgs from America (col)
Study head            MoSL
  MoSL. Handbook 1953
Thomas Jefferson        MeB
  Myers. Art
  Upjohn
Thomas Macdonough     DN
  DN. Mellon coll
Two girls sewing
  CtY. Handbook
Washington at Dorchester Heights
  Richardson. Ptg in America
Webb sr               OYB
  OYB. Catalogue 1951
William Cooper of Cooperstown
  CtY. Yale alumni
William Ellery Channing
  Flexner. Light of distant skies
William Redwood       RNR
  Roos
        Portrait of the artist
Goodridge, S. Gilbert Stuart
Neagle, J. Gilbert Stuart
Peale, C. W. and Peale, Rembrandt. Gilbert Stuart
**STUART, James Reeve, 1834-1915**
Sword, pistols, and teacup    MB
  MB. Karolik coll
Stubb and Starbuck by B. Robinson
**STUCKER, F.**
Albany Schoharie stagecoach
  Ford. Pictorial folk art
Studebaker, John Mohler, 1833-1917
  Powell, H. M. T. J. M. Studebaker in his wagon tire shop at Hangtown, California, 1853
Studio tapestry by L. Gatch
Studios
  Beckmann, M. Studio corner
  Bennett, R. Red studio

Burkhardt, H. G. Studio of G
Carr, L. Remington's studio
Chase, W. M. Alice in the Shinnecock studio
Chase, W. M. Duveneck in the studio
Chase, W. M. Self-portrait (Artist in his Fifth avenue studio) 1915
Chase, W. M. Tenth street studio
Demuth, C. H. Studio interior
Eakins, T. William Rush and his model
Eakins, T. William Rush carving his allegorical figure of the Schuylkill river
Eastman, W. Studio table
Frankenstein, J. P. The artist in his studio
Giacometti, A. The studio
Greene, B. The studio
Grosz, G. Model in the studio
Hamilton, J. M. Paul Wayland Bartlett in his Paris studio
Hofmann, H. Studio no 1 in grey
Hovenden, T. Self-portrait
Kaplan, J. Interior
Matteson, T. H. Sculptor's studio
Mintz, R. A. Artist's studio
Mommer, P. Studio interior
Pittman, H. Studio in Charleston
Ricci, J. In the studio
Rosenthal, T. E. The cardinal's portrait
Soyer, M. David Burliuk in his studio
Soyer, R. In the studio
Watkins, F. C. The studio
Weir, J. F. Artist's studio
Wood, G. Turner alley studio
The study by G. R. Davis
The study by G. L. Mueller
Study for a soldier by R. Lebrun
Study head by G. Stuart
Study in black and green by J. W. Alexander
Study in brown by N. E. Craig
Study in curves by W. M. Chase
Study in red—morning news at the camp by E. Johnson
Study in space V by L. Feininger
Study of a head after Couture by J. A. M. Whistler
Study of a house by J. La Farge
Study table by W. M. Harnett
STUEMPFIG, Walter, 1914-
    End of day                                    MAP
        CoS. New accessions USA, 1956
    Float on the Schuylkill
        CtY. Yale alumni
    Manayunk
        CSFP. Annual ex, 1947/48
        Time. 300 years (col)
    The railroad bridge
        MoSL. Contemporary Amer ptg
    The reprimand                                 PPhM
        CoS. New accessions USA, 1948
    Sculling                                      NJMo
        NJMo. Forty years
    Spring song
        Chew. 250 years of art
    Strathmere
        CSFP. Annual ex, 1950/51
    Street music                                  InIJ
        Bazin
        InIJ. 105 ptgs
    The tempest                                   OT
        OT. Contemp Amer ptgs

Three alone
    PPC. International ex, 1952
Thunderstorm II                                   MM
    MM. 100 Amer ptrs
    Pierson
    PPC. Ptg in the U.S. 1949
Trajan and the children                           NBuA
    NBuA. Contemporary ptgs
Two houses                                        DC
    DC. 20 biennial ex, 1947
    Gruskin
    Mendelowitz
    Wight. Milestones (col)
Via Partenope
    NAD. Annual ex, 1952
The wall                                          PA
    MMA. Contemp ptrs
West Wildwood                                     CSFP
    CoS. New accessions USA, 1950
    CSFP. Handbook
Stuka by G. L. Mueller
Stump speaking by G. C. Bingham
STURGIS, Katharine, 1904-
    Pigeon cove, Rockport, Massachusetts MB
    MB. Ptgs in water color
STURGIS, Mabel Russell, b 1865
    Heavy sea, Manchester                         MB
    MB. Ptgs in water color
Sturtevant, Mrs Eugene. See Clark, Mary Rebecca
Stuyvesant, Augustus Van Horne, 1838-1918
    Baker, G. A. (attributed works). Augustus Van Horne Stuyvesant sr
    Williams, A. A. V. H. Stuyvesant
Stuyvesant, Catharine Livingston (Reade) 1775-1862
    Durand, A. B. Mrs Nicholas William Stuyvesant
Stuyvesant, Gerard, 1805-1859
    Hicks, T. Gerard Stuyvesant
Stuyvesant, Mrs Gerard. See Stuyvesant, Susan Rivington (Van Horne)
Stuyvesant, Gerardus, 1690-1777
    McIlworth, T. Gerardus Stuyvesant
Stuyvesant, Harriet LeRoy (Steward) 1842-1872
    Baker, G. A. (attributed works) Mrs A. V. H. Stuyvesant
    Fagnani, G. Mrs A. V. H. Stuyvesant
    Unidentified artist. Mrs A. V. H. Stuyvesant (as a child)
Stuyvesant, Margaret (Livingston) 1738-1818
    Unidentified artist. Mrs Petrus Stuyvesant
Stuyvesant, Nicholas William, 1722-1780
    McIlworth, T. Nicholas William Stuyvesant
    Unidentified artist. Nicholas William Stuyvesant
Stuyvesant, Nicholas William, 1769-1833
    Unidentified artist. Nicholas William Stuyvesant
Stuyvesant, Mrs Nicholas William. See Stuyvesant, Catharine Livingston (Reade)
Stuyvesant, Peter, 1592-1672
    Couturier, H. (attributed works) Governor Stuyvesant
    Unidentified artist. Governor Peter Stuyvesant
Stuyvesant, Peter Gerard, 1778-1847
    Unidentified artist. Peter Gerard Stuyvesant

Stuyvesant, **Petrus,** 1727-1805
  Stuart, G. Petrus Stuyvesant
**STUYVESANT, Susan Rivington (Van Horne)** 1812-1899
  The trumpeter                          NNHS
    Vail. Stuyvesant ports
      **Portrait of the artist**
  Staigg, R. M. Mrs Gerard Stuyvesant
**Stuyvesant family**
  Unidentified artist. Gerard Stuyvesant family group
**STYKA, Tadé,** 1889-1954
  Tigers
    NSP. Sportscapes
Subercaseaux, Ramón, fl 1880
  Sargent, J. S. Señor Subercaseaux in a gondola in Venice
**Subjective** landscape by R. Rosenborg
**Submerged** by H. Hofmann
**Substance** and sustenance by N. Tschacbasov
**Subterranean** by R. Pousette-Dart
**Suburb** in Havana by W. De Kooning
**Suburban** figure by K. Finch
**Subway** by C. Enders
**Subway** by H. Koerner
**Subway** by G. Tooker
**Subway** lights by L. MacIver
**Subway** platform by R. Soyer
**Subway** scene by I. Bishop
**Succession** of feelings by S. Sekula
**Succubus** by P. Mangravite
**Sudbury,** Massachusetts, Old homestead at by Unidentified artist
**Suddarth, Martha Morris,** fl 1840
  Toole, J. Mrs Martha Morris Suddarth
**Suddarth, Mary Jane.** See Toole, Mary Jane (Suddarth)
**Suddarth, Richard Pleasants,** fl 1840
  Toole, J. Richard Pleasants Suddarth
**Suddarth, Tempe McCutchen,** fl 1840
  Toole, J. Tempe McCutchen Suddarth
**Sudden** windstorm over the Vega by H. G. Keller
**Suffering** softens stones by Y. Tanguy
**Suede** and tiger stripe by C. A. Morris
**Sugar** levee, New Orleans by V. V. Sebron
**Sugar** loaf mountain by A. Fisher
**Sugar** mill on Bayou Teche, Oliver plantation by A. Persac
**Sugaring-off** by A. M. R. Moses
**Sugaring-off** in Maple orchard by A. M. R. Moses
**Suicide** in costume by F. C. Watkins
**Suicide** of Judas by J. Brewton
**Suites** illimitées by Y. Tanguy
**Sulking** boy by G. B. Luks
**SULLIVAN, Charles,** 1794-1867
  Marietta earth works
    Ford. Pictorial folk art
Sullivan, Elizabeth (Russell) 1779-1854
  Malbone, E. G. Mrs John L. Sullivan
Sullivan, John Langdon, 1777-1865
  Malbone, E. G. J. L. Sullivan
Sullivan, Mrs John Langdon. See Sullivan, Elizabeth (Russell)
Sullivan, John Lawrence, 1858-1918
  Bellows, G. W. Introducing John L. Sullivan

**SULLIVAN, Patrick,** 1894-
  Fourth dimension
    MnMW. Reality and fantasy
Sullivan, Sarah (Russell) 1786-1831
  Malbone, E. G. Mrs Richard Sullivan
Sullivan street abstraction by G. C. Ault
Sully, Jane Cooper. See Darley, Jane Cooper (Sully)
Sully, Sarah (Annis) 1770-1867
  Sully, T. Thomas Sully and Mrs Sully
  Trumbull, J. Mrs Thomas Sully
**SULLY, Thomas,** 1783-1872
  Andrew Jackson, 1845                     DN
    Time. 300 years (col)
  Andrew Jackson (Long coll)
    DC. Privately owned
  Charles Stewart                          DN
    Pierson
  Elizabeth Wignall                        OYB
    OYB. Catalogue 1951
  Fanny Kemble as Bianca                   PA
    Flexner. Amer ptg
    Flexner. Light of distant skies
    Flexner. Sport history
  Frances Kemble, sketch                   MB
    Larkin
    Larkin rev ed
  George Cadwalader
    Chew. 250 years of art
  Jean T. David                            OCl
    Pierson
  John Biddle                              MM
    NYG. Fine art
    UNESCO. Prior to 1860
    UNESCO. Prior to 1860 3d ed
  John Connelly                            ATeS
    ATeS. Collection
  John Myers                               MB
    MB. Karolik coll
  Lady with a harp: Eliza Ridgely          DN
    Flexner. Light of distant skies
    PA. Annual ex, 1955
    Pierson
  Levi Fletcher
    CtY. Yale alumni
  Mary Sicard David                        OCl
    Pierson
  Miss C. Parsons as the Lady of the Lake
                                           KLU
    NUM. Art across America
  Mrs Edward Hudson                        MiD
    MiD. Treasures
    PA. Annual ex, 1955
  Mrs Henry Robinson                       InIJ
    InIJ. 105 ptgs
  Mrs James Montgomery                     MM
    NYG. Fine art
    UNESCO. Prior to 1860
    UNESCO. Prior to 1860 3d ed
  Mrs John Boucher Morris
    MdBMu. Rendezvous
  Mrs John Redman Coxe
    Chew. 250 years of art
  Mother and son (Mrs William H. W. Darley and Francis Thomas Sully Darley)                               MM
    Mendelowitz
    Pierson
  Passage of the Delaware (Washington at the passage of the Delaware)    MB
    Mendelowitz
    Pierson
    Richardson. Ptg in America
  Queen Victoria
    Taylor. Fifty centuries, 1954 ed (col)

Rebecca Cornell Biddle          NJMo
  NJMo. Your Montclair art museum
Samuel Coates
  Barker. Amer ptg
  ICA. From colony to nation
  Pierson
  Walker. Ptgs from America
Self-portrait          MM
  MdBMu. Rendezvous
Self-portrait          PH
  Roos
Thomas Biddle          PA
  PA. Annual ex, 1955
Thomas Handasyd Perkins          MBA
  Pierson
Thomas Jefferson          CtY
  CtY. Portrait index
Thomas Sully and Mrs Sully          CtY
  CtY. Portrait index
Torn hat          MB
  Roos
  UNESCO. Prior to 1860 3d ed
  UNESCO. Prior to 1860 5th ed
Victor René Value and his daughter Char-
  lotte          MB
  MB. Karolik coll
Washington at the passage of the Dela-
  ware. See Passage of the Delaware
William Edmonds Horner
  PA. Annual ex, 1955 (detail)
William Henry Hoffman
  MdBMu. Rendezvous (replica)
SULLY, Thomas, 1783-1872 and SULLY,
  Thomas Wilcocks, 1811-1847
Thomas Biddle          DN
  DN. Mellon coll
Sulphurous evening by C. E. Burchfield
Sultan's tomb, Fez, Morocco by G. O. Hart
Summit of Antelope valley by E. J. Kosa
Summer by V. Candell
Summer by A. G. Dove
Summer by O. Dozier
Summer by C. S. Du Back
Summer by S. Francis
Summer by P. Guston
Summer by W. Kahn
Summer by B. Karfiol
Summer by D. E. Lee
Summer by E. Magafan
Summer by R. Natkin
Summer by G. Peterdi
Summer by M. B. Prendergast
Summer by G. Prestopino
Summer by A. Rogoway
Summer by J. H. Twachtman
Summer by A. Walkowitz
Summer by M. Weber
Summer afternoon by C. E. Burchfield
Summer afternoon by R. Parker
Summer afternoon by S. Serisawa
Summer bounty by D. Nichols
Summer bouquet by H. V. Poor
Summer breezes by R. Philipp
Summer day by M. Beckmann
Summer day by R. Eshoo

Summer day by M. B. Prendergast
Summer day by A. C. Runquist
Summer day by J. H. Twachtman
Summer days by G. O'Keeffe
Summer 8, 1957 by M. Tobey
Summer flowers by A. B. Carles
Summer flowers with two chairs by H. Pip-
  pin
Summer holiday by J. Corbino
Summer house by M. Goldberg
Summer in the Catskills by T. Doughty
Summer landscape by S. Davis
Summer landscape by G. H. Durrie
Summer night by B. Browne
Summer night by W. Homer
Summer night, East side park by J. Myers
Summer night, Provincetown, Massachusetts
  by J. Whorf
Summer night, Riverside drive by G. W.
  Bellows
Summer orchard by A. G. Dove
Summer outing on the rocks by M. B. Pren-
  dergast
Summer shower by M. Sterne
Summer squall by W. Homer
Summer still life by E. Berman
Summer storm by Y. Johnston
Summer storm by Y. Kuniyoshi
Summer storm by R. Rauschenberg
Summer storm on Sunday afternoon by A.
  Shulkin
Summer thoughts in winter by K. Schrag
Summer twilight by S. Davis
Summer vista by K. Matthew
Summer wind by A. Brook
Summer's end by C. W. Rain
Summer's end by M. Schapiro
Summer's fruitful pasture by A. P. Ryder
Summertime by W. M. Chase
Summertime by M. Kantor
Summertime by J. Pollock
Summertime by B. Shahn
The sun by K. Knaths
Sun after rain by M. Phillips
Sun and rocks by C. E. Burchfield
Sun bath by J. Glasco
Sun bathers by W. Peirce
Sun chariot by M. Samant
Sun dance by G. Catlin
Sun dance by F. Remington
Sun filled fields by K. Schrag
Sun games by T. Stamos
Sun, isles and sea by J. Marin
Sun King and merganser by M. Peterson
Sun on the lake by B. Krauskopf
Sun setting through the catalpas by C. E.
  Burchfield
Sun sinking in Tyrzona by C. Cloar
Sun sinking into the sea by K. Schrag
Sun trap by J. W. Boynton
Sun treader—portrait of Carl Ruggles by
  T. H. Benton

Sun valley by Martyl
Sun worshipper by J. La Farge
Sun worshippers by C. M. Russell
Sun-a-get, a Pottawattomie chief by J. O. Lewis
Sunbath by J. Glasco
Sunburst by W. Thon
Sunday by A. M. R. Moses
Sunday afternoon by Z. L. Sepeshy
Sunday football by B. Shahn
Sunday in the country by G. H. Durrie
Sunday in Union square by J. Sloan
Sunday morning by G. Beal
Sunday morning by A. B. Durand
Sunday morning by H. Packman
Sunday morning breakfast by H. Pippin
Sunday morning in Gordon park, Cleveland by H. G. Keller
Sunday morning in the mines by C. C. Nahl
Sunday morning in Virginia by W. Homer
Sunday on Main street by E. Hopper
Sunday painters by A. A. Dehn
Sunday painting by B. Shahn
Sunday promenade by M. B. Prendergast
Sunday school room by A. N. Wyeth
Sunday sun by P. Cadmus
Sunday walk by E. D. Glackens
Sunday, women drying their hair by J. Sloan
Sunflower by R. F. Gates
Sunflower by K. Knaths
Sunflower by R. H. Laessig
Sunflower patterns by H. G. Keller
Sunflowers by H. G. Keller
Sunflowers and goldfinches by R. F. Gates
Sunken ledges by C. H. Woodbury
Sunlight and shadow by W. M. Chase
Sunlight and shadow by A. S. Wall
Sunlight on brownstones by E. Hopper
Sunlight on the coast by W. Homer
Sunlight on the Piazzetta, Venice by M. B. Prendergast
Sunny blue sea by C. Hassam
Sunny morning by F. C. Watkins
Sunny morning on the Hudson by T. Cole
Sunny side of the street by P. Evergood
Sunrise by R. A. Blakelock
Sunrise by S. Davis
Sunrise I, 1937 by A. G. Dove
Sunrise II, 1937 by A. G. Dove
Sunrise III, 1937 by A. G. Dove
Sunrise at Uponohu, Society islands by J. La Farge
Sunrise fishing in the Adirondacks by W. Homer
Sunrise in the stratosphere by D. Porter
Sun's path by H. G. Keller
Sunset by L. Feininger
Sunset by M. J. Heade
Sunset by J. Marin
Sunset by M. B. Prendergast
Sunset by G. Prestopino

Sunset and sea fog by M. B. Prendergast
Sunset and white trees by L. Harmon
Sunset, Black rock, Connecticut by M. J. Heade
Sunset by the river by Unidentified artist
Sunset, Casco bay by J. Marin
Sunset fires by L. Feininger
Sunset, Gloucester by L. J. Liberté
Sunset, High bridge by E. Lawson
Sunset hour by A. P. Ryder
Sunset in the fields by H. B. McCarter
Sunset in the mountains by H. W. Rice
Sunset: Lake Champlain by M. J. Heade
Sunset Mount Carmel, Connecticut by G. H. Durrie
Sunset on a quiet sea by M. Avery
Sunset on Long beach by M. J. Heade
Sunset over the marshes by M. J. Heade
Sunset, Saco Bay by W. Homer
Sunset: tropical marshes by M. J. Heade
Sunshine and shadow by G. Hetzel
Super table by S. Davis
Supplication by F. Castellón
Supplying camp with buffalo meat by A. J. Miller
The Supreme Court of California by B. Shahn
Surf at Ogunquit, Maine by E. Decombes
Surf birds by M. Graves
Surf fisherman by E. F. Spruce
Surf, Point Lookout by E. W. Dickinson
Surf reflected upon higher space by M. Graves
Surf, ten mile by I. E. Nordfeldt
Surf under moonlight by F. J. Waugh
Surgery by S. Radulovic
Surprise attack by C. M. Russell
Surprise party by M. Hoff
Surprised wader by P. Evergood
The surround by A. J. Miller
Surround of buffalo by Indians by A. J. Miller
Surveyor's wagon in the Rockies by A. Bierstadt
Surviving trace of something by W. A. Gaw
Survivor by G. Grosz
Survivors by R. Ray
Survivors by K. Zerbe
Susan by A. S. Andersen
Susanna and the elders by T. H. Benton
Susanna and the elders by B. Shahn
Susannah and the elders by W. Shirlaw
Suspended discs by G. L. K. Morris
Suspended forms by E. E. Boccia
Suspension bridge at Niagara falls by Unidentified artist
Suspension bridge for swallows by K. Sage
Suspension of forms by C. R. Holty
Susquehanna river
  Cropsey, J. F. Starrucca viaduct, Susquehanna valley
  Mifflin, L. The Susquehanna below Wrightsville, Pennsylvania, View of

Montalant, J. O. The Susquehanna
Shaw, J. On the Susquehanna
Strickland, W. View on the Susquehanna
**Sutliff, Betsy (Mulford)** 1792-1871
Ames, E. Mrs Henry Sutliff
**SUTTON, W.** fl 1820
Young girl with music book
Ford. Pictorial folk art

### Attributed works

Girl with a cat MSM
Ford. Pictorial folk art
**Swamp** country by A. Blanch
**Swamp** folk by A. Blanch
**SWAN, Barbara,** 1922-
Interior
MBIC. View 1960
**Swan** island by V. Flannery
**Swans**
Audubon, J. J. Trumpeter swan
Graves, M. Moor swan
Jones, J. Landscape with swans
Prendergast, M. B. The swans
Whorf, J. Swans
**Sweet** hour of prayer by P. S. Sample
**Swift, Joseph Gardner,** 1783-1865
Jarvis, J. W. Gen Joseph Gardner Swift
**Swimming** hole by T. Eakins
**Swimming** off West Washington market by
R. Marsh
The **swing** by W. J. Glackens
**Swing** landscape by S. Davis
**Swinging** chairs by R. Marsh
**Swimmers** and sunbathers by M. Avery
**SWINNERTON, James E.** 1875-
After the shower
Carlson. Gallery (col)
Deserted Navajo home
Carlson. Gallery (col)
Deserted Navajo trading post
Carlson. Gallery (col)
Grand Canyon
Carlson. Gallery (col)
Moonrise—northern Arizona
Carlson. Gallery (col)
Navajoland
Carlson. Gallery (col)
**Swinton, Elizabeth (Ebsworth)**
Sargent, J. S. Mrs George Swinton
**Swinton, Elsie**
Sargent, J. S. Elsie Swinton
**Swiss** mountains by E. Decombes
**SWORD, James Brade,** 1839-1915
A good day's work—return from duck
hunt
NSP. Sportscapes
The strike—trout fishing
NSP. Sportscapes
The **sword** by K. Davies
**Sword,** pistols, and teacup by J. R. Stuart
Les **sylphides** by G. R. Davis
**Sylvan** episode by D. Lutz
**Sylvia** by W. M. Paxton
**Symbol** of the sun and moon by P. Riba
**Symbolical and allegorical themes**
Blashfield, E. H. Power of the law
Cole, T. Voyage of life: Childhood
Cole, T. Voyage of life: Youth
Cooper, J. Allegorical figures

Cox, K. The light of learning
Eakins, T. William Rush carving his alle-
gorical figure of the Schuylkill river
Hunt, W. M. Anahita, the flight of night
Hunt, W. M. Flight of night
Kennedy, T. J. Symbolical painting
La Farge, J. Athens
Morse, S. F. B. Allegorical landscapes
Pachner, W. Israel
Pachner, W. Maternità
Peale, Rembrandt. Court of Death
Sargent, J. S. Classic and romantic art
Shahn, B. Allegory
Thayer, A. H. Florence protecting the
arts
Unidentified artist. Allegory of freedom
Unidentified artist. Aurora
Unidentified artist. Civil war—Symbolical
panorama
Unidentified artist. Columbia
Unidentified artist. Miss Liberty
West, B. Air, Water, Earth, Fire
**Symbols** by W. R. Garver
**Symbols** of our time by Ben-Zion
**Symbols** over the west by M. Tobey
**SYMONDS, Gardner,** 1863-1930
Silence and evening light OYB
OYB. Catalogue 1951
Symonds, **George Gardner.** See Symonds,
Gardner
**Symphony** by M. Oppenheimer
**Symphony** in brown and silver by J. A. M.
Whistler
**Symphony** in white by J. A. M. Whistler
**Symphony** in white no 2 by J. A. M. Whistler
**Synagogue** by H. Bloom
**Synagogue** by S. Drumlevitch
**Synagogue** by J. Friebert
**Synchroformic** no 4, staccato by J. Senn-
hauser
**Synchroformic** no 27 by J. Sennhauser
**Synchroformic** no 28, étude in yellows by
J. Sennhauser
**Synchromie** cosmique by M. Russell
**Synchromy** by S. MacDonald-Wright
**Synchromy** in green and orange by S. Mac-
Donald-Wright
**Synchromy** no 2 to light, 1912 by M. Russell
**Synchromy** no 3 by S. Macdonald-Wright
**Synchromy** no 3, color counterpoint by M.
Russell
**Synchromy** to form by M. Russell
**Synchromy** to form: orange by M. Russell
**Syracuse, New York**
Culverhouse, J. M. Clinton square, Syra-
cuse, N.Y.

### T

T by A. A. Gottlieb
T—1954 by J. D. Brooks
**Tabb, Mrs John,** fl 1850
Hubard, W. J. Mrs John Tabb
**Tabb, Maria Mason.** See Hubard, Maria
Mason (Tabb)
**Tabb, Martha (Tompkins)**
Hubard, W. J. Mrs Henry Wythe Tabb

Table by A. Blanch
Table by J. P. Jones
Table of fruit by G. A. Keniston
Table with bottles and cheese by R. D'Arista
Table with cyclamens by J. Binford
Table with fish and scales by C. Brown
Table with glasses and napkin by C. Brown
Table with glasses and roses by C. Brown
Table-talk by G. Grosz
Tabletop by B. Dyer
Tabletop by K. Knaths
**TACK, Augustus Vincent,** 1870-1949
  Aspiration                                      DP
    DP. Catalogue
  Passacaglia                                    DP
    DP. Catalogue
  Storm                                          DP
    DP. Catalogue
  Voice of many waters                           DP
    DP. Catalogue
**Taft, Robert Alphonso,** 1889-1953
  Shahn, B. Dewey, Vandenberg and Taft
**Taft, William Howard, president U.S.** 1857-
  1930
  Kendall, W. S. William Howard Taft
**Tagert, Joseph,** 1758-1849
  Neagle, J. Joseph Tagert
**TAGUE, Robert Bruce,** 1912-
  Attic windows
    NAD. Annual ex, 1955
**Tah-ro-hon,** an Iowa warrior by G. B. King
**Tailer, Elizabeth.** See Nelson, Elizabeth
  (Tailer)
**TAIT, Arthur Fitzwilliam,** 1819-1905
  American frontier life                         CtY
    Rathbone
  Barnyard                                       OYB
    OYB. Catalogue 1951
  Buffalo hunt
    Davidson v2
  Duck shooting
    Davidson v2
  On the warpath
    McCracken. Portrait of the old west
    (col)
  Saved—a hard chase
    NSP. Sportscapes
  Striped-bass fishing
    Davidson v2
  Trappers at fault looking for the trail
    Rathbone
  Young buck and doe
    NSP. Sportscapes
**TAIT, Arthur Fitzwilliam,** 1819-1905 and
  **GAY, Edward,** 1837-1928
  Deer at the lake
    NSP. Sportscapes
**TAIT, Arthur Fitzwilliam,** 1819-1905 and
  **HART, James McDougal,** 1828-1901
      Attributed works
  The Burden family enjoying the Hudson
    river near Troy                           NAI
    Jones. Rediscovered ptrs
**Taj** Mahal by W. G. Congdon
The **Taj** Mahal by E. S. Field
**TAKAI, Teiji**
  Metamorphosis
    WMAA. Contemp Amer ptg, 1959/60
**Take** my picture, mister by I. Rose

**TAKEHITA, Natsuko**
  Autumn landscape
    MM. Amer ptg today
**Taking** off by W. T. Murch
**Taking** sunflower to teacher by W. Homer
**Taking** the count, Study for head of referee
  by T. Eakins
**Taking** the hump rib by A. J. Miller
**Talcott family,** fl 1832
  Goldsmith, D. Talcott family
**Tales** of love by G. Ortman
**Talk** by W. W. Quirt
**Tall** building by C. W. Smith
The **tall** red by O. Osver
**Tallmadge, Benjamin,** 1754-1835
  Ames, E. Benjamin Tallmadge
**Tallmadge, Mrs Benjamin,** 1763-1805. See
  Tallmadge, Mary (Floyd)
**Tallmadge, Mrs Benjamin,** d 1838. See Tall-
  madge, Maria (Hallett)
**Tallmadge, Elizabeth (Clinton)** 1780-1825
  Ames, E. Mrs Matthias Burnett Tallmadge
**Tallmadge, Maria (Hallett)** d 1838
  Ames, E. Mrs Benjamin Tallmadge
**Tallmadge, Mary (Floyd)** 1763-1805
  Earl, R. Mrs Benjamin Tallmadge
**Tallmadge, Matthias Burnett,** 1774-1819
  Ames, E. Matthias Burnett Tallmadge
**Tallmadge, Mrs Matthias Burnett.** See Tall-
  madge, Elizabeth (Clinton)
**Talmudic** student by W. Gropper
**Talpa** by A. Dasburg
**Talpa** graveyard by V. I. Cuthbert
**TAM, Reuben,** 1916-
  The coast of fog
    WMAA. Contemp Amer ptg, 1959/60
  Dark wave
    IU. Contemp Amer ptg & sculp, 1953
    Pousette-Dart. Amer ptg
  Flounder                                       OYB
    OYB. Catalogue 1951
  Horizon conditions                            NUM
    NUM. Root bequest
  Moon and shoals                               MMA
    Pierson
  Noon on the reef
    DC. 21 biennial ex, 1949
  Ridge and forecast
    IU. Contemp Amer ptg & sculp, 1959
  The salt sea
    IU. Contemp Amer ptg & sculp, 1961
  Sprouting coconuts
    CSFP. Annual ex, 1952
    IU. Contemp Amer ptg, 1951
**Tambourine** by J. Myers
**Taming** of the shrew by M. Ray
**Tampa** fair by A. Blanch
**Tamworth,** View near; In the White moun-
  tains by T. Cole
**Tan** and black on red by M. Rothko
The **Tanagra** by T. P. Anshutz
**Tang** horse by C. C. Ross
**Tangerine** moon and wine dark sea by M.
  Avery
**TANGUY, Yves,** 1900-1955
  The armoire of Proteus
    MMA. Yves Tanguy
  At the fair
    MMA. Yves Tanguy

Black landscape. See The storm
The boat
  MMA. Yves Tanguy
Closed sea, wide world
  MMA. Yves Tanguy
Closing days
  CtY. Yale alumni
  MMA. Yves Tanguy (col)
Conversation
  MMA. Yves Tanguy
Dame à l'absence
  Genauer (col)
De mains pâles aux cieux lassés
  MnMW. Reality and fantasy
  PPC. International ex, 1950
Divisibilité indéfinie. See Indefinite divisibility
The doubter
  MMA. Yves Tanguy
L'eau nue
  MnU. 40 Amer ptrs
Elle viendra
  Pearson. Mod renaissance
Ennui and tranquillity
  Jean. Surrealist ptg
Extinction of the species
  MMA. Yves Tanguy
  Read. Art now, 1948 ed
Extinction of useless lights          MMA
  MMA. Yves Tanguy
Fear          WMAA
  CoS. New accessions USA, 1950
  Goodrich. Amer art (col)
  Mendelowitz
  MMA. Yves Tanguy (col)
Fear          NBuA
  Pierson
Five strangers          CtHW
  CtHW. Handbook
  MMA. Yves Tanguy
  Moderns and their world
Four o'clock in summer: hope
  Raynal. History v3 (col)
From one night to the other          CSFP
  CSFP. Annual ex, 1948/49
  CSFP. Handbook
Furniture of time          MMA
  Janson. Picture history (col)
  MMA. Soby collection
  MMA. Yves Tanguy (col)
Genesis
  Jean. Surrealist ptg (col)
  MMA. Yves Tanguy
Girl with red hair
  MMA. Yves Tanguy
The glance of amber
  Jean. Surrealist ptg
Gouache, 1931          MMA
  MMA. Yves Tanguy
He did what he wanted
  MMA. Yves Tanguy
Hérédité des caractères
  Pearson. Mod renaissance
Hunted sky
  MMA. Yves Tanguy
Illimited sequences
  PA. Annual ex, 1953
Indefinite divisibility (Divisibilité indéfinie)
  McCurdy
  MMA. Yves Tanguy (col)
  NBuA. Contemporary ptgs
  Pierson

Lady of eleven
  MMA. Yves Tanguy
A large picture which is a landscape
  MMA. Yves Tanguy (col)
The last days
  Cheney. Story 1959 ed
The lovers
  MMA. Yves Tanguy
Ma vie blanche et noire. See My life white and black
Le malheur adoucit les pierres. See Suffering softens stones
Mama, Papa is wounded          MMA
  MMA. Masters (col)
  MMA. Yves Tanguy (col)
  Myers
Mirage of time          MM
  MMA. Yves Tanguy
The mood of now          MMA
  MMA. Soby collection
  MMA. Yves Tanguy
The mountebanks
  IU. Contemp Amer ptg & sculp, 1955
Movements and acts
  MMA. Yves Tanguy
Multiplication of the arcs          MMA
  50 years of mod art
  Jean. Surrealist ptg
  McCurdy
  MMA. Yves Tanguy (col)
  Pierson
My life white and black (Ma vie blanche et noire)
  Bazin. History of art
  CSFP. Annual ex, 1947/48
  MMA. Yves Tanguy
Old horizon
  MMA. Yves Tanguy
Palace of the windowed rocks
  MMA. Yves Tanguy
The parallels          PPhM
  PPhM. Arensberg coll
The rapidity of sleep          ICA
  Jean. Surrealist ptg
  MMA. Yves Tanguy
  Pierson
Real numbers
  Jean. Surrealist ptg
Ribbon of extremes
  Jean. Surrealist ptg (col)
  MMA. Yves Tanguy
A risk in each hand
  MMA. Yves Tanguy
Rose of the four winds
  MMA. Yves Tanguy
  MnU. 40 Amer ptrs
La rue de la Santé
  Jean. Surrealist ptg
  MMA. Yves Tanguy
Saltimbanques
  MMA. Yves Tanguy
Shadow country
  Canaday
  MMA. Yves Tanguy
Sifter of gold
  MMA. Yves Tanguy
Slowly toward the north          MMA
  McCurdy
  MMA. Yves Tanguy (col)
Stone in the tree          ATeS
  ATeS. Collection
The storm (Black landscape)          PPhM
  MMA. Yves Tanguy
  PPhM. Arensberg coll

**TANGUY, Yves—**Continued
Suffering softens stones (Le malheur adoucit les pierres)    IU
  IU. Contemp Amer ptg, 1949
  IU. 20th century
  MMA. Yves Tanguy
Suites illimitées                PA
  Pousette-Darte. Amer ptg
Sun on cushion
  Read. Concise history
Time and again
  Rathbun
Tower of the sea                MoSLW
  MMA. Yves Tanguy
Transparent ones
  MMA. Yves Tanguy
Untitled, 1947                MMA
  MMA. Soby collection
Water-table
  Jean. Surrealist ptg
When they shoot me
  MMA. Yves Tanguy
Where are you
  Jean. Surrealist ptg (col)
  MMA. Yves Tanguy
Wine, honey and oil
  MMA. Yves Tanguy
The wish
  IU. Contemp Amer ptg & sculp, 1953
With my shadow
  MMA. Yves Tanguy
The witness
  MMA. Yves Tanguy
Your tapers taper
  Jean. Surrealist ptg

**Tanguy, Mrs Yves.** See Sage, Kay

**Tanks** by A. G. Dove

**TANNER, Henry Ossawa,** 1859-1937
Banjo lesson
  Larkin
  Larkin rev ed (detail)

**TANNING, Dorothea,** 1910-
Fête champetre
  CSFP. Annual ex, 1947/48
Juke box
  IU. Contemp Amer ptg & sculp, 1955
Eine kleine nachtmusik
  Jean. Surrealist ptg
Palaestra
  Baur. Revolution
Profanation of the host
  Jean. Surrealist ptg
A very happy picture
  ICA. Annual ex, 1947/48

**Taormina**
Croninshield, F. Taormina
Hotchkiss, T. H. Taormina, the island of Sicily
Senat, L. Street in Taormina
Silsbee, M. Taormina and Mt Aetna

**Taos** by J. Marin

**Taos** landscape, New Mexico by J. Marin

**Taos** plaza by A. Dasburg

**Tapping** a furnace by G. P. Ennis

**TARBELL, Edmund Charles,** 1862-1938
Girl crocheting                NCa
  Pierson
Josephine and Mercie            DC
  Larkin
  Larkin rev ed
Timothy Dwight                CtY
  CtY. Portrait index

**Target** with four faces by J. Johns

**Tarkington, Booth,** 1869-1946
Betts, L. Booth Tarkington

**Tarquinia** by J. E. Heliker

**Tarrasa** by A. Yunkers

**Tarring** nets by J. E. Levi

**Tasker, Levi B.** fl 1830
Davis, J. H. Levi B. Tasker

**TATTERSALL, George**
Road to the west
  Davidson v2

**Tattle** tale grey by D. Lord

**Tattoo** and haircut by R. Marsh

**Tattooed** by M. Tobey

**TAUBES, Frederic,** 1900-
Figure study
  IU. Contemp Amer ptg & sculp, 1957
Phantasy on the martyrdom of St Sebastian
  PPC. Ptg in the U. S. 1949
Portrait of a painter
  Gruskin

**Taurus** by F. S. Okada

**Taverns.** See Hotels, restaurants, etc.

**Taxco** street by R. Thompson

**Taxi** by L. MacIver

**Taxi** dance hall by R. Marsh

**Taxidermist's** window by E. A. Chaves

**TAYLOR,** fl 1850
American slave market            CtC
  Davidson v 1

**Taylor, Abigail (Starr)** 1768-1845
Earl, R. Mrs William Taylor and child

**Taylor, Archibald,** fl 1802
Malbone, E. G. Archibald Taylor

**Taylor, John** 1742-1829
Ames, E. John Taylor

**TAYLOR, John Williams,** 1897-
The levee no 2
  NAD. Annual ex, 1951
The ramparts                InIJ
  InIJ. 105 ptgs
Tin, sand and tide
  IU. Contemp Amer ptg, 1949
The tower
  IU. Contemp Amer ptg, 1948

**Taylor, Mrs John Williams.** See Ruellan, Andrée

**Taylor, Maria.** See Byrd, Maria (Taylor)

**Taylor, Maxwell Davenport,** 1901-
Lockman, D. M. Gen Maxwell D. Taylor

**Taylor, Nathaniel William,** 1786-1858
Emmons, A. H. Nathaniel William Taylor

**TAYLOR, Richard,** 1902-
Returning                MB
  MB. Ptgs in water color

**Taylor, William,** 1764-1841
Earl, R. Col William Taylor

**Taylor, Mrs William.** See Taylor, Abigail (Starr)

**TAYLOR, William Ladd,** 1854-1926
Electric automobile, Boston, 1892
  Davidson v2

**Taylor, Zachary, president U.S.** 1784-1850
Unidentified artist. Major General Zachary Taylor

**TCHELITCHEW, Pavel,** 1898-1957
Bathers
  Read. Art now

Blue clown                         MMA
  MMA. Soby collection
Bull fight
  Myers
Burial of an acrobat               MWi
  McCurdy
Cabbage head                       MMA
  MMA. Soby collection
Derby hill theme: Hiawatha         CtHW
  CtHW. Handbook
Fallen rider
  Bazin
Fatma                              MoKN
  CoS. New accessions USA, 1958
  MoKN. Handbook
Fish bowl
  Wight. Milestones
The green lion                     CSB
  CoS. New accessions USA, 1950
Head of winter                     MMA
  MMA. Masters (col detail)
Hide-and-seek                      MMA
  Canaday
  Mendelowitz
  MMA. Ptg and sculpture
  Newmeyer
Madame Bonjean                     MMA
  MMA. Soby collection
The mirror
  CtY. Yale alumni
Revolving head
  Pousette-Dart. Amer ptg
The riddle of Daedalus
  ICA. Annual ex, 1947/48
Tree into hand and foot (study for Hide
    and seek)                      MMA
  MMA. Masters
Twilight head
  IU. Contemp Amer ptg, 1949
  Roos
The whirlwind                      MM
  MM. 100 Amer ptrs
Tea for one by J. Sloan
Tea party by H. Sargent
Tea time by W. M. Chase
TEAGUE, Donald, 1897-
  Mid-ocean
    NAD. Annual ex, 1947, 2d half
  Shipyard, Singapore
    NAD. Annual ex, 1952
  Still life
    NAD. Annual ex, 1949, 2d half
  Work stock
    NAD. Annual ex, 1946, 2d half
Team of horses by A. G. Dove
Teel, Henry
  Wyeth, A. N. Henry Teel
Teenagers by R. Gikow
Telegraph hill, San Francisco by Unidenti-
    fied artist
Telegraph pole by A. G. Dove
Telephone by M. L. Schamberg
Telephone habit by G. Baumgarden
Telephones by C. Browning
Television by S. Davis
Teller, Margaret. See Stoutenburg, Mar-
    garet (Teller)
Telling fortunes by G. B. Luks
The tempest by L. E. Kupferman
The tempest by D. Newman

The tempest by A. P. Ryder
The tempest by W. Stuempfig
Temple, Augusta Grenville, fl 1803
  Malbone, E. G. Augusta G. Temple
Temple, Elizabeth (Bowdoin) lady, 1750-
    1809
  Malbone, E. G. Lady Elizabeth Temple
  Trumbull, J. Sir John Temple and his
    family
Temple, Sir John, 8th bart, 1732-1798
  Trumbull, J. Sir John Temple and his
    family
Temple at Philae by H. R. Newman
Temple fragment by L. Siegriest
Temple gold medal nude by W. J. Glackens
Temple of Segesta with the artist sketching
    by T. Cole
Temple of the mind by A. P. Ryder
Temptation of St Anthony by J. Covert
Temptatlan of St Anthony by L. Guglielmi
Temptation of St Anthony by J. Muller
Temptation of St Anthony by H. Pippin
Temptation of St Anthony by A. Rattner
Temptation in Tonopah by F. Martin
10 A.M. by J. Koch
Ten cents a ride by L. Bouché
Ten miles to Salem by G. H. Durrie
10 P.M. by H. C. King
Ten shots ten cents by R. Marsh
The tenant by C. di Marca-Relli
Ten Broek, Christina, 1718-1801
  Unidentified artist. Christina Ten Broek
Tenement by G. Biddle
Ten Eyck, Catharina. See Van Zandt,
    Catharina (Ten Eyck)
Ten Eyck, Matthew, fl 1733
  Vanderlyn, P. Matthew Ten Eyck
Ten Eyck, Tobias, fl 1740
  Unidentified artist. Tobias Ten Eyck
Ten Eyck family, member of
  Unidentified artist. Girl of the Ten Eyck
    family
TENNEY, Ulysses Dow
  David Daggett                    CtY
    CtY. Portrait index
Tennis. See Games and sports—Tennis
Tennyson by J. Johns
Tenochtitlan by L. Siegriest
Tension by moonlight by B. W. Tomlin
Tens-qua-ta-wa, the Shawnee prophet by
    J. O. Lewis
Tenth street studio by W. M. Chase
Tents at Lake O'Hara by J. S. Sargent
Tepees
  Catlin, G. Comanche village in Texas
  Catlin, G. Crow chief at his toilet
  Catlin, G. A Crow tepee
  Catlin, G. Sioux village
  Miller, A. J. Fort Laramie
  Miller, A. J. Large encampment north
    of the Cut rocks
  Miller, A. J. Shoshone Indian and his
    pet horse
  Stanley, J. M. Assiniboin encampment on
    the upper Mississippi

Terminal by S. Davis

Terminal by X. Gonzales

Terminal by E. Lanyon

Termination of a militia sham fight by D. C. Johnston

**Terrace** by J. Floch

**Terrace** at Windsor, View from the by B. West

Terrace, Central park by G. R. Beal

Terraced mound in a snow storm at sunset by J. J. Egan

TERRELL, Elizabeth, 1908-
  Fisherman               ATU
    ATU. Coll of Amer art

Terror by K. Zerbe

Terror in Brooklyn by L. Guglielmi

TERRY, Luther, 1813-1900
  Jacob's dream          NNHS
    MiD. Travelers in Arcadia

Tess by W. Sommer

Test-able by R. Crawford

TESTER, Jefferson, 1900-
  The critic
    ICA. Annual ex, 1945/46

Teton range by T. Moran

Texas landscape no 3 by D. Reich

Textile mill worker by B. Shahn

Textile mills by B. Shahn

Textile merchant by Unidentified artist

TEYRAL, Hazel (Janicki) 1918-
  Figures with mobiles
    IU. Contemp Amer ptg, 1950
  Fragment: three heads
    IU. Contemp Amer ptg, 1948
  Fragment: two figures
    IU. Contemp Amer ptg, 1949

TEYRAL, John, 1912-
  Algerian soldiers        OYB
    OYB. Catalogue 1951
  Night worker
    IU. Contemp Amer ptg, 1950
  Rockport window
    PPC. Ptg in the U.S. 1949
  Rudy: midget
    IU. Contemp Amer ptg, 1948

Teyral, Mrs John. See Teyral, Hazel (Janicki)

Thacher, Thomas, 1620-1678
  Pollard limner. Thomas Thacher, so-called

The Thames from Battersea bridge by J. A. M. Whistler

The Thames in ice by J. A. M. Whistler

Thanksgiving by D. E. Lee

Thanksgiving day by D. E. Lee

That red one by A. G. Dove

That which I should have done I did not do by I. L. Albright

Thatcher, Margaret Ann. See Walton, Margaret Ann (Thatcher)

Thatcher, Rhoda Ann. See Davis, Rhoda Ann (Thatcher)

That's my doll! by Unidentified artist

Thayendanegea. See Brant, Joseph

THAYER, Abbott Henderson, 1849-1921
  Florence protecting the arts    MeB
  Pierson

Margaret MacKittrick      InIJ
  InIJ. 105 ptgs
Meditation            OYB
  OYB. Catalogue 1951
Self-portrait (Blagden coll)
  CtY. Yale alumni
Self-portrait, c 1898       NAD
  NAD. Amer tradition
Stevenson memorial angel    DNC
  DNC. Gellatly coll, 1954
  Pierson
Stillman sisters          NBM
  Larkin
  Larkin rev ed
The virgin             DF
  Time. 300 years (col)
Young woman           MM
  Mendelowitz
  MM. 100 Amer ptrs
Young woman in a fur coat    CtNB
  NUM. Art across America

Thayer, Catherine M. See Wetherby, Catherine M. (Thayer)

Thayer, Deliverance, fl 1800
  Brewster, J. (attributed works) Deacon Eliphaz Thayer and his wife Deliverance

Thayer, Eliphaz, b 1750
  Brewster, J. (attributed works) Deacon Eliphaz Thayer and his wife Deliverance

Thayer, Sanford
  Elliott, C. L. Sanford Thayer

Thayer, Webster
  Shahn, B. Judge Webster Thayer

Thea by G. D. Brush

Theaters
  Cassatt, M. The loge
  Du Bois, G. P. Opera box
  Engel, T. The theatre
  Hopper, E. First row, orchestra
  Hopper, E. Sheridan theatre
  Hopper, E. Two on the aisle
  Searle, J. Interior of the Park theater, New York
  Shinn, E. Theatre
  Shinn, E. Theatre box
  Sloan, J. Carmine theatre
  Sloan, J. Little movie theater
  Smith, R. Old Holliday street theatre, Baltimore, 1839

THECLA, Julia
  I looked into a dream
    ICA. Annual ex, 1947/48
  Willow in the rain
    IU. Contemp Amer ptg, 1949
    PPC. Ptg in the U.S. 1949

Their only roof by H. Gottlieb

Theme and variations by A. Ozenfant

Theme of earth by W. Pachner

Theodore Roosevelt's cabin door by R. L. Goodwin

There is man in God by I. L. Albright

There were no flowers tonight by I. L. Albright

There were seven in eight by J. Pollock

Thetis bringing the armor to Achilles by B. West

Theus, Anne. See Lee, Anne (Theus)

THEUS, Jeremiah, 1719-1774
  Alexander Fraser
    Middleton. Jeremiah Theus

Barnard Elliott jr        SCGG
  Middleton. Jeremiah Theus
Charles Burnham Cochran
  Middleton. Jeremiah Theus
Christiana Broughton (copy of pastel by
  Henrietta Johnston)
  Middleton. Jeremiah Theus
Col Jones' grandchild (Sarah Jones)
  Middleton. Jeremiah Theus
Daniel Heyward
  Middleton. Jeremiah Theus
Daniel Horry
  Middleton. Jeremiah Theus
Daniel Ravenel        GST
  Middleton. Jeremiah Theus
  NUM. Art across America
Eleanor Ball
  Middleton. Jeremiah Theus
Elias Ball
  Middleton. Jeremiah Theus
Elizabeth Allen
  Middleton. Jeremiah Theus
Elizabeth Damaris Ravenel and her sister
  Middleton. Jeremiah Theus
Elizabeth Rothmaler        NBM
  Barker. Amer ptg
  Middleton. Jeremiah Theus
  Pierson
Elizabeth Smith
  Middleton. Jeremiah Theus
Gabriel Manigault        MM
  Middleton. Jeremiah Theus
Hutchinson boy
  Middleton. Jeremiah Theus
Isaac Holme
  Middleton. Jeremiah Theus
Isaac Motte (?)        DN
  Mendelowitz
James Habersham
  Middleton. Jeremiah Theus
Lionel Chalmers        MB
  Middleton. Jeremiah Theus
Little Alice Hayne
  Middleton. Jeremiah Theus
Mary Trusler
  Middleton. Jeremiah Theus
Maurice Keating
  Middleton. Jeremiah Theus
Mrs Algernon Wilson
  Middleton. Jeremiah Theus
Mrs Barnard Elliott jr
  Middleton. Jeremiah Theus
Mrs Daniel Heyward
  Middleton. Jeremiah Theus
Mrs Daniel Ravenel
  Middleton. Jeremiah Theus
Mrs Edward Richardson
  Middleton. Jeremiah Theus
Mrs Gabriel Manigault        MM
  Flexner. First flowers
  Middleton. Jeremiah Theus
Mrs Henry Izard
  Middleton. Jeremiah Theus
Mrs John Moore
  Middleton. Jeremiah Theus
Mrs Lionel Chalmers        MB
  Middleton. Jeremiah Theus
Mrs Paul Trapier III
  Middleton. Jeremiah Theus
Mrs Peter Manigault        SCCG
  Middleton. Jeremiah Theus
  Pierson

Mrs Rawlins Lowndes
  Middleton. Jeremiah Theus
Mrs Stephen Mazyck
  Middleton. Jeremiah Theus
Mrs Theus (traditionally Eva Rosanna
  Ainslie)
  Middleton. Jeremiah Theus
Mrs Thomas Grimball
  Middleton. Jeremiah Theus
Mrs William Hutson
  Middleton. Jeremiah Theus
Mrs William Lee
  Middleton. Jeremiah Theus
Mrs William Mazyck
  Middleton. Jeremiah Theus
Polly Ouldfield of Winyah        IBM
  Middleton. Jeremiah Theus
Ralph Izard as a boy
  Middleton. Jeremiah Theus
Rebecca Motte
  Middleton. Jeremiah Theus
Samuel Brailsford
  Middleton. Jeremiah Theus
Stephen Mazyck
  Middleton. Jeremiah Theus
Susannah Maybank
  Middleton. Jeremiah Theus
Thomas Grimball
  Middleton. Jeremiah Theus
William Mazyck
  Middleton. Jeremiah Theus
William Richardson        CtY
  CtY. Portrait index
  Middleton. Jeremiah Theus
William Wragg        MiD
  DC. Amer ptrs of the South
  Richardson. Ptg in America
Young William Branford
  Middleton. Jeremiah Theus

**Theus, Mrs Jeremiah,** fl 1755
  Theus, J. Mrs Theus (traditionally known
    as Eva Rosanna Ainslie)
**They** guard the night by R. Breinin
**They** pay to be seen by R. Marsh
**They** shall sail the seven seas by J. De Diego
**They** wait by Z. L. Sepeshy
**THIBAULT, Aimée,** 1780-1868
  Althea Lenox (?)        NNHS
    NNHS. Waldron Phoenix Belknap coll
  Lady of the Lenox family        NNHS
    NNHS. Waldron Phoenix Belknap coll
  Mrs Robert Maitland        NNHS
    NNHS. Waldron Phoenix Belknap coll
  Robert Lenox        NNHS
    NNHS. Waldron Phoenix Belknap coll
The **thicket** by D. Wingren
**Thiers, Louis Adolphe,** 1797-1877
  Healy, G. P. A. Louis A. Thiers
**Thieves** in the pantry by W. M. Harnett
**Things** and mess in classroom by J. Brown
**Things** I loved and did not keep by A. F.
  Radomski
**Things** on a table by H. L. McFee
**Think** of me, dear by L. Lewitin
The **thinker** by T. Eakins
**Third** avenue by F. J. Kline
**Third** avenue el by R. Crawford
**Third** avenue el by H. Gerardia
**Third** beach, Newport by J. F. Kensett
The **third** hand by H. Hofmann

Thirsty trapper by A. J. Miller
This architectural world by B. Greene
This is my playground by Y. Kuniyoshi
Thistles
   Ben-Zion. Large thistles
   Frary, M. Still life with thistles
Thomar, Portugal by J. S. Sargent
THOMAS, Howard, 1899-1959
   Fernandina
   Pierson
Thomas, Isaiah, 1749-1831
   Greenwood, E. A. Isaiah Thomas
   Sharples, J. Isaiah Thomas
THOMAS, J. fl 1810
   The ship Nancy, homeward bound   DN
   DN. Amer primitive ptgs, pt 2
THOMAS, John, 1927-
   Women on Victorian couch
   IU. Contemp Amer ptg & sculp, 1961
THOMAS, Mary Leath, 1905-1959
   We bought a fish   GAtM
   GAtM. Holbrook collection
THOMAS, Paul Middlebrook, 1875-
   Franklin Bowditch Dexter   CtY
   CtY. Portrait index
THOMPSON, A. E. fl 1847

Attributed works

   Wetumpka bridge, Alabama   MB
   MB. Karolik coll
   Pierson
THOMPSON, Cephas, 1775-1856
   Girl with dove   VWR
   VWR. Folk art (col)
THOMPSON, Jerome B. 1814-1886
   Harvest in Vermont
   Born
   Peep show   MB
   MB. Karolik coll
   A picnic in the woods of New England
      MB
   Pierson
   The picnic, near Mount Mansfield, Vermont   CSFD
   Pierson
THOMPSON, Ralston, 1904-
   The grudge   OYB
   OYB. Annual 1948
   OYB. Catalogue 1951
   Taxco street   OCiM
   CoS. New accessions USA, 1958
Thompson, Rosemary
   Watkins, F. C. Miss Rosemary Thompson
THOMPSON, Wordsworth
   Departing guests   NNHS
   NYG. Fine art (col)
Thompson-Neely house by J. Sharp
THON, William, 1906-
   After the fire
   IU. Contemp Amer ptg, 1948
   Aunt Thankful's farm
   Bazin
   The fountain
   IU. Contemp Amer ptg & sculp, 1951
   Light in autumn
   Time. 300 years (col)
   Maine quarry
   Pousette-Dart. Amer ptg
   Midnight quarry   WMAA
   Pierson

Night passage
   IU. Contemp Amer ptg, 1950
The outpost
   Gruskin (col)
Owl's head
   Genauer (col)
Padre Paolo of Pisa
   CSFP. Annual ex, 1948/49
Sea birds   MM
   Pierson
Sea gulls
   Gruskin (col)
Spring in Maine
   IU. Contemp Amer ptg, 1952
Spring mist
   IU. Contemp Amer ptg & sculp, 1955
Sunburst   OYB
   OYB. Annual 1956
   OYB. Supplement 1959
Vineyards in Tuscany
   NAD. Special ex, 1956
Thorndike sisters, fl 1841
   Unidentified artist. Thorndike sisters
Thornhill bar, Florida by W. Homer
Thornton, John, fl 1835
   Bingham, G. C. John Thornton
Thoroughbreds by C. C. Ross
Thorp, Aaron, fl 1826
   Ames, E. Aaron Thorp
Thorp, Mary (Dunn) fl 1826
   Ames, E. Mrs Aaron Thorp
THRALL, Donald, 1918-
   Entrance   OYB
   OYB. Annual 1951
   OYB. Catalogue 1951
The thread of life by G. C. Bingham
Threading light by M. Tobey
Threatened attack by A. J. Miller
Three by J. Pollock
3 A.M. by H. Maril
Three A.M., 1909 by J. Sloan
Three alone by W. Stuempfig
Three balls for five cents by J. Donaghy
Three bathers by D. Park
Three bathers by J. Strombotne
Three blues by J. Guerrero
Three boys on the shore by W. Homer
Three candidates for election by L. Gatch
Three children by J. F. Francis
Three children by W. M. Prior (manner of)
Three clowns by J. Berlandina
Three cows on hillside by M. Avery
Three dancers by Ben-Zion
Three dancers by M. Soyer
Three days of rain by C. E. Burchfield
Three doors by B. Shahn
Three doorways by M. Cone
Three figures by T. H. Benton
Three figures by J. Kramer
Three fishermen by R. Baker
Three forms by M. Rothko
Three friends by M. Avery
Three generations by C. M. Russell
Three gentlemen by J. Smibert
Three gold diggers by L. Carroll

Three horsemen by J. Corbino

Three horses in alarm by W. Sommer

Three jugs by M. Weber

Three kings by M. T. Kelly

Three literary gentlemen by M. Weber

The three-master by J. Marin

Three men by B. Shahn

Three men in a canoe by W. Homer

Three nudes by J. Marin

Three princesses by J. S. Copley

Three queens by S. P. Saffer

Three roses by A. Gorky

Three slickers by R. Iver

Three thousand miles to the point of beginning by K. Sage

Three towers by J. C. Atherton

Three trees by R. A. Blakelock

Three trees by C. E. Burchfield

Three trees by J. Twachtman

Threshing wheat by T. H. Benton

Threshold to success by P. Evergood

Throop, Deborah (Goldsmith). See Goldsmith, Deborah

Throop, Enos T. 1784-1874
   Ames, E. Enos T. Throop

Throop, George Addison, fl 1831
   Goldsmith, D. George Addison Throop

Throop, Mrs George Addison. See Goldsmith, Deborah

Through a frosty moon by A. G. Dove

Through a glass darkly by A. Bohrod

Through Coleman Hollow up the Allegheny
valley by J. Kane

Through the Luxembourg by M. Ray

Through the marshes by E. Berman

Through the pines, the ocean by W. Kienbusch

Through the window by F. D. Duncan

Through the woods by S. Laufman

Through to the sea by F. D. Duncan

Throughway by H. Gramatky

Thunderclap by C. E. Burchfield

Thunderstorm II by W. Stuempfig

Thunderstorm in the Rocky mountains by A.
Bierstadt

Thursby, Emma, 1845-1931
   Healy, G. P. A. Emma Thursby

THWAITES, Charles W. 1904-
   Portrait
      CSFP. Annual ex, 1946

Tibbits, George, 1763-1849
   Ames, E. George Tibbits

Tibbits, Sarah (Noyes) 1767-1846
   Ames, E. Mrs George Tibbits

Tiber below Perugia by G. Inness

Ticonderoga or Mount Defiance, View near
by T. Cole

Tidal by G. Peterdi

Tidal mill by A. Robertson

Tidewater by C. H. Carter

Tidewater shapes by J. E. Levi

TIFFANY, Louis Comfort, 1848-1933
   Old New York, c 1878          NBM
      Baur. Revolution
      U.S. National Capital sesquicentennial
      com

Tigers
   Austin, D. The tiger
   Austin, D. Tigress with three cubs
   Hirshfield, M. Tiger
   Pippin, H. Blue tiger
   Styka, T. Tigers

Tight dally and loose latigo by C. M. Russell

The tightrope by D. Austin

Tightrope dancer by M. Beckmann

Tilden children, fl 1840
   Mason, B. F. Julia, Ann and Harriet Tilden

Tilghman, Henrietta Maria. See Goldsborough, Henrietta Maria (Tilghman)

Tilghman, Mary
   Peale, C. W. Mary Tilghman

Tilghman, Richard, fl 1790
   Peale, C. W. Richard Tilghman

Tilghman, Tench, 1744-1786..
   Peale, C. W. Washington, Lafayette, and
   Tench Tilghman

TILLES, J. A. fl 1829
   Watch and fob          VWR
      VWR. Folk art (col)

Tilley, James, 1707-1765
   Copley, J. S. James Tilley, New England
   merchant

Tilted bowl by M. A. Haviland

Tilted horizon by J. Hultberg

Tilton family
   Davis, J. H. Tilton family

Tilyard, Charles Slade, 1820-1900
   Tilyard, P. Charles Slade Tilyard

TILYARD, Philip, 1787-1827
   Artist in his studio
      D.C. Amer ptrs of the South
   Charles Slade Tilyard
      MdBMu. Rendezvous
   First envoy from Santo Domingo     NBM
      DC. Amer ptrs of the South
   John Pendleton Kennedy
      DC. Privately owned

Timber line, Estes park, Colorado by G.
Peirce

Time by W. Gropper

Time and again by Y. Tanguy

Time and eternity by J. Haberle

Time and space by W. S. Schwartz

Time clock by W. T. Murch

Time echoes by S. Rosenberg

Time enclosure by C. A. Morris

A time for fear by J. Ernst

Time is money by F. Danton

Time of change by M. Graves

Time of change by N. Meitzer

The time of fire by W. De Kooning

Time table by W. T. Wiley

Time, tide and town by K. Knaths

Times square, abstraction no 1 by A. Walkowitz

Times square, abstraction no 2 by A.
Walkowitz

**Timescape** by J. Ernst
**Tin** by I. L. Albright
**Tin,** sand and tide by J. W. Taylor
**Tioga** point valley by J. O. Montalant
**Tired** by L. Rossbach
**Tired** violin by K. Knaths
**TIRRELL, George,** fl 1860
    View from waterfront, Sacramento, California
      Baur. Amer ptg
      Pierson
**'Tis** me O Lord by F. Martin
**Tishcohan** by G. Hesselius
**Titian's** goblet by T. Cole
**Tittering** female by W. W. Quirt
**Tivoli** by S. R. Gifford
**To** Edwin Booth by W. M. Harnett (attributed works)
**To** form synchromy by M. Russell
**To** Queequeg by P. Jenkins
**To** the ball by Y. Kuniyoshi
**To** the dock, Tadoussac by A. P. Lowrie
**To** the earth by R. W. Barnett
**To** the harbourmaster by J. Mitchell
**To** the rescue by W. Homer
**To** the sea by B. W. Tomlin
**To** the tomb by F. C. Watkins
**To** the yacht races by A. A. Abbot
**To** thine own self be true by S. M. Adler
**TOBEY, Mark,** 1890-
    Above the earth      ICA
      Baur. New art
      Cheney. Primer 1958 ed
    Agate world      WaS
      Cheney. New world history
      Cheney. Story 1958 ed
      Roberts. Mark Tobey (col)
    Allegro
      IU. Contemp Amer ptg & sculp, 1955
    Arena of civilization
      Roberts. Mark Tobey
    Awakening night      NUM
      Roberts. Mark Tobey (col)
    Broadway, 1936      MM
      Baur. New art
      Larkin rev ed (col)
      Pierson
    Burned over
      IU. Contemp Amer ptg, 1951
    Calligraphic
      Ponente. Mod ptg 1960 (col)
    Canals      WaS
      Read. Concise history
    Canticle      WMAA
      WMAA. Sara Roby
    City radiance
      Blesh
      ICA. Amer artists paint the city
      Ponente. Mod ptg, 1960
    Constellation
      Roberts. Mark Tobey (col)
    The cycle
      MnU. 40 Amer ptrs
    Dawn. See Prophetic light
    Desert town
      CSFP. Annual ex, 1952
    Drift for summer
      Baur. Nature
      MMA. Fourteen

    Drums, Indian and word of God
      MMA. Fourteen
    E pluribus unum      WaS
      MMA. Fourteen
      NBuA. Expressionism
    Edge of August      MMA
      Baur. New art (col)
      MMA. Masters
      WMAA. Contemp Amer ptg, 1953
    End of summer
      Roberts. Mark Tobey
    Forms follow man      WaS
      Roberts. Mark Tobey (col)
    Fossils
      Roberts. Mark Tobey
    Fountains of Europe      MB
      Eliot. Art of our time (col)
      Pierson
      Time. 300 years (col)
    Fragment of peace
      OCl. Some contemporary works
    Genesis
      Roberts. Mark Tobey
    Golden gardens
      OCl. Some contemporary works
    Gothic
      UNESCO. 1860-1955
      UNESCO. 1860-1959
    Harvest
      Ponente. Mod ptg, 1960 (col)
    Horn pipe
      NBuA. Expressionism
    Intersection
      Roberts. Mark Tobey (col)
    Journey in white
      50 years of mod art
    Lyric
      WMAA. Museum and its friends, 1959
    Marriage      DP
      DP. Catalogue
    Meditative series no 9, 1954
      Roberts. Mark Tobey (col)
      Seiberling
    Neon thoroughfare
      ICA. Amer artists paint the city
      Roberts. Mark Tobey
    New life (Resurrection)      WMAA
      Goodrich. Amer art (col)
    New York
      MMA. Fourteen
    New York tablet      NUM
      NUM. Root bequest
    1951
      Art since 1945
    Orpheus      WaS
      Pousette-Dart. Amer ptg
    Pacific circle
      Roberts. Mark Tobey (col)
    Pacific transition      MCH
      Pulitzer v2
    Partitions of the city      NUM
      MiA. Root coll
    Prehistoric playground
      CtY. Yale alumni
    Prophetic light (Dawn)
      MnMW. 60 Amer ptrs
    Red man—white man—black man      NBuA
      NBuA. Contemporary ptgs
    Remote field      MMA
      Larkin
      MMA. Fourteen

San Francisco street                          MiD
  ICA. Amer artists paint the city
  Richardson. Ptg in America
  Time. 300 years (col)
Space intangibles
  Hess. Abstract ptg (col)
Space ritual no 3
  OCl. Some contemporary works
Structure, 1946
  Hess. Abstract ptg
Summer 8, 1957
  Roberts. Mark Tobey (col)
Symbols over the west
  PPC. International ex, 1958
Tattooed
  Roberts. Mark Tobey (col)
Threading light                               MMA
  McCurdy
  Mendelowitz
Transit                                       MM
  Baur. New art
  MM. 100 Amer ptrs
  Time. 300 years
Tropicalism
  Art since 1945 (col)
  ICA. Annual ex, 1951
  Read. Concise history (col)
Tundra
  Baur. Revolution
  Hunter. Mod Amer ptg (col)
  IU. Contemp Amer ptg, 1949
  MMA. Fourteen
Universal field                               WMAA
  Goodrich. Amer art
  MnU. 40 Amer ptrs
  Pierson
Untitled, 1960
  PPC. International ex, 1961/62
White journey
  Roberts. Mark Tobey (col)
Window
  ICA. Annual ex, 1954
Yellow harvest
  Roberts. Mark Tobey (col)
**Tod, David**
  Crawford, J. S. Gov David Tod
**Todd, Robert Llewellyn,** 1792-1825
  Jouett, M. H. Robert Llewellyn Todd
**Tofellini** by P. Guston
The **toilers** by M. Weber
**Toilers** of the sea by R. Kent
**Toilers** of the sea by A. P. Ryder
La **toilette** by M. Cassatt
**Toiling** hands by P. Evergood
**Toledo** I by P. M. Gish
**Toledo** blade by W. M. Harnett
**Toledo,** Spain, View of by H. Mintz
**TOLEGIAN, Manuel J.** 1912-
  Afternoon at Tony's                      ATU
   ATU. Coll of Amer art
**Toll** rope by A. N. Wyeth
**Tolling** bell by P. Fine
**Tolling** bell by A. N. Wyeth
**Tolman, Joseph Robertson,** fl 1795
  Hathaway, R. Joseph Robertson Tolman
**Tom** Kenney comes home by F. A. Mechau
**Tom** Walker's flight by J. Quidor
**Tomato** patch by G. Fuller

**Tomatoes,** fruit, and flowers by Unidentified
  artist
**Tombstone** cutter by J. Levine
**Tombstones** by J. Lawrence
**TOMKINS, Margaret,** 1916-
  Fragrance of fear
   ICA. Annual ex, 1951
  Genesis
   WMAA. Annual ex, 1957
  Matriarchy
   VR. Biennial ex, 1948
  Sign of the sun
   OrPa. Ptgs & sculptures (col)
**TOMLIN, Bradley Walker,** 1899-1953
  Abstraction no 6, 1952-53                 MCH
   Pulitzer v 1
  Armor must change
   Baur. Bradley Walker Tomlin
  Arrangement                               IU
   Baur. Bradley Walker Tomlin (col)
   CoS. New accessions USA, 1950
   IU. Contemp Amer ptg, 1949 (col)
  Autocrats
   Baur. Bradley Walker Tomlin
   MnU. 40 Amer ptrs
  Burial                                    MM
   Baur. Bradley Walker Tomlin
   Baur. Revolution
   MM. 100 Amer ptrs
   WMAA. Juliana Force
  Death cry
   Baur. Bradley Walker Tomlin
  The goblet                                DP
   Baur. Bradley Walker Tomlin
   DP. Catalogue
  Green
   Baur. Bradley Walker Tomlin
  Maneuver for position
   Baur. Bradley Walker Tomlin
  Number I
   IU. Contemp Amer ptg, 1951
  Number 1, 1949                            WMAA
   Baur. Bradley Walker Tomlin (col)
   MnMW. 60 Amer ptrs (col)
   WMAA. New decade
  Number 1, 1951                            NUM
   Mendelowitz
   MMA. Fifteen
   NUM. Root bequest
  Number 1, 1952-53
   Baur. Bradley Walker Tomlin
   WMAA. New decade
  Number 1, 1956                            NUM
   NUM. Art across America
  Number 2, 1950
   Baur. Bradley Walker Tomlin
  Number 3, 1948
   Baur. Bradley Walker Tomlin
  Number 3, 1949
   Hess. Abstract ptg
   Pousette-Dart. Amer ptg
  Number 5, 1942
   Baur. Bradley Walker Tomlin
  Number 5, 1948
   NBuA. Expressionism
  Number 5, 1949
   Baur. Bradley Walker Tomlin
  Number 6, 1950
   Baur. Bradley Walker Tomlin
  Number 6, 1952
   Baur. Bradley Walker Tomlin

**TOMLIN, B. W.**—*Continued*
Number 7, 1950
  Baur. Bradley Walker Tomlin (col)
  Hess. Abstract ptg (col)
  MMA. Abstract
Number 7, 1951
  MnMW. Classic tradition
Number 8, 1949
  Baur. Bradley Walker Tomlin
  MnU. 40 Amer ptrs
Number 9, 1952    DP
  Baur. Bradley Walker Tomlin
Number 9: in praise of Gertrude Stein
                   MMA
  Art since 1945 (col)
  Baur. Bradley Walker Tomlin
  Hunter. Mod Amer ptg (col)
  MMA. Fifteen
  MMA. New Amer ptg (col)
Number 10, 1949
  MMA. Fifteen
Number 10, 1952-53    NUM
  Baur. Bradley Walker Tomlin
  Baur. New art
  Faulkner. Art today, 1956
  Ponente. Mod ptg, 1960 (col)
  WMAA. New decade
Number 11, 1952-53    MM
  Baur. New art (col)
Number 12, 1949
  Baur. Bradley Walker Tomlin
  PPC. International ex, 1952
Number 13, 1952-53
  Pierson
Number 15, 1953
  MMA. New Amer ptg
Number 18, 1950
  Baur. Bradley Walker Tomlin
  Baur. New art
  McCurdy
Number 18, 1952-53
  Baur. Bradley Walker Tomlin
Number 20, 1949    MMA
  Baur. Bradley Walker Tomlin (col)
  Baur. New art
  MMA. Fifteen
  MMA. Masters (col)
  MMA. New Amer ptg
  Pierson
  Read. Concise history
Outward preoccupation (Still life)
  Baur. Bradley Walker Tomlin
  Gruskin
Red box
  Baur. Bradley Walker Tomlin
Self-portrait, 1932    WMAA
  Baur. Bradley Walker Tomlin
Still life    WMAA
  Baur. Bradley Walker Tomlin
  Goodrich. Amer art
  Pierson
Tension by moonlight
  Baur. Bradley Walker Tomlin
To the sea
  Baur. Bradley Walker Tomlin (col)
  Rathbun
Two figures and easel
  Baur. Bradley Walker Tomlin
Untitled
  CSFP. Annual ex, 1950-51
**Tomlinson** court park by F. Stella
**Tomorrow** and tomorrow by F. Martin

**Tomorrow** is never by D. Tanning
**Tomorrow** morning by J. Ernst
**Tomorrow** we'll be sober by H. Bacon
**Tompkins, Daniel D.** 1774-1825
  Ames, E. Daniel D. Tompkins
  Jarvis, J. W. Daniel D. Tompkins
**Tompkins, Hannah (Minthorne)** 1781-1829
  Ames, E. Mrs Daniel D. Tompkins
**Tompkins children,** fl 1809
  Ames, E. Children of Gov Daniel D.
    Tompkins
**Tonal** rhapsody by C. G. Shaw
**Tondo** no 8, 1948 by F. Glarner
**TONEY, Anthony,** 1913-
  Bathers
    WMAA. Contemp Amer ptg, 1955
  Bridge
    IU. Contemp Amer ptg, 1951
**Tontine** coffee house, New York by F. Guy
**Tony's** house by E. Hopper
**TOOKER, George,** 1920-
  Artist's daughter
    ICA. Annual ex, 1959/60
  Chess game
    WMAA. New decade
  Government bureau    MM
    Pierson
  Guitar
    WMAA. Annual ex, 1958
  The gypsy
    CSFP. Annual ex, 1952
  Highway
    ICA. Annual ex, 1954
  In the summerhouse    WMAA
    WMAA. Sara Roby
  Red carpet
    WMAA. New decade
  Sleepers    WMAA
    CSB. Illusion
  Subway    WMAA
    Goodrich. Amer art
    ICA. Amer artists paint the city
    McCurdy
    Mendelowitz
    Pierson
    Pousette-Dart. Amer ptg
    WMAA. New decade
  The window
    WMAA. Annual ex, 1957
**Toole, Anne Leitch.** See Toole, Nannie
**Toole, George Henry,** b 1837
  Toole, J. George Toole
**Toole, Jennie,** 1841-1917
  Toole, J. Jennie Toole
**TOOLE, John,** 1815-1860
  Capture of Major André
    O'Neal
  George Toole (1)
    O'Neal
  George Toole (2)
    O'Neal
  Jennie Toole (1)
    O'Neal
  Jennie Toole (2)
    O'Neal
  John Mann
    O'Neal
  Martha Morris Suddarth
    O'Neal
  Mary Jane Toole
    O'Neal

Nannie Toole
  O'Neal
Richard Pleasants Suddarth
  O'Neal
Self-portrait (1)
  O'Neal
Self-portrait (2)
  O'Neal
Skating scene                    DN
  DN. Amer primitive ptgs, pt 2
Tempe McCutchen Suddarth
  O'Neal
Toole children
  O'Neal
Unknown sitter
  O'Neal
Vesuvius
  O'Neal
West Point
  O'Neal
Toole, Martha Jane. See Toole, Jennie
Toole, Mary Jane (Suddarth) 1817-1902
  Toole, J. Mary Jane Toole
Toole, Nannie, 1847-1862
  Toole, J. Nannie Toole
Toole children
  Toole, J. Toole children
Tops by D. Rosenthal
Topsail schooner in sheltered waters by
  J. S. Blunt
Torero and young girl by M. Cassatt
Torment, Puerto Rico by H. G. Keller
The tormentors by P. Guston
Torn hat by T. Sully
Torn in transit by J. Haberle
Torn sail by S. Wilson
The tornado by T. Cole
The tornado by J. S. Curry
Toro by L. Neiman
Torrey, Bethia. See Mann, Bethia (Torrey)
Torso and limbs by H. Bloom
The tortured ham by G. Grosz
The toss by F. Martin
Totem by J. Pollock
Tour of inspection by R. Crawford
Tournament by A. Gottlieb
Tournos by S. Davis
Touro, Isaac de Abraham, 1737-1782
  Stuart, G. Rev Isaac de Abraham Touro
Tousard, Anne-Louis de, 1749-1817
  Malbone, E. G. Col Anne-Louis de Tou-
  sard
TOVISH, Harold, 1921-
  Flayed arm
    MnMW. Reality and fantasy
Towards integrating sculptural influence by
  R. Sears
The tower by C. H. Demuth
The tower by K. Knaths
The tower by C. A. Morris
The tower by J. W. Taylor
The tower, Avallon by O. M. Pleissner
Tower of the sea by Y. Tanguy
Towers, Mrs John. See Towers, Susan
  (Coren)
Towers, Susan (Coren) fl 1796
  Peale, J. Mrs Susan Coren Towers

Town Gate tower II, 1925 by L. Feininger
Town hall (Zottelstedt) by L. Feininger
Town hall of Cammin by L. Feininger
Town house by F. Hillsmith
Town meeting by R. Haines
Town of Jim Thorpe, Pennsylvania by T.
  Asplund
Town on a river by Unidentified artist
Town square by S. Davis
Town square, Independence, Missouri by
  F. E. Warren
Townsend, Absolom, 1786-1861
  Ames, E. Absolom Townsend
Townsend, Catherine (Bronson)
  Sargent, J. S. Mrs John Joseph Town-
  send
Towson, Nathan, 1784-1854
  Peale, Raphaelle. Capt Nathan Towson
Toy battle by M. Jackson
Toy duck on wheels by L. MacIver
Toy in the sun by W. A. Baziotes
Toy world by W. A. Baziotes
Tracery of leaves by L. Lucioni
TRACY, John M. 1844-1892
  Grouse shooting (Hunter and two dogs)
    NSP. Sportscapes
  Pointers
    NSP. Sportscapes
Tracy, Patrick, 1711-1789
  Trumbull, J. Patrick Tracy
Traffic halt by H. Schuldt
Tragedy or Found drowned by L. M.
  Eilshemius
Tragedy is self-contained by W. W. Quirt
Tragic actor by B. Greene
Trail of the iron horse by C. M. Russell
Train leaving Auburn station at Rochester,
  New York by E. Sintzenich
Trajan and the children by W. Stuempfig
A tramp on Christmas day by A. M. R.
  Moses
Tramps hideout by D. G. Blythe
Trance by W. A. Baziotes
Tranquility by L. M. Eilshemius
Tranquility by M. Kantor
Tranquility by M. Weber
Tranquillity of previous existence by W. W.
  Quirt
Transcendental by F. Ruvolo
Transcending motion by F. Ruvolo
Transfiguration by A. Gottlieb
Transfluent lines by I. R. Pereira
Transforming gold by I. R. Pereira
Transients by J. W. Reilly
Transit by M. Tobey
Transition by K. L. Callahan
Transparent ones by Y. Tanguy
Transparent planes by I. R. Pereira
Transverse by J. Tworkov
Transverse parallels by I. R. Pereira
Transversion by I. R. Pereira
Transylvania university
  Jouett, M. H. Principal building of Tran-
  sylvania university

Trapeze, Winter garden, New York by E. Shinn

Trapier, Mrs Benjamin Foissin. See Heyward, Hannah Miles

Trapier, Elizabeth (Foissin) 1758-1836
    Theus, J. Mrs Paul Trapier III

Trapier, Hannah Miles (Heyward) See Heyward, Hannah Miles

Trapier, Mrs Paul, 1758-1835. See Trapier, Elizabeth (Foissin)

Trapier, Mrs Paul, fl 1801. See Shubrick, Sarah Alicia

Trapier, Sarah Alicia (Shubrick) See Shubrick, Sarah Alicia

The trapped by K. L. Callahan

The trapper by C. Deas

The trapper by R. Kent

Trappers by A. J. Miller

Trappers by A. M. R. Moses

Trappers by W. T. Ranney

Trappers and Indians communicating by signs by A. J. Miller

Trappers at fault looking for the trail by A. F. Tait

Trapper's bride by A. J. Miller

Trappers' encampment on the Big Sandy river by A. J. Miller

Trappers' return by G. C. Bingham

Trappers starting for the beaver hunt by A. J. Miller

Trapping beaver by A. J. Miller

Travelers meeting Minnetaree Indians by K. Bodmer

Treadmill by P. Evergood

Treasure map by H. Bloom

Treasures from China by C. C. Ross

TREBILCOCK, Paul, 1902-
    Mrs James M. Bovard
        PPC. Ptg in the U.S. 1949

Trecothick, Grizzell (Apthorp) fl 1748
    Feke, R. Mrs Barlow Trecothick

Tree by A. Leepa

Tree by L. MacIver

Tree by C. Schucker

Tree and sea, Maine by J. Marin

Tree forms by J. Marin

Tree house by D. Lord

Tree of foreboding by W. R. Keefe

Tree planting by G. Wood

Tree tops and veiled moon by K. Schrag

Trees by M. Avery

Trees by C. H. Demuth

Trees by S. Laufman

Trees against the sky by K. Schrag

Trees and barns, Bermuda by C. H. Demuth

Trees and sinking sun by K. Schrag

Trees in winter by G. H. Hallowell

Trees, light and movement by K. Schrag

TREIMAN, Joyce Wahl, 1922-
    Absolom
        WMAA. Young America 1957
    Arguing angels
        IU. Contemp Amer ptg & sculp, 1961
    Cactus and sundry
        IU. Contemp Amer ptg, 1952

Escape                                              ICA
    CoS. New accessions USA, 1952
    Pousette-Dart. Amer ptg
The human fold—flowering
    IU. Contemp Amer ptg & sculp, 1957
Nisus and Scylla
    ICA. Annual ex, 1957
Porch no 2
    WMAA. Annual ex, 1958
The wanderers
    IU. Contemp Amer ptg, 1951 (col front)

Trelawny, Edward John, 1792-1881
    West, W. E. Trelawny

Tremont street, Boston by P. Hardy

Tremont street, Boston by M. B. Prendergast

TRENHOLM, Portia Ash, 1813-1892
    Legareville, South Carolina                    VWR
        VWR. Folk art (col)

Trenton, Battle of, 1776
    Trumbull, J. Battle of Trenton
    Trumbull, J. George Washington at the Battle of Trenton

Trenton falls, New York by J. F. Kensett

Trenton, New Jersey. Commission chambers murals by E. Shinn

The trial by J. Levine

Trial of John Brown by H. Pippin

Trial scene by D. G. Blythe

Triatic by S. Davis

Tribute to the American working people by H. Sharrer

Trinity by D. Aronson

Trinity by C. Howard

Trio by K. Evett

Trio by W. Kuhn

Trio by B. Utter

Trio at the bar by L. B. Smith

Tripoli, Bombardment of by M. F. Corne

TRISCOTT, Samuel Peter Rolt, 1846-1925
    English cottage                                  MB
        MB. Ptgs in water color

Triumph by J. Hirsch

Triumphant child by W. Quirt

TRIVIGNO, Pat, 1922-
    Andante
        Pearson. Mod renaissance
    The captives
        CSFP. Annual ex, 1952
        IU. Contemp Amer ptg, 1950
        Pearson. Mod renaissance
    Gothic sentinels
        Pearson. Mod renissance
    Iberia
        IU. Contemp Amer ptg & sculp, 1961

TRIVILINI, Armond
    White wall
        NAD. Special ex, 1956

Trodden weed by A. N. Wyeth

Trojan gates by H. Frankenthaler

Trojan horse by J. De Diego

Trojan horse by M. H. Visser't Hooft

Trolley cars
    Glackens, W. J. The green car
    Hewes, M. The outing
    Prestopino, G. Trolley car
    Schell, F. H. Trolley excursion

**Trombone** player by R. J. Lee
**Troost, Benoist,** fl 1859
  Bingham, G. C. Dr Benoist Troost
**Tropes** de teens by S. Davis
**Tropical** landscape by M. J. Heade
**Tropical** squall by M. O. Sheets
**Tropical** sunset by F. E. Church
**Tropical** surf, Florida by K. Matthew
**Tropicalism** by M. Tobey
**TROTTER, McKie,** 1918-
  Two cities
    NNSG. Younger Amer ptrs
**TROTTER, Newbold Hough,** 1827-1898
  Held up by buffalo                              DNC
    Davidson v 1
    Rathbone
The **trotter** by Unidentified artist
**Trouble** by B. Shahn
**Trouble** hunters by C. M. Russell
**Trouble** in Frisco by F. Martin
**Trout**
  Graves, M. Trout in stream
  Homer, W. Leaping trout
**Trout** fishing by P. R. Goodwin
**Trout** fishing, Lake St John, Quebec by W.
  Homer
**Trout** pool by W. Whittredge
**TROYE, Edward,** 1808-1874
  Edward Troye and an unidentified boy
                                                  CtY
    CtY. Portrait index
    Richard Singleton
    Richardson. Ptg in America
**Truax, Susanna,** fl 1730
  Unidentified artist. Susanna Truax
The **truck** by W. Pachner
**Trumbull, Eunice (Backus)** 1749-1826
  Trumbull, J. Jonathan Trumbull jr with
    Mrs Trumbull and Faith Trumbull
**Trumbull, Faith,** 1769-1846
  Trumbull, J. Jonathan Trumbull jr with
    Mrs Trumbull and Faith Trumbull
**Trumbull, Faith (Robinson)** 1718-1780
  Trumbull, J. Jonathan and Faith Robin-
    son Trumbull
**Trumbull, John,** 1750-1831
  Trumbull, J. John Trumbull, poet and
    cousin of the artist
**TRUMBULL, John,** 1756-1843
  Alexander Hamilton                              DN
    DN. Mellon Coll
    UNESCO. Prior to 1860 5th ed
  Alexander Hamilton                              MB
    MB. Great Americans
    Sizer. John Trumbull
  Alexander Hamilton                              MSE
    Pierson
  Attack on Quebec                                CtY
    Sizer. John Trumbull
  Battle of Bunker's Hill                         CtY
    Barker. Amer ptg
    CtY. Portrait index
    Lee. Art then and now
    Mendelowitz
    Pierson
    Robb. Harper hist
    Roos
    Sizer. John Trumbull
    U.S. National Capital sesquicentennial
      com
    Walker. Ptgs from America

Battle of Princeton. See Death of General
  Mercer at the Battle of Princeton
Battle of Princeton (preliminary composi-
  tion)                                           CtY
  Flexner. Light of distant skies
Capture of the Hessians at Trenton (Bat-
  tle of Trenton)                                 CtY
  CtY. Portrait index
  Sizer. John Trumbull
  Time. 300 years (col)
Christopher Gore
  MB. New England miniatures
Daniel Morgan                                     CtY
  CtY. Portrait index
David Sproat                                      NNHS
  NNHS. Waldron Phoenix Belknap coll
Death of General Mercer at the Battle of
  Princeton (Battle of Princeton)   CtY
  CtY. Portrait index
  Flexner. Light of distant skies
  Roos
  Sizer. John Trumbull
Death of General Montgomery at the
  siege of Quebec                                 CtY
  CtY. Portrait index
  Flexner. Amer ptg
  Flexner. Light of distant skies
  Flexner. Short history
  Larkin
  Larkin rev ed
  Pierson
Declaration of Independence at Phila-
  delphia, July 4, 1776                           CtHW
  CtHW. Handbook
Declaration of Independence, July 4, 1776
                                                  CtY
  CtY. Portrait index
  Flexner. Light of distant skies
  Pierson
  Sizer. John Trumbull
  Time. 300 years (col)
Ebenezer Stevens                                  CtY
  CtY. Portrait index
Eleanor Parke Custis
  CtHW. Trumbull
Falls of Niagara taken from the road two
  miles below Chippawa. See Pan-
  oramas of Niagara Falls
George Washington                                 MM
  CtHW. Trumbull
George Washington at the Battle of
  Trenton                                         CtY
  CtY. Portrait index (col)
George Washington, detail of head of
  Washington at the battle of Trenton
                                                  CtY
  Sizer. John Trumbull
George Washington (Martha Washing-
  ton type)                                       MNS
  Sizer. John Trumbull
Giuseppe Ceracchi                                 MM
  Sizer. John Trumbull
Goldsbrow Banyar                                  NNHS
  Vail. Stuyvesant ports
Harriet Chew                                      CtY
  Sizer. John Trumbull
Jabez Huntington
  CtHW. Trumbull
Jabez Huntington                                  MB
  Sizer. John Trumbull
James Codwise                                     NNHS
  NNHS. Waldron Phoenix Belknap coll

**TRUMBULL, John**—*Continued*

Jeremiah and his son Daniel Wadsworth CtHW
  Pierson
Jeremiah Wadsworth
  Sizer. John Trumbull
John Adams CtY
  Sizer. John Trumbull
John C. Calhoun CtY
  CtY. Portrait index
John M. Trumbull, nephew
  Sizer. John Trumbull
John Trumbull, poet and cousin of the
  artist MiD
  MiD. Treasures
  Sizer. John Trumbull
John Vernet and his family CtY
  Larkin
  Larkin rev ed
  Pierson
Jonathan and Faith Robinson Trumbull
  ICA. From colony to nation
Jonathan Trumbull CtY
  CtY. Portrait Index
Jonathan Trumbull jr with Mrs Trum-
  bull and Faith Trumbull CtY
  Barker. Amer ptg
  CtY. Portrait index
  Flexner. Light of distant skies
  Pierson
  Sizer. John Trumbull
Jonathan Trumbull sr CtY
  Sizer. John Trumbull
Mrs Bartholomew Skaats (Schaets) IBM
  CtHW. Trumbull
Mrs James Codwise NNHS
  NNHS. Waldron Phoenix Belknap coll
Mrs John Trumbull, wife of the artist
  CtY
  Sizer. John Trumbull
Mrs Robert Lenox NNHS
  NNHS. Waldron Phoenix Belknap coll
Mrs Stephen Minot MB
  CtHW. Trumbull
Mrs Thomas Sully MAC
  Sizer. John Trumbull
Mrs Trumbull on her deathbed
  Sizer. John Trumbull
Oliver Ellsworth CtY
  CtY. Portrait
Panoramas of Niagara Falls (Falls of
  Niagara taken from the road two
  miles below Chippawa) NNHS
  Born
  Sizer. John Trumbull
Patrick Tracy
  Sizer. John Trumbull
Portrait of an artist, probably self-portrait
  CtHW
  CtHW. Trumbull
Priam returning the body of Hector MBA
  CtHW. Trumbull
Ralph Izard CtY
  CtY. Portrait index
Resignation of General Washington at
  Annapolis CtY
  CtY. Portrait index
  Sizer. John Trumbull
Robert Benson NNHS
  Flexner. Light of distant skies
Robert Lenox NNHS
  NNHS. Waldron Phoenix Belknap coll

Rufus Putnam CtY
  CtY. Portrait index
Self-portrait at 18 years
  Sizer. John Trumbull
Self-portrait at 21 years MB
  MB. Great Americans
  Sizer. John Trumbull
Self-portrait at about 56 years
  Sizer. John Trumbull
Signing the Declaration of Independence
  NNPL
  Ford. Edward Hicks
Sir John Temple NCa
  Flexner. Light of distant skies
Sir John Temple and his family CtY
  Sizer. John Trumbull
Sortie from Gibraltar OCiM
  CtHW. Trumbull
  ICA. From colony to nation
  OCiM. Guide
  Pierson
  Sizer. John Trumbull
Sortie from Gibraltar CtY
  CtY. Portrait index
Sortie of the British garrison from Gibral-
  tar MBA
  Richardson. Ptg in America
Surrender of General Burgoyne at Sara-
  toga CtY
  CtY. Portrait index
  Sizer. John Trumbull
Surrender of Lord Cornwallis at York-
  town CtY
  CtY. Portrait index
  Sizer. John Trumbull
Surrender of Lord Cornwallis at Yorktown
  DCap
  Richardson. Ptg in America
Surrender of Lord Cornwallis at York-
  town (Aiken coll)
  U.S. National Capital sesquicentennial
  com
Thomas Jefferson, detail from the Declara-
  tion of Independence CtY
  Sizer. John Trumbull
Thomas Youngs Seymour CtY
  Sizer. John Turnbull
Timothy Dwight CtY
  CtY. Portrait index
View of Niagara from upper bank on
  British side CtHW
  CtHW. Handbook
  CtHW. Trumbull
  Pierson
William Cochran
  CtHW. Trumbull

**Portrait of the artist**

Twibill, G. W. Col John Trumbull
Waldo, S. L. and Jewett, W. John Trum-
  bull
**Trumbull, Mrs John.** See Trumbull, Sarah
  Hope (Harvey)
**Trumbull, John M.** 1784-1859
  Trumbull, J. John M. Trumbull, nephew
**Trumbull, Jonathan,** 1710-1785
  Trumbull, J. Jonathan and Faith Robin-
  son Trumbull
  Trumbull, J. Jonathan Trumbull
**Trumbull, Mrs Jonathan,** 1718-1780. See
  Trumbull, Faith (Robinson)
**Trumbull, Jonathan,** 1740-1809
  Trumbull, J. Jonathan Trumbull jr with
  Mrs Trumbull and Faith Trumbull

Trumbull, Mrs Jonathan, 1749-1826. See
    Trumbull, Eunice (Backus)
Trumbull, Sarah Hope (Harvey) 1771-1824
    Trumbull, J. Mrs John Trumbull, wife of
        the artist
    Trumbull, J. Mrs Trumbull on her death-
        bed
The trumpeter by S. R. Van H. Stuyvesant
Trumpeter in the village by L. Feininger
Trumpeter swan by J. J. Audubon
Trusler, Mary, c 1723-1789
    Theus, J. Mary Trusler
Trussed sheep by A. Blaustein
Truth is upward by J. Carroll
TRYON, Dwight William, 1849-1925
    Springtime                                DF
    Time. 300 years (col)
TSCHACBASOV, Nahum, 1899-
    The clown
        Genauer
        IU. Contemp Amer ptg, 1949
        Roos
    Family with flowers                       OYB
        OYB. Supplement
    Flower still life
        IU. Contemp Amer ptg & sculp, 1955
    I, my own keeper
        IU. Contemp Amer ptg & sculp, 1957
    Lady with fan                             OYB
        OYB. Catalogue 1951
    The monkey
        IU. Contemp Amer ptg, 1948
    The offering
        NAD. Annual ex, 1948
    Profiles no 8
        IU. Contemp Amer ptg & sculp, 1953
    Substance and sustenance
        IU. Contemp Amer ptg, 1950
TSENG Yu-ho, 1923-
    Aquarelle: collage
        IU. Contemp Amer ptg & sculp, 1959
    Strings of amber
        IU. Contemp Amer ptg & sculp, 1961
Tuberoses by C. H. Demuth
TUCKER, Allen, 1866-1939
    Washington crossing the Delaware
                                            WMAA
        Pierson
TUCKER, Joshua, b 1800
    South east view of Greenville, South Caro-
        lina                                  VWR
        VWR. Folk art (col)
Tuckerman, Elizabeth. See Salisbury, Eliza-
    beth (Tuckerman)
Tudor, Emma Jane. See Gardiner, Emma
    Jane (Tudor)
Tug by L. Feininger
Tugboat O. M. Pettit by J. Bard
Tuileries gardens by M. B. Prendergast
Tulip buds by W. Kuhn
Tulips by M. Beckmann
Tulips by A. Dasburg
Tulips by S. Greene
Tulips in a white pitcher by E. E. Speicher
Tully, William, 1785-1859
    Ames, E. William Tully
Tumbling waters by S. Nichols
Tundo no 21 by F. Glarner

Tundra by M. Tobey
Tunk mountains, autumn, Maine by J. Marin
Turbulent forest by C. A. Morris
Turell, Ebenezer, 1701?-1778
    Smibert, J. Rev Ebenezer Turell
Turf house on the plains by C. Wimar
Turkey by A. B. Carles
Turkey buzzards
    Audubon, J. J. Turkey buzzard
    Wyeth, A. Soaring
Turkey shoot by J. W. Ehninger
Turkey shoot by T. H. Matteson
Turkeys
    Audubon, J. J. Wild turkey
    Moses, A. M. R. Catching the Thanks-
        giving turkey
Turkish page by W. M. Chase
Turkish page by F. Duveneck
TURMAN, William T. b 1867
    Gravel pit                                InTH
        InTH. Catalogue
TURNBULL, James Baare, 1909-
    Son of a sharecropper                     ATU
        ATU. Coll of Amer art
Turner, John B.
    Wood, G. John B. Turner, pioneer
TURNER, Ross Sterling, 1847-1915
    Dawn                                      MB
        MB. Ptgs in water color
    A garden is a sea of flowers              MB
        MB. Ptgs in water color
Turner alley studio by G. Wood
Turning the stake boat by T. Eakins
The turnkey by J. Levine
Turreted pitcher by W. Sommer
Turtle creek valley by J. Kane
Turtles
    Homer, W. The turtle pound
    Homer, W. Rum cay
Tuscany by E. C. Clark
TUTHILL, Abraham G. D. 1776?-1843
    Alida Livingston Woolsey
        Frankenstein. Two journeyman ptrs
    Anna Miretta Vail
        Frankenstein. Two journeyman ptrs
    Benjamin West
        Frankenstein. Two journeyman ptrs
    Ezekiel Walton
        Frankenstein. Two journeyman ptrs
    George Larned
        Frankenstein. Two journeyman ptrs
    Hezekiah Hutchins Reed
        Frankenstein. Two journeyman ptrs
    Hiram Pratt
        Frankenstein. Two journeyman ptrs
    Jackson, Solon, Mary Elizabeth and Anna
        Miretta Vail
        Frankenstein. Two journeyman ptrs
    Lewis Cass
        Frankenstein. Two journeyman ptrs
    Melancthon Taylor Woolsey
        Frankenstein. Two journeyman ptrs
    Mary Elizabeth Vail
        Frankenstein. Two journeyman ptrs
    Mrs Ezekiel Walton
        Frankenstein. Two journeyman ptrs
    Mrs Melancthon Taylor Woolsey
        Frankenstein. Two journeyman ptrs
    Mrs Nathaniel Platt
        Frankenstein. Two journeyman ptrs

**TUTHILL, A. G. D.**—*Continued*
Self-portrait
 Frankenstein. Two journeyman ptrs
Sylvester, Julia, Jane and Catherine
 Larned
 Frankenstein. Two journeyman ptrs
Thomas Reed
 Frankenstein. Two journeyman ptrs
Thomas Vail (?)
 Frankenstein. Two journeyman ptrs

**Tuttle, Esther,** fl 1835
 Davis, J. H. Esther Tuttle

**Tuttle, Henry Emerson,** 1890-
 Speicher, E. E. Henry Emerson Tuttle

**Tuttle, James,** fl 1836
 Davis, J. H. James and Sarah Tuttle

**Tuttle, Mrs James.** See Tuttle, Sarah

**Tuttle, Sarah,** fl 1836
 Davis, J. H. James and Sarah Tuttle
 Davis, J. H. (attributed works) Mrs
  Tuttle

**TWACHTMAN, John Henry,** 1853-1902
Blue brook water fall   OCiM
 Born
Coast scene       PR
 PR. Catalogue
Emerald pool       DP
 DP. Catalogue
End of winter      DNC
 Cheney. Story 1958 ed
Summer day       InIJ
 InIJ. 105 ptgs
Footbridge at Bridgeport  MdH
 MdH. Catalogue 1940
From the upper terrace   ICA
 Cheney. Story 1958 ed
Hemlock pool      MAP
 Pierson
 Robb. Harper history
Holly house, Cos Cob, Connecticut
          MWiC
 Pierson
Horseneck brook, winter
 PPC. Amer classics
Landscape       WMAA
 Born
March woodlands    MoSL
 MoSL. Handbook 1953
Rapids, Yellowstone park  MWM
 Cheney. Story 1958 ed
Reflections       NBM
 Baur. Revolution
 McCurdy
Sailing in the mist    PA
 Pierson
 Richardson. Ptg in America
Snowbound      ICA
 Larkin
 Larkin rev ed
 Pierson
Snow scene      DNC
 DNC. Gellatly coll, 1954
Summer        DP
 DP. Catalogue
 Pierson
Three trees      NBM
 Mendelowitz
Venice        NB
 CSB. Impressionism
The waterfall      MM
 MM. 100 Amer ptrs
Wild cherry tree    NBuA
 NBuA. Catalogue of the ptgs

**Twain, Mark.** See Clemens, Samuel
 Langhorne
**TWARDOWICZ, Stanley John,** 1917-
Lobster traps
 IU. Contemp Amer ptg, 1948
Number 38, 1957-58
 IU. Contemp Amer ptg & sculp, 1959
White on blue
 NNSG. Younger Amer ptrs
**Tweedy, Miss,** fl 1840
 Unidentified artist. Miss Tweedy of
  Brooklyn
**Twentieth** century baroque by R. O.
 Preusser
Twenty-cent movie by R. Marsh
**27** December 1959 by C. di Marca-Relli
**23** September, 1959 by C. di Marca-Relli
**Twenty-two** houses and a church by Un-
 identified artist
**TWIBILL, George W.** c 1806-1836
John Trumbull
 Cowdrey v 1
**Twilight** by R. A. Blakelock
**Twilight** head by P. Tchelitchew
**Twilight** landscape by P. Evergood
**Twilight** travelling by A. B. Davies
**Twin** heads by A. H. Maurer
**Twin** pine by W. A. Kienbusch
**Twin** sisters by Unidentified artist
**Two** by D. Hare
**Two** by J. Pollock
**Two** acrobats by C. H. Demuth
**Two** armies before a city by Unidentified
 artist
**Two** bathers by L. M. Eilshemius
**Two** bathers by B. Karfiol
**Two** birds by C. S. Price
**Two** boats by W. Homer
**Two** bridges by N. Spencer
**Two** brown and white puppies by Unidenti-
 fied artist
**Two** circles by A. Liberman
**Two** cities by M. Trotter
**Two** citizens engaged in a conversation by
 G. C. Bingham
**Two** classical studies by H. Warshaw
**Two-figure** composition by W. W. Quirt
**Two** figures by B. Browne
**Two** figures by J. Glasco
**Two** figures and easel by B. W. Tomlin
**Two** figures at a desk by M. Avery
**Two** fishermen by K. Knaths
**Two** flags by J. Johns
**Two** girls by I. Bishop
**Two** girls by A. H. Maurer
**Two** girls in New England woodland by
 M. B. Prendergast
**Two** girls sewing by G. Stuart
**Two** grouse in underbrush of laurel by
 Rubens Peale
**Two** guides by W. Homer
**Two** heads by B. Greene
**Two** heads by A. H. Maurer
**Two** heads by C. S. Price

Two houses by W. Stuempfig
Two little girls in blue by Unidentified artist
Two-master becalmed, Maine by J. Marin
Two men by E. Johnson
Two musicians by S. M. Grode
Two musicians by M. Weber
Two Negroes by G. Biddle
Two nudes by E. Cortor
Two nudes by R. Diebenkorn
Two nudes before Japanese screen by H. Katzman
Two on the aisle by E. Hopper
Two sides of red by D. Von Schlegell
Two sisters by R. Beauchamp
Two sisters by A. H. Maurer
Two sisters by R. Soyer
Two standing figures by B. Karfiol
Two standing women by W. De Kooning
Two trout by W. Homer
Two trout fishermen by P. S. Sample
Two tugs by C. Rosen
Two up by I. R. Pereira
Two ventilators by A. Osver
Two witnesses by B. Shahn
Two women by M. Beckmann
Two women by W. De Kooning
Two women by B. Greene
Two women by S. Macdonald-Wright
Two women by E. G. H Pinney
Two women by W. W. Quirt
Two women in front of a mirror by M. Hirshfield
Two women on a wharf by W. De Kooning
Two women with still life by W. De Kooning
Two women's torsos by W. De Kooning
Two worlds by S. Francis
Two yellow horses by W. Sommer
Two young ladies by A. M. Von Phul
TWORKOV, Jack, 1900-
    Blue cradle
        MMA. New Amer ptg
    Cradle
        MMA. New Amer ptg
    Crest
        MnMW. 60 Amer ptrs
    Duo I, 1956                                WMAA
        Goodrich. Amer art
    East barrier                               NBuA
        NBuA. Acquisitions 1959-1961
    Flowering white
        Hess. Abstract ptg
    Green landscape                            MbBM
        CoS. New accessions USA, 1954
        Hess. Abstract ptg
    Nausicaa
        PPC. International ex, 1952
    Pink Mississippi
        Art since 1945 (col)
        Hunter. Mod Amer ptg (col)
        Read. Concise ptg
    Redlake
        PPC. International ex, 1958
    Ridgeway
        IU. Contemp Amer ptg & sculp, 1961

Sirens in voice
    Pousette-Dart. Amer ptg
Transverse
    MMA. New Amer ptg (col)
Watergame
    Cheney. Story 1958 ed
The wheel                                      MMA
    Pierson
Tyler, Alice, fl 1842
    Healy, G. P. A. Alice Tyler
Tyler, John, president U.S. 1790-1862
    Healy, G. P. A. John Tyler
    Jarvis, J. W. John Tyler
Tyler, Mary Brown
    Bellows, G. W. Mrs T in cream silk
    Bellows, G. W. Mrs T in wine silk
Tynemouth sands by W. Homer
Tyng, Ann. See Smelt, Ann (Tyng)
Tyng, Elizabeth (Ross) 1751-1831
    Copley, J. S. Elizabeth Ross
Tyrol at Kufstein, Tyrol series, no 3 by J. Marin
Tyrolean mountains by J. Marin
Tyrolese crucifixion by J. S. Sargent

U

U. N. Conference room 3, 1956, Study for by S. Davis
U.S. mail boat by L. T. Bauman
U.S.S. Pensacola, 1946 by R. Crawford
Ud-je-jock, the Pelican by G. Catlin
UHLE, Bernard, b 1847
    An election day bonfire, Fifth and Chestnut streets, Philadelphia
        U. S. National Capital sesquicentennial com
ULBRICHT, John, 1926-
    La Veronica                                CoD
        CoS. New accessions USA, 1954
ULLRICH, Beatrice, 1907-
    Remembrance of things past                 ATU
        ATU. Coll of Amer art
Ulreich, Mrs Eduard Buk. See Nura
Ulreich, Nura (Woodson) See Nura
ULRICH, Charles Frederic, 1858-1908
    In the land of promise: Castle garden DC
        Davidson v2
        U. S. National Capital sesquicentennial com
The ultimate city by F. E. Warren
Ultra-marine by S. Davis
Ulysses by B. Newman
Umbrellas and parasols
    Prendergast, M. B. Dieppe
    Prendergast, M. B. Umbrellas in the rain, Venice
Umpferstedt by L. Feininger
Una and the lion by B. West
The unattainable by A. Gorky
Uncle Tom by H. Pippin
Uncle Tom and Little Eva by R. S. Duncanson
Uncompleted bridge by J. Ross
The undefeated by F. Martin

Under a cloud by A. P. Ryder
Under Cliff by T. Chambers
Under sea by E. Loran
Under the coco palm by W. Homer
Under the el by J. Levine
Under the falls, grand discharge by W. Homer
Under the greenwood by G. Inness
Under the horse-chestnut tree by M. Cassatt
Under the pier by L. Siegriest
Under the river by A. Pickens
Underpass by B. P. Arnest
Underpass by P. Blume
Underpass by S. Davis
Undersea mountain by E. Stasack
Undertow by W. Homer
Undulating arrangement by I. R. Pereira
Undulating fence by D. Macknight
Undulating landscape by F. Ruvolo
Unemployable by A. Friedman
Unexpected encounter by J. De Diego
Unformed figure by J. Pollock
Unicorns by A. B. Davies
Unicorns came down to the sea by K. Sage
UNIDENTIFIED artist
    See also Border limner; Freake limner; Gansevoort limner; Mason limner; Pierpont limner; Pollard limner
Abigail Hall
    MB. New England miniatures
Abraham and Isaac
    Pierson
Abraham Clark and his children          DN
    DN. Amer primitive ptgs pt 1
Abraham Van Cortlandt
    Belknap
Abram Gouverneur
    Belknap
Adam and Eve          DN
    DN. Amer primitive ptgs, pt 1
Adam Winne          DeWin
    Belknap
Adams family          VWR
    VWR. Folk art (col)
Adeline Harwood          DN
    DN. Amer primitive ptgs, pt 1
Adolphus Philipse          NNMC
    Belknap
Adoration of the Magi          NAI
    NAI. Hudson valley
Albert Crary
    Ford. Pictorial folk art
Allegory of freedom          DN
    DN. Amer primitive ptgs, pt 1
The all-seeing eye          CtHW
    Frankenstein. After the hunt
Alvah Cook          DN
    DN. Amer primitive ptgs, pt 1
American harvest (probably copy after Cropsey)
    Ford. Pictorial folk art
American madonna and child          NCHA
    Jones. New-found folk art
Angeline Eliza Shepard and her brother, Elisha Henry Shepard          CtHW
    CtHW. Handbook

Anna Cruger          NNMC
    Belknap
Anna Wendell Cuyler          NAI
    Jones. Rediscovered ptrs
Annie Robinson          DN
    DN. Amer primitive ptgs
Anthony Duane          NNHS
    NNHS. Waldron Phoenix Belknap coll
Anthony Rutgers
    Belknap
Anthony Van Schaick (formerly known as Sybrant Gozen Van Schaick)          NAI
    Belknap
    Jones. Rediscovered ptrs
    NAI. Hudson valley (as by Schuyler painter)
Aphia Salisbury Rich and baby Edward          DN
    DN. Amer primitive ptgs, pt 1
Apple gatherers          VWR
    Ford. Pictorial folk art
Ariaantje Coeymans. See Mrs David Verplanck
Ariaantje Schuyler Van Rensselaer          NAI
    Belknap
    NAI. Hudson Valley
Asahel Pomeroy
    ICA. From colony to nation
Attack of the rebel ram Manassas on the U.S.S. Pensacola, 1862          MeC
    Jetté. Amer heritage collection
Augusta, Maine, c 1825          MeC
    Jetté. Amer heritage collection
Augustus Cornelius Van Horne          NNHS
    Vail. Stuyvesant ports
Augustus Jay          NNHS
    Belknap
Aurora          DN
    DN. Amer primitive ptgs, pt 2
Baby in blue cradle          DN
    DN. Amer primitive ptgs, pt 2
Baby in pink and white          DN
    DN. Amer primitive ptgs, pt 1
Baby in red chair          VWR
    Lee. Art then and now
    Roos
    VWR. Amer folk art (col)
    VWR. Folk art (col)
    Walker. Ptgs from America
Baby reclining          DN
    DN. Amer primitive ptgs, pt 2
Baby with fruit          NCHA
    Jones. New-found folk art
Barbara Dean
    NYG. Fine art p20
Barclay children
    Belknap
Barent Rynders          NNHS
    Belknap
Barent Sports of Albany
    Belknap
Barn Bluff, Red Wing, Minnesota          NCHA
    Jones. New-found folk art
Basket of flowers          VWR
    VWR. Folk art (col)
Battle of White Oak swamp, Virginia 1862          NCHA
    Jones. New-found folk art
Beacon-on-the-Hudson
    Sears. Highlights
The Belle Creole at New Orleans
    U.S. National Capital sesquicentennial com

Belshazzar's feast                       NAI
  NAI. Hudson valley
Benjamin Smith                           DN
  DN. Amer primitive ptgs, pt 2
Bethlehem, Pennsylvania
  Davidson v 1
Blue eyes                                DN
  DN. Amer primitive ptgs, pt 1
  Time. 300 years (col)
The bountiful board                      VWR
  VWR. Folk art (col)
Bowl of fruit                            DN
  DN. Amer primitive ptgs, pt 1
  Ford. Pictorial folk art
Bowl of fruit (Halladay-Thomas coll)
  Ford. Pictorial folk art
Boy and girl                             DN
  DN. Amer primitive ptgs, pt 1
Boy and girl with dog                    MeC
  Jetté. Amer heritage collection
Boy in blue coat                         DN
  DN. Amer primitive ptgs, pt 2
Boy in plaid                             VWR
  VWR. Folk art (col)
Boy of the De Peyster family             NNHS
  Belknap
Boy of the Hallett family                ICA
  Belknap
Boy with a toy drum                      NNHS
  Ford. Pictorial folk art
Boy with finch                           VWR
  Ford. Pictorial folk art
  VWR. Folk art (col)
Boy with hammer and iron pot             NCHA
  Jones. New-found folk art
Boy with whip                            MeC
  Jetté. Amer heritage collection
British privateers with French prizes in
  New York harbor                        NNHS
  Flexner. First flowers (col)
Brother and sister                       DN
  DN. Amer primitive ptgs, pt 1
Buffalo hunter                           CSB
  Baur. Amer ptg
  Walker. Ptgs from America
Burning of Charles Town                  DN
  DN. Amer primitive ptgs, pt 1
Burning of Old South church, Bath,
  Maine                                  DN
  DN. Amer primitive ptgs, pt 2
Burning of the Tombs, New York
  city                                   NNMC
  Ford. Pictorial folk art
By the fireside                          MMA
  Lee. Art then and now
Cadwallader Colden family
  Ford. Pictorial folk art
Caleb Heathcote                          NNHS
  Larkin
  Larkin rev ed
Caleb Kempton
  Ford. Pictorial folk art
Camp Butler, Maryland, 1861              MB
  MB. Karolik coll
Captain Carnes of Salem                  MSP
  Davidson v 1
Captain Farnham of Farnham, Maine
                                         MeC
  Jetté Amer heritage collection
Captain George, Haverhill, Massachu-
  setts                                  NJP
  NJP. Amer folk art

The cat                                  DN
  DN. Amer primitive ptgs, pt 1
Cat and kittens                          DN
  DN. Amer primitive ptgs, pt 2
Catalina Schuyler                        NNHS
  Belknap
Catalynje Post                           DN
  Belknap
  DN. Amer primitive ptgs, pt 1
  Ford. Pictorial folk art
Catharina Schuyler                       DeWin
  Belknap
Catharine Hendrickson                    DN
  DN. Amer primitive ptgs, pt 1
Caught in the act
  Ford. Pictorial folk art
Ceremonies at a young ladies' seminary,
  1810-20
  Davidson v2
Charlotte Marsteller                     DC
  DC. Masterpieces
Cheese factory                           MeC
  Jetté. Amer heritage collection
Cheney family                            DN
  DN. Amer primitive ptgs, pt 2
Child and doll
  Ford. Pictorial folk art
Child holding eyeglasses                 NCHA
  Jones. New-found folk art
Child in blue
  Belknap
Child in blue dress                      NJN
  Ford. Pictorial folk art
Child in red dress
  Ford. Pictorial folk art
Child with dog                           VWR
  VWR. Folk art (col)
Child with rocking horse                 DN
  DN. Amer primitive ptgs, pt 2
Child with wheelbarrow                   MeC
  Jetté. Amer heritage collection
Children of Jacob Franks (1)
  NNHS. Waldron Phoenix Belknap coll
Children of Jacob Franks (2)
  NNHS. Waldron Phoenix Belknap coll
Christ and the woman of Samaria          VWR
  VWR. Folk art (col)
Christ at Emmaus                         NAI
  Flexner. First flowers
  Jones. Rediscovered ptrs
  NAI. Hudson valley
Christ on the road to Emmaus, versions
  I and II                               NAI
  NAI. Hudson valley
Christina Ten Broek                      NAI
  Belknap
Christmas party                          MB
  MB. Karolik coll
A city of fantasy                        DN
  DN. Amer primitive ptgs, pt 2
Civil war battle scene                   DN
  DN. Amer primitive ptgs, pt 2
Civil war—Symbolic panorama              NCHA
  Jones. New-found folk art
The cock                                 NCHA
  Jones. New-found folk art
Columbia                                 DN
  DN. Amer primitive ptgs, pt 1
Coming storm
  Sears. Highlights
Composite harbor scene with volcano DN
  DN. Amer primitive ptgs, pt 1

UNIDENTIFIED artist—*Continued*
Contemplation                                    VWR
  VWR. Folk art (col)
Coon hunt                                        DN
  DN. Amer primitive ptgs, pt 1
The courtship                                    MeC
  Jetté. Amer heritage collection
Creation scene
  Ford. Edward Hicks
Creole child
  Ford. Pictorial folk art
Crowning of King Jereboam                        NAI
  NAI. Hudson valley
Crow's nest from Bull hill. Hudson river
  looking toward West Point               NCHA
Crucifixion                                       MM
  Jones. New-found folk art
  Flexner. Light of distant skies
  Mendelowitz
Curls and scallops                               NCHA
  Jones. New-found folk art
Curse of gold
  Ford. Pictorial folk art
The dandy                                        VWR
  VWR. Folk art (col)
Daniel LeRoy                                     NNHS
  Vail. Stuyvesant ports
Daniel Russell
  Flexner. First flowers
Daniel Webster at his farm                        MB
  MB. Great Americans
  MB. Karolik coll
David Alling house and shop, Newark
                                                  NJN
  Ford. Pictorial folk art
David Davidse Schuyler                           NAI
  Belknap
  NAI. Hudson valley
David, Joanna and Abigail Mason
  Pierson
David Porter                                      MB
  MB. Great American
  MB. Karolik coll
David Provoost (?)                               NNHS
  Belknap
Deer hunt                                        DN
  DN. Amer primitive ptgs, pt 1
Dennison hill, Southbridge, Massachusetts
                                                  DN
  DN. Amer primitive ptgs, pt 2
De Peyster boy with deer                         NNHS
  Belknap
  Flexner. Amer ptg
  Flexner. First Flowers (col)
  Flexner. Short history
De Peyster girl with lamb (Margaret or
  Catherine)                                     NNHS
  Belknap
  Flexner. First flowers
The domino girl                                  DN
  DN. Amer primitive ptgs, pt 2
Dover baby                                       NJN
  Ford. Pictorial folk art
Eagle and snake
  Ford. Pictorial folk art
Easton, Pennsylvania
  McClintock
Edward Brodnax                                    VR
  Belknap
Edward Jaquelin II as a child
  Barker. Amer ptg
  Pierson

Edward Payson Crowell                            MSE
  MSE. Cat of ports, 1950
Egg salad                                         MB
  MB. Karolik coll
Elizabeth Eggington                              CtHW
  CtHW. Handbook
  Pierson
Elizabeth Paddy Wensley
  Flexner. First flowers
  Pierson
Elizabeth Fenimore Cooper
  Ford. Pictorial folk art
  Time. 300 years (col)
Emblem of peace
  Ford. Pictorial folk art
End of the hunt (End of the fox hunt)
                                                  DN
  Davidson v 1
  DN. Amer primitive ptgs, pt 1
  Flexner. First flowers
Enigmatic foursome                               NCHA
  Jones. New-found folk art
Eva and Catherina De Peyster
  Belknap
  Flexner. First flowers
Family burying ground                            DN
  DN. Amer primitive ptgs, pt 2
Fancy picture: fishing with waterfall MeC
  Jetté. Amer heritage collection
Farm scene                                        ICA
  Ford. Pictorial folk art
Farmhouse in Mahantango valley                    DN
  DN. Amer primitive ptgs, pt 2
Fashionable inn, New York, c 1825 MoKN
  Ford. Pictorial folk art
Father and son
  Ford. Pictorial folk art
Finding of Moses                                 NAI
  NAI. Hudson valley
Fire of the warehouse of Henry Webb
  and company, Baltimore, 1827  MdBH
  Davidson v2
The fish is on the other side
  Frankenstein. After the hunt
Five children of the Budd family                  DN
  DN. Amer primitive ptgs, pt 2
Five Points, New York, c 1829
  Davidson v2
Flag carried at the siege of Louisburg,
  1745                                           NNHS
  Flexner. First flowers
Flight into Egypt                                NAI
  Jones. Rediscovered ptrs
  NAI. Hudson valley
Flowers & fruit                                  DN
  Brussels. Exposition
  DN. Amer primitive ptgs, pt 1
Flowers, butterfly, and book                      MB
  MB. Karolik coll
Fort Snelling, c 1838 (also attributed to
  Eastman)                                     MnMI
  Davidson v 1
The four apostles writing the Gospels
                                                  NAI
  NAI. Hudson valley
Fourth Pennsylvania cavalry, 1861    DN
  DN. Amer primitive ptgs, pt 2
Frances Parke Custis                             VLW
  Belknap
Fruit and flowers                                DN
  DN. Amer primitive ptgs, pt 1
Fruit and melon                                  VWR
  VWR. Folk art (col)

Fruit in bowl      MeC
   Jetté. Amer heritage collection
Furniture shop and warehouse of Duncan
   Phyfe, Fulton street, New York   MM
   Davidson v 1
General Putnam's leap      NCHA
   Larkin
   Larkin rev ed
   Time. 300 years (col)
Gentleman farmer      VWR
   VWR. Folk art (col)
Gentleman from Montague, Massachu-
   setts      MeC
   Jetté. Amer heritage collection
Gentleman of the Beekman family (Wil-
   liam Beekman?)
   Belknap
Gentleman of the Hallett family (probably
   Joseph Hallett)      NNHS
   NNHS. Waldron Phoenix Belknap coll
Gentleman of the Schuyler family   NAI
   Belknap
George and Jane Bigelow
   Larkin
George Curwin      MSE
   Belknap
George Phillips      NNHS
   Belknap
   NNHS. Waldron Phoenix Belknap coll
George Washington family
   Kallir. Amer primitive ptgs
George Washington on white charger DN
   DN. Amer primitive ptgs, pt 1
George Washington, the Mason    DN
   DN. Amer primitive ptgs, pt 1
George Washington with horse   MeC
   Jetté. Amer heritage collection
Gerard De Peyster      NNHS
   Belknap
   NNHS. Waldron Phoenix Belknap coll
Gerard Stuyvesant family group   NNHS
   Vail. Stuyvesant ports
Gerrit Teunise Van Vechten (formerly
   known as Gerardus Beekman) NAI
   NAI. Hudson valley
Girl by the waterfall      VWR
   VWR. Folk art (col)
Girl in black pinafore      VWR
   VWR. Folk art (col)
Girl in blue
   Ford. Pictorial folk art
Girl in garden      VWR
   VWR. Folk art (col)
Girl in green      VWR
   Ford. Pictorial folk art
   VWR. Folk art (col)
Girl in red      MB
   MB. Karolik coll
Girl in ruffled collar      VWR
   VWR. Folk art (col)
Girl of the Ten Eyck family      NAI
   NAI. Hudson valley
Girl of the Van Rensselaer family
   Flexner. First flowers
Girl on balcony      VWR
   VWR. Folk art (col)
Girl with a gray cat      MB
   MB. Karolik coll
Girl with hoop      VWR
   VWR. Folk art (col)
Girl with the red shoes. See Magdalena
   Douw

Good Samaritan I, II, III, IV, V, VI
     VWR
   VWR. Folk art (col)
Governess and children      VWR
   Ford. Pictorial folk art
Gracie Beardsley Jefferson Jackman and
   her daughter      DN
   DN. Amer primitive ptgs, pt 2
Grapevine      VWR
   VWR. Folk art (col)
Gurdon Saltonstall      CtY
   CtY. Portrait index
Die gute mutter      MeC
   Jetté. Amer heritage collection
Hannah Alden      MeC
   Jetté. Amer heritage collection
Harlan Page      DN
   DN. Amer primitive ptgs, pt 1
Harmanus Wendell      NNMC
   Belknap
Harmony Child Wight
   Ford. Pictorial folk art
Haymakers      VWR
   Ford. Pictorial folk art
Headless horseman
   Ford. Pictorial folk art
Hendrick Remsen      NNHS
   NNHS. Waldron Phoenix Belknap coll
Henrietta Dorr, Chatham Center, New
   York      NJP
   NJP. Amer folk art
Henrietta Frances Cuthbert      VWR
   VWR. Folk art (col)
Henry A. Morehouse      VWR
   VWR. Folk art (col)
Henry Beekman
   Belknap
Henry Gibbs
   Larkin
Henry Wells      DN
   DN. Amer primitive ptgs, pt 1
High bridge across the Harlem river,
   c 1840      NNHS
   Davidson v2
High water in the bayou country   MoSL
   Rathbone
Hobby horse      DN
   DN. Amer primitive ptgs, pt 1
Home on the Mississippi, c 1850
   Davidson v 1
Horace Tuttle's livery stable    NCHA
   Jones. New-found folk art
Horses in a stream
   Sears. Highlights
Hudson river landscape      MeC
   Jetté. Amer heritage collection
Hudson river landscape with sailboats
     RPS
   Born
Hudson river scene      MMA
   Ford. Pictorial folk art
Hudson river view c 1800
   Ford. Pictorial folk art
Hunter family of Germantown, Pennsyl-
   vania      MeC
   Jetté. Amer heritage collection
Hunting scene      MM
   Ford. Pictorial folk art
In the heart of New Hampshire
   Sears. Highlights
Indian chief      DN
   DN. Amer primitive ptgs, pt 1

UNIDENTIFIED artist—*Continued*
Indian encampment DN
  DN. Amer primitive ptgs, pt 2
Indian Treaty of Greenville, 1795 (Signing
  the Treaty of Greenville) ICH
  Davidson v 1
  U. S. National Capital sesquicentennial
  com
Innocence DN
  DN. Amer primitive ptgs, pt 1
Interior of a butcher shop, c 1840 NJN
  Davidson v2
The ironers NCHA
  Jones. New-found folk art
Isaac blessing Jacob, versions I and II
                             NAI
  NAI. Hudson valley
Isaac De Peyster
  Belknap
Israel Munson CtY
  CtY. Portrait index
J. B. Sheldon DN
  DN. Amer primitive ptgs, pt 1
  Ford. Pictorial folk art
Jacob Franks
  Belknap
Jacob Myers
  Ford. Pictorial folk art
Jacob Von Kline DN
  DN. Amer primitive ptgs, pt 2
Jacobus Stoutenburg NNMC
  Belknap
  Flexner. First flowers
James A. De Peyster (?) NNHS
  Pierson
James Lenox NNHS
  NNSH. Waldron Phoenix Belknap coll
James Pierpont CtY
  Larkin rev ed
Jane Goelet NAI
  Belknap
  NAI. Hudson valley
Jean Macdonald Lee Myers VWR
  VWR. Folk art (col)
Jeremias Van Rensselaer NAI
  Belknap
Johannes De Peyster III NNHS
  Belknap
  NNHS. Waldron Phoenix Belknap coll
Johannes Rose
  Belknap
Johannes Schuyler NNHS
  Belknap
Johannes Wendell NAI
  Belknap
  NAI. Hudson valley
John Cruger NNMC
  Belknap
John Fitch
  Belknap
John Mix VWR
  VWR. Folk art (col)
John Perrin MSt
  Little. Country art
John Sanders
  Belknap
John Van Cortlandt NBM
  Belknap
  NNHS. Waldron Phoenix Belknap coll
  Pierson
John Whorf with bow and arrow NCHA
  Jones. New-found folk art

Jonathan Benham DN
  DN. Amer primitive ptgs, pt 2
Joseph and Anna Raymond DN
  DN. Amer primitive ptgs, pt 2
Joseph and his brethren VWR
  VWR. Folk art (col)
Joseph interpreting Pharaoh's dream
                             MMA
  Ford. Pictorial folk art
Joseph interpreting Pharaoh's dreams
                             VWR
  VWR. Folk art (col)
Judd's hotel, Philadelphia, c 1825 DN
  DN. Amer primitive ptgs, pt 2
Judd's house, Southold, Long Island MB
  MB. Karolik coll
Lady Berkeley
  Belknap
Lady from Hornell MiD
  Jones. Rediscovered ptrs
Lady from Montague, Massachusetts MeC
  Jetté. Amer heritage collection
Lady in a white dress MeC
  Jetté. Amer heritage collection
Lady in blue VWR
  VWR. Folk art (col)
Lady in red DN
  DN. Amer primitive ptgs, pt 1
Lady in white DN
  DN. Amer primitive ptgs, pt 2
Lady in white bonnet NCHA
  Jones. New-found folk art
Lady of the Beekman family (Mrs Wil-
  liam Beekman?)
  Belknap
Lady of the Hallett family (probably Mrs
  Joseph Hallett) NNHS
  NNHS. Waldron Phoenix Belknap coll
Lady of the lake VWR
  Ford. Pictorial folk art
Lady of the Van Rensselaer family
  NNHS. Waldron Phoenix Belknap coll
Lady Suffolk [a horse] MeC
  Jetté. Amer heritage collection
Lady with a rose MeC
  Jetté. Amer heritage collection
Lady with brown eyes DN
  DN. Amer primitive ptgs, pt 2
Lady with curls MeC
  Jetté. Amer heritage collection
Lady with lavender ribbons VWR
  VWR. Folk art (col)
Lady with plumed headdress DN
  DN. Amer primitive ptgs, pt 2
Land and seawater scape MeC
  Jetté. Amer heritage collection
Landscape with figures VWR
  VWR. Folk art (col)
Lavinia Van Vechten NBM
  Belknap
Leaving the manor house DN
  DN. Amer primitive ptgs, pt 2
Le Roy, New York MeC
  Jetté. Amer heritage collection
Letter of marque ship Bethel of Boston
                             MBH
  Davidson v 1
  U. S. National Capital sesquicentennial
  com
Lexington battle monument DN
  DN. Amer primitive ptgs, pt 1
Lincoln and his Cabinet, c 1860
  Kallir. Amer primitive ptgs

Little boy in red                          MB
 MB. New England miniatures
Little Falls, New York                    MeC
 Jetté. Amer heritage collection
Little girl and the cat                    DN
 DN. Amer primitive ptgs, pt 2
Little girl of the Schuyler family
 Ford. Pictorial folk art
Little girl with a flower book           NCHA
 Jones. New-found folk art
Little girl with a snowberry
 Ford. Pictorial folk art
Littleton, New Hampshire                   MB
 MB. Karolik coll
Lock Haven, Pennsylvania                   MB
 MB. Karolik coll
Lowell Mason                              MSE
 MSE. Cat of ports, 1950
Lucy Orcutt Leeds and her son
 Ford. Pictorial folk art
Lydia and Tabitha                         VWR
 VWR. Folk art (col)
Magdalen Beekman
 Flexner. First flowers (here by Patroon
 painter)
Magdalena Bogardus                        NAI
 Belknap
 NAI. Hudson valley
Magdalena Douw (Girl with the red
 shoes)                                  DeWin
 Belknap
 Mendelowitz
Mahantango valley farm                     DN
 DN. Amer primitive ptgs, pt 1
The maid of the grove                     MeC
 Jetté. Amer heritage collection
Making hay                                VWR
 VWR. Folk art (col)
A man, Portrait of (formerly attributed
 to Badger)                                DN
 Belknap
Man in a blue coat                        MeC
 Jetté. Amer heritage collection
Man in red                                 DN
 DN. Amer primitive ptgs, pt 1
Man with blue eyes                         DN
 DN. Amer primitive ptgs, pt 2
Mansion with soldiers                    NCHA
 Jones. New-found folk art
Margarita Van Vechten (formerly known
 as Miss Beekman)                         NAI
 NAI. Hudson valley (as by Schuyler
 painter)
Maria with dog under a tree               MeC
 Jetté. Amer heritage collection
Marine hospital, Chelsea, Massachusetts,
 1835-40
 U. S. National Capital sesquicentennial
 com
A mariner                                NCHA
 Jones. New-found folk art
Marriage at Cana                          NAI
 NAI. Hudson valley
Martha                                     DN
 DN. Amer primitive ptgs, pt 2
Martha                                    VWR
 VWR. Folk art (col)
Mary and David Dalzell of South Egre-
 mont, Massachusetts                      NJP
 NJP. Amer Folk art
Mary Briggs                               VWR
 VWR. Folk art (col)

Mary W. Roberts                           MeC
 Jetté. Amer heritage collection
Maryland family                           VWR
 VWR. Folk art (col)
Master Willoughby
 NYG. Fine art, p 16
 UNESCO. Prior to 1860
 UNESCO. Prior to 1860 3d ed
Meditation by the sea                      MB
 MB. Karolik coll
 Mendelowitz
 Walker. Ptgs from America
Melons and other fruit                    VWR
 VWR. Folk art (col)
The mill                                  VWR
 VWR. Folk art (col)
Mill of C. J. Hill & Son, Rochester,
 New York                                  NR
 Jones. Rediscovered ptrs
Mills residence, Ames, New York          MeC
 Jetté. Amer heritage collection
Miss Arnold knitting                       DN
 DN. Amer primitive ptgs, pt 1
Miss Daggett                               DN
 DN. Amer primitive ptgs, pt 1
Miss Dennison                              DN
 Brussels. Exposition
 DN. Amer primitive ptgs, pt 1
Miss Liberty                              VWR
 VWR. Folk art (col)
Miss Parke (possible Frances Parke)
 Belknap
Miss Tweedy of Brooklyn                   MiD
 Ford. Pictorial folk art
 Pierson
Mr Briggs                                 VWR
 VWR. Folk art (col)
Mr Carpenter
 Ford. Pictorial folk art
Mr Denison
 DN. Amer primitive ptgs, pt 1
Mr Goodrich, Hancock, Massachusetts
                                          NJP
 NJP. Amer folk art
Mr Murray                                  DN
 DN. Amer primitive ptgs, pt 2
Mrs A. V. H. Stuyvesant (as a child)
 Vail. Stuyvesant ports
Mrs Abram Gouverneur
 Belknap
Mrs Anthony Van Schaick (formerly
 known as Mrs Sybrant Gozen Van
 Schaick)                                 NAI
 Jones. Rediscovered ptrs
 NAI. Hudson valley
Mrs Arnold holding an apple                DN
 DN. Amer primitive ptgs, pt 1
Mrs Barent Rynders                       NNHS
 Belknap
Mrs Briggs                                VWR
 VWR. Folk art (col)
Mrs Daniel Phoenix                       NNHS
 NNHS. Waldron Phoenix Belknap coll
Mrs David Provoost (?)                   NNHS
 Belknap
 Flexner. First flowers
Mrs David Ver Planck                      NAI
 Belknap
 Jones. Rediscovered ptrs
 NAI. Hudson valley
Mrs Denison                                DN
 DN. Amer primitive ptgs, pt 1

UNIDENTIFIED artist—*Continued*
Mrs George Washington (after C. W
   Peale)
   Belknap
Mrs Hendrick Remsen                 NNHS
   NNHS. Waldron Phoenix Belknap coll
Mrs Henry S. Low
   MB. New England miniatures
Mrs J. B. Sheldon of Unionville, Ohio
                                    DN
   DN. Amer primitive ptgs, pt 1
   Flexner. Light of distant skies
Mrs Jacob Von Kline                 DN
   DN. Amer primitive ptgs, pt 1
Mrs Jacobus Stoutenburg            NNMC
   Belknap
   Flexner. First flowers
Mrs Jan Jansen Bleecker
   Belknap
Mrs Johannes Van Brugh             NNHS
   Belknap
Mrs John Casey and daughter        MoSL
   Ford. Pictorial folk art
   MoSL. Handbook 1953
Mrs John Nelson
   DC. Privately owned
Mrs Leonard Rogers                 NNHS
   Belknap
Mrs Mann Page II and baby John     VWC
   Belknap
   Flexner. First flowers
Mrs Murray                         DN
   DN. Amer primitive ptgs, pt 2
Mrs Myers with baby
   Ford. Pictorial folk art
Mrs Nicholas Ridgely
   Belknap
Mrs Noah Smith and family
   ICA. From colony to nation
Mrs Petrus Stuyvesant
   Vail. Stuyvesant ports
Mrs Philip Schuyler                NNHS
   Belknap
Mrs Rip Van Dam                    NNHS
   Belknap
Mrs Robert Elliston
   Belknap
Mrs Robert Lenox                   NNHS
   NNHS. Waldron Phoenix Belknap coll
Mrs Robert Lenox (possibly a copy of
   Inman portrait)                 NNHS
   NNHS. Waldron Phoenix Belknap coll
Mrs Robert Livingston
   Belknap
Mrs Robert Macbraire               NKS
   Belknap
Mrs Ruth Stanley Mix               VWR
   VWR. Folk art (col)
Mrs Samuel Browne jr               MB
   Belknap
Mrs Samuel Vetch                   NNMC
   Belknap
Mrs Sheldon
   Ford. Pictorial folk art
Mrs Starke's brother of Troy       NCHA
   Jones. New-found folk art
Mrs Sybrant Gozen Van Schaick. See Mrs
   Anthony Van Schaick
Mrs Thomas Lawrence                PH
   Belknap

Mrs Thomas Van Alstyne             NNHS
   Belknap
   Flexner. First flowers
   Pierson
Mrs Timothy Green
   MB. New England miniatures
Mrs William Axtell (possibly Mrs Abra-
   ham De Peyster jr)
   Belknap
Mrs William Goldborough and grandson
                                    MdBH
   Belknap
Mrs William Skinner
   Belknap
Mrs William Van Bergen             NNMC
   Belknap
Mrs Wynant Van Zandt               NNHS
   Belknap
   ICA. From colony to nation
Mohawk valley (formerly attributed to
   Durand)                         NCHA
   Born
Morgan addressing his friends      VWR
   VWR. Folk art (col)
Moses in the bulrushes             VWA
   Ford. Pictorial folk art
   VWR. Amer folk art
   VWR. Folk art (col)
Moses Levy                         NNMC
   Belknap
   Flexner. First flowers
Mother and child c 1810            NCHA
   Time. 300 years (col)
Mother and child in white          DN
   DN. Amer primitive ptgs, pt 1
Mother and child in white          NCHA
   Jones. New-found folk art
Mother and child in Windsor chair DN
   DN. Amer primitive ptgs, pt 1
Mount Vernon
   Ford. Pictorial folk art
Mount Vernon (after aquatint by Francis
   Jukes)                          NJN
   Ford. Pictorial folk art
Mountain landscape                 MMA
   Born
Mounting of the guard              DN
   DN. Amer primitive ptgs, pt 1
Mourning picture                   RPS
   Ford. Pictorial folk art
Mourning picture                   VWR
   Ford. Pictorial folk art
Mourning picture—Elizabeth Farr    VWR
   VWR. Folk art (col)
Mourning picture—left behind       VWR
   VWR. Folk art (col)
Mourning picture—Philo Day         VWR
   VWR. Amer folk art
   VWR. Folk art (col)
Mourning picture—Polly Botsford and
   her children                    VWR
   VWR. Folk art (col)
Mourning picture sacred to the memory of
   Jerhusha Williams
   Jetté. Amer heritage collection
Mourning scene
   Ford. Pictorial folk art
Murder of Jane McCrea              NCHA
   Time. 300 years (col)
Musicians in the snow              MB
   MB. Karolik coll

The Narrows from Fort Hamilton, New
   York Harbor                        NCHA
Jones. New-found folk art
Nathan Hawley and family               NAI
Jones. Rediscovered ptrs
The navigator                          VWR
VWR. Folk art (col)
The navigator's wife                   VWR
VWR. Folk art (col)
Negro child                            NCHA
Jones. New-found art
New England faces: husband and wife
                                       NCHA
Jones. New-found folk art
New England family group               MB
MB. Karolik coll
New England farm in winter             DN
DN. Amer primitive ptgs, pt 2
New England goddess                    RPS
Ford. Pictorial folk art
New England hillside                   MB
MB. Karolik coll
New England village                    DN
DN. Amer primitive ptgs, pt 1
New England village                    MB
MB. Karolik coll
New England village, possibly North-
   wood, New Hampshire                 MSt
Little. Country art
Nicholas William Stuyvesant            NNHS
Flexner. First flowers
Pierson
Vail. Stuyvesant ports
Nicholson Broughton
Pierson
Nitrate fleet at the Chinchas islands MSP
Davidson v 1
Northwestern town                      DN
DN. Amer primitive ptgs, pt 2
Old homestead at Sudbury, Massachu-
   setts                               MeC
Jetté. Amer heritage collection
Old lady with a Bible                  MB
MB. Karolik coll
Old lady with a plaid shawl            MB
MB. Karolik coll
Old mill
Sears. Highlights
The old plantation                     VWR
VWR. Amer folk art (col)
VWR. Folk art (col)
Oliver Wight
Ford. Pictorial folk art
On the lake
Ford. Pictorial folk art
Our flag in there
Ford. Pictorial folk art
Out for a drive                        NCHA
Jones. New-found folk art
Outdoor scene with feasting and danc-
   ing                                 CtHW
Ford. Pictorial folk art
Outing on the Hudson                   VWR
VWR. Folk art (col)
Oxbow (formerly attributed to Cole) OCl
Born
Palisades
Sears. Highlights
Paul and Virginia                      VWR
VWR. Folk art (col)
A peaceful village                     DN
DN. Amer primitive ptgs, pt 2

Pennsylvania Dutch lady                MB
MB. Karolik coll
Pennsylvania hospital                  VWR
VWR. Folk art (col)
Pennsylvania mill with Conestoga wagon
                                       NCHA
Jones. New-found folk art
Peter Farrington                       VWR
VWR. Folk art (col)
Peter Stuyvesant                       NNHS
Davidson v 1
Flexner. First flowers
Richardson. Ptg in Amer
Vail. Stuyvesant ports
Philip Schuyler                        NNHS
Belknap
Philipse manor at Yonkers, New York
Davidson v 1
Picking flowers                        NCHA
Jones. New-found folk art
Picking flowers                        VWR
VWR. Folk art (col)
Pierre Van Cortlandt                   NBM
Belknap
ICA. From colony to nation
NNHS. Waldron Phoenix Belknap coll
Pieter Schuyler
Belknap
Flexner. First flowers
Richardson. Ptg in America
Pieter Waldron
Belknap
Pineapple                              VWR
VWR. Folk art (col)
Pink roses                             DN
DN. Amer primitive ptgs, pt 1
Pioneer's camp
Ford. Pictorial folk art
The plantation                         DN
DN. Amer primitive ptgs, pt 1
Polly Maxon of Stephentown, New York
                                       NJP
NJP. Amer folk art
The Pool sisters                       MeC
Jetté. Amer heritage collection
Privateer hermaphrodite brig Rambler of
   Medford                             MSP
Davidson v 1
Privateer schooner Surprise of Baltimore
   capturing the British ship Star, 1815
                                       MdBH
Davidson v 1
Prodigal son gambling                  DN
DN. Amer primitive ptgs, pt 2
The prodigal son in misery             VWR
VWR. Folk art (col)
The prodigal son receiving his patrimony
                                       VWR
VWR. Folk art (col)
The prodigal son reclaimed             VWR
VWR. Folk art (col)
The prodigal son reveling with harlots
                                       VWR
VWR. Folk art (col)
Profile portrait of a lady             DN
DN. Amer primitive ptgs, pt 1
Profile portrait of a man              DN
DN. Amer primitive ptgs, pt 1
Profile portrait of lady in white cap DN
DN. Amer primitive ptgs, pt 2
Prospectors                            DN
DN. Amer primitive ptgs, pt 2

UNIDENTIFIED artist—*Continued*
Quilting party                                        MMA
  Barker. Amer ptg
  Ford. Pictorial folk art
  Walker. Ptgs from America
Quilting party                                        VWR
  VWR. Amer folk art (col)
Raft on river                                         InBU
  U.S. National Capital sesquicentennial
  com
Railroad engine, the Star
  Ford. Pictorial folk art
Rebecca at the well                                   VWR
  VWR. Folk art (col)
Red mill                                              NCHA
  Jones. New-found folk art
Rhode Island choir boy
  Ford. Pictorial folk art
Richard Ward
  Belknap
  NNHS. Waldron Phoenix Belknap coll
Richmond c 1822
  Davidson v 1
Rip Van Dam                                           NNHS
  Belknap
River landing                                         MB
  MB. Karolik coll
River landscape                                       VWR
  VWR. Folk art (col)
River view with shepherd and animals
  Ford. Pictorial folk art
Robert Lenox (after Jarvis)                           NNHS
  NNHS. Waldron Phoenix Belknap coll
Robert Livingston
  Belknap
Robert Macbraire                                      NKS
  Belknap
Robert Sanders
  Belknap
Runaway horse                                         WMAA
  Ford. Pictorial folk art
  Walker. Ptgs from America (col)
Running before the storm                              MB
  MB. Karolik coll
Ruth and Naomi                                        VWR
  VWR. Folk art (col)
The sad departure                                     DN
  DN. Amer primitive ptgs, pt 2
A sailor                                              DN
  DN. Amer primitive ptgs, pt 2
Sailors                                               ICA
  Ford. Pictorial folk art
Samuel Hart
  MB. New England miniatures
Samuel Houston as Marius                              TxA
  Roos
Samuel Mountfort Pitts sr (possibly by
  J. G. or L. E. Cole)                            MiD
  MiD. Ports of the Pitts family
Samuel Vetch                                          NNMC
  Belknap
Sarah Alden                                           MeC
  Jetté. Amer heritage collection
Sarah Hobbs
  Flexner. Light of distant skies
The Sargent family                                    DN
  DN. Amer primitive ptgs, pt 1
  Time. 300 years (col)
Schoolmaster and boys                                 VWR
  VWR. Folk art (col)

The schoolroom
  U.S. National Capital sesquicentennial
  com
Screaming eagle                                       NCHA
  Jones. New-found folk art
Schuyler family girl
  Belknap
The Senate, Albany, 1850                              NAI
  Jones. Rediscovered ptrs
The shepherd and his flock                            VWR
  VWR. Folk art (col)
Ship Bavaria
  Davidson v 1
Ship Hercules of Salem, 1809                          MSP
  Davidson v 1
Shrewsbury river near Seabright, New
  Jersey                                         MB
  MB. Karolik coll
Signing the Treaty of Greenville. See
  Indian Treaty of Greenville, 1795
Silas Ilsley                                          MeC
  MeC. Inaugural ex
  NUM. Art across America
Silver lake, New Hampshire
  Sears. Highlights
Sisters in red                                        DN
  DN. Amer primitive ptgs, pt 1
A smart turnout                                       CtHW
  CtHW. Handbook
Smith memorial
  Jones. New-found folk art
Son of Captain Samuel Hallett             ICA
  Belknap
Sophia Burpee                                         DN
  DN. Amer primitive ptgs
Southeast prospect of the city of New
  York c 1850                                    NNHS
  Born
The Southern Belle                                    MeC
  Jetté. Amer heritage collection
Spring fishing                                        VWR
  VWR. Folk art (col)
Stages of man                                         VWR
  VWR. Folk art (col)
Star spangled banner in the rocket's red
  glare over Fort McHenry, 1814
                    MdBH
  Davidson v2
Start of the hunt                                     DN
  DN. Amer primitive ptgs, pt 1
Stephen Decatur
  Ford. Pictorial folk art
Stephen Greenleaf jr
  Belknap
Still life with Johnson's dictionary
  CtY. Yale alumni
Still life with melons                                DN
  DN. Amer primitive ptgs
Still life with watermelon                            VWR
  VWR. Folk art (col)
Street in Brooklyn c 1840-60                          MiD
  Ford. Pictorial folk art
  Pierson
  Richardson. Ptg in America
Street in winter; evening                             MB
  MB. Karolik coll
Stylized landscape                                    DN
  DN. Amer primitive ptgs, pt 2
Stylized landscape                                    MeC
  Jetté. Amer heritage collection
Summer
  Sears. Highlights
Summer landscape: haymaking
  MB. Karolik coll

Sunset by the river
  Sears. Highlights
Susanna Truax                          DN
  Belknap
  DN. Amer primitive ptgs, pt 1
Suspension bridge at Niagara Falls
  Baur. Amer ptg
Sybrant Gozen Van Schaick. See Anthony
  Van Schaick
Telegraph hill, San Francisco, c 1849
  U.S. National Capital sesquicentennial
  com
Textile merchant                       DN
  DN. Amer primitive ptgs, pt 1
That's my doll!                        NCHA
  Jones. New-found folk art
Theatre scenic backdrop                RPHS
  Ford. Pictorial folk art
Thomas Lawrence                        PH
  Belknap
Thomas Savage                          MWM
  Belknap
  Davidson v 1
Thomas Van Alstyne                     NNHS
  Barker. Amer ptg
  Belknap
  Flexner. First flowers
  Larkin
  Larkin rev ed
  Pierson
Thorndike sisters
  MB. New England miniatures
Thrifty farm                           NCHA
  Jones. New-found folk art
Tobias Ten Eyck                        NAI
  Belknap
  NAI. Hudson valley
Tomatoes, fruit, and flowers           MB
  MB. Karolik coll
Tomb in memory of Richard Newhall
                                       MeC
  Jetté. Amer heritage collection
Town bridge                            VWR
  VWR. Folk art (col)
Town on a river                        NCHA
  Jones. New-found folk art
The trotter                            DN
  DN. Amer primitive ptgs, pt 2
True cross                             MMA
  Ford. Pictorial folk art
Twenty-two houses and a church    DN
  DN. Amer primitive ptgs, pt 1
Twin sisters                           DN
  DN. Amer primitive ptgs, pt 1
Two armies before a city               NCHA
  Jones. New-found folk art
Two boys in green tunics               NCHA
  Jones. New-found folk art
Two brown and white puppies       MeC
  Jetté. Amer heritage collection
Two children with a deer
  Belknap
Two little girls in blue               NCHA
  Jones. New-found folk art
Two young girls, 1835                  MeC
  Jetté. Amer heritage collection
A valley farm                          DN
  DN. Amer primitive ptgs, pt 2
Van Schaick hatchment                  NAI
  Jones. Rediscovered ptrs
  NAI. Hudson valley
Venice, c 1840                         NCHA
  Jones. New-found folk art

Venus drawn by doves                   VWR
  VWR. Folk art (col)
Victorian dairy farm, study in green
                                       NCHA
  Jones. New-found folk art
Victorian family                       NCHA
  Jones. New-found folk art
Victorian landscape                    MeC
  Jetté. Amer heritage collection
View of Baltimore, c 1840
  U.S. National Capital sesquicentennial
  com
View of Barnstable                     MAP
  Born
View of the Palisades
  Sears. Highlights
View of the Schuylkill waterworks, Phila-
  delphia (after William Henry Bart-
  lett)                                MiD
  Born
Village by the river                   DN
  DN. Amer primitive ptg, pt 2
A village street, Massachusetts, c 1845
                                       MeC
  Jetté. Amer heritage collection
Virgin Mary with Holy Ghost
  Mendelowitz
Walker family, father and son     NJP
  NJP. Amer folk art
Walker family, mother and daughter
                                       NJP
  Ford. Pictorial folk art
  NJP. Amer folk art
Walking the puppy                      NCHA
  Jones. New-found folk art
Wall painting from Connecticut
  Ford. Pictorial folk art
War horses                             NCHA
  Jones. New-found folk art
Warren Crosby
  Ford. Pictorial folk art
Washington and his staff at Fort Cum-
  berland, Maryland, 1794
  Davidson v2
The Washington, first double decker on
  the Mississippi
  Born
Watchmaker with his tools              MSt
  Little. Country art
Watercolor class
  U.S. National Capital sesquicentennial
  com
Watercolor on a religious theme   VWR
  Ford. Pictorial folk art
Watermelon                             MB
  MB. Karolik coll
Waterworks, Center square, Philadelphia
                                       PH
  Ford. Pictorial folk art
We go for the Union                    DN
  DN. Amer primitive ptgs, pt 1
Wesleyan academy, Wilbraham, Massa-
  chusetts                             MeC
  Jetté. Amer heritage collection
West Point, c 1850
  Ford. Pictorial folk art
West Point from above Washington valley
                                       MB
  MB. Karolik coll
Western frontier homestead             DN
  DN. Amer primitive ptgs, pt 2
Whaling                                DN
  DN. Amer primitive ptgs, pt 2

UNIDENTIFIED artist—*Continued*
Whaling scene
  Davidson v 1
Whaling scene—Triton of New Bedford
  MeC
  Jetté. Amer heritage collection
Wheat stack                          VWR
  VWR. Folk art (col)
Wife of Capt George, Haverhill, Massa-
  chusetts                           NJP
  NJP. Amer folk art
Wilkes-Barre and the Wyoming valley
  McClintock (col)
William Stoughton                    MCH
  Flexner. First flowers
  U. S. National Capital sesquicentennial
  com
William Van Bergen                   NNMC
  Belknap
Winter scene
  Born
Winter sports on the farm            NCHA
  Jones. New-found folk art
A woman                              ICA
  Ford. Pictorial folk art
Woman in a yellow dress (Pennsylvania)
  MeC
  Jetté. Amer heritage collection
Woman with apple                     OYB
  OYB. Supplement
Woman with sewing box                VWR
  VWR. Folk art (col)
Woodcutting in winter                MB
  MB. Karolik coll
Woodman spare that tree              MoSL
  Ford. Pictorial folk art
Woodshed interior                    MB
  MB. Karolik coll
Woodward children
  MB. New England miniatures (col)
Worth family mourning
  Ford. Pictorial folk art
Wynant Van Zandt                     NNHS
  Belknap
Wyoming valley (Conyngham coll)
  McClintock
Wyoming valley in 1850 (Wyoming his-
  torical society)
  McClintock
Yellow coach                         VWR
  VWR. Folk art (col)
Young girl in a red dress            MeC
  Jetté. Amer heritage collection
Young girl in white                  VWR
  VWR. Folk art (col)
Young ladies' seminary, Virginia
  Flexner. Light of distant skies
Young man in a gray linen suit       NCHA
  Jones. New-found folk art
Young man wearing white stock        DN
  DN. Amer primitive ptgs, pt 1
Zachary Taylor                       NNHS
  Ford. Pictorial folk art
The **uninvited** by G. Gutmann
**Union** square in spring by C. Hassam
**Union** square, night by M. Kantor

United States (frigate)
  Martens, J. W. Brooklyn Navy yard
    (Frigate USS United States)
The **United States** and the Macedonian by
  T. Chambers
United States Capitol
  Burton, C. The Capitol, Washington, 1824
United States cavalry defending a position
  by F. Remington
United States. Congress. House of repre-
  sentatives
  Morse, S. F. B. Old House of representa-
    tives, 1821-22
United States Military Academy, West
  Point
  Catlin, G. United States Military Acade-
    my, West Point
Universal field by M. Tobey
Universe by E. E. Wentz
Unknown Dane by W. M. Chase
Unmasked by R. Brackman
Unpainted horses by L. Bouché
Unscheduled stop by C. M. Russell
Untilled field by P. Bacon
Up the Hudson by G. W. Bellows
UPJOHN, Anna Milo
  Andrew Dickson White                CtY
    CtY. Portrait index
Upper deck by C. Sheeler
Upper House by W. Gropper
Upper pasture by M. Avery
Upright 3 by K. E. Fortess
Upright trees by A. Blanch
Uprooted tree by P. Pearlstein
Upside down table and mask by Y. Kuni-
  yoshi
**Uptown** by E. Model
URBAN, Albert, 1909-1959
  Painting, 1959                      MMA
    MMA. Sixteen
  Painting 1959                       NBuA
    NBuA. Acquisitions 1959-1961
  Painting, 1959 (Urban coll)
    MMA. Sixteen
  Phoenix no 2
    IU. Contemp Amer ptg & sculp, 1959
Urban by N. Lewis
Urban cathedral by J. Friebert
Urban landscape by A. Alcalay
Urchin's game by F. Martin
Urgent hour by G. Kamrowski
Uriel in the sun by W. Allston
Ursine park by S. Davis
Uruguay medicine man, South America by
  G. Catlin
Ut-Ha-Wah (Capt Vole) by W. J. Wilgus
UTLEY, Windsor, 1920-
  Aggressors
    OrPA. Ptgs & sculptures
UTTER, Bror, 1913-
  Pharmaceutic cabinet
    Pousette-Dart. Amer ptg
  Trio                                TxF
    CoS. New accessions USA, 1954

# V

V. J. day by V. Deezik
Vacant lot by B. Shahn
Vacationist by R. Gwathmey
Vagrants by C. A. Hall
Vail, Anna Miretta, fl 1840
  Tuthill, A. G. D. Anna Miretta Vail
Vail, Mary Elizabeth, fl 1840
  Tuthill, A. G. D. Mary Elizabeth Vail
Vail, Thomas, b 1760
  Tuthill, A. G. D. Dr Thomas Vail (?)
Vail children, fl 1818
  Tuthill, A. G. D. Jackson, Solon, Mary
  Elizabeth and Miretta Vail
Val d'Aosta, a stream over rocks by J. S.
  Sargent
Val d'Aosta, stepping stones by J. S.
  Sargent
Val d'Arconville by T. Robinson
Val Ticino, St Gothard route by R. Smith
Valentine, Mann Satterwhite, 1786-1865
  Hubard, W. J. Mann S. Valentine
Valentine, Mann Satterwhite, 1824-1892
  Hubard, W. J. Mann S. Valentine 2nd
  and the artist
The valentine by W. Allston
Valentine still life by H. A. Sawyer
Valhalla bridge by T. Donnelly
Vallé, Isabella (Sargeant)
  Sargent, J. S. Mrs Jules Vallé
The valley by E. Lawson
The valley by E. Ludins
Valley below by W. Lockwood
A valley farm by Unidentified artist
Valley landscape by J. Wilkinson
Valley of dry bones—triptych by A. Rattner
Valley of Mexico by C. W. Chapman
Valley ranch by P. L. Dike
Value, Charlotte Elizabeth, b 1830
  Sully, T. Victor René Value and his
  daughter Charlotte
Value, Victor René, 1790-1860?
  Sully, T. Victor René Value and his
  daughter Charlotte
Van Alen, Maria. See Van Alstyne, Maria
  (Van Alen)
Van Alen, Miss, fl 1720
  Vanderlyn, P. (attributed works) Miss
  Van Alen
Van Alstyne, Maria (Van Alen) fl 1695
  Unidentified artist. Mrs Thomas Van
  Alstyne
Van Alstyne, Thomas, 1688-1765
  Unidentified artist. Thomas Van Alstyne
Van Arnam, Judge, fl 1855
  Van Zandt, T. K. Judge Van Arnam in
  his sleigh
Van Bergen, Elinor (Van Dyke) fl 1720
  Unidentified artist. Mrs William Van
  Bergen
Van Bergen, William, fl 1720
  Unidentified artist. William Van Bergen
  of Catskill, New York
Van Brugh, Elizabeth. See Van Rensselaer,
  Elizabeth (Van Brugh)

Van Brugh, Margareta (Provoost) b 1673
  Unidentified artist. Mrs Johannes Van
  Brugh
Van Buren, Amelia C. fl 1889
  Eakins, T. Miss Van Buren
Van Buren, Martin, president U. S. 1782-
  1862
  Ames, E. Martin Van Buren
  Healy, G. P. A. Martin Van Buren
Van Cortlandt, Abraham, 1713-1746
  Unidentified artist. Abraham Van Cort-
  landt
Van Cortlandt, Anne (Stevenson) 1774-1821
  Ames, E. Mrs Pierre Van Cortlandt II
Van Cortlandt, Elizabeth. See Skinner,
  Elizabeth (Van Cortlandt)
Van Cortlandt, John, 1718-1747
  Unidentified artist. John Van Cortlandt
Van Cortlandt, Maria. See Van Rensselaer,
  Maria (Van Cortlandt)
Van Cortlandt, Philip, 1749-1831
  Ames, E. Philip Van Cortlandt
Van Cortlandt, Pierre, 1721-1814
  Unidentified artist. Pierre Van Cortlandt
Van Cortlandt, Pierre, 1762-1848
  Ames, E. Pierre Van Cortlandt II
Van Dam, Mrs Rip. See Van Dam, Sarah
  (Van Der Spiegel)
Van Dam, Rip, 1660?-1749
  Unidentified artist. Rip Van Dam
Van Dam, Sarah (Van Der Spiegel) 1663-
  1736
  Unidentified artist. Mrs Rip Van Dam
Van Dame, Bartholomew, fl 1836
  Davis, J. H. Bartholomew Van Dame
Vandenberg, Arthur Hendrick, 1884-1951
  Shahn, B. Dewey, Vandenberg and Taft
Vander Horst, Elizabeth. See Moore, Eliza-
  beth (Vander Horst)
VANDERLYN, John, 1775-1852
  Ariadne          PA
    Bazin
    Canaday
    Flexner. Amer ptg
    Flexner. Light of distant skies
    Flexner. Short history
    Larkin
    Larkin rev ed
    Mendelowitz
    MdBMu. Rendezvous
    Pierson
    Richardson. Ptg in America
    Roos
    Time. 300 years (col)
  Catherine H. Van Rensselaer    ATeS
    ATeS. Collection
  Death of Jane McCrea    CtHW
    Barker. Amer ptg
    CtHW. Handbook
    Flexner. Light of distant skies
    Pierson
  Falls of Niagara    NNPL
    Ford. Edward Hicks
  Falls of Niagara taken from under the
    Table rock    NNHS
    Born
  James Hillhouse    CtY
    CtY. Portrait index
  A lady and her son    NKS
    Pierson
    Richardson. Ptg in America

**VANDERLYN, John**—*Continued*
Marius amidst the ruins of Carthage
 CSFD
 Canaday
 Larkin rev ed (col detail)
 Pierson
Mrs Marinus Willett and child    MM
 Flexner. Light of distant skies
Niagara Falls    NKS
 Flexner. Light of distant skies
 Pierson
Panorama: palace and gardens of Ver-
 sailles (Panoramic view of the palace
 and gardens of Versailles)    MM
 Born
 Larkin rev ed (detail)
 Pierson
Robert R. Livingston    NNHS
 Larkin
 Larkin rev ed
 Pierson
Self-portrait    MM
 Mendelowitz
 Roos
Severyn Bruyn    NKS
 Larkin
 Larkin rev ed
Theodosia Burr
 DC. Privately owned
View in Rome    NKS
 Pierson
**VANDERLYN, Pieter,** 1687-1778
Helena Jansen Sleight    NKS
 Belknap

**Attributed works**

Catherine De Peyster
 Belknap
Cornelius D. Wynkoop
 Belknap
Matthew Ten Eyck
 Belknap
Miss Van Alen    DN
 Belknap
 DN. Amer primitive ptgs, pt 1
Mrs Petrus Vas    NAI
 Belknap
 Flexner. First flowers
 Jones. Rediscovered ptrs
 NAI. Hudson valley
**VAN DER POOL, James,** 1765-1799
A woman, Portrait of    NJN
 Ford. Pictorial folk art

**Attributed works**

A man, Portrait of    NJN
 Ford. Pictorial folk art
**Vander Sluis, George J.** 1915-
Grey and green
 IU. Contemp Amer ptg & sculp, 1961
**Van Der Spiegel, Sarah.** See Van Dam,
 Sarah (Van Der Spiegel)
**VANDERSPRITT, John**
Increase Mather    MBH
 Davidson v 1
**Vanderveer, Jane (Herbert)** fl 1819
 Williams, M. Mrs Jane Herbert Vander-
 veer
**Vanderveer, John G,** 1799-1883
 Williams, M. John G. Vanderveer
**Vanderveer, Mrs John G.** See Vanderveer,
 Jane (Herbert)

**VAN DUZER, Clarence Eugene,** 1920-
Pietà    OYB
 OYB. Annual 1956
 OYB. Supplement 1959
**Van Dyke, Elinor.** See Van Bergen, Elinor
 (Van Dyke)
**Vane, Henrietta Elizabeth Frederica,** fl 1783
 Stuart, G. Henrietta Elizabeth Frederica
 Vane
**VAN EVEREN, Jan,** 1875-1947
Abstraction    CtY
 CtY. Soc Anonyme
**Van Horne, Augustus Cornelius,** 1765-1853
 Unidentified artist. Augustus Cornelius
 Van Horne
**Van Horne, David**
 Dunlap, W. David Van Horne
**Van Horne, Susan Rivington.** See Stuy-
 vesant, Susan Rivington (Van Horne)
**Vanishing** city by A. Alcalay
**Vanity** by W. Auerbach-Levy
**Vanity** fair by H. Koerner
**Vanity** of an artist's dream by C. B. King
**Van Ness, William W.** 1776-1823
 Jarvis, J. W. William W. Van Ness
**Van Reid, Jane L.** fl 1810
 Stettinius, S. E. (attributed works) Jane
 L. Van Reid
**Van Reid, Wellington,** fl 1810
 Stettinius, S. E. (attributed works) Wel-
 lington Van Reid
**Van Rensselaer, Anne,** b 1719
 Watson, J. (attributed works) Anne Van
 Rensselaer
**Van Rensselaer, Ariaantje (Schuyler)** 1720-
 1763
 Unidentified artist. Ariaantje Schuyler
 Van Rensselaer
**Van Rensselaer, Catherine,** 1734-1803. See
 Schuyler, Catherine (Van Rensselaer)
**Van Rensselaer, Catherine H.**
 Vanderlyn, J. Catherine H. Van Rens-
 selaer
**Van Rensselaer, Elizabeth (Groesbeek)**
 1707-1729
 Watson, J. (attributed works) Mrs
 Stephanus (?) Van Rensselaer
**Van Rensselaer, Elizabeth (Van Brugh)**
 b 1712
 Duyckinck, G. (attributed works) Mrs
 Henry Van Rensselaer
**Van Rensselaer, Mrs Henry.** See Van Rens-
 selaer, Elizabeth (Van Brugh)
**Van Rensselaer, Jacobus,** 1713-1754?
 Watson, J. (attributed works) Gentleman
 of the Van Rensselaer family (prob-
 ably Jacobus Van Rensselaer)
**Van Rensselaer, Jan Baptist,** fl 1658
 Watson, J. (attributed works) Van Rens-
 selaer gentleman (known as Jan
 Baptist Van Rensselaer)
**Van Rensselaer, Jeremias,** 1705-1745
 Unidentified artist. Jeremias Van Rens-
 selaer
**Van Rensselaer, Mrs Kiliaen,** b 1680. See
 Van Rensselaer, Maria (Van Cort-
 landt)
**Van Rensselaer, Mrs Kiliaen,** 1720-1763. See
 Van Rensselaer, Ariaantje (Schuyler)
**Van Rensselaer, Maria (Van Cortlandt)**
 b 1680
 Watson, J. (attributed works) Mrs Kiliaen
 Van Rensselaer III

**Van Rensselaer, Solomon,** 1774-1852
  Ames, E. Solomon Van Rensselaer
**Van Rensselaer, Stephanus,** 1707-1747
  Watson, J. (attributed works) Gentleman
    of the Van Rensselaer family (prob-
    ably Stephanus Van Renssalaer)
**Van Rensselaer, Mrs Stephanus (?).** See
    Van Rensselaer, Elizabeth (Groes-
    beek)
**Van Rensselaer, Stephen,** 1764-1839
  Ames, E. Stephen Van Rensselaer
**Van Rensselaer family, Member of**
  Unidentified artist. Girl of the Van Rens-
    selaer family
**Van Rensselaer family, Member of,** fl 1725
  Unidentified artist. Lady of the Van
    Rensselaer family
**Van Schaick, Anthony,** 1682-1756
  Unidentified artist. Anthony Van Schaick
**Van Schaick, Mrs Anthony,** b 1685?
  Unidentified artist. Mrs Anthony Van
    Schaick
**Van Schaick, Sybrant Gozen.** See Van
    Schaick, Anthony
**Van Schaick** hatchment by Unidentified
    artist
**Van Vechten, Gerrit Teunise,** b 1703
  Unidentified artist. Gerrit Teunise Van
    Vechten
**Van Vechten, Lavinia,** fl 1720
  Unidentified artist. Lavinia Van Vechten
**Van Vechten, Margarita,** b 1705
  Unidentified artist. Margarita Van
    Vechten
**Van Zandt, Catharina (Ten Eyck)** 1692-1772
  Unidentified artist. Mrs Wynant Van
    Zandt
**VAN ZANDT, Thomas K.** fl 1844-1870
  Judge Van Arnam in his sleigh      NAI
    Jones. Undiscovered ptrs
**Van Zandt, Wynant,** 1683-1757
  Unidentified artist. Wynant Van Zandt
**Vanzetti, Bartolomeo,** 1889-1927
  Shahn, B. Bartolomeo Vanzetti
  Shahn, B. Sacco and Vanzetti in coffins
  Shahn, B. Vanzetti and Sacco
**VARGA, Margit,** 1908-
  Connecticut farm      ATU
    ATU. Coll of Amer art
  Country carnival
    IU. Contemp Amer ptg, 1952
  Road to Danbury
    Gruskin (col)
**Variation** on a theme by S. Zingale
**Variations** by J. Xceron
**Variations** in pink and grey—Chelsea by
    J. A. M. Whistler
**Variations** on a still life by B. Browne
**Variations** on a theme: the wreck by E.
    Fiene
**Variations** on the Avignon Pietà, no 2 by W.
    Pachner
**Varick, Richard,** 1753-1831
  Inman, H. Col Richard Varick
**Vartoosh,** Portrait of by A. Gorky
**Vas, Elsje (Rutgers) Schuyler,** b 1674
  Vanderlyn, P. (attributed works) Mrs
    Petrus Vas
**Vase** and flowers by P. Evergood
**Vase** of flowers by C. S. Price
**Vase** of mixed flowers by M. J. Heade

**Vase** with flowers by W. Chaiken
**Vases** by A. Ozenfant
**VASILIEFF, Nicholas,** 1892?-
  Black table
    IU. Contemp Amer ptg & sculp, 1961
  Girl with cat
    IU. Contemp Amer ptg & sculp, 1955
  Mrs V, Portrait of
    IU. Contemp Amer ptg & sculp, 1953
  On the porch      IU
    IU. Contemp Amer ptg & sculp, 1957
    IU. 20th century
  Pink tablecloth      DC
    CoS. New accessions USA, 1958
  Still life with fish      IU
    CoS. New accessions USA, 1956
  Still life with lobster
    PPC. International ex, 1952
**VASS, Gene,** 1922-
  Deux personnages      NBuA
    NBuA. Acquisitions 1957-58
  Eleventh street      NBuA
    NBuA. Acquisitions 1959-1961
  Hell Gate tie
    IU. Contemp Amer ptg & sculp, 1961
**Vaudeville** by C. H. Demuth
**Vaudeville** by J. Lawrence
**Vaudeville** musicians by C. H. Demuth
**VAUGHAN, David A.**
  The welder
    CSFP. Annual ex, 1946
**VAVRUSKA, Frank,** 1917-
  Cows in a tropical landscape
    ICA. Annual ex, 1947/48
**VEDDER, Elihu,** 1836-1923
  Bed of the torrent Mugnone, near Flor-
    ence
    MiD. Coll in progress
    WiMiA. Amer ptg 1760-1960
  A corner of Capri
    MiD. Travelers in Arcadia
  Fiesole      MiD
    MiD. Treasures
  Ideal head
    Pierson
    Richardson. Ptg in America
  Italian landscape      MB
    MiD. Travelers in Arcadia
  Lair of the sea serpent      MB
    Pierson
    Richardson. Ptg in America
  The lost mind      MM
    MiD. Travelers in Arcadia
    Pierson
  The philosopher      NJN
    Mendelowitz
  Rome      MeB
    Pierson
  The sphinx on the seashore
    MiD. Coll in progress
**Veiled** bouquet by H. Pittman
**Vellanti, Ailene**
  The mother
    NAD. Annual ex, spring 1950
**Venetian** bead stringers by J. S. Sargent
**Venetian** girl by F. Duveneck
**Venetian** Gothic art building on the old Yale
    campus by P. B. Wight
**Venetian** interior by J. S. Sargent
**Veni,** vidi, vici by D. Fredenthal

**Venice**
Boit, E. D. Rio di San Barnaba, Venice
Boit, E. D. Rio di San Lorenzo, Venice
Boit, E. D. Venice: afternoon on the Campo San Trovaso
Boit, E. D. Venice: afternoon on the Grand Canal
Boit, E. D. Venice: fisherman's quarter on the Giudecca
Boit, E. D. Venice: looking toward the Grand Canal
Boit, E. D. Venice: morning on the Grand Canal
Boit, E. D. Venice: off San Giorgio
Boit, E. D. Venice: showery morning on the Zattere
Chase, W. M. City streets, Venice
Chase, W. M. View of Venice
Congdon, W. G. Piazza San Marco
Congdon, W. G. Piazza, Venice
Congdon, W. G. Venice no 1
Congdon, W. G. Venice no 1, 1950
Congdon, W. G. Venice no 2
Inness, G. Venice: S. Giorgio Maggiore
Longfellow, W. P. P. Sala del Collegio, Ducal palace, Venice
MacIver, L. Venice, 1949
Moran, T. View of Venice
Prendergast, M. B. Bridge and steps, Venice
Prendergast, M. B. Bridge in Venice
Prendergast, M. B. Café Florian, Venice
Prendergast, M. B. Campo Santa Maria Formosa, Venice
Prendergast, M. B. Easter procession, St Mark's, Venice
Prendergast, M. B. Festival day, Venice
Prendergast, M. B. The Lagoon, Venice
Prendergast, M. B. Market place, Venice
Prendergast, M. B. Piazza di San Marco, Venice
Prendergast, M. B. Ponte della Paglia
Prendergast, M. B. Procession, Venice
Prendergast, M. B. Riva San Biagio, Venice
Prendergast, M. B. St Mark's Venice
Prendergast, M. B. Santa Maria Formosa, Venice
Prendergast, M. B. Sunlight on the Piazzetta, Venice
Prendergast, M. B. Umbrellas in the rain, Venice
Prendergast, M. B. Venice
Sargent, J. S. Cafe on Riva degli Schiavoni, Venice
Sargent, J. S. Corner of the church of St Staë, Venice
Sargent, J. S. Festa della regatta, Palazzo Barbaro
Sargent, J. S. Scuola di San Rocco, Venice
Sargent, J. S. Street in Venice
Sargent, J. S. Venice: La Digana
Sargent, J. S. Venice: I Gesuati
Sargent, J. S. Venice: La Salute
Sargent, J. S. Venice: under the Rialto bridge
Smith, F. H. Venice: canal scene I
Smith, F. H. Venice: canal scene II
Unidentified artist. Venice, c 1840
Whistler, J. A. M. Lagoon, Venice: Nocturne in blue and silver

**Venice** lace makers by H. Bacon
**Venus.** See Mythological themes
**Verdant** rise by R. Eshoo
**Verde** by C. Woods
**Verdict** of the people by G. C. Bingham
**Verdure** by H. Bayer
**VERELST, Willem,** fl 1734-1756
Oglethorpe presenting Tomo-Chi-Chi and the Indians to Lord Trustees of the colony of Georgia
Davidson v 1
**VERES (Mrs Margo Clark)**
Davy Emmet Crocky (Emmett Kelly) NSP. Sportscapes
**Verge** by R. Lytle
**Verlaine, Paul**
Lindner, R. Paul Verlaine
**Vermilion** cliffs by G. C. Delano
**Vermont**
Durand, A. B. View of Rutland, Vermont
Holt, H. Fading light, Stowe valley
Hopper, E. First branch of the White river, Vermont
Sloane, M. Vermont hamlet
Solomon, H. Vermont autumn
Thompson, J. B. Harvest in Vermont
Williams, F. B. Down from Mount Mansfield, Vermont
**Vermont** lawyer by H. Bundy
**Vernal** by S. Laufman
**Vernet, John,** fl 1806
Trumbull, J. John Vernet and his family
The **Veronica** by J. De Feo
La **Veronica** by J. Ulbricht
**Verplanck, Ariaantje (Coeymans)** 1672-1743
Unidentified artist. Mrs David Verplanck
**Verplanck, Mrs David.** See Verplanck, Ariaantje (Coeymans)
**Verplanck, Eliza (Fenno)** See Fenno, Eliza
**Verplanck, Mrs Gulian Crommelin.** See Fenno, Eliza
**Verplanck, Samuel,** 1739-1820
Copley, J. S. Samuel Verplanck
**Versailles**
Robinson, F. V. Versailles
Vanderlyn, J. Panorama: palace and gardens of Versailles
**VERSTILLE, William,** 1755-1803
Noah Webster
MB. New England miniatures
Solomon Ingraham
MB. New England miniatures
**Vertical** by W. P. Morehouse
**Vertical** by C. A. Morris
**Vertical** black by L. Calcagno
**Vertical** composition by F. Lebrun
The **very** great lion hunters by W. W. Quirt
A **very** happy picture by D. Tanning
**Vessels** of magic by M. Rothko
**Vesuvius** by J. Toole
**Vetch, Margaret (Livingston)** 1681-1758
Unidentified artist. Mrs Samuel Vetch
**Vetch, Samuel,** 1668-1732
Unidentified artist. Samuel Vetch
**Veteran** in a new field by W. Homer
**Veteran's** dream by C. Williamson
**Via** delle Corso, Rome by M. B. Prendergast

**Via** Partenope by W. Stuempfig

**Via** Porta Romana II by F. Bultman

**Vianna** do Castello, Portugal by J. S. Sargent

**Vibration** by S. Franks

**VICENTE, Esteban,** 1904-
Composition, 1951
  Hess. Abstract ptg
Composition no 6, 1959
  WMAA. Museum and its friends, 1958
Growth, 1951
  Hess. Abstract ptg
Number 3, 1952
  IU. Contemp Amer ptg & sculp, 1953
Number 6
  IU. Contemp Amer ptg, 1952
Number 9, 1959     MnMW
  MnMW. 60 Amer ptrs

**VICKREY, Robert,** 1926-
Abandoned wharf
  IU. Contemp Amer ptg & sculp, 1959
The barker
  IaDa. 30th anniversary
Conversation
Newmeyer
  WMAA. New decade
Doorway
  ICA. Annual ex, 1951
**Fear**     WMAA
Pierson
  WMAA. Sara Roby
Fear     PMB
  WMAA. New decade
Gravel
  CSB. Illusion
Halloween mask
  WMAA. New decade
Hopscotch
  MiD. Coll in progress
  WiMiA. Amer ptg 1760-1960
The labyrinth.     WMAA
  Goodrich. Amer art
  McCurdy
  MnMW. Reality and fantasy
Late afternoon     OYB
  OYB. Supplement 1959
The poster
  IU. Contemp Amer ptg & sculp, 1955

**Victim** by S. W. Hayter

**Victoria,** queen of Great Britain, 1819-1901
Sully, T. Queen Victoria

**Victoria** by W. Kuhn

**Victorian** building by Mingle

**Victorian** dairy farm, study in green by Unidentified artist

**Victorian** family by Unidentified artist

**Victorian** interior I, 1945 by H. Pippin

**Victorian** interior II, 1945 by H. Pippin

**Victorian** landscape by Unidentified artist

**Victorian** tapestry by P. L. Dike

**VIDAR, Frede,** 1911-
Canal in Brooklyn
  IU. Contemp Amer ptg, 1949
Manila no 4
  IU. Contemp Amer ptg, 1948

**View** from my window by E. Quincy

**Vigil** at the beach by T. C. Quirk

**Villa** dei misteri by A. Osver

**Villa** di Marlia: a fountain by J. S. Sargent

**Villa** di Marlia, Lucca by J. S. Sargent

**Villa** di Marlia: the balustrade by J. S. Sargent

**Villa** Falconiere by J. S. Sargent

**Villa** la Mouette by E. W. Dickinson

**Villa** Maria by C. Grant

**Villa** Rotunda by J. C. Atherton

The **village** by A. Blanch

**Village** above the river by L. Siegriest

**Village** church by L. Feininger

**Village** church by E. Ganso

**Village** church (Nieder-Reissen) by L. Feininger

**Village** dog by V. Candell

**Village** in the mountains by M. Kahn

**Village,** Maine by J. Marin

**Village** of the dead by G. Catlin

**Village** post office by T. W. Wood

A **village** street, Massachusetts, c 1845 by Unidentified artist

La **Villette** by W. J. Glackens

**Vinal, John,** 1736-1823
Furness, J. M. John Vinal

**Vinal, Mrs John**
Feke, R. Unknown woman (Mrs John Vinal?)

**VINCENT, Andrew McDuffie,** 1898-
McKenzie motif     OrPA
  OrPA. Ptgs & sculptures

**Vincent, Hannah.** See Everett, Hannah (Vincent)

**VINCENT, Tom,** 1930-
Crucifixion
  OYB. Annual 1959

**Vines** and cypresses by J. S. Sargent

**Vineyards** in Tuscany by W. Thon

**VINSON, Charles**
Paper flowers and paper
  OYB. Annual 1954

**Vintage** of uncertainties by A. Salemme

**Vinton, Frederick Porter,** 1846-1911
Sargent, J. S. Frederick Porter Vinton

**Violet** at seven by J. S. Sargent

The **virgin** by A. H. Thayer

**Virgin** Mary with Holy Ghost by Unidentified artist

**Virginia** City building by L. B. Siegriest

**Virginia** deer by J. J. Audubon

**Virginia** in the grotto by P. Evergood

**Virginia's** constitutional convention of 1829-30 by G. Catlin

The **virgins** by J. Muller

**Visa** by S. Davis

**Visione** nobilissima by H. Hofmann

The **visit** by P. Guston

The **visit** by J. Koch

The **visit** by M. Weber

**Visit** to an Indian camp by A. J. Miller

**Visitation** of the buffalo gun by F. Remington

**Visiting** neighbors by J. A. Weir

**VISSER'T HOOFT, Martha H.** 1906-
Fish in bottle
  PPC. Ptg in the U.S. 1949

VISSER'T HOOFT, M. H.—*Continued*
Southern tier                             NBuA
  NBuA. Acquisitions 1959-1961
Trojan horse
  IU. Contemp Amer ptg, 1952
Un vista by R. S. Neuman
Vita nova by L. Feininger
Vital storm by K. L. Callahan
Viterbo by J. E. Heliker
Viva Mexico by E. Berman
Vixen by D. Austin
Vocalization by J. K. Covert
VOGEL, Donald S. 1917-
  Still life
    IU. Contemp Amer ptg & sculp, 1957
A voice from the cliffs by W. Homer
Voice of many waters by A. V. Tack
Voice of the desert by W. R. Leigh
Voice of the nightingale by J. Stella
Voices of spring by H. Hofmann
The volante at Habana by N. V. Calyo
Vollersroda by L. Feininger
Von Habermann, Hugo, fl 1875
  Chase, W. M. Hugo Von Habermann
Von Hoesslin, Georg, fl 1878
  Duveneck, F. George Von Hoesslin
Von Kline, Jacob, fl 1845
  Unidentified artist. Jacob Von Kline
Von Kline, Mrs Jacob, fl 1845
  Unidentified artist. Mrs Jacob Von Kline
Von Kories, Yvette
  Speicher, E. E. Yvette Von Kories
Von Pfister, Alexander, fl 1803
  Malbone, E. G. Alexander Von Pfister
VON PHUL, Anna Maria, 1786-1823
  Boy in beaver hat                       MoSLH
    Rathbone
  Two young ladies                        MoSLH
    Rathbone
  Young gentleman of fashion              MoSLH
    Rathbone
VON SCHLEGELL, David, 1920-
  Flayed hills
    IU. Contemp Amer ptg & sculp, 1957
  Two sides of red
    MBIC. View 1960
VON WICHT, John G. F. 1888-
  Harbor festivity                        WMAA
    Pousette-Dart. Amer ptg
  Paganini
    WMAA. Annual ex, 1948
  Pertaining to harbour
    WMAA. Contemp Amer ptg, 1952
VON WIEGAND, Charmion
  Eight allegories of fate
    WMAA. Annual ex, 1955
VON WITTKAMP, Andrew L. fl 1850
  Black cat on a chair                    MB
    MB. Karolik coll
VOORHIES, Charles, 1901-
  Road to Alcumenar
    OrPA. Ptgs & sculptures
Vote for me by S. Raffo
Vox humana by J. D. Graham
The voyage by L. Feininger
The voyage by E. Giobbi
The voyage by R. B. Motherwell

Voyage of life: Childhood by T. Cole
Voyage of life: Manhood by T. Cole
Voyage of life: Youth by T. Cole
Voyage of the gods by E. J. Stevens
Voyage to Hell Gate from Communipaw by
  J. Quidor
Voyage to Matera by S. Sherman
Voyager's return by A. Gottlieb
Voyageurs by C. Deas
VYTLACIL, Vaclav, 1892-
  Fish cleaner
    IU. Contemp Amer ptg, 1949
  Fish composition
    DC. 21 biennial ex, 1949
  Forest number 4
    IU. Contemp Amer ptg, 1951
  Granada gardens
    IU. Contemp Amer ptg & sculp, 1957
  Images of Pompeii                       PA
    Pousette-Dart. Amer ptg
  Sky and boats
    IU. Contemp Amer ptg, 1950
  Wood interior                           DP
    DP. Catalogue
    Pierson
  Wood interior                           NJMo
    NJMo. Forty years

# W

W. 1954 by A. Gottlieb
W. C. T. U. parade by B. Shahn
Waa-Na-Taa, chief of the Sioux by J. O.
  Lewis
Wade, Frances. See Bleecker, Frances
  (Wade)
Wade, James, 1789-1868
  Ames, E. Dr James Wade
Wadsworth, Daniel
  Trumbull, J. Jeremiah and his son Daniel
    Wadsworth
Wadsworth, Jeremiah, 1743-1804
  Trumbull, J. Jeremiah and his son Daniel
    Wadsworth
  Trumbull, J. Jeremiah Wadsworth
Wadsworth, Mrs Daniel. See Trumbull,
  Faith
WAGGUNO, fl 1858
  Fruit and goldfinch                     DN
    DN. Amer primitive ptgs, pt 1
WAGNER, Gordon
  Sky festival                            CoD
    Cos. New accessions USA, 1960
WAGNER, Jacob, 1852-1898
  Neponset river, Milton                  MB
    MB. Ptgs in water color
WAGNER, Joseph E. 1917-
  Morning of November first               OYB
    OYB. Catalogue 1951
Wagner, Mrs Geoffrey. See Browning, Col-
  leen
Wagon boss by C. M. Russell
Wainwright, Rufus, fl 1840
  Mason, B. F. Rufus Wainwright
Wainwright, Mrs Rufus, fl 1840
  Mason, B. F. Mrs Rufus Wainwright

Wainwright children, fl 1840
  Mason, B. F. Rufus and Gardner Wain-
    wright
Waiter by G. P. Du Bois
Waiting by I. Bishop
Waiting by C. H. Demuth
Waiting by A. Gottlieb
Waiting figure by B. Greene
Waiting for a chinook by C. M. Russell
Waiting for a job by G. Grosz
Waiting for his turn by K. Schmidt
Waiting for the audition by R. Soyer
Waiting for the mail by R. Strang
Waiting for the stage by R. C. Woodville
Waiting in Bethlehem by W. Sommer
Waiting in the moonlight by F. Remington
Waiting room by R. Soyer
Wake of the ferry by J. Sloan
Wake of the hurricane by N. Spencer
Waking up by J. G. Clonney
Walden pond by L. E. Kupferman
Waldo, Cornelius, 1684-1753
  Badger, J. Cornelius Waldo
Waldo, Mrs Cornelius. See Waldo, Faith
    (Savage)
Waldo, Deliverance Mapes, fl 1826
  Waldo, S. L. Deliverance Mapes Waldo
    and her son
Waldo, Elizabeth. See Austin, Elizabeth
    (Waldo)
Waldo, Faith (Savage) 1683-1760
  Badger, J. Mrs Cornelius Waldo
Waldo, George Mapes, 1827-1831
  Waldo, S. L. Deliverance Mapes Waldo
    and her son
Waldo, Griselda (Oliver) b 1737
  Copley, J. S. Mrs Samuel Waldo jr
Waldo, Samuel, 1696-1759
  Feke, R. Gen Samuel Waldo
Waldo, Mrs Samuel. See Waldo, Griselda
    (Oliver)
WALDO, Samuel Lovett, 1783-1861
  Andrew Jackson                          MM
    Mendelowitz
  Deliverance Mapes Waldo and her son
                                          MB
    MB. Karolik coll
  James Gould                             CtY
    CtY. Portrait index
    Pierson
  Man with a watch fob                    MB
    MB. Karolik coll
    Richardson. Ptg in America
  Self-portrait                           MiD
    MiD. Treasures
WALDO, Samuel Lovett, 1783-1861 and
    JEWETT, William, 1795-1873
  Frederick Wolcott                       CtY
    CtY. Portrait index
  John Trumbull                           CtY
    CtY. Portrait index
    Pierson
  Lady in a dark blue dress               MB
    MB. Karolik coll
Waldron, Pieter, fl 1720
  Unidentified artist. Pieter Waldron
Wales, Abby Langdon (Frothingham)
    fl 1820
  Goodridge, S. Mrs Thomas B. Wales

WALES, George Canning, 1868-1940
  Clipper ship Competitor                 MB
    MB. Ptgs in water color
  Racing to market                        MB
    MB. Ptgs in water color
Wales, Mrs Thomas B. See Wales, Abby
    Langdon (Frothingham)
A walk in the poppies by T. Stamos
Walk-in-the-Water (steamship)
  Mathies, J.L.D. Wreck of the steamer
    Walk-in-the-Water
Walk in town by K. F. Roesch
WALKER, Charles Howard, 1857-1936
  Albert IV the Wise                      MB
    MB. Ptgs in water color
  Elizabeth of Tirol                      MB
    MB. Ptgs in water color
  Godfrey of Bouillon                     MB
    MB. Ptgs in water color
  Joanna of Castile                       MB
    MB. Ptgs in water color
  Philip the Good                         MB
    MB. Ptgs in water color
  Section of the Parthenon                MB
    MB. Ptgs in water color
Walker, Clara. See Allen, Clara (Walker)
WALKER, Clay, 1924-
  Security of the mother                  OYB
    OYB. Annual 1959
    OYB. Supplement 1959
WALKER, Gene Alden
  Mal du pays
    PPC. Ptg in the U. S. 1949
  Tetralogy portrait—Percy MacKaye
    NAD. Annual ex, 1949, 1st half
  Young Aurora
    IU. Contemp Amer ptg, 1948
Walker, Lucretia Pickering. See Morse,
    Lucretia Pickering (Walker)
WALKER, William Aiken, 1838-1921
  Charleston harbor from the Battery during
    the bombardment of Fort Sumter,
    April 13, 1861
    Davidson v2
  Cotton picker's home
    Davidson v1
  Dollarfish and sheepshead               MB
    MB. Karolik coll
  Scene along the lower Mississippi, 1883
    Davidson v2
Walker family, fl 1790
  Unidentified artist. Walker family, father
    and son of Middle Haddam, Connecti-
    cut
  Unidentified artist. Walker family, mother
    and daughter of Middle Haddam, Con-
    necticut
Walker greets Mooney by B. Shahn
Walker greets mother of Mooney by B.
    Shahn
WALKOWITZ, Abraham, 1880-
  Bathers: eight foreground figures        MB
    MB. Ptgs in water color
  Bathers: four foreground figures         MB
    MB. Ptgs in water color
  Bathers: three foreground figures        MB
    MB. Ptgs in water color
  Color symphony
    WMAA. Pioneers
  Family group                             MB
    MB. Ptgs in water color

WALKOWITZ, Abraham—*Continued*
New York
  Cheney. Primer 1958 ed
New York, 1917        WMAA
  Goodrich. Amer art
New York, improvisation, 1913        WMAA
  McCurdy
Oriental head
  Cheney. Expressionism 1948 ed
People in the park        DP
  Cheney. Story 1958 ed
Rocky coast        MB
  MB. Ptgs in water color
Summer        MM
  Brown. Amer ptg
Three dance abstractions: Isadora Duncan
                              CtY
  CtY. Soc Anonyme
Times square, abstraction no 1        MB
  MB. Ptgs in water color
Times square, abstraction no 2        MB
  MB. Ptgs in water color
WALL, A. Bryan, d 1937
Shepherd and his flock        PW
  Chew. 250 years of art
WALL, Alfred S. fl 1835-1890
Sunlight and shadow        PPC
  Chew. 250 years of art
WALL, William Allen, 1801-1885
New Bedford in 1807
  Davidson v 1
WALL, William Coventry, 1810-1886
Homestead mill near Pittsburgh
  U. S. National capital sesquicentennial
  com
Pittsburgh after the fire of 1845 (Ruins of
  Pittsburgh)        PPC
  Chew. 250 years of art
  Davidson v2 (detail)
WALL, William Guy, 1792-1864
Hudson river from West Point        CtNL
  NYG. Fine art
View from Fishkill, New York        NNHS
  Born
View near Fishkill        NNPL
  Larkin
  Larkin rev ed
View near Fort Montgomery        NNHS
  Flexner. Light of distant skies
View of Ogdensburg
  Jones. Rediscovered ptrs
The wall by J. Erickson
The wall by R. Gleitsman
The wall by L. Grebenak
The wall by W. T. Murch
The wall by W. Stuempfig
Wall of spikes by E. Berman
Wall street, half past 2 o'clock, October 13,
  1857 by J. H. Cafferty and C. D.
  Rosenberg
Wall with green door by G. O'Keeffe
WALLER, Frank, 1842-1923
Metropolitan museum in Fourteenth
  street, 1881        MM
  Davidson v2
  Larkin
  Larkin rev ed
Wallscape by J. L. Lasker
Walsh, Ann, 1800-1811
  Ames, E. Ann Walsh

WALSH, Edward
Fort Erie from Buffalo creek, site of the
  city of Buffalo, c 1810        NNPL
  Davidson v2
WALTER, Joseph, 1783-1856
Arrival of the Great Western at New
  York, 1838        NNPL
  Davidson v1
U.S. National Capital sesquicentennial
  com
WALTERS, S.
A Collins line steamship
  Davidson v 1
WALTERS, Susane, fl 1852
Memorial to Nicholas Catlin        DN
  DN. Amer primitive ptgs, pt 1
Walton, Cornelia (Beekman) 1708-1786
  Wollaston, J. Mrs William Walton
Walton, Ezekiel, fl 1811
  Tuthill, A. G. D. Gen Ezekiel Walton
Walton, Mrs Ezekiel, fl 1811
  Tuthill, A. G. D. Mrs Ezekiel Walton
WALTON, Henry, fl 1842
De Mott Smith, aged 8
  Jones. Rediscovered ptrs
Emeline Boynton, aged 32
  Jones. Rediscovered ptrs
Harriet Elizabeth Boynton, age 2 years
  Jones. Rediscovered ptrs
Henry Boynton, age 39
  Jones. Rediscovered ptrs
Sarah Louisa Spencer        VWR
  VWR. Folk art (col)
View of Ithaca, Tompkins county, New
  York, 1838
  Jones. Rediscovered ptrs
Walton, Mrs Jonathan. See Walton, Mar-
  garet Ann (Thatcher)
Walton, Margaret Ann (Thatcher) d 1843
  Ames, E. Mrs Jonathan Walton
Walton, Mrs William. See Walton, Cornelia
  (Beekman)
Wanamaker block by F. J. Kline
Wandelaer, Pau de, fl 1725
  Gansevoort limner. Pau de Wandelaer
The wanderer by W. Day
The wanderers by J. W. Treiman
Wandering Jew by P. Burlin
Wanderlust by P. Bacon
Wanton, Joseph, 1705-1780
  Smibert, J. Joseph Wanton
Wapiti by W. J. Hayes
Wapping on Thames by J. A. M. Whistler
War among the arthropods by F. Carbone
War dance of the Sauks and Foxes by P.
  Rindisbacher
War [dog] dance in the interior of a Konza
  lodge by S. Seymour
War horses by Unidentified artist
War news from Mexico by R. C. Woodville
War prisoners by L. Eades
War series: another patrol by J. Lawrence
The war spirit at home: celebrating the
  victory at Vicksburg by L. M. Spencer
Warblers
  Heil, C. E. Bay-breasted warbler on apple
  blossom
  Heil, C. E. Chestnut-sided warbler on
  barberry

**WARD, Charles Caleb,** fl 1870
Circus is coming
Davidson v2
**Ward, Hugh C.** fl 1870
Bingham, G. C. Hugh C. Ward
**Ward, James,** 1769-1859
Stuart, G. James Ward
**Ward, Richard,** 1689-1763
Unidentified artist. Richard Ward
**Warehouse** by R. Morgan
**Warehouse** mannequins by W. De Kooning
**Warmth** of memory by L. W. Coleman
**WARNER, Catherine Townsend,** 1785-1828
Mourning picture—George Washington
VWR
VWR. Folk art (col)
**Warner, Elizabeth (Pitts)** See Pitts, Elizabeth
**Warner, Mary,** 1757-1780?
Blackburn, J. Mary Warner
Copley, J. S. Mary Warner
**Warner, Mary MacPhedris (Osborne)** fl 1761
Blackburn, J. Mrs Jonathan Warner
**WARRE, Henry J.** 1819-1898
Fort Vancouver, 1845
U.S. National Capital sesquicentennial com
**WARREN, Ferdinand E.** 1899-
Lunar magic OYB
OYB. Annual 1954
OYB. Supplement
Night baseball game Cardinals vs. Dodgers
GAtM
GAtM. Holbrook collection
Town square, Independence, Missouri
DC. 21 biennial ex, 1949
The ultimate city
NAD. Annual ex, 1951
**Warren, Gretchen (Osgood)**
Sargent, J. S. Mrs Fiske Warren and her daughter Rachel
**WARREN, Harold Broadfield,** 1859-1934
Aegina from the Acropolis, Athens MB
MB. Ptgs in water color
Corner of the Parthenon, Athens MB
MB. Ptgs in water color
The Parthenon, Athens MB
MB. Ptgs in water color
The Propylaea, Athens MB
MB. Ptgs in water color
**Warren, James,** 1726-1808
Copley, J. S. James Warren
**Warren, Joseph,** 1731-1775
Copley, J. S. Joseph Warren
**Warren, Mercy (Otis)** 1728-1815
Copley, J. S. Mrs James Warren
**Warren, Rebecca.** See Brown, Rebecca (Warren)
**Warrior** by C. di Marca-Relli
**Warriors'** long trail by C. M. Russell
**WARSHAW, Howard,** 1920-
Blue hands
NNSG. Younger Amer ptrs
Child's skull
CtY. Yale alumni
Reclining figure
IU. Contemp Amer ptg, 1951
Spectator
MAA. Contemp Amer ptg, 1953

Two classical studies
PPC. International ex, 1955
The witnesses
IU. Contemp Amer ptg & sculp, 1959
**Warwick** mine, exit no 1 by A. Frasconi
**Wase, Phillip**
Bellows, G. W. Mr and Mrs Phillip Wase
**Wash** day by A. M. R. Moses
**Washburn, Cadwalader**
Chase, W. M. Cadwalader Washburn
**Washerwomen** by E. Melcarth
**Washington, Bailey**
Peale, J. Surgeon Bailey Washington, U.S.N.
**Washington, George, president U.S.** 1732-1799
Ames, E. George Washington
Bingham, G. C. Washington crossing the Delaware, 1872
De Grailly, V. Washington's headquarters, Newburgh-on-the-Hudson
Heath, J. (after G. Stuart) George Washington
Hicks, E. Washington crossing the Delaware
Kemmelmeyer, F. George Washington reviewing the western army at Fort Cumberland
Leutze, E. Washington crossing the Delaware
Peale, C. W. George Washington
Peale, C. W. Washington, Lafayette and Tilghman at Yorktown
Peale, Rembrandt. George Washington
Peale, Rembrandt. George Washington (porthole portrait)
Pickett, J. George Washington under the Council tree
Reed, R. L. Washington and Lafayette at the battle of Yorktown
Rivers, L. Washington crossing the Delaware
Rowell, A. J. George Washington
Sanford, M. M. Washington at Princeton
Smith, R. Original tomb of Washington, 1836
Stuart, G. George Washington
Stuart, G. George Washington (Athenaeum type)
Stuart, G. George Washington (Lansdowne type)
Stuart, G. George Washington (Miller-Cake-J. Stewart portrait)
Stuart, G. George Washington (Vaughan type)
Stuart, G. Washington at Dorchester Heights
Sully, T. Passage of the Delaware
Trumbull, J. George Washington
Trumbull, J. George Washington (Martha Washington type)
Trumbull, J. George Washington (detail of head of Washington at the Battle of Trenton)
Trumbull, J. George Washington at the Battle of Trenton
Trumbull, J. Resignation of Gemeral Washington at Annapolis
Unidentified artist. General Washington on white charger

**Washington, George, president U.S.**—*Continued*
  Unidentified artist. George Washington family
  Unidentified artist. George Washington with horse
  Unidentified artist. Washington and his staff at Fort Cumberland, Md. 1794
  Unidentified artist. Washington, the Mason
  Warner, C. T. Mourning picture—George Washington
  Willson, M. A. George Washington on horseback
  Wright, J. George Washington
**Washington, Martha (Dandridge) Custis, 1732-1802**
  Stuart, G. Martha Washington
  Unidentified artist. Mrs George Washington (after C. W. Peale)
**Washington family**
  Savage, E. The Washington family
**Washington, D.C.**
  Boit, E. D. The Capitol, Washington
  Burton, C. United States capitol, 1824
  Heriot, G. The Capitol after the British assault on Washington, 1815
  Latrobe, B. H. East front of the President's house with the addition of the north and south porticos, 1807
  Matthew, K. Capitol reflections
**Washington** arch, spring by C. Hassam
**Washington** crossing the Delaware by L. Rivers
The **Washington**, first double decker on the Mississippi by Unidentified artist
**Washington** monument, Washington square, N.Y. by A. S. Mira
**Washington** square by W. J. Glackens
**Washington** square, New York by D. Kingman
**Washington's** tomb by F. Guy
**Washington's** tomb at Mount Vernon by W. De Grailly
**Washington's** tomb at Mount Vernon by W. M. Prior
**Washington's** tomb, Mt Vernon by W. H. Bartlett
The **Wasp** and the Frolic by T. Birch
**Watch** and fob by J. A. Tilles
**Watch** factory by N. Spencer
**Watching** by A. Gottlieb
**Watching** for the smoke signal by C. M. Russell
**Watching** the cargo by G. C. Bingham
**Watching** the clock by K. Sage
**Watching** the settlers by C. M. Russell
**Watchmaker** with his tools by Unidentified artist
**Water** by C. Sheeler
**Water** by R. Strang
**Water** fan by W. Homer
**Water** front by E. Ludins
The **water** girl by C. M. Russell
**Water** lily by M. J. Heade
**Water** mill prospect by L. Rivers
**Water** of the flowery mill by A. Gorky
**Water-table** by Y. Tanguy
**Water** waltz by J. Guerin
**Waterbury** bridge: number one by D. Margules

**Waterfall** by A. G. Dove
**Waterfall** by A. Gorky
**Waterfall** by B. Miller
**Waterfall** by M. B. Prendergast
The **waterfall** by J. H. Twachtman
**Waterfall**, Morse pond by M. Hartley
**Waterfront** (New York) by K. Matthew
**Watergame** by J. Tworkov
The **watering** place by A. Fisher
**Watering** pots by T. Robinson
**Watermelon** by Unidentified artist
**Watermelon** and fruit by J. Peale (attributed works)
**Watermelon** and fruit by Raphaelle Peale
**WATERS, E. A.**
  Lady of the lake                          VWR
    Ford. Pictorial folk art
**Waters, John, 1774-1844**
  Malbone, E. G. John Waters
**Waters, Joseph Gilbert, 1796-1878**
  Osgood, C. Joseph Gilbert Waters
**Waterton, Charles, 1782-1865**
  Peale, C. W. Charles Waterton
**Waterworks,** Center square, Philadelphia by Unidentified artist
**WATKINS, Franklin Chenault, 1894-**
  Angel                                      MiD
    MMA. Watkins
  Angel posed
    MMA. Watkins
  The angel will turn a page in a book   DP
    DP. Catalogue
    MMA. Watkins
  Autumn recollections                       DP
    DP. Catalogue
  Beloved dead                             ATeS
    ATeS. Collection
    MMA. Watkins
    Pousette-Dart. Amer ptg
  Birth of spring
    Chew. 250 years of art
  Blue chair                               MoKN
    MMA. Watkins
  Boris Blai                                MMA
    Cheney. Story 1958 ed
    MMA. Watkins
  Crucifixion
    MMA. Watkins
  Death
    Baur. New art
    MMA. Watkins
    PPC. International ex, 1950
  Death, Study for
    MMA. Watkins
  Death in the orchard
    MMA. Watkins
  Descent no 1, 1947
    MMA. Watkins
  Dr George Kamperman
    Baur. Revolution
  Fanciful meeting long ago
    MMA. Watkins
  Fire eater                                PPhM
    Baur. New art (col)
    Gruskin
    MMA. Watkins
    NYG. Fine art
    Pierson
    Wight. Milestones
  Flowers in Pennsylvania Dutch teapot
    WiMiA. Amer ptg 1760-1960

Gabriel                                  MM
  MM. 100 Amer ptrs
Henry P. McIlhenny
  MMA. Watkins
J. Stogdell Stokes                       PPhM
  MMA. Watkins
Joseph G. Butler                         OYB
  OYB. Supplement 1959
Justice Owen J. Roberts                  PPhUn
  Baur. New art
  MMA. Watkins
  Pierson
Make the monkey jump
  IU. Contemp Amer ptg & sculp, 1959
Misses Maude and Maxine Meyer de
    Schauensee
  MMA. Watkins (col)
Mrs C. E. Etnier
  MMA. Watkins
Mrs John F. Steinman
  MMA. Watkins
Mrs Joseph S. Clark jr
  PA. Annual ex, 1954
Musician
  MMA. Watkins
Negro spiritual
  MMA. Watkins
Paul P. Cret
  MMA. Watkins
The picnic
  MMA. Watkins
Prudence
  PPC. Ptg in the U.S. 1949
R. Sturgis Ingersoll
  MMA. Watkins
Remember me
  MMA. Watkins
Resurrection                             IBM
  MMA. Watkins
Resurrection (McIlhenny coll)
  MMA. Watkins (col)
Resurrection no 1, 1947
  MMA. Watkins
Resurrection no 2, 1947
  MMA. Watkins
Resurrection, Study for, 1947
  MMA. Watkins
The return
  MMA. Watkins
Robert Raeburn White, esq
  Gruskin
Rosemary Thompson
  MMA. Watkins
Self-portrait
  WiMiA. Amer ptg 1760-1960
The sideboard                            WMAA
  Goodrich. Amer art (col)
Soliloquy                                WMAA
  Baur. New art
  Goodrich. Amer art
  MMA. Watkins
  Pierson
Solitaire                                MNS
  MMA. Watkins
  Time. 300 years (col)
Springtime                               CSB
  MMA. Watkins
Still life                               MiD
  MiD. Treasures
Still life (Wenger coll)
  MMA. Watkins
The studio                               NBuA
  MMA. Watkins
  NBuA. Contemporary ptgs

Suicide in costume                       PPhM
  Canaday
  MMA. Watkins
Sunny morning
  WiMiA. Amer ptg 1760-1960
Thomas Raeburn White
  Baur. New art
  MMA. Watkins
  Richardson. Ptg in America
To the tomb
  MMA. Watkins
WATKINS, Mary Bradley
  The blue and the strawberry roan       DP
  DP. Catalogue
Watson, Sir Brook, bart, 1735-1807
  Copley, J. S. Brook Watson
Watson, Elizabeth (Oliver) 1737-1767
  Copley, J. S. Mrs George Watson
Watson, Elkanah, 1758-1842
  Ames, E. Elkanah Watson
  Copley, J. S. Elkanah Watson
Watson, Mrs George. See Watson, Elizabeth
    (Oliver)
WATSON, John, 1685-1768
  Lewis Morris of New Jersey             NBM
    Belknap
    Flexner. First flowers
    Pierson
  William Burnet                         NNHS
    Belknap
  William Burnet                         NAI
    NAI. Hudson valley
              Attributed works
  Anne Van Rensselaer                    NNHS
    Belknap
  Gentleman of the Van Rensselaer family
    (probably Jacobus Van Rensselaer,
    also known as Kiliaen Van Rensselaer)
                                         NAI
    Belknap
  Gentleman of the Van Rensselaer family
    (probably Stephanus Van Rensselaer)
                                         NNHS
    Belknap
    NNHS. Waldron Phoenix Belknap coll
  Johannes Schuyler and his wife Elizabeth
    Staats Wendell                       NNHS
    Belknap
    Pierson
  Mrs Kiliaen Van Rensselaer             NNHS
    Belknap
    NNHS. Waldron Phoenix Belknap coll
  Mrs Stephanus(?) Van Rensselaer
    Belknap
  Van Rensselaer gentleman (known as Jan
    Baptist Van Rensselaer)              NAI
    Belknap
    NAI. Hudson valley
WATSON, Robert, 1923-
  The bridge
    CSFP. Annual ex, 1952
  The guardian
    NAD. Annual ex, 1955
  Interior
    IU. Contemp Amer ptg & sculp, 1955
Watson and the shark by J. S. Copley
Watts, Francis O. fl 1805
  Brewster, J. Francis O. Watts with bird
WAUGH, Frederick Judd, 1861-1940
  A bit of the Cape
    NYG. Fine art (col)
  Breakers at floodtide                  OYB
    OYB. Catalogue 1951

**WAUGH, F. J.**—*Continued*
Coast of Maine                                    NJN
  NYG. Fine art
Great seas                                        InTH
  InTH. Catalogue
Open sea
  NYG. Fine art
Pounding surf                                     PPC
  NYG. Fine art
Surf under moonlight                              PR
  PR. Catalogue
Windward shore                                    IaIU
  NYG. Fine art

**WAUGH, Samuel B.** 1814-1885
Immigrants' arrival at New York, 1847
                       NNMC
  Davidson v2

The **wave** by W. De Kooning
The **wave** by M. Hartley
The **wave** by C. A. Morris
The **wave** by G. O'Keeffe
The **wave** by E. F. Spruce
**Wave** breaking by E. F. Spruce
**Wave** motif by E. Kelly
**Waves** by E. F. Spruce
**Waves** of love and of the sea by K. Schrag
**Waving** the flag by G. Grosz
**Wayland, Francis,** 1826-1904
  Weir, J. F. Francis Wayland
**WAYNE, June C.** 1918-
The advocate
  IU. Contemp Amer ptg & sculp, 1955
The ladder
  ICA. Annual ex, 1951
Law court
  IU. Contemp Amer ptg & sculp, 1953
The messenger
  IU. Contemp Amer ptg & sculp, 1957
The sanctified
  CSFP. Annual ex, 1952
**Ways** and means by S. Davis
**Wayside** inn by A. F. Bellows
**We** bought a fish by M. L. Thomas
**We** gather together by M. Kahn
**We** go for the Union by Unidentified artist
**Weaning** the calf by W. Homer
**Weary** by E. Higgins
**Weary** by W. Homer
**Weather** vane by A. G. Dove
**Weather** vane and sofa by Y. Kuniyoshi
**Weatherbeaten,** or Stormbeaten by W.
  Homer
**Weatherbee, Mrs**
  Fuller, G. Old age (Mrs Weatherbee)
**Weavers** of a spell by H. Janicki
The **web** (Croton dam) by C. Sheeler
**Webb, Mr.** fl 1791
  Stuart, G. Webb sr
**Webb, Clifton,** 1893-
  Bellows, G. W. Robin (Portrait of Clifton
    Webb)
**Webb, James Watson,** 1802-1884
  Chase, W. M. Gen James Watson Webb
**Webb, Samuel Blachley (or Blatchley)** 1753-
  1807
  Peale, C. W. Samuel B. Webb

**Webber, Mrs Jeremiah**
  Blythe, D. G. Mrs Jeremiah Webber and
    son
**WEBBER, John,** fl 1750-1793
View in Nootka sound                              CtY
  U.S. National Capital sesquicentennial
    com
**WEBER, Hugo,** 1918-
Dark stretch
  NNSG. Younger Amer ptrs
**WEBER, Max,** 1881-1961
Acrobats
  Goodrich. Max Weber
  WMAA. Museum and its friends, 1959
Adoration of the moon                             WMAA
  Baur. New art
  Goodrich. Amer art (col)
  Goodrich. Max Weber (col)
  NJN. Weber
  Pierson
After an ice storm                                DP
  DP. Catalogue
Alone                                             FaW
  Goodrich. Max Weber
The antique                                       CtY
  CtY. Soc Anonyme
At the lake
  Goodrich. Max Weber
At the mill                                       NJN
  Goodrich. Max Weber
  NJN. Weber
Avenue of trees
  MnU. 40 Amer ptrs
Bach orchestra
  NJN. Weber
The bathers [1]
  Goodrich. Max Weber
The bathers [2]                                   MdBM
  NJN. Weber
Beautification                                    MM
  MM. 100 Amer ptrs
  Taylor. Fifty centuries, 1954 ed (col)
Beautification                                    InBU
  NUM. Art across America
Blue New York
  NJN. Weber
Broken tree
  Cheney. New world history
Chinese restaurant                                WMAA
  Baur. New art
  Goodrich. Amer art (col)
  Goodrich. Max Weber
  Hunter. Mod Amer ptg (col)
  Larkin
  Larkin rev ed
  McCurdy
  Mendelowitz
  MMA. Abstract (col)
  NBuA. Expressionism
  NJN. Weber
  Pierson
  Rathbun
  Rosenblum
  WMAA. Juliana Force
The comb
  PA. Annual ex, 1956
Composition—three figures
  Brown. Amer ptg
Composition with three figures
  Brown. Amer ptg
  Goodrich. Max Weber
Conversation
  Pearson. Mod renaissance

A cup of tea
  Goodrich. Max Weber
Dauntless bird
  IU. Contemp Amer ptg, 1949
  Pousette-Dart. Amer ptg
Decoration with cloud                    MMA
  Baur. Revolution
  Cheney. Story 1958 ed
Deserted farm                            OCl
  OCl. Handbook
Drapeau                                  GAtM
  GAtM. Holbrook collection
Draped head                              DP
  DP. Catalogue
Early American abstract
  CtY. Yale alumni
Eight figures
  Pearson. Mod renaissance
Family reunion
  Goodrich. Max Weber
  IU. Contemp Amer ptg, 1951
  Pearson. Mod renaissance
Figure study                             NBuA
  NBuA. Acquisitions 1959-1961
  NJN. Weber
Figure with bird
  DC. 27 biennial ex, 1961
Flower piece                             TxF
  UNESCO. 1860-1949
  UNESCO. 1860-1955
  UNESCO. 1860-1959
Flute soloist
  Roos
The forest
  Barker. From realism
Friendship
  Goodrich. Max Weber
Geranium                                 MMA
  Baur. New art
  Goodrich. Max Weber
  McCurdy
  MMA. Masters (col)
  MMA. Ptg and sculpture
  Pierson
  Raynal. History v3 (col)
Gesture
  Baur. Revolution
  Cheney. Expressionism 1948 ed
  Flexner. Amer ptg
  Flexner. Short history
  Goodrich. Max Weber
  NJN. Weber
Good news
  Goodrich. Max Weber
Good news
  NBuA. Expressionism
Grand central terminal
  DC. De gustibus
Group of figures
  Goodrich. Max Weber
Guitar player                            IBM
  Genauer (col)
The harem
  NJN. Weber
Hasidic dance
  Baur. New art
  Baur. Revolution
  Goodrich. Max Weber
  MMA. Contemp ptrs
  Pierson
  WMAA. Museum and its friends, 1958
Head of a woman
  NJN. Weber

Heads
  NJN. Weber
Interior of the fourth dimension
  NJN. Weber
Interior with figures
  WMAA. Annual ex, 1958
Interior with men
  Blesh
Invocation
  Biddle. Yes and no
Joel's cave
  NJN. Weber
Landscape, 1928                          NJN
  NJN. Weber
Latest news                              MoKN
  Time. 300 years (col)
Leaning figure
  IU. Contemp Amer ptg & sculp, 1959
Mothers and children
  Lewisohn
Multiple portrait
  IU. Contemp Amer ptg & sculp, 1961
Muses
  Goodrich. Max Weber
Music                                    NBM
  CoS. New accessions USA, 1950
  Goodrich. Max Weber
  Lee. Art then and now
  Munsterberg
Music of the Orient
  IU. Contemp Amer ptg & sculp, 1957
Musical evening                          CLA
  CLA. 35 ptgs
New York
  MMA. Abstract
  NBuA. Fifty ptgs
New York at night
  Brown. Amer ptg
  MMA. Abstract
  MnMW. Classic tradition
La Parisienne
  NJN. Weber
Pleasures of summer
  Goodrich. Max Weber
The rabbi
  Brown. Amer ptg
  Goodrich. Max Weber
Red cap                                  WMAA
  Larkin
  Larkin rev ed
Refugees                                 KW
  Goodrich. Max Weber
  NJN. Weber
Repose no 2, 1950
  NJN. Weber
Rush hour, New York
  Goodrich. Max Weber
  Hess. Abstract ptg
  MMA. Abstract
  Pierson
  Rosenblum
Russian ballet
  Goodrich. Max Weber
Sabbath
  NJN. Weber
Seeking work
  Gruskin (col)
  McCurdy
Solo
  NJN. Weber
Still life                               ATeS
  ATeS. Collection
Still life                               ICA
  CoS. New accessions USA, 1946

WEBER, Max—*Continued*
Still life, bread and peppers
  NJN. Weber
Still life, Egyptian pot
  Brown. Amer ptg
Still life with flowers
  NYG. Fine art
  UNESCO. 1860-1949
  UNESCO. 1860-1955
  UNESCO. 1860-1959
Still life with palette
  CSFP. Annual ex, 1952
  Goodrich. Max Weber
Still life with two tables
  Goodrich. Max Weber
String music
  Goodrich. Max Weber
  MnMW. Contemporary (col)
  WMAA. Neuberger collection
Summer                                       WMAA
  Bazin
  Goodrich. Amer art
  NYG. Fine art
  UNESCO. 1860-1949
  UNESCO. 1860-1955
  UNESCO. 1860-1959
Three jugs                                   DP
  Cheney. Primer 1958 ed
Three literary gentlemen                     MLL
  Baur. New art (col)
  Baur. Revolution
  Goodrich. Max Weber
  IU. Contemp Amer ptg, 1948
  Pierson
The toilers
  NJN. Weber
Tranquility
  Baur. New art
  Goodrich. Max Weber
  Pierson
The trio                                     WMAA
  DC. Halpert collection
  IU. Contemp Amer ptg & sculp, 1953
  WMAA. Sara Roby
Two musicians                                MMA
  Brown. Amer ptg
  MMA. Contemp ptrs
  NJN. Weber
  Read Concise history
The visit
  Baur. Revolution
  Goodrich. Max Weber
Whither now
  Wight. Milestones
Wind orchestra
  Goodrich. Max Weber
Winter twilight                              CSB
  Cheney. Story 1958 ed
  Goodrich. Max Weber
  Gruskin
  Pearson. Mod renaissance
  Pierson
  Robb. Art 1953 ed
  Robb. Harper history
Woman carrying picture                       MnMW
  Goodrich. Max Weber
Woman holding tablet
  MnU. 40 Amer ptrs
Women and tents
  WMAA. Pioneers
Young model
  Pearson. Mod renaissance
Zinnias                                      NJN
  NJN. Weber

WEBER, Paul, 1823-1916
  The artist sketching his friends
    Chew. 250 years of art
WEBER, Paul, 1823-1916 and SCHUES-
  SELE, Christian, 1824?-1879
  Skating at Kelly's dam. Germantown PH
    Chew. 250 years of art
Webster, Daniel, 1782-1852
  Healy, G. P. A. Daniel Webster
  Unidentified artist. Daniel Webster at his
    farm
Webster, Noah, 1758-1843
  Verstille, W. Noah Webster
Wedding dress by B. Kamihira
Weddings
  Krimmel, J. S. Country wedding
  Lee, D. E. Country wedding
  Stokes, J. S. Wedding in the Big Smoky
    mountains, 1872
  Woodville, R. C. Sailor's wedding
WEDIN, Elof, 1901-
  Black harbor, a grey moon               MNS
    CoS. New accessions USA, 1954
Weeds by N. Ziroli
Weeping girl by F. Martin
Weighing cotton by T. H. Benton
Weights of the Pacific by L. Mullican
WEINER, Bernard M. 1924-
  Bronx light                             OYB
    OYB. Annual 1958
    OYB. Supplement 1959
WEIR, John Ferguson, 1841-1926
  Artist's studio                         CtY
    Weir. Recollections
  Forging the shaft (replica)             MM
    Weir. Recollections
  Forging the shaft: a welding heat       MM
    Pierson
  Francis Wayland                         CtY
    CtY. Portrait index
  Gun foundry, Cold Spring, New York
    (Gun factory)
    Baur. Revolution
    U.S. National Capital sesquicentennial
    com
    Weir. Recollections
  Russell H. Chittenden                   CtY
    CtY. Portrait index
  Samuel Wells Williams                   CtY
    CtY. Portrait index
  The Theological of Yale university (Bacon,
    Barbour, Day, Dwight, Fisher, Harris)
                         CtY
    CtY. Portrait index
  View of the Highlands from West Point
                         NNHS
    Born
    Weir. Recollections

    **Portrait of the artist**
  Alexander, J. W. Professor John Fergu-
    son Weir
WEIR, Julian Alden, 1852-1919
  Building a dam, Shetucket               OCl
    OCl. Handbook
  The green bodice                        MM
    MM. 100 Amer ptrs
  Miss De L                               DC
    DC. 25 biennial ex, 1957
  Pan and the wolf                        DP
    DP. Catalogue

Red Bridge MM
Pierson
Still life InIJ
InIJ. 105 ptgs
Visiting neighbors DP
DP. Catalogue
Larkin
Larkin rev ed
Pierson
Willimantic, Connecticut ATeS
ATeS. Collection
Willimantic thread mill NBM
Born
Windham village MoSL
MoSL. Handbook 1953
WEIR, Robert Walter, 1803-1889
Bianca MB
MB. Karolik coll
Red Jacket NCHA
Jones. Rediscovered ptrs
Self-portrait NNHS
Weir. Recollections
View of the Hudson from West Point
Sears. Highlights (col)

**Attributed works**

Shipwreck at sea NAI
Jones. Rediscovered ptrs
Weir by J. E. Levi
The weir and the island by W. A. V. Kien-
busch
Weir's orchard by A. P. Ryder
WEISMANN, Donald L. 1914-
Ground-air control OYB
OYB. Annual 1957
OYB. Supplement 1959
WEISS, Hugh, 1925-
Italian village
IU. Contemp Amer ptg & sculp, 1953
Welcome home by L. Bosa
Welcome home by J. Levine
Weld, Mrs. Henry T. See Hoffman, Harriet
Emily
The welder by D. A. Vaughan
Welders by B. Shahn
Wellfleet, Cottages at by E. Hopper
WELLS, Cady, 1904-
The idols
IU. Contemp Amer ptg & sculp, 1953
Interlunar sea
ICA. Annual ex, 1947/48
Landscape from above
IU. Contemp Amer ptg, 1952
Penitente
WMAA. Annual ex, 1949
Wells, Eliza, fl 1840
Stanley, A. R. Eliza Wells
Wells, Henry, fl 1845
Unidentified artist. Henry Wells
Welsteed, William, fl 1753
Copley, J. S. Rev William Welsteed
WENCK, Paul
Grand Canyon, Arizona
NYG. Fine art
Rockies from Bear lake
NYG. Fine art
Wendell, Elizabeth Staats. See Schuyler,
Elizabeth Staats (Wendell)
Wendell, Harmanus, 1678-1732
Unidentified artist. Harmanus Wendell
Wendell, Johannes, b 1714?
Unidentified artist. Johannes Wendell

Wenona's leap by S. Eastman
Wensley, Elizabeth (Paddy) b 1641
Unidentified artist. Elizabeth Paddy
Wensley
Wentworth, Frances Deering (Wentworth)
Lady, 1746-1813
Copley, J. S. Lady Frances Wentworth
Wentworth, Hannah. See Atkinson, Hannah
(Wentworth)
WENTZ, Evelyn E.
Universe OYB
OYB. Annual 1951
WENTZ, Harry, 1876-
Rocks in the sea OrPA
Pierson
Wertheimer, Asher, 1844-1918
Sargent, J. S. Asher Wertheimer
Wertheimer, Mrs Asher
Sargent, J. S. Mrs Asher Wertheimer
Wertheimer, The Misses
Sargent, J. S. Daughters of Asher Wert-
heimer
WERTZ, Harry
Fisherman in red hat and shirt
NSP. Sportscapes
WESCOTT, Paul, 1904-
The harbor OYB
OYB. Annual 1959
OYB. Supplement 1959
Wesleyan academy, Wilbraham, Massachu-
setts by Unidentified artist
WEST, Benjamin, 1738-1820
The Adrian Hope family group MB
Pierson
Agrippina and her children mourning over
the ashes of Germanicus
Evans. Benjamin West
Agrippina landing at Brundisium with the
ashes of Germanicus CtY
Evans. Benjamin West
Flexner. Light of distant skies
Air, Water, Earth, and Fire (Dome of the
Royal academy of arts, London)
Evans. Benjamin West
The angel of the Lord announcing the
resurrection to the Marys at the
sepulchre NMB
Evans. Benjamin West
The apotheosis of Nelson
Evans. Benjamin West
The appeal of Coriolanus
Evans. Benjamin West
The archangel Gabriel
Evans. Benjamin West
Arthur Middleton, his wife and son PPhM
Canaday
The ascension of our Saviour ELT
Evans. Benjamin West
The battle of Crécy ELB
Evans. Benjamin West
Belisarius and the boy MiD
Evans. Benjamin West
Benjamin Franklin drawing electricity
from the sky
ICA. From colony to nation
Charles Willson Peale NNHS
Roos
The choice of Hercules ELV
Evans. Benjamin West
Christ healing the sick in the temple
Evans. Benjamin West
Christ on the Mount of Olives
Evans. Benjamin West

WEST, Benjamin—*Continued*
Christ rejected by the Jews          PA
  Evans. Benjamin West
  Flexner. Light of distant skies
Cleombrotus ordered into banishment by
    Leonidas II, king of Sparta    ELT
  Canaday
Conference of the treaty of peace with
    England, 1783                 DeWin
  Davidson v 1
  Richardson. Ptg in America
The conversion of St Paul           MNS
  Evans. Benjamin West
The conversion of St Paul (St Paul's
    church, Richmond, Virginia)
  Evans. Benjamin West
Cupid and Psyche                    DC
  Evans. Benjamin West
Cyrus liberating the family of Astyges
                                    ELB
  Evans. Benjamin West
Death of Epaminondas                ELK
  Evans. Benjamin West
Death of General Wolfe              CanO
  Canaday
  Davidson v 1
  Flexner. Light of distant skies
  ICA. From colony to nation
  Janson. Key monuments
  Larkin
  Larkin rev ed
  Lee. Art then and now
  Robb. Harper history
  U.S. National Capital sesquicentennial
    com
  Walker. Ptgs from America
Death of General Wolfe              ELK
  Evans. Benjamin West
Death of Lord Nelson, 1808
  Evans. Benjamin West
Death of Lord Nelson, 1811
  Evans. Benjamin West
Death of Socrates
  Evans. Benjamin West
  Flexner. Light of distant skies
Death of the Chevalier Bayard       ELK
  Evans. Benjamin West
Death on a pale horse (sketch)      PPhM
  Canaday
Death on the pale horse, c 1783     PPhM
  Evans. Benjamin West
  Pierson
Death on the pale horse, 1802       PPhM
  Evans. Benjamin West
Death on the pale horse, 1817       PA
  Barker. Amer ptg
  Evans. Benjamin West
  Flexner. Light of distant skies
  PA. Annual ex, 1955
Departure of Regulus                ELK
  Evans. Benjamin West
The destruction of the beast and the false
    prophet                        MnMI
  Evans. Benjamin West
Diana, wife of Thomas Wyld of Sheen
                                    NJMo
  NJMo. Forty years
Diomed and his horses stopped by the
    lightning of Jupiter
  Evans. Benjamin West
Elijah convincing the false prophets of
    Baol                           MAC
  Evans. Benjamin West

Elizabeth Peale                     PA
  Evans. Benjamin West
  Flexner. First flowers
An English gentleman                PW
  Chew. 250 years of art
General Kosciusko                   OOb
  NUM. Art across America
General Monk receiving Charles II on the
    beach of Dover
  WiMiA. Amer ptg 1760-1960
Guy Johnson                         DN
  DN. Mellon coll
  Evans. Benjamin West
  Flexner. Light of distant skies
  Janson. Picture history
  Time. 300 years (col)
Hagar and Ishmael                   MM
  Evans. Benjamin West
Hector parting with his wife and child at
    the Scæan gate                 NNHS
  Evans. Benjamin West
Jane Galloway                       PH
  Flexner. First flowers
Juno receiving the cestus from Venus
  Evans. Benjamin West
King Edward III entertaining his prison-
    ers after the battle of Calais
  Evans. Benjamin West
King Lear                           MB
  Evans. Benjamin West
Landscape with cow
  Flexner. First flowers
  Ford. Pictorial folk art
  Pierson
Mr and Mrs John Custance           MoKN
  MoKN. Handbook
Mrs Samuel Boudé                    DN
  DN. Amer primitive ptgs, pt 2
Mrs West and her son Raphael        OCl
  Evans. Benjamin West
  OCl. Handbook
Musidora
  MdBMu. Rendezvous
Narcissus
  Chew. 250 years of art
Omnia vincit amor                   MM
  Evans. Benjamin West
Penn's treaty with the Indians      PA
  Barker. Amer ptg
  Canaday
  Davidson v 1
  Evans. Benjamin West
  Flexner. Amer ptg
  Flexner. Light of distant skies
  Flexner. Short history
  Mendelowitz
  MiD. Ptg in America
  Pierson
  Richardson. Ptg in Amer (col)
  Roos
  Time. 300 years (col)
  U.S. National Capital sesquicentennial
    com
Penn's treaty with the Indians     NNPL
  Ford. Edward Hicks
Peter denying Christ
  Evans. Benjamin West
Prodigal son
  Taylor. Fifty centuries, 1954 ed (col)
Project for a monument: The apotheosis
    of Nelson                      NNCo
  Evans. Benjamin West
Queen Philippa interceding for the bur-
    gesses of Calais               MiD
  Evans. Benjamin West

Raising of Lazarus, 1780          CtHW
  Evans. Benjamin West
Raising of Lazarus (study) 1776
  Evans. Benjamin West
Return of Jephthah          ATeS
  ATeS. Collection
Rinaldo and Armida
  Evans. Benjamin West
Robert Fulton          NCHA
  ICA. From colony to nation
  Mendelowitz
St George and the dragon          PR
  PR. Catalogue
St Paul persecuting the Christians  MNS
  Evans. Benjamin West
St Paul's restoration to sight by Ananias
          MNS
  Evans. Benjamin West
St Paul shaking off the viper          ELT
  Evans. Benjamin West
Samuel Boudé          DN
  DN. Amer primitive ptgs, pt 2
Saul and the witch of Endor          CtHW
  CtHW. Handbook
  ICA. From colony to nation
  MiD. Ptg in America
  Richardson. Ptg in America
Saul and the witch of Endor          ELT
  Evans. Benjamin West
Seascape
  Flexner. First flowers
Self-portrait, 1756          CtY
  CtY. Portrait index
  Flexner. First flowers
  Pierson
Self-portrait, c 1770          DN
  Evans. Benjamin West (col)
Self-portrait c 1795
  Canaday
Self-portrait (Blaustein coll)
  MdBMu. Rendezvous
Stephen Carmick
  Chew. 250 years of art
Thetis bringing the armor to Achilles
          CtNB
  Evans. Benjamin West
Thomas Astle          MeC
  MeC. Inaugural ex
Thomas Mifflin          PH
  Flexner. First flowers (col)
  Pierson
Una and the lion          CtHW
  Evans. Benjamin West
Venus lamenting the death of Adonis PPC
  Evans. Benjamin West
View from the terrace at Windsor     ELT
  Evans. Benjamin West
William Henry          PH
  Flexner. First flowers
Woodcutters in Windsor Great park InIJ
  Evans. Benjamin West
  Flexner. Light of distant skies
  InIJ. 105 ptgs

          Attributed works

Bagshot heath, Surrey          MB
  MB. Ptgs in water color
Conway castle, North Wales          MB
  MB. Ptgs in water color
Lake in wooded country: sunset          MB
  MB. Ptgs in water color
Meadow and hills: sunset          MB
  MB. Ptgs in water color

Moorland landscape          MB
  MB. Ptgs in water color
Mountain landscape with cattle          MB
  MB. Ptgs in water color
Parkland and trees          MB
  MB. Ptgs in water color
Ploughland and distant hills          MB
  MB. Ptgs in water color
Rainstorm on the moors          MB
  MB. Ptgs in water color
Rocky moorland          MB
  MB. Ptgs in water color
Shooting birds          MB
  MB. Ptgs in water color
Stream and distant hills          MB
  MB. Ptgs in water color
Winding road with trees: sunset          MB
  MB. Ptgs in water color
Wolseley Park house, Staffordshire     MB
  MB. Ptgs in water color
Wooded landscape with castle          MB
  MB. Ptgs in water color

          Portrait of the artist

Allston, W. Benjamin West
Delanoy, A. Benjamin West
Pratt, M. Benjamin West
Stuart, G. Benjamin West
Tuthill, A. G. D.  Benjamin West
West, Benjamin, 1739-1809
Malbone, E. G. Benjamin West
West, Mrs Benjamin. See West, Elizabeth
  (Shewell)
WEST, Benjamin Franklin, 1818-1854
Whaling scene: Ship Julien and Bark
    Richard          MSP
  U.S. National Capital sesquicentennial
  com
West, Elizabeth (Shewell) fl 1765
Pratt, M. Mrs Benjamin West
West, B. Mrs West and her son Raphael
WEST, William Edward, 1788-1857
Edward John Trelawny
  MiD. Travelers in Arcadia
  Richardson. Ptg in America
Muses of painting, poetry and music  DC
  DC. Amer ptrs of the South
West by A. Ippolito
West Chester courthouse by H. Pippin
West Chester, Pennsylvania by H. Pippin
West church, Boston by M. B. Prendergast
West 57th street in 1902 by R. Henri
West Hartford, 1907 by W. J. Glackens
West Point, New York
  Chambers, T. View of West Point
  De Grailly, W. View from West Point
  Eilshemius, L. M. West Point, New York
  Toole, J. West Point
  Unidentified artist. West Point, c 1850
  Unidentified artist. West Point from
      above Washingon valley
  Whittredge. W. West Point on the Hud-
      son, View of
West point, Prout's neck by W. Homer
West rock, New Haven by G. H. Durrie
West Sand lake by J. H. Hidley
West side docks by R. Henri
West Wildwood by W. Stuempfig
The west wind by W. Homer
Westchester hills by W. J. Hays

Western air by R. B. Motherwell

Western festival by A. W. Garrett

Western frontier homestead by Unidentified artist

Western industrial by C. Sheeler

Western landscape by T. Moran

Western landscape by W. C. Sharon

Western landscape by J. M. Stanley

Western landscape by W. Whittredge

Western log cabin by A. J. Miller

Western roadstead by L. Feininger

Western sea by L. Feininger

Western sunset by A. Bierstadt

Western university of Pennsylvania
  Smith, R. Western university of Pennsylvania

WESTON, Harold, 1894-
  The arena                                    DP
    DP. Catalogne
  Loneliness                                   DP
    DP. Catalogue

Westward the course of empire takes its way by E. Leutze

Westwood children, fl 1805
  Johnston, J. Westwood children

Westwood hillside by C. C. Allen

Wet day, Paris by M. B. Prendergast

Wetherby, Catherine M. (Thayer) 1828-1912
  Wetherby, I. A. Catherine M. Thayer

WETHERBY, Isaac Augustus, 1819-1904
  Catherine M. Thayer                          NNHS
    Ford. Pictorial folk art
  Mary Eliza Jenkins
    Ford. Pictorial folk art
    Pierson

Wetherby, Mrs Isaac Augustus. See Wetherby, Catherine M. Thayer

Wetmore, Prosper M.
  Elliott, C. L. Prosper M. Wetmore

Wetumpka bridge, Alabama by A. E. Thompson (attributed works)

WEYGANDT, C. E. c 1860
  Easton
    McClintock

Whalers and whaling
  Salmon, R. W. South Sea whale fishing
  Unidentified artist. Whaling
  Unidentified artist. Whaling scene
  Unidentified artist. Whaling scene—Triton of New Bedford
  West, B. F. Whaling scene: Ship Julien and Bark Richard

Wharf in winter by S. Wilson

Wharf players, moonlight by C. F. Gaertner

Wharves by R. A. Florsheim

What a catch by J. G. Clonney

What are they going to do next (Disaster of the soul series) by J. De Diego

What atomic war will do to you by B. Deutsch

What is man by R. Ray

WHEAT, John Potter, 1920-
  Road to Golgotha
    NAD. Annual ex, 1949, 1st half
  September harvest
    UNESCO. 1860-1959

Wheat farmers by J. J. Jones

Wheat stack by Unidentified artist

The wheel by J. Tworkov

Wheeler, Catherine Sears. See Hardy, Catherine Sears (Wheeler)

Wheeler, Dora, b 1858
  Chase, W. M. Miss Dora Wheeler

Wheeler, Permelia Redmon
  Orear, L. R. Permelia Redmon Wheeler

WHEELOCK, Merrill Greene, 1822-1866
  On the Hudson                                MB
    MB. Ptgs in water color

Wheels of victory by P. Evergood

Wheelwright, John, 1594-1679
  Foster, J. John Wheelwright (?)

Wheelwright, Mary Cabot
  Duveneck, F. Mary Cabot Wheelwright

Whelan's pier, Roslyn by P. Gerry

When autumn is here by H. Pushman

When guns were slow by C. M. Russell

When guns were their passports by C. M. Russell

When horseflesh comes high by C. M. Russell

When horses turn back there's danger ahead by C. M. Russell

When law dulls the edge of chance by C. M. Russell

When meat was plentiful by C. M. Russell

When shadows hint death by C. M. Russell

When Sioux and Blackfeet meet by C. M. Russell

When the trail was long between camps by C. M. Russell

When they shoot me by Y. Tanguy

When tracks spell meat by C. M. Russell

When wagon trails were dim by C. M. Russell

When white men turn red by C. M. Russell

Where are the people I knew by Z. Sepeshy

Where are you by Y. Tanguy

Where sun and rain mate: landscape near Pali, Oahu, Hawaii by B. L. Culwell

Where will you spend eternity by C. Cloar

Wherefore now ariseth the illusion of a third dimension by I. L. Albright

Which is which by J. D. Chalfant

Which way to Sunbury? by A. Brook

Whipper, William, fl 1835
  Prior, W. M. (manner of) William Whipper

Whipple, Abraham, 1753-1819
  Savage, E. Abraham Whipple

Whipple, Catherine (Moffatt) 1723-1823
  Copley, J. S. Mrs William Whipple

Whippoorwills
  Audubon, J. J. Chuck-Will's widow
  Spruce, E. F. Whippoorwill, sandpiper

The whirlwind by P. Tchelitchew

WHISTLER, James Abbott McNeil, 1834-1903
  Arrangement in black (F. R. Leyland) DF
    Pearson, H. The man Whistler
  Arrangement in black and brown: the fur jacket                                   MWM
    Pearson, H. The man Whistler
    Sweet
  Arrangement in black and white: the young American (Maud)                    DF
    Pearson, H. The man Whistler

Arrangement in flesh-color and black. **See** Théodore Duret
Arrangement in grey and black (Artist's mother)
  Barr. What is mod ptg
  Canaday
  Cheney. Story 1958 ed
  Craven. Rainbow book
  Flexner. Amer ptg
  Flexner. Short history
  Janson. Key monuments
  Janson. Picture history
  Newmeyer
  Pearson, H. The man Whistler
  Roos
  Sweet
  UNESCO. 1860-1949
  UNESCO. 1860-1955
  UNESCO. 1860-1959
Arrangement in grey and black no 2, 1872. See Thomas Carlyle
Arrangement in pink and purple     OciM
  Bazin
  Sweet
Arthur Jerome Eddy     ICA
  Sweet
The artist in his studio     ICA
  Lewisohn
  Sweet
Artist's mother. See Arrangement in grey and black
At the piano
  Cheney. Story 1958 ed
  Rewald. History of impressionism
Battersea Reach     DC
  DC. Masterpieces
The Chelsea girl
  Sweet
Chelsea shop     ICA
  Sweet
Cicely Alexander (Miss Alexander; Harmony in grey and green     ELT
  Canaday
  Cheney. Story 1958 ed
  Gardner 1959 ed
  Gregory. The world of Whistler
  Pearson, H. The man Whistler
Coast of Brittany: alone with the tide     CtHW
  CtHW. Handbook
  Pierson
Comte Robert de Montesquiou-Fezensac
  Gregory. The world of Whistler
Courbet at Trouville, Harmony in blue and silver     MBI
  Rewald. History of impressionism
Cremorne gardens no 2     MM
  Sweet
The doorway, Venice
  Sweet
Falling rocket. See Nocturne in black and gold
Fire wheel. See Nocturne in black and gold
Frederick R. Leyland. See Arrangement in black
The fur jacket. Arrangement in black and brown
Gold scab
  PPC. Amer classics
Golden screen: caprice in purple and gold no 2, 1865     DF
  Cheney. Story 1958 ed

Grey and silver, Battersea Reach     ICA
  Sweet
Grey note—mouth of the Thames. See Little Scheveningen: grey note
Harmony in blue and silver. See Courbet at Trouville
Harmony in grey and green. See Cicely Alexander
Harmony in red: Lamplight
  Pearson, H. The man Whistler
Henry Graves, the printseller
  Sweet
Jo. See The little white girl
Jo in "Before the mirror." See The little white girl
Lady of the Lange Lijsen
  Pierson
  Sweet
Lagoon, Venice: nocturne in blue and silver     MB
  Baur. Amer ptg
Last of Old Westminster     MB
  Pierson
  Richardson. Ptg in America
Lillian Woakes     DP
  DP. Catalogue
Little Rose of Lyme Regis     MB
  Cheney. Story 1958 ed
  Riley. Your art heritage
Little Scheveningen: grey note (Grey note —mouth of the Thames)     MB
  MB. Ptgs in water color
  Pearson, H. The man Whistler
The little white girl (Jo; Jo in "Before the mirror"; Symphony in white no 2, 1864)     ELT
  Cheney. Story 1958 ed
  Craven. Treasury 1952 ed (col)
  Gregory. The world of Whistler
  Pearson, H. The Man Whistler
  Sweet
  UNESCO. 1860-1949
  UNESCO. 1860-1955
  UNESCO. 1860-1959
Mme Camille D'Avouille     MAP
  Sweet
Marine     OCiM
  Cheney. Story 1958 ed
Miss Alexander. See Cicely Alexander
Music room     DF
  Pierson
Nocturne in black and gold (The falling rocket)     MiD
  MiD. Treasures
  Pierson
  Richardson. Ptg in America (col)
  Sweet
Nocturne in black and gold (Fire wheel)
  Roos
Nocturne in blue and gold. See Old Battersea bridge
Nocturne in blue and green     ELT
  Cheney. Story 1958 ed
Nude     OYB
  OYB. Supplement 1959
Old Battersea bridge (Nocturne in blue and gold)     ELT
  Cheney. New world history
  Cheney. Story 1958 ed
  Janson. Picture history
  Robb. Harper history
  Roos

**WHISTLER, J. A. M.**
Old Battersea bridge—*Continued*
Sweet
Time. 300 years (col)
Upjohn
Old Battersea bridge (Symphony in brown and silver)      MAP
Pierson
Sweet
The Pacific
Lee. Art then and now
Portrait of Mrs Whistler. See Harmony in red: lamplight
La princesse du pays de la porcelaine   DF
Pearson, H. The man Whistler
Pierson
Richard Canfield            OCiM
Cheney. Story 1958
Rosa Corder
Gregory. The world of Whistler
Pearson, H. The man Whistler
Self-portrait, c 1858            DF
Rewald. History of impressionism
Self-portrait, 1867            MiD
MiD. Treasures
Sweet
Study of a head after Couture
Sweet
Symphony in brown and silver. See Old Battersea bridge
Symphony in white no 1. See The white girl
Symphony in white no 2. See The little white girl
The Thames from Battersea bridge OYB
OYB. Supplement 1959
The Thames in ice            DF
Born
Théodore Duret (Arrangement in flesh-colour and black)       MM
Cheney. Story 1958 ed
Mendelowitz
MM. 100 Amer ptrs
Pierson
Sweet
Taylor. Fifty centuries, 1954 ed (col)
Thomas Carlyle (Arrangement in grey and black no 2)       ScG
Cheney. New world history
Cheney. Story 1958 ed
Craven. Treasury 1952 ed
ICA. Sargent, Whistler and Mary Cassatt
McCurdy
Richardson. Ptg in America
Robb. Harper History
Roos
Time. 300 years (col)
Walker. Ptgs from America
Variations in pink and grey—Chelsea   DF
Walker. Ptgs from America
Wapping on Thames
CtY. Yale alumni
Sweet
The white girl            DN
Canaday
McKinney
NYG. Fine art
Pierson
Rewald. History of impressionism
Sweet (col)
UNESCO. 1860-1955
UNESCO. 1860-1959

The young American (Maud Franklin)·
See Arrangement in black and white
Young girl in blue
Bazin (col detail)
**Portrait of the artist**
Chase, W. M. James Abbott McNeill Whistler
Whistler, J. A. M. Artist in his studio
**Whistling** boy by W. M. Chase
**Whistling** boy by F. Currier
**Whistling** boy by F. Duveneck
**WHITAKER, Frederic,** 1891-
Pro Deo, pro populo
NAD. Annual ex, 1947, 2d half
**WHITCOMB, Susan,** fl 1847-1852
Mount Vernon (Residence of General Washington)       VWR
Flexner. Light of distant skies
VWR. Folk art (col)
**White, Alden Perley,** 1856-1933
Noyes, W. F. Alden Perley White (copy)
**White, Andrew Dickson,** 1832-1918
Upjohn, A. M. Andrew Dickson White
**WHITE, Charles,** 1918-
Hampton institute mural design    NJN
Larkin (detail)
Larkin rev ed (detail)
**White, Charlotte.** See Poor, Charlotte (White)
**WHITE, Doris A.**
Quiet street            OYB
OYB. Annual 1960
**White, John,** fl 1835
Bascom, R. H. M. Rev John White
**WHITE, John Blake,** 1781-1859
General Marion in his swamp encampment inviting a British officer to dinner
Cowdrey v 1
**White, Margaret (Rutherford)** fl 1883
Sargent, J. S. Mrs Henry White
**WHITE, Richard A.** 1917-
Untitled, 2-27-59, 1950
NNSG. Younger Amer ptrs
**White, Thomas Raeburn,** 1875-1959
Watkins, F. C. Thomas Raeburn White
**White** and gold by K. Okada
**White** architecture by C. Demuth
**White** bench by W. M. Chase
**White** bird by W. A. Baziotes
**White,** black and red by F. Mitchell
**White** callas by A. B. Carles
**White** Canadian barn by G. O'Keeffe
**White** castles on the Missouri by C. Wimar
**White** catamount by D. Austin
**White** center by M. Rothko
**White** city no 3 by L. L. Ribak
**White** cloud by J. R. Cox
**White** cloud by H. V. Poor
**White** cockatoo by W. M. Chase
**White** cockatoo by J. Pollock
**White** cow by E. F. Spruce
**White** cows by D. Burliuk
**White** factory by P. Blume
**White** field by T. Stamos
**White** flower by E. N. Bischoff
**White** flower by J. Carroll

White flower by G. O'Keeffe
White forms by F. J. Kline
White front by J. Albers
White garden by R. Pousette-Dart
The white girl by J. A. M. Whistler
White Hall plantation, Louisiana, c 1790 by
    C. Colomb
White horizon by A. P. Ryder
White horizontal by J. Pollock
White horse by G. W. Bellows
White horse by T. H. Benton
White horse by A. P. Ryder
White horses at the sand pit by H. G. Kel-
    ler
White house by R. Breinin
White iris by G. O'Keeffe
White journey by M. Tobey
White landscape by G. Peterdi
White light by J. Pollock
White light by W. W. Quirt
White lilac by S. Menkès
The white line by S. Francis
White lines by I. R. Miller
White lines by I. R. Pereira
White mare with foal by C. S. Price
White mist to greens by W. Meigs
White moon by M. Avery
White morning by I. Cavat
White morning by A. Dasburg
White mountains
    Cole, T. Notch of the White mountains
    Cole, T. View of Monte Video
    Cole, T. View of the White mountains
    Cropsey, J. F. White mountains in au-
        tumn
    Fisher, A. White mountains
    Macknight, D. Winter in the White moun-
        tains
    Marin, J. White mountain country, Dix-
        ville Notch
    Marin, J. White mountain country, New
        Hampshire
    Marin, J. White mountains, autumn
    Smith, R. In the falls of the Saco, Craw-
        ford's notch
    Spruce, E. F. White mountain
White nude with apple by A. B. Carles
White numbers by J. Johns
White Oak swamp, Virginia, Battle of, 1862
    Unidentified artist. Battle of White Oak
        Swamp, Virginia, 1862
White on black by J. Pollock
White on blue by S. J. Twardowicz
White painting by L. Calcagno
White painting by P. Guston
White painting by W. Ivey
White pelicans in Florida by G. Harvey
White pitcher by G. F. Hacker
White pitcher with field flowers by Ben-
    Zion
The white place in shadow by G. O'Keeffe
White Plume by A. J. Miller
White portico by J. A. Oneto
White rectangle by I. R. Pereira

White reverie by R. Pousette-Dart
White river at Sharon by E. Hopper
White rocks, Nova Scotia by J. E. Heliker
White sails by E. Lewandowski
White sands by C. R. Bentley
White shell by A. Ruellan
White ships by J. S. Sargent
The white squall by J. Evans
White still life by S. M. Adler
White structures by H. N. Cook
White table by B. Chaet
White tablet by C. A. Morris
White tails by C. M. Russell
White target by J. Johns
White town, Azemmour, Morocco by D.
    Macknight
White vase by K. Knaths
White violets and abandoned coal mine by
    C. E. Burchfield
White violets and coal mine by C. E. Burch-
    field
White wall by A. Trivilini
White water ahead by C. S. Chapman
The White way by J. Sloan
Whitefield, George, 1714-1770
    Wollaston, J. George Whitefield preach-
        ing
Whitefoord, Caleb, fl 1782
    Stuart, G. Caleb Whitefoord
Whitehouse, Hannah Goodwin. See Moul-
    ton, Hannah Goodwin (Whitehouse)
Whitehouse family
    Healy, G. P. A. Boating party on the
        Thames
The Whiteside church by A. M. R. Moses
Whitestone bridge by R. Crawford
Whither now by M. Weber
Whitman, Walt, 1819-1892
    Eakins, T. Walt Whitman
Whitney, Eben, fl 1807
    Woodside, J. A. Eben Whitney
Whitney, Eli, 1765-1825
    Morse, S. F. B. Eli Whitney
WHITNEY, L.
    American landscape              NJN
      Barker. Amer ptg
      Ford. Pictorial folk art
      Mendelowitz
      Pierson
Whittemore, Mrs John Howard, fl 1899
    Cassatt, M. Portrait of a grand lady (Mrs
        John Howard Whittemore)
Whittemore, Mary Anne. See Low, Mary
    Anne (Whittemore)
Whittemore, Rebecca Tufts, fl 1811
    Greenwood, E. A. Rebecca Tufts Whitte-
        more
Whittemore, William, 1761-1842
    Williams, H. William Whittemore
WHITTREDGE, Worthington, 1820-1910
    Apples                    MB
      MB. Karolik coll
    Boating party in Central park
      Born
    Camp meeting            MM
      Mendelowitz
      U.S. National Capital sesquicentennial
        com

WHITTREDGE, Worthington—*Continued*
Crossing the ford, Platte river, Colorado
                              NNCe
  Rathbone
Crow's nest                                   MiD
  Pierson
Deer, Mount Storm park, Cincinnati
                              MWM
  Barker. Amer ptg
  Baur. Amer ptg
  Pierson
  Drachenfels
  Sears. Highlights
Home by the sea                               MAP
  Pierson
House on the sea                              CLA
  Born
In the Rockies
  Rathbone
Landscape                                     OCiM
  OCiM. Guide
Long's peak, Colorado                         MB
  MB. Karolik coll
Old homestead by the sea                      MB
  MB. Karolik coll
On the Platte river                           MB
  MB. Karolik coll
Outskirts of the forest                       MB
  MB. Karolik coll
Self-portrait: the artist at his easel
  WiMiA. Amer ptg 1760-1960
Trout pool                                    MM
  Richardson. Ptg in America
View of West Point on the Hudson MB
  MB. Karolik coll
Western landscape
  WiMiA. Amer ptg 1760-1960
**Whoa** Emma by D. G. Blythe
**Whorf, John,** fl 1784
  Unidentified artist. John Whorf with bow
    and arrow
WHORF, John, 1903-1959
Algerian scene                                MB
  MB. Ptgs in water color
Algerian street scene                         MB
  MB. Ptgs in water color
Birches                                       MB
  MB. Ptgs in water color
Brightening Seine
  NYG. Fine art
Edge of the east water
  NSP. Sportscapes
Keeper of the bell                            OYB
  OYB. Catalogue 1951
River men                                     MB
  MB. Ptgs in water color
Sailboats                                     MB
  MB. Ptgs in water color
Setting out the decoys
  NSP. Sportscapes
Summer night, Provincetown, Massachu-
  setts                                      MB
  MB. Ptgs in water color
Swans                                         MB
  MB. Ptgs in water color
Winter by the sea
  NYG. Fine art
Winter, North end, Boston                     MB
  MB. Ptgs in water color
**Why** not use the L by R. Marsh
**Wichita** mountains from the Medicine Bluffs
  by H. Stieffel

Wickham, Catherine (Fry) See Fry, Cath-
  erine
Wickham, Elizabeth S. (McClurg)
  Stuart, G. Mrs John Wickham
Wickham, Mrs Samuel. See Fry, Catherine
WICKWIRE, Jere Raymond, 1883-
  William Lyon Phelps                        CtY
  CtY. Portrait index
Widener, Ella (Pancoast)
  Sargent, J. S. Mrs Joseph E. Widener
The **widow** by H. Hensel
The **widow** by J. E. Levi
The **widow** by H. Pittman
**Widow** Magee by G. B. Luks
WIEGHARDT, Paul, 1897-
  Oganda
    IU. Contemp Amer ptg & sculp, 1957
  Quiet colors
    IU. Contemp Amer ptg & sculp, 1955
WIGFALL, Benjamin L. 1931?-
  Chimneys
    Pousette-Dart. Amer ptg
WIGHE, A.
  Rural court scene, 1849                    RPS
    Davidson v2
Wight, Harmony Child
  Unidentified artist. Harmony Child Wight
Wight, Oliver, fl 1786
  Unidentified artist. Oliver Wight
WIGHT, Peter Bonnett, 1838-1925
  Venetian Gothic art building on the old
    Yale campus                              CtY
  Weir. Recollections
Wignall, Elizabeth, fl 1814
  Sully, T. Elizabeth Wignall
Wilcocks, Maria. See Ellis, Maria (Wil-
  cocks)
WILCOX, Lucia, 1906-
60-340
    PPC. International ex, 1961/62
Wilcox children, fl 1845
  Stock, J. W. Wilcox children
WILD, John Casper, 1806?-1846
  Cincinnati, 1835
    Davidson v2
  Dubuque, Iowa                             ICH
    Rathbone
  Fort Snelling                             MnSH
    Rathbone
  View of Davenport, Iowa and the Missis-
    sippi                                    IaDA
    Rathbone
  View of St Louis, c 1841                  ICH
    Rathbone
The **wild** bunch by I. L. Albright
**Wild** cherry tree by J. H. Twachtman
**Wild** flowers by H. R. Newman
**Wild** flowers by W. Williams
**Wild** flowers and grasses by H. L. McFee
**Wild** geese by W. Homer
**Wild** horse hunters by C. M. Russell
**Wild** horses by A. J. Miller
**Wild** horses by A. R. Saalburg
**Wild** iris by K. Schrag
**Wild** man's meat by C. M. Russell
The **wild** one by D. Fink
**Wild** roses by M. Hartley
**Wild** scenery by A. J. Miller
**Wild** turkey by J. J. Audubon

Wild West by G. W. Platt
**WILDE, John,** 1919-
Apotheosis of Marie-Henri Beyle
    Pierson
    WMAA. Annual ex, 1955
Further festivities at the Contessa San-
    severini's
    IU. Contemp Amer ptg, 1952
    MnMW. Reality and fantasy
Green peppers
    IU. Contemp Amer ptg & sculp, 1961
The pseudolucànus reconsidered
    IU. Contemp Amer ptg & sculp, 1955
Still life with Christmas candy    MiD
    CoS. New accessions USA, 1954
Still life with currants
    IU. Contemp Amer ptg & sculp, 1959
Wildeworld
    IU. Contemp Amer ptg & sculp, 1957
With a few of my favorites
    IU. Contemp Amer ptg & sculp, 1953
    (col)
Work reconsidered
    MM. Amer ptg today
Wildeworld by J. Wilde
**WILES, Irving Ramsey,** 1861-1948
John Gellatly    DNC
    DNC. Gellatly coll 1954
Wiley, John, fl 1771
    Williams, W. John Wiley, his mother and
    sisters
**WILEY, William Thomas,** 1937-
Firecrackers sold here
    WMAA. Young America 1960
Peaceable kingdom    CSFM
    IU. Contemp Amer ptg & sculp, 1961
Time table
    WMAA. Young America 1960
**WILGUS, William John,** 1819-1853
Ut-Ha-Wah (Capt Cole)    CtY
    CtY. Portrait index
**WILKES, Max S.**
Girl resting
    PA. Annual ex, 1949
Wilkes-Barre and the Wyoming valley by
    Unidentified artist
**WILKINSON, Jack,** 1913-
Valley landscape
    OrPA. Ptgs & sculptures
Wilkinson, Jemima, fl 1773
    Mathies, J. L. D. Jemima Wilkinson: the
    Publick Universal Friend
Will Schuster and blackman going shooting
    for rail by T. Eakins
Willett, Mrs Marinus, fl 1800
    Vanderlyn, J. Mrs Marinus Willett and
    child
William, Otho Holland, 1749-1794
    Peale, Raphaelle. Otho Holland William
William Rush carving the allegorical figure
    of the Skuylkill river by T. Eakins
Williams, Lady, fl 1783
    Earl, R. Lady Williams and child
**WILLIAMS, Alyn,** b 1865
Augustus Van Horne Stuyvesant  NNHS
    Vail. Stuyvesant ports
Williams, Ann (Wray) 1780-1817
    Jarvis, J. W. Mrs John Williams jr
Williams, Charles K. fl 1846
    Mason, B. F. Chief Justice Charles K.
    Williams
Williams, Elisha, 1694-1755
    Moulthrop, R. Elisha Williams

**WILLIAMS, Frederick Ballard,** 1871-1956
Down from Mount Mansfield, Vermont
    NJMo
    NJMo. Forty years
Williams, George, 1778-1852
    Stuart, G. George Williams
**WILLIAMS, Henry,** 1787-1830
Unknown man    MB
    MB. New England miniatures
William Whittemore
    MB. New England miniatures
Williams, Jerhusha
    Unidentified artist. Mourning picture
    sacred to the memory of Jerhusha
    Williams
Williams, John, 1752-1806
    Jarvis, J. W. Gen John Williams
Williams, John, 1783-1858
    Jarvis, J. W. Col John Williams, jr
Williams, Mrs John. See Williams, Ann
    (Wray)
**WILLIAMS, Keith Shaw,** 1905-1951
Seated nude
    NAD. Annual ex, autumn 1949
Williams, Mary Goddard, fl 1876
    Duveneck, F. The crimson gown
**WILLIAMS, Micah,** fl 1815
John G. Vanderveer    VWR
    VWR. Folk art (col)
Mrs Jane Herbert Vanderveer    VWR
    VWR. Folk art (col)
Williams, Norman, fl 1867
    Mason, B. F. (attributed works) Norman
    Williams
Williams, Mrs Oliver E.
    Prendergast, M. B. Mrs Oliver E. Wil-
    liams
Williams, Pamela. See Brown, Pamela
    (Williams)
Williams, Rose Adèle (Cutts) Douglas
    Healy, G. P. A. Mrs Stephen A. Douglas
Williams, Samuel, d 1841
    Allston, W. Samuel Williams
Williams, Samuel Wells, 1812-1884
    Weir, J. F. Samuel Wells Williams
Williams, Susan. See Proudfit, Susan (Wil-
    liams)
**WILLIAMS, Virgil**
Winnowing grain in California, 1872
    Davidson v2
**WILLIAMS, Walter,** 1920-
Poultry market    WMAA
    Pierson
Wild flowers
    WMAA. Annual ex, 1957
**WILLIAMS, William,** fl 1740-1794
Conversation piece
    Flexner. First flowers
David Hall
    Flexner. First flowers
Deborah Hall    NBM
    Barker. Amer ptg
    Flexner. First flowers (col)
    Larkin
    Larkin rev ed
    Pierson
Husband and wife in a landscape (Master-
    piece)    DeWin
    Mendelowitz
    Richardson. Ptg in America
John Wiley, his mother and sisters
    Flexner. First flowers
    Pierson

**WILLIAMS, William**—*Continued*
  Masterpiece. See Husband and wife in a landscape
  William Denning family
    Flexner. First flowers
    ICA. From colony to nation
    U.S. National Capital sesquicentennial com
  William Hall                DeWin
    Pierson

**Williams, William Stoddard,** 1762-1829
  Jennys, W. Dr William Stoddard Williams

**WILLIAMSON, Clara (McDonald)** b 1875
  Autumn outing
    PPC. International ex, 1955
  First Texas Central railroad
    Kallir. Amer primitive ptgs
  Night hunters
    IU. Contemp Amer ptg & sculp, 1957
  Standing in the need of prayer     TxD
    Ford. Pictorial folk art
    IU. Contemp Amer ptg & sculp, 1953
  Veteran's dream              TxD
    Lipman. Primitive ptrs

**Williamson, Thomas,** 1771-1846
  Hubard, W. J. Thomas Williamson

**Williamstown,** Massachusetts by A. M. R. Moses

**Willie** Gee by R. Henri

**Willimantic,** Connecticut, 1923 by J. A. Weir

**Willimantic** thread mill by J. A. Weir

**Willing, Anne (Shippen)** 1710-1791
  Feke, R. Mrs Charles Willing

**Willis** avenue bridge by B. Shahn

**Willoughby,** Master by Unidentified artist

**Willow** in the rain by J. Thecla

**Willow-Swamp,** Minnesota by B. J. O. Nordfeldt

**Willow** tree by A. G. Dove

**Willows** by T. Robinson

**WILLSON, Mr.** fl 1822
  Barnard Stratton of Amherst, New Hampshire            NCHA
    Jones. New-found folk art

**WILLSON, Mary Ann,** fl 1810-1826
  General Washington on horseback  RPS
    Brussels. Exposition
    Lipman. Primitive ptrs
  Mermaid
    Lipman. Primitive ptrs
  Pelican                 RPS
    Lipman. Primitive ptrs
  Prodigal son reclaimed by his father
    Lipman. Primitive ptrs

**Wilson, Mrs Algernon.** See Wilson, Sarah Procter (Daniell)

**WILSON, Bryan,** 1927-
  Hawk and quail
    IU. Contemp Amer ptg & sculp, 1961
  Ross snow geese
    Mendelowitz
    PPC. International ex, 1958

**WILSON, Mary R.** fl 1820
  Fruit in yellow bowl        VWR
    VWR. Folk art (col)

**WILSON, Milton,** 1923-
  The Great Goot
    OrPA. Ptgs & sculptures **(col)**

**WILSON, Reginald,** 1909-
  Pet rooster              ATU
    ATU. Coll of Amer art

**Wilson, Sarah Proctor (Daniell)**
  Theus, J. Mrs Algernon Wilson

**WILSON, Solomon,** 1896-
  Drugstore
    NAD. Annual ex, 1951
  East wind
    Gruskin
  Fishermen's festival
    IU. Contemp Amer ptg, 1948
  Floats and markers
    NAD. Annual ex. 1953
  Last stop
    IU. Contemp Amer ptg, 1950
  Old boats and beach
    IU. Contemp Amer ptg & sculp, 1955
  The pier
    IU. Contemp Amer ptg, 1949
  Repair shack interior
    DC. 21 biennial ex, 1949
  Schooner and scow         OYB
    OYB. Accessions
    OYB. Supplement 1959
  Torn sail
    PPC. Ptg in the U.S. 1949
  Town square
    IU. Contemp Amer ptg, 1951
  Wharf in winter
    OYB. Catalogue 1951

**WILT, Richard H.** 1915-
  Birthday cake            MiD
    CoS. New accessions USA, 1952
  Circus triptych           OYB
    OYB. Annual 1953
  Shambattle             OYB
    OYB. Catalogue 1951

**WIMAR, Carl,** 1828-1862
  The Adam Lemp Brewery     MoSL
    MoSL. Handbook 1953
  Attack on an emigrant train, 1856  MiA
    Davidson v 1
  Buffalo dance           MoSL
    McCracken. Portrait of the old west (col)
    MoSL. Handbook 1953
    Pierson
    Rathbone (col)
  Buffalo hunt          MoSLW
    McCracken. Portrait of the old west
    Rathbone
  Buffaloes crossing the Yellowstone             MoSLW
    Rathbone
  Buttes on the Missouri     MoSLH
    Rathbone
  Captive charger        MoSL
    Davidson v 1
    Rathbone
    Roos
  Cottonwoods on the Missouri   MoSLH
    Rathbone
  Indian camp fire
    Rathbone
  Indians approaching Fort Benton MoSLW
    Born
    Davidson v 1
    Rathbone
  Medicine bag          MoSL
    Rathbone
  On the warpath
    WiMiA. Amer ptg 1760-1960

Studies of a quartered buffalo MoSL
Rathbone
Turf house on the plains
Rathbone
Time. 300 years (col)
White castles on the Missouri MoSLH
Rathbone
**Wimar, Charles Ferdinand.** See Wimar, Carl
**Wind,** clouds and water by A. G. Dove
**Wind** clouds at sundown by L. Feininger
**Wind** from the sea by A. N. Wyeth
The **wind** of the sun by I. R. Pereira
**Wind** on land and sea, Maine by J. Marin
**Wind** orchestra by M. Weber
**Wind** river chain by A. J. Miller
**Wind** river country, Wyoming by A. Bierstadt
**Wind** river mountain by A. J. Miller
**Wind** river mountains, Wyoming, View from by A. Bierstadt
**Wind** rose by M. Hoff
**Wind,** sea and sails by C. Sheeler
**Wind,** wave and tree by K. Schrag
**Windham** village by J. A. Weir
**Winding** road by M. Sterne
**Winding** road with trees: sunset by B. West (attributed works)
The **windmill** by A. P. Ryder
The **window** by C. Browning
The **window** by H. Hofmann
The **window** by R. A. Mintz
The **window** by H. E. Niese
The **window** by M. Tobey
The **window** by G. Tooker
**Window** by the alley by C. E. Burchfield
**Window** cleaner by A. Rattner
**Window** cleaner no 3, 1951 by A. Rattner
**Window** composition by A. Rattner
**Window** with flowers by B. Connelly
**Window** in the Union club by G. P. Du Bois
**Window** shade by L. MacIver
**Windows** by T. Yerxa
**Windows,** Paris by E. W. Dickinson
**Windward** shore by F. J. Waugh
**Windy** corner by J. Myers
**Windy** day—Lowe's point by W. Zorach
**Wine,** honey and oil by Y. Tanguy
**Wing, Halsey,** fl 1832
Mason, B. F. Halsey Wing
**Wing, Mrs Halsey,** fl 1832
Mason, B. F. Mrs Halsey Wing
**Wingaersheek** beach by E. L. Novotny
**Wingaersheek** marsh by J. C. Pellew
**Wingahocking** at Shoemaker's lane, Germantown by R. Smith
**Winger** web by R. Koppe
**WINGREN, Dan,** 1923-
The thicket
PPC. International ex, 1955
**Wings** of the morning by H. E. Mattson
**Winne, Adam,** fl 1730
Unidentified artist. Adam Winne

**WINNER, William E.** c 1815-1883
Crazy Nora PH
Chew. 250 years of art
**Winnowing** grain by E. Johnson
**Winona** Falls by A. H. Wyant
**Winslow, Benjamin,** 1783-1863
Malbone, E. G. Benjamin Winslow
**Winslow, Isaac,** 1707-1777
Blackburn, J. Winslow family
Copley, J. S. Mr and Mrs Isaac Winslow
Feke, R. Isaac Winslow
**Winslow, Jemima (Debuke)** 1732-1790
Blackburn, J. Winslow family
Copley, John S. Mr and Mrs Isaac Winslow
**Winslow, Joshua,** 1727?-1801
Copley, J. S. Joshua Winslow
**Winsted,** Connecticut, 1877 by S. E. Harvey
**WINTER, Andrew,** 1892-1958
Bleak weather
NAD. Annual ex, autumn 1949
Breeches buoy
NAD. Annual ex, 1949, 1st half
**WINTER, C.**
Minstrel show MB
MB. Karolik coll
**Winter** by T. Birch
**Winter** by E. Lawson
**Winter** by R. Kent
**Winter** by H. Moller
**Winter** by G. Prestopino
**Winter,** a view of Monhegan, Maine by R. Kent
**Winter** afternoon by G. W. Bellows
**Winter** along the mills by G. Kachmer
**Winter:** an impediment in travelling by G. Harvey
**Winter** bouquet by C. E. Burchfield
**Winter** by the sea by J. Whorf
**Winter,** Central park, New York by E. Lawson
**Winter** coast by W. Homer
**Winter** cottonwoods east, V by G. O'Keeffe
**Winter,** Dirigo island by W. A. Kienbusch
**Winter** dunes by L. MacIver
**Winter** farm scene by G. H. Durrie
**Winter** forms by J. Maxwell
**Winter** holiday by P. S. Sample
**Winter** Hudson by J. C. Atherton
**Winter** idyl by B. Crane
**Winter** in the Catskills by D. E. Lee
**Winter** in the country, a cold morning by G. H. Durrie
**Winter** in the country, distant hills by G. H. Durrie
**Winter** in the country, getting ice by G. H. Durrie
**Winter** in the country, the old grist mill by G. H. Durrie
**Winter** in the valley by E. W. Redfield
**Winter** in the Verde valley by H. Strater
**Winter** journey by H. Koerner
**Winter** landscape by T. Doughty
**Winter** landscape by G. H. Durrie
**Winter** landscape by H. G. Keller
**Winter** landscape by W. Sommer

Winter landscape; gathering wood by G. H. Durrie

Winter landscape with skaters by F. R. Gignoux (attributed works)

Winter moonlight by C. E. Burchfield

Winter morning by A. L. Ripley

Winter nightfall in the city by C. Hassam

Winter, North end, Boston by J. Whorf

Winter on the river by E. Lawson

Winter port by E. D. Lewandowski

Winter rhythm by L. Pytlak

Winter road by L. Dodd

Winter rooftops by A. Osver

Winter scene by J. S. Blunt

Winter scene by G. H. Durrie

Winter scene by E. Shinn

Winter scene in Brooklyn by F. Guy

Winter scene in New England by G. H. Durrie

Winter scene in New Jersey by F. R. Gignoux

Winter scene, Jones' inn by G. H. Durrie

Winter scene on the Hudson by J. F. Cropsey

Winter scene outside of Bristol, Pennsylvania by T. Birch

Winter scene: the red fox by J. Hope

Winter shapes by K. Mattern

Winter silence by F. D. Ogden

Winter soldiers by M. Siporin

Winter solstice by C. E. Burchfield

Winter sports by F. R. Gignoux

Winter sun by H. Lundeberg

Winter trees by R. Gleitsmann

Winter twilight by C. E. Burchfield

Winter twilight by M. Weber

Winter visitor by P. S. Sample

Winter wharf by K. Knaths

Winter without snow by W. Zorach

Winter wood by L. Gatch

Winter's day by W. A. Lewis

A winter's day by A. M. R. Moses

Winter's dreamland by K. Matthew

Winter's end by W. E. Baum

The winters passed by C. Booth

Winter's playground by R. Gwathmey

Winterscape by C. Seliger

Winthrop, Hannah (Fayerweather) 1727-1790
    Copley, J. S. Mrs John Winthrop

Winthrop, John, 1714-1779
    Copley, J. S. Professor John Winthrop

Winthrop, Mrs John. See Winthrop, Hannah (Fayerweather)

Winthrop, Katherine. See Browne, Katherine (Winthrop)

Winthrop, Thomas Lindall, 1760-1841
    Malbone, E. G. Thomas L. Winthrop

Wintry park by B. Robinson

Wires down by C. E. Burchfield

Wisconsin
    Cikovsky, N. Wisconsin landscape
    Curry, J. S. Wisconsin landscape

Seifert, P. A. Jacob Bennett farm, Gotham, Wisconsin, c 1880

Seifert, P. A. Residence of E. R. Jones, Dodgeville, Wisconsin, 1881

Seifert, P. A. Residence of Lemuel Cooper, Plain, Wisconsin, 1879

Seifert, P. Wisconsin farm scene

Wisdom and destiny by H. G. Keller

Wise bird by G. S. Ratkai

The wise men by M. Dixon

The wish by Y. Tanguy

Wissahickon by R. Smith

Witchery by F. E. Conway

With a few of my favorites by J. Wilde

With my shadow by Y. Tanguy

With sloping mast and dripping prow by A. P. Ryder

With the Staatszeitung by W. M. Harnett

Within autumn by F. D. Duncan

Within the confines of window frame by M. Sokole

The witness by Y. Tanguy

Witness the whatless by P. Burlin

The witness tree by J. H. Fitzgerald

The witnesses by H. Warshaw

Woakes, Lillian
    Whistler, J. A. M. Miss Lillian Woakes

WOELLFER, Emerson S. 1914-
    Birds and orange sky
    Pierson
    Napoli forio
    IU. Contemp Amer ptg & sculp, 1959

WOISERI, L. J. Boqueta de, fl 1805
    New Orleans, 1803
    Davidson v2

Wolcott, Abigail. See Ellsworth, Abigail (Wolcott)

Wolcott, Frederick, 1767-1837
    Waldo, S. L. and Jewett, W. Frederick Wolcott

Wolcott, Oliver, 1760-1833
    Catlin, G. Oliver Wolcott
    Stuart, G. Oliver Wolcott

Wolf men by C. M. Russell

WOLFE, Jack, 1925?-
    Crucifixion
    WMAA. Young America 1957
    Purlieu
    MBIC. View 1960

Wolfe, James, 1727-1750
    West, B. Death of General Wolfe

Wolfe, Thomas Clayton, 1900-1938
    Gorsline, D. W. Thomas Wolfe

Wolfersberger, Elizabeth
    Stettinius, S. E. (attributed works) Mr and Mrs Wolfersberger

Wolfersberger, Philip
    Stettinius, S. E. (attributed works) Mr and Mrs Wolfersberger

Wolfert's will by J. Quidor

WOLFF, Robert Jay, 1905-
    Erewhon
    IU. Contemp Amer ptg & sculp, 1957

WOLLASTON, John, fl 1736-1767
    Abraham Barnes                           DC
        DC. Amer ptrs of the South
    Children of Warner Lewis
        Barker. Amer ptg

George Whitefield preaching      ELNP
    U. S. National Capital sesquicentennial
    com
Mrs Daniel Blake
    Flexner. First flowers
Mrs Samuel Gouverneur      DeWin
    Mendelowitz
Mrs Warner Lewis      VWC
    Pierson
Mrs William Allen      NBM
    Belknap
Mrs William Axtell (?)      NNHS
    ICA. From colony to nation
Mrs William Walton      NNHS
    Belknap
Philip Philipse      NNMC
    Larkin
    Larkin rev ed
Sir William Johnson      NAI
    NAI. Hudson valley
Thomas Appleford      NNHS
    NNHS. Waldron Phoenix Belknap coll
Warner Lewis      VWC
    Pierson
Warner Lewis II and Rebecca      VWS
    Pierson
**Wolseley** Park house, Staffordshire by B.
    West (attributed works)
**Wolverene** by J. J. Audubon
**Wolves**
    Audubon, J. W. Gray wolf or white Amer-
      ican wolf
    Kuhn, R. Wounded wolves
    Price, C. S. Wolves
**Woman** by I. L. Albright
A **woman** by W. M. Chase
**Woman** by W. De Kooning
A **woman** by T. Eakins
A **woman** by W. M. Prior (attributed works)
**Woman** by W. W. Quirt
**Woman** I, stage 1. Summer, 1950 by W.
    De Kooning
**Woman** I, stage 2 by W. De Kooning
**Woman** I, stage 3 by W. De Kooning
**Woman** I, stage 4 by W. De Kooning
**Woman** I, stage 5 by W. De Kooning
**Woman** I, stage 6 by W. De Kooning
**Woman** (Green) by W. De Kooning
**Woman** and bicycle by W. De Kooning
**Woman** and checkerboard by R. Diebenkorn
**Woman** and man by B. Greene
**Woman** and table by P. Wonner
**Woman** arranging her hair by M. B. Pren-
    dergast
**Woman** arranging her veil by M. Cassatt
**Woman** as landscape by W. De Kooning
**Woman** at piano by P. Evergood
**Woman** at Samaria by H. Pippin
**Woman** at work by J. Lawrence
**Woman** carrying picture by M. Weber
**Woman** cutting bread by A. Rattner
**Woman** dressing by B. Greene
**Woman** driving geese by W. Homer
**Woman** drying her hair by H. Katzman
**Woman** feeding birds by A. Blanch

**Woman** holding tablet by M. Weber
**Woman** in a white room by M. Hoff
**Woman** in a window by R. Diebenkorn
**Woman** in a yellow dress by Unidentified
    artist
**Woman** in black by M. Cassatt
**Woman** in black by W. M. Chase
**Woman** in chair by B. Shahn
**Woman** in doorway by C. E. Burchfield
**Woman** in landscape by W. De Kooning
**Woman** in white by W. M. Chase
**Woman,** ocher by W. De Kooning
**Woman** of Iowa by P. Evergood
**Woman** of sorrows by W. W. Quirt
**Woman** of the crucifixion by R. Lebrun
**Woman** on sofa by W. J. Glackens
**Woman** on trapeze by K. Zerbe
**Woman** reading by M. Cassatt
**Woman** reclining by M. Cassatt
**Woman** sewing by W. Homer
**Woman** sitting by W. De Kooning
The **woman** taken in adultery by H. Pippin
**Woman** watering plant by B. Currie
**Woman** with a dog by M. Cassatt
**Woman** with a fan by W. Jennys
**Woman** with a letter by G. Biddle
**Woman** with a purple hat by J. Binford
**Woman** with apple by Unidentified artist
**Woman** with black cat by G. Luks
**Woman** with cigarette by G. P. Du Bois
**Woman** with fighting dogs by J. Kirschen-
    baum
**Woman** with flower by W. Homer
**Woman** with folded arms by B. Greene
**Woman** with forget-me-nots by F. Duven-
    eck
**Woman** with green face by M. Avery
**Woman** with plants by G. Wood
**Woman** with sewing box by Unidentified
    artist
**Woman** with walking stick by C. H. De-
    muth
**Woman's** work by J. Sloan
**Women** admiring a child by M. Cassatt
**Women** and sea by J. Marin
**Women** and tents by M. Weber
**Women** forms and sea by J. Marin
**Women** on Victorian couch by J. Thomas
**Women's** dance by D. E. Brett
**Wonderful** object by F. Martin
**WONG, Frederick**
    Rain on Park south      OYB
      OYB. Annual 1960
**WONNER, Paul,** 1920-
    Landscape II, 1953
      NNSG. Younger Amer ptrs
    Woman and table
      IU. Contemp Amer ptg & sculp, 1961
**WOOD, Bernardine,** 1924-
    Still life with melons
      IU. Contemp Amer ptg & sculp, 1957
**Wood, Caroline Matilda.** See Burnham,
    Caroline Matilda (Wood)

**WOOD, Grant,** 1892-1942
  Adolescence
    Baur. New art
    IaDa. Wood
    KLU. Wood
  American Gothic                              ICA
    Baur. New art (col)
    Baur. Revolution
    Canaday
    Cheney. Story 1958 ed
    Craven. Treasury 1952 ed
    Faulkner. Art today, 1956
    Flexner. Amer ptg
    Flexner. Short history
    Gardner 1959 ed
    IaDa. Wood
    Lee. Art then and now
    Lewisohn
    McCurdy
    Mendelowitz
    Newmeyer
    NYG. Fine art
    Pierson
    Richardson. Ptg in America
    Roos
    Taylor. Fifty centuries, 1954 ed (col)
    Time. 300 years (col)
    UNESCO. 1860-1949
    UNESCO. 1860-1955
    UNESCO. 1860-1959
    Wight. Milestones
  Currants
    KLU. Wood
  Daughters of revolution
    Barr. What is mod ptg
    Baur. New art
    Walker. Ptgs from America
  Fall plowing
    KLU. Wood
  Iowa cornfield                               IaDa
    IaDa. Wood
    NUM. Art across America
  Italian farmyard
    KLU. Wood
  John B. Turner, pioneer
    KLU. Wood
  Midnight ride of Paul Revere                 MM
    Canaday
    Craven. Rainbow book
    Craven. Treasury 1952 ed
    MM. 100 Amer ptrs
    Pierson
    Time. 300 years (col)
  Nan
    KLU. Wood
  Old sexton's place
    KLU. Wood
  Parson Weems' fable
    Baur. New art
    KLU. Wood
  Return from Bohemia                          IBM
    KLU. Wood
  Self-portrait, 1932
    IaDa. Wood
    KLU. Wood
  Spring in the country                        InTH
    Bazin
  Spring in town                               InTH
    IaDa. Wood
    InTH. Catalogue
    KLU. Wood

  Spring landscape
    NYG. Fine art
    UNESCO. 1860-1949
  Spring turning
    KLU. Wood
  Stone City                                   NeO
    IaDa. Wood
    NYG. Fine art (col)
  Susan Angevine Shaffer
    KLU. Wood
  Tree planting
    IaDa. Wood
  Turner alley studio
    IaDa. Wood
  Woman with plants                            IaCR
    Baur. New art
    Craven. Treasury 1952 ed (col)
    UNESCO. 1860-1949
    UNESCO. 1860-1955
    UNESCO. 1860-1959
  Young corn
    KLU. Wood
    MnMW. Reality and fantasy
**Wood, Horatio C.**
  Eakins, T· Dr Horatio C. Wood
**WOOD, Joseph,** 1778-1832
  Thomas Say                                   CtY
    CtY Portrait index
                   **Attributed works**
  Oliver Hazard Perry
    MB. New England miniatures
**WOOD, Leonard,** 1860-1927
  Remington, F. Gen Leonard Wood
**WOOD, Thomas Waterman,** 1823-1903
  Moses, the Baltimore news vendor CSFP
    CSFP. Handbook
  Negress                                      CSFP
    CSFP. Handbook
  New England country store, 1873
    Davidson v 1
  Village post office                          NCHA
    Barker. Amer ptg
    Pierson
**Wood, Zipporah.** See Ames, Zipporah
    (Wood)
The **wood-boat** by G. C. Bingham
**Wood-boatmen** on a river by G. C. Bingham
**Wood** for winter by G. H. Durrie
**Wood** gatherers by R. Strang
**Wood** interior by V. Vytlacil
**Wood** of the Holy Cross by R. Le Brun
**Wood** road by A. P. Ryder
**Wood** rose by E. I. Maurice
**Woodbridge, Nathaniel Shaw**
  Earl, R. Nathaniel Shaw Woodbridge and
    his daughter Mary
**WOODBURY, Charles Herbert,** 1864-1940
  Canal scene, Holland                         MB
    MB. Ptgs in water color
  Sunken ledges                                MB
    MB. Ptgs in water color
**Woodbury, Mrs Charles Herbert.** See Wood-
    bury, Marcia Oakes
**WOODBURY, Marcia Oakes,** 1865-1913
  Triptych                                     MB
    MB. Ptgs in water color
The **woodchopper** by W. Homer
The **woodcutter** by W. Homer
**Woodcutters** in Windsor Great park by B.
    West

Woodcutting in winter by Unidentified artist

Wooded landscape with castle by B. West (attributed works)

Wooden box of catawba grapes by W. M. Harnett

Wooden horses by R. Marsh

Wooden Indian by M. Manigault

Woodgatherers: autumn afternoon by G. Inness

Wooding up the Mississippi by F. F. Palmer

Woodland scene by W. T. Aldrich

Woodland scene by E. W. Dickinson

Woodland stream by J. F. Cropsey

Woodland vista by G. Inness

Woodlands, seat of William Hamilton, near Philadelphia by W. Groombridge

Woodman spare that tree by Unidentified artist

Woodpeckers
  Audubon, J. J. Ivory-billed woodpecker
  Audubon, J. J. Pileated woodpecker
  Audubon, J. J. Woodpeckers
  Dove, A. G. Woodpecker
  Graves, M. Woodpeckers

Woodpile by H. Moller

WOODS, Conrad, 1932?-
  Verde
    IU. Contemp Amer ptg & sculp, 1959

Woods at sunset by R. A. Blakelock

Woods in winter by W. L. Palmer

Woodshed by A. N. Wyeth

Woodshed interior by S. M. Green

Woodshed interior by Unidentified artist

WOODSIDE, John Archibald, 1781-1852
  Children in a courtyard—the origin of drawing (copy of ptg by J. Paul)
    Chew. 250 years of art
  Country fair
    Barker. Amer ptg
    Davidson v 1
    Flexner. Light of distant skies
    U.S. National Capital sesquicentennial com
  Eben Whitney                          MeC
    Jetté. Amer heritage collection

Woodsman and fallen tree by W. Homer

Woodsman in winter by G. H. Durrie

Woodstock art conference by H. Hering

Woodstock pastoral by J. Levine

WOODVILLE, Richard Caton, 1825-1856
  Card players                          MiD
    Cowdrey v 1
    Pierson
  First step                            NNHS
    NYG. Fine art
  Mexican news
    Cowdrey v 1
  Politics in an oyster house           MdBW
    Mendelowitz
    MiD. Ptg in America
    Pierson
    Richardson. Ptg in America
    Roos
  Robert Gilmor II                      MdBM
    MdBMu. Rendezvous
  Sailor's wedding                      MdBW
    Davidson v 1
    Larkin

Larkin rev ed
  Waiting for the stage
    DC. Amer ptrs of the South
  War news from Mexico                  NAD
    Baur. Amer ptg
    Pierson

Woodward, Mary. See Hutson, Mary (Woodward)

WOODWARD, Stanley Wingate, 1890-
  Along the North shore                 MB
    MB. Ptgs in water color

Woodward children, fl 1830
  Unidentified artist. Woodward children

WOODWELL, Joseph R. 1843-1911
  Farmhouse at Scalp Level              PW
    Chew. 250 years of art

The wool winder by C. Gray

WOOLF, S. J.
  Franklin D. Roosevelt—beginning of his office
    NYG. Fine art

Woolsey, Alida Livingston, fl 1817
  Tuthill, A. G. D. Alida Livingston Woolsey

Woolsey, Melancthon Taylor, fl 1817
  Tuthill, A. G. D. Capt Melancthon Taylor Woolsey

Woolsey, Mrs Melancthon Taylor, fl 1817
  Tuthill, A. G. D. Mrs Melancthon Taylor Woolsey

WOOLSON, Ezra, fl 1842
  Jesse Kittredge Smith                 MSt
    Little. Country art

WOOLWORTH, Charlotte A. fl 1865
  Little dog                            WMAA
    Ford. Pictorial folk art

Woolworth building by J. Marin

Woolworth building in construction by J. Marin

Word, Mrs William Shaw
  Eakins, T. Mrs William Shaw Word

Work reconsidered by J. Wilde

Work stock by D. Teague

Workers and paintings by H. Sharrer

Workers' victory by P. Evergood

Workman's lunch by A. Rattner

A world I never made by I. Rose

World of wires by A. Osver

World tablet by T. Stamos

World's Columbian exposition—the fountains at night by W. Homer

World's greatest comics by B. Shahn

Worship at Eleusis by L. E. Kupferman

Worth family mourning by Unidentified artist

Worthy of liberty by C. W. Peale

Wounded animal by J. Pollock

Wounded beast by J. Pollock

Wounded buffalo by C. M. Russell

Wounded deer by C. Codman

Wounded gull by M. Graves

Wounded ibis by M. Graves

Wounded scoter by M. Graves

Wounded sea gull by M. Graves

Wounded wolf by R. Kuhn

Wragg, Elizabeth. See Manigault, Elizabeth (Wragg)

Wragg, Mary (du Bosc) fl 1708
   Johnston, H. Mrs Samuel Wragg
Wragg, Samuel, 1769-1842
   Malbone, E. G. Samuel Wragg
Wragg, William, fl 1740
   Theus, J. William Wragg
Wraith, wreath, and a final horn by A. H.
   Smith
Wray, Ann. See Williams, Ann (Wray)
The wreck by B. Greene
The wreck by W. Homer
Wreck of the Ancon in Loring bay, Alaska
   by A. Bierstadt
Wreck of the Iron Crown by W. Homer
Wreck of the St Christopher by J. De
   Martini
The wreck, or girl with red stockings by W.
   Homer
Wrecked building by C. Cloar
Wrecked schooner by W. Homer
Wrestlers. See Boxers and wrestlers
Wright, Henry Parks, 1839-1918
   Beckwith, J. C. Henry Parks Wright
WRIGHT, James Henry, 1813?-1883

                  Attributed works
   U.S. Ship Constellation                 MB
      MB. Karolik coll
WRIGHT, Joseph, 1756-1793
   George Washington                       OCl
      OCl. Handbook
   George Washington                       PH
      Pierson
   Self-portrait of the artist and family  PA
      MiD. Ptg in America
      Pierson
      Richardson. Ptg in America

                  Attributed works
   Benjamin Franklin                       CtY
      CtY. Portrait index
Wright, Stanton MacDonald-. See MacDon-
   ald-Wright, Stanton
Written in stone by C. A. Morris
Wyalusing by E. C. Frank
Wyalusing by J. O. Montalant
Wyan, Mary Gay. See Nelson, Mary Gay
   (Wyan)
WYANT, Alexander Helwig, 1836-1892
   Falls of the Ohio and Louisville    KyLS
      Barker. Amer ptg
   Forest stream, a study from nature  MnMI
      Born
   Lake George
      Sears. Highlights
   Mohawk valley                           MM
      Pierson
      Richardson. Ptg in America
   Mountain brook, Adirondacks         NBuA
      NBuA. Catalogue of the ptgs
   An old clearing                         MM
      Bazin
      Pierson
   On the upper Hudson
      Sears. Highlights
   Winona Falls                            MoSL
      MoSL. Handbook 1953
Wyckoff, Alexander Robertson, fl 1810
   Jarvis, J. W. Alexander Robertson
      Wyckoff

Wyckoff, George
   Bentley, L. George Wyckoff jr
Wyer, Alice, fl 1805
   Malbone, E. G. Alice Wyer
WYETH, Andrew Newell, 1917-
   Afternoon                              WiMiA
      IU. Contemp Amer ptg
      NHMC. Andrew Wyeth
   Albert's son
      WMAA. Contemp Amer ptg, 1959/60
   Arthur Cleveland                         DeW
      NHMC. Andrew Wyeth
      NUM. Art across America
   Benjamin's house                        CSFP
      CSFP. Handbook
   Blackberry picker
      Gruskin
   Brown Swiss
      PPC. International ex, 1958
   Chambered nautilus
      Time. 300 years (col)
   Christina Olsen
      Canaday
      CtY. Yale alumni
      NHMC. Andrew Wyeth
   Christina's world                        MMA
      Baur. New art (col)
      Baur. Revolution
      McCurdy
      Mendelowitz
      MMA. Masters
      NHMC. Andrew Wyeth
      Pierson
   The cloisters
      NHMC. Andrew Wyeth
      PPC. Ptg in the U.S. 1949
   Coot hunter                              ICA
      NHMC. Andrew Wyeth
   A crow flew by                           MM
      MM. 100 Amer ptrs
      Time. 300 years (col)
   Edge of the field                       MeC
      MeC. Inaugural ex
   General Knox mansion                    OYB
      OYB. Catalogue 1951
   Goose river                             NJMo
      NJMo. Forty years
   Hay ledge
      ICA. Annual ex, 1959/60
   Henry Teel
      NHMC. Andrew Wyeth
   Hoffman's slough
      Baur. New art
   House on Teel's island
      NAD. Annual ex, 1947, 2d half
   The hunter                               OT
      OT. Contemp Amer ptgs
   John Olsen's funeral                    CtNB
      NHMC. Andrew Wyeth
   Karl
      Baur. New art
      Cheney. Story 1958 ed
      NHMC. Andrew Wyeth (col)
      Pierson
   McVey's barn                            CtNB
      Baur. New art
      IU. Contemp Amer ptg, 1949
   Man from Maine
      PA. Annual ex, 1952
      Pousette-Dart. Amer ptg
   Memorial day                             MB
      MB. Ptgs in water color
   Mr River's garden                        MB
      MB. Ptgs in water color

Mother Archie's church          MAP
  NHMC. Andrew Wyeth
Nicholas
  PPC. International ex, 1955
Northern point          CtHW
  Baur. New art
  CtHW. Handbook
  Larkin rev ed
  Seiberling
  WMAA. Museum and its friends, 1959
Raccoon
  ICA. Annual ex, 1959/60
Road to friendship          MeR
  NHMC. Andrew Wyeth
Seed corn
  NHMC. Andrew Wyeth
Self-portrait          NAD
  Bazin
The sexton
  NHMC. Andrew Wyeth
Soaring          MB
  NHMC. Andrew Wyeth
  Pierson
  WMAA. Museum and its friends, 1958
Spindrift          NHMC
  NHMC. Andrew Wyeth
Spring beauty
  Barker. From realism
Sunday school room
  NAD. Annual ex, spring 1950
Toll rope
  PPC. International ex, 1952
Tolling bell          ATeS
  ATeS. Collection
Trodden weed
  Chew. 250 years of art
Wind from the sea
  ICA. Annual ex, 1954
  NHMC. Andrew Wyeth
Woodshed
  NHMC. Andrew Wyeth
Young America          PA
  Eliot. Art of our time (col)
  MM. Amer ptg today
  Time. 300 years (col)
WYETH, Newell Convers, 1882-1945
Buttonwood farm          PR
  PR. Catalogue
Wyld, Diana, fl 1766
  West, B. Diana, wife of Thomas Wyld of
    Sheen
WYLIE, Theophilus Adam
  Political scene in early Bloomington InBU
  Pierson
Wyndham sisters by J. S. Sargent
Wynkoop, Cornelius D. 1734-1792
  Vanderlyn P. (attributed works) Cornelius
    D. Wynkoop
Wyoming
  Albright, I. L. Roaring fork, Wyoming
  Bierstadt, A. Jenny lake, Wyoming
  Bierstadt, A. Wind river country, Wyo-
    ming
  Moran, T. Cliffs of the Green river, Wyo-
    ming
  Richardson, C. C. Wyoming desert
Wyoming valley by E. A. Christie
Wyoming valley by J. F. Cropsey
Wyoming valley by G. Grunewald
Wyoming valley by T. Hill
Wyoming valley by E. D. Lewis
Wyoming valley in 1850 by Unidentified ar-
  tist

X

X—1955 by H. Hofmann
X-1000 by N. J. Oliveira
XCÉRON, Jean, 1890-
  Beyond white
    IU. Contemp Amer ptg, 1951
    IU. 20th century
  Genesis
    IU. Contemp Amer ptg & sculp, 1953
  Ikon no 386          NNSG
    NNSG. Handbook
  Multiform
    IU. Contemp Amer ptg
  Painting 290
    IU. Contemp Amer ptg, 1950
  Painting 341, 1951          WMAA
    Pousette-Dart. Amer ptg
    WMAA. Contemp Amer ptg, 1952
  Painting 388
    IU. Contemp Amer ptg & sculp, 1957
  Radar          GAtM
    GAtM. Holbrook collection
  Variations
    PPC. International ex, 1950
Xmas morning by R. Philipp

Y

Yacht by L. Feininger
The yacht America leaving Boston harbor
  for England by J. E. Butterworth
Yacht race by L. Feininger
Yaddo by J. V. Harvey
Yaddo gardens by L. Gatch
Yale university
  Wight, P. B. Venetian Gothic art building
    on the old Yale campus
YAMAMOTO, Noriko, 1919-
  Semtua
    WMAA. Young America 1960
Yankee peddler by J. W. Ehninger
Yankee peddler at work by A. B. Durand
Yaquima bay, Oregon by M. M. Albright
Yates, Catherine (Brass) b 1735
  Stuart, G. Mrs Richard Yates
Yates, Helen Maria. See Paige, Helen Maria
  (Yates)
Yates, Joseph Christopher, 1768-1837
  Ames, E. Joseph C. Yates
  Malbone, E. G. Joseph Yates
Yates, Lawrence Reid, d 1796
  Stuart, G. Lawrence Yates
Yates, Richard, 1732-1808
  Stuart, G. Richard Yates
Yates, Mrs Richard. See Yates, Catherine
  (Brass)
Yates family, fl 1834
  Manchester, M. M. Conversation piece:
    A Yates family portrait
Ye Boston baked beans by H. E. Coville
Ye knights of old by W. M. Harnett
Yeamans, Mary. See Martin, Mary (Yea-
  mans)
The year eleven by A. Sessler
Yeats at Petitpas' by J. Sloan

YEKTAI, Manoucher, 1922-
Blue table
MnMW. 60 Amer ptrs
Yellow curtain
IU. Contemp Amer ptg & sculp, 1955
Yell of triumph by A. J. Miller
Yellow above by R. Scarlett
Yellow arc by C. A. Morris
Yellow blinds by C. H. Carter
Yellow-breasted chat by J. J. Audubon
Yellow chair by H. Pittman
Yellow coach by Unidentified artist
Yellow curtain by M. Yektai
The yellow fan by A. Brook
Yellow harvest by M. Tobey
Yellow hat by E. Manville
Yellow jacket by M. Avery
Yellow light by C. A. Morris
Yellow lines by I. R. Pereira
Yellow marsh, Sandwich by D. Macknight
Yellow meadow by M. Avery
Yellow oblongs by I. R. Pereira
Yellow over purple by M. Rothko
Yellow pitcher by H. L. McFee
Yellow, plus and minus by S. Chermayeff
Yellow river by W. De Kooning
Yellow room by F. C. Frieseke
Yellow rooster by E. F. Spruce
Yellow roses by W. M. Chase
Yellow seascape by R. Diebenkorn
Yellow sheep by I. Kriesberg
Yellow sky by M. Avery
Yellow sky by J. Hultberg
Yellow table by A. Rattner
The Yellowstone and Missouri rivers by K. Bodmer
Yellowstone park
Bierstadt, A. Geyser, Yellowstone park
Moran, T. Mist in the Yellowstone
Twachtman, J. H. Rapids, Yellowstone park
Yellowstone river near Fort Keough by H. Stieffel
YERXA, Thomas, 1935-
Atlantic
NAD. Annual ex, 1954
City child                                    OYB
NAD. Annual ex, 1957
OYB. Annual 1957
OYB. Supplement 1959
Still life
NAD. Annual ex, 1952
Windows
WMAA. Annual ex, 1958
Yesterday by I. L. Albright
Yesterday by R. O. Pozzatti
YEWELL, George Henry, 1830-1923
The bootblack                                 NNHS
MiD. Travelers in Arcadia
York by E. Kelly
York family by J. H. Davis
York in the lodge of the Mandans by C. M. Russell
Yosemite Falls
Zorach, W. Yosemite Falls

Yosemite valley
Bierstadt, A. In the Yosemite valley
Bierstadt, A. Valley of the Yosemite
Hahn, W. Yosemite valley
Hill, T. Bridal veil and El Capitan, Yosemite valley
Zorach, W. Rocky cliffs—Yosemite valley
YOST, Fred
Cape May wharf
OYB. Annual 1948
You can buy whiskey for twenty-five cents a quart by J. Lawrence
You can't come home again by A. Shulkin
Youle's shot tower, East river shore by J. F. Cropsey
YOUNG, Art
Trees
Brown. Amer ptg
Young, John, 1762-1840
Stuart, G. Judge John Young
Young, Mrs John. See Young, Maria (Barclay)
Young, Maria (Barclay) d 1811?
Stuart, G. Maria (Barclay) Young
Young America by A. N. Wyeth
Young American artist by J. D. Prendergast
Young artist, Portrait of by F. Knight
Young Aurora by G. A. Walker
Young birds by C. S. Price
Young boy by J. W. Jarvis
Young buck and doe by A. F. Tait
Young chief's mission by J. H. Sharp
Young Christ by D. Aronson
Young clown by W. Kuhn
Young colonial by R. Feke
Young corn by G. Wood
Young crow by C. E. Heil
Young couple drinking by P. Mangravite
Young Daniel Webster and the Constitution by B. Faulkner
Young gander ready for flight by M. Graves
Young gentleman of fashion by A. M. Von Phul
Young girl by J. Carroll
Young girl by E. Decombes
Young girl by W. Jennys (attributed works)
Young girl by A. H. Maurer
Young girl by Unidentified artist
Young girl in a red dress by Unidentified artist
Young girl in blue by J. A. M. Whistler
Young girl in flower by R. Feke
Young girl in green bonnet by M. Cassatt
Young girl in white by Unidentified artist
Young girl with music book by W. Sutton
Young girls by M. Cassatt
Young hammerer by J. W. Stock
Young hunter by C. W. Hare
Young hunter in woods by W. Homer
Young Joseph by D. Aronson
Young ladies' seminary, Virginia by Unidentified artist
Young lady by G. Duyckinck (attributed works)
Young lady in pink by E. G. Malbone
Young lovers by P. Mangravite

Young man by T. Eakins
Young man by Raphaelle Peale
Young man by W. M. Prior
Young man alone with his face by P. Burlin
Young man desiring position by G. Samstag
Young man from Arkansas by J. Farnsworth
Young man in a gray linen suit by Unidentified artist
Young man of the sea by J. Marin
Young man wearing white stock by Unidentified artist
Young men by the sea by M. Beckmann
Young merchants by W. Page
Young model by M. Weber
Young musician by D. G. Blythe
Young Omahaw, War Eagle, Little Missouri and Pawnees by C. B. King
Young owl and moth by M. Graves
Young pianist by A. Brook
Young woman by J. Chapin
Young woman by R. Soyer
Young woman by A. H. Thayer
Young woman in a fur coat by A. H. Thayer
Young woman in pink dress by T. Eakins
Young woman in white by R. Henri
Young woman of the Flathead tribe by A. J. Miller
Young woman reading by M. Cassatt
Young woman with bird by R. Brackman
Young woman with gloves by W. Brice
Young women picking fruit by M. Cassatt
Young worshipper of the truth by M. Hartley
**YOUNGERMAN, Jack,** 1926-
  Aquitaine                              MMA
    MMA. Sixteen
  Aztec III
    MMA. Sixteen
  Big black
    MMA. Sixteen
  Coenties slip
    MMA. Sixteen
  "Cuba Si"
    PPC. International ex, 1961/62
  Delfina                                NBuA
    NBuA. Acquisitions 1959-1961
  Naxos
    PPC. International ex, 1958
  Ram
    MMA. Sixteen
**Your** tapers taper by Y. Tanguy
**Youth** by B. Greene
**Youth** playing fife by T. Eakins
**Yule** log by V. Candall
**Yuma,** Arizona by L. M. Eilshemius
**YUNKERS, Adja,** 1900-
  Composition in black and ochre    NNSG
    NNSG. Handbook
  Gosier II
    IU. Contemp Amer ptg & sculp, 1961
  Tarrasa
    PPC. International ex, 1958
  Tarrasa XIII, 1958                     WMAA
    Goodrich. Amer art
  Untitled I, 1960
    MnMW. 60 Amer ptrs
**Yvanka** by B. Greene

# Z

**Zagorin, Mrs Perez.** See Sharrer, Honoré Desmond
**ZAJAC, Jack,** 1929-
  The anglers
    IU. Contemp Amer ptg, 1952
  Bird in the sun no 2, 1955
    WMAA. Young America 1957
  Resurrection
    WMAA. Young America 1957
  Seacoast                               CLA
    CoS. New accessions USA, 1954
  Seascape
    PPC. International ex, 1955
**ZALMAR,** 1925-
  Landscape with potted plant in foreground
    IU. Contemp Amer ptg, 1951
**ZELIFF, A. E.** fl 1850
  Barnyard                               DN
    DN. Amer primitive ptgs, pt 1
**Zen** Buddist by X. Gonzales
**Zenka** of Bohemia by R. Henri
**ZERBE, Karl,** 1903-
  Aging harlequin
    Baur. Revolution
  Apartment no 2
    Pousette-Dart. Amer ptg
  At night
    Pearson. Mod renaissance
  The birdcage                           InIJ
    InIJ. 105 ptgs
  Boston daily
    NAD. Annual ex, 1948
  Canal street no 2
    IU. Contemp Amer ptg & sculp, 1957
  China Town no 1                        MAP
    CoS. New accessions USA, 1954
  Collection X, no 2
    CSFP. Annual ex, 1952
  East of Lexington
    DC. 21 biennial ex, 1949
  Felix Adler
    Pearson. Mod renaissance
  Fortune seller
    IU. Contemp Amer ptg, 1949 (col)
  Gloucester alley                       NBuA
    NBuA. Contemporary ptgs
  Golden hat
    IU. Contemp Amer ptg, 1948
  Good angel tenanted
    IU. Contemp Amer ptg & sculp, 1959
  Good Friday
    IU. Contemp Amer ptg, 1950
    Pearson. Mod renaissance
  Harlem                                 MMA
    Pierson
  Harlequin                              WMAA
    Goodrich. Amer art
    Gruskin (col)
    Pierson
  The inventor
    IU. Contemp ptg & sculp, 1953
  Kokoschka, 1949
    MnMW. Expressionism 1900-1955
  Landscape with letters
    IC. Annual ex, 1954
  Landscape with scrap metal III        IU
    IU. Contemp Amer ptg & sculp, 1955
    IU. 20th century
    WMAA. Annual ex, 1955

ZERBE, Karl—*Continued*
Melancholia
  ICA. Annual ex, 1947/48     ICA
  Roos
Night
  MeC. Inaugural ex
Park street, Boston     DP
  DP. Catalogue
The parrot and decanter
  ICA. Annual ex, 1945/46
Pastorale     MM
  MM. 100 Amer ptrs
Rome—St Augustine
  Pearson. Mod renaissance
Rooster     GAtM
  GAtM. Holbrook collection
Ruins, Brantone     OYB
  OYB. Catalogue 1951
St Louis drawing room
  Wight. Milestones
St Philip's, Charleston     MoSL
  MoSL. Handbook 1953
Second floor front     NUM
  NBuA. Expressionism
  PPC. Ptg in the U.S. 1949
Street in Tepoztlan, Mexico     MB
  MB. Ptgs in water color
Survivors
  IU. Contemp Amer ptg, 1951
  PA. Annual ex, 1949
Terror
  Cheney. Story 1958 ed
Woman on trapeze     IBM
  Genauer

ZEREGA, Andrea Pietro, 1917-
In Montgomery county
  IU. Contemp Amer ptg & sculp, 1953
Zeretelli by M. Beckmann
ZIMMERMAN, Paul Warren, 1921-
Reminiscent Italia
  OYB. Annual 1950
The square
  NAD. Annual ex, 1954
Still life—delphinium
  IU. Contemp Amer ptg & sculp, 1961
ZINGALE, Santos, 1908-
Variation on a theme
  IU. Contemp Amer ptg & sculp, 1953
Zinnias by H. Katzman
Zinnias by M. Weber
Zinnias, larkspur and daisies by C. H. Demuth
Zion canyon by D. Macknight
Zirchow VII by L. Feininger
Zirchow VII by L. Feininger
ZIROLI, Nicola, 1908-
Self-portrait     OYB
  OYB. Annual 1955
  OYB. Supplement 1959
Weeds
  OYB. Annual 1956

ZOGBAUM, Rufus F. 1849-1925
Admiral Dewey at Manila bay, 1898
  U.S. National Capital sesquicentennial com
Zone by P. Guston
ZORACH, Marguerite (Thompson) 1888-
Hound
  Cheney. Expressionism 1948 ed
Moonset and sunrise
  WMAA. Pioneers

Portrait of the artist
Biddle, G. Woman with a letter
ZORACH, William, 1887-
The artist's son
  Baur. William Zorach
Five islands, Maine
  NYG. Fine art
Interior and exterior
  Baur. William Zorach
Leo Ornstein (Piano concert)
  Baur. William Zorach
  WMAA. Pioneers
  WMAA. Zorach
Mirage—ships at night
  Baur. William Zorach
  WMAA. Zorach
Morning glow, autumn
  Baur. William Zorach
  WMAA. Zorach
Piano concert. See Leo Ornstein
Popham beach no 1, Maine
  Baur. William Zorach
Robinhood marina
  Baur. William Zorach
  WMAA. Zorach
Rocky cliffs—Yosemite valley
  Baur. William Zorach
The roof playground
  Baur. William Zorach
Sailing by moonlight     DP
  DP. Catalogue
Sisters
  Baur. William Zorach
Spring no 1, 1913
  Baur. William Zorach
  WMAA. Zorach
Windy day—Lowe's point
  Baur. William Zorach
  WMAA. Zorach
Winter without snow     MB
  MB. Ptgs in water color
Yosemite Falls
  Baur. William Zorach
Yosemite Falls I
  Baur. William Zorach
Yosemite Falls II
  Baur. William Zorach
  WMAA. Zorach
Zorach, Mrs William. See Zorach, Marguerite (Thompson)
Zsissly. See Albright, Malvin Marr